# INTRODUCTION TO
# SOCIOLOGY

### SECOND EDITION

# PEARSON

We work with leading authors to develop the strongest learning experiences, bringing cutting-edge thinking and best learning practice to a global market. We craft our print and digital resources to do more to help learners not only understand their content, but to see it in action and apply what they learn, whether studying or at work.

Pearson is the world's leading learning company. Our portfolio includes Penguin, Dorling Kindersley, the Financial Times and our educational business, Pearson International. We are also a leading provider of electronic learning programmes and of test development, processing and scoring services to educational institutions, corporations and professional bodies around the world.

We enable our customers to access a wide and expanding range of market-leading content from world-renowned authors and develop their own tailor-made book. You choose the content that meets your needs and Pearson produces a high-quality printed book.

Every day our work helps learning flourish, and wherever learning flourishes, so do people.

To learn more please visit us at: www.pearsoned.co.uk/personalised

# INTRODUCTION TO
# SOCIOLOGY

SECOND EDITION

Compiled from:

SOCIOLOGY: A GLOBAL INTRODUCTION
Fifth Edition
John J. Macionis & Ken Plummer

AN INTRODUCTION TO IRISH SOCIETY: TRANSITIONS AND CHANGE
Dr Martin J. Power, Dr Eoin Devereux, Dr Amanda Haynes,
Dr Carmel Hannan, Dr Patricia Neville & Dr Cliona Barnes

Harlow, England • London • New York • Boston • San Francisco • Toronto • Sydney • Auckland • Singapore • Hong Kong
Tokyo • Seoul • Taipei • New Delhi • Cape Town • Sao Paulo • Mexico City • Madrid • Amsterdam • Munich • Paris • Milan

Pearson Education Limited
Edinburgh Gate
Harlow
Essex CM20 2JE

And associated companies throughout the world

Visit us on the World Wide Web at:
www.pearson.com/uk

First published 2013
This edition © Pearson Education Limited 2014

Compiled from:

SOCIOLOGY: A GLOBAL INTRODUCTION
Fifth Edition
John J. Macionis & Ken Plummer
ISBN 978 0 273 72791 0
© Prentice Hall Inc. 1997
© Pearson Education Limited 2002, 2012

AN INTRODUCTION TO IRISH SOCIETY: TRANSITIONS AND CHANGE
Dr Martin J. Power, Dr Eoin Devereux, Dr Amanda Haynes, Dr Carmel Hannan, Dr Patricia Neville & Dr Cliona Barnes
ISBN 978 0 85776 668 7
© Pearson Education Limited 2012

ISBN 978 1 78365 683 7

Manufactured in the United Kingdom

# Contents

# PART 1

# INTRODUCING SOCIOLOGY

# CHAPTER 1

# THE SOCIOLOGICAL IMAGINATION

IMAGINE YOU WERE BORN SOME 300 YEARS AGO, IN THE YEAR 1700. Although this is very recent in terms of the billions of years of the existence of planet earth, you would still be living in a remarkably different world. You would probably be living in a very small community and you would not have travelled anywhere except perhaps to a nearby town.

You would never have been to a shop, let alone a shopping centre. You would not have encountered the world of railways, cars, telephones, cameras, PCs, faxes, mobile phones, planes, videos, McDonald's, holiday tours, laptops or DVDs. And more than this, the idea of voting for your government, going to a university, choosing your religion, or even choosing your identity would all have been bizarrely rare. And a map of the world would have been very different. Welcome, then, to our twenty-first century world!

Now imagine again: this time that you were born and living in Afghanistan, one of the poorest and most conflict-torn places in the world today. Your life expectancy at birth would be no more than 44.5 years. By contrast, if you were born in Japan, your expectations would be nearly double this. Indeed, in Afghanistan, 150 children out of every thousand born die shortly after birth; in Japan (and Sweden), it is less than 3 per thousand. Your chances of extended education will be low: boys will have on average 8 years of education whereas it is double that in Japan (or the United Kingdom). The situation is worse for girls: they are likely to have only four years of schooling and less than 15 per cent will be literate. Some 53 per cent of people live below the poverty line and 40 per cent are unemployed. In Norway, by contrast, some 2.5 per cent are unemployed and poverty seems too low to be recorded! Media communications are also different: in Afghanistan, there are 500,000 internet users; in Japan there are 90 million.

But now have another leap of imagination: this time to a world that is yet to come – the world perhaps of your own grandchildren or great grandchildren. We cannot, of course, predict the future, but we can often see trends. For instance, 'babies in test tubes' and the new genetic engineering are now commonplace. The miniaturisation of electronics as new computers, cameras and I-phones become pocket size is ubiquitous in the rich world. Already these new technologies are being implanted into our bodies and secreted in public spaces. The home of the future will be driven by these. Medicine is prolonging many lives: and with many more people living longer and longer, some even predict that we may become immortal! Our music and media, shops and work situations, families and government structures are all changing beyond today's recognition. What once looked like science fiction a hundred years ago is the reality we now live in. Think up your own projections for the futuristic landscape of your old age!

The power of sociology is to demonstrate just how strong are the social forces that organise society in very, very different ways – and to demonstrate it in time (past societies, present societies and future societies) and space (across the 200 countries or so throughout the world). In this book, over and over again, you will see the variety of societies and the different opportunities that people have within them. Just where you were born – and when – has radically shaped much of what you know and what you can do. Having encountered sociology, you may never see the world with the same eyes again.

**tip** For more information and data on all this, and indeed for every country in the world, search online *The World Fact Book* compiled by the Central Intelligence Agency (CIA). For full details: type www.cia.gov/library/publications/the-world-factbook/index.html.

Note this is produced and kept up to date by the government of the United States of America.

*The first wisdom of sociology is this: things are not what they seem.*

Peter Berger

---

## In this chapter, we ask:

- **What is sociology?**
- **How can sociological perspectives help us understand everyday life?**
- **What do sociologists do?**
- **How did sociology develop?**

---

(Left) Pieter Brueghel the Younger, *The Battle between Carnival and Lent*, 1559

*Source: The Battle between Carnival and Lent* (oil on canvas). Brueghel, Pieter the Younger, (c. 1564–1638)/ Private Collection, Johnny Van Haeften Ltd, London/The Bridgeman Art Library.

*Note*: For more information, see: www.artcyclopedia.com/artists/bruegel_the_younger_pieter.html; http://wwar.com/masters/b/brueghel-pieter.html.

**Q** Brueghel's painting is a world classic. Examine it closely. What issues of social life does it depict? Can you imagine what a contemporary version of this would look like?

## What is sociology?

Welcome to sociology – the *systematic, sceptical and critical study of the social*. It studies the way people do things together. At the heart of sociology is a distinctive point of view. It should be more than you find in a good documentary on a social issue. It is certainly more than listings of facts and figures about society. Instead it becomes *a form of consciousness, a way of thinking, a critical way of seeing the social*. It takes a while, sometimes years, for this 'consciousness' to become clear. And it brings the potential to change your life forever.

So a health warning is needed. Sociology could change your life – maybe even damage it! Contrary to the popular view that sociology is just common sense, it often strains against the common sense. Once it becomes ingrained in your thinking, it will always be

asking for you to 'think the social', and it will entail *challenging the obvious, questioning the world as it is taken for granted*, and *de-familiarising the familiar*. This is personally enlightening, even empowering, but it can also make you a very critical person. It helps develop critical thinking and can help make critical citizens.

In this section, and subsequently in the whole book, we ask: what is distinctive about this way of seeing, this new consciousness? To get you going, the box below gives a few standard definitions to consider.

## Seeing the general in the particular

Peter Berger's short book *Invitation to Sociology* (1963) has tempted several generations of students into seeing this perspective. In it he characterised the

---

## So they ask me: what is sociology?

When you start to study sociology, people – friends, families, even strangers – will probably ask you what it is. You may well mumble something about 'the study of society', but that is very vague. Prepare a practical answer to give people. The following definitions might help you a little in this (but they all raise more questions than they resolve):

> The sociologist . . . is someone concerned with understanding society in a disciplined way. The nature of this discipline is scientific.
>
> (Peter Berger, *Invitation to Sociology*, 1963: 27)

Sociology is . . . first and foremost a *way of thinking* about the human world . . . [It asks how] does it matter that humans live always (and cannot but live) in the company of, in communication with, in an exchange with,

in competition with, in cooperation with other human beings? . . . Its questions 'defamiliarise the familiar'.

(Zygmunt Bauman, *Thinking Sociologically*, 1990: 8, 15)

The 'human world', or the 'world of humans', is the distinctive realm of human experience and existence . . . and the subject matter with which sociology is concerned.

(Richard Jenkins, *Foundations of Sociology*, 2002: 3)

The term has two stems – the Latin *socius* (companionship) and the Greek *logos* (study of) – and literally means the study of the processes of companionship. In these terms, sociology may be defined as the study of the bases of social membership. More technically, sociology is the analysis of the structure of social relationships as constituted by social interaction, but no definition is entirely satisfactory because of the diversity of perspectives.

(Nicholas Abercrombie, *Sociology*, 2004: 232)

The science or study of the origin, history and constitution of human society.

(*Shorter Oxford English Dictionary*)

Defined in dictionaries as the science or study of society. The term was coined by Comte (1830), linking the Latin *socius* (originally a people, tribe or city allied to Rome, but later a society) to the Greek *logos* (reason or knowledge). The term spread rapidly and is now used in virtually all languages to denote any relatively rigorous, reasoned study of society.

(Michael Mann, *Encyclopedia of Sociology*, 1983: 370)

A social science having as its main focus the study of the social institutions brought into being by the industrial transformations of the past two or three centuries . . . [It involves] an historical, an anthropological and a critical sensitivity.

(Anthony Giddens, *Sociology: A Brief but Critical Introduction*, 2nd edn, 1986: 9, 13) sociological perspective as a way of *seeing the general in the particular*. He meant that sociologists can identify general patterns of social life by looking at concrete specific examples of social life. While acknowledging that each individual is unique, in other words, sociologists recognise that society acts differently on various *categories* of people (say, children compared to adults, women versus men, the rich as opposed to the poor). We begin to think sociologically once we start to realise how the general categories into which we happen to fall shape our particular life experiences.

Each chapter of this book illustrates the general impact of society on the actions, thoughts and feelings of particular people. For example, seeing the world sociologically also makes us aware of the importance of gender – as we will see in Chapter 12. Every society attaches meanings (though often different meanings) to gender, giving women and men different kinds of work, family responsibilities, dress codes and even differing expectations across the life cycle. At the same time, the lives of men and women in modern Iraq, North America and China have very significant differences. And as societies change, so do these meanings: the expectations around men and women now, at the start of the twenty-first century, are very different from what they were at the start of the twentieth and they are often loaded with political conflict across many countries around the world. In this book, for instance, we will address the low pay of women (Chapter 15), their lack of power (Chapter 16), the violence against them (Chapter 12), the issues debated around Muslim women and the veil (Chapter 11), and the emergence of controversies around transgender and gay/homosexual/queer life (Chapter 12). Individuals experience the workings of society as they encounter advantages and opportunities characteristic of each sex.

The images on pages 6–7 suggest that there are many factors that shape our lives; Table 1.1 suggests some of the different 'levels' of reality we need to consider.

## Seeing the strange in the familiar

Especially at the beginning, using the sociological perspective amounts to *seeing the strange in the familiar*. As Peter Berger (1963: 34) says in his *Invitation to Sociology*, 'the first wisdom of sociology is this: things are not what they seem'. Or as Zygmunt Bauman (1990: 15) says in his *Sociological Thinking*, we need to 'defamiliarise the familiar'. For instance, observing

| Table 1.1 | The architecture of social life: the layers of reality |
|---|---|

- *Cosmic* – the widest presence in the universe/cosmos. This is a vast level of reality and we do not often look at it – but it is important to be aware of it as the infinitely complex presence behind the way we think about our humanly constructed social world.
- *World and globe* – the interconnectedness of the social and cultural across the world: the global flows and movements of economies, political systems, people, media messages, the internet, etc.
- *Social and cultural* – communities, societies, institutions and nation-states that have an existence independently of us, and that have definite structures and symbolic meanings over and above us.
- *Interactional* – the experience of the world in the immediate face-to-face presence and awareness of others: self, inter-subjectivity, and encounters with family, friends, groups and strangers in specific places.
- *Individual* – the inner world: the psychic world of human subjectivity and the inner biological workings of genetics, hormones, brain structure and the like.

sociologically requires giving up the familiar idea that human behaviour is simply a matter of what people *decide* to do and accepting instead the initially strange notion that society guides our thoughts and deeds.

Learning to 'see' how society affects us may take a bit of practice. Asked why you 'chose' your particular college or university, you might offer any of the following personal reasons:

I wanted to stay close to home.

This college has the best women's rugby team.

A law degree from this university ensures a good job.

My girlfriend goes to university here.

I wasn't accepted by the university I really wanted to attend.

What else could I do? I just drifted here.

Such responses are certainly grounded in reality for the people expressing them. But do they tell the whole story? The sociological perspective provides deeper insights that may not be readily apparent.

Thinking sociologically about going on to further or higher education, we might first realise that, for most people throughout most of the world and for most of history, university is all but out of reach. Moreover, had we lived a century or two ago, the 'choice' to go to university was only an option for the smallest elite.

But even in the here and now, a look around the classroom suggests that social forces still have much to do with whether or not one pursues higher education. Typically, college students are relatively young – generally between 18 and 24 years of age. Why? Because in our society going to university is associated with this period of life. But it needn't be – there are many 'mature students' and there is a 'University of the Fourth Age'. Likewise, higher education is costly, so college students tend to come from families with above-average incomes – young people lucky enough to belong to families from the service (middle) classes are some ten times more likely to go to university than are those from manual working-class families. And in many low-income societies such as Afghanistan, the length of time spend in education is drastically reduced. There are also significant variations by ethnicity and gender.

So, at the broadest level, sociology sets out to show the patterns and processes by which society shapes what we do.

# Individuality in social context: the strange case of suicide

The sociological perspective often challenges common sense by revealing that human behaviour is not as individualistic as we may think. For most of us, daily living seems very individual. We think we make our own choices, and have our own personal responsibilities – and we congratulate ourselves when we enjoy success and kick ourselves when things go wrong. Proud of our individuality, even in painful times, we resist the idea that we act in socially patterned ways. Yet much of social life is

**Society as a prison**
A key to sociological thinking is the basic idea that society guides our actions and life choices. In this painting, human beings are located at the centre of numerous social forces. Think about the forces that have shaped your own life – and consider how your life would be very different if you had been born into other languages, institutions or societies.

Maybe think of the 'walls of our imprisonment' – the constraints on our lives – as being linked to issues of:
- cultures (see Chapter 5)
- social divisions (see Part Three)
- economies (see Chapter 15)
- power structures (see Chapter 16)
- families (see Chapter 18)
- religion (see Chapter 19)
- education (see Chapter 20)
- media (see Chapter 22)
- science and technologies (see Chapter 23).

*Source: Withdrawn Man.*
© Paul Schulenburg/Stock Illustration Source.

**Multiple lives**
Differences are a key feature of social life. The power of society over the individual can easily be grasped by looking at the world through different cultures. (a) Teenage girl, Mali; (b) Teenage boy, England; (c) man, Egypt; (d) woman, Ivory coast; (e) Muslim woman
*Sources:* (a), (c), (d), (e) Getty Photodisk; (b) Pearson Education Ltd/BananaStock.

indeed shaped, even determined, by factors outside of our control.

Perhaps the most intriguing demonstration of how social forces affect human behaviour can be found in the study of suicide. It is a topic that has fascinated sociologists precisely because no act seems more individualistic – more driven by personal 'choice' – than the decision to take one's own life. This is why Emile Durkheim (1858–1917), a pioneer of sociology

writing a century ago who will reappear many times in this book, chose suicide as a topic of research. If he could show that an intensely individual act like suicide was socially shaped, then he would have made a strong case for sociological analysis. And many think he did! He showed that social forces help shape even the apparently most isolated act of self-destruction.

Durkheim began by examining suicide records in and around his native France. The statistics of his time (and 'statistics' was also a newly emerging field of study at this time) clearly showed that some *categories of people* were more likely than others to take their own lives. Specifically, Durkheim found that men, Protestants, wealthy people and the unmarried each had significantly higher suicide rates when compared with women, Roman Catholics and Jews, the poor and married people, respectively. Durkheim deduced that these differences corresponded to people's degree of *social integration: how they bonded, connected and tied into society*. Durkheim claimed that low suicide rates characterised categories of people with strong social ties; high suicide rates were found among those who were more socially isolated and individualistic. Working from this he developed a social classification (or typology) of different kinds of suicide. Too little integration – common at times of massive social change and social breakdown – could lead to *anomic suicide*; whilst too much integration could lead to *altruistic suicide*. A good example of this latter group would be suicide bombers, whose allegiance to a religion or a political group is so strong that they are literally willing to lay their lives down for it. (Durkheim also saw levels of regulation as another key to understanding suicide. He saw too little regulation leading to *egoistic suicide*, and too much to what he called *fatalistic suicide*; but we will not consider these here.)

Durkheim's analysis was poignant for the time he was writing, at the end of the nineteenth century. It was the time of the Great Transformation when the old order was breaking down (see pp. 17–19) and when industrialisation and market capitalism had led to a breakdown of the old integration. Suicide seemed to be on the rise everywhere. Durkheim started to make connections. And more: in the male-dominated societies studied by Durkheim, men certainly had more autonomy than women. Whatever freedom's advantages for men, concluded Durkheim, autonomy meant lower social integration, which contributed to a higher male suicide rate. Likewise, individualistic Protestants were more prone to suicide than Catholics and Jews, whose rituals fostered stronger social ties. The wealthy clearly have much more freedom of action than the poor but, once again, at the cost of a higher suicide rate. Finally, single people, with weaker social ties than married people, are also at greater risk of suicide.

Durkheim's study was very influential in helping people think about social influences and many of his correlations still hold. We discuss his work further in Chapters 2 and 4. But contemporary sociologists now claim that, as we have moved into the twenty-first century, and societies have continued to change, many

of the factors that Durkheim raised are no longer so significant. Two recent French sociologists – Christian Baudelot and Roger Establet (2008) – have examined world changes and concluded that, although suicide is shaped by social factors, these have changed somewhat since the time that Durkheim was studying. Suicide, for example, has declined amongst the wealthy and grown amongst the poor.

## The Chinese exception

Each year worldwide, approximately 1 million individuals die of suicide, 10–20 million attempt suicide and many more are affected by it. In some parts of the world, such as Iraq, suicide rates are very low; but Asia accounts for 60 per cent of the world's suicides. Table 1.2 shows a range of suicide rates across the world. Thus, for example, in almost every country of the world, men are more likely to commit suicide than women. Yet in China, this is not so. The statistics emerging from China on suicide – and they are quite hard to get, and we cannot be sure of their validity – suggest a very different pattern from the mainly Western one described by Durkheim. China, with 22 per cent of the world's people, accounts for some 40 per cent of suicides worldwide: a staggering higher rate. Indeed, suicide is the fifth largest cause of death in China, and each year more than a quarter of a million people take their own lives (and 2 million more attempt to do so). And whereas male suicides in the industrial West outnumber female suicides by roughly three or four to one, in China women's suicides outnumber men's. Likewise, whereas in the West suicide is linked to city life, in China it is three times higher in the countryside. Thus, suicide now accounts for a third of all deaths among women in the countryside. Sociologists, then, look at these statistics to detect broad social patterns that then need explaining.

## Methods and research: what sociologists do

Throughout this book you will find a selection of boxes which highlight key issues in sociology. One set of boxes are organised under the theme of *Methods and research* (look out for them). In these boxes, we will give you some idea of the kind of practical work that sociologists do – along with a sense of the methods they use. Often these boxes

## SUICIDE RATES AROUND THE WORLD: STUDY THE TABLE

Study this table and look at other countries on the original and fuller table which is accessible online.

| Table 1.2 | Selected suicide rates around the world per 100,000 population by country and gender (as of 2009) |

| Country | Year of latest data | Males | Females |
|---|---|---|---|
| Argentina | 2005 | 12.7 | 3.4 i |
| Australia | 2004 | 16.7 | 4.4 d |
| Brazil | 2005 | 7.3 | 1.9 |
| Canada | 2004 | 17.3 | 5.4 d |
| Chile | 2005 | 17.4 | 3.4 i |
| China (selected rural and urban areas) | 1999 | 13.0 | 14.8 |
| China (Hong Kong SAR) | 2006 | 19.3 | 11.5 i |
| Columbia | 2005 | 7.8 | 2.1 i |
| Croatia | 2006 | 26.9 | 9.7 d |
| Cuba | 2006 | 19.6 | 4.9 d |
| Cyprus | 2006 | 3.2 | 1.8 |
| Czech Republic | 2007 | 22.7 | 4.3 d |
| Denmark | 2006 | 17.5 | 6.4 d |
| Estonia | 2005 | 35.5 | 7.3 d |
| Finland | 2007 | 28.9 | 9.0 d |
| France | 2006 | 25.5 | 9.0 d |
| Germany | 2006 | 17.9 | 6.0 d |
| Greece | 1999 | 5.7 | 1.6 |
| Iceland | 2007 | 18.9 | 4.6 d |
| India | 1998 | 12.2 | 9.1 |
| Iran | 1991 | 0.3 | 0.1 [?] |
| Ireland | 2007 | 17.4 | 3.8 |
| Israel | 2005 | 8.7 | 3.3 |
| Italy | 2006 | 9.9 | 2.8 d |
| Japan | 2007 | 35.8 | 13.7 d |
| Kazakhstan | 2007 | 46.2 | 9.0 |
| Latvia | 2007 | 34.1 | 7.7 d |
| Lithuania | 2007 | 53.9 | 9.8 d |
| Norway | 2006 | 16.8 | 6.0 d |
| Portugal | 2004 | 17.9 | 5.5 i |
| Russian Federation | 2006 | 53.9 | 9.5 i |
| Spain | 2005 | 12.0 d | 16.8 i |
| Sweden | 2006 | 18.1 | 8.3 |
| United Kingdom | 2007 | 10.1 | 2.8 |
| United States of America | 2005 | 17.7 | 4.5 |
| Zimbabwe | 1990 | 10.6 | 5.2 |

i = increasing; d = decreasing

*Source*: This has been adapted from World Health Organization (2009) www.who.int/mental_health/prevention/suicide_rates/en/index.html.

Note in general that:
- The eastern Mediterranean region and the central Asian republics have the lowest suicide rates.
- World suicide *rates* are highest amongst men in Russia, Estonia, Hungary, Slovenia, Khazakistan and the Ukraine. They are also high in Japan and Sri Lanka.
- The largest *numbers* of all suicides worldwide occur in India and China (some 30%).
- 55% of suicides are aged between 15 and 44 years and 45% are aged 45 years and over.
- Youth suicide is increasing at the greatest rate.

1  Consider what patterns are revealed.
2  Why do you think there are these variations?
3  Can you really trust such statistics? Start making a list of problems with statistics. You will encounter a lot of statistics during this book but they should always be read critically (see pp. 94–5 and 289).

will sample key studies. In them we will explore what sociology is for and what sociologists do. Here we look briefly at some of the key roles that a sociologist performs in a modern society.

First, sociologists are *researchers*: they document the nature of the social times we live in. We need data about the human world – otherwise we would be living in the dark. You will find a lot of 'data' in this book, and ways of finding more, and sociology maps information on such things as population size, economic functioning, shifts in religious belief, the move to the cities, the functioning state of whole countries and regions – along with concerns over crime, migration patterns, family life and the nature of social class.

A second task of the sociologist is that of the *theorists*: they aim to foster deeper understanding of what is going on, and provide a way for sociological knowledge to become cumulative – wisdom can be passed on and developed from generation to generation. Data from research never just speaks for itself. We need more than information and data: we need wider understanding and the capacity to make connections, sense links with the rich heritage of thinkers from the past, and shun seeing facts in isolation and out of context. Sociologists develop wider ideas and help facilitate theoretical and analytical thinking about society. Random facts and information are of little value.

A third role is the sociologist as *critic* (and, often, change agent). As we have already seen, sociology fosters a critical attitude to social life, seeing that things are never quite what they seem, and common sense never quite that common. Sociologists question and interrogate the taken-for-granted society, and connect it to other possible worlds. They subvert the thinking as usual. Behind this, quite often sociologists seek progress and a 'better' world. Sociology developed as tool to build an emancipatory knowledge: to help us understand the world in order to advance it.

Next comes the sociologist as *educator and teacher* (and these days the media disseminator and the web coordinator of social knowledge). Amongst the many things that sociologists can do in this applied role is writing and teaching. But they also can provide governments (and world organisations and non-governmental organisations) with information that helps in planning future

pathways for society, and nowadays they also work in media of all kinds (from journalism to websites), helping society to find its way around social knowledge.

There are many other roles for sociologists. Sociologists can be *artists*, generating ideas that can inform and enhance human creativity. Sociological ideas feed into worlds of art, literature, music, poetry and film. Sociologists can be *policy shapers*, advising governments and groups on the nature of the social world. They can also be *commentators* and *public intellectuals*, providing a social diagnosis of the ills of our time. Sociologists can help make a contribution to the human world by clarifying options, sensing alternatives and signposting directions for the future.

They are also *dialogists*, creating organised dialogues across the multiple different voices to be heard in a society. At every level of social life we confront conflicts, and sociologists can facilitate listening to different voices and maybe evolving common ground as a basis for discussions. They look at global conflicts (e.g. wars between nation-states, and conflicts between men and women), at national conflicts (e.g. ethnic, religious), at local conflicts (e.g. community politics, splits between social movements), and even at personal conflicts (e.g. domestic violence, breakdown of trust between friends). In all this, they can help lay out different arguments and sources of tension, and seek greater understanding on both sides.

Finally, then, sociology has a wide and generic role in society: the sociologist becomes the *critical citizen in society*. This is the most general and possibly the most valuable role of the sociologist. Here we *can all help create a widespread social awareness and what might be called social thinking*, which is often in contradistinction to common sense, which usually sees the world in more individualising and 'natural' terms. Sociology helps people to challenge what is taken for granted, to look at their social world creatively, and to make the link between the private problems of individuals and the public problems of cultures. Sociologists can help people to make social connections and can foster aware citizens who know what is going on around them. Sociology *can help create critical, socially aware citizens*, who can make informed and knowledgeable decisions.

# What is public sociology?

Sociology involves multiple audiences and groups, as Figure 1.1 shows. It is an academic discipline to be studied (sometimes rather remotely) by students and lecturers in colleges and universities. But its subject matter also means that it is a matter of great general concern to the wider public. As you will see throughout this book, sociology's subjects are 'hot topics': the environment, pollution, family breakdown, religious conflicts, extreme differences of wealth and poverty, violence, terrorism, war, cyberspace, 'youth', women and men – and so on. Most people have views on such matters, and often like a good argument with friends and family about them. So sociology potentially has a very wide 'popular audience'. But can sociology help with all these issues?

Well, yes. Sociology's history can certainly show a strand of work that is indeed very aloof. But many sociologists have wanted to make their work more accessible and less 'ivory tower'. They have also shown a passion for social change. Marx, for example, was a revolutionary, wanting to see the overthrow of the entire social order to bring about greater equality and social justice. He wrote very academic books, but also produced very readable tracts – see his *Manifesto of the Communist Party* (Marx and Engels, 1894). Others have not been so extreme but, as you will see throughout this book, over and over again, many sociologists study the world in order to provide a better understanding and achieve an improved social world. They want to make a difference. They work with social movements, speak through the media, write books, engage with public policy formation. Sociology is not all moribund theory abstraction and neither is it senseless fact grabbing: it often shows a deep concern and engagement with the social world and how sociology's findings and ideas can be made more accessible. It lives at the interface between everyday life, public life and academic/intellectual work. Throughout this book there will be 'boxes' where you can consider some of the issues involved.

We will look at the ways in which public sociology can:

- Understand the audiences it is trying to reach – help us to see how the understanding of students, a television audience, a website reader, a social activist, a policy-maker, a social worker or a politician will start from different positions; and the sociologist may well have to approach these different audiences in different ways.
- Clarify language and definitions – help us to know which words to use, to understand 'new words' which keep appearing, and to appreciate the pitfalls of jargon and the advantages of clear speaking.
- Recognise positions – help us to see the moral and political positions which surround all arguments.
- Provide basic knowledge backgrounds – such as legal frameworks and information databases (now made so much easier through access to the internet).
- Assist in understanding research findings – so we know enough about the methods of researchers to make sense of their data.
- Present public debates – help us to understand the issues involved on various sides.
- Appreciate the different kinds of media that can present these issues – from television and film to debate and website blogging.
- Identify key spokespeople and organisations that work on these public issues.

You can find out a great deal about public sociology on Michael Burawoy's website, including the original article. *See*: http://burawoy.berkeley.edu. You can also hear him lecturing on public sociology on YouTube.

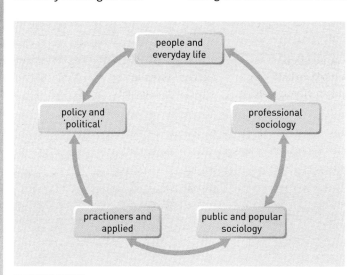

**Figure 1.1** The 5 Ps: the circle of sociological life
*Source*: Plummer (2010: 192).

## The sociologist as critical citizen: sociology in everyday life

## Sociology and social marginality

Sociological thinking is especially common among social 'outsiders'. Social marginality is something we all experience from time to time. For some categories of people, however, being an outsider is part of daily living. Great literature often speaks from an outsider's point of view: Shakespeare's Shylock in *The Merchant of Venice* or Albert Camus's *The Outsider*, for example. The more acute people's social marginality, the more likely they are to be keenly aware of their surroundings and to see the world from a different perspective. To an extent, sociology is an outsider discipline.

No Turkish guest worker in Germany or Pakistani in England lives for long without learning how much 'race' affects personal experience. But white people, because they are the dominant majority in these countries, think about 'race' only occasionally and often take the attitude that race affects only people of colour rather than themselves as well.

Much the same is true of women, gays and lesbians, people with disabilities, the homeless and the very old. All those who can be relegated to the outskirts of social life typically become more aware of social patterns that others take for granted. Turning the argument around, for any of us to develop a sociological perspective we must step back a bit from our familiar routines to look on our lives with a new awareness and curiosity. Sociology leads to a questioning of all that is taken for granted. Seeing the world through the eyes of others 'on the margins' can help us to see the way the world works more clearly. And it raises challenging questions about how margins and boundaries come about.

## Sociology and social crisis

Periods of massive social change or social crisis throw everyone a little off balance, and this, too, stimulates sociological vision. C. Wright Mills (1959), a noted US sociologist, illustrated this principle by recalling the Great Depression of the 1930s. As the unemployment rate in the United States soared to 25 per cent (as it did elsewhere – the depression was 'global'), people out of

work could not help but see general social forces at work in their particular lives. Rather than personalising their plight by claiming 'Something is wrong with me. I can't find a job', they took a more sociological approach, observing: 'The economy has collapsed. There are no jobs to be found!'

Conversely, sociological thinking often fosters social change. The more we learn about the operation of 'the system', the more we may wish to change it in some way. As women and men have confronted the power of gender, for example, many have actively tried to reduce the traditional differences that distinguish men and women.

In short, an introduction to sociology is an invitation to learn a new way of looking at familiar patterns of social life. At this point, we might well consider whether this invitation is worth accepting. In other words, what are the benefits of learning to use the sociological perspective?

## Benefits of the sociological perspective

As we learn to use the sociological perspective, we can readily apply it to our daily lives. Doing so provides four general benefits.

1 *It becomes a way of thinking, a 'form of consciousness' that challenges familiar understandings of ourselves and of others,* so that we can critically assess the truth of commonly held assumptions. Thinking sociologically, in other words, we may realise that ideas we have taken for granted are not always true. As we have already seen, a good example of a widespread but misleading 'truth' is that Europe is populated with 'autonomous individuals' who are personally responsible for their lives. Thinking this way, we are sometimes too quick to praise particularly successful people as superior to others whose more modest achievements mark them as personally deficient. A sociological approach becomes a way of thinking with an ingrained habit of asking awkward questions. It prompts us to ask whether these beliefs are actually true and, to the extent that they are not, why they are so widely held. Sociology challenges the 'taken for granted'.

2 *It enables us to assess both the opportunities and the constraints that characterise our lives.* Sociological thinking leads us to see that, for better or worse, our society operates in a particular way. It helps

## Looking across divides: sociology and other disciplines

Sociology is a branch of the academic field of social science and the humanities, and hence has many friends it can work alongside. Of course, sociology does have its own distinctive take on matters, as we show in the text, but it overlaps with many other fields. At points in this book you will sense sociologists' close affinity to historians, philosophers, anthropologists, students of literature and many others. This should not be seen as a problem. Connecting with these, not breaking from other ways of thinking, is a feature of twenty-first-century thought.

To start with, you may like to consider how sociology connects to:

- *History.* All social phenomena – from politics, economies, religions and wars to shopping, celebrities, cooking, lovemaking and space travel – have histories. All social actions must be located in time. Sociologists must ask: 'Just when did this happen, and what were the circumstances that led to it?'
- *Philosophy.* Behind all theories and research findings are ideas and assumptions which shape them – about 'human nature', 'freedom', the 'reality of the world' and even what 'knowledge really is'. Philosophy is the under-labourer of all knowledge: it digs around in these assumptions and can help us to clarify them. (But if we are not careful, it can lose us in language that does not help.) Sociologists must ask: 'Just what are the assumptions – of human nature, of choice, of social order – that lie behind sociological study?'
- *Anthropology.* This is the study of people's ways of life and is the cornerstone of understanding 'ethnocentrism' – *the practice of judging another culture by the standard of one's own culture.* Sociology must always recognise that people inhabit very different social worlds, and anthropology – especially the variant that is called 'cultural anthropology' – is a great helper in this. Sociologists must ask: 'How are social things organised in different ways across different cultures?'
- *Literature.* Novels – and drama, poetry, film, art, music – are all visions of human life. They create little worlds we can enter to appreciate the nature of the social and the human. Sociologists have a similar task – though they do not create imaginary worlds so much as study existing ones. But common themes and understandings are everywhere. Sociologists must ask: 'What are the different social worlds that humans inhabit and create. Can we imagine other worlds in other times and places?'

We could ask similar questions through economics, politics, art and biology. In addition, there are also newer disciplines – found mainly towards the end of the twentieth century – which can play prominent roles within sociology. Thus, look for help from *women's/feminist studies, media/film studies, cultural studies, cyber studies, ethnic and race studies, human rights, postcolonial studies, citizenship studies, queer studies* and the like. Most of these newer disciplines focus on a particular issue – women, gender, media and human rights – and tend to be more interdisciplinary. But they all assist in our thinking about the social.

Sociology has much to offer, but it does not stand on its own. A sample of introductions to other disciplines includes the following:

John Tosh, *The Pursuit of History*, 2009

Nigel Warburton, *Philosophy*, 4th edn, 2004

Peter Metcalf, *Anthropology*, 2005

Hans Bertens, *Literary Theory*, 2007

us to see the pattern and order that is found in all societies. Moreover, in the game of life, we may decide how to play our cards, but it is society that deals us the hand. The more we understand the game, the more effective players we will be. Sociology helps us to understand what we are likely and unlikely to accomplish for ourselves and how we can pursue our goals most effectively.

3 *It helps us to be active participants in our society.* Without an awareness of how society operates, we are likely to accept the status quo. We might just think that this is how all societies are, or how all people behave 'naturally'. But the greater our understanding of the operation of society, the more we can take an active part in shaping social life. For some, this may mean embracing society as it is;

others, however, may attempt nothing less than changing the entire world in some way. The discipline of sociology advocates no one particular political orientation, and sociologists themselves weigh in at many points across the political spectrum. But it does have a built-in 'critical' tendency. And evaluating any aspect of social life – whatever one's eventual goal – depends on the ability to identify social forces and to assess their consequences. Some 50 years ago, C. Wright Mills claimed that developing what he called the 'sociological imagination' would help people to become more active citizens. This major sociological thinker is highlighted in the box on p. 21. Other notable sociologists are featured throughout this book.

4  *It enables us to recognise human differences and human suffering and to confront the challenges of living in a diverse world.* Sociological thinking highlights both the world's remarkable social variety and its sufferings, real and potential. 'The British', for example, represent only a small proportion of the world's population, and, as the remaining chapters of this book explain, many human beings live in dramatically different societies. People everywhere tend to define their own way of life as proper and 'natural', and to dismiss the lifestyles of those who differ. But the sociological perspective encourages us to think critically about the relative strengths and weaknesses of all ways of life – including our own. It also encourages us to see the many forms of suffering that occur – poverty,

THINKERS & THEORY

# The Enlightenment and the Age of Reason

**Key idea: the world can be made better through the application of human reason.**

'Modern Sociology was born of Enlightenment Thinking. Its approximate boundaries are represented by – at its emergence – the work of Rene Descartes (1596–1650) born in France but spending much of his adult life in Holland, and, at its conclusion, the work of Immanuel Kant (1724–1804) living and working in Germany in the second half of the eighteenth century' (Evans, 2007: 23). Descartes wanted to know 'How do I know? And can I be certain?' He concluded with the famous aphorism: I think therefore I am. *Cogito ergo sum.* Kant characterised his difficult work as a bridge into eighteenth-century rationalism and empiricism.

The Enlightenment began in England (with Locke) and Scotland (with Adam Smith (1723–90) and David Hume

(1711–76)) and was developed in France in the eighteenth century (with Diderot, Voltaire and the Encyclopaediasts). In its broadest sense it takes in artists such as Hogarth, authors such as Jonathan Swift and maybe Jane Austen, and composers such as Mozart. Just as today we sense a new spirit of the times with the growth of the new information technology, this was also a time when new intellectul currents swept Europe. Rationality, science, progress and a certain questioning of religious dogma were among the hallmarks.

Jean-Jacques Rousseau (1712–78) said: 'Man is born free; and everywhere he is in chains.' This famous quote from Chapter 1 of *The Social Contract* opens up debates as to what human nature is and ultimately suggests that living under the 'general will' provides a remedy for the corruption by greed and meanness of the perfect state of nature into which man is born 'the noble savage'.

Voltaire (1694–1778) said: 'In this best of all possible worlds . . . all is for the best.' In his widely read work *Candide*, Voltaire suggests this is not true – indeed quite the opposite is

shown as 'our hero' Candide travels the world to face one horror after another. Life is not easy! It is better to cultivate one's own small garden and to ignore the rest, said Voltaire, ('Il faut cultiver son jardin'; Chapter 30).

Thomas Hobbes (1588–1679) said: 'No arts; no letters; no society; and which is worst of all, continual fear and danger of violent death; the life of man, solitary, poor, nasty, brutish and short.' Living through Britain's civil wars, Hobbes suggests in *Leviathan* that people should hand over power to a sovereign state and agree to live by its laws. The ruler's authority must be absolute, or there would be chaos.

John Locke (1632–1704) stated that knowledge depends upon our senses – we need to look at the material and empirical world. We need to recognise the supreme authority of the law; but it is conditional on an implied contract between subject and ruler. The ruler's authority is not absolute.

A good guide to the Enlightenment is: Paul Hyland, *The Enlightenment: A Sourcebook and Reader* (2003).

marital breakdown, illness, war and so on – and to see how such problems often arise because of the ways in which societies are organised.

## Some opening problems with the sociological perspective

While approaching the world sociologically brings many benefits, it also harbours some distinctive problems. Three can be mentioned at the outset.

1 *Sociology is part of a changing world*. One of the difficult things about studying sociology is that we are studying a moving object: society can change just as quickly as we study it! A 'finding' from one day may soon be proved wrong when situations and circumstances change. And, since it is a feature of the modern world that societies are changing extraordinarily rapidly, we can expect our knowledge about them to change rapidly too. For instance, many of the statistics you find in this book will be out of date by the time you read them.

2 *Sociologists are part of what they study*. 'I have seen society, and it is me.' As we are all part of society, we are all part of what we study. This cannot be otherwise, but it makes the tasks of a sociologist very difficult. Many other 'sciences' study objects that are separate from the human species, but sociologists do not. Since we are part of the very world we study, we may find it hard to distance ourselves from this world. A sociologist born in Europe may have all kinds of European assumptions which do not hold in Thailand or Brazil. With the best intentions in the world, much sociology remains *ethnocentric* – bound to a particular cultural view. Sociologists have to be *reflexive* and see themselves as part of the very things they study.

3 *Sociological knowledge becomes part of society*. The research and study that sociologists do – the books they write, the arguments they make – eventually become part of a society's knowledge about itself. Sociologists create ideas that can shape the ways in which societies work. Their work is *recursive* – it feeds back on to itself. Findings on crime – for example, that crime rates are soaring – can be reported in the media, and people then become more conscious of crime. As a result, even more crime is reported and sociologists may even study it more! There is an odd circle or cycle of knowledge at work in society and sociology, being part of this, has an impact on society.

## Social change and the Great Transformation 1

## The origins of Western sociology

Major historical events rarely just happen. They are typically products of powerful social forces that are always complex and only partly predictable. So it was with the emergence of sociology itself. Having described the discipline's distinctive perspective and surveyed some of its benefits, we can now consider how and why sociology emerged in the first place.

Although human beings have mused about society since the beginning of our history, sociology is of relatively recent origin. In many ways it was the product of the **Enlightenment**. The *French philosophes* were the cornerstone of such thinking, a 'solid, respectable clan of revolutionaries' (Gay, 1970: 9) that included Montesquieu, Rousseau and Voltaire. Such thinking signposted the arrival of the 'modern world'. The world-view of the Enlightenment highlighted, amongst other things, the following ideas:

1 Rationality and reason became a key way of organising knowledge.
2 Empiricism – we need facts and observations apprehended through the senses.
3 Science – linked especially to experimental scientific revolution.
4 Universalism – the search was on for general laws of the universe (and society).
5 Progress – the 'human condition' can be improved.
6 Individualism – the starting point for all knowledge.
7 Toleration – in the world of religious conflicts, beliefs of other nations and groups are not inherently inferior to European Christianity and different religions should be tolerated.
8 Freedom – the human condition was that of a choosing self.
9 Human nature was uniform: rational, individual and free.
10 Secularism – despite toleration, or because of it, the Enlightenment was often opposed to the Church (Hamilton, 1996).

Later – as we shall see – thinkers became very critical of this kind of thinking, but it is still pervasive in much of the modern Western world. (Watch out for the ideas of Foucault (Chapter 17) and Adorno (Chapter 22).)

## Auguste Comte: the French Revolution and positivism

**Key idea: the study of sociology is a science.**

What sort of person would invent sociology? Certainly someone living in times of momentous change. Auguste Comte (1798–1857) grew up in the wake of the French Revolution, which brought a sweeping transformation to his country. And if that wasn't sufficient, another revolution was under way: factories were sprouting up across continental Europe, recasting the lives of the entire population. Everyone living in this era became keenly aware of the state of society.

Auguste Comte (1798–1857) is usually seen as both the founder of sociology and of positivism in the social sciences. He sees them as the 'religion of humanity'. For an analysis of his work, see Mike Gane: *Auguste Comte* (2006)

*Source*: akg-images.

Drawn from his small home town by the bustle of Paris, Comte was soon deeply involved in the exciting events of his time. More than anything else, he wanted to understand the human drama that was unfolding all around him. Once equipped with knowledge about how society operates, Comte believed, people would be able to build for themselves a better future. He divided his new discipline into two parts: how society is held together (which he called social statics), and how society changes (social dynamics). From the Greek and Latin words meaning 'the study of society', Comte came to describe his work as sociology. He evolved an influential account of the stages of society – theological, metaphysical and positivist – and claimed that sociology should be part of this positivist, or scientific, phase (see pp. 63–5).

However, only in 1839 did the French social thinker Auguste Comte (introduced in the above box) coin the term *sociology* to describe a new way of looking at the world.

## Science and Western sociology

The nature of society was a major topic of enquiry for virtually all the brilliant thinkers of the ancient world, including the Chinese philosopher K'ung Futzu, also known as Confucius (551–479 BCE), and the Greek philosophers Plato (*c.* 427–347 BCE) and Aristotle (384–322 BCE).[1] Similarly, the medieval thinker St Thomas Aquinas (*c.* 1225–74), the fourteenth-century Muslim Ibn Khaldun and the French philosopher Montesquieu (1689–1755) all examined the state of human society.

[1] Throughout this text, the abbreviation BCE designates 'before the common era'. We use this terminology in place of the traditional BC ('before Christ') in recognition of religious plurality. Similarly, in place of the traditional AD (*anno Domini*, or 'in the year of our Lord'), we employ the abbreviation CE ('common era'). See also the timelines at the front of the book. This reaming is controversial, and does not seem to be widely used yet in Europe. It shows the relativity of categories. But to use a Christian-based chronology is seen by many as offensive in a world where billions are not Christian.

There have been many such social thinkers. Yet, as Emile Durkheim noted almost a century ago, none of these approached society from a truly sociological point of view.

> Looking back in history . . . we find that no philosophers ever viewed matters [with a sociological perspective] until quite recently . . . It seemed to them sufficient to ascertain what the human will should strive for and what it should avoid in established societies . . . Their aim was not to offer us as valid a description of nature as possible, but to present us with the idea of a perfect society, a model to be imitated.

(Durkheim, 1972: 57; orig. 1918)

What sets sociology apart from earlier social thought? Prior to the birth of sociology, philosophers and theologians mostly focused on imagining the ideal society. None attempted to analyse society as it really was. Pioneers of the discipline such as Auguste Comte, Emile Durkheim and Ferdinand Toennies (see below) reversed these priorities. Although they were certainly concerned with how human society could be improved, their major goal was to understand how society actually operates.

The key to achieving this objective, according to Comte, was developing a scientific approach to society. Looking back in time, Comte sorted human efforts to comprehend the world into three distinct stages: theological, metaphysical and scientific (1975; orig. 1851–54). The earliest era, extending through to the medieval period in Europe, was the *theological stage*. At this point, thoughts about the world were guided by religion, so people regarded society as an expression of God's will – at least in so far as humans were capable of fulfilling a divine plan.

With the Renaissance, the theological approach to society gradually gave way to what Comte called the *metaphysical stage*. During this period, people came to understand society as a natural, rather than a supernatural, phenomenon. Human nature figured heavily in metaphysical visions of society: Thomas Hobbes (1588–1679), for example, posited that society reflected not the perfection of God as much as the failings of a rather selfish human nature.

What Comte heralded as the final, *scientific stage* in the long quest to understand society was propelled by scientists such as Copernicus (1473–1543), Galileo[2] (1564–1642) and Isaac Newton (1642–1727). Comte's contribution came in applying this scientific approach – first used to study the physical world – to the study of society.

Comte was thus a proponent of **positivism**, defined as *a means to understand the world based on science*. As a positivist, Comte believed that society conforms to invariable laws, much as the physical world operates according to gravity and other laws of nature. Even today, most sociologists agree that science plays a crucial role in sociology. But, as Chapter 3 explains, we now realise both that human behaviour is often far more complex than natural phenomena and that science is itself more sophisticated than we thought before. Thus human beings are creatures with considerable imagination and spontaneity, so that our behaviour can never be fully explained by any rigid 'laws of society'. Likewise, the universe may be much more 'chaotic' and 'emergent' than we previously thought, making observations and laws much more difficult.

---

[2] Illustrating Comte's stages, the ancient Greeks and Romans viewed the planets as gods; Renaissance metaphysical thinkers saw them as astral influences (giving rise to astrology); by the time of Galileo, scientists understood planets as natural objects behaving in orderly ways.

# Change, transformation and sociology

Sociology was born out of the 'massive social transformation' of the past two centuries. Two great revolutions – the French Revolution of 1789 and the more general 'Industrial Revolution' traced to England in the eighteenth century – 'have all but totally dissolved the forms of social organisation in which humankind has lived for thousands of years of its previous history' (Giddens, 1986: 4). Striking transformations in eighteenth- and nineteenth-century Europe, then, drove the development of sociology. As the social ground trembled under their feet, people understandably focused their attention on society. Traditions were crumbling.

First came scientific discoveries and technological advances that produced a factory-based industrial economy. Second, factories drew millions of people from the countryside, causing an explosive growth of cities. Third, people in these burgeoning industrial cities soon entertained new ideas about democracy and political rights. Finally, the stable communities in which most people had lived for centuries started to decline. We shall briefly describe each of these four changes – though they all reappear for more detailed analysis during this book.

## 1 A new industrial economy: the growth of modern capitalism

During the European Middle Ages, most people tilled fields near their homes or engaged in small-scale *manufacturing* (a word derived from Latin words meaning 'to make by hand'). But by the end of the eighteenth century, inventors had applied new sources of energy – first water power and then steam power – to the operation of large machines, which gave birth to factories. England, the home of the Industrial Revolution, was transformed. The landscape changed radically as new cities were built. And now, instead of labouring at home, workers became part of a large and anonymous industrial workforce, toiling for strangers who owned the factories. This drastic change in the system of production generated huge poverty and mass suffering; it weakened families and 'demoralised societies'; it eroded traditions that had guided members of small communities for centuries. For many, the progress of the new machines was also the breakdown of any kind of society or social order as we previously knew it. The development of modern capitalism is considered in Chapter 4.

## 2 The growth of cities

Factories sprouting across much of Europe became magnets, attracting people in need of work. This 'pull' of work in the new industrialised labour force was accentuated by an additional 'push' as landowners fenced off more and more ground, turning farms into grazing land for sheep – the source of wool for the thriving textile mills. This 'enclosure movement' forced countless tenant farmers from the countryside towards cities in search of work in the new factories.

Many villages were soon abandoned; at the same time, however, factory towns swelled rapidly into large cities. Such urban growth dramatically changed people's lives. Cities churned with strangers, in numbers that overwhelmed available housing. Widespread social problems – including poverty, disease, pollution, crime and homelessness – were the order of the day. This was the world that Charles Dickens so vividly described in some of his nineteenth-century novels. Such social crises further stimulated development of the sociological perspective. We consider the rise of modern cities in Chapter 24.

## 3 Political change: control and democracy

During the Middle Ages, as Comte noted, most people thought of society as the expression of God's will. Royalty claimed to rule by 'divine right', and each person up and down the social hierarchy had some other part in the holy plan. Indeed, throughout history people have rarely seen themselves as being in control of their own lives. With economic development and the rapid growth of cities, changes in political thought were inevitable. Starting in the seventeenth century, every kind of tradition came under spirited attack. In the writings of Thomas Hobbes, John Locke (1632–1704) and Adam Smith (1723–90), we see a distinct shift in focus from people's moral obligations to remain loyal to their rulers, to the idea that society is the product of individual self-interest. The key phrases in the new political climate, therefore, were *individual liberty* and *individual rights*. Echoing the thoughts of Locke, the American Declaration of Independence asserts that each individual has 'certain unalienable rights', including 'life, liberty, and the pursuit of happiness'.

| Table 1.3 | Some early sociologists and how they viewed the social change of their time | | |
|---|---|---|---|
| **Sociologist** | **Earlier societies** | **Newer societies arriving** | **Explanatory dynamic?** |
| Smith and Montesquieu | Hunting, herding, agricultural | Commercial | Rise of free markets |
| Comte | Theological, metaphysical | Scientific, positivist | Science |
| Maine | Status | Contract | Changes in law |
| Spencer | Homogeneous – simple, militant | Heterogeneous – complex, industrial | Changes in population |
| Toennies | *Gemeinschaft* – community based | *Gesellschaft* – association based | Community shifts |
| Marx | Primitive communism, slavery, feudalism | Capitalism (but leading to socialism) | Economic exploitation |
| Durkheim | Mechanical solidarity | Organic solidarity | Population density and division of labour |
| Weber | Traditional | Rational-bureaucratic, secular | Changes in religion and economy (capitalism and its affinity with the Protestant ethic) |
| Simmel | Primitive production | Money and modernity | Circulation of money; Group size grows |

*Source*: Plummer (2010: 77).

The political revolution in France that began soon afterwards, in 1789, constituted an even more dramatic break with political and social traditions. As the French social analyst Alexis de Tocqueville (1805–59) surveyed his society after the French Revolution, he exaggerated only slightly when he asserted that the changes we have described amounted to 'nothing short of the regeneration of the whole human race' (1955: 13; orig. 1856). In this context, it is easy to see why Auguste Comte and other pioneers of sociology soon developed their new discipline. Sociology flowered in precisely those societies – France, Germany and England – where change was greatest.

## 4 The loss of Gemeinschaft: the eclipse of community

The German sociologist Ferdinand Toennies produced the theory of **Gemeinschaft** and **Gesellschaft** (see also Chapter 24). Toennies (1963; orig. 1887) saw the modern world as the progressive loss of Gemeinschaft, or human community. He argued that the Industrial Revolution had undermined the strong social fabric of family and tradition by fostering individualism and a business-like emphasis on facts and efficiency. European and North American societies gradually became rootless and impersonal as people came to associate mostly on the basis of self-interest – the condition Toennies dubbed Gesellschaft. Toennies' thesis was that traditional societies, built on kinship and neighbourhood, nourished collective sentiments, virtue and honour. Modernisation washes across traditional society like an acid, eroding human community and unleashing rampant individualism.

Through much of the twentieth century, at least some areas of the Western world approximated Toennies' concept of Gemeinschaft. Families that had lived for generations in rural towns and villages were tightly integrated into a hard-working, slow-moving way of life. Before telephones (invented in 1876) and television (introduced in 1939, widespread after 1950), families and communities entertained themselves, communicating with distant members by letter.

Before private cars became commonplace after the Second World War, many people viewed their home town as their entire world. Inevitable tensions and conflicts – sometimes based on race, ethnicity and religion – characterised past communities. According to Toennies, however, the traditional ties of Gemeinschaft bound people of a community together, 'essentially united in spite of all separating factors' (1963: 65; orig. 1887).

The modern world turned societies inside-out so that, as Toennies put it, people are 'essentially separated in spite of uniting factors' (1963: 65; orig. 1887). This is the world of Gesellschaft where, especially in large cities, most people live among strangers and ignore those they pass on the street. Trust is hard to come by in a mobile and anonymous society in which, according to researchers, people tend to put their personal needs ahead of group loyalty and a majority of adults claim that 'you can't be too careful' in dealing with people (Russell, 1993).

Toennies' work displays a deep distrust of the notion of 'progress', which he feared amounted to the steady loss of traditional morality. Toennies stopped short of claiming that modern society was 'worse' than societies of the past and he made a point of praising the spread of rational, scientific thinking. Nevertheless, the growing individualism and selfishness characteristic of modern societies troubled him. Knowing that there could be no return to the past, he looked to the future, hoping that new forms of social organisation would develop that would combine modern rationality with traditional collective responsibility.

 To develop timelines, see the inside cover of this book and examine:

Wikipedia Timeline of Sociology
http://en.wikipedia.org/wiki/Timeline_of_sociology

Hyper soc Timeline
www.timelineindex.com/content/view/160

Timeline of the American Sociological Association
www.asanet.org/cs/root/leftnav/asa_history/
a_history_of_asa_2005_appendix_1

## Timeline Western sociology: some early landmarks in thinking about society

### Before Western sociology

551–479 BCE   Confucius, *Analects of Confucius*
469–399 BCE   Socrates and Western philosophy
384–322 BCE   Aristotle, *Poetics*; *The Nicomachean Ethics*
360 BCE       Plato, *The Republic*
973–1048      Al-Biruni, Abu Rayhan Muhammad ibn Ahmad, *Qanun-i-Masoodi*
1332–1406     Ibn-Khaldun, *Muqaddimah*

### Renaissance and Enlightenment

1651   Thomas Hobbes, *Leviathan*
1739   John Locke, *An Essay Concerning Human Understanding*
1751   William Hogarth, *Gin Lane*
1755   Jean-Jacques Rousseau, *Discourse on Inequality*
1759   Voltaire, *Candide*
1776   Adam Smith, *Wealth of Nations*
1784   Immanuel Kant, *What is Enlightenment?*

### Origins and classics

1839   Comte defines sociology as a discipline – the term is invented.
       (published 1824 August Comte's *System of Positive Politics*: introduced the term 'sociology')
1846   Marx and Engels, *The German Ideology*: the theory of materialist history is outlined.
1987   Emile Durkheim, *Suicide* – suicide statistics show just how it varies socially.
1889   William E. Du Bois, *The Philadelphia Negro* – first major study of the American Negro.
1904   Max Weber, *The Protestant Ethic and the Spirit of Capitalism* – ideas shape history, and here religion shapes capitalism.
1900   Georg Simmel, *The Philosophy of Money* – changes in organisation of money shift human relations.

### *The rise of US sociology*

1912   Charles Horton Cooley, *Human Nature and Social Order*.
1905   American Sociological Society formed (becoming American Sociological Association in 1959).
1915–30   The tradition of the 'Chicago School' associated with Robert Park and the examination of urban life.
1918–20   W. I. Thomas and Florian Znaniecki, *The Polish Peasant in Europe and America* – highly regarded five volumes
       of innovative method, theory and data on migrants and city life.
1921   Park and Burgess, *Introduction to the Science of Sociology* – first major textbook from a major new sociology
       department at Chicago University with a stress on city conflict.
1929   Robert and Helen Lynd, *Middletown* – small-town community life (Muncie) in the USA observed closely and
       especially through its class system.
1934   George Herbert Mead, *Mind, Self and Society*.

### Mid-twentieth-century sociology

1944   Theodore Adorno and Max Horkheimer, *Dialectics of Enlightenment* – asks 'why mankind, instead of entering
       into a truly human condition, is sinking into a new kind of barbarism'.
1950   David Riesman et al.'s *The Lonely Crowd* – society has moved from tradition directed to outer directed.
1951   British Sociological Association founded.
1951   Indian Sociological Association founded.
1951   Talcott Parsons, *The Social System* – theoretical treatise about the integrated social order.
1956/59   Erving Goffman, *The Presentation of Everyday Life* – micro sociological argument about social life as drama.
1957   Peter Wilmott and Michael Young, *Family and Kinship in East London* – charts changes in community and family
       life in post-Second World War England.
1959   C. Wright Mills, *The Sociological Imagination* – left critique of grand theory and overworked methodology in sociology.

## C. Wright Mills: the sociological imagination

C. Wright Mills (1916–1962) was an outspoken, radical, and left wing sociologist of the mid twentieth century. His book *The Sociological Imagination* (1959) has been extremely influential on several generations of sociologists

*Source*: Archive Photos/Stringer/Getty Images.

Charles Wright Mills (1916–62) managed to cause a stir with almost everything he did. Even arriving for a class at New York's Columbia University – clad in a sweatshirt, jeans and boots, astride his motorcycle – he usually turned some heads. During the conservative 1950s, Mills not only dressed a bit out of the mainstream, but he also produced a number of books that challenged most of the beliefs the majority of us take for granted. He was an American Marxist and he acquired both adherents and adversaries.

As Mills saw it, sociology is not some dry enterprise detached from life. Rather, he held up sociology as an escape from the 'traps' of our lives because it can show us that society – not our own foibles or failings – is responsible for many of our problems. In this way, Mills maintained, sociology transforms personal problems into public and political issues. For Mills, 'The sociological imagination enables us to grasp history and biography and the relations between the two within society. That is its task and its promise . . .' (Mills, 1967: 4; orig. 1957).

In the following excerpt, Mills describes both the power of society to shape our individual lives, and the importance of connecting our lives (biographies) to history and society:

> When a society becomes industrialised, a peasant becomes a worker; a feudal lord is liquidated or becomes a businessman. When classes rise or fall, a man is employed or unemployed; when the rate of investment goes up or down, a man takes new heart or goes broke. When wars happen, an insurance salesman becomes a rocket launcher; a store clerk, a radar man; a wife lives alone; a child grows up without a father. Neither the life of an individual nor the history of a society can be understood without understanding both.
>
> Yet men do not usually define the troubles they endure in terms of historical change . . . The well-being they enjoy, they do not usually impute to the big ups and downs of the society in which they live. Seldom aware of the intricate connection between the patterns of their own lives and the course of world history, ordinary men do not usually know what this connection means for the kind of men they are becoming and for the kinds of history-making in which they might take part. They do not possess the quality of mind essential to grasp the interplay of men and society, of biography and history, of self and world . . .
>
> What they need . . . is a quality of mind that will help them to [see] . . . what is going on in the world and . . . what may be happening within themselves. It is this quality . . . that . . . may be called the sociological imagination. Always keep your eyes open to the image of man – the generic notion of his human nature – which by your work you are assuming and implying; and also to the image of history – your notion of how history is being made. In a word, continually work out and revise your views of the problems of history, the problems of biography, and the problems of a social structure in which biography and history intersect. Keep your eyes open to the varieties of individuality, and to the modes of epochal change. Use what you see and what you imagine as the clues to your study of the human variety . . . know that many personal troubles cannot be solved merely as troubles, but must be understood in terms of public issues – and in terms of the problems of history making. Know that the human meaning of public issues must be revealed by relating them to personal troubles and to the problems of individual life. Know that the problems of social science, when adequately formulated, must include both troubles and issues, both biography and history, and the range of their intricate relations. Within that range the life of the individual and the making of societies occur; and within that range the sociological imagination has its chance to make a difference in the quality of human life in our time.

(Mills, 1967: 3–5, 225–6; orig. 1957)

This triple focus, on *biography, history and structure*, is sociology's heritage (see Bipul Kumar Bhadra, 1998).

(Notice that in this excerpt Mills uses male pronouns to apply to all people. It is interesting – even ironic – that an outspoken critic of society like Mills reflected the conventional writing practices of his time as far as gender was concerned. But he was writing in the 1950s, before gender became a key issue for sociology.)

# Sociology and the significance of change

Living through the momentous changes brought about by the French Revolution and the Industrial Revolution must have been both exciting and dangerous. It is hard for the twenty-first-century person to grasp what it must have been like. But this was precisely the period that the earliest sociologists lived through and why they were driven to understand such changes and to consider where it may all have been heading. Sociology was born out of this firmament of change.

Yet sociologists reacted differently to the new social order then, just as they respond differently to society today. Some, including Auguste Comte and later Ferdinand Toennies, feared that people would be uprooted from long-established local communities and overpowered by change. So, in a conservative approach, Comte sought to shore up the family and traditional morality.

In contrast, Karl Marx (1818–83) worried little about the loss of tradition. But he could not condone the way industrial technology concentrated its great wealth in the hands of a small elite, while so many others faced hunger and misery. We examine his ideas at length in Chapter 4.

Clearly, Comte and Marx advanced radically different prescriptions for the problems of modernity. Yet they had in common the conviction that society rests on much more than individual choice. The sociological perspective animates the work of each, revealing that people's individual lives are framed by the broader society in which they live. This lesson, of course, remains as true today as it was a century ago.

## Social change and the Great Transformation 2

## The digital-information-network-cyborg society

Sociology may have been born of the Industrial Revolution but it has fast moved into the Cyber Revolution. In the twenty-first century, living in society – and studying it – is very different from the days of sociology's founders. The development of digital technologies, the spread of information technologies and the creation of new ways of communicating across the world since the later twentieth century has been an extraordinarily rapid development. In many countries across the world, it has become part of mainstream life in less than 20 years. Bearing in mind that the World Wide Web was not launched until 1991, already over 180 countries are connected and there are now over 100 million users in the United States alone. A new generation, the Net Generation, for whom the use of personal computers, information technology and the internet is taken for granted, is growing up. Brought up on Nintendo games and computers, they create a huge generation gap, often reversing adult–child roles as children come to know so much more about these things than either their teachers or their parents. Many 'users' are young, male and relatively wealthy: these are what Douglas Rushkoff (1999) calls the 'Digital Kids'. That said, more and more women are becoming involved; information technology is spreading through the classes and ethnicities; and it is moving through more groups across the world. One report in 2010 suggested that young people spent on average seven hours a day using the new technologies of various kinds; another recorded that there were at least 250 million Facebook sites in use by mid-2010. Growth in mobile phone use has been dramatic, as has growth in internet usage. Table 1.4 shows the numbers using the internet worldwide in 2009.

It is not quite clear yet what is the best term to use to describe this rapid change. Various suggestions have been made and we will use and discuss them variously though this book – as they highlight different aspects of the broad social change we are flagging here. They are:

- *The Digital Age*. This highlights the computerisation of life, the shift from analogue to digital, and the miniaturisation of these technologies which can now be found in all the smallest gadgets and gizmos of everyday life – from washing machines to watches to iPads and iPhones. Digitalisation is the key process here.

- *The Cyborg Age*. This highlights the ways in which human beings are more and more becoming adapted to and compelled to live with all manner of technologies, from transplants to space travel (see Chapter 20).

- *The Information Age*. This highlights the rapid growth of production and availability of all kinds of data and information. No society in history has been flooded with so much data that is available to so many. Wikipedia alone has in excess of 14 million articles – bigger than any encyclopedia ever imagined in the past.

| World regions | Population (2010 est.) | Internet users 31 Dec. 2000 | Internet users Latest data | Penetration ( % population) | Growth 2000–10 |
|---|---|---|---|---|---|
| **Table 1.4** | **World internet usage and population statistics: 2010** | | | | |
| Africa | 1,013,779,050 | 4,514,400 | **110,931,700** | 10.9% | 2,357.3% |
| Asia | 3,834,792,852 | 114,304,000 | **825,094,396** | 21.5% | 621.8% |
| Europe | 813,319,511 | 105,096,093 | **475,069,448** | 58.4% | 352.0% |
| Middle East | 212,336,924 | 9,284,800 | **63,240,946** | 29.8% | 1,825.3% |
| North America | 344,124,450 | 108,096,800 | **266,224,500** | 77.4% | 146.3% |
| Latin America/Caribbean | 592,556,972 | 18,068,919 | **204,689,836** | 34.5% | 1,032.8% |
| Oceania/Australia | 34,700,204 | 7,620,480 | **21,263,990** | 61.3% | 179.0% |
| **WORLD TOTAL** | 6,845,609,960 | 360,985,492 | **1,966,514,816** | **28.7%** | 444.8% |

*Notes*: (1) Internet usage and world population statistics are for 30 June 2010. (2) Demographic (population) numbers are based on data from the US Census Bureau. (3) Internet usage information comes from data published by Nielsen Online, the International Telecommunications Union, GfK, local regulators and other reliable sources.

*Source*: www.internetworldstats.com. Copyright © 2000–10, Miniwatts Marketing Group. All rights reserved worldwide.

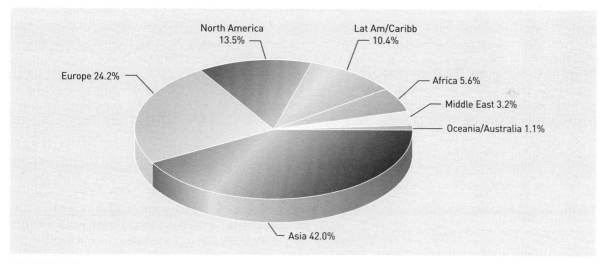

| **Figure 1.2** | Internet users in the world: distribution by regions, 2010 |
|---|---|
| | *Source*: Internet World Stats, www.internetworldstats.com/stats.htm © 2010, Miniwatts Marketing Group. |

- *The Network Society*. This highlights the ways in which new ways of communicating and relating have developed. Mobile phones have put us in 'perpetual contact' and Facebook (with some 500 million global users in mid-2010) has given us new ways of building friendship networks.

    (Both of these latter terms are used by the sociologist Manuel Castells in his major three volume book, *The Information Society* (see p. 200).)

- *The Virtual Age*. This highlights the mediated nature of reality. The twenty-first-century world is increasingly a world where reality is less direct and instead mediated through some technology – a mobile phone, a screen, a bar code.

## Sociology and the new information order

In the face of this, sociology is changing its nature. It is doing this in two ways:

• *New topics*. Sociologists now have a vast array of new fields to examine – from digital dating to digital democracies. The list in the *Living in the twenty-first century* box shows some of the new topics that are emerging in sociology and which will be featured in this book.

• *New methods*. Sociologists now have a vast array of new tools with which to study society – along with new problems in doing research. How do Google, YouTube, Wikipedia, Twitter and Facebook help sociology? This is a challenge for contemporary sociology. What is the role of the new technologies (digital television, web, mobile, MP3, digital imagery, cybercam, etc.), their formats (Wikipedia,

LIVING IN THE C21ST

# Living the digital life

The Information Age is no longer new. It is well settled into twenty-first-century life across the world and many now move seamlessly across 'real' and 'virtual' worlds, making them interconnected on a daily basis. The recognition of this has had profound effects on sociological thinking. Here, together, is a guide to some of the issues raised about digital life in this book.

| | |
|---|---|
| Studying sociology | Web search and Wikipedia (Chapter 1) |
| Globalisation | Network theory and global networks (Chapter 2) |
| Doing research | Transformation of research methods on line: Google, YouTube, network groups (Chapter 3) |
| Society | Post-industrial society (Chapter 4) |
| Culture | The arrival of texting; the flow of information; the culture of the internet (Chapter 5) |
| Organisations | Mobile phones, blogging, Facebook: the Network Society, Manuel Castells (Chapter 6) |
| Interactions | Cyber-self; internet communication; network groups like Facebook; 'Hi-Tech Harry Potters' (Chapter 7) |
| Inequalities | The digital divide (Chapters 8–14); the new ICT4 |
| Economy | The global economy; outsourcing; teleworking; 'Disneyisation' (Chapter 15) |
| Polity | Online social movements; digital democracies (Chapter 16) |
| Crime | The surveillance society; identity theft; cybercrimes (Chapter 17) |
| Families and personal life | Households and personal cultures: transformations of intimate life through internet and mobile phones (Chapter 18) |
| Religion | Cyber-churches; growth of e-religions (Chapter 19) |
| Education | The 'e-revolution'; digital ways of thinking; Wikiworld (Chapter 20) |
| Health | Cyber-health (Chapter 21) |
| Media | Digitalisation; iPods; YouTube; Baudrillard (Chapter 22) |
| Science | Donna Haraway; biotechnology; space travel; cyberworlds (Chapter 23) |
| Cities | The digital city (Chapter 24) |
| The environment | High costs of all this to the environment (Chapter 25) |
| Part 6: Resources | This whole section is designed to connect you up with the large number of electronic resources available to the student (e.g. websites, YouTube, electronic maps) and also give a few more tips on things like 'developing a critical cyber attitude' and 'thinking visually'. |

blogs, video-sharing websites, Google searches, etc.) and new social processes (e.g. e-education, i-labs, etc.) in social research? How can the new IT, which is clearly here to stay but is also likely to change in unexpected ways, be fruitfully and carefully used in doing sociology? We look at this more throughout the book but especially in Chapter 3 (and see the 'Big debate' on Wikipedia at the end of this chapter).

We now live in social worlds saturated with information about society and a startling array of ways of accessing it. We can access large amounts of social life at the press of a button – something our ancestors could not do. And we can find – on television, through photography, in film and documentary, in the everyday press and interviews, in the work and research of a myriad of pressure groups and non-governmental organisations – a staggering amount of stuff about society. In a way, everybody can now be their own sociologist: the material is there to be thought about. But thinking is just what is required. No data or information is just the automatic truth about society. The new technologies change patterns of communication and create new virtual worlds for many. They are profoundly shaping our relationship to information and knowledge. How does information technology shift the ways in which we do both our everyday life and our intellectual work? How does living in the Information Age shape the ways we now do sociology? These will be ongoing concerns in this book.

## Futures: a world brimming with change

Just as the changes brought by the nineteenth and twentieth centuries were momentous, so too are the changes that are happening now in the twenty-first century. This is an era which is being revolutionised by digital technologies, new media, new sciences such as the new reproductive technologies, and new transnational movements and global interconnections. It is an era when traditional families, religions, patterns of work and government are often being rethought. More and more, people are not given a clear blueprint on how to live their lives, as they often were in the past. Instead they have to ask: what kind of life do I want to lead? They become more individualised, less committed to common standards, more prone to self-reflection. It is an era when divisions and inequalities of class, ethnicity, age and gender have become more and more noticeable and often increased, and it is a world where significant new conflicts over religion and culture seem rife. All of these ideas will need defining, describing, analysing and explaining, and this is the continuing task for sociologists in the new century – as well as the task for this introductory book. Just as sociology was born of the Industrial Revolution, now it finds renewed excitement at the challenge of what we shall call the postmodern or information society.

In subsequent chapters of this book, then, we delve into some of these changes. We will look at the steady move to modernity and modern societies, and how these days this may be transforming into other kinds of (global, digital, postmodern) society. We will discuss the major issues that concern contemporary sociologists. These pivotal social forces include culture, inequality, social class, race, ethnicity, gender, the economy and the family. They all involve ways in which individuals are guided, united and divided in the larger arena of society. Sociology is a challenging discipline, highly relevant to a world brimming with change. This book sets out to explore a little of this. Welcome to the challenge.

# SUMMARY

1 Sociology is the systematic and critical study of society. It questions what people take for granted. It looks at social worlds as humanly produced.

2 The sociological perspective reveals 'the general in the particular' or the power of society to shape our lives. Because people in Western countries tend to think in terms of individual choice, recognising the impact of society on our lives initially seems like 'seeing the strange in the familiar' – 'defamiliarising the familiar'.

3 Public sociology tries to engage sociology with the wider world and the wider public. The circle of sociological life suggests groups involved in sociological knowledge. Sociologists have many roles and tasks to perform: as researchers, theorists, critics, educators, practitioners and critical citizens.

4 Socially marginal people are more likely than others to perceive the effects of society. For everyone, periods of social crisis foster sociological thinking.

5 There are at least four general benefits to using the sociological perspective. First, it challenges our familiar understandings of the world, helping us separate fact from fiction; second, it helps us appreciate the opportunities and constraints that frame our lives; third, it encourages more active participation in society; and fourth, it increases our awareness of social diversity locally and in the world as a whole.

6 There are three problems in studying sociology. First, societies change very rapidly; second, we are part of the societies we study; and third, sociology itself becomes a part of society.

7 Auguste Comte gave sociology its name in 1838. Whereas previous social thought had focused on what society ought to be, Comte's new discipline of sociology used scientific methods to understand society as it is. Sociology emerged as a reaction to the rapid transformation of Europe during the eighteenth and nineteenth centuries.

8 A first major transformation shows that four key dimensions of change – the rise of an industrial economy, the explosive growth of cities, the emergence of new political ideas and the decline of community – helped focus people's attention on the operation of society.

9 A second major transformation might be appearing, variously called the Digital, Cyborg, Information, Network or Virtual Age. Quite what it is to be called and what its features are will be raised throughout the book.

CONNECT UP: Turn to Part 6 of this book for key resources and link up with the book's website, which links to these resources
SEE: www.pearsoned.co.uk/plummer

## MYTASKLIST

# Ten suggestions for going further

## 1 Connect up with Part Six and the Sociology Web Resources

As you work through ideas and think about the issues raised in this chapter, look at the accompanying website and the resource centre at the end of this book which connects to it. There is a lot here to help you move on. To link up, see: www.pearson.co.uk/plummer.

- For a start, just spend some time surfing around and glancing over the final section of this book.

## 2 Review the chapter

*Briefly summarise (in a paragraph) just what this chapter has been about.* Consider: (a) What have you learned? (b) What do you disagree with? Be critical. And (c) How would you develop all this? How could you get more detail on matters that interest you?

## 3 Pose questions

(a) Consider how sociology differs from economics, politics, psychology, history, literature and journalism. Using the box on p. 4, try to define sociology and see what is distinctive about it.

(b) How does using the sociological perspective make us seem less in control of our lives? In what ways does it give us greater power over our surroundings?

(c) Give a sociological explanation of why sociology developed where and when it did. Examine whether it had 'biases' and, if so, what they were.

(d) Read or watch some science fiction, then write a futuristic account of the society in which your grandchildren will live, based upon your current knowledge of any new social trends.

(e) Discuss the nature of public sociology. What does the term mean? Scan the book to see what sorts of things are going to be discussed in these boxes.

## 4 Explore key words

Many concepts have been introduced in this chapter. There is a glossary of key concepts at the end of this book, but sometimes you will wish to explore the meanings of concepts more fully. For this, you will need a dictionary of sociology. There are many available. Among them are:

*The Penguin Dictionary of Sociology* (5th rev. edn, 2006)

*The Concise Oxford Dictionary of Sociology* (4th edn, 2009)

*The Cambridge Dictionary of Sociology* (1st edn, 2006)

Tony Lawson and Joan Garrod, *The Complete A–Z Sociology Handbook* (4th edn, 2009)

*The Concise Encyclopedia of Sociology* (1st edn, 2010)

## 5 Search the Web

Be critical when you look at websites – see the box on p. 940 in the Resources section.

There are now a large number of websites devoted to social science and to sociology. There is a major list in Part 6 of this book – usually with links on the book's website. For a general start look at:

The Internet Sociologist
www.vts.intute.ac.uk/he/tutorial/sociologist

This is one of a national series of tutorials written by qualified tutors, lecturers and librarians from across the UK. It is part of the Intute: Virtual Training Suite, funded by JISC.

The following sites may also be helpful:

Sociology Central
www.sociology.org.uk

The Sociolog
www.sociolog.com

SocioSite
www.pscw.uva.nl/sociosite

The SocioWeb
www.socioweb.com/~markbl/socioweb

## 6  Watch a DVD

Each chapter will suggest a few films that may be worth a look. As an opener, you might like to look at three 'classic' films that hold very different views of what society is like:

- Fritz Lang's *Metropolis* (1926): a futuristic account.
- Frank Capra's *It's a Wonderful Life* (1946): a tale of small-town America.
- David Lynch's *Blue Velvet* (1986): another tale of small-town America but one that is very different and not for the weak-hearted or squeamish (be warned: this last film is strong stuff and not recommended for all).

A comparison of the three kinds of society depicted would make for an interesting discussion! Look also at:

- Harold Ramis's *Groundhog Day* (1993): in which everybody pretty much does the same thing every day. It is a good way of thinking about the ways in which everyday life is often routine and taken for granted.

A good book that will help you to 'see' films sociologically is Jean-Anne Sutherand and Kathryn Fettey *Cinematic Sociology* (2010).

## 7  Read and think

Two classic introductions to the field, now read by millions of students and still worth a look at are:

Peter Berger, *Invitation to Sociology* (1963)

C. Wright Mills, *The Sociological Imagination* (1959)

There are many other recent ones: see for example:

Pamela Abbott, Claire Wallace and Melissa Tyler, *An Introduction to Sociology: Feminist Perspectives* (3rd edn, 2005) – an introductory text which provides a strong feminist perspective.

Zygmunt Bauman and Tim May, *Thinking Sociologically* (rev. edn, 2001) – a leading sociologist updates his views on what it means to be a sociologist.

Charles Lemert, *Social Things* (4th edn, 2008) – a very lively, often personal but also comprehensive coverage. Strongly recommended.

Ken Plummer, *Sociology: The Basics* (2010) – from one of the authors of this book, eight pathways into sociology are introduced for fostering a sociological imagination.

A useful guide to the Enlightenment is:

Paul Hyland, *The Enlightenment: A Sourcebook and Reader* (2003)

A good overview of Western society is:

Mary Evans, *A Short History of Society* (2006).

### Newspapers, magazines and journals

Much useful reading is contained in magazines or journals which come out at regular intervals, and all sociologists must read the news (but maybe on websites) regularly. In fact, sociologists can become very dependent on these for the latest findings. Key world newspapers (such as the *Guardian*, the *Washington Post* and *Le Monde*) all have their own websites.

*tip*  Make sure you read a good newspaper – one with world news and serious discussion. Search for its home page by its title, then make it an online favourite so you can look at it regularly.

Two very readable popular magazines for sociology students – even worth subscribing to – are:

- *Sociology Review*: Search Philip Allan Publishers. Published four times a year. Full of short, up-to-date articles on key issues in sociology and well illustrated. With a strong focus on the UK, this is useful for the emerging sociologist. See: www.philipallan.co.uk/sociologyreview/index.htm

- *New Internationalist*. Search New Internationalist. Published monthly. This takes a clear political stance and is packed full of valuable information on the 'global state' of the world. The magazine is a must for world activists for change. See: www.newint.org

## 8  Connect and integrate

Many of the ideas in this chapter can also be developed by looking at other chapters. For example:

- For more on the positivist method, see Chapter 3.
- For more on explanations of social change, see Chapter 4.
- For more on anomie and suicide, see Chapter 17.
- Get clear the ideas of *Public sociology* (p. 11) and *Living the digital life* (p. 24) – and follow these features as they appear throughout the book.
- But, of course, this is just the introductory chapter. Read the book!

## 9  Relax with a novel

A good start for thinking about Enlightenment thought is to read some classics of Enlightenment literature like Voltaire's *Candide* (1759) and Jonathan Swift's *Gulliver's Travels* (1726).

# 10 Engage in THE BIG DEBATE

## Debate Wikipedia and other digital tools for a digital generation

Sociology was born of the Industrial Revolution and used the growing tools of 'science' to develop. Now, in the twenty-first century, we live in the world of information science and high tech. Studying society now is very different from in the past. We are now fortunate enough to be able to access large amounts of social life at the press of a mouse, something our ancestors could never do. There are now a very large number of websites devoted to social science and to sociology – but a much vaster number which are simply devoted to social life in all its forms around the world. Quickly, and across the world, students now have access to sociology writings and world statistics online. You have access to almost any social 'scene', subculture or group you wish to know about (from alcoholics anonymous to asexuals; from xenophobia to extreme sports). You can enter the worlds of film, television and music too – saving them, filing them, editing them later. You can make digital images of anything instantly. You can chat with many specialist groups on Facebook. Indeed, you can blog and tweet your life away. It seems that the new young generation may spend as many as seven hours of each day living life through the new electronic gadgets.

All this means that the ways of doing sociology have changed. Even the way you read this book will be different – it has a website that accompanies it, and this will link you up immediately with thousands of online sites of interest. These are massive resources that were simply unavailable for students or sociologists before. As we have seen, sociology is becoming a very different enterprise. In every chapter of this book you will confront it head on. Old methods and old theories are changing: in many ways, you are the first true digital generation – the new pioneers with new challenges. These are exciting times for you. In this book you will find:

- key resources listed at the end of each chapter
- a major listing of websites and video-sharing resources in Part 6 of the book. This connects to our online website, which is very full and includes podcasts.

We no longer always use full addresses, as this is a fast-moving world and many will have changed.

But a few seconds on a search engine will usually take you there. You might want to create some home pages and 'favourites'.

So here you are, living in the digital world. And now, at the start of your course, is the time to debate some of the problems it raises. To start with, why not just look at the pros and cons of a number of the tools you are likely to use? As an exercise, spend some time surfing the net and looking for sociological entries on:

- *Google*: sensitises the first approximation of a field of inquiry and provides access to seemingly unlimited data resources.
- *Wikipedia*: raises issues about the democratisation of knowledge.
- *Amazon*: can suggest the books we want to read before we even know it ourselves.
- *YouTube*: shows the significance of a new visual (and blip) screen culture.
- *Blogs*: suggest that ongoing diaries, life stories and interviews are being made before our very eyes.
- *Facebook*: brings together new group styles that are shifting identities and patterns of communication.

 Remember, four matters are usually seen as important in evaluating material found on a website (Wilson and Carson, 2007). These concern:

- *The source*. Where does the information come from?
- *The objectivity of the author*. Might they have a particular point to push? Could it be 'propaganda'?
- *The logic of the argument*. Does it actually make sense?
- *Independent sources for the arguments or claims made*. Can you check them out elsewhere?

1 **Discuss Wikipedia.** This is the web's ever-expanding online encyclopedia. Many students rush to it these days. It seems to have all the answers, and can easily be cribbed for your essays! But this whole site also raises the question: *Just what is an encyclopedia and what is it for?* Conventionally, an encyclopedia provides stable answers to problems provided by experts in their fields. It does not change, so an encyclopedia often gets out of date quite quickly. But with Wikipedia, anyone can provide information and it will be as up to date as anyone wants to make it. It is also wide open to abuse: anyone could put anything on it! A lot of errors could be posted. And this raises the issue about what knowledge is. Is it to be fixed by experts – as in the past – or is it to be more

open, fluid and even democratic? But if this is to be the case, do you really want to risk filling up your minds with false, misleading information? This is a hot and contentious issue and now is the time for you to discuss it and ponder its implications.

Wikipedia raises major issues for the sociology of knowledge. Comparing it with any standard book encyclopedia will lead to a discussion of at least four critical issues. First, *how is this knowledge actually assembled – is it just there as a given, or is it selected by human agency?* And if it is the latter (which it is), then how does this social process take place. 'What are the social conditions for organising knowledge?' can become a topic for discussion.

Secondly, *what is the authority of the author for doing this?* Why should you trust an ageing professor who writes the entry to a standard published encyclopedia more than your friends who know nothing about it really but who can – if they want – submit entries? I know who I would trust more. A discussion of how knowledge, truth and authority are being questioned can follow.

Thirdly, *how can encyclopedias deal with the ways in which knowledge changes rapidly?* In their book forms, they often remain static for decades. Wikipedia opens up the possibility of an encyclopedia being dynamic and constantly responding to changes.

Fourthly, some of the above discussions could lead to a consideration of the democratisation of knowledge: *can ideas and knowledge be more usefully assembled through collective work than through individual expertise?* It would help here if you did a case study of the way in which Wikipedia entries are constructed – maybe constructing one, or modifying an entry. Guidelines for doing this can be found on Wikipedia itself, as well as in the useful handbook by John Broughton, *Wikipedia: The Missing Manual* (Cambridge: O'Reilly, 2008) – which perhaps your library should purchase.

To have an informed discussion on all these issues, look through some of the myriad back-up pages to Wikipedia, which show how entries are made, how changes can be made, and how records are kept for

all to see of who writes the entries and of all record modifications. Thousands of dedicated people all over the world are working to improve a fallible system, and it is good to understand this wider social process at work.

 For a really positive assessment of how Wikipeda mighty radically change the world for the better, see Juha Suoranta and Tere Vaden, *Wikiworld* (2010).

2 **Discuss Google searches** for something that interests you. Discuss the process of surfing with your friends, and share what you have come up with. Consider some of the problems that such data raise. Is all the information equally reliable, valid and truthful? Does it even make sense? Is it hurtful or even hateful in some way? What is its bias? What sources do you think you can rely on most?

3 **Discuss YouTube.** Now look at the lists of DVDs at the end of each chapter and see if you can track any of them down. Take this further: how central to social life now is the textual image? Is it becoming more important than books?

4 **Finally, read a book!** Consider whether reading books and articles is a better way to deal with issues than surfing. Does anyone in the class use an e-reader? Will books survive? Should they survive?

Later in the book we will suggest key issues to consider in using the digital world (see especially p. 939). Remember that the net is a public space – information on your site travels to you in complicated ways and leaves traces in many places. Watch out for sensitive and personal information and make sure it is restricted or encrypted. As we will see later in the book, many forms of 'deviance' have emerged around the net. And there are problems of surveillance, we will discuss in Chapter 17.

 Remember, since access to websites is open to anybody, anything could be said with no regard to truth, logic, rationality or even human kindness! So watch out and always scrutinise your data. *Develop a cyber critical attitude*: see p. 940.

# CHAPTER 2

# THINKING SOCIOLOGICALLY, THINKING GLOBALLY

IN THE MILLENNIUM YEAR OF 2000, the earth was home to some 6 billion people who lived in the cities and countryside of nearly 200 nations (by 2010 it had already grown another million). To grasp the social 'shape' of this world, imagine for a moment the planet's population reduced to a single settlement of 100 people. A visit to this 'global village' would reveal that more than half (61) of the inhabitants are from Asia, including 21 from the People's Republic of China and 17 from India. Next, in terms of numbers, we would find 13 from Africa, 12 from Europe, 8 from South America, 5 from North America and 1 from Oceania.

A study of this settlement would reveal some startling conclusions. People believe in very different 'gods': of the 100 people, 32 are Christian, 19 Muslim, 13 Hindus, 12 practise folk religions (like shamanism), 6 are Buddhists, 2 belong to other religions like Confucianism and the Bahai'i faith, 1 is Jewish and 15 are non-religious. There are some 6,000 languages but over half of the 100 speak Chinese, 9 English, 8 Hindi, 7 Spanish, 4 Arabic, 4 Bengali, 3 Portugese and 3 Russian.

The village is a rich place, with a vast array of goods and services for sale. Yet most people can do no more than dream of such treasures, because 80 per cent of the village's total income is earned by just 20 individuals.

Food is the greatest worry for the majority of the population. Every year, workers produce more than enough food to feed everyone; even so, half the village's people – including most of the children – go hungry. The worst-off 20 residents (who together have less money than the richest person in the village!) lack food, safe drinking water and secure shelter. They are weak and unable to work. Every day some of

them fall ill with life-threatening diseases. Another 50 do not have a reliable source of food and are hungry much of the time.

Villagers talk of their community's many schools, including colleges and universities. Of 38 school-aged villagers, 31 attend school but few (7.5) reach university. Half of the village's people can neither read nor write.

The sociological perspective reminds us of these many differences in the world. Our life chances and our very experiences of social life will differ dramatically according to what kind of society we are born into. Human lives do not unfold according to sheer chance; nor do people live isolated lives, relying solely on what philosophers call 'free will' in choosing every thought and action. On the contrary, while individuals make many important decisions every day, we do so within a larger arena called 'society' – a friendship, a family, a university, a nation, an entire world. The essential wisdom of sociology is that the social world guides and constrains our actions and life choices just as the seasons influence our choices of activities and clothing. It sets the framework in which we make decisions about our lives. And, because sociologists know a great deal about how society works, they can analyse and predict with insight and a fair degree of accuracy how we all behave. Many of the achievements we attribute to our personal abilities are products of the privileged position we occupy in the worldwide social system.[1]

[1] Global village scenario adapted from United Nations data. This is now widely taught in primary schools, and has been developed in posters and on T-shirts. In my view, it is still worth citing. See Smith and Armstrong (2003).

*Queremos un mundo donde quepan muchos mundos. We want one world, one that can accommodate many worlds.*

The Zapatistas, Chiapas, Mexico

*From now on, nothing that happens on our planet is only a limited local event.*

Ulrich Beck, *What is Globalization?* (2000)

*Globalization debates transform many existing sociological controversies. . . .*

John Urry, *Global Complexity* (2003)

---

## In this chapter, we ask:

- **What are the 'classical' ways of thinking about society and how are they being challenged and modified by a range of new perspectives?**

- **Why do we need a global perspective in sociology?**

- **What is meant by globalisation and how will it be developed as an idea in this book?**

---

(Left) Michael Simpson, *World in Sky*
*Source*: Getty Images/Taxi/Michael Simpson.

**Q** Where are you in this image? What does the image say about you and your position in the world? What does it say about the 7 billions of planet earth's population?

# How to think about society: a short tour of sociological theory

The task of weaving isolated observations into understanding brings us to another dimension of sociology: theory. Students are often put off by theory, believing it to be obscure and difficult. In fact, theory is what makes sociology different from, say, journalism or popular documentary television of social issues. For a **theory** is a *statement of how and why specific facts are related*. In a sense, we all theorise or generalise all the time. But sociology aims to do this more systematically (see Lee and Newby, 1983; Craib, 1992). Recall that Emile Durkheim observed that certain categories of people (men, Protestants, the wealthy and the unmarried) have higher suicide rates than others (women, Catholics and Jews, the poor and the married). He explained these observations by creating a theory: a high risk of suicide stems from a low level of social integration.

Of course, as Durkheim pondered the issue of suicide, he considered any number of possible theories. But merely linking facts together is no guarantee that a theory is correct. To evaluate a theory, as the next chapter explains, sociologists use critical and logical thinking along with an array of research tools to gather evidence. 'Facts', as we shall see, are always a bit of a problem – consider, for example, how the very idea of a suicide rate used by Durkheim brings problems. Just what does such a rate measure? Does it really record all the suicides? How can we really tell that a death has been a suicide? Nevertheless, sociologists do strive for 'facts', which often allow them to confirm some theories while rejecting or modifying others. As a sociologist, Durkheim was not content merely to identify a plausible cause of suicide; he set about collecting data to see precisely which categories of people committed suicide with the highest frequency.

Poring over his data, Durkheim settled on a theory that best squared with all the available evidence.

In attempting to develop theories about human society, sociologists face a wide range of choices. What issues should we study? How should we link facts together to form theories? What assumptions might underpin our theories? In making sense of society, sociologists are guided by one or more theoretical 'road maps' or perspectives. A **theoretical perspective** can be seen as *a basic image that guides thinking and research*.

We noted earlier that two of sociology's founders – Auguste Comte and Karl Marx – made sense of the emerging modern society in strikingly different ways. Such differences persist today as some sociologists highlight how societies stay the same, while others focus on patterns of change. Similarly, some sociological theorists focus on what joins people together, while others investigate how society divides people according to gender, race, ethnicity or social class. Some sociologists seek to understand the operation of society as it is, while others actively promote what they view as desirable social change.

In short, sociologists often disagree about what the most interesting questions are; even when they agree on the questions, they may still differ over the answers. Nonetheless, the discipline of sociology is far from chaotic. Like many disciplines, it has built-in controversies and has multiple perspectives, containing *an array of basic images that guide thinking and research*. See Figure 2.1 for a summary of various positions. Over the past hundred years, sociologists have developed three major theoretical ways of thinking about society. We will introduce these next – and they will reappear at various points in the book. They may be called the *classical perspectives* that have shaped sociology in the past. But, like any growing discipline, these are constantly being refined and developed, while at the same time newer ones are appearing alongside them. After outlining these mainstream, or classical, stances, we will turn to some *emerging perspectives*.

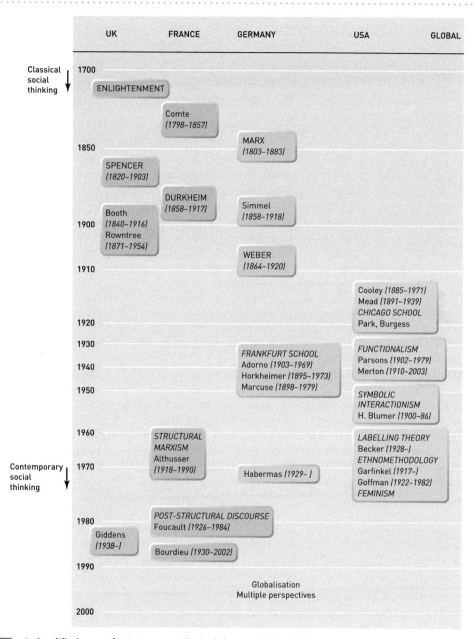

Figure 2.1 | A simplified map of Western sociological theory, 1700–2000

The sociological map shows some key Western sociologists – when they were born and where. When presented like this, it is easy to detect a very strong male bias.

*Source*: Plummer, with suggestions from Tabitha Freeman.

# Herbert Spencer: the survival of the fittest

The most memorable idea of the English philosopher Herbert Spencer (1820–1903) was his assertion that the passing of time witnesses 'the survival of the fittest'. Many people associate this immortal phrase with the theory of species evolution developed by the natural scientist Charles Darwin (1809–82). The expression was actually Spencer's, however, and he used it to refer to society, not to living creatures. In it, we find not only an example of early structural–functional analysis, but also a controversial theory that reflects the popular view in Spencer's day that society mirrored biology.

Spencer's ideas, which came to be known as social Darwinism, rested on the assertion that, if left to compete among themselves, the most intelligent, ambitious and productive people will inevitably win out. Spencer endorsed a world of fierce competition, thinking that as the 'fittest' survived, society would undergo steady improvements.

Society rewards its best members, Spencer continued, by allowing a free-market economy to function without government interference. Welfare, or other programmes aimed at redistributing money to benefit the poor, Spencer maintained, do just the opposite: they drag society down by elevating its weakest and least worthy members. For such opinions, nineteenth-century industrialists loudly applauded Spencer, and the rich saw in Spencer's analysis a scientific justification for big business to remain free of government regulation or social conscience. Indeed, John D. Rockefeller, who built a vast financial empire that included most of the US oil industry, often recited Spencer's 'social gospel' to young children in Sunday school, casting the growth of giant corporations as merely the naturally ordained 'survival of the fittest'.

But others objected to the idea that society amounted to little more than a jungle where self-interest reigned supreme. Gradually, social Darwinism fell out of favour among social scientists, though it still surfaces today as an influential element of conservative political thought. From a sociological point of view, Spencer's thinking is flawed because we now realise that ability only partly accounts for personal success, and favouring the rich and powerful does not necessarily benefit society as a whole. In addition, the heartlessness of Spencer's ideas strikes many people as cruel, with little room for human compassion.

For a positive appraisal of Spencer's life and work, see Mark Francis, *Herbert Spencer and the Invention of Modern Life* (2007).

## SOCIOLOGICAL THEORY:

### A MULTI-PARADIGMATIC DISCIPLINE WITH MANY THEORIES AND WAYS OF THINKING

A key challenge for sociology is to search for general ways of understanding social life. Sociologists are always developing sociological theories to help us make sense of this social world, and in this book you will be briefly introduced to a wide range of them. What you will find is that they tend to provide partial accounts – they take an angle, adopt a perspective and give you one way of seeing the world. Sociology is best seen as multi-paradigmatic and suggests a range of perspectives on social life. At its best it draws together a wide range of these perspectives to help provide the fullest picture.

We suggest you start your sociological theorising by trying to grasp the broadest 'image' of each theory. Table 2.1 provides some details of where you can find them discussed more in this book. Finally, if you want to take any theory further, look at some of the suggestions for further reading at the end of the chapter and book.

## Table 2.1

| Look at the social as: | Key theories and ideas to develop | Follow up in this book by looking at: |
| --- | --- | --- |
| A series of unfolding stages. | Evolutionary theories of society. | Early versions are Comte (Ch. 1); Spencer (Ch. 1). Modern variants such as 'multiple modernities' are discussed in Ch. 4. |
| An integrated whole where the parts and institutions work to hold it all together. Sometimes it falls apart and things do not function well. | Functionalism and neofunctionalism; ecological theory; modern social systems theory and cybernetics. | Classic version is Durkheim (Ch. 2 and 4); and Park (Ch. 24). Parsons' systems theory (Ch. 2); Mary Douglas and the natural order (Ch. 14); and Jeffrey Alexander (neofunctionalism and civic society, Ch. 26). |
| Composed of different groups with different interests which are in conflict. Dominant groups over exploited and dominated groups. These are commonly identified as class, race, gender, nation, sexual, disability and age interests. | Conflict theories of many and all kinds: which can include Marxism, feminism, anti-racist theories, queer theory, and postcolonial theories. They are also widely found in cultural studies, in the idea of hegemony and in notions of symbolic violence. | Can be found in Marx (Ch. 2 and 4); C. Wright Mills (Ch. 1); Du Bois (Ch. 11); Patricia Hill Collins (Ch. 11); Feminism (Ch. 2 and 12); queer theory (Ch. 12); Paulo Freire (Ch. 20); Intersections (Ch. 8). |
| Ways in which we orientate ourselves to meaning and interact with each other and develop culture and symbols – society is meaningful interaction. | Action theory, symbolic interactionism, phenomenological sociology, constructionism. | Most explicitly found in the works of Max Weber (Ch. 2 and 4); G. H. Mead (Ch. 7) and Goffman (Ch. 7). |
| The habits we create, change and live with in different arenas of life. | The psychology of William James on 'habits'; institutionalisation theory; the idea of habitus. | See especially Pierre Bourdieu (Ch. 8 and 10). |
| Drama, the roles we play and the selves we present. | Role theory, dramaturgy, theories of identity; ideas of performativity. Symbolic interactions. | See especially discussions of self and Goffman (Ch. 7) and Judith Butler (Ch. 12); Norman Denzin (Ch. 3). |
| Languages and discourses we live our lives through. Communication. | Social linguistics, conversational analysis, ethnomethodology, discourse analysis and hermeneutics. Symbolic interaction | Key recent influence is the work of Foucault (Ch. 17). Present in linguistics (Ch. 5), narrative and ethnomethodology (Ch. 7); Habermas. |
| A civilizing process | Configurational theory | Key proponent is Norbert Elias (see Ch. 7). |
| Creating a bridge between action and structure | See action–structure debate | See the big debate at the end of Ch. 2 and Giddens (Ch. 16). |
| Underlying forms of sociability and sociation | Formal sociology | See Simmel (Ch. 6). |
| Networks and flows | Network theory, mobilities theory. The term 'network' is used in a number of different ways: simple mapping of friends and contacts to a new cybernetic reality of high tech. | See discussions in Ch. 6. Note in particular the work of Manuel Castells. The work of Zygmunt Bauman on fluid society (Ch. 4) and of John Urry on mobilities (Ch. 26) see society as a flow. |
| Logo and brand | Many recent theories have been developed by a focus on a specific brand. | Most famous is George Ritzer's McDonaldisation of society (Ch. 6); see also Disneyisation etc. |
| Flourishing capabilities | Human capabilities theory, being developed by human development theorists like Nussbaum and Sen. | Discussed mainly in Ch. 9 and 14. |
| Global | Globalisation, world systems, cosmopolitanism. | See chart on p. 53. |

# The 'classical', traditional perspectives of sociology

Broadly, three perspectives dominated sociological thinking for a long while, and it is important to know about them. We will return to them in many chapters of this book. The three traditions are called by many different names but we will identify them very simply as *functionalism*, *conflict* and *action theory*. These terms are now old fashioned, but the ideas they capture are still very much alive today. Here, we briefly describe each.

## 1 The functionalist perspective: a world of balance

**Functionalism** is *a framework for building theory that sees society as a complex system whose parts work together and interconnect – often to promote solidarity and stability*. This perspective begins by recognising that our lives are guided by **social structure**, meaning relatively stable patterns of social behaviour. Social structure is what gives shape to the family, directs people to exchange greetings on the street, or steers events in a university classroom. Second, this perspective leads us to understand social structure in terms of its **social functions**, or consequences for the operation of society. All social structure – from family life to a simple handshake – contributes to the operation of society, at least in its present form.

Functionalism owes much to the ideas of Auguste Comte who, as we have already explained, sought to promote social integration during a time of tumultuous change. A second architect of this theoretical approach, the influential English sociologist Herbert Spencer (1820–1903), is introduced in the box on p. 36. Spencer was a student of both the human body and society, and he came to see that the two have much in common. The structural parts of the human body include the skeleton, muscles and various internal organs. These elements are interdependent, each contributing to the survival of the entire organism. In the same way, reasoned Spencer, various social structures are interdependent, working in concert to preserve society. The structural–functional perspective, then, organises sociological observations by identifying various structures of society and investigating the function of each one.

In France, several decades after Comte's death, Emile Durkheim continued the development of sociology. Durkheim did not share the social Darwinist thinking of his English colleague Spencer; rather, his work is primarily concerned with the issue of *social solidarity*, or how societies 'hang together'. Because of the extent of Durkheim's influence on sociology, his work is detailed in Chapter 4.

As sociology developed in the United States, many of the ideas of Herbert Spencer and Emile Durkheim were carried forward by Talcott Parsons (1902–79). The major US proponent of the functional perspective, Parsons treated society as a system, identifying the basic tasks that all societies must perform to survive and the ways they accomplish these tasks. All societies, he argued, need to be able to adapt, achieve their goals, maintain themselves and have members who are well socialised into their order. Without this, societies may begin to break down.

A contemporary of Parsons was the major US sociologist Robert K. Merton (1910–2003) , who expanded our understanding of the concept of social function in novel ways. Merton (1968) explains, first, that the consequences of any social pattern are likely to differ for various members of a society. For example, conventional families may provide crucial support for the development of children, but they also confer privileges on men while limiting the opportunities of women.

Second, Merton notes, people rarely perceive all the functions of a particular social structure. He described as **manifest functions** the *recognised and intended consequences of any social pattern*. By contrast, **latent functions** are *consequences that are largely unrecognised and unintended*. To illustrate, the obvious functions of higher education include providing people with the information and skills they need to perform jobs effectively. But perhaps just as important, although rarely acknowledged, is a university's function as a chance to meet potential partners. Another function may be to keep millions of young people out of a labour market where, presumably, many of them would not find jobs. And a third, less obvious function may well be to reinforce a system of prestige and inequality – by excluding those who do not go to universities from all sorts of work.

Merton makes a third point: not *all* the effects of any social structure turn out to be useful. Thus we designate as **social dysfunctions** any *social pattern's undesirable consequences for the operation of society*. And, to make matters still more complex, people may well disagree about what is useful or harmful. So some might argue that higher education promotes left-wing thinking that threatens traditional values. Others might dismiss such charges as trivial or simply wrong; higher education is dysfunctional for conferring further privileges on the wealthy (who disproportionately attend university), while poorer families find a university course beyond their financial reach.

## Critical comment

The most salient characteristic of the functional perspective is its vision of society as a whole being comprehensible, orderly and stable. Sociologists typically couple this approach with scientific methods of research aimed at learning 'what makes society tick'.

Until the 1960s, the functional perspective dominated sociology. In recent decades, however, its influence has waned. How can we assume that society has a 'natural' order, critics ask, when social patterns vary from place to place and change over time? Further, by emphasising social integration, functionalism tends to gloss over inequality based on social class, race, ethnicity and gender – divisions that may generate considerable tension and conflict. This focus on stability at the expense of conflict and change can give the functional perspective a conservative character. In the main, functionalism is a theory that is much less discussed and used these days.

## 2 The conflict perspective: a world of difference

The **conflict perspective** is *a framework for building theory that sees society as an arena of differences and inequalities that generate conflict and change*. This approach complements the functional perspective by highlighting not solidarity but division based on different interests and potential inequality. Guided by this perspective, sociologists investigate how factors such as social class, race, ethnicity, sex, disability and age are linked to unequal distribution of money, power, education and social prestige. We look at these in detail in Part Three of this book. A conflict analysis points out that, rather than promoting the operation of society as a whole, social structure typically benefits some people while depriving others.

Working within the conflict perspective, sociologists spotlight ongoing differences and conflict between dominant and disadvantaged categories of people – the rich in relation to the poor, white people as opposed to black, men versus women. Typically, those on top strive to protect their privileges; the disadvantaged counter by attempting to gain more resources for themselves.

To illustrate, a conflict analysis of our educational system might highlight how schooling perpetuates

inequality by helping to reproduce the class structure in every new generation. The process may start in primary schools and continue as secondary schools stream students. From a functional point of view, this may benefit all of society because, ideally, students receive the training appropriate to their academic abilities. But conflict analysis counters that streaming often has less to do with talent than with a student's social background, as well-to-do students are placed in higher streams and poor students end up in the lower ones.

In this way, privileged families gain favoured treatment for their children from schools. And, with the best schooling behind them, these young people leave university to pursue occupations that confer both prestige and high income. By contrast, the children of poor families are less prepared for college. So, like their parents before them, these young people typically move straight from secondary school into low-paying jobs. In both cases, the social standing of one generation is passed on to another, with schools justifying the practice in terms not of privilege but of individual merit (Bowles and Gintis, 1976; and see Chapter 20).

Social conflict extends well beyond schools. Later chapters of this book highlight efforts by working people, women, racial, ethnic, gay and lesbian minorities to improve their lives. In each of these cases, the conflict perspective helps us to see how inequality and the conflict it generates are rooted in the organisation of society itself.

Finally, many sociologists who embrace the conflict perspective attempt not just to understand society but to reduce social inequality. This was the goal of Karl Marx, the social thinker whose ideas underlie the conflict perspective. Marx did not seek merely to understand how society works. In a well-known declaration (inscribed on his monument in London's Highgate Cemetery), Marx asserted: 'The philosophers have only interpreted the world, in various ways; the point, however, is to change it.'

## Critical comment

The conflict perspective developed rapidly during the 1960s and the 1970s. Yet, like other approaches, it has come in for its share of criticism. Because this perspective highlights inequality and division, it glosses over how shared values or interdependence generate unity among members of a society. In addition, say critics, to the extent that the conflict approach explicitly pursues political goals, it can relinquish any claim to scientific objectivity. As the next chapter explains in detail, conflict theorists are uneasy with the notion that science can be 'objective'. They contend, on the contrary, that the conflict perspective as well as *all* theoretical approaches have political consequences, albeit different ones. Like functionalism, the language of conflict theory has gone more and more out of fashion in recent years.

One additional criticism, which applies equally to both the functional and conflict perspectives, is that they envisage society in very broad terms. 'Society' becomes a thing in itself, describing our lives as a composite of 'family', 'social class', and so on. A third theoretical perspective depicts society less in terms of abstract generalisations and more in terms of people's everyday, situational experiences.

THINKERS & THEORY

## The foundational three: a very brief introduction

Since the 1950s, when sociology really entered the university curriculum, the 'holy trinity' of Marx, Durkheim and Weber have been taught as the central founders of sociology. There is a good reason for this. Each provides a core understanding of the arrival of modern capitalist societies, the rapid changes that were going on with the Industrial Revolution and the key political transformation of the late eighteenth and nineteenth centuries. As the landscape of the world changed dramatically, so Marx, Durkheim and Weber provided key accounts to guide contemporary understanding. Their ideas still shape sociological analysis in the twenty-first century, so below we give a very brief introduction to them. Their ideas – and those of their

(a)

(b)

(c)

(d)

Some shapers of a modern sociology. With the rise of industrial capitalism, the nineteenth and twentieth centuries saw an explosion of significant thinkers about society. Above are just four of them: (a) Karl Marx (see Chapters 2 and 4); (b) Max Weber (see Chapters 2 and 4); (c) Emile Durkheim (see Chapters 1, 2 and 4); and (d) Herbert Spencer (see Chapter 2). What characteristics do they have in common?

*Source*: (a) © Pearson Education Ltd/The Illustrated London News Picture Library/Ingram Publishing/Alamy; (b) © The Granger Collection, New York; (c) © Bettmann/Corbis; (d) © Hulton-Deutsch Collection/Corbis.

contemporary followers – are discussed more fully throughout the book.

## Marx (1803–83)

Marx claimed that 'the history of all hitherto existing societies is the history of class struggle' (opening statement in *The Communist Manifesto*) and saw a flow of conflict between groups as the hallmark of histories everywhere. People are born into a history that is not of their making; but people also make history. People can change the world they are born into. In the nineteenth century, Marx saw that industrial capitalism (see Chapter 4) was developing into a system which would bring exploitation and a suffering lower class. As people became aware of their situation, so change – revolution – would come about; and create a new order of equality.

Marx's work has had a huge impact upon intellectual life, political activity and society. Few people have heard of Weber and Durkheim, but Marx became a household name in much of the twentieth century. He argued that 'the philosophers have only interpreted the world, the point is to change it' and claimed that 'The ideas of the ruling class are in every epoch the ruling ideas'. His work had a profound impact on the development of communist societies such as the Soviet Union and Mao's China. In the middle part of the twentieth century, more than a fifth of the world lived in communist societies inspired by him. Whilst these societies are now considered short-term failures which harboured deeply authoritarian structures and major genocidal tendencies,

many of his ideas have remained influential. In sociology, his work continues to flag the centrality of oppression and conflict in social life and the ubiquitous nature of inequality and exploitation.

Born in Germany, he eventually had to leave it because his relentless social criticism got him into trouble with the authorities. He lived much of his later life in relative poverty in Victorian London and was buried at Highgate Cemetery in 1883.

## Durkheim (1858–1917)

Durkheim saw societies as changing too. They were moving from societies based on great similarities to ones characterised by a rapid growth of division of labour. This increased differentiation (which he called a shift from mechanical society to organic society), which could become associated with a breakdown of integration and ultimate anomie – a state of normlessness. He suggested that new groups (guilds) could create a new sense of community and belonging. He was one of the main architects of the structural–functional tradition we locate throughout this book. His influence can be found today in the many theories of community and social bonding, as well as in studies of the power of symbols and rituals in everyday life.

Durkheim was the only one of our 'holy three' to work in a sociology department and identify as a sociologist. He outlined how sociology should study the social world – to '*treat social facts as things*', as matters that arise outside human consciousness and which shape the way we live in the world.

## Weber (1864–1920)

Weber saw societies as becoming increasingly dominated by rational thought. He highlighted the growth of bureaucracies (which we discuss in Chapter 6). While this brought benefits, it also brought an increasing 'disenchantment' with the world – men became trapped in an 'iron cage' in which they had little hope of change. Religions were likely to decline. Capitalism came about mainly because of shifts in the organisation of religion – the rise of an individualistic Protestant ethic (see Chapter 4).

Weber was very concerned with the ways in which human actions and meanings played their role in social life. His work ranged over many areas: music, religion, love, law, the economy, politics. He looked at a wide range of civilisations. He also engaged with politics (and his wife, Marianne, was a leading feminist of her time). He struggled with the balance between his personal political commitments and his view of sociology as being scientifically neutral – or value-free. He was the most pessimistic of our three thinkers. And, indeed, in his personal life he waged war with perpetual depression.

 Brush up on your Marx, Durkheim and Weber. If you want to understand how sociological ideas have developed, you could read:

John Hughes, Wes Sharrock and Peter Martin, *Understanding Classical Social Theory: Marx, Weber, Durkheim* (2nd edn, 2003)

Kenneth Morrison, *Marx, Durkheim, Weber: Formations of Modern Social Thought* (2006)

Most of the originals of these authors can be found online (see end of chapter).

# 3 The social action perspective: a world of meaning

Both the functional and conflict perspectives share a **macro-level orientation**, meaning *a focus on broad social structures that characterise society as a whole*. Macro-level sociology takes in the big picture, rather like observing a city from high above in a helicopter, noting how highways carry traffic from place to place and the striking contrasts between rich and poor neighbourhoods. Action theory, by contrast, starts with the ways in which people (or actors) orientate themselves to each other, and how they do so on the basis of meanings. This provides a *micro-level orientation*, meaning *a focus on the emerging meanings of social interaction in specific situations*. The distinction between macro and micro is an important one in sociology and it appears in a number of guises. The *Big debate* at the end of the chapter introduces some of these ideas.

One founder of the action perspective – a micro-theory that focuses on how actors assemble social meanings – is the highly influential Max Weber (1864–1920), a German sociologist who emphasised the need to understand a setting from the point of view of the people in it. Weber's approach is presented at length in Chapter 4, but here a few ideas can be introduced.

His approach emphasises how human meanings and action shape society. Weber understood the power of technology, and he shared many of Marx's ideas about social conflict. But he departed from Marx's materialist analysis, arguing that societies differ primarily in terms of the ways in which their members think about the world. For Weber, ideas – especially beliefs and values – have transforming power. Thus he saw modern society as the product not just of new technology and capitalism, but of a new way of thinking. This emphasis on ideas contrasts with Marx's focus on material production, leading scholars to describe Weber's work as 'a debate with the ghost of Karl Marx' (Cuff and Payne, 1979: 73–4).

In all his work, Weber contrasted social patterns in different times and places. To sharpen comparisons, he relied on the ideal type, an abstract statement of the essential, though often exaggerated, characteristics of any social phenomenon. He explored religion by contrasting the ideal 'Protestant' with the ideal 'Jew', 'Hindu' and 'Buddhist', knowing that these models precisely described no actual individuals. These 'ideal types' can then be contrasted with actual, empirical forms found in reality. Note that Weber's use of the word 'ideal' does not mean that something is 'good' or 'the best'; we could analyse 'criminals' as well as 'priests' as ideal types.

Closely allied to Weber is the American tradition of symbolic interactionism. The perspective emerges in the work of the philosopher George Herbert Mead (1863–1931), who looked at how we assemble our sense of self over time based on social experience. His ideas are explored in Chapter 7. The theory is also connected to the Chicago School of Sociology (explored more in Chapter 24), which examined city life in this way. The theory leads to careful observation of how people interact. **Symbolic interactionism**, then, is *a theoretical framework that envisages society as the product of the everyday interactions of people doing things together*. In order to understand such interactions, great emphasis is placed on studying everyday social life through tools such as life stories and observation. Sociology must proceed in this view through an intimate familiarity with everyday real-life events and not through abstract social theory.

How does 'society' result from the ongoing experiences of tens of millions of people? One answer, detailed in Chapter 7, is that society arises as a shared reality that its members construct as they interact with one another. Through the human process of finding meaning in our surroundings, we define our identities, bodies and feelings, and come to 'socially construct' the world around us.

Of course, this process of definition varies a great deal from person to person. On a city street, for example, one person may define a homeless woman as 'a no-hoper looking for a handout' and ignore her. Another, however, might define her as a 'fellow human being in need' and offer assistance. In the same way, one pedestrian may feel a sense of security passing by a police officer walking the beat, while another may be seized by nervous anxiety. Sociologists guided by the symbolic interaction approach, therefore, view society as a mosaic of subjective meanings and variable responses.

On this foundation, others have devised their own micro-level approaches to understanding social life. Chapter 7 presents the work of Erving Goffman (1922–82), whose *dramaturgical analysis* emphasises how we resemble actors on a stage as we play out our various roles before others. Other sociologists, including George Homans and Peter Blau, have developed *social exchange analysis*. In their view, social interaction amounts to a negotiation in which individuals are guided by what they stand to gain and lose from others. In the ritual of courtship, for example, people typically seek mates who offer at least as much – in terms of physical attractiveness, intelligence and social background – as they provide in return.

## Critical comment

The action perspective helps to correct a bias inherent in all macro-level approaches to understanding society. Without denying the usefulness of abstract social structures such as 'the family' and 'social class', we must bear in mind that society basically amounts to *people interacting*. Put another way, this micro-level approach helps convey more of how individuals actually experience society and how they do things together (Becker, 1986).

The trouble is that by focusing on day-to-day interactions, these theorists can obscure larger social structures. Highlighting what is unique in each social scene risks overlooking the widespread effects of our culture, as well as factors such as class, gender and race.

Table 2.2 summarises the important characteristics of the functional, conflict and action perspectives. As we have explained, each perspective is partially helpful in answering particular kinds of question. By and large, however, the fullest understanding of society comes from linking the sociological perspective to all three. Sociologists examine the social world by looking at *functions and dysfunctions, conflicts and consensus, actions and meanings*. The three theoretical perspectives certainly offer different insights, but none is more correct than the others, and all three have become increasingly modified in the light of newer theories.

| Table 2.2 | Three traditional perspectives: a summary | | |
|---|---|---|---|
| **Theoretical perspective** | **Orientation** | **Image of society** | **Core questions** |
| Functional | Macro-level | A system of interrelated parts that is relatively stable based on widespread consensus as to what is morally desirable; each part has functional consequences for the operation of society as a whole | • How is society integrated?<br>• What are the major parts of society?<br>• How are these parts interrelated?<br>• What are the consequences of each one for the operation of society? |
| Conflict | Macro-level | A system characterised by social inequality; each part of society benefits some categories of people more than others; conflict-based social inequality promotes social change | • How is society divided?<br>• What are the major patterns of social inequality?<br>• How do some categories of people attempt to protect their privileges?<br>• How do other categories of people challenge the status quo? |
| Symbolic interaction | Micro-level | An ongoing process of social interaction in specific settings based on symbolic communications; individual perceptions of reality are variable and changing | • How is society experienced?<br>• How do human beings interact to create, sustain and change social patterns?<br>• How do individuals attempt to shape the reality perceived by others?<br>• How does individual behaviour change from one situation to another? |

# The capitalist world: the neoliberal model

One of the key challenges for social theory is to grasp the changing nature of capitalism – which, in the twenty-first century, has become the dominant system organising principle of most societies. **Capitalism** is *the economic system in which resources and the means of producing goods and services are privately owned.* There are many kinds of capitalist economy, but commonly there will be three distinctive features:

1  *Private ownership of property.* A capitalist economy supports the right of individuals to own almost anything. The more capitalist an economy is, the more private ownership there is of wealth-producing property such as factories and land. The downside of this can be a mass accumulation of profits by relatively few people, which can generate polarisation and cleavages between groups – the 'haves' and the 'have nots'. A potential for conflict is generated.

2  *Pursuit of personal profit.* A capitalist society encourages the accumulation of private property and defines a profit-minded orientation as natural and simply a matter of 'doing business'. The classical Scottish Enlightenment economist Adam Smith (1723–90) claimed that the individual pursuit of self-interest helps an entire society prosper (1937: 508; orig. 1776). Others argue that it leads to the exploitation of the mass by the few, and consolidates a class system.

3  *Free competition, consumer sovereignty and markets.* A purely capitalist economy would operate with no government interference, sometimes called a *laissez-faire* approach. Adam Smith contended that a freely competitive economy regulates itself by the 'invisible hand' of the laws of supply and demand.

Capitalism takes many different forms across the world and we look at these in more detail in Chapter 15. But it is important to grasp how central the free market, the pursuit of profit and freed competition are in structuring much of world social life. The most prevalent system which was developed under the government of President Reagan in the USA and Prime Minister Margaret Thatcher is often called Reaganism, Thatcherism or more formally neoliberalism (the term used by the economist Friedrich Hayek who championed it). *Neoliberal market capitalism* involves highly competitive, decentralised, open markets. It is anti-trust and unions, and seeks the freest flows of capital markets. There should be minimum state involvement and planning and the maximising of returns to owners of capital. It champions the free individual – but is uncritical of the way it fosters poverty and injustice for large numbers of people.

For more on capitalism, see p. 503 *et seq*; and pp. 533–5. Read: Geoffrey Ingham, *Capitalism* (2008); and on neoliberalism, see David Harvey, *A Brief History of Neo-Liberalism* (2005).

# Contemporary perspectives in sociology: multiple perspectives, other voices and the postmodern

Although functionalism, conflict theory and action sociology are still common positions within sociology, many others have emerged over the past three decades. As we have seen, sociology is often seen as containing multiple perspectives, which means that it takes on many perspectives for looking at social life rather than just one. It is the sign of a lively subject that, as society changes, so too do some of the approaches being adopted within it.

Some of them are really just further developments of the above theories. Thus, they may, for example, focus on different aspects of 'action', such as language and conversation (**conversational analysis** is an approach which does this: see Chapter 7). Or they may develop the idea that societies are structures through a focus either on the system of signs and languages that often organise them (as **semiotics** does: see Chapter 5) or on the way the state works (as in Althusserian Marxism: see Chapter 22). We will say a little more about these theories when we discuss the mass media later in the book (Chapter 22).

Other developments, however, are seen by some to go deeper than this. A number of critics of sociology suggest that the discipline has now entered a stage of 'crisis' in which many of its older ideas and perspectives are seen as being too narrowly conceived. Broadly, the newer approaches highlight **different** *perspectives, standpoints, cultures* or *voices*: they are much more self-conscious that all of sociology has to come from a perspective, a position or a point of view. We can never grasp the 'full truth' of a society, a completely full picture of it, even though we should try. Hence we should be more open about the partial perspectives we adopt and understand where we stand in relation to these partial perspectives. Sociology will always be selective. Max Weber himself recognised this long ago when he said:

> There is no absolutely 'objective' scientific analysis of culture or . . . of 'social phenomena' independent of special and 'one-sided' viewpoints according to which . . . they are selected, analysed and organised.

(Weber, 1949: 72)

This recognition of *perspectives, points of view, different cultures* or *standpoints* from which analysis proceeds has become more and more important for modern sociology. And this means that it helps to be explicit and open about the perspective we take. At its most critical, many of the new perspectives suggest that the major perspective of the past has been that of white, Western, Anglo-American, heterosexual men. This may sound a cliché, but as you read this book you should look for authors and sociologists who lie outside this tradition. They will, sadly, be somewhat hard to find. Whether using a functionalist, conflict or (inter)action perspective, they all shared common assumptions derived from their male and Western position.

In contrast, the newer perspectives generally see a range of other voices that were missed out of sociology in the past. Taken together, they provide a lot more 'angles' from which to approach society as a whole. They help to enrich the openness of the discipline to the range of ways of seeing society. This does *not* mean that everything is relative and anything goes. Quite the opposite: it means that, by carefully and systematically unpacking different perspectives, we can come to see societies more deeply and in a more rounded way. The aim of sociology is still to be 'objective' even if, as we shall see in Chapter 3, this is much harder than sociologists used to think and even if we can only ever approximate truth.

Many of these newer approaches are very critical of the dominant, earlier approaches – what we have called the classical perspectives. At present, however, it may be most helpful to see them as complementing and challenging these earlier perspectives, but not as entirely replacing them. They do, however, disagree with these early theories whenever they suggest they are telling the whole story of society: only partial stories are now possible in this newer view. Some of these newer sociologies thus speak of the 'death of the metanarrative' – a term coined by the French philosopher Lyotard – as a way of rejecting any idea that there is one, and only one, 'Big Story of Sociology'.

What, then, are these new voices? They include women, racial and ethnic minorities, colonised peoples throughout the world, gays and lesbians, the elderly, disabled people and various other marginalised or overlooked groups. You may well belong to one or more of these many groups, and should read this book with this in mind.

Taken together, a number of criticisms of classical sociology can be briefly summarised as follows:

1   That sociology has mainly been by men for men and about men – and for 'men', read white and heterosexual and usually privileged and relatively affluent. As such, it has had a persistently limited, even biased approach.
2   That areas of significance to other groups – 'racism' for ethnic groups, 'patriarchy' for women, 'homophobia' for gays, 'colonisation' for many non-Western groups, 'disablement' for disabled people – have often been overlooked. You may like to think about what each of these terms means; they will be introduced later in this book.
3   That these areas of significance, when they have been included, have often been presented in a distorted fashion: often sociology has been sexist, racist, homophobic, etc.

Many voices have been missing in sociology, and they have led to a number of newer sociological stances that will be introduced throughout the book.

# An example: the case of a feminist sociology and the missing voice of women

To illustrate: the most apparent absence until the 1970s was that of women's voices. Until then, sociology had mainly been by men, about men and for men. All this started to change with the development of a second wave of feminism (see Chapter 12), which helped to

A multicultural world. Sociology used to be the study of white Western men by white Western men. This is no longer always so. It has become far more multicultural and listens more attentively to the voices of a whole array of different groups: (a) Pataxou Indians in Brazil; (b) a lesbian couple in New York; (c) a Navaho matriarch in Arizona
*Source*: (a) © Mike Goldwater/Alamy; (b) © Homer Sykes; Archive/Alamy; (c) © Eve Arnold; Magnum Photos.

foster both a *feminist sociology* and a *feminist methodology*. Broadly, these place either women or gender at the centre of their specific analysis. They do this because they see the need for a more political role for sociologists in trying to reduce or eliminate women's subordination and oppression in societies across the world. Although you will find a chapter in this book that looks at gender specifically (Chapter 12), you will also find that gender as an issue will be considered in nearly every chapter. Bringing a feminist gender perspective to any analysis helps to widen and deepen understanding (see Abbott and Wallace, 1992).

Once we enter a feminist sociology, however, we will find that there is no one or unified voice here either! To put it bluntly, not all women are the same across the globe! When we start suggesting that women are all the same, we start to engage in what has been called essentialist thinking – **essentialism** is the belief in essences that are similar. It is to suggest here that there is an 'essence' or pure core to what it is to be a woman. Yet we will find a plurality of women's stances too – ranging, as we shall see, from those who adopt

conflict perspectives to those who focus more on action perspectives; from those who highlight postcolonialist perspectives to those who focus on 'black' perspectives. For example, the experiences of a black woman living in poverty in Sierra Leone are very different from those of most white women studying in European universities.

Some do try to bring all these different voices together. But to do this, there has to be a major recognition that voices are not unified but fragmentary and multi-situated. As you will start to sense, this is no easy task!

## And other voices: postmodernism and a multi-paradigmatic sociology

Following on from all this, then, there are many new developments in sociology and you will encounter these throughout this book. For instance, Chapter 5 introduces ideas around multiculturalism; Chapter 7 introduces ideas around social constructionism; Chapter 11 debates postcolonial theory; Chapter 12 will extend feminist theory and introduce queer theory; Chapter 17 introduces ideas around Foucault's 'discourse theory'; Chapter 21 will introduce disablement theory; while Chapter 26 will further present some ideas around postmodern social theory. As in any introduction, we cannot take these newer ideas very far. But at least you will sense that sociology is a continuously growing and changing discipline of study that is always bringing new challenges to its students.

Some sociologists have started to suggest that in the twenty-first century a new generation of sociology is in the making, and that it is bringing what has sometimes been called a postmodern stance. Although sociology was born of the modern world – industrialisation, capitalism, the growth of big cities, the rise of democracies, the decline of traditional communities, etc. – it is now finding itself in a world where the features of modernity are accelerating: modernity is speeding up and going faster. It is what Giddens has called 'a runaway world' (Giddens, 1999). Over the past 30 years or so, there have been many rapid changes both within society and in our understanding of ways of approaching society. Sociology itself, therefore, has had to rethink some of its key ideas to at least accommodate these changes – which have been increasingly identified as 'postmodern' or a 'late modern turn' (see Giddens, 1992).

For some thinkers these changes have been so extreme as to question the very foundations of sociology. Two French thinkers, for example, have more or less proclaimed the death of sociology and suggested that we have moved into a postmodern world. Thus Baudrillard writes that:

> **It has all been done. The extreme limit of . . . possibilities has been reached. It has destroyed itself. It has deconstructed its entire universe. So all that are left are pieces. All that remains to be done is play with the pieces. Playing with the pieces – that is post-modern.**

(Baudrillard, 1984: 24)

This is an extreme position which will not be adopted in this book. Rather, this textbook will tell the story of the shift from a traditional form of society, one which was usually authoritarian with strong religious commitments to an overarching belief system, towards what we might see as *a more provisional world – one that is altogether less sure of itself*. Modernity has

In the early days of sociology, men dominated its concerns. Today, there has been the growth of a much more feminist-based sociology. Jane Addams (above) is often seen as a pioneer of sociology through her concern with city life in Chicago. Some have argued that she is the true founder of the Chicago School (see Chapter 24)
*Source*: © Bettmann/Corbis.

brought many changes; and in the twenty-first century this modern world is an accelerating one where there is an increased sensitivity to diversities and differences. In this view the world becomes less dominated by generalities and 'master narratives', and there is a turn towards 'local cultures' and their 'multiplicity of stories'. We could see postmodernism as:

> **. . . the liberation of differences, of local elements, of what could generally be called dialect. With the demise of the idea of a central rationality of history, the world of generalised communication explodes like a multiplicity of 'local' rationalities**

| Table 2.3 | Summary: six recent political influences on sociological thinking | |
| --- | --- | --- |
| Theory | Search for | Challenge |
| Feminism | Equality of sexes | Analyse gender differences |
| Anti-racism | Equality of ethnicities | Analyse nation and ethnicities |
| Queer theory | Equality of sexualities | Analyse sexualities |
| Post-colonialism and multiculturalism | Equality of cultures | Analyse different cultural positions and understandings |
| Postmodernism | Recognition of differences | Analyse differences, multiplicities and complexities |
| Globalisation | Interconnections across cultures | Globalisation and glocalisation as key social processes |

– ethnic, sexual, religious, cultural or aesthetic minorities – that finally speak up for themselves. They are no longer repressed and cowed into silence by the idea of a single pure form of humanity that must be realised irrespective of particularity and individual finitude, transience and contingency . . .

(Vattimo, 1992: 8–9)

All this leads to a new approach to sociology, but not one that has to reject its past. Rob Stones suggests that a postmodern sociology has three concerns:

Postmodernists argue . . . for respecting the existence of a plurality of perspectives, as against a notion that there is one single truth from a privileged perspective; local, contextual studies in place of grand narratives; an emphasis on disorder, flux and openness, as opposed to order, continuity and restraint.

(Stones, 1996: 22)

## Thinking globally: a global perspective in sociology

Part of this shift in voice and concern within sociology over recent years has involved recognising the position of different, local voices around the world. In recent years, as even the furthest reaches of the earth have become more easily accessible through advances in technology, many academic disciplines have been forced to incorporate a **global perspective**, *the study of the larger world and each society's place in it*. Instead of the overwhelming dominance in sociology of Western

voices, we can now pay attention to voices heard in all parts of the world – from various African states to those found in Latin American countries. They often see the world in radically different ways and it is important, if sociology is to develop, to take these voices seriously.

Many sociology textbooks in the recent past have tended to focus on one country only. While this certainly deepens understanding of *one* society, it is insular and limited. This book therefore tries to look outwards to a range of societies, while at the same time maintaining some kind of focus on Europe and the UK, the societies which most of its readers are likely to come from, and maybe therefore the societies that will probably interest the readers of this book most. But we have tried to avoid too much of a bias towards 'the West'.

## How does a global perspective enhance sociology?

Very often sociology looks too narrowly at specific cultures – usually of the West. Yet global awareness is a logical extension of the sociological perspective and greatly enhances it. Sociology's basic insight is that where we are placed in a society profoundly affects individual experiences – and the position of a society in the larger world system affects everyone. The opening story provided a brief sketch of our global village, indicating that people the world over are far from equal in their quality of life. Every chapter of this text will highlight life in the world beyond the borders of our own society. Here are three reasons to consider why global thinking should figure prominently in the sociological perspective.

THINKERS & THEORY

# Raewyn Connell: from men's studies to globalisation and southern theory

Raewyn Connell is one of Australia's leading sociologists, professor at the University of Sydney and globally influential. Her earliest work was on class and education, and she was extremely influential in the 1980s and 1990s in the development of 'men and masculinity' as a sociological problem of study. She suggested the importance of **'hegemonic masculinity'** – *the dominant way of being a man in society* – and the variety of global masculinities (ways of being men) that could be discovered (see Chapter 12).

Her work broadened out in the 1990s to study the development of sociology itself and she was not very happy with what she found. She discovered that sociology was not only a product of men, but of a certain kind of men. They were part of the Western, male Enlightenment; and as such they provided a rather specialised and limited view of the world. Her subsequent work turned to ideas about society that had been developed in different countries around the world. She examined the poetry and oral traditions in Africa and the development of an 'indigenous sociology'. The work of Al-Afghani and the Nigerian sociologist Akinsola Akiwowoo were considered. And then she reviewed developments and sociologists around the world: Raul Prebisch in Latin America, Ali Shariati in revolutionary Iran, Paulin Hountondji in Benin, Vienna Das and Ashes Nandi in India – and many others. Her aim was to introduce 'Western sociology' to a wider range of theorists and thinkers beyond the West, which should start to shape sociology in the future. Her book *Southern Theory* (2007) is a major challenge to the tradition of Western sociology and is likely to have a major impact on twenty-first-century sociology.

Raewyn Connell is a transsexual woman and was formally known as R. W. Connell or Robert Connell.

National flags provide unique symbolic identities in a global world. Here are the flags for Pakistan, Japan, South Africa, Nigeria, and Iran. Can you identify which is which?
*Source*: Corel Flags of the World.

1 *Societies the world over are increasingly interconnected.* A feature of the world over the past 300 years or so has been the ways in which countries have become more and more internationally connected, initially through 'the great explorers', then through colonialism, slavery and mass migrations, and nowadays through high finance, tourism and the electronic world. In recent times, the world has become linked as never before. Jet aircraft whisk people across continents in hours, while new electronic devices transmit pictures, sounds and written documents around the globe in seconds.

One consequence of this new technology, as later chapters explain, is that people all over the world now share many tastes in music, clothing and food. With their economic strength, high-income nations cast a global shadow, influencing members of other societies who eagerly gobble up American hamburgers, dance to British 'pop music' and, more and more, speak the English language.

Commerce across national borders has also propelled a global economy. Large corporations manufacture and market goods worldwide, just as global financial markets linked by satellite communications now operate around the clock. Today, no stock trader in London dares to ignore what happens in the financial markets in Tokyo and Hong Kong, just as no fisherman in Scotland can afford to ignore the European common fishing policy! But as the West projects its way of life on to much of the world, the larger world also reacts back. All of this is linked to the process of **globalisation**, *the increasing interconnectedness of societies*. This process will be discussed further in the next section and in many parts of this book.

2  *A global perspective enables us to see that many human problems we face in Europe are far more serious elsewhere.* Poverty is certainly a serious problem in Europe, and especially eastern Europe. But, as Chapter 9 explains, poverty is both more widespread and more severe throughout Latin America, Africa and Asia. Similarly, the social standing of women, children and the disabled is especially low in poor countries of the world. And, although racism may be pronounced in the UK,

it has even harsher forms throughout many parts of the world. Ethnic cleansings in Bosnia, 'Islamophobia', and hostility to German 'guest workers' are three examples that will be considered later (Chapter 11). Then, too, many of the toughest problems we grapple with at home are global in scope. Environmental pollution is one example: as Chapter 25 demonstrates, the world is a single ecosystem in which the action (or inaction) of one nation has implications for all others.

3  *Thinking globally is also an excellent way to learn more about ourselves.* We cannot walk the streets of a distant city without becoming keenly aware of what it means to live in western Europe at the beginning of the twenty-first century. Making global comparisons also leads to unexpected lessons. For instance, Chapter 9 transports us to a squatter settlement in Madras, India. There we are surprised to find people thriving in the love and support of family members, despite a desperate lack of basic material comforts. Such discoveries prompt us to think about why poverty in Europe so often involves isolation and anger, and whether material things – so crucial to our definition of a 'rich' life – are the best way to gauge human well-being.

In sum, in an increasingly interconnected world, we can understand ourselves only to the extent that we comprehend others.

Goma Zaire Rwandan refugee camp near Goma. Cholera victims July 1994. Baby sitting next to her sick mother
*Source*: © Jenny Mattthews/Alamy.

| Table 2.4 | Making the modern global world: Roland Robertson's six stages of globalisation |
|---|---|
| 1   1400–1750s (germinal) | Start of modern geography, Gregorian calendar, a bringing together of ideas about humanity |
| 2   1750s–1870s (incipient) | Emergence of nation states; transnational regulation and communication; nationalism versus internationalism |
| 3   1875–mid-1920s (take-off) | Growth of global communications; First World War; League of Nations; Olympics |
| 4   1920s–mid-1960s (struggle for hegemony) | United Nations formed in 1942; worldwide conflicts and growth of concern over common humanity; expansion of capital and capitalism |
| 5   1969–early 1990s (uncertainty) | Number of global 'problems', organisations and movement sharply increases – facing nuclear destruction and environment crisis |
| 6   Late 1990s (antagonism) | World Trade Organization; Kyoto Agreements, terrorism, the internet, global media, global capitalism |

*Source*: Based on Giulianto and Robertson (2009).

# Globalisation and sociology

Since the 1990s, sociologists have increasingly used the term 'globalisation' to capture the movements across world cultures. It has become one of the most influential of sociological ideas in the past two decades and it is still (in 2011) at the centre of many of its debates. The term itself is used across the globe: for the Germans it is *Globalisierung*; in Spain and Latin America it is *globalización*; and in France it is *mondialisation*! Yet even though it translates into many languages, its meaning is far from clear. It has now almost become a cliché and the term is often trotted out with little meaning. Most simply, we can start by defining **globalisation** as capturing *the increasing interconnectedness of societies*.

But hereafter we will find a lot of disagreement about the term. It brings different 'ideological baggage'. Some people embrace the term, seeing globalisation as everywhere and usually doing a lot of good. Thus it creates greater awareness of diversity and **hybridisation**; it stimulates international markets and wealth; it helps towards a more universal humankind – through awareness of common environmental problems, and international organisations like the United Nations. This is the dawning of the global age and it is to be celebrated. (David Held and others call those holding this view 'transformationalists' or 'hyperglobalisers'; Held et al., 1999: 10).

Critics, by contrast, suggest that there is nothing new about globalisation. History, they argue, shows that nations have a constant tendency to exploit, colonise and raid other cultures, and matters are getting worse. 'Global' in contemporary times usually means that dominant (capitalist) societies are taking over the finances and cultures of other societies (indeed, for some it means Americanisation, not globalisation!). Thus certain trading blocks and nation-states (largely in Europe, North America and the Pacific Rim) have become stronger, so there is no great tendency towards a greater universality at all. (These critics of globalisation are sometimes called 'sceptics'; see Hirst and Thompson, 2009).

The *Public sociology* box suggests a number of other definitions you may like to consider.

At the most basic, the term 'globalisation' can be grasped through the imagery of worldwide multicultural companies such as *Coca-Cola*, *McDonald's* and *Nike*. These companies exist across the globe – and in a number of ways. They *produce* goods across many countries; they *market* goods across many countries; and they *present* their logos and images which travel the globe ahead of them. Think of how McDonald's can be found across the world – even though it had its origins in the United States (see Chapter 5). Likewise, a Nike shoe – with its characteristic logo of the swoosh – is produced in many parts of the poorer world and yet sold everywhere. As we shall see, they are simultaneously loved by millions and hated by millions – as signs of convenience and the modern world, and as signs of corporate takeover of mass culture. We will have a lot more to say on all this in later chapters. They capture the economic, social and cultural impact of this process and simultaneously symbolise what may be good and bad about it. Globalisation is thus a controversial term.

PUBLIC SOCIOLOGY

# Some meanings of globalisation

Ideas of the 'global' and 'globalisation' are widespread in public debate and discussion. The term itself has been given many different meanings. Listen to discussions of globalisation and consider which position it might be coming from, and to get you going here are some recent discussions of its meaning:

- Globalization has something to do with the thesis that we all now live in one world ... (Anthony Giddens, *A Runaway World*, 1999: 7)
- Globalization is the widening, deepening and speeding up of worldwide interconnectedness in all aspects of contemporary life, from the cultural to the criminal, the financial to the spiritual. (David Held et al., *Global Transformations*, 1999: 14–16)
- Globalization ... denotes the processes through which sovereign national states are criss-crossed and undermined by transnational actors with varying prospects of power, orientations, identities and networks. (Ulrich Beck, *What is Globalization?*, 2000b: 11)
- The Global Age involves the supplanting of modernity with globality ... [This includes] the global environmental consequences of aggregate human activities; the loss of security where weaponry has global destructiveness; the globality of communication systems; the rise of a global economy; and the reflexivity of globalism, where people and groups of all kinds refer to the globe as the frame for their beliefs. (Martin Albrow, *The Global Age*, 1996: 4)
- Globalization is a transplanetary process ... involving increasing liquidity and growing multidirectional flows of people, objects, places, and information as well as the structures they encounter and create that are barriers to, or expedite, those flows. (George Ritzer, *Globalization: A Basic Text*, 2010: 519)

As we shall see (Chapter 16), major social movements have developed in the past few years to protest against it: in Seattle, in Prague, in London, in Genoa. For the time being we will just suggest a few of the key features of globalisation. We suggest that globalisation:

1 *Shifts the borders of economic transactions* – bringing a marked change in the pace of economic development in the world. Business companies, banking and investment now cross more national borders than ever before. In many instances these huge companies (TNCs or *transnational corporations*) have incomes and expenditures which are bigger than those of whole countries! Many argue that this has led to growing inequalities across the world, both within countries and between them. We will consider this in Chapters 9 and 16.

2 *Expands communications into global networks.* Television satellites, digital media, personal computers, mobile phones and all the information technologies help to 'shrink the world'. This has led to a major rethinking of ideas of *space and time*. We now no longer think mainly in terms of very local places. Instead we have entered a world where telephones, jet planes and now the internet make communications with others all over the globe instantaneous and hence very different from the past. Think especially of the phenomenal growth in the use of the mobile phone – handies, cellphones, etc. – and how this makes communications so much less restricted to face-to-face relations. Of course, telephones are not new, but the idea of being able to keep a phone on one's body wherever you are does make for a different pattern of communication. For growing numbers of people the whole world can be accessed instantly. Whereas a few hundred years ago it would take years for people to know what was happening in other parts of the world, now ideas can be moved instantly. We will consider this further in Chapters 22 and 23.

3 *Fosters a new, widespread 'global culture'.* Many urban areas come to look like each other, and many television programmes, much music, film and so on travels easily around the world. MTV has become a global youth form. And if you go to your local record store, the chances are you will now find quite a large section on global music! Not only do we have Hollywood but we have Bollywood. We will consider all this in Chapters 5 and 22.

4 *Develops new forms of international governance.* Some suggest that globalisation means the weakening of the nation-state. Though this is controversial, what is not in doubt is the growth of international agencies such as the United Nations, the European Court of Human Rights and the World Health Organization. These enact programmes that are publicly committed to what has been called 'the

democratisation of the world' – a growing belief that democracy as a political system will become dominant in the world. We consider this in Chapter 16.

5 *Creates a growing awareness of shared common world problems.* It is harder and harder to think of the world's problems as just the problems belonging to any one country. For instance, crime – as we shall see in Chapter 17 – has become increasingly global: drugs markets spread across continents, cyber-crimes push against the laws of any one country, international courts proclaim international justice. Likewise, the major impact of industrialisation on the environment becomes a compelling common problem in all countries (which is discussed in Chapters 24 and 25). Meanwhile, world poverty studies highlight growing inequalities both between and within nations; while debates on migration, refugees, wars and terrorism bring an international focus.

6 *Fosters a growing sense of risk* – what the German sociologist Ulrich Beck (1992) has called the *World Risk Society*. New technologies are generating risks which are of a quite different order from those found throughout earlier human history. Of course, past societies were risky and dangerous places too – whole populations could be wiped out by major earthquakes, floods or plagues, for example. Life for most people throughout history has been nasty, brutish and short. Nature brought with it its own dangers and risks. But Beck argues that new kinds of risk appear with the industrial world which are not 'in nature' but 'manufactured'.

These risks are associated with the many new technologies which generate new dangers to lives and the planet itself. These are humanly produced, may have massively unforeseen consequences, and may take many, many thousands of years to reverse. These 'manufactured risks' are taking us to the edge of catastrophe: to 'threats to all forms of life on this planet', to 'the exponential growth of risks and the impossibility of escaping them'. Risk, then, is associated with a globalising world that tries to break away from tradition and the past, and where change and the future become more valued. All these changes – from the railway to the computer, from genetic engineering to nuclear weapons – have unforeseen consequences that we cannot easily predict. The list of examples of new risks could be quite long: the changes in work and family patterns, fallout from the atomic bomb, the spread of networks of cars and planes throughout the planet,

the arrival of AIDS as a major world pandemic, the development of genetically modified crops, the cloning of animals (and people), the deforestation of the planet, 'designer children and surrogate mothering', the intensity of computer games and the new ways of relating (or not relating!) this might bring, and the arrival of new forms of terrorism where suicide bombers are willing to fly into major buildings (such as happened at the World Trade Center on 11 September 2001), and on and on. All have consequences which may be far reaching and are at present unpredictable. In some of the chapters that follow, we look at some of these main 'risks' and how they affect all countries and people. We consider this in many places, but especially in Chapters 23, 24 and 25.

7 *Leads to the emergence of 'transnational global actors' who 'network'.* From Greenpeace to Disneyworld, from the United Nations to tourism, from the Moonies to the women's movement, there are more and more people who move in networks that are not just bound to a fixed spatial community. Instead, they connect across the globe, making the global their local. They are global citizens.

## The globalisation guide

You can find more detail on globalisation throughout the book:

1 *Global economy*: Chapters 9 and 16.
2 *Global politics, war and terrorism*: Chapter 16.
3 *Global media, networks and communications*: Chapters 6, 22 and 23.
4 *Global inequalities*: Chapters 8–14
5 *Global people – migration, trafficking, refugees, the rich*: especially Chapter 11.
6 *Global education*: Chapter 20.
7 *Global technologies*: outer space, computer revolution: Chapter 23.
8 *Global culture/culture industries*: Chapters 5 and 22.
9 *Global conflicts, governance and social movements*: Chapter 16.
10 *Globalisation of crime*: Chapter 17.
11 *Global world problems*: Chapters 9, 24 and 25.
12 *Global environment and the risk society*: Chapters 23, 24 and 25.
13 *Global religions*: Chapter 19.
14 *Global cities*: Chapter 24.

See also Martell (2010) and Ritzer (2010).

In recent years, as ideas around globalisation have grown, many different stances have been taken on the relevance and usefulness of the idea. Two can be singled out here. *Globalisers* argue that there is a growing global economy which is transcending nations and providing the motor force of change. They tend to be the 'modernisers' and see the dynamic of international capitalism as a force for generating more and more wealth, from which more and more countries will be able to gain. By contrast, there are the *sceptics* who are critical of the globalisation thesis. They argue that there is much more economic independence among individual states than globalisers allow for. They also claim that there has been little real convergence of state policies across the globe. For them, real inequalities across countries can be shown to have actually grown. Sceptics often mirror a newer version of dependency theory (for example, Hirst and Thompson, 2009; Held et al., 1999).

# The globalisation of music: Hip Hop in Japan

In the past, except for the very rich and the world travellers, music has been limited to the local community and handed on by tradition. But today, music increasingly flows through worldwide cultures. Music has become part of the globalisation process. We can now find 'world music', cultures of international music celebrities, worldwide fan cultures, and the creation of music media companies worldwide that dominate music markets across the world. We can see examples of world music cultures everywhere: from global music festivals (often to raise money for charities) to 'global musicals' like *Les Misérables* – seen by 55 million people worldwide in some 40 countries and recorded in 21 languages. When the the Three Tenors (Domingo, Carreras and Pavarotti) performed at the 1990 FIFA World Cup in Italy in 1990, it led to a mass global phenomenon continuing well into 2005 and a new interest in classical music 'for the millions' (though the term has two different meanings!). Music is now part of the world economy and world media.

Central to all this, and indeed to much of globalisation, is the

You can see how widespread globalisation has been by looking at different musical forms and youth culture styles and dress. The rap of late 1970s black US ghettos turns into 1980s hip-hop and then travels the world, being modified in the process by different cultures. Depicted here is Japanese hip-hop

*Source*: © PYMCA/Alamy.

idea of **commodification** (*aspects of life are turned into things – commodities for sale*). Music has been turned into a

WORLD WATCH

sellable object. This has meant not just the selling of concerts, CDs, DVDs and music generally – but also an aggressive merchandising of adjuncts like posters, books, concert programmes and the like. Tickets for a world tour concert of the singer Barbara Streisand in 2007 were sold out at £500 a ticket! Globalisation leads to developed markets around the world for music. Up to 90 per cent of the global music market is accounted for by just five corporations: EMI Records, Sony, AOI Time Warner, BMG and Vivendi Universal. The latter is the largest with 29 per cent of the market share, and owning operations in some 63 countries. But it is interesting to note that certain areas of the world are not well marketed by the 'Big Five'. India resists their domination because it has its own very large industry (for example, in what has been called Bollywood). Africa's weak economic situation also means that, outside South Africa, the market does not seem attractive.

Global music appears to be increasingly Westernised. To some extent local cultures all over the world have been invaded by Western music – from 'classical concerts and opera'

(often seen as a sign of status), to modern rock, pop, MTV and all the spin-offs that largely reproduce the Western status quo. Some have claimed that this is a new form of colonialism, where local cultures lose their musical traditions at the expense of Western dominance. Nowhere is this more clearly seen than in the convergence of youth cultures and the convergence in their musical styles.

But global music is also shaped and adapted to local trends and cultures. Sociologists might call this 'the **glocalisation** of world music'. (Glocalisation *means the process by which local communities respond differently to global changes* – see Chapter 5.) Musical traditions are rarely 'pure': they get spliced into hybrid forms. Classical music goes 'light' with Classic FM; rap, itself a hybrid of African-American black music becomes Japanese hip hop. Japan has a vibrant hip hop scene which has borrowed heavily from Afro-American music and been remade in Tokyo clubs and recording studios. In a major study of this process, Ian Condry went to more than 120 hip hop performances in clubs in and around Tokyo, sat in on dozens of studio recording sessions, and

interviewed rappers, music company executives, music store owners and journalists. He shows how young Japanese combine the figure of the samurai with American rapping techniques and gangsta imagery, and how self-described 'yellow B-Boys' express their devotion to 'black culture'. Here there is mix (a blend, a hybridity) of black and yellow, classical Japanese and black America. Condry shows how rappers manipulate the Japanese language to achieve rhyme and rhythmic flow. This is a fascinating study (which could probably be redone in many other cultures). It shows how cultural musical globalisation often depends on grassroots connections and individual performers rather than just the control of big media corporation markets (though they may have initially started the popular concern). Hip hop is constantly made and remade in specific locations through local activities and for particular audiences (Condry, 2006). Local cultures embrace musical forms from other cultures while modifying them.

Look at YouTube for examples of 'Japan hip hop'. And see the website by Ian Condry at http://web.mit.edu/condry/www/jhh.

# Futures: a multi-paradigm discipline in a global world

This chapter has aimed to introduce you to some of the perspectives needed to think about society. We have suggested some classical ways (looking at society as functions, as structures, as actions, as conflicts, as consensus) and some emerging ways (looking at societies as an array of competing perspectives: from feminism to the postcolonial). We have suggested that some of the classical ways are now being questioned by

what might be seen as a postmodern perspective. These diverse positions suggest that sociology is not one position but many: sociologists call this **multi-paradigmatic**. This is a view we take throughout this book, and you will hence find a range of views – some of which many even conflict. Do not expect sociology to give you neat answers and tidy solutions!

Perhaps the most significant development in all this has been to push for sociology to focus on not just one country, but many. Here we have suggested that sociologists should take a global perspective and a helpful idea in doing this is globalisation. We will regularly return to all this throughout the book.

# SUMMARY

1 Building theory involves linking insights to gain understanding. Various theoretical perspectives guide sociologists as they construct theories.

2 The functional perspective is a framework for exploring how social structures promote the stability and integration of society. This approach minimises the importance of social inequality, conflict and change, whereas the conflict perspective highlights these aspects. At the same time, the conflict approach downplays the extent of society's integration and stability. In contrast to these broad, macro-level approaches, the action perspective is a micro-level theoretical framework that focuses on face-to-face interaction in specific settings. Because each perspective spotlights different dimensions of any social issue, the richest sociological understanding is derived from applying all three. Sociological thinking involves the action–structure debate.

3 Newer developments in sociological theory have highlighted how all sociology must work from perspectives or different voices. It is multi-paradigmatic. Classically, sociology has heard only the voices of white, Western, heterosexual men: other voices are now being heard. Feminist sociology is a prime example. Postmodernism suggests that a new social order is in the making that is accelerating social change and creating a more 'provisional' world. Postmodern sociology stresses the need to look at multiple perspectives, takes seriously the local elements, and tries to keep a provisional 'openness' in its ideas.

4 A key feature of the modern word is that it is organised through capitalism. It highlights private ownership of property, pursuit of personal profit and free competition.

5 A global perspective enhances the sociological perspective because, first, societies of the world are becoming more and more interconnected; secondly, many social problems are most serious beyond the borders of European countries; and, thirdly, recognising how others live helps us better understand ourselves. Globalisation is an emerging widespread process by which social relations acquire relatively distanceless and borderless qualities. Globalisation highlights the interconnectedness of business and TNCs, the development of global media, and the emergence of global cultures, international governance and world citizens.

# MYTASKLIST

# Ten suggestions for going further

## 1 Connect up with Part Six and the Sociology Web Resources

As you work through ideas and think about the issues raised in this chapter, look at the accompanying website and the resource centre at the end of this book which connects to it. There is a lot here to help you move on. To link up, see: www.pearson.co.uk/plummer.

## 2 Review the chapter

*Briefly summarise (in a paragraph) just what this chapter has been about.* Consider: (a) What have you learned? (b) What do you disagree with? Be critical. And (c) How would you develop all this? How could you get more detail on matters that interest you?

## 3 Pose questions

(a) Start keeping a list of sociologists you encounter throughout this book. Locate them historically, the name of the theory they are identified with, some examples of what they looked at and examined, and the key features and problems of their theories.

(b) What are the key theories discussed in this chapter? Be guided by some of these theoretical perspectives and ask yourself what kinds of question might a sociologist ask about (i) television, (ii) war, (iii) sport, (iv) colleges and universities, and (v) men and women?

(c) Start keeping a 'sociological glossary' of key new words you find in sociology. Try to make sure you can say (i) what the word means, (ii) what debates and research it is applied in, and (iii) whether you find it helpful or not: does it enable you to see society more sharply or does it confuse and hinder?

(d) Is globalisation a new phenomenon and is it really such a different world from that of the past? Consider what the term means and draw out some illustrations of it. How has your own life been touched by globalisation?

## 4 Explore key words

Many concepts have been introduced in this chapter. You can review them from the website or from the listing at the back of this book. You might like to give special attention to just five words and think them through – how would you define them, what are they dealing with, and do they help you see the social world more clearly or not? A useful additional dictionary for this chapter might be:

Andrew Jones *Dictionary of Globalization*, Polity (2006)

You may find it useful to have by you three books by John Scott:

*Sociology: The Key Concepts* (2006)

*Fifty Key Sociologists: The Formative Theorists* (2006)

*Fifty Key Sociologists: The Contemporary Theorists* (2006)

## 5 Search the Web

Be critical when you look at websites – see the box on p. 940 in the Resources section. For this chapter look at:

### Sociological theory

SocioSite www.sociosite.net/topics/theory.php – provides a general introduction.

### Durkheim

www.emile-durkheim.com
www.faculty.rsu.edu/~felwell/Theorists/Durkheim/index.htm
http://durkheim.itgo.com

### Marx

www.marxists.org
www.spartacus.schoolnet.co.uk/TUmarx.htm
http://plato.stanford.edu/entries/marx
www.bbc.co.uk/history/historic_figures/marx_karl.shtml

www.historyguide.org/intellect/marx.html
www.faculty.rsu.edu/~felwell/Theorists/Marx

## Weber

Verstehen: Max Weber's home page
www.faculty.rsu.edu/~felwell/Theorists/Weber/Whome.htm
Weberian sociology of religion
www.ne.jp/asahi/moriyuki/abukuma

## Feminism

Feminist theory website
www.cddc.vt.edu/feminism/enin.html

## Globalisation

Two introductory sites are:

The globalization website
www.sociology.emory.edu/globalization

Globalization 101: a student's guide
www.globalization101.org

See also:
Forces of globalisation
www.humanities.uci.edu/critical/html/Projects%20
+%20Events/Forces.html

International Forum on Globalization (IFG)
www.ifg.org

World Bank: globalisation
www.worldbank.org/globalization

World Commission on the Social Dimensions of Globalization
www.ilo.org/public/english/wcsdg

# 6  Watch a DVD

Look at the films of other cultures across the world
and see how they are interconnecting with your own.
One way into issues of globalisation is through international
film and video. A good source for such films is
http://worldfilm.about.com – a major site for world films.
   On globalisation, see: Tom Zaniello, *The Cinema of
Globalization: A Guide to Films about the New Economic
Order* (2007).
   For some opening examples, try:

- Ang Lee's *The Wedding Banquet* (1993): a romantic
  comedy about a gay Asian man in the USA who marries
  a Chinese girl to please his parents.
- Carlos Saura's *Blood Wedding* (1981): a powerful dance
  movie based on a Garcia Lorca story, starring Antonio
  Gades and Christina Hoyos.
- Bahman Ghobadi's *A Time for Drunken Horses* (2000): a
  film about the suffering and hard lot of Kurdish children.
- Marziyeh Meshkini's *The Day I Became a Woman* (2001):
  a disturbing portrayal of the role of women in Iran.

# 7  Think and read

## Introduction to social theory

Michele Dillon, *Introduction to Sociological Theory* (2009)
   is a clear and illustrated introductory tour. Shaun Best,
   *A Beginner's Guide to Social Theory* (2003) and E. C. Cuff,
   Wes Sharrock and D. Francis, *Perspectives in Sociology*
   (5th rev edn, 2006) outline most of the major positions.

Rob Stones (ed.), *Key Sociological Thinkers* (2nd edn, 2008)
   provides 21 short and readable essays on many of the
   key sociologists, past and present.

Charles Lemert (ed.), *Social Theory: The Multicultural and
   Classic Readings* (3rd edn, 2004) is a major compendium
   of articles that debates the full range of sociological
   theories – classical and newer. It is a very large volume!
   But for anyone very interested in the full range of
   sociological theory from the original authors it is an
   invaluable starting point.

## Introductions to globalisation

Zygmunt Bauman, *Globalization: The Human Consequences*
   (1998) and Anthony Giddens, *Runaway World: How
   Globalization is Reshaping Our Lives* (1999) provide two
   short, readable guides to the idea of globalisation.

Jan Nederveen Pieterse, *Globalization and Culture* (2004)
   and Malcolm Waters, *Globalization* (2000) are also short
   but more detailed and systematic treatments – a little
   more advanced.

George Ritzer, *Globalization: A Basic Text* (2010) and Luke
   Martell, *The Sociology of Globalization* (2010) are both
   major readable textbooks which introduce key ideas
   around globalisation.

David Held et al., *Global Transformations* (2nd edn, 2007).
   This is an altogether more advanced, very detailed and
   long account of globalisation. A shorter version is
   *Globalization/Anti Globalization: Beyond the Great Divide*
   (with Andrew McGrew) (2nd edn, 2007).

*Understanding Global Issues: The Facts behind the News* is a
very useful series of booklets which are issued regularly and
cover current global issues. Details can be accessed on its
website at: www.global-issues.co.uk/index.php

# 8  Relax with a novel

You will get the idea of a postmodern novel from reading:
John Fowles's *The French Lieutenant's Woman*, Umberto Eco's
*The Name of the Rose*, and Brett Easton's *American Pyscho*
(all are also films). Pico Iyer's *The Global Soul: Jet Lag,
Shopping Malls and the Search for Home* (2000) could be fun!

## 9 Connect to other chapters

- For more on Marx, Durkheim and Weber, see Chapter 4.
- For more on action and interaction, see Chapter 7.
- For more on feminism and queer theory, see Chapter 12.
- For more on globalisation, see all chapters but especially Chapters 9 and 22–25.

# 10 Engage in THE BIG DEBATE

## The sociological puzzle: do we make social life or does social life make us?

Which comes first: the chicken or the egg? This classic conundrum has a parallel question for sociology which has persisted throughout the discipline's history. It can be put like this: which comes first – society or the individual? And like the chicken and egg problem, there is no simple solution. Indeed, what has to be recognised is that one does not come first – eggs cannot simply come before chickens, any more than chickens can simply come before eggs. Both are needed. And it is the interaction of the two that has to be seen. You cannot, in short, have one without the other. And the same is true for individuals and societies. What sociologists do is look at both individuals and societies, and at their best they look at them together through dialectical thinking which requires looking at two seeming opposites (like individual and society) and how a new form emerges through them.

### Making it happen: individuals and action

One phase of sociological analysis is indeed to look at human beings. Not as a psychologist would – in terms of individual attributes like drives or personalities. Rather, the task is to look at the ways in which human beings are orientated towards action, to being world makers, creators of history and social life. Human beings make history, and sociology should look at the ways this happens.

For instance, if you want to understand how our current education system works, one task is to look at the ways in which people make it what it is. This means examining the ways in which legislators passed laws that provided the framework for schools, teaching, curriculum and exams. These did not just happen: they were made, and sociologists need to look at how they were made. Likewise, a pupil arrives in a class and, along with other students and teachers, sets about making the class happen. Sociologists like to get into the classrooms and observe this 'action' – to see just how human beings make the social world work.

### Pattern and prison: social structures as maps

Yet people are also born into worlds that are not of their own making. Indeed, as the sociologist Peter Berger says, 'society is the walls of our imprisonment' (Berger, 1963: 109). We are born into families, communities and nations over which we have little immediate control; our lives are heavily shaped by the class, gender and ethnicity we are born into; indeed, even the very language we think with and talk with helps set a pattern to our life. And we had no initial choice over which language we speak: it is given to us from early childhood. (It would be very odd, if you were born in England, if you were made to speak Swahili.) Thus, one moment of sociological analysis is to look at these broadest patterns of social organisation that shape our lives. Recurrent and habitual patterns of social life may be seen as structures. Think for a moment of the ways in which your own life is 'imprisoned'.

### Putting 'action' and 'structure' together

So, a structural approach tends to map out society as a whole, while an action approach tends to examine the ways in which individuals and small groups come to make their social worlds. Of course, ideally both will be done. This is a task for more advanced social theory.

British sociologist Anthony Giddens, for example, has introduced the idea of structuration to focus on both simultaneously, to suggest a process whereby action and structure are always two sides of the same coin (Giddens, 1984). For him, people engage in social actions that create social structures, and it is through these social actions that the structures themselves are produced, maintained and eventually changed over time. Language is a good example of this. Language is a structure of rules, but people speak, write and act it in different ways, changing it as they go along. Without the rules, they would be incomprehensible, so the structures are needed. But just slavishly adhering to the structure would allow for no change, no creativity, no humanity. Looking at both individuals and structures at the same time is what is required. This is no easy task.

As you read this book, keep this puzzle in mind. And take the discussion further.

### Continue the debate

1 Do you see yourself as 'determined' by social structure? Look at the image on p. 6 again (Society as a prison).
2 How much control do you have over your life? How far do you think you can change the world? Are you a world maker?
3 Look at attempts that have been made to resolve the problem between individual and society.

# CHAPTER 3

# STUDYING THE SOCIAL: AN INTRODUCTION TO SOCIOLOGICAL METHOD

SUDHIR VENKATESH STYLES HIMSELF AS A 'ROGUE SOCIOLOGIST'. He was a student and a budding sociologist at the University of Chicago in the late 1980s, but is now a major professor at New York's Columbia University. When at university he started long walks around the city and found himself intrigued by the neighbourhood that bordered his elite university. Right next to the elite Chicago University stands a major Chicago ghetto. Sudhir Venkatesh decided to study it.

There is a very long tradition of researching the life of this city (often called Chicago Sociology) and much of it has focused on delinquents, gangs and the race issue. For a decade in the 1990s, Sudir hung around with some of the most violent gangs of Chicago for his sociological studies. The Black Kings operated a hugely profitable drug ring – selling crack in the corridors of old buildings and extorting protection money from residents. They were not averse to violence. Sudhir got to know some of the dealers, the prostitutes, the pimps, the organisers, the cops and the officials – a good few of whom were corrupt and willing to take money from the gang for looking the other way. He watched them all 'misbehave' in many criminal situations and he became so accepted that for one day he was delegated with key decisions – acting as a 'Gang Leader for a Day'. He saw how they laundered money; he had to organise the selling and distribution of drugs; he lived the criminal life to see how it was done. His supervisors back at the university were not too keen on his approach – he seemed to be taking a lot of personal risks. After all the gang was quite a heavy one, even capable of killing! To start with Sudhir was indeed very uneasy, but bit by bit he started

to build up a strong bond with J.T., a gang leader, and he spent the better part of a decade inside the projects under JT's protection. Whilst he started the project thinking he would do a multiple-choice survey on urban poverty, he soon learnt that this was not a good way to get his data.

Sudhir was not the first to do this. William Whyte half a century before him had produced his famous study *Street Corner Society*, and many a young sociologist has spent their formative days studying 'youth cultures'. But Sudhir's work was written up in a way that made it very accessible – it reads like a good novel, with no academic jargon or references at all. Yet it bristles with sociological insights. It rapidly became a kind of sociological pop best seller – you will probably find it a local good bookshop in a Penguin paperback. This does not happen a lot in sociology.

You can find more about Sudhir Vankatesh and his projects on his website at: www.sudhirvenkatesh.org. Here you can:

* find reviews and press coverage for *Gang Leader for a Day*
* watch online video interviews with Sudhir Venkatesh
* listen to audio interviews with Sudhir Venkatesh

He is also on YouTube – reading extracts from his work.

*I have striven not to laugh at human actions, not to weep at them, not to hate them, but to understand them.*

Benedict Spinoza

*There is no best way to tell a story about society. Many genres, many methods, many formats – they can all do the trick. Instead of ideal ways to do it, the world gives us possibilities among which we choose. Every way of telling the story of a society does some of the job superbly but other parts not so well . . .*

Howard S. Becker

---

## In this chapter, we ask:

* **How can we do sociological research?**
* **What is the nature of sociological knowledge, evidence and 'truth'?**
* **What are the key tools of sociological research?**
* **What are the major political and ethical issues in research?**
* **What are the new developments in research methods?**

---

(Left) Leonardo da Vinci, *Vitruvian Man*, c. 1492

*Source*: Bridgeman Art Library Ltd/Galleria dell'Accademia, Venice, Italy/BAL.

*Note*: For more information go to: www.artcyclopedia.com/artists/leonardo_da_vinci.html; www.willamette.edu/cla/exsci/info/history/vitruvian.htm; http://leonardodavinci.stanford.edu/submissions/clabaugh/history/leonardo.html; and elsewhere in this chapter too.

**Q** Leonardo da Vinci (1452–1519) was one of the leading figures in Renaissance art. Why is this particular drawing so significant? Consider how you have seen it represented over and over again in the modern world. What does this suggest to you about studying social life?

Just how do social scientists get their data? The sociologist Sudhir Venkatesh went into the field and observed the daily life of a Chicago gang. Others interview, survey, give out questionnaires, draw upon documents of all kinds, set up focus groups. Some even monitor their own conduct. Such research may then get written up as stories and narratives; other researchers turn them into statistical reports. The ways of doing social science are many and varied. In this chapter we provide a brief review of some of the issues involved in 'doing social science'.

As we have seen, sociology involves a way of thinking; but it also involves a way of doing. It is a practice that looks at problems and then digs out the best 'data', 'evidence' or 'facts' that it can. This chapter will look at some of the ways sociologists actually go about studying the social world. It will ask about the very nature of 'knowledge'. It will highlight the methods that sociologists use to conduct research, and suggest appropriate questions to raise in assessing the value of any particular sociological study or 'finding'. Along the way, we shall see that sociological research involves not just procedures for gathering information but also controversies about whether that research should strive to be objective or to offer a bolder prescription for social change. Can it be neutral or is it bound up with politics and values? Sociologists are divided on all these issues.

The issues this chapter raises should help you think about the adequacy of the methods used in the sociological studies you read about. It should also enable you to start thinking about how you could conduct your own research – the chapter ends with some basic guidelines for you to plan your own project.

## The basics of sociological investigation

Sociological investigation begins with two simple requirements. The first was the focus of Chapters 1 and 2: *look at the world using the sociological perspective.* Suddenly, from this point of view, all around us we see curious patterns of social life that call out for further theoretical study. This brings us to the second requirement for sociological investigation: *be curious and critical by asking sociological questions.*

These two requirements – seeing the world sociologically and asking critical sociological questions – are fundamental to sociological investigation. Yet they are only the beginning. They draw us into the social world, stimulating our imagination. But then we face the challenging task of finding answers to our questions. To understand the kinds of insight sociology offers, it helps to divide the research process into the following three types of issue:

- *Theoretical/epistemological questions.* Here we ask about the *kind* of truth we are trying to produce. Do we, for example, want to produce a strong 'factual' scientific kind of truth with lots of evidence? Or do we wish to provide a wider theoretical understanding of what is going on? As we shall see, there are different versions of sociology and it helps to be clear which kind of sociology is being done.

- *Technical questions.* Here we ask questions about how to use tools and procedures which enable our 'findings' to be as good as they can be. There is the matter of the kinds of research tool to use – interviewing, observing, questionnaires, statistical calculations, for example; and then making sure they perform their tasks well and do not mislead us. We must always remember, though, that methods like this are a means to an end and should never be an end in themselves (sadly, a lot of social science forgets this and elevates the idea of methods to a fetish).

- *Ethical, political and policy questions.* Here we ask questions about the *point* of doing the research and consider what consequences it might have: for us, for our research subjects, and even for the wider world. All sociology is embroiled with politics and ethics: if it looks like it is being neutral, you may well want to be suspicious.

The discussion in this chapter will be framed by these questions. You can use them as a guide for thinking about your own research projects. But they are only a guide, and suggestions for taking them further will – as usual – be found at the end of the chapter.

## What is a sociological 'truth'? Matters of epistemology

A key question to ask of social investigation is a very hard one: 'What kind of truth am I trying to produce?' This raises questions of **epistemology**, *that branch of philosophy that investigates the nature of knowledge and truth.* Our opening concern is to realise that there are different kinds of 'truth'.

People's 'truths' differ the world over, and we often encounter 'facts' at odds with our own. Imagine being a volunteer with Voluntary Service Overseas (VSO) and arriving in a small, traditional village in Africa. With the job of helping the local people to grow more food, you take to the fields, observing a curious practice: farmers carefully planting seeds and then placing a dead fish directly on top of each one. In response to your question, they reply that the fish is a gift to the god of the harvest. A local elder adds sternly that the harvest was poor one year when no fish were offered as gifts.

From that society's point of view, using fish as gifts to the harvest god makes sense. The people believe in it, their experts endorse it, and everyone seems to agree that the system works. But, with scientific training in agriculture, you have to shake your head and wonder. The scientific 'truth' in this situation is something entirely different: the decomposing fish fertilise the ground, producing a better crop.

Our VSO worker example does not mean, of course, that people in traditional villages ignore what their senses tell them, or that members of technologically advanced societies reject non-scientific ways of knowing. A medical researcher using science to seek an effective treatment for cancer, for example, may still practise her religion as a matter of faith; she may turn to experts when making financial decisions; and she may derive political opinions from family and friends. In short, we all embrace various kinds of truth at the same time.

But science represents a very distinctive way of knowing, and one that has come to dominate in the modern Western world.

## Common sense versus scientific evidence

Scientific evidence sometimes challenges our common sense. Here are four statements that many people might assume to be 'true', even though each is at least partly contradicted by scientific research.

1 *Poor people are far more likely than rich people to break the law.* Watching a crime show on TV, one might well conclude that police arrest only people from 'bad' neighbourhoods. And, as Chapter 17 explains, poor people are arrested in disproportionate numbers. But research also reveals that police and prosecutors are likely to treat apparent wrongdoing by well-to-do people more leniently. Further, some researchers argue that our society drafts laws in such a way as to reduce the risk that affluent people will be criminalised.

2 *We now live in a middle-class society in which most people are more or less equal.* Data presented in Chapter 9 show that a very small group of people throughout the world control wealth. If people are equal, then some are much 'more equal' than others.

3 *Differences in the behaviour of females and males reflect 'human nature'.* Much of what we call 'human nature' is created by the society in which we are raised, as Chapter 5 details. Further, as Chapter 12 argues, some societies define 'feminine' and 'masculine' very differently from the way we do.

4 *Most people marry because they are in love.* To members of our society, few statements are so self-evident. But, surprising as it may seem, research shows that, in most societies, marriage has little to do with love. Chapter 18 explains why.

These examples confirm the old saying that 'It's not what we don't know that gets us into trouble as much as the things we *do* know that just aren't so.' We have all been brought up believing conventional truths, bombarded by expert advice, and pressured to accept the opinions of people around us. Sociology teaches us to evaluate critically what we see, read and hear. Like any way of knowing, sociology has limitations, as we shall see. But sociology gives us the tools to assess many kinds of information.

## A starting point: the positivist and humanistic traditions

The trouble is that precisely what is meant even by 'science' is not agreed upon by philosophers of knowledge. Traditionally, they take one of two views: positivist or humanist (often called interpretivist).

**Positivism** is *a logical system that bases knowledge on direct, systematic observation.* It usually seeks out law-like statements of social life that can be tested. The work of Durkheim on suicide introduced in Chapter 1 would be an instance of this. Scientific knowledge rests on **empirical evidence** (for Durkheim, recall, these were suicide rates), meaning *information we can verify with our senses.* But even here there is controversy among philosophers over the true nature of science, as we shall soon see.

The second position is interpretivism or humanism. **Humanist epistemology** sees that studying the human world is very different from studying the physical, biological or material world. There is a focus on the human and the symbolic. As such, social science must produce a different kind of knowledge, one that seeks to understand meanings. Research in this tradition will look at the empirical world (as in positivism) but will highlight the importance of understanding and interpretation.

Below, we will look at these two basic positions in a little more detail.

# The positivist baseline

Positivist sociologists apply science to the study of society in much the same way that natural scientists investigate the physical world. Whether they end up confirming a widely held opinion or revealing that it is completely groundless, sociologists use scientific techniques to gather empirical evidence. The following sections of this chapter introduce the major elements of positivist investigation.

## The ideal of objectivity

Assume that ten writers who work for a magazine in Amsterdam are collaborating on a story about that city's best restaurants. With their editor paying, they head out on the town for a week of fine dining. Later, they get together to compare notes. Do you think one restaurant would be everyone's clear favourite? That hardly seems likely.

In scientific terms, each of the ten reporters probably operationalises the concept 'best restaurant' differently. For one, it might be a place that serves Indonesian food at reasonable prices; for another, the choice might turn on a superb view of the canals; for yet another, stunning decor and attentive service might be the deciding factors. Like so many other things in life, the best restaurant turns out to be mostly a matter of individual taste.

Personal values are fine when it comes to restaurants, but they pose a challenge to scientific research. On the one hand, every scientist has personal opinions about the world. On the other, science endorses the goal of **objectivity**, *a state of personal neutrality in conducting research*. Objectivity in research depends on carefully adhering to scientific procedures in order not to bias the results. Scientific objectivity is an ideal rather than a reality, of course, since complete impartiality is virtually impossible for any researcher to achieve. Even the subject a researcher selects to study and the framing of the questions are likely to grow out of personal interest. But scientists cultivate detachment and follow specific methods to lessen the chance that conscious or unconscious biases will distort their work.

As an additional safeguard, researchers should try to identify and report their personal leanings to help readers evaluate their conclusions in the proper context.

The influential German sociologist Max Weber expected personal beliefs to play a part in a sociologist's selection of research topic. Why, after all, would one person study world hunger, another investigate the effects of racism, and still another examine one-parent families? But Weber (1958; orig. 1905) warned that, even though sociologists select topics that are *value-relevant*, they should conduct research that is *value-free* in their pursuit of conclusions. Only by being dispassionate in their work (as we expect any professional to be) can researchers study the world *as it is* rather than telling others how they think *it should be*. In Weber's view, this detachment was a crucial element of science that sets it apart from politics. Politicians, in other words, are committed to a particular outcome; scientists try to maintain an open-minded readiness to accept the results of their investigations, whatever they may be.

By and large, sociologists accept Weber's argument, though most concede that we can never be completely value-free or even aware of all our biases. Moreover, sociologists are not 'average' people: most are white people who are highly educated and more politically liberal than the population as a whole. Sociologists need to remember that they, too, are affected by their own social backgrounds.

One strategy for limiting distortion caused by personal values is **replication**, *repetition of research by other investigators*. If other researchers repeat a study using the same procedures and obtain the same results, they gain confidence that the original research (as well as their own) was conducted objectively. The need for replication in scientific investigation is probably the reason why the search for knowledge is called *research* in the first place.

In any case, keep in mind that the logic and methodology of science hold out no guarantee that we will grasp objective, absolute truth. What science offers is an approach to knowledge that is *self-correcting* so that, in the long run, researchers stand the best chance of overcoming their own biases and achieving greater understanding. Objectivity and truth, then, lie not in any particular research method, but in the scientific process itself.

## Some limitations of scientific sociology

The first scientists probed the operation of the natural world. Many sociologists use science to study the social world; however, the scientific study of people has several important limitations.

1 *Human behaviour is too complex to allow sociologists to predict precisely any individual's actions.* Astronomers calculate the movement of planets with remarkable precision, announcing years in advance when a comet will next pass near the earth. But planets and comets are unthinking objects; humans, by contrast, have minds of their own. Because no two people react to any event in exactly the same way, the best that sociologists can do is to show that categories of people typically act in one way or another. This is no failing of sociology; it is simply consistent with the nature of our task: studying creative, spontaneous people.

2 *Because humans respond to their surroundings, the mere presence of a researcher may affect the behaviour being studied.* An astronomer gazing at the moon has no effect whatever on that celestial body. But people usually react to being observed. Some may become anxious, angry or defensive; others may try to 'help' by providing the answers or actions they think researchers expect of them.

3 *Social patterns change constantly; what is true in one time or place may not hold true in another.* The laws of physics apply tomorrow as well as today; they hold true all around the world. But human behaviour is too variable for us to set down immutable sociological laws. In fact, some of the most interesting sociological research focuses on social diversity and social change.

4 *Because sociologists are part of the social world they study, being value-free when conducting social research can be difficult.* Barring a laboratory mishap, chemists are rarely personally affected by what goes on in test tubes. But sociologists live in their 'test tube' – the society they study. Therefore, social scientists face a greater challenge in controlling – or even recognising – personal values that may distort their work.

5 *Human behaviour differs from all other phenomena precisely because human beings are symbolic, subjective creatures.* Human beings – unlike planets or molecules – are always constructing meaning. And what marks us off from other animals is the elaborate symbolic systems we weave for ourselves. Therefore, sociologists cannot simply study societies from outside; they have to take on board ways of 'entering' these worlds of meaning.

# The humanistic stance: the importance of subjective interpretation

As we have explained, scientists tend to think of 'subjectivity' as 'bias' – a source of error to be avoided as much as possible. But there is also a good side to subjectivity, since creative thinking is vital to sociological investigation in three key ways.

First, science is basically a series of rules that guide research, rather like a recipe for cooking. But just as more than a recipe is required to make a great chef, so scientific procedure does not, by itself, produce a great sociologist. Also needed is an inspired human imagination. After all, insight comes not from science itself but from the lively thinking of creative human beings (Nisbet, 1970). The genius of physicist Albert Einstein or sociologist Max Weber lay not only in their use of the scientific method, but also in their curiosity and ingenuity.

Second, science cannot account for the vast and complex range of human motivations and feelings, including greed, love, pride and despair. Science certainly helps us gather facts about how people act, but it can never fully explain the complex meanings people attach to their behaviour (Berger and Kellner, 1981).

Third, we also do well to remember that scientific data never speak for themselves. After sociologists and other scientists 'collect the numbers', they face the ultimate task of *interpretation* – creating meaning from their observations. For this reason, good sociological investigation is as much art as science.

## Sociology and the humanities

The recognition of all these limitations leads many sociologists to adopt a somewhat different stance towards their study. They do not claim to be scientists as above, but instead try to make sociology a more humanistic discipline concerned with understanding. In his study of *Sociology as an Art Form*, Nisbet reflects 'How different things would be . . . if the social sciences at the time of their systematic formation in the nineteenth century had taken the arts in the same degree they took the physical science as models' (Nisbet, 1976: 16).

This corrective sociology may be called 'humanistic' and has at least four central criteria. It must pay tribute to *human subjectivity and creativity*, showing how individuals respond to social constraints and actively assemble social worlds. It must deal with concrete

**Being observed**. A basic lesson of social research is that being observed affects how people behave. Researchers can never be certain precisely how this will occur; while some people resent public attention, others become highly animated when they think they have an audience
*Source*: © Jenny Matthews/Alamy.

Does the camera ever tell the truth? How do people behave in front of cameras? What does this suggest to you as a major problem for all research?

human experiences – talk, feelings, actions – through their *social, and especially economic, organisation* (and not just their inner, psychic or biological structuring). It must show a naturalistic *intimate familiarity* with such experiences – abstractions untempered by close involvement are ruled out. And there must be a self-awareness by the sociologist of the ultimate *moral and political role* in moving towards a social structure in which there is less exploitation, oppression and injustice and more creativity, diversity and equality. A list like this is open to detailed extension and revision, but it is hard to imagine a humanistic sociology which is not so minimally committed to these criteria.

Table 3.1 summarises some of the wide-ranging contrasts between the positivistic and humanistic approaches to sociological investigation.

| Table 3.1 | **A bridgeable divide? Humanistic and positivist research contrasted** | |
|---|---|---|
| | **Towards the humanities** | **Towards the sciences** |
| Foci | Unique and idiographic<br>Human-centred<br>The inner: subjective, meaning, feeling, experience | General and nomothetic<br>Structure-centred<br>The outer: objective, 'things', events, facts |
| Epistemology | Phenomenalist<br>Relational/relativist<br>Perspectivist/pragmatist | Realist<br>Absolutist/essentialist<br>Logical positivist |
| Task | Interpret, understand<br>Describe, observe<br>Appreciate | Causal explanation<br>Measure<br>Theorise |
| Style | 'Soft', 'warm'<br>Imaginative<br>Valid, 'real', 'rich'<br>Personal research | 'Hard', 'cold'<br>Systematic<br>Reliable, 'replicable'<br>Large-scale funding |
| Theory | Inductive and grounded<br>'Storytelling' | Deductive and abstract<br>'Operationalism' |
| Values | Ethically and politically committed<br>Egalitarianism | Ethically and politically neutral<br>'Expertise and elites' |

*Source*: Adapted from Plummer, 2001a: 9.

# Emergent epistemologies

The traditional debates in sociology over epistemology have been between the positivist stance and the humanist stance. Unfortunately, matters are not quite as simple as this, as there are a number of other positions that are important. We will look further at science in Chapter 23. But here we briefly raise five others: realism, critical stances, standpoints, queer theory and postmodernism.

## 1  The realist stance: theorising science

**Realism** is *a theoretical system of concepts that are evolved to handle a particular problem* (like how the economy, our minds or even the solar system works). While it may also gather empirical evidence, this is not central to its research – since it argues that 'empirical evidence' is never straightforward. We can never be sure of 'facts'. What we need, therefore, are strong explanations – built up from theoretical tools that will help us do this. The work of Marx is usually seen as a realist theory. For him, the problem was how capitalism works. To explain this, he did not simply go out and talk with people or simply look at documents (although he did do both these things). Instead he developed the idea of the **mode of production**, *the way a society is organised to produce goods and services*. From this concept, he could start to evolve an understanding of how societies work and change.

## 2  Critical sociology

**Critical sociology** developed in reaction to positivist science, and is often inspired by Marx. It rejects the idea that society exists as a 'natural' system open to discovery. Critical sociologists suggest that not only should the social world be understood, it should ultimately be changed. They see the task of sociology as avowedly political, tying knowledge to action. They look at *all knowledge as harbouring political interests and the task of sociology as being critically to unmask what is actually going on.* Thus, for example, much sociology may suggest that we are free-thinking rational agents with choices: critical sociology would take this as a problem and try to show how all of this is shaped by social institutions. It subverts societies' dominant ideologies and beliefs. (For more on this, see Chapter 5, p. 163.)

## 3  Standpoint theory/standpoint epistemologies

Linked to the 'voices' raised in Chapter 1, **standpoint epistemologies** suggest that knowledge always comes out of specific kinds of social experience. *All knowledge is grounded in standpoints and standpoint theory enables groups to analyse their situation (problems and oppressions) from within the context of their own experiences.* The standpoint for most of social science has routinely been that of white, heterosexual, middle-class and middle-aged men – conventionally the dominant group in studying society. They have made their own standpoint appear to be 'the truth'.

But there is a range of other standpoints in the world: just as we saw in Chapter 2, there may be a feminist standpoint, which arises from the experiences and situations of women; a black standpoint, which arises from the situation of black people; or a gay standpoint, which arises from the experiences of lesbians and gays. The starting point, then, of this kind of epistemology is with the experience of these varied groups. The point is that starting from the (many different) daily activities of, for instance, lesbians enables us to see things in the social world that might otherwise have been invisible to us, not just about those lives but about heterosexual women's lives and men's lives, straight as well as gay (Harding, 1991: 252).

But problems can soon arise. For in taking, say, a feminist standpoint, it soon becomes clear that there is not just one position or stand to take – there is no universal (or essential) women's view. Women in low-income societies will almost certainly have different standpoints from those of middle-class white feminists in high-income societies. As we have already seen (Chapter 2), to work from a position which suggests there is only one standpoint of women would be to engage in **essentialism** – *the belief that qualities are inherent (essential to) specific objects*. A non-essentialising stance has to be taken which recognises how standpoints interweave (Collins, 1990; Harding, 1991).

## 4  Queer theory

**Queer theory** argues that *most sociological theory still has a bias towards 'heterosexuality' and that non-heterosexual voices need to be heard.* Such theorists would argue that all the topics discussed in this book – from stratification and ethnicity, to religion and economy – would be greatly enhanced if the position of 'non-heterosexual voices' were placed at the centre.

For example, it suggests that many religions have been organised around 'homophobic' persecutions; that a new form of economy is emerging that is based upon the spending power of young middle-class gay men – the pink economy; and that the experience of being lesbian or gay can differ significantly across different ethnic minority communities (Seidman, 1996). New insights can be provided for all the traditional concerns of sociology once we give a focus to a different group such as 'queers'. This is a position that is a little like standpoint theory. It is discussed further in Chapter 12.

## 5  Postmodern methodology

We could go on with other standpoints. As we have seen in Chapter 2, a number of different approaches have emerged within sociology over the past two decades which stress differing voices and an anti-essentialism. Most prominently, and most generally, there has been the arrival of what may be called postmodern methodology.

This suggests that any strong search for *the* truth (like the positivism discussed above) is part of the (now doomed) Enlightenment project of science. Postmodernists hold that this view of an absolute, scientific truth has now been discredited: truths are much more multiple, fluid, changing and fragmentary. Postmodern epistemology would highlight the following:

- The death of the meta-narrative, i.e. the end of any one big claim to truth.
- The need for local knowledges produced out of particular contexts, i.e. our truths must be located in specific situations.
- The need to be aware of the contexts which shape this knowledge. Part of this means a much greater self-awareness on the part of the researchers – knowing how they come to do this research and their involvement in it.
- The need to understand the ways in which this knowledge is then told – how it is represented through 'writing strategies'. This means an awareness of how knowledge is represented. Metaphors such as stories, discourses and narratives become part of this. Part may also be the visual turn – the importance given to film, video, cam-recording and the like as new tools for gathering data and new tools for presenting it.
- The need to know why this knowledge is being produced and how it will be used. Here sociological knowledge is rarely just 'knowledge for knowledge's sake': it is bound up with moral, political and ethical judgements. Sociology becomes a moral and political tale.

## A caution

We have to be careful. Ever since its birth, sociology has been locked into controversy as to its true character. A lot of recent debates are not in the end that recent – they have often been voiced, slightly differently, at earlier moments. The work of C. Wright Mills, for example, introduced in Chapter 1, was an earlier version of some of these ideas. What is important for you to sense at this stage is that the character of sociological knowledge itself has always been discussed and has led to many battles. These still continue today.

# Making sense of sociological data

Whichever epistemology is to be claimed, sociological research also always involves learning some 'tricks of the trade'. These are very practical matters – tools that are needed to make sure that you are doing the research as best you can.

## 1  Concepts, variables and measurement

A crucial element of all 'science' is the **concept**, *a mental construct that represents some part of the world, inevitably in a simplified form*. 'Society' is itself a concept, as are the structural parts of societies, including 'the family' and 'the economy'. Sociologists also use concepts to describe individuals, by noting, for example, their 'sex', 'race' or 'social class'.

A **variable** is *a concept whose value changes from case to case*. The familiar variable 'price', for example, changes from item to item in a supermarket. Similarly, people use the concept 'social class' to evaluate people as 'upper class', 'middle class', 'working class' or 'lower class'.

The use of variables depends on **measurement**, *the process of determining the value of a variable in a specific case*. Some variables are easy to measure, such as adding up income at tax time. But measuring many sociological variables can be far more difficult.

For example, how would you measure a person's 'social class'? You might be tempted to look at clothing, listen to patterns of speech, or note a home address. Or, trying to be more precise, you might ask about someone's income, occupation and education.

Researchers know that almost any variable can be measured in more than one way. Having a very high income might qualify a person as 'upper class'. But what if the income is derived from selling cars, an occupation most people think of as middle or even working class? And would leaving school at 16 make a person 'lower class'? To resolve such a dilemma, sociologists sensibly (if somewhat arbitrarily) combine these three measures – income, occupation and education – into a single composite assessment of social class, called socioeconomic status, which is described in Chapters 8 and 10.

Sociologists also face the challenge of describing thousands or even millions of people according to some variable of interest such as income. Reporting an interminable stream of numbers would carry little meaning and tell us nothing about the people as a whole. Hence sociologists use *statistical measures* to describe people efficiently and collectively. The box below explains how.

Measurement is always a bit arbitrary because the value of any variable depends, in part, on how one defines it. **Operationalising a variable** means *specifying exactly what one is to measure in assigning a value to a variable.* If we were measuring people's social class, for example, we would have to decide whether we were going to measure income, occupational prestige, education or something else and, if we measure more than one of these, how we will combine the scores. When reporting their results, researchers should specify how they operationalised each variable, so that readers can evaluate the research and fully understand the conclusions.

## 2 Reliability and validity of measurement

Useful measurement involves two further considerations. **Reliability** is *the quality of consistent measurement.* For a measure to be reliable, in other words, repeating the process should yield the same result. But consistency is no guarantee of **validity**, which is *the quality of measuring precisely what one intends to measure.* Valid measurement, in other words,

PUBLIC SOCIOLOGY

# Knowing your 'averages': three useful (and simple) statistical measures

We all talk about 'averages': the average price of a litre of petrol or the average salary for graduates. Sociologists, too, are interested in averages, and they use three different statistical measures to describe what is typical. They often say 'means, medians or modes'. What does this mean?

Assume that we wish to describe the salaries paid to seven members of a company: £23,000, £28,500, £27,800, £28,000, £23,000, £52,000 and £23,000.

The simplest statistical measure is **the mode**, defined as *the value that occurs most often in a series of numbers.* In this example, the mode is £23,000 because that value occurs three times, while each of the others occurs only once. If all the values were to occur only once, there would be no mode; if two values occurred three times (or twice), there would be two modes. Although the mode is easy to identify, sociologists rarely make use of it because this statistic provides at best only a crude measure of the 'average'.

A more common statistical measure, **the mean**, refers to *the arithmetic average of a series of numbers,* and is calculated by adding all the values together and dividing by the number of cases. The sum of the seven incomes is £205,300; dividing by 7 yields a mean income of £29,329. But notice that the

mean is actually higher than the income of six of the seven members. Because the mean is 'pulled' up or down by an especially high or low value (in this case, the £52,000 paid to one member who also serves as a director), it has the drawback of giving a distorted picture of any distribution with extreme scores.

**The median** is *the value that occurs midway in a series of numbers arranged in order of magnitude* or, simply, the middle case. Here the median income for the seven people is £27,800, because three incomes are higher and three are lower. (With an even number of cases, the median is halfway between the two middle cases.) Since a median is unaffected by an extreme score, it usually gives a more accurate picture of what is 'average' than the mean does.

means more than getting the same result time and again – it means obtaining a *correct* measurement.

To illustrate the difficulty of valid measurement, say you want to investigate how religious people are. A reasonable strategy would be to ask how often they attend religious services. But, in trying to gauge *religiosity* in this way, what you are actually measuring is *attendance at services*, which may or may not amount to the same thing. Generally, religious people do attend services more frequently, but people also participate in religious rituals out of habit or because of a sense of duty to someone else. Moreover, some devout believers shun organised religion altogether. Thus, even when a measurement yields consistent results (making it reliable), it can still miss the real, intended target (and lack validity). In sum, sociological research is no better than the quality of its measurement.

## 3  Relationships among variables

Once they achieve valid measurement, investigators can pursue the real pay-off, which is determining how variables are related. The scientific ideal is **cause and effect**, *a relationship in which we know that change in one variable causes change in another*. A familiar cause-and-effect relationship occurs when a girl teases her brother until he becomes angry. *The variable that causes the change* (in this case, the teasing) is called the **independent variable**. *The variable that changes* (the behaviour of the brother) is known as the **dependent variable**. The value of one variable, in other words, is dependent on the value of another. Why is linking variables in terms of cause and effect important? Because doing so is the basis of **prediction**: that is, *researchers using what they do know to predict what they don't know*.

Because science puts a premium on prediction, people may be tempted to think that a cause-and-effect relationship is present whenever variables change together. Consider, for instance, that the marriage rate in the United Kingdom falls to its lowest point in January, exactly the same month our national death rate peaks. This hardly means that people die because they fail to marry (or that they don't marry because they die). In fact, it is the dreary weather during January (and perhaps also the post-holiday blues) that causes both a low marriage rate and a high death rate. The converse holds as well: the warmer and sunnier summer months have the highest marriage rate as well as the lowest death rate. Thus, researchers often have to untangle cause-and-effect relationships that are not readily apparent.

To take a second case, sociologists have long recognised that juvenile delinquency is more common among young people who live in crowded housing. Say we operationalise the variable 'juvenile delinquency' as the number of times (if any) a person under the age of 18 has been arrested, and assess 'crowded housing' by looking at the total square footage of living space per person in a home. We would find the variables related: that is, delinquency rates are, indeed, high in densely populated neighbourhoods. But should we conclude that crowding in the home (the independent variable) is what causes delinquency (the dependent variable)?

Not necessarily. **Correlation** is *a relationship by which two (or more) variables change together*. We know that density and delinquency are correlated because they change together, as shown in Figure 3.1(a). This relationship *may* mean that crowding causes misconduct, but often some third factor is at work, causing change in both the variables under observation. To see how, think what kind of people live in crowded housing: people with less money, power and choice – the poor. Poor children are also more likely to end up with police records. Thus, crowded housing and juvenile delinquency are found together because *both* are caused by a third factor – poverty – as shown in Figure 3.1(b). In other words, the apparent connection between crowding and delinquency is 'explained away' by a third variable – low income – that causes them both to change. So our original connection turns out to be a **spurious correlation**, *an apparent, though false, association between two (or more) variables caused by some other variable*.

Unmasking a correlation as spurious requires a bit of detective work, assisted by a technique called **control**, *holding constant all relevant variables except one in order to see its effect clearly*. In the example above, we suspect that income level may be behind a spurious connection between housing density and delinquency. To check, we control for income (that is, we hold it constant) by using as research subjects only young people of the same income level and looking again for a correlation between density and delinquency. If, by doing this, a correlation between density and delinquency remains (that is, if young people living in more crowded housing show higher rates of delinquency than young people with the same family income in less crowded housing), we gain confidence that crowding does, in fact, cause delinquency. But if the relationship disappears when we control for income, as shown in Figure 3.1(c), we confirm that we have been dealing with a spurious correlation. Research has, in fact, shown that virtually all correlation between crowding and delinquency disappears if income is controlled. So we have now sorted out the relationship among the three variables, as illustrated in Figure 3.1(d). Housing density and juvenile delinquency have a spurious correlation; evidence shows that both variables rise or fall according to people's income.

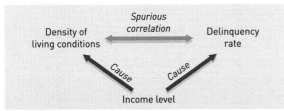

(a)

If two variables vary together, they are said to be correlated. In this example, density of living conditions and juvenile delinquency increase and decrease together.

(b)

Here we consider the effect of a third variable: income level. Low income level may cause both high-density living conditions and a high delinquency rate. In other words, as income level decreases, both density of living conditions and the delinquency rate increase.

(c)

If we control income level – that is, examine only cases with the same income level – do those with higher-density living conditions still have a higher delinquency rate? The answer is no. There is no longer a correlation between these two variables.

(d)

This finding leads us to conclude that income level is a cause of both density of living conditions and the delinquency rate. The original two variables (density of living conditions and delinquency rate) are thus correlated, but neither one causes the other. Their correlation is therefore spurious.

**Figure 3.1**  Correlation and cause: an example

To sum up, correlation means only that two (or more) variables change together. Cause and effect rests on three conditions: (1) a demonstrated correlation, but also (2) that the independent (or causal) variable precedes the dependent variable in time, and (3) that no evidence suggests a third variable is responsible for a spurious correlation between the two.

Natural scientists identify cause-and-effect relationships more easily than social scientists because the laboratories used for study of the physical world allow control of many variables at one time. The sociologist, carrying out research in a workplace or on the streets, faces a considerably more difficult task. Often, sociologists must be satisfied with demonstrating only correlation. In every case, moreover, human behaviour is highly complex, involving dozens of causal variables at any one time.

# 4 Issues of sampling

One of the key issues of research is to know just how representative of a wider group are the people you study. For example, if you want to speak about the population of Australia as a whole, it would be sheer folly just to interview Australian students on campus. They would not be representative. You would need a much wider sampling frame – maybe a list of everybody who lives in Australia. But clearly, obtaining such a list would be very costly, and contacting everybody on it would be prohibitively expensive and time consuming. Hence full-scale population surveys – the census found in many countries – usually take place only every ten years or so. The United States census for 2000 (which can be found on the website www.census.gov) and the UK census for 2001 are the most recent of such censuses and are discussed in the *Methods and research* box, below (see www.census.ac.uk).

Much more commonly, social scientists engage in *sampling*. Usually, a researcher begins a survey by designating a **population**, *the people who are the focus of research*. For example, if you wanted a random sample of your college or university, you would initially need a sampling frame of everybody attending it. Researchers then collect data from a **sample**, *a part of a population that represents the whole*. The now familiar national political surveys utilise a sample of some 1,500 people to gauge the political mood of the entire country. You use the logic of sampling all the time. If you look around a lecture room and notice five or six students nodding off, you might conclude that the class finds the day's lecture dull. Such a conclusion

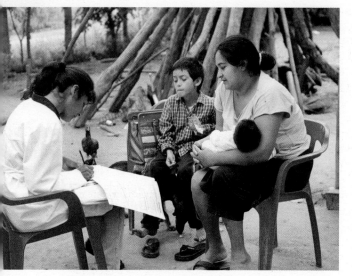

Argentine family answers questions during the nationwide Census

*Source*: Reuters/Corbis.

involves making an inference about *all* the people (the 'population') from observing *some* of the people (the 'sample'). But how do we know whether a sample actually represents the entire population? There are a number of different sampling strategies.

The main distinction made in sampling theory is usually between probability sampling and non-probability (convenience) sampling. The former is more sophisticated, for each of the elements of the sample has the same probability of being included. This is the only approach for a truly representative sample. It usually comes in two forms – simple random samples (something like every tenth person), or stratified random samples (where the population is divided into known strata or groups in advance, such as gender or age). In *random sampling*, researchers draw a sample from the population in such a way that every element in the population has the same chance of ending up in the sample. If this is the case, the mathematical laws of probability dictate that the sample they select will, in the vast majority of cases, represent the population with a minimal amount of error. Experienced researchers use special computer programs to generate random samples. Novice researchers, however, sometimes make the mistake of assuming that 'randomly' walking up to people on the street produces a sample representative of an entire city. This is a serious error, for such a strategy does not give every person an equal chance to be included in the sample. For one thing, any street – whether in a rich or a poor neighbourhood or in a 'university city' – contains more of some kinds of people than others. For another, any researcher is apt to find some people more approachable than others, again introducing a bias.

Examples of non-probability samples include *quota samples* and *snowball samples*. A quota sample represents the group of people it wants to make statements about. Thus interviewers may be told how many respondents with particular kinds of characteristic are needed for the study: if we know that the population has equal numbers of men and women, then interviewers are asked to interview equal numbers of each. If we know that it is likely to be an older group, then we make sure the sample contains an appropriate mix of ages. This is not a random sample, but one that is purposely constructed with people in their correct proportions or ratios.

Snowball sampling also does not aim at real representativeness and is usually associated with case studies and qualitative research, often in areas of research where respondents are hard to find. The basic method relies upon searching out more respondents from the respondents you interview, and building up a network of contacts through each interview. In a research project on drug users or alcoholics, for example, it is impossible to find a full sampling frame that lists 'all drug users', from which you can draw a random sample. Instead, a more common method is to make contact with some drug users and then ask about their friends and acquaintances and subsequently interview them. Such a method, of course, can never provide a truly representative sample, but it is convenient.

Although good sampling is no simple task, it offers a considerable saving in time and expense. We are spared the tedious work of contacting everyone in a population, while obtaining useful results.

# 5 Sociological thinking: the interplay of theory and method

Sociological investigators move back and forth between facts and theory. **Inductive logical thought** is *reasoning that transforms specific observations into general theory*. In this mode, a researcher's thinking runs from the specific to the general, something like this: 'I have some interesting data here; what are the data saying about human behaviour?'

A second type of logical thought works 'downwards' in the opposite direction. **Deductive logical thought** is *reasoning that transforms general theory into specific*

**METHODS & RESEARCH**

# The population census

A **census** is *a count of everyone who lives in the country*. It is seen as crucial for broad planning and the shaping of policies. Most countries try to have one, but the problems it can pose are formidable. India has a population in 2011 of around 1,210,000,000 (1.21 billion – the second largest population in the world) and its census started in 1872 – a history of 140 years. It conducted the most recent in 2011 – and every time it is a major challenge.

In the UK, the census has been held every ten years since 1801 (with the exception of 1841) when the population was 9 million. In 2001, it cost £255 million – but the 2011 census is well over half a million pounds. Run by the Office for National Statistics (ONS), it tries to count every person in the UK at the same moment. Although a lot of attention is given to the design of the questionnaire, it is getting longer and longer. By 2011 it

had become a 32 page booklet. And for the first time it was also accessible online. (There was also a follow-up survey – some 4,000 professional interviewers conducting some 32,000 ten-minute interviews.)

It was becoming clear that the scale of the census is heading towards trouble and the census of 2011 is predicted by many to be the last in the UK. It now is too unwieldy, too costly and too unreliable. Some statisticians often choose to ignore its data because its return rate was only 96 per cent, and indeed was much lower in some inner-city regions. Nowadays, the figures do not seem to tally: in 2001, there were some 900,000 people fewer than predicted – this was eventually put down to an increased emigration (possibly of young men). But there were other discrepancies. In Westminster, the population was revised downwards by a quarter, and in Manchester by a tenth. All this mattered because lower populations meant lower government grants.

Among the most commonly cited problems with the census are:

- *Undercounting*: some councils have complained that their populations are undercounted, and are suggesting a recount.
- *Cost*: as populations grow, the costs of a census can become prohibitive.
- *Distribution*: it is becoming harder both to get the forms to the right people and to get them to complete and return the forms.
- *Immigration*: there were more immigrants and some cannot read English.
- *Civil liberties*: there are suspicions about the nature of the questions in the census and how they impinge on civil liberties.
- *Ethics*: the questions asked are becoming more and more numerous – and more personally intrusive.

The census may be discontinued from 2011. Follow up the debates: on the UK census, see www.ons.gov.uk/census/2011-census/index.html; on the India census, see http://censusindia.gov.in; on wordwide census, see www.census.gov/ipc/www/cendates.

---

*hypotheses suitable for scientific testing.* This time, the researcher's thinking goes from the general to the specific: 'I have this hunch about human behaviour; let's put it in a form we can test, collect some data, and see if it is correct.' Working deductively, the researcher first states the theory in the form of a hypothesis and then selects a method by which to test it. To the extent that the data support the hypothesis, we conclude that the theory is correct; data that refute the hypothesis alert the researcher that the theory should be revised or perhaps rejected entirely.

Just as researchers commonly employ several methods over the course of one study, they typically make use of *both* types of logical thought. Figure 3.2 illustrates the two phases of scientific thinking: inductively building theory from observations and deductively making observations to test our theory.

Finally, it is worth noting that statistics, too, play a key part in the process of turning facts into meaning. Commonly, sociological researchers provide quantitative data as part of their research results. And precisely how they present their numbers affects the conclusions their readers draw. In other words, data presentation always provides the opportunity to 'spin' reality in one way or another.

Often, we conclude that an argument must be true simply because there are statistics to back it up. However, readers must use a cautious eye when encountering statistical data. After all, researchers choose what data to present, they offer interpretations of the statistics, and they may use tables or graphs to encourage others to reach particular conclusions. *The big debate* at the end of this chapter takes a closer look at these important issues.

**Figure 3.2**    Deductive and inductive logical thought

# The tools of sociological research

A **research tool** is *a systematic technique for conducting research*. The *Methods and research* box suggests a wide range of research tools that can be used by sociologists, and this section then briefly discusses a few of them. None is inherently better or worse than any other. Rather, in the same way that a carpenter selects a particular tool for a specific task, researchers choose a tool according to what they wish to learn. Each one of these requires their own skill – and there are numerous books published that provide such advice on all the above (see the guide at the end of the chapter).

To give some order to all of this, such data are often divided into *quantitative* materials involving statistics and requiring numeracy skills; and *qualitative* materials involving less measurable matter and requiring interpretive skills. Surveys and formal questionnaires are good examples of the former; and historical documents and fieldwork are good examples of the latter (but their paths often cross: there is statistical history and qualitative surveys). And although sociologists often make much of this divide (they split into 'the hard', with statistical tables, and the 'soft', without any tables), sociologists usually need both kind of data. The former help them make generalisations and often map trends – even when blind to inner meanings and idiosyncrasy; the latter help provide a deeper sense of meaning and

understanding – even if they fail to help map out broader trends. They are correctives to each other.

## Core tools

### 1 The experiment

The logic of positivist science is most clearly expressed in the **experiment**, *a research method for investigating cause and effect under highly controlled conditions*. This is used rarely by sociologists, but more commonly by psychologists and social psychologists. However, it is a pure form of research: it is *explanatory*, and asks not just what happens but why. Typically, researchers turn to an experiment to test a specific **hypothesis**, *an unverified statement of a relationship between variables*.

Ideally, we evaluate a hypothesis in three steps. First, the experimenter measures the dependent variable (the 'effect'); second, the investigator exposes the dependent variable to the independent variable (the 'cause' or 'treatment'); and third, the researcher again measures the dependent variable to see if the predicted change took place. If the expected change did occur, the experiment lends support to the hypothesis; if not, the hypothesis is discounted.

### 2 The survey

A **survey** is *a research method in which subjects respond to a series of items in a questionnaire or an interview*. Surveys are particularly well suited to studying attitudes that investigators cannot observe directly, including political and religious beliefs or the subjective effects of racism. Although surveys can shed light on cause and effect, most often they yield *descriptive* findings, as researchers seek to paint a picture of subjects' views on some issue.

### 3 Questionnaires

A **questionnaire** is *a series of written questions that a researcher supplies to subjects requesting their responses*. One type of questionnaire provides not only the questions but a series of fixed responses (similar to a multiple-choice examination). This *closed-ended format* makes the task of analysing the results relatively easy, yet narrows the range of responses in a way that might distort the findings. By contrast, a second type of questionnaire, using an open-ended format, allows subjects to respond freely, expressing various shades of opinion. The drawback of this approach is that the researcher later has to make sense out of what can be a bewildering array of answers.

METHODS & RESEARCH

# The research tool kit

Sociological data are the various bit of information that sociologists collect. In the past, the sociologist has been characterised as a person who uses interviews, surveys and statistics – but this is now a very limited view and only partially true. Research tools are used across a wide range of fields, and sociologists' work is much broader than this. Where possible, we signpost where you can find examples of research tools in this book.

30 research tools for sociologists

1. Artefacts and things (personal possessions, archaeological 'finds', consumer objects), e.g. p. 87
2. Art, e.g. pp. 930–5
3. Attitudes, e.g. pp. 152; 356
4. Autobiographies/life stories, e.g. pp. 77; 509; 613; 714
5. Auto/ethnographies/ personal experience, e.g. p. 86
6. Biography, e.g. pp. 823–5
7. Census, e.g. p. 73
8. Conversation analysis, e.g. p. 226
9. Cybermethods/netnography, e.g. pp. 24; 84–5
10. Diaries, e.g p. 78
11. Discourse analysis, e.g. p. 594
12. Documentary, e.g. p. 75
13. Ethnography, see Participant observation
14. Field research, see Participant observation
15. Experiments, e.g. pp. 178–80
16. Fiction, e.g. *mytasklist* (each chapter); Part 6
17. Film and video, e.g. p. 87; youth; Part 6
18. Historical research, e.g. pp. 186; 363
19. Interviews, e.g. p. 255
20. Letters, p.79
21. Longitudinal, panel and cohort, e.g. pp. 218–9; 825
22. Maps, e.g. p. 936
23. Narratives and stories, e.g. p. 824
24. Oral history, e.g. p. 506
25. Participant observation, e.g. pp. 61; 155; 225; 507; 699
26. Performance, e.g. pp. 86–7; 222
27. Photographs, e.g. pp. 79–82
28. Postcodes, e.g. p. 325
29. Statistics and surveys, e.g. pp. 8–9; 282–3; 288; 585–7
30. Video, see film

**Drama and documentary in sociology**

Nick Broomfield is a leading UK documentary film-maker. In a style he calls 'Direct Cinema', he uses non-actors to play themselves. In 2006, he completed a drama called *Ghosts* for Channel 4 which was inspired by the 2004 Morecambe Bay Cockling Disaster (You can read about this in the opening of Chapter 15). In this incident, 23 immigrants were drowned after being cut off by the tides. *Ghosts* won numerous awards and helped raise nearly half a million pounds to help the victims' families. In many ways it is a more striking document than a lot of mainstream sociology and really worth a look. You can find most of it on YouTube. Think about and discuss the value of documentary film, drama and performance as sociological methods

*See also*: http://www.nickbroomfield.com/home.html and especially: http://www.nickbroomfield.com/ghosts.html.

*Source*: Nick Broomfield, from the film *Ghosts*.

## 4 Interviews

An **interview** is *a series of questions a researcher addresses personally to respondents*. Interviews come in several forms. In a *closed-ended* interview, researchers would read a question or statement and then ask the subject to select a response from several alternatives. Generally, however, interviews are *open-ended* so that subjects can respond in whatever way they choose and researchers can probe with follow-up questions.

Closed-ended and open-ended interviews are both relatively formal. But there is another kind of informal conversational interview, which is more commonly used in the qualitative field research described in the next section. With this mode of interviewing, the goal is to encourage the respondent to participate fully and equally in discussion with the interviewer. Certain key themes provide the shape for the discussion, but there is no questionnaire as such, and the relationship between interviewer and respondent is much more casual, friendly and egalitarian. This mode of research is more suitable to gaining 'in-depth' understanding and for researching more sensitive topics. The 'conversations' are usually taped. This can lead to problems of a mass of data that are much less organised and accessible to analysis than the data found with more formal interviewing. See Table 3.2 for some key differences in interview forms.

| Table 3.2 | A continuum of interview forms |
|-----------|-------------------------------|
| **Positivist** | **Interpretative** |
| Interviews 'collect' data | Interviews 'construct' data |
| Standardised | Flexible |
| Mass | Formative |
| Focused | Open |
| Structured | Unstructured |
| Survey | Ethnographic |
| 'Objective' | Phenomenological/'subjective' |
| Passive | Active |
| Short | Long |

*Source*: Plummer (2001a).

## 5 Fieldwork, ethnography and participant observation

The most widely used strategy for humanistic field study is **participant observation**, *a method by which researchers systematically observe people while joining in their routine activities*. Researchers choose participant observation in order to gain an inside look at social life in settings ranging from nightclubs to religious seminaries. Cultural anthropologists commonly employ participant observation (which they call *fieldwork*) to study communities in other societies. They term their descriptions of unfamiliar cultures *ethnographies*; sociologists prefer to describe their accounts of people in particular settings as *case studies*.

At the outset of a field study, social scientists typically have just a vague idea of what they will encounter. Thus, most field research is *exploratory* and *descriptive*. Researchers might have hypotheses in mind, but it is just as likely that they may not yet realise what the important questions will turn out to be.

As its name suggests, participant observation has two facets. Gaining an 'insider's look' depends on becoming a participant in the setting – 'hanging out' with others, attempting to act, think and even feel the way they do. Compared to experiments and survey research, then, participant observation has fewer hard-and-fast rules. But it is precisely this flexibility that allows investigators to explore the unfamiliar and to adapt to the unexpected.

Unlike other research methods, participant observation requires a researcher to become immersed in the setting, not for a week or two, but for months or even years. For the duration of the study, however, the researcher must maintain some distance as an 'observer', mentally stepping back to record field notes and, eventually, to make sense of the action. The tension inherent in this method comes through in the name: 'playing the *participant*' gains for the researcher acceptance and access to people's lives; yet 'playing the *observer*' affords the distance and perspective needed for thoughtful analysis. The twin roles of 'insider' participant and 'outsider' observer, then, often come down to a series of careful compromises.

Most sociologists carry out participant observation alone, so they must remain mindful that results depend on the interpretations of a single individual.

## An aside: qualitative and quantitative research

Participant observation is typically **qualitative research**, meaning *investigation by which a researcher gathers subjective, not numerical, data*. (The informal conversational interviews we encountered earlier are also part of this approach.) Unlike experiments or surveys, participant observation and informal interviews usually involve little **quantitative research**, *investigation by which a researcher collects numerical data*. Some scientists disparage a 'soft' method such as participant observation as lacking in scientific rigour. Yet, much qualitative research has become very rigorous in recent years, even to the point of having computer programs such as *NVivo, Atlas, The Ethnograph* and *NUDIST* to enable a rigorous analysis of 'soft' data. Furthermore, its personal approach – relying so heavily on personal impressions – is also a strength: while a highly visible team of sociologists attempting to administer formal surveys would disrupt many social settings, a sensitive participant-observer can often gain considerable insight into people's natural day-to-day behaviour.

 For Advice on using qualitative software in research, see:

Computer assisted qualitative data analysis
http://caqdas.soc.surrey.ac.uk/index.html

## 6  Secondary and historical analysis

Not all research requires investigators to collect their own data personally. In many cases, sociologists engage in **secondary analysis**, *a research method in which a researcher utilises data collected by others*.

The most widely used statistics in social science are gathered by government agencies. The Office for National Statistics in the UK continuously updates information about the UK population, and offers much of interest to sociologists. Comparable data on Europe are available via *Eurostat*, from the Office for Official Publications of the European Communities in Luxembourg. Global investigations benefit from various publications of the United Nations and the World Bank. And much of the data of previous research is housed in archives such as the Social Science Research Data Archive at the University of Essex, UK. In short, a wide range of data about the whole world is as close as the university library. And most of these data sets, these days, are available on CD-Rom or on the World Wide Web.

Clearly, using available data – whether government statistics or the findings of individuals – saves researchers time and money. Therefore, this approach holds special appeal to sociologists with low budgets. Just as important, the quality of government data is generally better than what even well-funded researchers could hope to obtain on their own.

Still, secondary analysis has inherent problems. For one thing, available data may not exist in precisely the form one might wish; furthermore, there are always questions about the meaning and accuracy of work done by others. For example, in his classic study of suicide, Emile Durkheim realised that he could not be sure that a death classified as an 'accident' was not, in reality, a 'suicide' and vice versa. And he also knew that various agencies use different procedures and categories in collecting data, making comparisons difficult. In the end, then, using second-hand data is a little like shopping for a used car: bargains are plentiful, but you have to shop carefully to avoid being stuck with a 'lemon'.

# Emerging research tools: from life stories to visual sociology

So far, we have described the four most common tools used by sociologists to dig out data and understand the world. They are compared in Table 3.3. But there are others that are becoming increasingly common: we call them *documents of life* (see Plummer, 2001a). These are accounts of people's lives told by themselves – usually in words, but sometimes through other media such as video. The world is crammed full of these personal documents. People keep diaries, send letters, take photos, make their own video diaries, write memos, tell biographies, scrawl graffiti, publish their memoirs, write letters to the papers, leave suicide notes, inscribe memorials on tombstones, shoot films, paint pictures, make music and try to record their personal dreams. All of these expressions of personal life are hurled out into the world by the millions and can be of interest to anyone who cares to seek them out. They are all in the broadest sense 'documents of life', and are there to be gathered and analysed by sociologists. They come in a number of forms, which include the following.

## 1  Life stories

The life history method was established with the 300-page story of a Polish émigré to Chicago, Wladek Wisniewski, written in three months before the outbreak of the First World War. It was one volume of the massive study by W. I. Thomas and F. Znaniecki, *The Polish Peasant in Europe and America*, first published between 1918 and 1920. Wladek describes the early phases of his life in the Polish village of Lubotynborn as the son of a rural blacksmith, his early schooling, his entry to the baker's trade, his migration to Germany to seek work, and his ultimate arrival in Chicago and his plight there. Following the classic work, life histories became an important tool in the work of Chicago and

| Table 3.3 | Four classic research methods: a summary | | |
|-----------|---------|---------|---------|
| **Method** | **Application** | **Advantages** | **Limitations** |
| Experiment | For explanatory research that specifies relationships among variables; generates quantitative data | Provides greatest ability to specify cause-and-effect relationships; replication of research is relatively easy | Laboratory settings have artificial quality; unless research environment is carefully controlled, results may be biased |
| Survey | For gathering information about issues that cannot be directly observed, such as attitudes and values; useful for descriptive and explanatory research; generates quantitative or qualitative data | Sampling allows surveys of large populations using questionnaires; interviews provide in-depth responses | Questionnaires must be carefully prepared and may produce a low return rate; interviews are expensive and time consuming |
| Participant observation | For exploratory and descriptive study of people in a 'natural' setting; generates qualitative data | Allows study of 'natural' behaviour; usually inexpensive | Time consuming; replication of research is difficult; researcher must balance roles of participant and observer |
| Secondary analysis | For exploratory, descriptive or explanatory research whenever suitable data are available | Saves time and expense of data collection; makes historical research possible | Researcher has no control over possible bias in data; data may not be suitable for current research needs |

Polish sociologists. The authors have claimed this to be the best form of sociological method.

> **We are safe in saying that personal life records, as complete as possible, constitute the perfect type of sociological material, and that if social science has to use other materials at all it is only because of the practical difficulty of obtaining at the moment a sufficient number of such records to cover the totality of sociological problems, and of the enormous amount of work demanded for an adequate analysis of all the personal material necessary to characterise the life of a social group.**

(Thomas and Znaniecki, 1958: 1832–3)

## 2  Diaries

For Allport (1942: 95), the diary is the document of life *par excellence*, chronicling as it does the immediately contemporaneous flow of public and private events that are significant to the diarist. The word 'contemporary' is crucial here, for each diary entry – unlike life histories – is sedimented into a particular moment in time. In some recent research on sexual behaviour and AIDS, researchers have asked subjects to keep diaries of their sexual activities and they have then analysed them (Coxon, 1997).

## 3  'Logs' and 'time budgets'

Sorokin pioneered this method when he asked informants to keep detailed 'time-budget schedules' showing just how they allocated their time during a day (Sorokin and Berger, 1938). The anthropologist Oscar Lewis's particular method focused on a few specific families in Mexico, and the analysis of a 'day' in each of their lives. Of course, his actual familiarity with each family was in no way limited to a day. He 'spent hundreds of hours with them in their homes, ate with them, joined in their fiestas and dances, listened to their troubles, and discussed with them the history of their lives' (Lewis, 1959: 5). But in the end he decided that it would be analytically more valuable, for both humanistic and scientific purposes, to focus upon 'the day' as a unit of study. Thus each family – Martinez, Gomez, Gutierez, Sanchez and Castro – is first presented as a 'cast of characters' and then followed through one arbitrarily chosen but not untypical day of their life. Lewis believed that a study of a day had at least a threefold value: practically, it was small enough

## Asking questions of photographs

In a general study of photography, Akeret (1973) coins the term 'photoanalysis' and suggests the following useful scheme of questions to be asked. We suggest you keep this question list to hand – and add some of your own – when you look at some of the photos in this book.

What is your immediate impression (of the photograph)? Who and what do you see? What is happening in the photo? Is the background against which the photo was taken of any significance, either real or symbolic? What feelings does it evoke in you? What do you notice about physical intimacy or distance? Are people touching physically? How are they touching? How do the people in the photo feel about their bodies? Are they using their bodies to show them off, to hide behind, to be seductive, are they proud of their bodies, ashamed? What do you notice about the emotional state of each person? Is (s)he shy, compliant, aloof, proud, fearful, mad, suspicious, introspective, superior, confused, happy, anxious, angry, weak, pained, suffering, bright, curious, sexy, distant, etc.? Can you visualise how those emotions are expressed in facial dynamics and body movement? If there is more than one person in the photo, what do you notice about the group mood? Is there harmony or chaos? How do people relate? Are they tense or relaxed? What are their messages towards each other? Who has the power, the grace? Do you see love present? What do you notice about the various parts of each person? Look carefully at the general body posture and then the hands, the legs, the arms, the face, the eyes, the mouth. What does each part tell you? Are the parts harmonious or are there inconsistencies? Pay particular attention to the face, always the most expressive part of the person. Learn to read any photo as you would read a book from left to right then downwards. Go over it again and again, each time trying to pick out something you have missed. Ask yourself more general questions, as many as you can think of. What is obvious and what is subtle? What is the sense of movement or is there any? What memories and experiences does the photo stir in you? How do you identify with the people in the photo? How are you alike, how different? What moves you most about the photo? What do you find distasteful about it? Is there anything that disturbs you? Try to define the social and economic class of the people photographed. What is their cultural background? If it is a family, would you want to be a member of it? Would you want your children to play with theirs? If the photos are personal – of you, your family, friends or associates – try to remember the exact circumstances of the photo session. How have you changed since then? How have you remained the same? (Akeret, 1973: 35–6).

to allow for intensive observation; quantitatively, it permitted controlled comparisons across family units; and qualitatively, it encouraged a sensitivity to the subtlety, immediacy and wholeness of life.

## 4 Letters

Letters remain a relatively rare document of life in the social sciences. The most thoroughgoing use of letters is still to be found in Thomas and Znaniecki's *Polish Peasant* (see p. 77), where on discovering that there was extensive correspondence between Poles and Polish émigrés to America, an advertisement was placed in a Chicago journal offering to pay between 10 and 20 cents for each letter received. Through this method they were able to gain many hundreds of letters, 764 of which are printed in the first volume of their study, totalling some 800 pages and arranged in 50 family sequences. Each sequence is prefaced with a commentary that introduces the family members and the main concerns.

## 5 Visual sociology: photography

Invented at approximately the same time as sociology, photography has only occasionally figured in sociological research. It is true that in the earliest days of the *American Journal of Sociology*, photographs were a regular feature of its muck-raking, reformist articles: between 1896 and 1916, 31 articles used 244 photographs. Likewise many early fieldwork studies were illustrated with photographs. Thrasher's *The Gang*, for example, contains nearly 40 photos of boys and boy gangs. The lead has primarily come from anthropologists, and in particular the pioneering work of Gregory Bateson and Margaret Mead (1942), who provided a volume devoted entirely to photographic images from the culture of the Balinese. The photo

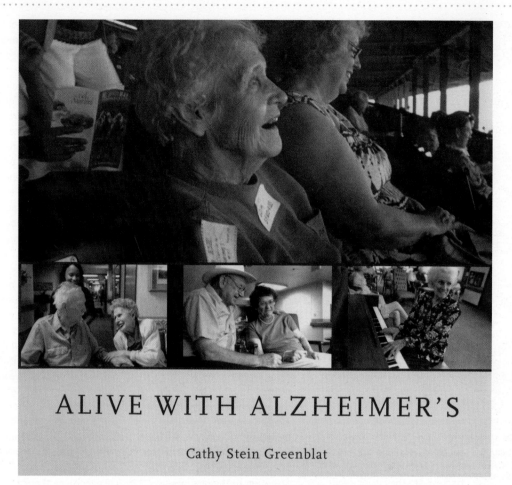

# ALIVE WITH ALZHEIMER'S

Cathy Stein Greenblat

Cathy Greenblat combines sociology with photography. Working to dispel myths and cut into common assumptions, her work focuses on care for the dependent elderly and for the end of life. She looks especially at those with Alzheimer's and dementia and shows how people with these illnesses are far from being 'empty shells' but come alive in diverse ways. Her work combines photographs with text – the images do not stand on their own; and she finds still photography a better medium to work in than film because, as she says, 'People need time to stop and reflect on the images, to deal with their emotions and thoughts at their own pace'. Her book *Alive with Alzheimer's* (2002) can be found online at her website: http://www.cathygreenblat.com/category.cfm?nL=0&nS=9

We also use some of her images in Chapters 13 and 21.

*Source*: Cathy Greenblat.

below is drawn from this book. Oddly, one of the most frequent places to find visuals is in sociology textbooks like this one. Indeed, throughout this book you will find many images: you may like to consider their value and use in sociology as you look at them (see the *Research in action* box above).

In the main, sociologists have not taken much interest in what should now be viewed as a major tool for investigation. Yet recently there has been growing interest in what has been called *visual sociology*.

Thus Cathy Greenblat takes photos of residents in an Alzheimer's home – her book shows their daily

round of ordinary activities (Greenblat, 2004); Mitch Dunier worked with Hakim Hassan to study the street vendors in New York City (Duneier, 2000) whilst Kevin Bales worked with documentary photographers to show the nature of contemporary slavery (2009). Douglas Harper is one of the leading developers of visual sociology. His work can be found in a range of studies looking at migrant labour in Hong Kong, agricultural change and human values, the sociology of the small shop, and *The Italian Way*, a study of food in family life in contemporary Italy. These books include innovative uses of photography as well as other qualitative methods, and highlight the ways in which

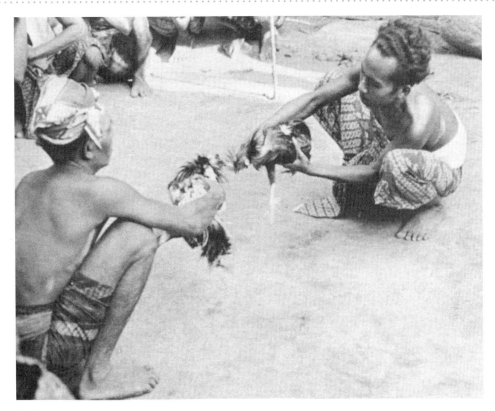

**Balinese cockfighting**

*Source*: Bateson and Mead (1942: 140). Reprinted by permission of the New York Academy of Sciences.

 **This image comes from one of the earliest attempts to use photography in field research. The authors – Gregory Bateson and Margaret Mead – were leaders in this field for much of the twentieth century. What does this picture depict? Why might it be significant? Consider the role of images in sociology.**

*See*: The Institute for Intercultural Studies: www.interculturalstudies.org/resources.

sociologists are starting at last to take the visual much more seriously in their research.

## 6 Visual sociology: film and video

The twentieth century has been called by Norman Denzin 'the cinematic century' (1995). Film, and later television, video and DVD, became prime modes for looking at social life. Yet few sociologists have seriously engaged with it as a tool for research.

It is the documentary film-makers and anthropologists who have been most adept at exploiting this medium to date. At the start of the century, ethnographers started to film various tribal peoples engaged in social rituals. In 1901 Spencer filmed Australian aborigines in kangaroo dances and rain ceremonies, while in 1914 Curtis filmed the Kwakiutl Indians. But the birth of the documentary film is commonly agreed to be Robert Flaherty's *Nanook of the North* (1922) about 'Eskimo' life.

Flaherty, a compassionate romantic appalled by the dehumanisation of modern technology, lived in 'Eskimo' country for 11 years, and shot his film under the most adverse conditions on the life of one specific individual – Nanook. In this film he reveals the constant struggle for life in a hostile environment. Sensitively, the power of the image is left behind.

One of Flaherty's most successful visual techniques was to follow an exotic act visually, showing it step by step as it developed, not explaining it in words. In one sequence we see Nanook tugging on a line leading into a hole in the ice. We are engaged in that act, and think about it. Eventually, the suspense is broken: our questions are answered when Nanook pulls out a seal. Flaherty creates the same visual involvement when Nanook makes the igloo, especially at the end of the sequence, when Nanook cuts a slab of ice for a window, sets it in place, and fixes a snow slab reflector along one side. For a time we are puzzled and, therefore, involved.

But when Nanook steps back, finished, we understand (Heider, 1976: 24).

In the main sociologists have either ignored the medium or used the documentaries created by film-makers like Frederick Wiseman. His films perhaps come closest to embodying sociological concerns: most deal directly with the ways in which individuals, in their social hierarchies, cope (or fail to cope) with the day-to-day pressures of social institutions. As he puts it:

**What I'm aiming at is a series on American institutions, using the word 'institutions' to cover a series of activities that take place in a limited geographical area with a more or less consistent group of people being involved. I want to use film technology to have a look at places like high schools, hospitals, prisons, and police, which seems to be very fresh material for film; I want to get away from the typical documentary where you follow one charming person or one Hollywood star around. I want to make films where the institutions will be the star but will also reflect larger issues in general society.**

(In Rosenthal, 1971: 69)

Hence Wiseman's 'documents' treat not 'lives' but 'institutions' – the police in *Law and Order* (1969), hospitals for the criminally insane in *The Titicut Follies* (1969), army life in *Basic Training* (1971) as well as films on *Welfare* (1975), *High School* (1968) and *Hospital* (1970).

# Feminist methodology: gender and research

One major development in sociology over the past 30 years has been the development of feminist methodology. Sociologists have (gradually) come to realise that gender often plays a significant part in their work. Margrit Eichler (1988) identifies the following five threats to sound research that relate to gender.

1 *Androcentricity*. Androcentricity (*andro* is the Greek word for 'male'; *centricity* means 'being centred on') refers to approaching an issue from a male perspective. Sometimes researchers enter a setting as if only the activities of men are important while ignoring what women do. For years, for example, researchers studying occupations focused on the paid work of men while overlooking the housework and childcare traditionally performed by women.

Clearly, research that seeks to understand human behaviour cannot ignore half of humanity.

Eichler notes that the parallel situation of *gynocentricity* – seeing the world from a female perspective – is equally limiting to sociological investigation. However, in our male-dominated society, this narrowness of vision arises less frequently.

2 *Overgeneralising*. This problem occurs when researchers use data drawn from only people of one sex to support conclusions about both sexes. Historically, sociologists have studied men and then made sweeping claims about 'humanity' or 'society'. Gathering information about a community from a handful of public officials (typically, men) and then drawing conclusions about the entire community illustrates the problem of overgeneralising. Here, again, the bias can occur in reverse. For example, in an investigation of child-rearing practices, collecting data only from women would allow researchers to draw conclusions about 'motherhood' but not about the more general issue of 'parenthood'.

3 *Gender blindness*. This refers to the failure of a researcher to consider the variable of gender at all. As we note throughout this book, the lives of men and women typically differ in virtually every setting. A study of growing old in Europe that overlooked the fact that most elderly men live with spouses while elderly women generally live alone would be weakened by its gender blindness.

4 *Double standards*. Researchers must be careful not to distort what they study by applying different standards to men and women. For example, a family researcher who labels a couple as 'man and wife' may define the man as the 'head of household' and treat him accordingly, while assuming that the woman simply engages in family 'support work'.

5 *Interference*. In this case, gender distorts a study because a subject reacts to the sex of the researcher in ways that interfere with the research operation. While studying a small community in Sicily, for instance, Maureen Giovannini found that many men responded to her as a woman rather than as a researcher, compromising her research efforts. Gender dynamics precluded her from certain activities, such as private conversations with men, that were deemed inappropriate for single women. In addition, local residents denied Giovannini access to places considered off-limits to members of her sex.

Of course, there is nothing wrong with focusing research on one sex or the other. But all sociologists, as well as people who read their work, should stay mindful about how gender can affect the process of sociological investigation.

## Feminist research

Sociology's pervasive attention to men in the past has prompted some contemporary researchers to make special efforts to investigate the lives of women. Advocates of feminist research embrace two key tenets: (1) that their research should focus on the condition of women in society, and (2) that the research must be grounded in the assumption that women generally experience subordination. Some proponents of feminist research advocate the use of conventional scientific techniques, including all those described in this chapter. Others maintain that feminist research must transform the essence of science, which they see as a masculine form of knowledge. Whereas scientific investigation has traditionally demanded detachment, feminists deliberately foster a sympathetic understanding between investigator and subject. Moreover, conventional scientists take charge of the research agenda by deciding in advance what issues to raise and how to study them. Feminist researchers, by contrast, favour a less structured approach to gathering information so that participants in research can offer their own ideas on their own terms (Stanley and Wise, 1983; Nielsen, 1990; Stanley, 1990; Reinharz, 1992).

Such alterations in research premises and methods have led more conventional sociologists to charge that feminist research is less science than simple political activism. Feminists respond that research and politics should not – indeed cannot – ever be distinct. Therefore, traditional notions that placed politics and science in separate spheres have now given way to some new thinking that merges these two dimensions.

## Twenty-first-century methods: new directions ahead

Although we can find traces of twenty-first-century developments in research methods and methodologies tracing back over generations and decades, there is a certain 'turning point' – even 'tipping point' – at the start of the twenty-first-century which has rendered some trends more and more significant for certain clusters of researchers. Eight major trends can be detected and in your studies it will be worth looking out for them.

## 1 'New' technologies and research

Most conspicuous is the development of the new technologies which are profoundly shaping the ways we do sociology. What once might have taken months to unearth can now be found at the click of a mouse. Major data sets can be created, stored, found and analysed through a large range of statistical and qualitative research packages. Large data sets such as those provided by the United Nations, the European Union and most governments can now be accessed instantly. Any research can usually start with a Google search or an Amazon book search and you will be on your way. Wikipedia can sometimes be a valuable resource and is usually a good first point of call. The ability to create images and videos – and store and present them easily – via web cam, digital camera, YouTube, PowerPoint and the rest has brought the visual world to sociology in a much more accessible way. Facebook can be homed into friends researching the same area. Blogs can provide access to research groups. Postcode searches can open up routes into lifestyle analysis. And so on. Table 3.4 suggests some of the ways in which the new technologies – not available a quarter of a century ago – are now to be found everywhere and shaping sociological research. Many of the older tools – interviews or surveys – are also being reshaped through these new technologies.

## 2 Global research

These new tools also aid in research that is going global. The internet is not bound to one country and so more and more research becomes accessible not just to one local community but to global ones. If you want to find people with a common experience – sickness, migration, work, families, sex or sport – you can find people to interview, blog, web cam or tweet online across many countries and even as they travel. It has made the possibilities of global research more and more possible – even for students. No longer is there the practical need for research to simply stay local – it can go global. But there is more than just a practical

| Table 3.4 | Digital culture and the transformation of twenty-first-century research | |
|---|---|---|
| **Research tasks** | **New digital research methods** | **A few examples (this is not meant to be comprehensive)** |
| Preliminary overview of the field | Do key word online searches, which will help you sketch out an area of research and see what already exists. | Search engines like Lycos (formed in 1994), Google (formed in 1998, and the world leader) and Bing (formed in 2009). The now ubiquitous Wikipedia which, despite its limitations, is 'good enough' for a starting point. |
| Accessing data | Get data. A core feature of the twenty-first-century world is its developing and managing of information which has never been possible before. You can now access both primary and secondary data online, with ease and little cost, as never before. | For secondary data, major statistical resources are provided by organisations, such as *Eurostats* (on the EU), *World Factbook* (CIA) and *United Nations Statistics*. But there are also databases for films (IMDb), literature (Project Gutenberg), and online archives for newspapers, sociology books, etc. (see Part Six of this book for much more on this). |
| Using internet tools for accessing original data | Do original research. Web 2 is highly interactive and enables you to gather data from your informants in many different ways. | Online and phone interviewing. Online ethnographies of networking groups from many spheres of social life (netnography). Analysing life stories and data found on blogs, Twitter and other sources. |
| Storing and managing the data you collect | Put in folders and files, and use table management. This is a core function of the information technologies. | Save your own data in well-organised and easily accessible files and folders on well-labelled and coded discs and memory sticks. Use programmes which analyse content of data. |
| Organising your research project | Plan frames and lists. Set up your research website, possibly including a blog where you can communicate with an emerging online research community working in similar areas. | Apart from setting up a website, this is where skills with Facebook, blogging and other network sites become important. |
| Constructing and managing bibliographies and reading | Nearly all sociologically relevant books and articles are electronically catalogued – often with abstracts, sometimes in e-book format. | Become familiar with the systems of your local library; use INTUTE; use search engines for recent books – and sites like Amazon. Keep all this catalogued in a database programme like EndNote. |
| Taking seriously the visual side of social life | Much sociology of the past has ignored the visual world but new technologies have created key ways of capturing and storing the world we live in through photographs and video. | The use of digital cameras makes on the spot image possible. Digital camera for ease of documentary work. Ubiqitous web cams. Visual websites like Flickr (for photo sharing). The value and use of YouTube. |

| Research tasks | New digital research methods | A few examples (this is not meant to be comprehensive) |
|---|---|---|
| Using programmes for the analysis of your data | Tools for inspecting your data range from simple table making (like Access and Excel) to the more elaborate but widespread softwares for data analysis. | NVivo 8 is the most common qualitative programme and it lets you combine detailed analysis with linking, searching, modelling and charting. The most common quantitative package is SPSS for Windows, which has become increasingly user-friendly over the last few years. |
| The presentation of your data | No longer do you have to stick with the straight essay and paper – there are many tools to help you enhance your presentation. | PowerPoint needs to be used creatively and imaginatively – never use it for plain text that you could put in a book or an essay. There are many programmes to help you design maps, charts and visuals of all kinds. Think of photos and how these lead you on to think. |

**Table 3.4** *continued*

reason for this turn to global research: there is an intellectual and political one.

As we have seen, globalisation is a key feature of the contemporary world. But it is also the case that much sociology has been seriously limited to European and North American ideas: the history of sociology is largely Western (see Chapter 2, p. 49). With the rise of postcolonial theory it has become more and more apparent that many more voices around the world need to be heard to challenge the rather limited one of current sociology. People in North America and Europe constitute a very small part of the world's population (Europe and North America together make up scarcely one-seventh of the world's population but almost all mainstream sociology has been by them, about them and for them). What we are starting to see are many developments – global ethnography, postcolonial research, standpoint theory – that give priority to the full range of cultures and society across the world, and adopting stances that take seriously as the baseline for research the world view and understandings of the people who inhabit these worlds.

## 3  Narrative research

More and more social researchers are beginning to understand that most of social life is actually conducted through narratives and stories. They take their lead from Roland Barthes (1915–80),

an important and influential French literary theorist, philosopher, critic and semiotician) when he says:

> **Narratives and stories are among the most powerful instruments for ordering human experience. Narrative can be expressed in oral or written language, still or moving pictures, or a mixture of these media. It is present in myths, legends, fables, tales, short stories, epics, history, tragedy, drama, comedy, pantomime, paintings, stained glass windows, movies, local news, and conversation. In its almost infinite variety of forms, it is present at all times, in all places, and in all societies. Indeed, narrative starts with the very history of mankind . . .**

(Barthes, 1975)

Human beings are *homo narrans* – narrating animals. We are story-telling animals and as we go through our lives we are ceaselessly narrating them. Even sociology itself can be seen as one form of story telling and narrative.

As more and more sociologists have come to understand this, they have started to speak of 'narrative reality' as one key focus for sociologists to study (see Gubrium and Holstein, 2009). This means that they are developing tools for understanding three things:

1  How do people come to tell stories of their lives?
2  How do these stories then take definite shapes, patterns and forms?
3  What are the social consequences of telling some stories – rather than others?

To do such work, narrative analysts draw from many disciplines – history, communications, semiology, literature and philosophy – to aid in the understanding of narrative construction.

## 4  Sensory research

Until recently, research methods have tended to neglect the senses. Most sociology has been spoken and written about lives without detailing how people feel, see, hear, smell and touch. As we will see in Chapter 7, some sociologists have recently started to take a major interest in the body and its emotions. Sarah Pink, for example, talks about *Doing Sensory Ethnography* (2009). As a result, sociologists have had to start to develop strategies for studying these things – to *get close to people's feelings*, *listen* to what they have to say, *attend* to how we and others perceive and see the world around us. Neglecting the senses in sociology has led to a very restricted, myopic account of the world – and sociologists are only just starting to rectify this. There is now a sociology developing which focuses on how we listen and hear (e.g. Back, 2007) and how we study a full range of senses – a sensory methodology (Pink, 2009).

Consider just one neglected sense: the eye and the visual. Clearly human beings organise social life in ways that are very dependent on what we see. Yet most sociology for its first 150 years never even bothered to look at photographs; few even today use videos; film is relegated to a side interest of a few. As we have suggested, the growth of many new visual technologies – as well as the massive increase of media in our lives – have made our lives more and more mediated lives: lives which are organised through mass media. How we see these media and how this in turn plays a role in social life has become more and more a key to understanding it. We will have more to say about media analysis in Chapter 22.

## 5  The reflexivity turn

Sociologists have long recognised that their presence in the social world partially shapes the nature of the social knowledge they 'find'. Think of the simplest interview – and how the interviewer plays some human role in shaping the outcome. People interact with each other and this shapes how knowledge gets produced. As sociologists come to understand their own position in shaping sociological findings, many find it more and more necessary to reflect upon their own role in the research. They ask questions about themselves – why are they interested in this research, what do they think

and feel about the people they are studying and the 'findings' they get, how does the research process have an impact on their own life and the life of the people they study? They try to include a sense of themselves in the very knowledge they produce – and write themselves into the findings.

Critics say that this is self-indulgent and distracts from the findings. But the argument that these researchers make is simply that no human knowledge can be devoid of its human creation and that it enhances our understanding of the knowledge to see how it was made by people.

## 6  Auto-ethnography in research

It is but a short step from this to the idea of auto-ethnography. This is the sociological version of autobiography, where there is a linking of the sociologist's own life to their research area. Here sociologists are willing to write in the first person and place their own self on the line: his or her voice has to come out, and be discussed and situated at the forefront of the analysis. Often this is claimed to be self-indulgent and it can lead to awkwardness and embarrassment. In doing this, however, the auto-ethnographer will explicitly connect to the wider aspects of studying the culture of which they are a part. Such tellings raise all kinds of methodological questions linked to the truth of the story and the life that tells it. They show how ideas are shaped in the very context which produces them.

## 7  Material culture and research on 'things'

Another range of new research focuses on what we could call 'the social life of things'. Here almost any material object in the world – a house, a photo, a concert, a house – can be examined through the relations in which it is enmeshed. Typically this kind of research examines the biography or history of the thing and traces its life through a series of events and people who have helped shape it. Table 3.5 outlines a few of the topics that have been studied.

## 8  Performance theory

One strand of new methods and approaches to research has been very critical of the over-reliance of sociology (and other branches of social science) on written texts and the pursuit of objective science.

| Table 3.5 | The sociology of consumer objects: a quick review | |
| --- | --- | --- |
| **Material object of consumption** | **The study** | **The book** |
| T-shirt | Traces the production of a T-shirt from start to end across the world economy | Pietra Rivoli, *The Travels of a T-shirt in the Global Economy* (2nd edn, 2009) |
| Tomatoes | Traces evolution of the tomato within the development of the capitalist market | Mark Harvey, Steve Quilley and Huw Benyon, *Exploring the Tomato* (2002) |
| Coca-Cola | Traces the globalisation of consumption through the famous soft drink: the role of the transnational company as it spreads the drink to Papua New Guinea | Robert J. Foster, *Coca-Globalization* (2008) |
| Nike | Traces the cycle of production, distribution and consumption of the famous shoe and its logo | Robert Goldman and Stephen Papson, *Nike Culture* (1998) |
| Sony Walkman | Now of historical interest as a major commodity that had mass sales but was morphed into other newer technologies | Paul du Gay et al., *Doing Cultural Studies: The Story of the Sony Walkman* (1996) |
| The McDonald's hamburger | The classic study which takes McDonald's as a paradigm for the shifts in bureaucratic social organisation | George Ritzer, *The McDonaldization of Society* (6th edn, in 2010) |

THINKERS & THEORY

# Norman Denzin: from life stories and film to performance radicalism

Norman Denzin has been very prominent in shaping new directions in qualitative research, primarily through his editorship of *The Handbook of Qualitative Research* (4th edn, 2011), which has provided a forum for all kinds of new developments – from poetry and drama to film and photography: all of which are now being encouraged as tools for sociology.

Denzin rose to prominence with his book *The Research Act* in the 1970s, where he demonstrated how social research should be analysed as a social process. Interviews and questionnaires are not simply neutral tools of research, but are deeply shaped by social encounters. In a sense he was writing a sociology of research methods.

In his later work he focused on children, emotion and alcohol, and found increasingly that life stories and film were key media for sociologists to work with. He claimed that film and cinema had become the media of the twentieth century and sociology neglected them at its peril. At the time he argued this, few sociologists were taking film seriously as a method.

More recently, Denzin has spearheaded the use of performance in sociology – suggesting that sociologists should write and perform dramas that come out of their ethnographic studies and which capture the rich emotional and political complexities of life. Social life always involves performance, and sociologists need both to enter the performing worlds of others and then to present them back to the world through their own performances which capture the stumbling difficulties of social life.

His latest book, *The Qualitative Manifesto: A Call to Arms* (2010), outlines a challenging new view of methods and champions what he calls 'social justice inquiry'. The social sciences should be value committed and should aim to improve the quality of life. A key factor here is the need to conduct research that will reduce inequalities and enhance social justice.

*See*: Norman Denzin, *The Research Act* (1970/1999); *Performance Ethnography* (2003); *The Qualitative Manifesto: A Call to Arms* (2010).

This critique wants to find better ways to capture and display the embodied lived experience – and to this end advocates using methods engaging with drama and performance. The claim is made that we live in a dramaturgical performance culture and we should be increasingly concerned with 'how to construct, perform and critically analyze performance texts' (Denzin, 2003: xi).

## Ethical, political and policy questions

As Max Weber observed long ago, a fine line separates politics from science. Most sociologists endorse Weber's goal of value-free research, but a growing number of researchers are challenging the notion that politics and science can – or should – be distinct. Many sociologists now argue that the ideal of 'value-free' research paints a 'storybook picture' of sociology. Every element of social life is political, they claim, in that it benefits some people more than others. In this view, sociology is saturated with values and politics from top to bottom. There is a long history, then, of discussing the role of politics, values and ideologies in sociology – and they are usually discussed using Max Weber's distinctions between value-free and value-relevant. Without detailing his work here, we can find three key issues:

1  *Value relevance*. In the early stages of research (choosing areas of research, etc.), values become crucial in making selections and phrasing problems. The tip here is to think about the value of your research and choose your area carefully – often on political and moral grounds.

2  *Value neutrality but ethical responsibility*. Whilst doing research, adequate objectivity has to be attained. The tip here is to follow a number of the guidelines of science whilst being aware, *at the same time*, that sociology always deals with human life and people, and there will be a need to think about your responsibilities towards the people you are studying.

3  *Value implications*. Most sociology can have an impact on the world and the sociologist has to think about this impact. The tip here is to think carefully about the implications of what you are going to say. Who will this impact and how? In particular, is there political fallout out here?

There are some who will suggest that values should be kept strictly out of sociology. Simply look at the great sociologists of the past – and indeed the key names of the present – and what you will almost invariably find is a passion drenched in languages of values. Much contemporary sociology is often quite explicit about its moral and political imagination: feminist sociology declares the need to remove women's inequalities; anti-racism sociology critiques racism; queer sociology destabilises gender and sexual categories; and postcolonial sociologies critique the supremacy of the European/American model that dominates thinking. Sociology asks: whose side are you on? Sociologists have to juggle their science with their politics, their ethics and their passions.

## Debating ethics and politics in sociology

Throughout this book you will encounter many political issues. Be sure to look at the boxes on *Public sociology* which often raise thorny issues and also turn to the Epilogue (p. 921) where some possible key ethical and political stances to help shape sociology are outlined. Many of the contemporary thinkers we encounter in this book are very politically engaged. Look at the boxes on Stuart Hall, Judith Butler, Donna Haraway, Martha Nussbaum, Raewyn Connell, Michel Foucault, Anthony Giddens, Norman Denzin, Patricia Hill Collins, Jürgen Habermas and Stanley Cohen, who are deeply partisan and explicitly political. They want, at the least, a world of greater justice.

 Look at the ethical codes of sociological professions. See, for example, the Code of the British Sociological Association at:

www.britsoc.co.uk/equality/Statement+Ethical+Practice.htm.

PUBLIC SOCIOLOGY

# Issues in ethics and politics

As a village schoolmaster said to anthropologist Nancy Scheper-Hughes:

> It's not your science I am questioning, but this: don't we have the right to lead unexamined lives, the right not to be analysed? Don't we have a right to hold on to an image of ourselves as different to be sure, but as innocent and unblemished all the same?

All researchers should be aware that research can be harmful as well as helpful to subjects or communities. The major professional associations of sociologists in the UK establish formal guidelines for the conduct of research. The prime directive here is that sociologists should strive to be both technically able and humanly ethical in conducting their research. Sociologists, for example, must disclose all their findings, without omitting significant data. Furthermore, they must point out various interpretations of data, and they are ethically bound to make their results available to other sociologists, some of whom may wish to

replicate the study. Yet what if this harms their subjects?

There are many ethical issues that face sociologists. Below are a few to consider:

- *Confidentiality*. In most sociology, research subjects need to be guaranteed confidentiality. Thus names of people are changed; schools studied get 'pseudonyms'.

- *Informed consent.* Respondents in research should know that they are involved in a research undertaking and roughly what this research is about.

- *Honesty*. As in life, so in research, 'honesty' would seem to be a fairly basic requirement! So a minimal canon of 'science' might well be seen as suggesting that the researcher should be as accurate, painstaking and honest as possible.

- *Deception*. A related form of dishonesty arises with deception. In sociology, the dilemma appears where the researcher conceals his or her identity and 'cons' his way into a new group – an issue that is often dubbed the overt/covert debate.

- *Exploitation*. A subject is asked by a sociologist to give up

hours – often hundreds of hours – of his or her life to tell their story. It might be very painful and involve a great deal of effort. And at the end of it all – for reasons of confidentiality – the subject must remain anonymous while the sociologist publishes. And certainly there have been prosecutions over such alleged abuses: the mother of one 'case study' – that of Genie, a 'wild child' found at the age of 13 to be living in complete isolation and subsequently studied in detail by psychologists – filed a suit against the researchers on the grounds that private and confidential information had been disclosed for 'prestige and profit' and that Genie had been subjected to 'unreasonable and outrageous' testing.

- *Hurt and harm*. A final worry is the hurt and harm that may befall the subject through the researcher's activities. Social science has produced many instances where communities have been upset by community studies on them – feeling they have been misrepresented; or where individual people feel they have told a story in good faith only for it to result in a kind of damaging or sensational exposure.

# Putting it all together: steps in planning a sociological project

Drawing together the elements of sociological investigation presented in this chapter, a typical project in sociology will include each of the following 14 steps. The emphasis here is upon planning the project well.

1 *Get yourself a research problem and define the topic of investigation.* Nothing is more important than getting yourself a good question. Being curious and looking at the world sociologically can generate ideas for social research anywhere. The issue you choose to study is likely to have some personal significance. But a social problem is not a sociological problem and you need to be clear how you can pose a sociological question.

2  *Start keeping a log and record files.* Keep a log of how you develop your research, how you change your views and problems, and how you make key decisions. This will be useful in helping you reflect, but it may also provide good source material for writing up the methodology chapter in your study – if you are to have one. Keep all your notes well organised, and plan this early.

3  *Find out what others have learned about the topic.* You are probably not the first person to develop an interest in a particular issue. Spend time in the library to see what theories and methods researchers have applied to your topic in the past. In reviewing existing research, note problems that may have come up before. Check on the findings.

4  *Assess the requirements for carrying out the research.* How much time and money will the research require? What special equipment or skills are necessary? Can you do the work yourself? What sources of funding are available to support the research? You should answer all these questions before beginning to design the research project.

5  *Specify the research questions.* Are you seeking to explore an unfamiliar social setting? To describe some category of people? Or to investigate cause and effect among variables? If your study is exploratory, identify general questions that will guide the work. If it is descriptive, specify the population and the variables of interest. If it is explanatory, state the hypothesis to be tested and carefully operationalise each variable. Make a long list of what puzzles you; and then work to narrow it to a firmer focus.

6  *Specify your theoretical orientation, and perhaps your disciplinary links.* You should try to locate your own research within certain traditions. For example, some research might be historical, some anthropological, and some more theoretical. And if it is to be theoretical, what kinds of theory will you use: to return to Chapter 1, would you find a functionalist, conflict or action approach most suitable?

7  *Consider ethical issues.* Not all research raises serious ethical issues, but you should be sensitive to this matter throughout your investigation. Could the research harm anyone? How might you design the study to minimise the chances of injury? Do you plan to promise anonymity to the subjects? If so, how will you ensure that anonymity will be maintained?

8  *Devise a research strategy or design.* Consider all major research strategies – as well as innovative combinations of approaches. Keep in mind that the appropriate method depends on the kinds of question you are asking as well as the resources available to support your research.

9  *Draw up a written research proposal in which you outline the above stages and say what you will be doing.* This is very valuable in providing a guide and checklist for doing the research.

10  *Do the research – gather and record your data.* The way you collect data depends on the research method you choose. Be sure to record all the information accurately in a way that will make sense later (it may be some time before you actually write up the results of your work). Remain vigilant for any bias that may creep into the research. Bias may be inevitable, but you should be aware of it.

11  *Interpret the data.* Scrutinise the data in terms of the initial questions and decide what answers they suggest. If your study involves a specific hypothesis, you should be able to confirm, reject or modify the hypothesis based on the data. In writing up your research report, keep in mind that there may be several ways to interpret the results of your study, consistent with different theoretical paradigms, and you should consider them all.

12  *Report your findings and conclusions.* As you write your final report, specify conclusions supported by the data. Consider the significance of your work both to sociological theory and to improving research methods. Of what value is your research to people outside sociology? Finally, evaluate your own work, noting problems that arose and questions that were left unanswered. Note ways in which your own biases may have coloured your conclusions.

13  *Share your results.* Consider submitting your research paper to a campus newspaper or magazine, or making a presentation to a seminar, a meeting of any people you have been involved in studying, or perhaps a meeting of professional sociologists. The important point is to share what you have learned with others and to let others respond to your work.

14 *Where possible, store your data in an archive.* You never know, at some point some other researchers may want to see your data, or even reuse it. So it is always wise to think about ways of storing it or keeping it available for others to see and use.

 **See the project 'Writing Across Boundaries'.** This is a project which gets various social scientists who have published quite a bit to reflect on the nature of their writing. It includes pieces by Howard Becker, Harvey Molotch, Marilyn Strathborn and Liz Stanley, myself and many others: see www.dur.ac.uk/writingacrossboundaries.

On this website you will also find resources relating to a variety of themes that engage writers in the social sciences. These include drafting and plotting; the data–theory relationship; narrative, rhetoric and representation; and hints and tips on writing.

# SUMMARY

1 Two basic requirements for sociological investigation are (1) viewing the world from a sociological perspective, and (2) being curious and asking questions about society.

2 Sociological research involves asking questions about three issues: (1) epistemology, (2) technical tools, and (3) ethics and politics.

3 Two major approaches to epistemology are positivism and humanism. Others include realism, critical sociology, standpoint theory, queer theory and postmodernism.

4 Measurement is the process of determining the value of a variable in any specific case. Sound measurement is both reliable and valid. A goal of science is discovering how variables are related. Correlation means that two or more variables change value together. Knowledge about cause-and-effect relationships is more powerful, however, because a researcher can use an independent variable to predict change in a dependent variable.

5 There are four major research tools. Experiments, which are performed under controlled conditions, attempt to specify causal relationships between two (or more) variables. Surveys, which gather people's responses to statements or questions, may employ questionnaires or interviews. Through participant observation, a form of field research, sociologists directly observe a social setting while participating in it for an extended period of time. Secondary analysis, or making use of available data, is often preferable to collecting one's own data; it is also essential in the study of historical questions. Other tools include 'documents of life', which are records of personal lives recorded by the subjects themselves. They help to gain an understanding of subjective experience, and include life histories, diaries and letters.

6 Visual sociology is a growing area of interest – as is the use of the personal computer in doing research.

7 Although investigators select topics according to their personal interests, the scientific ideal of objectivity demands that they try to suspend personal values and biases as they conduct research. Rejecting conventional ideas about scientific objectivity, some sociologists argue that research inevitably involves political values and that, with this in mind, research should be directed towards promoting desirable social change. Feminist methodologies take gender bias very seriously and aim to correct it.

8 Because sociological research has the potential to cause discomfort and harm to subjects, sociological investigators are bound by ethical guidelines.

CONNECT UP: Turn to Part 6 of this book for key resources and link up
with the book's website, which links to these resources
SEE: www.pearsoned.co.uk/plummer

## MYTASKLIST

# Ten suggestions for going further

## 1 Connect up with Part Six and the Sociology Web Resources

As you work through ideas and think about the issues raised in this chapter, look at the accompanying website and the resource centre at the end of this book which connects to it. There is a lot here to help you move on. To link up, see: www.pearson.co.uk/plummer.

## 2 Review the chapter

*Briefly summarise (in a paragraph) just what this chapter has been about.* Consider: (a) What have you learned? (b) What do you disagree with? Be critical. And (c) How would you develop all this? How could you get more detail on matters that interest you?

## 3 Pose questions

(a) What does it mean to state that there are various kinds of truth? What is the basic rationale for relying on science as a way of knowing? Is sociology a science? Should it be? And if so, what kind? Identify several ways in which sociological research is similar to – and different from – research in the natural sciences.

(b) What sorts of measure do scientists adopt as they strive for objectivity? Why do some sociologists consider objectivity an undesirable goal?

(c) Dissect any one sociological study in order to evaluate its methodology.

(d) If there can be a feminist methodology, can there also be an anti-racist methodology, or a gay/queer methodology?

(e) Examine the ways in which the internet and new technologies are changing the nature of social research.

## 4 Explore key words

Many concepts have been introduced in this chapter. You can review them from the website or from the listing at the back of this book. You might like to give special attention to just five words and think them through – how would you define them, what are they dealing with, and do they help you see the social world more clearly or not?

See: Victor Jupp, *The Sage Dictionary of Social Research Methods* (2006).

## 5 Search the Web

Be critical when you look at websites – see the box on p. 940 in the Resources section. Some useful sources for this chapter are:

The Qualitative Report
www.nova.edu/ssss/QR – an online journal that provides a major listing of qualitative research websites.

Data on the Net
http://3stages.org/idata – based at the University of California at San Diego, this is a useful site for quantitative data. It houses some 850 sources for gathering data.

National Statistics
www.statistics.gov.uk – the British government's website for all official statistics.

UK Data Archive
www.data-archive.ac.uk – this site, based at Essex University, is home for most of the major surveys and researches conducted in the UK.

## 6 Watch a DVD

- Akira Kurosawa's *Rashomon* (1951): a much celebrated introduction to the idea of different perspectives capturing a common reality.

It will be valuable now to watch *some classic documentary films* and consider whether they can offer more to understanding than conventional sociological research. For example, see:

- Robert Flaherty's *Nanook of the North* (1922): a classic early documentary about the Innu.
- Leni Riefenstahl's *Triumph of the Will* (1935): a controversial documentary made at the start of Hitler's rule.
- Tod Browning's *Freaks* (1932): a very disturbing introduction to deviance, not really a documentary. See also Chapter 14.

These give you a little sense of how new film-makers in the earliest days attempted to capture social life – and, indeed, how they often got this very wrong.

## 7 Think and read

C. Wright Mills, *The Sociological Imagination* (1959). This has already been introduced in Chapter 1. It has a very useful appendix on how to do sociology and is strongly recommended.

Alan Bryman, *Social Research Methods* (3rd edn, 2008). This is one of a large number of wide-ranging textbooks that cover the whole field.

Ann Gray, *Research Practice for Cultural Studies* (2003). A helpful guide to methods for cultural studies.

Robert Kozinets, *Netnography* (2010). A guide to researching online communities.

Karen O'Reilly, *Ethnographic Methods* (2nd edn, 2011). A useful guide to fieldwork in sociology.

Gillian Rose, *Visual Methodologies* (2nd edn, 2007). A good general introductory textbook on visual research.

Gerard Delanty, *Social Science: Philosophical and Methodological Foundations* (2005). A good background guide to the philosophical issues of social science.

## 8 Connect to other chapters

- Inspect some of the many tables and statistics throughout this book. Ask how they were produced and how valid and reliable they are. View them critically.
- See the life stories in the *speaking lives* boxes throughout this book. What are the problems with such stories?
- For more on the growth of multiple voices and feminism, see Chapter 2.

## 9 Relax with a novel

Several novels have tried to capture the life of a social researcher. See Alison Lurie's *Imaginary Friends* (1967), which looks at the researchers of a strange religious cult.

# 10 Engage in THE BIG DEBATE

### Damned lies and statistics: so do statistics tell the truth?

'Fact, fact, fact!' said the gentleman . . . 'You are to be in all things regulated and governed' . . . by fact. We hope to have, before long, a board of fact, composed of commissioners of fact. Who will force the people to be a people of fact, and of nothing but fact. You must discard the word Fancy altogether.

(Charles Dickens, Hard Times, Chapter 2)

You will soon notice that this book is littered with statistics. That is the sociologist's weakness, and you cannot trust him or her! As the English politicia Benjamin Disraeli once noted wryly: 'There are three kinds of lies: lies, damned lies, and statistics!' Every method of data collection is prone to error, and data do not speak for themselves. Throughout this book – as well as in much of the press – you will find a generous sprinkling of 'statistics' as well as 'statistical tables' that aim to summarise much data. Indeed, we live in a world that bombards us with 'scientific facts' and 'official figures' and it is well worth pausing to consider what such 'statistical evidence' means. People are so fond of saying: 'As the evidence shows . . . ' But what does it show?

As you find statistics in this book, ask yourself some of the questions below. You will soon learn that statistics should never be taken at simple face value and you will start to see that some seem more reasonable than others. Some of the questions you should ask of data include:

1  Are the statistics valid? Do they measure what they say they are trying to measure – like the 'suicide' rate, the 'crime' rate or 'human development'? If you simply think of the problems of just how 'suicide' (see Chapter 1), 'crime' (Chapter 17), 'class' (Chapter 10) or 'human development' (Chapter 4) can be defined (and indeed what they mean), you should soon see some of the problems.

2  Are the statistics possible to disaggregate or break down into different parts? Thus statistics can conceal differences between groups – such as men and women, or young and old, or region to region. Is it possible to break the statistics down to see these differences at work?

3  Are the statistics consistently measured over time? Statistics may be produced at different times using different measuring devices. Again, you need to check how the statistics were made in order to see if they were measuring the same things.

4  Who created this statistic? There is always someone who made the statistic – from a big world agency like the United Nations to the smallest undergraduate survey. Knowing a bit about them may help you see possible sources of error and bias.

5  Why was this statistic created? What were the author(s) trying to achieve by making these statistics? For example, if it is a poverty statistic produced by campaigners against poverty, it is good to know this. And if it is a measure of church memberships produced by devout Christians, it is good to know this too!

6  How was this statistic actually created? Was it, for example, part of a multi-million-pound bureaucratic enterprise involving the filling in of many forms by many different people across the world? If it was bureaucratically produced, how did the various contributors play their role – what rules guided them?

7  How is the statistic being used? Was the statistic produced as part of a political campaign and is it being used perhaps to get more resources? How statistics are used may give clues to hidden biases. There are usually plenty of statistics available for people on all sides of a political debate to use as ammunition to bolster their arguments. Watch out for over-use, under-use, misuse, political abuse and oversimplification.

8  Why was this statistic selected to be presented? Often the data we confront are not wrong; they just do not tell the whole story.

9  How is the statistic being presented? Very often graphs and charts can be used to 'spin' the truth. The picture tells only part of the story. A graph of the crime rate over only the last several years, for example, would reveal a downward trend; shifting the time frame to include the last few decades, however, would show a sharp increase.

Above all, initially be suspicious of all statistics. Put them through some of the above tests, and then make your mind up about them.

*Continue the debate*

1 Look at some of the statistics in this book. Consider where they have come from, why they are being used and just what it is they purport to measure.

2 When would you trust a statistic?

3 Why do you think people are so quick to accept 'statistics' as true?

4 Consider the opening quote from the hugely insightful Victorian novelist Charles Dickens. Do we now have this 'Board of Fact' and 'People of Fact' and is it a sign of our progress as a civilisation?

5 More questions are asked about statistics in Chapter 9. See the *Public sociology* box on p. 288.

6 See Joel Best, *Damned Lies and Statistics* (2001).

# Researching sport

Sport seems to be found in all societies and throughout history. In its many varieties, it is often among the most popular of social activities. The '10' box below suggests the ten most popular sports in the UK in 2008. Having read the first three chapters of this book, we can now ask just what sociology brings to our understanding of sport.

Chapter 1 asked questions about **the sociological imagination**; here, our concern lies with just how we can apply this imagination to 'sport' – indeed, just what is a sociology of sport? What is 'taken for granted' about sport? And how might it have been shaped or constructed by the great transformations of the nineteenth and twentieth centuries? Chapter 2 asked questions about different 'theoretical approaches', a nd here we consider their relevance to sport. And how has sport become globalised? Finally, Chapter 3 would help us pose questions about research and sport. In what follows, there are some hints on how you can develop all this.

**TOP 10**

**Active sports:[1] by sex, 2007/08**

England

| Men | % | Women | % |
|---|---|---|---|
| Indoor swimming and diving | 28 | Indoor swimming or diving | 35 |
| Snooker, pool, billiards[2] | 23 | Health, fitness, gym or conditioning activities | 22 |
| Cycling[3] | 21 | Keepfit, aerobics and dance exercise[6] | 16 |
| Health, fitness, gym or conditioning activities | 21 | Outdoor swimming or diving | 14 |
| Outdoor football[4] | 20 | Tenpin bowling | 13 |
| Golf, pitch and putt, putting | 18 | Cycling[3] | 13 |
| Outdoor swimming or diving | 16 | Jogging[5] | 8 |
| Tenpin bowling | 15 | Snooker, pool, billiards[2] | 7 |
| Darts | 12 | Badminton | 7 |
| Jogging[5] | 12 | Yoga | 6 |

1  Adults aged 16 and over.
2  Excludes bar billiards.
3  Includes for health, recreation, training or competition.
4  Includes 5-a-side and 6-a-side.
5  Includes cross-country and road running.
6  Includes exercise bike.

*Source: Social Trends 40* (2010) Table 13.12, p. 193.

# Sport is not what it seems: questioning the taken for granted

At the surface level, sport is just that – sport: good fun for healthy bodies perhaps. But sociology always invites you to look a little deeper and challenge what is taken for granted. You need to **defamiliarise yourself with the familiar**.

In this sense it may help to assume the guise of a Martian visitor to planet earth, who comes to see what is going on with no prior 'human' assumptions. The visitor would observe millions of people running, jumping, swimming, hitting each other, and chasing balls in various ways. For instance, just one thing our visitor could not help noticing pretty soon would be that little boys, adolescents, middle-aged men and older men too all seem preoccupied with 'balls'. They kick them around at the earliest of ages, organise into groups around them, build stadiums to them across the world, and dress in special clothing when they do this. Indeed, it all seems to generate a huge industry of 'goods to be sold'. They fight over the balls locally and internationally, they talk and write endlessly about them, and they create mass global gatherings screened across global television – from the favelas of Rio and São Paulo and the slums of Lagos to the Congo jungle and school playgrounds in India, everyone is talking about and kicking balls. And the visitor would also note a special gathering called 'The football World Cup Final' on 11 July 2010, which attracted a television audience of over 700 million people. Despite all the many seeming differences between people, they were all watching the same images, wherever they could.

**Beijing Olympics and the globalisation of sport**
The modern Olympic Games have been held every four years since 1896 (except during World Wars I and II). In 2008, there were some 11,028 competitors in the games held in Beijing, China with 204 nations participating. This is global sport at its most extreme. It is estimated that some 4.7 billion people watched the opening on television and some 7 million tickets were sold. You can watch the spectacular opening on YouTube. The London Olympics are scheduled for July–August 2012 and are bound to raise a lot of sociological debate. See: http://www.culturalolympics.org.uk/2010/06/sociology-and-the-2012-olympic-games/

*Source*: © Aflo Foto Agency/Alamy.

The visitor sees all this as very curious, and baffling: what is to be made of it all? One thing is clear, football is very important on planet earth in human societies: billions embrace it; indeed, they often seem to be obsessed with it; there is an intoxication by it; the media devote a huge amount of space to it; they fight over it. Football becomes a major symbol of many societies. So what then does a 'football' signify?

Although football is a major sport, it is not even our most popular sport. So what in the end is going on here? The visitor's first task must be to describe it. The second is to try to explain just what is going on. This is, in effect, the sociologist's task too.

# 1 Describing sport, researching sport

As we saw in Chapter 3, there are various ways of gathering materials and describing social worlds: we could collect statistics around sport to sense its social shape; we could interview people involved in sports – players, managers, funders, spectators – and find out what they do and why; we could observe the sports, see how people do things together and find out what it all seems to mean to them – and others; we could study documents that surround sports – press cuttings, books, films, fan magazines, photos, videos and websites; we could dig around in the historical archives and see how it developed; we could look at individual life stories and see the role sport has played in them. There is an enormous amount of descriptive work to do. In all of this, what we will be doing is social research.

Let's take just one example. French sociologist Loïc Wacquant's research on boxing on Chicago's South Side is a prime example of observational participation of a sport which connects to wider theory (his ideas have been shaped by the work of Bourdieu – see Chapter 8, p. 263). It is a case study with rich sociological implications. The book *Body and Soul: Notebooks of an Apprentice Boxer* (2004) is full of black boxers busily talking about boxing, many vivid descriptions of the actual boxing experience in the ring, and many photographs in the ring and around it. It is a 'hard-hitting' and very readable piece of sociology; and it will certainly give you a rich description of boxing as it is done.

Unusually, Wacquant is himself right there in the book (some sociologists would not approve of this). He signed himself up at a boxing gym in a black neighbourhood and spent three years immersed among local fighters, amateur and professional. Thus, a brainy white academic sociologist entered the world of black macho boxers! A scholar becomes a boxer. Here Wacquant hangs around at the Woodland boxing gym; learns 'bruising', 'shadow-boxing drills', 'sparring'; and ends up fighting in the Golden Gloves tournament. Never previously contemplating getting close to a ring, let alone climbing into it, he studied, lived and described boxing for three years.

Wacquant started with many popular assumptions about this sport as scary: very violent, utterly 'macho' and not a little dehumanising. Equally, it is sometimes seen as a sort of heroic style for black men – the world of Muhammad Ali and the like. It is a pretty rough and macho sport, but one which gives daily meaning to a lot of men. This is a study of sport. But it is much more: it looks at the way the body works in sport as a means of transcending the mundane; it is a study of personal transformation in the black American ghetto.

## Sport in the media

We live in a media world. Chapter 22 examines this in more detail. For the time being, you may like to consider the ways in which sport is ubiquitous in the media. Not only do sports have their own media forms (think of sports magazines, TV sports stations and sports programmes), but sport is also to be found in film, literature and on the internet.

Some interesting films on sport would include *Chariots of Fire* (competition and the male gazes), Scorseses's *Raging Bull* and Stallone's *Rocky* (is masculinity in crisis?) and *Field of Dreams* (with its famous line: 'If you build it, he will come'). *Rollerball* (1975) captures a (then) futuristic aggressive scenario. *Million Dollar Baby* (2004) confronts women's boxing and was very controversial in its death scene. *Hoop Dreams* (1994) is the classic documentary on two African-American college basketball players struggling to go professional.

Media also produce sports stars and celebrities. Consider the social significance of 'Beckham'. In the USA, consider 'the black bodies' of Michael Jordan and Mike Tyson.

Sport is also now to be found everywhere in cyberspace. On the web, you can look up any sport. Try extreme sports/alternative sports: for example, the world of boarders (of surf, on skate, on snow, in the sky), as well as bungy jumping, barefoot snow skiing, parachute skiing and much more.

In all of this, think of the ways in which sport permeates our everyday social worlds and consider the ways in which it shapes our social lives.

How does all this differ from what you read in the newspaper: why is it sociology? First, the data you gather need to be analysed as objectively as you can. Chapter 3 discusses some of the tools for appraising validity, reliability and representatives – as well as contrasting accounts of what social science is: positivistic, realist and interpretive. You might now like to consider the above examples and their links to all this.

## 2 Explaining sport: theory and sport

But all these 'little' or specific descriptions we have suggested above will probably be just that: little descriptions. These are very valuable, but we need a way to relate these to wider social understanding. Just how do they work in society and, more ambitiously, why do they take the forms that they do?

In Chapter 1 we saw the importance of structure and action; in Chapter 2 various positions – functionalist, conflict, interactionist, postmodern – were outlined. Can such theories be used to make sense of sport?

*Functionalism*. Put simply, we can see a traditional approach through the functionalist who explains sport as meeting certain 'needs', be they manifest or latent (see p. 38 for this distinction), as performing certain functions in making the society work and hold together. Among the key functions that sport could perform to make societies function or work well are:

- As an outlet for biologically active and healthy bodies.
- As a symbolic marker of certain groups. Thus sports mark out men from women, and various social classes: polo for the posh and wrestling for the lumpen.
- As a programmed channel for conflicts, competitions and social tensions. Sport manages to regulate conflicts which otherwise might erupt more violently in society.
- As a social ritual, or 'spectacle'. It gathers large numbers of people to celebrate and sometimes to attempt to reach a kind of transcendence of the banality of the daily round of work, sleep and everyday life.

We know that major sporting events capture enormous audiences and become global events (see below). It could be that they often condense major symbolic matters – of nationalism, gender, race.

*Action/Interaction*. Put simply, we look here at how people do things together and the meanings this generates. Here the emphasis becomes that of looking at specific situations and contexts. We look at the social worlds of sports – players, teams, managers, businesses, organisations, media professionals, spectators, families, communities – and inspect the ways in which 'action' builds these worlds and meaning is constructed. The work of Loïc Wacquant on boxers would be a very good example of such research. Our interest would mainly be with 'sport scenes' or subcultures (and we discuss them more in Chapter 5).

Sociologists have looked at the social worlds (ethnographies) of athletes, wrestlers, horse racing, pool hustlers, hockey players, baseball players, rugby players, racing cyclists, rock climbers, surfers, soccer hooligans, body builders, tennis clubs and 'little league baseball' teams – among many others. Here the explanation of sport is much less general than the functionalist. By looking closely at how people do their body movements and play out their sense of self and being in sports, we come to see the interaction of people as generating various meanings. Contexts can be used to explain sports. Thus sport can come to be seen as a celebration, as a means of self-control, as work, as play, as a mechanism of maintaining masculinity – or femininity – as sexuality, as a way of ordering time, as a means of generating thrills, as violence, as a transcendence of the everyday, as a means of escapism from the everyday, as a meaning for life! Consider for example:

- What are the social meanings of 'Formula 1' racing? It seems to be thrill-seeking, death-defying (or not: and that is the risk), very speedy, and the global rich flock to it at romantic places such as the Italian and Monaco Grand Prix. To top it all, they spray champagne over each other. It can bring 'glittering prizes' and the 'glamorous life'.
- In contrast, what meanings do 'runners' bring to their runs? Greg Smith (2003) shows how runners have to build up a different sense of time. When they train, when they plan their careers, and when they actually do their 'body work' of running, they build very different senses of time and what it means to them.
- For some, sport can mean narcissism and hyper-masculinity. Alan M. Klein looks at bodybuilding among men and a distinctive culture of masculinity. See his *Little Big Men: Bodybuilding subculture and gender construction* (1993).

*Conflict*. Other sociologists see sport as much more obviously linked to social conflicts. One approach here would be to see sport as a market involving consumerism, exploitation and the 'opium of the masses' (terms discussed in Chapters 15 and 19). Watching sport may well be a spectator sport, but it is also a consumer sport – a commodity sold for large sums of money. Commodification, as we have seen in the box on music in Chapter 2 (p. 54), involves turning things into objects for sale. There is the commodification of players and teams – sold for huge sums of money. There is the commodification of merchandise – shirts, balls, games, etc. And there is the commodification by media – the selling of sports in advertising and communication. For example, the sporting goods business is now huge and growing. In 2003, the US retail sales of sporting goods reached $45.8 billion.

# Social divisions in sport

In Part Three, we outline the main areas of social division and sport could be examined for its role in social inequalities. Here, we can see that sport is organised through class, gender, age, race, sexuality, disability and nation. There is much that could be said on all this and much research has been conducted in the growing field of the 'sociology of sport'. For the time being, just consider the ways in which sports can establish hierarchy and authority structures within themselves and the ways they reproduce the wider patterns of social divisions.

Thus, sports have been heavily organised by class and gender. Football belongs (at least initially) to working-class men, and it has a long history of being linked to 'macho' violence and 'hooliganism' (well studied by sociologists). More recently, it has become increasingly middle class, and there are now many women's teams. This reflects some of the wider shifts in class and gender that we will discuss in Chapters 10–13. Boxing and wrestling seem to have a concentration in the lower class. We can also see a strong ethnicity issue: many sports stars – especially in the USA – are 'black'. Some have argued that this concentration of black Americans has provided a success route for young people who might not otherwise have opportunities for success. Other groups too have new voices to be heard in sporting arenas: gays now have their own 'Gay Olympics', as do disabled people.

The 'Premiership' makes big money: some €2 billion during the 2008–9 season. It has regulated football hooligans, attracted funding at home, and expanded overseas. It lags behind major US leagues like the National Basketball Association (NBA) and the National Football League (NFL) (which made more than $6 billion in the same period). Television is crucial: events like the World Cup in South Africa in 2010 fetch deals in their billions for domestic TV rights. In 2007, the then new superstar Lewis Hamilton earned around £50 million a year (*Telegraph*: 17/06/07: 21). Young gifted and black, he was an advertiser's dream. The box provides details of the top-earning 20 football players in 2009.

# The transformation of sport

People make 'sports' throughout history, and 'sport', in turn, then makes them. Without going back too far in time, some see Renaissance Italy and France as the founding eras of what we could call 'modern sport' (as opposed to more traditional forms?); others see it as appearing with the growth of the modern world in eighteenth-century England. In any event, sport came to be seen as both a potentially civilising and a rationalising form of social life. It takes the

**Highest-paid footballers in the world, 2009**

1. Cristiano Ronaldo (Real Madrid, £11.3 million)
2. Zlatan Ibrahimovic (Barcelona, £10.4 million)
3. Lionel Messi (Barcelona, £9.1 million)
4. Samuel Eto'o (Internazionale, £9.1 million)
5. Kaka (Real Madrid, £8.7 million)
6. Emmanuel Adebayor (Manchester City, £7.4 million)
7. Karim Benzema (Real Madrid, £7.4 million)
8. Carlos Tevez (Manchester City, £7 million)
9. John Terry (Chelsea, £6.5 million)
10. Frank Lampard (Chelsea, £6.5 million)
11. Thierry Henry (Barcelona, £6.5 million)
12. Xavi (Barcelona, £6.5 million)
13. Ronaldinho (AC Milan, £6.5 million)
14. Steven Gerrard (Liverpool, £6.5 million)
15. Daniel Alves (Barcelona, £6.1 million)
16. Michael Ballack (Chelsea, £5.6 million)
17. Raul (Real Madrid, £5.6 million)
18. Rio Ferdinand (Manchester United, £5.6 million)
19. Kolo Toure (Manchester City, £5.6 million)
20. Wayne Rooney (Manchester United, £5.2 million)

*Source*: www.caughtoffside.com/2010/02/17/50-highest-paid-footballers-in-the-world-be-prepared-to-be-slightly-surprised.

more chaotic, violent and competitive worlds of the past (?) and 'civilises it' (see the box on Elias in Chapter 7, p. 233). With the rise of capitalism we see the growth of 'sports markets' (Guttmann and Allen, 'The development of modern sports', in Jay Oakley and Eric Dunning, *Handbook of Sports Studies*, London: Sage, 2000, 248–59). To take the history of football, David Goldblatt has shown how it moves from a chaotic folk ritual to a sector of the global entertainment industry.

The transformations of modern sport can be seen through six key terms (some of which we have already encountered and some of which will be discussed later):

- *Commercialisation* – more and more, sports are subject to market forces and develop large industries around them.

- *Globalisation* – sport is no longer bounded by one country (see below).

- *Professionalisation* – sports are not just played. Now they have 'elite groups' – the professional organisations which mark both standards (and boundaries) of skill. Sports are socially controlled and regulated.

- *Consumption* – more and more people, often across the world, spend large sums of money on sports and all its merchandise. Sport is objectified; sports people become consumers.

- *Spectacularisation* – more and more watch the sports across the globe. Sport becomes increasingly audience centred, and sport becomes a 'mediated simulacrum' (see p. 780 for the meaning of this term).

- *Postmodernisation* – sports worlds split into more and more different groups. There is now, for example, a large world of queer sport (including the Gay Olympics) and of disability sport (including the Paralympics and the Special Olympics). Sports themselves also become more 'X-treme' (the X Games: some 'respectable' – deep sea diving, ocean yacht racing, hot balloons; others less so – mud wrestling, etc.). Sport also becomes increasingly a media event.

## The globalisation of sport

Almost anywhere on earth, one of the quickest ways to enter a particular society or culture is to look at its world of sports. Initially we can think of sport as a very local thing: your local college football team, your local gym. Yet whereas, in the past, most sports were local – a few friends kicking a ball about, the rivalry between schools – they have increasingly become embedded in worldwide dimensions. Sport has become part of the globalisation process. We can now see sports as matters of global finance, international superstars, teams and supporters who travel the world, the development of international mass media coverage, the creation of an array of new logos known worldwide, advertising and commercial products. Think of the Olympics, the World Cup, Wimbledon, European football: sport is now part of the world economy, world media, world travel. The globalisation of sport has meant that sport is becoming truly international – and a big business. It has meant:

- *The commodification of sport*. Sport now means an aggressive merchandising of products, where multinationals sell replica team shirts, training shoes, wall posters, etc. In the USA alone, the retail sales of sporting goods reached $45.8 billion in 2003. Globalisation also leads to branding: company logos go on sports shirts, their adverts dominate sports fields, their sponsorship hooks them into the media, their shops and outlets are closely connected to the various games. Companies with a major impact on global sport include Murdoch's empire (Fox, Sky, Star), Nike, Time Warner, Kirch Group, Disney, Coca-Cola, ISL and NBC.

- *The creation of sports cities*. Cities bid for various world events not just because of the sporting activity but because of the ways in which this can rejuvenate their cities (in the 1984 Olympic Games based at Los Angeles, a profit of $215 million was made for the city; in 2006, the UK won a bid for the 2012 Olympic Games, which it is hoped will regenerate much of East London).

- *Global superstars and global identities*. Sporting events are now part of the global media world – sporting celebrities play a world role. From Tiger Woods and Michael Jordan (the sale of Nike shoes bearing his name totalled some $1.4 billion) to David Beckham, sports stars become worldwide superheroes and can command enormous salaries – teams and regions foster an international rivalry. David Beckham, for example, is much more than a football player: he is a brand. In 2003, David Beckham was bought by Real Madrid, for a transfer payment of £25 million to his original club (Manchester United, the richest soccer club in the world) in addition to the £4.2 million it paid Beckham. Real Madrid now starts to rival Man U as a brand! In 2006, he was bought as a 'coach' in Los Angeles to promote football – an alleged $250 million for a five-year contract. Vodafone and Pepsi used to pay him at least £2 million a year, and his wider impact is to increase the sale of some commodities to over £1 billion (see Cashmore, 2002).

And in addition, consider the ways in which:

- Global supporters become international travellers and sports stars become sporting migrants.

- International scandals from bribery to drug taking become commonplace.

- Sports violence becomes a feature of some sports – as teams become 'national icons' and their winning or losing becomes a kind of neo-nationalism. Other groups – women, the disabled, gays – come to hold their own international games.

## Sport: going further

Richard Giulianotti and Roland Robertson, *Globalization and Football* (2009)

Tim Delaney and Tim Madigon, *The Sociology of Sports* (2009)

D. Goldblatt, *The Ball is Round: A Global History of Football* (2006)

Jay Coakley and Eric Dunning, *Handbook of Sport Studies* (2002)

Loïc Wacquant, *Body and Soul: Notes of an Apprentice Boxer* (2007)

Ellis Cashmore, *Beckham* (2002)

# PART 2

# THE FOUNDATIONS OF SOCIETY

## FROM MACRO TO MICRO

# CHAPTER 4

# SOCIETIES

同　歡　共　樂

IN JUNE 2008, THERE WAS MUCH EXCITEMENT IN THE PRESS ABOUT THE SIGHTING OF AN 'UNKNOWN AND UNEXPLORED' AMAZON BASIN TRIBE. A plane flying over the Brazilian state of Acre (on the borders of Peru), saw dozens of people dotted around a clearing with two communal huts. When they returned later the same day, the impact of the earlier flight was clear. Most of the women and children had fled into the forest. Only three near-naked figures were now visible in the forest clearing – and they were aiming their bows at the sky. A third figure appeared to be a woman. This remarkable photograph has been seen as evidence of the existence of one of the world's last uncontacted tribes.

'We did the overflight to show their houses, to show they are there, to show they exist,' said José Carlos dos Reis Meirelles Junior, an expert on the remote tribal people who live beyond the boundaries of the modern world. 'This is very important because there are some who doubt their existence.'

Look at the photograph on page 106 (over). With planes flying over, it clearly looks as if the tribe sensed that the outside world brought danger.

And there is a long history of earlier societies and tribes being destroyed by 'newcomers' who plunder resources, bring aggression, and spread disease. There was every reason to fear these strangers. Across the borders of Peru, and across the world, similar tribes are under threat.

The Akuntsu tribe in neighbouring Rondônia is an example and tells a very sad story. Here a tiny tribe is now reduced to just five individuals who live in two small community houses made of straw. They hunt, cultivate small gardens and paint their bodies for ceremonies. They have their own language and culture. But soon they will be extinct.

And we will have lost another unique and distinct society.

 **tip** You can read and see more about all this, and watch a view of the Akuntsu through the website for Survival International: www.survivalinternational.org/tribes/akuntsu. This website is a useful guide to the smaller and neglected societies of the world.

### There is no such thing as society.

Margaret Thatcher, UK Conservative prime minister (1979–90)

### We are taking to help make the Big Society a reality.

David Cameron, UK Conservative prime minister (2010– )

(Left) *Happy Together As One*, Chinese School (1963)

Mao Zedong (1893–1976) (Mao Tse Tung) is one of the most important but controversial political figures of the twentieth century. In 1949, he established the People's Republic of China and became its first leader, spearheading the Cultural Revolution to rid China of old ways of thinking and unseat any 'ruling class', putting art and literature into the hands of the ordinary people: a 'perpetual revolution' that served the interests of the majority, not a tiny elite. Chinese art of this period advanced the principle that art must serve the workers and peasants, portraying the heroism of the Communists. The masses needed educating with true descriptions of valiant deeds and model conduct.

*Source*: Happy Together as One, August 1963 (colour litho), Chinese School (20th Century)/ Private Collection/© The Chambers Gallery/ London/The Bridgeman Art Library.

*See*: Chinese Art Portal: http://www. artzinechina.com/display.php?a=746

Chiu, M *Art and China's Revolution* 2008 Princeton University Press

 Look at this painting. What does it suggest to you about the nature of art under Chinese communist rule?

In 2010, there were around 200 major societies in the world (192 of them in the United Nations). But once you start to count small groups, numbers grow – for example, there are probably around 7,000 different languages in the world, which usually indicate different social groupings. Parts of the world – such as the Amazonian basin and the New Guinea highlands – have still not been fully explored. And, as we saw in the opening story, some new languages and societies are still being discovered.

Chapter 1 explained that sociology was born out of a concern with the decline of these traditional societies and the rapidly changing character of the newly arriving modern, industrial world: with where we have come from and where we are heading. New technologies, the advance of capitalism, the growth of cities and the rise of democratic politics all ushered in this new world. This chapter both reaches back into the different kinds of society that existed before the arrival of the modern world and looks forward into the changing shape of the contemporary world. Along the way, it offers some major reasons for the changes that have happened and that are even now accelerating. The central concept of **society** refers to *people who interact in a defined space and share culture*. In this sense, both Europe as a whole and specific countries such as Norway and England may be seen as societies.

**A society under threat**

Look at the opening story to this chapter. This is the photo taken from a plane of the trip described in the story. It is a photo that has captured the public's imagination. Several near-naked tribesmen can be seen firing arrows at the plane – thinking they are under threat. This remarkable photograph has been seen as evidence of the existence of one of the world's last uncontacted tribes. In Brazil today there are around 650,000 Indians in Brazil in over 200 tribes, who live scattered across the country speaking a huge number of languages, many of which are fast becoming extinct. Some of these tribes number thousands – the Guarani and Yanomami. But hidden deep in the Amazon rainforest, there may be an estimated 40 groups of truly isolated indigenous people. Centuries of exposure to disease, violence and dispossession has wiped out the vast majority.

The discovery of new tribes is a tricky business: the skill is to locate such tribes but without disturbing their ways of life and ensuring their survival

*See*: Survival International http://www.survivalinternational.org/.

*Source*: Reuters/Funai-Frente de Proteção Etno-Ambiental Envira/Handout (Brazil).

We shall start by describing the changing character of human society over the last 10,000–12,000 years. This is a very difficult task. The remainder of the chapter then analyses some of the main patterns of different kinds of society, and presents classic visions of society developed by three of sociology's founders, already introduced in earlier chapters. Karl Marx understood human history as a long and complex process of economic conflict. His concern was with the ways in which the economy generates *conflicts and inequalities* around the production of material goods in order to live (to eat and have shelter, for instance), and how these conflicts provided the motor force for change. Max Weber recognised the importance of productive forces as well, but he sought to demonstrate the power of *human ideas* (especially those found in religions) to animate society. Weber believed that rational thinking underlies modern society and promotes change. Finally, Emile Durkheim investigated patterns of *social solidarity*, noting that the bonds uniting traditional societies are strikingly different from those uniting their modern counterparts. All of them were concerned with the momentous changes taking place in European societies in their times, and with how the future would develop. At the end of the chapter we will turn to just what the 200 or so societies in the world today look like, and how they may be characterised. But we will be returning to much of this later in the book.

# Changing patterns of society

Sociologists who study the past (working with archaeologists and anthropologists) have learned quite a bit about our human heritage. Gerhard Lenski and Jean Lenski have chronicled the great differences among societies that have flourished and declined throughout human history. Just as important, the work of these researchers helps us better understand how we live today. The Lenskis call the focus of their research **sociocultural evolution**, *the process of change that results from a society's gaining new information, particularly technology* (Nolan and Lenski, 2010). Rather like a biologist examining how a living species evolves over millennia, a sociologist employing this approach observes how societies change over centuries as they gain a greater ability to manipulate their physical environments. It suggests that societies with rudimentary technology can support only a small

number of people, who enjoy few choices about how to live. Technologically complex societies – while not necessarily 'better' in any absolute sense – develop larger populations which are more likely to be characterised by diverse, highly specialised lives.

The greater the amount of technological information a society has in its grasp, the faster the rate at which it changes. Technologically less complex societies, then, change very slowly. By contrast, industrial, high-technology societies can start to change so quickly that people witness dramatic transformations in the span of their lifetimes. Again, consider some familiar elements of contemporary culture that would probably puzzle, delight, but most likely alarm people who lived just a few generations ago: fast food, faxes, mobile phones, computer 'cybersex', artificial hearts, laser surgery, test-tube babies, genetic engineering, computer-based virtual reality, fibre optics, smart bombs, the threat of nuclear holocaust, space shuttles, transsexual surgery, and 'tell-all' talk shows transmitted across the world to all countries! It is indeed a strange modern world we have arrived in – even when compared with the world of the recent past.

As a society extends its technological reach, the effects ripple through the cultural system, generating countless repercussions. When our ancestors first harnessed the power of the wind by using a sail, they set the stage for discovering kites, sailing ships, windmills and, eventually, aircraft. Consider, as more recent examples, the many ways modern life has been changed by atomic energy or the computer. Drawing on the Lenskis' work, we will describe five general types of society distinguished by their technology: hunting and gathering societies; horticultural and pastoral societies; agrarian societies; industrial societies; and post-industrial societies. We could equally well describe societies as distinguished by their political systems, or their kinds of community.

# 1 Hunting and gathering societies

**Hunting and gathering** refers to *simple technology for hunting animals and gathering vegetation*. From the emergence of our species until about 12,000 years ago, all humans were hunters and gatherers. Hunting and gathering societies remained common several centuries ago, but today they are in sharp decline as they are more and more ravaged by the advance of industrial societies. Still, estimates suggest there may still be – across some 70 countries – at least 370 million

**indigenous peoples** worldwide: *peoples with ties to the land, water and wildlife of their ancestral domain*. Many of these have been or still are hunter-gatherers. Today these include the Aka and Pygmies of central Africa, the Bushmen of south-western Africa, the Aborigines and Torres Strait Islanders of Australia, the Maori of New Zealand, the Kaska Indians of north-west Canada, and the Batek and Semai of Malaysia.

Most members of these societies looked continually for game and edible plants. Only in lush areas where food was plentiful would hunters and gatherers have much leisure time. Moreover, foraging for food demands a large amount of land, so hunting and gathering societies comprise small bands of a few dozen people living at some distance from one another. These groups were also nomadic, moving on as they depleted vegetation in one area or in pursuit of migratory animals. Although they periodically returned to favoured sites, they rarely formed permanent settlements.

Hunting and gathering societies are based on kinship. The family obtains and distributes food, protects its members, and teaches necessary skills to children. Most activities are common to everyone and centre on seeking the next meal; some specialisation, however, corresponds to age and sex. The very young and the very old contribute only what they can, while healthy adults secure most of the food. The gathering of vegetation – the most reliable food source – is typically the work of women, while men take on the less certain job of hunting. Although the two sexes have somewhat different responsibilities, then, most hunters and gatherers probably accorded men and women comparable social importance (Leacock, 1978).

Hunting and gathering societies have few formal leaders. Most recognise a shaman, or spiritual leader, who enjoys high prestige but receives no greater material rewards than other members of the society and must help procure food like everyone else. Other individuals who are especially skilful at obtaining food may also have high prestige; overall, however, the social organisation of hunters and gatherers is relatively simple and egalitarian.

Hunting and gathering societies rarely use their weapons – the spear, the bow and arrow, and stone knife – to wage war. Nonetheless, they are often ravaged by the forces of nature. Storms and droughts can easily destroy their food supply, and they stand vulnerable to accident and disease. Such risks encourage cooperation and sharing, a strategy that increases everyone's odds of survival. Even so, many

die in childhood, and perhaps half perish before the age of 20 (Brody, 2000; Lenski and Nolan, 2010).

During the twentieth century, technologically complex societies slowly closed in on the remaining hunters and gatherers, reducing their landholdings and depleting game and vegetation. Many of these 'indigenous' peoples, such as the Inuit in Canada and Alaska, are finding their cultures increasingly destroyed by the industrial West. In the first half of the twentieth century, Brazil alone lost some 87 tribes. They live under conditions where their human rights are abused and where they are under constant threat of extinction. Yet at the same time, there are signs that such cultures are also fighting back to protect their own ways of life. There is also now a Charter of Rights of Indigenous Peoples which was drawn up by the United Nations.

 There is a lot of information on the web about indigenous people. You could check out:

*Native Web*: www.nativeweb.com/resources

*Survival International*: www.survivalinternational.org

*Indigenous People*: www.indigenouspeople.net/sidemenu.html

*The UN Permananent Forum on Indigenous Issues*: www.un.org/esa/socdev/unpfii

*Indigenous Peoples: Issues and resources*: http://indigenouspeoplesissues.com

# 2 Horticultural and pastoral societies

Ten to twelve thousand years ago, a new technology began to change many hunting and gathering societies. **Horticulture** is *technology based on using hand tools to cultivate plants*. The most important tools of horticulturists are the hoe to work the soil and the digging stick to punch holes in the ground for seeds. Humans first used these tools in fertile regions of the Middle East and, later, in Latin America and Asia. Cultural diffusion spread knowledge of horticulture throughout most of the world by about 6,000 years ago.

Not all societies were quick to abandon hunting and gathering in favour of horticulture. Hunters and gatherers living amid plentiful vegetation and game probably saw little reason to embrace the new technology. The Yanomami of the Brazilian rainforest illustrate the common practice of combining horticulture with more traditional hunting and gathering. They are one of the last large isolated groups of indigenous peoples in the Americas.

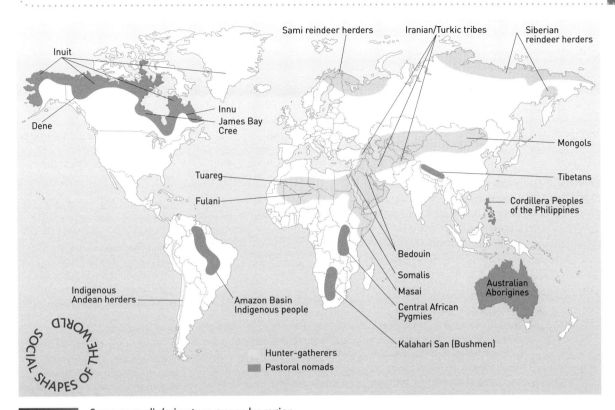

**Map 4.1**    Some nomadic/migratory groups by region

*See also*: genographic.nationalgeographic.com.

*Source*: Adapted from A. M. Khazanov, *Nomads and the Outside World*. Cambridge: Cambridge University Press, 1984: 185.

Then, too, people in particularly arid regions (such as the Middle East) or mountainous areas (such as in the Alps, where the Iceman lived) found horticulture to be of little value. Such people turned to a different strategy for survival, **pastoralism**, which is *technology based on the domestication of animals*. Still others combined horticulture and pastoralism to produce a variety of foods. Today, many horticultural–pastoral societies thrive in South America, Africa and Asia.

The domestication of plants and animals greatly increased food production, enabling societies to support not dozens but hundreds of people. Pastoralists remained nomadic, leading their herds to fresh grazing lands. Horticulturalists, by contrast, formed settlements, moving on only when they depleted the soil. These settlements, joined by trade, comprised multi-centred societies with overall populations often in the thousands.

Domesticating plants and animals generates a *material surplus* – more resources than are necessary to sustain day-to-day living. A surplus frees some people from the job of securing food, allowing them to create crafts, engage in trade, cut hair, apply tattoos or serve as priests. In comparison to hunting and gathering societies, then, horticultural and pastoral societies display more specialised and complex social arrangements.

Hunters and gatherers recognise numerous spirits inhabiting the world. Horticulturalists, however, practise ancestor worship and conceive of God as creator. Pastoral societies carry this belief further, viewing God as directly involved in the well-being of the entire world. This view of God ('The Lord is my shepherd', Psalm 23) is widespread among members of contemporary societies because Christianity, Islam and Judaism originated as Middle Eastern, pastoral religions.

Expanding productive technology also intensifies social inequality. As some families produce more food than others, they assume positions of relative power and privilege. Forging alliances with other elite families ensures that social advantages endure over generations, and a formal system of social inequality emerges. Along with social hierarchy, rudimentary government – backed by military force – is formed to shore up the power of elites. However, without the ability to communicate or to travel quickly, a ruler can control

**WORLD WATCH**

# What is 'Chinese society'?

The twenty-first century is tipped to become the Chinese Century. In 2010, China also became the world's second leading economic state (after the USA). Chinese society is one of the oldest and biggest societies in the world. In area, China is as large as the USA. In population it is about 1.3 billion – the largest population in the world (and increasing by about 14 million a year despite its policy of controlling family size). In land area, it is the fourth largest country. The first dynasty – the Xia dynasty – is conventionally thought to have begun in the twenty-first century BCE, and for a long while before the 'West' developed, it seems to have been one of a very few ancient civilisations. Strongly influenced by Confucianism, Taoism and Buddhism, Chinese society was not (and still is not) a religious society as we use the term 'religion' today (see Chapter 19). Confucianism is more of a moral code than a religion. Most people are influenced by these traditions, embedding belief rituals like ancestor worshipping in local communities and economies.

In the twentieth century, communism was the country's creed under Mao Tse Tung (1893–1976). More recently it has opened up markets internally and throughout the world, becoming semi-capitalist and partially 'democratised'. Major economic transformations towards a free market are under way (see Chapters 15 and 26). China, then, is a curious mixture of Confucian, socialist, capitalist and patriarchal societies (all terms that should become increasingly clear as you read this book!). It was once imperial, then republican, communist in the latter part of the twentieth century and now in the twenty-first century a hybrid of many shapes.

Indeed, today it is one of the most prominent societies in the world, predicted by many to become the most important country of the twenty-first century – as the USA was for the twentieth, and the UK was in the nineteenth (see Chapter 26, p. 902 for a discussion of this).

So what is Chinese society? This box shows some of its elements for you to consider and discuss.

## China as diverse

If it is defined by geography, we can soon see it as a society of vast diversity. We could at least speak of the 'five Chinas' (see Map 4.2).

**The margins**: mountainous; least populated and developed. The vast north of China is relatively lightly populated, partly because of inhospitable terrain and a climate that makes only around 10% of the area possible to cultivate.

**Xinjiang**: enclosed by mountain ranges to the north, south and west. Much of the province is barren.

**Tibet**: China's invasion of Tibet in 1950 and its bloody crackdown of an anti-government uprising in 1959 make Tibet one of China's most controversial regions.

**The hinterland**: dense population.

**Coastal strip**: flood plains and low land with the densest populations and the most economic activity. From China's largest city of Shanghai down to its tropical tourist island of Hainan, the coastal strip has been transformed by the pursuit of wealth.

**The rust belt**: was the industrial centre but there is now much unemployment.

## The 'state' of China

How can such a huge space be governed? In general, for much of its 12,000-year history, China has had a centralised imperial monarchy with between 17 and 22 'dynasties' between 1766 BCE and 1911 CE – from the Shang dynasty in 1766 BCE to the Qing

dynasty (which ended in 1911). The monarchy goes back through 4,000 years of history with 22 dynasties united by the 'First Emperor' of the Qin (Ch'in) in Shi Huangdi (Shih Huang-ti) (221–206 BCE) and consolidated by the Han dynasty (206 BCE to CE 220). The Chinese Empire may be seen to have lasted from 221 BCE to 1911–12 CE, although this was punctuated by long periods when a central government was lacking (Braudel, 1963). But with such a large land mass, it was also a very decentralised state. China has had a strongly agrarian society and has been administered for the last 2,000 years by a complex legal framework and large-scale bureaucracies. Warring and conflict were common.

Most of the twentieth century witnessed the rise of 'Marxist' ideas and the growth of communism. Although this seems like a radical change, it does need to be seen in the context of a very long history. In a sense, it is a simple blip in the twentieth century that certainly worked to modernise the country – albeit at high human cost.

## Chinese culture: 'Chineseness'

The belief system of China today is a curious mixture of three 'high traditions': Confucianism, Taoism and Buddhism. Ancestor worship is often part of this. But beliefs are ritualised in local forms.

Confucianism was closely linked with the teaching of the educated classes and aimed to explain the world, respecting its past and rejecting popular primitive beliefs and superstitions. It was constructed as a set of cosmological and ethical doctrines intended to serve the interests of the state, and for almost 2,000 years it functioned as the moral orthodoxy of the Imperial Order. As we will see in Chapter 19, it was originated by Confucius (Kong Fuzi) around 550 BCE. The *Yijing* (Book of Changes, fourth century BCE)

WORLD WATCH

China is a massive land space with a huge population. Different regions have very different levels of wealth and life styles. For example, the islands around its edge – Hong Kong, Macau and Taipei – have lower populations and the highest GDP's (40,000 yuan or more in 2007). By contrast, the large southern mass which includes Tibet and Sichuan had an average GDP between 10,000 and 14,000 a year.

**Map 4.2**    The Five Chinas

highlights the complementary aspects of the universe, which are in perpetual mutual opposition (day and night, cold and heat, love and hatred, anger and joy): 'One yin and one yang make the whole, Tao'. It integrates opposites via yin (the dark side, earth) and yang (the light side, heaven). It suggests an ethic in which the powerful gain moral serenity and inculcate respect and humility in the masses, and it functioned well to maintain hierarchy.

Taoism (Laozi, from Lao-Tse, 'the Master') was more mystical and recommended the many ways for a long life (through breathing, dieting and alchemy). Confucianism stressed tradition and harmony, whereas Taoism stressed individual freedom and rebellion.

Buddhism arose in India in the sixth and fifth centuries BCE and entered China around the second century BCE, causing conflicts and schisms with the more established Confucianism and Taoism.

## Timeline of China

*Early days*

- 18–12th centuries BCE: transition from a tribal to a feudal way of life
- 1766–1122 BCE: the first major dynasty: the Shang dynasty
- 1279–1368: Genghis Khan establishes the Mongol Yuan dynasty
- 4th century BCE: Kung Fu-Tzu Confucius (551–479 BCE). The I Ching Book. The Tao Te Ching: well-being, harmony and virtue
- 136 BCE: these ideas become central to the Chinese state

**COUNTRY FACT FILE**

CHINA
| | |
|---|---|
| Population | 1,338.6 million |
| Per capita GDP | $2,430 |
| Life expectancy | Male: 71.3 |
| | Female: 74.8 |
| Adult literacy | 93.3% |
| Key languages | Standard Chinese or Mandarin |
| Key religions | Daoist (Taoist), Buddhist |
| | ***Note:*** officially atheist |
| Key city | Beijing |
| Human development index | 0.663 (89th, 2010) |

**WORLD WATCH**

*Before the twentieth century*
- 221: Unification: Qin adopted title of First Emperor
- Great Wall constructed to repel 'barbarians' from the north (4,000 miles long and 2,000 years old)
- 2nd and 3rd centuries: spread of Taoism and neo-Taoism (conflicts with Buddhism and Confucianism)
- 1127–1279: 'second golden age' (printing press, compass invented)
- 1644–1911: The Qing (Ch'ing) Manchu dynasty
- 1839–60: Opium Wars with French and English

*The twentieth century*
- Chinese Revolution (1911): overthrow of Qing Manchu dynasty by nationalists and creation of republic
- The Long March (1934–5): conflict between nationalists and communists, with communists moving to north-west China under Mao Zedong (Mao Tse-tung)

- 1949: the People's Republic of China proclaimed; capital at Beijing (Peking)
- 1950s–1960s: the Great Leap Forward (established rural communes) and the Cultural Revolution
- 1976: Death of 'Chairman Mao'
- 1989: Tiananmen Square; world outrage at killing of student-led pro-democracy protesters. Official deaths: 200.
- 1990s: moves towards an expanding market and greater liberalism. Handover of former British colony Hong Kong in July 1997
- 2003: first manned spacecraft launched
- 2008: Beijing hosts World Olympic Games in great style
- 2010: Google ends its compliance with China's internet regulations and restrictions.

For a more detailed timeline and updates: search BBC China timeline at news.bbc.co.uk/1/hi/world/asia-pacific/1288392.stm

**Going further**

See Norman Stockman, *Understanding Chinese Society* (2000) and Robert E. Gamer, *Understanding Contemporary China* (3rd edn, 2008).

Watch the Oscar-winning film by Bernardo Bertolucci, *The Last Emperor* (1987), which shows the transformation of China from imperialism to communism through the life of the last absolute monarch. Read Jung Chang's *Wild Swans: Three Daughters of China* (1993) – a modern classic which tells the story of life in China through three generations of women. Philip Short's *Mao: A Life* (1999) is a human account of one of the twentieth century's major tyrants.

For more details see:
http://news.bbc.co.uk/1/hi/world/asia-pacific/2188605.stm
http://www.scotland.gov.uk/Topics/Government/International-Relations/china/Regional-Links (an interactive map of regions produced in Scotland!).

only a limited number of people, so empire building proceeds on a small scale.

The domestication of plants and animals surely made simpler societies more productive. But advancing technology is never entirely beneficial. Compared to hunters and gatherers, horticulturists and pastoralists display more social inequality and, in many cases, engage in slavery, protracted warfare and even cannibalism.

## 3 Agrarian societies

About 5,000 years ago – at about the time the Iceman roamed the earth – another technological revolution was under way in the Middle East that would eventually transform most of the world. This was the discovery of **agriculture**, *the technology of large-scale farming using ploughs harnessed to animals or more powerful sources of energy*. The social significance of the animal-drawn plough, along with other technological innovations of the period – including irrigation, the wheel, writing, numbers and the expanding use of metals – clearly suggests the arrival of a new kind of society.

Farmers with animal-drawn ploughs cultivated fields vastly larger than the garden-sized plots worked by horticulturists. Ploughs have the additional advantage of turning, and thereby aerating, the soil to increase fertility. Such technology encouraged agrarian societies to farm the same land for decades, which in turn led to humanity's first permanent settlements. Large food surpluses, transported on animal-powered wagons, allowed agrarian societies to expand to an unprecedented land area and population. As an extreme case, the Roman Empire at its height (about 100 CE) boasted a population of 70 million spread over some 2 million square miles (Lenski and Nolan, 2010).

As always, increasing production meant greater specialisation. Tasks once performed by everyone, such as clearing land and securing food, became distinct occupations. Specialisation made the early barter system obsolete and prompted the invention of money as a common standard of exchange. The appearance of money facilitated trade, sparking the growth of cities as economic centres with populations soaring into the millions.

Agrarian societies exhibit dramatic social inequality. In many cases, peasants or slaves constitute a significant

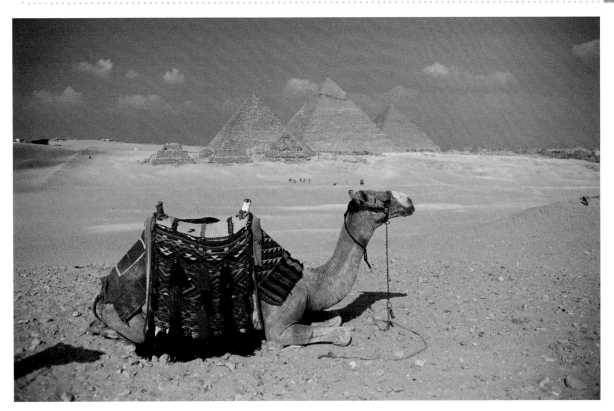

Of Egypt's 130 pyramids, the Great Pyramids at Giza are the largest. Each of the three major structures stands more than 40 storeys high and is composed of about 3 million massive stone blocks. Some 4,500 years ago, tens of thousands of people laboured to construct these pyramids so that one man, the pharaoh, might have a god-like monument for his tomb. Clearly social inequality in this agrarian society was extreme

*Source*: Getty Photodisk.

share of the population and labour for elites. Freed from manual work, elites can then devote their time to the study of philosophy, art and literature.

Among hunters and gatherers, and also among horticulturists, women are the primary providers of food. The development of agriculture, however, appears to have propelled men into a position of social dominance.

Religion reinforces the power of agricultural elites. Religious doctrine typically propounds the idea that people are morally obligated to perform whatever tasks correspond to their place in the social order. Many of the 'wonders of the ancient world', such as the Great Wall of China and the Great Pyramids of Egypt, were possible because emperors and pharaohs wielded virtually absolute power to mobilise their people to endure a lifetime of labour without pay.

In agrarian societies, then, elites gain unparalleled power. To maintain control of large empires, leaders require the services of a wide range of administrators. Consequently, along with the growing economy, the

political system becomes established as a distinct sphere of life.

Agrarian societies have greater specialisation and more social inequality. And, compared to horticultural and pastoral societies, agrarian societies differ more from one another because advancing technology can increase human control over the natural world.

## 4  Industrial societies

**Industrialism** is *technology that powers sophisticated machinery with advanced sources of energy*. Until the industrial era, the major source of energy was the muscle power of humans and other animals. At the dawning of the *Industrial Revolution*, about 1750, mills and factories relied on flowing water and later steam to power ever-larger and more efficient machinery.

Once this technology was at hand, societies began to change faster, as shown in Figure 4.1. Industrial

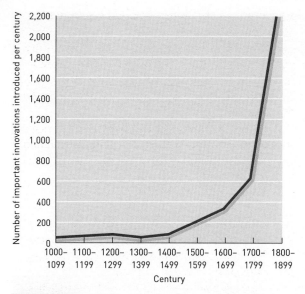

**Figure 4.1** The increasing number of technological innovations

This figure illustrates the number of technological innovations in western Europe after the beginning of the Industrial Revolution in the mid-eighteenth century. Technological innovation occurs at an accelerating rate because each innovation spins off existing cultural elements to produce many further innovations.

*Source*: Adapted from Lenski and Nolan (2006) p. 62, Fig. 3.1.

societies transformed themselves more in a century than they had in thousands of years before. As explained in Chapter 1, this stunning change stimulated the birth of sociology itself. During the nineteenth century, railways and steamships revolutionised transportation, and steel-framed skyscrapers recast the urban landscape, dwarfing the cathedrals that symbolised an earlier age.

As the twentieth century opened, the internal combustion engine further reshaped Western societies, and electricity was fast becoming the basis for countless 'modern conveniences'. Electronic communication, including the telephone, radio and television, was mass-producing cultural patterns and gradually making a large world seem smaller and smaller. More recently, transportation technology has given humanity the capacity to fly faster than sound and even to break the bonds of earth. Nuclear power has also changed the world for ever. And, during the last generation, computers have ushered in the *Information Revolution*, dramatically increasing humanity's capacity to process words and numbers.

Work, too, has changed. In agrarian societies, most men and women work in the home and on the land.

Industrialisation, however, creates factories near centralised machinery and energy sources. Lost in the process are close working relationships and strong kinship ties, as well as many of the traditional values, beliefs and customs that guide agrarian life.

Industrialism engenders societies of unparalleled prosperity. Although health in the industrial cities of Europe and North America was initially poor, a rising standard of living and advancing health-related technology gradually brought infectious diseases under control. Consequently, life expectancy increased, fuelling rapid population growth. Industrialisation also draws people from the countryside to the cities where the factories are built. So, while roughly one in ten members of agrarian societies lives in cities, three out of four people in industrial societies are urbanites.

Occupational specialisation, which expanded over the long course of sociocultural evolution, has become more pronounced than ever. Industrial people often size up one another in terms of their jobs, rather than according to their kinship ties as agrarian people do. Rapid change and movement from place to place also generate anonymity and cultural diversity, sparking the formation of numerous subcultures and countercultures, as described in Chapter 5.

Industrial technology recasts the family, too, diminishing its traditional significance as the centre of social life. No longer does the family serve as the primary setting for economic production, learning and religious worship. And, as Chapter 18 explains in detail, technological change also underlies the trend away from so-called traditional families to greater numbers of single people, divorced people, single-parent families, lesbian and gay couples and stepfamilies.

Early industrialisation concentrated the benefits of advancing technology on a small segment of the population, with the majority living in poverty. In time, however, the material benefits of industrial productivity spread more widely. Poverty remains a serious problem in industrial societies, but compared to the situation a century ago, the standard of living has risen fivefold, and economic, social and political inequality has declined. Some social levelling, detailed in Chapter 8, occurs because industrial societies demand a literate and skilled labour force. While most people in agrarian societies are illiterate, industrial societies provide state-funded schooling and confer numerous political rights on virtually everyone. Industrialisation, in fact, intensifies demands for political participation, as seen recently in South Korea, Taiwan, the People's Republic of China, the former Soviet Union, and the societies of eastern Europe.

# 5 Post-industrial societies

Many industrial societies now appear to be entering yet another phase of technological development. In the early 1970s, Daniel Bell (1976) coined the term **post-industrialism** to refer to *computer-linked technology that supports an information-based economy*. While production in industrial societies focuses on factories and machinery that generate material goods, post-industrial production focuses on computers and other electronic devices that create, process, store and apply information. It is the *information society, the network society, the cyber-society, the postmodern society* (all terms now in common sociological usage). At the individual level, members of industrial societies concentrate on learning mechanical skills; people in post-industrial societies, however, work on honing information-based skills for work involving computers, facsimile machines, satellites and other forms of communication technology.

As this shift in key skills indicates, the emergence of post-industrialism dramatically changes a society's occupational structure. Chapter 15 examines this process in detail, explaining that a post-industrial society utilises less and less of its labour force for industrial production. At the same time, the ranks of clerical workers, managers and other people who process information (in fields ranging from academia and advertising to marketing and public relations) swell rapidly. New skills – often less physical and more mental – are needed to handle fragmented work, multi-tasking and non-linear patterns of work.

The Information Revolution is, of course, most pronounced in industrial, high-income societies, yet the reach of this new technology is so great that it is affecting the entire world. As will be explained further in Chapters 6 and 23, the unprecedented worldwide flow of information originating in rich nations has the predictable effect of tying far-flung societies together and fostering common patterns of global culture. This extends the process of globalisation. And as we saw in Chapter 2, this also brings a society that some speak of as being postmodern (**postmodernism** is *the ways of thinking which stress a plurality of perspectives as opposed to a unified, single core*). It is a world where change is greatly speeding up, where classical boundaries across societies are breaking down, and a new sense of society is in the making.

At the same time, it is important to remember that all five of the different kinds of society we have outlined here still coexist (and there are others not discussed). There are still societies which focus on agriculture, and the industrial world still tends to dominate. But as this book will show over and over again, there is a sense that as the twenty-first century continues to unfold, many changes will accelerate – making the world of 3001 (if it comes to exist!), or even maybe the world of 2050, a quite different order from that we live in now.

Table 4.1 summarises how technology helps shape societies at different stages of sociocultural evolution.

## Technological determinism: a cautious word

While different kinds of technology may well create preconditions for different kinds of society, there are four cautions that need to be given.

First, the technology does not *determine* societies. There is no automatic connection between the kinds of technology a society has available and the form of that society. It takes people to decide how to use technologies – and they may use them in very different ways, developing different skills and meanings. In Nazi Germany, for example, the weight of modern technology was used to exterminate millions of people. The technologies of the Incas or the Egyptians were very sophisticated, but also involved systems of domination and slavery. As we will see later, modern information or computer societies need actions from people to use them – and they may be used for good or bad. Technology is neutral: it is people who shape technology.

Second, we must be very wary of saying that these five societies *evolve* from one to the next, as if there is some kind of automatic progress. In fact, in the twenty-first century all of these societies may be said to coexist. Many indigenous peoples may have hunting, pastoral or agrarian societies with highly evolved technologies of their own. It is often a 'Eurocentric' view that wants to see them as prior to or simpler than European culture. We will return to some of these problems when we discuss multiculturalism in the next chapter.

Third, we must recognise *the limits of technology*. While technology remedies many human problems by raising productivity, by eliminating disease and sometimes simply by relieving boredom, it provides no 'quick fix' for deeply rooted social problems. *Poverty* remains the plight of billions of people worldwide (see Chapter 9). Moreover, with the capacity to reshape the world, technology has created new problems that our ancestors could hardly have imagined. Industrial societies provide more personal freedom, often at the

| Table 4.1 | Kinds of society: a summary | | | | | |
|---|---|---|---|---|---|---|
| Type of society | Historical period | Productive technology | Population size | Settlement pattern | Social organisation | Examples |
| Hunting and gathering societies | Only type of society until about 12,000 years ago; still common several centuries ago; the few examples remaining today are threatened with extinction | Primitive weapons | 25–40 people | Often nomadic, but can be settled (Brody, 2000) | Family centred; specialisation limited to age and sex; little social inequality | Pygmies of central Africa Bushmen of south-western Africa Aborigines of Australia Semai of Malaysia Kaska Indians of Canada |
| Horticultural and pastoral societies | From about 12,000 years ago, with decreasing numbers after about 3000 BCE | Horticultural societies use hand tools for cultivating plants; pastoral societies are based on the domestication of animals | Settlements of several hundred people, interconnected through trading ties to form societies of several thousand people | Horticulturalists form relatively small permanent settlements; pastoralists are nomadic | Family centred; religious system begins to develop; moderate specialisation; increased social inequality | Middle Eastern societies about 5000 BCE Various societies today in New Guinea and other Pacific islands Yanomami today in South America |
| Agrarian societies | From about 5,000 years ago with large but decreasing numbers today | Animal-drawn plough | Millions of people | Cities become common, though they generally contain only a small proportion of the population today | Family loses significance as distinctive religious, political and economic systems emerge; extensive specialisation; increased social inequality | Egypt during construction of the Great Pyramids Medieval Europe Numerous non-industrial societies of the world |
| Industrial societies | From about 1750 to the present | Advanced sources of energy; mechanised production | Millions of people | Cities contain most of the population | Distinct religious, political, economic, educational and family systems; highly specialised; marked social inequality persists, diminishing somewhat over time | Most societies today in Europe and North America, Australia and Japan generate most of the world's industrial production |
| Post-industrial societies: Information Network Cyber Postmodern | Emerging in recent decades | Computers that support an information-based economy | Millions of people | Population remains concentrated in cities but now globalisation is the dominant experience | Industrial work downgraded to poorer societies. Information processing and other service work replace industrial production in rich societies. Consumption is key | Industrial societies noted above are now entering post-industrial stage |

cost of the sense of community that characterised agrarian life. Further, although the most powerful societies of today's world infrequently engage in all-out warfare, *international conflict* now poses unimaginable horrors. Should nations ever unleash even a fraction of their present stockpiles of nuclear weapons, human society would almost certainly regress to a technologically primitive state if, indeed, we survived at all.

Finally, another stubborn social problem linked to technology involves humanity's relation to the *physical environment*. Each stage in sociocultural evolution has introduced more powerful sources of energy and accelerated our appetite for the earth's resources at a rate even faster than the population is growing. We now face an issue of vital concern – one that is the focus of Chapter 24: can humanity continue to pursue material prosperity without subjecting the planet to damage and strains from which it will never recover?

In some respects, then, technological advances have improved life and brought the world's people closer together within a 'global village'. Yet in technology's wake are daunting problems of establishing peace, ensuring justice, and sustaining a safe environment – problems that technology alone can never solve.

# Explaining modern industrial society: the classical sociological accounts

There have been many attempts to explain how the modern industrial world was created. Sociology has its classic interpretations; and we saw at the start of this chapter three key visions of modern industrial society in the work of three of the key 'founders' of modern sociology: Karl Marx, Max Weber and Emile Durkheim. All three of their visions of society try to answer key questions:

- How do societies of the past and present differ from one another?
- How and why does a society change? What forces divide a society? What forces hold it together?
- Are societies getting better or worse?

The theorists profiled in this chapter all probed these questions, but they disagree on the answers. We shall highlight the similarities and differences in their views as we go along.

# Karl Marx: capitalism and conflict

The first of our classic visions of society comes from Karl Marx (1818–83). Few observed the industrial transformation of Europe as keenly as he did. Marx spent most of his adult life in London, then the capital of the vast British Empire. He was awed by the productive power of the new factories; not only were European societies producing more goods than ever before, but a global system of commerce was funnelling resources from around the world through British factories at a dizzying rate.

Marx saw that industry's riches were increasingly concentrated in the hands of a few. A walk almost anywhere in London revealed dramatic extremes of splendid affluence and wretched squalor. A handful of aristocrats and industrialists lived in fabulous mansions, well staffed by servants, where they enjoyed luxury and privileges barely imaginable by the majority of their fellow Londoners. Most people laboured long hours for low wages, living in slums or even sleeping in the streets, where many eventually succumbed to poor nutrition and infectious disease.

Throughout his life, Marx wrestled with a basic contradiction: in a society so rich, how could so many be so poor? Just as important, Marx asked, how can this situation be changed? He was motivated by compassion for humanity, and sought to help a society already badly divided forge what he hoped would be a new and just social order.

The key to Marx's thinking is the idea of **social conflict**, *struggle between segments of society over valued resources*. Social conflict can, of course, take many forms: individuals may quarrel, some towns have long-standing rivalries, and nations sometimes go to war. For Marx, however, the most significant form of social conflict involved clashes between social classes that arise from the way a society produces material goods.

## Society and production

Living in the nineteenth century, Marx observed the early stage of industrial capitalism in Europe. This economic system, Marx noted, transformed a small part of the population into *capitalists*, people who own factories and other productive enterprises. A capitalist's goal is profit, which results from selling a product for more than it costs to produce. Capitalism transforms most of the population into industrial workers, whom Marx called the **proletariat**, *people who provide labour necessary to operate factories and other productive enterprises.* Workers sell their labour for the wages they need to live. To Marx, an inevitable conflict between capitalists and workers has its roots in the productive process itself. To maximise profits, capitalists must minimise wages, generally their single greatest expense. Workers, however, want wages to be as high as possible. Since profits and wages come from the same pool of funds, ongoing conflict occurs. Marx argued that this conflict would end only when people abandoned the capitalist system.

All societies are composed of **social institutions**, defined as *the major spheres of social life, or society's subsystems, organised to meet basic human needs.* In his analysis of society, Marx contended that one specific institution – the economy – dominates all others when it comes to steering the direction of a society. Drawing on the philosophical doctrine of historical *materialism*, which asserts that how humans produce material goods shapes the rest of society, Marx claimed that all the other major social institutions – the political system, family, religion and education – operated under the influence of a society's economy. Marx argued that the economy is 'the real foundation. . . . The mode of production in material life determines the general character of the social, political, and spiritual processes of life' (1959: 43; orig. 1859).

Marx therefore viewed the economic system as the base or social *infrastructure* (*infra* is Latin for 'below'). Other social institutions, including the family, the political system and religion, which are built on this foundation, form society's *superstructure* (*supra* meaning 'above' in Latin). These institutions extend economic principles into other areas of life, as illustrated in Figure 4.2. In practical terms, social institutions reinforce the domination of the capitalists, by legally protecting their wealth, for example, and by transferring property from one generation to the next through the family.

Generally speaking, members of industrial–capitalist societies do not view their legal or family systems as hotbeds of social conflict. On the contrary, individuals come to see their rights to private property as 'natural'. Many people find it easy to think that affluent people have earned their wealth, while those who are poor or out of work lack skills or motivation. Marx rejected this kind of reasoning as rooted in a capitalist preoccupation with the 'bottom line' that treats human well-being as a market commodity. Poverty and unemployment are not inevitable; as Marx saw it, grand wealth clashing with grinding poverty represents

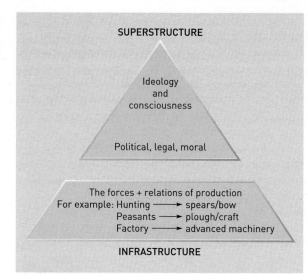

| Figure 4.2 | Karl Marx's model of society |

This diagram illustrates Marx's materialist view that the process of economic production underlies and shapes the entire society. Economic production involves both technology (industry, in the case of capitalism) and social relationships (for capitalism, the relationship between the capitalists, who control the process of economic production, and the workers, who are simply a source of labour). Upon this infrastructure, or foundation, are built the major social institutions as well as core cultural values and ideas. Taken together, these additional social elements represent the society's superstructure. Marx maintained that every part of a society operates in concert with the economic system.

merely one set of human possibilities generated by capitalism (Cuff and Payne, 1979).

Marx rejected capitalist common sense, therefore, as **false consciousness**, *explanations of social problems grounded in the shortcomings of individuals rather than the flaws of society.* Marx was saying, in effect, that industrial capitalism itself is responsible for many of the social problems he saw all around him. False consciousness, he maintained, victimises people by obscuring the real cause of their problems.

## Conflict in history

Marx studied how societies have changed throughout history, noting that they often evolve gradually, though they sometimes change in rapid, revolutionary fashion. Marx observed that change is partly prompted by technological advance. But he steadfastly held that conflict between economic groups is the major engine of change.

Early hunters and gatherers formed primitive communist societies. The word 'communism' refers to a social system in which the production of food and other material goods is a common effort shared more or less equally by all members of society. Because the resources of nature were available to all hunters and gatherers (rather than privately owned), and because everyone performed similar work (rather than dividing work into highly specialised tasks), there was little possibility for social conflict.

Horticulture, Marx noted, introduced significant social inequality. Among horticultural, pastoral and early agrarian societies – which Marx lumped together as the 'ancient world' – the victors in frequent warfare forced their captives into servitude. A small elite (the 'masters') and their slaves were thus locked in an irreconcilable pattern of social conflict (Zeitlin, 1981).

Agriculture brought still more wealth to members of the elite, fuelling further social conflict. Agrarian serfs, occupying the lowest reaches of European feudalism from about the twelfth to the eighteenth centuries, were only slightly better off than slaves. In Marx's view, the power of both the church and the state defended feudal inequality by defining the existing social order as God's will. Thus, to Marx, feudalism amounted to little more than 'exploitation, veiled by religious and political illusions' (Marx and Engels, 1972: 337; orig. 1848).

Gradually, new productive forces undermined the feudal order. Commerce grew steadily throughout the Middle Ages as trade networks expanded and the power of guilds increased. Merchants and skilled crafts workers in the cities formed a new social category, the *bourgeoisie* (a French word meaning 'of the town'). Profits earned through expanding trade brought the bourgeoisie increasing wealth. After the mid-eighteenth century, with factories at their command, the bourgeoisie became true capitalists with power that soon rivalled that of the ancient, landed nobility. While the nobility regarded this upstart 'commercial' class with disdain, the latter's increasing wealth gradually shifted the control of European societies to the capitalists.

Industrialisation also fostered the development of the proletariat. English landowners converted fields once tilled by serfs into grazing land for sheep to secure wool for the prospering textile mills. Forced from the land, serfs migrated to cities to work in factories, where they joined the burgeoning industrial proletariat. Marx envisaged these workers one day joining hands across national boundaries to form a unified class, setting the stage for historic confrontation, this time between capitalists and the exploited workers.

## Capitalism and class conflict

Much of Marx's analysis centres on destructive aspects of industrial capitalism – especially the ways in which it promotes class conflict and alienation. In examining his views on these topics, we will come to see why he advocated the overthrow of capitalist societies.

'The history of all hitherto existing society is the history of class struggles.' With this declaration, Marx and his collaborator Friedrich Engels began their best-known statement, the *Manifesto of the Communist Party* (1972: 335; orig. 1848). The idea of social class is at the heart of Marx's critique of capitalist society. Industrial capitalism, like earlier types of society, contains two major social classes – the dominant people and the oppressed – reflecting the two basic positions in the productive system. Capitalists and proletarians are the historical descendants of masters and slaves in the ancient world and of nobles and serfs in feudal systems. In each case, one class controls the other as productive property. Marx used the term **class conflict** (and sometimes *class struggle*) to refer to *antagonism between entire classes over the distribution of wealth and power in society*.

Class conflict, then, dates back to civilisations long gone (see Figure 4.3). What distinguishes the conflict in capitalist society, Marx pointed out, is how it has come out into the open. Agrarian nobles and serfs, for all their differences, were bound together by long-standing traditions and a host of mutual obligations. Industrial capitalism dissolved those ties so that pride and honour were replaced by 'naked self-interest' and the pursuit of profit in a blatant exercise of oppression. Marx believed that the proletariat, with no personal ties to the oppressors, had little reason to stand for its own subjugation.

But, though industrial capitalism brought class conflict out in the open, Marx realised that fundamental social change would not come easily. First, he claimed, workers must *become aware* of their shared oppression and see capitalism as its true cause. Second, they must *organise and act* to address their problems. This means workers must replace false consciousness with **class consciousness**, *the recognition by workers of their unity as a class in opposition to capitalists and, ultimately, to capitalism itself*. Because the inhumanity of early capitalism was plain for him to see, Marx concluded that industrial workers would inevitably rise up *en masse* to destroy industrial capitalism.

And what of the workers' adversaries, the capitalists? The capitalists' formidable wealth and power, protected by the institutions of society, might seem invulnerable.

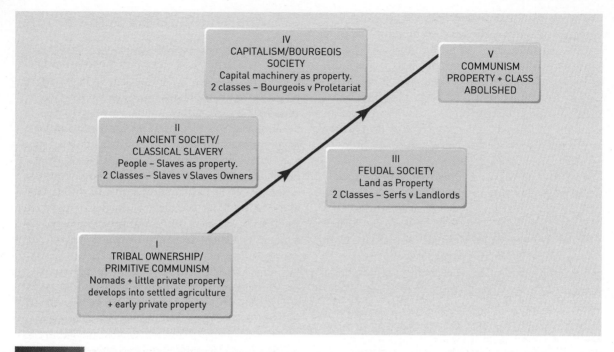

**Figure 4.3**    Marx's conflict model of change

But Marx saw a weakness in the capitalist armour. Motivated by a desire for personal gain, capitalists fear the competition of other capitalists. Thus Marx thought that capitalists would be reluctant to band together, even though they too share common interests. Furthermore, he reasoned, capitalists keep employees' wages low in their drive to maximise profits. This strategy, in turn, bolsters the resolve of workers to forge an alliance against them. In the long run, Marx surmised, capitalists would only contribute to their own undoing.

## Capitalism and alienation

Marx also condemned capitalism for producing **alienation**, *the experience of isolation resulting from powerlessness*. Dominated by capitalists and dehumanised by their jobs (especially monotonous and repetitive factory work), proletarians find little satisfaction in, and feel individually powerless to improve, their situation. Herein lies another contradiction of capitalist society: as human beings devise technology to gain power over the world, the productive process increasingly assumes power over human beings.

Workers view themselves as merely a commodity, a source of labour, bought by capitalists and discarded when no longer needed. Marx cited four ways in which capitalism alienates workers:

1 *Alienation from the act of working.* Ideally, people work both to meet immediate needs and to develop their long-range personal potential. Capitalism, however, denies workers a say in what they produce or how they produce it. Furthermore, much work is tedious, involving countless repetitions of routine tasks. The modern-day replacement of human labour by machines would hardly have surprised Marx; as far as he was concerned, capitalism had turned human beings into machines long ago.

2 *Alienation from the products of work.* The product of work belongs not to workers but to capitalists, who dispose of it for profit. Thus, Marx reasoned, the more workers invest of themselves into their work, the more they lose.

3 *Alienation from other workers.* Marx saw work itself as the productive affirmation of human community. Industrial capitalism, however, transforms work from a cooperative venture into a competitive one. Factory work often provides little chance for human companionship.

4 *Alienation from human potential.* Industrial capitalism alienates workers from their human potential. Marx argued that a worker 'does not fulfil himself in his work but denies himself, has a feeling of misery rather than well-being, does not freely develop his physical and mental energies,

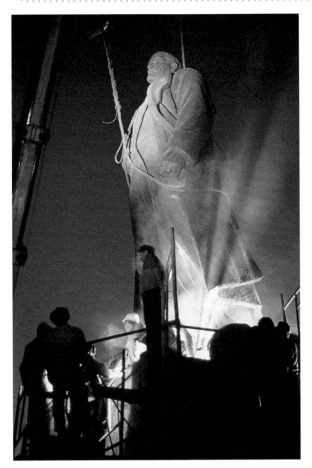

In the twentieth century, Marxism became one of the world's most influential social movements: at its peak it was shaping the economic and political life of nearly a third of the world's people, including those of China, the Soviet Union and eastern Europe. But the socialist regimes of eastern Europe and the former Soviet Union collapsed in the late 1980s. The political transformation of this world region is symbolised by the removal of statues of Vladimir Lenin (1870–1924), architect of Soviet Marxism, in city after city during the last few years

*Source*: Frank Spooner/Gamma.

but is physically exhausted and mentally debased. The worker, therefore, feels himself to be at home only during his leisure time, whereas at work he feels homeless' (1964b: 124–5; orig. 1844). In short, industrial capitalism distorts an activity that should express the best qualities in human beings into a dull and dehumanising experience.

Marx viewed alienation, in its various forms, as a barrier to social change. But he hoped that industrial workers would eventually overcome their alienation by uniting into a true social class, aware of the cause of their problems and galvanised to transform society.

## Revolution

The only way out of the trap of capitalism, contended Marx, was deliberately to refashion society. He envisaged a more humane and egalitarian productive system, one that would enhance rather than undermine social ties. He called this system *socialism*. Marx knew well the obstacles to a socialist revolution; even so, he was disappointed that he never lived to see workers in England overthrow industrial capitalism. Still, convinced of the basic immorality of capitalist society, he was sure that in time the working majority would realise that they held the key to a better future in their own hands. This transformation would certainly be revolutionary, perhaps even violent. What emerged from the workers' revolution, however, would be a cooperative socialist society intended to meet the needs of all.

The discussion of social stratification in Chapter 8 reveals more about changes in industrial–capitalist societies since Marx's time and why the revolution he championed has not taken place. Later chapters also delve into why people in the societies of eastern Europe recently revolted against established socialist governments. But, in his own time, Marx looked towards the future with hope (Marx and Engels 1972: 362; orig. 1848): 'The proletarians have nothing to lose but their chains. They have a world to win.'

# Max Weber: the rationalisation of society and the disenchantment of the world

With a broad understanding of law, economics, religion and history, Max Weber (1864–1920) produced what many regard as the greatest individual contribution to sociology. He generated ideas that were very wide ranging. Here, we limit ourselves to his vision of how modern society differs from earlier types of social organisation.

As we saw in Chapter 1, Weber's sociology can be seen as an action theory. Weber understood the power of the economic and technological, but he departed from Marx's materialist analysis. For him, ideas – especially beliefs and values – have transforming power. Thus he saw modern society as the product not just of new technology and capitalism, but of a new way of thinking. Growing out of changes in religious belief, the modern world can be characterised as an increasingly rational world. We have seen too that Weber also used **ideal types**, contrasting the ideal 'Protestant' with the ideal 'Jew', 'Hindu' and 'Buddhist'. We have already compared 'hunting and gathering societies' and 'industrial societies' as well as 'capitalism' and 'socialism'. Much of Weber's analysis focused upon the ideal types of rationality.

## Tradition and rationality

Rather than categorise societies in terms of technology or productive systems, Max Weber highlighted differences in the ways people view the world. In simple terms, Weber concluded that members of pre-industrial societies cling to *tradition*, while people in industrial–capitalist societies endorse *rationality*.

By **tradition**, Weber meant *sentiments and beliefs passed from generation to generation*. Thus traditional societies are guided by the past. Their members evaluate particular actions as right and proper precisely because these actions have been accepted for so long.

People in modern societies take a different view of the world, argued Weber, embracing **rationality**, *deliberate, matter-of-fact calculation of the most efficient means to accomplish a particular goal*. Sentiment has no place in a rational world-view, which treats tradition simply as one kind of information. Typically, modern people choose to think and act on the basis of present and future consequences, evaluating jobs, schooling and even relationships in terms of what we put into them and what we expect to receive in return.

Weber viewed both the Industrial Revolution and capitalism as evidence of a historical surge of rationality. He used the phrase **rationalisation of society** to denote *the historical change from tradition to rationality as the dominant mode of human thought*. Modern society, he concluded, has been 'disenchanted', as scientific thinking and technology have swept away sentimental ties to the past.

The willingness to adopt the latest technology, then, is one good indicator of how rationalised a society is.

Drawing on Weber's comparative perspective, we deduce that various societies place different values on technological advancement. What one society might herald as a breakthrough, another might deem unimportant, and a third might strongly oppose as a threat to tradition. Inventors in ancient Greece, for instance, devised many surprisingly elaborate

mechanical devices to perform household tasks. But since elites were well served by slaves, they viewed such inventions as mere entertainment. In Europe today, many small communities are guided by their traditions to staunchly oppose modern technology.

## Rationality, Calvinism and industrial capitalism

Is industrial capitalism a rational economic system? Here again, Weber and Marx were in debate. Weber considered industrial capitalism as the essence of rationality, since capitalists pursue profit in eminently rational ways. Marx, however, was critical of capitalism, arguing that it was the antithesis of rationality, and claiming that it failed to meet the basic needs of most of the people (Gerth and Mills, 1946: 49).

But, to look more closely at Weber's analysis, how did industrial capitalism emerge in the first place? Weber contended that industrial capitalism was the legacy of Calvinism – a Christian religious movement spawned by the Protestant Reformation. Calvinists, Weber explained, approached life in a highly disciplined and rational way. Moreover, central to the religious doctrine of John Calvin (1509–64) was *predestination*, the idea that an all-knowing and all-powerful God has preordained some people for salvation and others for damnation. With everyone's fate set before birth, Calvinists believed that people could do nothing to alter their destiny. Nor could they even know what their future would be. Thus the lives of Calvinists were framed by hopeful visions of eternal salvation and anxious fears of unending damnation.

For such people, not knowing one's fate was intolerable. Calvinists gradually came to a resolution of sorts. Why shouldn't those chosen for glory in the next world, they reasoned, see signs of divine favour in *this* world? Such a conclusion prompted Calvinists to interpret worldly prosperity as a sign of God's grace. Anxious to acquire this reassurance, Calvinists threw themselves into a quest for success, applying rationality, discipline and hard work to their tasks. This pursuit of riches was not for its own sake, of course, since self-indulgently spending money was clearly sinful. Calvinists also were little moved to share their wealth with the poor, because they saw poverty as a sign of God's rejection. Their ever-present duty was to carry forward what they held to be their personal *calling* from God (see Figure 4.4).

As they reinvested their profits for greater success, Calvinists built the foundation of capitalism. They

| An elective affinity between | | Figure 4.4 | The Protestant ethic and the spirit of capitalism |
| --- | --- | --- | --- |
| **The Protestant ethic** | **The spirit of capitalism** | | |
| Working hard as a sign of grace | Relentless profit and hard work | | |
| The 'Calling' and Earthly Duties | Rationality | | |
| Salvation and predestination via 'good works' | Time is money – invest for profit | | |
| Self-monitoring and self-control | Hard work profit motive | | |
| Sins of waste and idleness | Importance of hard work and saving | | |

piously used wealth to generate more wealth, practised personal thrift, and eagerly embraced whatever technological advances would bolster their efforts.

These traits, Weber explained, distinguished Calvinism from other world religions. Catholicism, the traditional religion in most of Europe, gave rise to a passive, 'otherworldly' view of life with hope of greater reward in the life to come. For Catholics, material wealth had none of the spiritual significance that so motivated Calvinists. And so it was, Weber concluded, that industrial capitalism became established primarily in areas of Europe where Calvinism had a strong hold.

Weber's study of Calvinism provides striking evidence of the power of ideas to shape society (versus Marx's contention that ideas merely reflect the process of economic production). But always sceptical of simple explanations, Weber knew that industrial capitalism had many roots. In fact, one purpose of this research was to counter Marx's narrow explanation of modern society in strictly economic terms.

As religious fervour weakened among later generations of Calvinists, Weber concluded, success-seeking personal discipline remained strong. A *religious* or, more precisely, *Protestant ethic* became simply a '*work*' ethic. From this point of view, industrial capitalism emerged as 'disenchanted' religion, with wealth now valued for its own sake. It is revealing that 'accounting', which to early Calvinists meant keeping a daily record of moral deeds, now refers simply to keeping track of money.

## Rational social organisation

Weber contended that, by unleashing the Industrial Revolution and sparking the development of capitalism, rationality had defined the character of modern society. Rational social organisation confers the following seven traits on today's social life.

1  *Distinctive social institutions.* Among hunters and gatherers, the family was the centre of virtually all activities. Gradually, however, other social institutions, including religious, political and economic systems, broke away from family life. In modern societies, institutions of education and healthcare have also appeared. The separation of social institutions – each detailed in a later chapter – is a rational strategy to address human needs more efficiently.

2  *Large-scale organisations.* Modern rationality is exemplified by a proliferation of large-scale organisations. As early as the horticultural era, political officials oversaw religious observances, public works and warfare. In medieval Europe, the Catholic Church grew larger still with thousands of officials. In modern, rational societies, the employees of national governments may number in the millions, and most people work for a large organisation.

3  *Specialised tasks.* Unlike members of traditional societies, individuals in modern societies pursue a wide range of specialised activities. The enormous breadth of occupations can be seen in any city's *Yellow Pages*, which typically runs to more than 1,000 pages.

4  *Personal discipline.* Modern society puts a premium on self-directed discipline. For early Calvinists, of course, such an approach to life was rooted in religious belief. Although now distanced from its religious origins, discipline is still encouraged by cultural values such as achievement, success and efficiency.

5  *Awareness of time.* In traditional societies, people measure time according to the rhythm of sun and seasons. Modern people, by contrast, schedule events precisely by the hour and minute. Interestingly, clocks began appearing in European cities some 500 years ago, just as commerce was starting to expand; soon, people began to think

(to borrow Benjamin Franklin's phrase) that 'time is money'.

6  *Technical competence*. Members of traditional societies evaluate one another largely on the basis of *who* they are – how they are joined to others in the web of kinship. Modern rationality, by contrast, prompts us to judge people according to *what* they are – that is, with an eye towards their skills and abilities.

7  *Impersonality*. Finally, in a rational society, technical competence takes priority over close relationships, rendering the world impersonal. Modern social life can be viewed as the interplay of specialists concerned with particular tasks, rather than people broadly concerned with one another. Weber explained that we tend to devalue personal feelings and emotions as 'irrational' because they are often difficult to control.

## Rationality and bureaucracy

Although the medieval church grew large, Weber argued that it was never entirely rational because its goal was to preserve tradition. Truly rational organisations, with the principal focus on efficiency, appeared only in the last few centuries. The organisational type that Weber called *bureaucracy* became pronounced along with capitalism as an expression of rationality.

Chapter 6 explains that bureaucracy is the model for modern businesses, government agencies, trade unions and universities. For now, note that Weber considered this organisational form to be the clearest expression of a rational world-view because its chief elements – offices, duties and policies – are intended to achieve specific goals as efficiently as possible. By contrast, the inefficiency of traditional organisation is reflected in its hostility to change. In short, Weber asserted that bureaucracy transformed all of society in the same way that industrialisation transformed the economy.

Still, Weber emphasised that rational bureaucracy has a special affinity to capitalism. He wrote:

> **Today, it is primarily the capitalist market economy which demands that the official business of public administration be discharged precisely, unambiguously, continuously, and with as much speed as possible. Normally, the very large capitalist enterprises are themselves unequalled models of strict bureaucratic organisation.**
>
> (1978: 974; orig. 1921)

## Rationality and alienation

Max Weber joined with Karl Marx in recognising the unparalleled efficiency of industrial capitalism. Weber also shared Marx's conclusion that modern society generates widespread alienation, though for different reasons. For Weber, the primary problem is not the economic inequality that so troubled Marx, but the stifling regulation and dehumanisation that comes with expanding bureaucracy. It leads to an increasing 'disenchantment with the world'.

Bureaucracies, Weber warned, treat people as a series of cases rather than as unique individuals. In addition, working for large organisations demands highly specialised and often tedious routines. In the end, Weber envisaged modern society as a vast and growing system of rules seeking to regulate everything and threatening to crush the human spirit.

An irony found in the work of Marx reappears in Weber's thinking: rather than serve humanity, modern society turns on its creators and enslaves them. In language reminiscent of Marx's description of the human toll of industrial capitalism, Weber portrayed the modern individual as 'only a small cog in a ceaselessly moving mechanism that prescribes to him an endlessly fixed routine of march' (1978: 988; orig. 1921). Thus, knowing well the advantages of modern society, Weber ended his life deeply pessimistic. He feared that the rationalisation of society would end up reducing people to robots.

## Emile Durkheim: the bonds that tie us together – from mechanical to organic

'To love society is to love something beyond us and something in ourselves.' These are the words of Emile Durkheim (1858–1917), another architect of sociology. This curious phrase (1974: 55; orig. 1924) distils one more influential vision of human society.

## Structure: society beyond ourselves

First and foremost, Emile Durkheim recognised that society exists beyond ourselves. Society is more than the individuals who compose it; society has a life of its own that stretches beyond our personal experiences. It was here long before we were born, it makes claims on us while we are alive, and it will remain long after we are gone. Patterns of human behaviour, Durkheim explained, form established *structures*; they are *social facts* that have an objective reality beyond the lives and perceptions of particular individuals. Cultural norms, values, religious beliefs – all endure as social facts.

And because society looms larger than individual lives, it has the *power* to shape our thoughts and actions, Durkheim noted. So studying individuals alone (as psychologists or biologists do) can never capture the essence of human experience. Society is more than the sum of its parts; it exists as a complex organism rooted in our collective life. A reception class in a primary school, a family sharing a meal, people milling about a country auction – all are examples of the countless situations that set an organisation apart from any particular individual who has ever participated in them.

Once created by people, then, society takes on a momentum of its own, confronting its creators and demanding a measure of obedience. For our part, we experience society's influence as we come to see the order in our lives or as we face temptation and feel the tug of morality.

## Function: society in action

Having established that society has structure, Durkheim turned to the concept of *function*. The significance of any social fact, he explained, extends beyond individuals to the operation of society itself.

To illustrate, consider crime. Most people think of lawbreaking as harmful acts that some individuals inflict on others. But, looking beyond individuals, Durkheim saw that crime has a vital function for the ongoing life of society itself. As Chapter 17 explains, only by recognising and responding to acts as criminal do people construct and defend morality, which gives necessary shape to our collective life. For this reason, Durkheim rejected the common view of crime as 'pathological'. On the contrary, he concluded, crime is quite 'normal' for the most basic of reasons: a society could not exist without it (1964a, orig. 1895; 1964b, orig. 1893).

## Personality: society in ourselves

Durkheim contended that society is not only 'beyond ourselves', it is also 'in ourselves'. Each of us, in short, builds a personality by internalising social facts. How we act, think and feel – our essential humanity – is drawn from the society that nurtures us. Moreover, Durkheim explained, society regulates human beings through moral discipline. Durkheim held that human beings are naturally insatiable and in constant danger of being overpowered by our own desires: 'The more one has, the more one wants, since satisfactions received only stimulate instead of filling needs' (1966: 248; orig. 1897). Having given us life, then, society must also instil restraints in us.

Nowhere is the need for societal regulation better illustrated than in Durkheim's study of suicide (1966; orig. 1897), detailed in Chapter 1. Why is it that, over the years, rock stars have been so vulnerable to self-destruction? Durkheim had the answer long before anyone made electric music: it is the *least* regulated categories of people that suffer the *highest* rates of suicide. The greater licence afforded to those who are young, rich and famous exacts a high price in terms of the risk of suicide.

## Modernity and anomie

Compared to traditional societies, modern societies impose fewer restrictions on everyone. Durkheim acknowledges the advantages of modern freedom, but he warned of a rise in **anomie**, *a condition in which society provides little moral guidance to individuals*. What so many celebrities describe as 'almost being destroyed by their fame' is one extreme example of the corrosive effects of anomie. Sudden fame tears people away from their families and familiar routines, disrupting society's support and regulation of an individual, sometimes with fatal results. Durkheim instructs us, therefore, that the desires of the individual must be balanced by the claims and guidance of society – a balance that has become precarious in the modern world.

## Evolving societies: the division of labour

Like Marx and Weber, Durkheim witnessed at first hand the rapid social transformation of Europe during the nineteenth century. Analysing this change, Durkheim saw a sweeping evolution in the forms of social organisation.

In pre-industrial societies, explained Durkheim, strong tradition operates as the social cement that

| Table 4.2 | The classic theorists briefly contrasted | | |
| --- | --- | --- | --- |
| | **Marx** | **Weber** | **Durkheim** |
| Type of society | Capitalism | Capitalism/rational bureaucratic | Organic solidarity |
| Source of change | Economic conflicts | Religion and ideas | Population density |
| The future | Revolutionary change – communism – optimistic | Disenchantment of the world – pessimistic | Breakdown and anomie, search for new guilds/communities |

binds people together. In fact, what he termed the *collective conscience* is so strong that the community moves quickly to punish anyone who dares to challenge conventional ways of life. Durkheim called this system **mechanical solidarity**, meaning *social bonds, based on shared morality, that unite members of pre-industrial societies*. In practice, then, mechanical solidarity springs from *likeness*. Durkheim described these bonds as 'mechanical' because people feel a more or less automatic sense of belonging together.

Durkheim considered the decline of mechanical solidarity to be a defining trait of modern society. But this does not mean that society dissolves; rather, modernity generates a new type of solidarity that rushes into the void left by discarded traditions. Durkheim called this new social integration **organic solidarity**, defined as *social bonds, based on specialisation, that unite members of industrial societies*. In short, where solidarity was once rooted in likeness, it now flows from *differences* among people whose specialised pursuits make them rely on one another.

For Durkheim, then, the key dimension of change is a society's expanding **division of labour**, or *specialised economic activity*. As Max Weber explained, modern societies specialise in order to promote efficiency. Durkheim fills in the picture by showing us that members of modern societies count on the efforts of tens of thousands of others – most of them complete strangers – to secure the goods and services they need every day.

So modernity rests far less on *moral consensus* (the foundation of traditional societies) and far more on *functional interdependence*. That is, as members of modern societies, we depend more and more on people whom we trust less and less. Why, then, should we put our faith in people we hardly know and whose beliefs may differ radically from our own? Durkheim's answer:

'Because we can't live without them'. In a world in which morality sometimes seems like so much shifting sand, then, we confront what might be called 'Durkheim's dilemma': the technological power and expansive personal freedom of modern society come only at the cost of receding morality and the ever-present danger of anomie.

Like Marx and Weber, Durkheim had misgivings about the direction society was taking. But, of the three, Durkheim was the most optimistic. Confidence in the future sprang from his hope that we could enjoy greater freedom and privacy while creating for ourselves the social regulation that had once been forced on us by tradition.

## Reviewing the theories

## How have societies changed?

We started with a view – sociocultural evolution, furthest developed by the North American sociologists Gerhard and Jean Lenski (Lenski and Nolan, 2010) – in which societies differ primarily in terms of changing technology. Modern society stands out in this regard because of its enormous productive power. Karl Marx also stressed historical differences in productive systems, yet pointed to the persistence of social conflict throughout human history (except perhaps among simple hunters and gatherers). For Marx, modern society is capitalist, and is distinctive because it brings that conflict out in the open.

Max Weber looked at this question from another perspective, tracing evolving modes of thought. Pre-industrial societies, he claimed, are guided by tradition, while modern societies espouse a rational world-view. Bureaucracies take on a key role. Finally, for Emile Durkheim, traditional societies are characterised by mechanical solidarity based on moral consensus. In industrial societies, mechanical solidarity gives way to organic solidarity based on productive specialisation.

## Why do societies change?

Marx's materialist approach pointed to the struggle between social classes as the 'engine of history', pushing societies towards revolutionary reorganisation. Weber's idealist view argues that modes of thought also contribute to social change. He demonstrated how rational Calvinism bolstered the Industrial Revolution, which in turn reshaped much of modern society. Finally, Durkheim pointed to an expanding division of labour as the key dimension of social change.

## What holds societies together?

Marx spotlighted social division, not unity, treating class conflict as the hallmark of human societies throughout history. From his point of view, elites may force an uneasy peace between the classes, but true social unity would emerge only if production were to become a truly cooperative endeavour. To Weber, members of a society share a distinctive world-view. Just as traditional beliefs joined people together in the past, so modern societies have created rational, large-scale organisations with their own organisational cultures that fuse and guide people's lives. Finally, Durkheim made solidarity the focus of his work, contrasting the morality-based mechanical solidarity of pre-industrial societies with modern society's more practical organic solidarity.

## What is European society?

Marx, Weber and Durkheim – discussed in this chapter – were not just seeking to understand the nature of industrial societies; they were Europeans largely in search of understanding industrial Europe. But it is hard to know quite what 'Europe' is. Before going on, make a list of ways you might define Europe, and ponder what are its common elements and what are its differences.

In one sense it is hard to see Europe as anything coherent. There are over 40 countries, and even more languages. They are scattered over diverse climates – from Scandinavia to the Mediterranean – and diverse cultures – from 'Spanish' to 'Nordic'. There are diverse histories, rituals, politics, economic systems and religions. Northern Europe has more individualistic values than southern Europe and Ireland (where religious values are

stronger). It is hard to see what the Nordic cultures of Denmark, Finland, Sweden and Norway have in common with the cultures of Spain, Italy or Portugal. And within each of these countries there are internal splits and differing ethnic groups (France has Algerians; Germany has guest workers; and the United Kingdom has Scots, Welsh and Irish alongside people of Asian and Afro-Caribbean descent). It is easy to ignore the diversity of this Europe and focus on the one voice of England (often with a diluted voice from North America). But clearly the English voice is not unanimous, and it is certainly not the French voice or the Norwegian one. Yet despite this, people speak of a European society. What can be meant by this?

One way is to search for some common elements. Maybe there are a few? A common history, common lands and geography and – perhaps – some broad common, cultural elements that could be seen as similar. It may indeed be what Benedict Anderson has called an 'imagined community', held together by a

common sense of history and culture (Anderson, 1989). In part this may be because most of these cultures have deep values that link to being the first industrialising countries, the first modern democratic cultures and the first Christian cultures. As we will see, these values are pervasive. Taken together, it may be, as Agnes Heller argues, that 'European culture is modernity – cumulative knowledge and progress, technology and wealth – along with nation states and ideas of freedom and equality' (Wintle, 1996: 11). It defines others through this 'own sense'.

Another way is to approach them as countries themselves seeking to be united. Since the Second World War (itself a curiously unifying factor), there have been persistent attempts to create a European Union. Starting with the Congress of Europe in 1948 at The Hague, the European Union has grown through many stages, as shown in Table 4.3. In 1951 Jean Monnet called the European Coal and Steel Community 'the first expression of the Europe that is being born'. But this involved

WORLD WATCH

| Table 4.3 | Some landmarks in the making of the European Union |

### 1945–1959 THE BEGINNINGS OF COOPERATION

**April 1951** Treaty of Paris establishes the European Coal and Steel Community (with France, West Germany, Italy, Belgium, the Netherlands and Luxembourg). The UK does not join.

**March 1957** Treaties of Rome, signed again by the above six, establish the European Economic Community and the European Atomic Energy Community. Also includes new parliament and new court and eliminates customs duties among member states.

**1 January 1958** Treaties of Rome become law. In effect, this is the start of the European Economic Community (EEC).

### 1960–1969 A PERIOD OF ECONOMIC GROWTH

**1964** Common agricultural policy established with uniform prices to start in 1967.

### 1970–1989 A GROWING COMMUNITY – THE FIRST ENLARGEMENT

**22 January 1972** The United Kingdom, Denmark, Ireland and Norway admitted to membership from January 1973. Conservative government in the UK with Prime Minister Edward Heath takes the UK into the EEC, but a referendum in Norway rejects membership.

**June 1975** Labour government in UK wishes to withdraw and holds a referendum: 67% of voters decide they want to stay in.

**December 1975** Elected European Parliament planned to start in 1979. No powers to introduce legislation, but powers to advise.

**1978** Members agree to ECU (European Currency Unit).

**1 January 1981** Greece becomes tenth member.

**January 1983** Common fishing policy.

**January 1985** First European passports issued. Jacques Delors is first president of European Commission.

**January 1986** Spain and Portugal join.

**February 1986** The Single Act; streamlining, with legalisation now passed by a majority.

### 1989–2000 THE FALL OF THE BERLIN WALL – A EUROPE WITHOUT FRONTIERS

**October 1990** Former East Germany becomes part of the Community.

Maastricht Treaty signed (see 1992 below).

**October 1991** European Free Trade Association (EFTA – Austria, Finland, Iceland, Liechtenstein, Norway, Sweden, Switzerland) agrees an extended cooperation project – the European Economic Area

(EEA) – within the Community and EFTA, creating an integrated trade area.

**November 1991** Associations with Poland, Hungary and Czechoslovakia (but stopping short of full membership).

**1992 The Treaty of Maastricht** ratified. A key step in the integration of the EU with a timetable for the single currency, the new status of EU citizenship, a single internal market and a common foreign and security policy.

**1 January 1995** Austria, Finland and Sweden join the EU, bringing membership to 15.

**June 1997 The Treaty of Amsterdam** concluded and launched in 1999: gave more power to the EU Parliament and 'tidied up' Maastricht 1990 (see above).

**March 1998** EU opens negotiations with Cyprus, Czech Republic, Estonia, Hungary, Poland and Slovenia. New agricultural policy – a ban on member states subsidising their own farmers.

**1 July 1998** European Central Bank inaugurated in Frankfurt.

**1 January 1999** Single monetary policy – the euro; responsibility of European System of Central Banks. Launched by participating countries: all EU except Denmark, Sweden and the UK.

**March 1999** The Amsterdam Treaty: EU's new constitution.

### 2000–NOW: CONTINUING EXPANSION

**1 January 2000** Circulation of euro banknotes and coins.

**Early 2002** Legal tender of national currencies withdrawn in most EU member states; the euro becomes the currency. UK, Denmark and Sweden do not adopt euro.

**1 May 2004** Enlargement of EU with ten new members, seven of which had lived under the Third Reich or Stalinist communism. Estonia, Latvia and Lithuania were part of the former Soviet Union. Poland, Hungary, Slovakia and the Czech Republic were satellites under the Warsaw Pact. Slovenia had been part of socialist Yugoslavia. In addition, there are the islands of Malta and Cyprus (EU25).

**2007: 50th anniversary of EU:** now has over 400 million people.

**2007** Romania and Bulgaria join (EU27). Croatia, the former Yugoslavic Republic of Macedonia and Turkey are current candidates to be accepted in the EU in the future.

**2009 The Treaty of Lisbon:** major changes updating Maastricht (finally approved in a second referendum in 2009).

*Source*: http://europa.eu.

only six countries: Belgium, France, Italy, West Germany, Luxembourg and the Netherlands. Map 4.3 aims to give some sense of the European Union's growth in the past, and also the projected plans for the future. Some now suggest that this is the most advanced and unified economic and political 'region' in the world, and that the twenty-first century may become the European Century. Others – as we shall see – strongly disagree.

Britain has always been a slightly 'awkward partner' in Europe. Until the election of a Labour government on 1 May 1997, successive Conservative governments were the embodiment of 'euroscepticism'. But since then, the UK government has adopted a more favourable stance.

## A note on Turkey

In 2005 historic talks started on the incorporation of Turkey into the EU. This would bring a much larger Muslim culture into the dominant European culture. As well as bridging to the East and being the only Muslim and non-Christian country, Turkey would add one of the largest populations and one of the poorest economies of the region. It would answer critics who see the EU as purely Christian. But initially some countries – such as Austria – have been opposed. The arrival of Turkey would bring about some striking changes but it will take some 10–15 years of discussion, with many hurdles in its way (for example, there is an 'absorption capacity' test to decide if the EU can fit Turkey in).

See: Alex Warleigh, *European Union: The Basics* (2nd edn, 2008); Gerard Delanty and Chris Mumford, *Rethinking Europe* (2005).

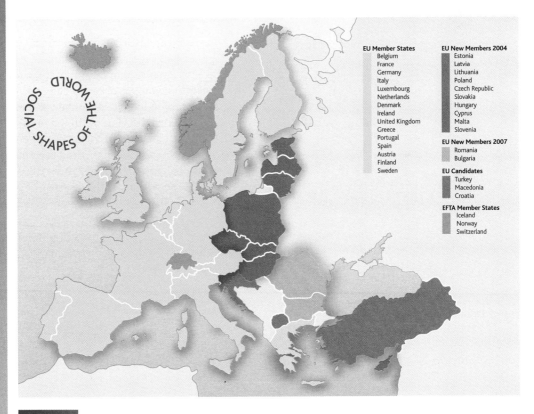

| EU Member States | EU New Members 2004 |
| --- | --- |
| Belgium | Estonia |
| France | Latvia |
| Germany | Lithuania |
| Italy | Poland |
| Luxembourg | Czech Republic |
| Netherlands | Slovakia |
| Denmark | Hungary |
| Ireland | Cyprus |
| United Kingdom | Malta |
| Greece | Slovenia |
| Portugal | |
| Spain | **EU New Members 2007** |
| Austria | Romania |
| Finland | Bulgaria |
| Sweden | **EU Candidates** |
| | Turkey |
| | Macedonia |
| | Croatia |
| | **EFTA Member States** |
| | Iceland |
| | Norway |
| | Switzerland |

SOCIAL SHAPES OF THE WORLD

**Map 4.3**    Greater Europe: the new enlarged European Union in 2007

# Where are societies heading?

Finally, there is the question of where society may now be headed (see the *Big debate* at the end of this chapter). For Marx, capitalism would generate the seeds of its own destruction: revolutionary change should bring about a new communist social order. In general, however, attempts to bring about a communist order during the twentieth century in the old Soviet Union and China were not successes. For Weber, there was a strong pessimistic streak: he saw the world as an Iron Cage, with growing rationality creating an ever-spreading 'disenchantment with the world'. Durkheim held out hope for new forms of association to emerge that would bind people together through their differences and resolve the problem of anomie. We will evaluate these views as we move through the book.

Like a kaleidoscope that shows us different patterns as we turn it, these approaches reveal an array of insights into society. Yet no one approach is, in an absolute sense, right or wrong. Society is exceedingly complex, and we gain the richest understanding from using all of these visions, as we do in the *Thinkers and theory* box on p. 135 and Map 4.4.

# The contemporary shape of world societies

We have looked at some of the range of world societies in the past and have considered some of the main explanations given for the rise of the modern industrial world. In this section, we take a very quick tour of the contemporary world, introducing a few key themes before exploring them more fully in later chapters. The box suggests some of the terms that sociologists use to describe this twenty-first century world, and you may also like to look at the map on the inside back cover, which suggests some of the major social regions of the world.

## The early twenty-first-century world

The world population reached 6.7 billion in mid-2007 and is projected to peak at 9 billion in 2070. At the start of the twenty-first century, world societies could be divided in several ways. (To update the population figures at any time search: popclocks at www.census/gov/main/gov/popclock.)

## Nation-states

There are around 200 well-identified nation-states (one indication of a society). There have been major shifts in power. The end of the 'Cold War', which dominated politics in the last half-century, led to the break-up of four multi-ethnic states: the USSR, Czechoslovakia, Yugoslavia and Ethiopia: over 20 new independent states emerged. But along with break-ups and fragmentations also came reunification: East Germany with West Germany, and Hong Kong with the People's Republic of China, as well as the growth of a much more unified Europe through the European Union (see the *World watch* box, above).

## Languages

There are up to 10,000 spoken languages. Since spoken languages indicate groups, it may be better to take the latter as an indicator of the range of societies functioning on planet earth. Thus, there are still a number of much smaller, usually indigenous, peoples who have maintained something of their own society. Thus, the languages of the native American Indians (numbering around 300), or of the Australian aboriginal peoples (about 250 are documented), help us sense something of the diversity of societies of the past and outside the 'nation state' systems of today (Crystal, 2010).

## First, Second and Third Worlds

There are a number of other ways of approaching world societies. After the Second World War, and until the collapse of the Soviet Union in 1991, it became a tradition to classify societies as 'First World' (the rich, industrialised countries), 'Second World' (less rich and often socialist) and 'Third World' (poor, 'developing'). Although widely used for decades, this 'three worlds' model has generally lost validity in recent years. It was a product of Cold War politics by which the capitalist West (the First World) confronted the socialist East (the Second World), while the rest of the world (the Third World) remained more or less on the sidelines. But the sweeping transformation of eastern Europe and the former Soviet Union in the early 1990s meant that there no longer existed a distinctive Second World. Just as important, the superpower opposition that defined the Cold War has faded in recent years.

This model also lumped together in the Third World more than 100 countries at different levels of development. Some relatively better-off nations of the Third World (such as Chile in South America) have ten times the per-person productivity of the poorest countries of the world (including Ethiopia in eastern Africa). Most countries now also contain their own 'fourth worlds' – a term introduced by the World Bank in 1978 to refer to the very poorest of countries, and even the very poorest within wealthier countries.

## High-, low- and middle-income societies

A very straightforward way of classifying societies is through their income and standard of living. Map 4.4(a) provides a visual guide to the relative economic development of the world's countries. **High-income countries** are defined as *the nations with highest overall standards of living* (there are roughly 65 of them). **Middle-income countries** are not as rich: they are *nations with a standard living of about average for the world as a whole* (about 75). The remaining countries are **low income**: nations with a *low standard of living in which most people are poor* (about 40).

### 1 High-income countries

High-income countries are *nations with highest overall standards of living*.[1] The largest and richest of these countries are known as the G8 ('group of eight') and embrace the USA, Japan, Germany, France, the UK, Italy, Canada and (more recently) Russia. They have been meeting since the 1970s to discuss the global economy. Taken together, these 40 societies generate most of the world's goods and services and control most of the planet's wealth. On average, individuals in these countries live well, not because they are particularly bright or exceptionally hard-working, but because they had the good fortune to be born in an affluent region of the world.

High-income societies are rich because theirs were the first economies to be transformed by the Industrial Revolution more than two centuries ago, increasing their productive capacity 100-fold. To grasp how this development enriched our own region of the world, consider that the typical European household may well spend more today just caring for their pets than the average European household did to meet all its needs during the Middle Ages. The nations of western Europe, including the UK, were where industrialisation first took hold about 1750. Canada and the United States are also rich nations; in North America, the Industrial Revolution was well under way by 1850. In Asia, one of the world's leading economic powers is Japan; recent economic growth also places Hong Kong and Singapore in this favoured category. Finally, to the south of Asia in the global region known as Oceania, Australia and New Zealand also rank as industrial, high-income nations.

Taken together, countries with the most developed economies cover roughly 47 per cent of the earth's land area – including parts of five continents – while lying mostly in the northern hemisphere. In 2008, the total population of these nations was about 1.5 billion, representing about 22 per cent of the earth's people. By global standards, rich nations are not densely populated; even so, some countries (such as Japan) are crowded, while others (such as Canada) are sparsely settled. Inside their borders, however, about three-quarters of the people in high-income countries congregate together in or near cities (see Chapter 24).

High-income countries reveal significant cultural differences – the nations of Europe, for example, recognise more than 30 official languages. But these countries share an industrial capacity that generates, on average, a rich material life for their people. Per capita income in these societies ranges from about US$10,000 annually (in Costa Rica and the Russian Federation) to more than US$41,000 annually (in the United States and Norway).[2] In fact, people in high-income societies enjoy some 80 per cent of the world's total income. And many individuals enjoy personal wealth that is far greater than many low-income societies. Two of the world's richest men in the world, William Gates III and Warren Buffett, are worth about $100 billion between them (Forbes lists, 2010).

[1] The text uses this terminology as opposed to the traditional, but outdated, terms 'First World', 'Second World' and 'Third World' for reasons described above. There are other classifications too, like *the North and the South*. In this classification, the North is usually identified with wealthier countries and the South with poorer ones. Alternatively, the world may be divided into *the West and the East*. Again the West signifies the more prosperous countries, but there is also a major cultural difference since the East also incorporates much of Asia, which has cultural and religious characteristics often discussed as 'Asian values'.

[2] High-income countries have per capita annual income of at least US$10,000. For middle- and low-income countries, the comparable figures are $2,500 to £10,000 and below $2,500. All data reflect the United Nations' concept of 'purchasing power parities', which avoids distortion caused by exchange rates when converting all currencies to US dollars. Instead, the data represent the local purchasing power of each nation's currency.

Finally, just as people in a single society perform specialised work, so various regions form a global division of labour. Generally speaking, high-income countries dominate the world's scientific efforts and employ the most complex and productive technology. Production in rich societies is capital-intensive, meaning high investments in factories and related machinery. High-income countries also stand at the forefront of new information technology; the majority of the largest corporations that design and market computers, for instance, are centred on rich societies. With the lion's share of wealth, high-income countries also control the world's financial markets: ups and downs on the financial exchanges of New York, London and Tokyo affect people throughout the world.

## 2 Middle-income countries

Individuals living in any of the roughly 90 nations at this level of economic development – including some of the countries of eastern Europe and most of Latin America – are more likely to live in rural areas than in cities, to walk or to ride bicycles, scooters or animals rather than to drive automobiles, and to receive only a few years of schooling. Most middle-income countries also have marked social inequality, so that while a few people are extremely rich (Hollywood superstars or sheiks of oil-producing nations in the Middle East, for example), many more lack safe housing and adequate nutrition.

These are the countries with per capita income ranging between US$2,500 and $10,000, or roughly the median for the world's *nations* (but higher than that of the world's *people*, since most *people* live in low-income countries). These nations have experienced limited industrialisation, primarily centred on cities. There has been a major population drift to the new cities, and what Mike Davis has called the Planet of Slums (see Chapter 24). Nevertheless, just under half still live in rural areas and engage in agricultural production. Especially in the countryside, schooling, medical care, adequate housing and even safe water are hard to come by, which represents a standard of living far below what members of high-income societies take for granted.

At the high end of this category are Uruguay (Latin America), Bulgaria (Europe) and Thailand (Asia), where annual per capita income is about $9,000. Bolivia (Latin America), Lesotho (Africa) and Vietnam (Asia) are at the low end with roughly $3,000 annually in per capita income.

One group of middle-income countries used to be part of the Second World. These countries, found in eastern Europe and western Asia, had mostly socialist economies until the changes of 1989 and 1991 swept their governments aside. Since then, these nations have begun to introduce market systems. This process, detailed in Chapter 16, has developed free market systems and but has yet to solve serious economic woes. These middle-income countries include Belarus, Ukraine and Romania, as well as Kazakhstan, Georgia and Turkmenistan.

In the second category of middle-income countries are most of the oil-producing nations of the Middle East (or, less ethnocentrically, western Asia). These nations, including Saudi Arabia, Oman and Iran, are very rich, but their wealth is so concentrated that most people receive little benefit and remain poor.

The third, and largest, category of middle-income countries can be found in Latin America and northern and western Africa. These nations (which might be considered the better-off countries of the Third World) include Peru and Brazil in South America as well as Namibia and Gabon in Africa. Both India and China have now entered the middle-income category, which includes much of Asia.

Taken together, middle-income countries span roughly 33 per cent of earth's land area and are home to about 3.8 billion people (about 58 per cent of humanity). Some very large countries (such as China) are far less crowded than other smaller countries (such as El Salvador), but compared to high-income societies, these are all densely populated.

## 3 Low-income countries

Finally, about half of the world's people live in the 50 to 60 low-income countries, which are *nations with little industrialisation, in which severe poverty is the rule*. Most of the poorest societies in the world are in Africa and Asia. Here again, a small number of people in each of these nations are rich; but the majority barely get by with poor housing, unsafe water, too little food, little or no sanitation and, perhaps most seriously of all, little chance to improve their lives. The population density for poor countries is generally high, though it is much higher in Asian countries (such as Bangladesh and Pakistan) than in more sparsely settled central African nations (such as Chad or the Democratic Republic of the Congo).

In poor countries, one-third of the people live in cities; most inhabit villages and farms as their families have done for centuries. In fact, half the world's people are farmers or peasants, and most of them live in the low-income countries. By and large, 'peasants' are staunchly traditional, following the folkways of their ancestors. Living without industrial technology, peasants are not very productive. Hunger, minimal housing and frequent disease all frame the lives of the world's poorest people.

This broad overview of global economic development gives us a foundation for understanding the problem of global inequality. For people living in affluent nations, the scope of human want in much of the world is difficult to grasp. From time to time, televised scenes of famine in very poor countries such as Ethiopia and Bangladesh give us a shocking glimpse of the absolute poverty that makes every day a life-and-death struggle. Behind these images lie cultural, historical and economic forces that we shall explore in the remainder of this chapter.

*Note*: To classify a country as 'low income' does not mean that only poor people live there. On the contrary, the rich districts of poor countries testify to the high living standards of some. Indeed, given the low wages paid to most urbanites in these countries, the typical well-to-do household is staffed by several servants and served by a gardener and chauffeur. But for the majority in the world's poor countries, poverty is the rule. Moreover, with incomes of only several hundred pounds a year, the burden of poverty is greater than it is among the poor in high-income societies.

A key reason for marked disparities in quality of life is that economic productivity is lowest in precisely the regions of the globe where population growth is highest. High-income countries are by far the most advantaged with 80 per cent of global income supporting just 22 per cent of the world's people. Middle-income nations contain about 58 per cent of the global population; these people earn about 12 per cent of the world's income. This leaves about 20 per cent of the planet's population with a scant 2 per cent of total global income (see Chapter 9, p. 287).

## Newly industrialising countries and China rising

The map of the world is constantly changing, and one of the most significant recent developments is the emergence of **newly industrialising countries** (often called NICs), *lower-income countries that are fast becoming high-income ones*. A cluster of (mainly) south-east Asian countries are making rapid economic progress. These countries include Hong Kong, Singapore, South Korea, Thailand and Taiwan. Some commentators have suggested that this new 'Asian Way' has been adopting different industrialisation patterns

from those traditionally found in the West, and that they are indeed likely to become the trailblazers for the twenty-first century (Naisbitt, 1997). Above all, as we saw in the box on p. 110, China has moved out of its recent communist past to become a world player on the economic stage.

## The Human Development Index

To focus on the economic alone, however, is to give a very skewed view of the world, and sociology is always interested in a wider array of factors. Some recent analysts, for example, have developed ways of classifying societies based upon a wider conception of how well a society works – how 'happy' it is, and how good its environmental track record is. These are often contentious debates and we return to them in the final chapters of this book (see Chapters 25 and 26).

The most significant new way of classifying and understanding societies has been through the development of the Human Development Index (or HDI). The HDI was first used in 1990 by the United Nations Development Programme (and is subsequently published annually in its *Human Development Report*). It is a composite figure bridging three main issues across all the countries for which relevant data are available:

- *longevity* – life expectancy at birth
- *knowledge and education* – adult literacy rate and enrolment in schooling
- *decent standards of living* – adjusted income per head.

Index values are decimals that fall between hypothetical extremes of 1 (highest) and zero (lowest). By this calculation, Norwegians enjoy the highest quality of life (HDI value 0.938), with residents of Australia, New Zealand and the USA close behind; at the other extreme, people in Zimbabwe and the Democratic Republic of the Congo have the world's lowest quality of life (0.140 and 0.239 respectively) (*Human Development Report*, 2010).

Of course, there are many critical problems in using such composite figures. Statistics need very careful interpretation, especially across cultures, and we discuss this more fully in Chapter 9. Bearing this in mind, some major points can be made from the 2010 listing.

- Of the 169 countries listed, 42 score very high HDIs, 43 score high HDIs, 42 have medium HDIs and 42 have low HDIs.
- Norway, Australia, New Zealand, the United States and Ireland rank as the top five; Zimbabwe, Congo, Niger, Burundi and Mozambique rank at the bottom.

(a) **The World Bank** ranked by income (gross national income, GNI, per capita)

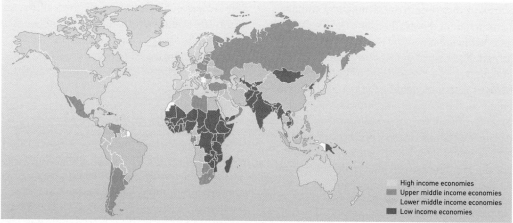

High income economies
Upper middle income economies
Lower middle income economies
Low income economies

(b) **UNDP** (UN Development Program) ranked by Human Development Index

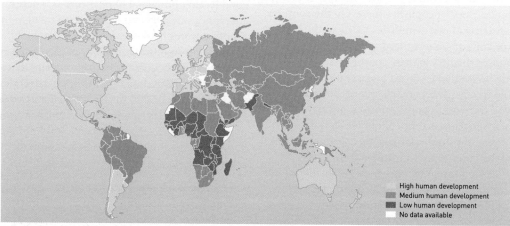

High human development
Medium human development
Low human development
No data available

(c) **UNICEF** (UN Children's Fund) ranked by under-five mortality rate (per 1,000 live births)

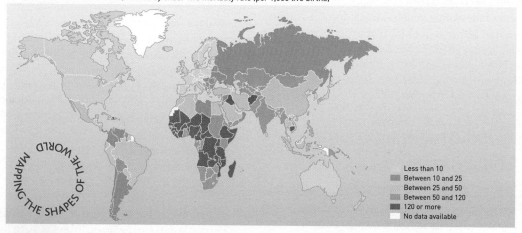

Less than 10
Between 10 and 25
Between 25 and 50
Between 50 and 120
120 or more
No data available

MAPPING THE SHAPES OF THE WORLD

**Map 4.4**

The world according to . . .
(a) the World Bank: ranked by income (gross national income, GNI per capita)
(b) UNDP (UN Development Programme): ranked by Human Development Index
(c) UNICEF (UN Children's Fund): ranked by under-five mortality rate (per 1,000 live births)

*Source: The World Guide*, 2007, 11th edn, Oxford: New Internationalist Publications, p. 60. Reprinted by kind permission of the New Internationalist. Copyright © New Internationalist, www.newint.org.

- The Netherlands is seventh; Japan is tenth; Israel is fifteenth; Denmark is nineteenth; Hong Kong is twenty-first; and the United Kingdom is twenty-sixth.
- China, Oman, Nepal, Indonesia and Saudi Arabia have made the most sustained advances in development over the past 40 years, but much of sub-Saharan Africa still lags far behind.

 **tip**

For more critical comments on the Human Development Index, see Chapter 9. For a summary table of all recorded countries, see Chapter 9, p. 284. For the latest *Human Development Report* online, access: http://hdr.undp.org/en/reports/global/hdr2010.

## THINKERS & THEORY

## Multiple modernities: theorising the twenty-first-century society

Over the past 50 years, sociologists have regularly claimed that we are moving into a new kind of society. How are we to characterise the times we live in? In Table 4.1 we refer to 'post-industrial societies'. Throughout this book, we use the terms 'postmodern' and 'late modern' most regularly – and often we will be using the term 'twenty-first century'. It is descriptive of the time period we are now in. But there are many different terms and concepts that can be used, and this box aims to introduce you to some of them. Each brings its own account of the new world we are moving into.

These are all controversial, and usually come from male theorists. They bring with them a high level of generalisation and suggest that very strong changes are happening. A general problem with most of them is that they write *apocalyptically*: that is, they talk of radical major changes that are coming our way and which are usually heralding 'the end of the world as we know it'. (Indeed, this is the title of one such book: Immanuel Wallerstein's *The End of the World as We Know it: Social Science for the Twenty*

*First Century* (1999)!) We need to be aware of these theoretical suggestions, but they all need to be seen as just that: suggestive – giving you ideas to think with – rather than conclusive.

- *The post-industrial society*. The first major suggestion and used widely between 1960 and 1990. Used by Daniel Bell, it refers to a productive system based on service work and high technology.

- *The post-history society*. Controversially put forward by Francis Fukuyama. In the wake of the collapse of communism, he argued that society had now reached its historical end point in the worldwide triumph of liberal capitalism. It was much criticised, and Fukuyama has now largely changed his position and argument.

- *The postmodern society*. Seen as a direct challenge to Enlightenment thinking and modernity. It takes many forms – especially in culture, where ideas of fragmentation, difference and pluralism are stressed. In a weaker form, it embraces nearly all the ideas below and recognises that the traditional, modern and postmodern worlds all live alongside each other.

- *Late modernity*. Associated with Anthony Giddens, David Harvey and Jürgen Habermas. Generally they do not agree with the ideas of the postmodernists, as they do

not see a break with the past modern world. Instead, they see late modern society as an intensification and speeding up of themes well developed in the modern world.

- *Reflexive modernity*. Closely linked to ideas of late modernity, but here the stress is on a society in which people become more aware (reflexive) about what is going on around them. For example, science no longer simply leads the way: people want to know more about what it means. They want to know about the environment, and about the risk generated by new technologies and the like.

- *Multiple modernities*. An idea developed by Eisenstadt to suggest that there are many past routes into the present world and many forms that contemporary modernity can take. There is no one way.

- *Liquid society*. A new form of society that is much more fluid than previous modern and traditional ones. Everything changes, everything flows, mobility is key. Zygmunt Bauman highlights the uncertainty (*Unsicherheit*) of this world; John Urry is concerned with its global flow and complexity.

- *Late capitalism*. A continuation of the themes first analysed by Marx and which can still be seen at work in so-called modern societies. But Marx's concerns have now become

THINKERS & THEORY

amplified and are speeding up on a worldwide stage.

- *The information age/the network society* (Castells). A new form of society dependent upon new information technologies and networking (see Chapter 6).

- *The risk society*. This is Ulrich Beck's term for a new form of risk where uncertainty permeates society because of changes in technology, globalisation and the environment. These risks are not like the old natural risks (which still continue) (see Chapter 23).

- *The surveillance society* (Foucault, Cohen). A new form of society dependent on communication and information technologies for administration and control processes, and which result in the close monitoring of everyday life (see Chapter 17).

The list is really getting quite long. Other terms you may come across include:

- post-national (Habermas)
- post-honour (Ahmed)
- world risk (Beck)
- the global age (Albrow)
- the cyber-society (Haraway)
- the human rights society
- the citizenship society
- the cosmopolitan society (Appiah, Beck)
- the mobile society (Urry)

- individualised society (Beck)
- empathic civilisation (Rifkin)

And more: you may also want to note more specific processes that are discussed throughout the book. Consider, for instance, 'The McDonaldsisation of society' (Ritzer), and the 'Disneyisation of society' (Bryman) in Chapter 6.

All these theories suggest a new world that is emerging full of rapid change, uncertainty, risk, openness and individualism. They have different emphases. Some are dark, pessimistic dystopias and others provide more optimistic, positive utopian images. We will return to all this throughout the book.

# Conclusion: change and societies

This chapter has aimed to introduce you to a range of different kinds of society from both the past and the present, and to suggest how they have come about and how they might be changing. For much of history, world societies have been dominated by hunting, gathering, horticultural and agrarian societies. What we have witnessed over the past few centuries has been a major shift into a capitalist, technological and 'modern' world. Such societies were the key focus of early sociologists such as Marx, Durkheim and Weber. Recently, many industrial societies seem to be entering yet another phase of society linked to computer technologies and globalisation.

As the book moves along, we shall try to appraise just what some of the more recent changes mean: whether indeed they do signpost a major new form of society in the making. The final chapter of this book will return to a further assessment of this issue.

**Aborigines with a laptop**

*Source*: © Robert Essel NYC/Corbis.

*Note*: Look at the art and culture of the Australian aboriginals through www.aboriginalaustralia.com.

**Q** Do these children really have laptops? Why are they smiling so much? Why are they marked the way they are? Do they have images of themselves on the laptop? Is this a fake photo just posed for the camera by child actors? Or are the aboriginals in some way being exploited here? What is going on?

# SUMMARY

**1** In the work of the Lenskis, five kinds of society have been outlined as linked to sociocultural evolution and technology. The earliest *hunting and gathering* societies were composed of a small number of family-centred nomads. Horticulture began some 12,000 years ago as people devised hand tools for the cultivation of crops. *Pastoral* societies domesticate animals and engage in extensive trade. *Agriculture*, about 5,000 years old, is large-scale cultivation traditionally using animal-drawn ploughs. This technology allows societies to grow into vast empires, making them more productive, more specialised and more unequal. *Industrial* societies began 250 years ago in Europe as people harnessed advanced energy sources to power sophisticated machinery. In *post-industrial*, *information* societies, enterprise shifts from the production of material things to the creation and dissemination of information; computers and other information-based technology replace the heavy machinery of the industrial era.

**2** Karl Marx's materialist analysis pointed to historical and contemporary conflict between social classes. Conflict in 'ancient' societies involved masters and slaves; in agrarian societies, it places nobles and serfs in opposition; in industrial–capitalist societies, capitalists confront the proletariat. Industrial capitalism alienates workers: from the act of working, from the products of work, from fellow workers, and from human potential. Once workers had overcome their own false consciousness, Marx believed they would overthrow capitalists and the industrial–capitalist system.

**3** Max Weber's idealist approach reveals that modes of thought have a powerful effect on society. Weber drew a sharp contrast between the tradition of pre-industrial societies and the rationality of modern, industrial societies. Weber feared that rationality, embodied in efficiency-conscious bureaucratic organisations, would stifle human creativity.

**4** Emile Durkheim explained that society has an objective existence apart from individuals. His approach relates social elements to the larger society through their functions. Traditional societies are fused by mechanical solidarity based on moral consensus; modern societies depend on organic solidarity based on the division of labour or productive specialisation.

**5** The contemporary world is composed of around 200 societies, which can be classified in various ways, including North and South, East and West, and low-, medium- and high-income societies.

**6** The Human Development Index (HDI) has become one way of looking at world societies. This is a United Nations measurement which collates three issues: longevity, knowledge (or education) and standard of living.

**7** Many terms have been introduced to discuss the nature of twenty-first-century societies. Amongst these are postmodern, post-history, post-industrial, late capitalism, late modern, self-reflexive, liquid, surveillance and information society.

CONNECT UP: Turn to Part 6 of this book for key resources and link up
with the book's website, which links to these resources
SEE: www.pearsoned.co.uk/plummer

# Ten suggestions for going further

## 1 Connect up with Part Six and the Sociology Web Resources

As you work through ideas and think about the issues raised in this chapter, look at the accompanying website and the resource centre at the end of this book which connects to it. There is a lot here to help you move on. To link up, see: www.pearson.co.uk/plummer.

## 2 Review the chapter

*Briefly summarise (in a paragraph) just what this chapter has been about.* Consider: (a) What have you learned? (b) What do you disagree with? Be critical. And (c) How would you develop all this? How could you get more detail on matters that interest you?

## 3 Pose questions

(a) Draw up a balance sheet of the pros and cons of various technologies, and then discuss whether technological change amounts to 'progress' (hint: see Gray, 2004).

(b) Examine the situation of any one contemporary indigenous people – such as the Innu. Is their way of life likely to survive into the future? (hint: see Samson, 2003).

(c) Contrast the theories of Marx, Durkheim and Weber on the emergence of the modern world. Which do you find most helpful – and why?

(d) Discuss some of the major features of contemporary world societies. What seem to be the major conflicts and issues for the twenty-first century?

(e) Which term do you think most adequately helps you describe and understand the world we live in at the start of the twenty-first century?

## 4 Explore key words

Many concepts have been introduced in this chapter. You can review them from the website or from the listing at the back of this book. You might like to give special attention to just five words and think them through – how would you define them, what are they dealing with, and do they help you see the social world more clearly or not?

## 5 Search the Web

Be critical when you look at websites – see the box on p. 940 in the Resources section. Some useful sources for this chapter are:

### Indigenous and tribal peoples

Indigenous Peoples: Issues and resources
http://indigenouspeoplesissues.com

Survival International
www.survivalinternational.org

The movement for tribal peoples – many of whom are in decline

### Europe

Eurostat
http://epp.eurostat.ec.europa.eu/portal/page

European statistics can be found in Eurostat, who also produce a Eurostat yearbook.

Europa
http://europa.eu

Europa is the European Union's server to the Parliament, the Council, the Commission, the Court of Justice, the Council of Auditors and other EU bodies. This server offers news, simple answers to key questions, the history of the EU, information on policies and institutions, and links to Eurostat, which is a great source of statistics. It is available in all EU languages.

## China

China Perspectives
http://chinaperspectives.revues.org

China country profile at the BBC
http://news.bbc.co.uk/1/hi/world/africa/country_profiles/1287798.stm

*China Daily* newspaper
www.chinadaily.com.cn

## Statistics on world societies

The most general source here is provided by the CIA and details every country in the world. See its World Fact Book at:
www.cia.gov/library/publications/the-world-factbook

See also:
The *Human Development Report*
http://hdr.undp.org/en/reports/global/hdr2010
This is a major source for world society statistics, and will have the most up-to-date Human Development Index results.

*The theories of Marx, Durkheim and Weber* can be explored further through the websites listed in Chapter 2 (see p. 57).

## 6 Watch a DVD

- James Cameron's *Avatar* (2009): this is currently the world's top film. In it we visit Pandora which is inhabited by the Na'vi, a humanoid race with their own language and culture. Those from earth find themselves at odds with each other and the local culture. It is seen by many as a metaphor for the invasion of capitalism over tribal life.
- Ingmar Bergman's *The Seventh Seal* (1956–57): looks at the forces of life and death through a medieval knight returning from the crusades. See also his *Wild Strawberries* (1957), which examines the meanings of life in society.
- Satyajit Ray's trilogy *The World of Apu* (1959) – *Pather Panchali, Aparajito* and *Apur Sansar*: examines the growth of a young Indian boy through childhood, rural youth and city adult life.
- Luis Buñuel's surrealist films – especially *The Discreet Charm of the Bourgeoisie* (1972), *The Phantom of Liberty* (1974) and *That Obscure Object of Desire* (1977): turn many of the assumptions about society on their head.
- Nicolas Roeg's *Walkabout* (1971): contrasts white and aboriginal children's world-views in the Australian outback.
- Bernardo Bertolucci's *The Last Emperor* (1987): tells the tale of Pu Yi, born in 1906 and the last absolute monarch of China.

## 7 Think and read

Patrick Nolan and Gerhard Lenski, *Human Societies: An Introduction to Macrosociology* (2010, 11th edn). A text which reviews different kinds of society.

The anthropologist Jared Diamond has written a number of books which compare the history and evolution of societies and which have become very popular. They are very readable. See his *Guns, Germs, and Steel: The Fates of Human Societies* (1979), *The Third Chimpanzee* (1992) and *Collapse: How Societies Choose to Fail or Succeed* (2005).

Krishan Kumar, *From Post-industrial to Post-modern Society: New Theories of the Contemporary World* (1995; 2nd edn, 2004). Reviews three current debates on the future of societies: the information society, post-Fordism and postmodernity.

Gary Browning, Abigail Halci and Frank Webster (eds), *Understanding Contemporary Society: Theories of the Present* (2000). Provides 33 short articles to introduce the reader to all the key aspects of modern and postmodern societies.

Eric Hobsbawm, *Age of Extremes: The Short Twentieth Century*, 1914–1991 (1994). This is a full account of the history of the world during the twentieth century, and leaves one at the very least being cautious about any simple view of progress.

### Europe

Alex Warleigh, *European Union: The Basics* (2nd edn, 2008). A handy quick tour of evolution, policies and controversies in the European Union.

Goran Therborn, *European Modernity and Beyond: The Trajectory of European Societies, 1945–2000* (1995). The most important sociological study of Europe to date by a leading Swedish sociologist.

Gerard Delanty and Chris Rumford, *Rethinking Europe: Social Theory and the Implications of Europeanization* (2005). A major attempt to understand Europe as a cosmopolitan world.

## 8 Relax with a novel

On China, see Jung Chang's *Wild Swans* (1993).

## 9 Connect to other chapters

- The work of Marx, Durkheim and Weber is discussed in many chapters of the book and themed on the website.

- Discussion on low-, medium- and high-income societies is developed in Chapter 9.
- Discussions on Europe feature in boxes throughout the book.

- Jump to the China box on p. 902 in Chapter 26. Review various discussions of China in Chapters 1 (suicide), 14 (economy), 16 (family) and 17 (prisons).

# 10  Engage in THE BIG DEBATE

## Progress: is society getting better or worse?

In Europe, generally, burdened by the sense of a long and troubled history, the fate of humankind is often looked upon with foreboding. Much of its intellectual tradition highlights critique, disenchantment, cynicism, despair and pessimism. Weber, for instance, wrote of the 'disenchantment of the world'. Freud, introduced in Chapter 7, saw civilisation as advancing at the cost of human happiness. And, perhaps most significant, the last 100 years have been the tragic century that witnessed two world wars and the Holocaust. Now, in the twenty-first century, we have entered the age of terror and the world remains in crisis.

A highly influential sociologist, Robert Nisbet (1989), once argued that one of the defining features of modernity had been a belief in progress, often in spite of problems. Indeed, the contemporary Swedish sociologist Goran Therborn also sees this as the key in distinguishing between premodernity, modernity and postmodernity. Progress is the definer of the modern world. He writes:

> Pre-modernity is looking back over its shoulder, to the past, to the latter's example of wisdom, beauty, glory, and to the experiences of the past. Modernity looks to the future, hopes for it, plans for it, constructs it, builds it. Post-modernity has lost or thrown away any sense of direction . . . Modernity ends when words like progress, advance, development, emancipation, liberation, growth, accumulation, enlightenment, embetterment, avant-garde, lose their attraction and their function as guides to social action.
>
> (Therborn, 1995: 4)

So can we see progress in the twenty-first century? Are we approaching a utopia or is a dystopia fast descending upon us?

To begin, we can point to some good reasons for society's belief in progress. Since the beginning of the twentieth century, for example, the scope of education has expanded to an unprecedented level. Moreover, even taking account of inflation, average income and national productivity have grown significantly. In addition, back in 1900, it was a rare home that had a telephone and, outside large cities, none had access to electricity. No one had even heard of television, and cars were still on the drawing boards. Today, almost every Western home is served by a telephone, a host of electric appliances, one or more television sets, and a DVD player; many also are equipped with satellite or cable TV. Most important of all, people born in 1900 lived an average of just 47 years; children born today can look forward to 30 additional years of life.

But some trends, especially during the last 25 years, have been troubling. It is true that some countries seem to be enjoying higher standards of living, and so on, but is this at the expense of others? Contrasts of inequality are massive, as Chapters 8–14 (Part Three) show. To give one figure from these chapters: 20 per cent of the world (some 1 billion people) lack the nutrition to work regularly, and 800 million are at risk for their lives. Add to this problems of cities, of pollution, of media, of environment, of risk, of crime, and so on. Rising crime rates have undermined people's sense of personal safety, even in their own homes. Our relative affluence, coupled with our capacity to move further and faster than ever before, seems to have eroded our sense of responsibility for others, unleashing a wave of individualism that often comes across as unbridled selfishness. As a result, not only is pessimism on the rise, but many people have been losing confidence in the direction of society.

So, which is it? Is society getting better or worse?

The theorists whose ideas we have examined in this chapter shed some light on this question. It is easy to equate 'high tech' with 'progress'. But we should make such assumptions cautiously, the Lenskis maintain, because history shows us, that while advancing technology does offer real advantages, it is no guarantee of a 'better' life. Marx, Weber and Durkheim also acknowledged the growing affluence of societies over time; yet each offered a pointed criticism of modern society because of a dangerous tendency towards individualism. For Marx, capitalism is the culprit, elevating money to godlike status and fostering a culture of selfishness. Weber's analysis claims that the modern spirit of rationality wears away traditional ties of kinship and neighbourhood while expanding bureaucracy, which, he warned, both manipulates and isolates people. In Durkheim's view, functional interdependence joins members of modern societies, who are less and less able to establish a common moral framework within which to judge right and wrong.

In the end, what human societies gain through technological advances may be offset, to some extent, by the loss of human community. We return to all these issues throughout the book, and make a further appraisal in the conclusion in Chapter 26.

### Continue the debate

1 Draw up a balance sheet of 'progress' in the modern world. Do you think life in the (post)modern world is getting better or worse? What evidence can you produce for your argument?

2 Is our society's increasing level of affluence good? What might Marx, Weber and Durkheim say?

3 Do you think people in low-income countries are aware of the 'advances' in the Western/Northern/ rich/high-income societies? Would they see them as advances?

A recent polemic on the idea of progress is the very readable book by John Gray, *Heresies: Against Progress and Other Illusions* (2004).

# CHAPTER 5
# CULTURE

**WE WERE FLYING INTO HONG KONG.** The air stewardess welcomed us to the land, but with a cryptic message. She informed us that Hong Kong was the land where half the people had mobile phones but the other half believed in ghosts! And here, in a nutshell, is the clash of two cultures – a 'modernising' West touching a 'superstitious' East.

Everywhere one turns in Hong Kong the contrast is visible. The bustling, dirty old temples where women cry and wail at the altars of their ancestors, offering money to their gods; the glittering, elaborate shopping malls soaring to the skies – some of the largest in the world – where consumerist capitalism is at its most spectacular. Spirituality versus materialism. Or the Chinese schoolchildren elaborately dressed in their formal 'Western' school uniforms complete with satchels – clambering over the ill-equipped peasant boats in the harbour to their own overcrowded houseboat homes. Or the Bank of Hong Kong – a monument to modern architecture, but built with full regard to *feng shui* (pronounced 'fung shway', Chinese words that mean 'wind and water') and potential 'evil spirits' and designed to keep them at bay. Here are rich and vibrant cultures pushing against each other.

Or consider another example: New York real-estate broker Barry Lewen, after six months of tough negotiations with a group of Taiwanese investors, is on the verge of signing what any broker would regard as a dream deal – the sale of a $14 million building on New York's Madison Avenue. But the investors soberly informed Lewen of 'one final concern'. Before any sale would go through, they explained, they would have to enlist the services of a master of *feng shui*. After flying to New York from Taiwan, this practitioner of the ancient Chinese art would inspect the building; only if he declared the structure to be acceptable would the sale be completed.

Several days later, a jet carrying the *feng shui* master landed at a New York airport and a car whisked him directly to the Madison Avenue building. A small crowd of anxious onlookers had assembled and they watched intently as he surveyed the setting, took account of the surrounding buildings, and, for 30 tense minutes, walked through the structure noting the shape and length of hallways, the location of doorways and lifts, and the presence of mirrors, fountains and even air conditioners. 'I can tell you there were a lot of sweaty palms,' recounts Barry Lewen. In the end, the master turned to the apprehensive audience, smiled, and formally approved the building. A wave of relief broke over the group.

To the West's way of thinking, the merit of a building is a matter of its location, its size and the state of its plumbing and other systems. Such concerns are also of great importance to the Chinese. But, historically, members of south-east Asian societies have also considered how physical space affects human feelings and emotions. From this point of view, a 'life force' or *qi* (pronounced 'chee') flows through all of nature – including buildings – so that the physical design of a home or office building will either help or hinder this flow. A 'good' building – that is, one that stands in harmony with nature – will enhance the luck, health and prosperity of the people living or working inside (Dunn, 1994). Understanding how such cultural differences work is a crucial part of sociology, and this chapter sets out to explore them.

*There is no such thing as a human nature independent of culture. Men without culture . . . would be unworkable monstrosities with very few useful instincts, fewer recognisable sentiments, and no intellect: mental basket cases.*

Clifford Geertz

*There is no way out of the game of culture.*

Pierre Bourdieu

## In this chapter, we ask:

- **What is the meaning of 'culture' and its major components?**

- **What are the key features of Muslim cultures?**

- **What is cultural studies?**

- **How is globalisation shaping culture?**

(Left) *The Tribunal of the Inquisition*, detail from mural cycle (mural), Rivera, Diego (1886–1957)/Palacio Nacional, Mexico City, Mexico/Index/The Bridgeman Art Library. © 2011 Banco de Mexico Diego Rivera Frida Kahlo Museums Trust, Mexico D.F. DACS

**Diego Rivera** (1886–1957) is often seen as Mexico's most important artist and became a folk hero in Latin America. He led a passionate life devoted to art and communism. He is most famous for his large-scale political murals where he critically examines social and political issues relating to the working class. This image is an extract from a large mural which depicts the past sufferings and joys of the Mexican people and the ways the masses have built a great civilisation. It suggests they can and will build glorious civilisations in the future.

*Source*: Index/The Bridgeman Art Library.

*Look at*: The Diego Rivera Virtual Web Museum: http://www.diegorivera.com/.

*See*: Luis-Martin Lozano and Juan Coronel Rivera *Diego Rivera: The Complete Murals* (2008).

**Q** Rivera can be seen as a Marxist artist. Think how artists try to capture a sense of their own societies, often vast civilizations? Can you find parallels to Rivera's depiction of Mexico in the artists of other cultures around the world?

While the 7 billion-plus people on the earth today are members of a single biological species, *Homo sapiens*, we display remarkable differences. Some differences may be arbitrary matters of convention – the Chinese, for example, wear white at funerals while people in European countries prefer black. Similarly, Chinese people associate the number 4 with bad luck, in much the same way that people in England think of the number 13. Or take the practice of kissing: most people in Europe kiss in public, most Chinese kiss only in private; the French kiss publicly twice (once on each cheek), while Belgians kiss three times (starting on either cheek); for their part, most Nigerians don't kiss at all. At weddings, moreover, North American couples kiss, Koreans bow, and a Cambodian groom touches his nose to the bride's cheek! If you have travelled much, you will know that it really helps to be aware of these differences.

Other cultural differences, however, are more profound. The world over, people wear much or little clothing, have many or few children, venerate or shunt aside the elderly, are peaceful or warlike, embrace different religious beliefs, and enjoy different kinds of art, music, food and sport. In short, although we are all one biological species, human beings have developed strikingly different ideas about what is pleasant and repulsive, polite and rude, beautiful and ugly, right and wrong. This capacity for startling *difference* is a feature of our species: the expression of human culture.

## What is culture?

Sociologists define **culture** as '*designs for living*': *the values, beliefs, behaviour, practices and material objects that constitute a people's way of life.* Culture is a toolbox of solutions to everyday problems. It is a bridge to the past as well as a guide to the future. One classic account puts it like this:

> Believing, with Max Weber, that *man is an animal suspended in webs of significance he himself has spun*, I take *culture to be those webs*, and the analysis of it to be therefore not an experimental science in search of law but an interpretative one in search of meaning . . .

(Geertz, 1995: 5, our italics)

To begin to understand what culture entails, it is helpful to distinguish between thoughts and things. What sociologists call **non-material culture** is *the intangible world of ideas created by members of a society*

that span a wide range from altruism to zen. **Material culture**, on the other hand, constitutes *the tangible things created by members of a society*; here again, the range is vast, running from armaments to zips, from mobile phones to pottery. They both involve cultural **practices** – *the practical logics by which we both act and think in a myriad of little encounters of daily life* (Bourdieu, 1990). Human beings make culture and it in turn 'makes us'. It becomes part of us – what we often (yet inaccurately) describe as 'human nature'. For sociologists, there is no such thing as human nature in itself: 'nature' is produced through our varying histories and cultures. This is often hard for students to grasp, but it is another example of where common sense gets challenged by sociology.

No cultural trait is inherently 'natural' to humanity, even though most people around the world view their own way of life that way. What is crucial to our human species is the capacity to create culture in our collective lives. Every other form of life – from ants to zebras – behaves in more uniform, species-specific ways. But to a world traveller, the enormous diversity of human life stands out in contrast to the behaviour of cats and other creatures, which is more or less the same everywhere. Most living creatures are guided by instincts, a biological programming over which animals have no control. A few animals – notably chimpanzees and related primates – have the capacity for limited culture: researchers have observed them using tools and teaching simple skills to their offspring. But the creative power of humans far exceeds that of any other form of life; in short, *only humans generate and then rely on culture rather than instinct to ensure the survival of their kind.* To understand how this came to be, we must briefly review the history of our species on earth.

## Culture, intelligence and the 'dance through time'

In a universe some 15 billion years old, our planet is a much younger 4.5 billion years of age. For a billion years after the earth was formed, no life at all appeared on our planet. Huge geological upheavals kept changing the earth's surface. Billions more years went by before dinosaurs ruled the earth and then disappeared. And then, some 65 million years ago, our history took a crucial turn with the appearance of the creatures we call primates.

What sets primates apart is their intelligence, based on the largest brains (relative to body size) of all living creatures. As primates evolved, the human line diverged from that of our closest relatives, the great apes, about 12 million years ago. But our common lineage shows through in the traits humans share with today's chimpanzees, gorillas and orangutans: great sociability, affectionate and long-lasting bonds for child-rearing and mutual protection, the ability to walk upright (normal in humans, less common among other primates), and hands that manipulate objects with great precision.

Studying fossil records, scientists conclude that, about 2 million years ago, our distant ancestors grasped cultural fundamentals such as the use of fire, tools and weapons, created simple shelters, and fashioned basic clothing. Although these Stone Age achievements may seem modest, they mark the point at which our ancestors embarked on a distinct evolutionary course, making culture the primary strategy for human survival.

To comprehend that human beings are wide-eyed infants in the larger scheme of things, Carl Sagan (1980) came up with the idea of superimposing the 15-billion-year history of our universe on a single calendar year. The life-giving atmosphere of the earth did not develop until the autumn, and the earliest beings who resembled humans did not appear until 31 December – the last day of the year – at 10.30 at night! Yet not until 250,000 years ago, which is mere minutes before the end of Sagan's 'year', did our own species finally emerge. These *Homo sapiens* (derived from Latin meaning 'thinking persons') have continued to evolve so that, about 40,000 years ago, humans who looked more or less like we do roamed the earth. With larger brains, these 'modern' *Homo sapiens* produced culture at a rapid pace, as the wide range of tools and cave art from this period suggests. (You can see Carl Sagan and his account visually on *YouTube*).

Still, what we call 'civilisation' (see below) only began in the Middle East (in what is today Iraq and Egypt) and China about 12,000 years ago. In terms of Sagan's 'year', this cultural flowering occurred during the final *seconds* before midnight on New Year's Eve. Our modern, industrial way of life, begun a mere 300 years ago, amounts to less than a second in Sagan's scheme. It is with this fraction of a second that most of this book is concerned. We are:

> latecomers to a global party that has been in progress for at least 3.5 billion years, since life began, and will continue till the death of the planet itself. It is a fabulous party, with billions of participants from all walks of life.

(Tudge, 1995: 76)

Human culture, then, is very recent and was a long time in the making. As culture became a strategy for survival, our ancestors descended from the trees into the tall grasses of central Africa. There, walking upright, they discovered the advantages of hunting in groups. From this point on, the human brain grew larger, allowing for greater human capacity to create a way of life – as opposed to simply acting out biological imperatives. Gradually, culture pushed aside the biological forces we call instincts so that humans gained the mental power *to fashion the natural environment for themselves*. Ever since, people have made and remade their worlds in countless ways, which explains today's extraordinary cultural diversity.

## What is civilisation?

**Civilisations** refer to *the broadest most comprehensive cultural entities*. Although there are many cultural groupings – 'Spanish culture', 'nudist culture', 'religious culture', 'gay culture', 'musical culture' – the idea of civilisation suggests the highest possible cultural grouping of peoples. A civilisation is a culture writ large. These have no clear-cut boundaries but are very long lived. They are totalities sensed over long periods (*the longue durée*, as it is often called).

Civilisations of the past include Ancient Sumerian, Egyptian, Classical, Mesoamerican, Christian and Islamic. Contemporary civilisations are often identified as:

- Chinese (or Sinic)
- Japanese (sometimes combined with China as Far Eastern civilisation)
- Indian or Hindu
- Islamic (originating in the Arabian peninsula in the seventh century CE) and including Arab, Turkic, Persian and Malay cultures
- Orthodox, centred in Russia and separate from western civilisation
- Western (emerging about 700 CE) in Europe, North America and maybe Latin America, although the latter is increasingly seen on its own as:
- Latin American (Catholic and more authoritarian)
- African

Religions are one of the key defining features of civilisations. Christianity, Islam, Hinduism and Confucianism are four leading religions linked to civilisations, and these are discussed in Chapter 19. In the twenty-first century, some social scientists talk about a new global culture emerging which will be seen as a 'universal' civilisation, but this is a hotly contested idea (Braudel, 1995; Huntington, 1996).

| Table 5.1 | The quick history of world societies: only seconds before midnight in Sagan's schema |
|---|---|

The Contemporary World (1989– )

The Short Twentieth Century (1914–1989)

The Modern Era (1789–1914)

The Early Modern World (16th–18th centuries)

The Middle Ages (5th–15th centuries)

The Ancient World (2500 BCE–900 CE)

First Empires (circa 7000 BCE–200 CE)

Prehistory: from the beginning to around 4000 BCE

*Source*: *National Geographic Visual History of the World* (2005).

## The major components of culture

Although the cultures found in all the world's nations differ in many ways, they all seem to be built on five major components: *symbols, language, values, norms and material culture*. In this section, we shall consider each in turn.

## 1 Symbols

Human beings not only sense the surrounding world as other creatures do, we build a reality of meaning. In doing so, humans transform elements of the world into **symbols**, *anything that carries a particular meaning recognised by people who share culture*. A whistle, a wall of graffiti, a flashing red light and a fist raised in the air all serve as symbols. We can see the human capacity to create and manipulate symbols reflected in the very different meanings associated with the simple act of winking the eye. In some settings this action conveys interest; in others, understanding; in still others, insult.

We are so dependent on our culture's symbols that we take them for granted. But entering an unfamiliar society also reminds us of the power of symbols; culture shock is nothing more than the inability to 'read' meaning in one's surroundings. We feel lost and isolated, unsure of how to act, and sometimes

Here are some well-known symbols. How do you make sense of them?
Human beings are symbol-manipulating creatures and the discipline that studies the nature of signs and symbols is semiotics. Since symbols are so important in understanding cultures, sociologists often have to draw from ideas in semiotics
*Source*: The Creative Symbol Collection, Ingram Publishing.

frightened – a consequence of being outside the symbolic web of culture that joins individuals in meaningful social life.

Culture shock is a two-way process. On the one hand, it is something the traveller experiences when encountering people whose way of life is unfamiliar. On the other hand, it is also what the traveller inflicts on others by acting in ways that may well offend them. For example, because the English consider dogs to be beloved household pets, travellers to northern regions of the People's Republic of China might well be appalled to find people roasting dogs as a wintertime meal. On the other hand, visitors to England from much of south-east Asia can be shocked to find how much alcohol they consume! Indeed, global travel provides almost endless opportunities for misunderstanding. When in an unfamiliar setting, we need to remember that even behaviour that seems innocent and quite normal to us may be anathema to others.

Symbolic meanings vary even within a single society. A fur coat, prized by one person as a luxurious symbol of success, may represent to another the inhumane treatment of animals. Cultural symbols also change over time. Jeans were created more than a century ago as sturdy and inexpensive clothing for workers. In the liberal political climate of the 1960s, this working-class

## Texting: the making of a new language

Languages are always changing and information technology has brought many new forms of communication and language: computing languages, message texting, tweeting. Here we consider briefly the case of texting.

Texting has developed as a new universal language over the past 20 years. The first text message (or 'telenote', as it was originally called) was sent on 3 December 1992 by Neil Papworth to colleagues at Vodafone and said 'Merry Christmas'. The commercial launch of SMS (short service messages) took place in 1995, and the first recorded monthly text message total was 5.4 million in April 1998. Ten years on – in 2009 – there was a daily average of 265 million text messages and 1.6 million picture messages being sent in the UK alone. The text message total was 96.8 billion, while over 600 million picture messages were sent across the whole year. It has been estimated that on average, some 4.7 million text messages are currently sent every hour in Britain. (Tweeting has had a similar success story, having grown to around 50 million world users.)

Are texters the modern vandals of our languages? From many quarters, the new language is roundly condemned. It is seen as a language for the lazy and the illiterate, and masks – even encourages – dyslexia, poor spelling and laziness. David Crystal, one of the world's leading linguists defends it. He argues that all languages are living and changing things and that this new language is just part of this. He goes further in seeing it a positive and exciting development. He writes:

Ever since the arrival of printing – thought to be the invention of the devil because it would put false opinions into people's minds – people have been arguing that new technology would have disastrous consequences for language. Scares accompanied the introduction of the telegraph, telephone, and broadcasting. But has there ever been a linguistic phenomenon that has aroused such curiosity, suspicion, fear, confusion, antagonism, fascination, excitement and enthusiasm all at once as texting? And in such a short space of time. Less than a decade ago, hardly anyone had heard of it.

There is now growing research on texting which is exploring such issues as:

Does texting erode young people's ability to write and read? Does texting result in lazy and sloppy writing? Does it mark the end of the long history of the formal languages? Does texting reduce creativity?

David Crystal's review leads him to conclude that:

Some people dislike texting. Some are bemused by it. But it is merely the latest manifestation of the human ability to be linguistically creative and to adapt language to suit the demands of diverse settings. There is no disaster pending. We will not see a new generation of adults growing up unable to write proper English. The language as a whole will not decline. In texting what we are seeing, in a small way, is language in evolution.

See www.text.it; David Crystal, txtng: thegr8 db8, Oxford University Press (2008).

aura made jeans popular among affluent students –
many of whom wore them simply to look 'different' or
perhaps to identify with working people. A decade later,
'designer jeans' emerged as high-priced 'status symbols'
that conveyed quite a different message. In recent years,
jeans remain as popular as ever; many people choose
them as everyday clothing. Still others seek out designer
labels to establish their difference from others. Jeans
do not have a fixed symbolic meaning. In sum,
symbols allow people to make sense of their lives, and
without them human existence would be meaningless.
Manipulating symbols correctly allows us to engage
others readily within our own cultural system.

The *study of the symbols and signs* is called
**semiotics**. Broadly, semiotics suggests that meanings
are never inherent in objects but are constructed
around them through a series of practices. The
American pragmatist Peirce, the French language
specialist de Saussure and the French philosopher
Roland Barthes have made special studies of the ways
in which any sign – a T-shirt, a flag, a pop song,
a menu, a word – can be given different meanings.
We return to this in Chapter 22.

## 2 Language

**Language**, the key to the world of culture, is *a system of
symbols that allows members of a society to communicate
with one another*. These symbols take the form of
spoken and written words, which are culturally variable
and composed of the various alphabets and ideograms
used around the world. Even conventions for writing
differ: in general, people in Western societies write
from left to right, people in northern Africa and
western Asia write from right to left, and people in
eastern Asia write from top to bottom. We cannot be
sure how many world languages there are but a good
estimate is that there are around 6,900 languages across
the world (Table 5.2).

There are three major world languages: Chinese,
English and Spanish (Table 5.3). Chinese is the official
language of 20 per cent of humanity (about 1.2 billion
people). English is the mother tongue of about 10 per
cent (600 million) of the world's people, with Spanish
the official language of 6 per cent (350 million). While
these are major languages, there are thousands of
minor ones – estimates usually vary from 5,000 to
6,000. About 3,000 are endangered: 473 of the
languages listed in the *Ethnologue* are classified as
nearly extinct – classified this way when 'only a few
elderly speakers are still living'. Linguists predict that

| Table 5.2 | Distribution of languages by area of origin | | |
|---|---|---|---|
| Area | Living languages | | No. of people |
| | No. | % | |
| Africa | 2,110 | 30.5 | 726,453,403 |
| Americas | 993 | 14.4 | 50,496,321 |
| Asia | 2,322 | 33.6 | 3,622,771,264 |
| Europe | 234 | 3.4 | 1,553,360,941 |
| Pacific | 1,250 | 18.1 | 6,429,788 |
| *Totals* | 6,909 | 100.0 | 5,959,511,717 |

*Source*: Used by permission, © S.I.L., adapted from *The Ethnologue*, 16th edn, M. Paul Lewis (ed.), pub. 2009.

| Table 5.3 | Major world languages | | |
|---|---|---|---|
| Rank | Language | No. of countries | No. of speakers (millions) |
| 1 | Chinese* | 31 | 1,213 |
| 2 | Spanish | 44 | 329 |
| 3 | English | 112 | 328 |
| 4 | Arabic* | 57 | 221 |
| 5 | Hindi | 20 | 182 |
| 6 | Bengali | 10 | 181 |
| 7 | Portuguese | 37 | 178 |
| 8 | Russian | 33 | 144 |
| 9 | Japanese | 25 | 122 |
| 10 | German, Standard | 43 | 90 |

\* There are varieties of language within these languages too.

*Source*: As Table 5.2.

half of our known living languages will die out during
this century, and 80–90 per cent will die off in the next
200 years. Large languages dominate smaller ones.

 Have a look at the websites on world languages
and the endangered languages. The *Ethnologue*
is the most detailed: www.ethnologue.com.

The United Nations has a website which
monitors the loss of culture – including endangered
languages – in countries around the world. See
UNESCO Intangible Cultural Heritage Site and its
Atlas of the World's Languages in Danger:
www.unesco.org/culture/ich/index.

At the same time languages are always changing and developing. There are small signs of some languages resisting extinction – language revivals aiming to rekindle interest in languages such as Welsh take place. And new forms start to appear: the growth of texting through the wide use of mobile phones has suggested – controversially – that a new kind of language may be appearing (see *Living in the twenty-first century*, p. 147).

English is also becoming a global tongue: it is a favoured second language in many of the world's nations. It is used as an official or semi-official language in over 60 countries, and is the main language of the World Wide Web, air traffic control, business conferences and pop music. But in many countries there is considerable concern about this. So much so that there is now a European Bureau of Lesser Used Languages (EBLUL) which tries to promote and conserve these less used languages (with a bulletin, *Contact*, published three times a year and a website at www.//eblul.org). And some countries, such as France and Wales, are trying hard to resist the weakening of their language by challenging English words. In any event, Chinese remains the most popular language and is likely to triple its number of speakers by 2050. The European Union itself is a Tower of Babel. The European Commission in Brussels employs 400 full-time staff to deal with translation problems. In 2007, there were 23 official languages.

## Dead language and ethnicity booms

In 2000, of the 262 or so million people in the USA aged 5 or over, some 215 million spoke only one language: English. But nearly 50 million spoke other languages at home (17.9 per cent of the population): 28 million spoke Spanish, 10 million spoke Indo-European languages, and about 6 million spoke Asian and Pacific Rim languages. There were nearly 12 million who were linguistically isolated (US Census, 2000).

Despite the dominance of the English language, from the mid-1960s onwards, North America and western Europe experienced something of an 'ethnicity boom' – a widespread awareness of different ethnicities having their own languages (the Census Bureau lists 25 languages, each of which is favoured by more than 100,000 people). In Europe, there are wide variations in language too, often generating conflicts. In Spain, Basque (Euskera) was banned during Franco's dictatorship from the mid-1930s: books written in it were publicly burnt. In the 1960s, policy changed, and

by March 1980 the first Basque Parliament was elected and Euskera became its official language. In Britain, although English dominates, both Welsh and Gaelic are more widely spoken than many presume and are given full support regionally, and there are speakers of Punjabi, Bengali, Urdu, Gujarati and Cantonese, not to mention German, Polish, Italian, Greek and Spanish. There is also 'Black English Vernacular' (BEV) linked to the use of a Creole English, used by the first blacks in America (Crystal, 2010).

## Language and cultural reproduction

For people everywhere, language is the major means of **cultural reproduction**, *the process by which one generation passes culture to the next*. Just as our bodies contain the genes of our ancestors, so our symbols carry our cultural heritage. Language gives us the power to gain access to centuries of accumulated wisdom.

Throughout human history, people have transmitted culture through speech, a process sociologists call the **oral cultural tradition**, *transmission of culture through speech*. Only as recently as 5,000 years ago did humans invent writing, and even then, just a favoured few ever learned to read and write. It was not until the twentieth century that nations (generally the industrial high-income countries) boasted of nearly universal literacy (see Chapter 22). Even so, in many industrial countries there are still a large number of people who are functionally illiterate – approximately one in five people in the UK have literacy and numeracy problems, which is an almost insurmountable barrier to opportunity in a society that increasingly demands symbolic skills. In low-income countries of the world, illiteracy rates range from 30 per cent (People's Republic of China) to as high as 80 per cent (Sierra Leone in Africa).

Language skills not only link us with others and with the past, they also set free the human imagination. Connecting symbols in new ways, we can conceive of an almost limitless range of future possibilities. Language – both spoken and written – distinguishes human beings as the only creatures who are self-conscious, mindful of our limitations and aware of our ultimate mortality. Yet our symbolic power also enables us to dream of a better world, and to work to bring that world into being.

## Is language uniquely human?

Creatures great and small direct sounds, smells and gestures towards one another. In most cases, these signals are instinctive. But research shows that some animals have at least a rudimentary ability to use symbols to communicate with one another and with humans.

Consider the remarkable achievement of a 12-year-old pygmy chimp named Kanzi. Chimpanzees lack the physical ability to mimic human speech. But researcher E. Sue Savage-Rumbaugh discovered that Kanzi was able to learn language by listening and observing people. Under Savage-Rumbaugh's supervision, Kanzi has amassed a vocabulary of several hundred words, and has learned to 'speak' by pointing to pictures on a special keyboard. Kanzi has correctly responded to requests like 'Will you get a nappy for your sister?' and 'Put the melon in the potty.' More intriguing, Kanzi's abilities surpass mere rote learning because he can respond to requests he has not heard before. In short, this remarkable animal has the language ability of a human child aged two years six months (Linden, 1993).

Despite such accomplishments, the language skills of chimps, dolphins and a few other animals are limited. And even specially trained animals cannot, on their own, teach language skills to others of their kind. But the demonstrated language skills of Kanzi and others caution us against assuming that humans alone can lay claim to culture.

## Does language shape reality?

Do the Chinese, who think using one set of symbols, actually experience the world differently from Swedes who think in Swedish or English who think in English? The answer is yes, since each language has its own, distinct symbols that serve as the building blocks of reality.

Edward Sapir (1929, 1949) and Benjamin Whorf (1956; orig. 1941), two anthropologists who specialised in linguistic studies, noted that each language has words or expressions with no precise counterparts in other tongues. In addition, all languages fuse symbols with distinctive emotions. Thus, as multilingual people can attest, a single idea often 'feels' different if spoken in, say, German rather than in English or Chinese (Gerhard Falk, personal communication to J. J. Macionis, 1987).

Formally, then, what we now call the **Sapir–Whorf hypothesis** states that *people perceive the world through the cultural lens of language.* Using different symbolic systems, a Filipino, a Turk and a Brazilian actually experience 'distinct worlds, not merely the same world with different labels attached' (Sapir, 1949: 162). They combine two principles, **linguistic determinism**, which suggests that *language shapes the way we think,* and **linguistic relativity**, which states that *distinctions found in one language are not found in another.* Whorf's classic case studies involved the Hopis, who had only one word for everything that flies – insects, planes, pilots – except birds; and the Inuit, who had many different words for snow.

The capacity to create and manipulate language also gives humans everywhere the power to alter how they experience the world. For example, many African Americans hailed it as a step towards social equality with white people when the word 'negro' was replaced by the term 'black' and, more recently, by 'African American' or 'person of colour'. Likewise, homosexuals redefined themselves as 'gay' during the 1970s, creating a more forceful, positive self-definition.

In short, a system of language guides how we understand the world but does not limit how we do so.

## 3 Values and beliefs

**Values** are *the standards people have about what is good and bad,* which vary from culture to culture. They are prescriptive: statements about what ought to exist in a language of ethical and moral terms, and are the broad principles that underlie **beliefs**, *specific statements that people hold to be true.* While values are abstract standards of goodness, beliefs are particular matters that individuals consider to be true or false.

Cultural values and beliefs not only colour how we perceive our surroundings, they also form the core of our moral world-view. We learn from families, schools and religious organisations to think and act according to approved principles, to pursue worthy goals, and to believe a host of cultural truths while rejecting alternatives as false.

### European values?

In a continent as large and diverse as Europe, of course, few cultural values and beliefs are shared by everyone. In fact, with a long history of immigration from the rest of the world, Europe may be seen as a cultural mosaic. Even so, there may be some broad shape to European life.

First, European values can be seen as the long accumulation of what might be called 'the Age of the Enlightenment' (Gay, 1970). That is, they hold broadly to the values of rationality, science and progress that came with the philosophers – the great writers and thinkers, mainly of the eighteenth century (for example, Voltaire, Hume, Diderot). This was a period marked by significant improvements in some lives due to reason, science and medicine. People started to sense that they were the makers of their own futures, that they could exert some rational control over their world, that they could bring about change and make it a better place.

Second, Europe has been dominated by versions of the Judaeo-Christian religion, and its subsequent struggle with secularisation. Much of its heritage cannot be understood without grasping the long struggles between Catholic groups and emerging Protestant ones, and the more recent weakening of both. The very calendar year and most of its key holidays – Christmas, Easter – are bound up with Christian values, culture and identity: 'To be a European is to celebrate Christmas and Easter' (Therborn, 1995: 234). Thus core Christian values might suggest:

> **You should love the Lord your God with all your heart, and with all your soul, and with all your mind. This is the first and great commandment. And a second is like it. You should love your neighbour as yourself. On these two commandments depend all the law and the prophets.**
>
> (Matthew, 22: 37–40)

Third, European values have been structured by the development of nation-states, and their belief in 'citizenship'. Here core values of rights and obligations can be laid out to suggest what a good citizen – a 'Spaniard', a 'German', a 'Scot' – is expected to do.

And finally, Europe may be seen as a culture that has generally highlighted a principle of hierarchy – that people should recognise their superiors and inferiors. Europe has deep roots in the values of a feudal and aristocratic system that turns into a class system (Therborn, 1995: 273).

## Asian values

At the turn of the twentieth century, a key global debate appeared which considered whether there were distinctive values in Asia. Some have argued that the 'East' differs from the 'West' over a number of key values such as:

- Belief in strong families
- Reverence for education

- Hard work a virtue
- Virtue of saving and frugality
- A social contract between the people and the state
- East Asians practise national teamwork
- Governments should maintain a morally wholesome environment
- Collective values and rejection of extreme forms of individualism.

Often these so-called Asian values have been used to justify authoritarian states, and critics say they are not in any sense 'distinctively Asian'. Asia is a region where about 60 per cent of the world's population lives – and it harbours many contrasting values deriving from sources as different as Confucianism and Islam (Mahbubani, 2004).

## World values?

The political scientist Ronald Inglehart has produced an important, if somewhat controversial, body of evidence about the different kinds of values held across the six continents in some 97 different countries throughout the world over the past 30 years (Inglehart, 2000). He clusters societies on a number of different value dimensions, but two take prominence: what he calls traditional versus secular-rational, and survival versus self-expression.

- Traditional societies appeal to an authority rooted in the past – often via religion or through autocratic leaders. Secular-rational societies tend to be much less religious and can be seen to have values that are much more individualistic.
- The survival/self-expression dimension involves themes which link to the arrival of so-called postmodern or postmaterialist societies.

Some cultures – usually what we have called low-income societies – emphasise *survival values*. For Inglehart, this means they report low levels of subjective well-being, relatively poor health, low interpersonal trust, relative intolerance towards outgroups, low support for gender equality, emphasis on materialist values, relatively high levels of faith in technology and science, relatively low concern with environmental activism, and relatively favourable attitudes to authoritarian government. *Self-expression values*, by contrast, focus on the reverse of these.

In industrial societies, one of the main variations was found between age groups. Among the oldest, top priority was given to economic and physical security, but the younger birth cohort espouses what Inglehart calls a post-materialist view, where matters such as the environment and feminism become more important. Such younger groups give more importance to belonging and self-expression.

 **tip** If you want to look at different attitudes across cultures, here are some sources:

- *World Values Surveys (WVS)*, first conducted in 1981. A new wave of surveys will be carried out in 2010–11. This will provide a 30-year time series for the analysis of social and political change. See: www.worldvaluessurvey.org.

- *Eurobarometer*, conducted in the expanding European countries since 1973. This is the website for the Public Opinion Analysis sector of the European Commission. See: http://ec.europa.eu/public_opinion/index_en.htm.

- More specific studies, such as *British Social Attitudes*. The 26th annual survey of British attitudes can be accessed at: www.natcen.ac.uk/study/british-social-attitudes-26th-report.

## Values: inconsistency and conflict

Cultural values can be inconsistent and even outright contradictory (Lynd, 1967; Bellah et al., 1985). For example, we sometimes find ourselves torn between the 'me first' attitude of an individualistic way of life and the opposing need to belong and contribute to some larger community. Similarly, we affirm our belief in equality of opportunity, only to turn around and promote or degrade others because of their ethnicity, gender or sexual preference. Value inconsistency reflects the cultural diversity of society and the process of cultural change by which new trends supplant older traditions.

## 4 Norms

In China, people curious about how much money colleagues are paid readily ask about their salaries. In Europe, people consider such a question rude. Such patterns illustrate the operation of **norms**, *rules and expectations by which a society guides the behaviour of*

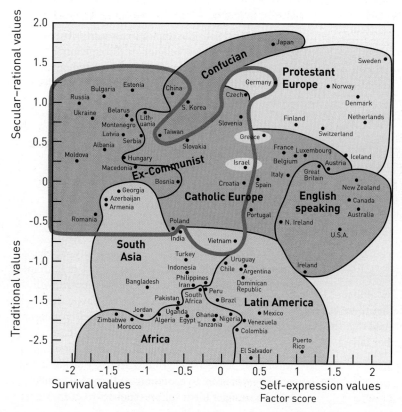

**Map 5.1** World values: cultural map of the world

The World Values Surveys were designed to provide a comprehensive measurement of all major areas of human concern, from religion and politics to economic and social life.
Two dimensions dominate the picture:
(1) traditional/secular–rational and
(2) survival/self-expression values.

*Source*: Inglehart-Weizel Cultural Maps of the World, www.worldvaluessurvey.org/statistics/some_findings.html.

For update: see www.worldvaluessurvey.org.

*its members.* Some norms are *proscriptive*, mandating what we should not do, as when Chinese parents scold young lovers for holding hands in public. *Prescriptive* norms, on the other hand, spell out what we *should* do, as when some European schools teach practices of 'safe sex'.

Most important norms apply virtually anywhere and at any time. For example, parents expect obedience from children regardless of the setting. Many normative conventions, by contrast, are situation-specific. In Europe, we expect audience applause at the end of a musical performance; we discourage it when a priest or a rabbi finishes a sermon. But, then, normative conventions change: increasingly, audiences at a rock concert can clap throughout the performance, and fundamentalist religious leaders expect a clapping congregation (happy-clappy!). Indeed, postmodern societies seem to change a considerable informalisation of norms. They are still there, but become more complicated.

## Mores and folkways

William Graham Sumner (1959; orig. 1906), an early US sociologist, recognised that some norms are more crucial to our lives than others. Sumner used the term **mores** to refer to *a society's standards of proper moral conduct.* Sumner counted among the mores all norms essential to maintaining a way of life; because of their importance, he contended that people develop an

PUBLIC SOCIOLOGY

# Cultural difference, value conflicts?

Many social scientists argue that culture is the key to understanding how societies grow and change. They explain the fact that some have become advanced industrialised nations and others have not by considering their core values. Core values are seen to shape society. We have already seen how Weber saw the rise of capitalism as having a strong affinity with Protestantism through the 'Protestant ethic'.

To have an effective public sociology, 'values' need to be made explicit. They often are not. Once values are openly on the table, they can be discussed and debated.

For example, Lawrence Harrison overtly states that there are real cultural value differences between what he terms 'progressive' and 'static' societies. Progressive societies are the more industrialised societies; static ones are those which have not changed a great deal.

Among the value differences he notes are:

1 *Education*: a key to progress for progressive cultures, but of marginal importance except for the elites in static cultures.

2 *Time orientation*: progressives look to the future, statics look to the past or the present.

3 *Work*: central for progressive societies, but often a burden in static cultures.

4 *Frugality*: a major value for progressive societies – leading to investment and financial security; often a threat to static cultures.

5 *Merit*: central to advancement in progressive cultures; connections and family are what count in static cultures.

6 *Community*: in progressive cultures, community extends beyond the locality and the family; in static cultures, the family circumscribes community.

7 *Ethics*: more rigorous in advanced societies;

corruption is greater in static societies.

8 *Justice and fair play*: universal impersonal expectations in progressive cultures; in static societies, justice is often a function of who you know and how much you can pay.

9 *Authority*: dispersed in progressive societies; concentrated in static societies.

10 *Secularism*: progressive societies find that religious influence on civic life dwindles; in static societies, religion has a substantial influence.

*Source*: Harrison and Huntingdon (2000: 299).

Capturing general values like this is fraught with difficulties. They are far too general and suggest a moral split between 'Modern Societies' (progressive) and much of the rest of the world (static). You may like to ponder the weaknesses and strengths of such a depiction. Is the author being ethnocentric? How might culturalist explanations of change differ from materialist ones?

emotional attachment to mores and defend them publicly. In addition, mores apply to everyone, everywhere, all the time. Violation of mores – such as our society's prohibition against sexual relations between adults and children – typically brings a swift and strong reaction from others.

Sumner used the term **folkways** to designate *a society's customs for routine, casual interaction.* Folkways, which have less moral significance than mores, include notions about proper dress, appropriate greetings and common courtesy. In short, while mores distinguish between right and wrong, folkways draw a line between right and *rude*. Because they are less important than mores, societies afford individuals a measure of personal discretion in matters involving folkways, and punish infractions leniently. For example, a man who does not wear a tie to a formal dinner party is, at worst, guilty of a breach of etiquette. If, however, the man were to arrive at the dinner party wearing *only* a tie, he would be challenging the social mores and inviting more serious sanctions.

## 5  Material culture

In addition to intangible elements such as values and norms, every culture encompasses a wide range of tangible human creations that sociologists term *artefacts.* The Chinese eat with chopsticks rather than knives and forks, the Japanese place mats rather than rugs on the floor, and many men and women in India prefer flowing robes to the tighter clothing common in much of Europe. An unfamiliar people's material culture may seem as strange to us as their language, values and norms.

## Cultural diversity: many ways of life in one world

When contractors and estate agents in New York take account of the Chinese art of *feng shui*, as noted in the opening to this chapter, we can see a nation of striking cultural diversity. In fact, between 1980 and 1990, the number of people in the United States with Chinese or other Asian ancestry more than doubled. Historical isolation makes Japan the most *monocultural* of all industrial nations; heavy immigration over centuries, by contrast, makes the United States the most *multicultural* of all industrial nations.

Between 1820 (when the US government began keeping track of immigration) and 2001, more than 67 million people travelled to the United States from other countries. At the end of the nineteenth century, as shown in Figure 5.1, most immigrants hailed from Europe; by the end of the twentieth century, a large majority of newcomers were arriving from Latin America and Asia.

Cultural variety has characterised most of the world, and not just the United States. We return to this in Chapter 11. In this section, we look at some ways of approaching these diversities and differences.

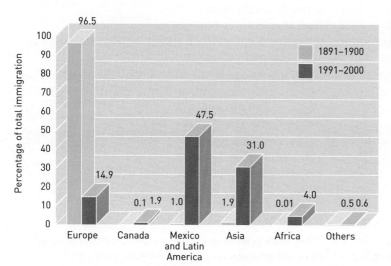

**Figure 5.1**  Recorded immigration to the United States, by region of birth, 1891–1900 and 1991–2000

*Source*: Adapted from US Immigration and Naturalization Service (2000).

## The tool box of culture: ten ways to start a research investigation of culture

|   | Think about | Question | Discipline linkage |
|---|---|---|---|
| 1 | Symbols | Examine key symbols. Look at the chain of signs and the process of signification. | Semiotics |
| 2 | Language | What are the words, the slang, the special meanings of terms in this culture? | Social linguistics |
| 3 | Values | Know the values that inform cultures and guide lives. | Attitude and value measurement and surveys |
| 4 | Norms | Look for taken-for-granted rules, as well as wider, more public laws. | Sociology of law, ethnomethodology |
| 5 | Material Cultures | See material objects as acting in relational networks with consequences. | ANT theory |
| 6 | Stories and narrative | Listen to the stories (narratives, myths, accounts, etc.) that people tell. | Narrative theory |
| 7 | Verstehen Role Taking | Understand the ways people come to see others: see the world through others' eyes. | Max Weber used the term 'Verstehen'; G. H. Mead developed the idea of role taking |
| 8 | Emotions & Empathy | Appreciate what others are feeling. | Sociology of emotion – Cooley, Scheler, Hochschild |
| 9 | Identities and roles | How do people come to see themselves (who are they) and what roles do they perform? | Dramaturgy – see Goffman; role/performance theory; modern identity theory |
| 10 | Bodies | What are the key projects in which people use their bodies? | Mind/body dualism debates; the new 'body theory' |

It is the challenge of ethography, field research and participant observation to examine these areas.

*Source*: Adapted from Plummer (2010: 108).

## High culture and popular culture

Much cultural diversity is seen to have roots in social class. In fact, in everyday life, we often reserve the term 'culture' for sophisticated art forms such as classical literature, music, dance and painting. We praise some people as 'cultured', because they presumably appreciate the 'finer things in life'. The term 'culture' itself has the same Latin root as the word 'cultivate', suggesting that the 'cultured' individual has cultivated or refined tastes. By contrast, we speak less generously of ordinary people, assuming that everyday cultural patterns are somehow less worthy. In more concrete terms, Mozart is seen as 'more cultured' than Rap,

French 'cuisine' as better than fish fingers, and polo as more polished than ping pong!

Such judgements imply that many cultural patterns are readily accessible to some but not all members of a society. Sociologists use the shorthand term **high culture**[1] to refer to *cultural patterns that distinguish a society's elite*; **popular culture**, then, designates *cultural patterns that are widespread among a society's population*.

[1] The term 'high culture' is derived from the more popular term 'highbrow'. Influenced by phrenology, the bogus nineteenth-century theory that personality was determined by the shape of the human skull, people a century ago contrasted the praiseworthy tastes of those whom they termed 'highbrows' with the contemptible appetites of others whom they derided as 'lowbrows'.

Common sense might suggest that high culture is superior to popular culture. After all, history chronicles the lives of elites much more than those of ordinary women and men. But sociologists are uneasy with such a sweeping evaluation: they generally use the term 'culture' to refer to *all* elements of a society's way of life. However, they do recognise too that culture is also used to define people's social standing – their tastes, their distinction. Indeed, the term **cultural capital** (invented by sociologist Pierre Bourdieu – see Chapter 8, p. 254) is often used to designate *the practices where people can wield power and status because of their educational credentials, general cultural awareness and aesthetic preferences.* It is an idea which helps reinforce class distinctions – setting apart those who are 'cultured', who have 'travelled a lot', who know about their good wines and the latest 'art works'. 'Cultural' capital is distributed very unevenly in societies. Its acquisition starts in families and schools. But its impact continues through life as a major marker of distinction (Swartz, 1997: 76).

## Subcultures and countercultures

Another set of differences are caught in the terms **subculture** (*cultural patterns that set apart some segment of a society's population*) and **counterculture** (*cultural patterns that strongly oppose those widely accepted within a society, contraculture*).

Rastafarians, young gays and lesbians, frequent-flyer executives, jazz musicians, old people in residential homes, homeless people, campus poets and offshore powerboat racers all display subcultural patterns. It is easy – but often inaccurate – to place people into subcultural categories. Almost everyone participates simultaneously in numerous subcultures, and we often have little commitment to many of them.

In some cases, however, important cultural traits such as ethnicity and religion do set off people from one another – sometimes with tragic results. Consider the former nation of Yugoslavia in south-east Europe. The turmoil there was fuelled by astounding cultural diversity. This *one* small country (which, before its break-up, was about half the size of England, with a population of 25 million) made use of *two* alphabets, professed *three* religions, spoke *four* languages, was home to *five* major nationalities, was divided into *six* political republics, and absorbed the cultural influences of *seven* surrounding countries. The cultural conflict that plunged this nation into civil war reveals that subcultures are a source not only of pleasing variety

but also of tensions and outright violence (see Chapter 16 and Sekulic et al., 1994).

Cultural diversity involves not just *variety* but also *hierarchy*. Too often, what we view as 'dominant' or 'highbrow' cultural patterns are those favoured by powerful segments of the population, while we relegate the lives of the disadvantaged to the realm of 'subculture'. This dilemma has led some researchers to highlight the experiences of less powerful members of our society in a new approach called multiculturalism (see the *Big debate* at the end of this chapter).

## Youth cultures

Cultural diversity also includes outright rejection of conventional ideas or behaviour – countercultures. An example of this would be the youth-orientated counterculture of the 1960s that rejected the cultural mainstream as too competitive, self-centred and materialistic. Instead, hippies and other counterculturalists favoured a cooperative lifestyle in which 'being' took precedence over 'doing' and the capacity for personal growth – or 'expanded consciousness' – was prized over material possessions such as homes and cars. Such differences led some people at that time to 'drop out' of the larger society. Counterculture may involve not only distinctive values, but unconventional behaviour (including dress and forms of greeting) as well as music. Many members of the 1960s counterculture, for instance, drew personal identity from long hair, headbands and blue jeans; from displaying a peace sign rather than offering a handshake; and from drug use and the energy of ever-present rock and roll music. We look at these further in Chapter 13.

## Cultural change

A wise human axiom suggests that 'All things shall pass'. Even the dinosaurs, which thrived on this planet for some 160 million years, exist today only as fossils. Will humanity survive for millions of years to come? No one knows. All we can say with certainty is that, given our reliance on culture, for as long as we survive, the human record will be one of continuous change.

Change in one dimension of a culture usually accompanies other transformations as well. For example, women's rising participation in the labour force has paralleled changing family patterns, including later age at first marriage, a rising divorce rate, and a growing share of children being raised in households without fathers. Such connections illustrate the principle of **cultural integration**, *the close relationship among various elements of a cultural system.*

But all elements of a cultural system do not change at the same speed. William Ogburn (1964) observed that technology moves quickly, generating new elements of material culture (such as 'test-tube babies') faster than non-material culture (such as ideas about parenthood) can keep up with them. Ogburn called this inconsistency *cultural lag*, the fact that cultural elements change at different rates, which may disrupt a cultural system. In a culture with the technical ability to allow one woman to give birth to a child by using another woman's egg, which has been fertilised in a laboratory with the sperm of a total stranger, how are we to apply the traditional notions of motherhood and fatherhood?

Cultural changes are set in motion in three ways. The first is *invention*, the process of creating new cultural elements. Invention has given us the telephone (1876), powered aircraft (1903) and the aerosol spray can (1941), all of which have had a tremendous impact on our way of life. The process of invention goes on constantly, as indicated by the thousands of applications submitted annually to the European Patent Office.

*Discovery*, a second cause of cultural change, involves recognising and understanding something not fully understood before – from a distant star, to the foods of another culture, to the athletic prowess of US women. Many discoveries result from scientific research. Yet discovery can also happen quite by accident, as when Marie Curie left a rock on a piece of photographic paper in 1898 and serendipitously discovered radium.

The third cause of cultural change is *diffusion*, the spread of cultural traits from one society to another. The technological ability to send information around the globe in seconds – by means of radio, television, facsimile (fax) and computer – means that the level of cultural diffusion has never been greater than it is today.

Certainly, our own society has contributed many significant cultural elements to the world, ranging from computers to jazz music. But diffusion works the other way as well: for example, much of what we assume is inherently 'British' actually comes from other cultures. Ralph Linton (1937) explained that many commonplace elements of our way of life – most clothing and furniture, clocks, newspapers, money, and often the food we eat – are derived from other cultures.

# Ethnocentricity and cultural relativity

We think of childhood as a time of innocence and freedom from adult burdens such as regular work. In poor countries throughout the world, however, families depend on income earned by children. So what people in one society think of as right and natural, people elsewhere find puzzling and even immoral. Perhaps the Chinese philosopher Confucius had it right when he noted that 'All people are the same; it's only their habits that are different.'

Just about every imaginable social habit is subject to at least some variation around the world, and such differences cause travellers excitement and distress in about equal measure. The tradition in Japan is to name road *junctions* rather than streets, a practice that regularly confuses Europeans, for example, who do the opposite; Egyptians move very close to others in conversation, irritating any foreign visitors who are used to maintaining several feet of 'personal space'; bathrooms have a water tap but lack toilet paper throughout much of Morocco, causing great agitation among Westerners unaccustomed to using one's left hand for bathroom hygiene!

Because a particular culture is the basis for everyone's reality, it is no wonder that people everywhere exhibit **ethnocentrism**, *the practice of judging another culture by the standards of one's own culture.* On one level, some ethnocentrism is inevitable if people are to be emotionally attached to a cultural system. On another level, however, ethnocentrism generates misunderstanding and sometimes conflict.

For example, take the seemingly trivial matter of people in Europe referring to China as the 'Far East'. Such a term, which has little meaning to the Chinese, is an ethnocentric expression for a region that is far east *of Europe*. For their part, the Chinese refer to their country with a word translated as 'Middle Kingdom', suggesting that, like us, they see their society as the centre of the world.

Is there an alternative to ethnocentrism? The logical alternative is to imagine unfamiliar cultural traits from the point of view of *them* rather than *us*. The casual observer of an Amish farmer in Pennsylvania tilling hundreds of hectares with a team of horses rather than a tractor might initially dismiss this practice as hopelessly backward and inefficient. But, from the Amish point of view, hard work is a foundation of religious discipline. The Amish are well aware of tractors; they simply believe that using such machinery would be their undoing.

This alternative approach, called **cultural relativism**, is *the practice of judging a culture by its own standards*. Cultural relativism is a difficult attitude to adopt because it requires that we not only understand the values and norms of another society but also suspend cultural standards that we have known all our lives. But, as people of the world come into increasing contact with one another, so we confront the need to understand other cultures more fully.

The world may need greater cultural understanding, but cultural relativity introduces problems of its own. Virtually any kind of behaviour is practised somewhere in the world; does that mean that everything is equally right? Just because Indian and Moroccan families benefit from having their children work long hours, does that justify such child labour? It is hard to appreciate and understand other cultures and yet maybe maintain some sense of a universal standard. There are no simple answers to such dilemmas.

Resist making a snap judgement, so that you can observe unfamiliar cultural surroundings with an open mind. Try to imagine the issue from *their* point of view rather than *yours*. After careful thought, try to evaluate an unfamiliar custom. After all, there is no virtue in passively accepting every cultural practice. But, in reaching a judgement, bear in mind that – despite your efforts – you can never really experience the world as others do. Then turn the argument around and think about your own way of life as others might see it. What we gain most from studying others is insight into ourselves.

## Muslim cultures: an example

Well over 1 billion people live in Muslim cultures across some 60 countries. They can be found in many Arab (e.g. Iraq, Egypt), Asian (e.g. Indonesia, Pakistan) and African (e.g. Algeria, Morocco) societies, as illustrated in Map 5.2. They can also be found partially almost everywhere else in the world (with large and growing minorities in Europe and America). Table 5.4 gives some indication of this. Muslim cultures are religion based and take on a wide variety of forms. All in all they serve around a quarter to a fifth of humanity.

| Table 5.4 | Approximate Muslim population in different countries |
|---|---|
| Saudi Arabia | 100% of 27.6 million |
| Turkey | 99.8% of 71 million |
| Afghanistan | Sunni Muslim 80%, Shi'a Muslim 19% of 31.88 million |
| Algeria | Sunni Muslim (state religion) 99% of 33 million |
| Morocco | 98.7% of 33.75 million |
| Iran | 98% of 65 million |
| Pakistan | 97% of 164.7 million |
| Iraq | 97% of 27 million |
| Egypt | 90% of 80 million |
| Syria | Sunni Muslim 74%, other Muslim (includes Alawite, Druze) 16% of 19 million |
| Indonesia | 86.1% of 234.7 million |
| Bangladesh | 83% of 150 million |
| Malaysia | 60.4% of 24.8 million |
| Lebanon | 59.7% of 3.9 million |
| Nigeria | 50% of 135 million |
| Kazakhstan | 47% of 15 million |
| India | 13.4% of 1.129 billion |
| UK | 2.7% of 60.77 million |
| Australia | 1.5% of 20 million |
| USA | 1% of 301 million |

*Source*: CIA, *The World Factbook*, www.cia.gov/library/publications/the-world-factbook.

## Core cultural elements

What are Muslim cultures? As we have seen, all cultures suggest languages, world-views, norms, rituals and rules as well as material artefacts (like dress). Religion is the core of Muslim culture (indeed, religion has frequently been a major tool for building dominant cultures throughout world history – see Chapter 19). At the heart of its orthodoxy is complete submission to the will of Allah.

The *key text* is the Koran, Quran or Qur'an – the non-negotiable authority in Muslim life and belief. It literally means 'recitation' and it is taken to be the Word of God. It tells the life of Muhammad, and speaks of the *sunna* – his behaviour, sayings, values – and the *Shariah* – the 'path' for Muslims. 'God is Great.' 'There is no god but God.'

Understanding *language* is crucial for all cultures. Not understanding the language will inevitably bring major misunderstandings. Much discussion by

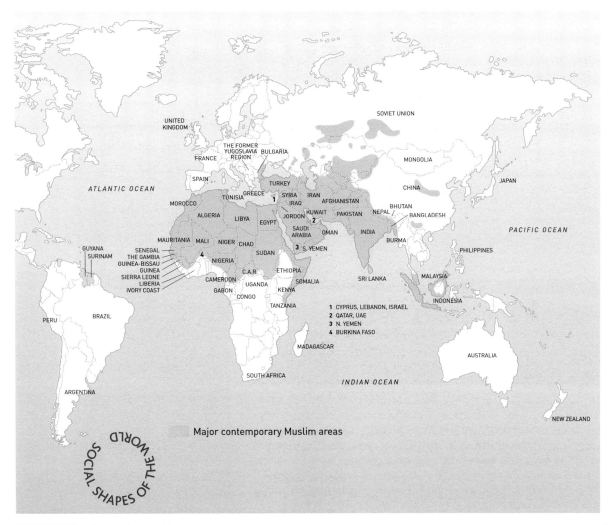

SOCIAL SHAPES OF THE WORLD

Major contemporary Muslim areas

1 CYPRUS, LEBANON, ISRAEL
2 QATAR, UAE
3 N. YEMEN
4 BURKINA FASO

**Map 5.2**    The Muslim worlds

*Source*: Ahmed (1988: 146–7). *Discovering Islam*, Akbar S. Ahmed. Copyright © 1986 Routledge. Reproduced by permission of Taylor & Francis Books.

Westerners fails because there is a lack of comprehension – there is no speaking across cultures.

There are strong *rules* that tell Muslims what they must do (as in all cultures). Here they rest on the five pillars (a little like the Ten Commandments in Judaic and Christian religions – see Chapter 19). These are:

1  *The Shahada* – the affirmation: there is no god but God, and Muhammad is the messenger of God.
2  *Salat* – the set prayers to be said five times a day facing the Ka'ba (the shrine at the centre of the mosque at Mecca).
3  *Sawn* – daily fasting at Ramadan.
4  *Zakat* – almsgiving, contributing wealth for the poor and charitable causes (usually one-fortieth of their annual income).

5  *Hajj* – the pilgrimage to Mecca (the birthplace of Muhammad), which all healthy Muslims should try to do at least once in their life.

The *law* embodies four major different legal schools – the *Malaski*, *Hanafi*, *Shafi'I* and *Hanbali*. Most Muslims today relate to one or other of these, and this can be seen in contrasting ways: for example, performing prayer, conducting personal relations or treating criminals.

As with all cultures, rituals are very important to the conduct of daily life. There should be regular almsgiving (Zakat) and daily prayer (Salah). There is fasting during the month of Ramadan, and there should be a pilgrimage to Mecca during one's life (Hajj).

Muslim cultures are also replete with their own **material cultures**. These can be found in art (see the

(a)

(b)

**(a)  White-veiled East Timorese Muslim women pray at Ramadan's end**
East Timorese Muslim women attend a mass prayer celebrating Eid al-Fitr
at An-Nur mosque. Muslims around the world celebrate Eid al-Fitr, which
marks the end of the fasting month of Ramadan.
**(b)  Veiled model presents a creation by Bahrain designer Maryam Wadlee**
A model takes to the catwalk in an outfit by Bahrain designer Maryam
Wadlee during the Gulf Night fashion show.
*Source*: (a) Corbis/Antonio Dasiparu/Epa; (b) Corbis/Wael Hamzeh.

opening image to Chapter 19, p. 658), calligraphy, books
(the Koran), architecture (such as the mosques – the
place of prostration), and in typical cultural dress and
appearance: men bearded, women veiled.

Islam is a monotheistic religion. It combines holy
law, a sacred text (the Koran), a prophet (Muhammad,
570–632 CE) and a prophetic revelation of individual
salvation that is all-embracing over daily life. We look at
it a little in Chapter 19. It began in the seventh century CE
with the prophet Muhammad, born in the town of Mecca
in what is now known as Saudi Arabia. Islam means
entering into a condition of peace and security with God
through allegiance and surrender to him. Muhammad
– like Christ for Christians – is seen as the perfect
example of living a life. Islam grew out of two declining
empires – the Byzantine and the Sassanian – and Islam
spread through the Middle East and Northern Africa.

# Variation and divisions

Muslim cultures do have common themes, as
suggested above. But they are also very different.
There is Morrocan Islam, Pakistani Islam, Malay
Islam and so on. South Asian Muslim cultures are not
always at home with Arab cultures. To suggest only
one Muslim culture, then, would be like suggesting
there is only one Christian culture: that Christians in
England are the same as Christians in Brazil, or that
Methodist Christians in England are like Catholic
Christians in Italy! Common themes, yes; but
great variety.

After the death of the Prophet Muhammad (632 CE),
the Muslim community split between the Sunni and
the Shi'ite. This is a key divide that is present in many
Muslim cultures and still works into conflicts today.

Sunni Muslims follow the customs of Muhammad. They originally thought that Muhammad's successor or caliph should be the best-qualified man. Today they base their lives on his sayings and actions. In contrast, the Shi'at Ali – the party of Ali – thought Muhammad's nearest relative should become their Imam. Sunni sees Islamic leadership in the consensus of the community rather than religious and political authorities. In general, they have more tolerant views based on the Koran (sometimes a parallel is drawn with Protestants in Christianity, as being a more flexible and less traditional approach). Shia – the 'partisans of Ali' – are the majority in Iran; there are more than 165 million and they generally hold strong views based on history and a strict interpretation of the Koran.

Politically too there are major splits across Muslim cultures. There are, for example, many radical groups that have appeared to fight the jihad (or holy war) across the world: the Muslim Brotherhoood in Egypt, the Islamic Revolution Front in Algeria, Hizbolllah in Lebanon, Hamas in the West Bank, and the now very well known Al Quaeda in Afghanistan. These more militant paths all have their own distinctive cultures – language, world-views, identities, knowledge.

## Asabiyya: understanding Muslim cultures

Living in a culture brings deep understanding that is not always easy to see with an outsider's eyes. Yes, we can look at the rules, see the buildings and dress, read the Koran. But cultures are much more finely grained than this – they rest on hidden assumptions and rules, items that go much deeper than the surface observables. Akbar Ahmed suggests that a key idea to grasp is that of Asabiyya – an honour found through group loyalty. The loss of honour may be a key idea to understanding the workings of Muslim culture (Ahmed, 2003: 14). Indeed, it is so important that he talks about the modern world as 'the post-honour society' (Bowker, 2006; Ahmed, 1988; 2003; Rosen, 2004).

## Understanding culture

Through culture, we make sense of ourselves and the surrounding world. Sociologists and anthropologists, however, have the special task of comprehending culture. They do so by using various theoretical paradigms.

## The classic approach from anthropology: the functions of a culture

The reason for the stability of a cultural system, as functionalists see it, is that core values anchor its way of life (Parsons and Bales, 1955; Parsons, 1964; orig. 1951; Williams, 1970). The assertion that ideas (rather than, say, the system of material production) are the basis of human reality aligns functionalism with the philosophical doctrine of *idealism*. Core values give shape to most everyday activities, in the process binding together members of a society. New arrivals, of course, will not necessarily share a society's core orientations. But, according to the functionalist melting-pot scheme, immigrants learn to embrace such values over time.

Thinking functionally is also helpful in making sense of an unfamiliar way of life. Recall, for example, the Amish farmer ploughing hundreds of acres with a team of horses. This practice may violate the more widespread cultural value of efficiency; however, from the Amish point of view, hard work functions to generate discipline, which is crucial to Amish religious life. Long days of teamwork, along with family meals and recreation at home, not only make the Amish self-sufficient but unify families and local communities.

Of course, Amish practices have dysfunctions as well. Farm living is hard work, and some people find strict religious discipline too confining, ultimately choosing to leave the community. Then, too, different interpretations of religious principles have generated tensions and sometimes lasting divisions within the Amish world (Hostetler, 1980; Kraybill, 1989; Kraybill and Olshan, 1994).

Because cultures are strategies to meet human needs, we would expect that societies the world over would have some elements in common. The term **cultural universals** refers to *traits that are part of every known culture*. Comparing hundreds of cultures, George Murdock (1945) found dozens of traits common to them all. One cultural universal is the family, which functions everywhere to control sexual reproduction and to organise the care and upbringing of children. Funeral rites, too, are found everywhere, because all human communities cope with the reality of death. Jokes are also a cultural universal, acting as a relatively safe means of releasing social tensions.

WORLD WATCH

# Disneyland: old cultures and new cultures in Europe

However unified Europe may or may not seem, it is clear that it harbours many different cultures with different ways of life and ways of doing things. Think of the following:

- *Breakfasts*. While in the UK it is cereals or a fry-up, in France they have croissants and in the Netherlands, cheese and ham.

- *The working day*. While in the UK to have a 'siesta' would be looked upon as outrageously lazy, in most Mediterranean countries the whole system shuts down after lunch for a couple of hours. Workers in Spain or Italy tend to be very casual and relaxed, even chaotic; in Germany, everything is much more formal.

- *Consuming*. The English tend to form queues, but this is not so in many European Union (EU) countries. Further, the English tend to accept the prices of goods from street sellers; not so in most of Europe. In UK bars you order drinks at the bar, pay straight away and do not tip; in most of the EU, you are served, pay at the end and leave a tip.

Yet these cultural differences – many and small – are starting to change. Increasingly, for instance, breakfasts offered at hotels throughout Europe would give a choice of cereals, fry-ups, croissants, cheese and ham, and even Japanese noodles. Cultural differences both are recognised and are breaking down.

## And the new cultures

Nowhere was this clearer than when Disney came to Paris. Disneylands all over the world have been a favourite topic of cultural studies (see Bryman, 1995: 81–2, for a listing). EuroDisney, covering about 1,500 acres 20 miles east of Paris and housing six themed hotels, opened on 12 April 1992. EuroDisney was derided by French intellectuals as a cultural Chernobyl, and the unions objected to an almost fascist concern with uniformity that is anathema to the French. 'No one on the Disney payroll is allowed to smoke, wear flashy jewellery, chew gum, tint their hair an unnatural shade, possess a visible tattoo, be fat or fail to subdue their sweat glands. Men must wear their hair short, and may not have a beard or a moustache' (B. Bryson, 1993: 17).

In its opening years it was a significant failure, losing as much as $60 million in one three-month period and raising fears of closure. Many reasons were put forward for this, including the high costs and the poor weather. But at the heart of the complaints was a fear that Disney had come to the wrong place. It was out of culture.

Thus, while the French value food, here it was all fast food. While the French have a lugubrious and nonchalant manner, here the workers had to be cheery and efficient. The French could not easily play the smiling hosts. There was a cultural resistance and cultural contagion. Slowly, EuroDisney has become more successful: there is a lot of money in it, after all. And traditional cultures look less and less stable in the light of McDisney Worlds.

In 2005, Disneyland opened its first Asian Experience on Lantau Island in megapolis Hong Kong. After more than a decade of negotiations, Disney has now received clearance to build its second Disneyland in China, this one in Shanghai. In 2010, it celebrated its 55th anniversary.

See Alan Bryman, *Disney and His Worlds* (London: Routledge, 1995); and *The Disneyization of Society* (London: Sage, 2004).

EuroDisney, Paris
*Source*: Corbis/Peter Turnley.

## Critical comment

The functional paradigm shows how culture operates as an integrated system for meeting human needs, yet by emphasising cultural stability, this approach downplays the extent to which societies change. Similarly, functionalism's assertion that cultural values are embraced by every member of a society overlooks the range of cultural diversity. Finally, the cultural patterns favoured by powerful people often dominate a society, while other ways of life are pushed to the margins. Thus, cultures typically generate more conflict than functional analysis leads us to believe.

# New developments: the cultural turn and cultural studies

Over the past 40 years, sociology has been challenged by a number of newer disciplines. One of these has been 'cultural studies'. In this section, we will briefly consider a number of routes into this.

# Early foundations of cultural studies: the culture industry and hegemony

Cultures are usually unequal, and some traits may benefit some members of society at the expense of others. Why do certain values dominate a society in the first place, and what are the ways in which people come to create their own alternative 'cultures of resistance'? Sociologists, often influenced by Marx, argue that values reflect a society's system of economic production. 'It is not the consciousness of men that determines their existence,' Marx proclaimed. 'It is their social existence that determines their consciousness' (1977: 4; orig. 1859).

The tradition of 'critical theory' was developed by the Frankfurt School in the 1930s. Theodor Adorno (1903–69), a leading proponent, suggested that the emerging 'mass culture' – of popular music and film, for example – weakened critical consciousness and manipulated the working masses. He studied the workings of the 'culture industry' and the ways in which it standardised culture, made people passive and served to make people uncritical. For Adorno, the 'culture industry perpetually cheats its consumers of

what it perpetually promises' (Adorno and Horkheimer, 1972: 120–3).

Another Marxist tradition was spearheaded by the Italian Antonio Gramsci (1891–1937). A militant in the Italian Communist Party, he spent ten years imprisoned by Mussolini. During this time he wrote his famous *Prison Notebooks* which developed the idea of **hegemony**, *the means by which a ruling/dominant group wins over a subordinate group through ideas*. 'Culture' in its many forms may thus serve as a mechanism for encouraging people to accept the existing social order uncritically – as a means of 'winning consent'. Through culture, coercive power may not be needed to maintain dominance. Watching a regular diet of soaps, daytime TV and sports programmes may be sufficient! This argument has been taken further by an English group of sociologists stimulated by the work of Stuart Hall (see *Thinkers and thinking* on p. 164).

# The UK tradition: class and resistance

The UK tradition can be (roughly) dated from three important books written by socialist historians and literary critics. They differ from much of the discussion of this chapter, which focuses upon 'culture' as an anthropological and sociological term. Instead, each of these books switched attention to the study of the values, beliefs, behaviour and material culture of the working class in England. The three books are Richard Hoggart's *The Uses of Literacy* (1957), Raymond Williams's *Culture and Society* (1987; orig. 1958), and E. P. Thompson's *The Making of the English Working Class* (1963). What each of these books does is show that working-class culture is an intelligible, active, even coherent and vibrant culture that has historical roots. These authors highlighted the active nature of the working class – how they made their culture.

*The Uses of Literacy* looks at both traditional working-class culture (and Hoggart's own experiences in Leeds as a child) and the wider development of 1950s popular culture among the young – magazines, jukebox coffee bars – suggesting problems with the latter over the former as a new 'mass culture' emerged. *Culture and Society* formulated 'a theory of culture as the study of relationships in a whole way of life' (Williams, 1987; orig. 1958). *The Making of the English Working Class* traced 'the growth of class consciousness, especially through trade unions, friendly societies, educational and religious movements, political organisations and periodicals – working-class intellectual traditions, working-class community pattern, and a working-class structure of feeling' (Thompson, 1963). What this tradition highlighted, then, was the way in which working-class groups both created their own cultures and resisted other (dominant) ones. Cultures were active, and there was a worry that 'mass culture' was swamping this long-time 'active' nature.

This tradition was taken up and pushed further in the work of Stuart Hall. With Stuart Hall, 'cultural studies' comes into its own. Drawing from Hoggart and others, Hall makes culture a much more political idea. Indeed, as he says, popular culture is 'an arena of consent and resistance. It is partly where hegemony arises, and where it is secured. It is not a sphere where socialism, a socialist culture – already fully formed – might be simply expressed. But it is one

## THINKERS & THEORY

# Stuart Hall: from culture to cultural studies

Born in Jamaica in 1932, Stuart Hall came to England in the early 1950s and eventually became director of the Birmingham Centre for Contemporary Cultural Studies (CCCS) and Professor of Sociology at the Open University. He retired in 1997. He has been one of the world's leading shapers of cultural studies, and has influenced a whole generation of young scholars studying class, race, gender and national cultures. We will see the impact of his work throughout this book, especially when we look at ethnicity, media, identity and class. His students have looked at the ways media 'represent' gender; how ethnic groups battle over their identities; and how dominant political forces – such as 'Thatcherism' – have been resisted through the creation of alternative cultures, rituals and identities. He was indeed a key intellectual to recognise the importance of **'Thatcherism'**, *a political belief grounded in economic individualism and the free market*, and showed how this political philosophy was part of an 'authoritarian populism' which gained wider support in the culture by appealing to materialist

Stuart Hall (1932–)
*Source*: Eamonn McCabe.

and individualist (populist) as well as traditional (Victorian) values. He produced a model of communication with four key moments: production, circulation, use (consumption) and reproduction (see Chapter 21).

His earliest work was explicitly drawn from Marx, but most of his later work does not look to the economy so much as culture. He sees always the importance of people's lived ideas, as they turn them into everyday cultures, though he always sees these cultures enmeshed in the wider workings of the state. Much of his earlier work draws from Althusser and Gramsci, and his more recent work from **poststructuralism** – we introduce this term later (but see the Glossary at the end of the book now).

In one of his key books, *Policing the Crisis* (Hall, 1978), he

and his colleagues looked at the crime of 'mugging' in England in the early 1970s (1972–3) and showed how black youth were scapegoated for such crimes as part of wider state responses to changes in the organisation of capitalism and the state. He was one of the first to suggest that the growth of new immigrant groups in the UK in the 1950s and 1960s, combined with the recession of the early 1970s, had hit immigrant groups hard. The attacks being made on them were part of a new kind of racist response, deflecting attention away from growing unemployment and declining wages.

One of his key themes has been the ways in which cultures are hybrids, which encourage a fusion of different forms. Hybrid cultures no longer have one form or one set of values, but are much more contradictory and complex. Likewise, people do not have one unitary identity or one sense of who they are. Rather, they speak from many positions, with ethnicity, gender, sexuality and class all coming into it. Globalisation has generated more extreme forms of racism as people try to defend their own national identity.

Stuart Hall Hall retired from the Open University in 1997 and is now a Professor Emeritus. The British newspaper *The Observer* called him 'one of the country's leading cultural theorists'. For a brief tour of his work, see James Procter, *Stuart Hall* (2004).

of the places where socialism might be instituted. That is why "popular culture" matters' (Hall, in Storey, 1996: 3).

## The North American tradition of cultural studies

A little after the development of the UK tradition, a distinctive US pattern of research started to develop from within mainstream sociology during the late 1980s and early 1990s. In general, it is much less abstractly theoretical and more empirically grounded in middle-range research – and usually with a much more scientific claim for its position. It deals more concretely in case studies – with much less concern for class analysis or taking critical stances. Its prime concern is with the analysis of meanings and symbols. It studies key objects like art collections, computers, AIDS, nuclear power and war memorials in order to grasp their place in the symbolic order (for examples, see Smith, 1998).

## The study of the global cultural industries

One important aspect of culture in the contemporary world is the development of commercial industries. David Hesmondhalgh (2007) has outlined seven core industries which constitute large parts of the economy and employ many people. They are:

1 *Broadcasting*: the radio and television industries.
2 *Film industries*: which include the dissemination of films on video and DVD.
3 *The content aspect of the internet industry* (i.e. that which is not simply to do with electronics).
4 *Music industries*: recording, publishing and live performance.
5 *Print and electronic publishing*, including books, newspapers and CD-Roms.
6 *Video, computer and digital games.*
7 *Advertising and marketing.*

Table 5.5 shows some of the biggest corporations that are directly involved in the production and dissemination of products and services that shape contemporary culture in many countries, if not worldwide. Sony produces a wide variety of cultural objects, from music to films to video games consoles. Microsoft and Apple are responsible for computer technology, software and computer entertainment

| Table 5.5 | 10 Large corporations with cultural industry interests (financial year 2010) | |
|---|---|---|
| Company | Total revenue (UK £m; approximate) | Gross profit (UK £m; approximate) |
| Sony Corp. | 54,000 | 11,000 |
| Apple | 40,000 | 15,000 |
| Microsoft | 38,000 | 30,000 |
| Vivendi | 25,000 | 12,000 |
| Walt Disney Co. | 23,000 | 4,000 |
| Coca Cola Co. | 21,000 | 13,000 |
| News Corporation CDI | 20,000 | 7,000 |
| Christian Dior SA | 18,000 | 11,000 |
| Time Warner Inc. | 16,000 | 6,000 |
| Google | 18,000 | 11,000 |

*Source*: Adapted from: http://money.msn.com/stocks; Access date: 20 May, 2011. Currency conversion according to exchange rates published on www.xe.com; 20 May, 2011.

products that have had a defining impact on electronic cultures in the Western world and beyond for several decades. Disney cartoons began to shape the imagination of children (and many adults) in the USA in the first half of the twentieth century, and since then they have spread rapidly around the globe. News Corporation owns newspapers and TV channels that shape the political attitudes of many people in the Western world. Vivendi is involved in television, music, film and videogame production, and Time Warner is active in television, cinema and news publications. Christian Dior is regarded as a leading provider of luxury fashion, while L'Oréal produces a wide range of cosmetics and hygiene items. Google, finally, has become one of the most successful internet search engines and providers of online content worldwide. We look more at this in Chapter 22.

A recent study by Scott Lash and Celia Lury (2007) has examined a range of these 'texts' or things as they have 'moved' across the world. They are interested in the ways in which these objects have become brands which almost take on a social life of their own. Their concern is with the biography of objects – with following them through the shifting and multiple journeys they follow.

# Circuits of culture: doing cultural studies research

In a celebrated discussion, Stuart Hall, Paul du Gay and others have suggested that any cultural item or object can be analysed through a circuit of culture which has five key features. Look at Figure 5.2, and then pick any cultural object that interests you. This can be a film like *Avatar*; a TV channel like Sky Arts; a TV programme like *The X Factor*; an item of clothing like a Nike shoe; or even a technology like an iPhone or iPad. Then think how you can present an analysis of it, following the questions below.

There are five moments in the process of the life of any cultural object – from fashion and food to houses and holidays. These five moments serve to establish:

- *Production*. How are raw materials, labour, time and technologies combined to create an object? This may include the inventor and founder of the object, but also the economics of its making as well as the cultures of work, the organisation of businesses and so on that generate it.

- *Representation*. What are the ways in which meanings are presented around the object (for example, images in magazines, on television and film, through logos)? This may be through spoken and written words, but also through photographs, videos, drawing, music and painting – in fact, any way of representing the 'object'.

It now becomes a set of signs and symbols, open to interpretation and the creation of meanings.

- *Identities*. What are the roles or positions from which people are recruited to buy this object? Certain styles of fashion (or houses, or food) appeal to certain kinds of people. Consuming certain items and not others may enhance style, create a sense of difference and allow for a new identity to be found.

- *Consumption*. What is involved in the exchange of services at the moment when objects are bought and consumed? It is very closely linked to production (but then, as we have shown, they are all linked), where we are concerned in part with marketing strategies, market research, advertising and design features. But the prime concern here is with the accumulation of material

goods and the proliferation of spaces for consumption – shops, malls, mail order, e-markets, etc. It is linked with social differentiation (how different groups consume different items) and the ways that consumption may change people's consciousness and perceptions.

- *Regulation*. What are the ways in which the public and private spheres of life are linked in the governance and control of production and consumption? This means looking at the employment rules, and any censorship rules, laws which may regulate the way it can be produced and consumed.

The study of culture circuits often leads especially to the study of cultural industries.

*Source*: Paul Du Gay, Stuart Hall, L. Janes, H. MacKay and K. Negus (eds), *Doing Cultural Studies: The Story of the Sony Walkman* (Buckingham: Open University Press, 1997).

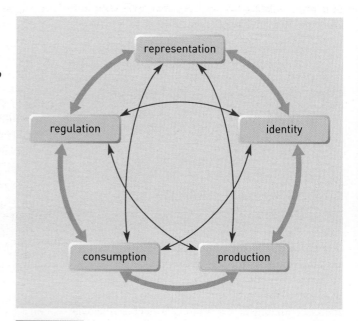

**Figure 5.2**    The circuit of culture

They take a range of 'objects' and follow them through the 'circuit of culture' (see Figure 5.2). Thus, they examine *Toy Story*, *Trainspotting* and the *Wallace and Grommit* animated films; the European Football Championship of 1996; the art movement BA of a group of British artists; and two major retail brands, Swatch and Nike. They devote a chapter to each and ask about its life history.

## Postmodernism and the new culture

If modernism suggests the need to 'make it new', then postmodernism suggests it has all been done, and all we can do is 'play with the pieces'. In recent times, and despite its controversial nature, postmodernism has become an influential world-view, and is heavily shaped by North America. A key to the postmodern is a sense of the fragments and the loss of any one unifying theme. Postmodern culture is usually seen to (a) celebrate the surface rather than depth; (b) be eclectic and pastiched; and (c) adopt ironic and even cynical tones.

Postmodern culture is usually seen to originate in the provinces of architecture and art. Thus, postmodern architecture borrows colourfully from past styles and is less concerned with obvious function. It is found in the work of Robert Venturi, Richard Rogers, I. M. Pei and Charles Moore. The Bonaventura Hotel in Los Angeles is perhaps the classic example. Here is a massive hotel in the heart of the downtown city area whose lobby seems to serve like a gigantic aircraft hanger-come-shopping mall!

Postmodernism suggests a wide variety of pastiched and differing styles. In art it is often linked to new playful forms, such as video art, body art and 'art installations'. Many of the new art galleries, such as the Tate Modern in London, the Guggenheim at Bilbao and the new Getty in Los Angeles, are also seen as prime examples. In literature, postmodernism becomes what writer John Barth has called 'the literature of exhaustion': it is often indulgently self-reflective and is often linked to contradiction, permutation, discontinuity, randomness and excess (Lodge, 1977: 228). Likewise, postmodern films (found in the work of directors such as Jim Jarmusch and David Lynch) often engage with a radical reordering of what are seen as traditional narrative forms. And in postmodern music (John Cage, John Adams, Michael Nyman) the form is usually bare and minimalist yet with striking technosonic effects.

## Looking ahead: globalisation, global cultures and hybridity

We have looked at a wide range of cultural phenomena in this chapter: culture is the stuff of our everyday life experience and sociology has found a major collaborator in its study. More than this, we also showed the impact of our concern with globalisation on cultures worldwide. We will conclude this chapter with a brief tour of the implications of globalising cultures.

Today, more than ever before, we can observe many of the same cultural patterns the world over. Walking the streets of Seoul (South Korea), Kuala Lumpur (Malaysia), Chennai (India), Cairo (Egypt) and Casablanca (Morocco), we find familiar forms of dress, hear well-known pop music, and see advertising for many of the same products we use at home. Just as important, English is rapidly emerging as the preferred second language of most of the world. So are we witnessing the birth of a global culture?

Yet as we have seen, the world is still divided into around 200 nation-states and thousands of different cultural systems. Many of these are in deep conflict. As recent violence in the former Soviet Union, the former Yugoslavia, the Middle East, Sri Lanka and elsewhere attests, many people are intolerant of others whose cultures differ from their own. Yet, looking back through history, we might sense that societies around the world now have more contact with one another, and enjoy more cooperation, than ever before. These global connections involve the flow of goods, information and people.

1 *The global economy: the flow of goods*. The extent of international trade has never been greater. The global economy has introduced many of the same consumer goods (from cars to TV shows to T-shirts) the world over.

2 *Global communications: the flow of information*. A century ago, communication around the world depended on written messages delivered by boat, train, horse and wagon, or, occasionally, by telegraph wire. Today's satellite-based communication system enables people to experience sights and sounds of events taking place thousands of miles away – often as they happen.

3 *Global migration: the flow of people*. Knowledge about the rest of the world motivates people to

move where they imagine life will be better. Moreover, today's transportation technology – especially air travel – makes relocating easier than ever before. As a result, most countries now contain significant numbers of people born elsewhere, and tourism has become one of the leading world industries.

These global links have partially made the cultures of the world more similar, at least in superficial respects. But they have also generated awareness of deep contrasts in world peoples. Some – usually poor and in low-income cultures – remain heavily restricted to a local world. But others have developed a much more flexible, global character. Ulf Hannerz describes this as a *cosmopolitan character*, who adopts:

> a stance towards diversity . . . towards the coexistence of cultures in the individual experience . . . a willingness to engage with the other . . . a stance of openness towards divergent cultural experiences . . . a search for contrasts rather than towards uniformity . . . a state of readiness, a personal ability to make one's way into other cultures, through listening, looking, intuiting and reflecting . . .

(Hannerz, 1990: 239)

Sociologists also talk of the hybridisation of cultures. Just as in plant biology, a hybrid is a crossover between different species, so **cultural hybridisation** refers to *the ways in which parts of one culture (language, practices, symbols) get recombined with the cultures of another*. Dutch sociologist Jan Nederveen Pieterse puts this strikingly:

> How do we come to terms with phenomena such as Thai boxing by Moroccan girls in Amsterdam, Asian rap in London, Irish bagels, Chinese tacos and Mardi Gras Indians in the United States, or Mexican schoolgirls dressed in Greek togas dancing in the style of Isadora Duncan? How do we interpret Peter Brook directing the Mahabharata, or Ariane Manouchkine staging a Shakespeare play in Japanese Kabuki style for a Paris audience in the Théatre Soleil?

(Pieterse, 1995: 53)

But there are three important limitations to the global culture thesis. First, the flow of goods, information and people has been uneven throughout the world. Generally speaking, urban areas (centres of commerce, communication and people) have stronger ties to one another, while rural villages remain more isolated. The greater economic and military power of North America and western Europe means that these regions influence the rest of the world more than the other way around.

Second, the global culture thesis assumes that people everywhere are able to afford various new goods and services. The grinding poverty in much of the world deprives millions of even the basic necessities of a safe and secure life.

Third, although many cultural traits are now found throughout the world, we should not conclude that people everywhere attach the same meanings to them. Do teenagers in Tokyo understand rap music the way their counterparts in New York or Los Angeles do? Similarly, we mimic fashions from around the world with little knowledge of the lives of people who first came up with them. In short, people everywhere look at the world through their own cultural 'lenses' (Featherstone, 1990). This process has been identified as **glocalisation**, *the ways in which global phenomena are responded to differently in local cultures*. Karaoke may have been sent round the world from Japan, but it takes on different meanings, songs and rituals when it is done in Thailand, London or San Francisco.

All this said, a hallmark of twenty-first century life is its hybridic and increasingly cosmopolitan nature.

# SUMMARY

**1** Cultures are 'designs for living' and refer to ways of life. They are partly material (tangible things like telephones or pottery), partly non-material (for example, ideas) and involve practices (the practical logics through which we act and think in everyday life). Several species display a limited capacity for culture, but only human beings rely on culture for survival.

**2** As the human brain evolved, the first elements of culture appeared some 2 million years ago; the development of culture reached the point we call 'the birth of civilisation' approximately 12,000 years ago.

**3** Humans build culture on symbols by attaching meaning to objects and action. Language is the symbolic system by which one generation transmits culture to the next. Values represent general orientations to the world around us; beliefs are statements that people who share a culture hold to be true. Cultural *norms* guide human behaviour: mores consist of norms of great moral significance; *folkways* guide everyday life and afford greater individual discretion. *Material culture* refers to tangible human creations.

**4** High culture refers to patterns that distinguish a society's elites; popular culture includes patterns widespread in a society. Subculture refers to distinctive cultural patterns adopted by a segment of a population; counterculture means patterns strongly at odds with a conventional way of life.

**5** Invention, discovery and diffusion all generate cultural change. When parts of a cultural system change at different rates, this is called cultural lag.

**6** Because we learn the standards of one culture, we evaluate other cultures ethnocentrically. An alternative to ethnocentrism, cultural relativism, means judging another culture according to its own standards. The conflict perspective envisages culture as a dynamic arena of inequality and conflict. Cultural patterns typically benefit some categories of people more than others.

**7** Cultures may be approached functionally (as a relatively stable system built on core values, cultural traits function to maintain the overall system). They may also be approached conflictually as webs of inequality, mass culture and hegemony.

**8** The past 30 years have seen the growth of cultural studies and the study of cultural industries.

**9** Increasingly we live in global cultures that generate hybrids and cosmopolitan characters.

CONNECT UP: Turn to Part 6 of this book for key resources and link up
with the book's website, which links to these resources
SEE: www.pearsoned.co.uk/plummer

# Suggestions for going further

## 1 Connect up with Part Six and the Sociology Web Resources

As you work through ideas and think about the issues raised in this chapter, look at the accompanying website and the resource centre at the end of this book which connects to it. There is a lot here to help you move on. To link up, see: www.pearson.co.uk/plummer.

## 2 Review the chapter

*Briefly summarise (in a paragraph) just what this chapter has been about.* Consider: (a) What have you learned? (b) What do you disagree with? Be critical. And (c) How would you develop all this? How could you get more detail on matters that interest you?

## 3 Pose questions

(a) Imagine you are a stranger arriving for the first time in your culture. Look at it with a stranger's ideas and try to see just how its values, symbols, languages, etc. give it a distinctive feel. Look at the book by Kate Fox: *Watching the English: The Hidden Rules of English Behaviour* (2005), which provides a fascinating account of the oddities of the English!

(b) Give instances of Eurocentrism found in this textbook (if you can find them!). Are there European values at work? Do you think European cultural values are changing? If so, how and why?

(c) Using some of the key concepts developed in this chapter – language, values, material culture, etc. – present an analysis of any one cultural group you know (such as a religious culture, a sports culture, a youth culture or a 'deviant' culture). (*Hint*: look back at Chapter 3 on ways of doing research, and do a web search for different groups, scenes.) The chapter uses Muslim culture as an example and you could use this as your example too.

(d) What is cultural studies? How does it differ from sociology? Which might be more helpful in studying human societies?

(e) Is the world becoming more culturally hybridic and cosmopolitan? Discuss clear examples.

## 4 Explore key words

Many concepts have been introduced in this chapter. You can review them from the website or from the listing at the back of this book. You might like to give special attention to just five words and think them through – how would you define them, what are they dealing with, and do they help you see the social world more clearly or not?

The classic book here is Raymond Williams, *Keywords* (1975). Also see Chris Barker, *The Sage Dictionary of Cultural Studies* (2004).

## 5 Search the Web

Be critical when you look at websites – see the box on p. 940 in the Resources section. For this chapter look at the following.

### Languages

The Ethnologue
www.ethnologue.com
Site for the study of all the world's known living languages.
The UNESCO endangered languages site
www.unesco.org/culture/ich/index.php?pg=00136

### Cultural attitude surveys

World Values Survey
www.worldvaluessurvey.org
Global Voice of the People
www.voice-of-the-people.net

British Social Attitudes
www.britsocat.com/Body.aspx?control=HomePage
European Social Survey
www.europeansocialsurvey.org
http://ec.europa.eu/public_opinion/standard_en.htm

## Cultural studies

Theory.org.uk
www.theory.org.uk
A well-established site for cultural theory fans (do not confuse it with theory.org).
Cultural Studies Central
www.culturalstudies.net
Another large and well-established site.

## Cultural anthropology

Human Relations Area Files
www.yale.edu/hraf
A major resource on different cultures.
Society for Cultural Anthropology
www.aaanet.or/sca/index.htm
Site for the American Anthropological Society, focusing on culture.

## 6  Watch a DVD

Wim Wender's *Buona Vista Social Club* (1991) ostensibly looks at the making of music in Cuba, but conveys much more about culture.

This may be a good time to watch some class DVDs that display youth cultures and look for their language, values, symbols, etc. Have a look at Nicholas Ray's *Rebel without a Cause* (1955), Dennis Hopper's *Easy Rider* (1969), John Badham's *Saturday Night Fever* (1977), Michael Lehman's *Heathers* (1989) and Catherine Hardwicke's *Thirteen* (2004). These are just a few and span some 50 years. Bring them up to date with *High School Musical* (parts 1–3) or *The Twilight Trilogy* (parts 1–3). All are based on US culture, have been very influential in their time and show the drifting cultural forms of youth cultures. Search for more and maybe think of drawing up a comparison.

## 7  Think and read

Martin J. Gannon, *Understanding Global Cultures: Metaphorical Journeys through 23 Nations* (4th edn, 2009) provides a series of short case studies of different cultures through an organising image such as 'The Japanese Garden', 'The Brazilian Samba', 'American Football', 'The Spanish Bullfight' and 'The Swedish *Stuga*'.

Ken Gelder, *Subcultures* ( 2008) provides a clear and historical account of subcultures.

Ken Gelder and Sarah Thornton (eds), *The Subcultures Reader* (2005, 2nd rev. edn) and D. Muggleton and R. Weinzierl (eds), *The Post-subcultures Reader* (2004) provide both classic readings around subcultures and the different forms of youth cultures and up-to-date challenges to classical work.

Akbar Ahmed, *Discovering Islam: Making Sense of Muslim History and Society* (1988), alongside his *Islam Under Siege* (2003), provides a good guide to Muslim culture and its contemporary conflicts.

The new field of cultural studies should not be confused with 'culture', which generally has a much broader set of concerns. Jeff Lewis, *Cultural Studies: The Basics* (2nd edn, 2008) and Chris Rojek, *Cultural Studies* (2007) are two useful short guides to the whole field. The latter suggests that the field of inquiry has moved through four 'moments': the 'National/Popular', the 'Textual/Representational', 'Global/Post Essentialism' and 'Governmentality/Policy'. Simon Duhring (ed.), *The Cultural Studies Reader* (2nd edn, 2006) includes articles by Adorno, Hall, Williams, Bourdieu and many others.

The essential reading on the culture industries is David Hesmondhalgh, *The Cultural Industries* (2nd edn, 2007), which gives detailed accounts of each industry.

Finally, Scott Lash and Celia Lury, *Global Culture Industry: The Mediation of Things (2007)* examines a range of cultural products.

## 8  Relax with a novel

You might read some books on 'culture clash'. E. M. Forster's *A Passage to India* (1924), also a film by David Lean (1985), and Henry James's *The Europeans* (1978 edn), also a Merchant-Ivory film (1978), would be interesting starts. And for a complete contrast, Gautam Malkani's coming-of-age novel *Londonstani* (Fourth Estate, 2005) captures modern youth culture – a mix of English, street cred, Punjabi, Urdu, profanity, mobile texting and 'gangsta rap'.

## 9  Connect to other chapters

- For more on semiology and how to do a mass media analysis, see Chapter 22.
- For more on cultural studies, see Bourdieu in Chapter 20.
- For more on religion and culture, see Chapter 19.

# 10  Engage with THE BIG DEBATE

### Whose culture is this? The problem of Eurocentrism, multiculturalism and postcolonialism in sociology

For some, Europe can be seen as the cradle of the modern world. Indeed, for the Swedish sociologist Goran Therborn:

> There is no doubt that Europe was the pioneer of modernity and the centre of it. Neither the Islamic, the Black African, the Hindu nor the East Asian Confucian world seems to have discovered the future as a new place, attainable but never visited before . . . Europe became the undisputed centre of modernity in terms of knowledge as well as in terms of power.
>
> (Therborn, 1995: 19)

It was the 'chief organiser' of this modern world. For Therborn, there are many features of this. Europe's 'modernity' brought new knowledge, new settlements around the world, new technologies and capital investment, as well as the development of all the 'isms' – socialism, communism, anarchism, liberalism, Protestantism, etc.

But 'a sense of Europe' can go back a long way. Some writers suggest that European culture can be defined by four elements that mark it off from the rest of the world:

- The Hellenistic and Roman Empires – rediscovered through the Renaissance – which helped establish a sense of art, politics and philosophy that shapes a characteristic 'humanistic' temper.
- Christianity, which for two millennia, and despite oppositions and internal schisms, has pervaded the European idea (and at times the very words 'Europe' and 'Christendom' were synonymous).
- The Enlightenment – the creation of a scientific, sceptical, creative intellectual climate helps to define it – as does the 'Europabild' literature.
- Industrialisation: while not alone, and these days overtaken by many other countries, it was the first region to foster the industrial world (Hay, 1968).

Yet there are serious problems with this commonly held 'Eurocentric' view. Taking a European view of the world often minimises the importance of other cultures: Asian, Latin American, African, etc. It also cultivates a view of Europe as an entity with a history of continuity, which on closer inspection is hard to sustain. Greek history, for example, is as much connected to the Middle East and the Orient. Indeed, the eminent historian Arnold Toynbee saw this continuity as a 'thoroughgoing misinterpretation of the history of Mankind' – a dangerous tendency that minimised the contribution of many other cultures. These days, this is recognised as the twin problem of 'multiculturalism' and 'postcolonialism'.

Originally emerging as an education policy in the United States, **multiculturalism** *recognises past and present cultural diversity and promotes the equality of all cultural traditions*. This movement represents a sharp turn from the view where cultures are defined through their European links. **Postcolonialism** *recognises how many cultures have been made through oppressor–subject relationships and seeks to unpack these, showing how cultures are made.*

For more than two centuries, historians have highlighted people of English and other European ancestry and chronicled events from their point of view. In the process, little attention has been paid to the perspectives and accomplishments of other cultures. Multiculturalists condemn this pattern as **Eurocentrism**, *the dominance of European (particularly English) cultural patterns*. Molefi Kete Asante, a leading advocate of multiculturalism, draws a historical analogy. Like the fifteenth-century Europeans who could not let go of the idea that the earth was the centre of the universe, many today find it difficult not to view European culture as the centre of the social universe (Asante, 1988: 7).

The European flag
*Source*: Corel Flags of the World

Few deny that our culture has wide-ranging roots. But multiculturalism is controversial because it demands that we rethink the norms and values at the core of our society. Not surprisingly, battles are now raging over how to describe culture. Some claim that Western thought has been dominated by **Orientalism** – *a process by which the West (Europe and America) has created an image of the East – or Orient – as a stereotype* (Said, 1978). Thus the Orient becomes 'mysterious', Turks become 'lustful', and Asians become 'inscrutable'. The others – Asians, Arabs – are seen through Western eyes in ways that are demeaning and dehumanising.

Frantz Fanon analysed the impact of white colonialism on blacks. He aimed through his writings to liberate the consciousness of the oppressed. In the first phase he sees how blacks may become assimilated to dominant white culture; a second phase sees the black writer disturbed; and a third sees the native writers turning themselves into awakeners of the people. But labels such as African, Muslim, American, 'Chinese' or, worse, 'Chineseness' are no more than starting points. The object then is to 'deconstruct' them – to take them apart and see what lies behind them.

Although multiculturalism and postcolonialism have found widespread favour in the last several years, they have provoked criticism as well. Opponents think they encourage divisiveness rather than unity by urging individuals to identify with their own category rather than with common elements. Similarly, rather than recognise any common standards of truth, say critics, multiculturalism maintains that we should evaluate ideas according to the race (and sex) of those who present them. Common humanity thus dissolves into an 'African voice' an 'Asian voice' and so on.

Critics say that multiculturalism and postcolonialism may not end up helping minorities, as proponents contend. They argue that multiculturalist initiatives (from African-American studies to all-black college accommodation) seem to demand precisely the kind of racial segregation we do not want. Then, too, an Asiacentric curriculum may well deny children a wide range of crucial knowledge and skills by forcing them to study only certain topics from a single point of view. Whose voices are to be heard?

Is there any common ground in this debate? Virtually everyone agrees that all people in Europe need to gain greater appreciation of the extent of cultural diversity. Eurocentric views distort an appreciation of the emergent global cultures, all with their differing languages, symbols, countercultures, etc.

Throughout much of history the world has been colonised by other countries and nations. Many countries have been invaded by others and had their cultures uprooted, transformed, even destroyed. And today, whenever we look at cultures, we tend to see them from the point of our own. This is now a burning issue for a new generation of sociologists: how to grasp the range of varying cultural perspectives that can be taken and to incorpoarte them into understanding. Some have referred to this as **cosmopolitanism** – *the philosophy that all people, despite their great differences, can still share a common humanity and community*.

## Continue the debate

1 Do you think there is a truly distinctive 'European' culture with history and roots? What does it look like, and what is its history? Does it have a coherence, or does it conceal many voices?

2 How does the multiculturalism debate shape our views on school curricula and language learning? What are the pros and cons of different curricula and languages?

3 Whose voices are being heard once you adopt a 'postcolonial' voice?

4 Explore the idea of 'cosmopolitanism' through websites, and see if you think it just might provide a soloution.

# CHAPTER 6

# GROUPS, ORGANISATIONS AND THE RISE OF THE NETWORK SOCIETY

**2008 SAW THE 40ᵗʰ ANNIVERSARY CELEBRATION OF THE BIG MAC AND A CONTINUING EXPANSION OF MCDONALD'S ECONOMIC SUCCESS AROUND THE WORLD.** The business began in 1940, with a restaurant opened by brothers Richard and Maurice McDonald in San Bernardino, California. By 1948, they had their 'Speedee Service System' and the fast-food industry had been born. Initially, it attracted little attention from the local community and went unnoticed by the world as a whole. Yet this seemingly insignificant small business would eventually spark a revolution in the restaurant industry and provide a global organisational model that would be copied by countless other businesses and even schools and churches.

The basic formula the McDonald brothers put into place – 'fast food' – was to serve food quickly and inexpensively to large numbers of people. They trained employees to perform highly specialised jobs, so that one person grilled hamburgers, while others 'dressed' them, made French fries, whipped up milkshakes, and presented the food to the customers in assembly-line fashion.

As the years went by, the McDonald brothers prospered, and they moved their single restaurant from Pasadena to San Bernardino. It was there, in 1954, that events took an unexpected turn when Ray Kroc, a travelling blender and mixer merchant, paid a visit to the McDonalds. Kroc was fascinated by the brothers' efficient system, and, almost immediately, he saw the potential for a greatly expanded system of fast-food restaurants. Initially, Kroc launched

his plans in partnership with the McDonald brothers. Soon, however, he bought out their interests and set out on his own to become one of the greatest success stories of all time.

Today, over 32,000 McDonald's restaurants serve more than 58 million customers a day across 119 countries. One in 200 people across the world visit a McDonald's daily. In the UK, more than 2.5 million people eat at a McDonald's everyday. It is the best-known 'brand' in the world – its major world markets being in the USA (34 per cent), Europe (42 per cent) and Asia/Pacific, Middle East and Africa (APMEA), which account for 18 per cent of revenues. In 2008, its annual revenue was $22.79 billion.

But McDonald's has been much criticized. In 1990, activists in London distributed leaflets entitled *What's wrong with McDonald's?*, criticising its environmental, health and employment record – resulting in a major live trial; and in 2001, Eric Schlosser's book *Fast Food Nation* alleged that McDonald's profited at the expense of people's health and its workers. Morgan Spurlock's 2004 documentary film *Super Size Me* said that McDonald's food was contributing to the epidemic of obesity in society

Despite criticisms from many, especially in the environmental movement, McDonald's continues to grow and adapt. The McPuff has been pioneered in China, McRice can be found in Indonesia and the McCafé developed in Australia is popular in Hong Kong, France and Germany. The Big Mac Index has been invented as a way of comparing a Big Mac's cost in various world currencies to

informally assess a currency's purchasing power parity.

*The disease which inflicts bureaucracy, and what they usually die from, is routine.*

J. S. Mill

*Bureaucracy is a giant mechanism operated by pygmies.*

Honore de Balzac

*Every revolution evaporates and leaves behind only the slime of a new bureaucracy.*

Franz Kafka

## In this chapter, we ask:

- **How do social groups shape our conduct?**
- **How are groups changing?**
- **What is the nature of organisations and the 'McDonaldisation' of society?**
- **How is social life changing in an age of mobile phones and Facebook?**

**Is this conformity or individuality?**

From a sociological point of view, the success of McDonald's reveals much more than the popularity of hamburgers. As this chapter will explain, one larger importance of this story lies in the extent to which the principles that guide the operation of McDonald's are coming to dominate much of social life in very many parts of the world. So much so, that sociologists have started to talk of the **McDonaldisation of society**, *a process by which the principles of the fast-food industry come to be applied to more and more features of social life.* Close, intimate groups are giving way to fast, efficient but distant ones. At the same time, the way that people communicate and get close to others is changing. No longer living in stable or well-bounded groups and communities, as we like to think people did in the past, many people now live their lives increasingly through networks. Through standard phones, mobile phones, the car, the email, the fax, we can now develop close relations with a complex network of people scattered over a wide area, even the globe. Often, people living on the other side of the world, and whom we have never seen, can become our 'friends'!

In this chapter, we will begin by examining one of the oldest ideas of sociology: that we live in *social groups*, the clusters of people with whom we associate in much of our daily lives. As we shall see, the scope of group life expanded greatly during the twentieth century. From a world built on kin and community – usually small, local, face-to-face and intense – the structure of many societies now turns on the operation of vast businesses, bureaucracies and formal organisations – usually large, impersonal and fleeting. And even more recently, we can 'log on' to our computer and surf, and we can Facebook and Twitter with a vast array of known (and unknown) individuals across the world. By 2011, 500 million people were using Facebook. In many parts of the world, social networking has become commonplace. Understanding how this changing and expanding scale of life has come to dominate society, and what it means for us as individuals, are the chapter's key objectives.

## Social groups

Virtually everyone moves through life with a sense of belonging; this is the experience of group life. A **social group** refers to *two or more people who identify and interact with one another.* Human beings continually come together to form couples, families,

circles of friends, gangs, neighbourhoods, churches, businesses, clubs, communities, transnational corporations and numerous large organisations. Whatever the form, groups encompass people with shared experiences, loyalties and interests. In short, while maintaining their individuality, the members of social groups also think of themselves as a special 'we'. In what follows, we shall introduce a few terms that help clarify our thinking about groups: primary and secondary groups, group conformity, reference groups and group size.

## A basic distinction: primary and secondary groups

Acquaintances commonly greet one another with a smile and the simple phrase 'How are you?' The response is usually a well-scripted 'Fine, thanks. How are you?' This answer, of course, is often more formal than truthful. In most cases, providing a detailed account of how you are really doing would prompt the other person to beat a hasty and awkward exit.

Sociologists classify social groups by measuring them against two ideal types based on members' level of genuine personal concern. This variation is the key to distinguishing *primary from secondary groups*.

Charles Horton Cooley (1864–1929) was a pioneering North American sociologist. He is most famed for his idea of the looking-glass self, discussed in Chapter 7. According to Cooley, a **primary group** is a *small social group whose members share personal and enduring relationships.* Bound together by primary relationships, individuals in primary groups typically spend a great deal of time together, engage in a wide range of common activities and feel that they know one another well. Although not without periodic conflict, members of primary groups display sincere concern for each other's welfare. This is the world of family and friends. The strength of primary relationships gives people a comforting sense of security. In the familiar social circles of family or friends, people feel they can 'be themselves' without constantly worrying about the impressions they are making.

Members of primary groups generally provide one another with economic and other forms of assistance as well. But, as important as primary ties are, people generally think of a primary group as an end in itself rather than as a means to other ends. In other words, we prefer to think that kinship or friendship links people who 'belong together', rather than people who expect to benefit from each other. For this reason, we readily call on family members or close friends to help us move into a new apartment, without expecting to pay for their services. And we would do the same for them. A friend who never returns a favour, by contrast, is likely to leave us feeling 'used' and questioning the depth of the friendship.

Moreover, this personal orientation means that members of a primary group view each other as unique and irreplaceable. We typically do not care who cashes our cheque at the bank or takes our money at the supermarket checkout. Yet in the primary group – especially the family – we are bound to specific others by emotion and loyalty. So even though brothers and sisters do not always get along, they always remain siblings.

In contrast to the primary group, the **secondary group** is *a large and impersonal social group whose members pursue a specific interest or activity*. In most respects, secondary groups have precisely the opposite characteristics of primary groups. *Secondary relationships* usually involve weak emotional ties and little personal knowledge of one another. Secondary groups vary in duration, but they are frequently short term, beginning and ending without particular significance. Students following a university course, for instance, who may not see one another after the term ends, exemplify the secondary group.

Weaker social ties permit secondary groups to include many more people than primary groups do. For example, dozens or even hundreds of people may work together in the same office, yet most of them pay only passing attention to one another. Sometimes the passing of time will transform a group from secondary to primary, as with co-workers who share an office for many years. Generally, however, the boundary separating members of a secondary group from non-members is far less clear than it is for primary groups.

Secondary groups lack strong loyalties and emotions because members look to one another only to achieve limited ends. So while members of primary groups display a *personal orientation*, people in secondary groups reveal a goal orientation. Secondary ties are not necessarily always aloof or cold, of course. Social interactions among students, co-workers and business associates are often quite pleasant, even if they are rather impersonal. The goal orientation of secondary groups encourages individuals to craft their behaviour carefully. In these roles, we remain characteristically impersonal and polite. The secondary relationship, therefore, is one in which the question 'How are you?' may be asked without really expecting a truthful answer.

In primary groups, members define each other according to *who* they are – that is, in terms of kinship or unique, personal qualities. Members of secondary groups, by contrast, look to one another for *what* they are or what they can do for each other. In secondary groups, in other words, we are always mindful of what we offer others and what we receive in return. This 'scorekeeping' comes through most clearly in business relationships. Likewise, the people next door typically expect that a neighbourly favour will be reciprocated. Table 6.1 summarises these characteristics. (Keep in

| Table 6.1 | Primary groups and secondary groups: a summary | |
| --- | --- | --- |
| | **Primary group** | **Secondary group** |
| Quality of relationships | Personal orientation | Goal orientation |
| Duration of relationships | Usually long term | Variable; often short term |
| Breadth of relationships | Broad; usually involving many activities | Narrow; usually involving few activities |
| Subjective perception of relationships | As ends in themselves | As means to an end |
| Typical examples | Families; circles of friends | Co-workers; political organisations |
| New technologies | Mobile phones can keep family and close friends in perpetual contact | Facebook can provide more 'loose' contacts and friends than ever before possible |

mind that these traits define two types of social group in ideal terms; actual groups in our lives may well contain elements of both.) By placing these concepts as ends of a continuum, sociologists have devised a basic but useful scheme for describing and analysing group life.

A long-standing sociological view suggests that rural areas and small towns tend towards a greater emphasis on primary relationships while large cities are typically more secondary. While this holds some truth, some urban neighbourhoods – especially those populated by people of a single ethnicity, religion or even sexual orientation – can be quite tightly knit. 'Jewish neighbourhoods', 'Polish communities' or 'gay communities' are usually strong in primary orientation, with local meeting places or bars to facilitate this.

Primary relationships may well predominate in low-income pre-industrial societies throughout Latin America, Africa and Asia, in which people's lives still often revolve around families and local villages. Especially in rural areas, strangers stand out in the social landscape. But even many of these countries now find that more and more of their populations live in cities where secondary relations have become much more common. In high-income industrial societies, in which people assume highly specialised social roles, secondary ties usually take precedence. Most people in England, for example, routinely engage in impersonal, secondary contacts with virtual strangers – people about whom they know very little and whom they may never meet again.

# Group conformity

In most of the Western world, people do not like to think they are 'conformists', that they follow the group. Most people like to think they are unique individuals, that they in some way stand out from the crowd. But think for a minute of the main groups you belong to – at school, university, in sport, at home. Think of your peer group and how you want (or even need) to be accepted by them. Maybe you do stand out as a less conformist person, but many social psychological studies have shown that group conformity is very likely. This section looks at two classic yet still widely cited social psychological studies that suggest this. Social scientists confirm the power of group pressure to shape human behaviour and report that it remains strong in adulthood as well as in adolescence.

## Asch's classic research

Solomon Asch (1952) conducted a classic investigation that revealed the power of group conformity. Asch recruited students for an alleged study of visual perception. Before the actual experiment, however, he revealed to all but one member in each small group that their real purpose was to impose group pressure on the remaining subject. Placing all the students around a table, Asch asked each, in turn, to note the length of a 'standard' line, as shown on Card 1 in Figure 6.1, and match it to one of three lines on Card 2.

| Figure 6.1 | Cards used in Asch's experiment in group conformity (Asch, 1952) |

Anyone with normal vision could easily see that the line marked 'A' on Card 2 was the correct choice. Initially, as planned, everyone made the matches correctly. But then Asch's secret accomplices began answering incorrectly, making the naive subject (seated at the table in order to answer next to last) bewildered and uncomfortable.

What happened? Asch found that one-third of all subjects placed in this situation chose to conform to the others by answering incorrectly. His investigation indicates that many people are willing to compromise their judgements to avoid the discomfort of being different from others, even from people they do not know. Think about yourself for a minute: do you think you would conform like this?

## Milgram's classic research

In an equally famous (even notorious) set of experiments, Stanley Milgram – a former student of Solomon Asch – conducted conformity experiments that were even more surprising. In Milgram's initial

Stanley Milgram's electric shock experiment is the most famous of all social psychological experiments. Conducted in the early 1960s, you can now download it on YouTube (search: Milgram experiment). There have also been many replications (see for example The Milgram Re-enactment (2002): http://www.roddickinson.net/pages/milgram/project-synopsis.php

*Source*: Manuscripts and Archives, Yale University Library, Stanley Milgram Papers (MS 1406). From the film *Obedience* copyright © 1968 by Stanley Milgram; copyright renewed 1993 by Alexandra Milgram, and distributed by Penn State Media Sales.

study (Milgram, 1963, 1965; Miller, 1986), a researcher explained to male recruits that they were about to engage in a study of how punishment affects learning. One by one, he assigned them the role of 'teacher' and placed another individual – an insider to the study – in a connecting room as the 'learner'.

The teacher saw the learner sit down in an ominous contraption resembling an electric chair with an electrode attached to one arm. The researcher then had the teacher read aloud pairs of words. In the next step, the teacher repeated the first word of each pair and asked the learner to recall the corresponding second word.

As mistakes occurred, the researcher instructed the teacher to shock the learner using a 'shock generator', a bogus but forbidding-looking piece of equipment with a shock switch and a dial marked to regulate electric current from 15 volts (labelled 'mild shock') to 300 volts (marked 'intense shock') to 450 volts (marked 'Danger: Severe Shock' and 'XXX'). Beginning at the lowest level, the researcher told the teacher to increase the shock by 15 volts every time the learner made a mistake. The shocks, explained the researcher, would become painful but cause no permanent damage. And so it went. At 75, 90 and 105 volts, the teacher heard audible moans from the learner; at 120 volts, shouts of pain; at 270 volts, screams of agony; and, after 330 volts, deadly silence.

The results show just how readily authority figures can obtain compliance from ordinary people. None of 40 subjects assigned in the role of teacher during the initial research even questioned the procedure before 300 volts had been applied, and 26 of the subjects – almost two-thirds – went all the way to 450 volts.

Milgram (1964) then modified his research to see if Solomon Asch had documented such a high degree of group conformity only because the task of matching lines seemed trivial. What if groups pressured people to administer electrical shocks? To investigate, he varied the experiment so that a group of three teachers, two of whom were his accomplices, made decisions jointly. Milgram's rule was that each of the three teachers would suggest a shock level when the learner made an error and they would then administer the lowest of the three suggestions. This arrangement gave the naive subject the power to lessen the shock level regardless of the other two teachers' recommendations.

The accomplices called for increasing the shock level with each error, placing group pressure on the third member to do the same. Responding to this group pressure, subjects applied voltages three to four times higher than in control conditions in which subjects acted alone. Thus Milgram's research suggests that people are surprisingly likely to follow the directions not only of 'legitimate authority figures', but also of groups of ordinary individuals.

### Zimbardo's research: the Stanford experiment

Back in August 1971, a somewhat scary and very controversial social psychological experiment was conducted on a group of students at Stanford University. It is now very well known, even notorious.

The experiment invited some 'normal' students to take part in a study which aimed to simulate prison conditions. In a basement in the psychology department at Stanford University in California, rooms were made out to be like prison cells. 'Normal' average students were divided into two groups: guards and inmates. They were then asked to live these roles for a couple of days – and were provided with 'uniforms' appropriate to their parts. Zimbardo wanted to see what they would do, but soon found he was horrified at the degree to which seemingly normal students turned seriously abusive to each other. The guards were extremely violent – physically, verbally and mentally – to the inmates. Yet previously the students had related well and had been their normal-time friends. They fell into their roles with the greatest of ease. And 'the guards' were so abusive to the 'inmates' that Zimbardo had to call the experiment off.

His study was part of a general concern and interest at that time (especially in the wake of the Nazi holocaust, where millions had been exterminated by seemingly normal people: see *European eye*, p. 186) with the ways in which people would follow authority. (Milgram's study, raised above, was another prime example of research with this interest.) What he found was scary. Normal people will do terrible things to other people if the situation demands it (Zimbardo, 2007).

## Reference groups

How do we assess our own attitudes or behaviour? Frequently, we make use of a **reference group**, *a social group that serves as a point of reference in making evaluations or decisions.*

A young lad who imagines the response of his 'mates' to a girl he is going out with is using his friends as a reference group. Similarly, a banker who assesses her colleagues' reactions to a new loan policy is using her co-workers as a standard of reference. As these examples illustrate, reference groups can be primary or secondary. In each case, the motivation to conform to a group means that the attitudes of others can greatly affect us. We also use groups that we do not belong to for reference. People preparing for job interviews typically notice how those in the company they wish to join dress and act, adjusting their personal performances accordingly.

### Stouffer's classic research

Samuel A. Stouffer (1949) and his associates conducted a classic study of reference group dynamics during the

Second World War. In a survey, researchers asked soldiers to evaluate the chances of promotion for a competent soldier in their branch of the service. One might guess that soldiers serving in outfits with a high promotion rate would be optimistic about their future advancement. Yet survey results supported the opposite conclusion: soldiers in branches of the service with low promotion rates were actually more optimistic about their own chances to move ahead.

The key to this paradox lies in sorting out the groups against which the soldiers measured their progress. Those in branches with low promotion rates looked around them and saw people making no more headway than they were. That is, they had not been promoted, but neither had many others, so they did not feel unjustly deprived. Soldiers in service branches with high promotion rates, however, could easily think of people who had been promoted sooner or more often than they had. With such people in mind, even soldiers who had been promoted themselves were likely to feel short-changed. So these were the soldiers who voiced more negative attitudes in their evaluations.

Stouffer's research demonstrates that we do not make judgements about ourselves in isolation, nor do we compare ourselves with just anyone. Instead, we use specific social groups as standards in developing individual attitudes. Whatever our situation in *absolute* terms, then, we assess our well-being subjectively, *relative* to some specific reference group (Merton, 1968).

## Group size: form over content

If you are the first person to arrive at a party, you can observe some fascinating group dynamics. Until about six people enter the room, everyone generally shares a single conversation. But as more people arrive, the group divides into two or more smaller clusters. It is apparent that size plays a crucial role in how group members interact. Numbers matter.

To understand why, consider the formal (and here, mathematical) connection between the number of people in a social group and the number of relationships among them. As Figure 6.2 shows, two people form a single relationship (a dyad); adding a third person generates three relationships (a triad); adding a fourth person yields six. Increasing the number of people one at a time, then, boosts the number of relationships much more rapidly, since every new individual can interact with everyone already there. Thus, five people produce ten

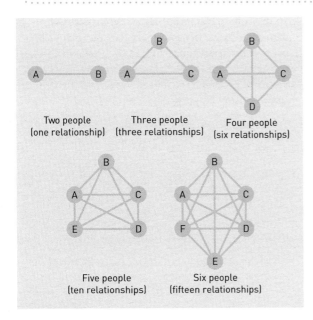

**Figure 6.2**    Group size and relationships

relationships and, by the time six people join one conversation, 15 'channels' connect them. This leaves too many people unable to speak, which is why the group usually divides at this point.

## The dyad

The German sociologist Georg Simmel (1858–1918), profiled in the *Thinkers and theory* box, built a sociology of forms in which he explored social dynamics in the smallest social groups. He used the term **dyad** to designate *a social group with two members*. Throughout the world, most love affairs, marriages and the closest friendships are dyadic.

What makes the dyad a special relationship? First, explained Simmel, social interaction in a dyad is typically more intense than in larger groups since, in a one-to-one relationship, neither member shares the other's attention with anyone else. Thus dyads have the potential to be the most meaningful social bonds we ever experience.

Second, Simmel explains, like a stool with only two legs, dyads have a characteristic instability. Both members of a dyad must actively sustain the relationship; if either one withdraws, the group collapses. Because of the importance of marriage to society, the marital dyad is supported with legal, economic and often religious ties. By contrast, a large group such as a charity run by volunteers is

inherently much more stable, as it can survive the loss of many members.

Marriage in our society is dyadic; ideally, we expect powerful emotional ties to unite husbands and wives. As we shall see in Chapter 18, however, marriage in other societies may involve more than two people. In that case, the household is usually more stable, though many of the marital relationships are weaker (Simmel, 1950; orig. 1902).

## The triad

Simmel also probed the **triad**, *a social group with three members*. A triad encompasses three relationships, each uniting two of the three people. A triad is more stable than a dyad because, should the relationship between any two members become strained, the third can act as a mediator to restore the group's vitality. This process of group dynamics helps explain why members of a dyad (say, a married couple) sometimes seek out a third person (a counsellor) to air tensions between them.

Nonetheless, two of the three can form a coalition to press their views on the third, or two may intensify their relationship, leaving the other feeling like a 'third wheel'. For example, two members of a triad who develop a romantic interest in each other will understand the old saying 'Two's company, three's a crowd'.

As groups grow beyond three members, they become progressively more stable because the loss of even several members does not threaten the group's existence. At the same time, increases in group size typically reduce the intense personal interaction possible only in the smallest groups. Larger groups are thus based less on personal attachments and more on formal rules and regulations. Such formality helps a large group persist over time, though the group is not immune to change. After all, their numerous members give large groups more contact with the outside world, opening the door to new attitudes and behaviour.

Does a social group have an ideal size? The answer depends on the group's purpose. A dyad offers unsurpassed emotional intensity, while a group of several dozen members is more stable, capable of accomplishing larger, more complex tasks, and is better able to assimilate new members or ideas. People typically find more *personal pleasure* in smaller groups, while deriving greater *task satisfaction* from accomplishments in larger organisations (Slater, 1958).

## Social diversity

Social diversity affects group dynamics, especially the likelihood that members will interact with someone of another group. Peter Blau (Blau, 1977; Blau et al., 1982) points out four ways in which the composition of social groups affects intergroup association.

1 *Large groups turn inwards.* Extending Simmel's analysis of group size, Blau explains that the larger a group, the more likely its members are to maintain relationships exclusively among themselves. The smaller the group, by contrast, the more members will reach beyond their immediate social circle.

   To illustrate, consider the efforts of many universities to include a wider range of students from overseas. Increasing the number of international students may add important dimensions to a campus, but, as their numbers rise, these students are eventually able to maintain their own distinctive social group. Thus intentional efforts to promote social diversity may well have the unintended effect of promoting separatism.

2 *Heterogeneous groups turn outwards.* The more internally heterogeneous a group is, the more likely its members are to interact with members of other groups. We would expect, for example, that campus groups that recruit members of both sexes and people of various ethnic and geographic backgrounds would promote more intergroup contact than those that choose members of only one social type.

3 *Social parity promotes contact.* An environment in which all groups have roughly equal standing

# Georg Simmel: a sociology of forms

When students encounter sociology, they invariably hear of the three giants – Marx, Durkheim, Weber – who have already been introduced several times in this book. They may hear of a fourth 'founding theorist', Georg Simmel (1858–1918), but rarely will they ever consider him in any detail. Yet his influence has been very profound.

Simmel adopted a distinctive and wide-ranging approach to sociology, studying many things from money and gender to cities and 'strangers'. He viewed society as interaction, and believed the task of the sociologist was to study the interactive webs into which people entered. He was keen to depict the ways in which changing numbers and scales of interactions brought about profoundly different relationships. In the text, you see how he contrasted simple dyads with triads and the difference this makes.

But he also looked at how social relations changed as cities emerged and relationships became more and more impersonal. He provided a sociological portrait of people's changing consciousness under **modernity**, and especially cities. He saw there was a downside to this: people kept their distance from each other. But there was also an upside: people became more tolerant and even sophisticated (see Chapter 24).

Simmel invented a style of sociology known as **formal sociology**: a sociology which studies the underlying forms of interaction in society. To do this, he distinguished between *content* and *form*. Social life is about content in so far as it studies such things as marriage, war, education and drug-taking. But for sociology to be systematic it needed more than studies of little areas of social life and their contents: instead it also needed to piece together the underlying social processes that they have in common.

Georg Simmel (1858–1918)

Thus, for instance, one common process found in social life is conflict: you can look at marriages, wars, education and drug taking and you will usually find elements of social interaction involving conflicts. Sociologists needed to study not just contents, then, but also forms.

A brilliant essayist, Simmel left his mark on much contemporary sociology which looks at forms of interaction.

For a short guide to Simmel's work, see David Frisby, *Georg Simmel* (London: Routledge, 2nd edn, 2002).

encourages people of all social backgrounds to mingle and form social ties. Thus, whether groups insulate their members or not depends on whether the groups themselves form a social hierarchy.

4  *Physical boundaries foster social boundaries.* Blau contends that physical space affects the chances of contacts among groups. To the extent that a social group is physically segregated from others (by having its own accommodation or dining area, for example), its members are less apt to engage other people.

## Organisations

Throughout human history, most people lived in small groups of family members and neighbours; this pattern was still widespread in Europe and the United States a century ago. Today, families and neighbourhoods persist, of course, but our lives revolve far more around **formal organisations**, *large, secondary groups that are organised to achieve their goals efficiently.*

Formal organisations, such as corporations and government agencies, differ significantly from families and neighbourhoods: their greater size renders social relationships less personal and fosters a planned, formal atmosphere. In other words, formal organisations operate to accomplish complex jobs rather than to meet personal needs.

When you think about it, organising a continent like Europe, with some 500 million members, is a remarkable feat. Countless tasks are involved, from collecting taxes and delivering the mail to the production and distribution of consumer goods. To meet most of these tasks, we rely on large, formal organisations. From national governments to private corporations, millions of people are employed in them. Such vast organisations develop lives and cultures of their own, so that as members come and go, the statuses they fill and the roles they perform remain unchanged over the years. Consider the following figures, which give some indication of the numbers of major organisations that now *exist across the world*: that is, are global. (Even this excludes hundreds of others, such as global religious organisations and global social movements.) There are:

- 77,200 major transnational corporations/companies (TNCs) such as Shell, Coca-Cola, Nestlé and Microsoft
- 10,000 single-country non-governmental organisations (NGOs) such as Médecins sans

Frontières (France) and Population Concern (UK) which have significant international activities
- 246 intergovernmental organisations (IGOs) such as the United Nations, NATO and the European Union
- 7,300 international non-governmental organisations (INGOSs), such as Amnesty International and the International Red Cross (Baylis and Smith: 2008: 332).

## Types of formal organisation

There are a number of classifications of organisations. A classic one was presented by Amitai Etzioni (1975), who identified three types, distinguished by why people participate: utilitarian organisations, normative organisations and coercive organisations.

Just about everyone who works for income is a member of a *utilitarian organisation*, which provides material rewards for its members. Large business enterprises, for example, generate profits for their owners and income in the form of salaries and wages for their employees. Joining utilitarian organisations is usually a matter of individual choice, though most people must join one or another utilitarian organisation to make a living.

People join *normative organisations* not for income but to pursue goals they consider morally worthwhile. Sometimes called *voluntary associations*, these include community service groups such as the Boy Scouts and Girl Guides (the Boy Scouts, with some 360,000 members in the UK aged between 6 and 25, celebrated its centenary in 2007; the Guide Movement had 477,000), political parties, religious organisations, and numerous other confederations concerned with specific social issues (such as Greenpeace and Liberty). In 2005, nearly half of adults aged 16 and over in England participated in some form of volunteering activity, and over two-thirds participated in an informal voluntary activity (*Social Trends*, 2007: 180). About 10 per cent of adults in Britain belonged to an environmental organisation or charity – the National Trust and the Royal Society for the Protection of Birds are the largest; Greenpeace comes a respectable third with 380,000 members.

In Etzioni's typology, *coercive organisations* are distinguished by involuntary membership. That is, people are forced to join the organisation as a form of punishment (prisons) or treatment (psychiatric hospitals). Coercive organisations have extraordinary physical features, such as locked doors and barred windows, and are supervised by security personnel (Goffman, 1961). These are settings that segregate people as 'inmates' or 'patients' for a period of time and sometimes radically alter their attitudes and behaviour. *Total institutions* transform a human being's overall sense of self.

From differing vantage points, any particular organisation may fall into all these categories. A psychiatric hospital, for example, serves as a coercive organisation for a patient, a utilitarian organisation for a psychiatrist and a normative organisation for a part-time hospital volunteer.

# The nature of bureaucracy

Formal organisations date back thousands of years. Elites who governed early empires relied on government officials to extend their power over millions of people and vast geographical regions. Chinese civilisation provides many examples of large formal organisations, allowing rulers to collect taxes, undertake military campaigns and construct monumental structures such as the Great Wall of China. In many countries a system known as 'oriental despotism' created huge administrative systems to build major public structures – such as the pyramids of Egypt.

The power of these early organisations was limited, however, not because elites lacked grandiose ambition, but by the traditional character of pre-industrial societies. Typically, cultural patterns placed greater importance on preserving the past or carrying out 'God's will' than on organisational efficiency. Only in the last few centuries did there emerge what Max Weber called a 'rational world-view', as described in Chapter 4. In the wake of the Industrial Revolution, the organisational structure called *bureaucracy* became commonplace in Europe and North America.

## Weber and bureaucracy

We have already seen how Max Weber introduced the idea of **bureaucracy** (see p. 41) – *an organisational model rationally designed to perform complex tasks efficiently*. In a bureaucratic business or government agency, officials deliberately enact and revise policy to make the organisation as efficient as possible. What specific traits promote organisational efficiency? Weber (1978; orig. 1921) identified six key elements of the ideal bureaucratic organisation.

1   *Specialisation.* Through most of human history, everyone pursued the basic goals of securing food and shelter. Bureaucracy, by contrast, assigns to individuals highly specialised duties.

2   *Hierarchy of offices.* Bureaucracies arrange personnel in a vertical hierarchy of offices. Each person is thus supervised by 'higher-ups' in the organisation while, in turn, supervising others in lower positions.

3   *Rules and regulations.* Cultural tradition holds scant sway in bureaucracy. Instead, operations are guided by rationally enacted rules and regulations. These rules control not only the organisation's own functioning but, as much as possible, its larger environment. Ideally, a bureaucracy seeks to operate in a completely predictable fashion.

4   *Technical competence.* A bureaucratic organisation expects officials to have the technical competence to carry out their official duties. Bureaucracies regularly monitor the performance of staff members. Such impersonal evaluation based on performance contrasts sharply with the custom, followed through most of human history, of favouring relatives – whatever their talents – over strangers.

5   *Impersonality.* In bureaucratic organisations, rules take precedence over personal whim. This impersonality encourages uniform treatment for each client as well as other workers. From this detached approach stems the notion of the 'faceless bureaucrat'.

6   *Formal, written communications.* An old adage states that the heart of bureaucracy is not people but paperwork. Rather than casual, verbal communication, bureaucracy relies on formal, written memos and reports. Over time, this correspondence accumulates into vast files. These files guide the subsequent operation of an organisation in roughly the same way that social background shapes the life of an individual.

These traits represent a clear contrast to the more personal character of small groups. Bureaucratic organisation promotes efficiency by carefully recruiting personnel and limiting the unpredictable effects of personal tastes and opinions. In smaller, informal groups, members allow one another considerable discretion in their behaviour; they respond to each other personally and regard everyone as more or less equal in rank. Table 6.2 summarises the differences between small social groups and large formal organisations.

| Table 6.2 | Small groups, formal organisations and networks: a comparison | | |
|---|---|---|---|
| | **Small groups** (e.g. family) | **Formal organisations** (e.g. school) | **Networks** (e.g. Facebook) |
| Activities | Members typically engage in many of the same activities | Members typically engage in distinct, highly specialised activities | Members again have common focus |
| Hierarchy | Often informal or non-existent | Clearly defined, corresponding to offices | Largely non-existent – web-like |
| Norms | Informal application of general norms | Clearly defined rules and regulations | Emergent norms over time (e.g. 'netiquette') |
| Criteria for membership | Variable, often based on personal affection or kinship | Technical competence to carry out assigned tasks | Self-selecting |
| Relationships | Variable, typically primary | Typically secondary, with selective primary ties | Fragmented, focused |
| Communications | Typically casual and face-to-face | Typically formal and in writing | Digitalised |
| Focus | Person orientated | Task orientated | Communications oriented |

## The informal side of bureaucracy

Weber's ideal bureaucracy deliberately regulates every activity. In actual organisations, however, human beings have the creativity (or the stubbornness) to resist conforming to bureaucratic blueprints. Sometimes informality helps to meet a legitimate need overlooked by formal regulations. In other situations, informality may amount to simply cutting corners in one's job (Scott, 1981).

In principle, power resides in offices, not with the people who occupy them. Nonetheless, the personalities of officials greatly affect patterns of leadership. For example, studies of corporations document that the qualities and quirks of individuals – including personal charisma and interpersonal skills – have a tremendous impact on organisational outcomes.

Authoritarian, democratic and *laissez-faire* types of leadership also reflect individual personality as much as any organisational plan. Then, too, in the 'real world' of organisations, leaders and their cronies sometimes seek to benefit personally through the abuse of organisational power. And perhaps even more commonly, leaders take credit for the efforts of their subordinates. Many secretaries, for example, have far more authority and responsibility than their official job titles and salaries suggest.

Communication offers another example of how informality creeps into large organisations. Formally, memos and other written communications disseminate information through the hierarchy. Typically, however, individuals cultivate informal networks or 'grapevines' that spread information much faster, if not always accurately. Grapevines are particularly important to subordinates because high officials often attempt to conceal important information from them.

Throughout the hierarchy, employees modify or ignore rigid bureaucratic structures for a host of reasons. A classic study of the Western Electric factory in Chicago revealed that few employees reported fellow workers who violated rules, as the company required (Roethlisberger and Dickson, 1939). On the contrary, workers took action against those who *did* blow the whistle on their colleagues, shunning them as 'squealers'. Although the company formally set productivity standards, workers informally created their own definition of a fair day's work, criticising those who exceeded it as 'rate-busters' and those who fell short as 'chisellers'.

Such informal social structures suggest that people act to personalise rigidly defined social situations. This leads us to take a closer look at some of the problems of bureaucracy.

EUROPEAN EYE

# Bureaucracy's darkest hour: killing 11 million people in the Nazi genocide

One of the most significant events of twentieth-century history was Hitler's Final Solution: the mass extermination of over 11 million people – 6 million Jews, often called 'The Holocaust', along with millions of others (gypsies, gays, 'impure races') – throughout the Second World War. There have been many other genocides in history. The book *Century of Genocide* (Totten et al., 1997) looks at eyewitness accounts of large numbers of people slaughtered during the twentieth century in Armenia, Bangladesh, Burundi, Cambodia, East Timor, Indonesia, Rwanda, south-west Africa and the Ukraine. Some have involved larger numbers of people – Rummel (1996) suggests that over 60 million people were killed in the Soviet Gulag state. But the Holocaust must be seen as unique because it involved the systematic, huge-scale extermination of large numbers of people through bureaucratic means in concentration camps such as Auschwitz in a mechanical way. People were 'rounded up'; trains took them to the death camps; there they were stripped, numbered, herded and led, finally, to the gas chambers or other execution.

Zygmunt Bauman, in his powerful sociological study *Modernity and the Holocaust* (1989), shows that 'we live in a type of society that made the Holocaust possible' (p. 88). For him, the modern world facilitated the mass exterminations.

The numbers slaughtered in the Holocaust are hard to calculate, but figures of at least 11 million deaths are common. These deaths reveal the inhumanity of people to people, and the power of social organisation and social groups. It is also a major test case for those who believe in human progress. There are approximately 250 Holocaust museums and centres around the world where you can learn more

*Source:* © World History Archive/Alamy.

Drawing from Max Weber's analysis of bureaucracy and Durkheim's analysis of the division of labour, he suggests that these very characteristic features of modern society made the Holocaust possible. People could exterminate large numbers of others simply because they were distant links in a work chain, following the abstract rules that most jobs now dictate. There was an abrogation of personal responsibility, fostered by bureaucracy that made it all possible then – and indeed possible again now.

People become dehumanised, and moral standards become irrelevant to the success of the technical operation.

When society seemed to be at its most advanced, and most civilised, the dark atrocities of mass extermination became a routine, bureaucratic commonplace. The challenge for sociology is to see this extreme horror – even 'evil' – as part of the routine workings of modern societies. The twentieth century was, in fact, a century of genocides.

*See:* Bauman (1989); Rummel (1996); Totten et al. (1997); Mann (2005) and Goldhagen (2009).

## Problems of bureaucracy

Despite our reliance on bureaucracy to manage countless dimensions of everyday life, many members of our society are ambivalent about this organisational form. The following sections review several of the problems associated with bureaucracy, ranging from its tendency to dehumanise and alienate individuals to the threats it poses to personal privacy and political democracy.

### 1 Bureaucratic alienation

Max Weber saw that bureaucracy could be a model of productivity. Nonetheless, he was keenly aware of bureaucracy's potential to *dehumanise* those it purports to serve. That is, the same impersonality that fosters efficiency simultaneously denies officials and clients the ability to respond to each other's unique, personal needs. On the contrary, officials must treat each client impersonally as a standard 'case'.

The impersonal bureaucratic environment, then, gives rise to *alienation*. All too often, Weber contended, formal organisations reduce the human being to 'a small cog in a ceaselessly moving mechanism' (1978: 988; orig. 1921). The trend towards more and more formal organisation, therefore, left him deeply pessimistic about the future of humankind. Although formal organisations are designed to benefit humanity, he feared that humanity might well end up serving formal organisations.

### 2 Bureaucratic inefficiency and ritualism

Then there is the familiar problem of inefficiency, the failure of a bureaucratic organisation to carry out the work it was created to perform. Perhaps the greatest challenge to a large, formal organisation is responding to special needs or circumstances. Anyone who has ever tried to replace a lost driving licence, return defective merchandise to a discount store or change an address on a magazine subscription knows that bureaucracies can sometimes be maddeningly unresponsive.

The problem of inefficiency is captured in the concept of *red tape* (a phrase derived from the red tape used by eighteenth-century English administrators to wrap official parcels and records). Red tape refers to a tedious preoccupation with organisational routines and procedures. Sociologist Robert Merton (1968) points out that red tape amounts to a new twist on the already familiar concept of group conformity. He coined the term **bureaucratic ritualism** to designate *a preoccupation with rules and regulations to the point of thwarting an organisation's goals*. Ritualism impedes individual and organisational performance as it stifles creativity and imagination. In part, ritualism emerges because organisations, which pay modest, fixed salaries, give officials little or no financial stake in performing efficiently. Then, too, bureaucratic ritualism stands as another expression of the alienation that Weber feared would arise from bureaucratic rigidity (Whyte, 1957; Merton, 1968).

### 3 Bureaucratic inertia

If bureaucrats sometimes have little motivation to be efficient, they certainly have every reason to protect their jobs. Thus, officials typically strive to perpetuate their organisation even when its purpose has been fulfilled. As Weber put it, 'once fully established, bureaucracy is among the social structures which are hardest to destroy' (1978: 987; orig. 1921).

**Bureaucratic inertia** refers to *the tendency of bureaucratic organisations to perpetuate themselves*. Formal organisations, in other words, tend to take on a life of their own beyond their formal objectives. Occasionally, a formal organisation that meets its goals will simply disband; more commonly, an organisation stays in business by redefining its goals so that it can continue to provide a livelihood for its members.

For example, consider the history of the US National Association for Infantile Paralysis, the sponsor of a fundraising campaign known as the March of Dimes (Sills, 1969). This organisation came into being as part of the drive to find a cure for polio. The goal was accomplished in the early 1950s when Dr Jonas Salk developed the polio vaccine. Subsequently, however, the March of Dimes did not close down; rather, it redirected its efforts towards other medical problems, such as birth defects, and continues to this day.

### 4 Bureaucratic abuse of power: oligarchy

Early in the twentieth century, Robert Michels (1876–1936) pointed out the link between bureaucracy and political **oligarchy**, *the rule of the many by the few* (1949; orig. 1911). According to what Michels called 'the iron law of oligarchy', the pyramid-like structure of bureaucracy places a few leaders in charge of vast and powerful government organisations.

Max Weber credited bureaucracy's strict hierarchy of responsibility with increasing organisational efficiency. By applying Weber's thesis to the organisation of government, Michels reveals that this hierarchical structure concentrates power and thus endangers democracy. While the public expects organisational officials to subordinate personal interests to organisational goals, people who occupy powerful positions can – and often do – use their access to information and the media, plus numerous other advantages, to promote their personal interests. Furthermore, bureaucracy also insulates officials from public accountability, whether in the form of a corporate president who is 'unavailable for comment' to the local press or a national president seeking to control information by claiming 'executive privilege'. Oligarchy, then, thrives in the hierarchical structure of bureaucracy and undermines people's control over their elected leaders (Tolson, 1995).

## The 'total institution' as a specific form of organisation

A specific form of organisation involves being confined – often against a person's will – in prisons, concentration camps or mental hospitals. But parallels can also be drawn to life in (many) army camps, boarding schools, old people's homes, homes for the disabled, etc. These are specific forms of bureaucracies in that they are **total institutions**, *settings in which people are isolated from the rest of society and manipulated by an administrative staff.*

Erving Goffman (1961), whose work we will look at in more detail in the next chapter, observed life in a mental hospital in the early 1960s. He saw broad similarities with life in the mental hospital and other kinds of organisation. From his research, he suggested that total institutions have a number of key characteristics. First, staff members supervise all spheres of daily life, including where residents ('inmates') eat, sleep and work. Second, a rigid system provides inmates with standardised food, sleeping quarters and activities. Third, formal rules and daily schedules dictate when, where and how inmates perform virtually every part of their daily routines. Life regulated, lived in common, creates a major divide between inmate and staff.

Most of all, inmates may well experience what Goffman calls a 'mortification of the self'. Total institutions impose such regimentation often with the goal of a radical resocialisation, altering an inmate's sense of self through deliberate manipulation of the environment. The power of a total institution to resocialise is also enhanced by its forcible segregation of inmates from the 'outside' by means of physical barriers such as walls and fences topped with barbed wire and guard towers, barred windows and locked doors. Cut off in this way, the inmate's entire world can be manipulated by the administrative staff to produce lasting change – or at least immediate

compliance – in the inmate. Goffman's work can be read in tandem with the work of Zimbardo, described above.

## Parkinson's Law and the Peter Principle

Finally, and on a lighter note, we acknowledge two additional insights concerning the limitations of bureaucratic organisations. The concerns of C. Northcote Parkinson and Laurence J. Peter are familiar to anyone who has ever been a part of a formal organisation.

Parkinson (1957) summed up his understanding of bureaucratic inefficiency with the assertion: *Work expands to fill the time available for its completion.* There is enough truth underlying this tongue-in-cheek assertion that it is known today as Parkinson's Law. To illustrate, assume that a bureaucrat working at the Driver and Vehicle Licensing Centre processes 50 driving licence applications in an average day. If one day this worker had only 25 applications to examine, how much time would the task require? The logical answer is half a day. But Parkinson's Law suggests that if a full day is available to complete the work, a full day is how long it will take.

Because organisational employees have little personal involvement in their jobs, few are likely to seek extra work to fill their spare time. Bureaucrats do strive to *appear* busy, however, and their apparent activity often prompts organisations to take on more employees. The added time and expense required to hire, train, supervise and evaluate a larger staff make everyone busier still, setting in motion a vicious cycle that results in *bureaucratic bloat*. Ironically, the larger organisation may accomplish no more real work than it did before.

In the same light-hearted spirit as Parkinson, Laurence J. Peter (Peter and Hull, 1969) devised the Peter Principle: *Bureaucrats rise to their level of incompetence.* The logic here is simple: employees competent at one level of the organisational hierarchy are likely to earn promotion to higher positions. Eventually, however, they will reach a position where they are in over their heads; there, they perform poorly and thus are no longer eligible for promotion.

Reaching their level of incompetence dooms officials to a future of inefficiency. Adding to the problem, after years in the office they have almost certainly learned how to avoid demotion by hiding behind rules and regulations and taking credit for work actually performed by their more competent subordinates.

**A 'total institution'?**
Children with shaved heads and yellow uniforms sit in rows in a classroom of an orphanage for juvenile delinquents in Bucharest, Romania

*Source*: © Bernard Bisson/Sygma/Corbis.

# Social science and the problem of 'evil'

One of the most persistent questions asked by all societies concerns the nature of good and evil. Usually this takes us into the realm of religion – and, as we shall see in Chapter 17, one of the key functions of religion is indeed to define the good life and mark out the boundaries of the bad. But in the twenty-first-century world, social scientists also have contributions to make to this debate.

They can *first* help to show the enormous relativity of what is considered 'good and bad', 'saintly and evil' by different societies at different times, and even different groups in the same societies. 'Evil terrorists' for some countries are the saviours and heroes of others. *Second*, social scientists can document the widespread existence of seemingly bad acts: the My Lai massacre in Vietnam, the genocide in Rwanda, the bombing of the New York Twin Towers on 9/11, and a host of day-to-day nasty things that people do to each other. *Third*, they can publicly discuss the

nature of the origins of evil – a debate which is often raised in everyday discussions in the media, in pubs, at meetings of all kinds around the world. Can social science help us understand 'evil'?

Public sociology takes the works of social scientists considering these issues into public life. For example, the works of Zygmunt Bauman (see *European eye*, p. 186) and the social psychologist Philip Zimbardo (see p. 179) are two relevant observers. Bauman shocks us by telling us that the horrendous horrors of something like the Holocaust, where millions were exterminated in the gas chambers by ordinary people (surely an evil?), were really fostered by the routine conditions of modern technology and bureaucracy. Modern societies can dehumanise and impersonalise personal relations in such terrible ways that ordinary, everyday folk can routinely slaughter their fellow citizens. Mass murder becomes banal. Good people become bad people.

And this is what Zimbardo has shown us in the more controlled situation of a social psychological experiment. It shows us how ordinary folk – you and us – if put into difficult situations may well also abuse, damage and possibly even kill each other. Again, bad things can be easily done by good people. Here, dehumanisation and moral disengagement happen both in the social laboratory and in social life.

The sociological suggestion, then, is that we should not focus on people as evil, but rather we should look at the situations and contexts that facilitate bad acts. We could all do it. This insight might help us look at the world differently. Zimbardo, for example, became a witness for the trials around the abuses by the American Military Police at the Abu Ghraib Prison in Iraq in 2004.

Many will recall the photos of extreme abuse of Iraqi prisoners

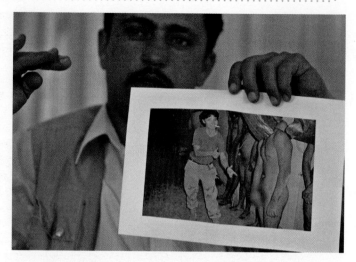

This image, obtained by The Associated Press, shows Pfc. Lynndie England holding a leash attached to a detainee in late 2003 at the Abu Ghraib prison in Baghdad, Iraq. The photo generated worldwide controversy at the start of the UK/US war with Iraq

*Source*: © Oleg Popov/Reuters/Corbis.

that became prominent in newspapers and on television (see the image above: but they are all online). The Iraqi prisoners were stripped, beaten, put on leashes and made to have (simulated) sex with their captives. Photos, surprisingly, were taken of these acts and eventually were leaked to the global media. It is clear these Muslims were thoroughly degraded and abused by the US Army. People around the world asked just how could such dreadful acts be perpetrated and photographed by seven normal and likeable young men and women. Was it simply a matter

of rogue soldiers and bad apples? Was it simply an isolated incident by bad people? Zimbardo thought not. It was neither an isolated incident, nor due to just a few freakish soldiers. He suggests it was built into the very command chain of the army. He saw his Stanford experiment being replicated in Abu Ghraib, and said so loud and clear to the US courts prosecuting the young soldiers. This is an important social role for social scientists to play.

*See*: Philip Zimbardo, *The Lucifer Effect: How Good People Turn Evil* (2007).

*See also*: Baumeister (2001); Lemert (1997).

# Weber revisited: the 'McDonaldisation' of society

Weber's discussion of organisation was written in the early part of the twentieth century. Some 80 years on, the North American sociologist George Ritzer suggested that the 'bureaucratisation of society' has proceeded further and deeper. He took the case of

McDonald's restaurants as his illustration, but drew much wider implications.

Consider for a moment the nature of McDonald's, introduced at the start of this chapter. Have you ever eaten in one? Chances are the answer is 'yes'. Indeed, everywhere in the world your authors have travelled, they have not been far from a McDonald's! And sometimes in the most surprising of places. While visiting Hong Kong, both of us visited the former

McDonald's is well known throughout the Western World, but it is also a global phenomenon. The restaurant chain had 1,135 outlets across mainland China by the end of 2009. In 2010, there were 130 McDonald's restaurants in South Africa. There is also now McDonald's Arabia

Source: © Iain Masterton/Alamy.

Portuguese colony of Macau – a little nub jutting from the Chinese coast. Few people here speak English, and life on the streets seems a world apart from the urban rhythms of London, Amsterdam or Los Angeles – where you would certainly expect to find a McDonald's. But strolling the old streets, we turn the corner and stand face to face with the famous McDonald's logo! But the most amazing thing is that the food – the burger, fries and drinks – looks, smells and tastes (almost) the same as it does thousands of miles away in Sydney!

As noted in the opening to this chapter, McDonald's has enjoyed enormous success. From a single store in the mid-1950s, McDonald's now operates over 33,000 restaurants throughout much of the world,

with 744 opening in 2006. There are more than 850 pairs of golden arches in Japan, for example, and the world's largest McDonald's opened for business in China's capital city of Beijing in April 1992, with some 700 seats, 29 cash registers and 40,000 customers on its first day! (In 2006, it took a $21.6 billion revenue.)

But while McDonald's may be everywhere and has become a symbol of the modern world, this is not Ritzer's point. For him, McDonaldisation suggests that the organisational principles that underlie McDonald's are steadily coming to dominate our entire society. Our culture is becoming 'McDonaldised' – a way of saying that we now model many aspects of life on the famous restaurant chain. Parents buy toys at worldwide chain stores such as Toys R Us; more vacations take the form of resort and tour packages; television presents news in the form of ten-second sound bites; sports become packaged into ever larger stadia and broadcasts; and religion is to be found in megachurches and cyberchurches. McDonaldisation has even had an impact on education: universities devise mass courses based on pre-packaged 'modules'; admissions officers size up students they have never met by glancing over their grades; lecturers assign ghost-written textbooks and evaluate students with tests mass-produced for them by publishing companies; and even sociology may start to become McDonaldised – as McSociology! (B. Smart, 1999). The list goes on and on.

## McDonaldisation: four principles

What do all these developments have in common? According to George Ritzer, the 'McDonaldisation of society' involves four basic organisational principles:

1  *Efficiency*. Ray Kroc, the marketing genius behind the expansion of McDonald's, set out with the goal of serving a hamburger, French fries and a milkshake to a customer in 50 seconds. Today, one of the company's most popular items is the Egg McMuffin, an entire breakfast in a single sandwich. In the restaurant, customers clear their own trays or, better still, drive away from the pickup window taking the packaging and whatever mess they make with them.

   Efficiency is now a value virtually without critics in our society. Almost everyone believes that anything that can be done quickly is, for that reason alone, good.

2  *Calculability*. The first McDonald's operating manual declared the weight of a regular raw hamburger to be 1.6 ounces, its size to be

3.875 inches across, and its fat content to be 19 per cent. A slice of cheese weighs exactly half an ounce. Fries are cut precisely nine-thirty-seconds of an inch thick.

Think about how many objects around the home, the workplace or the university campus are designed and mass-produced uniformly according to a calculated plan. Not just our environment but our life experiences – from travelling on motorways to sitting at home watching television – are now more deliberately planned than ever before.

3  *Uniformity and predictability.* An individual can walk into a McDonald's restaurant anywhere and receive the same sandwiches, drinks and desserts prepared in precisely the same way. Predictability, of course, is the result of a highly rational system that specifies every course of action and leaves nothing to chance.

4  *Control through automation.* The most unreliable element in the McDonald's system is human beings. People, after all, have good and bad days, sometimes let their minds wander, or simply decide to try something a different way. To eliminate, as much as possible, the unpredictable human element, McDonald's has automated its equipment to cook food at fixed temperatures for set lengths of time. Even the cash register at a McDonald's is little more than pictures of the items so as to minimise the responsibility of the human being taking the customer's order.

The scope of McDonaldisation is expanding throughout the world. Automatic banking machines are replacing banks, highly automated bakeries now produce bread with scarcely any human intervention, and chickens and eggs (or is it eggs and chickens?) emerge from automated hatcheries. In supermarkets, laser scanners are phasing out (less reliable) human checkout operators. Much shopping now occurs in large precincts, in which everything from temperature and humidity to the kinds of store and product are subject to continuous control and supervision (Ritzer, 1993; 2010). Recently the term 'Starbucksisation' has been introduced to update their idea.

## Can rationality be irrational?

No one would challenge the popularity or the efficiency of McDonald's and similar organisations (although there has been a lot of critical comment of late and its sales are falling in parts of the world). But there is another side to the story. Max Weber viewed the increasing rationalisation of the world with alarm, fearing that the expanding control of formal organisations would take away spontaneity and human creativity – crushing the human spirit. As he saw it, rational systems were efficient, but at the terrible cost of dehumanisation and disenchantment. Each of the four principles noted above depends on controlling human creativity, discretion and autonomy. George Ritzer contends that McDonald's food is not particularly good for people; nor is the company's extensive use of packaging good for the natural environment. Taking a broader perspective, Ritzer echoes Weber's concern, asserting that 'the ultimate irrationality of McDonaldization is that people could lose control over the system and it would come to control us' (1993: 145). In his book he therefore spends some time discussing ways in which people could resist the McDonaldisation process. This includes avoiding daily routines as much as possible, avoiding classes where tests are short answer and graded by a computer, and eating in local, non-standardised restaurants.

## Changing organisational forms

After the Second World War, most formal organisations in Europe were typically conventional bureaucracies, run from the top down according to a stern chain of command. Today, especially as businesses face growing global competition, rigid structures are breaking down. One important element of this trend is the increasing use of the *self-managed work team.* Members of these small groups have the skills necessary to carry out tasks with minimal supervision. By allowing employees to operate within autonomous groups, organisations enhance worker involvement in the job, generate a broader understanding of operations and raise employee morale. A few corporations (such as Procter & Gamble) have had autonomous work units since the 1960s. In recent years, many more are following suit.

Even though it is difficult to compare the performance of organisations with disparate goals and operations, research indicates that self-managed work teams do boost productivity while heading off some of the problems – including alienation – of the traditional bureaucratic model. In the business world, many companies have found that decentralising responsibility in this way also raises product quality and lowers rates of employee absenteeism and turnover.

# The audit culture

Management has been among the fasting-growing occupations over the past century. More and more work requires more and more administration and management. Frederick William Taylor (1856–1915) heralded the growth of what was called *scientific management* – where, it was argued, the 'best ways' of organising work would be practised: a systematic matching of pay, abilities, tasks and rules in the work process. This 'Taylorism' established the 'time and motion' studies of work life. (It was much criticised by the Human Relations School for its lack of concern with actual work process and human experience.)

*Total quality management* (TQM) takes up where Taylorism left off. It started in Japan, was introduced in the USA in the 1970s and quickly became a major movement – by the 1980s entering most government agencies and travelling to the United Kingdom where it was widely adopted. *Quality assurance* (QA) depends upon a full-scale rationalisation of the work process; aims and objectives spelled out with targets and ways of evaluating their success. Strengths, weaknesses, opportunities and threats should be examined.

Feedback from customers should be monitored regularly and with corrective actions following. To do all this, major departments of evaluation and monitoring – the inspectorates – should be established with carefully trained and skilled assessors. This new public management has come to organise education, health and policing in the late twentieth and early twenty-first centuries. Thus Ofsted was formed in 1992, QAA in 1996, and the Commission for Health Improvements and the Commission for Social Care Inspectorate in 2004. They have led to national Audit Commissions, Cycles of Inspections, and an elaborate new terminology: performance indicators, audits, benchmarks, methodologies, SWOTs, feedback forms, accreditation, baseline inspections, annual monitoring, best values, best practice. Such procedures are put in place to improve the performance of education, medicine and policing. TQM makes organisations work more efficiently and effectively.

Yet critics of TQM make five major observations. They argue that it is:

- *Bureaucratic*. All the problems that Max Weber raised about the dysfunctionality of bureaucracies, discussed in the text, come into play.

- *Demoralising*. Those who experience this constant monitoring feel that their workload has been taken over by matters that are not connected to their professional concerns. Teachers want to teach; nurses want to nurse; police want to police: nobody wants to administer. Dejection happens because people are not doing the work they wish to be doing.

- *Deskilling*. The experience of work now becomes rigidly ruled by 'assessments'. Practitioners in various areas complain that this robs them of their own creativity, originality and spontaneity. Lecturers, nurses and the police are required to follow rules.

- *Disciplining and controlling*. Increasingly, management gets people to write things down, making them conform to certain clear norms, and then gains access to all this self-commenting. It becomes what some have called a 'technology of government' – a way of regulating social life.

- *Costly*. Direct costs can be high but tell little of the costings in time and skill from the professionals who have to incorporate this as part of their workload (for example, teachers get no extra money but have to devote hundreds of hours to this extra work).

*See*: Strathern (2000); Travers (2007); Power (1997).

## Humanising bureaucracies

**Humanising bureaucracy** means *fostering a more democratic organisational atmosphere that recognises and encourages the contributions of everyone.* Research by Kanter (1989) and others suggests that 'humanising' bureaucracy produces both happier employees and healthier profits. Based on the discussion so far, we can identify three paths to a more humane organisational structure.

1 *Social inclusiveness.* The social composition of the organisation should, ideally, make no one feel 'out of place' because of gender, race or ethnicity.

The performance of all employees will improve to the extent that no one is subject to social exclusion.

2 *Sharing of responsibilities.* When organisations ease rigid organisational structures, they spread power and responsibility more widely. Managers cannot benefit from the ideas of employees who have no channels for expressing their opinions. Knowing that superiors are open to suggestions encourages all employees to think creatively, increasing organisational effectiveness.

3 *Expanding opportunities for advancement.* Expanding opportunity reduces the number of employees stuck in routine, dead-end jobs with little motivation to perform well. The organisation should give employees at all levels a chance to share ideas and try new approaches, defining everyone's job as the start of an upward career path.

Kanter's work takes a fresh look at the concept of bureaucracy and its application to business organisations. Rigid formality may have made sense in the past, when organisations hired unschooled workers primarily to perform physical labour. But today's educated workforce can contribute a wealth of ideas to bolster organisational efficiency – if the organisation encourages and rewards innovation.

There is broad support for the idea that loosening up rigid organisations improves performance. Moreover, companies that treat employees as a resource to be developed rather than as a group to be controlled stand out as more profitable. But some critics challenge Kanter's claim that social heterogeneity necessarily yields greater productivity. In controlled comparisons, they maintain, it is homogeneous work groups that typically produce more, while heterogeneous groups are better at generating a diversity of ideas and approaches. Optimal working groups, then, appear to be those that strike a balance: team members bring to the decision-making process a variety of backgrounds and perspectives, yet are similar enough in outlook and goals to coordinate their efforts effectively.

## The Japanese situation and the drift to postmodern organisations

We have described efforts to 'humanise' formal organisations. Interestingly, however, organisations in some countries have long been more personal than those in others. For instance, organisations in Japan, a nation that had remarkable economic success in the mid-twentieth century, developed within a culture of strong collective identity and solidarity. For much of the mid-twentieth century, Japanese companies were built on personal relationships, resembling primary groups, and reflected that society's more collective orientation. Most Japanese companies hired employees for life and played a broad role in their life – helping with mortgages, sponsoring social activities and planning social events for them. They would train employees in all phases of the work operations, and give them a much closer involvement with managers in decision making. They worked through a collective 'group' structure, unlike the more individual and competitive achievement found in the USA or the UK. They were also amazingly productive.

This has come to an end. When the Japanese economy faltered in the 1990s, employees were loathe to lay off their workers, whom they saw more as 'family'. Bit by bit, the system changed – and organisationally it is now more like the American one. Maybe a third or so of Japanese employees are now temporary, are paid lower wages and have less secure work conditions.

Stuart Clegg (1990) has taken this argument further, suggesting that the early Japanese firms approximated to what he calls the 'postmodern firm'. Such organisations were much more flexible and fluid than firms of the past. Strict demarcations were weakened, and they employed the 'just in time' (JIT) system of production. Here, goods are produced as required – there is no mass stocking of parts. And this in turn makes the system more adaptable and flexible. Postmodern organisations break with traditional models, adopting new, creative patterns of operation. In a sense they are usually hybrids of modern and postmodern modes of organising (see Table 6.3).

| Table 6.3 | Contrasting organisational forms: from modern to postmodern |
| --- | --- |
| **Modern organisations** | **Postmodern organisations** |
| More mechanical | More organic |
| Hierarchical | Network |
| Specialised | Unspecialised |
| More rigid | More flexible |

# Declining communities and rising networks: the rise of the network society

Groups and organisations have proved to be very useful concepts for sociologists to develop. But as relationships change – from primary groups to secondary groups, from secondary groups to formal organisations, from formal organisations to postmodern organisations – so many sociologists have claimed that these changes have been detrimental. Many argue that there has been a decline in traditional communities – the *Gemeinschaft* of Toennies that we discussed in Chapter 1 (see p. 19) – along with a growth in impersonal relations through organisations and the audit culture. There has been a marked decline in small face-to-face groups.

## Robert Putnam: bowling alone

This view has recently been put forward most forcefully by Robert Putnam. Surveying the lives of North Americans over the past 25 years, he notes that there has been a significant decline in social bonding within families, friends and community: a decline in church membership, a fall in membership of recreational and volunteer groups, and less engagement with team sports groups. This is what he means by **social capital** – an important sociological concept which captures *those connections among individuals over time which create social bonds.* These are our friendships and social networks, and being generally well integrated into these enhances our sense of well-being and belonging. For Putnam, societies depend on a kind of 'generalised reciprocity' where bonds link each other and there is a concern for each other's welfare. I may help someone today, and tomorrow someone may help me.

But Putnam argues (from a lot of data) that US society has shown a serious decline in social capital since the 1950s. Many people have become more and more disconnected from society, feeling less and less involved. Communities with less social capital generally have lower educational performance, more suicide, more crime, poorer health and a lesser sense of well-being (see also Chapters 8 and 21 on health and inequalities). This is an old story repeated by many sociologists for over a century. Many facts have

contributed to this, including urban sprawl, the increased number of women working and the rise of a new consumer generation. But, all in all, he claims that Americans have been 'pulled apart from one another and our communities' (Putnam, 2001: 180).

## New developments: personal communities and social networks

Others, however, are less sure. Human relationships are always changing as societies change, and what we are now starting to see are new forms of social bonds that might better be viewed as personal communities and social networks. Formally, a personal community may be seen as people's intimate and active ties with friends, neighbours and workmates as well as kin (Wellman, 1988), while social networks may be seen as webs of social ties that link people who identify with one another. Liz Spencer and Ray Pahl, in a study of friendships, see friends and friend-like ties as an important (and neglected) source of social glue. From intensive interviews with people, they have developed a set of ideas around friendships – their repertoires (the range of friendships people have); their modes (the way people make and maintain friendships over time); and their patterns of suffusion (the extent to which boundaries between friends and family become blurred). From this they have explored the idea of personal communities and they ways in which such groupings give a sense of solidarity and belonging to social life (Spencer and Pahl, 2006). In their book they spend some time looking at the ways in which these personal communities can be mapped; they get their interviewees to follow these maps. You may like to try their instructions (see the *Methods and research* box) and draw your own friendship map.

## Social networks

Think of a network as a 'fuzzy' group that brings people into contact without a group's sense of boundaries and belonging. If we consider a group as a 'circle of friends', then we might describe a network as a 'social web' expanding outwards, often reaching great distances and including larger numbers of people. The most basic pattern of a network – between only two people, such as two people who are merely standing in the same room – can be represented as in Figure 6.4. People are now increasingly bonding differently.

# Mapping your personal community, social network and frienships circle

Spencer and Pahl (2006) asked people to list those who were important to them now, and to arrange their names in order of importance on a map, placing them in an appropriate place in relation to the centre. Two contrasting personal communities (where P is the participant) are shown in Figure 6.3.

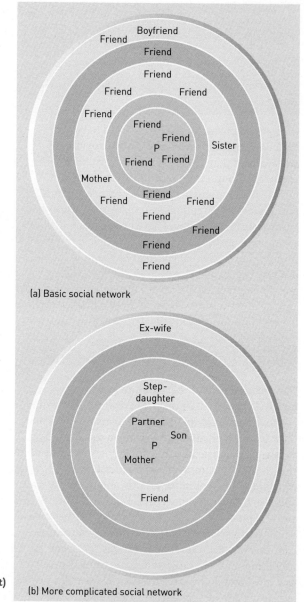

(a) Basic social network

(b) More complicated social network

| Figure 6.3 | Two contrasting personal communities (P = participant) |

*Source*: Spencer and Pahl (2006: 52).

This could be a very basic relationship between two people – maybe both standing in the same room

| Figure 6.4 | A basic social network |

Social networks go beyond ideas of groups, or even organisations. Groups and organisations usually presume some kind of boundary, often with face-to-face interactions going on within them. Networks, by contrast, envisage a field of connections and relations: a set of *nodes* (key points) and a set of *ties* (or links) that connect some or all of these nodes. The nodes could be people, or groups, or even nation-states. A more complex social network is represented in

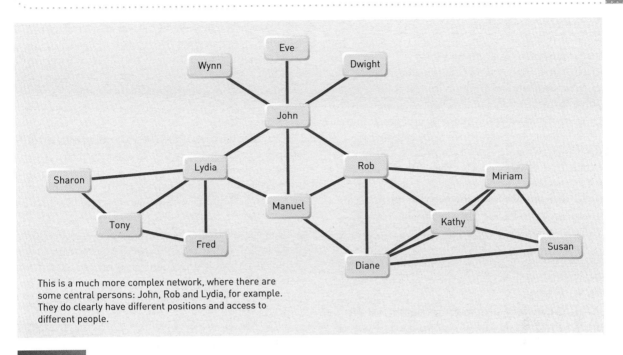

This is a much more complex network, where there are some central persons: John, Rob and Lydia, for example. They do clearly have different positions and access to different people.

**Figure 6.5** A more complex social network

Figure 6.5. Here there are some central people – John, Rob and Lydia, for example – but they have different positions and access to different people.

Social network analysis, then, looks at underlying patterns and links that shape such social networks. For example, we could look at the *number* of ties, the *diversity* of ties, the *frequency* and *intensities* of interactional ties, the *directions* of interactional ties, the *content* of the ties, and the *quality* of ties. We could build up maps of friendships which interconnect; see how bounded communities or families relate beyond themselves; or even locate patterns of people who have been part of the same network of sexual partners (an area of research that has been of value in studying AIDS: see Chapter 21).

Some such networks may then be seen as densely knit (most nodes are connected) and tightly bounded (most stay within the same subset of nodes). Or by contrast they may be seen as very thin and loose (Wellman, 1999). 'Contemporary Western communities rarely are tightly bounded, densely knit groups of broadly based ties. They usually are loosely bounded, sparsely knit, ramifying networks of specialised ties' (Wellman, 1999: 97). From this, we can now talk of network communities. Living in a specific geographical area or space no longer defines your community of personal interactions – instead it is now defined through phones, cars, the internet, public transport

systems and the like. These can connect you to a wide range of people. Living in a residential community may now mean that you are not really living in a specific, geographically bounded community but in an altogether wider network community. As you connect more and more through your network, so the older style of direct face-to-face communications ceases to have the same kind of meaning. And as a result of this, each of us may well come to live in our own network. We come to live with our own personal maps of the spaces we inhabit.

All this may signify important changes in patterns of contact and communication, which we discuss further in Chapters 8 and 22. Some network contacts are solid, traditional and regular, as among college friends who, years later, stay in touch (by personal contact, or mail and telephone). But, more commonly, a network includes people we *know of* – or who *know of us* – but with whom we interact infrequently, if at all. Social networks amount to 'clusters of weak ties' (Granovetter, 1973).

Network ties may be weak, but they serve as a significant resource. For example, many people rely on their networks to find jobs. Even the scientific genius Albert Einstein needed a hand in landing his first job. After a year of unsuccessful interviewing, he obtained employment only when the father of one of his fellow students put him in touch with an office manager who hired him. This use of networks to one's advantage suggests that, as the saying goes, *who you know* is often just as important as *what you know*.

Networks are based on people's colleges and universities, clubs, local communities, political parties and informal cliques. Some networks encompass people with considerably more wealth, power and prestige than others do, which is the essence of describing someone as 'well connected'. And some people have denser networks than others – that is, they are connected to more people, which is also a valuable social resource. Typically, the most extensive social networks are maintained by people who are young, well educated and living in urban areas.

Gender, too, shapes networks. Although the networks of men and women are typically the same size, women include more relatives in their networks, while those of men are filled out with more co-workers. Women's networks, therefore, may not carry quite the same clout as the 'old boy' networks do. Even so, research indicates that, as gender inequality lessens, this difference is diminishing over time.

# Technology and networks: mobile phones and network groups

Technologies have played a major role in the changing shape of networking. Just how have the telephone, email, mobile phones and SNS (social networking sites) shifted our networks and communication styles?

Take the mobile telephones as a key example. To appreciate networking, just consider that any one of the millions and millions of phones in the world can connect anybody, within seconds, to any other phone – in homes, businesses, automobiles, even in the middle of a football field. Such instant communication is beyond the imagination of those who lived in the ancient world. Of course, the telephone system depends on technological developments such as electricity, fibre optics and computers. But the system could not exist without the organisational capacity to keep track of every telephone call – noting which phone called which other phone, when and for how long – and presenting all this information to billions of telephone users in the form of regular bills. So it is connected to bureaucracies too. But it starts to enable a very different mode of building up relations.

Mobile phones make for even more complex networks and they are the fastest-spreading technology of all time. Within just a few years, many people have come to take them for granted. Mobile networks in 2007 covered 80 per cent of the world's population; double the level in 2000. There were 1 billion users by 2004, 2 billion by 2006, and in 2010 there were nearly 5 billion – approaching 70 per cent of the world's population. This is an extraordinary change in a decade and a half and many claim that it is reworking the way we live.

Consider the case of the UK. According to official statistics, in 2005, 82 per cent of children aged 12–15 had their own mobile phones (the most popular reason for having a phone was 'texting'); and some 85 per cent of adults used mobile technology regularly (*Social Trends*, 2007: 172–3). A survey conducted as early as 2006 suggested that in fact some 90 per cent of children had a mobile by the time they went to secondary school at 12, and it 'provides them with a social network, a sense of security and access to entertainment. But most importantly it provides them with a sense of belonging to their peer group' (*Mobile Life Youth Report*, 2006). 'Texting' was already a major activity: the average 11- to 17-year old received or made an average of 9.6 texts a day (in contrast, for adults the figure is 3.6). By 2010, mobiles (and texting) are firmly and ubiquitously embedded in the lives of the young (and most of the older), and are not likely to go away in their lifetimes unless a new technology replaces them (which, of course, probably will happen).

The impact of the mobile phone has been worldwide. Even in low-income and poorer countries, mobile phones have become widespread. Whereas landline telephones were costly and inaccessible, mobile phones are much cheaper. In 2010, some 40 per cent of Nigerians and 30 per cent of Bangladeshis had mobile phones, whilst India had the fourth largest uptake in the world – with some 650 million mobile phones in operation (around 60 per cent of the population – and many more than have a good sanitation!). (Sources: *Social Trends*; *GSM Statistics, 2010*; *indiatelecom*.)

Mobiles signify a shift in patterns of contact and communication. We can now have relationships on the phone anywhere, anytime. Of course, it depends a great deal whether you carry the phone around with you all the time, and whether it is switched on or off! But when it is both these things (on and with you), we shift to a new mode of contact probably unique in our history: that of *perpetual contact*. Slowly, new rules for conducting phone calls are emerging. Just as you have access to everyone on the phone, so they have access to you. This means that several things have happened in networking contacts. First, there has been a breakdown of the old split between home and street, etc. – people can now talk anywhere. Secondly, it is intrusive – it can interrupt other streams of life. Thus while going shopping, being in lectures, eating in a restaurant, having sex, or simply talking with someone else, the mobile can ring or you can ring it and the network of interaction abruptly shifts. Thirdly, it is fast: people are on tap and online for any time. All this and more has meant that new rules are having to be evolved as to how we can manage this perpetual contact (Katz and Aakhus, 2002). More than this: sociologists are now arguing that *mobile communication is reshaping social cohesion.* Keeping phones with us permanently by our side keeps us in touch with significant others all the time. Families may even be strengthened as children are always in touch with parents (Ling, 2008).

## Social networking: Facebook and our internet friends

Along with mobile phones, another new technology to shift group organisation and personal life significantly has been the rise of the social networks group (SNG). Social networking websites started as early as 1985, bringing together communities to interact with each other and share information through chat rooms. Mail bulletin boards helped to stretch out to various kinds of web groups (and friendship sites such as Friends Reunited). Friends support networks started out with My Space in 2003, but this was soon overtaken by Facebook, which had over 500 million active users in July 2010. Facebook, Bebo and Twitter are widely used worldwide; but there are many different sites for different countries: Orkut and Hi5 in South America and Central America, and Friendster, Mixi, Multiply, Orkut, Wretch, Renren and Cyworld in Asia.

In the UK, social networking doubled between 2007 and 2009. The proportion of users rose for all age groups, but the largest rises were among those aged 25 to 34 (38 percentage points) and those aged 35 to 44 (28 percentage points). Women were more likely than men to have set up a social networking site profile. Users of social networking sites reported that they used them to talk to friends and family whom they see a lot (78 per cent), those they rarely see (75 per cent), and to look for old friends and people they have lost contact with (47 per cent) (*Social Trends*, 2010). On a global scale, Facebook claims that 50 per cent of active users log on to the site each day. This would mean at least 175 million users every 24 hours. Twitter also claims that it now has 75 million user accounts, but only around 15 million are active users on a regular basis. In the first quarter of 2010, 4 billion tweets per quarter were posted.

Social network groups have certainly changed the meaning of personal relationships and, indeed, the meaning of communities (for they are often called online *communities*). Unlike traditional communities, they do not involve direct face-to-face communication but are mediated through technology. We will see later the importance of what are increasingly called *mediated lives.* Unlike traditional communities, they are not local and bound to a place but usually global and break down any firm sense of place. And unlike

Mobile phones can be used anywhere – even in the most surprising places

*Source:* © Al Rod/Corbis.

# Manuel Castells: the network society and the Information Age

Manuel Castells is Emeritus Professor of Sociology at the University of California, Berkeley. Born in Spain in 1942, he studied law and economics at the University of Barcelona from 1958 to 1962. He was a student activist against Franco's dictatorship and had to escape to Paris, where he eventually gained his PhD in Sociology from the University of Paris in 1967. His first book, *La Question Urbaine*, was translated into ten languages and became a classic around the world, and he became known as one of the intellectual founders of the 'New Urban Sociology'.

Castell's trilogy, *The Information Age*, is considered to be one of the most sustained and readable accounts of the rise of the information society and the new networks that come with it. He analyses the ways in which economic and social transformations in capitalism connect to the information technology revolution, and have brought about a new world social order in the twenty-first century.

**Manuel Castells (1942–)**

*Source*: Permission from Manuel Castells.

His three books look at the rise of new communications, the creation of new identities, and the shifting political contours of the world in the twenty-first century – especially the role of social movements. Long and detailed as the books are, Castells tries to make himself intelligible (he does not use incomprehensible jargon) and provides much data, evidence and illustration for his arguments (it is not a work of abstract theory). The volumes have come to be regarded as one of the major statements of changing times and what sociology in the twenty-first century should have to deal with. Unlike Marx's view of the mode of production, for Castells it is the new telecommunications – the informational mode of

development – that is reordering our very sense of time and space. It creates a capitalist network economy.

Crucial to Castell's work is the idea of networks and flows. Networks provide a series of hubs and points – people, cities, businesses, states – connected by flows of different sorts – information, money, people. With these 'flows' time changes: there is a speeding up of time but also a lack of standard sequencing. Time becomes a 'perpetual present' – the past comes back to us in sound bites, and the future arrives almost before we've experienced it. In this new world, our sense of space and time becomes dramatically reordered: the local now goes global; the past and the future are the present. We can be everywhere and nowhere at the same time – sitting at our computers. All this has great importance for the way we think about ourselves (our identities), our political actions (through social movements), and our ways of living (through work and families). International forms of money, international forms of crime, environmental issues – all change under this new order and Castells discusses each. The Information Age touches all globally.

A very useful guide to all this can be found in David Bell's *Cyberculture Theorists* (2007).

most traditional communities, they are unrestricted in numbers – friendships and communities usually have some kind of restricted size, but social network groups can be very large (often Facebook leads to thousands of new friends) and seemingly unbounded. As a result of these differences, many critics claim these social network sites are not communities at all, but can instead lead to 'impoverished communication'.

In contrast, defenders claim that social networks bring personalised 'methodologically individuated communities'. In many ways, they take on the characteristics of the subcultures we described in Chapter 5 (see p. 155). They generate their own languages, values, rules and norms; they build their own software and programs if needed; they provide shared resources – emotional and informational. They give members a sense of self and esteem – indeed, they become major mechanisms for creating common, shared identities and social bonds. Wellman refers to this as a 'networked individualism' in which each person sits at the centre of their own personal community. From this community they can engage with others, including involvement in local or even global politics. Defenders of SNGs would see them as simply the evolution of another form of group and social solidarity – another ingenious way of bringing people together in a large and complex world (Baym, 2010).

## An uncontrolled matrix?

The new information technology has generated a global network of unprecedented size in the form of the internet, mobile phones and networking groups. We now dwell in this. Its origins seem right out of the 1960s Cold War film *Dr Strangelove*: its character demonstrated in the 1990s trilogy *The Matrix*. Five decades ago, US government officials and scientists were trying to imagine how to run the country after an atomic attack, which, they assumed, would instantaneously eliminate telephones and television. The brilliant solution was to devise a communication system with no central headquarters, no one in charge and no main power switch – in short, an electronic web that would link the country in one vast network. But by 1999, when the first part of *The Matrix* was released, this vast network has indeed taken over. The machines now run everything and use humans merely as an energy source. An illusory simulated reality constructs the world of 1999 and all people can do is try to resist it, or 'unplug' it.

## Looking ahead: the network society

Spanish sociologist Manuel Castells (1996) uses the term 'network society' to capture the new kind of society we are moving into – one based on computers and information technologies, and characterised by new networks of relating (see *Thinkers and theory* above).

In the twenty-first century, we can clearly see how older patterns of group life and communication are being partially replaced by 'networking'. This brings with it a potential for self-expansion and a new logic of thinking (think of how you read a book and how you search the Web to capture the different logics at work here). It also, of course, means that life gets lived at a faster pace and in a more fragmented way. Real changes in our ways of relating to each other may be taking place. For Castells the new information technology brings five features:

1 Information as the raw material to act on: our access to information and our use of it starts to change.
2 The pervasiveness of information technologies: scarcely an item in daily use is not touched by it – from hand-held 'palm top' computing to automobile satellite technology mapping. Every institution – from medical recording to educational processes – requires the new technologies.
3 The network logic of any system using them: no longer simply linear and straightforward.
4 Flexibility: open to rapid changes and adjustments.
5 Convergence of technologies: the ways in which computers etc. can now connect to photo, sound, time and personal technologies. Complete interconnected systems may soon scan whole bodies, settings and areas (Castells, Vol. 1, 1996: 21).

Power is no longer concentrated in institutions like the state: it now diffuses through global networks. We shall return to this regularly and in more detail in later chapters (see Chapters 8, 15 and 23 especially). All the themes touched upon in this book must now be placed alongside this new 'culture of virtuality' in a globalising world. Thus, we shall see in later chapters how this is shaping the economy, power, all forms of media, and even issues like class, gender and education. We will take stock of this idea of a 'network society' in the closing chapters of this book.

# SUMMARY

1 Social groups – important building blocks of societies – foster personal development and common identity as well as performing various tasks. Primary groups tend to be small and person orientated; secondary groups are typically large and goal orientated. The process of group conformity is well documented by researchers. Because members often seek consensus, work groups do not necessarily generate a wider range of ideas than do individuals working alone. Individuals use reference groups to form attitudes and make decisions.

2 Georg Simmel characterised the dyad relationship as intense but unstable; a triad, he noted, can easily dissolve into a dyad by excluding one member.

3 Peter Blau explored how the size, internal homogeneity, relative social parity and physical segregation of groups all affect members' behaviour. Formal organisations are large, secondary groups that seek to perform complex tasks efficiently. According to their members' reasons for joining, formal organisations are classified as utilitarian, normative or coercive. Bureaucratic organisation expands in modern societies to perform many complex tasks efficiently. Bureaucracy is based on specialisation, hierarchy, rules and regulations, technical competence, impersonal interaction and formal, written communications. Ideal bureaucracy may promote efficiency, but bureaucracy also generates alienation and inefficiency, tends to perpetuate itself beyond the achievement of its goals and contributes to the contemporary erosion of privacy.

4 The trend towards the 'McDonaldisation of society' involves increasing automation and impersonality. It is defined by growing efficiency, predictability, calculability and control through automation.

5 Humanising bureaucracy means recognising people as an organisation's greatest resource. To develop human resources, organisations should spread responsibility and opportunity widely. One way to put this ideal into action is through self-managed work teams. Reflecting the collective spirit of Japanese culture, formal organisations in Japan are based on more personal ties than are their counterparts in the United States and Europe.

6 We are now living in the network age. Mobile phones, social networking and the internet are relational webs that link people. The internet is a vast electronic network linking millions of computers worldwide. Mobile phones and social networking groups are starting to change group relations.

## MYTASKLIST

# Suggestions for going further

## 1 Connect up with Part Six and the Sociology Web Resources

As you work through ideas and think about the issues raised in this chapter, look at the accompanying website and the resource centre at the end of this book which connects to it. There is a lot here to help you move on. To link up, see www.pearson.co.uk/plummer.

## 2 Review the chapter

*Briefly summarise (in a paragraph) just what this chapter has been about.* Consider: (a) What have you learned? (b) What do you disagree with? Be critical. And (c) How would you develop all this? How could you get more detail on matters that interest you?

## 3 Pose questions

(a)  Identify various (i) primary and secondary groups, (ii) formal and informal organisations, and (iii) networks in your own life. What do you like or dislike about each type of setting?

(b)  Examine the nature of bureaucracies in the worlds you live in. Are they essentially male worlds? Are they really dehumanising? Can you write 'in praise' of them?

(c)  What is the 'McDonaldisation of society'? Discuss whether it can be seen as a sign of a progressing society, or whether it should be resisted. Should it nowadays perhaps be called the 'Starbucksisation of society'?

(d)  Draw up your own social network and contrast it with that of a friend. How might such networks differ across different cultures?

(e)  Does the 'network society' suggest a really different way of relating to people than that found in the past? Consider how you use your mobile phone and

Facebook. How does this differ from interaction in the past?

## 4 Explore key words

Many concepts have been introduced in this chapter. You can review them from the website or from the listing at the back of this book. You might like to give special attention to just five words and think them through – how would you define them, what are they dealing with, and do they help you see the social world more clearly or not?

## 5 Search the Web

Be critical when you look at websites – see the box on p. 940 in the Resources section. For this chapter look at:

The McDonaldisation website
www.mcdonaldization.com
This gives a very good overview of the issues, but has not been kept up to date.

Social psychological experiments: Milgram
www.stanleymilgram.com
The purpose of this website is to be a source of accurate information about the life and work of the social psychologist Stanley Milgram.

Zimbardo
www.zimbardo.com
The homepage of Professor Phillip G. Zimbardo. An extremely useful website devoted to Zimbardo's work. When we looked at it in July 2007, it was very up to date. It also includes a slideshow of the famous experiment (as well as the video).

The Holocaust
www.history1900's.about.com/library/holocaust/blholocaust.htm
A clear and simple site which would lead you to many others.

On information technology, see the sites listed in Chapter 23.

## 6 Watch a DVD

Look at a range of films that have different kinds of group relations as their key backdrop and compare them. Why not look at:

- Frank Darabont's *The Shawshank Redemption* (1994): life in a prison.
- Nunally Johnson's *Man in a Grey Flannel Suit* (1957): life as an organisation man in the mid-1950s.
- Walter Hill's *The Warriors* (1979): life in a gang in New York.
- Steven Spielberg's *Schindler's List* (1993): life in the Holocaust.
- Larry and Andy Wachowki's *The Matrix* (1999): the Matrix is an all-engulfing simulated reality which pacifies and subdues the human population. It generated two follow-up films made in 2003, a cult following and a huge games industry around it. It suggests a life through cyber-relations at the end of the twentieth century.
- Morgan Spurlock's *Super Size Me* (2004): chronicles a month in the life of Morgan Spurlock, who eats nothing but McDonald's food and becomes dangerously ill as a result.
- David Fisher's *The Social Network* (2010): charts the rise of facebook.

## 7 Think and read

George C. Homans, *The Human Group* (1992; orig. 1950). This is the classic sociological investigation of the group, the setting for much of our lives.

Robert Putnam, *Bowling Alone: The Collapse and Revival of American Community* (2001). This is the most recent significant study in the USA to discuss the changing nature of groups and communities.

Philip Zimbardo, *The Lucifer Effect: How Good People Turn Evil* (2007). The controversial study described in the chapter, and here it is applied to Abu Ghraib.

George Ritzer, *The McDonaldization of Society* (1st edn, 1993; 6th edn, 2010). A highly readable and lively account of the McDonald's phenomenon and how it provides a blueprint for contemporary organisational life. The book has spawned a number of linked books. Later editions discuss 'Starbucksisation'.

Stuart R. Clegg, *Modern Organisations: Organisation Studies in the Postmodern World* (1990). An important review of earlier studies of organisations which also suggests the postmodern organisation. There are some intriguing case studies too of the French bread industry, the Italian fashion industry and 'post-Confucian' Asian enterprises.

Max Travers, *The New Bureaucracy: Quality Assurance and Its Critics* (2007). Readable account of quality management and the audit culture, applied to health, education and policing in the UK.

John Scott, *Social Network Analysis: A Handbook* (2nd edn, 2000a). Reviews the whole field of network research.

Manuel Castells, *The Rise of the Network Society*, Vol. 1 of *The Information Age* (1996). The now classic study mentioned in the chapter. There is a new introduction to the 2nd edition published in 2010.

Frank Webster, *Theories of the Information Society* (3rd edn, 2006). An important and critical evaluation of major information society theorists, including Daniel Bell, Manuel Castells and Jürgen Habermas.

Nancy K. Baym, *Personal Connections in the Digital Age* (2010). A useful overview of the ways in which digital media are changing our lives.

## 8 Relax with a novel

If Weber is the great theorist of bureaucracy, then the early twentieth-century Czech novelist Franz Kafka (1883–1924) is its poet laureate. See Franz Kafka, *The Trial* and *The Castle* (both originally published in English in 1937). The word 'Kafkaesque' suggests society as a pointless and irrational organisation into which a bewildered individual has strayed.

This may also be a good time to read William Golding's *The Lord of the Flies* (1954), which has also been made into a film, twice.

## 9 Connect to other chapters

- For more on genocide, see Chapters 11 and 16.
- Cyberworlds and new technologies are featured further in Chapters 7, 22 and 23.
- For more on Goffman, see Chapter 7.
- For educational bureaucracies, see Chapter 20.
- For prisons, see Chapter 17.

# 10 Engage with THE BIG DEBATE

## Mobile phones and Facebook: what are they doing to our personal life?

It would seem that the intimate face-to-face relationships of the primary group have long been breaking down. We have all been familiar with the more impersonal and transitory relationships of the secondary group for a long time. Indeed, most of us have come to accept that, while there is a part of our life where the primary group matters most, for much of our daily activities, from work to shopping to entertainment, we depend more and more on secondary groups. The ways of relating in the world have changed.

But it may well be that this is radically changing again. Indeed, many of the themes found in this text suggest that a new set of relationships are starting to happen. We now personally communicate with each other and relate to each other in ways that contrast sharply with the past. Perhaps you should start your discussion by considering what these changes have been.

One way of thinking about these is to look at your relationships with the world of high-tech gadgetry: Facebook, mobiles, texting, iPods, games, your PC. Now think about how much time you spend doing these things, usually away from face-to-face contact with people. For many, this will be a lot of time (studies have suggested that young people spend 7 hours a day on electronic gadgets!). Indeed, look around any city and you are likely to see people rushing somewhere while 'on their mobile phone'. Sit in a café and out comes the laptop. Everybody on trains seems to have ears plugged – they are all wired up. People have eyes down and are busy texting – or playing the latest game. Watch increasingly for those who get out their iPhones and iPads. More and more people (in the rich world, of course) do their work, their play, their shopping and their relationships all through computing technologies. Our daily lives are digitalised.

But think for a minute how this is changing our personal lives and group involvement. Consider some of the changes:

- Personal face-to-face talking relationships are replaced by distanced writing relationships on the screen or in texting: face-to-face contact ceases in this medium.

- Close primary groups and even secondary groups give way to global groups: providing you are connected up to the Web or your mobile, you can talk with anybody in the world. Intimacy can now spread across the globe (and it does, literally, through computer sex lines – or cybersex).

- Straightforward linear thinking – as in most writing – becomes taken over by 'hypertext' where the reader jumps around, splices the text, and moves in and out of different 'MUDS' (multi-user domains). Ways of thinking start to shift.

- Identities are no longer given in face-to-face interaction (for example, as a man or a woman), but assembled through the machine. In a literal sense, you can make yourself anybody you wish. You can become your email address, your 'facebook', or your new 'second life'.

This is just a preliminary list. You may like to continue it and we will look at it a little more in the next chapter. But the big question becomes: what will happen when we all start to conduct our lives like this, as many argue we already do? A new generation is arriving which will know nothing else.

There may be many downsides to this. What happens when people cannot afford a computer (and most of the world not only cannot afford it, but also remain illiterate)? Surely this will divide the world into a new form of stratification – the cyberclasses and the non-cyberclasses?

There again, what happens when people can afford it? Some researchers are starting to suggest that there has been an increase in shyness and an inability to communicate with others since the computer has arrived. We avoid primary groups and face-to-face relationships, and are only comfortable with machines and text talk. We can do so much more in virtual reality than we can do in 'real life'!

So there are pluses and minuses to the arrival of this new technology.

### Continue the debate

1 How might the new information technology change our relationships? Have mobile phones, for example, provided more and better relationships than the past could offer? Draw up a list of the dangers and merits.

2 What is cybersex? How can people have sex with or on a computer? Is this the way ahead for all our sexual problems? (See Chapter 23, p. 818)

3 Does the new technology lead to a growing inequality?

*See*: Nancy Baym, *Personal Connections in the Digital Age* (2010).

# CHAPTER 7

# MICRO-SOCIOLOGY: THE SOCIAL CONSTRUCTION OF EVERYDAY LIFE

ON A COLD WINTER DAY IN 1938, a social worker walked anxiously to the door of a rural Pennsylvania farmhouse. Investigating a case of possible child abuse, the social worker soon discovered a five-year-old girl hidden in a second-floor storage room. The child, whose name was Anna, was wedged into an old chair with her arms tied above her head so that she could not move. She was dressed in filthy garments, and her arms and legs – looking like matchsticks – were so frail that she could not use them.

Anna's situation can only be described as tragic. She was born in 1932 to an unmarried and mentally impaired woman of 26 who lived with her father. Enraged by his daughter's 'illegitimate' motherhood, the grandfather did not even want the child in his house. Anna therefore spent her first six months in various institutions. But her mother was unable to pay for such care, so Anna returned to the hostile home of her grandfather.

At this point, her ordeal intensified. To lessen the grandfather's anger, Anna's mother moved the child to the attic room, where she received little attention and just enough milk to keep her alive. There she stayed – day after day, month after month, with essentially no human contact – for five long years.

Upon learning of the discovery of Anna, sociologist Kingsley Davis (1940) travelled immediately to see the child. He found her at a county home, where local authorities had taken her. Davis was appalled by Anna's condition. She was emaciated and feeble. Unable to laugh, smile, speak or even show anger, she was completely unresponsive, as if alone in an empty world.

After four years of care, Anna learned to walk, talk in short phrases and care a little for herself. She died on 6 August 1942 at the age of 10.

*If we had a keen vision and feeling of all ordinary human life, it would be like hearing the grass grow and the squirrel's heart beat, and we should die at the roar which lies on the other side of silence.*

George Eliot, *Middlemarch*, 1872

*We dwell in the minds of others even when we do not know this.*

Charles Horton Cooley, *Human Nature and the Social Order*, 1902

## In this chapter, we ask:

- **What is micro-sociology?**

- **How do we become social and develop biographies across the life course?**

- **How is everyday life constructed and negotiated?**

- **How is everyday life changing in the twenty-first century?**

- **How are our identities, bodies and emotions socially formed?**

(Left) Painting of a masked ball by Lincoln Seligman that features on a wall of the Berkley Hotel, London

*Source*: Berkley Hotel Mural – 1, Seligman, Lincoln (Contemporary Artist)/Private Collection/The Bridgeman Art Library.

*See*: www.lincolnseligman.co.uk.

 What does the nature of the masked ball suggest about social life? Read on . . .

This classic story of Anna is a sad but instructive case of a human being deprived of virtually all social contact. Although physically alive, Anna hardly seemed human. Her plight reveals that, isolated in this way, an individual develops scarcely any capacity for thought, emotion and meaningful behaviour. In short, without social experience, an individual is not a social human being.

This chapter explores what Anna was deprived of – the means by which we become fully human. It looks at how we become social; how our bodies and emotions become social; how identities are formed; and how we assemble our everyday lives. In doing this, we move to a different kind of problem and a different level of analysis from those encountered so far. Up till now our discussions have been looking at the big picture: of society, cultures and organisations, along with the broad changes that have been taking place in them as first industrialisation and more recently the information revolution have brought new forms of society. This is **macro-sociology** – *the study of large-scale society*.

By contrast, we now turn to what may be seen as the building blocks of a society – the human actions in little social worlds that enable social life to get done. We are interested here in everyday life – how people go shopping, make breakfasts, go to work, use mobile phones, make love, fight wars, lie, cheat and steal! All the wonders of daily life are here. This is **micro-sociology** – *the study of everyday life in social interactions*. We will start by seeing just how our everyday realities are 'socially constructed'. From this, we will look at the ways in which we come to assemble our sense of who we are through what can be called the socialisation process. We will then look at five key ideas that help organise our everyday lives: *interaction, identity, bodies, emotion* and *biography*.

## The social construction of reality

Nearly 100 years ago, the Italian playwright Luigi Pirandello (1867–1936) skilfully applied the sociological perspective to social interaction. In *The Pleasure of Honesty*, Angelo Baldovino – a brilliant man with a chequered past – enters the fashionable home of the Renni family and introduces himself in a most peculiar way:

**Inevitably we construct ourselves. Let me explain. I enter this house and immediately I become what I have to become, what I can become: I construct myself. That is, I present myself to you in a form suitable to the relationship I wish to achieve with you. And, of course, you do the same with me.**

(Pirandello, 1962: 157–8)

This curious introduction suggests that each human being has some ability to shape what happens from moment to moment. 'Reality', in other words, is not as fixed as we may think.

The phrase **social construction of reality** was introduced by Peter Berger and Thomas Luckmann (1967) to identify *the process by which people creatively shape reality through social interaction*. Human worlds are socially produced, changed and modified. This idea stands at the foundation of the symbolic-interaction paradigm, as described in earlier chapters, and is the hallmark of what is now called the social constructionist perspective. As Angelo Baldovino's remark suggests, especially in an unfamiliar situation, quite a bit of 'reality' remains unclear in everyone's mind. So as Baldovino 'presents himself' in terms that suit his purposes, and as others do the same, a complex reality emerges, though few people are so 'up front' about their deliberate efforts to foster an impression.

Social interaction, then, amounts to negotiating reality. Most everyday situations involve at least some agreement about what is going on, but participants perceive events differently. We have to take seriously people's different perspectives on the world, and how they come to define the situations they are in. One core issue to consider here is how the way in which people define situations helps shape the world they live in. W. I. Thomas, the founding sociologist from the University of Chicago (1966: 301; orig. 1931), succinctly expressed this insight in what has come to be known as the **Thomas theorem**: *situations we define as real become real in their consequences*.

## Becoming social: the process of socialisation

How do we come to be social beings, acquiring our own perspectives on the world? Sociologists suggest that it is through a process of **socialisation**, *a lifelong social experience by which individuals construct their personal biography, assemble daily interactional rules and come to terms with the wider patterns of their* *culture.* Unlike other living species whose behaviour may be largely biologically set, human beings rely on social experience to learn the nuances of their culture in order to survive.

## Questions for an account of socialisation

Socialisation theory can ask five broad questions, which may be summarised as follows:

1 *Who is being socialised?*
2 *By whom?*
3 *How?*
4 *Where?*
5 *When?*

The first question raises the issue of the nature of the person being socialised and ultimately asks about *human nature.* Is this something people are born with or are they the product of their environment? This is the classic 'nature/nurture' argument. The second question looks at the role of *agents of socialisation.* This might start out with the formative role of mothers, fathers and siblings as *primary* socialisers, but it soon moves on to other agents such as friends, peers, teachers, significant others and indeed even the mass media (see Chapter 22). The 'how' question asks about the processes through which people become socialised. *These are development theories, which look at the many mechanisms through which we become human, and include what is known as psychodynamic and interactionist approaches.* Finally, the last questions aim to locate the life in time and place – at how socialisation varies across different cultures and across history. We look at some of these questions in more detail below.

## How do we develop – nature, nurture or both?

Virtually helpless at birth, the human infant depends on others for care and nourishment as well as learning. Although Anna's short life makes these facts very clear, most people mistakenly believe that human behaviour is the product of biological imperatives: for many, instincts, evolution and genes are seen as the core of human behaviour. 'It's genetic' is one of the most common claims made these days. But sociologists cast much doubt on the overstated power of the gene, as we shall see.

Initially it was Charles Darwin who argued, plausibly, that each species evolves over thousands of generations as genetic variations enhance survival and reproduction. Biologically rooted traits that enhance survival emerge as a species' 'nature'. As Darwin's fame grew, people assumed that humans, like other forms of life, had a fixed, instinctive 'nature' as well.

Such notions are still with us. People sometimes claim, for example, that our economic system is a reflection of 'instinctive human competitiveness', that some people are 'born criminals', or that women are more 'naturally' emotional while men are 'inherently' more rational. Indeed, almost anything social – from race differences to illness, from wealth to intelligence – is explained by some as genetic. We often describe familiar traits as *human nature*, as if people were born with them, just as we are born with five senses. More accurately, however, our human nature leads us to create and learn cultural traits, as we shall see.

People trying to understand cultural diversity also misconstrued Darwin's thinking. Centuries of world exploration and empire building taught western Europeans that people around the world behaved quite differently from themselves. They attributed such contrasts to biology rather than culture. It was a simple – although terribly damaging – step to conclude that members of technologically simple societies were biologically less evolved and, therefore, less human. Such a self-serving and ethnocentric view helped justify colonial practices, including land seizures and slavery, since it is easier to exploit others if you are convinced that they are not truly human in the same sense that you are.

In the twentieth century, social scientists launched a broad attack on naturalistic explanations of human behaviour. Psychologist John B. Watson (1878–1958) devised a theory called **behaviourism**, which held that *specific behaviour patterns are not instinctive but learned.* Thus people the world over have the same claim to humanity, Watson insisted; humans differ only in their cultural environment. In a classic observation, Watson remarked that 'human nature' was infinitely malleable:

> **Give me a dozen healthy infants . . . and my own specified world to bring them up in, and I will guarantee to take any one at random and train him [or her] to become any type of specialist that I might select – doctor, lawyer, artist, merchant, chief, and yes, even beggar-man and thief – regardless of his [or her] talents, penchants, tendencies, abilities, vocations, and race of his [or her] ancestors.**

(Watson, 1930: 104)

Anthropologists weighed in on this debate as well, showing how variable the world's cultures are. An outspoken proponent of the 'nurture' view, anthropologist Margaret Mead summed up the evidence:

> **The differences between individuals who are members of different cultures, like the differences between individuals within a culture, are almost entirely to be laid to differences in conditioning, especially during early childhood, and this conditioning is culturally determined.**
>
> (Mead, 1963: 280; orig. 1935)

Today, social scientists (and many biologists who specialise in genetics too) are cautious about describing any type of behaviour as *simply* instinctive or genetic. Of course, this does not mean that biology plays no part in human behaviour. Human life, after all, depends on the functioning of the body. We also know that children share many biological traits with their parents, especially physical characteristics such as height, weight, hair and eye colour, and facial features. Intelligence and various personality characteristics (for example, how one reacts to stimulation or frustration) have some genetic component, as does the potential to excel in such activities as art and music. But whether a person develops an inherited potential depends on the opportunities associated with social position.

Sociologists generally work from the assumption that nurture is far more important than nature in determining human behaviour. We should not think of nature as opposing nurture, though, since we express our human nature as we build culture. For humans, then, nature and nurture are inseparable. A useful term to deal with all this is *human capabilities*. These suggest *the features which are central to a human life to function well*. In some ways they should be seen as our basic entitlements. Without them, we cannot function well in social life. They can be seen as 'opportunities for functioning' in the world (see the box on Martha Nussbaum, Chapter 14, p. 471).

## Feral children/isolated children

For obvious ethical reasons, researchers cannot subject human beings to experimental isolation. Consequently, much of what we know about this issue comes from rare cases of abused children like Anna. After her discovery, Anna benefited from intense social contact and soon showed improvement. Visiting her in the county home after ten days, Kingsley Davis (1940) noted that she was more alert and even smiled with

obvious pleasure. During the next year, Anna made slow but steady progress, showing greater interest in other people and gradually learning to walk. After a year and a half, she could feed herself and play with toys.

But it was becoming apparent that Anna's five years of social isolation had left her permanently damaged. At the age of eight her mental and social development was still less than that of a two-year-old. Not until she was almost ten did she begin to grasp language. Of course, since Anna's mother had learning difficulties, perhaps Anna was similarly disadvantaged. The riddle was never solved, because Anna died at the age of ten from a blood disorder, possibly related to her years of abuse (Davis, 1940, 1947).

A second, quite similar case involves another girl, found at about the same time as Anna and under strikingly similar circumstances. After more than six years of virtual isolation, this girl – known as Isabelle – displayed the same lack of human responsiveness as Anna. Unlike Anna, though, Isabelle benefited from a special learning programme directed by psychologists. Within a week, Isabelle was attempting to speak, and a year and a half later, her vocabulary included nearly 2,000 words. The psychologists concluded that intensive effort had propelled Isabelle through six years of normal development in only two years. By the time she was 14, Isabelle was attending sixth-grade classes, apparently on her way to at least an approximately normal life (Davis, 1947).

A final case of childhood isolation involves a 13-year-old California girl victimised in a host of ways by her parents from the age of two (Curtiss, 1977; Pines, 1981; Rymer, 1994). Genie's ordeal included extended periods of being locked alone in a garage. Upon discovery, her condition mirrored that of Anna and Isabelle. Genie was emaciated (weighing only 59 pounds) and had the mental development of a one-year-old. She received intensive treatment by specialists and thrived physically. Yet even after years of care, her ability to use language remains that of a young child, and she lives today in a home for developmentally disabled adults.

The story of Victor is also a famous film, *L'Enfant Sauvage* by Francois Truffaut (1970).

All the evidence points to the crucial role of social experience in personal development. Human beings are resilient creatures, sometimes able to recover from even the crushing experience of abuse and isolation. But there is a point – precisely when is unclear from the limited number of cases – at which social isolation in infancy results in irreparable developmental damage.

Victor, often known as the wild boy of Aveyron, is probably the most discussed case of a feral child. He was first sighted in 1797 in woods near Toulouse (in the Aveyron region of France). He lacked speech and it is thought that he had grown up wild in the woods. He came to live with the French doctor Jean Marc Gaspard Itard, who attempted to teach him to speak, but Victor only ever learnt two words: milk and God. He died in 1828. Truffaut has made a very famous film about him: *L'enfant sauvage (The Wild Boy)* (1970). Extracts can be found on YouTube. See also http://www.imdb.com/title/tt0064285/

*Source*: artwork from *Education d'un homme sauvage* (J. M. G. Itard, Paris, 1801). CCI Archives/Science Photo Library.

## Becoming biographies? Two theories of socialisation

Socialisation results in a personal **biography**, *a person's unique history of thinking, feeling and acting* (see Interlude 4, pp. 823–6). We build a biography through interacting with others throughout all our lives: as biography develops, we participate in a culture while remaining, in some respects, distinct individuals. But in the absence of social experience, as the case of Anna shows, a biography can hardly start to emerge at all.

Social experience is vital for society just as it is for individuals. Societies exist beyond the life span of any person, and thus each generation must teach something of its way of life to the next. Broadly speaking, then, socialisation amounts to the ongoing process of cultural transmission. Socialisation is a complex, lifelong process. In what follows, we highlight two major theories of human development. There are many others (which can be accessed via the website).

## Sigmund Freud: the importance of the unconscious and emotional structuring

Sigmund Freud (1856–1939) lived in Vienna at a time when most Europeans considered human behaviour to be biologically fixed. Trained as a physician, Freud gradually turned to the study of personality and eventually developed the celebrated theory of psychoanalysis.

The cornerstone of this theory is the workings of the repressed **unconscious**: people's lives are partly shaped by emotional *experiences*, traumas and 'family romances' *which then become too difficult to confront and so become hidden from the surface workings of life, while still motivating our actions*. The unconscious goes deep: it is repressed and cannot be easily recovered. (Psychoanalysis and 'dream analysis' are two 'roads to the unconscious'.) In any event the unconscious often means that we really do not know why we do certain things.

Many aspects of Freud's work bear directly on our understanding of how we become social.

### Life and death

Freud contended that biology is diffuse but plays an important part in social development, though not in terms of the simple instincts that guide other species. Humans, Freud theorised, respond to two general needs or drives. We have a basic need for pleasure and bonding, which Freud called the life instincts, or *eros* (from the Greek god of love). Second, opposing this need, are aggressive drives, which Freud termed the death instincts, or *thanatos* (from the Greek meaning 'death'). Freud postulated that these opposing forces, operating primarily at the level of the unconscious mind, generate deeply rooted inner tensions.

Sigmund Freud (1856–1936). Freud is the great theorist of the unconscious, but with a few exceptions (such as Parsons, the Frankfurt School and some feminisms) he has not had a major impact on sociology

*Source*: Pearson Education Ltd/The Illustrated London News Picture Library/Ingram Publishing/Alamy.

## Id, ego, superego

These basic drives need to be controlled and Freud incorporated them and the influence of society into a model of personality with three parts: id, ego and superego. The **id** (Latin for 'that') represents the *human being's basic drives*, which are unconscious and demand immediate satisfaction. Rooted in our biology, the id is present at birth, making a newborn a bundle of needs demanding attention, touching and all kinds of nervous and sexual experience. They are a 'cauldron of seething excitation' and they seek the release of their desires. But society does not tolerate such a self-centred orientation, so the id's desires inevitably encounter resistance. Because of this cultural opposition, one of the first words a child comprehends is 'no'.

To avoid frustration, the child learns to approach the world realistically. This accomplishment forms the second component of the personality, the **ego** (Latin for 'I'), which is *a person's conscious efforts to balance innate, pleasure-seeking drives with the demands of society*. It is dominated by what Freud calls the reality principle. The ego arises as we gain awareness of our distinct existence; it reaches fruition as we come to understand that we cannot have everything we want. We start to adjust and adapt to the vagaries of everyday life.

Finally, the human personality develops the **superego** (Latin, meaning 'above' or 'beyond' the ego), which is the *operation of culture within the individual*. With the emergence of the superego, we can see *why* we cannot have everything we want. The superego consists of cultural values and norms – internalised in the form of conscience – that define moral limits. The superego begins to emerge as children recognise parental control; it matures as they learn that their own behaviour and that of their parents – in fact, everyone's behaviour – reflects a broader system of cultural demands. It is a conscience and it creates new tensions, generating guilt and guilty thoughts.

## Personality development

The id-centred child first encounters the world as a bewildering array of physical sensations and need satisfactions. With the gradual development of the superego, however, the child's comprehension extends beyond pleasure and pain to include the moral concepts of right and wrong. Initially, in other words, children can feel good only in the physical sense; but, after three or four years, they feel good or bad as they evaluate their own behaviour according to cultural standards.

Conflict between id and superego is ongoing, but, in a well-adjusted person, these opposing forces are managed by the ego. Unresolved conflicts, especially during childhood, typically result in personality disorders later on.

As the source of superego, culture operates to control human drives, a process that Freud termed *repression*. Some repression is inevitable, since any society must coerce people to look beyond themselves. Often the competing demands of self and society are resolved through compromise. This process, which Freud called *sublimation*, transforms fundamentally selfish drives into socially acceptable activities. Sexual urges, for example, may lead to marriage, just as aggression gives rise to competitive sports.

## Freud and the Oedipus Complex

Central to Freud's thought, and to his theory of socialisation, is his concept of the Oedipus Complex: a metaphor for the emotional and psychic struggles and conflicts that a young child experiences with its mother and father. The term is derived from the Greek tragedy in which Oedipus marries his mother and murders his father, and looks at the passionate 'little love affairs' that children have with their families in the earliest years of life.

Broadly, Freud suggests that newborn children initially feel a strong closeness and attachment to the mother, and that the father is experienced as something of a threat to this attachment. The child thus starts to harbour hostile feelings towards the father, for which it feels increasingly guilty. This little dilemma can be experienced very profoundly. Freud uses the term 'castration complex' to suggest a powerful threat to the child. And in order to resolve this threat, the child starts to identify with the father instead.

The Oedipus Complex is the key to getting the id and all its desires under control: the father becomes part of the superego as an authority figure. Freud is outlining a basic predicament in becoming social: how to cope with all our desires and become a socialised adult with a conscience. And he does this through seeing a struggle in emotional identification.

### Critical comment

Freud's work sparked controversy in his own lifetime, and some of that controversy still smoulders today. The world he knew vigorously repressed human sexuality, so that few of his contemporaries were prepared to concede that sex is a basic human need. More recently, Freud has come under fire for his depictions of humanity in allegedly male terms, thereby devaluing the lives of women. But Freud also provided a foundation that influenced virtually everyone who later studied the human personality. Of special importance to sociology is his notion that we internalise social norms and that childhood experiences have a lasting impact on socialisation. More than this, in his book *Civilisation and its Discontents* (2004; orig. 1930), he saw a distinct parallel between social and individual developments. Just as human beings develop through instinctual repression, so civilisation as a whole advances through controls. Civilisation, then, depends upon repression but in the process it generates many problems.

Freud is considered an intellectual giant of the twentieth century – probing deeply the dynamics of the repressed unconscious human life. He is not a sociologist but his ideas have shaped many aspects of sociology. You will find a lot about his work on the internet, but a straightforward guide is: Sigmund Freud: His Life and Work, at: www.freudfile.org.

# George Herbert Mead and the social self

Our understanding of socialisation stems in large part from the life work of George Herbert Mead (1863–1931), who is introduced in the *Thinkers and theory* box on p. 214. Mead (1962; orig. 1934) described his approach as *social behaviourism*, calling to mind the behaviourism of psychologist John B. Watson described earlier. Both recognised the power of the environment to shape human behaviour. But Watson focused on outward behaviour, while Mead highlighted inward *thinking*, which he contended was humanity's defining trait.

## The self

Mead's central concept is the self, *the human capacity to be reflexive and take the role of others*. Mead's genius lay in seeing that the self is inseparable from society, and bound up with communication. It is a connection explained in a series of steps.

First, Mead claims that *the self emerges from social experience*. The self is not part of the body in itself, and it does not exist at birth. But it emerges through communication with others and this is distinctly what makes us human. Mead rejected simple ideas about biological drives, and argued that the self develops *only* through social experience. In the absence of social interaction, as we saw above in the cases of isolated children, the body may grow but no self will emerge.

Secondly, Mead explained how *social experience involves communication and the exchange of symbols*. Using words, a wave of the hand or a smile, people create meaning, which is a distinctively human experience. We can use reward and punishment to train a dog, after all, but the dog attaches no meaning to these actions. Human beings, by contrast, make sense of actions by inferring people's underlying intentions. In short, a dog responds to *what you do*; a human responds to *what you have in mind* as you do it. People have to 'take the role of the other' in order to make sense of action.

Return to our friendly dog for a moment. You can train a dog to walk to the porch and return with an umbrella. But the dog grasps no meaning in the act, no intention behind the command. Thus, if the dog cannot find the umbrella, it is incapable of the human response: to look for a raincoat instead.

Thirdly, says Mead, *to understand intention, you must imagine the situation from another person's point of view.* Using symbols, we can imaginatively place ourselves in another person's shoes and thus see ourselves as that person does. This capacity allows us to anticipate how others will respond to us even before we act. A simple toss of a ball requires stepping outside ourselves to imagine how another will respond to our throw. Social interaction, then, involves seeing ourselves as others see us – a process that Mead called *taking the role of the other.* The self, then, is reflective and reflexive.

## The looking-glass self

In social life, other people represent the mirror or looking glass in which we perceive ourselves. Charles Horton Cooley (1864–1929), one of Mead's contemporaries, used the phrase **looking-glass self** to designate *the image people have of themselves based on how they believe others perceive them* (1964; orig. 1902). He claimed that we can only live social lives through entering the minds of others. Whether we think of ourselves as clever or clumsy, worthy or worthless, depends in large measure on what we think others think of us. This insight goes a long way towards explaining Carol Gilligan's (1982) finding that young women lose self-confidence as they come of age in a society that discourages women from being too assertive.

## The I and the Me

Our capacity to see ourselves through others implies that the self has two components. First, *the self is subject* as we initiate social action. Humans are innately active and spontaneous, Mead claimed, dubbing this subjective element of the self the *I* (the subjective form of the personal pronoun). But secondly, *the self is object* because, taking the role of another, we form impressions of ourselves. Mead called this objective element of the self the *Me* (the objective form of the

# George Herbert Mead: the self is born of society

George Herbert Mead (1863–1933) was a leading US philosopher and some of his key ideas are described here. Based at the University of Chicago, he has been identified as a leading pragmatist. His work *Mind, Self and Society* (1962; orig. 1934) was published after his death from notes taken by students, and provides his major theory of the self.

Few people were surprised that Mead became a college professor. He was born to a Massachusetts family with a strong intellectual tradition, and both his parents were academics. His father was both a preacher and a teacher at a number of colleges, and his mother served for a decade as president of Mount Holyoke College.

But Mead also had a hand in shaping his own life, rebelling against the strongly religious atmosphere of his home and community. After completing college, he restlessly travelled throughout the Pacific Northwest, surveying for the railroad and reading voraciously. He gradually settled on the idea of studying philosophy, an academic endeavour he pursued at Harvard and in Europe.

Mead took a teaching position at the new University of Chicago. But his outlook still veered from the conventional. He rarely published, going against a long-standing tradition among academics. Mead's reputation and stature grew only after his death, when colleagues and former students collected and published his lecture notes. Mead drew together a wide range of ideas to help launch the new field of social psychology.

Never content with life as it was, Mead was an active social reformer. To him, the course of

**George Herbert Mead (1863–1933)**
*Source*: The Granger Collection, New York.

an entire society was as ongoing and changeable as the life of any individual. This insight follows from his basic contention: society may have the power to shape individuals, but people also have the capacity to mould their society.

For an up-to-date guide to Mead's work, see Filipe Carreira da Silva, *G. H. Mead* (2007).

personal pronoun). All social experience begins with someone initiating action (the I-phase of self) and then guiding the action (the Me-phase of self) by taking the role of the other. Social experience is thus the interplay of the I and the Me: our actions are spontaneous yet guided by how others respond to us.

Mead stressed that thinking itself constitutes a social experience. Our thoughts are partly creative (representing the I), but in thought we also become objects to ourselves (representing the Me) as we imagine how others will respond to our ideas. Table 7.1 draws out some of these contrasts.

| Table 7.1 | The Meadian 'I' and 'ME' | |
|---|---|---|
| **The I phase** | **The ME phase** | |
| Subject | Object | |
| Impulsive | Determined | |
| Knowing | Known | |
| Acts in world | Attitudes of others | |
| Social experience is the interplay of I and Me in process | | |

## Development of the self

According to Mead, gaining a self amounts to learning to take the role of the other. Like Freud, Mead regarded early childhood as the crucial time for this task, but he did not link the development of the self to biological maturation. Mead maintained that the self emerges over time with increasing social experience.

Infants respond to others only in terms of *imitation*. They mimic behaviour without understanding underlying intentions. Unable to use symbols, Mead concluded, infants have no self.

Children first learn to use language and other symbols in the form of *play*, especially role playing. Initially, they model themselves on key people in their lives – such as parents – whom we call *significant others*. Playing 'mummy and daddy', for example, helps children imagine the world from their parents' point of view.

Gradually, children learn to take the roles of several others at once. This skill is the key to moving from simple play (say, playing catch) involving one other to complex *games* (like baseball) involving many others. Only by the age of seven or eight have most children acquired sufficient social experience to engage in team sports that demand taking the role of numerous others simultaneously.

Figure 7.1 shows the logical progression from imitation to play to games. But a final stage in the development of the self remains. A game involves taking the role of others in just one situation. But members of a society also need to see themselves as others in general might. In other words, we recognise that people in any situation in society share cultural norms and values, and we begin to incorporate these general patterns into the self. Mead used the term **generalised other** to refer to *widespread cultural norms and values we use as references in evaluating ourselves*.

Of course, the emergence of the self is not the end of socialisation. Quite the contrary: Mead claimed that socialisation continues as long as we have social experience, so that changing circumstances can reshape who we are. The self may change, for example, with divorce, disability or unexpected wealth. And we retain some control over this process as we respond to events and circumstances and thereby play a part in our own socialisation. Mead's theory was really the start of the perspective we introduced in Chapter 2: symbolic interactionism.

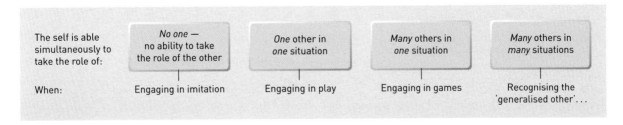

**Figure 1.2**     Building on social experience

George Herbert Mead described the development of the self as the process of gaining social experience. This is largely a matter of taking the role of the other with increasing sophistications, broadening out from specific others to greater complexity.

**Will the real Cindy Sherman reveal herself?**
Cindy Sherman (b. 1954) is a leading postmodern, feminist photographer. Starting in 1977 Cindy Sherman has photographed herself dressed up and playing the roles of others. In early works she often focused on B star celebrities and fairytale characters; in more recent works she focuses on older women. But always, she dresses up and then captures herself as another self. She shows a play of selves – using her own body and photographing it as a wide array of women; and is a lively example of role playing and identity changing in life and art (though she does not cite either Erving Goffman or Judith Butler). Her art embodies two developments in the art world: the impact of postmodern theory on art practice; and the rise of photography and mass-media techniques as modes of artistic expression. For more on her work, see her website at: http://www.cindysherman.com/
*Source*: © Louie Psihoyos/Corbis.

*Critical comment*

The strength of Mead's work lies in exploring the nature of social experience itself. He succeeded in explaining how symbolic interaction is the foundation of both the self and society. Yet some critics disparage Mead's view as radically social because it acknowledges no biological element in the emergence of the self (in fact this is false criticism, as he certainly did highlight bodily processes and 'impulses'). Mead's concepts of the I and the Me are often confused with Freud's concepts of the id and the superego. But Freud rooted the id in the biological organism, while Mead saw the I as impulsive and the Me as regulative. Freud's concept of the superego and Mead's concept of the Me both reflect the power of society to shape personality. But for Freud, superego and id are locked in continual combat. Mead, however, held that the I and the Me work closely and cooperatively together, in a dialectical process (Meltzer, 1978).

# The life course and generations

While both Freud and Mead focus on the earlier (or primary) socialisation stages of lives, 'life course' is a term that enables us to look right across the whole structure of a person's life – and the secondary socialisation that this usually involves. Although each stage of life is linked to the biological process of ageing, the life course itself is largely a social construction. People in different societies may experience a stage of life quite differently, or not at all. Yet each stage of any society's life course presents characteristic problems and transitions that involve learning something new and unlearning familiar routines. Note, too, that just because societies organise human experience according to age, this in no way negates the effects of other features

of stratification we are examining, such as class, race, ethnicity and gender. Thus, the general patterns we have described are all subject to further modification as they apply to various categories of people.

## Understanding life course development

The most basic feature of development is the changing sequencing and phasing of a life course. We are all familiar with *chronological age* and its common sequencing from babyhood, through childhood, youth, middle age, old age and so on. These have commonly been called the 'seasons of a life' (Levinson et al., 1978, 1996; Kortre and Hall, 1999), as illustrated in Figure 7.2. But these categories are themselves a problem – ageing, for example, is now quite frequently broken into a 'third age' (65–74) and a 'fourth age'

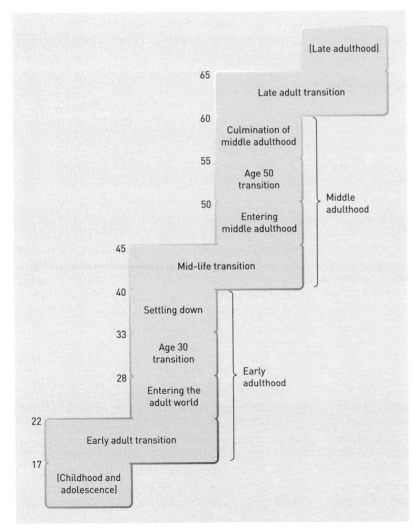

**Figure 7.2** The seasons of life
Daniel Levinson's research into human development depicts the lifespan as a series of critical transitions

*Source*: Adapted from Levinson et al. (1978: 57).

(75+), or into the younger elderly (65–75), the older elderly (75–85), and the very old (see Chapter 13). Indeed, as we find more and more people living longer and longer, the category of 'centenarian' will become more and more common. So we must note that age phase categories themselves change: 'childhood', 'middle age' and 'youth' are now seen by sociologists and historians to be recent historical inventions – they are certainly not found in all societies (for example, Shweder, 1998). We understand now that 'life phases' themselves change across history.

Lives also need to be located on a *historical timeline* and through their demographic features. A life occurs within a definite historical time span. A line of key world events (a bit like the timeline which opens this book) can be drawn which 'situates' a life firmly within its specific cultural history. South African lives, Australian lives and Peruvian lives will have a differing sense of key dates and experiences within their cultures. In Figure 7.3, we have listed just a few Anglo-American themes: clearly a life that has been through two world wars (those born before 1914) has a different historical matrix from one that has not been through any (those born after 1945). Likewise, lives that have grown up with the key singers of their time – for example, Bing Crosby, Elvis Presley, Take That or Eminem – may use these figures and their works as a way of thinking about their lives in the future.

From this we can locate *birth cohorts*: people born in the same year, or in a cluster of named years. A **cohort** is *a category of people with a common characteristic, usually their age*. Age cohorts are likely to have been influenced by the same economic and cultural trends, so that members typically display similar attitudes and values (Riley et al., 1988). The lives of women and men born early in the twentieth century, for example, were framed by an economic depression and two world wars – events unknown to their children or grandchildren. For their part, younger people today are living in a world where Playstations, high-tech information and websites have become taken for granted in their lives (in ways which older cohorts cannot really grasp). An *age cohort generation*, then, is a group of people born in a specified period of years, who are hence tied together through a particular shared historical time period. The most obvious examples would include the 'children of the Great Depression' (see Elder, 1974), the 'baby boomers', the 'hippy generation', 'Thatcher's children', 'Generation X' and the 'digital kids' (Rushkoff, 1999) and the 'millennial generation'. This is a most important way of locating a group of people – akin to

locating them in class and gender (see Chapter 13). With some tongue in cheek, we might call today's generation the high-tech Harry Potter generation'!

A *generation cohort perspective* is the more subjective sense that people acquire of belonging to a particular age reference group through which they may make sense of their 'memories' and 'identities' (they share a common perspective and say things like 'We all lived through the war together', 'In our days, feminism was more active', 'I was part of the Peace Movement in Vietnam', 'I am an older gay – part of the Stonewall generation'). The former category is structural – it locates a person in the society overall; the latter is more subjective – it shows who people identify with over time. Both nevertheless take the researcher into an important awareness of historical time – and how different lives are shaped throughout by different historical baselines and different historical roots. To put it bluntly: a child of the Thatcher or Reagan Generation cannot have experienced the Second World War at first hand as their grandparents inevitably would have; and such factors need to be located in looking at a life. Often these critical locations are to be found in a person's 'youth' period. Shared generational and historical experiences come to play a key role in a *life history* approach.

All this is closely linked to mapping lives as a 'life trajectory' or as a 'life course' – 'a pathway defined by the ageing process or by movement across the age structure' (Elder, 1985). It is common here to see a tripartite life course, characterised by an early period of preparation, a middle part of work (including domestic work), and a final part for 'retirement'. We used to be able to think very straightforwardly of this – long periods of work were followed by retirement, punctuated by raising children, maturation and growth, followed by disengagement and decline. For men the emphasis was most on work; for women the emphasis most on raising children. But nowadays the shape of life courses is changing: heterogeneity, fragmentation and discontinuities have happened for many and the sequencing is no longer quite so clear. Not all cultures have the same 'shape' to this life course; again, it can change historically.

Some contemporary writers are talking about the postmodernisation of the life course – how the formal patterns found in the past are breaking down, with people 'dipping in and out' of phases in a much less regularised and institutionalised fashion. We have what German sociologist Ulrich Beck refers to as the 'individualisation of the life course'. As traditional industrial ways of life become destroyed, so individuals

(a) Life cohorts

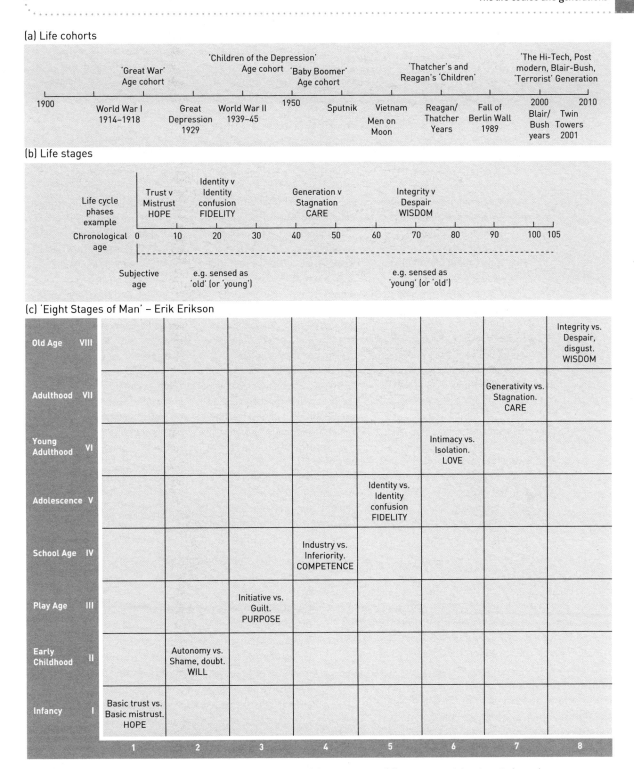

Figure 7.3    Mapping a life: life cohorts and life stages: (a) life cohorts; (b) life stages; (c) Erikson's (1980) 'Eight Stages of Man'

*Source*: Adapted from Plummer (2001a: 126–7).

# The high-tech Harry Potter generation

The Harry Potter series of seven novels by English author J. K. Rowling can be seen as a sociological phenomenon. The books are long. They chronicle the adventures of Harry Potter and his friends Hermione Granger and Ron Weasley at the Hogwarts School of Witchcraft and Wizardry. The books are about 'schooldays', 'growing up', 'magic and reality' and 'death'. First published in 1997, the books have gained enormous worldwide popularity – and have led to a spin-off series of films, merchandise and recently a theme park. The books have been translated into over 67 languages, selling well over 400 million copies (Rowling is one of the most translated and fastest-selling authors in history); and the films are listed among the top grossing films of all time.

Sociologists are very interested in the ways in which 'childhood' can be constructed in different ways in different cultures. Children make sense of their social worlds through all the artefacts they find around them – from parents, friends and schools to literature and other media forms. Children's stories, children's television and children's films often provide 'keys' to understanding the experiences of different generations. The books and films that children grow up with can tell a great deal about the adult worlds that children later move into. The modern world has witnessed the experience of children and young people growing up with 'media' events. The film *Miss Potter* (2006) shows the success of the author Beatrice Potter, and her illustrated books – which became the best-sellers of their time. In the 1950s, Enid Blyton became a key author of children's books for a whole generation. And across cultures, different children's stories come into being.

Cohorts of different generations come to identify certain events (wars, depressions, coronations, prime ministers) and certain cultural objects (books, films, music, sports, celebrities) with their own specific generations. We can speak of the 'Beatles generation', the 'Star Trek generation', the 'Thatcher generation' and so on. It identifies a group of people who move through their lives with a common experience. The Harry Potter generation may well become an identifiable tag for those who experience a critical life stage between 1997 and 2007. It is high-tech because this same generation is also the first generation to completely assimilate and take for granted the world of high technology that could only be imagined or struggled with before. Harry Potter is not just a book: he comes in multiple digital forms, websites, games and DVDs. A book is no longer a straightforward book. The reality of this generation is different from those before it.

*See:* Wikipedia entry on Harry Potter; Plummer (2001a); Edmunds and Turner (2002). The writings of George Beahm provide tours of youthful cult reading – including more recently *Bedazzled: The Stephenie Meyer's Twilight Phenomenon* (2009).

find they have to construct their own life plans and course: the routines and rituals of the past have gone too. As Beck says: 'individuals must produce, stage and cobble together their biographies themselves . . . the individual is actor, designer, juggler and stage director of his own biography, identity, social networks, commitment and convictions' (Beck, 1997: 95).

Within a life trajectory, we can then go on to identify *critical life events* and *life cycle crises*. These may range from major events such as death and divorce to less significant ones. There is a very substantial amount of writing and analysis of these themes, spearheaded by Erik Erikson's classic work on the Eight Stages of Man, but now developed in many directions. Again, though, we must distinguish between scientific accounts which try to capture some sense of an 'objective' series of phases lying, so to speak, within a life; and the more subjective awareness of subjects of their own sense of crises, their subjective identification with age, and the process of subjective reminiscences.

Move on to Chapter 13 to examine childhood, youth and the elderly as the stages of the life cycle; look too at Interlude 4 (p. 823).

# Constructing situations: Erving Goffman and drama

Erving Goffman (1922–1982), profiled in the *Thinkers and theory* box on p. 222, was the twentieth century's leading micro-sociologist. He studied what he called the **interaction order** – *what we do in the immediate presence of others* (Goffman, 1982: 2). One of the major ways he enhanced our understanding of everyday life was by noting that people routinely behave much like actors performing on a stage. By imagining ourselves as directors scrutinising what goes on in some situational 'theatre', we engage in what Goffman called **dramaturgical analysis**, *the investigation of social interaction in terms borrowed from theatrical performance*. Everyday social life becomes theatre. Dramaturgical analysis offers a fresh look at two now-familiar concepts. In theatrical terms, people come to play parts and roles as if in a play, and scripts emerge to supply dialogue and action for each of the characters. Moreover, in any setting, a person is both actor and audience. Goffman described each individual's 'performance' as the **presentation of self**, *an individual's effort to create specific impressions in the minds of others*. Presentation of self, or *impression management*, contains several distinctive elements (Goffman, 1959, 1967). We can see daily life as a series of stagecraft rules.

## Performances

As we present ourselves in everyday situations, we convey information – consciously and unconsciously – to others. An individual's performance includes dress (costume), any objects carried along (props) and tone of voice and particular gestures (manner). In addition, people craft their performance according to the setting (stage). We may joke loudly in the street, for example, but assume a more reverent manner upon entering a church. In addition, individuals design settings, such as a home or office, to enhance a performance by invoking the desired reactions in others.

Consider, for example, how a doctor's surgery conveys information to an audience of patients. Doctors enjoy prestige and power, a fact immediately grasped by patients upon entering the surgery or health centre. First, the doctor is nowhere to be seen. Instead, in what Goffman describes as the 'front region' of the setting, the patient encounters a receptionist who functions as a gatekeeper, deciding if and when the patient can meet the doctor. A simple survey of the waiting room, with patients (often impatiently) awaiting their call to the inner sanctum, leaves little doubt that the medical team controls events.

The doctor's private examination room or surgery constitutes the 'back region' of the setting. Here the patient confronts a wide range of props, such as medical books and framed degrees, which together reinforce the impression that the doctor has the specialised knowledge necessary to be in charge. In the surgery, the doctor may remain seated behind a desk – the larger and grander the desk, the greater the statement of power – while the patient is provided with only a chair.

The doctor's appearance and manner convey still more information. The common hospital doctor's costume of white lab coat may have the practical function of keeping clothes from becoming soiled, but its social function is to let others know at a glance the doctor's status. A stethoscope around the neck or a black medical bag in hand has the same purpose. A doctor's highly technical terminology – frequently mystifying – also emphasises the hierarchy in the situation. The use of the title 'Doctor' by patients who, in turn, are frequently addressed only by their first names, also underscores the physician's dominant position. The overall message of a doctor's performance is clear: 'I will help you only if you allow me to take charge.'

## Non-verbal communication

Novelist William Sansom describes a fictional Mr Preedy – an English holidaymaker on a beach in Spain:

> He took care to avoid catching anyone's eye. First, he had to make it clear to those potential companions of his holiday that they were of no concern to him whatsoever. He stared through them, round them, over them – eyes lost in space. The beach might have been empty. If by chance a ball was thrown his way, he looked surprised; then let a smile of amusement light his face (Kindly Preedy), looked around dazed to see that there were people on the beach, tossed it back with a smile to himself and not a smile at the people . . .
> . . . [He] then gathered together his beach-wrap and bag into a neat sand-resistant pile (Methodical and Sensible Preedy), rose slowly to stretch his huge frame (Big-Cat Preedy), and tossed aside his sandals (Carefree Preedy, after all).

(1956; quoted in Goffman, 1959: 4–5)

THINKERS & THEORY

# The dramatic world of Erving Goffman

Universal human nature is not a very human thing. By acquiring it, the person becomes a kind of construct, built up not from psychic propensities but from moral rules that are impressed from without . . .

Erving Goffman, *Interactional Ritual* (1967: 45)

Erving Goffman (1922–82) is generally considered to be the most influential of twentieth-century micro-sociologists and carved out a world of analysis that was distinctly his. A Canadian, he was trained at the University of Chicago and his first major field trip was to the Shetland Isles in Scotland for his PhD – for the book that eventually became his first classic, *The Presentation of Self in Everyday Life* (1959). Observing life closely on those islands, he started to develop a framework for seeing social life as a kind of drama. Just like people on a stage, people in everyday life could be seen as actors playing out roles and giving impressions

Erving Goffman (1922–82)

*Source*: © American Sociological Association. www.asanet.org.

to others that enabled the others to make sense of what was going on. This was the *drama-turgical perspective*.

Throughout his work – which often changed direction and was idiosyncratically written – his main concern was with *the interaction order*: what people do in the presence of others. He studied how behaviour in public places works – how people walk through doors and down streets. He looked at how people develop 'interaction rituals': 'the world in truth is a wedding' is one of his famous lines, in which he suggests that much of the most routine everyday interaction has important ritual elements to it.

He looked at the ways in which identities became spoilt – how some people became stigmatised and had to work hard to present themselves as 'normal'.

Along the way, Goffman literally produced a new language for thinking about the everyday. He produced an array of 'mini-concepts' which help us see how daily life is composed, terms such as 'face-work', 'cooling the mark', front and back regions, moral careers, information control, impression management, passing, own and wise, frames, keying, role distance, role playing, role attachments, civil inattention, situational adjustments, people as 'vehicular units', total institution, avoidance rituals, presentation rituals, tie signs.

In the light of this, and your reading of some of Goffman's work, you might like to write your own 'dramaturgical handbook'. Think about who are the key players in your life and where you interact with them, and map out some of your own ways of presenting yourself and making 'interaction rituals'. Is this a useful framework for thinking about how life is constructed?

*See*: Greg Smith, *Erving Goffman* (2006).

---

Through his conduct, Mr Preedy offers a great deal of information about himself to anyone caring to observe him. Notice that he does so without uttering a single word. This illustrates the process of **non-verbal communication**, *communication using body movements, gestures and facial expressions rather than speech*.

Virtually any part of the body can be used to generate *body language*: that is, to convey information to others. Facial expressions form the most significant element of non-verbal communication. Smiling and other facial gestures express basic emotions such as pleasure, surprise and anger the world over. Further, people project particular shades of meaning with their

faces. We distinguish, for example, between the deliberate smile of Kindly Preedy on the beach, a spontaneous smile of joy at seeing a friend, a pained smile of embarrassment and a full, unrestrained smile of self-satisfaction that we often associate with the 'cat that ate the canary'.

Eye contact is another crucial element of non-verbal communication. Generally, we use eye contact to initiate social interaction. Someone across the room 'catches our eye', for example, sparking a conversation. Avoiding the eyes of another, on the other hand, discourages communication. Hands, too, speak for us. Common hand gestures in our culture convey, among other things, an insult, a request for a lift, an invitation for someone to join us, or a demand that others stop in their tracks. Gestures also supplement spoken words. Pointing in a menacing way at someone, for example, intensifies a word of warning, just as shrugging the shoulders adds an air of indifference to the phrase 'I don't know', and rapidly waving the arms lends urgency to the single word 'Hurry!'

But, as any actor knows, the 'perfect performance' is an elusive goal. In everyday performances, some element of body language often contradicts our intended meaning. A teenage boy offers an explanation for getting home late, for example, but his mother doubts his words because he avoids looking her in the eye. The movie star on a television talk show claims that her recent flop at the box office is 'no big deal', but the nervous swing of her leg belies her casual denial. In practical terms, carefully observing non-verbal communication (most of which is not easily controlled) provides clues to deception, in much the same way that a lie detector records tell-tale changes in breathing, pulse rate, perspiration and blood pressure.

Yet detecting lies is difficult, because no single bodily gesture directly indicates deceit in the way that, say, a smile indicates pleasure. Even so, because any performance involves so many expressions, few people can confidently lie without allowing some piece of contradictory information to slip through, arousing the suspicions of a careful observer. Therefore, the key to detecting deceit is to scan the whole performance with an eye for inconsistencies and discrepancies.

In sum, lies are detectable, but training is the key to noticing relevant clues. Another key to spotting deception is knowing the other person well, the reason that parents can usually pick up deceit in their children. Finally, almost anyone can unmask deception when the liar is trying to cover up strong emotions.

## Gender and personal performances

Because women are socialised to be less assertive than men, they tend to be especially sensitive to non-verbal communication. In fact, gender is a central element in personal performances. Based on the work of Nancy Henley, Mykol Hamilton and Barrie Thorne (1992), we can extend the present discussion of personal performances to spotlight the importance of gender.

## Demeanour

Demeanour – that is, general conduct or deportment – reflects a person's level of social power. Simply put,

powerful people enjoy far greater personal discretion in how they act; subordinates act more formally and self-consciously. Off-colour remarks, swearing or casually removing shoes and putting feet up on the desk may be acceptable for the boss, but rarely for employees. Similarly, people in positions of dominance can interrupt the performances of others with impunity, while others are expected to display deference by remaining silent (Smith-Lovin and Brody, 1989; Henley et al., 1992).

Since women generally occupy positions of lesser power, demeanour is a gender issue as well. As Chapter 12 explains, about half of all working women in Europe and the United States hold clerical or service jobs that place them under the control of supervisors who are usually men. Women, then, craft their personal performances more carefully than men and display a greater degree of deference in everyday interaction.

## Use of space

How much space does a personal performance require? Here again, power plays a key role, since using more space conveys a non-verbal message of personal importance. According to Henley et al. (1992), men typically command more space than women do, whether pacing back and forth before an audience or casually lounging on the beach. Why? Our culture traditionally has measured femininity by how *little* space women occupy (the standard of 'daintiness'), while gauging masculinity by how *much* territory a man controls (the standard of 'turf').

The concept of **personal space** refers to *the surrounding area to which an individual makes some claim to privacy*. In the United Kingdom, for example, people typically position themselves several feet apart when speaking; throughout the Middle East, by contrast, individuals interact within a much closer space.

Throughout the world, gender further modifies these patterns. In daily life, men commonly intrude on the personal space of women. A woman's encroachment into a man's personal space, however, is likely to be construed as a sexual overture. Here again, women have less power in everyday interaction than men do.

## Staring, smiling and touching

Eye contact encourages interaction. Typically, women employ eye contact to sustain conversation more than men do. Men have their own distinctive brand of eye contact: staring. By making women the targets of stares, men are both making a claim of social dominance and defining women as sexual objects.

Although frequently signalling pleasure, *smiling* has a host of meanings. In a male-dominated world, women often smile to indicate appeasement or acceptance of submission. For this reason, Henley, Hamilton and Thorne maintain, women smile more than men; in extreme cases, smiling may reach the level of nervous habit.

Finally, *touching* constitutes an intriguing social pattern. Mutual touching conveys feelings of intimacy and caring. Apart from close relationships, however, touching is generally something men do to women (though rarely, in our culture, to other men). A male doctor touches the shoulder of his female nurse as they examine a report, a young man touches the back of his woman friend as he guides her across the street, or a male skiing instructor looks for opportunities to touch his female students. In these examples – as well as many others – touching may evoke little response, so common is it in everyday life. But it amounts to a subtle ritual by which men express their dominant position in an assumed hierarchy that subordinates women.

## Idealisation

Complex motives underlie human behaviour. Even so, according to Goffman, we construct performances to *idealise* our intentions. That is, we try to convince others (and perhaps ourselves) that what we do reflects ideal cultural standards rather than more selfish motives.

Idealisation is easily illustrated by returning to the world of doctors and patients. In a hospital, consultants engage in a performance commonly described as 'making the rounds'. Approaching the patient, the doctor often stops at the foot of the bed and silently examines the patient's chart. Afterwards, doctor and patient converse briefly. In ideal terms, this routine involves a doctor making a personal visit to enquire about a patient's condition.

In reality, something less exemplary is usually going on. A doctor who sees several dozen patients a day may remember little about most of them. Reading the chart gives the doctor the opportunity to rediscover the patient's identity and medical problems. Openly revealing the actual impersonality of much medical care would undermine the culturally ideal perception of the doctor as deeply concerned about the welfare of others.

Idealisation is woven into the fabric of everyday life in countless ways. Doctors, university lecturers and other professionals typically idealise their motives for entering their chosen careers. They describe their work as 'making a contribution to science', 'helping others', 'answering a calling from God', or perhaps 'serving the community'. Rarely do such people concede the less honourable, though common, motives of seeking the income, power, prestige and leisure that these occupations confer.

Taking a broader view, idealisation underlies social civility, since we smile and make polite remarks to people we do not like. Such small hypocrisies ease our way through social interactions. Even when we suspect that others are putting on an act, rarely do we openly challenge their performance, for reasons we shall explain next.

## Embarrassment and tact

The eminent professor consistently mispronounces the dean's name; the visiting dignitary rises from the table to speak, unaware of the napkin that still hangs from her neck; the president becomes ill at a state dinner. As carefully as individuals may craft their performances, slip-ups of all kinds frequently occur. The result is *embarrassment*, which, in dramaturgical terms, means the discomfort that follows a spoiled performance. Goffman describes embarrassment simply as 'losing face'.

Embarrassment looms as an ever-present danger because, first, all performances typically contain some measure of deception and, secondly, most performances involve a complex array of elements, any one of which, in a thoughtless moment, may shatter the intended impression.

Interestingly, an audience usually overlooks flaws in a performance, thereby allowing an actor to avoid embarrassment. If we do point out a mis-step ('Excuse me, but do you know that your fly is open?'), we do it discreetly and only to help someone avoid even greater loss of face. In Hans Christian Andersen's classic fable *The Emperor's New Clothes*, the child who blurts out that the emperor is parading around naked is telling the truth, yet is scolded for being rude.

But members of an audience usually do more than ignore flaws in a performance, Goffman explains; typically, they help the performer recover from them. *Tact*, then, amounts to helping another person 'save face'. After hearing a supposed expert make an embarrassingly inaccurate remark, for example, people may tactfully ignore the comment as if it were never spoken at all. Alternatively, mild laughter may indicate

## Researching everyday life

LIVING IN THE C21ST

For over a century, the main task of anthropologists has been to visit and live with different cultures around the world so that the intricacies of their daily routines and 'ways of living could be understood'. In *Watching the English* (2005), the anthropologist Kate Fox turned the tables and conducted some fieldwork on the English. She became the observer of the quaint ways of these strange people – showing how they form queues, drink in pubs, talk about social class all the time. Like all cultures, the English have developed very distinctive patterns of everyday life.

The sociologist Susie Scott is interested in examining all the everyday things we do in a society. She looks at our eating and drinking habits, how we fill in our days, how we shop and develop leisure interests, how we become embarrassed, fall in love – and do a thousand mundane things in our everyday life. Again, what she finds is that most of these everyday things have a broad pattern. She suggests that a number of theories are useful in approaching everyday life – some of these we have mentioned in this chapter (dramaturgy, symbolic interactionism, psychoanalysis) and others we have discussed elsewhere (functionalism, structuralism and cultural studies).

In one chapter, for example, she looks at the meanings and rituals we employ when we go shopping. What are the different meanings of shopping? There are many: it can be duty or a pleasure, a virtue or a vice. It can be an escape from the norms of everyday life. It can serve as a site of identity performance – whereby we 'demonstrate who we are, what we like, and with whom we identify' (Scott, 2009: 141). For some shopping becomes a lifestyle; for others it is a very practical means to an end.

The inspiration for much contemporary study of everyday is Erving Goffman, who is discussed in the text and in the box on p. 222.

*See*: Susie Scott, *Making Sense of Everyday Life* (2009); Kate Fox, *Watching the English* (2005).

---

that they wish to dismiss what they have heard as a joke. Or a listener may simply respond, 'I'm sure you didn't mean that', acknowledging the statement but not allowing it to destroy the actor's performance.

Why is tact such a common response? Because embarrassment provokes discomfort not simply for one person but for *everyone*. Just as the entire audience feels uneasy when an actor forgets a line, people who observe awkward behaviour are reminded of how fragile their own performances often are. Socially constructed reality thus functions like a dam holding back a sea of chaotic possibility. Should one person's performance spring a leak, others tactfully assist in making repairs. Everyone, after all, jointly engages in building culture, and no one wants reality to be suddenly swept away.

In sum, Goffman's research shows that, while behaviour is spontaneous in some respects, it is more patterned than we like to think. Almost 400 years ago, William Shakespeare captured this idea in memorable lines that still ring true:

> All the world's a stage,
> And all the men and women merely players:
> They have their exits and their entrances;
> And one man in his time plays many parts . . .

(*As You Like It*, II)

## Ethnomethodology and conversational analysis

Rather than assume that reality is something 'out there', the symbolic-interaction paradigm posits that reality is created by people in everyday encounters. But how, exactly, do we define reality for ourselves? What is the logic through which we make sense of everyday life? Answering this question is the objective of other theoretical approaches: *ethnomethodology* and *conversational analysis*.

### Ethnomethodology

The term itself has two parts: the Greek *ethno* refers to people and how they understand their surroundings; 'methodology' designates a set of methods or principles. Combining them makes **ethnomethodology**, *the study of the way people make sense of their everyday lives*. Ethnomethodology is largely the creation of the Californian-based sociologist Harold Garfinkel (1967), who challenged the then-dominant view of society as a broad, abstract 'system' (recall the approach of Emile Durkheim, described in Chapters 1, 2 and 4). Garfinkel wanted to explore how we make sense of countless familiar situations by looking at the practical reasoning we employ in everyday situations. On the surface, we engage in intentional speech or action; but these efforts rest on deeper assumptions about the world that we usually take for granted.

Think, for a moment, about what we assume in asking someone the simple question, 'How are you?' Do we mean physically? Mentally? Spiritually? Financially? Are we even looking for an answer, or are we 'just being polite'?

Ethnomethodology, then, delves into the sense-making process in any social encounter. Because so much of this process is ingrained, Garfinkel argues that one effective way to expose how we make sense of events is purposely to *break the rules*. Deliberately ignoring conventional rules and observing how people respond, he points out, allows us to tease out how people build a reality. Thus, Garfinkel (1967) directed his students to refuse to 'play the game' in a wide range of situations. Some students living with their parents started acting as if they were boarders rather than children. Others entered stores and insisted on bargaining for items. Some recruited people into simple games (like tic-tac-toe or noughts-and-crosses), only to intentionally flout the rules. Still others initiated conversations while slowly moving closer and closer to the other person. It was a matter of making the everyday 'strange', of 'breaching' commonsense assumptions; and this was done to show just how everyday life depends upon our ongoing sense of 'trust' with each other. Life is fragile, yet it has a rule- and game-like quality which human beings daily recognise, produce and reproduce.

## Conversational analysis

Taking this one step further, some sociologists argue that the guiding feature of everyday interaction is language (see Chapter 5). To understand society and the everyday life through which it is made, we need to look at language and the rules through which we speak. In a sense, societies are languages.

**Conversational analysis** provides *a rigorous set of techniques to technically record and then analyse what happens in everyday speech*. It sets about listening to and observing language, recording it, transcribing it, often videotaping it. Everywhere people are talking, conversational analysts are interested in understanding their talk. Thus they look everywhere – at courts,

hospitals, street conversations, political speeches, suicide notes, statistics making, children's play, television – to see how people construct their daily talk. They see this talk and conversation as a *topic* to investigate in its own right: they are not interested in what people actually say in terms of its contents (which they call resource). Rather, they are interested in its forms and rules, which they see as the underlying feature of social interaction. Human realities are accomplished through talk.

As one example, conversational analysts are concerned with the *sequencing* of talk: sentences generally follow on from one another. 'Normal' interaction depends upon this, and everyday life can only really be accomplished if people are willing to follow certain 'sequencing rules'. One of these, for instance, is *turn taking*: people bide their time, and take turns at being hearers and tellers to talk to others. Another is the *adjacency pair* through which most greetings, openings and closings of conversations have an unstated rule that as one speaks a line, so another makes the most appropriate conventional response to it. Thus, for example, a standard opening line may be: how are you? And this requires a response, usually of the form: very well, thank you. Everyday life is in this way deeply regulated by social rules (Heritage, 1987).

## Digitalised life: new features of daily interaction

We have already seen how pervasive the technologies of computers and mass media are in the twenty-first century (see Chapter 1, Table 1.4 for an overview). Here we suggest that these technologies have had growing and very significant influences on how the several billions of people now live their everyday lives on planet earth. Here as a quick illustration are some ways that everyday life has changed in the recent decades because of the new media. You may want to think how much you now take for granted these changes which were unknown features of life to your grandparents in their youth. *Amongst the new feature of interaction are:*

1 Being in *perpetual contact* with a wide range of people – mainly because of mobile phones which can be close to the body all the time. This means we can gain access to people and information at great

*speed*. Whereas tasks used to take weeks or months, now everything seems capable of being done in an instance. People get irritated when people do not reply to their emails for a day or so; a Google search is expected to deliver an immediate answer to any problem at once; and books, flowers and shopping of all kinds have to be delivered at the latest by the following day. Everyday life has been speeded up. (We now live in a *High Speed Society* (Hartmut and Scheuerman, 2009), and a *Fast Food Nation* (Schlosser, 2002), and it has generated a response in the 'go slow movement').

2   Being able to have *immediate global access* to people all over the world and get a response through phone, email, twitter and web cam. Daily life becomes potentially global: families at other ends of the earth can speak and even see each other on a daily basis. Wherever you are, you are never alone with a mobile phone. This has not only shifted the closesness of families and friends, but also brought strangers from all over the world into close proximity. People need never be far away from other people.

3   Being able to access friends, new communities, shared networks of interest – and complete strangers – at the click of a mouse. A massive global world of other people and friends has become possible for those who want it. *New patterns of community, friendship, dating – and sex – are all in the making* (see Chapter 6).

4   *New modes of speaking and communicating* are appearing with texting, tweeting, photograph sharing and YouTube/web cam presentations. None of these was possible before the 1990s.

5   Being able publicly to *display identities* to others through the new media, often *making public what used to be held to be very private*. The Goffman presentation of self we discussed earlier now becomes an online self. People can make up new identities online (though there does seem to be a lot of evidence that large numbers choose *not* to do this).

6   Closely linked to all of the above, our lives become – more and more – *mediated lives*. We live lives through the media, the internet, the mobile phone; and the technologies become in a sense 'our lives'.

7   Being able to *manage all kinds of everyday practical matters* from home and online: managing bank accounts, travel and holiday bookings, and shopping of all kinds. New technologies change the routines of everyday life.

8   The development of new status systems both in terms of who owns what technologies (owning the latest gadget can become very important to status), but also in terms of being able to present oneself properly online (through blogs, web pages, photos, etc). Status may now be achieved by the numbers of friends we have on Facebook!

9   The development of new rules and behaviour patterns – what Maria Bakardjieva has called the 'little behavior genres' of the internet – appear, alongside 'the micro-regulation of the internet'. New worlds of everyday habits appear which we are only just beginning to grasp.

(On all this, see Baym, 2010; Bakardjieva, 2005; Katz and Aakhus, 2002; Ling, 2008; Miller and Slater, 2000.)

# The sociologies of identity, emotion and the body

In recent years, three subjects have become 'hot topics' for some sociologists to study: the body, identity and emotions. Each of these topics takes an area of life that we have typically taken for granted and almost seen as natural: of who we are, what our bodies are, and what our feelings are – and then challenges them to a sociological analysis. Typically in the past these topics have been the concerns of psychologists, doctors, psychiatrists: but this recent research now clearly shows that all three are also profoundly shaped by the social. The social invades the personal. In the following section, we look at each briefly in turn.

## A sociology of identity

Identity has become a key concept within contemporary sociology, although it is far from new. For Richard Jenkins, **social identity** is '*our understanding of who we are and of who other people are, and, reciprocally, other people's understanding of themselves and of others*' (Jenkins, 1996). As a sociological concept, it serves as a crucial bridge in social life between human beings and wider cultures. Identity refers to sameness (from Latin *idem*, the same; after the Latin *identitas*, and similar to the word 'identical'); the word entered the English language around 1570. It highlights the quality or condition of being the same; of oneness and continuity. As Jeffrey Weeks says:

Identity is about belonging, about what you have in common with some people and what differentiates you from others. At its most basic it gives you a sense of personal location, the stable core to your individuality. But it is also about your social relationships, your complex involvement with others.

(Weeks, 1991: 88)

Far from being a new idea, then, it implies a sense of meaning and a sense of categorisation and difference: we mark out our identity and sameness with some by highlighting the differences between ourselves and others. It implies a necessary 'other' who is not 'us'. Zygmunt Bauman, a leading contemporary theorist, puts this strikingly when he says:

woman is the other of man, animal is the other of human, stranger is the other of native, abnormality the other of norm, deviation the other of law abiding, illness the other of health, insanity the other of reason, lay public the other of expert, foreigner the other of state subject, enemy the other of friend . . .

(Bauman, 1991: 8)

Identity as a concept, then, looks both inwards and outwards. On the one hand, it speaks to the most microscopic of events – the inner world of how we feel about ourselves. (Freud may be our partial guide here.) It suggests that there is an inner flow of being that is social. On the other hand, it also looks outwards to the most macro of organisations – to the nation-state and the global world. We can speak of Catholic identity through our identification with the Catholic Church, or Celtic identity through our identity with Ireland. Communities of many different kinds – Catholic, Celtic, Chinese – provide meanings from which we can come to fashion our sense of who we are and who we are not.

By its very terminology, then, identity theory implies some sense of sameness, commonality, continuity: if not actually present, the search is nevertheless at least on for an identity – a project of knowing who one is or what one's nation is. At the strongest extremes this is a jingoistic, brazen, self-assertive 'I am this: British, Black, Gay, and Male'. The category behind the identity is presumed and is often stridently clear. I am what I am. At the opposite extreme, the identity has so far dissolved that it is permanently unsettled, destabilised, under provisional construction, very much a project and never a thing. We are not quite sure who we are, or at any event who we are is open to frequent change.

But even in this most extreme form it has to recognise the need for and the power of categories and boundaries in the organisation of the social: it is just that these continuities and sameness are much more pluralised, shifting and fragmented than they were previously thought to be. In what follows, we will look a little more at some of these key contrasts.

## Changing meanings of identity

In the past, small, homogeneous and slowly changing societies provided a firm (if narrow) foundation for building meaningful identity. In many societies throughout history, the idea of identity has not really been a problem. In traditional worlds, 'premodern identities' may often be taken for granted. People know who they are, and often define themselves through traditions and religion. They find what seems to be 'a natural place' in the order of things. Identities are shared and communal, given as part of the world, the cosmos and nature. Such identities remain quite common today. For example, in the tight-knit Amish communities that flourish in parts of the United States (well depicted in the film *Witness*, 1985), young people are taught 'correct' ways to think and behave. Not everyone born into an Amish community can tolerate these demands for conformity, but most members establish an identity that is well integrated into the community (see Hostetler, 1980; Kraybill and Olshan, 1994).

As capitalism developed, there appeared an increased concern with human individuality, which starts to make the issue of individual identity more and more important. The modern (industrial, capitalist) period becomes a time of enormous self-reflection upon just who one is. An individual identity starts to emerge which seems a unified, singular and unique, integral individual, endowed with reason and a possible essential core of human beingness. This is what has been seen as the 'birth' of the modern human subject with a quest for personal self-understanding and identity.

But modern societies, with their characteristic diversity and rapid change, offer only shifting sands on which to build a personal identity. Left to make our own life decisions, many of us – especially those with greater affluence – confront a bewildering array of options. Autonomy has little value without standards for making choices, and people may find one path no more compelling than the next. Not surprisingly, many people shuttle from one identity to another, changing

RESEARCH IN ACTION

## The 'who am I?' test

Sociologists working in the 1950s devised the simplest of tools for measuring self and identity, which has been called the 'Who am I?' or 'Twenty Statements' test. The authors – Kuhn and McPartland (1954)

– suggest to students that they should write the first 20 statements that come to mind in answer to the question 'Who am I?' They stress that there are no right and wrong answers. You might like to try it.

*There are 20 numbered blanks in the table below. Please write 20 answers to the simple question 'Who am I?'*

*in the blanks. Just give 20 different answers to this question. Answer as if you were giving the answers to yourself, not to somebody else. Write the answers in the order they occur to you. Don't worry about logic or 'importance'. Go along fairly fast, for time is limited.* Now look at *The big debate* on p. 239.

| | | | |
|---|---|---|---|
| 1 | 6 | 11 | 16 |
| 2 | 7 | 12 | 17 |
| 3 | 8 | 13 | 18 |
| 4 | 9 | 14 | 19 |
| 5 | 10 | 15 | 20 |

their lifestyle, relationships and even religion in search of an elusive 'true self'. Beset by the widespread 'relativism' of modern societies, people without a moral compass have lost the security and certainty once provided by tradition.

To David Riesman (1970; orig. 1950), pre-industrial societies promote what he calls **tradition-directedness**, *rigid conformity to time-honoured ways of living.* Members of traditional societies model their lives on what has gone before, so that what is 'good' is equivalent to 'what has always been'. Tradition-directedness, then, carries to the level of individual experience Toennies' *Gemeinschaft* and Durkheim's mechanical solidarity (see Chapters 1 and 4). Culturally conservative, tradition-directed people think and act alike because everyone draws on the same solid cultural foundation. Amish people exemplify tradition-direction; in Amish culture, tradition ties everyone to ancestors and descendants in an unbroken chain of righteous living.

Many members of diverse and rapidly changing societies define a tradition-directed personality as deviant because it seems so rigid. Modern people, by and large, prize personal flexibility, the capacity to adapt and sensitivity to others. Riesman describes this type of social character as **other-directedness**, *a receptiveness to the latest trends and fashions, often expressed in the practice of imitating others.* Because their socialisation occurs within societies that are constantly in flux, other-directed people develop fluid identities marked by superficiality, inconsistency and

change. They try on different 'selves', almost like so many pieces of new clothing, seek out 'role models' and engage in varied 'performances' as they move from setting to setting (Goffman, 1959). In a traditional society, such 'shiftiness' marks a person as untrustworthy, but in a changing, modern society, the chameleon-like ability to fit in virtually anywhere stands as a valued personal trait.

In societies that value the up-to-date rather than the traditional, people anxiously solicit the approval of others, looking to members of their own generation rather than to elders as significant role models. 'Peer pressure' can sometimes be irresistible to people with no enduring standards to guide them. Our society urges individuals to be true to themselves. But when social surroundings change so rapidly, how can people determine to which self they should be true? This problem lies at the root of the identity crisis so widespread in industrial societies today. 'Who am I?' is a nagging question that many of us struggle to answer. In truth, this problem is not so much psychological as sociological, reflecting the inherent instability of modern mass society.

Most recently, we have seen the arrival of postmodern identities. These are altogether less unified identities and much more fragmented. Identity now becomes **decentred**, *a process by which a centre, core or essence is destabilised and weakened.* This connects to many of the changes we have already identified – globalisation, feminism, proliferating new voices – and generates the search for 'new frameworks' of self-understanding. Giddens talks about all this as a reflexive self-identity:

> . . . because of the 'openness' of social life today, the pluralisation of contexts of action and the diversity of 'authorities', life style choice is increasingly important in the constitution of identity and daily activity. Reflexively organised life planning . . . becomes a central feature of the structuring of self-identity.

(Giddens, 1991: 5)

What we find is that the very idea of personal identity can be thrown into doubt.

As we shall see later (Chapters 22 and 23), the presence of the new information technologies and the new media also leads to what has been called a 'culture of simulation'. This is a kind of virtual reality through which we come to live increasingly in worlds of media images and cyberspaces. The question now being asked is in what way this might be leading to new kinds of 'simulated identity' and 'cyber identity', as even the modern boundaries get eroded. On the internet, it is suggested, people can – if only for a while – become whoever they wish.

Table 7.2 briefly charts some of these shifts in the meanings of identities.

# The sociology of bodies

Bodies – perhaps more than anything else – seem to be straightforwardly biological, 'natural' and given. Indeed, at first sight, bodies do not seem to be the most obvious area for sociologists to study. After all, so the argument goes, bodies are biological and individual:

| Table 7.2 | **The shifting nature of identities** | |
|---|---|---|
| **Traditional** | **Modern** | **Postmodern** |
| Given | Determined and structured | Chosen |
| Taken-for-granted | Polarised/dichotomous | Multiple/fragmenting |
| Powerful but hidden | Predictable | Chaotic |
| Essential | Essentialising | De-essentialising |

sociologists are surely only interested in the cultural and the social. But if we think about our own bodies for a bit and use our newly discovered sociological imagination (see Chapter 1), we will soon discover that our bodies are indeed social (see Figure 7.4).

## The social body

Traditionally, we may look at bodies through what has been called a 'Cartesian dualism' that divides bodies from non-bodies and mind from matter. René Descartes (1591–1650) is often considered the founder of modern philosophy, and at the heart of his arguments was the conclusion that mind is a non-corporeal substance, distinct from a material or bodily substance. The taken-for-granted assumption is that of the 'natural body'. True, it may become weakened in all sorts of ways (and medicine is largely there to help repair it), but the body is 'natural'.

This view is no longer tenable for sociologists. The boundaries and borders of bodies with nature and technologies have significantly dissolved. We are instead, according to the sociologist Chris Shilling, involved in **body projects**, *the process of becoming and transforming a biological entity through social action*. We work on our bodies in myriad ways – from clothing, washing and hygiene to medical and fitness regimes.

## The scaling and commodification of bodies – poor bodies/rich bodies

Bodies change across space and time, and much of this may also be linked to bodies in poor and rich countries. What we could call 'poor bodies' may be linked to dirt (sanitation), disease, death, danger and diet (or lack of it), while bodies in high-income countries ('rich bodies') engage with 'body projects' such as dieting, exercise, training, body modification – from tattoos and haircuts to plastic surgery, transgender surgery and on to cyborgs (Shilling, 2003). If intimacies are grounded in bodies, then the scaling of bodies give very different meanings and responses in rich and poor worlds.

Linked to globalisation is the growth of trafficking in body parts. Everything from skin, bone and blood to organs and genetic materials of 'the other' is now up for sale, and this global trafficking is almost invariably in one direction: from the poorest to the richest. Often justified in terms of 'choices', this is part of a process of bodily commodification. As two people remarked in seeming desperation:

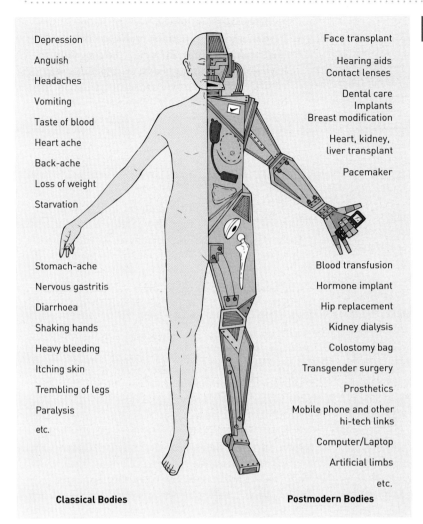

Figure 7.4

The social body: from classical bodies to postmodern bodies

**Classical Bodies**

Depression

Anguish

Headaches

Vomiting

Taste of blood

Heart ache

Back-ache

Loss of weight

Starvation

Stomach-ache

Nervous gastritis

Diarrhoea

Shaking hands

Heavy bleeding

Itching skin

Trembling of legs

Paralysis

etc.

**Postmodern Bodies**

Face transplant

Hearing aids
Contact lenses

Dental care
Implants
Breast modification

Heart, kidney,
liver transplant

Pacemaker

Blood transfusion

Hormone implant

Hip replacement

Kidney dialysis

Colostomy bag

Transgender surgery

Prosthetics

Mobile phone and other
hi-tech links

Computer/Laptop

Artificial limbs

etc.

I am willing to sell any organ of my body that is not vital to my survival and which could help save another person's life in exchange for an amount of money that will allow me to feed my family.

(Ad placed in the *Diaro de Pernambuyco*, Recife, Brazil, by Miguel Correira de Oliveira, aged 30)

Please, I need money to get dentures, and am a senior desparet [sic] for money. Want to sell a very good kidney. Am desparet for money for teeth. Am a senior citizen in excellent medical shape, but need $ for dentures. My husband and I have no dental plan.

(Email from E. B., Oak Hills, California, cited in Scheper-Hughes and Wacquant, 2002: 42)

Nancy Scheper-Hughes has chronicled the rise in this process of bodily commodification and the sale of organs, and puts it dramatically:

Continuous throughout these transactions across time and space is the division of society into two populations, one socially and medically included and the other excluded, one with and one utterly lacking the ability to draw on the beauty, strength, reproductive, sexual, or anatomical power of the other . . . Commercialised transplant medicine has allowed global society to be divided into two decidedly unequal populations – organ givers and organ receivers. The former are an invisible and discredited collection of anonymous suppliers of spare parts; the latter are cherished patients, treated as moral subjects and as suffering individuals. *Their* names and their biographies and medical histories are known, and their proprietary rights over the body parts of the poor, living and dead, are virtually unquestioned.

(Scheper-Hughes and Wacquant, 2002: 4)

## Open and closed bodies

Sociologist Deborah Lupton (1998: 72) has indeed suggested a movement from a body that was predominantly 'open' in premodern times to one that has become increasingly 'closed' and regulated in modern times. Basically, what she means to capture with this idea is a major shift from societies where the body was ever present to one where we increasingly try to regulate and control it. In an analysis of medieval and early modern German culture, the historian Christel Roper describes how the body was seen as:

> a container for a series of processes: defecation, sexual pollution, vomiting. Fluids course about within the body, erupting out of it, leaving their mark on the outside world. The body is not so much a collection of joints and limbs, or a skeletal structure, as a container of fluids, bursting out in every direction to impact on the environment.
>
> (Roper, 1994: 23)

This was a messy world of strange fluids, smells and diseases – the body an ever-present source of chaos.

But with the enlightenment (see Chapter 1), the sociologist Norbert Elias (see the box on p. 233) suggests that we became increasingly preoccupied with taming and regulating our bodily functions and processes. They became increasingly civilised and under control. The most apparent examples of this today would be dieting, fitness regimes, medical regimes for the elderly and sick as well as plastic surgery. On this latter concern alone, Adele Clarke estimates that it is a $1.75 billion a year industry in the United States, with about 1.5 million people undergoing plastic surgery of some kind (Clarke, 1995: 147).

But there are more extreme examples which are becoming of interest. Thus, the Human Genome Project – discussed in Chapter 23 – raises the issue of genetics and the body. Basically, when every gene in the body has been identified, will this lead to radical transformations of our bodies as we undergo gene replacement?

Sociologists are also starting to discuss **cyborgs**, *creatures which connect human and biological properties to technological ones.* Anyone drugged to feel better, reprogrammed to resist disease or given an artificial organ or limb, is technically a cyborg. By this definition, currently some:

> 10% of the US population are estimated to be cyborgs in the technical sense, including people with electronic pacemakers, artificial joints, drug implant systems, implanted corneal lenses and

artificial skin. A much higher percentage participate in occupations that make them into metaphoric cyborgs, including the computer keyboard operator joined in cybernetic system with the screen, the neurosurgeon guided by fibre optic microscopy during an operation, and the teen game player in the local video arcade.
>
> (Hayles, 1995: 321)

## Health and illness

The sociology of health and illness – discussed more fully in Chapter 21 – may also be seen as looking at the way in which the body breaks down and needs to be socially repaired. Medical regimes are required to organise all this work around disease, decay and death. The final inability to repair the body results in death, and the need then is to find some socially organised way of dealing with dead bodies.

Sarah Nettleton has suggested a number of reasons for the growing sociological interest in the body. First has been the recent attempts by women to gain control over their bodies from male-dominated professionals (evidenced in the Boston Women's Health Book Collective, *Our Bodies, Ourselves* (1978; orig. 1971)). Second has been the growth of the new reproductive technologies (described in Chapter 18), which are shifting the meaning of foetus, birth and body. Thirdly, the 'greying of the population' (highlighted in Chapter 13) means that larger numbers of people will have to come to terms not only with the 'ageing body' but also the possibility of taking their own life. Fourthly, consumer patterns (see Chapter 15) are increasingly concerned with body products: everything from 'the fitness industry' to the 'cosmetics industry'. Fifthly, the arrival of AIDS in the early 1980s served to remind us of the limits of medical technology. And finally, ethical issues around the body – from abortion to research on embryos – are opening up debates about the boundaries between life and death (Nettleton, 1995: 102–3).

# The sociology of emotions in everyday life

Emotions would seem to be another one of those topics that is far removed from sociological analysis. Emotions, after all, are something we feel within; they are personal, psychological, private. But think about it again. For in recent years, sociologists have turned their

## Norbert Elias: the civilising of bodies and societies

The German–English sociologist Norbert Elias (1897–1990) made important contributions to the study of both sociology and social change. A refugee from Hitler's Germany, his studies of *The Civilizing Process* (originally published in Germany in 1939) suggest how from the Middle Ages onwards in most of Europe, people came to exert greater self-control over their behaviour and their bodies. Through a series of studies of ways of eating, sleeping, dressing, spitting, having sex, defecating, dying and eliminating, he charts the changing ways of life.

Medieval life was unpredictable, highly emotional, often chaotic and indulgent, and there were few codes around bodily functions. Court society slowly started to change all this, by bringing about etiquette for body management, locations for defecation, and sleeping. Restraint appeared in codes such as those managing table manners. The state developed side by side with a 'civilised' system of self-control. The civilised society has self-discipline, self-control, higher shame and embarrassment, etc.

Chris Shilling (1993) summarises three key processes involved in civilising: socialisation, rationalisation and individualisation. People are taught to hide natural functions – like defecating and urinating; rationalisation makes us less emotional; individualisation suggests that we come to see ourselves and our bodies as distinctively separate.

All of this is part of Elias's wider approach to sociology, developed in his *What is Sociology?* (1978b; orig. 1970), and known as 'figurational sociology'. Interactions between individuals and societies are his area of study: 'the network of inter-dependencies among human beings is what binds them together' (1978a: 261; orig. 1939).

Elias's work has been influential on a range of scholars who study everyday life processes. Stephen Mennell, for instance, has studied food.

*Source*: Elias (1978a; orig. 1939).

attentions to a full array of feelings, and suggested that there may indeed be social patterns to these too.

Think for a moment about your own emotions and those of your friends. Do you show them with ease, or do you perhaps try to conceal them? Do you talk about your feelings at all? And do you show different patterns of feeling from those of your friends? Maybe boys show aggression more than girls? There are surely moments when you are permitted to cry (at weddings and funerals) and moments when you may want to but know it is not appropriate (at job interviews or in gang conflicts). There are places when it seems right to 'disclose' your feelings (to loved ones, in therapy groups) and other times when it would be clearly odd to do so (perhaps to shop assistants or public officials). There is once again a certain social pattern around our feelings, and it is this which sociologists look for.

Arlie Hochschild (1983) has been prominent in introducing an important way of thinking about emotions in sociology. One of her early studies was concerned with the everyday work of airline stewardesses. This is becoming an increasingly common job – and it requires working under great pressure. Global traffic, tight confinements, 'air rage passengers', 'waitressing' and the like make it quite a taxing job. But as Hochschild spends time observing the training of these flight attendants, she realises that they are being trained to do a different kind of job. She comments:

> The young trainee sitting next to me wrote on her notepad, 'Important to smile. Don't forget to smile'. The admonition came from the speaker in the front of the room, a crew-cut pilot in his early fifties, speaking in a Southern drawl: 'Now girls, I want you to go out there and really *smile*. Your smile is your biggest asset. I want you to go out there and use it. Smile, *really* smile. Really *lay it on*.'

(Hochschild, 1983: 4)

A core of their training, she found, was that they should be 'nice to people'. This is one of many jobs which involve service work where a central task is to smile, to be courteous, and to show your 'niceness' to others. Indeed, so basic is it that if a stewardess was not nice to you, she might well lose her job (unless, of course, there were very good reasons for this behaviour: for example, you had attacked her!) From this study, Hochschild introduces several key ideas. First, she shows how emotions are socially constructed and presented. In this she continues to draw upon the work of Goffman, mentioned above. Here we are dealing not so much with self-management as with

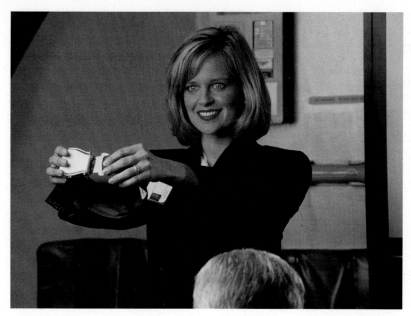

Arlie Hochschild's *The Managed Heart* (1984) helped shape the new sociology of emotions. Her fieldwork was amongst air hostesses where she observed them being trained to look cheerful and be happy. These days many forms of work require that we sell our emotions and smiles: we are paid to be nice

*Source*: Pearson Education Ltd/Photodisc/Jack Hollingsworth.

emotional management. But in any event, how you present your feelings also plays a role in forming and showing your self and identity. Secondly, she suggests that the task for a sociologist is to locate the *feeling rules* that are found in specific situations and that enable people to match their feelings with the expectations of a situation; feeling rules act as guides as to how to perform. Finally, she pioneered an important new concept: **emotional labour**, *the management of feeling to create a publicly observable facial and bodily display* (Hochschild, 1983: 7). In a way this is a new form of work involving more and more people. It involves the selling not of a skill or a craft, but of a particular emotional style. Emotion work is another form of emotional labour, but it is done in private: caring, for example, within the home; or sometimes maybe during sex with a partner (Duncombe and Marsden, 1993).

In Duncombe and Marsden's (1993) study of love and intimacy in heterosexual coupledom, they stress the importance of emotional work inside relationships. From their findings, they report the unhappiness of women at men's general unwillingness to do the emotional work needed to sustain a relationship. The women felt 'psychically deserted'. Rather pessimistically, they conclude that 'men's difficulties in expressing intimate emotions will emerge as a major source of the "private troubles" underlying the "public issues" of rising divorces and family breakdown, or the instability of cohabitation among couples who may often be parents' (Duncombe and Marsden, 1993: 233).

## Concluding reflection: the puzzles of individual and society – again

In sociology, a continuous (and endless) tension exists between the individual and society. We have already seen it in the debate over action and structure (see the *Big debate* at the end of this chapter) and it haunts much of sociological research. The social, as we have seen, implies some sense of collective life, of togetherness, whilst the individual implies that in some sense individual people can become cut off, and separate from, other 'individuals'. And the puzzle is how they can be brought together.

So here are some big questions. How can there be individuals within society and a society with individuals? How can the individual dwell in the social and the social dwell in the individual? How can individuals function as individuals within a society that must take away their individuality if it is to run well for all the other individuals too, and in an orderly fashion? How can a society develop a cohesion and a collectivity whilst fostering an individuality and cultivating a unique humanity? How can we have communities and bonding which do not overreach themselves into totalitarianisms and despotism? How can we have creative and caring individuals who do not overreach themselves into selfish, narcissistic egoists? How, in short, can we develop and maintain a balance of individuality and sociality in life and society? Most sociologists ultimately address this issue in some way or another; it is the big social question. If 'individuals' triumph, we can so often sense a crumbling anarchy of egoism and selfishness taking over; if the 'social' triumphs, we can so often sense a painful loss of individuality as we are stalked by collective terrors.

A good starting point might be to think about the balance of the individual and the social in a personal life – even your own. Individual human beings are quite likely to follow their own personal desires and interests – will be selfish – unless there are good reasons not to. There is a huge amount of evidence from biology and history of the selfish gene or of self-interest. We can challenge the details, but with everything equal I follow my self-preservation and interests. I want what is best for me. But – and this soon dawns on any thinking individual – to get this requires a bonding with others. To be on my own will be to *not* function. Without others, social life as we know it cannot function. One of the first features of becoming social is the development of the awareness of others. Our lives are henceforward shaped by these others. Following our own interests requires, in fact, that we attend to others – not all others, but some: and usually those nearest and dearest. Life becomes a struggle of attaching to others and then rejecting and losing them. At a small-scale level of social life, we are constantly bonding and breaking away. It is this making of bonds and their dissolution as we create our own individuality which is a key preoccupation of sociology.

## Conclusion: micro-sociology

This chapter has served as only the briefest of introductions to a number of issues that are often termed micro-sociology, and which focus on everyday life and its social construction. We have suggested the importance of a lifelong socialisation process in helping to shape who we become during our lives; and of the importance of situations in building up the social notions of identity, body and emotion. Even as we may like to think of ourselves as 'free individuals', micro-sociology shows us how, even in the smallest moments of everyday feelings and encounters, the social is present, helping to shape the outcomes.

# SUMMARY

**1** The phrase 'social construction of reality' conveys the important idea that we all build the social world through our interaction. The Thomas theorem states: 'Situations defined as real become real in their consequences.'

**2** For individuals, socialisation is the process of building our humanity and particular identity through social experience. For society as a whole, socialisation is the means by which one generation transmits culture to the next. The permanently damaging effects of social isolation reveal the importance of social experience to human development.

**3** A century ago, people thought most human behaviour was guided by biological instinct. Today, the nature–nurture debate has tipped the other way as we understand human behaviour to be primarily a product of a social environment. So-called human nature is actually the capacity to create variable cultural patterns.

**4** Sigmund Freud envisaged the human personality as composed of three parts. The id represents general human drives (the life and death instincts), which Freud claimed were innate. The superego embodies cultural values and norms internalised by individuals. Competition between the needs of the id and the restraints of the superego are mediated by the ego. To George Herbert Mead, socialisation is based on the emergence of the self, which he viewed as partly autonomous (the I) and partly guided by society (the Me). Mead contended that, beginning with imitative behaviour, the self develops through play and games and eventually recognises the 'generalised other'. Charles Horton Cooley used the term 'looking-glass self' to underscore that the self is influenced by how we think others respond to us.

**5** Dramaturgical analysis studies how people construct personal performances. This approach casts everyday life in terms of theatrical performances, noting the settings of interaction, the use of body language and how performers often idealise their intentions. Ethnomethodology seeks to reveal the assumptions and understandings that people have of their social world.

**6** The life course itself is largely a social construction. People in different societies may experience a stage of life quite differently, or not at all. Lives can be located through such ideas as a 'historical timeline' and birth cohorts. Life stages may be changing as the formal patterns found in the past are breaking down, with people 'dipping in and out' of phases in a much less regularised and institutionalised fashion.

**7** Identity concerns our understanding of who we are. Identity refers to sameness and serves to link a sense of who we are to a wider culture. Identities change across time and space, from traditional societies where identities are shared and communal, given as part of the world, the cosmos and nature, to postmodern societies where identities are seriously questioned and challenged. Bodies were predominantly 'open' and ever present in premodern times, whereas they have become increasingly 'closed' and regulated in modern times. The body is social and 'body projects' involve the process of becoming and transforming a biological entity through social action.

**8** Sociologists look at body projects – and consider the ways in which a biological entity is transformed through social actions. Some examples would include the ways in which bodies may be scaled, open or closed, and civilised.

**9** Emotions are socially constructed and presented. The sociologist looks at *feeling rules* that are found in specific situations and that enable people to match their feelings with the expectations of a situation; and at emotional labour.

# MYTASKLIST

# Ten suggestions for going further

## 1 Connect up with Part Six and the Sociology Web Resources

As you work through ideas and think about the issues raised in this chapter, look at the accompanying website and the resource centre at the end of this book which connects to it. There is a lot here to help you move on. To link up, see: www.pearson.co.uk/plummer.

## 2 Review the chapter

*Briefly summarise (in a paragraph) just what this chapter has been about.* Consider: (a) What have you learned? (b) What do you disagree with? Be critical. And (c) How would you develop all this? How could you get more detail on matters that interest you?

## 3 Pose questions

(a) Using the questions raised about the socialisation process as your guide, consider your own life experiences of socialisation.
(b) Take any social situation – a meeting with friends, a visit to the doctor, a shopping trip, a fight – and using ideas from this chapter, suggest how it is 'socially constructed'.
(c) Starting with your hair, move down your body to your feet – considering each body part. How far is each of these body parts made 'social'?
(d) Examine the ways in which the body is being changed by machines of all kinds.
(e) Are men less emotional than women, or do they just construct their emotions in different ways?
(f) Look at the table, which names many 'meanings of the self'. Look at them and see if you can guess what they mean. Then think of your own self and which terms if any apply to you. How do you come to make sense of your own self?

### The multiple meanings of the self: where do you fit?

| | | | |
|---|---|---|---|
| Essential | Core | Unified | Stable |
| Substantial | Spiritual | Material | Social |
| Dramaturgical | Presented | Impression management | Constructed |
| Working | Distancing | Embracing | Engulfing |
| Narrated | Embodied | Emotional | Multiple |
| Narcissistic | Contradictory | Fragmented | 'In crisis' |
| Saturated | Mediated | Consumerised | Global |
| Individualised | Cyborg/ digitalised | Disciplined | Regulated |
| Political | Moral | Hybridic | Diasporic |
| Traditional | Modern | Postmodern | Homeless |

## 4 Explore key words

Many concepts have been introduced in this chapter. You can review them from the website or from the listing at the back of this book. You might like to give special attention to just five words and think them through – how would you define them, what are they dealing with, and do they help you see the social world more clearly or not?

## 5 Search the Web

Be critical when you look at websites – see the box on p. 940 in the Resources section. Some useful sources for this chapter are as follows:

### Freud

The Freud Archives
http://users.rcn.com/brill/freudarc.html

There are many websites on Freud, but this one contains a biography, his writings, photos, and libraries and museums.

## Symbolic interactionism

Society for the Study of Symbolic Interaction
www.espach.salford.ac.uk/sssi/index.php
The website of the Society for the Study of Symbolic Interaction. A good source for developing ideas about symbolic interactionism.

## Feral children

www.feralchildren.com/en/index.php
The website 'feral children' provides a detailed listing of all known feral children, including links to original documents.

## Ethnomethodology and conversational analysis

http://www2.fmg.uva.nl/emca
Information, resources, event listings, and weblinks on ethnomethodology and conversation analysis.

## 6 Watch a DVD

### Case studies of extremely deprived children

- François Truffaut's *The Wild Boy of Aveyron* (1970): a delightful film about a French 'wolf boy' named Victor.
- Werner Herzog's *The Enigma of Kasper Hauser* (1974): a classic about a German boy.
- The story of Helen Keller is told in her *The Story of My Life* (1902) and in Arthur Penn's film *The Miracle Worker* (1962) and William Gibson's play *The Miracle Worker* (1962) (with Anne Bancroft and Patty Duke – both of whom won Oscars).

### Interaction issues

- Hal Ashby's *Being There* (1979): a comedy in which Peter Sellers plays an illiterate gardener, unable to present himself properly, eventually coming to be seen as some kind of hero.
- Harold Ramis's *Groundhog Day* (1993): life lived over and over again in the same way. This really is an interaction ritual.
- Woody Allen's *Zelig* (1983): like most of Woody Allen films this one raises the problems of human interaction. *Zelig* is good on multiple identities and the film is full of technical trickery to achieve this.
- Sacha Baron Cohen's *Borat: Cultural Learnings of America for Make Profit* (2006): outrageously challenges all everyday assumptions.

### The body

- David Cronenberg's *The Fly* (1986): a classic horror film remade to be even more gruesome, but interesting concerning the social body, as a man's body becomes that of a fly.
- James Glickenhaus's *The Exterminator* (1970) and later spin-offs with Arnold Schwarzenegger were popular in the early 1990s and bring to the screen the issues of cyborgs, as does Fritz Lang's *Metropolis* (1926).

## 7 Think and read

Alfred R. Lindesmith, Anselm L. Strauss and Norman K. Denzin, *Social Psychology* (8th edn, 1999; orig. 1949). This is a classic textbook to introduce this whole field, with strong links to symbolic interactionism.

John P. Hewitt and David Shulman, *Self and Society* (10th edn, 2010). Provides an account of the symbolic-interactionist tradition on which much of this chapter is based.

Erving Goffman, *The Presentation of Self in Everyday Life* (1959). Goffman's first and best-known book.

Peter L. Berger and Thomas Luckmann, *The Social Construction of Reality: A Treatise in the Sociology of Knowledge* (1967). A more advanced study that elaborates on the argument that individuals generate meaning through their social interaction.

Susie Scott, *Making Sense of Everyday Life* (2009). Useful introduction to the sociology of everyday life – briefly discussed in the box on p. 225.

Anthony Giddens, *Self Identity and Late Modernity* (1991). An important study that suggests how socialisation processes are changing in the modern world.

Robin Woofitt and Ian Hutchby, *Conversational Analysis: Principles, Practices and Applications* (1998) and Celia Kitzinger, *Feminism and Conversational Analysis* (2003). Two useful guides to conversational analysis with different emphases.

Nancy Scheper-Hughes and Loic Wacquant (eds), *Commodifying Bodies* (2002). A lively collection of essays that details the ways in which bodily parts and bodies are sold or turned into sellable commodities.

Anthony Elliott and Charles Lemert, *The New Individualism* (2009, rev. edn). An account of contemporary selves – worth a look.

## 8 Relax with a novel

Read also Luke Rheinehart's *The Dice Man* (1971, reissued 2000) for an account of a man who creates his identity based upon the throw of a dice. The work of George Eliot, especially *Middlemarch* (1871–2), conveys a great deal about emotion and interaction. See also Candace Clark's *Misery and Company: Sympathy in Everyday Life* (1977).

## 9 Connect to other chapters

- Discussions on the body connect to many chapters, but see Chapter 12 on gender, Chapter 13 on ageing and Chapter 21 on health.
- Link the discussion of Mead to that of symbolic interactionism in Chapter 2.

# 10 Engage in THE BIG DEBATE

## Who am I? identity crisis in our time

To start: Ask yourself the question: **Who am I?** The table on p. 229 provides a very simple 'Who am I?' test (also known as the Twenty Statement test). You might like to start this discussion by privately indicating twenty answers to yourself. Just who are you? How do you define yourself?

Let's now think about some of your responses.

- Did they indicate your membership in a particular country (Australian), or a particular culture (Muslim, Goth)? These are identities we have touched upon in this part of the book.
- Did they indicate your class ('stinking rich', 'bottom billion'?), your gender (female, transgendered?), your sexuality (gay?), your ethnicity (black, Muslim?), your disablement (blind, educational difficulties?), your age (centenarian or child?)? These are identities connected to the inequalities which we discuss in Chapters 8–14.
- Did they indicate your work situation, your politics, your family position, your religion, your educational position (e.g. student), your health (e.g. a person with AIDS), or even science and technology (you may be a 'test tube baby' or a 'person with a liver transplant'). These are identities connected to the central institutions of society and which we discuss in Chapters 15–23.

All these could be seen as pretty clear and strong identities which people often have and which are linked to key concerns in society.

Consider, though, what other identities you may have that do not fit this. Here is a rag-bag of identities that people may have:

> I am what I am. I am a happy person. I am an angst-ridden person in deep despair. I am in love. I am a Jewish queer. I am a Muslim atheist. I am a feminist man. I am an Asian Australian. I am a Catholic abortionist. I am a cyberspace queen.

In the modern world, the claim is that we came to develop new but strong identities. When we faced difficult times – as in our youth – we might have faced an 'identity crisis', but most of the time we roughly knew who we were and could, over a bit of time, sort out our identity. But now, as we drift into the new social order of the twenty-first century, it is claimed that our identities are much less stable, clear or coherent. Indeed, many are now living in a permanently unsettled identity crisis. Indeed, they are de-decentred and fragmented (see Table 7.2). As you provided your list of identities, did you find that you were more 'modern' or 'postmodern' in your identity list?

Many sociologists have addressed these kinds of concern. For the whole of the twentieth century, books were being written that tried to characterise the sorts of identity and identity crises we were facing. There are books that talk of *the narcissistic self* (Lasch), *the protean self* (Lifton), *the mutable self* (Zurcher), *the saturated self* (Gergen), *the abstract self* (Ziejerderveld). We also have *the cosmopolitan self, the homeless self, the individualised self, the fragmented self* and many more. Some writers have also taken to hyphenating identities: Asian-gay, Muslim-British, feminist-man. These immediately suggest some kind of tension within the identity. Other writers suggest global identities: global souls (Picolo), global citizens, people with global human rights, etc. Some talk of hybridic identities. Just who are the Japanese hip hop people we met in Chapter 2? (see Condry, *Hip Hop Japan*, 2006). Just who are the European queers in the European Song Contest that we will meet briefly in Chapter 22? And, perhaps more significant than any other at the start of the twenty-first century, just who are the identities we present and fashion on the net? Who and what are our cyber-identities?

A closing thought: the sociologist Zygmunt Bauman once said: 'If the modern "problem of identity" was how to construct an identity and keep it solid and stable, the post-modern "problem of identity" is primarily how to avoid fixation and keep the options open' (Bauman, 1996: 19).

### Continue the debate

1 In what ways do you think notions of self and identity have really changed over the past 100 years?
2 Is it possible for you to be identity-less?
3 Consider how many of the new social movements discussed throughout this book (see Chapter 16, p. 565) raise issues of identity – or what has been called 'the politics of identity'.

# Researching food

## From macro to micro

*The history of the world, my sweet, is who gets eaten and who gets to eat.*

Stephen Sondheim's *Sweeney Todd*

Part Two of this book has been looking at some building blocks for doing sociology: *society*, *culture*, *organisations* and *interaction*. There has been a move *from macro to micro* as we move from the widest social processes to the smallest. Any social phenomena can be analysed through these building blocks – crime, families, wars, bicycling. In this interlude we have selected one issue: food. There can be a sociology of anything – so why not food?

A *sociology of food* examines how food connects to the macro–micro flow, and how all life depends on this. It examines how food is enormously varied across societies, cultures, organisations and interactions. Among the questions it asks are:

1 *Society*. How has 'food' changed across societies – past and present? How can we understand these food changes in societies? We might even ask if societies today are 'progressing' in their eating habits!

2 *Culture*. How does food become a 'design for living' with its own values, beliefs, behaviour practices and material objects that constitute a people's way of life? What meanings, values and practices are linked to it?

3 *Organisation and network*. What are food networks? How does 'food' get organised in social life? How is it produced, distributed, sold and consumed through networks and organisations?

4 *Interaction*. How does food change across the life cycle? How does food involve the presentation of a self? How does it link to language, body and emotion? What role does it play in the story of our lives?

You will not be surprised by now to learn that there is a vast amount of writing and research on the sociology of food. Here there is only space to get you going, and to introduce just a few of these issues.

## 1 Food and society

Food is usually seen as very high on a basic list of items needed to survive (and so it should be: nutritionists today tell us that our bodies need some 1,300 calories a day to live: but Western societies usually take in much more than that in a day). High on the list of real human needs has to be 'food' – without food we die (*needs* are necessities that people require in order to live – usually food, shelter and clothing; *wants* are our socially generated desires – things that people would like to have but which are not necessary).

The history of societies can, in part, be seen as the evolution of food – no food, no society. The classic descriptions of major societies given in Chapter 4 are in reality partial descriptions of food production. In early societies, one key task involved roaming around the earth to find food sources (hunter-gatherers). Once food stocks were depleted, there was a need to move on. But once the idea of cultivating food was struck upon, societies could become more settled. Geographic differences in local vegetation systems and animals were more or less available for 'domestication'. Water systems needed to be developed; plants needed to be grown in settled areas; animals reared. The rise of food production varied around the world. But where food production was developed and advanced, many other skills could be developed: writing, germ control, technology, political systems.

Many writers have examined the history of food, and suggested that the evolution of industrial society can be seen as part of a wider civilising process (see the box on Elias, p. 233). Stephen Mennel, *All Manners of Food* (1984) has traced this history.

# Think and discuss

## Are there stages in the evolution of food?

1 Hunting and gathering.
2 Horticultural and pastoral – domestication of animals.
3 Agrarian – large-scale farming.
4 Industrial – the rise of mass production/ technological food.
5 Post-industrial – postmodern fusion and McDonaldsisation.

For a fascinating full account of the rise of food chains in society and the emergence of different kinds of societies, see Jared Diamond's *Guns, Germs and Steel: The Fates of Human Societies* (1997). You can also download much of it on YouTube. Food for Jared is a key shaper of evolution. He is not a sociologist, and sociologists are often critical of his view.

## Food in late modern society

Most recently, food has taken on ever new forms. Tim Lang and Michael Heasman, in their book *Food Wars* (2004), comment that 'the 20th century witnessed arguably one of the most significant food revolutions since settled agriculture began around 10,000 years ago' (p. 139). Since then we have seen radical changes in the ways food is grown, processed, distributed and consumed.
We can see this in such changes as:

1 *Growing food* (agro-farming and biotechnology): much food is now grown with the aid of chemicals and hybrid plants, and animals are reared on factory farms.

2 *Processing food*: food is processed through high technologies and cheap labour across the world.

3 *New distribution systems across the world* (e.g. airfreight, heavy-lorry networks and satellite tracking).

4 *Retailing and marketing*: increasingly in the hands of monopolies and large **transnational corporations** (for more on TNCs, see Chapter 15).

5 *Consumption*: the creation of new tastes and brands. We now eat breakfast bars, pick at taco crisps from a bag and Mexican dips in jars, slurp alco-pops, and eat a wide variety of global food that comes pre-packed and chilled or frozen in the supermarket. And all foods now come 'branded' through advertising. In 2002 alone, there were 13,600 new food products introduced to the world (75 per cent were sweets, breakfast cereals, bakery products, dairy products, beverages and condiments – Lang and Heasman, 2004: 140). Stand in your local supermarket and just try to count the number of foods available to you in one aisle! Eating is shopping.

In all of this we can see the growth of large TNCs dominating the organisation of food (see Chapter 15) and the significance of the globalisation of food. A worldwide food economy of considerable size and economic power has been created. And with this has come a major set of concerns about 'food' in our diets and the environment – many Western diseases are linked to modern eating problems.

### TOP 10
### Food companies, 2008

| Ranking | Previous ranking | Company name | 2008 food sales |
|---|---|---|---|
| 1 | 4 | Nestle (USA and Canada) | $26.477 |
| 2 | 1 | Tyson Foods Inc. | 26,325 |
| 3 | 2 | Pepsico Inc. | 25,346 |
| 4 | 3 | Kraft Foods Inc. | 23,956 |
| 5 | 5 | Anheuser-Busch InBev | 15,571 |
| 6 | 6 | Dean Foods Co. | 12,455 |
| 7 | 7 | General Mills Inc. | 12,100 |
| 8 | 8 | Smithfield Foods Inc. | 10,726 |
| 9 | 10 | Kellogg Co. | 8,457 |
| 10 | 13 | Coca-Cola Co. | 8,205 |

*Source*: Based on Foodprocessing.com, August 2009.

Following on from this, it is now suggested that there is a 'nutrition transition' taking place in high-income societies (linked to rising wealth). High-income societies have generated a series of health problems for themselves through their eating habits. But now it seems that these problems are starting to spread to low-income societies – because of the ways in which global marketing trends have been established. We discuss some of these problems in Chapter 21.
To conclude: food, then, is bound up with the processes and development of societies and may even be seen to underlie the creation of societies.

LIVING IN THE C21ST

# Still starving – as we get fatter

According to the United Nations Food and Agriculture Organization (FAO), which measures 'undernutrition', 1.02 billion people are undernourished. That means that roughly one in six people do not get enough food to be healthy and lead an active life. Hunger and malnutrition are in fact the number-one risk to the health worldwide – greater than AIDS, malaria and tuberculosis combined. Nearly all of the undernourished are in developing countries. This hunger, which we discuss further in Chapter 9, pp. 313–14, is seen to be due to a mix of the neglect of agricultural development, increases in prices of food, political conflicts and war, and economic crises. But whatever the reasons, there are dire consequences and children are its most common 'victims'. One out of four children – roughly 146 million – in developing countries are underweight and poor nutrition plays a role in at least half of the 10.9 million child deaths each year – 5 million deaths. Under-nutrition magnifies the effect of every disease, including measles and malaria.

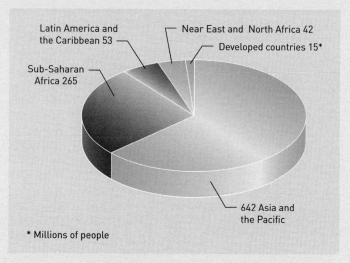

* Millions of people

**More than 1.02 billion hungry people**

*Source*: http://www.fao.org/hunger, Food and Agriculture Organization of the United States.

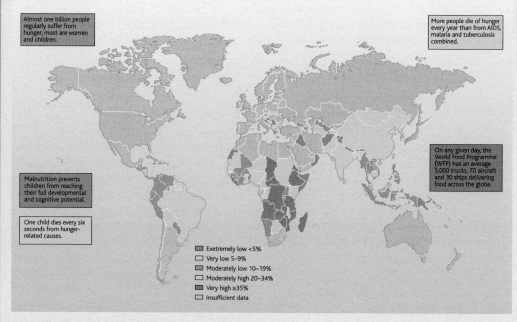

The World Hunger Map 2009

*Note*: for the latest edition, click www.wfp.org/hunger/map.

*Source*: United Nations World Food Programme.

LIVING IN THE C21ST

## The Western problems of obesity and anorexia

By stark contrast, the Western world has very different concerns linked to eating. Here the problems of 'obesity' and 'anorexia' are widely recognised, and Western governments increasingly talk about them and initiate health education programmes around them. Some 60 per cent of the US population and two-thirds of men and over half of women in the UK are estimated to be *overweight*. In England, the proportion of the adult population classified as obese increased from 16 per cent in 1994 to 25 per cent in 2008 (*Social Trends*, 2010). At the same time, there has been a growth of the problem of chronic *underweight* – though not through malnutrition. Found especially among the young, and girls in particular (though it is increasing among boys), underweight issues affect 5–7 per cent of the UK population.

Weight problems also bring serious health issues: being overweight can pose problems of diabetes, heart disease, hypertension and some forms of cancer; being underweight can pose problems of emaciation and diarrhoea, and in extreme cases the symptoms can lead to starvation and a cessation of menstruation. Both can ultimately be life-threatening. The most extreme forms of being underweight are anorexia (a sustained and deliberate restriction of food intake) and bulimia (where food may be consumed in binges but is subsequently 'thrown up'). The most extreme form of being overweight is obesity.

## Obesity

The International Obesity Task Force (IOTF) revealed that 1.7 billion of the world's population was overweight or obese. In the UK, obesity levels have trebled in the past 20 years. In 2007, 24 per cent of adults (aged 16 or over) in England were classified as obese (www.ic.nhs.uk/pubs/opad09). In Europe, one in four adults will be obese by 2010 (*Tackling Obesity in England*, National Audit Office, 2001). In the United States, nearly two-thirds of adults (64.5 per cent) are overweight, with three in ten (30.5 per cent) being obese.

Several social factors seem to be shaping the 'crisis of obesity'. First, Western society is increasingly sedentary. Many people sit for long hours at work with a subsequent decline of exercise. Rising affluence has brought the growth of conveniences such as cars, computers and televisions, all of which remove activity and generate passivity. Secondly, we have witnessed the development of fast foods. Each year, billions of meals are eaten at 'quick service' catering outlets around the world; each day one in five Americans eats in a fast-food restaurant (Millstone and Lang, 2003: 95) and the consumption of fizzy drinks has almost doubled in the past 15 years. These foods are high in fats and sugar. There are, however, signs that this is beginning to change.

Curiously, obesity is not restricted to industrialised or high-income societies. In 1999 a United Nations survey found that in Brazil and Colombia the figure was around 40 per cent – comparable to much of Europe. In China, the consumption of high-fat foods has soared. Traditional diets feature grains and vegetables, but as incomes in developing societies rise, these give way to meals high in fat and sugar, which is the main source of the problem. It is a bitter irony that as low-income societies are trying to reduce hunger, the World Health Organization estimates that over 115 million people in low-income societies also suffer from obesity (and 300 million overall).

## Anorexia and bulimia

Anorexia and bulimia bring an abnormally low bodyweight. In the UK about 1 per cent of female adolescents have anorexia and about 4 per cent of college-aged women have bulimia. Only about 10 per cent of people with anorexia and bulimia are male. This gender difference may reflect our society's different expectations for men and women. Men are supposed to be strong and powerful; they feel ashamed of skinny bodies.

Many have suggested that these eating disorders are part of a wider preoccupation with the body and 'looking good'. The impact here is especially on younger women and girls, who may feel the need to look attractive and slender (though younger men are increasingly being influenced too). Susan Bordo (1993) sees these women as in some ways protesting against the cultural ideals of femininity.

# 2  Food and culture

Food is certainly a material resource necessary for living. But in all cultures it plays a very important role in shaping a 'way of life'. Just think for a moment of cultures and you may well think of their foods. The Italians and their pasta, the Indians and their curries, the British and their fish and chips, the Scottish and their haggis, and the Swedes with their herrings! These are all stereotypes; but they flag the fact that the world is made of a multiplicity of different forms of ethnic eating. Food is built into cultural systems. Interestingly, in a postmodern, global world, we might say that the traditional forms of ethnic cuisine may be breaking down and being modified, becoming more and more blended together. This is 'fusion food' – implying the fusion of global cultures. Sociologists might call this the **hybridisation of food** (we have encountered the idea of hybridisation before: see Chapter 2).

## Food as distinction

In looking at food in culture, sociologists look for the symbolic role of food. It often stands for much more than simple eating. The French sociologist Pierre Bourdieu, for instance, discusses it as a major way of establishing class and 'distinction' in French society.

Bourdieu was a leading French sociologist whom we consider later in the book (see Chapter 20). His prime interests were social class and French society. In his book *Distinction* he uses statistical data to examine both the material and the cultural dimensions of food and eating. The working class, he suggests, treat food as it is, while the bourgeoisie give it all kinds of value and significance – way beyond its basic nutrition For the bourgeoisie, food requires skilful presentation; it is an aesthetic, and it is part of the 'art of living'. He also suggests that 'It is part of men's status to eat and to eat well (and also to drink well); it is particularly insisted that they should eat on the grounds that "it won't keep", and there is something suspect about a refusal.' Women put the food on the table and eat less. In much of social life, Bourdieu suggests, the primary function of food – nutrition – is replaced by a social and aesthetic ritual (Bourdieu, 1984: 197–200).

## Food as rules and regulations

We can also see that food is bound up with rules and regulations. All societies have food rules on what can or cannot be eaten, and often just how (and just when, where and why) food can be eaten. Usually this is bound up with religious codes and norms (see Chapter 19). Consider as a striking example the range of different foods that become prohibited in different cultures, and usually because of religious symbolism. The pig, for instance, is a taboo in Judaism and Islam. Here there is a sense of the violation of boundary categories (which we return to in Chapter 13 when we discuss the boundaries of 'normal bodies'). Some animals can be eaten, but some others are wholly taboo. Few Westerners eat horse or insects or snakes. But these can be common foodstuffs for some cultures at some times (Harris, 1968). Most religions also provide rules and rituals around when we should eat – there are 'fasts' and 'festivals' that are prescribed. There are 613 rules in Leviticus and Deuteronomy about eating food.

## Media food and foodways

Food, then, is built into cultural practices and materials – what we might call 'foodways'. In the modern/postmodern world, food enters our magazines, newspapers, television programmes, films, arts and literature. An interesting example in recent times has been the growth of the television chef and the cookbook. Of course, cookery books have been around for a long time, and they provide fascinating accounts of the cultures of their time. The books of today – and there are many of them – are also a key to changes in our mores. Modern food cultures inhabit worlds of mass marketing, mass media and highly 'spectacular' entertainment formats.

Jamie Oliver is a UK 'celebrity chef' who started in 1998 with his own book and television programme, *The Naked Chef*. With a cheerful 'Essex-lad' style, he moved from being a cheeky young male cook to being a cook guru with an MBE. During the 2000s, his television programmes dealt more and more with social issues. First, he developed a programme for unemployed youth whom he trained up for his Fifteen restaurant; and then he waged war on the 'bad diets' of school dinners in *Jamie's School Dinners*. Most recently he has taken his campaign to the USA, where diets seem even worse than with UK children (and his reception even more strained). Probably each culture now has to have its own Jamie Oliver. His cookbooks regularly top the best-sellers, and his programmes are shown in over 40 countries, including the USA's Food Network, where he became the second most popular presenter.

Food in most Western countries is moving from being a necessity to a 'hobby pastime'. Everyday food is more and more 'bought out' through restaurants, fast-food chains, chilled foods and frozen food. It is bought and eaten 'on the go'. One in five Americans eat in a fast-food restaurant every day. Food has become fast and convenient. But, at the same time, for some, an interest in cooking and eating has grown as a hobby. We may not spend a lot of time in our kitchens, but we love buying cookery magazines and books,

TV chef Jamie Oliver deals with social issues as well as menus. His TV series *Ministry of Food* revealed both the class nature of food and the poor diets of many people in the UK. For a while he became the government's adviser on school food and nutrition

*See*: www.jamieoliver.com/tv.

*Source*: Corbis SRC/Peter Dench.

# 'Foodies' on TV

## Notes for a history of food programmes on UK television

**1950s**: In the UK, Fanny (and Johnny) Craddock were the first noted 'telecooks'. They were very formal, adopting aristocratic principles, elegance and evening dress (see also Philip Harben). Marguerite Patten, in her history of food in the twentieth century, calls them 'television cookery demonstrations' (2001: 160): the cooks toured provincial theatres and city halls.

**1960s**: Graham Kerr, 'The Galloping Gourmet', brought a 'loosening of earlier formality', joking

a lot and sometimes behaving a little naughtily. He was the breakthrough from Fanny Craddock's formality. 'Good food' and 'eating out' were also celebrated by Robert Carrier, Jane Grigson and Elizabeth David.

**Late 1970s**: Widespread growth of interest in international cuisines. To help you cook your Indian meal or Chinese meal at home, there were Ken Hom (a Chinese cookery programme and book) and Madhur Jaffrey (with Indian cookery). Keith Floyd displayed 'drunken masculinity' and an altogether more relaxed style of cooking, light years away from the Fanny Craddock of the 1950s. Delia Smith maintained standards and a degree of formal elegance. The best-selling cookbook blockbuster became well established, along with the growth of 'Cookery Book Clubs'.

**1980s:** The age of *Masterchef* and the tele 'chef contest', along with *The Food and Drink Show*. Cookery series have tie-in books, courses, and food and drink promotions of all kinds. There are very informal 'magazine style' television programmes on every aspect of food and drink.

**1990s:** Celebrity chefs galore. Television now comes of age with many celebrity chefs, and eventually its own TV food channels. Two Fat Ladies, Ainsley Harriott, Rick Stein and Gary Rhodes.

**And onwards:** Jamie Oliver, Gordon Ramsey, Nigella Lawson, Nigel Slater and James Martin. Television food has been fully postmodernised. Food is entertainment and has become very informal, much more personal and full of reflection and personalities. It is also very commercial. Cookbooks usually top the best-sellers for weeks. Television food is also fragmented, fusioned and global. The earlier formats have broken down completely. You can now watch 24 hours-a-day food channels. 'Food' has come a long way from the formal, elegant and tightly measured world of Fanny Craddock to the informal, chatty, 'throw-it-all-in-as-easily-as-you-can' sensuality of Nigella Lawson.

nutrition experts, transport systems that carry food around, law-makers who regulate foods, and educational policies around good nutrition and eating. We inhabit multiple networks of food.

A feature of the modern organisation of food is its required speed. This really is the time of fast food. It has been suggested that one in five Americans eat in a fast-food restaurant each day and that in the UK, the use of pre-prepared meals has become ubiquitous. An entirely new food system is being introduced in the modern world. We now eat fast, on the hoof; and we shop in hypermarkets: in the UK, it has been estimated that half the food consumed by the country's 60 million mouths is sold from just 1,000 stores. Although in Chapter 6 we have used the term 'McDonaldisation' to refer to a process in which the principles of the McDonald's food company are applied to many things that are not linked to food (like schools, clothes and business), it does of course also apply to food. As we have seen, McDonald's restaurants are found in over 100 countries, serving millions of people every day.

Of course, along with this are a wide range of eating problems and disorders. Much of our eating – fast and convenient as it may be – brings nutrition problems (Lang and Heasman, 2004: 210).

 Here are two films which are very critical of the food industry. You can also watch selections of them on YouTube.

Eric Schlosser, *Fast Food Nation* (book, 2001; film, 2006).

Robert Kenner, *Food, Inc.* (2008) – and several accompanying books with this title.

watching food programmes on the 'food channel', going on cookery courses, and knowing the latest styles of food and the latest talking points. Many people see cooking now as a 'de-stressing activity' (Lang and Heasman, 2004: 208).

To conclude, food is a key to culture. It performs crucial symbolic roles and helps give meaning to our lives. In the contemporary world, it is embedded in our languages, our rituals, our media worlds and even our politics and values.

## 3  Food and organisation

The production and use of food always involves some kind of chain – or network – of people who produce, distribute and ultimately consume food. As we have seen, these networks may be changing in the modern world – and they are for food.

The networks or social worlds of food include the obvious: food shops, restaurants, bars. But they also link to chains involved in the full range of production, distribution and consumption of food. To give just a few interconnecting networks: we need to understand the networks and social organisation of the world of work, agriculture and farming, food manufacturers, scientists working on food, health and

## The global food chain and you

Think about what you have eaten in the last few days. Hamburgers, curries, apples, orange juice, coffee, tea, coke, beans, bread, chocolates, cod, chips, chicken, muesli, a Chinese take-away? Do you know where each item was produced? The chances are that many minimally processed products that you may have eaten, such as fresh fruit and vegetables, were imported from countries on the other side of the globe. More heavily processed products, from chocolates to frozen meals, probably included ingredients produced and processed by many groups of people from many different countries, some of whom have prospered by selling the product you ate, and some of whom themselves are worrying about when they might get their next meal. If you were to trace the processes of producing each of the items you consumed in your last meal, Harvey reflects, you would discover:

a relation of dependence upon a whole world of social labour conducted in many different places under very different relations and conditions of production. That dependency expands even further when we consider the materials and goods used in the production of goods we directly consume. Yet we can in practice consume our meal without the slightest knowledge of the intricate geography of production and the myriad social relationships that puts it upon our table

(Harvey, 1989)

For better or worse, the food products we use each day have become part of a cycle of international exchange that is reshaping the way people around the world live and work.

For a series of special issues on 'foods', see *New Internationalist* (1998): on coffee, 271; on cocoa, 304; on bananas, 317; on fish, 325.

## 4 Food and interaction

Food is a central feature of everyday life. In all societies and at all times, food is biologically necessary, but at the same time it also emerges into our daily social interactions. Consider any day and think of the number of times you simply engage with food. Think of breakfast: these days people eat their breakfast 'on the hop', but they haven't always done this; nor did they always have cereals. Nowadays we think nothing of 'snacking' our way through the day. Think of the junk food you eat (or not), the drinks you choose (a coffee from Starbucks or diet coke), the dinners, the meals out. Consider how this might differ across history, and country, and even your own life cycle. Indeed, how does food change across the life cycle? Consider the rituals of baby eating, through to teen junk food, and on, finally, to 'food for the elderly'. Consider your daily encounters around food: how do you share food with others, what are the spaces in which you do this, how do you pace your food and what kinds of conventions – even rituals – guide you along? Food may also become a part of our identity – we define ourselves as certain kinds of 'eaters' and by what kinds of 'food' we like. In the twentieth century there are an array of labels available that we can apply to ourselves: as vegetarians, vegans, anorexics, binge drinkers, gourmets. Food can help to define who we are, and who we are not. And we can link our eating to our ethnicity, gender and class. There is Indian food, Chinese food, fusion food. There is 'posh food' and 'bad food'. Food also plays a role in the social meanings of our bodies: indeed, some say 'we are what we eat'. How we eat is reflected in the way we look. And food can even be an emotion: for some,

food is the new sex. Here are three aspects of food to consider when thinking about this.

## Food as interaction ritual

This can be most clearly seen in 'the meal'. Here people share food with each other. We sit with other people, share food, take turns in speaking around food, and sometimes use meals as a major way of celebrating. And if not actually celebrating a birthday, a wedding or the like, then it is tacitly celebrating life and living together. 'The family that eats together stays together.' 'Sharing food' has a long history (over half a million years), and a wide variety of forms, from family meals to large public banquets, from TV dinners to the 'dining out' experience, from the 'take-away' to the 'night out with friends' (Jones, 2007). But it goes beyond the meal: consider, for example, kitchens. Here we can look at the complicated interactions among kitchen workers – servers, dishwashers, pantry workers, managers, restaurant critics and customers. Kitchens show the effects of organisational structure on individual relations (Fine, 1995).

## The body and food

Food and eating interactions are also at the centre of the new concern in many Western societies about the body, self-control, health and identity. We give meanings to food from the earliest years of our life. Deborah Lupton has explored the many ways in which we construct sociocultural and personal meanings of food and eating: in the context of childhood and the family, as well as in the social construction of foodstuffs as being linked to 'being a man' and 'being a woman' – male food and girlie food (Lupton, 1996). We shall see in Chapter 21 how obesity has become a major public issue, which in turn may be linked back to the meanings of the body, and especially that of the beautiful woman's body. And this in turn may well link to the issues of gender we discuss in Chapter 12, where we talk about the 'beauty myth'.

## The food biography

Consider the story of your life which includes food. Just how has food changed over your life, from childhood to now, and who has helped you fashion those changes? Nigel Slater, the English cook, has written a lovely little book called *Toast: The Story of a Boy's Hunger* (2003), where he recalls his childhood involvements in ice cream, jam tarts, 'cheese on toast', crisps – and hundreds more foods.

## Looking ahead

Over time, sociologists and others have outlined a number of key factors that affect food. These include:

- Environment (see Chapter 25) – using (and abusing) natural resources.
- Health (see Chapter 21) – many foods become acceptable because they are considered 'healthy' (yogurts, berries, food supplements). These are links between diet, nutrition, disease and public health.
- Economics and business (see Chapter 14) – poverty and the work of producing food, from inputs to consumption.
- Family dynamics (see Chapter 18) – from family meals to fast foods; shifts in the arrangements for food.
- Politics (see Chapter 16) – governance; regulations of the food economy.
- Religion (see Chapter 19) – a prime concern: religions nearly always lay down food taboos, and build food rituals into their religious ceremonies. Protestantism is quite weak on this, but consider the rules for orthodox Jews, Hindus, etc. Food is always bound up with taboos.

We will not return to food in this book. But as you read further and think more, you should be able to draw upon the analysis started here and build your own deeper understanding of the sociology of food. Maybe it generates good topics for projects?

## Food: going further

Here are some of the classic academic studies on food:

- Claude Levi Strauss, *The Raw and the Cooked* (1983). Classic cultural anthropology. Food is taken as symbolic of the division between the 'natural' and the 'cooked', i.e. products of human creation. The book is not just about food!
- Stephen Mennel, *All Manners of Food* (1985). The classic historical/sociological study of food in Western history and its role in the civilising process.
- Deborah Lupton, *Food, Body and the Self* (1996). A more recent account of the role of food in our bodies, emotions and identities.
- George Ritzer, *The McDonaldization of Society* (6th edn, 2010). In fact, not so much about food as about the ways in which the process of McDonaldisation applies to much of contemporary social life.
- Gary Alan Fine, *Kitchens* (1995). Ethnography of what goes on behind the scenes.

*See also*: Tim Lang and Michael Heasman, *Food Wars* (2004); Eric Millstone and Tim Lang, *The Atlas of Food: Who Eats, What, Where, When, Why* (2003); James Watson and Mellisa Caldwell, *The Cultural Politics of Food and Eating* (2004). These are all lively accounts of the contemporary 'politics of food' debate.

# PART 3

# THE UNEQUAL WORLD

## DIFFERENCE, DIVISION AND SOCIAL STRATIFICATION

# CHAPTER 8

# INEQUALITY, SOCIAL DIVISIONS AND SOCIAL STRATIFICATION

IT IS A CENTURY SINCE ON 10 APRIL 1912 the ocean liner *Titanic* slipped away from Southampton docks on its maiden voyage across the North Atlantic to New York. A proud symbol of the new industrial age, the towering ship carried 2,300 passengers, some enjoying more luxury than most travellers even today could imagine. By contrast, poor immigrants crowded the lower decks, journeying to what they hoped would be a better life in the USA.

Two days out, the crew received radio warnings of icebergs in the area but paid little notice. Then, near midnight, as the ship steamed swiftly and silently westwards, a lookout was stunned to see a massive shape rising out of the dark ocean directly ahead. Moments later, the *Titanic* collided with a huge iceberg, almost as tall as the ship itself, which split open its starboard side as if the grand vessel were nothing more than a giant tin can.

Sea water surged into the ship's lower levels, and within 25 minutes people were rushing for the lifeboats. By 2 a.m. the bow of the *Titanic* was submerged, and the stern reared high above the water. Clinging to the deck, quietly observed by those in the lifeboats, hundreds of helpless passengers solemnly passed their final minutes before the ship disappeared into the frigid Atlantic.

The tragic loss of more than 1,600 lives made news around the world. Looking back dispassionately at this terrible accident with a sociological eye, however, we see that some categories of passengers had much better odds of survival than others. In an age of conventional gallantry, women and children boarded the boats first, so that 80 per cent of the casualties were men. Class, too, was at work. Of people holding first-class tickets, more than 60 per cent were saved, primarily because they were on the upper decks, where warnings were sounded first and lifeboats were accessible. Only 36 per cent of the second-class passengers survived, and of the third-class passengers on the lower decks, only 24 per cent escaped drowning. On board the *Titanic*, class turned out to mean much more than the quality of accommodation: it was truly a matter of life or death.

Years later, the story of the *Titanic* still fascinates. In 1997 it was filmed (for the third time) and became the biggest box office success of all time. It was also staged as a musical. There are many threads to be analysed in the *Titanic* story: but one of them is always the extreme divisions of social class that destroyed many lives.

*All animals are equal, but some are more equal than others.*

George Orwell, *Animal Farm* (1945)

(Left) *Abandoned* Luigi Nono (1850–1918)

Luigi Nono (1850–1918) was an Italian painter of the Venetian school. (He was also grandfather of the celebrated avant-garde composer Luigi Nono). His works often captured the tragic element of life, with paintings of *Sick child*, *Burial of a child* and here, *Abandoned*. He died at the end of the first world war.

Source: *Abandoned*, 1903 by Nono, Luigi (1850–1918) Museo d'Arte Moderna di Ca'Pesaro, Venice, Italy/Bridgeman Art Library.

See: Lilie Chouliaraki *The Specatorship of Suffering*. London: Sage, 2006

**In this chapter, we ask:**

- **What is social stratification and inequality?**
- **How are inequalities patterned through divisions of economy, gender, sexuality, age and ethnicity?**
- **How do we explain the prevalence and persistence of these divisions?**
- **What is the future of inequalities – especially the emerging digital divide?**

**Q** How do we relate to images of the distant sufferer – here 'the abandoned'? How might art cultivate a disposition of care for and engagement with the sufferings of others?

The fate of the *Titanic* dramatically illustrates the consequences of social inequality for the ways in which people live and die. Social diversity and differences are everywhere part of society. But when such differences start to become socially significant – as we can see on the *Titanic* – sociologists start to speak of **social divisions**: human *differences that are rendered socially significant*. While differences may be found everywhere and can often be inconsequential (such as the differences between stamp collectors, sports people and cooks), differences between people that are given strength and made significant start to play crucial roles in the shaping of a society. The chapters in this part of the book will be examining different aspects of these differences; this chapter starts with a more general look.

## Introduction: what is social stratification and inequality?

Most (and probably all) societies exist with systems of social division and social stratification, through which entire categories of people are elevated above others, providing one segment of the population with a disproportionate amount of money, power and prestige. Sociologists use the concept of **social stratification** to refer to a *system by which a society ranks categories of people in a hierarchy*. Five basic principles tend to organise them everywhere.

1   *Social stratification is a characteristic of society, not simply a reflection of individual differences*. It is a system which confers unequal access to resources. Members of industrial societies consider social standing as a reflection of personal talent and effort, though we typically exaggerate the extent to which people control their destinies. Did a higher percentage of the first-class passengers survive the sinking of the *Titanic* because they were smarter or better swimmers than the second- and third-class passengers? Hardly. They fared better because of their privileged position on the ship. Similarly, children born into wealthy families are more likely than those born into poverty to enjoy health, achieve academically, succeed in their life's work and live well into old age. Neither rich nor poor people are responsible for creating social stratification, yet this system shapes the lives of them all.

2   *Social stratification persists over generations*. To understand that stratification stems from society rather than individual differences, note how inequality persists over time. In all societies, parents confer their social positions on their children, so that patterns of inequality stay much the same from generation to generation.

Some individuals do experience **social mobility**, *change in one's position in a social hierarchy*. Social mobility may be upwards or downwards. Our society celebrates the achievements of a David Beckham or a Madonna, who rose to prominence from modest beginnings. But we also acknowledge that people move downward as a result of business setbacks, unemployment or illness. More often, people move *horizontally* when they exchange one occupation for another that is comparable. For most people, however, social standing remains much the same over a lifetime.

3   *Social stratification is universal but variable*. Social stratification seems to be found everywhere. At the same time, *what* is unequal and *how* unequal it is varies from one society to another. Among the members of technologically simple societies, social differentiation may be minimal and based mostly on age and sex (though these factors still matter in most societies today as well).

4   *Social stratification involves not just inequality but beliefs*. Any system of inequality not only gives some people more resources than others but defines certain arrangements as fair. Just as what is unequal differs from society to society, so does the explanation of why people should be unequal. Sociologists have introduced ideas such as ideology and hegemony to help us understand this. Virtually everywhere, however, people with the greatest social privileges express the strongest support for their society's system of social stratification, while those with fewer social resources are more likely to seek change.

5   *Social stratification engenders shared identities* as belonging to a particular social category different from others. Identity serves to mark off one social division from another, often being closely linked to different kinds of culture as well. In all systems of social division, people have a sense of their location – and may accept, negotiate or even resist it. For Marx, for example, a sense of class consciousness was very significant; and class identities could have been harbingers of major social change (Payne, 2000; Braham and Janes, 2002).

# Types of inequality

Goran Therborn (2006: 6–9) suggests that there are three fundamental kinds of inequality. These are:

1 *Inequalities of health, life and death.* These are basically linked to the biological organism – sometimes called *vital inequality.* Birth and death rates – as well as illness and disease – are significantly shaped by social factors (see Chapter 21).

2 *Existential inequalities.* These involve the differential recognition of human individuals as persons. Stigma is the opposite of positive esteem and recognition, and this kind of inequality is linked to the study of stigma.

3 *Resource inequalities.* These are the differences between people in their capacity to act. Humans are very different in their capabilities and abilities to act in the world. Having adequate resources – money, knowledge, friends and family – helps shape life opportunities.

# The intersecting forms of social divisions and the processes of inequality

For a long time, sociologists focused primarily upon one major system of stratification: that which dealt with social and economic positions. Broadly, this is how people are ranked in terms of their economic position, their power and their prestige. It included systems of slavery, caste and the modern class system. But more recently, sociologists have also recognised that social divisions and their linked inequalities are organised through a range of key social structures, such as gender, ethnicity, sexuality, disability and age. It is constructive in any sociological analysis to examine the structures of inequalities through which social life gets organised. Whatever social thing you are looking at – schools, social work or senility – always try and ask questions about how it interconnects with at least some of the inequalities shown in Table 8.1.

Within such divisions and stratification systems, Iris Marion Young has identified a number of key processes at work. These include:

| Table 8.1 | The intersecting orders of inequalities | | |
|---|---|---|---|
| | **Social structures and social orders (channels of opportunities)** | **Supporting ideas and identities (discourses/positionalities)** | **Chapter where more fully discussed** |
| 1 | Class order: how does work, income, wealth shape life? | Classism and class consciousness | See Chapters 9 and 10 |
| 2 | Gender order (and patriarchy): how does being a man or woman shape social life? | Sexism and gender identity | See Chapter 12 |
| 3 | Racial formation (ethnicity and race): the role of ethnic and cultural difference in social life | Racialisation, racism and ethnic identity | See Chapter 11 |
| 4 | Age stratification and generational orders: how are lives stratified by generation and age? | Ageism and generational self | See Chapter 13 |
| 5 | Nations: what is the significance of local and national cultures? | Nationalism and national identity | See Chapter 16 |
| 6 | The sexual order | Heterosexism, homophobia and heteronormativity: sexual identity | See Chapter 12 |
| 7 | The disability and health order | Sickness and 'disablement' ideologies: health/ability identity | See Chapter 14 |

*Source:* Adapted from Plummer (2010) Table 7.3.

- *Social exclusion and marginalisation*: a process by which 'a whole category of people is expelled from useful participation in social life' (Young, 1990: 53). Here, people are pushed from the mainstream of participation in society. We will see this when we talk about the idea of the exclusive and inclusive society in Chapter 10.

- *Exploitation*: a process by which there is 'the transfer of the results of the labour of one social group to benefit another' (Young, 1990: 49).

- *Powerlessness*: a process by which people come to lack the authority, status and sense of self that many professionals tend to have (Young, 1990: 57).

- *Cultural imperialism*: 'the universalization of a dominant group's experience and culture, and its establishment as the norm' (Young, 1990: 59). We will see this when we discuss ideas around the postcolonial in Chapter 11.

- *Violence*: directed at members of a group simply because they belong to that group (Young, 1990: 62). Thus, we will discuss violence against women and homophobia against gays in Chapter 12.

## Overview

Part Three of this book looks at aspects of these systems, gives examples and raises some debates around them.

This chapter considers some contrasting patterns of social-economic stratification and ponders why it is so widespread. Chapter 9 then looks at the wider world, raising such issues as global poverty, widening inequalities and the uneven development of societies across the globe. Chapter 10 then examines how social and economic stratification works in specific 'high-income' countries such as the UK and the United States (where poverty, for example, curiously continues to exist on a massive scale). Chapter 11 turns to the ethnic stratification system and discusses matters of race and migration. While it will focus specifically on Europe, we will also see that 'race stratification' goes deep in all cultures of the world. Chapter 12 will draw from feminist and queer sociology to introduce the ideas of patriarchy and heterosexism and see how gender acts as a major system of stratification. Chapter 13 looks at age stratification, focusing especially on children as well as the social exclusion of those in later life. As populations skew to more and more older people, a major change is in the air. Finally, Chapter 14 looks at disablement, focusing on a range of ways in which people are excluded and stereotyped through their bodies, mental faculties and general health.

Of course, one key problem with these varying systems of stratification is how they all interconnect. Sociologists have recently started to call this the problem of **intersectionality**: *the ways in which different forms*

METHODS & RESEARCH

# On interviews and suffering

Pierre Bourdieu (1930–2002) was one of the leading French sociologists of the late twentieth century (he is featured in the *Thinkers and theory* box on p. 263 and will be often mentioned during this book). Although much of his research may be described as theoretical, one of his major books, *The Weight of the World* (1999) (originally published in 1993 as *La Misère du Monde*) is a remarkable instance of the sociological interview at work. The book contains around 70 interviews and commentaries with men and women who have confided 'their lives and the

difficulties they have had in living those lives'. In general, they have been denied a socially respected and valuable existence – suffering from racism, or poverty, or marginalisation; and they have not been able to adjust to rapid changes around them. We could say they lead 'damaged lives' because of inequalities.

These are no ordinary social science interviews, which can be flat, dull and overly structured. Instead, these interviews are more detailed and are often reproduced in the book as direct interviews with the interview questions included. They are placed side by side with interviews from people who hold different social positions – even though they live on the same

housing estate or work at the same place. Each interview is also given an interpretation, in which the interview has been examined and listened to repeatedly by the researcher(s) in order to make sense of it.

Complex and multilayered representations, unlike those found in the press and much journalism, can often lead the reader to sense some kind of social explanation of the social sufferings that many people experience. They also lead us to see the 'multiplicity of co-existing, and sometimes directly competing, points of view' (Bourdieu et al., 1999: 3). This study is a fine example of the interview at work in tracking the personal experience of inequalities.

*of inequality and division interact with each other.* We will discuss this as we go along. It is one of the major issues of current sociology to learn how to make these linkages adequately.

## Closed and open systems of stratification: slavery, estate, caste and class

Here we locate four of the major systems of stratification which have been found throughout history. In describing social stratification in particular societies, sociologists often stress the degree of social closure and mobility that is allowed in the society. 'Closed' systems allow little change in social position, while 'open' systems permit some mobility (Tumin, 1985).

## Slavery

**Slavery** is *a form of social stratification in which people are owned by others as property.* Chattel slavery turns human beings into things to be bought or sold. Many early civilisations such as Egypt and Persia (now Iran), as well as the ancient Greeks and Romans, relied heavily on slave labour. Slaves could be worked to death in the building of huge pyramids or in massive public works such as irrigation systems.

But it was not just a pervasive feature of 'classical worlds'. Between the fifteenth and nineteenth centuries, there was a major slave trade into the New World. It has been estimated that the total population of the African continent in 1500 was 47 million. As S. I. Martin chronicles:

> **Over the next 350 years, between 10 and 15 million Africans arrived in chains in the New World. Four to six million more are believed to have died during their capture or the rigours of the Atlantic crossing – a total of between 14 and 21 million people. This excludes the 17 million Africans thought to have been abducted as a result of the trans-Saharan slave trade. History has seen few disruptions on such a scale.**

(Martin, 1999: 21)

The forms that slavery has taken have been highly variable. The legal rights and autonomy of slaves varied. In classical Athens, for example, slaves could often hold positions of great responsibility even though they were owned by their masters. But the slaves who worked building pyramids, or excavating mines, or on plantations, were much more regulated and treated as less than human. People captured in warfare often became slaves.

### Modern slavery

The British Empire abolished slavery in 1833, and the American Civil War brought slavery in the United States to an end in 1865. Although slavery no longer exists in its classical forms, it does still persist in a variety of forms in many parts of the world today (the United Nations has investigated claims that some 100,000 people in Mauritania in West Africa were being kept in slavery). However, English social scientist Kevin Bales (2004) suggests that traditional and modern slavery differ. For him, one key difference is that modern slavery is not about direct ownership but about control through violence, usually with major elements of economic exploitation. This could include:

- *Forced labour*, where governments forcibly recruit labour. This often involves children who may be forced to leave home.
- *Debt bondage*, where people labour to pay off a debt that they will probably never be able to repay and which may be inherited by subsequent generations.
- *Prostitution*, where women (and children) may move between countries in the hope of work, only to find themselves part of the human chain of sex traffic from which it may be hard to escape.
- *Servile marriage*, where women are given in marriage without the right to refuse.

It is estimated that there are 27 million slaves alive today – probably more than at any point in history. This number is also greater than the total population stolen from Africa during four centuries of the transatlantic slave trade (Bales, 2009). As other forms of slavery appear through the selling of immigrants to other countries, and the selling of body parts – usually from those in poorer countries to those needing body parts in the richer countries (see Scheper-Hughes, 2000), so estimates of modern slavery are indeed increasing. Indeed, some agencies working in this field suggest that numbers may well be much greater than Bales estimates – with perhaps more than 200 million people in modern slavery. Sometimes slavery can appear in the most unlikely places: one estimate has suggested that there are some 3,000 households in Paris holding slaves!

Usually, modern slaves are found among the poor, the uneducated and the low-status groups

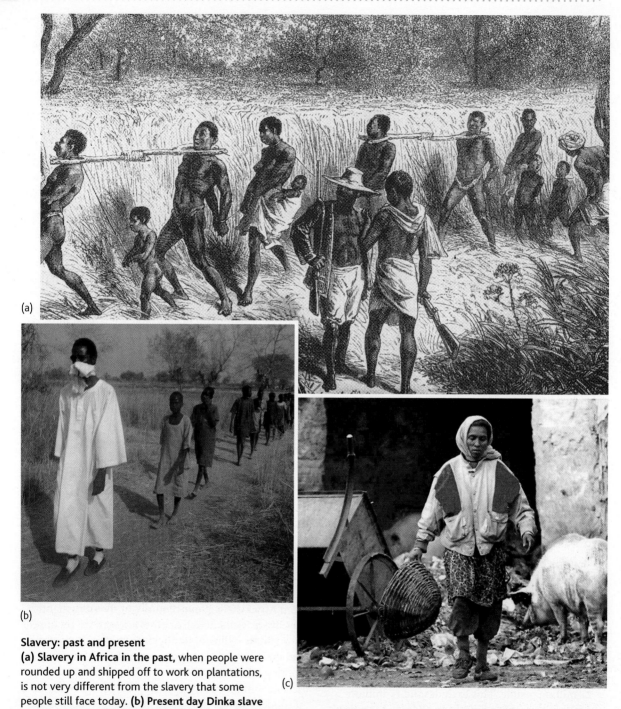

**Slavery: past and present**
**(a) Slavery in Africa in the past,** when people were rounded up and shipped off to work on plantations, is not very different from the slavery that some people still face today. **(b) Present day Dinka slave trade in Sudan. (c) New Delhi, India,** 18 February: a sweeper, one of India's reported hundreds of millions of untouchables and lower-caste Hindus who perform menial labour, walks by a pig picking through garbage in New Delhi

*Source*: (a) Popperfoto/Getty Images; (b) David Orr/Sygma/Corbis; (c) AFP/Getty Images.

of a society: frequently, of course, these are women and children. In all cases, slavery is a closed system of stratification, robbing a life of much hope of control or change.

**tip** See *Documenting Disposable People*, a photographic essay of contemporary slavery in the world with an introduction by Kevin Bales (2010). This is an example of visual sociology.

# The estate system

Medieval Europe was a feudal system based on ideas of an **estate**, *a system based on a rigidly interlocking hierarchy of rights and obligations*. Estates were created politically and supplied an orderly chain of rights and obligations throughout society. Thus, usually a chain of obligations ran through three major groups – nobility, clergy and commoners. Land was controlled by powerful lords who enlisted the military to protect their land in return for rights over a part of it. Peasants were then dominated by the local nobility, while having some control over their own pieces of land. The tenants were vassals (dependants) of the lord; the lord was linked to the monarch, and so forth.

# The caste system

The **caste system** has complex meanings (Sharma, 1999) but is usually seen as a form of *social stratification based on inherited status or ascription*. A pure caste system, in other words, is 'closed' so that birth alone determines one's social destiny with no opportunity for social mobility based on individual efforts. Caste systems rank categories of people in a rigid hierarchy. Some scholars believe that the concept can only really be applied to the system found in India – a system that is now under change. Others see it as a more widespread system, one which could embrace the Deep South in America in the post-slavery period, South Africa under apartheid, elements of the system of relationships in contemporary Thailand, and even the gypsies in England.

The most frequently cited example of a caste system is that of India, or at least India's traditional Hindu villages in which most people still live. The Indian system of caste is usually discussed in terms of *varna*, a Sanskrit word that means 'colour' (see Figure 8.1). It denotes four major categories: Brahmins (priests and writers) who claim the highest status, Kshatriyas (warriors and rulers), Vaishyas (the merchants and landowners) and Sudras (artisans and servants). People outside the system become 'untouchables' and often have the most unpleasant work – handling sewage, burning corpses, scavenging. It is estimated that there are some 150 million untouchables in India (about 20 per cent of the population), whereas the Brahmins at the top make up just 3 per cent.

Each local community develops its own language and ways of building up what is, in effect, an endogamous

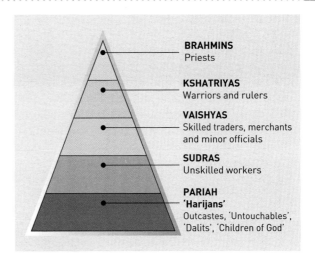

**BRAHMINS**
Priests

**KSHATRIYAS**
Warriors and rulers

**VAISHYAS**
Skilled traders, merchants and minor officials

**SUDRAS**
Unskilled workers

**PARIAH**
'Harijans'
Outcastes, 'Untouchables', 'Dalits', 'Children of God'

**Figure 8.1**    Classic depiction of the caste system

(or closed) community which lays down a very broad system of positioning. This guides people into very clear rules about washing, eating or communicating with other people. It suggests ideas of ritual purity, pollution and exclusion. In the past it was largely a fixed system – no movement between castes was possible. The most controversial group (in Western eyes at any rate) were the 'untouchables', who performed polluted work.

'Dalits' means oppressed or ground-down peoples and refers to the former 'untouchables'. Traditionally they performed 'impure' functions, – such as handling sewage and corpses, – were forced to live in the worst parts of Indian villages and towns, and were denied access to common resources like wells, shops, schools and Hindu temples. This system of savage exclusion was formally abolished over half a century ago, but today there are still some 150 million people (about 20 per cent of the population) living in around 450 castes. In the UK, research has suggested there may still be some 50,000 Dalits who suffer from 'caste' and experience discrimination in jobs, healthcare, politics, education and schools – but such figures are hard to evaluate (see Gorringe, 2006).

## Race and caste

It could be argued that race is often used as a tool for the caste system (though many disagree). In the southern plantations of the USA after slavery, for example, it has been argued that the division between 'blacks' and 'whites' into strictly segregated groups was so extreme that it amounted to a version of a caste system (Dollard, 1937; repr. 1998). Likewise, it might also be argued that caste played a key role in South Africa until recently. In this nation's former policy of apartheid, the 5 million South Africans of European ancestry enjoyed a commanding share of wealth and power, dominating some 30 million black South Africans. In a middle position were another 3 million mixed-race people, known as 'coloureds', and about 1 million Asians. The *World watch* box on p. 259 details the problems of dismantling South Africa's racial caste system.

## The nature of a caste system

In a caste system, birth determines the fundamental shape of people's lives in four crucial respects. First, traditional caste groups are linked to occupation, so that generations of a family perform the same type of work. In rural India, although some occupations (such as farming) are open to all, castes are identified with the work their members do (as priests, barbers, leather workers, street sweepers and so on). In South Africa, whites still hold most of the desirable jobs, with most blacks consigned to manual labour and other low-level service work.

No rigid social hierarchy could persist if people regularly married outside their own categories, as then most children would have uncertain rank. To maintain the hierarchy, then, a second trait of caste systems is mandating that people marry others of the same ranking. Sociologists call this pattern *endogamous* marriage (*endo* stems from Greek, meaning 'within'). Traditionally, Indian parents select their children's marriage partners, often before the children reach their teens. Until 1985, South Africa banned marriage and even sex between the races. Even now, interracial couples are rare since blacks and whites continue to live in separate areas.

Thirdly, caste guides everyday life so that people remain in the company of 'their own kind'. Hindus in India enforce this segregation with the belief that a ritually 'pure' person of a higher caste will be 'polluted' by contact with someone of lower standing. Often this leads to 'caste feuds', with bitter attacks and murders usually on lower-caste citizens. Apartheid in South Africa also led to much bitter conflict.

Finally, caste systems rest on powerful cultural beliefs. Indian culture is built on Hindu traditions that mandate accepting one's life work, whatever it may be, as a moral duty. Although apartheid is no longer a matter of law, South Africans still

cling to notions distinguishing 'white jobs' from 'black jobs'.

## Caste and agrarian life

Caste systems are typical of agrarian societies because the lifelong routines of agriculture depend on a rigid sense of duty and discipline. Thus, caste still persists in rural India, half a century after being formally outlawed, even as its grip is easing in the nation's more industrial cities, where most people exercise greater choice about their work and marriage partners. Similarly, the rapid industrialisation of South Africa elevated the importance of personal choice and individual rights, making the abolition of apartheid increasingly likely. Note, however, that the erosion of caste does not signal the end of social stratification. On the contrary, it simply marks a change in its character, as the next sections explain.

## The class system

Agrarian life relies on the discipline wrought by caste systems; industrial societies, by contrast, depend on developing specialised talents. Industrialisation erodes caste in favour of **social class**, *social stratification resulting from the unequal distribution of wealth, power and prestige.* Unlike caste, estate and slavery, it is a system that claims to be more open and based on individual achievement. A class system is seen to be more 'open' in that people who gain schooling and skills may experience some social mobility in relation to their parents and siblings. Mobility, in turn, blurs class distinctions. Social boundaries also break down as people immigrate from abroad or move from the countryside to the city, lured by greater opportunity for education and better jobs (Lipset and Bendix, 1967). Typically, newcomers take low-paying jobs, thereby pushing others up the social ladder.

People in industrial societies come to think that everyone is entitled to 'rights', rather than just those of particular social standing. This has not always been the case. The principle of equal standing before the law steadily assumes a central place in the political culture of industrial class systems. Class systems are no different from caste systems in one basic respect: people remain unequal. But social stratification now rests less entirely on the accident of birth. Class systems, for instance, may allow more individual freedom in work careers (when they are available) and in such things as the selection of marriage partners.

WORLD WATCH

# From 'race as caste' to social class: a report from South Africa

At the southern tip of the African continent lies South Africa. Long inhabited by black people, the region attracted white Dutch traders and farmers in the mid-seventeenth century,

Nelson Mandela, leader of the African National Congress (ANC), who was imprisoned by the white apartheid government for 27 years, at his inauguration 10 May 1994. He was elected president in South Africa's first all-race election. His ninetieth birthday was celebrated on 18 July 2008. Mandela has had a strong world moral voice, when new presidents have been elected to power. He has since become a major advocate for a variety of social and human rights organisations. Read Mandela's *Long Walk to Freedom* (1994) and see Clint Eastwood's film *Invictus* (2009)

*Source*: WALTER DHLADHLA/AFP/ Getty Images.

who became known as the Boers, the Dutch for farmers. Early in the nineteenth century, a second wave of colonisation saw British immigrants push the Dutch inland in the Boer Wars (1899–1902). By the early 1900s, the British had taken over the country, proclaiming it the Union of South Africa. In 1961, the United Kingdom gave up control and recognised the independence of the Republic of South Africa.

But freedom was a reality for only the white minority. Years before, to ensure their political control over the black majority, whites had instituted a policy of apartheid, or racial separation. Apartheid was made law in 1948, denying blacks national citizenship, ownership of land and any formal voice in the government. In effect, black South Africans became lower caste, receiving little schooling and performing menial low-paid jobs. Under his system, even 'middle-class' white households had at least one black household servant. The prosperous white minority defended apartheid, claiming that blacks threatened their cultural traditions or, more simply, were inferior beings. But resistance to apartheid rose steadily, prompting whites to resort to brutal military repression to maintain their power.

Steady resistance – especially from younger blacks, impatient for a political voice and economic opportunity – gradually forced change. Adding to the pressure were criticism and boycotts from many nations. By the mid-1980s the tide began to turn as the South African government

granted limited political rights to people of mixed race and Asian ancestry. Then came the right for all people to form labour unions, to enter occupations once restricted to whites, and to own property. Officials also began to dismantle the system of laws that separated the races in public places. The rate of change increased in 1990 with Nelson Mandela's release from prison. In 1994, the first national election open to all people of all races elected Mandela the president, ending centuries of white minority rule.

The suffering of people under apartheid remains one of the twentieth century's epic stories of 'man's continuing inhumanity to man'. In order that these experiences should not be easily forgotten, a Truth and Reconciliation Commission was established which compiled the evidence of over 20,000 witnesses to the regime, breaking the silence that surrounded the many gross violations of human rights committed during those years.

Despite this awareness of its past and the current dramatic political change, however, social stratification in South Africa is still partially based on race. Even with the right to own property, one-third of black South Africans have no jobs, and the majority remain poor. The worst-off are some 7 million *ukublelekka*, which means 'marginal people' in the Xhosa language. Soweto-by-the-Sea may sound like a summer getaway, but it is home to thousands of *ukublelekka* who live crammed into shacks made of packing cases, corrugated metal, cardboard and other discarded materials. There is no electricity for lights or refrigeration. Without plumbing, people use buckets to haul sewage, and women line up to take a turn at a single water tap that serves more than 3,000 people. Any job is hard to come by, and those who do find work are lucky to earn $200 a month. Crime has become a major problem. South Africa's current president, Jacob Zuma, who was elected in 2009, leads a nation still twisted by centuries of racial caste. In 2010, however, it assumed global significance when it hosted the month-long World Cup, which attracted world attention.

Today, researchers have suggested that South Africa is probably more unequal than it was under apartheid. Jeremy Seekings and Nicoli Natrass, examining the country from the mid-twentieth century to now, conclude that there has been a shift from race to class as the key organising feature. They suggest that South Africa is now riven between 'insiders' and 'outsiders'. 'Insiders' are increasingly multiracial and enjoy access to 'good jobs' and high incomes. But 'outsiders' lack skills and employment and live 'outside' the mainstream of South African society. To make matters worse, the country now has one of the highest homicide rates in the world.

*Source*: Christie, 2000; Truth and Reconciliation Commission, 2000; Howarth and Norval, 1998; Seekings and Nattrass, 2006.

**COUNTRY FACT FILE**

SOUTH AFRICA

| | |
|---|---|
| Population | 49.01 million |
| Per capita GDP | $10,100 |
| Life expectancy | 60.4 |
| Adult literacy | 88.0 |
| Key languages | IsiZulu 23.8%, IsiXhosa 17.6%, Afrikaans 13.3%, Sepedi 9.4% |
| Key religions | Zion Christian 11.1%, Pentecostal/ Charismatic 8.2%, Catholic 7.1%, Methodist 6.8% |
| Key city | Pretoria |
| Human development index | 0.597 (110th, 2010) |

# Stratification at work: the cases of Japan and Russia

## Stratification in Japan

Social stratification in Japan mixes the traditional and the contemporary. Japan is at once the world's oldest continuously operating monarchy and a modern society in which wealth follows individual achievement.

### Feudal Japan

As early as the fifth century CE, Japan was an agrarian society with a rigid caste system composed of nobles and commoners and ruled by an 'imperial family'. Despite the people's belief that the emperor ruled by divine right, limited government organisation forced the emperor to delegate much authority to a network of regional nobles or *shoguns*.

Below the nobility stood the *samurai*, or warrior caste. The word *samurai* means 'to serve', indicating that this second rank of Japanese society comprised soldiers who cultivated elaborate martial skills and pledged their loyalty to the nobility. To set themselves off from the rest of the commoners, the *samurai* dressed and behaved according to a traditional code of honour.

As in Great Britain, the majority of people in Japan at this time were commoners who laboured to eke out a bare subsistence. Unlike their European counterparts, however, Japanese commoners were not the lowest in rank. The *burakumin*, or 'outcasts', stood further down in that country's hierarchy, shunned by lord and commoner alike. Much like the lowest caste groups in India, 'outcasts' lived apart from others, engaged in the most distasteful occupations and, like everyone else, had no opportunity to change their standing.

### Modern Japan

Important changes in nineteenth-century Japan – industrialisation, the growth of cities and the opening of Japanese society to outside influences – combined to weaken the traditional caste structure. In 1871, the Japanese legally banned the social category of 'outcast', though even today people look down on women and men who trace their lineage to this rank. After Japan's defeat in the Second World War, the nobility, too, lost legal standing, and, as the years have passed, fewer and fewer Japanese accept the notion that their emperor rules by divine right.

Thus social stratification in contemporary Japan is a far cry from the rigid caste system in force centuries ago. Analysts describe the modern-day Japanese population in terms of social gradations, including 'upper', 'upper-middle', 'lower-middle' and 'lower'. But since classes have no firm boundaries, they disagree about what proportion of the population falls in each.

Today's Japanese class system also reveals this nation's fascinating ability to weave together tradition and modernity. Because many Japanese people revere the past, family background is never far from the surface in assessing someone's social standing. Therefore, despite legal reforms that ensure that everyone is of equal standing before the law and a modern culture that stresses individual achievement, the Japanese continue to perceive each other through the centuries-old lens of caste.

This dynamic mix echoes from the university campus to the corporate boardroom. The most prestigious universities – now gateways to success in the industrial world – admit students with outstanding scores on rigorous entrance examinations. Even so, the highest achievers and business leaders in Japan are products of privilege, with noble or *samurai* background. At the other extreme, 'outcasts' continue to live in isolated communities cut off from opportunities to better themselves.

Finally, traditional ideas about gender still shape Japanese society. Despite legal reforms that confer formal equality on the sexes, women are clearly subordinate to men in most important respects. Japanese parents are more likely to push sons than daughters towards university and the nation thus retains a significant 'gender gap' in education. As a consequence, women predominate in lower-level support positions in the corporate world, only rarely assuming leadership roles. In this sense, too, individual achievement in Japan's modern class system operates in the shadow of centuries of traditional privileges.

## Class in the Russian Federation

The Russian Federation, which rivalled the USA as a superpower while it existed as the Soviet Union, was born out of revolution in 1917. The feudal system, ruled by a hereditary nobility, came to an abrupt end as the Russian revolution transferred most farms, factories and other productive property from private ownership to state control.

### A classless society?

This transformation was guided by the ideas of Karl Marx, who argued that private ownership of productive property was the basis of social classes (see Chapter 4). As the state gained control of the

PUBLIC SOCIOLOGY

## The Spirit Level

Richard Wilkinson and Kate Pickett are researchers with a cause. Their book *The Spirit Level* became an academic best-seller in 2009. Their research claims that inequality is socially divisive, and that inequality is the most important explanation of the prevalence of poor health and a wide range of social problems across the world. Drawing on data from the United Nations, the World Bank, the World Health Organization and the US Census, they argue that inequality causes shorter, unhealthier and unhappier lives; it increases the rate of teenage pregnancy, violence, obesity, imprisonment and addiction; and it weakens relationships. They look at research from many countries around the world and conclude that what matters in our healthy lives is where we stand in relation to others. Simply being poor is not the issue; what matters is our relative position in the society.

The USA, for example, has 'the highest homicide rates, the highest teenage pregnancy rate, comes in 28th in the league of life expectancy *and* it has the biggest income differences'. In contrast, Japan, Sweden and Norway, with much lower inequalities, also seem to have many fewer social problems. Aware that this is a simple correlation and not necessarily a cause (see p. 70), the authors spend some time developing a theory that links these facts together. For more, see: the Equality Trust at www.equalitytrust.org.uk, which includes a three-minute animated film.

See also Wilkinson's online paper, 'What difference does *inequality* make?', www.thpc. scot.nhs.uk/Presentations/Wellbeing/Wilkinson.pdf, and Chapter 21 of this book, p. 731.

economy, Soviet officials claimed that they had engineered a remarkable achievement: humanity's first classless society.

Analysts outside the Soviet Union were sceptical about this claim of classlessness. The occupations of the people in the former Soviet Union, they pointed out, clustered into a four-level hierarchy. At the top were high government officials, or *apparatchiks*. Next came the Soviet intelligentsia, including lower government officials, university lecturers, scientists, physicians and engineers. Below them stood the manual workers and, in the lowest stratum, the rural peasantry.

Since people in each of these categories enjoyed very different living standards, the former Soviet Union was never classless in the sense of having no social inequality. But one can say, more modestly, that placing factories, farms, colleges and hospitals under state control did rein in economic inequality (although not necessarily differences of power) compared to capitalist societies such as the members of the European Union.

The 1917 Russian Revolution radically recast the society as prescribed by Karl Marx (and revolutionary Russian leader Vladimir Lenin). Then in the 1980s, the Soviet Union underwent another sweeping transformation. Economic reforms accelerated when Mikhail Gorbachev came on the scene in 1985. His economic programme, popularly known as *perestroika*, meaning 'restructuring', sought to solve a dire problem: while the Soviet system had succeeded in minimising economic inequality, everyone was relatively poor and living standards lagged far behind those of other industrial nations. Simply put, Gorbachev hoped to stimulate economic expansion by reducing inefficient centralised control of the economy.

Gorbachev's reforms soon escalated into one of the most dramatic social movements in history, as popular uprisings toppled one socialist government after another throughout eastern Europe and, ultimately, brought down the Soviet system itself. In essence, people blamed their economic plight as well as their lack of basic freedoms on a repressive ruling class of Communist Party officials.

From the Soviet Union's founding in 1917 until its demise in 1991, the Communist Party retained a monopoly of power. Near the end, 18 million party members (6 per cent of the Soviet people) still made all the decisions about Soviet life while enjoying privileges such as vacation homes, chauffeured cars and access to prized consumer goods and elite education for their children (Theen, 1984). The second Russian revolution, then, mirrors the first in that it was nothing less than the overthrow of the ruling class.

The transformation of the Soviet Union into the Russian Federation demonstrates that social inequality involves more than economic resources. Soviet society lacked the income disparity typical of European states and the United States. But elite standing in the former Soviet Union was based on power rather than wealth. Thus, even though Mikhail Gorbachev and Boris Yeltsin earned far less than a US president, they wielded great power.

And what about social mobility in Russia? Evidence indicates that during the twentieth century there was more upward social mobility in the Soviet Union than in Great Britain, Japan or the United States. Why? For one thing, Soviet society lacked the concentrated wealth that families elsewhere pass from one generation to the next. Even more important, industrialisation and rapid bureaucratisation during the twentieth century pushed a large proportion of the working class and rural peasantry upwards to occupations in industry and government. Nevertheless, this pattern has begun to change as dynasties, sometimes linked with organised crime, have formed in Russia in the last few years.

Now, with new laws sanctioning individual ownership of private property and business, some experts monitoring the changing Russian scene predict further structural social mobility along with greater economic inequality. Professionals and businessmen are being pushed aside by officials and representatives of the bureaucratic structures. Today, about a third of the country's revenues, according to Rosstat (Russia's Federal Statistic Service), are distributed to the country's richest 10 per cent of the population, and the country's poorest 10 per cent get only 1.9 per cent of total revenues.

Often, as the Russian experience attests, widespread societal changes affect people's individual social standing in a process sociologists call **structural social mobility**, a *shift in the social position of large numbers of people due more to changes in society itself than to individual efforts*. Half a century ago, industrialisation in the Soviet Union created a vast number of new factory jobs that drew rural people to cities. Similarly, the growth of bureaucracy propelled countless Soviet citizens from ploughing to paperwork. Now, with new laws sanctioning individual ownership of private property and business, some experts monitoring the changing Russian scene predict further structural social mobility along with greater economic inequality. But, equal or not, everyone hopes to enjoy a higher standard of living.

# Pierre Bourdieu: reproducing inequalities and dominance

**Pierre Bourdieu (1930–2002)**
*Source:* © Nogues Alain/Corbis Sygma.

For many, Pierre Bourdieu (1930–2002), a French sociologist, is considered to be one of 'the greatest sociologists of our era' (Burawoy). Although he produced at least 35 books on topics as diverse as sport, art, culture, education, photography, peasants and masculinity, he is most noted for his contribution to the study of inequality and class. His major concern was with unmasking the way domination works (what he called 'symbolic violence'). He was puzzled by the fact that whilst people live in massively unequal systems, they usually seem to come to accept them and take them for granted. He asked: how do systems of privilege, dominance and hierarchy reproduce themselves across generations – without much resistance from those below? At the heart of his work are four core ideas: *symbolic dominance and violence*, *capital*, *fields* and *habitus*. These are hard to define but briefly:

- *Symbolic dominance* means the exercise of dominance through culture and its mystification. Symbols and meanings organise our life and much class conflict is over these very symbols, languages and meanings.

- *Habitus* refers to our learned social habits: they are relatively permanent and routine ways of life which often shape our life chances. They are learned dispositions which lead people to behave in certain ways.

- *Fields* refers to relatively autonomous spaces in which social relationships get organised. Those relations are often economic, social, cultural and symbolic (but this does not exhaust the type). They are the arenas where competition and conflicts of social life get worked through.

- *Capital* refers to the resources we have to live with. Forms of capital can be exchanged. Bourdieu is most noted for developing a typology of these resources. Economic capital is the most obvious and Marx wrote about it – it refers to our economic resources (wealth, income, work). But there are others as Table 8.2 indicates. Those with high social capital know all the right people; those with cultural capital know all the right things; those with symbolic capital have the right respect.

In Bourdieu's most central and famed book, *Distinction* (1981 originally, 1984 in English), he uses a detailed questionnaire about consumer activities on a large 1960s French sample to investigate cultural tastes. Cultural tastes are enduringly linked to class position and

| Table 8.2 | Bourdieu's forms of capital | |
|---|---|---|
| **Form of capital** | **Definitions and features** | **How you can recognise it** |
| Economic capital | Ownership of wealth (and means of production) | Wealth, income, property |
| Social capital | Membership and involvement in social networks and the 'unceasing effort of sociability' | Good connections |
| | | Networking |
| | | Patronage – who you know |
| Cultural capital | Gained through family and education | Educational credentials |
| | | Knowledge of arts and culture |
| Symbolic capital | Prestige, status and social honour | Reputation, respect |

capture the profound sense of social difference and distance we often feel when faced with different cultures. In particular, he is concerned with our tastes for particular music (whether popular or classical, for instance), foods, art and so forth, and with the ways items may move into and out of our scale of tastes. These can all be seen as *ways of maintaining social distance and reproducing class relations*. Each family teaches its children a certain cultural capital and a certain ethos. Starting in the pre-school years, children have different access to cultural capital. For instance, children taken by parents around the world have experiences of many different cultures with their different languages, manners, foods, arts and etiquettes. They build up experiences of travel, diversity and languages which other children may never know. Cultural capital, then, is much more than formal education; it is found often in personalities who 'know things', about art or food or films or history – who have a stock of cultural knowledge. Different tastes are cultivated in different groups – it all depends upon the groups you hang around with. It is found in the reproduction of everyday life.

We will encounter Bordieu in several places in this book. His ideas have been 'used' by many contemporary sociologists, but he is not always easy to understand. There are many guides to him: try Richard Jenkins, *Pierre Bourdieu* (revised edition, 2002).

# The persistence of inequalities in social life

Looking around the world at the extent of social inequality, we might wonder how societies persist without distributing their resources more equally. Caste-like systems in early Great Britain and Japan lasted for centuries, concentrating land and power in the hands of several hundred families. Even more striking, for 2,000 years most people in India accepted the idea that they should be privileged or poor because of the accident of birth. Many still do today. As we shall see in this section of the book, today class systems pervade the world; and in many countries, the majority of their populations still live in abject poverty. Women often live in fear of violence. Ethnic minorities everywhere are discriminated against. Everywhere one looks throughout the world, we find inequalities and stratification.

As Ken Plummer has commented elsewhere:

The history of human societies can well be read as a history of billions of people going quietly to their graves with lives of almost unspeakable suffering delivered upon them from the raging inequalities of the differences given to them by the society where they were born . . . There are always it seems the rich and the poor, the slave owner and the slave, the black and the white, the migrant and the host, the educated and the ignorant, the diseased and the healthy, the man and the woman, the gay and the straight, the able and the disabled, the terrorist and the terrorised, the pathological and the normal, us and them – indeed the good, the bad and the ugly. And sociology cannot fail to see this. In human societies, differences are used as moral markers to establish how some are better than others. Moral worth is often attached to this labeling as boundaries are established of the normal and the pathological. The elite are superior; the mass are downcast. Borders become hierarchically arranged and a ranking or pecking order is established: outsiders, underclasses, dangerous people, marginals, outcasts – the scapegoats – are invented. And sociologists ask: just how are these 'outsiders' and ranking orders created, maintained and changed? This is the problem of social exclusion, the social other; and social stratification.

(Plummer 2010: 153–5)

The question we have to ask here is just why human beings have managed to sustain such systems over long periods of history. Typically, sociologists suggest four broad and interconnected answers.

# 1 Ideology

A first broad explanation suggests the significance of **ideology**: *cultural beliefs that serve to legitimate key interests and hence justify social stratification*. Any beliefs – for example, the claim that the rich are clever while the poor are lazy – are ideological to the extent that they bolster the dominance of wealthy elites and suggest that poor people deserve their plight. A millennium ago, a rigid estate system in Europe rested on church teachings that such arrangements reflected the will of

God. More specifically, the church endorsed as divinely sanctioned a system by which most people laboured as serfs, driving the feudal economy with their muscles. According to the church, nobility was charged with responsibility for defending the realm and maintaining public order. To question this system meant challenging the church and, ultimately, defying God. The religious justification that supported the medieval estate system for centuries is expressed in the following stanza from the nineteenth-century English hymn 'All Things Bright and Beautiful':

> The rich man in his castle,
> The poor man at his gate,
> He made them high and lowly
> And ordered their estate.

The Industrial Revolution opened the way for newly rich industrialists to topple the feudal nobility. In the process, industrial culture advanced a new ideology. Capitalists mocked the centuries-old notion that social hierarchy should depend on the accident of birth. Under God's law, the new thinking went, the most talented and hard-working individuals should dominate society. The rise of industrial capitalism transformed wealth and power into prizes won by those who display the greatest talent and effort. Class systems celebrate individualism and achievement, so that social standing serves as a measure of personal worthiness. Thus poverty, which called for charity under feudalism, became under industrial capitalism a scorned state of personal inadequacy. The same thinking recast the poor from objects of charity into unworthy people lacking ability and ambition. The ideological shift from birth to individual achievement as the basis of social inequality was well established by the time early nineteenth-century German writer Johann Wolfgang von Goethe quipped:

> Really to own
> What you inherit,
> You first must earn it
> With your merit.

Clearly, medieval and modern justifications for inequality differ dramatically: what an earlier era viewed as fair, a later one rejected as wrong. Yet both cases illustrate the pivotal role of ideology – cultural beliefs that define a particular kind of hierarchy as fair and natural. Justifications for social stratification, then, are culturally variable across history and from place to place.

More recently, the social geographer Danny Dorling has mapped out some of our contemporary ideologies in detail (Dorling 2010). Amongst the key ideological themes which prop up systems of inequality are the views that:

1. *Elitism is efficient.* For example, children and adults are divided into types and their education is funded differently. Glittering prizes are awarded for the best because they are the best. Behind this lurk ideas about IQ potential, genius children and the genetic foundations (superiority) of elite groups.

2. *Exclusion is necessary.* For example, the exclusions of certain groups in societies (typically 20 per cent of society or so – the foreigners, scroungers, criminals, etc.) can always be justified as necessary in protecting the lifestyles and wishes of the majority. Prisons, for example, can become major dumping grounds; cities can develop 'no-go' areas.

3. *Prejudice against 'the lower orders' is natural*: suspicions against immigrants, the feckless poor, security scroungers, etc. are justifiable.

4. *Greed is good:* wanting to make a lot of money is a good thing and ruthlessness is even encouraged (as seen in the current success of the television programme *The Apprentice*).

As these ideas circulate and reproduce themselves widely in contemporary culture, so we become unknowingly immersed in a culture where inequalities become widened, deepened and acceptable. At the heart of each of these statements, Dorling claims, is a justification of the perpetuation of inequalities.

## 2 Habitualisation

A second explanation of the perpetuation of inequalities highlights the habitualisation of inequalities in everyday life. This is a central idea of Bourdieu, as discussed in the box. For him, cultural reproduction does not involve the reproduction of the culture of all segments of society, only that of the dominant classes. People in each class transmit a distinctive 'habitus' (classifications, perceptions, ways of talking, moving and generally carrying oneself) down the generations, but schools pick up only on the habitus of the most powerful classes. He argues that the educational system has systematic biases against working-class knowledge and skills. Bourdieu observed underlying patterns of class domination in education, art and 'culture' generally. He suggested that the primary roles of education are **social reproduction**, *the maintenance of power and privilege between social classes from one generation to the next*, and **cultural reproduction**, *the process by which a society transmits dominant knowledge from one generation to another.*

## A research measure for inequality: the Gini coefficient

This is the most popular of several measures of inequality because it provides a simple single summary statistic to show a pattern of income distribution. In a fully equal society, the poorest 25 per cent would earn 25 per cent of the total income, the poorest 50 per cent would receive 50 per cent of the total income – and so on. In an unequal society like ours, the richer groups earn as much as 80 per cent of the total income, whilst the poorest 25 per cent may earn as little as 1 or 2 per cent. These discrepancies are measured by the Gini coefficent. This measures incomes for different groups in a society and then matches them with an ideal 'equal pattern' like above. A rank can then be provided so that we can compare societies or groups on how 'equal' their income distribution is. Having a Gini coefficient value of 0.00 indicates that each household has the same income; a coefficient of 1.00 indicates perfect inequality. This measure is used in Wilkinson's study (see Public sociology, p. 261).

## 3 Subjugation

A third explanation suggests that the subjection of many subordinate groups makes them too downtrodden to challenge the dominant orders. Truly poor and socially excluded people often lack the power and resources to challenge the existing social order. They have to bear the burdens of the poor, which ill equips them for change and action. Economic deprivation defines their existence and leaves a mark. Marx, of course, believed that these exploited groups would become the revolutionary challenge; that they would rise up against their rulers. But he overlooked just how weak and disempowered such groups generally become. At the very least, as we shall see, outcast groups may also be more likely to suffer from illness, physical and mental.

## 4 Coercion and violence

A final but major explanation suggests the role of coercion, power and violence: we should not overlook the coercive power of ruling groups. Ultimately, elites have a lot at stake – a lot to lose – and one way or another they play a key role in regulating the poor through armed forces, police and prisons. The ultimate regulation of the unequal order is the power of the coercive state (more on this in Chapter 16).

## Explaining social stratification

Why are societies stratified at all? In the next few sections we look at a few rival theories – one which suggests stratification may be functional; another which claims that societies work through exploitation and conflict; and a third – Weberian – which sees stratification as multidimensional. There are others.

## 1 Stratification as functional

One answer, consistent with the functional perspective, is that social inequality plays a vital part in the operation of all societies. It is, so to speak, 'needed'. Over 50 years ago, Kingsley Davis and Wilbert Moore (1945) set out such an argument by asserting that social stratification has beneficial consequences for the operation of a society. How else, asked Davis and Moore, can we explain the fact that some form of social stratification has been found everywhere? Davis and Moore described our society as a complex system involving hundreds of occupational positions of varying importance. Certain jobs – say, changing spark plugs in a car – are fairly easy and can be performed by almost anyone. Other jobs, such as transplanting a human organ, are quite difficult and demand the scarce talents of people who have received extensive (and expensive) education. Positions of high day-to-day responsibility that demand special abilities are the most functionally significant.

In general, Davis and Moore explained, the greater the functional importance of a position, the more rewards a society will attach to it. This strategy pays off, since rewarding important work with income, prestige, power and leisure encourages people to do these things. In effect, by distributing resources unequally, a society motivates each person to aspire to the most significant work possible, and to work better, harder and longer. The overall effect of a social system of unequal rewards – which is what social stratification amounts to – is a more productive society.

Davis and Moore conceded that every society could be egalitarian. But, they cautioned, rewards could be equal only to the extent that people were willing to let *anyone* perform *any* job. Equality also demands that someone who carries out a job poorly be rewarded on a par with another who performs well. Logic dictates that such a system offers little incentive for people to make their best efforts, and thereby reduces a society's productive efficiency.

## Meritocracy

The Davis–Moore thesis implies that a productive society is a **meritocracy**, *a system of social stratification based on personal merit*. Such societies hold out rewards to develop the talents and encourage the efforts of everyone. In pursuit of meritocracy, a society promotes equality of opportunity while, at the same time, mandating inequality of rewards. In other words, a pure class system would be a meritocracy, rewarding everyone based on ability and effort. In addition, such a society would have extensive social mobility, blurring social categories as individuals move up or down in the social system depending on their performance.

For their part, caste societies can speak of 'merit' (from Latin, meaning 'worthy of praise') only in terms of persistence in low-skill labour such as farming. Caste systems, in short, offer honour to those who remain dutifully 'in their place'.

Although caste systems waste human potential, they are quite orderly. And herein lies a clue to an important question: why do modern industrial societies resist becoming pure meritocracies by retaining many caste-like qualities? Simply because, left unchecked, meritocracy erodes social structure such as kinship. No one, for example, evaluates family members solely on the basis of performance. Class systems in industrial societies, therefore, retain some caste elements to promote order and social cohesion.

## Critical comment

The Davis–Moore thesis is a conservative one (as most functional arguments are). While Davis and Moore pointed out that *some* form of stratification exists everywhere, they could not explain why these systems can be so very different – from harsh and rigid ones, to much more flexible ones. Nor did Davis and Moore specify precisely what reward should be attached to any occupational position. They merely pointed out that positions a society deems crucial must yield sufficient rewards to draw talent away from less

important work. Can we even measure functional importance? Surgeons may perform a valuable service in saving lives, but a related profession, nursing, is vastly less well paid. Many popular footballers, pop singers and 'stars' can earn more in a few nights than most primary school teachers and childminders earn in their working lives – and the latter are responsible for raising the next generation!

Further, the Davis–Moore thesis exaggerates social stratification's role in developing individual talent. Our society does reward individual achievement, but we also allow families to transfer wealth and power from generation to generation in caste-like fashion. Additionally, for women, ethnic groups, the disabled and others with limited opportunities, stratification still raises barriers to personal accomplishment. Social stratification functions to develop some people's abilities to the fullest while barring others from ever reaching their potential.

Thirdly, by contending that social stratification benefits all of society, the Davis–Moore thesis ignores how social inequality promotes conflict and, sometimes, even outright revolution. This assertion leads us to the social-conflict paradigm, which provides a very different explanation for the persistence of social hierarchy (Tumin, 1953).

# 2 Marxist and neo-Marxist ideas on stratification and conflict

Conflict analysis argues that, rather than benefit society as a whole, social stratification provides major advantages to some people at the expense of others. This theoretical perspective draws heavily on the ideas of Karl Marx (whose approach to understanding social inequality was introduced in Chapter 4).

Writing (with Engels) in the original manifesto of the Communist Party (1848), Marx identified two major social classes corresponding to the two basic relationships to the means of production: individuals either (1) own productive property or (2) labour for others. In medieval Europe, the nobility and the church owned the productive land; peasants toiled as farmers. Similarly, in industrial class systems, the capitalists (or the *bourgeoisie*) own and operate factories, which utilise the labour of workers (the *proletariat*). Figure 4.3 on p. 120 suggests that these polarities occur throughout history.

Marx noted great differences in wealth and power arising from the industrial–capitalist productive system, which, he contended, made class conflict inevitable. In time, he believed, oppression and misery would drive the working majority to organise and, ultimately, to overthrow capitalism. A process would take place in which the poorer classes would become more pauperised, polarised and aware of their class position. This would lead to a class consciousness of their true economic exploitation.

Marx's analysis was grounded in his observations of capitalism in the nineteenth century, when great industrialists dominated the economic scene. In North America, for example, Andrew Carnegie, J. P. Morgan and John Jacob Astor (one of the few very rich passengers to perish on the *Titanic*) lived in fabulous mansions filled with priceless art and staffed by dozens of servants. According to Marx, the capitalist elite draws its strength from more than the operation of the economy. He noted that, through the family, opportunity and wealth are passed down from generation to generation. Moreover, the legal system defends this practice through inheritance law. Similarly, exclusive schools bring children of the elite together, encouraging informal social ties that will benefit them throughout their lives. Overall, from Marx's point of view, capitalist society *reproduces the class structure in each new generation.*

## Critical comment

Exploring how the capitalist economic system generates conflict between classes, Marx's analysis of social stratification has had enormous influence on sociological thinking in recent decades. Because it is revolutionary – calling for the overthrow of capitalist society – Marxism is also highly controversial.

One of the strongest criticisms of the Marxist approach is that it denies one of the central tenets of the Davis–Moore thesis: that motivating people to perform various social roles requires some system of unequal rewards. Marx separated reward from performance, endorsing an egalitarian system based on the principle of 'from each according to ability; to each according to need' (1972: 388; orig. 1845). Critics argue that severing rewards from performance is precisely the flaw that generated the low productivity characteristic of the former Soviet Union and other socialist economies around the world.

Defenders of Marx rebut this line of attack by pointing to considerable evidence supporting Marx's general view of humanity as inherently social rather than unflinchingly selfish. They counter that we should not assume that individual rewards (much less monetary compensation alone) are the only way to motivate people to perform their social roles. Table 8.3 compares the functional and conflict paradigms.

In addition, although few doubt that capitalist society does perpetuate poverty and privilege, as Marx asserted, the revolutionary developments that he considered inevitable have failed to materialise. The next section explores why the socialist revolution that Marx predicted and promoted has not occurred, at least in advanced capitalist societies.

| Table 8.3 | Two explanations of social stratification: a summary | |
|---|---|
| **Functional paradigm** | **Conflict paradigm** |
| Social stratification keeps society operating. | Social stratification is the result of social conflict. |
| The linkage of greater rewards to more important social positions benefits society as a whole. | Differences in social resources serve the interests of some and harm the interests of others. |
| Social stratification encourages a matching of talents and abilities to appropriate positions | Social stratification ensures that much talent and ability within society will not be utilised at all. |
| Social stratification is both useful and inevitable. | Social stratification is useful to only some people; it is not inevitable. |
| The values and beliefs that legitimise social inequality are widely shared throughout society. | Values and beliefs tend to be ideological; they reflect the interests of the more powerful members of society. |
| Because systems of social stratification are useful to society as a whole and are supported by cultural values and beliefs, they are usually stable over time. | Because systems of social stratification reflect the interests of only part of society, they are unlikely to remain stable over time. |

*Source*: Adapted in part from Stinchcombe, 1963: 808.

## Why no Marxist revolution?

Despite Marx's prediction, capitalism is still thriving. Why have workers in the UK and other industrial societies not overthrown capitalism? Some while ago, Ralf Dahrendorf (1959) pointed to four reasons:

1 *The fragmentation of the capitalist class.* The 120 years since Marx's death have witnessed the fragmentation of the capitalist class in Europe. A century ago, *single families* typically owned large companies; today, *numerous stockholders* fill that position. The diffusion of ownership has also stimulated the emergence of a managerial class, who may or may not be major stockholders (Wright, 1985; Wright et al., 1992). We will find more evidence of this in the next chapter (see Scott, 1991).

2 *White-collar work and a rising standard of living.* A 'white-collar revolution' has transformed Marx's industrial proletariat. As Chapter 15 details, the majority of workers in Marx's time laboured either on farms or in factories. They had **blue-collar or manual occupations**, *lower-prestige jobs involving mostly manual labour*. By contrast, most workers today hold **white-collar occupations**, *higher-prestige work involving mostly mental activity*. These occupations include positions in sales, management and other service work, frequently in large, bureaucratic organisations.

While many of today's white-collar workers perform repetitive tasks like the industrial workers known to Marx, evidence indicates that most do not think of themselves in those terms. Rather, most white-collar workers now perceive their social positions as higher than those of their blue-collar parents and grandparents. One key reason is that workers' overall standard of living in Europe rose fourfold over the course of the twentieth century, even as the working week decreased. As a result of a rising tide of social mobility, society seems less sharply divided between rich and poor than it did to people during Marx's lifetime (Wright and Martin, 1987).

3 *More extensive worker organisation.* Employees have organisational strengths that they lacked a century ago. Workers have won the right to organise into trade unions that can and do make demands of management backed by threats of 'working to rule' and strikes. Although union membership started to decline seriously in the 1980s, research suggests that well-established unions can still enhance the economic standing of the workers they represent.

Further, today's negotiations between labour and management are typically institutionalised and peaceful, a picture quite different from the often-violent confrontations common before the mid-twentieth century.

4 *More extensive legal protections.* Since Marx's death, the government has extended laws to protect workers' rights and has given workers greater access to the courts for redressing grievances. Government programmes such as National Insurance, health and safety, disability protection and social security also provide workers with substantially greater security and financial resources than the capitalists of the nineteenth century were willing to grant them.

Taken together, these four developments mean that, despite persistent stratification, many societies have smoothed out some of capitalism's rough edges. Consequently, social conflict today may be less intense than it was a century ago.

We could also add that Marx's time was starting to see the growth of the mass press, but he could hardly have foreseen the major escalation in all media forms. As Chapter 22 will suggest, we increasingly live our lives in a 'mediated society' where the media infuses all we do. Of course, some of this adopts a critical and reflective stance. But the growth of pop music, mass film, television, gameboys, computer games and the like can mean that we have started to 'amuse ourselves to death' (Postman, 1986). As we have become media-saturated with entertainment, so many people have lost the critical edge for thinking about the nature of their class position.

## The critical case

Many sociologists continue to find value in Marx's analysis, often in modified form (Miliband, 1969; Domhoff, 1983; Stephens, 1986). They respond with their own set of five key points, defending Marx's critical analysis of capitalism but suggesting ways in which it needs to be modified over a hundred years later.

1 *Wealth remains highly concentrated and inequalities have increased.* Capitalism remains an extensively exploitative system with wealth in the hands of the few. In Europe, about half of all privately controlled corporate stock is owned by just 1 per cent of individuals, who persist as a capitalist class. Why does such extreme inequality continue to grow?

2 *The global system of capitalism.* Tellingly, much of the production of goods in the twenty-first century

has shifted from the high-income countries to low-income countries. As we will see in the next chapter, it is in these low-income countries that workers can be paid very little for their labour. The sweatshops of nineteenth-century England are now, literally, 'the sweatshops of the world'. Marx's model may still hold for societies once the global dimension is taken into consideration.

3  *Work remains degrading and dehumanising*. Not only has the white-collar revolution delivered little in the way of higher income, but also much white-collar work remains monotonous and routine, especially the low-level clerical jobs commonly held by women. But many new jobs have arrived which are temporary, low paid and lacking a career structure (see Chapter 15, pp. 513–17).

4  *Labour activity has been weakened*. Trade unions may have advanced the interests of the workers during the earlier twentieth century, and regular negotiation between workers and management may now be a frequent activity. Many of the concessions won by workers in the past came about precisely through the class conflict that Marx described. But by the late twentieth century, union activity had been weakened and much labour throughout the world in now non-unionised (see Chapter 15, p. 516).

5  *The law still favours the rich*. Workers have gained some legal protections over the course of the twentieth century. Even so, the law still defends the overall distribution of wealth in Europe. Just as important, 'average' people cannot use the legal system to the same advantage as the rich do.

## 3  Max Weber: class, status and power

Max Weber, whose approach to social analysis is described in Chapter 4, agreed with Karl Marx that social stratification sparks social conflict, but differed from Marx in several important respects. Weber considered Marx's model of two social classes too simple. Instead, he viewed social stratification as a more complex interplay of three distinct dimensions. First is economic inequality – the issue so vital to Marx – which Weber termed 'class position'. Weber's use of 'class' refers not to crude categories but to a continuum on which anyone can be ranked from high to low. A second continuum, *status*, measures

social prestige. Finally, Weber noted the importance of *power* as a third dimension of social hierarchy.

### The socioeconomic status hierarchy

Marx believed that social prestige and power derived from economic position; thus he saw no reason to treat them as distinct dimensions of social inequality. Weber disagreed, recognising that stratification in industrial societies has characteristically low status consistency. An individual, Weber pointed out, might have high standing on one dimension of inequality but a lower position on another. For example, bureaucratic officials might wield considerable power yet have little wealth or social prestige.

So while Marx viewed inequality in terms of two clearly defined classes, Weber saw something more subtle at work in the stratification of industrial societies. Weber's key contribution in this area, then, lies in identifying the multidimensional nature of social rankings. Sociologists often use the term **socioeconomic status** (SES) to refer to *a composite ranking based on various dimensions of social inequality*.

A population that varies widely in class, status and power – Weber's three dimensions of inequality – creates a virtually infinite array of social categories, all of which pursue their own interests. Thus, unlike Marx, who focused on conflict between two overarching classes, Weber considered social conflict as highly variable and complex.

### Inequality in history

Weber also made a key historical observation, noting that each of his three dimensions of social inequality stands out at a different point in the evolution of human societies. Agrarian societies, he maintained, emphasise status or social prestige, typically in the form of honour or symbolic purity. Members of these societies gain such status by conforming to cultural norms corresponding to their rank.

Industrialisation and the development of capitalism level traditional rankings based on birth, but generate striking material differences in the population. Thus, Weber argued, the crucial difference among people in industrial–capitalist societies lies in the economic dimension of class.

In time, industrial societies witness a surging growth of the bureaucratic state. This expansion of government, coupled with the proliferation of other types of formal organisation, brings power to the fore in the stratification system. Power is also central to the organisation of socialist societies, as we see in their extensive government regulation of many aspects of life. The elite members of such societies are mostly high-ranking officials rather than rich people.

This historical analysis underlies a final disagreement between Weber and Marx. Looking to the future, Marx believed that social stratification could be largely eliminated by abolishing private ownership of productive property. Weber doubted that overthrowing capitalism would significantly diminish social stratification in modern societies. While doing so might lessen economic disparity, Weber reasoned, the significance of power based on organisational position would only increase. In fact, Weber imagined, a socialist revolution might well *increase* social inequality by expanding government and concentrating power in the hands of a political elite. Recent popular uprisings against entrenched bureaucracies in eastern Europe and the former Soviet Union lend support to Weber's argument.

## Critical comment

Weber's multidimensional analysis of social stratification retains enormous influence among sociologists, especially in Europe. Some analysts (particularly those influenced by Marx's ideas) argue that while social class boundaries have blurred, striking patterns of social inequality persist in the industrial world.

As we shall see in Chapter 10, the enormous wealth of the most privileged members of our society contrasts sharply with the grinding poverty of millions who barely meet their day-to-day needs. Moreover, the upward social mobility that historically fuelled optimism in this country all but came to a halt in the 1970s, and evidence points to an increase in economic inequality during the 1980s. Against this backdrop of economic polarisation, the 1990s were marked by a renewed emphasis on 'classes' in conflict rather than on the subtle shadings of a 'multidimensional hierarchy'.

# Inequalities and The Equality Act 2010

Inequalities cover a wide range of social life and, in the contemporary world, some governments have been concerned about the problems it raises. As sociologists have mapped out the intersecting grounds of inequalities (Table 8.1 on p. 253), so some governments have tried to take seriously the idea of inequality in legislation. In 2010, the then Labour government in the UK passed a major new piece of legislation called The Equality Act. Bringing together the majority of existing equality laws, it also aimed to increase protection for minority groups and victims of discrimination by strengthening the law in some areas. (It is estimated that 90–95 per cent of the new legislation simply consolidates previous legislation.)

Previously, each area of social division, such as class, race and gender, had its own separate legislation and support organisation (such as the Race Equality Commission, disbanded in 2007). Now all the various forms of discrimination have been brought together under the heading 'protected characteristics'. Here the issues of age, disability (which includes mental health and people diagnosed as clinically obese), race, religion or belief, sex, sexual orientation, gender reassignment (people who are having or who have had a sex change, transvestites and transgender people), marriage and civil partnership, and pregnancy and maternity are all brought together in one Act. Seven different types of discrimination are included: from direct discrimination and victimisation to harassment and 'associative discrimination'. This latter category is discrimination against someone because they

are associated with another person with a protected characteristic – such as carers of disabled people and elderly relatives, who can claim they were treated unfairly because of duties that they had to carry out at home relating to their care work. It also covers discrimination against someone because, for example, their partner is from another country.

*Age* is still the only protected characteristic by which you can justify direct discrimination, because you can argue that treating someone differently because of their age is necessary to meet a legitimate aim. You can also still have a default retirement age of 65 (unless/until the retirement age legislation changes, which it may do in the coming years).

 Full details of this new legislation can be found at: www.legislation.gov.uk/uksi/2010/2317/pdfs/uksi_20102317_en.pdf and a summary at: www.equalities.gov.uk/equality_bill.aspx.

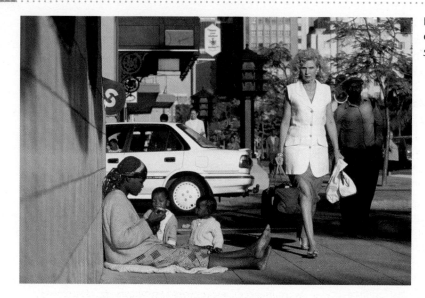

Pedestrian passing a beggar and children, Durban, South Africa

*Source*: © David Turnley/Corbis.

## Inequality theory as normative theory?

This chapter's explanations of social stratification also involve value judgements. The Davis–Moore thesis, which cites universal social stratification, interprets this pattern as evidence that inequality is a necessary element of social organisation. Class differences, then, reflect both variation in human abilities and the importance of occupational roles. From this point of view, the spectre of equality is a threat to a society of diverse people, since such uniformity could exist only as the product of the relentless and stifling efforts of officials like Vonnegut's fictitious 'Handicapper General' (see the *Big debate*, p. 277).

The conflict theory of Marx interprets universal social inequality in a very different way. Rejecting the notion that inequality is in any sense necessary, Marx condemned social hierarchy as a product of greed and exploitation. Guided by egalitarian values, he advocated social arrangements that would enable everyone to share all important resources equally. Rather than undermining the quality of life, Marx maintained that equality would enhance human well-being.

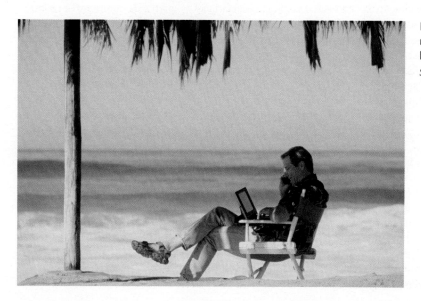

Everyday wealth? A man with a mobile phone and laptop on a tropical beach

*Source*: © Strauss/Curtis/Corbis.

# Stratification and technology in global perspective

We can weave together a number of observations made in this chapter by considering the relationship between a society's technology and its type of social stratification. Gerhard and Jean Lenski's model of sociocultural evolution, detailed in Chapter 4, puts social stratification in historical perspective and also helps us to understand the varying degrees of inequality found around the world today (Nolan and Lenski, 2010).

## Hunting and gathering societies

Simple technology limits the production of hunting and gathering societies to only what is necessary for day-to-day living. No doubt some individuals are more successful hunters or gatherers than others, but the group's survival depends on all sharing what they have. With little or no surplus, therefore, no categories of people emerge as better off than others. Thus social stratification among hunters and gatherers, based simply on age and sex, is less complex than among societies with more advanced technology.

## Horticultural, pastoral and agrarian societies

Technological advances generate surplus production, while intensifying social inequality. In horticultural and pastoral societies, a small elite controls most of the surplus. Agrarian technology based on large-scale farming generates even greater abundance, but marked inequality means that various categories of people lead strikingly different lives. The social distance between the elite hereditary nobility and the common serfs who work the land looms as large as at any time in human history. In most cases, lords wield god-like power over the masses.

## Industrial societies

Industrialisation reverses the historical trend, prompting some decrease in social inequality. The eclipse of tradition and the need to develop individual talents gradually erode caste rankings in favour of greater individual opportunity. Then, too, the increasing productivity of industrial technology steadily raises the living standards of the historically poor majority. Specialised, technical work also demands the expansion of schooling, sharply reducing illiteracy. A literate population, in turn, tends to press for a greater voice in political decision making, further diminishing social inequality. As already noted, continuing technological advances transform much blue-collar labour into higher-prestige white-collar work. All these social shifts help to explain why Marxist revolutions occurred in agrarian societies – such as Russia (1917), Cuba (1959) and Nicaragua (1979) – in which social inequality is most pronounced, rather than in industrial societies, as Marx predicted more than a century ago.

Initially, the great wealth generated by industrialisation is concentrated in the hands of a few – the pattern so troubling to Marx. In time, however, the share of all property in the hands of the very rich declines somewhat. According to estimates, the proportion of all wealth controlled by the richest 1 per cent of US families peaked at about 36 per cent just before the stock market crash in 1929; during the entrepreneurial 1980s, this economic elite owned one-third of all wealth (Williamson and Lindert, 1980; Beeghley, 1989).

Finally, industrialisation diminishes the domination of women by men, a pattern that is strongest in agrarian societies. The movement towards social parity for the sexes derives from the industrial economy's need to cultivate individual talent as well as a growing belief in basic human equality.

## The Kuznets curve

The trend described above can be distilled into the following statement. *In human history, technological progress first sharply increases but then moderates the intensity of social stratification.* So if greater inequality is functional for agrarian societies, then industrial societies benefit from a more egalitarian climate. This historical shift, recognised by Nobel Prize-winning economist Simon Kuznets (1966), is illustrated by the Kuznets curve, shown in Figure 8.2.

Current patterns of social inequality around the world generally square with the Kuznets curve. Industrial societies have somewhat less income inequality – one important measure of social stratification – than nations that remain predominantly agrarian. Specifically, mature industrial societies, such as those in the European Union, Australia and the United States, exhibit less income inequality than the less industrialised countries of Latin America, Africa and Asia.

**Figure 8.2** Social stratification and technological development: the Kuznets curve
The Kuznets curve reveals that greater technological sophistication is generally accompanied by more pronounced social stratification. The trend reverses itself, however, as industrial societies gradually become more egalitarian. Rigid caste-like distinctions are relaxed in favour of greater opportunity and equality under the law. Political rights are more widely extended, and there is even some levelling of economic differences. The Kuznets curve may also be usefully applied to the relative social standing of the two sexes.

Yet income disparity reflects a host of factors beyond technology, especially political and economic priorities. Societies that have had socialist economic systems (including the People's Republic of China, the Russian Federation and the nations of eastern Europe) display relatively little income inequality. Keep in mind, however, that an allegedly egalitarian society such as the People's Republic of China has an average income level that is quite low by world standards; further, on non-economic dimensions such as political power, China's society reveals pronounced inequality.

And what of the future? Although the global pattern described by the Kuznets curve may be valid, this analysis does not necessarily mean that industrial societies will gradually become less and less stratified. In the abstract, members of our society endorse the principle of equal opportunity for all; even so, this goal has not been and may never become a reality. The notion of social equality, like all concepts related to social stratification, is controversial, as the final section of this chapter explains.

## Looking ahead: inequalities, stratification and divisions in the twenty-first century

Social scientists have long taken an interest in inequalities. They seem to have been present in almost all societies throughout all of history, be this through class or caste or slavery, or be it through race or sexuality or gender. Apart, perhaps, from a few very early traditional societies, it is hard not to conclude that the history of society is indeed the history of inequality.

Today, the twenty-first century is no different. Some suggest that inequalities are greater now than ever – and growing. In the long course of history, this seems unlikely. But certainly in recent times, where the measurement of such issues has become a little more reliable, we can find evidence that inequalities have indeed grown.

We can perhaps see the world most basically as split into three kinds of experience. One is that of the truly wealthy and high-status groupings – a few million or so in a world of seven billion, who fly way above most ordinary mortals with incomes that top the GDP of many of the smaller countries, and lifestyles that are hermetically sealed off from the everyday lives of the rest of us. Few sociologists have ever been seriously allowed to enter these worlds, and we know little about them.

Then, at the other extreme, there are a billion or so (somewhere between a fifth and a sixth of the world's population) – one writer calls them 'the bottom billions' – who live on incomes that amount to less than one US dollar a day. They are truly low on most social indicators such as health, literacy, political engagement, access to communications and, of course, wealth. Often homeless and living lives in the most desperate of situations, these are damaged lives, brutalised lives, even 'wasted lives' (Bauman, 2004). Sociologists have not written as much about these experiences as cultural anthropologists and developmental theorists have. Most sociology stays relatively safely away from them.

And then there are a third grouping: 'us' if you like, maybe in one sense 'the majority'. But within our social world, major social divisions continue to exist too. There are huge demonstrable inequalities across it. And it is these inequalities which sociologists seem mainly to study: the organisation of social class in modern relatively high-income societies. But all of this is heavily 'intersected' with ethnicity, gender, age, sexuality and disability. We will look at these 'intersections' in Chapters 11–14.

# SUMMARY

1 Sociologists are never far away from issues of stratification and inequality, since they so seriously shape social life. The following chapters pick up on a range of these issues. Social stratification refers to categories of people ranked in a hierarchy. There are four major stratification systems: socioeconomic, ethnic, gender and age. Stratification is (a) a characteristic of society, not something that merely arises from individual differences; (b) persistent over many generations; (c) universal, yet variable in form; and (d) supported by cultural beliefs.

2 Slavery, estate and caste are major forms of stratification. Slavery still exists today. Caste systems, typical of agrarian societies, are based on ascription and rest on strong moral beliefs, shaping a person's entire life, including occupation and marriage. Class systems, common to industrial societies, reflect a greater measure of individual achievement. Because the emphasis on achievement opens the way for social mobility, classes are less clearly defined than castes.

3 Historically, socialist societies have claimed to be classless, based on their public ownership of productive property. While such societies may exhibit far less economic inequality than their capitalist counterparts, they are notably stratified with regard to power.

4 Social stratification persists for two reasons – support from various social institutions and the power of ideology to define certain kinds of inequality as both natural and just.

5 The Davis–Moore thesis states that social stratification is universal because it contributes to the operation of society. In class systems, unequal rewards motivate people to aspire to the occupational roles most important to the functioning of society. Critics of the Davis–Moore thesis note that (a) it is difficult to assess objectively the functional importance of any occupational position; (b) stratification prevents many people from developing their abilities; and (c) social stratification often generates social conflict.

6 Marx recognised two major social classes in industrial societies. The capitalists, or bourgeoisie, own the means of production in pursuit of profits; the proletariat, by contrast, offer their labour in exchange for wages. The socialist revolution that Marx predicted has not occurred in industrial societies such as Germany or the United States. Some sociologists see this as evidence that Marx's analysis was flawed; others, however, point out that our society is still marked by pronounced social inequality and substantial class conflict.

7 Max Weber identified three distinct dimensions of social inequality: economic class, social status or prestige, and power. Taken together, these three dimensions form a complex hierarchy of socioeconomic standing.

8 Gerhard Lenski and Jean Lenski explained that, historically, technological advances have been associated with more pronounced social stratification. A limited reversal of this trend occurs in advanced industrial societies, as represented by the Kuznets curve.

9 Social stratification is a complex and controversial area of research because it deals not only with facts but with values that suggest how society should be organised. Two ideas of the twentieth century may help to reorganise stratification in the twenty-first century: cyberpower and human rights.

## MYTASKLIST

# Ten suggestions for going further

## 1 Connect up with Part Six and the Sociology Web Resources

As you work through ideas and think about the issues raised
in this chapter, look at the accompanying website and the
resource centre at the end of this book which connects to it.
There is a lot here to help you move on. To link up, see:
www.pearson.co.uk/plummer.

## 2 Review the chapter

*Briefly summarise (in a paragraph) just what this chapter has
been about.* Consider: (a) What have you learned? (b) What
do you disagree with? Be critical. And (c) How would you
develop all this? How could you get more detail on matters
that interest you?

## 3 Pose questions

(a) Look at Table 8.1. How are social divisions and
    social stratification evident in your university
    or college? Locate your own position in the
    stratification system. Compare it with those of
    friends and family.
(b) Consider the mix of class, ethnicity, gender, sexuality,
    disability and age as systems of stratification. Are
    they all equally important? Can they be usefully
    combined?
(c) Compare some slavery systems from the past (like the
    plantation system of the USA) with those at work in
    the world today. (*Hint*: see Bales, 2000.)
(d) Discuss systems of stratification found in any two
    countries today.
(e) In what respects have the predictions of Karl Marx
    failed to materialise? In what respects does his analysis
    ring true?

## 4 Explore key words

Many concepts have been introduced in this chapter. You
can review them from the website or from the listing at the
back of this book. You might like to give special attention to
just five words and think them through – how would you
define them, what are they dealing with, and do they help
you see the social world more clearly or not?

## 5 Search the Web

Be critical when you look at websites – see the box on p. 940
in the Resources section. For this chapter look at the following:

### General sites concerned with inequalities

Global Policy Forum on Inequality
www.globalpolicy.org/social-and-economic-policy/
global-injustice-and-inequality.html

The Equality Trust (mainly UK)
www.equalitytrust.org.uk/about

Working Group on Extreme Inequality (mainly USA)
http://extremeinequality.org

Focus on the Global South
www.focusweb.org

Online Atlas of the Millennium Development Goals
http://devdata.worldbank.org/atlas-mdg

### Slavery

On modern slavery, see Anti-Slavery International:
www.antislavery.org

Contemporary 'Sexual Slavery' Links
www.brandeis.edu/projects/fse/slavery/slav-index.html
which connects to the Feminist Sexual Ethics Project

For websites on Marx, look back to Chapter 2.

## 6 Watch a DVD

• Von Stroheim's silent classic *Greed* (1924): about lives
  ruined by the desire for money.

- Les Blair's *Jump the Gun* (1997): looks at the working class in Johannesburg.
- Arthur Howes' *Nuba Conversations* (1999): looks at poverty, refugees and the Sudan.
- Srdjan Dragojevic's *The Wounds* (1999): portrays two of the most horrifically memorable under-age criminals amidst the devastating backdrop of the war in Bosnia.

## 7  Think and read

A short tour of the whole field is to be found in Ken Plummer, *Sociology: The Basics* (2010: Ch. 7).

Evelyn Kallen, *Social Inequality and Social Injustice* (2004). A very valuable account that looks at the links between inequalities and rights, and discusses a series of major cases such as the rights of children, women's rights, lesbian and gay rights and aboriginal rights.

Goran Therborn, *Inequalities of the World* (2006). A good general introduction is followed by a series of country case studies.

Daniel Dorling, *Injustice: Why Social Inequality Persists* (2010). Looks at key reasons why we cannot get rid of inequalities.

Geoff Payne (ed.), *Social Divisions* (2006). Introduces the idea of social divisions and has major chapters on each kind, including some not discussed here.

Shaun Best, *Understanding Social Divisions* (2005). An extensive discussion of different theories and findings around a wide range of social divisions.

Jodi O'Brien and Judith Howard (eds), *Everyday Inequalities: Critical Inquiries* (1998). A useful collection of empirical readings which show how inequalities of gender, class and race permeate everyday life.

Peter Braham and Linda Janes (eds), *Social Differences and Divisions* (2002). Covers a wide range of divisions from class to ethnicity in a lively Open University text.

Kevin Bales et al., *Modern Slavery* (2009). A major contemporary account of slavery: readable and also very disturbing to those who thought slavery was a thing of the past. This is an update of his earlier work and is supported by the 'reader', *Understanding Global Slavery: A Reader* (2005) and a photographic exhibition, *Documenting Disposable People* (2008).

## 8  Connect to other chapters

- Connect to Marx and Weber in Chapter 4.
- Connect to discussion of class in Chapter 10.
- Link Davis and Moore back to functionalism in Chapter 2.
- Link slavery to ideas on sexual slavery in Chapter 12.

## 9  Relax with a novel

- Maxim Gorky, *Mother* (1907)
- Toni Morrison, *Beloved* (1987)
- Benjamin Disraeli, *Sybil or the Two Nations* (1845)
- Edmund Wilson, *To the Finland Station* (1940)

## 10  Engage with THE BIG DEBATE

### Are the rich worth what they earn?

For an hour of work, a residential care worker in southern England can earn about £5.80 an hour and a 16-year-old care worker, maybe £4.00; a university teaching assistant can earn a little more at about £13; and a computer programmer earns between £15 and £30. These wages seem insignificant in comparison to the hundreds of thousands of millions earned annually by television celebrities like Simon Cowell (£165 million), actors like Rowan Atkinson (Mr Bean) (£70m), celebrity hosts like Jonathan Ross (18m for a three-year contract), sports stars like David Beckham (£145m), Lewis Hamilton and Joe Lewis, and music chart-toppers like Sir Paul McCartney (valued at £475m), Madonna (valued at £275m) and Sir Elton John (at £185m). Newcomers like Keira Knightley and Orlando Bloom have already amassed around £15 million. A few years back, the Duchess of York paid off a personal debt in excess of £1 million (a debt greater than the lifetime earnings of many Britons) by writing children's stories and working the talk show and lecture circuits in the United States.

The Davis–Moore thesis states that rewards reflect an occupation's value to society. But are the activities of pop stars and celebrity hosts really worth as as much to our society as the work of all teachers in several primary schools? In short, do earnings really reflect people's social importance?

Salaries in industrial–capitalist societies such as the UK are a product of the market forces of supply and demand. In simple terms, if you can do something better than others, and people value it, you can command greater rewards. According to this view, movie stars, top athletes, skilled professionals and many business executives have rare talents that are much in demand; thus, they may earn many times more than the typical worker in the UK.

But critics claim that the market is really a poor evaluator of occupational importance. First, they claim, the British economy is dominated by a small proportion of people who manipulate the system for their own benefit. Corporate executives pay themselves multi-million-pound salaries and bonuses even in years when their companies flounder. Japanese executives, by contrast, earn far less than their counterparts in this country, yet most Japanese corporations have comfortably outperformed their rivals in the UK.

A second problem with the idea that the market measures people's contributions to society is that many people who make clear and significant contributions receive surprisingly little money for their efforts.

Hundreds of thousands of teachers, counsellors and healthcare workers contribute daily to the welfare of others for very little salary.

Using social worth to justify income, then, is hazardous. Some defend the market as the most accurate measure of occupational worth; what, they ask, would be better? But others contend that what is lucrative may or may not be socially valuable. From this standpoint, a market system amounts to a closed game which only a handful of people have the money to play.

### Continue the debate

1 Track down *The Sunday Times Rich List*, published each year, and discuss its contents. Find out the earnings of your favourite sports and media stars.
2 Look around you and consider how much cleaners and even teachers are likely to be earning.
3 Debate the significance of these disparities. Is inequality inevitable? Do you lead a 'privileged life' or an 'excluded life'? In what ways? Whither the growing inequalities?

# CHAPTER 9

# GLOBAL POVERTY/GLOBAL INEQUALITY

(Above) Yellow houses: a street in Sophiatown, South Africa 1940

*Source*: Yellow Houses: a street in Sophian town, *c.* 1940 (board), Sekoto, Gerald (1913–93)/© Johannesburg Art Gallery, South Africa/The Bridgeman Art Library. Courtesy of the Gerald Sekoto Foundation.

*See*: www.art.co.za/gerardsekoto/default.htm; http://the-artists.org/artist/Gerard_Sekoto.html.

**Q** Sekoto was a prominent artist in South Africa. Look at the websites and then consider how his art must have been shaped by his social situation. Do you think it is generally true that art is shaped by social situations? (And if so, might this also be true of sociology?)

AFGHANISTAN IS ONE OF THE POOREST AND MOST CONFLICT-RIDDEN COUNTRIES IN THE WORLD. **It has the highest rate of emigration of anywhere in the world – as people try to get out of it.** Some 70 per cent of its 28 million people live below the international poverty line. Its life expectancy of 45 years is among the lowest in the world. Its literacy rate is 28 per cent. It ranks low in the United Nations ranking of human development – at position 155 (in 2010). And its progress over time has been measured as at the bottom of many world league tables – it comes next to bottom in gender equality, child poverty, freedom and democracy measures, and health. The only league table it tops is that of drugs: 80 per cent of western Europe's heroin comes from Afghanistan!

What kind of country is Afghanistan? Eighty per cent of the country is mountainous, housing many clans, tribes and ethnic groups. Ethnically, the largest group is Pashtun (42 per cent), but there are many others with long histories of disagreements: Tajik (27 per cent), Hazara (9 per cent) Uzbek (9 per cent) and many others. For 300 years the Pashtun ruled Kabul but they lost this in 1992. Violence and civil war followed – but then civil war between tribes and wars with neighbours has long been part of Afghanistan's history. Basically Afghanistan is a pre-industrial tribal society which has been at war with it neighbouring countries for centuries. It is now also at the heart of the world conflict over terrorism.

Yet because of its geographical location, it is strategically important for many countries. Landlocked and lying at the heart of central Asia, it is bordered by Pakistan, Iran, India, China and the former Soviet republics of Turkmenistan, Uzbekistan and Tajikistan. For 2,500 years it has been the crossroads of many countries, conflicts and armies. It still is. For example, between 1842 and 1880, the British twice invaded Afghanistan to force Kabul to subordinate its foreign policy to British interests – both times with heavy losses. Britain gradually withdrew and subsequently, for much of the middle twentieth century, Afghanistan was under the influence

of the Soviet Union. In 1973, it became a republic. After a violent struggle, the communist Democratic Republic of Afghanistan was proclaimed in 1978 – attempting to modernise rapidly. This was followed by a 10-year Soviet occupation, resulting in the killing of between 600,000 and 2 million Afghans, mostly civilians. Many further conflicts followed. In 1992, the Islamic State of Afghanistan was established. Today, it is the prime home of the Taliban – a leading Islamic revolutionary organisation.

These days we hear a great deal about Afghanistan. After the 9/11 New York attack on the Twin Towers in New York, where 2,995 were killed, including the 19 hijackers, British and American troops invaded. By spring 2002, the Afghan Taliban regime had been officially defeated – the terrorists it harboured were supposedly on the run. But since then a long, drawn-out conflict has continued with thousands being killed on all sides. The last thing a poor country like this needed was such conflict, increasing its poverty day by day. It now has more people fleeing it than any other country in the world.

On 1 December 2009, US President Barack Obama announced that he would escalate US military involvement by deploying an additional 30,000 soldiers over a period of six months. He also proposed to begin troop withdrawals 18 months from that date. Several elections have also been held in Afghanistan since 2001, most recently in September 2010. There were around 2,500 candidates for the Afghan Parliament but there was severe disruption from the Taliban, who attacked all involved in the elections, including voters, killing 11 civilians and 3 Afghan National Policemen.

This is one of the poorest countries in the world: it is also one of the most conflict-ridden ones. We will return to this issue in Chapter 16. But we begin this chapter with Afghanistan as a key illustration of world inequalities and poverty.

*See*: Ceri Oeppen and Angela Schlenkhoff (eds), *Beyond the 'Wild Tribes': Understanding Modern Afghanistan and Its Diaspora* (2010).

**COUNTRY FACT FILE**

AFGHANISTAN

| | |
|---|---|
| Population | 29m (2009) |
| Per capita GDP | −0.4 (2009) |
| Life expectancy | 44.19 male 44.61 female |
| Adult literacy | 43.1% |
| Key languages | Afghan Persian or Dari (official) 50%, Pashto (official) 35% |
| Key religions | Sunni Muslim 80%, Shia Muslim 19% |
| Key city | Kabul |
| Human development index | 0.349 (155th, 2010) |

*Source*: World Bank and Human Development Report (2010).

*Poverty is an awful, eventually degrading thing and it is rare that anything good comes from it. We rise in spite of adversity, not because of it . . .*

The letters of Thomas Wolfe

*Eradicating poverty is an ethical, social and economic imperative of mankind.*

Copenhagen Declaration, World Summit for Social Development, 1995

## In this chapter, we ask:

- **What is the nature of the unequal world we live in now? What is the scale of poverty and inequality across the world?**

- **How can we understand and measure such poverty and inequality?**

- **Who are the key groups involved in this inequality?**

# Global stratification

Social stratification is found in all countries across the world. Everywhere, there are pronounced economic inequalities. There are major gender divisions. There is social exclusion based on ethnicity and race, which often results in displaced persons and refugees. There is an age stratification system at work by which both the young and the old can experience inequality. And there are processes excluding all manner of people with difference and disability. These are the key components of global stratification and we touch on them all throughout the book. In this chapter, however, the main focus will be on the poverty and economic inequalities found across the world. Why does nearly half the world still live in deep poverty? Why, in the face of great wealth in some countries and the extraordinary lives of a few million 'truly rich', do such huge discrepancies persist in the twenty-first century? Table 9.1 documents in stark form the global discrepancies.

# The inequalities of the world we live in

## 1 Life cycle and population

### Infant mortality

- 1 pregnant woman in 5,000 each year dies in the UK, but 1 in 10 pregnant women will not survive in the poorest countries.

### Childhood

- 240,000 children under the age of 5 die each day due to poverty.
- 'Child labour' involves some 250 million working children (61 per cent in Asia, 32 per cent in Africa and 7 per cent in Latin America).
- Child marriage is pervasive: in some countries over half of all girls are married by the time they reach age 18 (the figure is 74 per cent in the Democratic Republic of the Congo, 70 per cent in Niger, and around 50 per cent in Bangladesh and Afghanistan).
- There are some 100 million children who work on the streets.
- There are some 10 million refugees and 5 million internally displaced people.

### Old age

- In 2010, one out of every ten persons was 60 years or above; by 2050, one out of five will be 60 years or older. There were roughly 759 million people aged 60 or above, projected to rise to 2 billion by 2050.
- Throughout the world, older people often face discrimination in hiring, promotion and access to job-related training.
- In OECD countries, an average of 13.3 per cent of persons aged over 65 are poor, compared to 10.6 per cent of the general population, according to data for the mid-2000s (OECD, 2009).
- Older women are more likely to be poor than are older men.

## 2 Income, wealth and poverty

- 1.4 billion people (one in four) in the developing world were living on less than US$1.25 a day in 2005 (down from 1.9 billion (one in two) in 1981, but still huge).
- Over 3 billion (almost half the world) live below the World Bank's $2.50/day poverty line.
- Some 80 per cent of the population lives on less than $10 a day.
- The gross domestic product of the 41 heavily indebted poor countries (567 million people) is less than the wealth of the world's seven richest people combined.

## 3 City and environment

- In 2010 there were around 800,000 living in slum conditions.

## 4 Health, nutrition, AIDS, sanitation and disability

### Disease

- Some 35,000 children die each day from preventable or easily treatable diseases.

### AIDS

- An estimated 40 million people are living with HIV/AIDS (with 3 million deaths in 2004).

### Sanitation

- Some 2.4 billion people lack basic sanitation.

### Nutrition

- Over 20 per cent of the world's population (about 1.3 billion people) lack the nutrition they need to work regularly, living in absolute poverty.
- Most people in low-income countries not only do more physical labour, but also consume less than 2,000 calories daily.

## 5 Education and literacy

- 72 million children of primary school age in the developing world were not in school in 2005.
- Nearly a billion people entered the twenty-first century unable to read a book or sign their name.

## 6 Gender, family and sexuality

### Gender

- Across the world, at least one in every three women has been beaten, coerced into sex or abused – usually by someone she knows.
- As many as 5,000 women and girls are killed annually in so-called 'honour' killings (many of them for the 'dishonour' of being raped).
- An estimated 4 million women and girls are bought and sold worldwide each year, into marriage, prostitution or slavery.
- Worldwide, some 130 million girls and young women have undergone female genital mutilation (FGM).
- Each year, women undergo an estimated 50 million abortions, 20 million of which are unsafe, and some 78,000 women die and millions suffer in the process.

### Sexuality

- Around 70 countries have laws which criminalise homosexual acts, and a number of these – Iran, Afghanistan, Saudi Arabia and Chechnya among them – have the death penalty for gay sex.
- Torture is common to extract confessions of 'deviance', gays are raped to 'cure them of it', and they are sometimes killed by death squads.

## 7 Ethnicity, migration, hybridity, war and displaced people

- At the end of 2008 there were some 42 million displaced people worldwide. These included 15.2 million refuges, 827 asylum seekers and 26 million internally displaced persons (IDPs).
- Children make up about half of war refugees, while millions die and are often the main targets in war (being seen as the next generation of 'enemies'). Many are used as mine sweepers or spies and for kamikaze attacks. And many others are recruited or coerced into being soldiers: some 300,000 minors are recruited as active combatants by rebel groups and armies in some 41 countries – especially in Asia and Africa.
- Some 27 million people across the world live in modern slavery.

## 8 Crime, drugs, abuse, trafficking and violence

- Organisations combating child poverty in the world estimate that poverty forces some 100 million city children in poor countries to beg, steal, sell sex or serve as couriers for drug gangs in order to provide income for their families.

# Keeping up to date with the world's inequalities through the internet

Statistics like the above soon become outdated. Here is a small selection of key words to add to your 'favourites' list, which will help you keep up to date. The links can be found on the book's website. Always be aware, though, that *all statistics bring problems*, and need thinking about critically.

- For general data on all of the world's societies: search *The World Bank*; *The CIA Factbook*; *United Nations*; *NationMaster*; *New Internationalist*.
- Size of populations and their growth: search *United Nations World Population Reports (UNFPA)*.
- Size of cities and rural areas: search *The State of the World's Cities*; *Urban agglomerations*; *United Nations urban agglomerations*.
- Basic economic development of the world's countries: search *United Nations*; *OECD*.
- World poverty statistics: search *World Bank poverty net*; *Global issues*.
- The Human Development Index for each country in the world: search *UN Human Development Index*.
- World poverty: search *Poverty*; *One world*; *Human development*; *Global issues*.
- Environmental damage and degradation: search *World Watch*; *People Planet*; *UN climate change*; *World Environment Organization*; *DEFRA UK*.
- Human rights and abuse across the world: search *Amnesty International*; *Human Rights Watch*.
- Genocides across the world: search *Genocide Watch*.
- Migrations, refugees and displaced people across the world: search *United Nations High Commissioner for Refugees (UNHCR)*.
- Political freedom and democracy across the world: search *Freedom House*.
- Diverse religions, their sizes and beliefs across the world: search *Adherents*.
- Different languages across the world: search *Ethnologue*.
- Different values across the world: search *World Values Survey*.
- Maps of the world: search *World atlas*; *Google maps*; *Worldmapper*.

| Table 9.1 | Human Development Index (HDI): 2010 rankings |

| Very high human development | High human development | Medium human development | Low human development |
|---|---|---|---|
| 1 Norway | 43 Bahamas | 86 Fiji | 128 Kenya |
| 2 Australia | 44 Lithuania | 87 Turkmenistan | 129 Bangladesh |
| 3 New Zealand | 45 Chile | 88 Dominican Republic | 130 Ghana |
| 4 United States | 46 Argentina | 89 China | 131 Cameroon |
| 5 Ireland | 47 Kuwait | 90 El Salvador | 132 Myanmar |
| 6 Liechtenstein | 48 Latvia | 91 Sri Lanka | 133 Yemen |
| 7 Netherlands | 49 Montenegro | 92 Thailand | 134 Benin |
| 8 Canada | 50 Romania | 93 Gabon | 135 Madagascar |
| 9 Sweden | 51 Croatia | 94 Suriname | 136 Mauritania |
| 10 Germany | 52 Uruguay | 95 Bolivia (Plurinational | 137 Papua New Guinea |
| 11 Japan | 53 Libyan Arab Jamahiriya | State of) | 138 Nepal |
| 12 Korea (Republic of) | 54 Panama | 96 Paraguay | 139 Togo |
| 13 Switzerland | 55 Saudi Arabia | 97 Philippines | 140 Comoros |
| 14 France | 56 Mexico | 98 Botswana | 141 Lesotho |
| 15 Israel | 57 Malaysia | 99 Moldova (Republic of) | 142 Nigeria |
| 16 Finland | 58 Bulgaria | 100 Mongolia | 143 Uganda |
| 17 Iceland | 59 Trinidad and Tobago | 101 Egypt | 144 Senegal |
| 18 Belgium | 60 Serbia | 102 Uzbekistan | 145 Haiti |
| 19 Denmark | 61 Belarus | 103 Micronesia (Federated | 146 Angola |
| 20 Spain | 62 Costa Rica | States of) | 147 Djibouti |
| 21 Hong Kong, China (SAR) | 63 Peru | 104 Guyana | 148 Tanzania (United Republic of) |
| 22 Greece | 64 Albania | 105 Namibia | 149 Côte d'Ivoire |
| 23 Italy | 65 Russian Federation | 106 Honduras | 150 Zambia |
| 24 Luxembourg | 66 Kazakhstan | 107 Maldives | 151 Gambia |
| 25 Austria | 67 Azerbaijan | 108 Indonesia | 152 Rwanda |
| 26 United Kingdom | 68 Bosnia and Herzegovina | 109 Kyrgyzstan | 153 Malawi |
| 27 Singapore | 69 Ukraine | 110 South Africa | 154 Sudan |
| 28 Czech Republic | 70 Iran (Islamic Republic of) | 111 Syrian Arab Republic | 155 Afghanistan |
| 29 Slovenia | 71 The former Yugoslav | 112 Tajikistan | 156 Guinea |
| 30 Andorra | Republic of Macedonia | 113 Viet Nam | 157 Ethiopia |
| 31 Slovakia | 72 Mauritius | 114 Morocco | 158 Sierra Leone |
| 32 United Arab Emirates | 73 Brazil | 115 Nicaragua | 159 Central African Republic |
| 33 Malta | 74 Georgia | 116 Guatemala | 160 Mali |
| 34 Estonia | 75 Venezuela (Bolivarian | 117 Equatorial Guinea | 161 Burkina Faso |
| 35 Cyprus | Republic of) | 118 Cape Verde | 162 Liberia |
| 36 Hungary | 76 Armenia | 119 India | 163 Chad |
| 37 Brunei Darussalam | 77 Ecuador | 120 Timor-Leste | 164 Guinea-Bissau |
| 38 Qatar | 78 Belize | 121 Swaziland | 165 Mozambique |
| 39 Bahrain | 79 Colombia | 122 Lao People's | 166 Burundi |
| 40 Portugal | 80 Jamaica | Democratic Republic | 167 Niger |
| 41 Poland | 81 Tunisia | 123 Solomon Islands | 168 Congo (Democratic Republic |
| 42 Barbados | 82 Jordan | 124 Cambodia | of the) |
| | 83 Turkey | 125 Pakistan | 169 Zimbabwe |
| | 84 Algeria | 126 Congo | |
| | 85 Tonga | 127 São Tomé and Príncipe | |

*Source*: The HDI rankings featured above were published in the *Human Development Report 2010*. You can access the full report at: http://hdr.undp.org/en/reports/global/hdr2010.

*See also*: pp. 133–4 and 287–8.

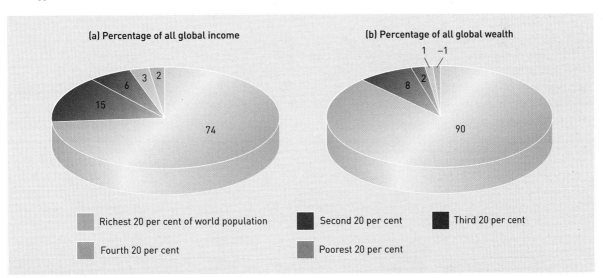

As this table shows, and the chapter will amplify, the human toll of global poverty is enormous. Consider three contrasts. At the end of the Second World War, the United States obliterated the Japanese city of Hiroshima with an atomic bomb. The worldwide loss of life from starvation reaches the Hiroshima death toll *every three days*. Given the magnitude of this problem, easing world hunger is one of the most serious responsibilities facing the world today. Secondly, the annual loss of life stemming from poverty is ten times greater than that resulting from all the world's current armed conflicts. In what follows, we look at this problem of world poverty in more detail. Thirdly, one author, Thomas Pogge, claims that world poverty produces substantially more harm than the fascists ever did (more each year, and this over much longer periods), and that the cost of ending poverty is tiny in comparison to the cost of ending fascist rule. He claims:

**The problem is so large that it causes one third of all human deaths and blights well over half of all human lives with hunger, disease, oppression, exclusion, and abuse. Yet global inequality has increased to such an extent that such poverty is now avoidable at a cost that would barely be felt in the affluent countries.**

(Pogge, 2010: 72)

The most basic starting point for thinking about global inequality is the issue of world poverty. Depending on how poverty is defined, somewhere between 1.3 billion and 3 billion people live in poverty – nearly half of the world's population. Furthermore, although many countries are indeed becoming wealthier, in general inequalities between countries seem to have been growing. Figure 9.1(a) divides the total global *income* by fifths of the population: the richest 20 per cent of the global population receive some 74 per cent of all income. At the other end of the social scale, the poorest 20 per cent of the world's people, by contrast, struggle to survive on just 1 per cent of global income. Because global income is so concentrated, the average member of a rich society (such as most people in Europe) lives extremely well by world standards. In fact, the living standard of most people below the poverty threshold far surpasses that of the majority of the earth's people. In terms of *wealth*, as Figure 9.1(b) shows, global inequality is even greater. A rough estimate suggests that the richest 20 per cent of the world own more than 90 per cent of the planet's wealth. About half of all wealth is owned by just 2 per cent of the world's population; about 40 per cent, by the richest 1 per cent.

**Figure 9.1** Distribution of global income and wealth
Global income is very unequal, with the richest 20 per cent of the world's people earning almost 40 times as much as the poorest 20 per cent. Global wealth is even more unequally divided, with the richest 20 per cent owning 90 per cent of private wealth and the poorest half of the world's people having barely anything at all.

*Source*: Macionis, John J., *Sociology*, 13th, © 2010. Printed and electronically reproduced by permission of Pearson Education, Inc., Upper Saddle River, New Jersey. Based on UNDP (2008) and Davies et al. (2006, 2008).

# How can inequalities be measured?

Measuring inequalities across cultures is no easy task and in this section we look at a range of ways in which poverty and inequality have been studied. As we saw in Chapter 4, there have been a number of ways to classify societies – and many have been based on wealth and income. Throughout much of the twentieth century the major divide was seen to be the First, Second and Third Worlds. This has now been superseded by two major measures. The first is based on economic factors and depends largely on measuring the gross national product (GNP) and the gross domestic product (GDP); the latter depends on a complex series of scales which aim to measure the quality of life, known as the Human Development Index.

## Poverty as money: economic measures of poverty

### GNP and GDP

The standard way of measuring a country's economic productivity is through GNP and GDP. GDP or **gross domestic product** refers to *all the goods and services on record as produced by a country's economy in a given year*. Income earned outside the country by individuals or corporations is excluded from this measure; this is the key difference between GDP and **gross national product** (GNP), which *includes foreign earnings*.

For countries that invest heavily abroad, GDP is considerably less than GNP; for countries in which other nations invest heavily, GDP is much higher than GNP. For countries that both invest heavily abroad and have considerable foreign investment at home, the two measures are roughly comparable.

## Purchasing power parity

It is possible to measure per capita GDP in terms of what the United Nations Development Programme (UNDP, 2001) calls 'purchasing power parities' (PPP), the value of people's income in terms of what it can buy in a local economy. For a long while, the measure of poverty was fixed at $1 a day. Currently, it is fixed at $1.5 a day. However, living on $1.5 a day does not mean being able to afford what $1.5 would buy when converted into a local currency, but the equivalent of what $1.5 would buy in the United States: for example, a newspaper, a local bus ride or a small bag of rice. Per capita PPP figures for rich countries such as Norway, Australia and Canada are very high – in the range of $40,000. For middle-income countries, including Iran, China and Ukraine, it is much lower – in the $4,000–8,000 range. And in the world's low-income countries, per capita annual income is no more than just a few hundred dollars (the average is $1,400 – but in Niger, the poorest country in the world, it is $680). In the African nations of Zaïre or Ethiopia, a typical person labours all year in order to earn what the average worker in the United States reaps in just several days. These are huge discrepancies (*World Development Report*, 2010). Figure 9.2 shows different levels of income by economic development.

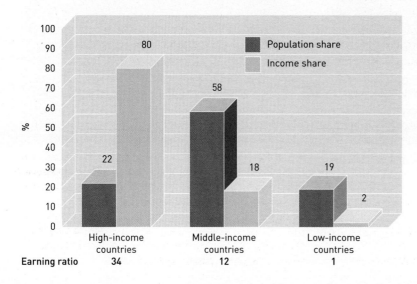

**Figure 9.2**  Relative share of income and population by level of economic development

*Note*: For every dollar earned by people in low-income countries, people in high-income countries earn $34.

*Source*: Macionis, John J., *Sociology, 13th*, © 2010. Printed and electronically reproduced by permission of Pearson Education, Inc., Upper Saddle River, New Jersey. Based on United Nations Development Programme (2008).

## High to low incomes

Ranking countries on the basis of their economies has led to a more general distinction between high income, medium income and low income societies. **High-income countries** are defined as *the nations with highest overall standards of living* (there are roughly 65 of them); **middle-income countries** are not as rich: they are *nations with a standard living which is about average for the world as a whole* (about 75); and the remaining countries are **low income**: nations with a *low standard of living in which most people are poor* (about 40). We looked at this in Chapter 4 (see p. 131).

# Poverty and the measurement of life quality: the Human Development Index

Measurements that focus only on income and wealth can ignore many other factors that play a crucial role in life. Low income is a key feature of poverty: but inequalities can also range on such things as housing, literacy and health. What we are talking about here is the very controversial subject of quality of life, and how that can be measured. For the Nobel Prize-winning economist Amartya Sen, we need to take into account human capabilities for living fulfilled and even flourishing lives. As he says: 'poverty must be seen as the deprivation of basic capabilities rather than merely as lowness of incomes' (Sen, 1999: 20). This 'capabilities' approach underpins the human development model which we introduced briefly in Chapter 4, and it suggests that if the people of a country are healthier and better educated, and have access to public services without discrimination, that country is making progress in reducing poverty. Poverty is linked to a sense of entitlement to a well-functioning life (Sen, 1999: 162). More and more, then, researchers try to go beyond the economic. The Human Development Index (HDI) brings together measures of income, education and life expectancy as a composite measure. We introduced this in Chapter 4 and it would be useful to revise it here (see pp. 133–4).

# Relative versus absolute poverty

The members of rich societies typically focus on the *relative poverty* of some of their members, highlighting how those people lack resources that are taken for granted by others. Relative poverty, by definition, cuts across every society, rich or poor.

But especially important in a global context is the concept of **absolute poverty**, a lack of resources that is life threatening (often measured as a per capita income equivalent to less than one international dollar a day). Human beings in absolute poverty commonly lack the nutrition necessary for health and long-term survival. To be sure, some absolute poverty exists in Europe. Inadequate nutrition that leaves children or elderly people vulnerable to illness and even outright starvation is a reality in the UK. But such immediately life-threatening poverty strikes only a small proportion of the population. In low-income countries, by contrast, one-third or more of the people are in desperate need.

Relative or absolute poverty? By and large, rich nations such as the United Kingdom wrestle with the problem of *relative poverty*, meaning that poor people get by with less than we think they should have. In poor countries such as Somalia, absolute poverty means that people lack what they need to survive. Here people gather in Baidoa, Somalia, to bury in a common grave family members who died from starvation
*Source*: © Chris Steele-Perkins/Magnum Photos.

Since absolute poverty places people at risk of death, we can see the extent of this problem by examining the median age at death around the world. In other words, by what age have half of all people born in a society died? Map 9.1 shows that death in high-income countries, on average, occurs among the elderly beyond the age of 75. Death occurs somewhat earlier in middle-income nations, reflecting a lower standard of living. But in many low-income countries of Africa and western Asia, the greater extent of absolute poverty is brought home by the fact that half of all deaths occur among children under the age of ten.

PUBLIC SOCIOLOGY

# Problems with poverty and inequality measurement: what does a statistical table mean?

Throughout this book you will regularly come across aggregate statistics and league tables, such as the Human Development Index produced by the United Nations Development Programme. In this chapter, you have the figures for the HDI given in Table 9.1 as well as a vast number of statistics collated for the box on pp. 282–3, which draws from many sources. Look at them. Similar statistics are used all the time by social scientists. You have already been warned to look at statistics cautiously and carefully (see Chapter 3, pp. 94–5).

In using sociology in public debate, it is important to have some skill in handling statistics. Here are four tips:

1  *Know what the statistic claims to measure* – it is rarely simple. Think whether it really measures what it says. Thus, the Human Development Index is complex. Invented in 1990, it is these days seen as a very important measurement and is widely used. But it is a composite measure of (a) *longevity* – life expectancy at birth; (b) *knowledge* – adult literacy rate and enrolment in schooling; and (c) *decent standards of living* – adjusted income per head. Each one of these rates brings its own problems of measurement (discussed in the appendix of the Human Development Reports).

2  *Consider the population sample to which the statistic applies.* Is it a statistically representative sample, or a very special selected one? If it is national statistics, is it part of a national census – or not?

3  *Then consider the times when the data were gathered.* Often when international statistics are composed, the data come from different years. And they are invariably 'out of date' by the time they reach publication. Since social changes can be very rapid, statistics can get out of date very quickly. Meanwhile populations grow, economies go into crisis, governments fail.

4  *Can the statistics of different countries really be compared?* Different countries very often have differing degrees of sophistication in measurement. Statistics cannot be so easily produced in many low-income societies, which may be in famine or suffer a natural disaster or civil conflict. Just how can statistics be fully reliable when produced under these circumstances?

5  *Watch out for spurious accuracy.* Many statistics sound very precise – they often give numbers that are very large and precise: for example, that the population of a country is 4,789,872. This is rubbish and the pseudo precision is nonsense. It might have been the population for a few seconds once, but numbers are never accurate and things change. By the time they reach this textbook, statistics are all wildly out of date as well. So look for general trends rather than specifics. Equally common are glib generalisations – using statistics which are really based on inadequate samples and bad measurements.

In any event, *statistics must always be used with care*. Challenge just what statistics mean and how they were produced. Most of the statistics used in this book have been produced by so-called 'reliable sources'; even so, they need careful and critical scrutiny. (See: *UNDHP Human Development Report*, annual.)

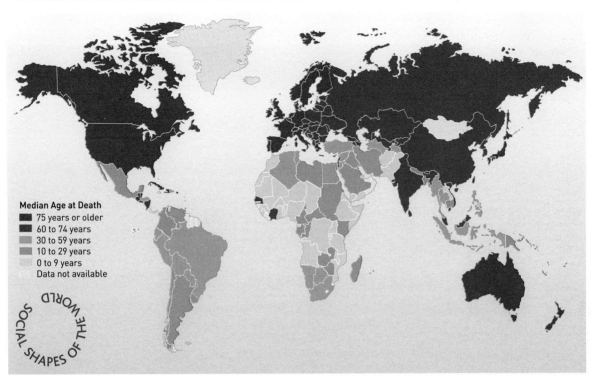

**Median Age at Death**
- ■ 75 years or older
- ■ 60 to 74 years
- ▨ 30 to 59 years
- ▨ 10 to 29 years
- ▨ 0 to 9 years
- ▨ Data not available

SOCIAL SHAPES OF THE WORLD

**Map 9.1**  Median age at death in global perspective
This map identifies the age below which half of all deaths occur in any year. In high-income countries, it is the elderly who face death – that is, people aged 75 or older. In middle-income countries, including most of Latin America, most people die years or even decades earlier. In low-income countries, especially in Africa and parts of Asia, it is children who die, with half of all lives ending before individuals reach 10 years of age.

*Source*: Based on World Bank (1993).

# The globalisation of the 'super rich' and the localisation of the 'bottom billion'

## The super rich

There are around 1,000 billionaires in the world. In 2010, the business magazine *Forbes* could list 937 of them – about 500 of them worth over $2 billion each (see Table 9.2). This may amount to an estimated combined wealth of $3.6 *trillion*. Surprisingly, after the financial crisis of 2009, the numbers of billionaires shot up! The average worth of the world's billionaires is now $3.5 billion. These figures are hard to imagine but, simply put, a billionaire is someone with wealth of at least a thousand million US dollars. It is wealth that most minds on the planet cannot even begin to comprehend. Many billionaires are wealthier than whole countries. Often they live lives that are cut off from the rest of the world – with private homes on private islands reached by private planes and mega yachts. The most striking inequality of the world lies in the fact that the *richest 1 per cent of adults in the world own 40 per cent of the planet's wealth*.

Billionaires can be found all over the world. The United States used to account for nearly half the names on the billionaire list, but now its share is just 40 per cent – or 403 billionaires. China (including Hong Kong) has the most billionaires outside the USA with 89. Russia has 62 (*Forbes*, 'The world's billionaires', 3 October 2010).

| Table 9.2 | The richest people in the world: the top 20 billionaires, 2010 | | | | |
|---|---|---|---|---|---|
| **Rank** | **Name** | **Citizenship** | **Age** | **Net worth ($bn)** | **Residence** |
| 1 | Carlos Slim Helu and family | Mexico | 70 | 53.5 | Mexico |
| 2 | William Gates III | USA | 54 | 53.0 | USA |
| 3 | Warren Buffett | USA | 79 | 47.0 | USA |
| 4 | Mukesh Ambani | India | 52 | 29.0 | India |
| 5 | Lakshmi Mittal | India | 59 | 28.7 | UK |
| 6 | Lawrence Ellison | USA | 65 | 28.0 | USA |
| 7 | Bernard Arnault | France | 61 | 27.5 | France |
| 8 | Eike Batista | Brazil | 53 | 27.0 | Brazil |
| 9 | Amancio Ortega | Spain | 74 | 25.0 | Spain |
| 10 | Karl Albrecht | Germany | 90 | 23.5 | Germany |
| 11 | Ingvar Kamprad and family | Sweden | 83 | 23.0 | Switzerland |
| 12 | Christy Walton and family | USA | 55 | 22.5 | USA |
| 13 | Stefan Persson | Sweden | 62 | 22.4 | Sweden |
| 14 | Li Ka-shing | Hong Kong | 81 | 21.0 | Hong Kong |
| 15 | Jim Walton | USA | 62 | 20.7 | USA |
| 16 | Alice Walton | USA | 60 | 20.6 | USA |
| 17 | Liliane Bettencourt | France | 87 | 20.0 | France |
| 18 | S. Robson Walton | USA | 66 | 19.8 | USA |
| 19 | Prince Alwaleed Bin Talal Alsaud | Saudi Arabia | 55 | 19.4 | Saudi Arabia |
| 20 | David Thomson and family | Canada | 52 | 19.0 | Canada |

*Source*: Forbes, www.forbes.com/lists/2010/10/billionaire. This provides the full list of the world's 937 billionaires in March 2010.

WORLD WATCH

# The troubles in Africa

Africa is a vast continent housing many different societies and cultures. After Asia, it is the second largest and most populous continent in the world, and in 2005 it had more than 900 million people living in 46 countries (53 including all the island groups). It has a very long history, and is widely considered to be the country of human origins: the land of the earliest discovered human skeletal remains.

But throughout the world, it is often seen as 'the other' – a dark, mysterious continent, a 'black hole' and a land of great poverty and tragedy. This is, of course, a dangerous stereotype in itself, for Africa is a continent with many different countries, each with its own history and concerns. But most of these countries were colonised in the eighteenth and nineteenth centuries and were dominated by European civilisations (see Map 9.2). Many were at the heart of the 'slave trade'. Today, most

African countries harbour deep poverty, widespread starvation and famine, economic stagnation and an AIDS crisis. It is also the most aid-dependent region in human history (Lockwood, 2005).

On the Human Development Index (HDI) scale, most of Africa's countries are at the lowest end (see Table 9.1). It has the ten poorest countries in the world. And indeed the $-a-day headcount measure of poverty has been rising in recent years: almost 75 million more people in Africa were living in poverty at the end of the 1990s than a decade earlier (Lockwood, 2005: 6). There are, nevertheless, huge disparities within countries: Ghana and Tanzania are generally doing much better than others. Four issues can be highlighted:

- For many African countries, *poverty* is extreme, as this chapter shows in more detail.
- Many African countries are *torn with internal conflicts and wars*. This makes them highly unstable and also prone to corruption. On average, all low-income countries face a 14 per cent chance of falling into civil war in any five-year period; the economist Paul Collier notes: 'Young men, who are the recruits for rebel armies, come pretty cheap in an environment of hopeless poverty. Joining a rebel movement gives these young men a small chance of riches.'

- Most African economies are *economically marginalised*. While it is not cut off from global trade (indeed, it is large and important), Africa has not shared in the global boom in higher-value trades. Its markets are in primary commodities, not 'richer ones'. It is always at the low end of world economic systems. On top of this, much of Africa is highly aid dependent. Economist Matthew Lockwood comments that Africa has a long history of low growth and failed development, and has come

**Starving African child**
*Source*: © Picture Contact BV/Alamy.

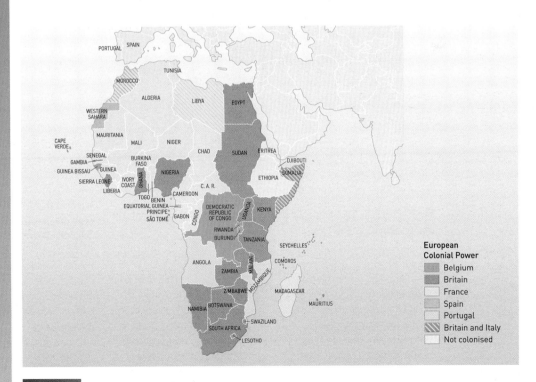

| Map 9.2 | Africa's colonial history |

WORLD WATCH

| Table 9.3 | How many children have been orphaned by AIDS? |
|---|---|

| Number of orphans due to AIDS, alive in 2007 | | AIDS orphans as a percentage of all orphans, 2005 | |
|---|---|---|---|
| South Africa | 1,400,000 | Zimbabwe | 77% |
| Uganda | 1,200,000 | Botswana | 76% |
| Nigeria | 1,200,000 | Swaziland | 66% |
| Zimbabwe | 1,000,000 | Lesotho | 64% |
| Tanzania | 970,000 | Malawi | 57% |
| Ethiopia | 650,000 | Zambia | 57% |
| Zambia | 600,000 | South Africa | 49% |
| Malawi | 560,000 | Kenya | 46% |
| Côte d'Ivoire | 420,000 | Uganda | 45% |

*Source*: www.avert.org/aids-orphans.htm.

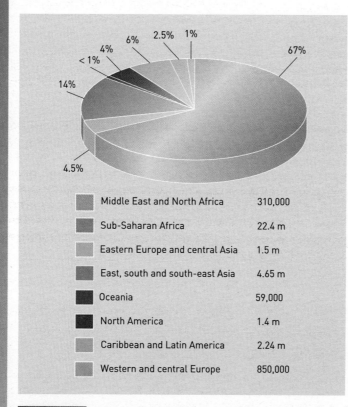

| Colour | Region | Value |
|---|---|---|
| | Middle East and North Africa | 310,000 |
| | Sub-Saharan Africa | 22.4 m |
| | Eastern Europe and central Asia | 1.5 m |
| | East, south and south-east Asia | 4.65 m |
| | Oceania | 59,000 |
| | North America | 1.4 m |
| | Caribbean and Latin America | 2.24 m |
| | Western and central Europe | 850,000 |

| Figure 9.3 | Distribution of people living with HIV around the world, 2008 |
|---|---|

*Source*: www.avert.org/worldstatinfo.htm.

### TOP 10
### Poorest countries

| | GDP per capita (US$) |
|---|---|
| Burundi | 90 |
| Ethiopia | 110 |
| Congo | 120 |
| Liberia | 140 |
| Malawi | 150 |
| Myanmar | 160 (est.) |
| Guinea-Bissau | 190 |
| Sierra Leone | 210 |
| Eritrea | 220 |
| Rwanda | 220 |

*Source*: Adapted from *Pocket World in Figures*, Profile Books: 18.

to develop 'an extraordinary dependence on aid for physical and human investment'.

- Most African countries – especially those in the sub-Saharan region – have very high rates of *HIV/AIDS* (discussed also in Chapter 21). AIDS is a massive burden.

It is firmly established across the continent and it has an impact on nearly every aspect of society. As we shall see in Chapter 21, life expectancy has plummeted. In some countries, 60 per cent of 15-year-olds cannot expect to live to 60.

As the *Top 10* list and Figure 9.3 illustrate, the poorest countries in the world and the highest rates of HIV/AIDS in the world are both found in Africa. There is also a widespread problem of AIDS orphans. Table 9.3 shows the numbers of African AIDS orphans, by country. In some countries, children who have been orphaned by AIDS comprise half or more of all orphans nationally.

*See*: Matthew Lockwood: *The State They're In: An Agenda for International Action on Poverty in Africa* (2005); Susan Hunter *Who Cares? AIDS in Africa* (2003).

# The bottom billion

The United Nations can claim that global poverty has been falling in a lot of countries. In China and India there is growth, and substantial poverty reduction seems to be under way (United Nations, 2007). But alongside this welcome trend, the UN notes that there is uneven and unequal development – some are getting richer, but others are getting poorer. In general, the economic crisis which started in 2008 has made the situation much worse. There are about 50 or 60 'failing' or 'trapped' countries – around 1 billion people, one-sixth of the world (Collier, 2007). These are generally small nations and include Afghanistan, Haiti, Malawi and countries in central Asia. But 70 per cent of these 'failing states' are in Africa. Sub-Saharan Africa alone has some 450 million people living in poverty.

## Key dimensions of global poverty

In this section, we briefly outline some of the key factors that correlate highly with poverty. Many poorer countries have a tendency towards:

1  *Less technology.* Almost two-thirds of people in low-income countries farm the land; the productive power of industrial technology is all but absent in these poorest nations. Energy from human muscles or beasts of burden falls far short of the force unleashed by steam, oil, gas or nuclear fuels – the power sources that propel complex machinery. Moreover, the focus of poor societies on farming, rather than on specialised production, inhibits development of human skills and abilities.

2  *High population growth.* As Chapter 24 explains in detail, countries with the least-developed economies have the world's highest birth rates. Despite the death toll from poverty, the populations of poor countries in Africa, for example, double every 25 years. There, more than half the people have yet to enter their child-bearing years, so the wave of population growth will roll into the future. Even an expanding economy cannot support vast population surges. During 1993, for example, the population of Kenya swelled by 4 per cent; as a result, even with some economic development, living standards actually fell.

3  *Traditional cultural patterns.* Poor societies are typically very traditional. Kinship groups pass folkways and mores from generation to generation. Adhering to long-established ways of life, people resist innovations – even those that promise a richer material life. The members of poor societies often accept their fate, although it may be bleak, in order to maintain family vitality and cultural heritage. Such attitudes bolster social bonds, but at the cost of discouraging development.

4  *Great inequalities.* While most societies distribute their wealth very unequally, in low-income societies the consequences are severe. In the farming regions of Bangladesh, for example, 10 per cent of the landowners own more than half the land area, while almost half of farming families hold title to little or no land of their own (Hartmann and Boyce, 1982). As another example, the richest 10 per cent of Central Americans control about three-quarters of that region's land.

5  *High gender inequality.* As we have already explained, poor societies subordinate women even more than industrial societies do. Moreover, women with few opportunities typically have many children and the needs of a growing population, in turn, restrain economic development. As a result, many analysts conclude that raising living standards in much of the world depends on improving the social standing of women.

6  *Colonised global power relationships.* A final cause of global poverty lies in the relationships among the nations of the world. Historically, wealth flowed from poor societies to rich nations by means of **colonialism**, *the process by which some nations enrich themselves through political and economic control of other countries.* Historical patterns of trade, some analysts claim, spurred certain nations to prosper economically while others simultaneously were made poor. The societies of western Europe colonised much of Latin America for more than 300 years and also controlled parts of Asia, notably India, for centuries. Africa, too, endured up to a century of colonisation.

During the twentieth century, about 130 former colonies gained their independence, leaving only a small number of countries as colonies today. As we shall see, however, a continuing pattern of domination has emerged. **Neocolonialism** (*neos* is a Greek word for 'new') amounts to *a new form of global power relationship that involves not direct* *political control but economic exploitation by multinational corporations.* **Multinational corporations**, *in turn, are large corporations that operate in many different countries.* As Chapter 15 explains, the power of today's multinational corporations to dominate a poor nation often rivals that of colonial countries in centuries past.

## Poverty traps: the structural bases of poverty

The economist Stephen C. Smith sees poverty as 'a cruel trap: A billion human beings today are bound in poverty traps, in almost unrelenting misery' (Smith, 2005: ix). A poverty trap arises from the structure of the society – it cannot be escaped without sustained and deep effort to change that society. Sociologists often call this 'structural poverty'. It is not that people are lazy or foolish. Rather, the society is structured in a way that makes it very hard for them to get out of their poverty. Smith suggests that there are many such traps. Among them are:

1   *Family child labour traps*: children often have to work to support their families (more than 100 million in 2003).

2   *Illiteracy traps*: there is little access to the resources that could educate, and hence improve working chances.

3   *'Working capital' traps*: the poor have no credit and no money. This means that no plans can be made for the future. Every 'crisis' is in the current moment and has to be dealt with in the here and now.

4   *'Unsuitable risk' traps*: the poor pay more. The poor cannot afford to pay for any kind of insurance – and their work is often chaotic, dependent on the vagaries of weather, etc. Any purchases in markets can be expensive because the poor have no power to 'shop around'.

5   *'Debt bondage' traps*: when credit is given, it often comes from unscrupulous money-lenders who make the situation worse, which means they can never get out of debt.

6   *'Information' traps*: long hours of work mean little time or energy to look for other work.

7   *Under-nutrition and health traps*: which can easily lead to being laid off work, and can also create the need for women and children to act as carers, who cannot then work or study.

8   *Low skill traps*: the problems are compounded. With little education, poor health, etc. there is little opportunity for training and hence better jobs.

9   *High fertility traps*: more children are a likelihood; but children often die early. So women can spend much time in pregnancy.

10  *Farm erosion traps*: whatever land they work on, or own, is subject to climate problems.

Many of these problems are common to all the poor across the world, not just among those in low-income societies. Stephen Smith's list of these traps is relentless. To the above he adds more: for instance, criminality traps, mental health traps and powerlessness traps.

## Puzzles for dealing with world poverty

### 1 Trade

Economies are expanding through globalisation and this generates expansion.

*But*: protectionism is needed so that economies can develop with their own strengths.

### 2 Debts and aid

Countries need more funds from rich countries. The HIPC (Heavily Indebted Poor Countries) programme considers ways in which debts can be written off.

*But*: aid often feeds corruption and does not reach true needs.

### 3 Governance and corruption

Political systems need to become more and more open and democratic.

*But*: the countries have such deep ethnic hatreds that this is hard to achieve.

# Dealing with world poverty: the UN Millennium Development Goals

The world is galvanised into action about world poverty, although there never really seems to be enough. Action occurs through government aid programmes, through the work of non-governmental organisations (NGOs), and through direct action groups. Among the key international organisations are the International Monetary Fund (IMF) and the World Bank. Through the Bretton Woods Agreement, 184 organisations seek to maintain stability in the financial world. The World Bank has major programmes to fight poverty and improve the living standards of people in low-income societies. Together they run the HIPC (Heavily Indebted Poor Countries) programme. The United Nations runs many programmes around poverty – including UNICEF, WHO and the UN Development Programme (see Chapter 16). But at the heart of its current programme is the UN Millennium Development Goals: adopted by 189 nations at a summit in 2000, it had eight targeted goals including halving extreme poverty, universal education for children, ending child and maternal mortality and stopping the spread of HIV/AIDS (see Table 9.4, p. 296).

 For up-to-date commentaries on the Millennium Development Goals, see: www.guardian.co.uk/global-development/millennium-development-goals.

 There are also many campaigns for specific 'issues around poverty', such as:

- the Campaign for Child Survival: www.childsurvivalcampaign.org
- the Global Alliance for Vaccines and Immunisation: www.gavialliance.org
- the Campaign against Malaria, and Malaria No More: www.malarianomore.org
- AIDS Orphans: www.avert.org/aidsorphans.com.

# Problems with the UN Millennium Development Goals

The core goal among the Millennium Development Goals (MDG) – to which 191 member states of the UN committed themselves in 2000 – was: 'to halve, by the year 2015, the proportion of the world's people whose income is less than one dollar a day and the proportion of people who suffer from hunger'. Regarding eight issues, clear targets have then been set for success (see Table 9.4). A large amount of money and energy has been put into the MDG project and it has become the flag-bearer of the wish for a better and more equal world in the twenty-first century.

Yet many critics suggest that the MDG project has become aexpensive window dressing and is not dealing adequately with the deep problems of global inequality. For the critic Thomas Pogge, behind the 'pro-poor rhetoric', we find *Politics as Usual* (2010). He claims that a close scrutiny shows that goals have been diluted. Four outstanding problems can be raised here.

- First, it is claimed that the targets of the MDG have been set far too low. The global international poverty level (IPL), for example, was initially set at US$1 a day (raised in 2005 to $1.25). Most of the key statistics have been based on this and it was calculated initially on the basis of the same purchasing power as $1 had in the USA. But that $1 buys very little indeed. More than that: it defines poverty as primarily a matter of income. There are many other factors – such as sanitation, housing and literacy – that move way beyond income. Living with good sanitation, housing and literacy but with below $1 of income is living in a very different kind of poverty from living with $1 but none of these things. (In fairness, however, the MDG is concerned with these things too.)

- Second, there are real problems about measuring poverty. The project thinks we can 'count the poor'. However, many of the countries we are looking at cover large masses and huge populations, many of whom are illiterate and living in desperate conditions with little food and sanitation. How can good measurement and recording practices go on under these circumstances?

| Table 9.4 | The Millennium Development Goals: A sample of targets and progress, 2010 |

| | Goal | Sample targets | 2010 Progress report |
|---|---|---|---|
| | 1 Eradicate extreme *poverty and hunger* | Halve, between 1990 and 2015, the proportion of people whose income is less than $1 a day | The global economic crisis has slowed progress, but the world is still on track to meet the poverty reduction target (see Figure 9.4 as an example) |
| | | Halve, between 1990 and 2015, the proportion of people who suffer from hunger | Financial crisis has reduced progress in ending hunger in most regions |
| | 2 Achieve universal *primary education* | Ensure that, by 2015, children everywhere, boys and girls alike, will be able to complete a full course of primary schooling | Hope is dimming for universal education by 2015, even as many poor countries are making tremendous strides |
| | 3 Promote *gender equality* and *empower women* | Eliminate gender disparity in primary and secondary education, preferably by 2005, and in all levels of education no later than 2015 | For girls in some regions, education remains elusive |
| | 4 Reduce *child mortality* | Reduce by two-thirds, between 1990 and 2015, the under-five mortality rate | Child deaths are falling, but not quickly enough to reach the target |
| | 5 Improve *maternal health* | Reduce by three-quarters, between 1990 and 2015, the maternal mortality ratio | Data show signs of progress, with some countries achieving significant declines in maternal mortality ratios. However, the rate of reduction is still well short of the 5.5 per cent annual decline needed to meet the target |
| | 6 Combat *HIV/AIDS, malaria and other diseases* | Halt by 2015 and begin to reverse the spread of HIV/AIDS | The spread of HIV appears to have stabilised in most regions, and more people are surviving longer |
| | 7 Ensure *environmental sustainability* | Integrate the principles of sustainable development into country policies and programmes and reverse the loss of environmental resources | The rate of deforestation shows signs of decreasing, but is still alarmingly high |
| | | Halve, by 2015, the proportion of the population without sustainable access to safe drinking water and basic sanitation (see the box on p. 298) | The world is on track to meet the drinking water target, though much remains to be done in some regions |
| | 8 Develop a global partnership for development | Address the special needs of the least developed countries, landlocked countries and small island developing states | Aid continues to rise despite the financial crisis, but Africa is short-changed; only five donor countries have reached the UN target for official aid |

*Note*: 8 goals, 21 targets and 60 official indicators are being monitored.

*Source*: Compiled by the authors from UN, *The Millennium Goals Report 2010*. For the full report, see: www.unfpa.org/webdav/site/global/shared/documents/publications/2010/mdg_report_2010.pdf.

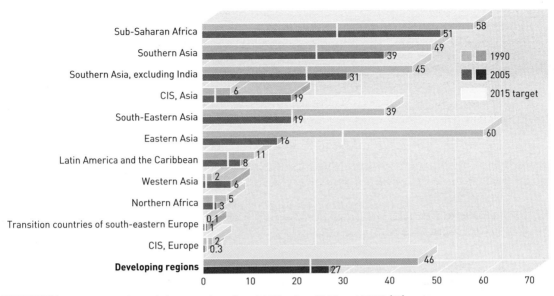

| Region | | |
|---|---|---|
| Sub-Saharan Africa | 51 | 58 |
| Southern Asia | 39 | 49 |
| Southern Asia, excluding India | 31 | 45 |
| CIS, Asia | 6 / 19 | |
| South-Eastern Asia | 19 | 39 |
| Eastern Asia | 16 | 60 |
| Latin America and the Caribbean | 8 | 11 |
| Western Asia | 2 / 6 | |
| Northern Africa | 3 | 5 |
| Transition countries of south-eastern Europe | 0.1 / 1 | |
| CIS, Europe | 2 / 0.3 | |
| Developing regions | 27 | 46 |

1990    2005    2015 target

**Figure 9.4** Proportion of people living on less than $1.25 a day, 1990 and 2005 (%)
*Source: UN Millennium Development Report 2010, p. 6.*

Official agencies spend fortunes on their statistical work in poorer countries, but much of it lies in the sophisticated handling of data in faraway government offices. The nitty-gitty data themselves simply may not be very good.

• Closely allied to this is the time problem. As world expectations change, and indeed as conditions in countries change with various economic crises, can measurement measures easily hold across time? Most significantly, populations over the 15 years of the project will all increase significantly, and as the goal is for a proportion rather than an absolute number of people to escape poverty, it seems likely that even if the proportion goal is met, the actual numbers in poverty may increase significantly due simply to rising populations.

• Fourthly, there is an ideological element to all of this. Time and time again in reading the reports, we can be led to a sense of celebration that progress is being made on most objectives (at least until the financial crisis of 2008–9). It is in the interest of funders and career developers to tell good stories of progress with the project. But critics are sceptical.

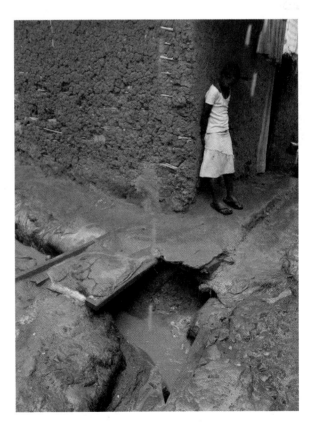

Some 40 per cent of people have no access to sanitation. This lack of hygienic facilities experienced by 2.6 billion people is a fundamental cause of disease which leads to 2 million deaths – mainly children – each year (see over)
*Source: © HJB/Alamy.*

WORLD WATCH

# How the other half shits

Across the world of nearly 7 billion people, some 40 per cent of people have no access to sanitation. This lack of hygienic facilities experienced by 2.6 billion people is a fundamental cause of disease which leads to 2 million deaths – mainly of children – each year. Every year, around 60 million children in the developing world are born into households without access to sanitation; and children living in such households are twice as likely to get diarrhoea as those with a toilet. It is the seventh Millennium Development Goal to halve, by 2015, the proportion of the population without sustainable access to safe drinking water and basic sanitation.

| Table 9.5 | The worst places in the world for sanitation provision | |
|---|---|---|

**As a percentage of population lacking access**

| Country | Ranking | Percentage lacking sanitation |
|---|---|---|
| Afghanistan | 1 | 92 |
| Chad | 2= | 91 |
| Eritrea | 2= | 91 |
| Burkina Faso | 4= | 87 |
| Ethiopia | 4= | 87 |
| Niger | 4= | 87 |
| Cambodia | 7 | 83 |
| Ghana | 8= | 82 |
| Guinea | 8= | 82 |
| Namibia | 10= | 75 |

**As a total number of people lacking access to sanitation (above 10 million)**

| Country | Ranking | Total population lacking sanitation |
|---|---|---|
| China | 1 | 732,480,000 |
| India | 2 | 728,357,000 |
| Indonesia | 3 | 99,045,000 |
| Bangladesh | 4 | 84,912,000 |
| Nigeria | 5 | 72,072,000 |
| Ethiopia | 6 | 65,772,000 |
| Pakistan | 7 | 63,468,000 |
| Brazil | 8 | 45,975,000 |
| Democratic Republic of Congo | 9 | 39,130,000 |
| Vietnam | 10 | 32,409,000 |

*Source*: Water Aid, *The State of the World's Toilets*; www.wateraid.org/uk.

*See also*: *New Internationalist*, 'We need to think about toilets', August 2008.

Organisations combating child poverty in the world estimate that poverty forces some 100 million city children in poor countries to beg, steal, sell sex or serve as couriers for drug gangs in order to provide income for their families. Such a life almost always means dropping out of school and places children at high risk of illness and violence. Many street girls, with little or no access to medical assistance, become pregnant – a case of children who cannot support themselves having still more children.

Some 100 million of the world's children have deserted their families altogether, sleeping and living on the streets as best they can. Roughly half of all street children are found in Latin America. Brazil, where much of the population has flocked to cities in a desperate search for a better life, has millions of street children – many not yet teenagers – living in makeshift huts, under bridges or in alleyways. The public response to street children is often anger directed at the children themselves. In Rio de Janeiro, police try to keep the numbers of street children in check. When this unrealistic policy fails, however, death squads may sweep through a neighbourhood, engaging in a bloody ritual of 'urban cleansing'. In Rio, several hundred street children are murdered each year. Often, too, children can become orphaned at an early age. Some may also be sold into slavery. We look at this further in Chapter 13.

Boy scavenging on rubbish dump, Manila
*Source*: Pearson Education Ltd/Digital Vision.

## Who are the global poor?

Figure 9.4 (p. 297) suggests the areas where inequalities can be found to have made most impact. In this section, we highlight four key groups who become most vulnerable to poverty. Although there are others, our main focus will be on children, women, refugees and the elderly.

## 1 Children and poverty

Poverty hits children hardest, and the extent and severity of child poverty are greatest in low-income countries. As we have already explained, death often comes early in poor societies, where families lack adequate food, safe water, secure housing and access to medical care. In many cases, too, children in poor countries leave their families because their chances to survive are better on the streets.

## 2 Refugees and the displaced

There are a large number of people who have no 'home' in the world – who have been displaced. In 2009, the United Nations estimated that there were:

- 43.3 million forcibly displaced people worldwide
- 15.2 million who were refugees
- 983,000 asylum seekers
- 27.1 million internally displaced persons (IDPs).

**Displaced peoples** are *those who often find themselves homeless in their own land*. This may be due to civil war, or to some environmental catastrophe through which they lose whatever home and possessions they may have had. An estimated 50 million people live off land that is rapidly deteriorating. After a time they will be unable to live or work off it, requiring them to move on. In 2009, there were estimated to be some 27 million people in this situation worldwide. **Refugees** are people who '*flee their own country for political or economic reasons, or to avoid war and oppression*' (*New Internationalist*, 1998: 221).

Muddy brown floodwaters by shanty town huts, Dhaka, Bangladesh, South Asia
*Source*: Pearson Education Ltd/Digital Vision.

They are a central feature of the global world, and they usually experience a well-founded fear of persecution (Marfleet, 2006). In leaving their 'home', often with no choice, they leave behind most of their worldly possessions.

Asylum seekers flee their own country and seek sanctuary in another state. The number of claims has been increasing in recent years, but in 2009 there were nearly a million seeking asylum whose claims had not yet been adjudicated. Many came from Afghanistan, Colombia, Ethiopia, Myanmar and Zimbabwe seeking international protection.

Table 9.6 shows where the refugees are most likely to come from and go to. Most stay within their region of origin and by far the largest movements are in Asia and Sub-Saharan Africa. Afghanistan has – for over 30 years – been the country with the greatest numbers leaving: one in four of all refugees and nearly 3 million in 2009. Neighbouring Pakistan is the country which received most refugees. Many are children (around 40 per cent in 2009). About a third live in camps and half flee to new urban areas.

There are also large movements from Iraq, Somalia, the Sudan and the Democratic Republic of Congo (DRC). Renewed armed conflict and human rights violations in DRC and Somalia led to new refugee outflows and the movement of 277,000 people primarily to the Republic of the Congo (94,000) and Kenya (72,500).

Refugees are always politically controversial. On the one hand, they symbolise humanitarian need; and on the other, they raise in potent ways issues of racism and the symbolic boundaries of a nation-state (see Chapter 11). Refugees test the willingness of governments and their people to provide asylum. They can also lead to human trafficking, where people are sold their illegal passage into a new country. Some have estimated this to be the largest industry in the world (see Chapter 16).

The United Nations High Commission for Refugees (UNHCR) was established in 1950–1 to provide a major world structure for responding to the needs of refugees and to provide standards of protection under international law. Initially it

| Table 9.6 | The world flow of refugees, 2010 | | |
|---|---|---|---|
| **WHERE THE REFUGEES GO TO . . .** | | **WHERE THE REFUGEES COME FROM . . .** | |
| Country/territory of asylum | Total refugees and people in refugee-like situations | Country of refugee/asylum seeker | Total refugees and people in refugee-like situations |
| Pakistan | 1,740,711 | Afghanistan | 2,887,123 |
| Iran (Islamic Rep. of) | 1,070,488 | Iraq | 1,785,212 |
| Syrian Arab Rep. | 1,054,466 | Somalia | 678,309 |
| Germany | 593,799 | Dem. Rep. of the Congo | 455,852 |
| Jordan | 450,756 | Sudan | 368,195 |
| Kenya | 358,928 | Viet Nam | 339,289 |
| Chad | 338,495 | Myanmar | 406,669 |
| China | 300,989 | Eritrea | 209,168 |
| United States of America | 275,461 | Serbia | 195,626 |
| United Kingdom | 269,363 | China | 180,558 |

*Source*: This is a simplified table of figures based on data in UNHCR, Global Trends, 2010.

focused on the displacement of Europeans caused by the Holocaust, the Second World War and the onset of the Cold War. It employed 33 staff and had a budget of $300,000. Over the years it has come to deal with the displacement of large groups of the world's population. It now has a budget of over $1 billion, employs 5,000 staff, has offices in 120 countries around the world and produces a major annual report (see, for example, *2009 Global Trends Refugees, Asylum-seekers, Returnees, Internally Displaced and Stateless Persons* (online).

## 3  The ageing

We will see in Chapter 13 how the twenty-first century is confronting a major increase in elderly people. It is often believed that this 'age explosion' is predominantly to be found in Western societies. But in fact the figures are substantial for low-income societies. They are often ignored and rendered invisible in debates about international policy and aid: and if noticed, they can be seen as unproductive, uncreative, sick, dependent and passive. But ageing is occurring at a far greater pace in low-income societies and it raises severe problems. We consider this in Chapter 13 (see Harper, 2006: Ch. 8).

## 4  Women and poverty

Women in Sikandernagar, one of India's countless rural villages, begin work at 4.00 in the morning, lighting the fires, milking the buffalo, sweeping floors and walking to the well for water. They care for other family members as they rise. By 8.00, when many people in Europe are just beginning their day, these women move on to their 'second shift', working under the hot sun in the fields until 5.00 in the afternoon. Returning home, the women gather wood for their fires, all the time searching for whatever plants they can find to enrich the evening meal. The buffalo, too, are ready for a meal and the women tend to them. It is well past dark before their 18-hour day is over.

In rich societies, the work women do is typically unrecognised, undervalued and underpaid; women receive less income for their efforts than men do. In low-income countries, this pattern is even more pronounced. Women do most of the work in poor societies, and families depend on women's work to provide income. At the same time, just as tradition keeps many women from school, it also accords them primary responsibility for child-rearing and maintaining the household. In poor societies, the United Nations estimates, men own 90 per cent of the

# What the poor say

According to the World Bank, 'the poor are the true poverty experts'. In a major study, *Voices of the Poor* (2000), Deepa Narayan heard the voices of approximately 60,000 poor men and women from over 60 countries around the world. With striking similarity, poor people describe repeatedly and in distressing detail the impact of poverty. The large majority of poor people included in *Voices* said they are worse off now, have fewer economic opportunities, and live with greater insecurity than in the past. Here are a few of the things they said (look at the website for full details):

*Poverty is pain; it feels like a disease. It attacks a person not only materially but also morally. It eats away one's dignity and drives one into total despair.* A poor woman, Moldova

*Children are hungry, so they start to cry. They ask for food from their mother and their mother doesn't have it. Then the father is irritated, because the children are crying, and he takes it out on his wife. So hitting and disagreement break up the marriage.* Poor people in Bosnia

A group of young men in Jamaica ranked lack of self-confidence as the second biggest impact of poverty: *Poverty means we don't believe in self, we hardly travel out of the community . . . so frustrated, just locked up in the house all day.*

*My children were hungry and I told them the rice is cooking, until they fell asleep from hunger.* An older man, Egypt

*Poor people cannot improve their status because they live day by day, and if they get sick then they are in trouble because they have to borrow money and pay interest.* Tra Vinh, Vietnam

*Security is knowing what tomorrow will bring and how we will get food tomorrow.* Bulgaria

*There is no control over anything, at any hour a gun could go off, especially at night.* A poor woman in Brazil

*The rich is the one who says: 'I am going to do it' and does it. The poor, in contrast, do not fulfil their wishes or develop their capacities.* A poor woman in Brazil

*Poverty is like living in jail, living under bondage, waiting to be free.* A young woman in Jamaica

*It is neither leprosy nor poverty which kills the leper, but loneliness.* Ghana

*When you are poor, nobody wants to speak with you. Everyone's sorry for you and no one wants to drink with you. You have no self-esteem and that's why some people start drinking.* A middle-aged man in Bulgaria

*Now there are hungry children, and before it was not so evident. There are children that knock on your door and ask for bread, children without shoes. This one would never see before.* La Matanza, Argentina

*If we knew that there would be an end to this crisis, we would endure it somehow. Be it for one year, or even for ten years. But now all we can do is sit and wait for the end to come.* A woman from Entropole, Bulgaria

In slums in Malawi, the physical conditions were so bad and hopeless that the poor said *the only way we can get out of poverty is through death.*

*The sewage runs in your front door, and when it rains, the water floods into the house and you need to lift the things . . . the waste brings some bugs, here we have rats, cockroaches, spiders, and even snakes and scorpions.* A resident of Nova California, a slum in Brazil

In the Kyrgyz Republic, poor people said that they were forced to take many risks to survive, including stealing (with the risk of getting caught) or borrowing money (with the risk of becoming indebted). *The rich do not have to take this risk, they have money to protect themselves, and they also have power.*

*You grow up in an environment full of diseases, violence and drugs . . . you don't have the right to education, work or leisure, and you are forced to 'eat in the hands of the government' . . . so you are easy prey for the rulers. You have to accept whatever they give you.* A young woman, Padre Jordano, Brazil

Poor people describe four pervasive and systemic problems that affect their lives adversely almost everywhere: *corruption, violence, powerlessness* and *insecure livelihood.*

*Source:* www.worldbank.org/poverty/ data/trends/poorsay.htm.

Woman on rubbish dump, Manila
*Source*: Pearson Education Ltd/Digital Vision.

land, representing a far greater gender disparity in wealth than is found in industrial nations. Clearly, multilayered systems of tradition and law subordinate women in poor societies. Caught in a spiral of circumstance that promises little hope for change, women are disproportionately the poorest of the poor. More than 500 million of the world's 800 million people living in absolute poverty and at risk for their lives are women.

Women in poor countries have limited access to birth control (which raises the birth rate), and they typically give birth without the assistance of any trained health personnel. There is a stark contrast between high- and low-income countries in this regard. Overall, gender inequality is strongest in low-income societies, especially in Asia where cultural traditions overwhelmingly favour males. This pattern of denigrating women affects virtually every dimension of life and has produced a stunning lack of females in some regions of the world (Kishor, 1993) (see Chapter 13). We look a little more at this below.

## Global gender issues

In global perspective, gender inequalities are usually found at their most extreme where people are poorest. Although there is great variation across countries, many women face subordination and discrimination in many areas of life. On most measures of development, low-income women fare worse than men (Seager, 2009). Briefly:

- *Education*: two-thirds of illiterates in the world are women; 60 per cent of children deprived of education are girls. Girls have much less opportunity to move beyond a primary education.

- *Wealth*: the majority of the world's women do not equally own or inherit property or land. In African countries, widespread discrimination exists against women inheriting or owing land and wealth – and this is supported by religion, law and custom.

- *Travel*: often the state restricts travel for women, who frequently need the permission of a male relative. At the same time, low-income women are the prime target for sex trafficking.

- *Reproduction*: women in low-income societies face serious problems through pregnancy. Pregnancy kills and harms as the box summarises.

## Transformations into modernity

In recent decades, the situation of low-income women has been changing. To start with, most of the world's governments are now committed – on paper at last – to full equality for women: 185 countries are signatories to the UN Convention on the elimination of all forms of discrimination against women (as of January 2008). In many areas of social life, change has been taking place: families are changing (they are getting smaller, with more families headed by women), mothers are having

## Spotlight

### Birth and its control in low-income societies

- *Pregnancy kills*. Maternal health disparities between rich and poor countries and between the rich and poor within countries is very great. The risk of a woman dying in sub-Saharan Africa as a result of pregnancy or childbirth is 1 in 22, as compared to 1 in 7,300 in developed regions. Every year, 536,000 women die from pregnancy-related causes.

- *Pregnancy harms*. Over 300 million women worldwide suffer from complications of pregnancy and delivery. At least 2 million women live with obstetric fistula in the developing world, and more than 50,000 new cases occur each year. Obstetric fistula is a key example of inequitable access to maternal health care and, until recently, one of the most hidden. Caused by obstructed labour, it generally presents itself in the early post-partum period. Fistula tends to affect the most marginalised members of society: young, poor, illiterate women living in remote areas.

- *Contraceptives save lives*. Fulfilling the unmet need for modern family planning in the developing world would reduce unintended pregnancies from 75 to 22 million. Having fewer children reduces the economic burden on poor families, and when fertility rates fall, more women join the labour force.

*Source*: UNFPA, www.unfpa.org/public/home/factsheets (accessed 2010).

unpaid work in high-income countries revealed that in all the countries covered, men spent a longer period of their working day in market-oriented work, while women spent more time than men in cooking, cleaning and childcare (UNDP, 1995; Razavi and Staab, 2008).

As economic opportunity draws men from rural areas to cities in search of work, women and children must fend for themselves. Some men sell their land and simply abandon their wives, who are left with nothing but their children. More: the waning strength of the family and neighbourhood leaves women who are deserted in this way with little assistance. The same holds true for women who become single through divorce or the death of a spouse. In the past, kin or neighbours readily took in a woman who found herself alone. But today old ties may start to get weakened and consequently the number of poor households headed by women is increasing. Rather than enhancing women's autonomy, a new spirit of individualism has actually eroded the social standing of women.

Economic development – as well as the growing influence of Western movies and mass media – may well undermine women's traditional roles as wives, sisters and mothers in favour of defining women as objects of men's sexual attention. The cultural emphasis on sexuality, familiar to most Westerners, now encourages men in poor countries to abandon ageing spouses for younger, more physically attractive partners. The same stress on sex contributes to the world's rising tide of sex trafficking prostitution, noted in Chapter 12 (see the box on pp. 396–7).

Transformation into a modern world, then, does not affect men and women in the same ways. In the long run, the evidence suggests, it does give the sexes more equal standing. In the short run, however, the economic position of many women actually declines, as women are forced to contend with new problems that were virtually unknown in traditional societies.

## Crisis for women

V. Spike Peterson and Anne Sisson Runyan, in their textbook on *Global Gender Issues* (3rd edition, 2010), outline and discuss three critical issues that women in developing/low-income societies confront. They call these the *crisis of representation*, the *crisis of insecurity* and the *crisis of sustainability*.

fewer children, and increasingly women work outside the home for pay (though typically paid much less than men). The rise of a 'third world women's movement' has also become prominent in campaigning for the rights of women.

Still, even when economic development takes place, it does not follow that women do better. There may be new opportunities to attend school and to work outside the home, to reduce birth rates and to weaken traditional male domination, but along the way new problems occur. Labour is often the only resource at the disposal of poor women to meet their basic needs, and a lack of access to decent work is a major cause of poverty. Data on the gender division of paid and

- The *crisis of representation* suggests that women are devalued in the way they are presented: 'third world women' are constructed in Western eyes as victims and robbed of a sense of agency and activity in their lives. Here is the challenge of thinking about the ways in which poor women are framed and discussed in public media.

- The *crisis of insecurity* is related to the violence and threats that women experience – from conflicts and wars (locally and internationally – where 'war rape' becomes commonplace) to the dangers experienced in unemployment, crime, domestic and sexual violence, and the starkness of brutal poverty. Over and over again, the stories women tell of their lives in poverty are ones of massive insecurity and a sense of risk and danger.

- Finally, the *crisis of sustainability* refers to the ways in which women's households and communities are often under threat. The ability to care for their children and reproduce their communities is under the severe threats of poverty and the violence that often surrounds it. More, today, there is a significant international migration of poor women for caregiving work, as both domestic and public-sector workers, across the world. The high demand for global care workers thereby becomes a threat to their own families, as they leave to look after the families of rich mothers in the West.

## Political responses

We can detect a range of responses to women's crises in low-income society. One, the modernist response, has aimed to incorporate women directly into the process of modernisation – increasing women's productivity, helping to strengthen their households. A second has aimed to develop women's projects – building women-centred projects. In most such projects, men are more or less excluded. A third approach has aimed to bring men and women together to discuss ways of enhancing their lives and creating equalities between them.

 On international projects, the Women's Development Programme and 'gender mainstreaming', see: Womenwatch: www.un.org/womenwatch.

# Spotlight
## The Global Gender Gap Index

Across the globe, women do not fare as well as men. To try to capture this, social scientists speak of the **gender gap index (GGI)**: *a measure of the levels of inequality between men and women in access to resources.* This is measured by a combination of four key indicators:

1 economic participation and opportunity
2 educational attainment
3 health and survival
4 political empowerment.

Recent research has measured this 'gap' for 115 countries (about 90 per cent of the world's population), and the highest and lowest are shown below. Out of the 115 countries covered in the report since 2006, more than two-thirds have posted gains in overall index scores, indicating that the world in general has made progress towards equality between men and women, although there are countries that continue to lose ground.

For more details on the gender gap, look at: World Economic Forum Gender Gap.

| Table 9.7 | The Global Gender Gap Index: 2009 rankings | |
|---|---|---|
| **Top 10 countries** | | |
| 1 | Iceland | 0.8276 |
| 2 | Finland | 0.8252 |
| 3 | Norway | 0.8227 |
| 4 | Sweden | 0.8139 |
| 5 | New Zealand | 0.7880 |
| 6 | South Africa | 0.7709 |
| 7 | Denmark | 0.7628 |
| 8 | Ireland | 0.7597 |
| 9 | Philippines | 0.7579 |
| 10 | Lesotho | 0.7495 |
| **Bottom 10 countries** | | |
| 125 | Qatar | 0.5907 |
| 126 | Eygpt | 0.5862 |
| 127 | Mali | 0.5860 |
| 128 | Iran | 0.5839 |
| 129 | Turkey | 0.5828 |
| 130 | Saudi Arabia | 0.5651 |
| 131 | Benin | 0.5643 |
| 132 | Pakistan | 0.5458 |
| 133 | Chad | 0.5417 |
| 134 | Yemen | 0.4609 |

*Notes:* The UK is ranked 15th, the USA 31st, China 60th, Greece 86th, Japan 101st and India 114th. Note that the differences are often very small and the measurements are far from precise. So tight rankings like this are open to much doubt. Nevertheless, they do provide an overall indication. See World Economic Forum, *The Global Gender Gap Report 2009*, Table 3a, p. 8 (www.weforum.org).

# Global inequality: how is it to be explained?

What accounts for the severe and extensive poverty in low-income countries? There have been many attempts to understand the shape and experiences of world inequalities – often called 'development theory' in the past. All of these also have major implications for social change and social policy. Here we briefly outline six major arguments; Table 9.8 provides a simple summary chronology with some names and key concepts to look out for.

*Modernisation theory* is possibly the most common and commonsensical explanation. It is a basic progress theory which suggests that uneven world development can be linked to the advance of industrial societies overtaking traditional life. It imports many assumptions about progress and evolution, and argues that as we have acquired more scientific knowledge, developed new technologies and made economic advances through capitalism, so some societies have left behind ways of life that have inhibited their growth. Some cultures and their traditions cause societies to lag behind. In this sense, traditional societies can be seen as 'underdeveloped'. As they become more modernised, so their uneven development and inequalities will decline. The most famous and widely known theory of this form was Rostow's 'limits of growth', which suggested that societies moved through four key phases: a traditional stage, a take-off stage, a drive to technological maturity and a stage of high mass consumption.

Extreme contemporary versions of this are contemporary *neoliberal theories of development*. Here the free market of capitalism effectively means that money goes where it will – the motor engine of social change is profit. As we have seen before (Chapter 2; see also Chapter 16), neoliberal capitalism fosters an open, competitive market, in which the profit motive is prime. And as some countries advance, they gain advantages over others. This open competition inevitably means that some go to the wall – and in this case, even the largest of nation-states can fall behind. We see a version of the 'survival of the fittest' with the rich getting richer and the poor getting poorer. Aware of some of the human problems this brings – mass poverty, world hunger, bad sanitation for the vast majority of the world, damaged lives – many of these accounts also suggest the need for international organisations which will provide international programmes of aid and support to 'undeveloped' countries. But in the end, according to these theories it is only economic growth – and the success of capitalism – which will save the poor.

Both these accounts have been strongly criticised and have led to *dependency and underdevelopment theories*. The kernel of these theories is exploitation. So-called 'underdeveloped' countries have become underdeveloped not because of failure – with technology, or in the market – but because of a long history in which they have been colonised, exploited and excluded by other more dominant countries. Africa is a very good example. Here is a continent that was ravaged by both slavery and colonialism during the seventeenth and eighteenth centuries, from which it has taken centuries to recover. The ravages of the colonial past and slavery have left deep scars. Much of the world has been enslaved to the market dominance of successful capitalist countries – England and Europe especially in the nineteenth century, and the United States in different ways in the twentieth century. They have remained underdeveloped precisely because they have been made dependent upon the dominant markets of capitalism. This theory has been most identified with Andre Gunder Frank's *Capitalism and Underdevelopment in Latin America* (1967).

Closely connected to this is the wider approach of **world systems theory**. This draws from a key distinction of core and periphery – an idea which is also found in underdevelopment theories. It suggests that there is only one world connected by a complex network of economic exchange relationships. It also draws heavily from Marxist ideas, suggesting a 'world-economy' (with its origins in sixteenth-century western Europe and the Americas) in which the 'dichotomy of capital and labor' and an endless 'accumulation of capital' by competing agents lead to conflict and change. In this world system, many societies have remained at the 'periphery' with an unequal share in the market structure. There is *unequal international division of labour* at its heart. Thus the relations of periphery societies with core societies place them in positions of great inequality and differences in economic power. Core societies are developed countries, and the periphery are the dependent developing countries. The leading Marxist theorist Immanuel Wallerstein is the author of *The Modern World System* (1974).

These theories dominated thinking during between the 1960s and 1980s and still have a major in influence. But more recent accounts of the contemporary unequal world have turned to

Children stand outside their small home in the impoverished El Pantonal neighbourhood in Tegucigalpa, Honduras, on11 October 2001. United Nation figures show that 74% of the Honduran population live below the poverty line. Today, the World Bank officially approves a $75 million package that aims to reduce poverty by 25% over fifteen years in the Central American nation

*Source*: © Reuters/Corbis.

some version of *globalisation*. As we have seen before (e.g. in Chapter 2), this word means many things, and for some it is actually little more than a new version of neoliberalism and the 'flattening' of the world (Friedman, 2006). The world is now seen as thoroughly interconnected with capitalism, and the new technologies have played a key role here. Old barriers and borders between nations have broker down to facilitate the flow of goods, capital, services, labour and outsourcing. There is global trade, international flows of capital and foreign investments, the mass migration of workers, and the integration of national and regional economies into the international economy through international agencies like the International Bank for Reconstruction and Development (World Bank), the International Monetary Fund (IMF) and the World Trade

Organization (WTO). It brings large trading blocks and huge global economic giants like China and the USA. And with it there is a continuing apparent downside: the great financial crisis of 1998–9, growing inequalities, continuing global poverty, the creation of sweatshops and international labour trafficking, continuing slavery, mass waste and dumping, and environmental crisis. Side by side with the construction of lush hotels and holiday resorts and the billionaire lifestyle nestles the world of slums and abject poverty.

Key elements in each of the above theories can help you try to make sense of the global inequalities around you. Ultimately, the contemporary world – with its 7 billion people and 200 states – is a web of *global complexity*: it is becoming harder and harder to make strong generalisations about it, and it is

| Table 9.8 | A summary of changing theories of development and inequalities | |
|---|---|---|
| **Starting period** | **Perspectives** | **Influential ideas** |
| 1700s | Classical early political economy | Free market capitalism and Adam Smith's guiding hand |
| 1800s | Evolutionism | Social Darwinians<br>Progress and evolution |
| 1850s | Colonial economics | Trusteeship/exploitation |
| 1850s | Marxist analysis | Exploitation, colonialism, imperialism |
| 1950s | Modernisation theory | Stages of growth: Rostow, p. 306 |
| 1970s | Dependency theory (neo-Marxist) | Gunder Frank, p. 306<br>Decolonisation, anti-imperialism, indigenisation<br>Unequal division of labour: Wallerstein |
| 1970s | World systems theory | |
| 1980s | Neoliberalism | Global finance, economic growth, trickle down, deregulation, privatisation<br>Market cultures, consumerism |
| 1980s | Globalisation | Interconnectedness of world<br>Often linked to latest phase of neoliberalism |
| 1980s | Human development | Capabilities, human flourishing<br>Key example: East Asia: Nussbaum and Sen, p. 417 |
| 1990s | ICT4D (Information and Communication Technology for Development) | The tele-centre and the mobile phone<br><br>Digital divide, cyber-apartheid |
| 2000s | Millennium Development Goals | Structural and eclectic reforms: p. 296 |
| 2010s | Normative theories – global complexities | Human rights, capabilities and complexities of global worlds |

*Source*: Modified from an idea by Jan Nederveen Pieterse, 2009a: 7).

necessary to see the deep interconnectedness of a range of multiple social processes, working within a (now) global capitalist process, which are always moving and always changing.

## A normative theory of inequality and global change

What is missing from all of the above theories of development is an explicit moral and evaluative stance on the world we would like to see. What kind of future world do we wish to see in the future? It is at this point, of course, that many sociologists and social researchers hand their work over to the philosophers and the politicians. They do not see it as part of their work to make value judgements. But in some ways this

is slightly dishonest. Do we simply want to understand the massive world inequality so that we can leave it as it is; or do we study it because we want to make the world a better place? And if we want a better place, what might this better place look like?

Some recent theories have also brought a growing concern in development theories for specifying the kind of world we want to live in: they are normative theories. They come in various forms. Some specify that all societies should meet basic human needs (Paul Streeten). Some seek to enable *human capabilities and human rights* to flourish (in the work of Sen and Nussbaum and the development of the Human Development Index). Others have established target goals for developing societies, as in the United Nations project of establishing the *Human Millennium Goals* (HMG).

## Two approaches to poverty reduction

Jonathan Sachs – in his book *The End of Poverty: How We Can Make It End in our Lifetime* (2005) – has called for 'on the ground solutions for ending poverty' (p. 23). He sees the lack of capital, resources and support for the poor as the key issues. The extreme poor lack 'health, nutrition and skills for work along with access to any kind of business, knowledge or public institutional structures which could alleviate their conditions' (p. 245). For Sachs, the solutions to world poverty require key investments – in people and infrastructure – that can give impoverished communities around the world, rural and urban, the tools for **sustainable development**. He suggests listening to the poor, hearing what they want and what they do. He argues that for a small cost (a tiny cost to the world – but too high for the villagers), poverty could be severely reduced. He asks about local ways to handle such issues as: nutrition-depleted soils, malaria, lack of access to safe drinking water and latrines, and the unmet need for basic transport, electricity, cooking fuels and communications. He argues for funding agricultural inputs; investments in basic health; investments in education; power, transport and communications; and safe drinking water and sanitation. These can all be specific local projects which would radically change the lives of the poor.

In contrast, Paul Collier, in his book *The Bottom Billion* (2007), argues that aid is often ineffective, globalisation can make the situation worse, and what is needed is a strong plan (from the G8) of preferential trade policies, new laws against corruption and new international charters. He stresses Africa's history of repeated coups d'état and civil wars. He cites studies which show how cash earmarked by the government for spending on poverty can disappear before it reaches its targets. The abundant natural resources in Africa do not lead to a 'trickle down' – the theory that the spending power of the rich benefits the poor. Rather more frequently, growth leads to corruption and theft. Collier concludes:

> The politics of the bottom billion is not the bland and sedate process of the rich democracies but rather a dangerous contest between moral extremes. The struggle for the future of the bottom billion is not a contest between an evil rich world and a noble poor world. It is within the societies of the bottom billion.

The real solutions to the struggles of the world's poorest people are more complex, and harder to sell to enthusiastic campaigners, than the aid-solves-everything, 'Make Poverty History' approach.

*See:* Sachs, 2005; Collier, 2007.

## Global inequality: looking ahead

Among the most important trends of recent decades is the development of a global economy. While some see this as generating markets of increased wealth and productivity, others see it as simply exacerbating inequality around the world. Profitable investments, many of them in poor nations, and lucrative sales have brought greater affluence to those who already have substantial wealth. And increasing industrial production abroad has cut factory jobs, exerting downward pressure on wages. The net result: gradual economic polarisation.

It is true that in some regions of the world, such as the 'Pacific Rim' of eastern Asia, market forces are raising living standards rapidly and substantially. Many Latin American nations (such as Colombia and Chile) have also recorded strong economic growth in recent years. Meanwhile, however, other poor societies, especially in Africa, are experiencing economic turmoil that frustrates hopes for market-based development.

The poor countries that have surged ahead economically have two factors in common. First, they are relatively small. Combined, the Asian nations of South Korea, Taiwan, Hong Kong, Singapore and Japan cover only about one-fifth of the land area and population of India. The economic problems that smaller countries face are more manageable; consequently, small societies more effectively administer programmes of development. Secondly, these 'best-case' nations have cultural traits in common, especially traditions emphasising individual achievement and economic success.

In other areas of the world, where powerful cultural forces inhibit change and individualism, even smaller nations have failed to turn economic opportunities to their advantage. Social inequality is striking in this global context. The concentration of wealth among high-income countries, coupled with the grinding poverty typical of low-income nations, may well constitute the most important dilemma facing humanity in the twenty-first century. To some analysts, globalisation holds the keys to ending world poverty; to others, it is the cause of this tragic problem.

# SUMMARY

1 The chapter provides many statistics on world poverty and inequality. Depending on how poverty is defined, somewhere between 1.3 billion and 3 billion people live in poverty – nearly half of the world's population. The richest 20 per cent of the global population receives some 74 per cent of all income. At the other end of the social scale, the poorest 20 per cent of the world's people, by contrast, struggle to survive on just 1 per cent of global income.

2 Two major measures of inequality are widely used. The first is based on economic factors and depends largely on measuring the gross national product (GNP) and the gross domestic product (GDP); the latter depends on a complex series of scales which aim to measure the quality of life, known as the Human Development Index.

3 Absolute poverty refers to a lack of resources that is life threatening (often measured as a per capita income equivalent to less than one international dollar, or one and a half dollars, a day). Human beings in absolute poverty commonly lack the nutrition necessary for health and long-term survival.

4 The UN Millennium Development Goals were adopted by 189 nations at a 2000 Summit. The eight goals targeted include halving extreme poverty, universal education for children, ending child and maternal mortality, and stopping the spread of HIV/AIDS.

5 Four groups of world poor are given special attention: children, women, the elderly and refugees.

6 Across the globe, women do not fare as well as men. The gender gap is a measure of the levels of inequality between men and women.

7 The poverty found in much of the world is a complex problem reflecting limited industrial technology, rapid population growth, traditional cultural patterns, internal social stratification, male domination and global power relationships.

8 There are many theories to explain the problem of world poverty and inequalities. Modernisation theory maintains that successful development hinges on acquiring advanced productive technology and sees traditional cultural patterns as the key barrier. Dependency theory claims that global wealth and poverty are directly linked to the historical operation of the capitalist world economy. The dependency of poor countries on rich ones is rooted in colonialism.

9 Both modernisation and dependency approaches offer useful initial insights into the development of global inequality. Recent theories have stressed globalisation, global complexity and the development of human capabilities.

CONNECT UP: Turn to Part 6 of this book for key resources and link up
with the book's website, which links to these resources
SEE: www.pearsoned.co.uk/plummer

## MYTASKLIST

# Ten suggestions for going further

## 1 Connect up with Part Six and the Sociology Web Resources

As you work through ideas and think about the issues raised in this chapter, look at the accompanying website and the resource centre at the end of this book which connects to it. There is a lot here to help you move on. To link up, see: www.pearson.co.uk/plummer.

## 2 Review the chapter

*Briefly summarise (in a paragraph) just what this chapter has been about.* Consider: (a) What have you learned? (b) What do you disagree with? Be critical. And (c) How would you develop all this? How could you get more detail on matters that interest you?

## 3 Pose questions

(a) For all the advances of globalisation and industralisation, it seems that poverty is still with us on a massive scale and inequalities still seem to be growing. Why do you think this is? What could (or should) be done about it? Do you think that more economic aid from high-income societies will help low-income societies?

(b) Do you think advertising (for coffee from Colombia or exotic vacations to Egypt or India) provides an accurate picture of life in low-income countries? Why or why not? Do you think most people in Europe have a realistic understanding of the extent and severity of poverty in the world?

(c) Using website resources, chart the range of refugees and displaced people in the world, looking at the cause of their displacement, where (if anywhere)

they have relocated, the problems they experience as 'asylum seekers', and what their future looks like.

(d) Read the quotes in the *Speaking lives* box on p. 302 and, if you can, watch one of the films listed below. Now engage in a *verstehen* exercise: try to understand the meanings and experiences of what it is like to be severely poor.

## 4 Explore key words

Many concepts have been introduced in this chapter. You can review them from the website or from the listing at the back of this book. You might like to give special attention to just five words and think them through – how would you define them, what are they dealing with, and do they help you see the social world more clearly or not?

Try looking at *The A to Z of World Development* – a very useful illustrated dictionary, compiled by Andy Crump and edited by Wayne Ellwood (New Internationalist, 1998). It is now a little out of date.

## 5 Search the Web

Be critical when you look at websites – see the box on p. 940 in the Resources section. Some useful sources for this chapter are as follows:

World Bank
www.worldbank.org

United Nations
www.undp.org/poverty

These are two major world resources for looking at poverty. They are updated with the latest figures, articles and plans for action, as well major sections in which the poor speak for themselves.

Global Monitoring Report
www.un.org/millenniumgoals
Keeps an up-to-date check on the Millennium Development Goals.

Oxfam
www.oxfam.org.uk
Oxfam is a development, relief and campaigning
organisation that works with others to overcome poverty
and suffering around the world.

United Nations Refugee Agency
www.unhcr.org/basics
A really useful website on all matters linked to refugees and
displacements of peoples.

On Africa and its neglect in cyberspace, see:
AllAfrica Internet Guide
www.goafrica.co.za
AllAfrica aggregates and indexes content from over 125
African news organisations, plus more than 200 other sources,
which are responsible for their own reporting and views.

## 6  Watch a DVD

- Ermanno Olmi's *The Tree of Wooden Clogs* (1978):
  a stunning depiction of poverty in rural Italy in the
  nineteenth century.
- Jibril Diop's Mambety's *Hyenas* (1992): a classic allegory
  of international aid.
- Soraya Mire's *Fire Eyes* (1993): a documentary about
  female genital mutilation.
- Tsitsi Dangarembga's *Everyone's Child* (1996): this film
  is a call for action on behalf of Africa's millions of
  parentless children.
- Soulymane Cissé's *Yeelen* (1987): film about traditional
  African culture.
- Miguel Littin's *The Promised Land* (1973: Chile), Hector
  Babenco's *Pixote* (1981: Brazil) and Victor Gaviria's
  *Rodrigo D: No Future* (1989: Medellin, Columbia):
  all vividly capture poverty.

## 7  Think and read

Vandana Desai and Robert B. Potter, *The Companion to
Development Studies* (2nd edn, 2008). A very useful
collection of short pieces on every aspect of the
developing world.

York W. Bradshaw and Michael Wallace, *Global Inequalities*
(1996). Discusses basic data region by region, as well as
the major explanations of global inequalities. A new
edition is promised for 2009.

Peter and Susan Calvert, *Politics and Society in the Third World*
(3rd edn, 2007). A comprehensive tour.

Deepa Narayan, *Voices of the Poor: Can Anyone Hear Us?*
(2000). A highly readable introduction, brimming with
personal experiences of poverty and inequalities in
low-income countries.

Jeffrey Sachs, *The End of Poverty: How We Can Make it
Happen in our Life time* (2005); Stephen Smith,
*Ending Global Poverty: A Guide to What Works* (2005);
Paul Collier, *The Bottom Billion* (2007); Amartya Sen,
*Development as Freedom* (1999). Four contrasting books
that examine the issues around poverty and what
should be done.

Paul Marfleet, *Refugees in a Global Era* (2006). A useful
text which looks at the global disordered world of
people making long, risky journeys to flee their own
countries.

## More information

Two annual publications provide a wide range of data
on the comparative economic development of the world's
nations:

United Nations Development Programme, *Human
Development Report*. This is published annually.

The World Bank, *World Development Report*. This is
published annually.

The magazine *New Internationalist*, published in Oxford,
provides a wealth of data on inequalities and the global
situation. *The World* CD-Rom and book are also available
from New Internationalist. The 11th edition was published
in 2007. A new website version seems to be forthcoming.

## 8  Relax with a novel

There is a wide-ranging and important literature on the
tensions and conflicts found in 'developing' or low-income
societies. See the following:

Ben Okri, *The Famished Road* (1991)
Alan Paton, *Cry, The Beloved Country* (1948)
Chinua Achebe, *Things Fall Apart* (1958)
V. S. Naipul, *A Bend in the River* (1979)
Isabel Allende, *Of Love and Shadows* (1987)
Vikram Seth, *A Suitable Boy* (1993).
Gabriel Garcia Marquez, *One Hundred Years of Solitude*
(1967).
And at a different level: see Joseph Conrad, *Heart of Darkness*
(1902).

## 9  Connect to other chapters

- Poverty is discussed further in Chapter 10.
- The discussion of refugees should also be linked to
  migration and racism in Chapter 11.
- Consider women's situation more fully in Chapter 12.
- More on children and poverty in Chapter 13.
- Link to AIDS in Chapter 21.

# 10 Engage with THE BIG DEBATE

## Will the world starve?

Hunger casts its menacing shadow not only over regions of Asia, but also over much of Latin America, most of Africa and even parts of North America. Throughout the world, hundreds of millions of adults do not consume enough food to enable them to work. And some 10 million of the world's children die each year because they do not get enough to eat. Meanwhile, in the Western world, many people suffer from obesity and spend their money on slimming aids! (See pp. 242–3.)

At the start of a new century, what are the prospects for eradicating the wretched misery of so many human beings enduring daily hunger?

It is easy to be pessimistic. For one thing, the population of poor countries is currently increasing by 90 million people annually – equivalent to adding another Mexico to the world every year. Poor countries

## Hunger in the developing world 2010: World Food Programme headlines

| | |
|---|---|
| Total in hunger | 1.2 billion people go hungry every day |
| Total undernourished | In Asia and the Pacific, 642 million are suffering from chronic hunger; in Sub-Saharan Africa, 265 million. |
| Developed countries | 15 million hungry in total |

*Source*: United Nations World Food Programme, www.wfp.org/about.

can scarcely feed the people they have now; looking ahead a generation into the future, how will they ever feed double their current populations?

In addition, as detailed in Chapter 25, hunger forces poor people to exploit the earth's resources by using short-term strategies for food production that will lead to long-term disaster. For example, to feed the swelling populations of poor tropical countries, farmers are cutting down rainforests in order to increase their farmland. But, without the protective canopy of trees, it is only a matter of time before much of this land turns to desert.

Taken together, rising populations and ecological approaches that borrow against the future raise the spectre of hunger and outright starvation escalating well beyond current levels. Regarded pessimistically, the world's future is bleak: unprecedented hunger, human misery and political calamity. But there are also some grounds for optimism. Thanks to the Green Revolution, food production the world over is up sharply over the last 50 years, even outpacing the growth in population. Taking a broader view, the world's economic productivity has risen steadily, so that the average person on the planet has more income now to purchase food and other necessities than ever before.

This growth has increased daily calorie intake as well as life expectancy, access to safe water and adult literacy, while infant mortality is going down. In fact, looking at these social indicators, we can see the gap between rich and poor countries actually narrowing. So what are the prospects for eradicating world hunger – especially in

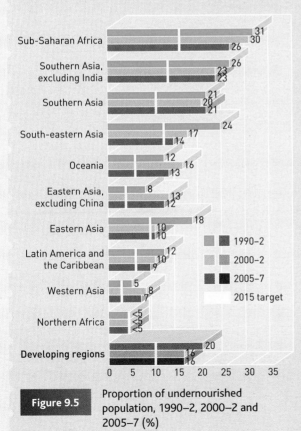

| Figure 9.5 | Proportion of undernourished population, 1990–2, 2000–2 and 2005–7 (%) |

*Source*: United Nations (2010: 12).

low-income nations? Overall, we see less hunger in both rich and poor countries: that is, a smaller share of the world's people faces starvation now than, say, in 1960. But as global population increases, with 90 per cent of children born in middle- and low-income countries, the number of lives at risk is as great today as ever before. Moreover, even though living standards are rising, there has not been any narrowing of the economic gap between rich and poor countries.

Also bear in mind that aggregate data mask different trends in various world regions. The 'best case' region of the world is eastern Asia, where incomes (controlled for inflation) have tripled over the last generation. It is to Asia that the 'optimists' in the global hunger debate typically turn for evidence that poor countries can and do raise living standards and reduce hunger. The 'worst case' region of the world is Sub-Saharan Africa, where living standards have actually fallen over the last decade, and more and more people are pushed to the brink of starvation. It is here that high technology is least evident and birth rates are highest. Pessimists typically look to Africa when they argue that poor countries are losing ground in the struggle to keep their people well nourished.

Television brings home the tragedy of hunger every year or so when news cameras focus on starving people in places such as Ethiopia, Somalia and Afghanistan. But hunger – and the early death from illness that it brings on – is the plight of millions all year round. The problem is not that there is too little food in the world – there is, in principle, enough food for the world to eat (Smith, 2005: 5). Indeed, there are more people in the world suffering from being overweight than those experiencing calorie deprivation. Rather, the issue is: 'How to give the poor enough command over resources to meet their nutrition and other basic needs on a regular basis?' (Smith, 2005: 5).

The world does have the technical means to feed everyone; the question is: do we have the moral determination to do so?

### Continue the debate

1  What are the primary causes of global hunger?
2  Do you place responsibility for solving this problem on poor countries or rich ones? Why?
3  Do you expect the extent of global hunger to increase or decrease? Why?

*See*: United Nations World Food Programme: www.wfp.org.

# CHAPTER 10

# CLASS, POVERTY AND WELFARE: THE CASE OF THE UK

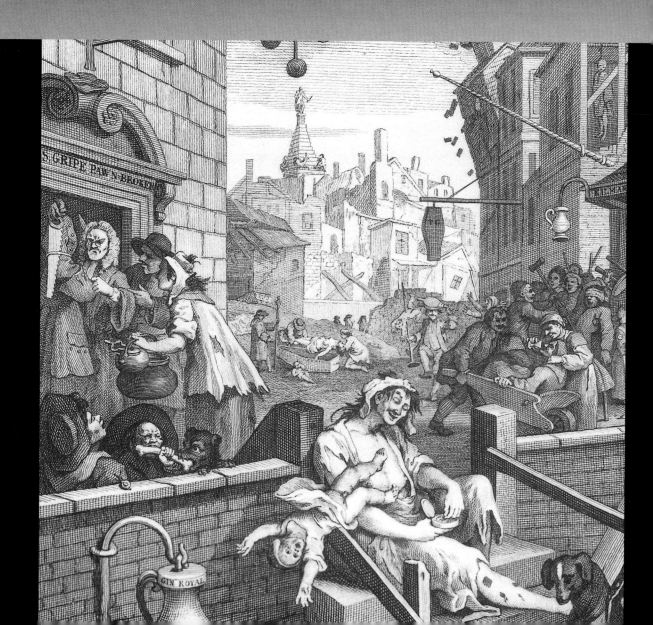

ALL CONTEMPORARY SOCIETIES HAVE CLASS STRUCTURES, though not every society treats class as an issue of premium social importance. In the United States, racial divides are often foremost in people's minds and people tend to see themselves as being much less class bound. Any visitor to the UK, by contrast, will soon hear people talk about class. Indeed, they may soon see it: with elite educational institutions from public schools to Oxford and Cambridge universities, gentlemen's clubs, and the famous houses of the landed aristocracy. At the other extreme, the homeless sleeping in streets and slum housing can mark out 'the lower classes'. As Valerie Walkerdine and her colleagues (2001) suggest:

> Class is not something that is simply produced economically. It is performed, marked, written on minds and bodies. We can 'spot it a mile off' even in the midst of our wish for it no longer to be there.
>
> (cited in Roberts, 2001: 9)

To get a good idea of what class is all about, consider two extremes in the UK. First consider the election of the new UK government (the Conservative–Democratic Alliance) in 2010. Under the co-leaders David Cameron and Nick Clegg, the cabinet of 29 was established as usual to provide the key group of people to run the country. In that cabinet, some 23 of them had wealth well over a million pounds and some 20 of them had been to the same university group – Oxford and Cambridge. They are in a sense a distinctly privileged group – with more wealth than most people in the country, but also have a different social and cultural capital, being from the UK's most prestigious (and elite) universities. What class would you put them in?

Next try to watch some episodes of Paul Abbott's semi-autobiographical Channel 4 drama about a wayward Manchester family, the Gallaghers, in the series *Shameless*. Very funny and very shocking, it displays a dysfunctional, working-class family running wild on a modern housing estate. It relentlessly and unapologetically depicts them as a 'horrifying, irredeemable bunch of work-shy, Asbo-inviting chavs, hooked on handouts, the neighbours from hell'.

Yet *Shameless* seems to have universal appeal. David Threlfall, who plays Frank Gallagher, has suggested that we all experience an excitement in seeing this dysfunctional family go into places that we, in our safe homes, would never dare enter. 'People love the Gallaghers because they know they're not them. They think, "There but for the grace of the Gallaghers go I."'

'It doesn't just attract the lower end of society,' Threlfall says. 'I've had people from right across the social spectrum tell me they get it. Sometimes reporters ask, "Don't you think you're being a bit patronising about working-class people?" To which I say, "Bollocks, you middle-class journalist!" If it was condescending, I'd know because people on the estates where we film would come and tell me.' *Shameless* has already been commissioned for an eighth series (to transmit in 2011). What class would you put these people in? (*Source*: James Rampton, 'Still Shameless', *Independent*, 21 December 2007).

In this chapter, we will examine the nature of classes, wealth and poverty in industrial capitalist societies, with a major focus on the UK. The chapter will ask how we can identify classes, present a brief 'portrait' of class life as it is lived in the UK, and examine

poverty. Finally, we will consider the emergence of 'welfare states' as a means of dealing with some of the problems that inequalities generate.

### *It's the same the whole world over*
### *It's the poor what gets the blame*
### *It's the rich what gets the pleasure*
### *Ain't it all a bloody shame.*

Billy Bennett, Traditional English Music Hall, 1930.

---

## In this chapter, we ask:

- **What is the nature of class and its measurement?**

- **How can we 'measure' poverty in the UK?**

- **What is the nature of 'welfare states' and citizenship as means of dealing with some of the problems that inequalities generate?**

---

(Left) William Hogarth's engraving *Gin Lane* shows the depravity of the poor of London when trying to forget their situation by turning to drink
*Source*: The Art Archive.

**Q** William Hogarth's engravings are major social comments on life in eighteenth-century England, and his work is worth a sociological study of its own. Examine this image carefully and look up a wide range of his work at: http://exhibits.library.northwestern.edu/spec/hogarth/index.html and www.artchive.com/artchive/H/hogarth.html. The entry in Wikipedia is also helpful and locates this image.

# The nature of social class

In this chapter, social class is the key issue. To give it a firmer focus, the prime concern will be with the system of class found in the United Kingdom – long considered one of the most class-ridden societies in the world. It has also been of great interest to sociologists. As we shall see, modern class systems are dynamic, fluid, always changing. An underlying split amongst sociologists here is between those who focus upon class as primarily economic (linked to income, wealth, work and poverty) and those most concerned with status and culture (linked to lifestyles, symbols and identity). Traditionally, the former take a *Marxist view* and the latter a *Weberian view* which looks more at class, status and power and is multidimensional. But as we will see, the divisions are more complicated than this.

## Marx: the economic position

Karl Marx defined class in terms of those who own the means of production and those who do not (with a residual class in between). Any Marxist definition of class must give a priority to the ownership of capital and patterns of work. Thus, the leading North American class theorist Erik Olin Wright (1985, 1992) elaborated on Marx's model by dividing ownership into three categories: those *controlling resource allocation*; those *controlling the means of production*; and those *controlling labour power*. Wright defines all low-level employees as working class, and suggests that the rest in the middle occupy a contradictory position in which they may identify with either the capitalists or the working classes. Others break down Marx's original distinctions further into six (Warner and Lunt, 1941) or even seven (Coleman and Rainwater, 1978) categories. The separation of management and 'capital', and the failure of radical class consciousness to emerge among working people, have made such class definitions difficult to translate into numbers that we can meaningfully measure and compare.

## Weber: the multidimensional position

Other scholars endorse Max Weber's contention that, rather than clear-cut classes, people are ranked in a multidimensional status hierarchy. Those elaborating on Weber often examine socioeconomic status (SES) as a composite measure of social position. This can involve class, status and power, embracing work, wealth and income, status dimensions (lifestyle), consciousness and identity as well as where a person stands politically.

This is clearly a complex equation; and such definitions run into many problems because of the relatively low level of status consistency in societies. Especially around the middle of hierarchies, ranking on one dimension may often contradict one's position on another. A government official, for example, may have the power to administer a multimillion-pound budget, yet earn only a modest personal income. Similarly, members of the clergy typically enjoy ample prestige but only moderate power and low pay.

Perhaps most commonly, class these days is defined through people's *work situation* (their work tasks and the degree of control they have over their working timetables

Five elderly women onlookers are lined against a wall outside the famous Ascot race course on Ladies' Day, an annual event on the English sporting and social calendar in June. Each are standing and watching as two posh couples arrive for the day's racing dressed in showy dresses for the ladies and formal top hat and tails for the men. Each wears their red Ascot badge allowing them entry to this exclusive event attended by the Royal Family and the hoi polloi of English society. Here we see the two sides of the class system but in a humorous scene. See also the photo that opens Chapter 20

*Source*: © Richard Baker/In Pictures/Corbis.

and methods) and *market situation* (people's life chances, which depend upon such things as their income and opportunity for promotion). John Scott (1997), for example, breaks down capitalist classes into three types: entrepreneurs, who own and control their own businesses; internal capitalists (top career managers); and finance capitalists, who own and manage big finance companies and big business (Scott, 1997).

## Key dimensions of class and social inequality in the UK

The most direct way into thinking about class is to examine three key features of the economic system: work, income and wealth. Here we look only at the last two (work is examined in Chapter 15 on the economy).

## Income

A first important dimension of inequality involves **income**, *occupational wages or salaries and earnings from investments*. There are enormous discrepancies here, as Figure 10.1 suggests. Here we see a table of percentiles ranked at ten per cent intervals. The lowest 1 per cent of the population have incomes of £5,668 per year; the top 1 per cent highest are paid well over £1,200,000 a year and 90 per cent earn less than £46,488 a year. The chart shows an enormous inequality of incomes.

### Average and low incomes

In more detail, between April 2008 and April 2009, the average weekly pay for employees in the UK grew by 2 per cent, reaching £489 (£531 for men; £426 for women). There were major discrepancies: health professionals and corporate managers earned median weekly pay of £1,031 and £745 respectively, while employees in sales occupations only reached a median income of £278. Likewise, available data show notable discrepancies between men's and women's full-time weekly earnings, with women earning up to £100 less than men in similar positions. If one had a degree, then average earnings were much higher. There were also regional differences. Median full-time weekly earnings reached £627 in London, but ranged from only £436 to £514 in other parts of the country. At

the time of going to press this income was falling: in April 2010, the average total pay (including bonuses) in the UK had dropped to £455 per week. The lowest income in the UK is formally fixed by the minimum wage which came into being in April 1999. Set initially at £3.60 in 1999 for those aged 22 and over (£3.00 for those aged 18–21), there are currently four levels of minimum wage. From 1 October 2010, these were:

- £5.93 – the main rate for workers aged 21 and over
- £4.92 – the 18–20 rate
- £3.64 – the 16–17 rate for workers above school leaving age but under 18
- £2.50 – the apprentice rate, for apprentices under 19, or 19 or over and in the first year of their apprenticeship.

The age at which you become entitled to the main rate was reduced from 22 to 21 on 1 October 2010. The apprentice rate was introduced on the same date.

Even so, many get less than this outside of the legal system. And you may also like to contrast this income with earnings in low-income societies that we discussed in the previous chapter, where a routine weekly income is rarely above £20). Table 10.1 shows weekly earnings by occupational group. (Note too the differentials for women.)

### The rich

At the other extreme are the rich. Since 1988, the *Sunday Times* has produced an annual Rich List. This shows that the number of millionaires in the UK increased by more than 80 per cent between 2001 (230,000) and 2004 (425,000). In 2004 it reached 425,000, but the global recession of 2008 and 2009 led to the number of millionaires shrinking to 242,000. In 2010 the list suggested a major recovery: in just one year there had been a 30 per cent increase in the collective wealth of the 1,000 multimillionaires – the biggest annual improvement in the 22 years of the Rich List.

### Inequalities

As some people are getting significantly richer, many others are on very low wages and getting poorer. It is not just that actual incomes in a major industrial country are often very low indeed, but also the fact that the gap between high incomes and low incomes is growing. This gap bodes badly for concerns about equality and class. In the UK in the 1980s, inequalities were growing faster than in any other country in the

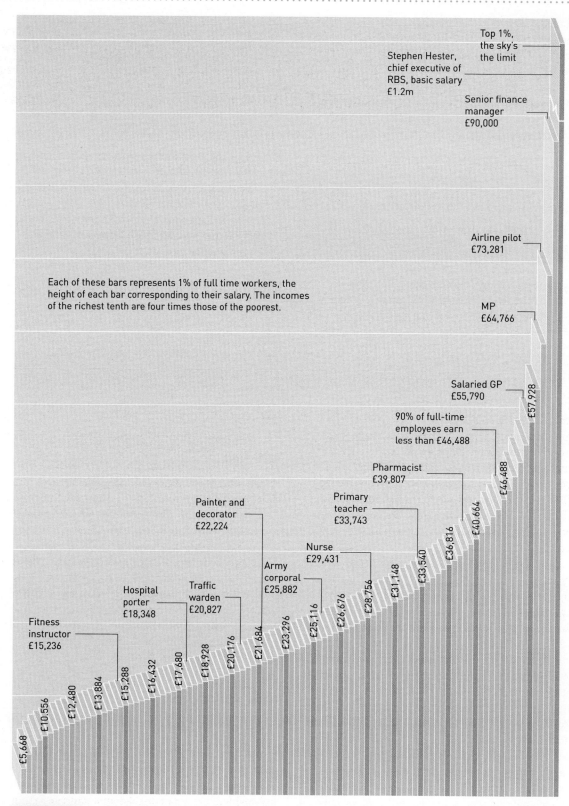

Each of these bars represents 1% of full time workers, the height of each bar corresponding to their salary. The incomes of the richest tenth are four times those of the poorest.

Top 1%, the sky's the limit

Stephen Hester, chief executive of RBS, basic salary £1.2m

Senior finance manager £90,000

Airline pilot £73,281

MP £64,766

Salaried GP £55,790

90% of full-time employees earn less than £46,488

Pharmacist £39,807

Primary teacher £33,743

Painter and decorator £22,224

Nurse £29,431

Army corporal £25,882

Traffic warden £20,827

Hospital porter £18,348

Fitness instructor £15,236

£5,668  £10,556  £12,480  £13,884  £15,288  £16,432  £17,680  £18,928  £20,176  £21,684  £23,296  £25,116  £26,676  £28,756  £31,148  £33,540  £36,816  £40,664  £46,488  £57,928

**Figure 10.1**  Income disparities in the UK

*Source*: *The Guardian*, 20 November 2010. Copyright Guardian News & Media Ltd 2010.

| Table 10.1 | Median gross weekly earnings by occupation: employees on adult rates, whose pay was unaffected by absence | | |
|---|---|---|---|
| | Full time | | |
| **April 2009** | **Men** | **Women** | **All** |
| £ per week | | | |
| **All employees** | **531.1** | **426.4** | **488.7** |
| 1 Managers and senior officials | 773.4 | 602.7 | 712.9 |
| 2 Professional | 733.1 | 655.1 | 695.6 |
| 3 Associate professional and technical | 581.5 | 516.0 | 551.1 |
| 4 Administrative and secretarial | 409.3 | 363.6 | 373.7 |
| 5 Skilled trades | 459.7 | 323.0 | 452.1 |
| 6 Personal service | 364.6 | 316.8 | 325.8 |
| 7 Sales and customer service | 311.0 | 285.9 | 296.2 |
| 8 Process, plant and machine operatives | 427.8 | 305.7 | 414.0 |
| 9 Elementary occupations | 344.0 | 271.3 | 322.5 |

Source: ONS, *Annual Survey of Hours and Earnings*, 2009, p. 10.

OECD except New Zealand. By the early 1990s growth was more stable, but since then the gap has started to grow again. The research of the Joseph Rowntree Foundation and the Child Poverty Action Group (CPAG) suggests that a great deal of poverty still exists in the UK. The number of people living in low-income households rose by 1.3 million between 2007 and 2009 and has remained constant in comparison with the year 2000. The number of children in low-income households with at least one employed adult, at 2.1 million, is the largest ever measured. We will look at this further below. (See websites for Joseph Rowntree Foundation, Child Poverty Action Group and the Department of Work and Pensions; see also *Social Trends*, 2010).

While the UK may have less income inequality than, say, Venezuela, Kenya or Sri Lanka, income inequality in these countries is higher than in many other industrial societies. Figure 10.2 shows a comparison of incomes within the EU in 2007 (see also Chapter 9).

## Wealth

Income is one component of a person's **wealth**, *the total value of money and other assets, minus outstanding debts*. Assets contributing to wealth include such items as houses, property, jewels, cars, artworks, boats, shares in a stock market, deposited money and racehorses. While the richest 1 per cent of Britons controlled 69 per cent of the national wealth in 1911, today the wealthiest 1 per cent of individuals own between one-fifth and one-quarter of the total wealth, and one-quarter of the adult population owns nearly three-quarters of the total wealth. By 2009, the Office for National Statistics found that the less wealthy 50 per cent of households in Britain only held 9 per cent of wealth. In contrast, the most affluent 20 per cent of households had accumulated 62 per cent of wealth (*Social Trends*).

Even though the wealth base has broadened, the wealthiest people still command considerable resources. According to the Sunday Times Rich List 2010, the wealth of the 1,000 richest individuals in Britain rose by more than £77 billion in 2009, in spite of a global economic crisis. Some examples among the richest 25 people in Britain include the industrialist Lakshmi Mittal and family (at £22.4 billion in 2010), Sir Richard Branson (the entrepreneur who founded the various Virgin companies, with a personal fortune estimated at between £2 billion and £3 billion; and the Duke of Westminster, wielding wealth of £6.7 billion.

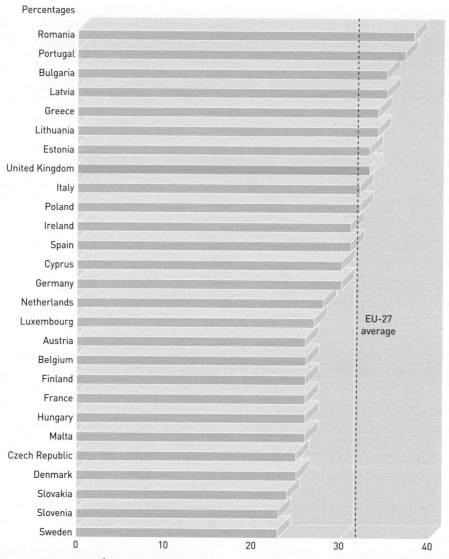

Percentages

| | |
|---|---|
| Romania | |
| Portugal | |
| Bulgaria | |
| Latvia | |
| Greece | |
| Lithuania | |
| Estonia | |
| United Kingdom | |
| Italy | |
| Poland | |
| Ireland | |
| Spain | |
| Cyprus | |
| Germany | |
| Netherlands | |
| Luxembourg | |
| Austria | |
| Belgium | |
| Finland | |
| France | |
| Hungary | |
| Malta | |
| Czech Republic | |
| Denmark | |
| Slovakia | |
| Slovenia | |
| Sweden | |

EU-27 average

0    10    20    30    40

**Figure 10.2**    Income inequality:[1] EU comparison, 2007

[1] As measured by the Gini coefficient, which can take values between 0 and 100, with 0 representing complete equality and 100 representing complete inequality.

*Source: EU Survey of Income and Living Standards, Eurostat in Social Trends, 40 (2010), Fig. 5.15, p. 69.*

Author J. K. Rowling has assets of £519 million, and former Beatle Sir Paul McCartney has some £475 million. Such wealth gives the mega-rich considerable influence, from the field of national politics to minor business transactions.

The super-rich also tend to reinforce and protect each other's interests. As John Scott notes (Scott, 1991, 1996, 1997), the elite 0.1 per cent of industrial populations often share similar backgrounds, swap directorships of high-performing companies, and are dominant shareholders in the leading businesses.

*tip* You can update information on the minimum wage online. See: www.hmrc.gov.uk/nmw/#b.

You can update on the rich through the *Sunday Times* Rich List, published annually, usually in April. Just search online for Sunday Times Rich List.

# Inequalities, resources and social class

The study of inequalities and social class is ultimately about our access to different resources (or capital) to live with. Some people have an abundance of access to these resources; while others have almost no access. The most obvious 'resource' is capital or wealth or economic resources. But it goes beyond this, and these days (often following the influence of the French sociologist Pierre Bourdieu, who we met in Chapter 8), sociologists locate a wider array of resources. Below is a list of key resources and you might like to think about your own opportunities in relation to them:

- **Economic resources**: how much income, wealth, financial assets and inheritance do you have access to? How much does your work provide for your needs?

- **Social resources**: how much support do you have from family, friends, community and networks?

- **Cultural resources**: how much access do you have to the knowledge, information, skills, education of your society?

- **Symbolic resources**: how much access do you have to people giving you legitimacy and privileging your life over others?

- **Political resources**: how much autonomy do you have in your life? Are you able to control much of your day or do others control it for you?

- **Bodily resources**: in what ways does your body seem to limit or control your life? How far do others regulate your body?

- **Personal resources**: how much has your own unique life and life history helped you generate the personal skills needed for you to move easily in the world?

*Source*: Adapted from Plummer, 2010: 175.

# Social class in the UK

Goran Therborn has suggested that *social class is one of the key defining features of modern Europe*, as Europe was the first major arena of industrialisation. More than anywhere in the world, class is to be found here (1995: 68). Europe as a whole, he contends, first experienced the rise of a manual working class through the industrialisation period, followed much more recently by a decline in this section of the population. Nowadays, 'less than a third of the economically active population is engaged in industrial labour' (1995: 76), marking the shrinking size of the working-class population. And there is a widespread view – amongst both politicians and the public – that class is less important than it was.

Yet, all main political parties in the UK, at least rhetorically, claim to want to create conditions for upward social mobility – a world where we can all 'make it'. Indeed, both of the last two Conservative prime ministers, John Major (1990–7) and Margaret Thatcher (1979–90), came from 'humble' origins: he, the son of a circus acrobat and garden gnome salesman; she, the daughter of a grocer from Grantham. The current Con–Lib coalition in the UK, by contrast, brings leaders David Cameron and Nick Clegg to power, with much more obviously privileged backgrounds.

There are various ways of visualising these class patterns. Most conventionally, the class structure is seen as a ladder – here the steps suggest mobility as people move upwards. More often it is seen as a pyramid – here the base would be a large working class, a smaller middle class and a tiny upper class. But recent class studies suggest this is not an adequate image. It may be better to see class through the image of a ball – with a large middle class in the centre and smaller working and upper classes at the ends. The middle class may account for around 50 per cent of western European societies – but it is growing as traditional manual occupations decline. Figure 10.3 provides an image of this.

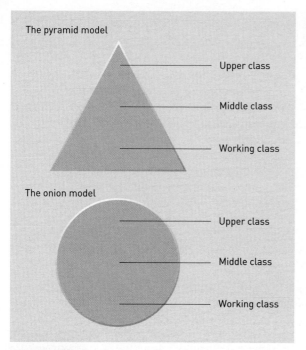

**Figure 10.3**    The shapes of class

| Table 10.2 | The likely shape of class in the UK? |
|---|---|
| Upper class | 0.2–0.1% |
| Lower upper class | Less than 10% |
| Upper middle and service class | 15% |
| Lower middle class | 20% |
| Skilled working class | 20% |
| Unskilled working class | 30% |
| Underclass | 5% |

*Source*: Based on Runciman (1990).

Runciman (1990) has produced such a map. He has documented that the approximate proportions of people at the different levels of the British class structure are as shown in Table 10.2. In the next sections, we will examine some of these distinctions and groups.

# 1  The upper classes

In industrialised countries, the upper classes make up anything from 5 to 10 per cent of the population, and include a small cadre of the super-rich (around 0.2 per cent). Traditionally, the upper classes have been linked to old aristocratic traditions and to significant ownership of property (especially land). But this 'old' money is increasingly being joined by 'new' money. We might distinguish two groups: the upper-uppers and the lower-uppers.

## Upper-uppers

Membership of the upper-upper class is almost always the result of ascription or birth. In much of Europe, many large landed estates have passed from generation to generation for centuries. The British aristocracy owns 40 per cent of British land: with the monarch at the head, they include dukes, marquesses, earls and viscounts. These families possess enormous wealth, primarily inherited rather than earned. Most of them have *old money*. Set apart by their wealth, members of the upper-upper class live in a world of exclusive affiliations. Children typically attend private schools with others of similar background, completing their formal education at high-prestige colleges and universities.

Europe remains highly stratified. Not only do the rich have controlling stakes in most businesses, but they also benefit from the most schooling, enjoy the best healthcare and consume the greatest share of almost all goods and services (Scott, 1991). Such privileges contrast sharply with unemployment throughout much of Europe, and the poverty of millions of people who struggle from day to day simply to buy food and keep a roof over their heads.

Sociologists have long debated just what social class is, and we have encountered some of these debates in Chapter 8. Some are very theoretical – building on the ideas of Marx and Weber developed in the previous chapter. Some adopt the large-scale survey approach – attempting to measure 'classes'. Still others provide descriptive case studies. We will look at some of this research as we go along. In what follows, we will show some of the major ways in which class has been measured, discuss broad features of different classes and consider whether people are generally moving between classes. We will not, however, be concerned with the detailed complexities of the debates. It will be sufficient for our purposes to provide the broadest contours.

# Measuring social class through your postcode

Market research seems to be taking over from sociology in its ability to identify social class groups. Using postcodes and examining spending patterns, market research has developed ever complex but clear systems of classifying different social–economic groups. *Mosaic* is based on analysis of the latest trends in UK society: it suggests 155 Mosaic person types aggregate into 67 household types and 15 groups, to create a three-tier classification that can be used at the individual, household or postcode level. Here we see a few of the new categories emerging.

For more details of this emerging methodology, see: Mosaic UK 2009 http://strategies.experian.co.uk/Products/Demographic%20Classifications/~/media/Files/Brochures/Mosaic%20UK%202009%20brochure.ashx

*Source: Optimise the value of your customers and locations, now and in the future – Mosaic UK – the consumer classification of the United Kingdom,* © 2010 Experian Ltd. All rights reserved.

| Group | Description | %👤 | %🏠 | Type | Description | %👤 | %🏠 |
|---|---|---|---|---|---|---|---|
| A | Alpha Territory | 4.28 | 3.54 | A01 | Global Power Brokers | 0.32 | 0.30 |
| | | | | A02 | Voices of Authority | 1.45 | 1.18 |
| | | | | A03 | Business Class | 1.83 | 1.50 |
| | | | | A04 | Serious Money | 0.68 | 0.56 |
| B | Professional Rewards | 9.54 | 8.23 | B05 | Mid-Career Climbers | 2.90 | 2.30 |
| | | | | B06 | Yesterday's Captains | 1.80 | 1.84 |
| | | | | B07 | Distinctive Success | 0.48 | 0.48 |
| | | | | B08 | Dormitory Villagers | 1.81 | 1.29 |
| | | | | B09 | Escape to the Country | 1.41 | 1.31 |
| | | | | B10 | Parish Guardians | 1.14 | 1.00 |
| C | Rural Solitude | 4.84 | 4.40 | C11 | Squires Among Locals | 1.01 | 0.85 |
| | | | | C12 | Country Loving Elders | 1.32 | 1.31 |
| | | | | C13 | Modern Agribusiness | 1.61 | 1.36 |
| | | | | C14 | Farming Today | 0.53 | 0.53 |
| | | | | C15 | Upland Struggle | 0.36 | 0.34 |
| D | Small Town Diversity | 9.21 | 8.75 | D16 | Side Street Singles | 1.21 | 1.17 |
| | | | | D17 | Jacks of All Trades | 2.60 | 1.99 |
| | | | | D18 | Hardworking Families | 2.87 | 2.63 |
| | | | | D19 | Innate Conservatives | 2.53 | 2.96 |
| E | Active Retirement | 3.41 | 4.34 | E20 | Golden Retirement | 0.52 | 0.67 |
| | | | | E21 | Bungalow Quietude | 1.42 | 1.79 |
| | | | | E22 | Beachcombers | 0.57 | 0.60 |
| | | | | E23 | Balcony Downsizers | 0.90 | 1.29 |
| F | Suburban Mindsets | 13.16 | 11.18 | F24 | Garden Suburbia | 2.82 | 2.14 |
| | | | | F25 | Production Managers | 2.31 | 2.63 |
| | | | | F26 | Mid-Market Families | 3.75 | 2.70 |
| | | | | F27 | Shop Floor Affluence | 2.82 | 2.73 |
| | | | | F28 | Asian Attainment | 1.45 | 0.98 |
| G | Careers and Kids | 5.34 | 5.78 | G29 | Footloose Managers | 1.11 | 1.67 |
| | | | | G30 | Soccer Dads and Mums | 1.34 | 1.34 |
| | | | | G31 | Domestic Comfort | 1.24 | 1.09 |
| | | | | G32 | Childcare Years | 1.46 | 1.52 |
| | | | | G33 | Military Dependants | 0.19 | 0.17 |
| H | New Homemakers | 3.99 | 5.91 | H34 | Buy-to-Let Territory | 1.08 | 1.79 |
| | | | | H35 | Brownfield Pioneers | 1.13 | 1.38 |
| | | | | H36 | Foot on the Ladder | 1.48 | 2.37 |
| | | | | H37 | First to Move In | 0.30 | 0.37 |
| I | Ex-Council Community | 10.60 | 8.67 | I38 | Settled Ex-Tenants | 2.08 | 2.06 |
| | | | | I39 | Choice Right to Buy | 1.90 | 1.72 |
| | | | | I40 | Legacy of Labour | 3.46 | 2.68 |
| | | | | I41 | Stressed Borrowers | 3.15 | 2.20 |
| J | Claimant Cultures | 4.52 | 5.16 | J42 | Worn-Out Workers | 1.82 | 2.30 |
| | | | | J43 | Streetwise Kids | 0.90 | 1.05 |
| | | | | J44 | New Parents in Need | 1.80 | 1.80 |
| K | Upper Floor Living | 4.30 | 5.18 | K45 | Small Block Singles | 1.26 | 1.77 |
| | | | | K46 | Tenement Living | 0.62 | 0.80 |
| | | | | K47 | Deprived View | 0.36 | 0.50 |
| | | | | K48 | Multicultural Towers | 1.09 | 1.11 |
| | | | | K49 | Re-Housed Migrants | 0.97 | 0.99 |
| L | Elderly Needs | 4.04 | 5.96 | L50 | Pensioners in Blocks | 0.89 | 1.31 |
| | | | | L51 | Sheltered Seniors | 0.67 | 1.12 |
| | | | | L52 | Meals on Wheels | 0.51 | 0.86 |
| | | | | L53 | Low Spending Elders | 1.98 | 2.68 |
| M | Industrial Heritage | 7.39 | 7.40 | M54 | Clocking Off | 2.18 | 2.25 |
| | | | | M55 | Backyard Regeneration | 2.40 | 2.06 |
| | | | | M56 | Small Wage Owners | 2.81 | 3.09 |
| N | Terraced Melting Pot | 6.54 | 7.02 | N57 | Back-to-Back Basics | 2.50 | 1.97 |
| | | | | N58 | Asian Identities | 1.06 | 0.88 |
| | | | | N59 | Low-Key Starters | 1.60 | 2.72 |
| | | | | N60 | Global Fusion | 1.38 | 1.44 |
| O | Liberal Opinions | 8.84 | 8.48 | O61 | Convivial Homeowners | 1.74 | 1.68 |
| | | | | O62 | Crash Pad Professionals | 1.41 | 1.09 |
| | | | | O63 | Urban Cool | 1.25 | 1.10 |
| | | | | O64 | Bright Young Things | 1.36 | 1.52 |
| | | | | O65 | Anti-Materialists | 1.12 | 1.03 |
| | | | | O66 | University Fringe | 1.10 | 0.93 |
| | | | | O67 | Study Buddies | 0.87 | 1.14 |

## Lower-uppers

Most upper-class people actually fall into the *lower-upper class*. From most people's point of view, this group is every bit as privileged as the upper-upper class. The major difference, however, is that lower-uppers are the 'working rich' who depend on earnings rather than inherited wealth as the primary source of their income. They include what we have come to call the 'fat cats', whose incomes often rise to extraordinary heights. The lower-upper class also includes 'the jet-set rich' – the very visible and very famous, such as the footballer who accepts a million-pound contract to play in the Premiership; the computer whiz who designs a program that sets a standard for the industry; or the musician whose work tops the charts – these are the lucky and talented achievers who reach the level of the lower-upper class. Celebrities such as Elton John and Andrew Lloyd Webber are included here, but there are also the entrepreneurial rich, including such people as Richard Branson, Alan Sugar, the Guinness family (the brewers) and the Sieff family (Marks & Spencer). Entrepreneurial capitalists, rentiers, executive and finance capitalists generally make the majority of their money through wise investments of stocks and bonds.

Especially in the eyes of members of 'society', the lower-upper class are merely the 'new rich' who can never savour the status enjoyed by those with rich and famous grandparents. Thus, while the new rich typically live in the biggest homes, they often find themselves excluded from the clubs and associations of old-money families.

## 2  The middle classes

The middle classes used to be the 'middle group' between poor and rich, who gained income through trade and manufacturing. Weber predicted their growth and Marx their demise. In fact, however, the middle classes have made up a larger and larger proportion of most of the class structure of Europe. Middle-class occupations have material and cultural advantages over working-class employment, generally offering more security, higher pay and higher prestige. The middle class encompasses far more racial and ethnic diversity than the upper class. While many upper-class people (especially upper-uppers) know each other personally, such exclusiveness and familiarity do not characterise the middle class. We can identify three general shades of middle class: the upper (or traditional) middle class, the service class and the lower middle class. It is a large and highly fragmented group, characterised by considerable lifestyle diversities (see Savage et al., 1992).

# Class measurements in the UK

So far we have looked at a number of variables and issues in identifying class. To examine the challenges of defining class more directly, we will now look at three classifications in use in the UK.

## 1  The Registrar General's Index of Social Class

This provided a straightforward classification of social classes which was widely used in the twentieth century. Originally introduced in the census of 1911, this scale ranked occupations and skills of similar social standing, from 'professionals' to 'unskilled manuals'. Table 10.3 illustrates the six categories in this scale. It ceased to be used, however, with the arrival of the new NS-SEC scale which was introduced into the 2001 census and which is discussed below.

Although the index has been very widely used, it does bring a great many problems. Among the most prominent have been:

- A huge chunk of the population is now in classes 3a and 3b, mainly because of occupational changes in the twentieth century.
- Pay scales and prestige within the same category are often quite different, or again have changed over time. For example, a starting teacher may earn £20,000 or a major lawyer £300,000-plus. It makes the category nonsensical.

- Women were allocated class based on their nearest male relative, but large numbers of women now work (there were fewer when the 1911 classification was introduced).

For these and other reasons, in the latter part of the twentieth century, sociologists in the UK struggled to find better measurements such as the Essex University Class Scale (Marshall et al., 1988) and the Surrey Occupational Scale (1986).

## 2  John Goldthorpe's modification

John Goldthorpe, one of the most prominent British class analysts of the late twentieth century, modified the Registrar General's scale. Goldthorpe groups workers into three

*METHODS & RESEARCH*

| Table 10.3 | The twentieth-century Registrar General scale categories | | |
|---|---|---|---|
| **Class** | **Letter** | **Name of class** | **Examples** |
| 1 | A | Professional | Solicitors, accountants, surgeons, university lecturers |
| 2 | B | Managerial and technical | Managers, teachers, nurses |
| 3a | C1 | Skilled non-manual | Estate agents, secretaries, sales clerks |
| 3b | C2 | Skilled manual/craft | Bricklayers, electricians, drivers |
| 4 | D | Partly skilled manual | Postal carriers, pub/bar staff |
| 5 | E | Unskilled manual | Cleaners, labourers |

main categories of work, and further subdivides each group. He suggests that there are the following broad groupings:

- A *service class* made up of (a) professional and managerial workers; (b) supervisors of non-manual workers.
- An *intermediate class* made up of (a) routine non-manual workers; (b) small proprietors; (c) supervisors of manual workers; (d) lower-grade technicians.

- A *working class* made up of (a) skilled; (b) semi-skilled; (c) unskilled manual workers.

Such a 'class scale' makes allowances for three factors that determine the general social power that people gain from their occupation: prestige, income and wealth.

### 3 The National Statistics Socio-Economic Classification (NS-SEC)

This is a more recent classification system. It was announced in December 1998 and was used for the first time in a major way in the UK census in 2001. It draws upon a number of features from the Goldthorpe scale above. Instead of just ranking occupations, it highlights (a) job security, (b) promotion opportunity, and (c) ability and opportunity to work on one's own and make decisions. It is shown in Table 10.4.

| Table 10.4 | Eight-, five- and three-class versions of the NS-SEC scale, and their nested relationship | |
|---|---|---|
| **Eight classes** | **Five classes** | **Three classes** |
| 1 Higher managerial and professional occupations | 1 Managerial and professional occupations | 1 Higher occupations |
| 1.1 Large employers and higher managerial occupations | | |
| 1.2 Higher professional occupations | | |
| 2 Lower managerial and professional occupations | | |
| 3 Intermediate occupations | 2 Intermediate occupations | 2 Intermediate occupations |
| 4 Small employers and own account workers | 3 Small employers and own account workers | |
| 5 Lower supervisory and technical occupations | 4 Lower supervisory and technical occupations | 3 Lower occupations |
| 6 Semi-routine occupations | 5 Semi-routine and routine occupations | |
| 7 Routine occupations | | |
| 8 Never worked and long-term unemployed | Never worked and long-term unemployed | Never worked and long-term unemployed |

*Note:* The number of classes used depends upon both the analytical purposes at hand and the quality of available data.

*Source:* Based on Office for National Statistics.

## The upper-middle class

The more powerful end of this category, also dubbed the traditional middle class, earns above-average incomes. Family income may be even greater if both wife and husband work. High income allows upper-middle-class families gradually to accumulate considerable property, a comfortable house in a fairly expensive area, several cars and investments. A majority of upper-middle-class children receive university educations, and postgraduate degrees are common. Many go on to high-prestige occupations (as doctors, engineers, lawyers, accountants or business executives). Lacking the power of the upper class to influence national or international events, the upper-middle class nonetheless often plays an important role in local political affairs.

## The service class

The service class includes people who provide highly valued and well-paid services to employers, including middle-level bureaucrats, management of health, welfare and education services, technically trained secretaries and business consultants. This group also

LIVING IN THE C21ST

# The parade of class: what a difference a class makes

Imagine an hour-long parade of people with heights matched to income. What a parade it would be! For more than 25 minutes, all the toddlers and 'vertically challenged' would march by. Three-quarters of an hour would pass before we saw people of average height or taller. Suddenly, for the last minute we would be stunned to see people who would be 20 metres or so tall. Then in the final seconds, huge, colossal figures would start to emerge, their heads lost in the clouds. Just a few massive people, and yet such vast numbers of small ones. One of the world's richest men, Bill Gates, could stand as tall as 10 miles.

This is an example of the colourful language used in several recent reports on inequality. It makes a point. More prosaically, we can say that most Western societies are characterised by extremes of inequality: huge numbers with low incomes and a few with large incomes. But statistics conceal the experiences. At one end there is the life of luxury – a level of wealth that most of us can only imagine. But at the other extremes are what

sociologist Richard Sennett has called 'the hidden injuries of class'. These are the deep scars often thrust upon a life because of no work or demeaning work over which one has little control; because of poor housing or no housing; because money is tight and there are no assets; and, maybe worst of all, because of a deep sense of being outside society, at the bottom of the heap.

Why do sociologists spend so much time talking about class? The answer is that there is little doubt that *social class has a major impact on nearly every dimension of our lives*. While class alone does not define our sense of place in society, class is one of the most significant influences on our lives. Our class impacts us *objectively*: that is, in our health, our education, our possessions and our lifestyle. But it also impacts us *subjectively*: that is, in the way we see ourselves, our language, our values, our ideas, our 'cultural capital'. Here are a few examples of the impact of class on various aspects of life in the UK:

- *Infant mortality* (see also Chapter 24). Working-class children may be three times more likely to die in their first year of life than children of professional parents.

- *Health* (see also Chapter 21). Working-class people may be three times more likely to have long-term serious illness than people of the higher classes.

- *Death* (see also Chapters 21 and 24). A child of an unskilled manual worker may well die around seven years earlier than a counterpart born to professional parents.

- *Divorce* (see Chapter 18). The risk of divorce is four times higher among manuals than among professionals.

- *Education* (see Chapter 20). Just 1 per cent going to university come from the unskilled manual class, while some 78 per cent come from social class I.

- *Public safety* (see Chapter 21). Crime rates were lowest in affluent suburban and rural areas and highest in council estates and low-income areas.

- *Job security*. There is much less job security for working-class occupations than for middle-class professions.

- *Unemployment*. While around 14 per cent in social class V may be out of work, unemployment is much smaller in class I (around 3 per cent).

- *Home ownership*. While some 90 per cent of professionals were owner-occupiers, only around 40 per cent of unskilled manual workers were.

Note: The above is only a schematic and is meant only to provide a general sense that there are differences; the list does not specify years or detail. For further discussion, see the relevant chapters.

Source: *Social Trends* (2007); Acheson (1998); Scott (2000b).

includes many people who work in media, teaching, fashion and therapy professions. Service-class people enjoy a lot of autonomy in their work, usually exercise and delegate authority, and tend to have secure careers (see Goldthorpe, 1982; Lash and Urry, 1987). David Lockwood (1992) further subdivides this group into professionals, who rely on cultural capital (knowledge); managers; and petty bourgeois (traders and small property owners). People in this class also tend to own property (though in less fashionable districts), to own vehicles (though less expensive models) and to have relatively high levels of education, though they are more likely to work to pull maximum advantage from state-sponsored education and to have attended second-tier colleges and universities.

## The lower-middle class

The rest of the middle class falls close to the centre of the class structure. People in the lower-middle class typically work in less prestigious white-collar occupations (such as bank clerks, middle managers or sales clerks) or in highly skilled blue-collar jobs (including electrical work and carpentry). Commonly, lower-middle-class households earn incomes around the national average. Income at this level provides a secure, if modest, standard of living. Lower-middle-class people generally accumulate some wealth over the course of their working lives, mostly in the form of a house. People in this class generally complete some post-secondary school qualifications, though not necessarily university degrees. They are sometimes seen as 'intermediate classes': that is between the working and middle class.

## 3 The working classes

Two distinct phases have marked out the working class. What we might call *traditional* working-class life used to be defined in terms of strong identities based in communities associated with a particular field of labour, such as were found in traditional mining communities (Dennis et al., 1956), steel communities (Beynon et al., 1991), fishing communities, and so forth. But to name these communities is to sense their demise. In the UK, the old coalfields around Durham or the steel furnaces blasting out around Middlesbrough have gone and the fishing communities around the country are rapidly shrinking. With them went jobs, income, security and communities. After long periods of unemployment and demoralisation, some people benefit from new patterns of work that

emerge. But these patterns are very different, often involving relocation and work that is much more fragmented. We have moved from work in the mine to work in McDonald's. And with that, traditional working-class communities are in steep decline.

But a new working class has also emerged. This is one that will own their own homes, live in suburbs and be more affluent, with cars and DVD players. It is even unlikely that they will see themselves as working class. Indeed, Beverley Skeggs' ethnographic research on young women from working-class backgrounds in a northern town suggests that being working class now carries a stigma and the concern is to be seen as respectable (Skeggs, 1997).

Working-class occupations generally yield a household income somewhat below the national average. Working-class families thus find themselves vulnerable to financial problems, especially when confronted by unemployment or illness. Besides generating less income, working-class jobs typically yield less personal satisfaction. Tasks tend to be routine, requiring discipline but rarely imagination, and workers are usually subject to continual supervision. Such jobs also provide fewer benefits, such as private medical insurance and pension schemes. About half of working-class families own their homes, usually in lower-cost districts.

## Social exclusion and the idea of an underclass

## Social exclusion

In recent years, an important concept has entered the sociological language: that of social exclusion. The term probably has its origins in France, *les exclus* (the excluded) being those who fell though the net of social protection in the 1970s – lone parents, disabled, the uninsured unemployed (Burchard, 2000: 385). It is related in part to ideas of the underclass, as it highlights people being cut off from the mainstream of society. It has been used both in the United Nations (where it highlights a lack of access to the basic institutions of civil society, a lack of citizenship) and in Europe, where it has been widely adopted.

There have been several attempts to chart the main indicators of social exclusion. The Rowntree/New Policy Institute developed a substantial listing – embracing income, children, young adults, adults and the elderly, and whole communities (Gordon and

Townsend, 2000: 367). The Institute for Public Policy Research (IPPR) highlighted exclusion over four domains – income poverty, exclusion from the labour market, exclusion in education, and health. The Poverty and Social Exclusion (PSE) Survey distinguished four dimensions of exclusion: impoverishment, or exclusion from adequate income or resources; labour market exclusion; service exclusion; and exclusion from social relations.

In 1997, in the UK, a Social Exclusion Unit or Task Force (SEU) was set up under the Labour government to focus on specific groups, such as street homeless and pregnant teenagers. It closed in 2006, and created a tighter unit to focus on a much more specific and smaller group that had been identified in its work. This smaller group was identified as 'high harm, high risk and high lifetime cost'. The aim of the new policy was to intervene in the lives of these people as soon as they appeared at risk of exclusion, breakdown or criminal behaviour (*Guardian*, 13 June 2006).

## The underclass

The **underclass** is a more difficult term. For some sociologists, it comprises those people '*under the class structure*', *those who are economically, politically and socially marginalised and excluded*. Typically, these people live between unemployment and the labour market of casual and temporary work. They usually live on state benefits or charitable aid. Encompassing frail pensioners, single 'trapped' parents and the long-term unemployed, the term covers those who are in a sense 'outside' the system of work and even class. In 1987, Dahrendorf estimated that about 5 per cent of the British population fell within the underclass – and that this percentage was growing rapidly.

The idea of an underclass has a long and controversial history. Marx spoke of the *lumpenproletariat* (the social scum of vagrants, misfits, dregs). Booth (1901–2), Rowntree (1902) and Mayhew (1861) described the 'dangerous classes' of 'paupers, beggars and outcasts with a repugnance to regular labour'. There is a long history of distinguishing undeserving, disreputable poor from 'respectable' people trapped in a 'cycle of deprivation' (Morris, 1994). This is discussed in the *Big debate* at the end of this chapter. All these writings point to a heavily stigmatised group at the bottom of the heap, excluded from work, living in dire poverty. The least generous observers suspect the underclass of turning to crime and, as we shall discuss more later, this view often associates racial and underclass issues.

The novel *Angela's Ashes* depicts the harrowing childhood of Frank McCourt in the 1930s and 1940s in Limerick, Ireland. Later turned into a film, the starkness of poverty is dramatically conveyed – the overcrowded and basic housing, the lack of sanitation, the deprivation of food. Such stark poverty has often been depicted in literature

*Source*: Ronald Grant Archive. Courtesy Dirty Hands Prods/RGA.

The American sociologist Charles Murray has been a recent champion of the idea of 'underclass'. Looking at the United States, in his book *Losing Ground* (1984) he charted what he saw as the failure of welfare policies, where he argued that more and more people had become dependent on the state. In the late 1980s he brought these ideas to the UK and they became serialised in The *Sunday Times* (26 November 1989). For Murray, this underclass lived in a different world, raised its children differently and had different values. He pondered: 'How is a civilised society to take care of the deserving without encouraging people to become undeserving? How does it do good without engendering vice?'

In Europe, the problem of the underclass is often linked to problems of migration. Workers who cannot find work in their own countries want to go to others where work may be found. But in this process – as new arrivals, often with different ethnic backgrounds – all they can find is casual work. Algerians in France, Turks in Germany, Moroccans in Spain and Bangladeshis in the UK often confront both formal and informal barriers against their entering the regular labour market. People who have illegally joined family and friends in the European Union face an even more tenuous position, as they cannot even apply for benefits to meet basic needs. The drive for daily survival focuses the attention of underclass people more on the present. Without much prospect of work, people in the underclass live on the margins of society.

Although many people experience the conditions implied by the term 'underclass', the academic use of this term is problematic. 'Underclass' is often used as an abusive 'catch all' phrase that lumps together many different kinds of experience, and then proceeds to stigmatise them. It is the most recent term – in a long line – for blaming the poor for their poverty. So sociologists have to be very careful how they come to use it.

## Poverty: the lower ends of inequality in capitalist society

Sociologists address the concept of poverty in two different ways. **Relative poverty** refers to *the deprivation of some people in relation to those who have more.* Relative poverty is universal and unavoidable; even a rich society has some members who live in relative poverty. It depends on the values and standards of living that a particular society sets; those falling below it are 'poor'. In contrast, absolute poverty is a deprivation of resources that is life threatening. It depends upon a universally agreed minimum for adequate nutrition and living. Much of the poverty we discussed in the previous chapter – the lives of perhaps 800 million people, one in seven of the earth's entire population – is like this.

Yet even in Europe, one of the most affluent regions in the whole world, as defined by its gross domestic product, people still go hungry, become homeless, live in poor housing and endure poor health because of the wrenching reality of poverty.

## Measuring poverty

Some of the earliest attempts to measure poverty were conducted in Britain in the latter part of the nineteenth century. Aware of the shocking conditions brought about through rapid industrialisation in major cities such as Manchester and London, the philanthropist and businessman Charles Booth set about a door-to-door survey in large areas of London, enumerating the numbers of people occupying each dwelling and measuring poverty in terms of their income. Poverty, for Booth, was taken to be absolute and objective: it was the amount of money people had to live on. If it fell below a certain breadline of nutritional needs, it meant that people were poor.

A little later, Seebohm Rowntree conducted three surveys between 1899 and 1951 in the city of York and concluded in the last study that poverty had more or less been eradicated in the UK by 1951. He defined absolute poverty in subsistence terms: 'nothing must be bought but that which is absolutely necessary for the maintenance of physical health and what is bought must be of the plainest and most economical description'. Subsequent researchers developed more sophisticated modes of measurement (see Scott, 1994, for an excellent review of the work of Booth and Rowntree).

Since the mid-1950s, poverty in the UK has been studied by Peter Townsend, who defines it as 'the lack of the resources necessary to permit participation in the activities, customs and diets commonly approved by society' (Townsend, 1979: 81). After a major survey, using a national random sample, Townsend concluded that poverty and deprivation almost certainly begin to occur at a level which is over 50 per cent above the official government definition of poverty for means-tested social assistance rates. Social assistance rates are fixed by governments at minimum levels;

(a) New York: keeping warm is always a problem to those living in the street and fashionable Fifth Avenue is no different. With her legs wrapped in newspaper, a woman enjoys the warmth from the grating. The fashions in the window have little meaning for her; (b) Doré's London in Victorian times

*Source*: (a) © Bettmann/Corbis; (b) plate from Doré: *A London Pilgrimage*.

Townsend and many subsequent researchers see this as far too low and basic, failing to take into account the relative need for 'participation' in a society.

A little later, Mack and Lansley took Townsend's ideas of relative poverty one step further. For a television series called *Breadline Britain*, they investigated the 'British standard of living' by conducting a public opinion poll. They asked people what they regarded as necessary for a good standard of living. Then, documenting the level of missing necessities experienced by a national quota sample of over 1,000 people (see Table 10.5), they defined the poor as those 'excluded from the way of life that most people take for granted' (Mack and Lansley, 1985: 15). They found that the number of poor people, especially children, increased in Britain between 1983 and 1990.

The Mack and Lansley approach consistently moves the poverty line upwards over time, as expectations of living standards shift (Table 10.5). These days, for instance, students increasingly need computers for their work. You might ask yourself whether a student who is unable to afford to buy a computer is poor. This approach has recently been developed further and applied across Europe (Gordon and Townsend, 2000).

Given the complexities of these more sophisticated sociological approaches, it is most common, these days, for poverty to be measured relatively through income. Until 1987, poverty was measured as living below whatever was the government's current supplementary benefit level. (It moves under various names in various countries. Currently, in the UK it is the income support level/employment support level.) Nowadays, households below-average income (HBAI) is the most common measure.

As we have seen, in the measurement of world poverty the most common indicator is to measure those who live below an income of US$1 a day (recently changed to $1.50); and this itself is a problem for analysts (see pp. 286–8). In the UK (and much of Europe) the standard measurement is 60 per cent

| Table 10.5 | Mack and Lansley's 'lack of necessities' as a poverty measure | | |
|---|---|---|---|
| Necessity | 1983 Percentage of households unable to afford | Necessity | 1990 Percentage of households unable to afford |
| 1 Holiday | 21 | 1 Regular savings | 30 |
| 2 Two pairs of shoes | 9 | 2 Holiday | 20 |
| 3 Meat or fish every other day | 8 | 3 Decent decoration | 15 |
| 4 Hobby | 7 | 4 Outing for children | 14 |
| 4 Damp-free house | 7 | 5 Insurance | 10 |
| 4 Warm coat | 7 | 5 Out-of-school activities | 10 |
| 4 Weekly roast | 7 | 7 Separate bedrooms | 7 |
| 8 Leisure equipment for children | 6 | 7 Hobby | 7 |
| 8 New clothes | 6 | 7 Telephone | 7 |
| 8 Washing machines | 6 | 10 Best outfit | 8 |
| | | 10 Entertaining of children's friends | 8 |

*Source*: Adapted from Frayman (1991: 6), reprinted in Scott (1994).

below median income. The most commonly used data in the UK are at the *Households Below Average Income (HBAI)* data source (which you can find at www.dwp.gov.uk). In the UK, the **poverty line** is defined in terms of *60 per cent of the median household income*. This means that in 2003–4, the poverty line could be calculated at the following (note though that this does not include housing costs):

| | |
|---|---|
| Single person | £98 |
| Couple | £178 |
| Couple with two children (5–11) | £262 |
| Lone parent with two children | £182 |

Given the complexities of measuring poverty, estimates of it are notoriously variable and 'poverty figures' can be quite wide ranging. Rowntree in 1950 found only 1.5 per cent of York living in poverty, but he was applying very strict absolute standards. Under the more lenient relative standards of recent times, poverty is found to be anywhere between a tenth and a third of the population. Thus, Townsend's major study of 1969 (published in 1979) found that 21.8 per cent of the population were below 140 per cent of the Supplementary Benefit line, and 22.9 per cent below his deprivation standard. In 1993, the Low Pay Unit estimated that a third of the population lived in poverty; the OECD suggested there were 12 million poor in the UK (a quarter of Europe's 50 million people living in poverty); and 10 per cent of people claimed income support (5.6 million people) (Skellington, 1996: 105–11).

The Labour governments of 1997–2010 set themselves a series of major targets to radically reduce relative poverty. At the time they came to power, research suggested that around a quarter (26 per cent) of the British population were living in poverty (as measured in terms of low income and multiple deprivation necessities). For a while, poverty seemed to decline, through such measures as a national minimum wage, working families tax credit, pension credit and winter fuel payments. In 2003, the Joseph Rowntree Foundation could declare that 'poverty fell by about a million'. By the time labour lost office in 2010, however, poverty had surged back upwards. The Rowntree Foundation found that the number of low-income households had risen continuously during the latter part of the 2000s, returning to numbers previously measured ten years before. Likewise, the Institute for Fiscal Studies has pointed out that poverty levels have risen continuously since 2005 and now slightly exceed the numbers measured at the beginning of the past decade. According to the Child Poverty Action Group, in 2008 13.5 million people in the UK, or 23 per cent of the population, were considered poor, in the sense that their income amounted to less than 60 per cent of the national median income after housing costs had been paid.

# Spotlight

## Poverty in the UK, 2010

Poverty in the UK is usually measured as households with below 60 per cent of contemporary median net disposable income. Between 1945 and the early 1970s there was a narrowing of the gap between richest and poorest. Since then there has been a widening of the gap (with a slight narrowing in the early 2000s).

- *Children*. In 2008/9, there were 2.8 million children living in UK households with below 60 per cent of contemporary median net disposable household income before housing costs and 3.9 million after housing costs.

- *Working-age adults*. In 2008/9, there were 5.8 million working-age adults living in UK households with below 60 per cent of contemporary median net disposable household income before housing costs, and 7.8 million after housing costs.

- *Pensioners*. In 2008/9, there were 2.3 million pensioners living in UK households with below 60 per cent of contemporary median net disposable household income before housing costs, and 1.8 million after housing costs.

So, officially in 2008/9 between 10.9 and 13.5 million people were likely to be living at 60 per cent below the average income of the country (around 23 per cent of the population). This is the official poverty line. This comprises:

- 53 per cent who are in households which include at least one child
- 34 per cent who are in households of people of working age without children
- 13 per cent who are in pensioner households.

The cost to UK society of poverty and the many other social problems to which it is related is huge. While it is not easy to quantify all the consequences of poverty, here are some of the annual costs directly or indirectly connected to child poverty:

- £3 billion spent on children by local authority services
- more than £500 million to support homeless families with children
- around £300 million on free school dinners
- around £500 million on primary healthcare for deprived children
- knock-on costs in lost taxes and extra benefits claimed by adults with poor job prospects, linked to educational failure at school.

*Source*: Department of Work and Pensions, http://research.dwp.gov.uk/asd/hbai.asp (released 20 May 2010). For updates see: Joseph Rowntree Foundation, www.jrf.org.uk/reporting-poverty/facts-figures; Child Poverty Action Group www.cpag.org.uk. More generally, see: Pat Thane (ed.), *Unequal Britain* (2010).

## A note on poverty in Europe

In the European Union, poverty and social exclusion have generally been rising, despite a series of programmes to combat them. In 1975, poverty was recorded at some 38 million people and by the 1990s at some 50 million. In 2007 around 17 per cent of people in the EU-27 lived in a household with less than 60 per cent of the respective national median income and were considered to be 'at risk of poverty'. As Figure 10.2 on p. 322 shows, the highest levels of inequality were recorded in Romania, Portugal and Bulgaria, while the lowest were recorded in the Nordic states, the Czech Republic, Slovakia, Slovena and Hungary. In the majority of countries, social benefits reduce the proportion of people at risk of poverty by between 25 and 60 per cent. Thus, benefit payments were instrumental in lifting approximately 35 per cent of persons with low income above the poverty line. The household types most at risk of poverty are single parents with dependent children, single elderly people and single females.

Overall, there are significant inequalities in Europe. Broadly, the 20 per cent of the EU with the highest incomes received five times the income of those 20 per cent with the lowest incomes.

## Who are the poor?

Although no single description covers all poor people, poverty is pronounced among certain categories of the population. In particular, it is likely to hit people who are disadvantaged in other ways: low-wage earners, the unemployed, disabled people. With this in mind, who are the poorest groups in the UK? In summary, for 2007/8, the risk of income poverty was highest for:

1 Children: more than 30 per cent of children are facing the risk of poverty.
2 Ethnicity: 19 per cent of white people were poor; in contrast, the risk of poverty among Bangladeshi, Pakistani, and Black non-Caribbean people lay at between 50 and 60 per cent.
3 Lone parents: approximately 50 per cent were income poor.
4 Pensioners: more than 20 per cent of single pensioner households faced the risk of poverty.
5 Disabled: the poverty risk for households with one or more disabled members ranged from nearly 30 to more than 50 per cent.

## Age: children and the elderly

A generation ago, the elderly were at greatest risk of poverty. They still remain at risk, but studies now conclude that a 'new poverty' has emerged among the young and children. In the UK, the number of elderly needing assistance fell from 1.8 million in 1974 to 1.4 million in 1991. Today, the burden of poverty falls most heavily on children. Thus, numbers of children under 16 needing assistance in the UK rose from 800,000 in 1974 to 2.3 million in 1991 and 3.9 million in 2007. According to the Child Poverty Action Group, more than 30 per cent of children in 2008 lived in households considered poor after housing costs were accounted for. The Rowntree study suggested that the poverty rates of children were higher among those:

- in households without any workers
- in lone-parent families
- with a larger number of siblings
- with household members suffering a long-standing illness
- of non-white ethnicity
- living in local authority housing
- in households in receipt of Job Seeker's Allowance or Income Support.

The same story is true in much of the rest of Europe. In the United States, it is even more extreme. In 2008, 14.1 million children or 19 per cent of all children were poor. Among Hispanic and African American children, more than 30 per cent were living in poverty. According to the National Poverty Center, children represent a disproportionately large share of the poor in the USA. They account for 35 per cent of the poor population, while only representing 25 per cent of the country's population in general.

## Race and ethnicity

Studies also strongly suggest that 'multiple deprivations' affect ethnic minorities, leading to significantly higher levels of poverty. The Joseph Rowntree Foundation's (1995) study of poverty in the UK was 'particularly concerned . . . at what is happening to the non-white population'. One in three of the non-white population was in the poorest fifth of the population. Most significant here were alarming rates of unemployment (worst of all among people of Pakistani and Bangladeshi origin) and the difficulties of ethnic women and children, not least Afro-Caribbean single-parent families. Many of these groups were contributing to an emerging underclass (see above). Recent work by Lucinda Platt (2002; 2007) suggests little change.

Ethnicity is important across the world when looking at poverty. In the United States, for example, in absolute numbers, two-thirds of all poor people are white. But in relation to their overall numbers, African-Americans are almost three times as likely as white people to be poor. In 2008, 24.7 per cent of African-Americans (8.7 million people) lived in poverty, compared to 21.2 per cent of Latinos (9.4 million), 10.6 per cent of Asians (1.3 million), and 9.2 per cent of non-Hispanic white people (21.4 million). Thirty per cent of African-American children are poor (US Census Bureau, 2008).

## Gender and family patterns

The term **feminisation of poverty** describes *the trend by which women represent an increasing proportion of the poor*. Many years ago, Peter Townsend (1987) identified four groups of women that made up the 'female poor'. These are:

- single (including divorced) women with children
- elderly women pensioners
- 'carers' who look after children or other dependants
- women with low earnings.

This *feminisation of poverty* is part of a larger change: the rapidly increasing number of households – at all class levels – headed by single women. This trend, coupled with the fact that households headed by women are at high risk of poverty, explains why women (and their children) represent an increasing share of the European poor. Black women appear in all these categories, and for them poverty becomes even more likely.

## Disablement

Disabled people may be severely affected by poverty. Often they have been excluded from the routine activities of everyday life – they may be less likely to have (well-paid) employment. They usually have lower average income levels and in addition have to meet the 'extra costs' of impairment (Townsend, 1979; Barnes et al., 1999: 134).

# The 'Death of Class' debate

The past 50 years or so have seen so many changes in the socioeconomic environment that it would be surprising if there had not also been changes in the nature of class. Sociologists have for a long time disagreed about both its importance and how it should be studied. While some argue that 'class remains the sociological key to understanding the structure of society' (Scott, 1994: 19) and have argued that its significance is still central, others have contended that 'class as a concept is ceasing to do any useful work for sociology' (Pahl, 1989). Which is it?

# The end of class?

Some sociologists argue that we have become more and more of a classless society and that the concept of class cannot incorporate the scope of the changes that are happening in the (post)modern world. It is not a question of whether inequalities persist – all agree that they do (and many suggest they are widening). But it is often more a matter of whether and how these inequalities can be traced back to class as *the* key issue.

For instance, as we have previously seen, in so much early sociology, women were excluded. Much of 'class theory' naively ignored gender, and much of it may well therefore be misconceived. Certainly, bringing women into the picture shifts the focus of class questions, such as how child-bearing, child-rearing, and 'domestic labour' and housework fit into the labour structure. Moreover, women as a group generally earn less than men – even at comparable levels of education and experience. While overt sex discrimination is illegal in the European Union (as well as in most other industrialised countries), women remain more likely to be 'ghettoised' into lower-paid occupations such as social work, auxiliary nursing, child care and routine secretarial roles (see Chapter 12 for further details). All this means, at the very least, that gender has to be an important factor in understanding inequality. And, as we shall see in the next chapter, the same can also be said of ethnicity.

One (ex?) Marxist, André Gortz (1982), significantly called his book *Farewell to the Working Class*. If class is seen as primarily economic, involving some sense of class awareness and consciousness, and if it is seen as an important force for bringing about social change, then critics argue it has clearly declined in significance. Thus, the power (or lack of it) linked to different groups and social movements – ethnic groups, the disabled, women, the elderly, etc. – has become much more prominent. Matters of consumption and lifestyle have become more and more important in people's lives. The role of new social movements in bringing about social change (see Chapter 16) also now seems

more important generally than class in shaping change (Waters, 1997). Further, wider changes in society – the spread of share ownership, the growth of social mobility through education, the flexibility of what has been called post-Fordist production (see Chapter 15) – have all contributed to a reworking of the class order.

Perhaps the most widespread argument on the 'death of class' is that there has been a general 'levelling-up' of the classes. Traditional working-class communities such as those associated with mining or the steel industry have vanished and new working-class lives have become heavily shaped by home ownership and consumerism. The 'working class' no longer harbours the strong community that it once did. Indeed, there has been a clear failure of working-class-based action and a decline of working-class identity and trade unionism. During the Thatcher period, there was a major dealignment of politics, so that there is no longer even a clear working-class vote attached to the Labour Party (Crewe, 1992).

## The embourgeoisement thesis

One of the first major studies in the UK to examine the shifting nature of class was in the work of David Lockwood, John Goldthorpe, Frank Beckhoffer and Jennifer Platt, who looked at the changing nature of class among Luton car workers in the 1960s (Goldthorpe et al., 1968). Their study was explicitly designed to examine the so-called 'embourgeoisement' thesis that 'we are all in the middle class now'. It examined an early version of the theory of the decline of class: that the traditional 'proletarian' working class was losing its old identity, becoming more affluent and looking more and more like the middle classes. In the main, this study rejected such a thesis. True, it certainly showed major changes in class: the car factory workers were comparatively well paid, could spend money on major consumer goods, and were becoming home-owners. But the middle class had advanced in line with this. Further, the car workers still usually voted Labour and did not really adopt middle-class lifestyles. They had become a new kind of working class – much more private and home-centred, seeing their work as a means to make money but with little sense of the job satisfaction found in middle-class work (Goldthorpe et al., 1968). So the argument to be made here is not that class was weakening or vanishing, but that it was changing with the times.

This study, however, was conducted over half a century ago. The world has moved on. More recent studies have suggested that key divides now occur around *consumption* and *lifestyles* which cut right across old class lines. In the 1980s, Ray Pahl, looking at working-class households in Kent, saw the working class as becoming more and more divided – often between those in regular work and those drifting in and out of unemployment. Strikingly, he suggests that 'if the cathedral of the nineteenth century was the factory chimney, that of the twentieth century is the shopping mall' (Pahl, 1984; J. Pahl, 1989).

More important, perhaps, are the new divides between those who rely on the market and those who rely on the state; between those who own their houses and those who rent them; between those who work and those who are unemployed; between 'work-rich' and 'work-poor' households. Classes now need to be linked to the 'texture' of cultures and the key role of (largely middle-class) social movements, such as the Green Movement.

In this view, then, class analysis has become so complicated that the nature of what we are studying ceases to be clear. Myriad variables are important to studying inequality, and 'class' as a concept can no longer handle this range. 'Class' can no longer be simply linked to the workplace as it is being replaced by 'lifestyle', 'differences' and all sorts of other inequalities linked to ethnicity, gender, sexuality, age and disability (see subsequent chapters). The failure of class analysis to seriously incorporate these concerns made it weaker and weaker. Indeed, some argue that 'class analysis' has become an area of academic study, of restricted relevance to only a few ivory tower academics! Others take a very different view.

# The continuing importance of class

Indeed, many sociologists – John Goldthorpe, John Scott, David Rose and many others – still take class as the central feature of societies. The nature of class may be changing, they claim, but it remains the central organising feature of industrial countries. John Scott argues that 'Class differences persist and have in many respects become sharper' (Scott in Payne, 2000: 38). Class here is not in dispute, but its changing character may be. These class theorists often point to a number of key changes, including the following:

1  The decreasing importance of the manual/non-manual labour distinction as manual work declines.

2  The collapse of a very traditional working class (for example, around mining communities).
3  The growth and diversity of the middle class, including the expansion of the service sector.
4  The identification of an underclass who are largely outside the class system and, indeed, society.
5  The introduction of both gender and ethnicity into various class schemas as a complicating factor.

While these sociologists do try to incorporate many of the issues raised by those who have suggested the end of class, they conclude that class is still the most important factor. Class, and class analysis, are far from dead. Indeed, this chapter should have clearly shown that although class patterns are changing, they are deep and widespread. 'Classlessness' may have been exaggerated, for there remains a very clear, powerful and strong upper class. People still strongly identify with class groups; and new divisions and polarisations continue to appear.

# The cultural turn and fractured identities

Many of the newer theorists try to take a conciliatory role between the older theories of class and newer accounts. Sympathetic to postmodernism and cultural studies, they suggest that the idea of any one overarching 'truth' about class is now unlikely. Older theorists of class sometimes placed a belief in the importance of class and class consciousness that may have made it too central, restricting their vision. Now class needs to be seen as cultural as well as economic, and closely linked to the wider social divisions found in contemporary society. In the work of Harriet Bradley, Beverley Skeggs and Mike Savage, the way ahead lies in the idea of recognising that we all now inhabit complex and changing cultures (see Chapter 5), embodying fractured identities (see Chapter 7) – identities that are not unitary or essential, but variable and changing and plural. People's sense of social location in social worlds is no longer simply a matter of class: their lives are bound into all the variations of inequality that this section of the book is discussing – class, yes, but also ethnicity, gender, age and other factors such as disability or sexuality. Bradley, Skeggs and Savage suggest that identities around class are now highly fractured.

Class, then, remains an important area of sociological analysis. Recent analyses and research, however, suggest that it continues to change its forms, and must be considered alongside a whole array of new identities and social changes.

# Citizenship and the rise of welfare states

An important development of modern, industrial capitalist societies has been the evolution of welfare states. A narrow definition of this would be 'the involvement of the state in social security and social services' (Cochrane and Clarke, 1993: 4). More broadly, some definitions of the welfare state include a commitment to full employment and a whole arena of welfare policies to do with education, health and families. Welfare states are therefore very much bound up with improving the quality of life for a society's citizens and reducing the problems generated through inequalities.

Most modern industrialised nations are welfare states – they increasingly have to deal with public problems and deal with them through public expenditure. In Britain, in 1981, 56.3 per cent of the government's budget was spent on welfare; in 1993, it was 64.1 per cent. This was despite having an anti-welfare government for much of this time. (Much of the rise, though, was due to costs of increased unemployment, etc.)

Some industrial societies, such as Sweden, have highly developed welfare states, while others, such as the United States, have only minimal ones. Nevertheless, it is a characteristic feature of modern societies that they have to devote large sums to welfare.

A central question in understanding the workings of welfare states concerns the extent to which they are run by governments or through markets (see Chapter 15). When the market dominates, we often talk of the **marketisation** of the welfare state – here it is run by *an economic system based on the principles of the market, including supply, demand, choice and competition.* Thatcherism (discussed in Chapter 16) attempted to bring marketisation into all spheres of life, including much of the welfare state. Thus, as we shall see, both education (Chapter 20) and health (Chapter 21) were to move to the principles of the market. Even prisons, as we shall see in Chapter 17, have moved towards markets and privatisation.

## The citizenship approach

The growth of state involvement with the 'welfare' of its citizens parallels the growth of industrial societies. In the optimistic version, this is a story of growing 'citizenship rights'. The key thinker in this area is the British sociologist T. S. Marshall (1893–1981), who argued that with industrialisation, citizenship emerged in three ways. These were:

1  *Civil*: the rights necessary for individual freedom – liberty of the person, freedom of speech, thought and faith, the right to own property and to conclude valid contracts, and the right to justice. The key institutions to implement this would be the civil and criminal courts of justice.

2  *Political*: the right to participate in the exercise of political power, as a member of a body invested with political authority or as an elector of such a body. This included such institutions as parliament and local elective bodies, along with the extension of political suffrage.

3  *Social*: the whole range from the right to a modicum of economic welfare and security, to the right to share to the full in social heritage and to live the life of a civilised being according to the standards prevailing in the society. Educational and social welfare institutions are the key here.

For Marshall, each of these sets of rights appears in distinct periods. In the Middle Ages, they were 'wound together' but weak. Civil rights emerged most clearly in the eighteenth century, political rights in the nineteenth and social rights in the twentieth century.[1] Many do not agree with the precise periodisation and remark that Marshall's model was developed through one case study only – that of the UK. When applied to other countries it does not fit so well. Bryan Turner (1990), for example, has suggested that the foundations of citizenship differ for France, Germany and Sweden. Marshall's model does raise a series of key issues about the emerging rights and responsibilities in modern societies.

## A Marxist approach

Marxists see the welfare state differently: instead of seeing it as a benign set of institutions that foster security and equality, they argue that it helps contribute to the smooth running of the capitalist order. In order for capitalism to work, it needs a well-trained labour force that is reasonably healthy and secure. The welfare state ensures this. Marxists suggest that advanced capitalism needs welfare to 'buy off' working-class dissent and maintain social order with a secure workforce (Piven and Cloward, 1972).

---

[1]  There is talk, at the beginning of the twenty-first century, of the emergence of a fourth cluster of citizen rights centred around 'intimate citizenship' (Plummer, 2003).

# The three worlds of welfare capitalism

In 1990, Costa Esping-Andersen published a much-discussed study of different kinds of welfare regime. For him, 'The welfare system is not just a mechanism that intervenes in . . . inequality; it is, in its own right, a system of stratification' (1990: 23). He argued that there were three major kinds of welfare system, though they are a little like ideal types (see Chapter 1). They can be evaluated as systems of **decommodification**, whereby the focus is on *the degree to which welfare services are free from the market*. (Commodification, by contrast, turns welfare issues into sellable things and needs markets.) The three main 'worlds' he locates are:

1 *Social democratic.* This argues for universal rights, equality and a kind of 'universal solidarity' in favour of the welfare state. It is largely anti-market. It takes on many family responsibilities and is a universalist model. Scandinavian countries largely adopt this approach.

2 *Corporatist/'Bismarck'.* Here, welfare is mainly organised through work itself, through business, tradition, church and existing powers. This approach does not enourage redistribution. While the state may deliver welfare, its aim is the maintenance of traditional families. This is a conservative model, found in Austria, France, Germany and Italy.

3 *Liberal.* This intervenes in the market as little as possible and gives benefits that are subject to strict entitlement rules. It is a basic safety-net approach, showing a direct line of inheritance from the old Poor Laws. It leads to market-based insurance for the wealthy and means testing for the poor. Private schemes are encouraged. Examples are the United States, Australia and Canada. The UK used to be close to the social democratic model, but under Thatcherism moved closer and closer to the market/liberal model.

Esping-Andersen derived this classification from his own research into pensions, unemployment insurance and sickness benefits. He examined levels of benefit, protection against risks and strictness of rules that govern access across a number of countries. It was on this basis that he could classify societies thus:

- Lowest scores for welfare – liberal: the USA and UK.
- Intermediate scores for welfare – corporatist: France, Germany, Italy and Switzerland.
- Highest scores for welfare – social democratic: Scandinavia, Belgium and the Netherlands.

More recently, Leibfreid (2001) has added a fourth group: the 'Latin Rim countries' – Spain, Greece, Portugal, southern Italy and part of France – which have 'rudimentary welfare states'.

# The welfare state in the UK

The UK is quite close to the liberal model but is, at least historically, a bit of a mixture of all three. Its roots go back to the Poor Law in Elizabethan and Tudor England, where government started to impose an elementary framework on what had previously been the task of churches and charities. But this rudimentary care of the sick broke down with mass industrialisation and the arrival of capitalism. In 1834 the Poor Law Amendment Act set up a national Poor Law Commission to oversee the development of a system with links eventually growing to state education and healthcare. All this shapes the 'state' links to a society's population, and especially its 'poor' and 'working class'.

Bit by bit, a system that was heavily *laissez-faire* gave way to a system that is more central and state controlled. By the start of the twentieth century, legislation such as the Pensions Act of 1908 and the National Insurance Act of 1911 provided cover for sickness and unemployment for some workers, introducing the 'insurance principle' into British social security.

The period 1945–75 may be seen as the years of the 'classic welfare state'. It was spearheaded by the work of William Beveridge in several major reports. Waging war on the 'five great evils' of 'Want, Disease, Ignorance, Squalor and Idleness', his plan for social security was to abolish Want – but only if the others could simultaneously be abolished (Beveridge, 1942: paragraph 8). This was a time when there was a commitment to a mixed economy, to full employment and to a welfare state that would provide universal rights. At this stage, the welfare state in the UK was closest to the social democratic model described above. In education, health, childcare and welfare provisions, the UK seemed to be moving towards this social democratic welfare state. There were 'means-tested' systems, but the broad principles stressed universality.

This was also the period when the National Health Service came into existence – a time very different from our own, when most people rented their houses, nobody had televisions but instead listened to the wireless, few had overseas holidays, only a minority had telephones, nobody had computers, and few had cars so most were dependent upon public transport. Social democratic thinkers believed the welfare state

# The Social Charter: social policies in the European Union

In May 1989, the European Community Charter of the Fundamental Social Rights of Workers – commonly known as the Social Charter – was approved. It was subsequently incorporated as the 'Social Chapter' into the Maastricht Treaty in 1991 (see Chapter 4). The Charter's main provisions included the following rights and guarantees of workers who hold citizenship in EU countries.

The rights were:

- to work in the EU country of one's choice
- to a fair wage
- to continuing improvements in living and working conditions
- to adequate social protection and social security
- to belong to a trade union (or professional body) and to be represented in collective bargaining
- to satisfactory healthcare and safe working conditions.

The guarantees were:

- equal treatment for men and women in the workplace, and 'enabling men and women to reconcile their occupational and family obligations'
- consultation between employers and workers
- protection of children and adolescents; with a minimum working age of 15, fair pay and reasonable hours
- a minimum decent standard of living for the elderly
- changes to make it easier for the disabled to become part of the workforce.

Until 1997, the UK opted out of the Social Chapter. In practice, the UK did recognise many of the conditions, but the former Conservative government objected to the regulations of maximum hours and minimum wages, as well as to fathers being given a statutory three months' unpaid leave after the birth of a child. The Conservatives argued that these provisions would increase industrial costs to a level that would make the UK less competitive with the United States, Japan and the newly industrialising countries. The Labour government elected in 1997 rejected these arguments and signed up to the Social Chapter.

Like most such mission statements, these ideal goals are not always followed in practice. Although there is a clear statement that men and women should be treated equally, in practice there remain significant pay and opportunity differentials. Additionally, the charter does not always allow for consistent enforcement. Some issues, including a 48-hour maximum working week and a common retirement age for men and women, are laid down centrally, but other matters, including the power to set the age of retirement, remain at the discretion of national governments.

Through the Social Protection in Europe Directive (1993), all EU countries must provide a basic level of support in unemployment benefits, pensions, cover for work accidents, health cover and maternity benefits. A predictable pattern emerges: a high level of protection in Sweden, as is the case for Luxembourg and the Netherlands; a low level of protection in Spain, Portugal, Ireland, Greece and the UK; and middle levels of support in France, Germany, Finland, Denmark, Belgium and Austria.

would create citizenship for all and would combat inequality. But by the mid-1970s – as unemployment surged forward and huge economic changes were in the offing – it was clear that it had not been especially successful in redistribution. Indeed, a number of commentators saw most of the benefits of the system going to the middle classes (Le Grand, 1982).

A new period was ushered in from the mid-1970s onwards. Most notably, from 1979 there emerged a much more 'anti-welfare state' approach. It was, as Prime Minister Margaret Thatcher bluntly put it, a rejection of the Nanny State. Monetarist theory (to be outlined in Chapter 15) was put into practice

and at the same time the 'classic' welfare state began to be 'marketised'.

When the New Labour government was elected in 1997 with a landslide majority, many believed that it would reverse the marketisation policies of the Thatcher years. While it set up a Social Exclusion Unit which aimed to target specific groups in need (such as the homeless) and to provide integrated services for them, in the main it continued with a policy in which the market was given a major focus. The new Coalition government elected in 2010 showed clear signs of accelerating this marketisation strategy.

# Looking ahead: class in the twenty-first century

This chapter has raised many problems about class and its role in modern industrial societies. We have seen that there are many problems involved in knowing just what it is; and at the same time we have heard both from sociologists who regard it as the key feature of modern societies and from others who see it as a factor in decline.

For the authors of this book, it seems impossible to deny the continuing role that class plays in social life. It is tangibly present through poverty, low incomes, extremes of wealth, prestige systems and status, and differing degrees of control over work and life. However, it is changing and new patterns of class are in the making.

At the same time, one of the most important lessons of recent times is that class on its own is a weak concept. It needs to be placed in specific circumstances and connected to other key issues such as social exclusion, gender, ethnicity and age: it is these which the subsequent chapters will examine.

# SUMMARY

1 Social inequality involves disparities in a host of variables, including income, wealth and power. Marxists would adopt an approach to measuring class that focuses upon the ownership of the means of production, while Weberians tend to focus on a range of variables, including work and market situation.

2 Occupation is a common way in which class is measured. The Registrar General's classification is the most commonly used such classification in the UK. This has recently been updated to the National Statistics Socio-Economic Scale (NS-SES). Income and wealth are other ways in which social class is often measured.

3 The upper class, which is small (about 5 per cent), includes the richest and most powerful families. Members of the upper-upper class, or the old rich, derive their wealth through inheritance over several generations; those in the lower-upper class, or the new rich, depend on earned income as their primary source of wealth. The middle class includes 40–45 per cent of the population. The upper-middle class may be distinguished from the rest of the middle class on the basis of higher income, higher-prestige occupations and more schooling. The working class, sometimes called the lower-middle class, includes about one-third of the UK population. With below-average income, working-class families have less financial security than those in the middle class. Only one-third of working-class children reach college and most eventually work in blue-collar or lower-prestige white-collar jobs. There is a growing 'underclass' – people outside society and the class system.

4 Social class affects nearly all aspects of life, beginning with health and survival in infancy and encompassing a wide range of attitudes and patterns of family living.

5 Since the early 1970s, changes in the economy have reduced the standard of living for low- and moderate-income families. One important contemporary trend is a decline in manufacturing industries, paralleling growth in low-paying, service-sector jobs.

6 An important aspect of modern capitalist societies has been the development of welfare states alongside the idea of 'citizenship'.

## MYTASKLIST

# Ten suggestions for going further

## 1 Connect up with Part Six and the Sociology Web Resources

As you work through ideas and think about the issues raised in this chapter, look at the accompanying website and the resource centre at the end of this book which connects to it. There is a lot here to help you move on. To link up, see: www.pearson.co.uk/plummer.

## 2 Review the chapter

*Briefly summarise (in a paragraph) just what this chapter has been about.* Consider: (a) What have you learned? (b) What do you disagree with? Be critical. And (c) How would you develop all this? How could you get more detail on matters that interest you?

## 3 Pose questions

(a) Assess your own social class. What factors would you have to take into account? Look at measurements that sociologists have invented. How well do you fit with these? Does your family have consistent standing on various dimensions of social stratification? Why do most people find talking about their own social position awkward?

(b) Identify some of the effects of social stratification on health, values, politics and family patterns.

(c) Is class dead? If so, why?

(d) What categories of people are at high risk of poverty in Europe? Does any evidence support the assertion that the poor are responsible for their situation? Does any evidence suggest that society is primarily responsible for poverty?

(e) Compare three 'welfare states'. Why is public assistance for the poor more controversial in some countries than in others?

## 4 Explore key words

Many concepts have been introduced in this chapter. You can review them from the website or from the listing at the back of this book. You might like to give special attention to just five words and think them through – how would you define them, what are they dealing with, and do they help you see the social world more clearly or not?

## 5 Search the Web

Be critical when you look at websites – see the box on p. 940 in the Resources section. For this chapter look at the following:

The Poverty Site
www.poverty.org.uk
This site monitors what is happening to poverty and social exclusion in the UK. The material is organised around 100 statistical indicators covering all aspects of the subject, from income and work to health and education. It is run by the Joseph Rowntree Foundation.

Child Poverty Action Group
www.cpag.org.uk
CPAG provides information about low-income families and the policies that affect them. It produces regular newsletters and fact lists.

Low Pay Commission
www.lowpay.gov.uk
This provides commentary, debate and the most recent figures, especially on the minimum wage.

Policylibrary.com
www.policylibrary.com/welfare
A useful guide to social policy issues.

## 6 Watch a DVD

Daryll Zanuck's *The Grapes of Wrath* (1940) is a classic film about the Depression and Alan Parker's *Angela's Ashes* (2000) is a striking depiction of poverty in Ireland. There is a fascinating cluster of early films about social class in Britain set in the 1950s – often seen as 'kitchen sink dramas' from 'angry [working class] young men'. These include: *Look Back in Anger*, *The Loneliness of the Long Distance Runner*, *Saturday Night and Sunday Morning*, and *Taste of Honey*. The films of Mike Leigh, such as *High Hopes* (1988), *Secrets and Lies* (1996) and *Vera Drake* (2004), convey both the humour and desperation of working-class life.

## 7 Think and read

### General sociology texts on class

Wendy Bottero, *Stratification: Social Division and Inequality* 9 (2005). A readable and comprehensive introduction to the UK class system examining all the key debates.

Tony Bennett, Mike Savage, Elizabeth Bortolaia Silva, Alan Warde, Modesto Gayo-Cal, David Wright, *Culture, Class, Distinction* (2009). Engages head-on with the recent critiques of class from postmodernist and other angles, and provides a replication of Bourdieu's classic study.

Fiona Devine and Mary C. Waters, *Social Inequalities in Comparative Perspective* (2004). A valuable recent series of essays on class systems in a range of (mainly Western) countries.

Tim Butler and Paul Watt, *Understanding Social Inequality* (2007). Uses contemporary theories to make sense of class, poverty and inequality in the UK.

### Discussions on poverty

Ruth Lister, *Poverty* (2004) A very valuable overview.

Tess Ridge and Sharon Wright (eds), *Understanding Inequalities, Poverty and Wealth: Policy and Prospects* (2008). A useful collection of readings and arguments in a student-friendly text.

Lucinda Platt, *Understanding Inequalities* (2011). The most recent critical overview of inequalities in the UK.

### The rich

George Irwin, *Super Rich: The Rise of Inequality in Britain and the United States* (2008).

### Exclusion, inclusion and welfare states

Ruth Levitas, *The Inclusive Society? Social Exclusion and New Labour* (2nd edn, 2005). Good on social exclusion.

C. Esping-Andersen, *The Three Worlds of Welfare Capitalism* (1990). Now the classic study of modern welfare which distinguishes three types (and clearly favours the Scandinavian model).

James Russell, *Double Standards: Social Policy in Europe and the United States* (2nd edn, 2010).

## 8 Relax with a novel

- Alan Parker's *Angela's Ashes* (2000): the compelling novel by Frank McCourt about grinding poverty in early-twentieth-century Ireland is also a vivid and striking film depiction of poverty.
- *The Grapes of Wrath* (1940): John Steinbeck's classic novel of the Depression. It was turned into a major, moving and classic film by John Ford in 1940.
- *Down and Out in Paris and London* (1933): George Orwell's classic account of tramps and derelicts working in kitchens and out of them. In a way, it is an early example of a kind of participant observation study.

## 9 Connnect to other chapters

- Link discussion of poverty and its measurement back to Chapter 9.
- Think about links to ethnicity, gender and age to be discussed in Chapters 11–13.
- Return to Marx and Weber in Chapters 2 and 4 and think of how this links to class.
- Think about issues of method. See Chapter 3 and ask: how do you know you are measuring class and poverty in a valid and reliable way?
- Link class to issues of identity, as discussed in Chapter 7.

# 10  Engage with THE BIG DEBATE

## Why does poverty still exist in high-income countries?

That the richest regions on earth – Europe and North America – are home to tens of millions of poor people and massive inequalities raises serious questions. Of course, many of the people counted among the officially poor in industrialised countries are better off than the poor in other countries – in the UK 30–40 per cent of people own their homes and nearly 30 million (half the population) own cars. But it is also the case, as noted earlier, that malnutrition and outright hunger are quite widespread, along with violence, illness and a host of other problems that accompany economic deprivation.

Debate these two approaches to the problem of poverty.

### Position 1: Blaming the poor – cycles of deprivation and cultures of poverty

One side of the issue is based on the following view: *The poor are primarily responsible for their own poverty.* Since the creation of the English Poor Laws, some thinkers in industrial nations have drawn distinctions between the 'deserving' and the 'undeserving' poor. Believing that social standing primarily reflects talent and individual effort, these people contend that industrial societies offer considerable opportunities to anyone able and willing to take advantage of them. The poor, then, are those who cannot or will not work, people with fewer skills, less schooling or simply lower motivation. While some people (historically, widows, orphans and the disabled) command our compassion as 'worthy poor', this line of reasoning leads us to condemn many people as, in one way or another, responsible for their own fate, and hence undeserving.

Some researchers have offered a different view, suggesting that a *culture of poverty* holds down the poor, fostering resignation to poverty as a matter of fate. Anthropologist Oscar Lewis (1961), who investigated the poor *barrios* of Latin American cities, is one of the early proponents of this view. Although Lewis doubted that most poor people could do much about their plight, he did not blame them individually for their poverty. Instead, he claimed that the *barrio* environment socialised children to believe that there is little point in aspiring to a better life. The result is a self-perpetuating cycle of poverty, as one generation transmits its way of life to the next. In the UK, this has been a widely influential model too.

Research in the United States led Charles Murray (1984) to much the same conclusion. Especially in areas of intense poverty such as the inner cities, claims Murray, a lower-class subculture has taken hold, eroding personal ambition and achievement. One element of this subculture, as he sees it, is a present-time orientation that encourages living for the moment. While a future orientation guides most better-off people to study, plan, work hard and save, Murray saw poor people as failing to look beyond the moment. In living for the present, he concluded, the poor perpetuate their own poverty and, therefore, reap what they deserve.

### Position 2: Blaming society – social exclusion and structural divisions

The other side of the issue can be summed up as follows: *Society is primarily responsible for poverty.* This alternative position, argued by William Ryan (1976), holds that social structures – not people themselves – distribute the resources unequally and are, therefore, responsible for poverty. Looking at societies around the world from this point of view, we see that those that distribute wealth very unequally (such as the United Kingdom) also have high levels of relative poverty, while societies that strive for more economic equality (such as Sweden and Japan) lack such extremes of social stratification.

Poverty, Ryan insists, is not inevitable. Low income, not personal deficiencies, cause the problem. Ryan interprets any lack of ambition on the part of poor people as a consequence rather than a cause of their lack of opportunity. He therefore dismisses Lewis's analysis as little more than 'blaming the victims' for their own suffering. In Ryan's view, social policies that empower the poor would give them real economic opportunity and yield more economic equality.

### Weighing the evidence

Each of these explanations of poverty has won its share of public support, and each has advocates among policy-makers. As Murray sees it, society should pursue equality of opportunity, especially for the young, but otherwise people should take responsibility for themselves, and their success will correspond to their talents and interests.

Ryan takes a more activist approach, asserting that public policy should reduce poverty through more equitable redistribution of income. Programmes such as comprehensive child care, for example, could help poor mothers gain job skills; indeed, the living standard of every poor person could be raised by a tax-funded, guaranteed minimum income for every family.

Certainly, both of these views could be put into practice, and many societies periodically lean towards one or the other. Typically, conservative policies are sympathetic towards the first, while left-leaning and liberal strategies are usually more in tune with the second.

## Continue the debate

1. What are the major groups in the communities of poor people? Is it reasonable to divide some of them into 'deserving' and some into 'undeserving' categories?
2. Why do you think poverty in Europe seems to be constantly on the increase?
3. Discuss strategies for reducing poverty.

# CHAPTER 11

# RACISM, ETHNICITIES AND MIGRATION

BOSNIA, A FEDERAL STATE OF THE FORMER YUGOSLAVIA, is a country marked by multicultural and ethnic differences. Its chronicler, Noel Malcolm, has said: 'There is no such thing as a typical Bosnian face: there are fair-haired and dark-haired Bosnians, olive-skinned and freckled, big-boned and wiry-limbed. The genes of innumerable people have contributed to this human mosaic' (1996: 1). In its 1,000-year history it has been touched by all the great empires of the European past: Rome, Charlemagne, the Ottomans and the Austro-Hungarians. It has harboured most of the major faiths: Western Christianity, Eastern Christianity, Judaism and Islam. And it has been home to migrants from all over Europe bringing their own languages and culture. It has long been home to Slavs (who arrived 1,000 years ago), and Muslims and Croats whose own states bordered it (Croatia and Serbia). In 1991, the three main groups were Muslims (44 per cent), Serbs (31 per cent) and Croats (17 per cent).

Yet 1992 marked Bosnia's destruction. A bloody civil war erupted between the Serbs (Orthodox Christians), the Croatians (Catholics) and the Bosnian Muslims. Estimated to have cost the lives of some 500,000, unleashing some three and a half million refugees, it also involved the systematic rape of thousands of Muslim women, the destruction of much of the country's infrastructure, and the desecration of its great ancient mosques and churches. Whole cities were destroyed, as each group claimed its territories and aimed to 'cleanse' other ethnic groups. The biggest and most hideous ethnic cleansing was of the Bosnian Muslims, attacked by the Serbs. After much humanitarian intervention, a settlement was reached in 1995 (known as the Dayton Agreement).

Although it was a 'local war', it eventually provoked international intervention. But even this could not prevent a large and devastating civil war. It has come to symbolise the modern 'ethnic' war complete with its horrendous atrocities and ethnic cleansings. Neighbouring groups hate each other and are willing to do the most terrible things. Today, most wars are not between nation-states. They are tribal conflicts between different ethnic groupings. It may be that the days of the big wars are over. What we are seeing is a proliferation of civil wars and 'tribal conflicts'. Currently there are some 30 civil wars taking place all over the world and the map later in the chapter documents some of these (see p. 370). This chapter probes both the differences of peoples and the hatreds that this generates.

*See:* Noel Malcolm, *Bosnia* (2002); pp. 368–9 and 553.

(Left) Ron Waddams, *We the Peoples . . .* 1984 (acrylic on board)

*Source:* We the Peoples . . . 1984 (acrylic on board), Wadams, Ron (Contemporary Artist)/Private Collection,/The Bridgeman Art Library.

*See* more of Waddams' work online at: http://www.larrenart.org.uk.

**Q** What do you see here? The artist uses elements from the near and distant past to create contemporary expression of spiritual and humanitarian concerns. Many of the works are reflections on living without conflict, and refer to the aims of the United Nations Charter.

*Race, as a meaningful criterion within the biological sciences, has long been recognised to be a fiction. When we speak of 'the white race' or 'the black race', 'the Jewish race' or 'the Aryan race', we speak in biological misnomers and, more generally, in metaphors . . .*

Henry Louis Gates

## In this chapter, we ask:

- **What are the meanings of race, ethnicity and racialisation?**

- **How can we start to explain prejudice and racism?**

- **What are the major patterns and problems around migration?**

- **What is the ethnic situation in the UK?**

Globally, the pattern of inequality and conflict based on colour, ethnicity and culture is becoming ever more pronounced. The extermination of Jews and other minorities, such as gypsies and homosexuals, in the Holocaust may mark the twentieth century's extreme low point (see Chapter 8), but ethnic strife still continues. Indeed, with the collapse of the former Soviet empire, Ukrainians, Moldavians, Azerbaijanis and a host of other ethnic peoples in eastern Europe are struggling to recover their cultural identity after decades of Soviet subjugation. In the Middle East, deep-rooted friction divides Arabs and Jews, while blacks and whites strive to establish a just society in South Africa. In Turkey there is conflict between the government and Kurdish nationalists; in Sudan between north Muslim Arabs and southern blacks, both Christian and animist – going on since the 1950s; in Sri Lanka between Hindu Tamils and Buddhist Sinhalese; in Rwanda between Hutus and Tutsis (see below); in Iraq between Sunni and Shi'ite. And, of course, in Israel between Jews and Palestinians. The list goes on and on (see the map in Chapter 16 on conflict zones).

In the African nations, the Asian countries, the Arab states, in the Balkans, and elsewhere in the world, racial and ethnic rifts frequently flare into violent confrontation. Every year or so we hear of new conflicts. There are, for example, major ethnic tensions in most large, urban cities, exploding intermittently as with the Los Angeles 'riots' of 1992 or, more recently, in the autumn of 2005, with the conflict waged in many French suburbs for over two weeks. In just two nights, over 2,000 cars were burned in large and small towns – Nantes in the west, Avignon in the south, and Evreux in Normandy (*Guardian*, 7 November 2005: 20). It was suggested that some 6,000 cars were destroyed in 12 nights. This was seen mainly as a conflict between black African youths aged 14–25, along with others from poor big-city suburbs, and the state: it was conflict between marginalised youth and France as a society. Between 7 and 10 per cent of France is ethnic and

The Rwandan Genocide was the 1994 mass murder of an estimated 850,000 people in the small East African Nation of Rwanda. The Rwandan military and Hutu militia groups systematically set out to murder all the Tutsis they could reach, regardless of age or sex, as well as the political moderates among the Hutu. Here a man looks at photographs of genocide survivors (see pp. 363–5)

*Source*: © Radu Sigheti/Reuters/Corbis.

**Map 11.1**

**The former Yugoslavia**

Yugoslavia as a country dissolved in the early 1990s into five independent countries and has been a site of many conflicts. We now have: Bosnia and Herzegovina (1992), Croatia (1992), Macedonia (1991–4), and Serbia and Montenegro (also known as the Federal Republic of Yugoslavia) which separated in 2006. Kosovo unilaterally declared its independence from Serbia in 2008.

See the introduction to this chapter and page 553.

*70 per cent of this is Muslim*. The national policy is generally assimilationist and integrationist, but this policy was seen to be not working. Further, the migration of displaced peoples everywhere across the globe nearly always generates cultural conflicts. Worldwide, ethnic antagonisms remain, fomenting hatred and mistrust, and propelling violence and war.

This chapter examines the meaning of ethnicities, and the racism and conflicts that often accompany them. It critically examines how these social constructs have shaped our history and suggests why they continue to play such a central part – for better or worse – in the world today.

# The social significance of nation, race and ethnicities

Most people living on the earth today live in nation-states. But this is a phenomenon of recent history. Ethnic groups made claims to their territories and right up to the sixteenth century people lived with these territorial limits. But between the sixteenth and nineteenth century, as we shall see later in more detail, nation-states as we now know them started to congeal (see Chapter 16, p. 545). Little by little, people came to identify themselves as belonging to 'nations'. In the words of Benedict Anderson, nation-states started to develop as **imagined communities**: *a socially constructed community, one which is imagined by the people who perceive themselves as part of that group*. The trouble is that behind this 'imagined community' lie many old ethnic divisions and conflicts seething away.

**Ethnicity** refers basically *to a shared historical and cultural heritage*. People frequently use the terms 'race' and 'ethnicity' imprecisely and interchangeably. Using the 'correct' language in the study of race and ethnicity can be very difficult. Some commentators prefer the language used by different ethnic groups themselves: the word 'black' (in the UK) or 'people of colour' (in the United States). The trouble here is that there is no agreement within these groups: some, often more political, people prefer one word; others may prefer another. For example, 'Asian' English-American black feminist Indian Kum-Kum Bhavnani suggests that 'black' is used in Britain as a political category for racialised groups – all those non-white groups who experience racism. This would include Pakistani, Bangladeshi and Indian groups. The word would then become a unifying force for a 'black movement'. But others do not agree. Tariq Modood argues that 'black' is not suitable for Asians in the UK because it generates a false sense of essential unity and is itself used inconsistently (it sometimes means only people of African descent). Indeed, he argues that most Asians do not use the term, and that what is really needed is a language of Asian pride with its own historical and cultural roots (Bhavnani, 1993; Modood, 1994). Using the 'right' language can be very difficult.

## Race and racialisation

'Race' itself is a very muddled, and even dangerous, concept. The idea of **race** came into use between the latter part of the eighteenth and the mid-nineteenth centuries: it is thus a modern idea. It usually refers to *a category of people who share biologically transmitted traits that members of society deem socially significant*. People may classify each other into races based on different physical characteristics, such as skin colour, facial features, hair texture and body shape. These differences are superficial; individuals of all races are members of a single biological species. People the world over display a bewildering array of racial traits. This variety is the product of migration and intermarriage over the course of human history, so that many genetic characteristics once common to a single place are now evident throughout the world. The most striking racial variation appears in the Middle East (that is, western Asia), which has long served as a 'crossroads' of human migration. Striking racial uniformity, by contrast, characterises more isolated peoples such as the island-dwelling Japanese. But no society lacks genetic mixture, and increasing contact among the world's people will ensure that racial blending accelerates in the future.

Nineteenth-century thinkers, such as A. de Gobineau (1816–82) in his *Essay on the Inequality of the Human Races* (1915; orig. 1853), developed a three-part scheme of racial classification. Labelling people with relatively light skin and fine hair as *Caucasian*, those with darker skin and coarser, curlier hair *Negroid*, and those with yellow or brown skin and distinctive folds on the eyelids *Mongoloid*, a 'race science' was established, in which, for example, Caucasians were seen as people of greater intelligence and higher morality! Sociologists consider such theories and categories not just as very misleading (since we now know that no society is composed of biologically pure individuals) but also politically dangerous (in fuelling the fires of racism). Indeed, this has led most sociologists to reject the very idea of race and to look elsewhere for better concepts to understand these issues.

Nevertheless, people around the world do seem quick to classify each other racially. This *process of ranking people on the basis of their presumed race* sociologists now call **racialisation**: it is at the heart of this system of inequality and social exclusion. As will be explained later, people may also defend racial hierarchy with assertions that one category is inherently 'better' or more intelligent than another, though no sound scientific research supports such beliefs. But, because so much is at stake, it is no wonder that societies strive to make racial labelling much clearer than the 'facts' permit. Early in the twentieth century, for example, many southern states in the United States legally defined as 'coloured' anyone who had as little as one-thirty-second African ancestry (that is, one African-American great-great-great-grandparent). Today, with less of a caste distinction in the United States, the law enables parents to declare the race of a child, if they wish to do so at all.

## Ethnicity and its problems: ten key words to think with

1 *Race/ethnicity*: race usually refers to a *presumed* significant biological difference between groups, whereas ethnicity refers to differences based on cultural, religious and historical heritage which confer distinctive identities. All societies are composed of cultures linked to many different ethnic histories.

2 *Racialisation*: refers to the social processes by which people are ranked, sorted and classified on the basis of their presumed race. Often such rankings devalue certain 'race' groups over others and are organised through political processes.

3 *Racial formation*: refers to a social structure which is organised around race, ethnicity and racialisation, although they change across history and across lives. It involves language and material conditions – and in lives we can see speak of racial projects: ways of organising and dealing with resources along racial lines (see Omi and Winant, 1995).

4 *Racism*: refers to the belief that *the genetic factors* which constitute race are a primary determinant of human traits and capacities, and that racial differences produce an inherent superiority of a particular race. The *new racism* suggests that *cultural factors* may also be the basis of this superiority and discrimination.

5 *Multiculturalism*: recognises both past and present cultural diversity and promotes the potential equality of all cultural traditions (see the *Big debate* in Chapter 5, p. 172). It refers to differences found across a culture based on race and ethnicity, and more generally, cultural differences. It is applied as a policy in a range of areas of social life, but especially in education. It argues for an ability to live with difference and to promote different cultural traditions as equally acceptable within a culture.

6 *Diaspora*: the movements (and scatterings) of different cultures and ethnicities across the world. Most nations (see Chapter 16) can be seen as composed of many different groups who have migrated and moved from country to country throughout history.

7 *Othering*: a process in which groups come to define themselves through the recognition of people outside their group as 'the other' – which usually means they are outsiders to be stigmatised.

8 *Politics of recognition*: a politics which gives priority to the importance of acknowledging human differences and according equal respect to these differences. It is often contrasted with a politics of redistribution, which is more concerned with equality. They are not in fact incompatible.

9 *Colonialism*: the process by which some countries/ nations enrich themselves through political and economic control of other countries.

10 *Intersectionality*: the connections between race and other forms of domination and exclusion, such as class, gender, sexuality, age and disability (as discussed in this section of the book).

For a full and lively collection of readings on all these issues, see Les Back and John Solomos (eds), *Theories of Race and Racism: A Reader* (2nd edn, 2009).

## Ethnicity, multiculturalism and the diaspora

Ethnicity is a valuable term, but not when it is applied only to groups that differ from us: everybody on the planet is part of a complex ethnicity. Members of an *ethnic category* have common ancestors, a language or a religion that, together, confer a distinctive social identity. The forebears of Pakistani, Indonesian, Caribbean, Hong Kong or Chinese Europeans – to name just a few – may well retain cultural patterns rooted in particular areas of the world. There are over a million foreign students in French schools (and three-quarters of a million in Germany) where German, English, Spanish, Italian, Portuguese, Arabic,

Hebrew, Russian, Japanese, Dutch, Chinese and Turkish are taught. In Britain, there exist around 100 minority languages – about a quarter of them taught in English schools, and in the United States, more than 30 million people speak a language other than English in their homes (Crystal, 2010).

But it goes deeper than just language. Most Europeans and Americans of Spanish, Italian and Polish ancestry are Roman Catholic, while others of Greek, Ukrainian and Russian ancestry are members of the Eastern Orthodox church. There are more than 6 million Jewish Americans (with ancestral ties to various nations) who share a distinctive religious history. Similarly, several million women and men in Europe have a Muslim heritage. Almost every country in the world is composed of multiple ethnicities, each harbouring its own culture and history. Chapter 5 has given you a more detailed discussion of this for Muslim cultures (see p. 158). In a loose sense, **multiculturalism** is a term used to indicate an awareness of this range of different cultures (see below).

Race and ethnicity may overlap, but one has a firm sense of biological difference (now very muddled) and the other relies on understanding cultural heritage. The two can sometimes go hand in hand. Gujarati Hindus, for example, can have distinctive physical traits and – for those who maintain a traditional way of life – cultural attributes as well. But ethnic distinctiveness should not be viewed as racial. For example, Jews are sometimes described as a race although they are distinctive only in their religious beliefs as well as their history of persecution (Goldsby, 1977).

Finally, ethnicity involves even more variability and mixture than race does, for most people identify with more than one ethnic background (a person might claim to be, say, German and English). Many Asians in the UK, for example, identify with quite specific ethnic cultures in Asia, as well as 'being British'. Often this leads to hyphenated identities such as 'Asian-British', 'Afro-Caribbean' or 'Black-African' (see Chapter 7 on identities). Ethnic communities can also vary greatly: from Punjabi Hindus (who speak Punjabi) and Gujarati Muslims (who speak Gujarati) who come from Indian states (Punjab and Gujarat); to those from Pakistan (such as Mirpuri Muslims), Bangladesh (such as Bengali Muslims) and East Africa (such as Uganda or Kenya). Table 11.1 provides a listing of key groupings.

Moreover, people may intentionally modify their ethnicity over time. Many West Indian immigrants to England have gradually shed their cultural background, becoming less 'West Indian' and absorbing new ethnic traits from others. In a reversal of this pattern, others have highlighted their background through 'Rastafarianism' (see below). Likewise, many people with native Irish ancestry have recently taken a renewed interest in their traditional ethnicity, enhancing this dimension of their identity. In short, ethnicity is about varying cultures (see Chapter 5) which are themselves changeable and fluid. Much of this leads to discussions of migration patterns, hybridities and diasporas – so we understand the paths along which different ethnicities have travelled in the world.

Studying these different ethnicities and cultures leads us to an awareness of diasporas. **Diaspora** refers to *the dispersal of a population from its 'homeland' into other areas*. Table 11.2 helps clarify what this term means.

## Minorities

A racial or ethnic **minority** is *a category of people, distinguished by physical or cultural traits, who are socially disadvantaged*. Distinct from the dominant 'majority', in other words, minorities are set apart and subordinated. The breadth of the term 'minority' has expanded in recent years beyond people with particular racial and ethnic traits to include people with physical disabilities; as the next chapter explains, some analysts view all women as minorities as well. Gays and lesbians have also been placed in a minority framework.

Minorities have two major characteristics. First, they share a *distinctive identity*. Because race is highly visible (and virtually impossible for a person to change), minority men and women typically have a keen awareness of their physical distinctiveness. The significance of ethnicity (which people can change) is more variable. Some people (many Reform Jews among them) have downplayed their historic ethnicity, while others (including many Orthodox Jews) have retained their cultural traditions and have lived in distinctive ethnic enclaves.

A second characteristic of minorities is *subordination*. As the remainder of this chapter will demonstrate, racialised minorities typically have less income, lower occupational prestige and more limited schooling than their counterparts in the majority. Class, race and ethnicity, as well as gender, are not mutually exclusive issues but are overlapping and reinforcing dimensions of social stratification.

While not all members of any minority category are disadvantaged, race or ethnicity often serves as *a master status or core identity* that overshadows personal accomplishments.

| Table 11.1 | 'Asians in Britain': contrasting groups | | |
| --- | --- | --- | --- |
| **Place of origin** | **Religion** | **First language** | **Community known as** |
| **(a) Indian subcontinent** | | | |
| *(i) India* | | | |
| Punjab State | mainly Sikhs<br>some Hindus | Punjabi | Punjabi Sikh<br>Punjabi Hindu |
| Gujarat State | mainly Hindus<br>some Muslims | Gujarati<br>(some Kutchi) | Gujarati Hindu<br>Gujarati Muslim<br>(Kutchi Muslim) |
| *(ii) Pakistan* | | | |
| Punjab | Muslims | Punjabi (some Urdu) | Punjabi Muslim |
| Mirpur (Azad Kashmir) | Muslims | Punjabi (Mirpuri dialect) | Mirpuri |
| NW Frontier<br>Province (very few) | Muslims | Pashto | Pathan |
| *(iii) Bangladesh* | | | |
| Sylhet District | Muslims | Bengali | Bengali Muslim |
| **(b) East Africa** | | | |
| Most have come from Uganda, Kenya, Tanzania, some from Malawi, Zambia; the families of most East African Asians originated in: | | | |
| (i) Gujarat State (main group) | Hindus<br>some Muslims | Gujarati<br>(some Kutchi) | EA Gujarati Hindu<br>EA Gujarati Muslim<br>(EA Kutchi Hindu)<br>(EA Kutchi Muslim) |
| (ii) Punjab State (India) | Sikhs<br>Hindus | Punjabi | EA Punjabi Sikh<br>EA Punjabi Hindu |
| (iii) Punjab (Pakistan) | Muslims | Punjabi<br>(some Urdu) | EA Punjabi<br>Muslim |

*Source*: Based on Coombe and Little (1986: 38).

| Table 11.2 | Some key features of diasporas |
| --- | --- |

1. A dispersal and scattering of people from an original 'homeland'.

2. A strong ethnic consciousness around the homeland and strong empathy with co-members.

3. This consciousness includes a collective memory and idealisation of an imagined community.

4. There is a discontent with the host land.

5. Frequently, a social movement is built with the idea of 'returning to the homeland'.

6. There is the possibility of a good life in the new land if it has a tolerance of pluralism.

*Source*: Based on Robin Cohen, *Global Diasporas* (2008: 17).

# Prejudice and racism

We have to ask why people hold such negative views of others based on their race or ethnicity. Three ideas help here: prejudice, stereotyping and racism.

## Prejudice

**Prejudice** is *a rigid and irrational generalisation about an entire category of people*. A prejudice is an attitude – a prejudgement – that one applies indiscriminately and inflexibly to some category with little regard for the facts. People commonly hold prejudices about individuals of a particular social class, sex, sexual orientation, age, political affiliation, race or ethnicity.

Prejudices can be positive or negative. Our positive prejudices tend to exaggerate the virtues of people like ourselves, while our negative prejudices condemn those who differ from us. Negative prejudice runs along a continuum, ranging from mild aversion to outright hostility. Because attitudes are rooted in culture, everyone has at least some measure of prejudice. Most people recognise that white people commonly hold prejudiced views of minorities, but minorities, too, harbour prejudices, sometimes of whites and often of other minorities.

## Stereotypes

Prejudices combine to form a **stereotype** (*stereo* is derived from Greek meaning 'hard' or 'solid'), described as *a prejudicial, exaggerated description applied to every person in a category of people*. Because many stereotypes involve emotions such as love and loyalty (generally towards members of in-groups) or hate and fear (towards out-groups), they are exaggerated images that are hard to change even in the face of contradictory evidence. For example, some people have a stereotypical understanding of the poor as lazy and irresponsible spongers who would rather rely on welfare than support themselves (NORC, 1994). As Chapter 10 explained, however, this stereotype distorts reality because most poor people tend to be children, women, working adults or elderly people.

Stereotypes have been devised for virtually every racial and ethnic minority, and such attitudes may become deeply rooted in a society's culture. In the United States, for example, half of white people stereotype African-Americans as lacking motivation to improve their own lives (NORC, 1994: 236). Such attitudes assume that social disadvantage is a matter of personal deficiency, which, in most cases, it is not. Moreover, stereotypes of this kind ignore the fact that most poor people in the United States are white and that most African-Americans work as hard as anyone else and are not poor. In this case the bit of truth in the stereotype is that black people are more likely than white people to be poor (and slightly more likely, if poor, to receive welfare assistance). But by building a rigid attitude out of a few selected facts, stereotypes grossly distort reality.

## Racism

A powerful and destructive form of prejudice, **racism** refers to *the belief that one racial category is innately superior or inferior to another*. Racism has pervaded world history. The ancient Greeks, the peoples of India and the Chinese – despite their many notable achievements – were all quick to view 'others' as inferior. Racism has also been widespread in our own history: indeed, it is probably found in every society in the world today. Thus in Australia, targeted groups include aboriginals, Pacific Islanders and Chinese, while in Denmark the Somalians and other refugee groups are objects of racism. It is hard to find cultures that do not have some form of race tension or conflict.

## Racism and social domination

Historically, the assertion that one specific category of people is innately inferior to another has served as a powerful justification for subjecting the targets of these taunts to *social* inferiority. By the end of the nineteenth century, European nations and the United States had forged vast empires, often ruthlessly and brutally subjugating foreign peoples with the callous claim that they were somehow less human than the explorers who enslaved them.

In the twentieth century, racism was central to the Nazi proclamation that a so-called Aryan super-race of blond-haired, blue-eyed Germans was destined to rule the world. Such racist ideology encouraged the systematic slaughter of anyone deemed inferior, including some 6 million European Jews and millions of Poles, gypsies, homosexuals and people with physical and mental disabilities.

More recently, racial conflict has intensified in western Europe with the immigration of people from former colonies as well as from eastern Europe seeking a higher standard of living. In Germany, France, Britain and elsewhere, growing public intolerance of immigrants has fuelled a resurgence of Nazi-style rhetoric and tactics. The United States, too, is experiencing increasing racial tensions in cities and on college campuses. Racism – in thought and deed – remains a serious social problem everywhere as people still contend that some racial and ethnic categories are 'better' than others.

## Explaining racism

If prejudice does not represent a rational assessment of facts, what are its origins? Social scientists have come up with various answers to this vexing question, citing the importance of frustration, personality, culture and social conflict.

**THINKERS & THEORY**

# W. E. B. Du Bois: race and conflict

One of sociology's pioneers, who has not received the attention he deserves, is William Edward Burghardt Du Bois (1868–1963). Born to a poor Massachusetts family, Du Bois showed extraordinary aptitude as a student. After graduating from

**William Edward Burghardt Du Bois (1868–1963). As well as being a founding sociologist, he was an intellectual leader of the black community in America, a civil rights activist, a historian and a Pan-Africanist. He helped shape a black standpoint sociology. Note that many sociologists have been actively involved in social movements for change**

*See*: Edward J. Blum. *W. E. B. Du Bois, American Prophet*. Philadelphia, University of Pennsylvania Press, 2007.

*Source*: africanpictures/akg-images.

high school, he went to college, one of only a handful of the young people in his small town (and the only person of African descent) to do so. After graduating from Fisk University in Nashville, Tennessee, Du Bois realised a childhood ambition and enrolled at Harvard, repeating his junior and senior years and then beginning graduate study. He earned the first doctorate awarded by Harvard to a person of colour.

Du Bois believed that sociologists should direct their efforts to contemporary problems, and for him the vexing issue of race was the paramount social concern. Although he was accepted in the intellectual circles of his day, Du Bois believed that US society consigned African-Americans as a whole to an existence separate and apart. Unlike white people, who can make their way in the world simply as 'Americans', Du Bois pointed out, African-Americans have a 'double consciousness', reflecting their status as Americans who are never able to escape identification based on colour.

Politically speaking, his opposition to racial separation led Du Bois to serve as a founding member of the National Association for the Advancement of Colored People (NAACP). Du Bois maintained that his research, too, should attempt to address pressing racial problems. Later in his life, Du Bois reflected (1940: 51):

**I was determined to put science into sociology through a study of the condition of my own group.**

**I was going to study the facts, any and all facts, concerning the American Negro and his plight.**

After taking a position at the University of Pennsylvania in Philadelphia, Du Bois set out to conduct the research that produced a sociological classic, *The Philadelphia Negro: A Social Study* (1967; orig. 1899). In this systematic investigation of Philadelphia's African-American community at the turn of the century, Du Bois chronicled both the strengths and weaknesses of people wrestling with overwhelming social problems. Running against the intellectual current of the times (especially Spencer's social Darwinism), Du Bois rejected the widespread notion of black inferiority, attributing the problems of African-Americans to white prejudice. But his criticism extended also to successful people of colour, whom he scolded for being so eager to win white acceptance that they abandoned all ties with those still in need. 'The first impulse of the best, the wisest and the richest', he lamented, 'is to segregate themselves from the mass' (1967: 317; orig. 1899).

At the time *The Philadelphia Negro* was published, Du Bois was optimistic about overcoming racial divisions. By the end of his life, however, he had grown bitter, believing that little had changed. At the age of 93, Du Bois left the United States for Ghana, where he died two years later.

*Source*: Based, in part, on Baltzell (1967; orig. 1899) and Du Bois (1967; orig. 1899).

# 1 Scapegoat theory of prejudice

*Scapegoat theory* holds that prejudice springs from frustration. Such attitudes, therefore, are common among people who are themselves disadvantaged (Dollard et al., 1939). Take the case of a white woman frustrated at the low wages she earns working in a textile factory. Directing hostility at the powerful people who operate the factory carries obvious risks; therefore, she may well attribute her low pay to the presence of minority co-workers. Prejudice of this kind may not go far towards improving the woman's situation, but it serves as a relatively safe way to vent anger and it may give her the comforting feeling that at least she is superior to someone.

A **scapegoat**, then, is *a person or category of people, typically with little power, whom people unfairly blame for their own troubles*. Because they are often 'safe targets', minorities are easily used as scapegoats. The Nazis blamed the Jewish minority for all of Germany's ills in the 1930s. And today some Europeans attribute troubles at home to the presence of Turkish, Pakistani or other immigrants from abroad.

# 2 Authoritarian personality theory

Theodore W. Adorno and his colleagues (1950) claimed that extreme prejudice was a personality trait of particular individuals. They based this conclusion on research showing that people who displayed strong prejudice towards one minority were usually intolerant of all minorities. Such people exhibit *authoritarian personalities*, rigidly conforming to conventional cultural values, envisaging moral issues as clear-cut matters of right and wrong, and advocating strongly ethnocentric views. People with authoritarian personalities also look upon society as naturally competitive and hierarchical, with 'better' people (such as themselves) inevitably dominating those who are weaker.

By contrast, Adorno found, people tolerant towards one minority were likely to be accepting of all. They tend to be more flexible in their moral judgements and believe that, ideally, society should be relatively egalitarian. They feel uncomfortable in any situation in which some people exercise excessive and damaging power over others.

According to these researchers, authoritarian personalities tend to develop in people with little education and harsh and demanding parents. Raised by cold and insistent authority figures, they theorised, children may become angry and anxious people who seek out scapegoats whom they come to define as their social inferiors.

# 3 Cultural theory of prejudice

A third approach holds that, while extreme prejudice may be characteristic of certain people, some prejudice is common to everyone because such attitudes are embedded in culture.

For more than 40 years, Emory Bogardus (1968) studied the effects of culturally rooted prejudices on interpersonal relationships. He devised the concept of *social distance* to gauge how close or distant people feel in relation to members of various racial and ethnic categories. Interestingly, his research shows that people throughout the United States share similar views in this regard, leading Bogardus to conclude that such attitudes are culturally normative.

Bogardus found that members of US society regarded most positively people of English, Canadian and Scottish background, welcoming close relationships with and even marriage to them. There was somewhat less of a premium on interactions with people of French, German, Swedish and Dutch descent. The most negative prejudices, Bogardus discovered, targeted people of African and Asian descent.

If prejudice is widespread, can we dismiss intolerance as merely a trait of a handful of abnormal people, as Adorno asserted? A more all-encompassing approach recognises that some bigotry is within us all as we become well adjusted to a 'culture of prejudice'.

# 4 Oppression of minorities

A fourth view claims that powerful people utilise prejudice as a strategy to oppress minorities. To the extent that the public looks down on Turkish guest workers in Germany, illegal Latino immigrants in the southwest United States, or refugees in the UK, employers are able to pay these people low wages for hard work. Similarly, elites benefit from prejudice that divides workers along racial and ethnic lines and discourages them from working together to advance their common interests (Geschwender, 1978).

# 5 The postcolonial plight and the new 'cultural' racism

While older forms of 'scientific' racism (with their focus on biological races as inferior) still continue, an important theory to have an impact upon race thinking recently has been **postcolonial theory**. This refers to *the wide critiques of (usually 'white') Western cultures that are made by people who have been colonised in the past.* As is well known, from the sixteenth century onwards (but especially during the nineteenth century) European colonial empires such as those of the British, Portuguese, Spanish, French, Belgian and Dutch were established all over the world. The indigenous peoples of Asia, Africa and the Americas became subject to cultural conquest – often enslavement and genocide, too. But in an even wider sense, postcolonialism can bring an understanding of the wider world historical process by which people have invaded other cultures throughout history. It is a feature of many societies that as one culture invades another, so it attempts to settle its own values and beliefs over it – from the Incas, the Ottomans and the Chinese through to the British in North America with the native Indian tribes. It is a major world process that leads to the blurring and fragmentation of different groups across the world, each of which generally creates its own sense of the threatening 'other' within its midst.

Postcolonialism challenges the superiority of 'white' or dominant thinking and listens to the voices of peoples who have been hidden from sight through this process of colonialisation. These are people who, in effect, have 'lost their voice' (see Chapter 2). At the heart of this critical position is the recognition of just how much 'the West' (in this case, principally western Europe and the United States) came to dominate the world throughout the nineteenth and early twentieth centuries. As Edward Said, a leading figure in the postcolonial movements, has commented:

> By 1914 . . . Europe held a grand total of roughly 85% of the earth as colonies, protectorates, dependencies, dominions and commonwealths. No other set of colonies in history was as large, none so totally dominated, none so unequal in power to the Western metropolis.

(Said, 1993: 3)

Such colonisation has left its mark on the world.

What these newer ideas highlight are the ways in which ethnicities depend upon different senses of collectivity and belonging among groups. They stress the ways in which boundaries – often defined as 'the nation' or 'us' – are created, maintained, challenged and transformed between different ethnic groups (Jenkins, 1997: 16–24). State policies (for example, on immigration) are often closely connected to identifying these groupings, which are frequently identified through 'race' and 'colour', and then made the source of boundary definition. Nationalism often takes on an importance in such discussions: just what does 'being British', 'being German', 'being Scandinavian' or even 'being European' mean?

The categories are far from simple. Take the case of 'being British'. Although claims may be made by some about the purity of the category, sociologist Stuart Hall has suggested that it is very much a 'mongrel category': 'Our mongrel selves and most cultures are inextricably multicultural – mixed ethically, religiously, culturally and linguistically' (Hall, 1992a). Thus, 'being British' – historically encompassing descent from many waves of European immigrants as well as peoples of the 'Celtic fringe' of Scotland, Ireland and Wales – must at the very least engage with major migrations from Asia, the West Indies, etc., with the history of the Commonwealth, and with many countries across the world that have some legacy of colonisation. To quote Paul Gilroy, a leading sociologist of ethnicity and race:

> We increasingly face a racism which avoids being recognized as such because it is able to line up 'race' with nationhood, patriotism, and nationalism. A racism which has taken a necessary distance from crude ideas of biological inferiority now seeks to present an imaginary definition of the nation as a unified cultural community. It constructs and defends an image of national culture – homogeneous in its whiteness yet precarious and perpetually vulnerable to attack from enemies within and without.

(Gilroy, 1987: 87)

## Discrimination

Closely related to prejudice is the concept of **discrimination**, *any action that involves treating various categories of people unequally.* While prejudice refers to attitudes, discrimination is a matter of behaviour. Like prejudice, discrimination can be either positive (providing special advantages) or negative (placing obstacles in front of particular categories of people). Discrimination also varies in intensity, ranging from subtle to blatant.

Prejudice and discrimination often – but not always – occur together. A personnel manager prejudiced against members of a particular minority may refuse to employ them. Robert Merton (1976) describes such a person as an *active bigot*. Fearing legal action, however, another prejudiced personnel manager may not discriminate, thereby becoming a *timid bigot*. What Merton calls *fair-weather liberals* may be generally tolerant of minorities yet discriminate when it is expedient to do so, such as when a superior demands it. Finally, Merton's *all-weather liberal* is free of both prejudice and discrimination.

Not all kinds of discrimination are wrong. Individuals discriminate all the time, preferring the personalities, favouring the looks or admiring the talents of particular people. Discriminating in this basic sense of *making distinctions* is necessary to everyday life and rarely causes problems. But discriminating on the basis of race or ethnicity is another matter.

All societies praise some forms of discrimination: in other words, while condemning others. Universities, for example, systematically favour applicants with greater abilities over those with less aptitude. This kind of discrimination is entirely consistent with our culture-based expectation that the greatest rewards go to people with more ability or those who work harder.

But what if a university were to favour one category of people (Christians, say) over another (Jews), regardless of individual talent? Unless the university had a religious mission (making a specific religion directly relevant to performance in school), such a policy would discriminate in a manner both morally wrong and against the law.

In historical terms, principles of fair play change along with economic development. In low-income countries, people routinely favour members of their families, clans, religious groups and villages. Traditional people typically recognise a moral duty to 'look after their own'. In high-income industrial societies, by contrast, cultural norms elevate the individual over the group, so that achievement rather than ascription guides our code of fairness. Many organisations, therefore, seek out the most qualified applicant while forbidding 'nepotism' or 'conflict of interest', by which employees would favour a relative or reject someone based on race or sex.

## Institutional discrimination

We typically think of prejudice and discrimination as the hateful ideas or actions of specific individuals. But far greater harm results from **institutional**

**discrimination**, which refers to *bias in attitudes or action inherent in the operation of society's institutions*, including schools, hospitals, the police and the workplace. Until the US Supreme Court's *Brown* decision in 1954, the principle of 'separate but equal' legally justified the institutional discrimination by which black and white children in the United States attended different schools. In effect, the law before *Brown* upheld institutional racism in the form of an educational caste system. Institutional discrimination remains one of US society's most intractable problems. Despite the *Brown* decision, relatively little has changed since 1954: while no US schools remain officially 'black' or 'white', most students still attend schools in which one race or the other predominates overwhelmingly. Indeed, in 1991, a court decision recognised that neighbourhood schools would never provide equal education as long as the US population was divided into racially segregated neighbourhoods, with most African-Americans living in city centres and most white people (and Asian-Americans) living in geographically and politically separate suburbs.

In the UK, the report by Sir William Macpherson into the murder of Stephen Lawrence suggested that police conduct during the case had been seriously lacking and that institutional racism was at work in the British police. On 22 April 1993, a young black man, Stephen Lawrence, was murdered by a gang of white youths as he waited at a bus stop. After the murder, there were complaints from the family that the murder had not been properly investigated and that indeed the police had behaved in a racist fashion. The Macpherson Report was a detailed investigation of the events around the crime, and concluded that although individual police officers may not have been deliberately prejudiced, the Metropolitan Police Service itself was 'institutionally racist'. Macpherson defined this as:

> **The collective failure of an organisation to provide an appropriate and professional service to people because of their colour, culture, or ethnic origin. It can be seen or detected in processes, attitudes and behaviours which amount to the discrimination through unwitting prejudice, ignorance, thoughtlessness and racist stereotyping which disadvantage minority ethnic people.**

(Macpherson, 1999: 6.43)

The report has been influential in generating public debate on police policy and racism in the UK.

# Oppression, prejudice and discrimination: the vicious cycle

Oppression, prejudice and discrimination frequently reinforce each other. W. I. Thomas offered a simple explanation of this fact, noted in Chapter 7. The Thomas theorem states: *if situations are defined as real, they are real in their consequences* (1966: 301; orig. 1931). Because people socially construct reality, stereotypes become real to those who believe them and sometimes even to those who are victimised by them. Power also plays a role here, since some categories of people have the ability to enforce their prejudices to the detriment of others.

Prejudice by whites against people of colour, for example, does not produce *innate* inferiority but it can produce *social* inferiority, consigning minorities to poverty, low-prestige occupations and poor housing in racially segregated neighbourhoods. If white people interpret social disadvantage as evidence that minorities do not measure up to their standards, they unleash a new round of prejudice and discrimination, giving rise to a *vicious cycle* whereby each perpetuates the other, as illustrated in Figure 11.1, even from generation to generation.

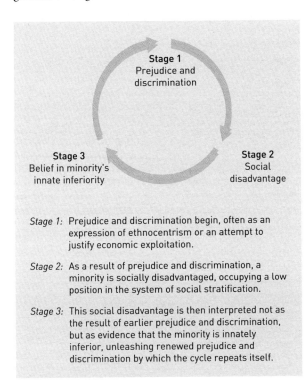

Stage 1: Prejudice and discrimination begin, often as an expression of ethnocentrism or an attempt to justify economic exploitation.

Stage 2: As a result of prejudice and discrimination, a minority is socially disadvantaged, occupying a low position in the system of social stratification.

Stage 3: This social disadvantage is then interpreted not as the result of earlier prejudice and discrimination, but as evidence that the minority is innately inferior, unleashing renewed prejudice and discrimination by which the cycle repeats itself.

**Figure 11.1**    Prejudice and discrimination: the vicious cycle

# Majority and minority: patterns of interaction

Social scientists describe patterns of interaction among racial and ethnic categories in terms of four models: multiculturalism, assimilation, segregation and genocide.

## 1 Multiculturalism and pluralism

**Pluralism** is *a state in which racial and ethnic minorities are distinct but have social parity*. In a pluralist society, categories of people are socially different, but they share basic social resources more or less equally. Most Western societies are – to differing degrees – pluralistic in several respects. They provide schooling and other services to all categories of people, and generally promise them equal standing before the law. Moreover, large cities contain dozens of 'ethnic villages' where people proudly display the cultural traditions of their immigrant ancestors. In London there are Arab, Chinese, Maltese, Greek, Italian, Jewish, 'West Indian' and, of course, differing Asian communities. In New York there is Spanish Harlem, Little Italy and Chinatown; in Philadelphia, Italian 'South Philly'; in Miami, 'Little Havana'; in Chicago, 'Little Saigon'; as well as Latino East Los Angeles.

Pluralism – living with difference – is one goal of the recent trend towards multiculturalism. As described in Chapter 5, this scholarly and political initiative seeks to promote an ability to live with difference and to accept as equal the many cultural traditions that make up our national life.

But, in other respects, much of the West remains far from pluralistic. In the United States, for instance, while most people appreciate and value their cultural heritage, only a small proportion of minorities want to live and interact only and exclusively with their 'own kind' (NORC, 1994). Further, in many cases, racial and ethnic identity is forced on people by others who shun them as undesirable. For example, people in many communities in the Appalachian Mountains of the eastern United States remain culturally distinctive because others snub them as 'hillbillies'. And worse: in recent years, rising levels of immigration have stretched many people's tolerance for social diversity. One reaction against the new immigrants has been a social movement seeking to establish English as the official language of the United States – hardly a strategy to bolster pluralism.

Switzerland presents a much sharper example of pluralism. In this European nation of almost 7 million people, German, French and Italian cultural traditions run deep. The Swiss have been relatively successful in maintaining pluralism (albeit, but critically, involving little difference in colour), officially recognising all three languages. Just as important, the three categories have roughly the same economic standing (Simpson and Yinger, 1972).

## 2 Assimilation

**Assimilation** is *the process by which minorities gradually adopt patterns of the dominant culture.* Assimilation involves changing modes of dress, values, religion, language or friends. This is the so-called 'melting pot' model in which various nationalities have fused into an entirely new way of life. At the turn of the nineteenth century, one immigrant expressed this perception in these words:

> America is God's Crucible, the great melting-pot where all races of Europe are melting and reforming. Here you stand, good folks, think I, when I see them at Ellis Island [the historical entry point for many immigrants in New York], here you stand with your fifty groups, with your fifty languages and histories, and your fifty blood-hatreds and rivalries. But you won't be long like that, brothers, for these are the fires of God . . . Germans and Frenchmen, Irishmen and Englishmen, Jews and Russians, into the Crucible with you all! God is making an American!

(Zangwill, 1921: 33; orig. 1909)

The melting-pot image is misleading as a matter of historical fact. Rather than everyone 'melting' into some new cultural pattern, minorities typically adopt the traits (the dress, accent and sometimes even the names) of the dominant culture established by the earliest settlers.

Not surprisingly, elites tend to favour the assimilation model, since it holds them up as the standard to which others should aspire. Many immigrants, too, have been quick to pursue assimilation in the hope that it will free them from the prejudice and discrimination directed against distinctive foreigners and encourage upward social mobility. But multiculturalists find fault with the assimilation model because it tends to paint minorities as 'the problem' and define them (rather than the elites) as the ones who need to do all the changing.

Certainly some assimilation has occurred. In the UK, while Afro-Caribbean and Asian cultures may be strong, they have also taken on many key features of British society. In the United States, as fast as some urban 'ethnic villages' disappear, new ones emerge, the product of a steady and substantial stream of immigrants. Almost 30 per cent of today's New Yorkers are foreign born – the highest percentage in 50 years. No wonder some analysts argue that race and ethnicity endure as basic building blocks of US society (Glazer and Moynihan, 1970).

As a cultural process, assimilation involves changes in ethnicity but not in race. For example, many Americans of Japanese descent have discarded their traditional way of life but still maintain their racial identity. However, racial traits do diminish over generations as the result of **miscegenation**, *biological reproduction by partners of different racial categories.* Miscegenation (typically outside marriage) has occurred throughout US history despite cultural and even legal prohibitions. Norms against miscegenation are now eroding and, while the share of officially recorded interracial births in the United States is still just 4 per cent, it is rising steadily.

## 3 Segregation

**Segregation** refers to *the physical and social separation of categories of people.* Some minorities, especially religious orders like the Amish of Pennsylvania, have voluntarily segregated themselves. Mostly, however, majorities segregate minorities involuntarily by excluding them. Various degrees of segregation characterise residential districts, schools, occupations, hospitals and even cemeteries. While pluralism fosters distinctiveness without disadvantage, segregation enforces separation to the detriment of a minority.

South Africa's system of apartheid (described in Chapter 8) illustrates racial segregation that has been both rigid and pervasive. Apartheid was created by the European minority it served, and white South Africans historically enforced this system through the use of brutal power. All this is changing dramatically, as the *World watch* box in Chapter 8 (p. 259) indicated. Likewise, in the United States, racial segregation has a long history. Centuries of slavery gave way to racially separated lodging, schooling and transportation. Decisions such as the 1954 *Brown* case have reduced overt and *de jure* (Latin meaning 'by law') discrimination in the United States. However, *de facto* ('in fact') segregation continues.

**Greater London poster**
Promoting an image of London's multicultural diversity

*Source*: Equality and Human Rights Commission. This poster was originally published by the Commission for Racial Equality, which is now part of the new Equality and Human Rights Commission: www.equalityhumanrights.com.

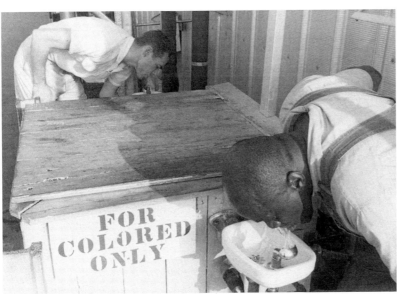

Only a full century after the abolition of slavery did the US government take action to dismantle the 'Jim Crow' laws that continued to separate people of European and African ancestry. Until the early 1960s, these laws formally segregated hotels, restaurants, parks, buses and even drinking fountains. More than three decades later, de facto racial segregation in housing and schooling remains a reality for millions of people of colour in the United States

*Source*: © Bettmann/Corbis.

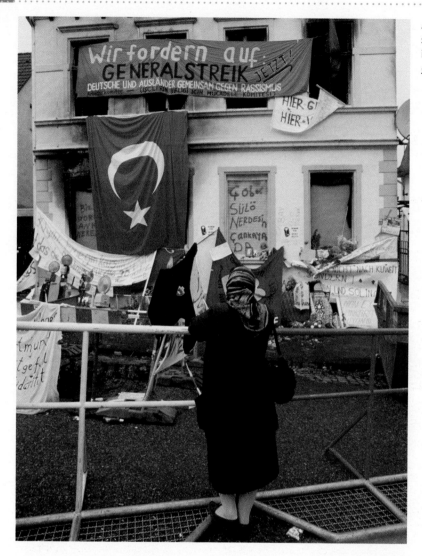

A woman looks at a burned house, site of the slayings of five Turkish immigrants by Neo-Nazis in Germany
*Source:* © Peter Turnley/CORBIS.

In the 1960s, Karl and Alma Taeuber (1965) assessed the residential segregation of black people and white people in more than 200 cities in the United States. On a numerical scale ranging from zero (a mixing of races in all neighbourhoods) to 100 (racial mixing in no neighbourhoods), they calculated an *average* segregation score of 86.2. Subsequent research has shown that segregation has decreased since then, but only slightly; even African-Americans with high incomes continue to find that their colour closes off opportunities for housing (Wilson, 1991; NORC, 1994).

We associate segregation with housing but, as Douglas Massey and Nancy Denton (1989) point out, racial separation involves a host of life experiences beyond neighbourhood composition. Many African-Americans living in inner cities, these researchers concluded, have

little social contact of any kind with the outside world. Such *hypersegregation* affects about one-fifth of all African-Americans but only a small fraction of comparably poor whites (Jagarowsky and Bane, 1990).

In short, segregation generally means second-class citizenship for a minority. For this reason, many minority men and women have struggled valiantly against such exclusiveness. Sometimes the action of a single person can make a difference. On 1 December 1955, Rosa Parks boarded a bus in Montgomery, Alabama, and sat in a section designated by law for black people. When a crowd of white passengers boarded the bus, the driver asked Parks and three other African-Americans to give up their seats. The three did so, but Rosa Parks refused. The driver left the bus and returned with police, who arrested her for violating the racial segregation laws. A court later convicted

# Spotlight

## The ways we exclude others: processes of social division

Throughout this part of the book we are discussing many processes in which people get excluded from society. Here are some key processes to think about, find illustrations of and discuss:

1  Social exclusion
2  The dominance and subordination of groups
3  Exploitation
4  Marginalisation
5  Stereotyping
6  Discrimination
7  Stigmatisation
8  Ghettoisation
9  Segregation
10  Colonisation
11  Violence
12  Pauperisation
13  Disempowerment
14  Silencing of voices
15  'Othering'
16  Dehumanisation
17  Genocide

Parks and fined her $14. Her stand (or sitting) for justice sparked the African-American community of Montgomery to boycott city buses, ultimately bringing this form of legal segregation to an end (King, 1969).

# 4 Genocide

**Genocide** is *the systematic annihilation of one category of people by another.* A more recent term for this is **ethnic cleansing**, a term used especially in the Bosnian conflict **described** at the start of this chapter. Some prefer **eliminationism** (Goldhagen, 2009). This racist and ethnocentric brutality violates nearly every recognised moral standard; nonetheless, it has occurred time and again in the human record.

Genocide figured prominently in centuries of contact between Europeans and the original inhabitants of the Americas. From the sixteenth century on, the Spanish, Portuguese, English, French and Dutch forcefully colonised vast empires. These efforts decimated the native populations of North and South America, allowing Europeans to gain control of the continent's wealth. Some native people fell victim to calculated killing sprees; most succumbed to diseases carried by Europeans, to which native peoples had no natural defences (Matthiessen, 1984).

# History in sociology: examining genocide

One strand of ways of doing sociology requires a critical inspection through history. Michael Mann's book *The Dark Side of Democracy* (2005) traces the history of genocides, and provides case studies of state murder such as the Nazis, Stalin and Mao. He tries to piece together these cases into a broader theory – an explanation of these atrocities.

Although murderous ethnic 'cleansing' is found throughout history (he describes the conflicts in the Assyrian, Greek and Roman societies, Goths, Mongols, Chinese and the Middle East, along with Ghenghis Khan, Attila and Ivan the Terrible), Mann suggests that it is distinctly modern – it has become a routine feature of the democratic process. Built largely out of ethnic conflicts, in the twentieth century he suggests it led to some 70 million refugees.

In 2003, to different degrees, these conflicts could be found in Bosnia, Kosovo, Macedonia, Algeria, Israel, Iraq, Chechnya, Azerbaijan, Afghanistan, Pakistan, India, Sri Lanka, Kashmir, Burma, Tibet, Chinese Xinjiang, the Southern Philippines, Indonesia, Bolivia, Peru, Mexico, the Sudan, Somalia, Senegal, Uganda, Sierra Leone, Rwanda, Nigeria, Congo, the Basque Country and Burundi. Inter-ethnic conflicts were multiple: Russians and Chechens, Sunni and Shi'ite Muslims, various Afghan tribes. Many involve substantial killings. It is estimated that in the last four years of its 12-year life, the Nazi regime killed some 20 million.

Mann highlights four linked networks of power which organise this terrorism and tyranny. He calls these ideological (concerned with value and rituals), economic (concerned with material interests), military (concerned with lethal violence) and political (central and concerned with the territorial regulation of life). He outlines those societies that are changing to democratisation as being in greater turmoil. Here enemy minorities – fairly old ethnic groups – are more easily found. These are largely in the South. Those in the North have become much more stable, though they have been through a major period of conflict in the past (between Catholics and Protestants, for example). These days such conflicts are less common.

*See: Michael Mann, The Dark Side of Democracy: Explaining Ethnic Cleansing (2005).*

Claims of genocides continue in the twenty-first century. In 2008–2010, a crisis emerged between Georgia and Russia. Both countries accused each other of military build up near the separatist regions of South Ossetia and Ankhazia. Increasing tensions led to the outbreak of the 2008 South Ossetia war. In this photo, a South Ossetian woman looks at the bodies of Georgian soldiers on August 13, 2008 in Tskhinvali. Georgians accused Russian tanks still present inside the Georgian town of Gori of destroying buildings and shooting at people. The president accused the opposing forces of setting up 'internment camps' inside South Ossetia to carry out a policy of 'ethnic cleansing' of the local population. The tem 'genocide' is possibly now overused: the numbers dead in this situation have been very hard to estimate

Trace current debates on: Genocide Watch: http://www.genocidewatch.org/.

*Source*: AFP/Getty Images.

R. J. Rummel, in his book *Death by Government* (1996), has coined the concept of **democide** to capture *mass murders by governments*. He argues that 'democracies commit less democide than other regimes' but shows how during the twentieth century some 169 million people have been the victims of state murders. He suggests that the Soviet Gulag state murdered the most – some 61 million – closely followed by the communist Chinese (35 million), the Nazi genocide state (21 million) and the Chinese Nationalist regime (some 10 million). Unimaginable horrors befell large numbers of outcast people. But Rummel's calculations do not stop here. He suggests that 5 million were murdered by Japan's military; 2 million were slaughtered by Pol Pot in Cambodia between 1975 and 1980: a quarter of the population perished in the Cambodian 'killing fields'; nearly 2 million were murdered in Turkey; and many more in Vietnam, Poland, Pakistan, North Korea and Mexico.

## Migration, ethnicity and race

We live in a world of some 200 million migrants – maybe 10–14 million of them refugees. About 3 per cent of the world's population are on the move (UN Development Report, 2009). Migration patterns – the movements of people in and out of societies – offer crucial clues to the workings of

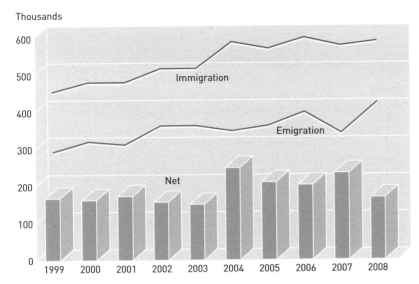

Thousands

**Figure 11.2**   Long-term international migration, UK, 1999–2008

*Source*: Long-Term International Migration (LTIM), International Passenger Survey (IPS), www.statistics.gov.uk.

societies. Not only do they help in understanding demographic patterns (discussed in Chapter 24), they focus attention upon the dynamics of different groups in a society. They highlight some of the major global inequalities across countries and the world. Often these 'migratory' groups become singled out in the processes of racialisation and discrimination. Bauman (1998) has distinguished between two major forms of global mobility. The *Vagabonds* are the mass of impoverished travellers who are on the move because they have to be (through government genocide, poverty or finding their country inhospitable). In contrast, the *Tourists* are those on the move because they want to be – who want to travel and who can afford to do so. In this chapter our main concern is with the former grouping.

There have always been migratory movements: sometimes voluntary, sometimes planned, sometimes forced. There has been exile, forcible repatriation and evacuation thoughout history. In the past, the distances travelled were often short, but with new modes of travel, vast distances have often been covered. Sometimes there have been enforced geographical dispersals of a people (for example, Jews). These are the **diasporas**. Sometimes peoples have been assimilated and absorbed into a host culture. Sometimes there is a refusal to have permanent settlers.

Until recently, four main patterns of migration have been identified:

- The *classical model*, which fits the United States, Canada and Australia. Generally such countries encourage migration and see immigrants as future citizens.

- The *colonial model*, which fits France, the Netherlands and the UK. Generally, migration to these countries has been heavily skewed to their colonies, giving them a kind of privileged position in as much as immigrants have potential citizenship rights.

- The *'guest worker' model*, which fits Germany and Belgium. Generally, migration here is temporary and without potential citizen rights. As with the other models, migration is usually for work – but in this case, conditions of employment and potential security of work are much weaker.

- The *'illegal' models*. Most countries have some illegal migration. It is characterised especially by people living outside the official society – and often, therefore, being forced to take the lowest-paid, most temporary and demanding work.

Traditionally, sociologists have suggested various phases through which migrants may pass. These phases of migration hold best for the classical pattern outlined above, but they are common in the others too. In phase 1 there is temporary labour migration of young workers who send their earnings back home, and have a strong feeling that they still belong to the homeland. In phase 2 there is often a prolonging of stay and the development of some new social networks. In phase 3 there is often a family reunion – issues of long-term settlement can now start to appear, along with the development of new ethnic communities. And in phase 4 (and depending on government policies) there is permanent settlement. This model is only an ideal type: it is much less relevant to certain groups of migrants, such as refugees or the highly skilled.

# Contemporary trends in migration

Recently Castles and Miller have suggested that migration is rapidly changing its forms in the twenty-first century. They suggest six key developments (2009: 10–12):

- *The globalisation of migration*: more and more countries are affected by migratory movements.

- *The acceleration of migration*: there are growing numbers in all major regions.

- *The differentiation of migration*: a wide array of types are found – refugees, labour migrants, permanent settlers – all at the same time. Sex trafficking has also become prominent.

- *The feminisation of migration*: many more women are playing a much larger role (until recently, it was mainly men who migrated in the first instance). Examples are Filipinos to the Middle East and Thais to Japan.

- *The politicisation of migration*: raising many issues from religious belief to domestic politics, as well as issues of national and international security. Migration raises political controversies all round the world.

- *The proliferation of migration transition*: traditional lands of emigration become lands of transit migration and immigration as well (e.g. Spain, Mexico, Turkey and South Korea).

This growth in global migration results in many cultures confronting more and more ethnic diversity. And as ethnic diversification grows, we find an increase in levels of racism.

## European patterns of migration

The history of Europe is the history of its migratory peoples. These migratory peoples may rapidly become outsider ethnic groups. So it is as well to remember that people originating from places as far flung as Africa, India and the Caribbean have lived in Europe for hundreds of years.

During the twentieth century, the European pattern may be seen as occurring in three main waves. Wave 1 was the 'European Exodus'. In the decades surrounding the turn of the nineteenth and twentieth centuries, it is estimated that 'around 52 million Europeans left their

countries and 72 per cent of them settled in North America' (Soysal, 1994: 17).

Wave 2 was the 'European Inflow', shortly after the Second World War, which saw a large number of immigrants in Europe. There were two main kinds of recruitment: one was of colonial workers – the inflow from former colonies – usually for work. This was true of the UK (with immigrants coming from Ireland, the West Indies and parts of southern Asia and East Africa). France experienced migration from former Southern colonies: by 1970, there were 90,000 Tunisians, 140,000 Moroccans and over 600,000 Algerians. In the Netherlands, some 300,000 Indonesians (formerly the Dutch East Indies) resettled (Castles and Miller, 1993: 72). The second kind of flow was from guest workers – they were 'guests' visiting temporarily and not, strictly speaking, immigrants seeking to become permanent citizens. They were expected to leave when their work came to an end and they had no political or economic rights: they were not citizens. Migrant workers constituted large portions of the manual working population in many European countries.

These workers may be seen as an **industrial reserve army** – *a disadvantaged section of labour that can be supplied cheaply when there is a sudden extra demand*. Throughout much of Europe, such migrant workers were brought in to swell the labour force and were central to the reconstruction of Europe.

Wave 3 came after 1973, when there was a marked decline in migration to Europe. In the UK, for instance, new legislation started to restrict migration. Currently, about 15 million migrants in Europe are 'foreigners' – that is, they have no formal citizenship status (Soysal, 1994: 22). Foreign workers vary greatly: in 1990, they made up 2 per cent of the labour force in Denmark but 18 per cent in Switzerland. The Swedish have classically lacked much migration. In 1975, a new policy emerged that stressed equality between immigrants and Swedes, freedom of cultural choice for immigrants and cooperation between the native Swedish majority and various ethnic minorities (Soysal, 1994: 47).

More recently there have been significant changes in the migration patterns in the EU. The Maastricht Treaty (see Chapter 4, p. 128) meant that less developed nations such as Poland, Bulgaria and Romania entered the EU between 2004 and 2007; and that the whole area became a *borderless* continent for its members. This meant that EU members were free to move from country to country.

In the UK, for instance, it was estimated that some half a million new migrants arrived from within the EU (mainly from Poland) – often seeking low-paid work.

## Refugees and migration in crisis

Throughout the world, through wars, genocides, conflicts and disasters, people are compelled to leave their homes. Sometimes this leads to refugee settlements, and sometimes long journeys to find a 'new home' – at least for a while. The photos below indicate some of the most recent humanitarian crises.

Afghanistan has a population of around 28 million – with several million living in refugee camps in Pakistan and Iran. From the 1930s to the 1970s it had a stable monarchy. This was overthrown by Marxist rebels and the USSR in the 1970s, which in turn were overthrown in 1992 through the establishing of an Islamic republic. In 1996, this was overthrown by the Taliban – a fundamentalist faction of Islam.

(a) An Afghan refugee family waits at a refugee camp before their departure from Islamabad to Afghanistan, 6 May 2004. Thousands of Afghan refugees have returned to their homeland as part of the UNHCR repatriation programme

(b) Members of five families from Fallujah rest at a relative's home after fleeing the American siege of their city. They brought 39 people in all and among them was 17-year-old Sajidah Hameed, who was to be married in four days. Her fiancé was among the estimated 600 people from Fallujah, Iraq, who were killed in fighting with American troops (April 2004)

(c) Médecins Sans Frontières hospital on the Sudanese border. Nutrition centre for children, Tine, Chad, April 2004

(d) Iraqi Kurds on Isik Veren Mountain, Turkey

*Source*: (a) © Faisal Mahmood/Reuters/Corbis; (b) © Ed Kashi/Corbis; (c) © Patrick Robert/Corbis; (d) © Peter Turnley/Corbis.

# Living through ethnic cleansing

*Stevan Weine spent many years talking with Bosnians who had witnessed ethnic cleansing. Below is one of the testimonies he gathered.*

For the first ten days they didn't give us any food. Then they fed us once a day at 6.00. They gave us three minutes to come from our building to the kitchen. Some of us were more than 50 metres away, and we had no chance to reach the kitchen. Those who came had three minutes to eat. Those who did not had no food. The guards formed a line that we had to run through to get to the kitchen. As we ran they beat us with guns, wheels, and tools.

After eleven days I asked them to let me go to the washroom just to wash my face. When I got there I didn't see that two men from Koïarac also came inside along with some soldiers from special units. The soldiers started to beat them. When they saw me they took me to a place with a big sink and started to beat me. They told me to lick the floor of this washroom for 20,000 people which was dirty with urine and sewage. They broke my ribs. I vomited for one month. I vomited blood.

Sometimes they put us in a 4 x 4 meter room – 700 people. They told us to lie down and they closed the windows and the doors. It was summer.

We lay like sardines in a can. Those on top were in the best position. Every morning, some on the bottom were dead. Every morning a guard came with a list and called people's names. Those they brought out never came back.

One day they came at 3 a.m. and they brought out 174 people. I was one of them. They lined us up behind a building they called the White House. Ten soldiers came with automatic weapons and they started to shoot us. Only three of us survived.

The worst event was when I watched one young man as they castrated him. Right now I can hear his cry and his prayers to be killed. And every night it wakes me. He was a nice young man. His executioner was his friend from school. He cut his body and he licked his blood. He asked him just to kill and to stop all that suffering. All day and all night we heard his prayers and his crying until he died. This is something that I cannot forget. It gives me nightmares and makes sleep almost impossible. I can't remember the people who were the executioners. For me all of them in those uniforms were the same. I can't remember who was who.

At the end of our first meeting, H. said I am all tears. When I speak about that even though my eyes are open I see all those images in front of me.

The second meeting begins tentatively, with H. saying, it is difficult to talk about anything when all the days were similar. So we review the last meeting's testimony with him and ask some questions to restart the dialogue.

Here in my neighborhood there is a man who was with me in the camp. He was a prisoner, like me, but he had the duty to beat us in order to save his own skin. And he did that very well. He wasn't alone. I know many examples of people like him. They had to do that just to survive. But I preferred it when he beat me. I always stayed on my feet. He didn't beat as hard as the others. I remember also one other man. He was a Muslim. He was very violent. He killed many prisoners. Finally we prisoners killed him by our own hands.

'You were there when that happened?'

Yes I was there. They moved him from our camp but then after some time they brought him back. And they pushed him inside a crowd of prisoners because they knew what would happen. All of us participated in that. One thousand people. And nobody could say 'I killed him' because all of us did. I didn't directly participate in the killing. But I was in the same room. I do not feel guilty. I wished to be in that group – the execution group – and I wished to participate in killing him. But I was really very weak.

I have to say something about the first prisoner who beat us and any other person who had to do the same job he did. Some people came to my house in Chicago to ask me to sign a note condemning him. I didn't do that because I do not think he is guilty. He helped many people. He didn't beat us like the Serbs did. He saved many, many lives. He needed to do that to save his own life.

Our region had very rich soil, and we had many farm animals. Day after day the Serbs brought our animals, and Muslim butchers had to slaughter them and put them in freezer trucks. Every day for two and a half months freezer trucks took that meat somewhere. Almost everything went into Serbia. The Serbs passed through our region especially to find gold and money. If someone wished to take all your property, he came and asked you to sign a paper that was something like a will, and you left him everything you had – car, truck, house, and everything inside. And for that he gave you a piece of bread. But if he went to your house and he couldn't find everything you signed over to him, he would then kill your family and come back into the camp and kill you.

I want to tell you something else. We had a special platoon. About a hundred prisoners had the duty of taking the bodies of murdered people, putting them in trucks, and bringing them to a special place with pits to dispose of them. They knew where they put all the Muslim bodies. One day before our camp was closed, before the Red Cross came, the soldiers killed all of them. Serbs killed all one hundred Muslims just to wipe out all witnesses. I was not in that group because I was too weak and too thin.

*Source:* Weine (1999: 35–6).

The events of 11 September 2001 identified the Taliban as protecting Osama bin Laden and a bombing campaign was started by US and British forces. By 2010, the country was one of the poorest and most conflict-torn countries on earth. It is not surprising that it had generated the largest number of refugees (see Table 9.6 on p. 301).

Sudan has a population of 38 million and is the largest country in Africa. The majority of its population are Arab Muslims (22 million – over 50 per cent), who are in the north; by contrast, groups in the south (rich in oil) (and rival groups including the Dinka (11.5 per cent), the Nuba (8.1 per cent), the Zande and the Nuer) tend to be Christian or Animist. From 1898 to 1956, the British colonised much of the area. Since that time there has been constant strife/war between the non-Muslim 'black' population of the south and the Arab Muslim-controlled government of the north; 30,000 people are believed to have died in the war, and several million from the south are now homeless. It is considered to be one of the worst humanitarian crises the world has seen.

Rwanda is quite a small country (population 7 million) tucked away in east central Africa (bordered by Uganda, Tanzania, Burundi and the Congo). It has a life expectancy of around 38.5. It was originally inhabited by the Twa, and became home to the Hutu. The Tutsi appeared in the fourteenth century and came to rule in the fifteenth. There is a long history of periodic rules first by Hutu and then by Tutsi. In 1962 the Hutu took rule again, and waged wars and genocide, massacring over 500,000 Tutsi. And then as the Tutsi fought back, it left some 2 million refugees, mainly Hutu, to flee to neighbouring countries.

# North America: who is the majority in the land of migration?

Although Europe may be seen as a continent of migration, the figures of ethnic groups present in Europe are small when compared with those found in the United States, truly the modern land of migration. Table 11.3 shows just how many groups have settled in the United States, and any visit to Ellis Island off New York – the place where most of the migrating people first arrived – would soon confirm the enormity of this migration pattern.

With such a vast pattern of migration, the argument is now made that 'white' groupings are becoming a minority. During the 1980s, Manhattan, the central borough of New York City, gained a minority-majority. This means that people of African, Asian and Latino descent, together with other racial and ethnic minorities, became a majority of the population. The same transformation has taken place in 186 counties across the United States (some 6 per cent of the total). As early as 2050, according to some projections, minorities will represent a majority of the country.

## THE WORLD AS A CONFLICTUAL DIASPORA

*Despite wide global movement, only 3% of the world's people*
*are living in a different country from where they were born (Smith. 2008:32)*

**WORLD REFUGEES**

*Europe:* Refugees from Iraq, Serbia and Turkey are largest groups. Europe hosts 16% of refugees with Germany (600,000) and the UK (270,000) hosting most.

**WORLD REFUGEES**

*Americas:* Smallest numbers of refugees. The USA with 275,000 refugees is the region's largest host. Columbians are the largest group of refugees (mainly to Ecuador).

**MIGRATION FLOWS**

*Canada*: Historically one of the most liberal and open societies for migration.
*The Black Atlantic*: black cultures right across the Atlantic basin - this implies movements rather than a specific place (see Gilroy, 1993).
*Mexico*: It is estimated that more than 10% of Mexico's total population (around 116 million) live in the USA - about 6 million illegally (Ritzer, 2010: 304).

**MIGRATION FLOWS**

*USA*: The United States is truly the modern land of migration.
Only 37% of global migration involves movement from poor to rich countries.

**ETHNIC CONFLICTS/TRIBAL WARS**

Many countries have deep-seated internal ethnic rivalries and tribal warfares. In Afghanistan, for example, there are continuing conflicts between the Pashtuns of the south and the Kabul regime, which is controlled by the northern Tajiks, Uzbeks and Hazara. But there are also conflicts in many other places, such as:
Mexico: Zapatista
Soviet Union: Georgia
Sri Lanka: Sinhalese-Tamil
Yugoslavia: Bosnia, Kosovo

**WORLD REFUGEES**

*Africa:* Over 2 million refugees live in Africa, with Somalia and DR Congo as key areas.
*Middle East and North Africa*
Around 2 million refugees. Occupied territories contain 4.8 million Palestinians.

NORTH AMERICA

ATLANTIC OCEAN

EUR

AFR

SOUTH AMERICA

**Map 11.2**    The world as a conflictual diaspora

**MIGRATION FLOWS**

*Europe*: The Maastricht Treaty (see Chapter 4) set out a timetable for European integration and the new status of EU citizenship. It created a borderless community with members having citizenship across member countries. Large numbers moved from poorer countries to richer ones in search of work.

**WORLD REFUGEES**

*Afghanistan*: In 2010, some 2.9 million refugees were living in 71 host countries.

**MIGRATION FLOWS**

*Arab countries*: In most Arab Gulf countries the labour force consists of up to 80% migrant workers. The major sending countries are the Philippines, Indonesia, Sri Lanka, Nepal and Bangladesh. These countries also supply labour for Japan, South Korea, Taiwan, Malaysia and Thailand. About 10% of the population of Philippines, 8 million people, are engaged in work away from their home country.

**WORLD REFUGEES**

*General figures*
In 2010, 43.3 million people were forcibly displaced around the world, including 27.1 million internally displaced people (IDP) and 15.6 million refugees. This is the highest number of displaced people worldwide since the 1990s.
*Key movements*
The key drivers of these trends are continuing conflicts in countries such as Afghanistan, Somalia and the Democratic Republic of Congo. Conflicts in places such as Iraq and Sudan are also prominent. Colombia's 3.3 million internally displaced persons are the highest number in the world. African nations account for 40% of the world's internally displaced population.
*Resettlement*
Four out of every five refugees are housed in the developing world, with Europe only accounting for the resettlement of 16% of the global population.
*The internally displaced*
27.1 million people were displaced in their own country in 2009. Columbia, Congo and Pakistan have witnessed the largest numbers.

**GLOBAL ETHNICITIES**

The USA is a land of migration and ethnic diversities: the Rainbow Coalition (see Table 11.3).
China, Australia and mainland Europe are the most homogenous (under 10% diversity: Smith, 2008: 23).
India, many central African states and Indonesia have 50% ethnic diversity: non-single ethnic or national groups are more than 50% of the population. Indonesia identifies over 300 ethnic groups speaking some 700 languages (see Smith, 2008: 22-3).

| Table 11.3 | The Rainbow Coalition: racial and ethnic categories in the United States, 2007 | |
|---|---|---|
| **Racial or ethnic classification*** | **Approximate US population** | **Share of total population (%)** |
| **Hispanic descent** | **45,427,437** | **15.1%** |
| Mexican | 29,166,981 | 9.7 |
| Puerto Rican | 4,120,205 | 1.4 |
| Cuban | 1,611,478 | 0.5 |
| Other Hispanic | 10,528,773 | 3.5 |
| **African descent** | **38,756,452** | **12.8** |
| Nigerian | 225,284 | 0.1 |
| Ethiopian | 159,809 | 0.1 |
| Somalian | 90,363 | < |
| Other African | 38,280,996 | 12.7 |
| **Native American descent** | **2,365,347** | **0.8** |
| American Indian | 1,922,043 | 0.6 |
| Alaska Native Tribes | 110,556 | < |
| Other Native American | 332,748 | 0.1 |
| **Asian or Pacific Island descent** | **13,667,962** | **4.4** |
| Chinese | 3,045,592 | 1.0 |
| Asian Indian | 2,570,166 | 0.9 |
| Filipino | 2,412,446 | 0.8 |
| Vietnamese | 1,508,489 | 0.5 |
| Korean | 1,344,171 | 0.4 |
| Japanese | 803,092 | 0.3 |
| Cambodian | 218,624 | 0.1 |
| Other Asian or Pacific Islander | 1,765,382 | 0.6 |
| **West Indian descent** | **2,231,842** | **0.7** |
| **Arab descent** | **1,545,982** | **0.5** |
| **Non-Hispanic European descent** | **198,696,006** | **65.9** |
| German | 50,756,529 | 16.8 |
| Irish | 36,495,800 | 12.1 |
| English | 28,178,670 | 9.3 |
| Italian | 17,849,848 | 5.9 |
| Polish | 9,976,358 | 3.3 |
| French | 9,616,662 | 3.2 |
| Scottish | 6,019,281 | 2.0 |
| Dutch | 5,071,425 | 1.7 |
| Norwegian | 4,655,711 | 1.5 |
| **Two or more races** | **6,509,013** | **2.2** |

* People of Hispanic descent may be of any race. Many people also identify with more than one ethnic category. Therefore, figures total more than 100 per cent.

< indicates less than 1/10 of 1 per cent.

*Source*: US Census Bureau (2008).

# Ethnicity in the UK

So far, we have drawn a rather broad map, suggesting that racism is a continuing feature across the world. We will now consider the specific case of the UK. Table 11.4 below presents the broad sweep of racial and ethnical diversity in the UK, as recorded by the 2001 Census. Every country in the world can be analysed in terms of its ethnic dimensions.

## Brief history: ethnicity, migration and conflict

The timeline on p. 374 outlines some of the significant developments and conflicts in ethnic relations in the UK over many years. We can go back a long way. Since the Anglo-Saxon invaders of the sixth and seventh centuries drove Celtic-speaking Britons into Wales, Cornwall and the Scottish highlands, England has been more ethnically homogenous than most of the rest of Europe. Nevertheless, there have been 'blacks' in England for hundreds of years (as many as 20,000 in the eighteenth century), who were often sailors or servants of white masters. Black communities often grew around seaports such as Liverpool. In the nineteenth century, migrants to the cities were from the less wealthy or developing areas of the UK, such as Ireland, Wales and Scotland. London, Manchester, Liverpool and Glasgow had large settlements from Ireland (by 1851, half a million Irish had settled in England and Wales). Jews started migrating in significant numbers around the time of the First World War and there was an acceleration during the 1930s. Nearly all the major migration during this latter period came from western European countries.

In modern times, the critical period for migration to the UK followed the Second World War. This was a part of massive immigration into Europe from all over the world – estimated to involve around 30 million people. At this time, after the war, there was a marked labour shortage which made many countries seek new reserves of labour. It was also a time when the colonies – so critical at an earlier period – were coming to an end. In England, the new Commonwealth (India, Pakistan and the West Indies) was important and provided a major recruiting base for migration and labour.

Initially, the largest postwar immigrant group coming to Britain were the Irish – nearly 900,000.

| Table 11.4 | Population of Great Britain by ethnic group and age, 2008 (%) | | | |
|---|---|---|---|---|
| | Under 16 | 16–64 | 65 and over | All people |
| White | | | | |
|   White British | 18 | 65 | 17 | 100 |
|   White Irish | 7 | 68 | 25 | 100 |
|   Other White | 14 | 75 | 12 | 100 |
| Mixed | 51 | 47 | 2 | 100 |
| Asian or Asian British | | | | |
|   Indian | 20 | 72 | 8 | 100 |
|   Pakistani | 34 | 62 | 4 | 100 |
|   Bangladeshi | 36 | 61 | 4 | 100 |
|   Other Asian | 23 | 73 | 5 | 100 |
| Black or Black British | | | | |
|   Black Caribbean | 20 | 66 | 13 | 100 |
|   Black African | 33 | 64 | 2 | 100 |
|   Other Black | 37 | 57 | 6 | 100 |
| Chinese | 12 | 83 | 5 | 100 |
| Other ethnic group | 20 | 75 | 4 | 100 |
| All ethnic groups | 19 | 65 | 16 | 100 |

*Source: Social Trends*, 40 (2010), Table 1.4, p. 4.

## Timeline Ethnic divides in the UK

### Prior to the 1950s

| | |
|---|---|
| 1066 | Norman invasion of Britain from northern France. |
| 1362 | English language legally recognised. |
| 1707 | Union of Scotland and England. |
| 1807 | Slave trade abolished in the British Empire. |
| 1834–8 | Slavery abolished in the British Empire. |
| 1892 | Dadabhai Naoroji is the first Asian elected to the House of Commons. |
| 1919 | Anti-black riots in Liverpool. |
| 1921 | Anglo-Irish Treaty established Eire; six northern counties with a Protestant majority to remain as part of the UK. |
| 1930–40s | Around 60,000 Jews come to Britain to escape Nazis and the war. |

### The modern period: from the 1950s

| | |
|---|---|
| 1948 | British Nationality Act: distinguished British subjects who were citizens of the UK, and those from the Commonwealth and colonies. Both groups could enter and work in the UK; the arrival of the ship *Empire Windrush* with 492 West Indians on board. |
| 1955 | Churchill wanted slogan 'Keep Britain white'. |
| 1958 | First 'race riots' in Notting Hill, London. |
| 1962 | Commonwealth Immigrants Act: withdrew right of entry to Commonwealth immigrants under most considerations. |
| 1965 | Race Relations Act (under the Labour government): an early attempt to ban discrimination in public places, or to incite racial hatred; Race Relations Board set up. |
| 1968 | 'Troubles' start in Northern Ireland; the Provisional Irish Republican Army (IRA) formed. Commonwealth Immigrants Act; Race Relations Act extended the 1965 Act to employment and housing, but not to police. Enoch Powell's 'Rivers of Blood' speech. |
| 1971 | Immigration Act: aliens could now enter only with a work permit; aliens could apply for citizenship after four years; distinctions between patrials and non-patrials. |
| 1972 | Expulsion of Ugandan Asians: 27,000 accepted by Britain. |
| 1976 | Race Relations Act: Commission for Racial Equality formed and indirect discrimination (e.g. via advertising) made illegal; Anti-Nazi League formed. Notting Hill Carnival formed. |
| 1981 | British Nationality Act: British citizenship could pass to children only if their parents were born in the UK. |
| 1980s | Inner-city 'race conflicts' at Brixton, Merseyside, Hackney; Lord Scarman reported on these conflicts in 1982, identifying key tension between police and local black youth; police relations with young black people were identified as significant. |
| 1983 | Black sections in Labour Party. |
| 1985 | More inner-city clashes. Conflict in Tottenham led to death of a policeman (Broadwater Farm Estate). |
| 1988 | Immigration Act: dependants of men who settled before 1973 could no longer join them, unless evidence of non-dependency. |
| 1991 | Census questions on ethnicity (3 million people, 5.5 per cent of population identified). |
| 1993 | Asylum and Immigration Act: certain countries to be refused asylum automatically; murder of black teenager Stephen Lawrence. |
| 1997 | Nine Black and Asian MPs returned at general election. |
| 1999 | Macpherson Report in the wake of the inquiry into Stephen Lawrence, who was murdered in 1995. |
| 2000 | The Race Relations (Amendment) Act: strengthened duty to promote race and equality. |
| 2000–1 | More race tensions in Bradford, Burnley and Oldham. |

## The new millennium: multiethnic Britain in terrorist times?

**2000**  The Commission on the Future of Multi-Ethnic Britain (Parekh Report) from Runnymede Trust. Suggested we should – among other things – understand the transitional nature of all identities; achieve a balance between cohesion, difference and equality; address and eliminate all kinds of racism; and build a 'human rights culture'.

**2001**  '9/11' terrorists attacks (and later 7/7): created new climate of racism linked to terrorist fears, which especially impacted the Muslim communities. New migrant groups from Iraq, Afghanistan and Zimbabwe: 'victims' of internal conflicts, and harbingers of world conflicts to come.

**2002**  Highest figure of 'asylum applications' to the UK (103,000 people: 24 per cent of EU total).

**2004**  Workers' Registration Scheme: required new migrants to register for work on arrival.

**2005**  Suicide bombings in London by four British Muslims intensified debates about multiculturalism.

**2006**  The Terrorism Act: latest in a line of legislation since '9/11' which centred on terrorism and the growth of terrorist fears. This legislation authorised 28 days' detention without trial for terrorist suspects. An array of new offences around terrorism were created.

**2006**  New eastern European migrants: around 375,000 people from eastern Europe came to the UK to work. Six out of ten are Polish. Most have stayed in the south of England and work in construction, agriculture, catering, retail and healthcare.

**2007**  Exacerbated by the attacks of 9/11 and 7/7: background of forced migration, global terrorism and social segregation. Equality and Human Rights Commission took over from the Commission for Racial Equality.

*Note:* The Equality and Human Rights Commission can be found at: www.equalityhumanrights.com.

New Commonwealth immigrants came independently during the 1950s. Often, their arrival in England was a shock: the 'Mother Country' was grey and dreary, and very, very cold! Added to this was an unexpected turn towards racism, as UK society encountered, for the first time in its modern history, a 'mass' migration of 'black' workers. Famously, in 1948, the first of many ships, the *Empire Windrush*, carrying many Commonwealth immigrants, arrived in Britain. Many others followed. London Transport had directly recruited large numbers of these new immigrants. Many immigrants subsequently followed from Pakistan and India. From this time on, racism became a much more visible feature of the English landscape, with debates about the colour bar and the need to ban migrants from certain jobs. From the 1960s onwards, starting with the Commonwealth Immigrants Act of 1962, much stricter controls were introduced to regulate immigrant entry. The past 50 years in the UK can be depicted as a constant series of conflicts and tensions, as the timeline shows.

## Cultures of ethnicities: generations and movements

The number of people from ethnic minorities in the UK has grown from a few tens of thousands in 1950 to more than three million now. The population of Great Britain is made up predominantly of people from a White British ethnic background: in 2008, around 83 per cent of the population belonged to this ethnic group. The pattern of migration into Great Britain from the 1950s onwards has produced a number of distinct ethnic minority groups within the general population. In 2008, the second largest ethnic group was Other White (5 per cent) – for example, those born overseas – followed by Indian (2 per cent) and Pakistani (also 2 per cent). The remaining ethnic minority groups accounted for around 8 per cent of the population.

Table 11.4 shows the age structure of the population, which varies across the different ethnic groups. The Mixed ethnic group – for example, people who identify with both of their parents' differing ethnicities, had the youngest age profile in Great Britain in 2008, with more than half (51 per cent) of people in this group aged under 16. Only 2 per cent of people in the Mixed ethnic group were aged 65 and over. The Other Black group also had a young age profile, with 37 per cent of people in this group being aged under 16. The majority of people in the Chinese group in Great Britain in 2008 were aged between 16 and 64 (83 per cent). Only 12 per cent of people in the Chinese group were under 16, and 5 per cent were aged 65 and over.

Understanding *multiple ethnic diversities* accompanied by *multiple different racisms* is usually a key to grasping an ethnic situation anywhere: there is never one unitary racism or one unified ethnic group. Still, in the UK ethnic groups are commonly divided into crude groupings such as 'South Asian', 'Caribbean' 'Polish' or 'Irish' – even though these terms are crude and conceal a wealth of further differences (and conflicts). Within these groupings there are many subgroupings of class, age, gender and sexual orientation. Some ethnic groupings develop their own strong communities and identities; others do not.

Ethnic groupings bring elements of their culture of origin to a hybrid arrangement of other cultures. This is a growing, and crucial, feature of modern global societies which mix and transform earlier cultural elements with newer ones. There are now a great many studies that document diverse aspects of these cultures.

South Asian communities may be seen in many parts of the UK, but they are often structured by their roots in religion. Most Bangladeshis and Pakistanis are Muslim; Indians may be Sikh, Hindu or Muslim. Much as in the migration model outlined above, we can trace various phases of development. A pioneer phase sees a small number of early migrants arriving and establishing small south Asian communities. Despite the major culture shock from the confrontation with UK culture, the old culture is maintained. From this there follows a phase of mass migration, where the diverse cultural patterns from home are imported and developed. Family, religious codes and dress all play a key solidifying role. There follows a major phase of family reunion, with a substantial second generation being born into the community. Throughout, there is a tension between the old culture and the new. New divisions start to appear: Sikhs from one region (such as Jullunder Doab) with Muslims from another (such as Mirpur district in Kashmir). By now, we have a third generation – and even a fourth generation is starting to appear. Here the realities of 'being Asian' and 'being British' become very different: new generations create new cultural responses – new music styles, new dress codes, new responses to religion compared to their parents (and grandparents) – even as they face new kinds of racism.

One key part of some Asian cultures is the Muslim faith (discussed in Chapter 5). In recent years, since the New York terrorist attack on 9/11, tensions have been heightened in Muslim communities in the UK and the world as they are perceived to be involved in terrorist activities. A new pattern of racism has emerged: *Islamophobia* (see the *Big debate* at the end of the chapter) along with new controversies such as the debate on the Muslim veil (see the *Public sociology* box on p. 377). Here again we find multiple splits within

the community and many new responses (some younger women now wear the very veils that their parents had fought to reject).

The same is true of Caribbean cultures: again, there is a mix of elements. Religion plays a strong role, but so too do elements of recovering an earlier culture. At the same time, much of this is mixed with elements from the dominant cultures. There are several notable strands, including Pentecostal culture and Rastafarianism.

*Pentecostal culture* has its roots in the Caribbean and the United States, and grew in England from the 1950s onwards. The first assemblies were in 1954 in Wolverhampton. There is a strong regard for the British way of life, while at the same time a strong moral system is imposed that is slightly at odds with much of the contemporary culture. Pentecostalists are not allowed to drink, swear, have any kind of sex outside marriage or even wear jewellery.

*Rastafarian culture* has its origins in Jamaica in the early 1930s after the demise of Marcus Garvey, who suggested 'Africa for the Africans'. 'Rastas' adopted Haile Selassie, one-time Emperor of Ethiopia, as the messiah and argued that Babylon was the system of European colonialism that enslaved Africans. There was a conspiracy to keep blacks suppressed. The culture surfaced in the UK in the 1970s and is easily distinguished by its dreadlocks hairstyle; many white youths copied the style during the 1970s and 1980s.

In practice, there is a diversity of culture. Early sociological studies depicted this diversity: in a now classic study of male youth in the St Paul's area of Bristol, the late Ken Pryce (1986; orig. 1979) looked at six lifestyles, with a mix of Afro-Caribbean and UK culture. This was a participant observation that indicated, above all, the range of male youth forms that were developing. Broadly, he distinguished between those who held an expressive-disreputable orientation and those who valued a stable, law-abiding orientation.

Six types were identified at that time. In the first groupings were:

- Hustlers: males, marginal and hedonistic (Yardies are a more recent and tougher version).
- Teenyboppers: delinquents and/or Rastafarians.

In the second (more law-abiding) grouping were:

- Proletarian respectables: those who adopt more conventional lifestyles.
- Saints: the Pentecostals, as defined above.
- Mainliners: white-collar black people.
- In-betweeners: an older, law-abiding group, who also have a passion about their 'black culture'.

# Debating the Muslim veil

In 2010 the French government passed a bill to make it illegal to wear garments such as the niqab or burka, which incorporate a full-face veil, anywhere in public. It envisaged fines of €150 (£119) for women who break the law and €30,000 and a one-year jail term for men who force their wives to wear the burka. The niqab and burka are widely seen in France as threats to women's rights and the secular nature of the state.

The debate over women and 'the veil' has achieved an almost central role in many Western cultures. There have been controversies about it in schools and the workplace; in the UK, government minister Jack Straw urged a 'public debate' in 2006; and it has featured in press, news and TV talk shows as a major issue.

How can a sociologist help in such a passionate public debate? Does a sociologist have helpful things to say? Consider that a sociologist could bring to work (a) some evidence (empiricism); (b) some critical thoughts (theory); and (c) a systematic standpoint (analysis).

## Empiricism

What are the social facts of the veil? Most religions prescribe some dress for women: in Judaism, Christianity and Islam the concept of covering the head is or was associated with propriety. The veil has a long history, and fieldwork suggests that the veil is a very important, though not the most essential, feature of contrasting Muslim cultures across the world. Since there are over a fifth of the world's population engaged in this practice, it cannot be lightly dismissed. Veiling is far from one simple act. There are many kinds of veil – the *khimar* is a type of

headscarf while the *niqāb* and *burqa* are two kinds of veil that cover most of the face except for a slit or hole for the eyes. The sociologist can document the history and the different cultures in which it is used. Very often the kind of veiling practice depends on the kind of culture it is lodged in – and it is often linked to Sunni/Shi'ite divides.

## Theory

One debate concerns the ways in which the veil fits into Muslim lives – what does it mean to Muslim women, and men? What too does it mean to a European? Research shows multiple and ambiguous meanings. There are major diversities of practice, meaning and significance across different Muslim cultures and the challenge for sociologists is to make clear these multiple histories and meanings. To some it is crucial, to others marginal; some even deny its role. For some it is a deep religious expression; for some it signifies what a woman must do; for some it may be seen as a personal threat, a fear or a danger; for some a sign of subordination, even slavery; to yet others a means of Muslim identity; to yet more a sign of resistance to the 'West'. There is a wide range of dress – from dark and total, to light and almost 'fashionable'. And different groups respond in different ways. What is clear to the sociologist is that there is no absolute fixed meaning on which all agree. Veiling is multiply symbolic and contested. Part of the sociologist's job is to see what this contest is about.

## Analysis

The contest strikes in at least three key areas:

1 *The gender debate*: here it can be seen as part of the struggle

about the Western view of men and women that is strongly linked to Western feminism. The veil represents women's subordination, and is the iceberg tip of this subordination. More deeply, Islam is a religion which regulates women's lives and keeps women out of public space, public life, etc. Some Muslim women argue to the contrary – that the veil helps them to assert their identity. Still others organise major campaigns against it. So there is conflict across many groups which needs to be grasped.

2 *The modernity debate*: part of the struggle here is the divide between tradition, symbolised by the veil, and the West – a modern view of individualism and freedom. The veil symbolises a 'clash of cultures' and their views of where the future is headed. It symbolises being a Muslim woman in a Western-dominated world.

3 *The assimilation/minority debate*: here the concern is whether different groups should be assimilated into a culture and whether it helps for them to make themselves stand out through their differences.

What is important throughout this is the sociological recognition that things are not quite what they seem – that there is no one simple account of this social phenomenon and that it is indeed a critical symbol of our times. Carefully unpacking these ideas – and bringing rich complexity and awareness of differences – is one task for sociological analysis which could help informed citizen debate and critical thinking.

*See*: Joan Wallach Scott: *The Politics of the Veil* (2007). There is plenty to see on YouTube on this: for example, French Muslim woman denied citizenship for wearing the veil, www.youtube.com/watch?v=JoKOVjIM2_Q.

More recent studies such as those by Les Back (1996) and Rupa Huq (2006) trace the new emerging styles and growing diversities of ethnic cultures. They show how new generations of 'Brits' generate Asian-styled bhangra and post-bhangra cultures (bhangra is a dance which originated in the Punjab region) and Afro-Caribbean-styled rap and hip hop cultures, even as they mix and merge with 'Brit culture'. Ethnic cultures now criss-cross class, gender, sexuality and age, and become an everyday feature for many of 'British cultures', having one foot in a 'culture of origin' and another foot in 'diverse British cultures'. Ethnic cultures are dynamic: they are always changing and on the move. Each generation pushes its culture on in different ways and, as young generations become older generations, so the culture moves again. We can see some of this in films like Ayub Khan-Din's *East is East* (1999) and the sequel *West is West* (2010).

## Ethnicity and class

In general, those of Caribbean, Pakistani and Bangladeshi descent tend to occupy the lowest position in the labour market and to experience the highest levels of unemployment (Mason, 2000a: 106).

We have seen that, although there is no official poverty line in the UK (Chapter 10), something like 15–25 per cent of the population may well be living in poverty. There are few specific data on ethnicity, but one commentator has remarked that:

> Every indicator of poverty shows that black people and other ethnic minorities are more at risk of high unemployment, low pay, shift work and poor social security rights. Their poverty is caused by immigration policies which have often excluded people from abroad from access to welfare, employment patterns which have marginalised black people and other ethnic groups into low paid manual work, direct and indirect discrimination in social security and the broader experience of racism in society as a whole.

(Oppenheim, 1993: 130)

## Ethnicity and age

A Joseph Rowntree Foundation report of 1995 (see Chapter 10) was alarmed at the disparities that were appearing between ethnic youth and others. In the late 1980s, while 12 per cent of young whites were unemployed, the figure was higher for young ethnic groups: 25 per cent of Afro-Caribbeans, 16 per cent of

Indians, 27 per cent of Pakistanis and Bangladeshis (aged 16–24) (Skellington, 1996: 102).

## Ethnicity and gender

If stratification systems appear across race, class and gender lines – which this book suggests they do – then black women are more likely to be at the centre of all three systems of stratification (if age is added, then elderly black women may be the most vulnerable of all).

There has been a growing amount of research on black women in the UK in recent years, which suggests among other things that black women:

- make up something like a quarter of the minority labour force (Phizacklea, 1995)
- are often heavily concentrated in the worst work: poorly paid, bad conditions, temporary, hard work, long hours, often unregistered home work, often subject to unemployment (Allen and Walkowitz, 1987)
- are often unpaid workers in family businesses (Anthias and Yuval Davis, 1993)
- are often in single households – over 30 per cent of British West Indian households are single parents (Anthias and Yuval Davis, 1993: 117)
- may perform well in school and university, only to find they have less access to work and are less well paid
- are over-represented in the prison population.

White feminism is often critical of the family, and the subordination of women within it. This can mean an implicit attack on Muslim women, whose lives are often circumscribed by the family, and on Afro-Caribbean women, who are often seen to be single mothers. This has resulted in a significant debate amongst black women, who sometimes feel they have become the objects of white feminism, which is critical of their family life and their subordination to it.

# Racisms and ethnic antagonisms in Europe

Racism, of various kinds and under various names, runs deep throughout history. We have examined some of its complex roots above. It is not really suprising, then, that racism is found throughout Europe. As Figure 11.2 shows, Europe is a culture in which there are many ethnic diversities. And much of this diversity makes for distinct antagonism. There are five features to note.

First, racism is generally on the increase. Nearly all countries in the European Union report increased numbers of racist incidents and attacks on foreigners and individuals belonging to ethnic, racial or linguistic minorities. In France, this has involved numerous attacks on people of North African origin, as well as anti-Semitism. In Germany, the objects have mainly been Turkish, as well as gypsies (the Sinti and Roma). There also appears to be a worrying resurgence of anti-Semitism and 'Holocaust denial' spearheaded by new skinhead gangs. In part, the latter is explained through the growing tensions arising from the reunification of East and West Germany. Further, European football matches regularly produce concern about the levels of racist violence. And each year there are many deaths across Europe that are caused by racism (see the box below on skinheads and Roma).

Secondly, problems of displaced people throughout Europe have led to many issues around 'asylum seekers'. Leaving their home countries because of intolerable social, economic and political conditions, such asylum seekers may then find themselves confronting further racism and discrimination in the country of destination. Often, they are placed in camps that resemble prisons, and find themselves without family, support or funds. Governments, which are cautious of the political implications of allowing too many asylum seekers into their countries, often deploy subtle and tacit racist selection procedures.

A third development is the extremes of ethnic purging and cleansing that have been taking place across eastern Europe. The horrors of the events of Bosnia (which were told at the start of this chapter) are but one of many such conflicts which have been taking place over religions and borders as the old cultures of Russia and Yugoslavia break down. In Europe we now have the 'Serbian Question', the 'Albanian Question', the 'Macedonian Question', the 'Hungarian Question' and the 'Roma Question' (Kocsis, 2001).

A fourth development is the emergence of a more sophisticated kind of racism, one often called the 'new racism' or 'cultural racism'. This new racism no longer makes the old (and not very respectable) arguments (usually about biological inferiority), but highlights instead *cultural* differences as those that really matter. Just how incompatible this 'different culture' is with the dominant one becomes a key issue. Closely allied with this is the recognition of multi-racisms: for example, white people who are racist to some groups can like or even admire other ethnic groups. There are then racisms or plural racisms (Modood, 2005).

Finally, there is an emerging mentality that is specific to Europe. In England, it takes the form of 'little England'; in Europe more generally, it is 'Fortress Europe'. There is a growing concern to exclude the poorer countries on the fringe of Europe, which includes some of the eastern European countries, as well as those in Africa and eastern Asia. And there has been a growing intolerance of migrating groups – especially what have become known as 'bogus asylum seekers'.

# Contemporary conflict across Europe

Two concerns have driven much racism in Europe so far in the twenty-first century. One has been the rise of and scare about terrorism. The other has been the scares over immigration. Both connect to issues of racism.

Since the 9/11 bombings at the World Trade Center in New York, the world has been alerted to 'terrorists'. But much of this scare is also linked to issues of racism. After all, the main perpetrators of the Trade Center outrage were Muslim, and this has led to conflicts about Muslims and their religion. Across the world, there have been recurrent attacks and fears about more. In addition to this, there has also been a growing tide of concern over immigration. By 2002, electoral rebellion over the issue of immigration was threatening the party systems of Austria, Belgium, Denmark, France and the Netherlands.

The Dutch were also incensed by the 2002 assassination of Pim Fortuyn, a gay anti-immigration politician. The Netherlands has been proud for a long while of its 'tolerance' of minorities. It has welcomed tens of thousands of Muslim asylum seekers allegedly escaping persecution. But in 2004, the killing of Theo van Gogh (a famous and polemical film-maker – and a descendant of the painter Vincent van Gogh) raised the possibility of assassinations as part of the European jihad and al Qaeda. Osama bin Laden, the leader, now facilitates actions from European jihadist networks across Europe that assemble for specific missions. The Dutch General Intelligence and Security Service (AIVD) says that radical Islam in the Netherlands encompasses 'a multitude of movements, organisations and groups'. Some are non-violent and share only religious dogma and a loathing for the West. But AIVD stresses that others, including al Qaeda, are also 'stealthily taking root in Dutch society' by recruiting estranged Dutch-born Muslim youths.

According to Robert S. Leiken, two types of jihadist can be found in Europe. *Outsiders* can be seen as typically referring to asylum seekers or students, who gained refuge in liberal Europe from crackdowns against Islamists in the Middle East. *Insiders* are a group of demoralised, cut-off, marginalised citizens – often second- or third-generation children of immigrants. They are often unemployed and form something like an underclass – in Paris or Marseilles, in Amsterdam or Bradford. All have grievances against their society, and the current crisis of terrorism fuels their passions.

With the Muslim headscarf controversy raging in France and England, talk about the connection between asylum abuse and terrorism rising in the United Kingdom, and the Dutch outrage over the van Gogh killing, western European racism now raises many issues. A major concern is the debate over liberalism and multiculturalism. Many of the new ethnic cultures that have become settled within European borders in recent decades are now feeling unsettled by some of the challenges of the new century.

## Ethnic antagonisms in the UK

**Britain is now two entirely different worlds, and the one you inherit is determined by the colour of your skin.**

(Salman Rushdie, 1982: 418)

There has been a long history of ethnic antagonisms in the UK, but several main issues can be highlighted.

First, *public conflicts* – even riots. In the 1950s, shortly after the arrival of a major wave of West Indians, there were the Notting Hill Riots – in this case, with whites attacking blacks. But by the 1980s the rioting and conflicts had changed. Now it was the blacks themselves who protested, in a series of riots throughout the 1980s, mainly involving young people against the police – in Brixton (April 1981), St Paul's in Bristol, Handsworth, and Toxteth in Liverpool. They were considered serious enough for a committee of inquiry, chaired by Lord Scarman. In an influential report, he located the problems of black inner-city youth whose lives had become marginalised. He noted the tension between black youth and the police, the plight of inner-city

## THINKERS & THEORY

# Patricia Hill Collins: standpoints at the intersections of gender and race

Patricia Hill Collins (born 1 May 1948) is Distinguished University Professor of Sociology at the University of Maryland, College Park, and former President of the American Sociological Association Council. She is a prominent thinker on race, gender and inequality. She was one of the first sociologists to point simultaneously to the *intersections* of gender and race (see this chapter), and to develop what has

come to be called *standpoint theory* (see Chapter 3). She draws on her own experience as an African-American woman and makes a key sociological point about connecting sociological theory to personal life. Both of these help to shape a different kind of sociology. Her key ideas are published in her classic book *Black Feminist Thought: Knowledge, Consciousness and the Politics of Empowerment*, originally published in 1990.

Her work is striking because in addition to her personal experiences, she uses a wide range of sources such as fiction, poetry, music and oral history – which is relatively unusual for sociologists. She sees contributions to social theory coming from poets and writers like Alice Walker and Audre Lorde. The core of her book focuses upon case studies of 'black womanhood' and black women's historical oppression

in family, motherhood and work. Throughout she places black women's experience at the centre of her analysis and is concerned with the ways in which black women can empower themselves through a deeper understanding of their situation. In later books, she has examined discrimination against women in black communities and the role of black women as 'outsiders within'; the relationship between black nationalism, feminism and women in the hip-hop generation; and the problems of public education.

*See also: Fighting Words: Black Women and the Search for Justice* (1998); *Black Power to Hip Hop: Racism, Nationalism, and Feminism* (2006); and *Another Kind of Public Education: Race, Schools, the Media and Democratic Possibilities* (2009).

# The Roma in Europe

Around 8 million gypsies or Roma live in Europe. They pose major issues of human rights. They are largely scattered in small communities throughout the former communist societies and around the Mediterranean. For example, in Slovakia they make up as much as 10 per cent of the population; in Hungary and the Czech Republic it is estimated that they comprise around 3 per cent; and in Romania they number some 2 million people – the largest national population in the world.

The terms used to describe them are often hard to define: 'pikeys', 'travellers', 'Gypsies', 'Roma', 'Bohemians', 'Manush' and 'Burugoti' can be used, though they do not all mean the same thing. One thing they have in common is that wherever they are found, they are usually badly treated. They also figure low on most social indicators – usually among the very poorest of a society, under-educated, short-lived, dependent on welfare, segregated, in poor health, and removed from political life. They are also among the most imprisoned. They are hugely discriminated against – from where they can live, to life in school, to being the victims of neo-Nazi thugs.

In one major incident, a Romani teenager, Mario Goral, was attacked by a group of skinheads in the central town of Slovakia, Ziar nad Hronom. Some 30 skinheads attacked a pub frequented by Roma with Molotov cocktails, crowbars and knives. They doused Mario with gasoline and polystyrene and set him on fire. He died a few days later. Only after his death did the Slovak government condemn the attack. And writing anonymously in the Presov evening newspapers, the skinheads explained who they were to the general public:

The skinheads wanted to protect Presov against Gypsies – Roma. Who else

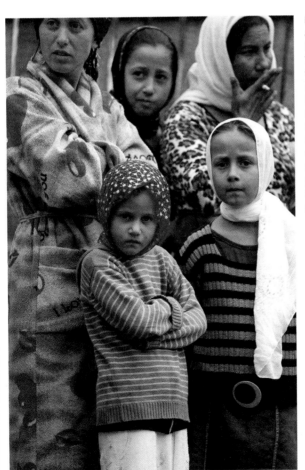

Romanian Roma women Julieta Moise, left, and Maria Bacanu, right, stand with children in Barbulesti, Romania, September, 2010. The European Union had just announced that it will take legal action against France over its expulsion of more than 1,000 gypsies in recent weeks after their improvised settlements were destroyed and they were rounded up to be flown home. But as France carries out mass expulsions in a broadly condemned policy of ethnic targeting, some returnee gypsies are saying home-grown poverty is better than the seething hostility they face on French streets

*Source*: AP/Press Association Images.

WORLD WATCH

but the Gypsies create a mess in the city, steal, and participate in the black market? Now you can think that we are very racist. But you can hardly find a man who would not be ashamed of a Gypsy ... We want Slovaks to live in Presov, in Slovakia. We want a white Slovakia, because if nothing changes, then it will be a catastrophe for Presov and for Slovakia.

(*The Economist*, 12 May 2001: 29–32)

Anti-Roma violence continues. Since January 2008, in Hungary, the Czech Republic and the Slovak Republic, such violence has gained significant prominence in the media. The attacks involve firebombing, shooting, stabbing, beating and other acts of violence. They have taken the lives of eight people and have left dozens of others with serious injuries. Many of the attacks have targeted families and children. They are happening in an increasingly racist climate. These countries have seen a

strengthening of extremist and openly racist groups, which spread hate speech and organise anti-Romani marches through the very same villages where people are being attacked. Breaking EU rules, in September 2010, the French government deported some 1,000 Roma to Romania and Bulgaria. The controversies continue for one of Europe's most stigmatised minorities.

For updates: see European Roma Rights Centre, www.errc.org.

living, and the exclusion experienced by black youth. Troubles erupted again in the summer of 2001, when further conflicts broke out in the north of England – in Bradford, Oldham, Leeds and Burnley. As usual, these conflicts primarily involved young men, but this time they flared up mainly in poor Muslim communities where there was also a menacing threat from right-wing campaigners such as the National Front.

A second issue is *racial attacks*. There is a long history of violence directed towards 'blacks' – what will be described in Chapter 17 as **hate crimes**. Many instances of these crimes have involved young people again, and the police. The Runnymede Trust estimated that between January 1970 and November 1989, some 74 people died as a result of racial attacks (Skellington, 1996: 83). Since then it has documented a further 61 cases (and each case is discussed on its website). The level of violence on the street appears to have escalated.

Third, has been the widespread existence of *racial discrimination*. Formally, this is now illegal in the UK and in many other countries. In practice, it often works on a more informal and covert level. A number of surveys have found discrimination in the work situation. Studies from the Policy Studies Institute (formerly Political and Economic Planning, PEP) have regularly documented high levels of discrimination (see Daniel, 1968; Modood et al., 1997). Often, the studies show blatant discrimination – with white and black stooges applying for similar jobs, only to find that the black population is more discriminated against.

All of the above signals a long-term and growing series of complex problems. Migration and ethnic diversity can bring fears, prejudice, racism – and the possibilities of more and more ethnic conflict and ethnic cleansing, even ethnic war. Stuart Hall

(1992b: 308–9) has suggested three main responses to ethnic divides in a multicultural society. These are:

- A defensive strengthening of local/dominant cultural identities. People feel threatened and resolve this through a reassertion of absolute values. In the UK, this can mean an 'aggressive little Englandism'.
- A defensive strengthening of the minority culture identities. With the experience of racism and exclusion, the culture of origin is used to construct a strong counter-identity. This can be found in the UK as Rastafarianism (reasserting 'Africa' and the Caribbean) and the revival of Muslim fundamentalism (in the Pakistani community).
- The creation of new 'mixed' identities – a possible consequence of globalisation, giving a broader sense of identity. In the UK, the identity 'black' can be used by both Afro-Caribbean and Asian communities. Paul Gilroy (1994) talks of 'the Black Atlantic' as a cultural network spanning many countries (Africa, the Caribbean, the Americas, the UK) where people may have African descent even though they have come to modify it greatly in new cultures.

## The future of ethnic relations: multiple racisms, multiple ethnicities

This chapter has highlighted the multiple ethnicities – each taking generational forms – across all cultures. Often these are connected to deep conflicts and hostilities between groups. Most societies have their ethnic tensions, and in some that tension leads to the death of thousands, even millions.

We started by reviewing a number of major explanations of prejudice and discrimination. Often, such prejudices are seen as the individual quirks of a few people in prejudiced cultures. But this chapter has tried to show that these processes are deeply social and work right across the world: they are based upon shifting patterns of ethnic migration, the creation of diasporas and the existence of multiple ethnic cultures organised on generational, class and gender lines which are struggling to defend their own ways of life. Each culture comes to identify some people as different from and outside the culture. These are often connected to

economic problems, and these 'others' come to serve major scapegoating functions and can mark out boundaries of national identities. They can be used to reassert the importance and dominance of majority populations.

Ethnic divides seem wide and deep. As we saw in the opening story of Bosnia, many contemporary wars are connected to such divides. In the twenty-first century, new patterns of racism are being generated around new migration patterns and the ubiquitous growth of 'terrorist fears' after the 9/11 attacks. An understanding of the social processes at work in the construction of these hostilities – and of the ways we may transcend them to live together with our differences – seems ever more urgent.

# SUMMARY

**1** Race involves a presumed cluster of biological traits. A century ago, scientists identified three broad, overarching racial categories: Caucasians, Mongoloids and Negroids. However, there are no pure races and these categories are in disrepute. Ethnicity is a matter not of biology but of shared cultural heritage. Racialisation is the process of naming different races. Minorities, including those of certain races and ethnicities, are categories of people who are socially distinctive and who have a subordinate social position.

**2** A prejudice is an inflexible and distorted generalisation about a category of people. Racism, a powerful type of prejudice, is any assertion that one race is innately superior or inferior to another. Discrimination is a pattern of action by which a person treats various categories of people unequally. Institutional discrimination refers to the fact that the law and other social institutions, in contrast to individuals, can treat different categories of people unequally.

Pluralism refers to a state in which racial and ethnic categories, although distinct, have equal social standing. Assimilation is a process by which minorities gradually adopt the patterns of the dominant culture. Segregation means the physical and social separation of categories of people. Genocide involves the extermination of a category of people.

**3** Migration patterns have played a significant role in shaping most cultures. Future patterns of migration are likely to be more global, and involve more women.

**4** The main ethnic groups in the UK number about 7 per cent of the population. They are an ethnically heterogeneous group but include south Asians (from India, Bangladesh and Pakistan) and Afro-Caribbeans. Forty-eight per cent are under the age of 24.

**5** Ethnic antagonisms are widespread and increasing in Europe. Attacks, harassment and discrimination are features of minority ethnic living in Europe.

## MYTASKLIST

# Ten Suggestions for going further

## 1 Connect up with Part Six and the Sociology Web Resources

As you work through ideas and think about the issues raised in this chapter, look at the accompanying website and the resource centre at the end of this book which connects to it. There is a lot here to help you move on. To link up, see: www.pearson.co.uk/plummer.

## 2 Review the chapter

*Briefly summarise (in a paragraph) just what this chapter has been about.* Consider: (a) What have you learned? (b) What do you disagree with? Be critical. And (c) How would you develop all this? How could you get more detail on matters that interest you?

## 3 Pose questions

(a) Discuss patterns of ethnic inequality in any one European culture.
(b) What is meant by 'racialisation'? How does it connect to the idea of 'race'?
(c) What are the major patterns of migration in postwar Europe? Should there be limits on immigration?
(d) Examine what is meant by the 'new racism'. Give examples.

## 4 Explore key words

Many concepts have been introduced in this chapter. You can review them from the website or from the listing at the back of this book. You might like to give special attention to just five words and think them through – how would you define them, what are they dealing with, and do they help you see the social world more clearly or not?

## 5 Search the Web

Be critical when you look at websites – see the box on p. 940 in the Resources section. For this chapter look at the following:

Minority Rights International
www.minorityrights.org
An international NGO, based in London, which promotes the rights of ethnic, religious and other minorities. Contains a great deal of information.

### Migration

Two main (United Nations) agencies acting on behalf of the world's refugees and migrants are:

United Nations High Commissioner for Refugees (UNHCR)
www.unhcr.ch

Global Commission for International Migration
www.gcim.org

See also:

Centre of Migration
www.compass.ox.ac.uk

The Age-of-migration website for the book by Castles and Miller (see below) has a useful set of links at:
www.age-of-migration.com/uk/resources/weblinks.html

History of International Migration
www.let.leidenuniv.nl/history/migration
www.swap.ac.uk/Links/links.asp?sid=__Jacsb21&screen=2
A major source of links on issues of migration and refugees.

### Race and racism

Institute of Race Relations
www.irr.org.uk
The Institute of Race Relations (IRR) was established as an independent educational charity in 1958 to carry out research and publish and collect resources on race relations throughout the world.

Runnymede Trust
www.runnymedetrust.org
The Runnymede Trust is an independent policy research organisation focusing on equality and justice through the promotion of a successful multi-ethnic society.

European Network Against Racism
www.enar-eu.org/en

European Monitoring Centre on Racism and Xenophobia
http://eumc.eu.int

European Commission against Racism and Intolerance (ECRI)
www.coe.int/T/e/human_rights/ecri/1-ECRI

## 6 Watch a DVD

There are many films to see on racism. Here is a list of some classics worth seeing:

- Udayan Prasad's *My Son the Fanatic* (1997): a father is confronted by his Islamic fundamentalist son in Bradford.
- Tony Gatlif's *Gadjo Dilo* (1999): gives an ethnographer's eye on gypsy life and racism in Romania.
- Robert Mulligan's *To Kill a Mockingbird* (1962): the classic novel of racism in the Deep South of the United States came to be a major film.
- Stephen Frear's *My Beautiful Laundrette* (1985): Asian community in the UK meets gay life in a laundrette. Controversial in its day.
- Damien O'Donnell's *East is East*: very funny but telling look at discrimination within Asian communities in the UK.
- Alan Parker's *Mississippi Burning* (1988) tells the true story of the Ku Klux Klan and the murders of civil rights workers.
- John Singleton's classic *Boyz N the Hood* (1991): about surviving the pressures of family and street life in south-central Los Angeles. Set a model for black American films.
- Wayne Wang's *Chan is Missing* (1982): a 1982 film of two taxi drivers searching the streets of San Francisco. Something of a cult film.
- Gurinda Chadas' *Bend it like Beckam* (2002): fusion of Hindi culture meets Western culture meets feminism and gay, and all through football!
- Terry George's *Hotel Rwanda* (2004): harrowing account of the Tutsi conflict in Rwanda.
- Nick Broomfield's *Ghosts* (2007): the Chinese immigrants discussed at the start of Chapter 15 are here 'documented' to show the abuses of the global migrant worker's life.

## 7 Think and read

Tariq Modood, *Multicultural Politics* (2005). A foremost UK sociologist engaged with the debate over multiculturalism raises many of the key issues.

The Parakh Report, *The Future of Multi-Ethnic Britain* (2000). A sustained analysis of a modern multi-ethnic society with key recommendations for a 'human rights culture'.

David Mason, *Race and Ethnicity in Modern Britain* (2nd edn, 2000a). A short, clear introduction to the whole field. Now a little out of date.

Christian Karner, *Ethnicity and Everyday Life* (2007). Examines ethnicity as a structure of action, a way of seeing and a structure of feeling.

Patricia Hill Collins, *Black Feminist Thought* (2nd edn, 2000). A now classic and important statement of theoretical issues concerning black feminism.

Stephen Castles and Mark J. Miller, *The Age of Migration: International Population Movements in the Modern World* (4th edn, 2009). A major textbook which discusses migration movements on a global level, and shows how they lead to ethnic minorities.

Philip Marfleet, *Refugees in a Global Era* (2006). A critical review of the whole social process of migration.

Martin Shaw, *What is Genocide?* (2007). An important book that builds a sociology of the most extreme form of discriminating hatred and scapegoating: genocide.

Finally: three recent books that will help you engage with current debates are: Paul Gilroy, *After Empire: Melancholia or Convivial Culture* (2004); Kwame Anthony Appiah, *Cosmopolitanism: Ethics in a World of Strangers* (2006); Akbar Ahmed, *Journey into Islam: The Crisis of Globalization* (2007).

### More information

Internationally, the Minority Rights Group publishes the *World Directory of Minorities*, which details 1,000 minorities (and their various persecutions). *The International Migration Review* (Center for Migration Studies, New York) is a regular and valuable source of information on migration patterns. *Race Today*, *Ethnic and Race Relations*, and *Race and Class* are all journals that highlight matters of race; the first is the most accessible to students. For up-to-date 'briefing papers' on issues of concern to the multi-ethnic society in the UK, look at the Runnymede Trust's website (see above).

## 8 Relax with a novel

Four good classic US novels on race and racism are Ralph Ellison's *Invisible Man* (1999); Maya Angelou's *I Know Why the Caged Bird Sings* (1993); James Baldwin's *Giovanni's Room* (1956); and Alice Walker's *The Colour Purple* (1982).

## 9 Connect to other chapters

- For links to culture and language, see Chapter 5.
- For links to world poverty, see Chapter 9.
- For links to religion, see Chapter 19.
- Ethnicity is also discussed in the chapters on crime (17), family (18) and education (20).

# 10 Engage with THE BIG DEBATE

## Dangerous extremists: Islamic fundamentalists or Islamophobes?

As we have seen in Chapter 5, Muslim cultures are widespread in the world and involve around a sixth of the world's population. Further, as we shall see in Chapter 19, Islam is the dominant faith in some 40 states throughout the world, and is seen by many to be the fastest-growing religion. In the UK, there has been a significant growth over the past decade to around 2.4 million Muslims – partly due to the birth rate and immigration, but also because of 'conversions' to the faith. Overall, Muslims account for some 3 per cent of European faith.

In the twenty-first century, Islam has come to symbolise key questions about ethnicity, prejudice and tolerance. This can be seen from the prominence given to the debate over the Salman Rushdie affair and the Iranian *fatwah* (death threat) imposed upon him (see the opening vignette to Chapter 19). It is seen in the controversy in France and elsewhere over the veil (see the box on p. 377). And it is seen in the Gulf Wars waged against Iraq in 1992 and 2003. Some have even claimed that this is a new 'Holy War' between East and West, where the traditional forces of the anti-Western, anti-rational and anti-modern Islamic religions are in spiritual and moral combat with the modernising but decadent West. Benjamin Barber (1995), for one, sees this as a clash of civilisations, a conflict between the *jihad* (holy war) and the materialism symbolised by McDonaldisation (see Chapters 5, 6 and 19). It is a conflict which may also be linked to ethnicity and some see it as the major world conflict in the twenty-first century. In the aftermath of the World Trade Center bombings in 2001, such tensions have become more and more acute.

And with it has arrived Islamophobia. On the one hand, some Westerners argue that Islam is a dangerous force in the world. It is seen as a fundamentalist religion (see Chapter 19), holding strongly to traditionalist views, emphasising religious texts and looking back to its past to affirm its puritan vision. It is seen to hold particular prejudices against many modern concerns of the West: the liberation of women, the 'open and free society', the decline of religion, the acceptance of diversity such as homosexuality and 'sexual freedom'. And it is seen to favour an absolutist religious state where nothing can exist outside the religion. Indeed, of the 40 or so states where Islam is dominant, few can be called democratic. All of this clashes with the modern values of the Western state.

Such claims certainly do have some basis in fact, but the critics argue that such statements are extreme: the Islamic faith actually comes in a number of varieties, and many of its supporters do not adopt these extreme positions. Just as Christianity has a number of its own divides, so too do the Muslims. Most are not extreme. Indeed, as we have seen, a key divide lies between Shi'ism and the Shi'ites (who hold more traditional and rigid views) and the Sunnis (who accept more diversity and change). In the UK, for instance, the majority of Muslims must be distinguished from small extreme groups like Al-Muhajiroun which calls for Islamic government in the UK (*Khilafah*).

It is the more extreme views which get reported most often, and it is these ideas which form the basis of a new form of prejudice called 'Islamophobia' – *a hatred of all things Muslim*. Where once the Jews or blacks or 'Asians' were prime objects of attack, increasingly Muslims have become the new objects of prejudice and discrimination. Not only is the incidence of violent attacks against Muslims increasing, but prejudicial views are being widely held. Few, for example, blamed the Catholics for IRA bombings in Ireland: the IRA was recognised as a more extreme group. So why blame Muslims for much of what is, in fact, only an extreme edge?

In 1996, the Runnymede Trust – a major organisation which promotes and researches a multicultural society in the UK – announced a commission to look into what it considered as the most rapidly growing form of prejudice. It was concerned to look at such things as anti-Islamic and anti-Muslim attitudes; the relations between Islam and secular outlooks and other world faiths; the treatment of Islam and Muslim concerns in the media; and the contributions of British Muslims to government and society. The Trust highlighted a major emerging form of prejudice in Western societies, one that is likely to become more and more recognised. Since then the term has come into wide use.

These divides raise serious issues around prejudice and discrimination. How far can a multicultural society which claims to accept religious and ethnic diversity pursue such outright attacks upon different religions? At the same time, how far can a religious strand which rejects tolerance and diversity be allowed to propagate its views? This is a classical dilemma of freedom for those who may advocate unlimited freedom.

### Continue the debate

1 What is Islamophobia, and what might cause it?
2 Consider some possible scenarios of what might happen in Europe and the West in the future.
3 Will more and more Muslims be co-opted into Western secular individualism? Will more and more Muslims stay with their own faith, while accepting multicultural values? Or will a strong defence of Islamic fundamentalism lead to growing ethnic conflicts?
4 What is multiculturalism? Does it work?

*See*: Tariq Modhood, *Multicultural Politics* (2005), especially Part II: The Muslim Challenge; Runnymede Trust (1997); Barber (1995). Visit Islamophobia Watch: www.islamophobia-watch.com.

# CHAPTER 15

# ECONOMIES, WORK AND CONSUMPTION

**ON A HOT SUMMER'S DAY IN 2000**, a large sealed container lorry arrived at Dover in the UK. As the lorry door was opened by immigration inspectors, it was clear that something terrible had happened. For a start there was no chilled air – which would have been usual for a lorry full of food. Indeed, there seemed to be no air at all. And there was a very strange smell. Soon the worst was uncovered: the lorry contained 58 dead young illegal Chinese migrants. Only two had survived the journey.

Kei Su Di, aged 20, was one of the two survivors. He had left his family in China 11 days earlier, having paid the first installment of a £20,000 fee. Travelling in groups, he and his hopeful companions flew from Beijing to Belgrade, and eventually reached Rotterdam where they were all packed tightly into a lorry for the concealed and illegal journey to the UK. Tomato racks were placed at the front to conceal the illegal travellers. Each person had no more space than the size of a newspaper; they had no food or water; there were little bags for excrement; and the ventilation was off so that any noise from within the lorry could not be heard. In the end, their silenced screams as they suffocated to death are hard to imagine.

Of the 58 dead found in the container lorry, 23 came from one county (Changle) in China, and the rest from neighbouring counties. In search of a better life, they had found the equivalent of 10 years' pay to give to organised criminals (the 'Snakeheads') to 'export' them to a land of opportunity. Full of hope, their families had waved them goodbye . . .

On a cold winter's night in 2004, a group of illegal Chinese immigrants trawled the wild and unruly beach at Morecambe (near Blackpool) in search of cockles to be sold on the market. They worked nine hours for a pound in the bitter cold. The beach was notoriously dangerous – even experienced fishermen would not use it. Suddenly, they found themselves engulfed by the incoming tide and 19 of them were drowned in the darkness – not knowing which way to run or turn, or how to escape. It was subsequently found that they were living 40 to a house in the most squalid conditions.

Here are two tragic incidents involving crime and illegal migration. But odd as this may seem, this is also now part of the economy. Behind both tragedies there appears to have been a gang – The Snakeheads (named after the sliding movement of a snake) – that preys on poor migrants. In the case of the illegal lorry, they charged migrants around £20,000 each to transport them across Russia to Europe, and in 2000 it was estimated they netted some £4 billion. This is human trafficking on a large scale. It has become a hugely profitable industry, probably worth US$30 billion each year. Europe may well account for some 6–7 million illegal immigrants each year. Likewise, the migrant cockle workers were desperate for some money and, although they earned very little and they put their lives at great risk, they seemed to have no other options. Here is the rough side of our economy at work (see the film *Ghosts* (2007) and www.guardian.co.uk/refugees).

Source: *Guardian*, 19 June 2000, 6 April 2001; *The Week*, 1 July 2000; *Sunday Telegraph*, 8 February 2004.

*Global capitalism affects whatever it touches, and it touches virtually everything . . .*

Arlie Hochschild

## In this chapter, we ask:

- **What is the economy and how is it changing?**

- **What are the key different kinds of economic system?**

- **How does capitalism work?**

- **What is the nature of work and corporations in post-industrial capitalist economies?**

- **What is the nature of consumption in modern capitalism?**

Ford Madox Brown, *Work*, a detail

Source: Preliminary study for *Work*, 1863, 1852–65 (oil on canvas) (see also 62924 & 100701), Brown, Ford Madox (1821–93)/ © Manchester Art Gallery, UK/ The Bridgeman Art Library.

Discover more about the painter and his works at: www.european-artgallery.com/artist_page.cfm?painter=105 and www.manchestergalleries.org/the.collections/search-the-collection.

 This painting shows a whole range of people from various social strata going about their daily tasks. How many kinds of work can you see in this painting, how are they organised, and does the painting have much to say about social class?

It may seem odd to start a chapter on economies with two curious accounts of the death of Chinese illegal immigrants. But economies, for sociologists, are not simply about economics. For while **economies** may comprise of *social institutions that organise the production, distribution and consumption of goods and services*, such goods and services are diverse (such as here, the illegal sale of immigration) and connected to all the other social institutions, such as families (who raised money for the migrants to travel and then had to cope with their deaths), politics (where governments restrict migration and the flow of peoples), crime (where illegal immigrants were forced to work for nine hours for £1 by gang leaders) and media (which turned the deaths into a major issue). They are all interconnected. *Economies are never just economies.*

Hence in this chapter, we will explore the social significance and workings of economies, investigating the changing character of work in today's world, showing how economies are interdependent with other features of societies, suggesting that they are now more closely interconnected internationally than ever before. An opening section will look at the emergence of modern economic systems – and highlight the growth of capitalism. The chapter is then organised though the three key phases of economic organisation: (a) production, (b) distribution and (c) consumption of goods (such as food, clothing and shelter) and services (such as the work of religious leaders, doctors, police officers and telephone operators). Throughout the chapter, we will keep a close eye on social change and life in the twenty-first century.

Table 15.1 shows the largest and smallest economies of 2010. Of great interest is the rapid rise of China to second place in the world's economies. As we have suggested elsewhere (Chapters 4 and 26), this is perhaps a sign of the world to come.

| Table 15.1 | The largest and smallest economies in the world, by GDP, for 2009/10 | | | | | | |
|---|---|---|---|---|---|---|---|
| **The largest economies in the world, by GDP (US$bn)** | | | | **The smallest economies in the world, by GDP (US$bn)** | | | |
| Rank | Country | Human development rank 2010 | GDP 2010 | Rank | Country | Human development rank 2009 | GDP 2010 |
| 1 | USA | 4 | 14,799.56 | 1 | Kiribati | Not ranked | 0.152 |
| 2 | China | 89 | 5,364.87 | 2 | São Tomé and Príncipe | 127 | 0.203 |
| 3 | Japan | 11 | 5,272.94 | 3 | Tonga | 85 | 0.301 |
| 4 | Germany | 10 | 3,332.80 | 4 | Dominica | 88 | 0.375 |
| 5 | France | 14 | 2,668.79 | 5 | Samoa | Not ranked | 0.54 |
| 6 | UK | 26 | 2,222.63 | 6 | Comoros | 140 | 0.564 |
| 7 | Italy | 23 | 2,121.12 | 7 | St Kitts and Nevis | 60 | 0.565 |
| 8 | Brazil | 73 | 1,910.50 | 8 | St Vincent and the Grenadines | 93 | 0.581 |
| 9 | Canada | 8 | 1,556.035 | 9 | Grenada | 74 | 0.645 |
| 10 | Russia | 65 | 1,507.59 | 10 | Democratic Republic of Timor-Leste | 162 | 0.659 |

*Source*: Human development data adapted from HDR Statistical Tables, downloadable at http://hdr.undp.org/en/statistics/data; access date 4 September 2010. GDP data adapted from IMF World Economic Outlook database, at www.imf.org/external/ns/cs.aspx?id=28; access date 7 September 2010.

# Changing economies: the 'Great Transformations' and the development of capitalism

As Chapter 4 explained, members of the earliest human societies relied on hunting and gathering to live off the land. In these societies, production, distribution and consumption of goods were all usually primarily dimensions of family life. What is distinctive about the modern world is the growth of technologies, and with it the accompanying development of a capitalist economic system. It is part of the 'Great Transformation' we discussed in Chapter 1.

## The Agricultural Revolution

The development of agriculture about 5,000 years ago brought change to these societies. Agriculture emerged as people harnessed animals to ploughs, increasing the productive power of hunting and gathering more than tenfold. The resulting surplus freed some people in society from the demands of food production. Individuals began to adopt specialised economic roles: forging crafts, designing tools, raising animals and constructing dwellings. A division of labour started to become more and more important as size increased.

With the development of agriculture under way, towns emerged, soon to be linked by networks of traders dealing in food, animals and other goods. These four factors – agricultural technology, productive specialisation and division of labour, permanent settlements and trade – were the keys to an expansion of the economy.

In the process, the world of work became less obviously bound up with families, though production still occurred close to home. In medieval Europe, for instance, most people farmed nearby fields. Both country and city dwellers often laboured in their homes – a pattern called *cottage industry* – producing goods sold in frequent outdoor 'flea markets' (a term suggesting that not everything was of high quality).

## The Industrial Revolution

By the middle of the eighteenth century, a second technological revolution was proceeding apace, first in England and soon afterwards elsewhere in Europe and North America. The development of industry was to transform social life even more than agriculture had done thousands of years before. Industrialisation introduced five notable changes to the economies of Western societies.

1 *New forms of energy*. Throughout history, people derived energy from their own muscles or those of animals. Then, in 1765, James Watt pioneered the development of the steam engine. Surpassing muscle power 100 times over, steam engines soon operated large machinery with unprecedented efficiency.

2 *The centralisation of work in factories*. Steam-powered machinery soon rendered cottage industries obsolete. Factories – centralised and impersonal workplaces separate from the home – proliferated. Work moved from the private sphere to the public sphere – that is, people 'went out to work'.

3 *Manufacturing and mass production*. Before the Industrial Revolution, most work involved cultivating and gathering raw materials, such as crops, wood and wool. The industrial economy shifted most jobs into manufacturing, which turned raw materials into a wide range of saleable products. For example, factories mass-produced timber into furniture and transformed wool into clothing.

4 *Division of labour and specialisation*. Typically, a single skilled worker in a cottage industry fashioned a product from beginning to end. Factory work, by contrast, demands division of labour and specialisation so that a labourer repeats a single task over and over again, making only a small contribution to the finished product. Thus as factories raised productivity, they also lowered the skill level of the average worker. Despoiling occurred.

5 *Wage labour*. Instead of working for themselves or joining together as households, industrial workers entered factories as wage labourers. They sold their labour to strangers, who often cared less for them than for the machines they operated. Supervision became routine and intense. Incomes were usually pitifully low and workers were hence subject to great exploitation.

The impact of the Industrial Revolution gradually rippled outwards from the factories to transform all of society. While working conditions were very poor for many, greater productivity steadily raised the standard of living as countless new products and services filled an expanding marketplace. The benefits of industrial technology were shared very unequally. Some factory owners made vast fortunes, while the majority of industrial workers hovered perilously close to poverty. Children, too, worked in factories or deep in coal mines for pennies a day. Women factory workers, among the lowest paid, endured special hardships.

In Europe and North America, workers gradually formed trade unions to represent their collective interests in negotiations with factory owners. From the late nineteenth century onwards, governments in the West were forced to outlaw child labour, push wages upwards, improve workplace safety and extend schooling and political rights to a larger segment of the population.

## The Information Revolution and the post-industrial society

The nature of production itself also started to change. By the middle of the twentieth century, many Western countries were being transformed. Automated machinery reduced the role of human labour in production, while bureaucracy simultaneously expanded the ranks of clerical workers and managers. Service industries – such as public relations, healthcare, education, media, advertising, banking and sales –

started to employ the bulk of workers. Distinguishing the post-industrial era, then, is a shift from industrial work to service jobs.

Driving this economic change was a third technological transformation: the development of the computer and the new technologies we have encountered in previous chapters (see Chapters 1, 3, 4 and 6). The *Information Revolution* in Europe, the United States, much of newly industrialising Asia and elsewhere started to generate new kinds of information and new forms of communication, changing the character of work just as factories did two centuries ago. This Information Revolution unleashed three key changes.

1  *Tangible products to ideas.* The industrial era was defined by the production of goods; in the post-industrial era, more and more work revolves around creating and manipulating symbols. Computer programmers, writers, financial analysts, advertising executives, architects and all sorts of consultants represent the workers of the Information Age.

2  *Mechanical skills to literacy skills.* Just as the Industrial Revolution offered opportunities to those who learned a mechanical trade, the Information Revolution demands that workers have literacy skills – the ability to speak, write and use computer technology. People who can communicate effectively enjoy new opportunities; those who cannot face declining prospects.

A street cleaner sweeps a road near a coal-fired power plant at an industrial park in Shizuishan, China's northern Ningxia Hui Autonomous Region, 7 December 2009, just before the biggest climate meeting in history, with 15,000 participants from 192 nations, took place in Copenhagen seeking to agree curbs on greenhouse gas emissions and raise billions of dollars for the poor in aid and clean technology

*Source*: Corbis/REUTERS/Jason Lee.

3 *Decentralisation of work away from factories.* Just as industrial technology (steam power driving massive machines) drew workers together into factories, computer technology now permits many people to work almost anywhere. Indeed, laptop computers and facsimile (fax) machines linked to telephone lines now make the home, a car or even a plane a 'virtual office'. New information technology, in short, is reversing the industrial trend and bringing about a return of home-based 'cottage industries'. The virtual workplace and 'telecommuting' is becoming a reality for many.

The need for face-to-face communication as well as the availability of supplies and information still keep most workers in the office. On the other hand, today's more educated and creative labour force no longer requires – and often resists – the close supervision that marked yesterday's factories.

## Sectors of the economy

The three 'revolutions' just described also reflect a shifting balance among the three sectors of a society's economy. The **primary sector** *generates raw materials directly from the natural environment* and includes agriculture, animal husbandry, fishing, forestry and mining. It predominates in pre-industrial societies. The **secondary sector** *transforms raw materials into manufactured goods* and includes the refining of petroleum and the use of metals to manufacture tools and automobiles. It grows quickly as societies industrialise. The **tertiary sector** *generates services rather than goods* and includes teachers, shop assistants, cleaners, solicitors, IT experts and media workers.

The tertiary sector grows with industrialisation and dominates the economies of high-income nations as they enter the post-industrial era. Now accounting for some 70 per cent of economic output in high-income countries, it accounts for only 48 per cent in low-income societies. This marks one of the most significant changes in modern economies.

Figure 15.1 shows these differences strikingly. Here we see that in low-income countries 25 per cent of the workforce is engaged in the primary sector, compared to just 2 per cent in high-income societies. When it comes to the tertiary sector of services, some 72 per cent of the labour force is 'in service' in high-income societies, but only 47 per cent in much poorer ones. Old economic patterns of agriculture and even manufacturing are giving way to an increasingly service and information-based economy (World Bank, 2008). Table 15.2 gives the detailed breakdown for the UK and the changes between 1978 and 2008. You can see the significant growth in financial, health and education services – and a massive decline in the manufacturing base.

## The nature and variety of capitalism

As we have seen, the contemporary world is predominantly **capitalist**. It is *an economic system in which resources and the means of producing goods and services are privately owned.* It brings three key features (see the Timeline on p. 501):

1 Private ownership of property.
2 Pursuit of personal profit.
3 Free competition, consumer sovereignty and markets.

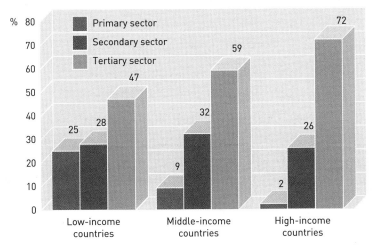

**Figure 15.1**   The size of economic sectors, by income level of country

*Source:* Macionis, John J., *Sociology, 13th*, © 2010. Printed and electronically reproduced by permission of Pearson Education, Inc., Upper Saddle River, New Jersey. Estimates based on World Bank (2008).

| Table 15.2 | Employee jobs: by industry[1] in the UK | | | | | | |
| --- | --- | --- | --- | --- | --- | --- | --- |
| **United Kingdom** | | | | | | | **Percentages** |
| | 1978 | 1988 | 1998 | 2008 | 2009 | Change 1978 to 2008 | Change 2008 to 2009 |
| Agriculture and fishing | 1.7 | 1.4 | 1.3 | 1.0 | 1.0 | −0.7 | – |
| Energy and water | 2.8 | 1.8 | 0.8 | 0.7 | 0.7 | −2.1 | – |
| Manufacturing | 28.5 | 20.7 | 17.0 | 10.5 | 10.0 | −18.0 | −0.6 |
| Construction | 5.7 | 5.1 | 4.4 | 4.8 | 4.8 | −0.8 | – |
| Distribution, hotels and restaurants | 19.5 | 21.3 | 23.8 | 23.6 | 23.5 | 4.1 | −0.1 |
| Transport and communications | 6.5 | 5.9 | 5.7 | 5.9 | 5.8 | −0.7 | −0.1 |
| Finance and business services | 10.5 | 14.8 | 18.1 | 21.4 | 20.8 | 10.9 | −0.6 |
| Public administration, education and health | 21.1 | 24.5 | 24.2 | 26.9 | 28.1 | 5.8 | 1.2 |
| Other services[2] | 3.8 | 4.5 | 4.7 | 5.3 | 5.4 | 1.5 | 0.1 |
| All industries (=100%) (millions) | 24.3 | 23.7 | 24.7 | 27.2 | 26.5 | 2.9 | −0.7 |

[1] Date are at June each year and are not seasonally adjusted. See Appendix, Part 4: Standard Industrial Classification 2003 (SIC2003).
[2] Community, social and personal services including sanitation, dry cleaning, personal care, and recreational, cultural and sporting activities.

*Source: Short-Term Employment Surveys*, Office for National Statistics in *Social Trends*, 40 (2010), p. 49.

The shape of capitalism has shifted across time and across countries. Capitalism has a long history. We can find evidence of merchants making money through investing in goods in Genoa and Venice during the twelfth century. But the arrival of a distinctively modern capitalism is usually linked to the rise of the industrial world, first in the cotton mills in England at the turn of the eighteenth century, and then throughout Europe and the United States. In this factory-based capitalism, workers sold their labour for wages and in the process capitalist owners made profits.

It was the eighteenth century thinker Adam Smith (now featured on English banknotes) who argued that the market system is dominated by consumers, who select goods and services that offer the greatest value. He developed ideas around what has come to be called 'market capitalism' and which is indentified with neoliberalism. Producers compete with one another by providing the highest-quality goods and services at the lowest possible price. Thus, while entrepreneurs are motivated by personal gain, everyone benefits from more efficient production and ever-increasing value. In Smith's time-honoured phrase, from narrow self-interest comes the 'greatest good for the greatest number of people'. Smith claimed that a free market and a competitive economy would regulate themselves by the 'invisible hand' of the laws of supply and demand. Government control of an economy would inevitably upset the complex market system, reducing producer motivation, diminishing the quantity and quality of goods produced, and short-changing consumers.

Pure, ideal capitalism is non-existent. The United States may have the purest form – private markets are more extensive than in Europe – yet even there the guiding hand of government does play a role in economic affairs. Through taxation and various regulatory agencies, the government influences what companies produce, the quality and costs of merchandise, the products that businesses import and export, and the consumption and conservation of natural resources. The federal government also owns and operates a host of businesses, including the US Postal Service, the Amtrak railway system and the Nuclear Regulatory Commission (which conducts atomic research and produces nuclear materials). The entire US military is also government-operated. Federal officials may step in to prevent the collapse of businesses, as in the 'bailout' of the savings and loan industry. Further, government policies mandate minimum wage levels, enforce workplace safety standards, regulate corporate mergers, provide farm price supports, and funnel income in the form of social security, public assistance, student loans and veterans' benefits to a majority of people.

Capitalism comes in many forms: Japan and the United States, for instance, work very differently. Generally, modern capitalism has moved through three phases. The first was a *liberal capitalism*, which dominated Britain and the United States in the early and middle nineteenth century and involved a free market, a 'facilitative' state and a legal framework which helps to maintain capitalism. Second was an *organised capitalism*, which involved an administered market and a more 'directive state'. There was, for example, in the UK between 1946 and 1979 much

more 'state' intervention as governments often shaped economic policies. More recently a *disorganised/post-Fordist capitalism* has emerged, which involves an increase in the service sector, more global and dispersed operations and a decline of nation-states (Lash and Urry, 1987). Throughout the short modern history of capitalism it has been persistently subject to periods of booms and bust (see *Timeline*).

## Disorganised capitalism: Fordism and post-Fordism

Fordism was associated with the American car manufacturer Henry Ford, who, at the start of the twentieth century, developed the assembly line to produce cheap cars that could be purchased by the

## Timeline Twentieth-century modern capitalism and its crises

Capitalism takes many forms and the last 200 years have seen a varying history of booms, depressions and crises of different scales. There is nothing new about this cycle of 'boom and bust' – in 1720 there was the famous South Sea Bubble. It is often seen to approach a ten-year cycle.

*The 'Roaring Twenties'*
- leading to the Wall Street Crash of 1929 and the Great Depression of the 1930s. It led ultimately to 'New Deal capitalism', which focused on the '3 Rs': *relief* for the unemployed and poor; *recovery* of the economy to normal levels; and *reform* of the financial system to prevent a repeat depression.

*Postwar prosperity*
- starting in the 'You never had it so good' 1950s (a phrase of UK Prime Minister Harold Macmillan) and carrying on through the 'swinging sixties'.

*The 'stagflation' of the 1970s*
- accompanied by the neoliberalism of UK Prime Minister Margaret Thatcher (Thatcherism) and President Ronald Regan (Reaganism). Here the free market became the dominant force, with officially less and less state intervention. Despite changes of governments it set a pattern of social life which influenced much of the world and continued until the 'bust' of 2008.

*Fall of Soviet Union in 1991 and global capitalism*
- the rise of China, India and the newly industrialised countries of southeast Asia (NICs) and the boom years of the 1990s and the early twenty-first century. This was a period of conspicuous consumption, living on credit, substantial loans and debts, a belief in economic growth – and massive inequalities.

*2008 financial crisis*
- the credit crunch, the crisis of subprime mortgages; banks had to be bailed out with massive debts; recession followed.

For a straightforward account of these booms and busts, see Andrew Gamble (2009).

masses. **Fordism** is *an economic system based on mass assembly-line production, mass consumption and standardised commodities*. It depends upon dedicated machinery and tools producing identical components; centralised unskilled labour used intensively on specific tasks; and low-cost production of vast quantities of goods. Workers do repetitive work over long periods: the work is usually of mind-blowing tedium. They are paid reasonably well and this increases their consumer spending. Fordism is technically limited and not very flexible. A classic study by Huw Beynon looked at the Ford motor plant in Liverpool in the late 1960s and documented this moving assembly line where about 16,000 different components had to be 'screwed, stuck or spot welded' as the car moved and slipped down the line (Beynon, 1973: 105). The relentless pressure is more amusingly documented in Charlie Chaplin's classic silent film *Modern Times*.

While Fordist production techniques continued through much of the twentieth century, newer and more flexible ones emerged alongside them (especially in Japan and southeast Asia). This newer process involved:

- shifts in production: more flexible systems of production
- more flexible time: part-time, temporary and self-employed workers
- decentralisation of labour into smaller, less hierarchical units
- the 'casualisation of labour', where work becomes less stable and secure
- 'just-in time' (that is, last-minute) rapid production
- movement from standardised goods to goods including options

- gradual replacement of 'mass marketing and advertising' by 'niche marketing', targeted at specific 'style' groups
- globalisation, with a new international division of labour.

Often called **post-Fordism**, this *new economic system is based on flexibility (rather than standardisation), specialisation and tailor-made goods* (see Table 15.3 for comparison). We have already seen some of this at work in organisational forms in Chapter 6 (where they were identified as 'postmodern'). These modes are not just to be found in work practices, but in consumption in the home as well. As we shall see, much of this new pattern has meant a system which is much more casual in its employment of workers.

# The global revolution: globalisation and the global economy

As technology draws people around the world closer together, another important economic transformation seems to be taking place. As we saw in Chapter 2, globalisation has become a key feature of the late modern world: we have witnessed the emergence of a **global economy**, *economic activity spanning many nations of the world with little regard for national borders*. The development of a global economy has six main consequences.

First, we are seeing a global division of labour by which each region of the world specialises in particular kinds of economic activity. Agriculture occupies more than 70 per cent of the workforce in low-income

| Table 15.3 | **A comparison of ideal types of production system: from Fordist to post-Fordist** | |
|---|---|---|
| | **Fordist** | **Post-Fordist** |
| Product | Standardised – all the same | Specialised – better quality? |
| Labour | Fragmented | Integrated |
| | Few tasks | Many tasks |
| | Little discretion | Flexible |
| Management | Centralised | Decentralised |
| Technology | Fixed machines | Multi-purpose/electronic |
| Contracts | Relatively secure | For most: insecure |

countries, while industrial production is concentrated in the middle- and high-income nations of the world. The economies of the richest nations, including Europe, now specialise in service-sector activity.

Secondly, we are seeing workers in the poorer countries working long hours for little pay in what have been called 'the sweatshops of the world'. They produce goods that can be sold in high-income countries. In a single day, workers may produce hundreds of garments in poor working conditions. Just one garment sold to high-income societies would sell for the equivalent of their wages for five days (Klein, 2000: 353). Often, too, these workers are compelled to travel long distances, leaving families behind, in order even to find such opportunities for work. Note, too, that very frequently this labour is that of children. The International Labour Organization suggests that some 250 million children work in low-income societies, a number that excludes child work hidden from the statisticians, such as domestic labour (often by girls). This brings the total nearer 500 million, and this does not include the children who work in high-income societies.

Thirdly, an increasing number of products pass through the economies of more than one nation. Consider, for instance, that workers in Taiwan may manufacture shoes, which a Hong Kong distributor sends to Italy, where they receive the stamp of an Italian designer; another distributor in Rome forwards the shoes to New York, where they are sold in a department store owned by a firm with its headquarters in Tokyo.

A fourth consequence of the global economy is that national governments no longer control the economic activity that takes place within their borders. In fact, governments cannot even regulate the value of their national currencies, since money is now traded around the clock in the financial centres of Tokyo, London and New York. Global markets are one consequence of satellite communications that forge information links among the world's major cities. Indeed, this gives rise to *global cities* (see Chapter 24).

The fifth consequence of the global economy is that a small number of businesses, operating internationally, now control a vast share of the world's economic activity. One estimate concludes that the 600 largest multinational companies account for fully half of the earth's entire total economic output (Kidron and Segal, 1991). The world is still divided into approximately 200 politically distinct nations. But, in light of the proliferation of international economic activity, 'nationhood' has lost much of its former significance.

Finally, a major consequence of this modern global capitalist system is the *extraordinary inequality of wealth* – the top few against the bottom billion. Look back to Chapter 9 to review the wealth of the super-rich when compared with the abject poverty of over half the world.

# Capitalism and its alternatives

Contemporary economies of the world have conventionally been seen through two abstract models – *capitalism* and *socialism*. Few societies have economies that are purely one or the other: most European countries are, to varying degrees, *mixed economies*. Sweden and the other Scandinavian countries are generally seen as a version of a more socialist approach – interventionist, corporatist and planned. But they are in the process of being pulled towards the German model, which is more inclined towards a social market. The system in the UK was mixed until the advent of Thatcherism in 1979, since when it has moved more and more towards a privatised market system (the neoliberal model).

## Socialism

**Socialism** is *an economic system in which natural resources and the means of producing goods and services are collectively owned*. In its ideal form, a socialist economy opposes each of the three characteristics of capitalism we have described above. Thus, socialism brings:

1 *Collective ownership of property*. An economy is socialist to the extent that it limits the right to private property, especially property used in producing goods and services. Laws prohibiting private ownership of property are designed to make housing and other goods available to all, not just to those with the most money. Karl Marx asserted that private ownership of productive property spawns social classes, as it generates an economic elite. Socialism, then, seeks to lessen economic inequality while forging a classless society.

2 *Pursuit of collective goals*. The individualistic pursuit of profit also stands at odds with the collective orientation of socialism. Socialist values and norms condemn what capitalists celebrate as the

entrepreneurial spirit. For this reason, private trading is branded as illegal 'black market' activity.

3 *Government control of the economy.* Socialism rejects the idea that a free-market economy regulates itself. Instead of a *laissez-faire* approach, socialist governments oversee a *centrally controlled* or *command economy.* Socialism also rejects the idea that consumers guide capitalist production. From this point of view, consumers lack the information necessary to evaluate products and are manipulated by advertising to buy what is profitable for factory owners rather than what they, as consumers, genuinely need. Commercial advertising thus plays little role in socialist economies.

The People's Republic of China and a number of nations in Asia, Africa and Latin America – some two dozen in all – model their economies on socialism, placing almost all wealth-generating property under state control. But the extent of world socialism has declined in recent years as societies in eastern Europe and the former Soviet Union have forged new economic systems increasing the sway of market forces.

## Socialism and communism

Some people equate the terms *socialism* and *communism.* More precisely, as the ideal spirit of socialism, **communism** is *an economic and political system in which all members of a society are socially equal.* Karl Marx viewed socialism as a transitory stage on the path towards the ideal of a communist society that had abolished all class divisions. In many socialist societies today, the dominant political party describes itself as communist, but nowhere has the pure communist goal been achieved.

Why? For one thing, social stratification involves differences of power as well as wealth. Socialist societies have generally succeeded in reducing disparities in wealth only through expanding government bureaucracies and subjecting the population to extensive regulation. In the process, government has not 'withered away' as Karl Marx imagined. On the contrary, socialist political elites have usually gained enormous power and privilege. Marx would probably have agreed that a communist society is a *utopia* (from Greek words meaning 'not a place'). Yet Marx considered communism a worthy goal and might well have disparaged reputedly 'Marxist' societies such as North Korea, the former Soviet Union, the People's Republic of China and Cuba for falling far short of his ideal.

## Capitalism and socialism: the big issues

Which economic system works best? In practice, most societies now work from a mix of capitalism and socialism to different degrees, although capitalism has become stronger and stronger. In 1989 and 1990, the nations of eastern Europe (seized by the Soviet Union after the Second World War) rejected their socialist regimes. And today, China is also moving towards a market economy. But what was it like before these dramatic changes? We can look at this through three dimensions: economic productivity (or GDP), economic equality and civil liberties.

### 1 Economic productivity

Important elements of GDP, such as the proportion of the international export market a country controls, varied dramatically among capitalist countries. As a group, however, capitalist countries generated more goods and services than socialist countries. Averaging the economic output of industrialised nations at the end of the 1980s yielded a per capita GDP of about US$13,500. The comparable figure for the former Soviet Union and the nations of eastern Europe was about $5,000. This means that capitalist countries outproduced socialist nations by a ratio of 2.7 to 1 (United Nations Development Programme, 1990). Recent comparisons of the differences between capitalist South Korea (at $22,985 per capita GDP) and socialist North Korea (at $1,700) finds an even sharper contrast (United Nations Development Programme, 2008).

### 2 Economic equality

How resources are distributed within a society stands as a second crucial issue. A comparative study completed in the mid-1970s calculated income ratios by comparing the earnings of the richest 5 per cent of the population and the poorest 5 per cent (Wiles, 1977). This research found that societies with predominantly capitalist economies had an income ratio of about 10 to 1; the corresponding figure for socialist countries was 5 to 1. This comparison of economic performance reveals that *capitalist economies produced a higher overall standard of living but also generated greater income disparity.* Or, put otherwise, *socialist economies created less income disparity but offered a lower overall standard of living.*

## 3 Civil liberties and personal freedom

A third issue to consider in evaluating socialism and capitalism is the personal freedom and civil liberties that each offers its citizens. Capitalism emphasises *freedom to* pursue one's self-interest. It depends on the freedom of producers and consumers to interact in a free market, with minumum interference by the state. By contrast, socialist societies emphasise *freedom from* basic wants. Equality is the goal which requires state intervention in the economy, and this in turn limits some of the choices of citizens. There are, then, major tensions between freedom from and freedom to, between freedom and equality.

This tension has not been resolved between the two systems. In the capitalist West, many freedoms are ostensibly guaranteed, but are these freedoms worth as much to a poor person as a rich one? On the other hand, in Cuba or North Korea – two of the last remaining socialist states – economic equality is bought at the expense of the rights of people to express themselves freely.

# Varieties of twenty-first century capitalism

At the start of the twenty-first century, capitalism is to be found throughout the world. Although it is in crisis, it is usually seen as the dominant contemporary form of economic organisation. It does, however, take on a range of different forms, shaped by history, governments (see Chapter 16) and cultures (see Chapter 5). For example, three kinds are regularly distinguished as:

- *Neoliberal market capitalism*: decentralised, open markets; an anti-trust or union tradition; fluid capital markets; individualism; minimum state involvement and planning; maximising returns to owners of capital; linked with the 'liberal democracy' political system (e.g. predominantly the United States, and the United Kingdom to a lesser extent, as it is also shaped by the EU – see social market capitalism, below).

- *Social market capitalism*: social partnerships, more organised markets, dedicated bank-centred capital markets; state interventions; linked with 'social democracy' (e.g. much of western Europe and the Scandinavian countries).

- *Developmental capitalism*: guided markets, tight business networks, strong bureaucracy, highly technological, reciprocity between state and firms; state plays quite a strong role; linked with 'developmental democracy' (e.g. Japan, the NICs and the Association of South-East Asian Nations) (Dicken, 2010).

Many of the nations of western Europe – including Sweden and Italy – have merged socialist economic policies with a democratic political system. Analysts call this **democratic socialism**, *an economic and political system that combines significant government control of the economy with free elections*. Under democratic socialism, the government owns some of the largest industries and services, such as transportation, the mass media and healthcare. In Sweden and Italy, about 12 per cent of economic production is state controlled or 'nationalised'. That leaves most industry in private hands, but nevertheless subject to extensive government regulation. High taxation (aimed especially at the rich) funds various social welfare programmes, transferring wealth to less advantaged members of society.

Along the Pacific Rim, in Japan, South Korea and Singapore, yet another blend of capitalism and socialism is found: **state capitalism**: *an economic and political system in which companies are privately owned, although they cooperate closely with the government*. Systems of state capitalism are all capitalist nations, but their governments work closely with large companies, supplying financial assistance or controlling imports of foreign products to help businesses function as competitively as possible in world markets. During this century, China has also conspicuously opened itself to the market system – while still keeping central state control (see Chapter 26).

Since the fall of the old socialist regimes in the late 1980s, eastern Europe (including the German Democratic Republic (GDR), Czechoslovakia, Hungary, Romania and Bulgaria) has also moved towards market-led or capitalist systems. In 1992, the Soviet Union itself dissolved. Ten years later, three-quarters of its state enterprises were partly or entirely under private ownership. There were many reasons for these sweeping changes. In part, socialist economies underproduced compared to capitalist societies, and living standards were often very low. And while members were formally equal, they often experienced large restrictions on freedom and heavy-handed states which regulated the media. New elites based on power usually appeared.

So far the market reforms in eastern Europe are very uneven. Some countries (Slovakia, the Czech Republic)

# The degradation and alienation of work in the Western world

Many people have spoken up about the conditions of work in all countries of the world. In film, in novels and in many autobiographies, you can find the voices of people talking about their work experiences. In this chapter, we have two boxes to capture this. Here we look at two studies of Western voices. In the next box (p. 509), we look at the voice of a Guatemalan girl worker. Look on the internet to find many other voices.

## Oral history

In the 1970s, the oral historian Studs Terkel conducted many interviews about the experience of work. Many of these showed how dull, repetitive jobs can generate alienation for men and women.

Phil Stallings was a 27-year-old car worker in a Ford assembly plant in Chicago.

I start the automobile, the first welds. From there it goes to another line, where the floor's put on, the roof, the trunk, the hood, the doors. Then it's put on a frame. There is hundreds of lines. . . .

I stand in one spot, about two- or three-feet area, all night. The only time a person stops is when the line stops. We do about thirty-two jobs per car, per unit. Forty-eight units an hour, eight hours a day. Thirty-two times forty-eight times eight. Figure it out. That's how many times I push that button.

The noise, oh it's tremendous. You open your mouth and you're liable to get a mouthful of sparks. [Shows his arms.] That's a burn, these are burns. You don't compete against the noise. You go to yell and at the same time you're straining to manoeuvre the gun to where you have to weld.

You got some guys that are uptight, and they're not sociable. It's too rough. You pretty much stay to yourself. You get involved with yourself. You dream, you think of things you've done. I drift back continuously to when I was a kid and what me and my brothers did. The things you love most are what you drift back into.

It don't stop. It just goes and goes and goes. I bet there's men who have lived and died out there, never seen the end of the line. And they never will – because it's endless. It's like a serpent. It's just all body, no tail. It can do things to you . . .

(Terkel, 1977: 151)

Twenty-four-year-old Sharon Atkins was a college graduate working as a telephone receptionist for a large midwestern business.

I don't have much contact with people. You can't see them. You don't know if they're laughing, if they're being satirical or being kind. So your conversations become very abrupt. I notice that in talking to people. My conversation would be very short and clipped, in short sentences, the way I talk to people all day on the telephone . . .

You try to fill up your time with trying to think about other things: what you're going to do on the weekend or about your family. You have to use your imagination. If you don't have a very good one and you bore easily, you're in trouble. Just to fill in time, I write real bad poetry or letters to myself and to other people and never mail them. The letters are fantasies, sort of rambling, how I feel, how depressed I am . . .

I never answer the phone at home.

(Terkel, 1977: 60)

## Participant observation

More recently, Barbara Ehrenreich (2001) in the USA and Polly Toynbee (2003) in the UK have experimented with going undercover in the world of low-paid women's work. They worked in cafés and fast-food restaurants, acted as cleaners and maids, as well as working in factories. Both were highly educated middle-class women, but on low incomes they did not fare well. They felt stigmatised; they had difficulty finding a place to live or ways of getting to work; and of course they worked long hours, often with gruelling work. And there was more to the work than they thought. Barbara Ehrenreich remarks towards the end of her book:

How did I do as a low-wage worker? If I may begin with a brief round of applause: I didn't do half bad at the work itself, and I claim this as a considerable achievement. You might think that unskilled jobs would be a snap for someone who holds a Ph.D. and whose normal line of work requires learning entirely new things every couple of weeks. Not so. The first thing I discovered is that no job, no matter how lowly, is truly 'unskilled.' Every one of the six jobs I entered into the course of this project required concentration, and most demanded that I master new terms, new tools, and new skills – from placing orders on restaurant computers to wielding the backpack vacuum cleaner. None of these things came as easily to me as I would have liked; no one ever said, 'Wow you're fast!' or 'Can you believe she just started?'

Whatever my accomplishments in the rest of my life, in the low-wage work world I was a person of average ability – capable of learning the job and also capable of screwing up.

(Ehrenreich, 2001: 193–4)

are faring well; others (such as the Russian Federation itself) have brought out many of the weakest points of capitalism, with growing poverty and inequality, high competitiveness and social decline (Burawoy, 1997).

To conclude: countries in eastern Asia, western Europe, eastern Europe and elsewhere illustrate that there are many ways in which governments and companies can work cooperatively. Blends of socialism and capitalism are becoming a common pattern.

## Global capitalism: triumph or crisis?

For many, then, it looks as if capitalism is here to stay: it is seen as the dominant (and for many, the only way) of organising the economy across the world. There are now very few societies that support a strict socialist/communist model (North Korea, Cuba and a few states in Africa and Latin America). All rivals are usually dismissed. Nowhere is this view clearer than in Francis Fukuyama's much discussed book *The End of History* (1989). For him, history came to an end with the triumph of Western capitalism. The Soviet bloc had collapsed and we are now living in an age of permanent capitalism.

By contrast, the political philosopher John Gray in his book *False Dawn* (2002) argues that the unfettered global free market economy is not likely to stay. In the long run of world history, contemporary capitalism will be seen as a mere blip. With modern capitalism we increasingly find social instability, growing social inequalities and economic unpredictability across the world. This may not be tenable into the distant future. Indeed, Gray argues that 'the free market is a rare, short-lived phenomenon', a specific product of English nineteenth-century social engineering, from whose cycles of boom and bust we still have much to learn.

Gray does not, however, see the future as bringing a return to the socialist models of the past. Indeed,

at present, he offers few solutions to 'the deepening international anarchy' in which free markets spiral out of control. At the start of the twenty-first century, it is unclear to Gray and many others in which direction our economies are now heading.

## The changing nature of work

Work seems to be a precondition of social life. Three billion people on this planet labour for wages. They sell their labour for money. And most spend some 70 to 80 per cent of their lives working in order to meet their everyday needs and wants. They live and work in every imaginable place – from the salt mines of Russia to the most remote Chilean village. Their work conditions and their work experiences vary enormously. Men and women, old and young, work – but their experiences may be hugely different. Yet at the same time, others are unemployed – around 160 million are seeking employment. And many millions (as we saw in the opening stories) travel from their homeplaces to find employment and are often stigmatised 'migrant workers'. A much smaller number of people employ these people. The wealthiest of these 'business people' and employers – like Bill Gates and Rupert Murdoch – control finances that are equal to that of small countries (cf. Castree et al., 2004: xi). In this section, we look at some of the basic characteristics of work and just how it may be changing in the twenty-first century.

## Work in Europe and the UK

First, here are a few details about the numbers who work. In 2009, about 65 per cent of the EU-27's population aged between 15 and 64 were employed. In 12 member states, over 67 per cent were employed (in

Germany, Denmark, Cyprus, the Netherlands, Austria, Slovenia, Finland, Sweden, the United Kingdom, Iceland and Norway). But the employment rate remained below 60 per cent in Spain, Italy, Hungary, Malta, Poland, Romania and Croatia. Table 15.4 shows a detailed breakdown of this for you to consider – showing also the gender differences between employment for men and women. Across Europe, the working week in 2007 approximated 42 hours – but there were variations, the number of hours being lowest in Norway, Luxembourg, Lithuania, Ireland and Denmark, and highest in the UK, Austria, the Czech Republic, Poland and Slovenia.

Looking at the UK in 2009, there were 31.4 million people over 16 in work. Around 18 million people were economically inactive. Figure 15.2 shows the ways this was patterned over the life cycle (age) and between men and women. Across the country, there are also large variations: in 2008, working-age employment rates were highest in Scotland, at 76 per cent, while in Northern Ireland only 70 per cent of working-age persons were employed. In England, London had a relatively low employment rate of 70 per cent, while the highest employment rate was to be found in the southeast, at 79 per cent.

Contrary to a popular stereotype, the number of hours worked per week has been going up in recent years – we are not becoming a 'leisure society'. Looking at Europe, people working full time in Italy worked 37 hours per week (the lowest in the EU), whilst those in the UK worked 42 hours (one hour less than the countries with the highest number of hours worked) (*Social Trends*, 2004: Chapters 4 and 5).

Age clearly also affects labour force participation. Typically, both women and men join the workforce in their teens and early twenties. During their child-bearing years, however, women's participation lags behind that of men. After about the age of 45, the working profiles now differ, with women more likely to continue in work and men less likely. There is a marked withdrawal from the labour force as people approach the age of 65. After that point in life, only a small proportion of each gender continues to perform steady income-producing work.

| Table 15.4 | Employment rates: by gender, EU comparison, 2008 | | | | | | |
|---|---|---|---|---|---|---|---|
| | | | | | | | Percentages |
| | Men | Women | All | | Men | Women | All |
| Denmark | 81.9 | 74.3 | 78.1 | Spain | 73.5 | 54.9 | 64.3 |
| Netherlands | 83.2 | 71.1 | 77.2 | Lithuania | 67.1 | 61.8 | 64.3 |
| Sweden | 76.7 | 71.8 | 74.3 | Bulgaria | 68.5 | 59.5 | 64.0 |
| Austria | 78.5 | 65.8 | 72.1 | Luxembourg | 71.5 | 55.1 | 63.4 |
| United Kingdom | 77.3 | 65.8 | 71.5 | Belgium | 68.6 | 56.2 | 62.4 |
| Finland | 73.1 | 69.0 | 71.1 | Slovakia | 70.0 | 54.6 | 62.3 |
| Cyprus | 79.2 | 62.9 | 70.9 | Greece | 75.0 | 48.7 | 61.9 |
| Germany | 75.9 | 65.4 | 70.7 | Poland | 66.3 | 52.4 | 59.2 |
| Estonia | 73.6 | 66.3 | 69.8 | Romania | 65.7 | 52.5 | 59.0 |
| Slovenia | 72.7 | 64.2 | 68.6 | Italy | 70.3 | 47.2 | 58.7 |
| Latvia | 72.1 | 65.4 | 68.6 | Hungary | 63.0 | 50.6 | 56.7 |
| Portugal | 74.0 | 62.5 | 68.2 | Malta | 72.5 | 37.4 | 55.2 |
| Ireland | 74.9 | 60.2 | 67.6 | | | | |
| Czech Republic | 75.4 | 57.6 | 66.6 | EU-27 average | 72.8 | 59.1 | 65.9 |
| France | 69.8 | 60.7 | 65.2 | | | | |

*Source*: Eurostat, *Labour Force Survey*, © European Union, 2008.

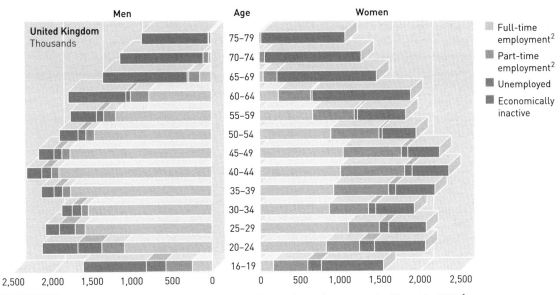

**Figure 15.2** Economic activity and inactivity status: by gender and age over the life cycle, 2009[1]

[1] Data are at Q2 and are not seasonally adjusted.
[2] The *Labour Force Survey* asks people to classify themselves as full or part time, based on their own perceptions.

*Source: Labour Force Survey*, Office for National Statistics in *Social Trends*, 40 (2010), Fig. 4.2, p. 45.

# The story of an eight-year-old agricultural worker in Guatemala

The story of Rigoberta Menchú has become a famous life story in social science. She tells the story of her life in her book *I, Rigoberta Menchú* – the life of a Guatemalan peasant who experiences revolutionary change. After the success of her book, she went on to become a leading political figure. In the extract below, she talks of her early work experiences in the family and on the fields.

I worked from when I was very small, but I didn't earn anything. I was really helping my mother because she always had to carry a baby, my little brother on her back as she picked coffee. It made me very sad to see my mother's face covered in sweat as she tried to finish her load, and I wanted to help her. But my work wasn't paid, it just contributed to my mother's work. I either picked coffee with her or looked after my little brother, so that she could work faster. My brother was two at the time . . . I remember that, at the time, my mother's work was making food for forty workers. She ground maize, made tortillas, and put the nixtamal on the fire and cooked beans for the workers' food. That's a difficult job . . . All the dough made in the morning has to be finished the same morning because it goes bad. My mother had to make the number of tortillas the workers would eat. She was very appreciated by the workers because the food she gave them was fresh.

I was five when she was doing this work and I looked after my little brother. I wasn't earning yet. I used to watch my mother, who often had the food ready at three o'clock in the morning for the workers who started work early, and at eleven she had the food for the midday meal ready. At seven in the evening she had to run around again making food for her group. In between times, she worked picking coffee to supplement what she earned. Watching her made me feel useless and weak because I couldn't do anything to help her except look after my brother. That's when my consciousness was born. It's true. My mother didn't like the idea of me working, of earning my own money, but I did. I wanted to work, more than anything to help her, both economically and physically. The thing was that my mother was very brave and stood up to everything well, but there were times when one of my brothers or sisters was ill – if it wasn't one of them it was another – and everything she earned went on medicine for them. This made me very sad as well . . .

When I turned eight, I started to earn money on the finca. I set myself the task of picking 35 pounds of coffee a day . . . my brothers and sisters finished work at about seven or eight in the evening and sometimes offered to help me, but I said: 'No, I have to learn because if I don't learn myself, who's going to teach me?' I had to finish my

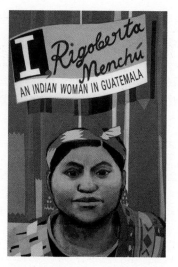

Rigoberta Menchú

Source: *I, Rigoberta Menchú: An Indian Woman in Guatemala*, Verso, New Left Books, designed, illustrated and reprinted by permission of Sophie Herxheimer.

workload myself. Sometimes I picked barely 28 pounds because I got tired, especially when it was very hot. It gave me a headache. I'd fall asleep

under a coffee bush, when suddenly I'd hear my brothers and sisters coming to look for me.

In the mornings we'd take turns to go off into the scrub to do our business. There are no toilets in the finca. There was only this place up in the hills where everyone went. There were about 400 of us living there and everyone went to this same place. It was the toilet for all those people. We had to take it in turns. When one lot of people came back, another lot would go. There were a lot of flies on all that filth up there and everyone went to this same place. There was only one tap in the shed where we lived, not even enough for us to wash our hands.

Source: Menchú (1984); see also Menchú (1998).

# The decline of agricultural work

When the twentieth century began, about 40 per cent of the industrial world's labour force were engaged in farming. By its end, the figure was nearer 2 per cent, and many agricultural workers worked part time. Even though today's agriculture involves fewer people, it is often more productive. A century ago, a typical farmer grew food for five people; today, one farmer feeds 75. This dramatic rise in productivity also reflects new types of crop, pesticides that increase yields, more efficient machinery and other advances in farming technology. While in southern Europe holdings remain small (4 to 7 hectares in Greece, Portugal and Italy), in the north the holdings are much larger (in the UK, the average is 68 hectares).

This process signals the eclipse of 'family farms', which are declining in number and produce only a small part of our agricultural yield, in favour of large *corporate agribusinesses*. But, more productive or not, this transformation has wrought painful adjustments for farming communities across the country, as a way of life is lost.

# From factory work to service work

Industrialisation swelled the ranks of factory workers during the nineteenth century, but by 1911 more than 45 per cent of the United Kingdom workforce had service jobs (with 40 per cent in industry and some 15 per cent in agriculture) (Coleman and Salt, 1992: 375). Jobs in the service industries have continued to increase: between 1978 and 2000 by 36 per cent, from 15.6 million in 1978 to 21.2 million (and those in manufacturing industry fell by 39 per cent from 7.0 million to 4.2 million). Overwhelmingly, then, jobs in the industrialised world have moved to the service sector.

'Teleworking' has become well established as a form of work. Between 1997 and 2002, the number of such workers grew by 70 per cent and in spring 2001 there were 2.2 million teleworkers (equivalent to 7.4 per cent of the total UK workforce). Some of these work mainly in their own home or in various locations using home as a base, but others work at 'call centres'. In the second quarter of 2009, 84,000 people worked as call centre agents and operators in the UK, and 52,000 worked as telephone salespersons.

Not surprisingly, workers are often young and female, and the conditions in such call centres can be the modern equivalent of the old steel mills, with 'customer service representatives' (CSRs) being expected to take as many as 20 calls an hour, or even two calls a minute. It is a new service industry that is relentless. And as with so much work in high-income countries, much of this work is farmed out to low-income countries such as India.

In addition, note the growth of the new information technology (IT) sector. The trend towards a 'knowledge society' signposts a real shift in patterns of work. By mid-2009, the IT sector was prevalent and pervaded all forms of work: 189,000 persons worked as IT technicians in the UK, and 141,000 were employed as IT strategy and planning professionals. An additional 297,000 were working as managers in fields related to information and communications technology.

The growth of service occupations is one reason for the widespread description of Europe as a middle-class society. Nevertheless, as explained in Chapter 10, much service work – including sales positions, secretarial work and jobs in fast-food restaurants – yields little of the income and prestige of professional white-collar occupations, and often provides fewer rewards than factory work. In short, more and more jobs in this post-industrial era provide only a modest standard of living. This is illustrated in Table 15.5.

## The dual labour market

The change from factory work to service jobs represents a shifting balance between two categories of work. The **primary labour market** includes *occupations that provide extensive benefits to workers*. This favoured segment of the labour market contains the traditional white-collar professions and high management positions. These are jobs that people think of as *careers*. Work in the primary labour market provides high income and job security and is also personally challenging and intrinsically satisfying. Such occupations require a broad education rather than specialised training, and offer solid opportunity for advancement.

But few of these advantages apply to work in the **secondary labour market**, *jobs providing minimal benefits to workers*. This segment of the labour force is employed in the low-skilled, blue-collar type of work found in routine assembly-line operations, and in

low-level service-sector jobs, including clerical positions. The secondary labour market offers workers much lower income, demands a longer working week and affords less job security and opportunity to advance. Not surprisingly, then, workers in the secondary labour market are most likely to experience alienation and dissatisfaction with their jobs. These problems most commonly beset women and other minorities, who are over-represented in this segment of the labour force. In spring 1996, only 8 per cent of male employees worked part time, while some 45 per cent of women did (*Social Trends*, 1997: 71).

Most new jobs in our post-industrial economy fall within the secondary labour market, and they involve the same kind of unchallenging tasks, low wages and poor working conditions characteristic of jobs in factories a century ago. Moreover, job insecurity is on the rise as the economy shuttles an unprecedented share of workers from one temporary position to another.

## Gender, women and work

One of the most striking features of the modern world is that more and more women are working across the world, accounting for around 36–40 per cent of the world's labour force. Men, by contrast, become increasingly unemployed, both when young and as they get older.

In the UK, for example, working men and women have different patterns of work at most ages. Young men (16–19) are least likely to be in work; men in their thirties and forties are most likely to work, with around 82 per cent employed full time in 2009; and at later ages, men's work activity sharply declines. For women, full-time employment was at its highest for women aged 25 to 29, with 53 per cent in full-time employment in 2009, and fell to 42 per cent for women aged 35 to 39. Part-time employment then becomes more common. There has been a steady growth of women in the labour market, from roughly 30 per cent in 1945 to 45 per cent by the end of the twentieth century. Over the last 40 years the numbers have grown from 10 million (in 1971) to 13 million in 1999. By 2009 employment rates for men and women had significantly converged, but they had not equalised (*Social Trends*, 2009). Part-time employment continues to be more common among women than among men, particularly in younger age groups. Indeed, the characteristics of women's work are often very different from those of men:

**Table 15.5    Highest- and lowest-paid occupations, and average hourly pay (£), excluding overtime, for employee jobs, United Kingdom, 2009**

| Lowest paid | £ |
|---|---|
| 1  Sales occupations | 7.46 |
| 2  Elementary administration and service occupations | 7.55 |
| 3  Elementary trades, plant and storage-related occupations | 8.39 |
| 4  Caring personal service occupations | 8.72 |
| 5  Textiles, printing and other skilled trades | 8.86 |
| 6  Customer service occupations | 8.95 |
| 7  Skilled agricultural trades | 8.98 |
| 8  Transport and mobile machine drivers and operatives | 9.58 |
| 9  Leisure and other personal service occupations | 9.62 |
| 10  Process, plant and machine operatives | 10.30 |

| Highest paid | £ |
|---|---|
| 1  Health professionals | 31.89 |
| 2  Corporate managers | 23.19 |
| 3  Teaching and research professionals | 21.27 |
| 4  Business and public service professionals | 21.12 |
| 5  Science and technology professionals | 19.66 |
| 6  Culture, media and sports occupations | 16.45 |
| 7  Business and public service associate professionals | 16.38 |
| 8  Protective service occupations | 16.05 |
| 9  Managers and proprietors in agriculture and services | 15.67 |
| 10  Health and social welfare associate professionals | 14.97 |

*Source*: Adapted from Annual Survey of Hours and Earnings 2009, Table 2.6a; www.statistics.gov.uk/downloads/theme_labour/ASHE-2009/tab2_6a.xls, access date 4 September 2010.

- They work more often for wages (as opposed to salaries).
- They are usually paid less than men.
- Often their work has less status.
- Job insecurity is greater.
- They are more likely to become unemployed in many countries.
- Advances into administrative and managerial positions are often blocked by what has been called 'the glass ceiling'.

Further, a process of **occupational gender segregation** *works to concentrate men and women in different types*

*of job*. According to *Social Trends*, men in 2009 were most likely to be employed as managers or senior officials, while women were most likely to be employed in administrative and secretarial work; 16 per cent of women worked in personal service occupations, such as hairdressing and childcare, and 11 per cent worked in customer service occupations. These occupations were much less likely to be found among men (3 and 5 per cent, respectively). Women's work is also often characterised by what Arlie Hochschild has called a 'second shift' (maybe even more precisely, a triple shift). After a day's work in the factory or the office, the woman usually returns home to do the domestic work, raise the children and cook the meals (we consider this in Chapters 12 and 17). All this is unpaid work.

## 'Doing the dirty work'

This unpaid and often hidden work – domestic labour – has another aspect. There is also a significant amount which is paid and visible: largely that which is performed by women employed by middle-class men and women. Such work is often disproportionately performed by racialised groups and migrant workers.

Bridget Anderson (2000), in her study of migrant domestic workers in five European cities (Athens, Barcelona, Bologna, Berlin and Paris) in the mid-1990s, found that such work not only brought low pay and long hours, it could amount to a kind of 'slavery'. Women from poor countries would be asked to do impossible lists of work tasks; to care for children and families; to have very little time away from the home where they worked; and to be treated in subservient ways. Often they found it difficult to break away from the middle-class family that 'bought' them.

## The sweatshops of the world

This global labour goes further. In lower-income countries, women are often compelled to work in the 'sweatshops of the world'. The term 'sweatshop' was introduced around the 1880s during the Industrial Revolution to describe the subcontracting system of labour. Miriam Ching Yoon Louie comments:

> Sweatshop workers toil at the bottom of a pyramid of labour exploitation and profit generation. Workers' immediate bosses are subcontractors, often men of their own ethnicity. Manufacturers and retailers sit at the top of the pyramid over the contractors who act as buffers, shock absorbers and shields . . . Like the nineteenth-century sweatshop middle-men, many of today's subcontractors survive the competition by 'sweating' their workers out of wages, hours, benefits and safety rights.

(Louie, 2001: 4)

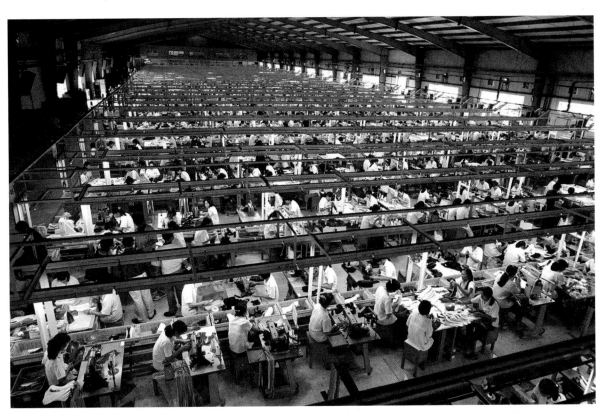

In the poorer countries all over the world, workers are exploited to produce goods for the richer nations, as in this Korean enterprise where many Burmese work on textile production

*Source*: Richard Vogel/AP/PA Photos.

Such sweatshops are especially common in the garment industry. With exceptionally low incomes (much less than a pound a day), work conditions are subject to little or no regulation, are casual and temporary, and are often hazardous. Much of women's work here is uncounted, so official figures can mean very little. These women are also 'on the move', migrating to where the work is. For example, each year about 100,000 women leave Asia's developing countries to work in newly industrialising economies. Although the world's agricultural force is shrinking rapidly, it is also becoming feminised – some 40 per cent of agricultural workers worldwide are women. For many women around the world, globalisation is a concrete process of exploitation. As Christa Wichterich writes in *The Globalized Woman*:

> **Female textile-workers from Upper Lusatia in Eastern Germany are losing their jobs to women in Bangladesh; Filipinas clean vegetables and kitchens in Kuwait; Brazilian prostitutes offer their services around Frankfurt's main railway station; and Polish women look after old people at rock-bottom prices in various parts of Germany. Women in the Caribbean key in commercial entries for North American banks. In the Philippines, families who make a living by sorting through refuse cannot sell their plastic wares whenever a shipment of unbeatably cheap waste, collected by Germany's recycling scheme, arrives. And what is for the next meal is decided not by local women, but by multinationals specialising in novelty food and genetically modified crops.**

(Wichterich, 2000: viii)

## Business process outsourcing

A rapidly growing sector of work has been the spreading of industries from high-income societies to lower-income societies: we have already seen this in the manufacturing of many commodities above, but we also find it now in the re-routing of telephone calls to call centres set up in poorer parts of the world where educated workers can be paid much less. In India, business process outsourcing (BPO) has grown by 60 per cent a year since 2000 and employs over a million people. It employs graduates for long hours, having trained them in English to answer calls. Workers make about £140 in a month, way below the UK or US salaries for equivalent work, but more than a farm worker in India would make in six months.

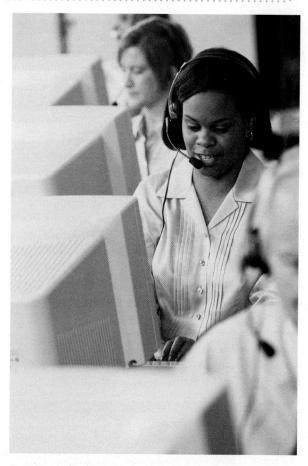

Female telephone operator working in a call centre, giving advice over the phone.
*Source*: Pearson Education Ltd/Eyewire.

## The spread of part-time and flexible work

Over the past decade, part-time work has become more common – especially for women. In the UK in 2009, there were some 7.5 million part-time jobs, of which 5.6 million were done by women. One consequence of this can be the undermining of job security. Several decades ago, workers could confidently assume that hard work and playing by the rules all but guaranteed that their jobs would be there until they were ready to retire. This is no longer the case.

In the short run, at least, the dislocation for workers is tremendous. Companies scrambling to 'remain competitive' in the global economy are 'downsizing' and decentralising to gain 'flexibility'. These trends mean not only cutting the number of people on the payroll – managers as well as secretaries – but also replacing long-term employees with temporary workers. By hiring 'temps', companies no longer have to worry about providing insurance, paid vacations or pensions. And, if next month workers are no longer needed, they can be released without further cost.

## Self-employment

**Self-employment** – *earning a living without working for a large organisation* – was once commonplace in Europe. Families owned and operated farms, and self-employed urban workers owned shops and other small businesses or sold their skills on the open market. With the onset of the Industrial Revolution, however, the economy became more centralised so that self-employment diminished. But more recently this has been changing. The number of self-employed people in the UK increased throughout the 1980s to peak at 3.6 million in 1990. In spring 1996 there were 3.3 million, three-quarters of whom were men. By 2009, the rate of self-employment was 13.7 per cent. In the European Union as a whole, 18.8 per cent of all employment was self-employment. Particularly high rates of self-employment were found in Greece and Romania, at more than 30 per cent. In contrast, in Sweden, Estonia, Luxembourg and Denmark, rates of self-employment lay below 10 per cent.

Most self-employed workers work in agriculture, fishing and construction, and are more likely to perform blue-collar than white-collar work. Society has always painted an appealing picture of working independently: no time clocks to punch, no one looking over your shoulder. For minorities who have long been excluded from particular kinds of work, self-employment has been an effective strategy for broadening economic opportunity. Further, self-employment holds the potential – though it is rarely realised – of earning a great deal of money. But for all its advantages, self-employment is vulnerable to fluctuations in the economy, which is one reason that only one-fifth of small businesses survive for more than ten years. Another common problem is that the self-employed generally lack pension and healthcare benefits provided for employees by large organisations.

## The underground economy

Running parallel with the economic activity monitored and regulated by governments is the **underground economy**, *economic activity generating income that is unreported to the government as required by law.* On a small scale, most people participate in the underground economy on a regular basis. One family makes extra money from a car boot sale; another allows its teenage children to baby-sit for the neighbours without reporting the income received. Taken in total, such activities amount to millions of pounds in lost taxes annually. But much of the underground economy (or 'black economy') is attributable to criminal activity, which can run into billions of pounds. We opened with the story of 'people trafficking', which may well be a hidden economy of many billions of pounds, but to this we can add the sale of illegal drugs and weapons, trafficking of stolen goods, bribery, extortion, illegal gambling and money laundering. Some countries, including parts of the Russian Federation and parts of Latin America, face larger problems with illicit activity than others. But the dimensions of this form of work are also clearly global: there is a globalised underground economy.

## Non-work

In 2009, 72.7 per cent of the working-age population were employed. This means that nearly 1 in 5 of those of working age were unemployed. Some 37 per cent of working-age individuals in the UK (18 million people) were economically inactive: that is, not working because of being a student, having a disability, retirement, or having duties of care towards family members. The main reasons for economic inactivity were being a student and long-term sickness or disability. Together, these reasons covered nearly two in three of the economically inactive population.

In 2009, 16.9 per cent of UK households (3.3 million) were workless. According to the Office for National Statistics, this is the highest rate measured since 1999. About 4.8 million people lived in these households, among them 1.9 million children. Some sociologists have started to suggest that a future trend may well be the rise of the workless society, but others suggest that a main trend is rather towards increasingly fragmented and casual work patterns.

Recent trends are undoing workplace bonds with remarkable speed and at all levels of the labour force. Like workers at the dawn of the industrial era centuries ago, many of today's secretaries, engineers, bank staff and even corporate executives are finding their job security vanishing before their eyes. For the foreseeable future, there is probably no going back to the traditional notion of lifetime employment with one company.

# Changes in trade unions

The changing economy has been accompanied by a declining role for **trade unions**, *organisations of workers collectively seeking to improve wages and working conditions through various strategies, including negotiations and strikes*. Membership in trade unions increased rapidly in Europe through the earlier part of the twentieth century, peaking at 13 million people in the UK in 1979 (around 55 per cent). But by the mid-1990s it had dropped to 9 million (around 35 per cent); by 2000 it had fallen to 29 per cent. In 2009, there were 7.1 million trade union members in the UK (*Social Trends*, 2010). Figure 15.3 maps the rise and fall of the unions in the UK – a pattern repeated in many countries of the world.

During the 1980s, the British government under Margaret Thatcher was firmly committed to weakening the power of trade unions. Blaming unions for strikes and industrial unrest, the Thatcher government introduced much legislation (like the 1980 Employment Act and the 1984 Trade Union Act) which made secret ballots on industrial action compulsory, prohibited 'secondary picketing' by restricting union members to picket only at their own place of work, and made industrial action in support of workers employed elsewhere illegal. The Thatcher government also reduced consultation with union officials. Symbolically, too, this was the time of the 1985 miners' strike, in

which pit closures became a key issue and which was used by Thatcher as a key defining moment to bring the unions down. Add to this the increases in unemployment during this period and it is clear that the unions' strength was considerably undermined. Hyman sees all this as a process of 'coercive pacification' in which employers and government suppress and weaken union activities (Hyman, 1989).

But the decline of unions is not an isolated British phenomenon. In the United States, in absolute numbers, union membership peaked during the 1970s at almost 25 million people. Since then, it has declined steadily. In 2009, 12.3 per cent of all wage and salary workers in the USA were union members.

While a similar trend has emerged throughout Europe, in a few countries, particularly Denmark, trade union membership has actually increased. Roughly 80 per cent of workers in the Scandinavian countries belong to unions, and employer–union cooperation is high. In Europe as a whole about 40 per cent belong to unions, while in Canada and Japan the proportion is about one-third (Western, 1993, 1995).

The relative decline of unions stems from a number of trends already noted. First, industrial countries have lost tens of thousands of jobs in the highly unionised factories as industrial jobs have been 'exported' overseas. Many plant managers have succeeded in forcing concessions from workers, including, in some

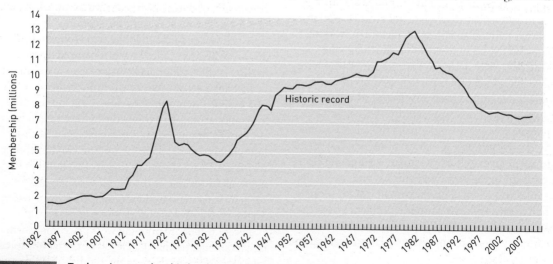

**Figure 15.3**   Trade union membership levels in the UK, 1892–2009

*Source: Labour Force Survey*, Office for National Statistics; Department for Employment (1892–1974); Certification Office (1974–2007/8) in Archur, J. (2010) *Trade Union Membership 2009*, Dept for Business, Innovation and Skills, Chart 1.1, p. 3.

cases, the dissolution of trade unions. Moreover, most of the new service-sector jobs being created today are not unionised, and hardly any temporary workers belong to a trade union. Young people are much less likely to be unionised than older workers.

Falling job security may well make union membership a higher priority for workers in the years to come. But to expand their membership, unions will also have to adapt to the new global economy. Instead of seeing foreign workers as a threat to their interests, in short, union leadership will have to forge new international alliances.

# The quality and experience of work: from dehumanisation to 'decent work'

To conclude this section, it may be helpful for you to consider the nature of employment relations in the modern workplace, and to ponder the kind of work that you would like and the situation more generally of most people in the world. Among the issues to consider are:

- *Autonomy*: does the worker have some autonomy, or does management strictly control and regulate?

- *Training*: does the worker get training for specific skills, or is there no training and a presumption of no skill?

- *Wages*: does the worker get a reasonable wage? A good wage? A fair wage? An exploitative wage? A low wage?

- *Hours*: does the worker have fixed and limited hours, or are they long and variable?

- *Promotion*: good opportunities or no prospects?

- *Security*: permanence, fixed contracts, temporary or job insecurity?

- *Status*: full time or temporary?

- *Non-wage perks*: does the worker have access to a company pension (or a company car), or are there no non-wage perks?

- *Facilities*: just what is the work environment like – does it have good facilities, or are they poor?

- *Health support*: does the work environment provide 'health and safety' or not?

- *Worker representation*: does the worker have some kind of voice, a union, in which they can debate problems and grievances, or not?

Putting the questions as bluntly as this, we can see that the world is, and always has been, very divided. There are those for whom the experience of work is positive: they have autonomy, feel their work is valued, and work the hours they need. But for others (and this is probably most of the world's population), work overwhelmingly brings low skills, low wages, long hours, no autonomy and insecurity; it is short lived and has no supports or prospects. This work is often described as degraded and dehumanised – people become objects of work and lose their human dignity. It was a major theme of Marx's theory that under capitalism the condition of labourers and their work would become increasingly unbearable. Looking around the world today, there is plenty of evidence that much work is indeed dehumanised and degraded.

At the simplest level, consider yet more statistics. There are about 200 million children (below 15) who work. Some 12.3 million people endure 'forced labour'. Only 20 per cent of the world's population get any kind of social security. About 86 million people have to leave their home countries for work. And for around one in five of the world, the hours worked in a week are over 48, and many work a seven-day week.

In the light of all this, the idea of 'decent work' as a worldwide goal for labour systems has been introduced. The International Labour Organization (originally founded in 1919 and now a branch of the United Nations) comments:

> Decent work sums up the aspirations of people in their working lives. It involves opportunities for work that is productive and delivers a fair income, security in the workplace and social protection for families, better prospects for personal development and social integration, freedom for people to express their concerns, organize and participate in the decisions that affect their lives, and equality of opportunity and treatment for all women and men'.

(www.ilo.org/global/Themes/Decentwork)

## Ulrich Beck: a brave new world of work in a globalised risk society

*THINKERS & THEORY*

German sociologist Ulrich Beck (1944–) is a Professor of Sociology at Munich University and the London School of Economics. Since 1986, when he published his key first book *The Risk Society* in German, he has produced a large volume of influential work around the new world order.

For Beck, old work society is going. The old order – first modernity – was characterised by 'collective lifestyles, full employment, the national state and the welfare state, and an attitude of heedless exploitation of nature' (Beck, 2000a: 18). The new world order sees the decline of paid employment, globalisation, and new crises around the environment, gender and technologies.

He characterises this newly emerging society variously as:

(a) A 'second modernity' which is replacing the age of simple modernity linked to capitalist industrialisation.

(b) A 'global risk society' which brings growing uncertainty. Risk now derives less from the natural dangers of the past (like earthquakes or floods) and more from the new technologies that we have created (from computer dependency to new genetic modification) (see Chapter 19). Life becomes insecure, uncertain and risky.

(c) A 'reflexive modernity', in which people become more and more aware of the problems inherent in the first modernity. Life becomes more aware of the problems of living. The idea of 'sustainability', discussed in Chapter 24, is an example.

(d) An 'individualised society'. Whereas the safe structures of modernity had involved stable families, protected and stable jobs, strong local communities and class loyalty, now the world becomes much less stable and thoroughly individualised. The world becomes more individualised rather than collective, life now becomes a 'do-it-yourself' biography, work becomes more 'chopped up' and consumption becomes pervasive.

(e) A 'cosmopolitan society' is one which looks beyond the borders and boundaries of nation-states and fixed identities. Beck looks towards a future where 'in a radically insecure world, all are equal and everyone is different'.

He has books on each of these themes.

Much of Beck's writing anticipates the way experiences of work will change in this new society. Life in the 'second modernity' can be characterised by an increase of global capitalism, a decline of unions and a major shift in the flexibility of the labour process. In one book, *The Brave New World of Work* (2000a), he discusses eleven different scenarios of work, all of which flag the end of full employment as we have thought about it in the first modernity (see Beck, 2000: Chapter 4). This is a world where standard work is increasingly being replaced by non-standard forms of work. He suggests that the situation of work in Brazil anticipates much of what the

Ulrich Beck (1944–)
*Source*: Permission from Ulrich Beck.

rest of the Western world may soon come to experience. He sees such a society as having four main groups: the super-rich, the overworked middle class, the working poor and those with no work at all, who live in local poverty. This is the blueprint for relations in the future. A significant group will be the 'super-rich'. But a huge group will have little work: they will have time in abundance – but no resources. Work is not available to them. They live in localised poverty. Many may well live in prisons. So Beck asks: *What happens when the work society runs out of work?* (2000: 62).

He suggests that with the decline of unionism, we can now look to the start of a new politics to emerge outside the formal realm of politics. Women's perspectives will become increasingly important (as their experience of work is very different); and we could expect a move from paid work to what he calls 'civil labour' – forms of work that are self-organised and which develop art, culture and politics.

As he concludes: 'Cosmopolitans of the World Unite!' (2000: 176).

# Unemployment

Every industrial society has some unemployment. Much of it is temporary. Few young people entering the labour force find a job right away; some workers temporarily leave the labour force while seeking a new job, to have children or because of a strike; others suffer from long-term illnesses; still others may lack skills to work.

But the economy itself also generates unemployment, often called structural unemployment. Jobs disappear as occupations become obsolete, as businesses close in the face of foreign competition and as recessions force layoffs and bankruptcies. Since 1980, for example, the 'downsizing' of US businesses has eliminated some 5 million jobs – a quarter of the total – in that country's 500 largest corporations.

Unemployment rates vary over time, as they do from country to country. The number of unemployed people worldwide reached 212 million in 2009, up 34 million or an unprecedented 19 per cent since 2007. The unemployment rate in the 27 countries of the European Union was 8.9 per cent, US unemployment stood at around 9.3 per cent and in Japan it was 5.1 per cent.

## Unemployment in Europe

Unemployment rates and experiences both differ and fluctuate greatly across Europe, as Table 15.6 shows.

Overall, in 2009, the EU-27 had an average unemployment rate of 8.9 per cent, high in Slovakia, Estonia, Lithuania, Spain and Ireland, much lower in Denmark, Cyprus, Luxembourg, the Netherlands, Austria and Slovenia. The long-term unemployed are much more prominent in the eastern European countries. In absolute terms, Russia had a large rate of unemployment, at between 8 and 9 per cent in early 2010, while Norway has a much more modest 3.3 per cent. Figure 15.4 also shows the greater likelihood of women to be unemployed.

## Unemployment in the UK

From the late 1940s to the 1970s in the UK, it was generally assumed that unemployment should never rise above 1 million. But since that time there have been quite dramatic swings: 3 million by 1985, down again to 1.5 million by the early 1990s, up again to 2.5 million people (8.5 per cent of the workforce) in 1994, and in 2001 the Blair government formally announced that it had fallen below the symbolic figure of 1 million. This figure crept up again so that in spring 2003 there were 1.48 million unemployed. Of course, this unemployment rate reflected large regional differences, with the lowest rate in the southeast and southwest (around 3.8 per cent) and the highest in the north of England (around 6.5 per cent) and Greater London (7 per cent) (*Social Trends*, 2003: 63). In 2009 and early 2010, the number of unemployed individuals in the UK continuously surpassed 2.3 million (at 7.6 per cent).

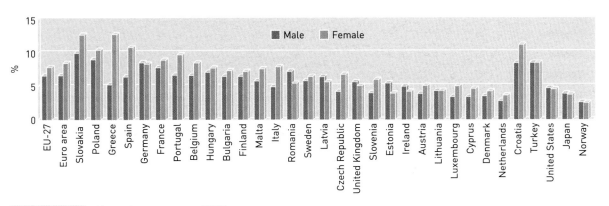

**Figure 15.4**  Unemployment rates, 2007

*Note*: The figure is ranked on the average of male and female.

*Source*: Eurostat *Europe in Figures: Eurostat Yearbook 2009*, © European Union, 2009.

**Table 15.6** Unemployment rates in Europe, 1999–2009

| | 1999 | 2000 | 2001 | 2002 | 2003 | 2004 | 2005 | 2006 | 2007 | 2008 | 2009 |
|---|---|---|---|---|---|---|---|---|---|---|---|
| EU-27 | : | 8.7 | 8.5 | 8.9 | 9.0 | 9.1 | 8.9 | 8.2 | 7.1 | 7.0 | 8.9 |
| Euro area | 9.3 | 8.4 | 8.0 | 8.4 | 8.8 | 9.0 | 9.0 | 8.3 | 7.5 | 7.5 | 9.4 |
| Belgium | 8.5 | 6.9 | 6.6 | 7.5 | 8.2 | 8.4 | 8.5 | 8.3 | 7.5 | 7.0 | 7.9 |
| Bulgaria | : | 16.4 | 19.5 | 18.2 | 13.7 | 12.1 | 10.1 | 9.0 | 6.9 | 5.6 | 6.8 |
| Czech Republic | 8.6 | 8.7 | 8.0 | 7.3 | 7.8 | 8.3 | 7.9 | 7.2 | 5.3 | 4.4 | 6.7 |
| Denmark | 5.2 | 4.3 | 4.5 | 4.6 | 5.4 | 5.5 | 4.8 | 3.9 | 3.8 | 3.3 | 6.0 |
| Germany | 8.2 | 7.5 | 7.6 | 8.4 | 9.3 | 9.8 | 10.7 | 9.8 | 8.4 | 7.3 | 7.5 |
| Estonia | : | 13.6 | 12.6 | 10.3 | 10.0 | 9.7 | 7.9 | 5.9 | 4.7 | 5.5 | 13.8 |
| Ireland | 5.6 | 4.2 | 3.9 | 4.5 | 4.6 | 4.5 | 4.4 | 4.5 | 4.6 | 6.3 | 11.9 |
| Greece | 12.0 | 11.2 | 10.7 | 10.3 | 9.7 | 10.5 | 9.9 | 8.9 | 8.3 | 7.7 | 9.5 |
| Spain | 12.5 | 11.1 | 10.3 | 11.1 | 11.1 | 10.6 | 9.2 | 8.5 | 8.3 | 11.3 | 18.0 |
| France | 10.4 | 9.0 | 8.3 | 8.6 | 9.0 | 9.3 | 9.3 | 9.2 | 8.4 | 7.8 | 9.5 |
| Italy | 10.9 | 10.1 | 9.1 | 8.6 | 8.4 | 8.0 | 7.7 | 6.8 | 6.1 | 6.7 | 7.8 |
| Cyprus | : | 4.9 | 3.8 | 3.6 | 4.1 | 4.7 | 5.3 | 4.6 | 4.0 | 3.6 | 5.3 |
| Latvia | 14.0 | 13.7 | 12.9 | 12.2 | 10.5 | 10.4 | 8.9 | 6.8 | 6.0 | 7.5 | 17.1 |
| Lithuania | 13.7 | 16.4 | 16.5 | 13.5 | 12.5 | 11.4 | 8.3 | 5.6 | 4.3 | 5.8 | 13.7 |
| Luxembourg | 2.4 | 2.2 | 1.9 | 2.6 | 3.8 | 5.0 | 4.6 | 4.6 | 4.2 | 4.9 | 5.2 |
| Hungary | 6.9 | 6.4 | 5.7 | 5.8 | 5.9 | 6.1 | 7.2 | 7.5 | 7.4 | 7.8 | 10.0 |
| Malta | : | 6.7 | 7.6 | 7.5 | 7.6 | 7.4 | 7.2 | 7.1 | 6.4 | 5.9 | 7.0 |
| Netherlands | 3.2 | 2.8 | 2.2 | 2.8 | 3.7 | 4.6 | 4.7 | 3.9 | 3.2 | 2.8 | 3.4 |
| Austria | 3.9 | 3.6 | 3.6 | 4.2 | 4.3 | 4.9 | 5.2 | 4.8 | 4.4 | 3.8 | 4.8 |
| Poland | 13.4 | 16.1 | 18.3 | 20.0 | 19.7 | 19.0 | 17.8 | 13.9 | 9.6 | 7.1 | 8.2 |
| Portugal | 4.5 | 4.0 | 4.1 | 5.1 | 6.4 | 6.7 | 7.7 | 7.8 | 8.1 | 7.7 | 9.6 |
| Romania | 7.1 | 7.3 | 6.8 | 8.6 | 7.0 | 8.1 | 7.2 | 7.3 | 6.4 | 5.8 | 6.9 |
| Slovenia | 7.3 | 6.7 | 6.2 | 6.3 | 6.7 | 6.3 | 6.5 | 6.0 | 4.9 | 4.4 | 5.9 |
| Slovakia | 16.4 | 18.8 | 19.3 | 18.7 | 17.6 | 18.2 | 16.3 | 13.4 | 11.1 | 9.5 | 12.0 |
| Finland | 10.2 | 9.8 | 9.1 | 9.1 | 9.0 | 8.8 | 8.4 | 7.7 | 6.9 | 6.4 | 8.2 |
| Sweden[1] | 6.7 | 5.6 | 5.8 | 6.0 | 6.6 | 7.4 | 7.6 | 7.0 | 6.1 | 6.2 | 8.3 |
| United Kingdom | 5.9 | 5.4 | 5.0 | 5.1 | 5.0 | 4.7 | 4.8 | 5.4 | 5.3 | 5.6 | 7.6 |
| Croatia | : | : | : | 14.8 | 14.2 | 13.7 | 12.7 | 11.2 | 9.6 | 8.4 | 9.1 |
| Turkey | : | : | : | : | : | : | 9.2 | 8.7 | 8.8 | 9.7 | 12.5 |
| Norway | 3.0 | 3.2 | 3.4 | 3.7 | 4.2 | 4.3 | 4.5 | 3.4 | 2.5 | 2.5 | 3.1 |
| Japan | 4.7 | 4.7 | 5.0 | 5.4 | 5.3 | 4.7 | 4.4 | 4.1 | 3.9 | 4.0 | 5.1 |
| United States | 4.2 | 4.0 | 4.8 | 5.8 | 6.0 | 5.5 | 5.1 | 4.6 | 4.6 | 5.8 | 9.3 |

[1] Break in series, 2001.

*Source*: Eurostat, http://epp.eurostat.ec.europa.eu/statistics_explained/index_php/File:Table_unemployment_rates.PNG, © European Union, 2010.

# Who are the unemployed?

Writing of the UK (but the data are probably generalisable across Europe), Adrian Sinfield (1981) suggests that five major groups are more likely to become or remain unemployed:

- those who experience redundancies due to economic change
- unskilled youth trying to make the transition from school to work
- older workers who face enforced retirement
- unemployed women
- the long-term unemployed.

# Experiencing unemployment

Unemployment can wreak havoc on lives and families. Many studies have suggested that there is an initial shock, followed for a short while by denial and optimism (in which there may be a sense of being on holiday for a little while), but this is soon followed by distress and anxiety. If the unemployment continues for a long time, it may lead to resignation and adjustment. It has also been linked to ill health, premature death, attempted and actual suicide, marriage breakdown, child battering, racial conflicts and football hooliganism. A subculture of despair can emerge, sometimes linked to the development of an underclass (see Chapter 10). For women who see work as an escape from the home, unemployment can be especially harsh (Jahoda et al., 1972; orig. 1933). Generally, unemployment affects those with least resources most.

# Problems of measuring unemployment

Measuring unemployment is no easy task. Although there are official figures, they can conceal the difficulties in recording practices and the major differences within countries. In many countries, but especially lower-income ones, it can be almost impossible to count the numbers out of work.

Government unemployment statistics, based on monthly national surveys, generally understate unemployment for three reasons. First, to be counted among the unemployed, a person must be actively seeking work; 'discouraged workers', those who have given up looking for a job, are omitted from the statistics. Second, many people unable to find jobs for which they are qualified settle, at least for a while, for 'lesser' employment: a secretary works as a 'temp' several days a week, or a former university lecturer drives a taxi while seeking a new teaching position. Such people are counted among the employed, though they might better be described as *under*employed. Third, changes in policies towards the unemployed or in the procedures for measuring unemployment can conceal and distort the 'true picture'. In the UK, for instance, between 1982 and 1996 there were at least 14 changes that tended towards lowering the figures. For example, since 1982, only those eligible for benefits are included in the unemployment figures; and since 1988, most people in the UK under the age of 18 have been ineligible for benefits (income support), resulting in 90,000 being taken off the register. There are many tricks that can conceal unemployment – such as youth training schemes which conceal unemployment by taking young people out of the unemployment statistics. On the other hand, statistics also overlook the fact that many people officially out of work receive income 'under the table' from odd jobs or even from illegal activity. But, even considering off-the-books income, the actual level of unemployment is probably several percentage points above the official figure.

# The world of corporations

At the core of today's capitalist economy lies the market, which is composed centrally of **corporations**, *organisations with a legal existence, including rights and liabilities, apart from those of their members.* By incorporation, an organisation becomes an entity unto itself, able to enter into contracts and own property. More and more these corporations transcend nation-states: as we have seen, they are transnational corporations (or TNCs) and they are the primary 'movers and shapers' of the world economy. A **transnational corporation** is *a firm which has the power to coordinate and control operations in more than one country, even if it does not own them* (Dicken, 2010).

The practice of legal incorporation accelerated with the rise of large businesses a century ago because it offered company owners two advantages. First, incorporation shields them from the legal liabilities of their businesses, protecting personal wealth from lawsuits arising from business debts or harm to consumers. Second, profits earned by corporations receive favourable treatment under the tax laws of Europe. The largest corporations are typically owned not by single families but by millions of stockholders, including other corporations. This dispersion of corporate ownership has spread wealth to some extent, making more people small-scale capitalists. Moreover, day-to-day operation of a corporation falls to white-collar executives, who may or may not be major stockholders themselves. Typically, however, a great deal of corporate stock is owned by a small number of the corporation's top executives and directors (Dicken, 1998).

## Capitalist markets

Capitalist economies can vary greatly in their approach to the market. In the purest form, the market is simply a situation where there is private ownership of companies competing freely and equally with other companies. But as many commentators have noted, such a fully free system is rare. There are many reasons for this. Among these are the facts that governments often intervene in markets; some companies can become so large that they dominate certain markets; and companies can become heavily bureaucratic so that they are not open to quick adjustment to market situations.

## Economic concentration

While many companies are small, with assets worth less than £750,000, the largest corporations dominate the global economy (see Table 15.7). In 2010 for example, Wal-Mart employed well over 2 million people across the world, while the largest world corporation was car maker General Motors (GM), with more than £413 billion in revenue (*Fortune*, 2010). This one company has higher revenue than many countries. It may also have more influence!

# Spotlight
## Global corporations

The world's dominant corporations are clustered in very few countries – the top 50, for example, originate from only 12 countries (China, USA, Spain, the UK, Netherlands, France, Russia, Brazil, Germany, Italy, Switzerland and Japan). There are two major lists of the world's biggest corporations. In the US, *Fortune* magazine ranks the top 500 by *revenue*. In the UK, the *Financial Times* ranks them on *shareholder value*. (You can also rank companies by country, work force, or industry.)

- *The World Top 10* in *Fortune* regularly highlights: Wal-Mart, Royal Dutch Shell, Exxon Mobil, BP, Toyota Motor, Japan Post Holdings, Sinopec, State Grid, AXA, China National Petroleum, Chevron, General Electric.

- *The World Top 10* in the *Financial Times* highlights: Petro China, Exxon Mobil, Apple Inc., Microsoft, Wal-Mart, BHP Billiton, General Electric, and the Industrial and Commercial Board of China.

- *The UK Top 10* in the *Financial Times* (with the London Stock Exchange) regularly feature: BHP Billiton, Royal Dutch Shell, HSBC, Vodafone, BP, Rio Tinto, GlaxoSmithKline, Unilever, British American Tobacco and BG Group.

- *Green Lists*. Note that there are also Green Lists – companies that have the best environmental credentials. This frequently includes for the UK: Kingfisher, the BT Group, Biffs, BP, Unilever, Severn Trent, BSkyB Group, BHP Billiton, M&S Group. Across the world, the highest ranked include: Vestas Wind Systems, Ericsson, MTR, and Svenska Cellulosa, Kingfisher, BT and Westpac Banking.

The latest details on all these companies can usually be found easily through a Google search. Company reports are usually quite obscure but can be found online too.

## The capitalism of Wal-Mart

A number of mega-companies rival each other for top place in the world market. Wal-Mart is one of these. It is one of the largest companies in the USA, and is fast becoming one of the largest in the world (in the UK it trades as ASDA). It is seen by many as one 'template' for the modern capitalist organisation (Lichtenstein, 2006: 3).

Wal-Mart is today one of the largest profit-making enterprises in the world. It operates more than 5,000 stores worldwide, has sales of over $400 billion a year (with revenues larger than those of Switzerland), employs more than 2 million workers, has sales around $1 trillion a year, and its owners – the Walton family – own shares and assets of over $120 billion. It is to be found all over the US landscape, and it is now opening up stores everywhere around the world.

It can be found in Mexico City and Tokyo, China and Germany. Its biggest claim for success is that it provides low prices, cheap enough for poor families to survive on. But it also claims to serve its communities: revitalising the community, creating 'happy workers' and doing good philanthropic works. On the surface, it looks like a model of 'happy' capitalism – providing work and cheap goods for average and poor families.

But Wal-Mart is not without its critics. They ask: at what hidden costs do these 'cheap' prices come? The film *Wal-Mart: The High Cost of Low Price* (2005) (and the book that accompanies it by Gregg Spott (2006)) sets out to reveal the global problems of this mega transnational corporation. Indeed, it shows how Wal-Mart is at the centre of a number of court cases, legal conflicts and protest movements across the globe. If you look at the criteria for 'decent work' outlined in this chapter,

Wal-Mart itself would claim that it meets these. But critics suggest that very few are met. They suggest there is a 'high cost' to pay for the 'low prices'. The critics claim, among other things, that 'associates' (workers) earn low wages for long working hours. Across the world, conditions of work can be particularly bad by Western standards. In China, for example, workers often work seven days a week for long hours and pay of $3 a day. They also live in 'dorms'. Both gender and race discrimination takes place in the workplace. Little (or no) health insurance is provided. And often Wal-Mart is claimed to lead to the breakdown of small communities (local shops inevitably close), while also creating dangerous areas (the car parks of the malls are not adequately monitored and can become the scenes of crimes).

*See*: Nelson Lichtenstein (ed.), *Wal-Mart: The Face of 21st Century Capitalism* (2006).

## Conglomerates and corporate linkages

Economic concentration has spawned **conglomerates**, *giant corporations composed of many smaller corporations*. Throughout much of the twentieth century, small companies were gobbled up by larger ones. Some industries, such as tobacco, came to be dominated by three or four major firms. Since the 1980s, however, there has been some shift in this process, as some companies have decided to downsize and shift some of their functions to other firms.

Conglomerates emerge as corporations, enter new markets, spin off new companies or carry out takeovers of existing companies. Forging a conglomerate is also a strategy to diversify a company, so that new products can provide a hedge against declining profits in the original market. Faced with declining sales of tobacco products, for example, R. J. Reynolds merged with

Nabisco foods, forming a conglomerate called RJR–Nabisco. Coca-Cola's soft drinks market is still growing, but this company now produces fruit drinks, coffee and bottled water, as well as movies and television programmes. Besides conglomerates, corporations are also linked through mutual ownership, since these giant organisations own each other's stock. In today's global economy, many companies have invested heavily in other corporations commonly regarded as their competitors. Chapter 22 looks a little more at how big media corporations such as Disney and TimeWarner link and diversify.

One more type of linkage among corporations is the *interlocking directorate*, a social network of people serving simultaneously on the boards of directors of many corporations. These connections give corporations access to valuable information about each other's products and marketing strategies. Laws forbid linkages of this kind among corporations that compete directly with one another. Yet beneficial linkages persist among non-competing corporations with common interests – for example, a corporation building tractors may share directors with one that manufactures tyres. Indirect linkages also occur when, for example, a member of General Motors' board of directors and a director of Ford both sit on the board of Exxon/Esso (Weidenbaum, 1995).

Corporate linkages do not necessarily run counter to the public interest, but they certainly concentrate power and they may encourage illegal activity. Price fixing, for example, is legal in much of the world (the Organisation of Petroleum Exporting Countries (OPEC) meets regularly to try to set oil prices), but not in Europe. By their nature, however, corporate linkages invite price fixing, especially when only a few corporations control an entire market.

## Corporations and competition

The capitalist model assumes that businesses operate independently in a competitive market. But while smaller businesses and self-employed people may indicate a competitive sector, they are usually at considerable disadvantage since the corporate core is largely non-competitive. Large corporations are not truly competitive because, first, their extensive linkages mean that they do not operate independently and, second, a small number of corporations come to dominate many large markets.

With the exception of some public utility providers (in the UK this used to include water), no large company can establish an actual **monopoly**, *domination of a market by a single producer*. The law does permit lesser economic concentration called **oligopoly**, *domination of a market by a few producers*. Oligopoly results from the vast investment needed to enter a new market such as the car industry. Certainly, the successful entry of foreign-owned corporations into the European car markets shows that new companies can successfully challenge the biggest corporations. But all large businesses strive to limit competition simply because it places profits at risk.

Although capitalism favours minimal government intervention in the economy, corporate power is now so great – and competition among corporations sometimes so limited – that government regulation may be the only way to protect the public interest. Yet, governments are also the corporate world's single biggest customer, and national governments frequently intervene to bolster struggling corporations. In short, corporations and governments typically work together to make the entire economy more stable and profitable.

## Corporations and the global economy

Corporations have grown in size and power so fast that they are now responsible for most of the world's economic output. In the process, the largest corporations – centred in Europe, Japan and the United States – have spilled across national borders and now view the entire world as one vast marketplace. As noted in Chapter 9, multinationals are large corporations that produce and market products in many different nations.

Corporations become multinational in order to make more money, since most of the planet's resources and three-quarters of the world's people are found in less developed countries. Worldwide operations, then, offer access to plentiful materials and vast markets. In addition, labour costs are far lower in poor countries of the world. A manufacturing worker in Taiwan labours all week to earn what a German worker earns in a single day or less.

The impact of multinationals on poor societies is controversial, as Chapter 9 explained in detail. On one side of the argument, modernisation theorists argue that multinationals unleash the great productivity of the capitalist economic system, which will boost economic development (Rostow, 1978; Berger, 1986). Cadbury-Schweppes alone, for example, far out-produces any one of the least-productive nations in the world. Corporations offer poor societies tax revenues, capital investment, new jobs and advanced technology – taken together, what modernisation theorists call a certain recipe for economic growth.

On the other side of the argument, dependency theorists who favour a socialist economy claim that multinationals only intensify global inequality (Wallerstein, 1979). Multinational investment, as they see it, may create a few jobs in poor countries but it also stifles the development of local industries, which are a better source of employment. Further, critics charge, multinationals generally push developing countries to produce expensive consumer goods for export to rich nations rather than food and other necessities that would bolster the standard of living in local communities. From this standpoint, multinationals establish a system of neo-colonialism, making poor societies poorer and increasingly reliant on rich, capitalist societies.

While modernisation theory hails the virtues of an unregulated market as the key to a future of progress and affluence for all the world's people, advocates of dependency theory call for the replacement of market systems by government regulation of economic affairs.

# Consumption in modern economies

Until very recently the dominant approach to the economy taken by sociologists has concerned the production of goods, with a focus on either businesses or workers and work. So far this has been the main focus of this chapter too. But sociologists have increasingly come to recognise the importance of not just what we produce, but what – and how – we consume. Indeed, as there has been a growing move in society *from production to consumption*, so there has been the growth of *a sociology of consumption*. Shopping and consuming has now become a major social practice of everyday life; and in some markets – such as the 'youth market' – it has become almost the number one social activity. 'Going shopping', 'Born to shop', 'Shop till you drop', 'I am what I consume' are common slogans.

Throughout most of history, the shop has been the 'open air market'. In Hong Kong or in Thailand's busy street markets today, there is a sense of historical continuity, of the bustle of the market. But with the arrival of the huge department store and the rise of advertising in the nineteenth century, new worlds of conspicuous consumption were slowly created. Goods moved from being merely functional commodities such as food to eat, and became instead major markers of lifestyles and identities. The question now posed concerns whether consumers are sovereigns or dupes – *are we driven to consume through our needs and choices, or are we perhaps driven to consume through the manipulation of our needs?*

## The branding of commodities

The modern capitalist world is dominated by internationally known brand names such as Nike, Starbucks, Mitsubishi, Shell, Wal-Mart, Virgin, McDonald's, Calvin Klein, Sony, IBM, Coca-Cola and Toshiba. What we find here is that brands, not products, become more and more central. Thus people no longer ask for a soft drink, they want a Coke; they do not want trainers but Nikes; they do not want underwear but Calvin Kleins. This branding depends on promotion and advertising: the growth in global advertising spending now outpaces the growth of the world economy by one-third (Klein, 2000: 9, 11). New markets are constantly being generated – Baby Gap for Kids, for example. Overall, however, many are strongly linked to the youth market, creating what has been called 'The Global Teen':

> **Despite different cultures, middle class youth all over the world seem to live their lives as if in a parallel universe. They get up in the morning, put on their Levis and Nikes, grab their caps, backpacks and Sony personal CD players, and head for school.**

(Klein, 2000: 119)

The Branded World is organised through style, logos and image. Thus 'Tommy Hilfiger pioneered a clothing style that transforms its faithful adherents into walking, talking, lifesized Tommy dolls, mummified into fully branded Tommy worlds' (Klein, 2000: 28). Brands start to have their own superstores and sometimes even their own city space and 'branded villages' (e.g. Disney's Celebration Town in Florida). They sponsor sports, arts, music, education – each time getting their brand identified with culture. And 'stars' are paid large sums to lend their names to the goods: Tiger Woods (with a $90 million contract with Nike over five years), Michael Jordan, Puff Daddy, Martha Stewart, Austin Powers, Michael Jackson.

There are major downsides to all this. Commodities become very predictable – it is a world of 'theme park shopping', and a kind of self-censorship creeps in to stop diversity. Major companies are merged till they regulate the markets, and goods are produced largely in the sweatshops of low-income countries. Here the labour force has no unions and is utterly temporary: lines of young women hunch over their hard work for a dollar a day and with no job security. There is a floating workforce where 'temps' develop an odd kind of loyalty to their 'brand'.

Further, our identities – who we are – come to be shaped by everything we buy: designer clothes (or otherwise), the 'latest' film and music band (or 'golden oldies'), the 'coolest' (or plain) food, the holiday, the car and so on. We are what we buy. And this has fuelled the worlds of logos. For some people, logos matter more than the quality of the goods (see the discussion of 'Nike culture' in Goldman and Papson, 1998). Advertising, logos and consumption serve up images of the good life to which we start to aspire.

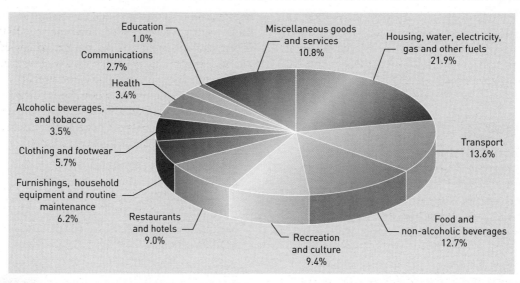

| **Figure 15.5** | Consumption expenditure of households on goods and services, EU-27, 2006 (% of total household consumption expenditure) |

*Note*: Figures do not sum to 100% due to rounding.

*Source*: Eurostat *Europe in Figures: Eurostat Yearbook 2009*, © European Union, 2009.

# 'Born to shop': the growth of consumer societies

Many suggest, then, that Western societies are cultivating 'consumer societies'. Indeed, shopping has become the second most popular leisure activity in Britain, after watching television (*Social Trends*, 2010). Think of your own life and how purchases – buying clothes, CDs, computers, tickets to sporting events and so forth – may play a part in it. Look at Figure 15.5. Consider the following:

- *The massive growth of shopping malls* with 'megastores' such as Virgin Records, hypermarkets like Tesco, chain stores such as Argos, retail parks and the endless proliferation of DIY stores across the country. Each Tesco store in Britain had a minimum area of 10,670 square metres in the 1990s (compared with 3,048 in the 1970s). In some parts of eastern Europe, such as Poland, there has been a massive expansion of 'hyper malls'.

- *The arrival of shopping not as a merely functional activity* (for example, to buy the necessary food for a meal) *but as a major leisure form in itself.* Malls and shopping centres are key public spaces to 'hang around' in, and shops are designed for us to wander in voyeuristically, looking and enjoying the sights. Many people often go just to look, not to purchase, and can spend hours and hours doing this.

- *The growth of more and newer forms of commodities.* We now 'need' commodities that we could not even imagine some 50 years ago: sports clothes geared to every sport; new bathroom commodities such as shower gels, foot creams and electric toothbrushes; new electronic gadgets ranging from computer toys and video games to mobile phones and multimedia computers; new forms of entertainment such as multiplex cinemas and leisure complexes; new modes of eating out, from fast-food to up-market dining; holidays that take us to theme parks, on world cruises and to 'resort hotels'; and cars owned individually.

- *The attachment of our identities to our shopping.* Especially in the major 'youth markets', our identities can be constructed around the kinds of shop we go to and the sorts of commodity we buy. Caught in early phrases such as 'conspicuous consumption' and in more recent phrases such as 'I shop, therefore I am', much consumption heralds the types of people we are.

- *The spread of credit cards.* In the UK, at least one-third of all consumption is based on credit; there were 25 million credit cards in the UK by 1998 and, in 2002, purchases of around £100 billion were made through credit cards. The figures are higher for many other countries, especially the United States (Ritzer, 1995).

# Think and discuss
## Debt and online shopping

### We live with debt and credit cards

The volume of automated payments and debit card transactions in the UK in 2008 were both approximately nine times greater than they were in 1985. Debit card payments accounted for the largest volume of non-cash payments in 2008 with 5.3 billion transactions, followed by automated payments transactions (3.4 billion) and credit and charge card transactions (1.8 billion).

### We are more and more shopping online

When interviewed in the UK between January and March 2009, 64 per cent of all recent internet users in the UK had purchased goods or services over the internet at least once. Of these, 83 per cent (26 million) had purchased items within the three months prior to interview. Men were more likely to have purchased goods and services over the internet in 2009 than women (69 per cent and 60 per cent respectively).

*Source: Social Trends, 2010.*

- *Teleshopping and netshopping.* Going online means that an array of armchair services become available – from shopping and banking to travel and public services. Hundreds of channels with interactive shopping services come on stream through the television and the internet, and all goods are purchasable through credit cards.

## Mass consumption, cultural dopes and a shallow world

The rise of so much consumption has given sociologists much to discuss. In the first place, some argue that the 'consumerist' culture is having a deleterious effect on the quality of life. Socialist critic Jeremy Seabrook (1996) sees consumerism accelerating since 1945, and destroying traditional cultures and solidarities. The 'loads-a-money' culture promotes self-gratification, and with the market dominating, leads to a general flattening of life – destroying differences and communities. This is seen to lead to the weakening of creativity and the decline of participatory communities as people now go to the impersonal shopping mall and not 'the corner shop', and it generates a crass materialism. We have seen something of this in our earlier discussion of George Ritzer's McDonaldisation thesis (Ritzer, 1993, and see Chapter 6). Indeed, in a later book, Ritzer has discussed more fully the dangers of what he calls 'cathedrals of consumption' (Ritzer, 2004a).

We have also seen the dangers inherent in what we could call the 'brand name society', where what is on sale is not so much a commodity as a logo. The importance of the sign – the Nike swoosh, the Virgin 'V', the Tommy Hilfiger colours – turns shoppers into walking advertising systems.

## Consumption: a sovereign world of choice, distinctiveness and creativity?

Others, by contrast, argue that the new consumerism has been a major advance for most. It has become the means for a higher standard of living, as well as a chance not to deaden culture but to enhance it. Goods and brands may spread through the world, but they are used differently and become different things. With the packaging of CDs in vast megastores, for instance, global music has developed – and the sheer range of music available now has increased dramatically. The same is true of food, with supermarkets now making available ingredients and recipes unheard of 20 years ago. Far from flattening culture, consumerism has enriched it, giving us a greater choice and a better control of our lives. There has been a growing mass participation in creative activities, from DIY to music, from cooking to reading, and from painting to all kinds of 'hobby'.

## Inequalities and consumption

Many years ago the sociologist Thorstein Veblen recognised what he called conspicuous consumption, through which people (usually elites) can enhance their status through commodities, from clothes and houses to cars and other material symbols of wealth (Veblen, 1953; orig. 1899). Consumption and its display are not available to all and thus can become a marker of inequality.

In Veblen's view, consumption patterns lead to three ways of excluding people. The first is through money:

The modern marketplace: shopping malls and megastores are now a common sight throughout much of the world. Asia is home to eight of the world's ten largest shopping malls, six of which have been built since 2004. See Chapter 24, p. 842

*Source:* © Viviane Moos/Corbis.

many people simply cannot afford to purchase new or high-quality goods and services, and suffer 'economic exclusion' as a result. Others may be excluded spatially; without a car or good public transport they cannot easily get to shopping centres and other places of consumption. Often, indeed, if restricted to using small local shops, they will find they pay more and have less choice. Finally, some people will be excluded because they lack the knowledge and skills to consume. Being a skilful consumer these days may well require knowledge of the metric system, computing or international food, for example.

Of course, many people resist these pervasive forms of consumption: they do not want to be part of a high-consumption world and may actively prefer to support local shops, while being indifferent, or in some cases even hostile, towards international brand names. To some extent, this is what the new worldwide 'anti-globalism' protests are about (for example, Klein, 2000). Still, for some, not being able to shop

and consume in this way can be experienced as a form of social exclusion.

The new consumption patterns may make life difficult for many. Elderly people, for instance, may find small local shops closing, while the new megastores – should they want to use them – are inaccessible. The elderly are less likely to drive and their state of health may make time and travel hard; and even the design of stores, with high shelves, big trolleys, masses of people and constant commotion, makes them seem very inhospitable places.

## Disneyisation

One recent and useful lens through which to understand the way contemporary consumption works has been provided by an analysis of the marketing strategies of Walt Disney. Most people have some idea of what a Disney theme park is like, and indeed large numbers of people have visited one.

Alan Bryman, taking his lead from Ritzer's discussion of McDonaldisation (see Chapter 6), has suggested that **Disneyisation** is *the process by which the principles of the Disney theme parks are coming to dominate more and more sectors of American society as well as the rest of the world* (Bryman, 2004: 1). Disneyisation lies at the heart of modern consumption (and capitalism?), in that it has started to shape many shopping experiences, providing a platform for purchases. In his book, Bryman suggests that four main principles lie behind Disneyisation. These are:

- *Theming*, putting the sales object into a story line to which it is not necessarily related. Thus a restaurant takes on the theme of rock music (for example, Hard Rock Café) or movies (Planet Hollywood), a hotel takes on the theme of a place (New York, Venice, ancient Rome or Egypt in Las Vegas) or shopping takes on a historical theme (Liverpool's Albert Docks, London's Tobacco Dock, and Barcelona's Port Vaill).

- *Hybrid consumption*, in which one type of shopping becomes linked in with another very different kind, making them increasingly hard to distinguish. Airports and sports stadia, for example, become shopping malls too.

- *Merchandising*, the promotion and sale of goods which bear copyrighted images and logos. Thus films such as *Pirates of the Carribean*, *Shrek*, *Star Wars* and *Spider-Man* also generate not just DVDs, CDs and videos but T-shirts, greeting cards, toys, books, video games and tie-ins with food and clothing markets. Often the merchandise makes much more money than the original product!

- *Performative or emotional labour*, in which the frontline service industry is seen less as a job and more as a performance. Often this involves 'dressing up' and performing a role in line with the attire; usually it involves smiling and being friendly – acting as if the tasks being done are fun and friendly and not really work at all.

When you next go shopping, remember this is the most popular leisure activity, and ponder if any of this fits.

## Looking ahead

This chapter has suggested that although industrial capitalism may have become the dominant economic form throughout most of the world over the past 200 years, it continues to change. The chapter has looked at the rise of fragmentation in both work and production (post-Fordism); the flow of companies across the world (globalisation); the increasing use of women's labour; the changing patterns of service work; the rise of major markets of mass consumption, which seem to be generating ever-increasing demand for consumer goods; and the ever fluctuating nature of capitalism's unstable market which led to the credit crunch of 2008–9.

Sociologists are not fortune-tellers and cannot predict the future. It would have been hard for them to predict, in the late eighteenth century, the rise of the new information economy that appears to be emerging in the early twenty-first. But this chapter does at least suggest that, just as capitalism has been flexible in the past, so it may well continue to adjust to the changes of the future.

# SUMMARY

**1** The economy is the major social institution by which a society produces, distributes and consumes goods and services. It is not just economic, but social.

**2** In technologically simple societies, the economy is subsumed within the family. In agrarian societies, most economic activity takes place outside the home. Industrialisation sparks significant economic expansion built around new energy sources, large factories, mass production and worker specialisation. The post-industrial economy is characterised by a productive shift from tangible goods to services. Just as the technology of the Industrial Revolution propelled the industrial economy of the past, so the Information Revolution is now advancing the post-industrial economy.

**3** The primary sector of the economy generates raw materials; the secondary sector manufactures various goods; the tertiary sector focuses on providing services. In pre-industrial societies, the primary sector predominates; the secondary sector is of greatest importance in industrial societies; the tertiary sector prevails in post-industrial societies.

**4** Social scientists describe the economies of today's industrial and post-industrial societies in terms of two models. Capitalism is based on private ownership of productive property and the pursuit of personal profit in a competitive marketplace. Socialism is based on collective ownership of productive property and the pursuit of collective well-being through government control of the economy. Although most European economies are predominantly capitalist, the European community and national governments are broadly involved in economic life. Governments play an even greater role in the 'democratic socialist' economies of some western European nations and the 'state

capitalism' of Japan. The Russian Federation has gradually introduced some market elements into its formerly centralised economy; the nations of eastern Europe are making similar changes.

**5** The emergence of a global economy means that nations no longer produce and consume products and services within national boundaries. Moreover, the 600 largest corporations, operating internationally, now account for most of the earth's economic output.

**6** The nature of work is changing. Agricultural work is generally in decline and there is a move from factory work to service work. There is a spread of part-time and flexible work, a relative decline in trade union activity, and the growth of international labour markets which bring about 'sweatshop' labour. New forms of work, such as 'teleworking', are growing rapidly.

**7** Unemployment has many causes, including the operation of the economy itself. The European unemployment rate is generally at least 5 per cent.

**8** Transnational corporations (TNCs) form the core of the world's economies. They produce and distribute products in most nations of the world, although the distribution of wealth resulting from this activity is hugely unequal.

**9** The consumer society has become crucial to the working of modern capitalism. The Western world is increasingly buying goods and services in large, centralised establishments, a pattern that has sapped the strength of small, locally based industries.

**10** Disneyisation suggests four principles that help shape contemporary consumption: theming, hybrid consumption, mechandising and performative labour.

CONNECT UP: Turn to Part 6 of this book for key resources and link up
with the book's website, which links to these resources
SEE: www.pearsoned.co.uk/plummer

# MYTASKLIST

# Ten suggestions for going further

## 1 Connect up with Part Six and the Sociology Web Resources

As you work through ideas and think about the issues raised in this chapter, look at the accompanying website and the resource centre at the end of this book which connects to it. There is a lot here to help you move on. To link up, see: www.pearson.co.uk/plummer.

## 2 Review the chapter

*Briefly summarise (in a paragraph) just what this chapter has been about.* Consider: (a) What have you learned? (b) What do you disagree with? Be critical. And (c) How would you develop all this? How could you get more detail on matters that interest you?

## 3 Pose questions

(a) Make a critical analysis of your last 'shopping expedition'. Drawing from ideas in this chapter, discuss what you bought, the processes by which those items were produced, the people and agencies that benefited from your purchases, and why you felt motivated to purchase those goods and services. Consider whether you were involved in the process described in the chapter as 'Disneyisation' and, if so, in what ways.

(b) Look at the people who work on your campus. What are their official designations – cleaners, teaching assistants, secretaries, professors, etc? From the tables in the text, guess how much they earn. What sort of contracts do they have? How much autonomy do they have over their working day?

(c) Identify several ways in which the Industrial Revolution reshaped the economies of Europe. How is the Information Revolution transforming these economies once again?

(d) What key characteristics distinguish capitalism, socialism and democratic socialism? Compare these systems in terms of productivity, economic inequality and support for civil liberties.

## 4 Explore key words

Many concepts have been introduced in this chapter. You can review them from the website or from the listing at the back of this book. You might like to give special attention to just five words and think them through – how would you define them, what are they dealing with, and do they help you see the social world more clearly or not?

For this chapter, a dictionary of economics would be useful. See:

John Black, *A Dictionary of Economics* (2nd edn, 2009)

Graham Bannock et al., *The Penguin Dictionary of Economics* (2004)

## 5 Search the Web

Be critical when you look at websites – see the box on p. 940 in the Resources section. For this chapter look at the following:

Statistics on work patterns, unemployment, consumption and the economy generally can be found in sources already mentioned: search under

  Social Trends (UK)
  Eurostats (Europe)
  World Bank Fact Book (World)

See also:

United Nations Conference on Trade and Development (UNCTAD)
www.unctad.org
Useful for all kinds of data about global trade.

International Labour Organization (ILO)
www.ilo.org
A UN organisation devoted to advancing opportunities for women and men to obtain decent and productive work. A useful statistical resource and offers many new stories of work around the world.

International Monetary Fund
www.imf.org

New Economics Foundation (NEF)
www.neweconomics.org/about
An independent think-and-do tank that inspires and demonstrates real economic well-being and is developing the new economics.

Institute for Economic Affairs
www.iea.org.uk
The IEA's goal is to explain free-market ideas to the public, including politicians, students, journalists, business people, academics and anyone interested in public policy.

The Work Foundation
http://theworkfoundation.com
The Work Foundation is a not-for-profit organisation that brings all sides of working organisations together to find the best ways of improving both economic performance and the quality of working life.

Trades Union Congress
www.tuc.org
Information on unions in the UK.

Two useful magazines are:

Fortune Magazine
www.fortune.com
One of the world's leading business magazines. Among many other things, you can access lists of the top companies, lists of some of the best companies to work for, and a list of the 40 richest under-forties in the USA.

The Economist
www.economist.com/index.html
A weekly magazine focusing on international news and business affairs.

See also:

Interbrand
www.interbrand.com/books_papers.asp
A website devoted to discussion and details on brand names.

See also the websites of:

Naomi Klein, www.naomiklein.org/main
Paul Krugman, http://krugman.blogs.nytimes.com

## 6 Watch a DVD

- Park Kwang-Su's *A Single Spark* (1998): a tale of trying to improve working conditions in South Korea's garment shops, with powerful images of the sweatshops (world distribution: Fortisimo Films, Rotterdam).
- Charlie Chaplin's *Modern Times* (1936): classic silent comedy, which shows the Fordist production line.
- Joseph Santley's *Rosie the Riveter* (1944): five women who work during the Second World War.
- Ken Loach's *Bread and Roses* (2001): illegal immigrant Hispanic janitors work in Los Angeles to send money back home. On very low incomes and poor work conditions, they unionise. Strong stuff.
- *Ghosts* (2007): Chinese immigrants to the UK die on Morecombe Bay while working. A harrowing tale, which we introduced in the opening to this chapter.

## 7 Think and read

Geoffrey Ingham, *Capitalism* (2008) and David Harvey, *A Brief History of Neoliberalism* (2005) are good at setting the background economic scene. On the 1990s economic crisis, see Andrew Gamble, *The Spectre at the Feast* (2009).

Rudi Volti, *An Introduction to The Sociology of Work and Occupations: Globalization and Technological Change into the Twenty-First Century* (2008). Lively and global.

Noel Castree, Neil MCoe, Kevin Ward and Michael Samers, *Spaces of Work: Global Capitalism and Geographies of Labour* (2004). Critical of globalisation and capitalism, a book that brings the 'new geography' to issues surrounding work.

Peter Dicken, *Global Shift: Transforming of the World Economy* (6th edn, 2010). A major study of the world economy, now in its fifth edition. *The* classic. It is stuffed full of diagrams and charts and is very comprehensive, although it is not an easy or introductory read!

Naomi Klein, *No Logo* (2000) and *Shock Doctrine: The Rise of Disaster Capitalism* (2008). *No Logo* is a popular and very lively read on the ways in which modern economies depend upon brand names. The 'bible' of the anti-capitalist movement.

Ulrich Beck, *The Brave New World of Work* (2000a). This comes from one of the world's leading contemporary sociologists and is a polemic about where work may be heading in the future – what he calls the 'Brazilianization of work'.

Finally:
Benjamin R. Barber, *Consumed* (2007), George Ritzer, *Cathedrals of Consumption* (2004a) and Alan Bryman,

*The Disneyization of Society* (2004) are three useful books on consumption.

## 8 Relax with a novel

See: *The Ragged Trousered Philanthropists* by Robert Tressel and Peter Miles.

## 9 Connect to other chapters

- Link to chapters on social divisions in Part Three. How do class, gender and ethnicity link to work? What might happen if you are disabled? Or gay?
- For more on women and work, see gender in Chapter 12 and families in Chapter 18.
- For more on consumption and identity, see Chapter 5.

## 10 Engage with THE BIG DEBATE

### The crisis and the crash: will capitalism survive?

The 2007–8 'credit crunch' was one of the more serious financial crises faced by the world. It stemmed from an unstable mortgage market in America whereby mortgage lenders approved high-risk mortgage loans to people with poor credit records. Problems ensued. When it just involved poor people, it passed relatively unnoticed. But by 2007, it was found to be a problem for major banks like Bear Stearns in the United States, and Northern Rock in England. Bit by bit, a major world financial crisis ensued, which will now shape the world for the next decade or longer. Here we suggest a full-scale debate on the nature of contemporary capitalism.

### The rise of Thatcherism, Reaganism and the neoliberal model

Neoliberalism has dominated the world economic order now for over 30 years. When Margaret Thatcher came to power as Prime Minister in the UK in 1979, she started to revolutionise the way in which both the economy and the government were to be run. So influential was she that a whole ideology – **Thatcherism** – was named after her. Broadly, this is a *system of political beliefs based on free markets, individualism and minimum state intervention*. Her ideas are also known as neoliberalism, and were shaped particularly by the libertarian Milton Friedman (1912–2006), famed for the saying that 'there was no such thing as a free lunch'. (A **libertarian** is someone who *takes individual freedom as the prime political value*.) In the USA, Thatcher's leadership coincided with the presidency of Ronald Reagan (1911–2004, presidency 1981–9) and Reaganism. What they both achieved was to radically shift the grounds of government debate to a focus on the importance of market mechanisms and reduced government intervention. Between 1946 and 1979,

for example, very few people in the UK discussed health or education provision through market models (though in the USA, they did!). But it is a sign of Thatcher's influence that nowadays many countries across the world, and not just the UK, have come to stress the importance of markets in many areas of life.

The debate is not a new one, however. Thatcher just 'modernised' it, 30 years ago, for the UK. Historically, most European societies have had a mix of market and government intervention – hence, mixed economies. From 1946, and with the exception of the Thatcher years (1979–90), the British government has regularly intervened in the economy, both through the welfare state and for a while with its extensive programme of nationalisation (now ceased). The Scandinavian countries also had a pronounced 'welfare' and interventionist background. By contrast, US society has relied on 'the market' for most economic decisions: the market sets prices, as potential buyers and sellers bid for goods and services upwards or downwards in a changing balance of supply and demand.

### The march of the neoliberal model

With Thatcherism all the previously nationalised industries (including telephones, water, gas, electricity and rail) were privatised, and a programme of internal markets was introduced into the welfare state (especially in healthcare and schools).

Defenders praise the market for encouraging choice, diversity and flexibility: in so doing, the market coordinates the efforts of countless people, each of whom – to return to Adam Smith's crucial insight – is motivated only by self-interest. Economists like Milton Friedman (revised edn, 1990) argue that a more or less freely operating market system has provided many members of capitalist societies with an unprecedented economic standard of living.

They also claim that virtually any task that government undertakes, it performs inefficiently. They claim that the products we enjoy – such as computers,

| Table 15.8 | Capitalism: for and against |
| --- | --- |
| **Capitalism is a good force** | **Capitalism is a problem** |
| Free markets are crucial. | There is no such thing as a free market. |
| Governments should not intervene in the market. | Implicitly, they always intervene – regulating international trade, fostering migration policies, passing factory and workplace Acts. When the credit crunch happened, ultimately governments bailed banks out for billions. |
| Free markets mean freedom of individuals to choose. | Freedom to choose is only for a few. Many and especially the poor have little choice. |
| Free markets generate wealth. | But the wealth is unevenly distributed and the system favours the rich getting richer and the poor getting poorer. |
| Everybody gets richer – as wealth trickles down to the poor. | The rich are made richer, but there is no guarantee for the poor. In fact, the poor often get poorer and inequalities increase. Why do we have so many people across the world living in abject poverty? |
| Markets serve personal and private interests – people get what they want. | But public goods are not private interests: the needs of all – the collective good – is not fostered under capitalism (e.g. good environment, safety and protection, travel, education, health and security). |

household appliances and the myriad offerings of supermarkets and shopping centres – are primarily products of the market. By contrast, the least-satisfying goods and services available today, and Friedman places schools, public transport and health services among these, are those operated by governments. Thus, while some government presence in the economy is necessary, supporters of free markets maintain that an economy that operates with minimal state regulation serves the public interest well.

### Critics of the neoliberal model

Other analysts, however, all but dismiss the market and see it as a negative force. For one thing, critics point out, the market has little incentive to produce goods and services that generate little profit, which include just about everything consumed by poor people. Government-directed public housing, for example, stands as a vital resource that no profit-seeking developer would offer independently.

Second, critics look to government to curb what they see as the market system's self-destructive tendencies. The formation of economic monopolies, for example, can threaten the public interest. Government can perform a host of regulatory functions, intervening in the market to control inflation, to enhance the well-being of workers (by creating workplace health and safety standards) and to benefit consumers (through product quality controls). Indeed, the power of global corporations is so great, conclude the critics, that even government cannot effectively defend the public interest. And as we shall see in Chapter 25, with increasing environmental degradation being heaped upon the planet, often through self-interested corporations, surely there is a need for international governments to provide regulation?

Finally, critics support government's role in curbing what they see as another market flaw: magnifying social stratification. As we have seen, capitalist economies characteristically concentrate income and wealth; a government system of taxation (which typically would apply higher rates to the rich) counters this tendency in the name of social justice. For a number of reasons, then, the market operating alone does not serve the public interest.

Does the market's 'invisible hand' feed us well or pick our pockets? Although many – perhaps most – people view the market as good, they also support some government role in economic life to benefit the public.

Indeed, government assists not only citizens but business itself by providing investment capital, constructing roads and other infrastructure, and shielding companies from foreign competition. Yet the precise balance struck between market forces and government decision-making continues to underlie much of the political debate around the world.

Look now at Table 15.8, which debates the case for and against capitalism.

## Continue the debate

1 Why do defenders of the free market assert that 'the government that governs best is the government that governs least'?

2 Does a market system meet the needs of all? Does it serve some better than others?

3 What is your impression of the successes and failures of Thatcherism? Compare it with socialist economic systems.

4 Will capitalism remain the dominant economic system in the twenty-first century? What are the alternatives to capitalism?

*Source:* Gray (2002).

If you are interested in contemporary social-economic debate, look at:

Ha-Joon Chang, *23 Things They Don't Tell You about Capitalism* (2010)
Andrew Gamble, *The Spectre at the Gate* (2009)
David Harvey, *The Enigma of Capital* (2009)
Tim Jackson, *Prosperity Without Growth* (2009)

# CHAPTER 16

# POWER, GOVERNANCE AND SOCIAL MOVEMENTS

THE PEOPLE CALLED IT 'The Battle of Seattle'. It started in early December 1999 on the streets of Seattle, which was for a short while to be the home of a major political conflict over world finance. The World Trade Organization (WTO) had come to town for a major international conference, and the people were not happy with it. The WTO came into being in 1995 (originally set up under the General Agreement on Trade and Tariffs, GATT) and claimed to be the only 'global international organisation dealing with the rules of trade between nations'. 'The goal is to help producers of goods and services, exporters, and importers conduct their business . . . Its main function is to ensure that trade flows as smoothly, predictably, and freely as possible.' Based in Geneva, in 2000 it had around 500 staff and a budget of some $83 million. In 2010, it had over 150 nation members accounting for nearly all of world trade.

But the people said it was 'undemocratic': it had been formed from the powerful, global financial elite and did not represent the people of the world. Accused of neglecting the environment, poorer countries, child labour and exploitation, while championing free trade, it came to symbolise the new global world of high finance and transnational corporations. And the people protested. Some 30,000 protestors took to the streets. At its heart was a political attack on capitalism and the widespread global influence of corporations. There was a sense of global awareness that much of what the 'First World' consumes makes for the tragedies of the 'Third World'. But it was wider than this: in a sense it was a coming together of all the 'causes' of the late twentieth century: the Greens, animal rights, anti-slavery, disarmament and non-violence, the New Age, lifestyle politics, eco-feminism, labour rights, civil rights, human rights. There have been many critiques and movements against contemporary world capitalism – which has seen as unprecedented changes characterised variously as 'turbo-capitalism' (Edward Luttwak)

market fundamentalism (George Soros), 'casino capitalism' (Susan Strange), 'cancer-stage capitalism' (John McMurtry) and 'McWorld' (Benjamin Barber). In this chapter we look at a range of diverse political responses to the world we live in.

See: Massimiliano Andretta and Donatella della Porta (eds), *The Global Justice Movement* (2007).

**The early days of the anti-globalisation or global justice movement**

| | |
|---|---|
| 1994: | Formation in Mexico of 'People's Global Action' ('Ya Basta'). |
| 1999: | Battle of Seattle; 1,200 NGOs combined. |
| 2000s: | Summits challenged in Quebec, London, Barcelona, Sweden, Genoa and New York |
| 2005 | 31st G8 Summit in Edinburgh. |

*Man is a political animal.*

Aristotle

## In this chapter, we ask:

- What are the different kinds of power and the nature of democracies?

- How has politics become globalised?

- How are women excluded from power?

- What is the political organisation of Europe?

- How can we explain the workings of power?

- How does power work 'beyond the rules'? Revolutions, war and terrorism

- What is the significance of social movements in the twenty-first century?

- What is the significance of human rights regimes?

(Above) Demonstrators gather to protest against the World Trade Organization (WTO) during its 1999 conference in Seattle. What started out as a peaceful protest turned into a violent clash between demonstrators and riot police, with many injuries, over 500 arrests and major damage to the downtown area

*Source*: © Christopher J. Morris/Corbis.

(Left) Lenin addresses the workers to encourage them to support him

*Source*: Vladimir Ilyich Lenin (1870–1924) *Addressing the Red Army of Workers on 5th May 1920*, 1933 (oil on canvas), Brodsky, Isaak Israilevich (1883–1939)/Private Collection, RIA Novosti/The Bridgeman Art Library.

*See*: www.marxists.org/archive/lenin/index.htm as a general source on Marxism; also www.aha.ru~mausoleu; www.stel.ru/museum; http://azer.com/aiweb/categories/magazine/al142_folder/142_lenin_art.html.

 Soviet art rejected the trends of twentieth-century art in much of the Western world. What might this image tell you about Soviet power?

This chapter investigates the dynamics of power and focuses on it mainly as a process within societies and among nations. Formal **politics** is *the social institution that distributes power, sets a society's agenda and makes decisions*, and **governance** is *the exercise of political, economic and administrative authority in the management of a country's affairs at all levels*. We will be looking mainly at the more formal exercise of power in this chapter, but first we should recognise that power has much wider implications.

## Power

Power is actually to be found as much in everyday encounters (see Chapter 7) as it is in formal politics and governance. This is *informal power*. You can encounter it in face-to-face interactions, inside families, between men and women, in the workings of institutions such as schools and prisons, in child–adult relations. But precisely because it can be found everywhere, sociologists often have difficulty defining it. It is most obviously seen when people take decisions that affect others' lives, but it can be more subtle: as when people prevent certain issues from ever even being discussed; or where it tacitly shapes desires and wishes, often against our will. Michel Foucault is most extreme, for he sees power as everywhere, and to be found in all relationships (Foucault, 1977). It does not simply come from the top; it is not simply about the formal institutions of power. He looks at all social life to find the power mechanisms at work in it. We look a little further at his ideas in Chapter 17.

## Max Weber's classic ideas on power and authority

Perhaps the classic sociological statement on power is to be found in the work of Max Weber (1978; orig. 1921), whom we have regularly encountered before. He declared power to be the ability to achieve desired ends despite resistance from others. Force – physical might or psychological coercion – may be a basic expression of power, but no society can exist for long if power derives only from force, because people will break rules they do not respect at the first opportunity. Social organisation, therefore, depends on generating some sense of legitimacy and consensus. As we have seen earlier, sociologists use concepts such as ideology and hegemony to deal with this non-coercive power.

The key to social stability is exercising power within a framework of legitimacy. This insight led Weber to focus on the concept of **authority**, *power that people perceive as legitimate rather than coercive*. When parents, teachers or police perform their work well, their power can generally win respect as authority. The source of authority, Weber continued, differs according to a society's economy. He distinguished three types: traditional, rational–legal and charismatic.

**Traditional authority** is *power legitimised through respect for long-established cultural patterns*. The might of Chinese emperors in antiquity was legitimised by tradition, as was the rule of nobles in medieval Europe. In both cases, hereditary family rule within a traditional, agrarian way of life imbued leaders with almost god-like authority. In the modern world, traditional authority is being challenged more and more.

**Rational–legal authority** is *power legitimised by legally enacted rules and regulations*. It is legitimised by **government**, *formal organisations that direct the political life of a society*. Weber viewed bureaucracy as the organisational backbone of rational, industrial societies. Rationally enacted rules not only guide government in more and more countries today, but they also underlie much of our everyday life. The authority of classroom teachers and lecturers, for example, rests on the offices they hold in bureaucratic schools and universities. Compared to traditional authority, then, rational–legal authority flows not from family background but from organisational position. Thus, while a traditional monarch rules for life, a modern prime minister or president accepts and relinquishes power according to law, with authority remaining in the office.

**Charismatic authority** is *power legitimised through extraordinary personal abilities that inspire devotion and obedience*. Charisma, a concept to be detailed in Chapter 19, designates exceptional personal qualities that people take to be a sign of divine inspiration. Unlike tradition and rational law, then, charisma has less to do with social organisation and is more a trait of individual personality. The extraordinary ability of charismatics to challenge the status quo is deeply ingrained in global history: Vladimir Lenin guided the overthrow of feudal monarchy in Russia in 1917, Mahatma Gandhi inspired the struggle to free India from British colonialism after the Second World War, and Martin Luther King, Jr, galvanised the Civil Rights Movement in the United States. In more recent years, charismatic women, including Indira Gandhi of India, Benazir Bhutto of Pakistan, Golda Meir of Israel and Margaret Thatcher of the United Kingdom, have gained international political prominence.

A Theocratic State Celebrated: Iran is a major theocratic state. Here Iranians are carrying images of the late Islamic leader Ayatollah Ruhollah Khomeini and his successor incumbent leader Ayatollah Ali Khamenei at a rally celebrating the 31st anniversary of Islamic Revolution at the Azadi (liberty) Square in Tehran, capital of Iran, 11 February 2010
*Source*: © Ahmad Hala bisaz/Xinhua Press/Corbis.

# Religion as power: theocracy in Iran

A **theocracy** (from the Greek θεοκρατία, meaning 'the rule of God') is a *form of government where a god or religion is recognised as the supreme ruler*. The Islamic state of Iran and the Vatican in Rome are the only theocracies that are ruled by a religious figure (the Grand Ayatollah and the Pope). But there are many other countries that are partially theocratic – Saudi Arabia, Sudan, the Republic of Yemen, Afghanistan, the United Arab Emirates, Pakistan, Malaysia and Mauritania are all Islamic theocracies. The Vatican City is the only Christian theocracy. Most theocracies are usually authoritarian in nature and ruled by an absolute king (e.g. Saudi Arabia), a president (e.g. Sudan), a prime minister, or both (e.g. Pakistan). Some are called *constitutional theocracies*. Very controversially, some see Israel as a theocracy based on the Jewish faith.

Here we will briefly consider the case of Iran. Iran is one of the world's oldest civilisations: Persia and part of Mesopotamia. Its roots stretch back to the dawn of civilisation around 3,500 BCE. Today, it is a modern oil-exporting economy. And it is a theocracy: the Islamic Republic of Iran. Islam became its religion around 637 with the death of Muhammad and has continued to be so to this day. This new religion was linked with the growth of science, and Iran became for a while a leading, advanced civilisation. The invasion of Genghis Khan and the Mongols in the thirteenth century led to mass slaughter. Later, as Western industrialisation took place, its central role in the world started to decline.

Iran has had a long and difficult history of political conflict. The great split between Sunni and Shi'a took place in the lifetime of Muhammad's son-in-law. But the religious-based conflicts

LIVING IN THE C21ST

continue today. Modernisation started in the 1950s with the 'help' of the United States: Mohammad Mossadegh (1882–1967) was the democratically elected, fairly secular prime minister of Iran from 1951 to 1953, and was responsible for many reforms as well as the development of the oil industry. He was overthrown in a *coup d'état* backed by the US Central Intelligence Agency. Mossadegh resisted and was put under house arrest. The Shah returned in 1953 and became king of kings in 1976, and Americanisation proceeded until the Islamic revolution of 1979.

This was the defining moment in modern history of Iran. With serious economic problems, the people revolted and the Shah fled the country. The Khomenei returned from exile and the world's first Islamic republic was declared. Iran has remained an Islamic republic ever since. With this, the Mullahs appointed Khomenei as supreme ruler: a society was constructed through religion. The Islamic republic is a mixture of theocracy and democracy. It has presidential elections every five years or so;

and yet all government is tightly regulated by a religious council and a supreme leader (Vali-e-Faqih) who controls all branches of government, the judiciary and the revolutionary guard. Originally ruled by Ayatollah Khomeini, Iran is now ruled by Ayatollah Ali Khamenei. The religious council is composed of a number clerics.

The period 1997–2005 was marked by the presence a more liberal president, Muhammad Khtamai; but he was encircled by the religious establishment. An ultra conservative new president, Mahmoud Ahmadinejad, was elected in 2005 (and gained a much disputed second term in 2009).

Iran is generally a prospering country – doing well on the Human Development Index. Life expectancy has increased from 59 years in 1980 to 71 in 2005. It now has one of the lowest birth rates in the world. At the same time, it is a highly repressive society and fares very badly on human rights.

 A key book on Iran is Sami Zubaida: *Islam, The People and the State* (revised edn, 2009).

For a sense of the country, see Nasrin Alavi, *We are Iran* (2006). It is a patchwork of diverse Iranian voices found on Iranian blogs – telling it as it is.

An excellent documentary was produced by the BBC and Rageh Omar in 2007. It is well worth a look and you can see most of it on YouTube: search *Rageh Inside Iran*.

**COUNTRY FACT FILE**

IRAN

| | |
|---|---|
| Population | 66.4 million |
| Per capita GDP | $4,030 |
| Life expectancy | 69.65 male 72.72 female |
| Adult literacy | 83.5% |
| Key languages | Persian, Persian dialects 58% |
| Key religions | Shi'a Muslims (89%) Sunni Muslims (9%) |
| Key city | Tehran |
| Human development index | 0.702 (70th, 2010) |

## Types of political system

Political systems display marked variety. Some societies such as the Nuer in Africa, studied by the anthropologist E. E. Evans-Pritchard (1951), have been 'headless', having no leaders. But more generally, throughout much of history, imperial systems or empires – the Chinese, the Japanese, the Islamic, the Roman – have dominated politics, functioning as separate worlds having little contact with each other. Life under these systems was often capricious. It is only in the latter part of the second millennium that we start to see the emergence of what we take for granted today: the nation-state, with a clearly defined territory, military support and nationalist creed. Historically, the

idea that people imagine a community connected to their nation is probably not that common. But it has been a defining feature of the modern world.

Generally speaking, the world's major contemporary political systems fall into four categories: totalitarianism, authoritarianism, monarchy and democracy. Theocracies are often seen as fifth (see *Living in the twenty-first century* above).

## 1 Totalitarianism

The most restrictive political form is **totalitarianism**, *a political system that extensively regulates people's lives.* Although some totalitarian governments claim to represent the will of the people, most seek to bend people to the will of the government. As the term itself implies, such governments represent total concentrations of power and prohibit organised opposition of any kind. Denying the populace the right to assemble for political purposes and controlling access to information, these governments thrive in an environment of fear and social atomisation. Socialisation in totalitarian societies is intensely political, seeking not just outward compliance but inward commitment to the system. In North Korea, pictures of leaders and political messages over loudspeakers are familiar elements of public life that remind citizens that they owe total allegiance to the state. Government-controlled schools and mass media present only official versions of events.

Government indoctrination is especially stringent whenever political opposition surfaces in a totalitarian society. In the aftermath of the 1989 pro-democracy movement in the People's Republic of China, for example, officials demanded that citizens report all 'unpatriotic' people – even members of their own families. Further, Chinese leaders subjected all students at Beijing universities to political 'refresher' courses. Totalitarian governments span the political spectrum from the far right (including Nazi Germany) to the far left (North Korea).

## 2 Authoritarianism

Some nations give their people little voice in politics. **Authoritarianism** refers to *a political system that denies popular participation in government*. An authoritarian government is not only indifferent to people's needs; it lacks the legal means to remove leaders from office and provides people with little or no means even to express their opinions. Polish sociologist Wlodzimierz Wesolowski sums up authoritarianism this way: 'The authoritarian philosophy argues for the supremacy of the state [over other] organised social activity' (1990: 435). The absolute monarchies in Saudi Arabia and Kuwait are highly authoritarian, as are military juntas, found today in Congo and Ethiopia, where political dissatisfaction has been widespread. (This is not always the case, however, as the *World watch* box shows in the case of the 'soft authoritarianism' of the small Asian nation of Singapore.)

## 3 Monarchy

**Monarchy** is *a political system in which a single family rules from generation to generation*. Today's British monarchy traces its lineage back roughly 1,000 years.

During the medieval era, absolute monarchy, in which hereditary rulers claimed a virtual monopoly of power based on divine right, flourished from England to China and in parts of the Americas. In some nations, today monarchs still exercise virtually absolute control over their people. The system is legitimated by tradition.

Yet as democracies and egalitarianism have spread throughout many parts of the world, so monarchs have gradually passed from the scene in favour of elected officials. Europe's remaining monarchs – in the UK, Spain, Norway, Sweden, Belgium, Denmark and the Netherlands – now preside over *constitutional monarchies*. They serve as symbolic heads of state, while actual governing is the responsibility of elected politicians: the monarch may formally reign, but elected officials actually rule. Still, in 2003, around 30 nations were political monarchies where families passed power from generation to generation.

## 4 Democracies

The historical trend in the modern world has favoured **democracy**, *a political system in which power is exercised by the people as a whole*, though quite how this power is to be exercised has always been a key problem. Members of democratic societies rarely participate directly in decision-making; *representative democracy* places authority in the hands of elected leaders, who are accountable to the people (under *participatory democracy* people would represent themselves and take their own decisions). The system is legitimated by rational–legal authority, and a rational election process places leaders in offices regulated by law.

### Democracy and its problems

But democratic political systems are much more than just leaders and followers; they are often built on extensive bureaucracy and economic power. Considerable formal organisation is necessary to carry out the expanding range of government activities undertaken by democratic societies. As it grows, government gradually takes on a life of its own, revealing an inherent antagonism between democracy and bureaucracy. The federal government of the United States, for example, employs more than 3 million people (excluding the armed forces), making it one of the largest bureaucracies in the world. Another 15 million people work in some 80,000 local governments. In the UK, some 2.6 million people are employed by local authorities alone.

**WORLD WATCH**

# 'Soft authoritarianism' or planned prosperity? A report from Singapore

Singapore, a tiny nation on the tip of the Malay Peninsula with a population of just over 3 million, seems to many to be an Asian paradise. Surrounded by poor societies that grapple with rapidly growing populations, squalid, sprawling cities and surging crime rates, the affluence, cleanliness and safety of Singapore make the European visitor think more of a theme park than a country.

In fact, since its independence from Malaysia in 1965, Singapore has startled the world with its economic development; today, the economy is expanding rapidly and per capita income now rivals that of the United States. But, unlike Europe or the United States, Singapore has scarcely any social problems such as crime, slums, unemployment or children living in poverty. In fact, people in Singapore do not even contend with traffic jams, graffiti on underground trains or litter in the streets.

The key to Singapore's orderly environment is the ever-present hand of government, which actively promotes traditional morality and regulates just about everything. The state owns and manages most of the country's housing and has a stake in many businesses. It provides tax incentives for family planning and completing additional years of schooling. To keep traffic under control, the government slaps hefty surcharges on cars, pushing the price of a basic saloon car up to around £25,000.

Singapore made international headlines in 1994 after the government accused Michael Fay (from the United States) of vandalism and sentenced him to a caning – a penalty illegal in most Western countries. Singapore's laws also permit police to detain a person suspected of a crime without charge or trial and to mandate death by hanging for drug dealing. The government has outlawed some religious groups (including Jehovah's Witnesses) and bans pornography outright. Even smoking in public brings a heavy fine. To ensure that city streets are kept clean, the state forbids eating on the subway, imposes stiff fines for littering and has even outlawed the sale of chewing gum.

In economic terms, Singapore defies familiar categories. Government control of scores of businesses, including television stations, telephone services, airlines and taxis, seems socialist. Yet, unlike socialist enterprises, these businesses are operated efficiently and very profitably. Moreover, Singapore's capitalist culture celebrates economic growth (although the government cautions its people about the evils of excessive materialism) and this nation is home to hundreds of multinational corporations.

Singapore's political climate is as unusual as its economy. Members of this society feel the hand of government far more than their counterparts in Europe. Just as important, a single political organisation – the People's Action Party – has ruled Singapore without opposition since the nation's independence 30 years ago.

**COUNTRY FACT FILE**

**SINGAPORE**

| | |
|---|---|
| Population | 4,450,000 (2006) |
| Urban population | 100% |
| Per capita GDP | $31,400 (2006 est.) |
| Life expectancy | 79.4 years (2005–10); male 76 years, female 80 years (2000) |
| Literacy | Over 93% (2004) |
| Languages | Malay, English, Chinese (Mandarin) and Tamil (official languages) |
| Religions | Buddhism, Islam, Christianity, Taoism and Hinduism, Sikh and Jewish minorities |
| Main cities | Singapore: around 3 million |
| Human development index | 0.846 (27th, 2010) |

Clearly, Singapore is not a politically democratic country. But most people in this prospering nation seem content – even enthusiastic – about their lives. What Singapore's political system offers is a simple bargain: government demands unflinching loyalty from the populace; in return, it provides a high degree of security and prosperity. Critics charge that this system amounts to a 'soft authoritarianism' that stifles dissent and gives government unwarranted control over people's lives. Most of the people of Singapore, however, know the struggles of living elsewhere and, for now at least, consider the trade-off a good one.

*Source*: Based on Branegan (1993).

The great majority of these bureaucrats were never elected and are unknown to the public they purport to serve. To elect them would seem impractical, given their numbers and the need for specialised training. But, ironically, while the public focuses attention on a small number of elected leaders, most everyday decision-making is carried out by career bureaucrats who are not directly accountable to the people (Scaff, 1981).

## Democracy and freedom: contrasting approaches

Despite their distinctive histories and cultural diversity, virtually all industrialised nations in the world claim to be democratic and politically free. Map 16.1 shows the countries of the world where 'free' systems exist. By the end of 2003, according to Freedom House (a New York-based organisation that tracks global political trends), more people in the world were 'free' than 'not free' for the first time in history (see Table 16.1). In 2007, its latest worldwide political survey found

that the percentage of countries designated as 'free' has remained flat. Setbacks for freedom have happened in a number of countries in the Asia-Pacific region, with a more modest decline in Africa, and a solidification of authoritarian rule in the majority of countries of the former Soviet Union. Some countries – Guyana, Haiti and Nepal – became more free; and Thailand and the Congo (Brazzaville) less free.

| Table 16.1 | The extent of global freedom: 30-year global trend, 1973–2003 | | |
|---|---|---|---|
| | Free countries | Partly free countries | Not free countries |
| 1973 | 43 | 38 | 69 |
| 1983 | 54 | 47 | 64 |
| 1993 | 75 | 73 | 38 |
| 2003 | 89 | 55 | 48 |

*Source*: Freedom House.

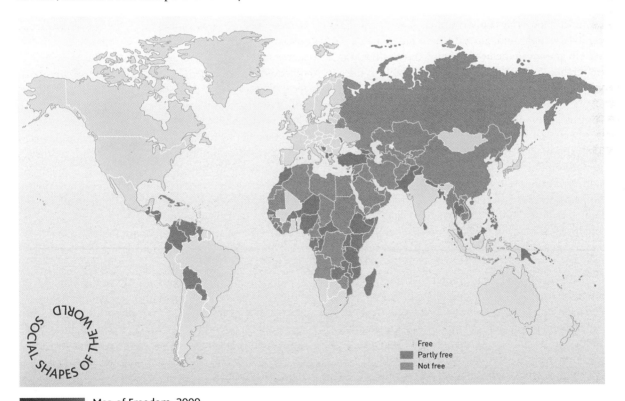

Free
Partly free
Not free

| Map 16.1 | Map of Freedom, 2009 |

*Source*: Map of Freedom, 2009, http://www.freedomhouse.org.

*Freedom House* is an independent watchdog organisation that supports the expansion of freedom around the world. Freedom House supports democratic change, monitors freedom, and advocates for democracy and human rights. Since its founding in 1941 by prominent Americans concerned with the mounting threats to peace and democracy, Freedom House has been a vigorous proponent of democratic values and a steadfast opponent of dictatorships of the far left and the far right. Its website is a useful source of information on the extent and change of 'global freedom' – though some of its statistics are contested by other groups. See www.freedomhouse.org.

Measuring 'freedom' is always a problem: and here it is defined in terms of national ratings on political rights and civil liberties – and since countries mean different things by these terms, these are very hard to measure. So these conclusions need to be tempered, as usual, with caution. Still, overall, it looks like there is a worldwide movement towards democratisation. Again, though, we must be careful and ask just what is meant by this political freedom.

The political life of the West is largely shaped by the free-market economic principles of capitalism. Supporters argue that the operation of a market system affords individuals the personal freedom to pursue whatever they perceive as their self-interest. Thus, the argument continues, the capitalist approach to political freedom translates into personal liberty – freedom to vote for one's preferred leader or otherwise act with minimal interference from government.

Yet, as the last chapter explained, capitalist societies are marked by a striking inequality of wealth. Such economic disparity, critics counter, gives some people far more choices and opportunities than others. Thus, capitalism looks undemocratic in so far as such a system attends to the needs of only the wealthy and highlights choices that may not be available to the poor and less well off.

Supporters of a socialist economic system, by contrast, point out that socialist politics strives to meet every citizen's basic needs for housing, schooling, a job and medical care. Thus, the socialist approach to political freedom emphasises freedom from basic want. For example, there is little of the hunger and homelessness we associate with the capitalism of the United States in more socialist nations such as Norway and Sweden. Many in the Scandinavian countries would regard their systems as more free because of this.

But critics of socialism counter that such systems are more likely to be unresponsive to people's needs and aspirations as well as heavy-handed in their suppression of any political opposition. During the 1990s, for example, people living under socialist governments in eastern Europe overthrew that system in favour of a free market that would, presumably, reduce political repression (and, hopefully, raise living standards: something that is now in doubt).

These contrasting views of freedom raise an important question: are economic equality and political liberty compatible? To foster economic equality, socialism tends to infringe on individual initiative. Capitalism, on the other hand, provides broad political liberties, which, in practice, mean little to the poor.

Many of the countries of Europe may be seen generally to favour positions which can be called **social democratic**. This is *a mix of capitalist and socialist/welfare economies and politics*. Scandinavian countries pay high taxes and have strong welfare systems, middle European countries have lower commitments, southern European systems are less comprehensive, and the UK system highlights welfare and social services with quite high tax levels, but also has income-dependent benefits.

## The rise of nation-states and the globalisation of politics

Most people living on the earth today live in **nation-states** – *political apparatuses over a specific territory with their own citizens backed up by military force and a nationalistic, sovereign creed*. But this is a new phenomenon of recent history. It has far from typically been the case in the past, where land masses have been ruled diversely by tribal chiefs, kings, emperors and sultans – despots who ruled by force and theocracies held together by religion. Ethnic groups made claims to their territories and, right up to the sixteenth century, people lived with these territorial limits set through land stewardship. Nation-states as we now know them congealed between the sixteenth and nineteenth centuries. Starting with the Treaty of Westphalia (1648), criteria started to be set out to demarcate local domestic territories and recognise independent nations. Thereafter the old empires – the Russian Empire, the Austro-Hungarian Empire, the British Empire – started to collapse, and new nation-states started to appear. Nationalism is hence also a new and modern phenomenon. Modern nation-states subsequently became the core of the systems of catastrophic wars built around nationalism in the twentieth century.

A nation-state sounds like a contradiction. A *state* is a political organisation with effective rule, sovereignty and governance over a limited geographic area – claiming a monopoly on authority, controlling armies and civil service, and believing it can use violence 'legitimately'. By contrast, a *nation* suggests a human and cultural community – connected often with religions, languages, ethnicities and a shared way of life. The nation is something to make sacrifice for, even lay one's life down for, and usually generates strong identities (I am German; I am Thai; I am a Maori). Often these are less real than **imagined communities** – an influential term developed by Benedict Anderson to suggest how nationalism is linked to the emergence of a 'print-capitalism' and the growing rejection of ideas of the monarchy and divine rule. (There has been much recent sociological research on the nation-state and its workings by Michael Mann, Anthony Smith and Saskia Sassen; along with a concern about the democratisation or not of these states).

## Globalisation and politics

In Chapter 15, we pointed to the emergence of a global economy, meaning that finance flows routinely across national boundaries, along with products and services. In a similar way, we can point to the parallel development of a global political system. As we have seen, for the past 300 years or so, the dominant mode of governing has been through the nation-state, and we still think primarily in terms of these nation-states – such as Norway, China or Australia. At the same time, politics has clearly become part of a globalisation process. In some ways, there is a long history of 'international governance': ancient Greece and Renaissance Italy are two earlier examples. But today we can see at least five ways in which country politics have become interlinked:

1   The steady growth of political interconnectedness over large regions – notably the European Union comprising some 27 states, and the Association of South East Asian Nations (ASEAN: Indonesia, the Philippines, Malaysia, Singapore, Brunei, Thailand, Vietnam, Laos, Myanmar and Cambodia) – signposts a continuing regional interconnectedness (see: www.aseansex.org).

2   A worldwide layer of global government has been introduced since 1945, with the development of the United Nations. A major raft of political institutions, from UNICEF and UNHCR to UNESCO and WHO, have developed within it, and now play significant roles in world policies (for these and other abbreviations see the list on pp. 952–3; their website addresses are all straightforwardly found: do a Google search for the initials given above).

3   Multinational corporations (discussed in Chapter 15) now represent a political order of a quite different kind. They have enormous power to shape social life throughout the world. From this point of view, politics is dissolving into business as corporations grow larger than governments. *Of the 100 largest economies in the world, 51 today are corporations, not countries* (Brecher et al., 2000: 128).

4   The Information Revolution has put national politics on to the world stage. Even as early as 1989, hours before the Chinese government sent troops to Tiananmen Square to crush the 1989 pro-democracy movement, officials 'unplugged' the satellite transmitting systems of news agencies in an effort to keep the world from watching as events unfolded that day. Despite their efforts, news of the massacre was flashed around the world minutes after it began via the fax machines in universities and private homes. In short, just as individual nations can no longer control their own economies, so no national government can fully manage the political events that occur within its borders. And when suicide bombers attacked New York's Twin Towers on 11 September 2001, the whole world watched on more or less as it happened. Current information technology brings politics to homes and businesses across the globe in a flash.

5   New social movements have also been involved in the new Information Revolution and turned their activities into global campaigns and actions. As we shall see below, new forms of power have been developing linked to social movements. Green movements such as World Action for Rainforests (at www.rainforestweb.org) and the Women's Environmental Network (at http://web.wen.org) and hundreds of others are now global 'eco-warriors'. They are playing a significant role in putting issues of the green agenda on the actions list of international government (Scarce, 2006).

There are many recent examples of global politics. The 'Make Poverty History' campaign, which accompanied the G8 Gleneagles Summit in 2005, demanded 'trade justice', 'drop the debt' and 'more and better aid' for low-income societies. Over 500 organisations from some 84 nations participated, and a proliferation of websites for communication developed. At the time, the campaign was claimed to have been a huge political success; in practice, it closed down a year later amidst much criticism. In December 2009, tens of thousands of people staged protests in Copenhagen and around the world to push for stronger international commitments at the climate change conference in the Danish capital.

## Gender and power

Throughout history, women have been excluded from most positions in the political system. Moreover, until very recently, women rarely appeared in studies or research connected to politics and governance. Simply posing the question 'where are the women?' in studies of any aspect of the political system soon reveals their lack of representation. Consider the seemingly simple issue of the right to vote: women in general acquired this right very late – sometimes a century after men had gained it. Moreover, the proportion of women in governments across the world is low, well below 40 per cent at best.

A few women, though, have risen to prominence: Indira Gandhi (in India during the 1960s through to the 1980s), Margaret Thatcher (a Conservative and very influential free marketer in England 1979–90), Mary Robinson (President of Ireland 1992–6), Sirimavo R. D. Bandaranaike (Prime Minister of Sri Lanka in the 1960s, 1970s and 1990s), Angela Merkel (Chancellor of Germany, elected autumn 2005), Ellen-Johnson-Sirleaf (first elected female president in Africa in 2006 – Liberia), Benazir Bhutto of Pakistan (assassinated in 2007) and Julia Gillard (first female prime minister of Australia in 2010). But simply to name them is to suggest how few of them there are: in 2009, there were 13 women who could be counted amongst the 200 or so world leaders.

Looking at the membership of world parliaments and national assemblies tells a similar story. Very few have any kind of equality between men and women. There has been growth, however: in 1995, national assemblies comprised, on average, 11.5 per cent women;

World leaders gather to discuss the global financial crisis at the G20 Summit in London on 2 April 2009. It is interesting to see how few women are world leaders. They are Angela Merkel (Germany) and Cristina Fernandez de Kirchner (Argentina)
*Source*: © Olivier Hoslet/epa/Corbis.

| Table 16.2 | Meetings of the global women's movement | | |
|---|---|---|---|
| | Date | Location | Delegates |
| 1st | 1975 | Mexico | 6,000 |
| 2nd | 1980 | Copenhagen | 7,000 |
| 3rd | 1985 | Nairobi | 15,000 |
| 4th | 1995 | Beijing | 8,000 |
| 5th | 2000 | Beijing +5 | |
| 6th | 2005 | Beijing +10 | |
| 7th | 2010 | Beijing +15 | |
| | 2 July 2010 | UN Entity for Gender Equality and the Empowerment of Women established* | |

\* See UN Women: www.unwomen.org.

by May 2008, it was 18.4 per cent. Rwanda had nearly 50 per cent women, as did Sweden. The USA had only 15 per cent and the UK around 20 per cent. The same is true at a global level: the United Nations has not been able to achieve 50:50 equality even though it has committed to doing so. And most of its women are concentrated at lower occupational levels. In short, wherever you look, there are many fewer women than men in politics (Peterson and Runyan, 2010: 109 et seq.).

Both first- and second-wave feminism may have brought about some changes (see Chapter 12). Most significantly, we can start to see something like the emergence of a transitional women's movement in the past few decades. Often prompted by organisations such as the United Nations, a number of International Women's Conferences have been held, though these often revealed significant conflicts between 'First World' and 'Third World' women. Priorities and approaches differ greatly across cultures.

In the most general terms, these organisations have recognised that standard development models, such as the Human Development Index discussed in Chapters 4 and 9, do not reveal the extent or nature of gender imbalances in the status of women when compared to men across the world. The United Nations Development Programme (UNDP) has championed eight major areas where the position of women needs to be further equalised. These are:

1 Autonomy of the body (for example, controls over reproduction and sexuality, and the problem of violence).

2 Autonomy within family and household (for example, freedoms to marry, divorce and have custody of children in case of divorce).

3 Political power (for example, increased role in decision-making in unions, governments, parliaments, etc.).

4 Social resources (for example, access to health and education).

5 Material resources (for example, access to land, houses and credit).

6 Employment and income (for example, fair distribution of paid and unpaid labour).

7 Time (for example, relative access to leisure and sleep).

8 Gender identity (for example, problems with the rigidity of the sexual division of labour).

In all these areas, across the world, women tend to be in a strikingly less powerful position than men. As we saw in Chapter 13, there is now a global gender gap report which enables global tracking of the shifting fortunes of women's equality across the globe.

 For more on women in politics, see Websites on Women and Politics at: www.ipu.org/wmn-e/web.htm.

# Political organisation in Europe

Although this has not always been the case, all the countries of western and central Europe may currently be seen as liberal democracies with a plurality of political parties and an electoral process. Spain, Germany, Greece and Italy have all at times been run by authoritarian governments. Portugal and Spain were right-wing dictatorships until the mid-1970s. The situation in eastern Europe is somewhat more complex. The Soviet Union dominated this bloc and most countries were communist until 1989. Since then, and often with much difficulty, they have been in the process of becoming democracies too.

In most countries there is usually both a national system of government and a local one. This can sometimes cause major tensions, when different parties hold the balance of power in one but not the other. But in general, the political parties of Europe have been stable.

# The European Union

Most European countries are standing at the threshold of major change. They have their own (usually long-standing) political system as a nation-state. The nation-states of Europe are the independent nations – with their own territories, military forces, sense of national identity, and forms of citizenship and government, such as Parliament in the UK and the Bundestag and Bundesrat in Germany.

But increasingly important is the fact that many of the nation-states have become member states of the European Union (Norway and Switzerland are major exceptions), sending their elected representatives to the European Parliament at Strasbourg. As the map of Europe (Map 4.3) in Chapter 4 shows, there are a number of countries within Europe that have recently joined and others that are lining up to join. Figure 16.1 shows the main political parties in the European Parliament elected in June 2009. The centre-right European People's Party (EPP) remains the most powerful group in the 2009–14 European Parliament, with 263 out of the 736 MEPs (Members of the European Parliament). The Social Democrats (PES) have 163 seats; and the Liberal ALDE group has 66 seats. The Greens retained their fourth place with 52. Europe's voters generally shifted to the right: in four of the EU's six biggest nations (Germany, France, Italy and Poland), centre-right ruling parties performed unexpectedly well, whilst centre-left governments in Britain and Spain did badly. Nationalist and anti-immigration parties made gains in the Netherlands, Denmark, Finland, Austria, Greece, Romania and Hungary.

In the June 2009 elections, there was widespread apathy. The turnout continued to fall – it was 50 per cent in 1999; 45 per cent in 2004; and 43 per cent in 2009. In Britain, two-thirds of voters stayed away from the polls (Table 16.3). Voters often cast votes for fringe parties and parties in opposition to their own governments. Table 16.4 reveals this in detail.

The EU has developed a whole panoply of European institutions. Among these are:

- *The Commission*: with at least one member for each country; it proposes new laws and implements them.

- *The Council*: each country has one seat; this is the main decision-making body.

- *The Parliament*: in 2009, there were 736 MEPs; they are allocated proportionally to population.

- *The Court of Justice*: monitors the EU laws and watches member states' compliance.

- *The European Court of Human Rights*: established in 1959.

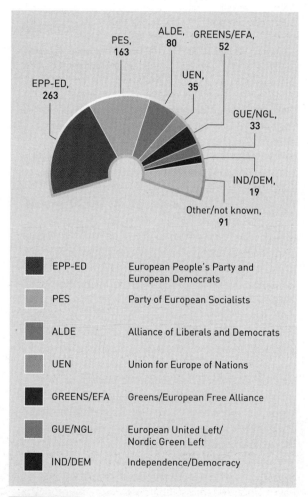

| | EPP-ED | European People's Party and European Democrats |
| | PES | Party of European Socialists |
| | ALDE | Alliance of Liberals and Democrats |
| | UEN | Union for Europe of Nations |
| | GREENS/EFA | Greens/European Free Alliance |
| | GUE/NGL | European United Left/ Nordic Green Left |
| | IND/DEM | Independence/Democracy |

**Figure 16.1**  Major political parties in the New European Parliament (Elected in June 2009)

*Note:* For a full breakdown of political parties, see www.parties-and-elections.de/eu.html.

*Source: European Parliament Elections 2009, Research Paper 09/53,* 17 June 2009, p. 25.

| Table 16.3 | Turnout in elections to the European Parliament, 1979 to 2009, by EU country | | | | | | | | | | | |
|---|---|---|---|---|---|---|---|---|---|---|---|---|
| | 1979 | 1981 | 1984 | 1987 | 1989 | 1994 | 1995 | 1996 | 1999 | 2004 | 2007 | Prov. 2009 |
| Belgium | 91 | | 92 | | 91 | 91 | | | 91 | 91 | | 86 |
| Denmark | 48 | | 52 | | 46 | 53 | | | 50 | 48 | | 60 |
| Germany | 66 | | 57 | | 62 | 60 | | | 45 | 43 | | 43 |
| Ireland | 64 | | 48 | | 68 | 44 | | | 50 | 59 | | 55 |
| France | 61 | | 57 | | 49 | 53 | | | 47 | 43 | | 40 |
| Italy | 86 | | 82 | | 81 | 74 | | | 70 | 72 | | 66 |
| Luxembourg | 89 | | 89 | | 87 | 89 | | | 87 | 91 | | 91 |
| Netherlands | 58 | | 51 | | 47 | 36 | | | 30 | 39 | | 37 |
| United Kingdom | 32 | | 33 | | 36 | 36 | | | 24 | 39 | | 35 |
| Greece | | 81 | 81 | | 80 | 73 | | | 70 | 63 | | 52 |
| Spain | | | | 69 | 55 | 59 | | | 63 | 45 | | 44 |
| Portugal | | | | 72 | 51 | 36 | | | 40 | 39 | | 37 |
| Sweden | | | | | | | 42 | | 39 | 38 | | 44 |
| Austria | | | | | | | | 68 | 49 | 42 | | 42 |
| Finland | | | | | | | | 58 | 30 | 39 | | 40 |
| Czech Rep | | | | | | | | | | 28 | | 28 |
| Estonia | | | | | | | | | | 27 | | 43 |
| Cyprus | | | | | | | | | | 73 | | 59 |
| Lithuania | | | | | | | | | | 48 | | 21 |
| Latvia | | | | | | | | | | 41 | | 53 |
| Hungary | | | | | | | | | | 39 | | 36 |
| Malta | | | | | | | | | | 82 | | 79 |
| Poland | | | | | | | | | | 21 | | 27 |
| Slovenia | | | | | | | | | | 28 | | 28 |
| Slovakia | | | | | | | | | | 17 | | 20 |
| Bulgaria | | | | | | | | | | | 29 | 37 |
| Romania | | | | | | | | | | | 29 | 27 |
| EU total | 62 | | 59 | | 58 | 57 | | | 50 | 45 | | 43 |

Source: European Parliament, www.elections2009-results.eu/_turnout_en.html. TNS opinion in conjunction with the European Parliament.

Note: In Belgium, Luxembourg, Cyprus and Malta voting is compulsory; this was also the case in Italy up to 1992.

| Table 16.4 | MEPs by country and political group 2009 (provisional) | | | | | | | | |
|---|---|---|---|---|---|---|---|---|---|
| * | EPP-ED | PES | ALDE | UEN | GRN/EFA | GUE/NGL | IND/DEM | Others | Total |
| Austria | 6 | 5 | 0 | 0 | 1 | 0 | 0 | 5 | 17 |
| Belgium | 6 | 5 | 5 | 0 | 3 | 0 | 0 | 3 | 22 |
| Bulgaria | 6 | 4 | 5 | 0 | 0 | 0 | 0 | 2 | 17 |
| Cyprus | 2 | 1 | 0 | 0 | 0 | 2 | 0 | 1 | 6 |
| Czech Rep | 2 | 7 | 0 | 0 | 0 | 4 | 0 | 9 | 22 |
| Denmark | 1 | 4 | 3 | 2 | 2 | 1 | 0 | 0 | 13 |
| Estonia | 1 | 1 | 3 | 0 | 0 | 0 | 0 | 1 | 6 |
| Finland | 4 | 2 | 4 | 0 | 2 | 0 | 0 | 1 | 13 |
| France | 30 | 14 | 6 | 0 | 14 | 4 | 1 | 3 | 72 |
| Germany | 42 | 23 | 12 | 0 | 14 | 8 | 0 | 0 | 99 |
| Greece | 7 | 9 | 0 | 0 | 1 | 3 | 2 | 0 | 22 |

| Table 16.4 | *continued* | | | | | | | | |
| | | | | | | | | | |
| * | EPP-ED | PES | ALDE | UEN | GRN/EFA | GUE/NGL | IND/DEM | Others | Total |
|---|---|---|---|---|---|---|---|---|---|
| Hungary | 15 | 4 | 0 | 0 | 0 | 0 | 0 | 3 | 22 |
| Ireland | 4 | 2 | 1 | 3 | 0 | 1 | 1 | 0 | 12 |
| Italy | 34 | 0 | 7 | 9 | 0 | 0 | 0 | 22 | 72 |
| Latvia | 1 | 0 | 1 | 3 | 1 | 0 | 0 | 2 | 8 |
| Lithuania | 4 | 3 | 2 | 2 | 0 | 0 | 0 | 1 | 12 |
| Luxembourg | 3 | 1 | 1 | 0 | 1 | 0 | 0 | 0 | 6 |
| Malta | 2 | 3 | 0 | 0 | 0 | 0 | 0 | 0 | 5 |
| Netherlands | 5 | 3 | 6 | 0 | 3 | 2 | 2 | 4 | 25 |
| Poland | 28 | 7 | 0 | 15 | 0 | 0 | 0 | 0 | 50 |
| Portugal | 10 | 7 | 0 | 0 | 0 | 5 | 0 | 0 | 22 |
| Romania | 13 | 11 | 5 | 0 | 1 | 0 | 0 | 3 | 33 |
| Slovakia | 6 | 5 | 0 | 1 | 0 | 0 | 0 | 1 | 13 |
| Slovenia | 3 | 2 | 2 | 0 | 0 | 0 | 0 | 0 | 7 |
| Spain | 23 | 21 | 2 | 0 | 2 | 1 | 0 | 1 | 50 |
| Sweden | 5 | 5 | 4 | 0 | 2 | 1 | 0 | 1 | 18 |
| United Kingdom | 0 | 14 | 11 | 0 | 5 | 1 | 13 | 28 | 72 |
| All MEPs | 263 | 163 | 80 | 35 | 52 | 33 | 19 | 91 | 736 |

* For explanations of these headings, see p. 548.

*Source*: European Parliament, www.elections2009-results.eu/en/national_parties_en.html. TNS opinion in cooperation with the European Parliament.

# Explaining power: the classic analysis of power in society

Sociologists and political scientists have long debated how formal power is distributed. Power is among the most difficult topics of scientific research because decision-making is complex and often occurs behind closed doors. It might be brutally visible in authoritarian societies, but in 'democratic' ones it is much harder to locate. From this mix of facts and values, three competing models of power have traditionally been discussed: the pluralist model, the power elite model and the ruling class (or Marxist) model (see Table 16.5).

## The pluralist model

Formally, the **pluralist model** is *an analysis of politics that views power as dispersed among many competing interest groups*. This approach is closely tied to structural–functional theory. Pluralists claim, first, that politics is an arena of negotiation. With limited resources, no organisation can expect to realise all its goals. Organisations, therefore, operate as veto groups,

achieving some success but mostly keeping opponents from reaching all their goals. The political process, then, relies heavily on negotiating alliances and compromises that bridge differences among numerous interest groups and, in the process, produce policies that generate broad-based support. In short, pluralists believe that power is widely dispersed throughout society and that the political system takes account of all constituencies.

A second pluralist assertion holds that power has many sources, including wealth, political office, social prestige, personal charisma and organisational clout. Only in exceptional cases do all these sources of power fall into the same hands. Here, again, the conclusion is that power is widely diffused (Dahl, 1961, 1982).

## Research results

Supporting the pluralist model, Nelson Polsby (1959) found that in New Haven, Connecticut, key decisions on various issues – including urban renewal, the nomination of political candidates and the operation of the schools – were made by different groups. Polsby also noted that few of the upper-class families listed in New Haven's Social Register were also economic leaders. Thus, Polsby concluded, no one segment of society rules all the others.

Robert Dahl (1961) investigated New Haven's history and found that, over time, power had become increasingly dispersed. Dahl echoed Polsby's judgements, concluding that 'no one, and certainly no group of more than a few individuals, is entirely lacking in [power]' (1961: 228).

The pluralist model implies that 'democracies' are indeed reasonably democratic! They grant at least some power to everyone. Pluralists assert that not even the most influential people always get their way, and even the most disadvantaged are able to band together to ensure that some of their political interests are addressed.

# The power elite model

The **power elite model** is *an analysis of politics that views power as concentrated among the rich*. This second approach is closely allied with the social-conflict paradigm. The term 'power elite' is a lasting contribution of C. Wright Mills (1956), who argued that the upper class holds the bulk of society's wealth, prestige and power. The power elite constitutes the 'super-rich' or, in Marxist terms, the capitalists who own and control the lion's share of the economy. These families, broadly linked through business dealings as well as marriage, are able to turn the national agenda towards their own interests.

Mills, writing about the power elite in the United States, claimed that historically that country has been dominated by three major sectors – the economy, the government and the military. Elites circulate from one sector to another, consolidating their power as they go. Alexander Haig, for example, has held top positions in private business, served as White House chief of staff under Richard Nixon, was secretary of state under Ronald Reagan, made a bid for the White House in 1988 as a presidential candidate, and is a retired army general. Haig is far from the exception: a majority of national political leaders enter public life from powerful and highly paid positions – 10 of 13 members of the Clinton cabinet were reputed to be millionaires – and most return to the corporate world later on.

Power elite theorists challenge claims that the United States is a political democracy; the concentration of wealth and power, they maintain, is simply too great for the average person's voice to be heard. Rejecting pluralist assertions that various centres of power serve as checks and balances on one another, the power elite model contends that those at the top encounter no real opposition.

## *Research results*

Over more than 60 years, social scientists have conducted research that helps to evaluate these opposing views of government. Supporting the power elite position, Robert and Helen Lynd (1937) studied Muncie, Indiana (which they called 'Middletown', to indicate that it was a typical city). They documented the fortune amassed by a single family – the Balls – from their business manufacturing glass canning jars and showed how the Ball family dominated many dimensions of the city's life. If anyone doubted the Balls' prominence, the Lynds explained, there was no need to look further than the local bank, a university, a hospital and a department store, which all bear the family name. In Muncie, according to the Lynds, the power elite more or less boiled down to a single family.

Floyd Hunter's (1963; orig. 1953) study of Atlanta, Georgia, provided further support for the power elite model. Atlanta, concluded Hunter, had no one dominant family, but there were no more than about 40 people who held all the top positions in the city's businesses and controlled the city's politics.

# The ruling class: a Marxist model

For Marxists, political equality is 'one of the great myths of our time' (Miliband, 1969; Miliband and Panitch, 1993). Basically, the state always works in the interests of the dominant, ruling, economic class: it favours and supports 'capital'. Although there may be many different groupings – elected parliaments, judiciaries, local government, pressure groups – which create a semblance of balance, checks and equality, in practice they simply serve as masks for what is really happening. There have been many prominent sociologists who have adopted variants of this position. Three will be introduced here.

The Italian Marxist Antonio Gramsci (1891–1937) was a leader in the Italian Communist Party. Imprisoned from 1926 till his death by Mussolini's fascist government, his theory appears in his *Prison Notebooks*. For Gramsci, 'the state = political society + civil society'. The ruling class must gain the consent of the working class. No government can rule by force alone for long. He called this process **hegemony**, *the means by which a ruling/dominant group wins over a subordinated group through ideas*. To make hegemony work, dominated groups have to be taken into consideration, their interests noted and concessions given to them. Because dominated groups are always

| Table 16.5 | Three models of contemporary politics and society | | |
|---|---|---|---|
| | **Pluralist** | **Power elite** | **Ruling class** |
| Distribution of power | Highly dispersed | Concentrated | Concentrated |
| Is it democratic? | Yes: every vote counts; no one group dominates | No: a small share of people dominate economy, armed services and government | No: concentration of wealth and power |
| Voter apathy | Some people are just not interested, but all could have a voice | How can ordinary folk stop 'big government'? Apathy is perfectly understandable | Apathy is alienation. Most people are powerless |

partially aware of their subordinated position, these concessions become vital to the smooth working of the state (Gramsci, 1971).

Ralph Miliband (1969) provided a lot of detail about the social background of cabinet ministers, senior police, top judges and the like, showing how they act in the interests of capital. Either these people occupy elite positions in the bourgeoisie, or through education and culture they have come to identify with this group. Much work of the media disguises the real nature of the power, providing a process of legitimation.

Nicos Poulantzas (1969) adopts a wider (and much more abstract) approach. Individual politicians are not of interest to him. Instead, he looks at the state as part of a society, independent of people. It, so to speak, rolls on all on its own. The ruling class does not govern directly, but its interests are served through the autonomous functioning of a state which rises above sectional interests and maintains a myth of public interests and national unity. For Poulantzas, the state works through a repressive apparatus – army, police, etc. – using coercive power, and an ideological apparatus – church, schools, media and family – which 'manipulates' values and beliefs. Poulantzas's theory is very abstract, and indeed he has been criticised for being too general and for seeing too little role (or indeed no role!) for people to play in shaping their own lives. More than this: he does not provide any evidence for his theories, and some have argued that the theory is impossible to prove or disprove.

## Who rules Britain?

John Scott has studied the power structures in the UK, asking: who rules Britain? He suggests that 'there is in

Britain today a ruling class' (1991: 4). While there is an economically dominant class at the top of the class structure, there is also a series of overlapping status circles at the top. Here there are strong alignments between educational backgrounds: 'private schooling remained the most important route to political success' (1991: 134). He suggests that Britain is run by an 'inner circle' of finance capitalists who represent a 'city' point of view. They fuse banking and industry, and play a key role in articulating capitalist industries within the power elite (Scott, 1991: 150–1; and see Chapter 10).

# Power beyond the rules

Politics is always a matter of disagreement about goals and the means to achieve them. Yet a political system tries to resolve controversy *within* a system of rules. The most heated debates in the European Union today surround efforts to harmonise these rules across the many disparate countries. But political activity often exceeds – or tries to do away with – established practices. It goes beyond the accepted rules. Here we look at six ways this happens.

## 1 Revolution

**Political revolution** is *the overthrow of one political system in order to establish another.* In contrast to reform, which involves change within a system and rarely escalates into violence, revolution implies change of the system itself, sometimes sparking violent action.

No type of political system is immune to revolution; nor does revolution invariably produce any one kind of government. Colonial rule by the British monarchy in the United States was overthrown by the revolutionary war. The French revolutionaries in 1789 also overthrew a monarch, only to set the stage for the return of monarchy in the person of Napoleon. In 1917, the Russian Revolution replaced monarchy with a socialist government built on the ideas of Karl Marx (overturned, again, in 1992).

Despite their striking variety, revolutions share a number of traits, according to political analysts (de Tocqueville, 1955, orig. 1856; also Brinton, 1965; Skocpol, 1979):

1  *Rising expectations.* Although common sense would dictate that revolution is more likely when people are grossly deprived, history shows that revolution generally occurs when people's lives are improving. Rising expectations, rather than bitter resignation, fuel revolutionary fervour.

2  *Unresponsive government.* Revolutionary zeal gains strength to the extent that a government is unwilling or unable to reform, especially when demands for change are made by large numbers of people or powerful segments of society.

3  *Radical leadership by intellectuals.* The English philosopher Thomas Hobbes (1588–1679) observed that political rebellion is often centred in universities. During the 1960s, throughout Europe

WORLD WATCH

## Violence beyond the rules: a report from the former Yugoslavia

The conflicts and wars within and around Yugoslavia during the 1990s have led to a number of new, highly unstable mini-states and groupings. We have already seen what this has meant in Bosnia (see pp. 347, 349 and 367–8). In many ways the extent of destruction and displacement of peoples reached catastrophic levels during this period. This is a deeply troubled region, and Serbs, Croats and Muslims have all committed war crimes – tens of thousands of deaths, rapes and serious injuries, plus an incalculable loss of property.

War is violent, but it also has rules. Many of the current norms of warfare emerged from the ashes of the Second World War, when German and Japanese military officials were brought to trial for war crimes. Subsequently, the United

Nations has added to the broad principles of fair play in war that have become known as the 'Geneva Conventions' (the first of which dates back to 1864). One of the most important principles of the rules of war is that, whatever violence soldiers inflict upon each other, they cannot imprison, torture, rape or murder civilians; nor can they deliberately destroy civilian property or wantonly bomb or shell cities to foster widespread terror. Even so, a growing body of evidence reveals that all these crimes have occurred as part of the protracted and bloody civil war in the former Yugoslavia. And they have gone 'beyond the rules'.

### The United Nations and the future of interventions

Late in 1993, therefore, a United Nations tribunal convened in the Netherlands to assess the evidence and consider possible responses. After the Second World War, the Allies successfully prosecuted (and, in several cases, executed) German officers for their crimes against humanity based on evidence culled from extensive Nazi records. This time, however, the task of punishing

offenders proved to be far more difficult. For one thing, there appeared to be no written records of the Balkan conflict; for another, United Nations officials feared that arrests might upset the delicate diplomatic efforts at bringing peace to the region.

Even so, since beginning their investigations in 1993, the United Nations has indicted more than 50 military officers on all sides of the conflict for war crimes. And in 2000, the former Yugoslavian president Slobodan Milosevic was arrested, and charged at the International Tribunal in The Hague with atrocities committed by troops under his command in Kosovo, and by others that linked him with atrocities in the Croatian War of 1991, and the Bosnian conflict of 1992–5. Milosevic conducted his own defence in the five-year-long trial, which ended without a verdict when Milosevic died on 11 March 2006 in the War Criminal Prison in The Hague.

Many observers suspect that – despite a staggering toll in civilian deaths – very few of those responsible will ever be convicted.

*Source:* Adapted from Nelan (1993) and various news reports.

and the United States, students were at the forefront of much of the political unrest that marked that tumultuous decade. Students also played a key role in China's pro-democracy movement, as they did in the toppling of socialist governments in eastern Europe.

4　*Establishing a new legitimacy.* The overthrow of a political system rarely comes easily, but it is more difficult still to ensure a revolution's long-term success. Some revolutionary drives are unified merely by hatred of the past regime and fall victim to internal division once new leaders are installed. Revolutionary movements must also guard against counter-revolutionary drives spearheaded by past leaders; frequently, revolutionaries ruthlessly dispose of these former leaders.

## 2 'Terrorism'

**Terrorism**, *violence or the threat of violence employed by an individual or a group as a political strategy*, is nothing new. But since the suicide bombings of the World Trade Center in New York and the Pentagon in Washington on 11 September 2001, terrorism has taken centre stage in international politics. The United States government, led by President Bush, declared 'war' on all forms of terrorism and in October 2001 started its major mission in bombing the Taliban regime in Afghanistan, which was suspected of protecting the prime terrorist organisation, al Qaeda, and the prime suspect, Osama bin Laden. This 'war' was followed by the invasion of Iraq in March 2003. A sense of perpetual conflict, wars and 'terrorism' has defined the first decade of the twenty-first century. It has led to heated discussion as to what is and what is not terrorism – along with growing concerns over new biological weapons of terrorism (such as anthrax) and the threat of attack on nuclear installations.

Like revolution, terrorism is a political act beyond the rules of established political systems. Paul Johnson (1981) offers four insights about terrorism. First, explains Johnson, terrorists try to cast violence as a legitimate political tactic, even though virtually every society condemns such acts. Terrorists also bypass (or are excluded from) established channels of political negotiation. Terror is thus a weak organisation's strategy to harm a stronger foe. For example, the

# Wanted by Interpol
## BIN LADEN, Usama

Pictures of Saudi-born Osama bin Laden are posted on Interpol's wanted list, 15 September 2001. He was the presumed architect of the suicide bombings of 11 September 2001 and became 'the world's most wanted man'. He was killed by American forces on 2 May 2011, aged 54. He was 'hiding' in Pakistan

*Source:* © Reuters/Corbis.

Terrorist suicide bombings, New York City, 11 September 2001
*Source*: © David Turnley/Corbis.

people who held Western hostages in the Middle East until 1991 may have been morally wrong to do so, but they succeeded in directing the world's attention to that region of the globe.

Second, Johnson continues, terrorism is a tactic employed not only by groups but also by governments against their own people. **State terrorism** refers to *the use of violence, generally without the support of law, against individuals or groups by a government or its agents.* While contrary to democratic political principles, state terrorism figures prominently in authoritarian and totalitarian societies, which survive by inciting fear and intimidation. From the left-wing regimes in North Korea and the former Soviet Union to the extreme right-wing regimes in Nazi Germany and Zaïre, states have routinely employed terror against their own citizens. More recently, Saddam Hussein has ruled Iraq in the same manner.

Third, although democratic societies reject terrorism in principle, democracies are especially vulnerable to terrorists because they afford extensive civil liberties to their people and have minimal police networks. This susceptibility helps to explain the

tendency of democratic governments to suspend civil liberties if officials perceive themselves to be under attack. Hostage taking and outright killing provoke widespread anger, but devising an effective response to such acts poses several thorny problems. Because most terrorist groups are shadowy organisations with no formal connection to any established state, targeting reprisals may be impossible. Yet the failure to respond can encourage other terrorist groups. Then, too, a forcible military reaction to terrorism may broaden the scope of violence, increasing the risk of confrontation with other governments.

Finally, terrorism is always a matter of definition. Governments claim the right to maintain order, even by force, and may brand opponents who use violence as 'terrorists'. Similarly, political differences may explain why one person's 'terrorist' is another's 'freedom fighter'.

## Old and new terrorism

We can make a distinction between old and new styles of terrorism. In the past, terrorism was linked to nationalism and the struggles over national boundaries. It is usually focused on its enemies and their destabilisation or destruction. It is fairly local.

By contrast, new-style terrorism is enhanced by the new information technology. It is much more dispersed, more global, and much less formally structured. A famous example would be the fundamentalist al Qaeda. Their object of attack is 'the world' – or 'the West'. It aims to rescue the world from the decadence of the West – its modernism – and to reconstruct it in the sight of Allah. It was created in 1989 through Osama bin Laden and others in Afghanistan. It is now said to operate in 40 to 50 countries across the world.

The new terrorism is seen to have emerged largely since 11 September 2001, and can be characterised by four key features:

1 *Organisational decentralisation*. Terrorist organisations no longer organise themelves in pyramidic, hierarchical structures. They are much more likely to take the form of loose clusterings organised through chains, hub-and-spoke networks, or a series of contact points.

2 *Operational asymmetry*. The acts of violence become unanticipated and unconventional. Objects are attacked which may, on the surface, seem to have little relevance, and attacks may happen quite unpredictably.

3 *Religious centrality*. Struggles are seen as between forces of good and evil, with religious belief and religious extremism as a core motivating factor.

4 *Weapons of mass destruction*. The stakes are raised with the new terrorism: high-yield weapons come to be employed and deaths can potentially be catastrophically large. These weapons include biological, chemical, radiological and nuclear agents (Martin, 2004).

## 3 Corruption and state crimes

Corruption and state crimes range from the relatively mild to the extreme and cover a wide range of abuses and crimes costing trillions of pounds. Included here are bribery, nepotism, patronage, embezzlement and cronyism. In the UK, there has been a long history of parliamentary scandals and corruption: in 2009 there was a prolonged scandal over multiple abuses by MPs which related to costs of maintaining two residences, one in the constituency and one in London. They

included renting second homes, overclaiming for tax, evading tax, claiming expenses they were not entitled to, subsidising the property balance and more generally overclaiming for food, travel and all kinds of purchases. In many countries, corruption goes much further than this and includes state involvement in organised and corporate crime, avoidable 'natural' disasters, facilitating criminal enterprises such as drug trafficking, money laundering, human trafficking, torture, criminal policing, war crimes and genocide.

Corrupt governments have enriched themselves in many ways, such as by plundering natural resources (oil and mineral) or foreign aid, which can be spent on armaments or material rewards (from extravagant buildings to clothes). A corrupt dictatorship is the extreme case: and often results in decades of suffering for the vast majority of its citizens. A classic case of a corrupt, exploitive dictator is Marshal Mobutu Sese Seko, who ruled the Democratic Republic of the Congo (which he renamed Zaire) from 1965 to 1997. Another classic case is Nigeria, especially under the rule of General Sani Abacha, who was *de facto* president from 1993 until his death in 1998. He is reputed to have stolen some US$3–4 billion.

Transparency International (TI) is an international non-governmental organisation which aims to raise public awareness in part through the annual construction of a Corruption Perceptions Index. The boxes show the top ten least and most corrupt governments in 2010. To form this index, TI compiles surveys that ask business people and analysts, both in and outside the countries they are analysing, their perceptions of how corrupt a country is. Since so much corruption is hidden, the CPI has been criticised as potentially very unreliable.

**TOP 10**
**Least corrupt countries**

Highest score is least corrupt

| | | |
|---|---|---|
| 1 | Denmark | 9.3 |
| 1 | New Zealand | 9.3 |
| 1 | Singapore | 9.3 |
| 4 | Finland | 9.2 |
| 4 | Sweden | 9.2 |
| 6 | Canada | 8.9 |
| 7 | Netherlands | 8.8 |
| 8 | Australia | 8.7 |
| 8 | Switzerland | 8.7 |
| 10 | Norway | 8.6 |

*Source*: Reprinted from Corruption Perceptions Index 2010.

## TOP 10
### Most corrupt countries

Lowest score is most corrupt

| | | |
|---|---|---|
| 1 | Somalia | 1.1 |
| 2 | Myanmar | 1.4 |
| 2 | Afghanistan | 1.4 |
| 4 | Iraq | 1.5 |
| 5 | Uzbekistan | 1.6 |
| 5 | Turkmenistan | 1.6 |
| 5 | Sudan | 1.6 |
| 8 | Chad | 1.7 |
| 9 | Burundi | 1.8 |
| 10 | Equatorial Gurinea | 1.9 |

*Source:* Reprinted from Corruption Perceptions Index 2010.

A total of 178 countries are ranked in this survey on a scale from 10 to 0 with New Zealand best at 9.3 and Somalia worst at 1.1. Hong Kong is ranked 13th, the UK 20th, the USA 22nd, Poland 41st, South Africa 54th, Brazil 69th, Syria 127th, Uganda 127th, Pakistan 143rd and Russia 154th. For the full results see: www.transparency.org/policy_research/surveys_indices/cpi/2010.

## 4  War

Perhaps the most critical political issue is war. War is as old as humanity. In recorded history, since 3600 BCE, it has been estimated that some 14,500 major wars have been waged, killing some 4 billion people.

# War and peace: a militarised world

WORLD WATCH

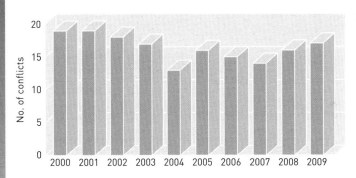

Major armed conflicts, 2000–9

### Nuclear warheads (estimates), 2010

| Country | Deployed warheads | Total warheads |
|---|---|---|
| USA | 2,468 | 9,600 |
| Russia | 4,630 | 12,000 |
| United Kingdom | 160 | 225 |
| France | 300 | 300 |
| China | nk | 240 |
| India | nk | 60 to 80 |
| Pakistan | nk | 70 to 90 |
| Israel | nk | 80 |
| Total | 7,560 | 22,600 |

**WORLD WATCH**

### The most and least peaceful states: Global Peace Index 2010

| The most peaceful countries | | | The least peaceful countries | | |
|---|---|---|---|---|---|
| Rank | Country | Score | Rank | Country | Score |
| 1 | New Zealand | 1.188 | 145 | Pakistan | 3.050 |
| 2 | Iceland | 1.212 | 146 | Sudan | 3.125 |
| 3 | Japan | 1.247 | 147 | Afghanistan | 3.252 |
| 4 | Austria | 1.290 | 148 | Somalia | 3.390 |
| 5 | Norway | 1.322 | 149 | Iraq | 3.406 |

### The five top arms-producing companies in the world, excluding China, 2008

| Rank | Company | Country | Arms sales in US$ |
|---|---|---|---|
| 1 | BAE Systems | UK | 32,420 |
| 2 | Lockheed Martin | USA | 29,880 |
| 3 | Boeing | USA | 29,200 |
| 4 | Northrop Grumman | USA | 26,090 |
| 5 | General Dynamics | USA | 22,780 |

*Source*: Stockholm International Peace Research Institute, *SIPRI Yearbook 2010: Armaments, Disarmament and International Security* (Oxford University Press: Oxford 2010), Figure 2A.1, Table 8.1, Table 28.1, Table 6A.1.

In the twentieth century alone, it has been estimated that well over 100 million people died as a result of war. Many people think of war as extraordinary, yet it is periods of peace that are actually rare (*New Internationalist*, 1999: 18; Roxborough, 2004).

Mary Kaldor (2007), Martin Shaw (2003) and others have distinguished between different types of war throughout history. In the past, wars were usually waged with mercenary or conscript armies using weapons from swords to (more recently) firearms. Many of the twentieth-century wars were not like this. Funded on a large scale through the mobilisation of the whole economy, mass armies deployed massive firepower, tanks and aircraft. The two world wars of the twentieth century were sites of major destruction, including the dropping of the atomic bombs on Nagasaki and Hiroshima. A key feature of late-twentieth-century warfare, then, was the potential destructiveness of today's nuclear arsenals and the ways in which more and more civilans come to be killed. Table 16.6 suggests ways in which these 'old wars' evolved.

At present over 30 wars are being waged across the earth with millions of casualties. Most of these armed conflicts of recent times tend to take place within states rather than between them. The Bosnia–Herzegovina war described at the start of Chapter 11 is a major example of what have been called 'new wars'. They are mixtures of war, organised crime and mass violations of human rights with civilian deaths, and do not follow any obvious rules of modern warfare. Indeed, they seem almost anarchic – attacking people and property at local, private levels. Rape and genocide are commonplace. Mary Kaldor argues that these new wars require international intervention and regulations for their resolution, which she calls a 'cosmopolitan approach' (Kaldor, 2007). Martin Shaw sees them as **degenerate wars**, whereby there is '*a deliberate and systematic extension of war against an organized armed enemy to war against a largely unarmed civilian population*' (Shaw, 2003: 5). Such is typical of more and more modern wars.

## The costs of war

The costs of armed conflicts extend far beyond battlefield casualties. Together, the world's nations spend some £3.5 trillion annually for military

| Table 16.6 | The evolution of 'old wars' | | | |
|---|---|---|---|---|
| | 17th and 18th centuries | 19th century | Early 20th century | Late 20th century |
| Type of polity | Absolutist state | Nation-state | Coalitions of states; multinational states; empires | Blocs |
| Goals of war | Reasons of state; dynastic conflict; consolidation of borders | National conflict | National and ideological conflict | Ideological conflict |
| Type of army | Mercenary/professional | Professional/conscription | Mass armies | Scientific–military elite/ professional armies |
| Military technique | Use of firearms, defensive manoeuvres, sieges | Railways and telegraph, rapid mobilisation | Massive firepower; tanks and aircraft | Nuclear weapons |
| War economy | Regularisation of taxation and borrowing | Expansion of administration and bureaucracy | Mobilisation economy | Military–industrial complex |

*Source*: Based on Kaldor (2006).

U.S. soldiers carry the body of an American soldier, who was killed in a roadside bomb attack in Afghanistan's Kandahar province, to a medical evacuation helicopter. Pararescuemen and pilots from the 46th and 26th Expeditionary Rescue Squadrons responded to the attack which killed two American soldiers and wounded three others
*Source*: AP Photo/David Guttenfelder.

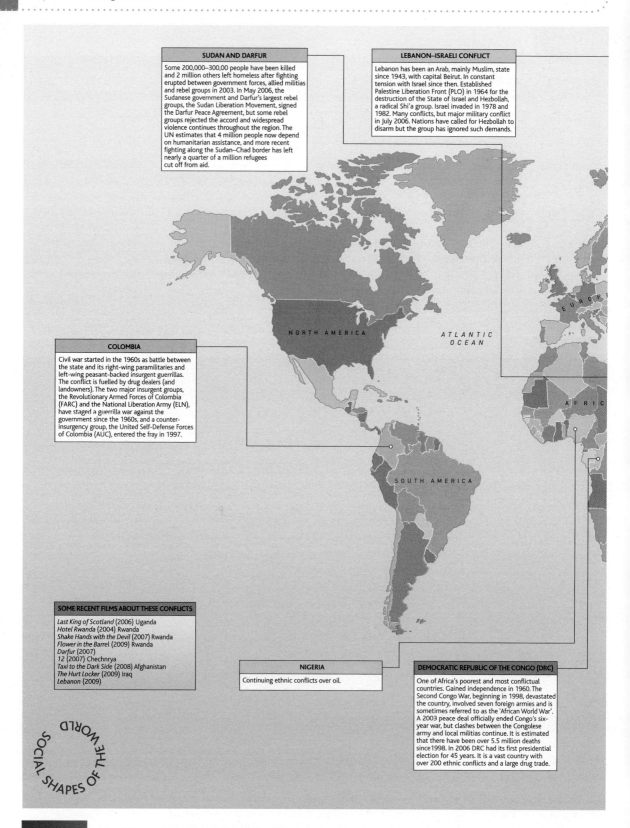

**SUDAN AND DARFUR**

Some 200,000–300,00 people have been killed and 2 million others left homeless after fighting erupted between government forces, allied militias and rebel groups in 2003. In May 2006, the Sudanese government and Darfur's largest rebel groups, the Sudan Liberation Movement, signed the Darfur Peace Agreement, but some rebel groups rejected the accord and widespread violence continues throughout the region. The UN estimates that 4 million people now depend on humanitarian assistance, and more recent fighting along the Sudan–Chad border has left nearly a quarter of a million refugees cut off from aid.

**LEBANON–ISRAELI CONFLICT**

Lebanon has been an Arab, mainly Muslim, state since 1943, with capital Beirut. In constant tension with Israel since then. Established Palestine Liberation Front (PLO) in 1964 for the destruction of the State of Israel and Hezbollah, a radical Shi'a group. Israel invaded in 1978 and 1982. Many conflicts, but major military conflict in July 2006. Nations have called for Hezbollah to disarm but the group has ignored such demands.

**COLOMBIA**

Civil war started in the 1960s as battle between the state and its right-wing paramilitaries and left-wing peasant-backed insurgent guerrillas. The conflict is fuelled by drug dealers (and landowners). The two major insurgent groups, the Revolutionary Armed Forces of Colombia (FARC) and the National Liberation Army (ELN), have staged a guerrilla war against the government since the 1960s, and a counter-insurgency group, the United Self-Defense Forces of Colombia (AUC), entered the fray in 1997.

**SOME RECENT FILMS ABOUT THESE CONFLICTS**

*Last King of Scotland* (2006) Uganda
*Hotel Rwanda* (2004) Rwanda
*Shake Hands with the Devil* (2007) Rwanda
*Flower in the Barrel* (2009) Rwanda
*Darfur* (2007)
*12* (2007) Chechnrya
*Taxi to the Dark Side* (2008) Afghanistan
*The Hurt Locker* (2009) Iraq
*Lebanon* (2009)

**NIGERIA**

Continuing ethnic conflicts over oil.

**DEMOCRATIC REPUBLIC OF THE CONGO (DRC)**

One of Africa's poorest and most conflictual countries. Gained independence in 1960. The Second Congo War, beginning in 1998, devastated the country, involved seven foreign armies and is sometimes referred to as the 'African World War'. A 2003 peace deal officially ended Congo's six-year war, but clashes between the Congolese army and local militias continue. It is estimated that there have been over 5.5 million deaths since 1998. In 2006 DRC had its first presidential election for 45 years. It is a vast country with over 200 ethnic conflicts and a large drug trade.

SOCIAL SHAPES OF THE WORLD

**Map 16.2**    'Troublespots': some world conflicts in focus

## CHECHNYA

Became independent from Russia in 1991. Russia has invaded twice, recapturing the would-be breakaway republic at a cost of approximately 500,000 lives, mostly Chechen civilians. The second Russian offensive in 1999 installed a Moscow-friendly government and was a serious blow to the Chechan independence movement. Counterattacks took place at the Dubrovk Moscow Theatre in 2002, with 850 people held hostage (and 52 people killed) and the Beslan School Siege (2004), where 344 civilians were killed, of whom 186 were children.

## GAZA AND PALESTINE: ISRAELI–ARAB CONFLICTS

Zionists settled in Israel in the 1880s, and after the Second World War there was mass migration (the Exodus) by Jews to the Jerusalem area. Two states in Palestine – one Jewish, one Arab – were enforced by the United Nations in 1947. Continuing tension between Arabs and Jews since then. Conflicts include Israeli-Arab wars of 1949-9, Suez (1956) and the Six Day War of 1967. Rarely out of the news as a major world troublespot, most recently with its 2006 conflict with Lebanon and the bombarding of HAMAS (Islamic resistance movement) in December 2008. 1.5 million people are packed into Gaza, many of whom have been killed.

## AFGHANISTAN

Following the 11 September 2001 attacks, the USA conducted a military campaign to destroy the al Qaeda terrorist network and overthrow the Taliban government that protected it. NATO forces now occupying the country continue to face a determined Taliban insurgency. But there is continuing internal conflict between the Pashtuns of the south and the Kabul regime, which is controlled by the northern Tajiks, Uzbeks and Hazara. By mid-2010, it is estimated that well over 10,000 civilians had been killed along with 2,000 members of the armed forces. A gradual withdrawal of US and UK forces is planned.

## KASHMIR

Ongoing conflict over disputed territory between India and Pakistan.

## GULF/IRAQ WARS

20th March 2003: US missile attacks on Iraq (Baghdad) mark start of armed hostilities (but a long history of US military intervention before).

## SRI LANKA AND THE TAMIL TIGERS

The Liberation Tigers of Tamil Eelam (LTTE), also known as the Tamil Tigers, have waged a violent secessionist campaign against the Sri Lankan government since 1970, a fight that has claimed more than 65,000 lives. The LTTE seeks independence for the northeast region of the island, the traditional home of the Tamil ethnic group. A 2002 Norwegian-brokered ceasefire is officially still in place, but international monitoring groups say it only exists on paper; the two sides have violated the agreement more than 3,000 times, but 2006 was a relatively peaceful year, at least as far as civilian casualties went.

## RWANDA

Conflicts between the Tutsi tribe and the Hutu go back to the 16th century. In 1959, a Hutu revolt led to overthrow of Tutsi rule. Independence in 1962, followed by rebellions and coups. In 1944 inter-ethnic violence escalated, with an estimated 800,000 Tutsis slaughtered in ten days (10% of the population).

## SOMALIA–ETHIOPIA

A long-running civil war since 1988 in which 300,000 have died. UN and US troops have been involved. Recent developments risk the war moving into neighbouring Eritrea.

## MIDDLE EAST AND NORTH AFRICA UPRISINGS

In early 2011, many internal rebellions started against long-standing dominant (largely authoritarian) regimes in Arab countries of the Middle East including Egypt, Syria, Libya, Tunisia and Bahrain. In March, the UN intervened in Libya as violence escalated.

## UGANDA

Former British colony gained independence in 1962. Coup led by General Odi Amin Dada in 1971 and decades-long civil war. Over 1.4 million Ugandans were uprooted in an insurgency dating back to 1987 (see the film *The Last King of Scotland*).

RUSSIA

CHINA

ARABIA

INDIA

PACIFIC
OCEAN

INDONESIA

AUSTRALIA

purposes. Such expenditures, of course, divert resources from the desperate struggle for survival by millions of poor people throughout the world. Moreover, a large proportion of the world's top scientists concentrate on military research; this resource, too, is siphoned away from other work that might benefit humanity.

In recent years, defence has been the largest single expenditure of most governments. The average proportion of GDP that the world spends on defence is around 3 per cent, but many countries spend more than that. In the United States, for example, defence accounts for 18 per cent of all federal spending. By September 2010, the Iraq War was estimated to have cost $900 billion.

The United States became a superpower as it emerged victorious from the Second World War with newly developed nuclear weapons. The atomic bomb was first used in war by US forces to crush Japan in 1945. But the Soviet Union countered by exploding a nuclear bomb of its own in 1949, unleashing the 'Cold War', by which leaders of each superpower became convinced that their counterparts were committed to military superiority. Ironically, for the next 40 years, both sides pursued a policy of escalating military expenditures that neither nation wanted or could afford.

With the collapse of the Soviet Union in 1991, much of the Cold War dissipated. Even so, before the Iraq conflict started, US military expenditure remained high. Some analysts have argued that, all along, the US economy has relied on militarism to generate corporate profits (Marullo, 1987). This approach, closely allied to power elite theory, maintains that the United States is dominated by a **military–industrial complex**, *the close association among the federal government, the military and defence industries.* The roots of militarism, then, lie not just in external threats to US security; they also grow from within the institutional structures of US society.

But another reason for persistent militarism in the post-Cold War world is regional conflict. Since the collapse of the Soviet Union, for example, localised wars have broken out in Bosnia, Chechnya and Rwanda, and tensions still run high in a host of other countries, including Iraq and a divided Korea. Even wars of limited scope have the potential to escalate, involving other countries, and the danger of regional conflicts is growing as more and more nations gain access to nuclear weapons. The main cost, though, at the present time focuses on Iraq.

# 5 Nuclear weapons

Despite the easing of superpower tensions, the world still contains almost 25,000 nuclear warheads perched on missiles or ready to be carried by aircraft. This arsenal represents destructive power that one can barely imagine: five tons of TNT for every person on the planet. Should even a small fraction of this stockpile be detonated in war, life as we know it would cease on much of the earth. Albert Einstein, whose genius contributed to the development of nuclear weapons, reflected: 'The unleashed power of the atom has changed everything save our modes of thinking, and we thus drift toward unparalleled catastrophe.' In short, nuclear weapons have rendered unrestrained war unthinkable in a world not yet capable of peace.

At present, although the UK, France and China all have substantial nuclear capability, the vast majority of nuclear weapons are based in the United States and the Russian Federation. Other countries – Israel, India, Pakistan, North Korea – also possess some nuclear weapons, while others (including Iran) may be in the process of developing them. Some nations have stopped the development of such weapons, including Argentina, Brazil and South Africa (Shaw, 2003; Roxborough, 2004; see also Chapter 23).

*tip* A very valuable website for facts and figures on 'war and peace' is that of the Stockholm International Peace Research Institute at www.sipri.org/yearbook/2010/05.

# 6 Information warfare

As earlier chapters have explained, the Information Revolution is changing almost every dimension of social life. Currently, military strategists envisage future conflict played out not with rumbling tanks and screaming aircraft but with electronic 'smart bombs' that would greatly reduce an enemy country's ability to transmit information. In such 'virtual wars', soldiers seated at workstation monitors would dispatch computer viruses to shut down an aggressor's communication lines, causing telephones to fall silent, air traffic control and railway switching systems to fail, computer systems to feed phoney orders to field officers, and televisions to broadcast 'morphed' news bulletins, prompting people to turn against their leaders.

Like the venom of a poisonous snake, the weapons of 'information warfare' can quickly paralyse an adversary, perhaps triggering a conventional military engagement. Another, more hopeful, possibility is that new information technology might not just precede conventional fighting but prevent it entirely. Yet so-called 'infowar' also poses new dangers, since, presumably, a few highly skilled operators with sophisticated electronic equipment could also wreak havoc on communications in Europe and the rest of the world.

# New politics: the rise of social movements

Politics is always on the move: things change. At the start of the twenty-first century, it is often claimed that a new politics is in the making. There are many signs of this: the partial break-up of nation-states, globalised politics, the creation of major new political units such as the European Union, the arrival of 'new wars', and, as the *Big debate* at the end of the chapter suggests, the collapse of traditional divides between left and right. In addition, we could consider the seeming growth of political apathy and voter discontent; the embracing by some of what has been called 'post-materialist values'; and the potential for digital democracies, whereby voting systems are modified through the widespread use of computers. Some sociologists, such as Ulrich Beck, now believe we have entered a period of *sub-politics*, where the world of major political institutions built up in modernity is increasingly under question through a politics that takes place in everyday life. Formal politics becomes less and less effective as sub-politics develops (Beck, 1997). One feature of this may be the rise and proliferation of new social movements (NSMs), which, while having a long history, are far more common today than in the past and take on a different form.

## Development of social movements

Mass mobilisation and social movements began to take shape in Western countries during the later eighteenth century – symbolised massively by the French Revolution. During the nineteenth century a durable set of elements started to appear that spread across the world (through colonisation, migration and trade), whereby more and more groups and populations engaged in new forms of political action. Charles Tilley (1929–2008) was a sociologist who spent much of his life showing the rise of social movements in parallel with the development of the ballot box. In his book *Social Movements 1768–2004* (Tilley, 2004), he suggests that these new social movements combine three things:

1 They develop public campaigns, getting organised to make collective claims on targeted audiences.

2 They combine whole repertoires of political actions, ranging from public meetings, processions and rallies through to demonstrations, petitions and the creation of special purpose associations.

3 And ultimately they display and present themselves to the public as good causes and worthy people. They are united, with large numbers of committed supporters.

Social movements have perhaps become the key feature of modern political life. What is interesting to note about them is that not only do they provide the momentum for political change, they also provide a sense of meaning in life. Very often people build their sense of who they are (their identities) from these very movements. Identity has become a basis for social action and change. The list of such organisational movements and identities is very long and very

## The new social movements

The importance of NSMs is marked at the start of the twenty-first century. During the course of this book, we look at a number of them. For starting points, see:

- the women's movement: Chapter 12

- the gay and lesbian movement: Chapter 12
- the AIDS movement: Chapter 21
- the green movement: Chapter 25
- ethnic movements: Chapter 11
- the elderly movement: Chapter 13
- the disability movement: Chapter 13

- religious movements: Chapter 19
- the anti-capitalist movement: the opening to this chapter
- the human rights movement.

They all have websites. Search for them all through 'Social Movements and Culture', www.wsu.edu/-amerstu/smc/gay.htm.html.

striking. Amongst them are the women's movement, gay, lesbian, bisexual and transgender (LGBT) movements, environmental movements, student movements, anti-globalisation movements, the 'right to life' movement, the animal rights movement, the Landless People's Movement, the indigenous people's movements, the human rights and civil rights movements, the disability movement, the AIDS movement, and rights of all kinds. All these have been studied by sociologists and often made central to a grasp of contemporary political life.

## Stages of social movements

Researchers have identified four phases in the life of the typical social movement (shown in Figure 16.2): emergence, coalescence, bureaucratisation and decline (Blumer, 1969; Mauss, 1975). In Stage 1, emergence, social movements build on the perception that all is not well. Some, such as the gay and lesbian rights movement and the women's movement, are born of widespread dissatisfaction. Others emerge only as a small vanguard group, which increases public awareness of some issue.

By the second stage, coalescence, the movement must define itself and develop a strategy for 'going public'. Leaders must determine policies, decide on tactics, build morale and recruit new members. At this stage, the movement may engage in collective action such as rallies or demonstrations to attract media attention in the hope of capturing public notice. Additionally, the movement may form alliances with other organisations to gain necessary resources.

To become an established political force, a social movement must bureaucratise: that is, develop formal structures (Stage 3). As procedures become formal, the movement depends less on the charisma and talents of a few leaders and relies more on a capable staff. Social movements which avoid this stage, such as the campaigns organised to produce legislation against 'dangerous dogs' and handgun ownership in Britain, have short lives, fading when leaders lose energy or even die. Bureaucratisation can also weaken a movement by blunting the radical and innovative edge. On the other hand, the well-established Greenpeace, despite its changing leadership, offers a steady voice on behalf of environmentalists.

Social movements are inherently dynamic, so a decline (Stage 4) need not signal a demise. Eventually, however, most social movements do wither. This may occur when members achieve their primary goals, or because of organisational factors, such as poor leadership or exhaustion of resources, or because hostile public or governmental reaction (sometimes literally) beats activists into submission. 'Selling out' is another possible outcome, when organisational leaders may use their positions to enrich themselves.

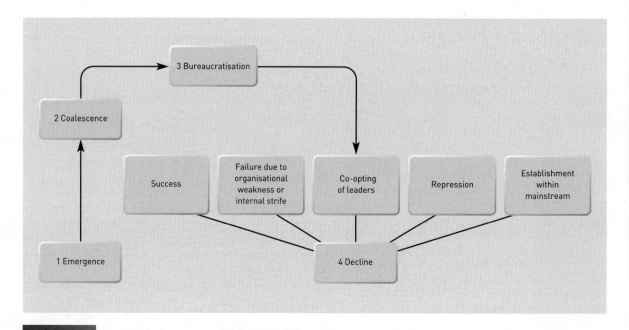

**Figure 16.2**    Stages in the life of social movements

# New social movements and new politics

Alan Touraine, Alberto Melucci, Klauss Offe and others suggest that the new post-industrial or information societies are fostering a growing awareness of differences through subcultures and counter-cultures, and that these are generating new social movements around a wide range of public issues. In recent decades, for example, gays, lesbians, bisexuals and transgendered people have organised to combat oppression and discrimination. A green movement has emerged to challenge environmental destruction. Disability alliances have been formed to champion the rights of the disabled. There has been a powerful women's movement, a men's movement, an age-activist movement, AIDS and various health movements. More recently, as the opening story told, there has been a worldwide anti-capitalist movement bridging many different groups, from respectable lobbying groups to out-and-out anarchists. Like any social movement that challenges convention, they often spark counter-movements as others try to block their goals. In contemporary societies, almost every significant public issue gives rise to both a social movement favouring change and an opposing counter-movement to resist change and reinforce the status quo.

Although social movements have been around for a long time, the so-called 'new social movements' generally broaden the range of what is considered political. They are much less concerned with the traditional issues of politics such as class and work (and the old trade unions and class movements). Their membership tends to be younger. Organisationally, they tend to be much more informal, more fragmented, less hierarchical, with little interest in formal power. They employ a wider range of tactics for change – often illegal and direct. They do not usually pursue mainstream or conventional values, but are part of what we have already noted as 'post-materialist values' where the issue is much more the quality of life (see Chapter 5 on post-materialist cultural values). They are part of what Giddens has called the new politics of lifestyles (1990: 158).

Today's most notable social movements are concerned with global ecology, the social standing of women and gays, reducing the risks of war, animal rights, and the rejection of a worldwide global capitalism. One feature of these movements is their national and international scope. The power of the state continues to expand in post-industrial societies. Not surprisingly, then, as global political connections multiply, social movements respond by becoming international in scope. One clear strength of NSMs is their growing recognition of the global scale of response needed to deal with the development of a global economic and political system, and to spotlight the power of the mass media to unite people around the world in pursuit of political goals.

A million women rise, protest and march proclaiming 'Together we can fight male violence'. London, 2010
*Source*: © Janine Wiedel Photolibrary/Alamy.

Critics argue that this approach exaggerates differences between past and present social movements. The women's movement, for example, focuses on many of the same issues, including workplace conditions and pay, that consumed the energies of labour organisations for decades.

# Explaining social movements

There have been many attempts to explain the nature of social movements in the contemporary world. Often they are pitched as rival explanations in opposition to each other. In this section we will briefly outline nine of these major explanations. In our view, they should not be seen as rivals. Instead, we think they can all be viewed as partial explanations focusing on different aspects or problems. Any full explanation is likely to draw upon each contribution.

1   *Conflict and suffering.* Marx's ideas have remained some of the most useful for approaching the ways social movements work. His concern, as we have seen, was with the class movement and the development of class consciousness and identity as a necessary condition for bringing about social movement. He outlined the conditions in which the working class became poorer and poorer under the new capitalist industrialisation, and how this led in turn to a growing awareness of themselves as a social class that could come together and seek radical change.

2   *Structural strain.* These early explanations often developed functional theory and suggested that social movements arise because of a problem, threat or breakdown in the social structure: for example, the French Revolution arose because of the increasing poverty of the peasants. The more recent concern over world finance or the environment can be located in the breakdown of the banking system and the ecological order respectively. The focus here is upon the breakdown in the social world to which a social movement becomes a response. Useful as this may be for a starting point, it fails actually to address the nature of social movements.

3   *Movements as process and collective behaviour.* It was the symbolic interactionist Herbert Blumer who turned his attention to the movements as a collective social process. He argued that social movements should be seen as processual, symbolic and interactive. They emerged out of collective behaviour and could be traced through definite stages. In his work, he detected five key stages which have shaped much thinking since. Figure 16.2 is a modified version of this.

4   *Symbolic politics.* Blumer's ideas also led to the view that social movements could be seen not simply as *instrumental* in bringing about change but also as performing distinct *symbolic* roles. Thus, for example, in Joseph Gusfield's study of the campaigns and temperance movements against alcohol in the United States in the 1930s, he could argue that these should not be seen simply as instrumental drives to prevent people from drinking, but as more of a symbolic mechanism to promote and enhance the status of a middle class under threat. Behind many social movements there were key issues of class and status at work, of declining elites and emerging new groups.

5   *Organisational resources and their mobilisation.* Arising in the 1970s, another major attempt to explain the rise of social movements focused sharply on the nature of their organisations. To be a successful asocial movement in effect required the successful mobilisation of good organisational resources. Resources are understood here to include: knowledge, money, media, labour, solidarity, legitimacy, and internal and external support from the power elite. A successful movement would have leaders with good skills, access to good administrative and organisational support, and of course access to funds and finance to help lobby and organise. In a sense, the more access a group had to financial support, the stronger it could grow.

6   *Identity politics.* Closely connected to this was the firm focus on the development of new identities as a basis for organising social movements. Growing in part during the time of the countercultural movements of the late 1960s and 1970s, movements emerged where a clear identity became a core focus. The black movement with a strong race identity, the women's movement with a strong identity of women, and the lesbian and gay movement with a strong sexual identity became key examples. Here the fashioning of a strong identity (usually with claims to rights attached to it) became the key organising explanation of social movements.

7 *Claims making' 'frames'*. As part of the wider social constructionist turn in social theory, social movements can be examined in terms of the kinds of claim they make for change. A key explanation now becomes the ways in which social movements develop rhetoric and languages to put their case – and how these 'claims' come to be accepted or not.

8 *Globalisation of social movements*. Most recently with the rise of theories of globalisation theories, it is becoming increasingly clear that social movements can rarely be approached in terms of simple local communities: very often their causes, organisations, identities and claims move across the globe. We see this most strikingly in the 'Make Poverty History' movement, the postcolonial movements and the worldwide environmental movements.

9 *Digitalisation of social movements*. The globalisation of movements has also involved digital developments – websites, blogging, twitter and the rest have made worldwide communications easy and widespread.

# Social movements and social change

Social movements exist to encourage – or to resist – social change. Sometimes we overlook the success of past social movements and take for granted the changes that other people struggled so hard to win. Early workers' movements, for example, battled for decades to end child labour in factories, to limit working hours, to make the workplace safer and to establish the right to bargain collectively with employers. Legislation protecting the environment is also the product of successful social movements throughout the twentieth century. The women's movement has yet to attain full social equality for the sexes, but it has significantly extended the legal rights and economic opportunities of women. In fact, younger people can be surprised to learn that, early in the twentieth century, few women worked for income and none was permitted to vote.

Past social movements have shaped society in ways that people now take for granted. Just as movements produce change, so change itself sparks social movements. New social movements have been shaped by widespread dissatisfaction with the existing political system and debates. They bring new issues (especially issues linked to the environment, gender, peace, sexuality, race and world development) and a broader conception of participatory politics, and often dissolve the clear distinction between public and private (see Chapter 22). As leading German sociologist Klauss Offe says, 'the conflicts and contradictions of advanced industrial society can no longer be resolved by the state or by increasing bureaucracy' (Offe, 1985). New social movements are seen as the answer.

This broad view leads to one overarching conclusion: we can draw a direct link between social movements and change. In one direction, social transformations, such as the Industrial Revolution and the rise of capitalism, sparked the emergence of various social movements. Going the other way, the efforts of workers, women, racial and ethnic minorities and gay people have sent ripples of change throughout industrial societies. Thus social change is both the cause and the consequence of social movements.

Social movements have become a growing feature of globalised post-industrial life. The scope of social movements is likely to grow, for two reasons. First, the technology of the Information Revolution has drawn the world closer together than ever before. Today anyone with a satellite dish, personal computer or fax machine can stay abreast of political events, often as they happen. Secondly, as a consequence of new technology as well as the emerging global economy, social movements are now uniting people throughout the entire world. As we saw in the opening tale to this chapter, with the realisation that many problems are global in scope has come the understanding that they can be effectively addressed only on an international scale.

 There are many reports on human rights across the globe that are worth looking at in order to keep up to date with current concerns. Try:

*Human Rights Watch*: www.hrw.org

*Amnesty International*: http://thereport.amnesty.org and in the UK, *Annual Reports on Human Rights*: http://centralcontent.fco.gov.uk/resources/en/pdf/human-rights-reports/human-rights-report-2009 (which started in 1997 and ran until 2010: at the time of going to press, we have learned that the current UK government is thinking of scrapping it).

# Anthony Giddens: the global politics of 'life choice', 'Third Way' and environmental regulation

Anthony Giddens is one of the UK's leading sociologists. In his many early books he examined the classical social theories of sociologists (Marx, Durkheim and Weber), and ultimately produced his own theory of the link between action and structure – a theory known as **structuration theory**, which we briefly introduced in Chapter 1. In his later books, starting around the late 1980s, he becomes more concerned with the arrival of globalisation and what he calls 'late modern society'. This is a society where the pace and scope of change deepens and accelerates – we break free from traditions, our sense of time and space gets reordered, and globalisation becomes a central process. Social life is lifted out ('disembedded') from local traditional contexts and becomes more open and fluid. In 1999 he summarised his major ideas for a worldwide audience in a series of talks he gave as the Reith Lectures (the BBC's most prominent annual lecture series). They were published in a short book, *Runaway World* (1999).

Giddens senses that contemporary identities are changing as we become more aware of having to choose who we are. Traditional institutions such as the family are also changing as relations between members become more equal, open and democratised. Above all, he senses a major change in the political order. What was ushered in with modernity was an 'emancipatory politics' – its main focus was on justice, freedom and equality. It was embodied in the ideals of the French Revolution and the American War of Independence. These political values remain to this day, but now they are not new but widespread. He believes they will continue. In addition a new set of concerns have arrived which make politics more concerned with questions about how we should live our lives in a late modern world. This is what he calls 'the politics of life choice', and it is this new politics which is becoming more prominent. He espouses a utopian realism in which new models of life and participation are to be evolved in helping us live in a new kind of social order (Giddens, 1990).

Giddens suggests that the old social democratic 'welfare consensus' that was found in many industrial countries till the late 1970s has collapsed. The classic distinctions of 'left' and 'right' have broken down. The changes have come about partly because of the rise of free-market philosophies associated with Thatcherism and Reaganism – capitalist neoliberalism (identified in the previous chapter and often seen as uncaring and inadequate) along with the fall of the old Soviet Union and what some claim to be 'the death of socialism' (Giddens, 1998: 3).

Giddens talks of this new politics as the **Third Way** – *a framework that adapts politics to a changed world, transcending old-style social democracy and neo-liberalism*. He identifies a number of dilemmas of the late modern world and suggests that:

> The overall aim of third way politics should be to help citizens pilot their way through the major revolutions of our time: globalization, transformations in personal life and our relationships to nature ... third way politics should preserve a core concern with social justice.
>
> (Giddens, 1998: 64)

He outlines the new 'Third Way values' in a series of slogans: 'Equity', 'Protection of the vulnerable', 'Freedom as autonomy', 'No rights without responsibilities', 'No authority without democracy', 'Cosmopolitan pluralism' and 'Philosophic conservatism' (1998: 66). He suggests a Third Way programme which would involve a radical centre, a new democratic state, an active civil society, a democratic family, a new mixed economy, equality as inclusion, positive welfare, the social investment state, the cosmopolitan nation and cosmopolitan democracy (1998: 70).

## Way beyond left and right: international environmentalism

Most recently, Giddens has become concerned about the turn to the right in politics and indeed the growth of far-right parties. In his latest writings, he suggests that the third way was a major source of change in the 1990s, but today we must go beyond this – beyond left and right. His key concern has become the politics of the environment, which is not a simple left and right issue at all. He sees climate change and global heating as an urgent and serious problem which requires international agreements alongside effective global policy planning and action. This is a real challenge and the 'rich' governments (often the highest polluters) should foster new structures to deal with this. (We look more at this in Chapter 25.)

Unlike many sociologists, Giddens plays an active role in world politics and publishes less and less. His advice has been sought by political leaders from Asia, Latin America and Australia, as well as from the USA and Europe. He had a major impact upon the evolution of New Labour in the UK and took part in the original Blair–Clinton dialogues from 1997 onwards. Nowadays, he is a major crusader on the need for international coordination, planning and policy around the environment.

*Source*: Giddens (1990, 1991, 1998, 1999, 2004, 2009).

See Giddens on YouTube – you will find many lectures by him.

# The globalisation of 'human rights regimes'?

A final major development we will consider in the political landscape of the early twenty-first century is the arrival of the international language of 'human rights'. Increasingly, after the horrors of the Holocaust and other atrocities, a major trend in world politics has been towards 'rights'. Yet such a language is far from new. Three waves of human rights in recent history have been distinguished (Klug, 2000).

The *first wave* started in the late eighteenth century in the West against a background of totalitarianism and a lack of religious freedom: the search was on for liberty, justice and equality before the law. The 1789 French Declaration of the Rights of Man and Citizen spoke of 'the natural, inalienable and sacred rights of man', while the 1776 US Declaration of Independence from the colonial power of Britain claimed that:

> We hold these truths to be self evident, that all men are created equal; that they are endowed by their creator with certain inalienable Rights; that among these are life, liberty and the pursuit of happiness.

The prime task of this wave of rights was freedom from state tyranny and religious persecution, and it led to the American Bill of Rights and the French Declaration of Rights.

The *second wave* started around the Second World War and an evolving United Nations (UN). International human rights treaties and declarations came to be enacted and enforced by international courts and monitoring bodies. Rights talk here focused especially on dignity, equality and community. It is enshrined in what most would consider the central document of human rights of our times – the Universal Declaration of Human Rights (UDHR), which is built into the UN Charter. 'Human dignity' is the core value behind such rights. The declaration established a potentially universal language of freedom and equal rights – even for those many countries like South Africa which were not able to achieve it at that time. Each of the main covenants has been ratified by some 140 out of 190 states, and the numbers are growing.

The *third wave* started to appear at the end of the Cold War (early 1990s) against a background of increasing globalisation and a new millennium looking for common values. It champions mutuality and participation. Here, more and more countries establish their own rights programmes, and 'human rights regimes' begin to seem part of a major international political network. There are now, for instance, over 200 human rights NGOs in the United States, and a similar number in the UK and Europe. They are growing fast. Political scientist Benjamin Barber (1995) can now talk of a 'world of citizens without frontiers'. Most countries – even when they are riddled with the denial and corruption of human rights – still make claims to use versions of this language (which should, of course, alert us to some of the major problems with such a language: it can and does mean all things to all people!).

British sociologist Martin Albrow, in *The Global Age*, talks of a new kind of citizenship – *global citizenship* – which 'begins in people's daily lives, is realized in everyday practices and results in collective action up to the level of the globe' (Albrow, 1996: 177). He sees the model for this as the international working-class movement in the nineteenth century, but now sees many roots into this through citizens who are, as he puts it, 'performing the state'. Here are global actions at the local level. Many of these claims now come conspicuously from new social movements – the green movement of eco-warriors, the gay/lesbian/queer/transgender movement, the women's movement – and they are epitomised in what has come to be called the Battle of Seattle, introduced in the opening to this chapter. These may not reinforce national systems of governance and may indeed even run counter to them.

**WORLD WATCH**

# Global governance: the United Nations

The United Nations had 191 members in 2003, and has a regular budget of about $1.25 billion. It stands, among other things, 'as a focal point for global security issues, a world forum for debate, a network for developing universal norms and standards, and a vehicle for administering humanitarian assistance around the world' (Krasno, 2004: 3). Since its inception in 1945, it has come to symbolise the long-sought-for goal of universal government and harmony. It divides into six main committees which deal with (a) politics and security issues, (b) economic and financial issues, (c) social, humanitarian and cultural issues, (d) trusteeship issues, (e) legal issues, and (f) administration and budget. The Millennium Declaration was adopted by member states in 2000, and called for the eradication of poverty, access to clean water, sanitation and access to clean energy sources (see Chapter 25).

*See*: Jean Krasno, *The United Nations: Confronting the Challenges of a Global Society* (2004).

**US President George W. Bush addresses the 57th session of the United Nations General Assembly at the UN headquarters, New York**

*Source*: © Brooks Kraft/Corbis.

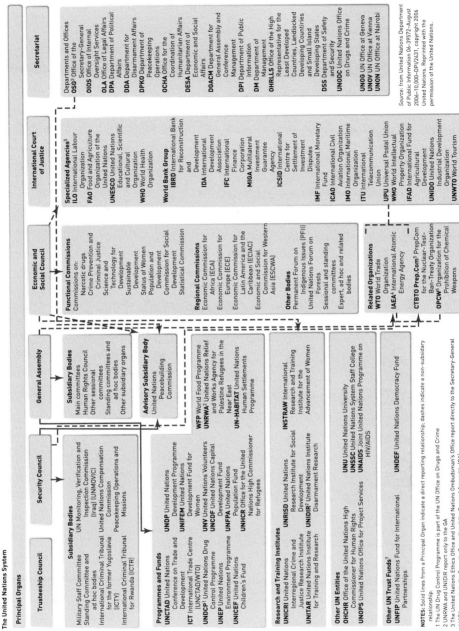

The United Nations System

WORLD WATCH

**Principal Organs**

| Trusteeship Council | Security Council | General Assembly | Economic and Social Council | International Court of Justice | Secretariat |

**Security Council**

**Subsidiary Bodies**
Military Staff Committee
Standing Committee and ad hoc bodies
International Criminal Tribunal for the former Yugoslavia (ICTY)
International Criminal Tribunal for Rwanda (ICTR)

UN Monitoring, Verification and Inspection Commission (Iraq) (UNMOVIC)
United Nations Compensation Commission
Peacekeeping Operations and Missions

**Programmes and Funds**
**UNCTAD** United Nations Conference on Trade and Development
  **ICT** International Trade Centre (UNCTAD/WTO)
**UNDCP**[1] United Nations Drug Control Programme
**UNEP** United Nations Environment Programme
**UNICEF** United Nations Children's Fund

**UNDP** United Nations Development Programme
  **UNIFEM** United Nations Development Fund for Women
  **UNV** United Nations Volunteers
**UNCDF** United Nations Capital Development Fund
**UNFPA** United Nations Population Fund
**UNHCR** Office for the United Nations High Commissioner for Refugees

**WFP** World Food Programme
**UNRWA**[2] United Nations Relief and Works Agency for Palestine Refugees in the Near East
**UN-HABITAT** United Nations Human Settlements Programme

**Research and Training Institutes**
**UNICRI** United Nations Interregional Crime and Justice Research Institute
**UNITAR** United Nations Institute for Training and Research

**UNRISD** United Nations Research Institute for Social Development
**UNIDIR**[2] United Nations Institute for Disarmament Research

**INSTRAW** International Research and Training Institute for the Advancement of Women

**Other UN Entities**
**OHCHR** Office of the United Nations High Commissioner for Human Rights
**UNOPS** United Nations Office for Project Services

**UNU** United Nations University
**UNSSC** United Nations System Staff College
**UNAIDS** Joint United Nations Programme on HIV/AIDS

**Other UN Trust Funds**[7]
**UNFIP** United Nations Fund for International Partnerships

**UNDEF** United Nations Democracy Fund

**General Assembly**

**Subsidiary Bodies**
Main committees
Human Rights Council
Other sessional committees
Standing committees and ad hoc bodies
Other subsidiary organs

**Advisory Subsidiary Body**
United Nations Peacebuilding Commission

**Economic and Social Council**

**Functional Commissions**
Commissions on:
Narcotic drugs
Crime Prevention and Criminal Justice
Science and Technology for Development
Sustainable Development
Status of Women
Population and Development
Commission for Social Development
Statistical Commission

**Regional Commissions**
Economic Commission for Africa (ECA)
Economic Commission for Europe (ECE)
Economic Commission for Latin America and the Caribbean (ECLAC)
Economic and Social Commission for Western Asia (ESCWA)

**Other Bodies**
Permanent Forum on Indigenous Issues (PFII)
United Nations Forum on Forests
Sessional and standing committees
Expert, ad hoc and related bodies

**Related Organizations**
**WTO** World Trade Organization
**IAEA**[4] International Atomic Energy Agency
**CTBTO Prep.Com**[5] PrepCom for the Nuclear-Test-Ban-Treaty Organization
**OPCW**[6] Organization for the Prohibition of Chemical Weapons

**International Court of Justice**

**Specialized Agencies**[3]
**ILO** International Labour Organization
**FAO** Food and Agriculture Organization of the United Nations
**UNESCO** United Nations Educational, Scientific and Cultural Organization
**WHO** World Health Organization

**World Bank Group**
**IBRD** International Bank for Reconstruction and Development
**IDA** International Development Association
**IFC** International Finance Corporation
**MIGA** Multilateral Investment Guarantee Agency
**ICSID** International Centre for Settlement of Investment Disputes

**IMF** International Monetary Fund
**ICAO** International Civil Aviation Organization
**IMO** International Maritime Organization
**ITU** International Telecommunication Union
**UPU** Universal Postal Union
**WMO** World Meteorological Organization
**WIPO** World Intellectual Property Organization
**IFAD** International Fund for Agricultural Development
**UNIDO** United Nations Industrial Development Organization
**UNWTO** World Tourism Organization

**Secretariat**

Departments and Offices
**OSG**[9] Office of the Secretary-General
**OIOS** Office of Internal Oversight Services
**OLA** Office of Legal Affairs
**DPA** Department of Political Affairs
**DDA** Department for Disarmament Affairs
**DPKO** Department of Peacekeeping Operations
**OCHA** Office for the Coordination of Humanitarian Affairs
**DESA** Department of Economic and Social Affairs
**DGACM** Department for General Assembly and Conference Management
**DPI** Department of Public Information
**DM** Department of Management
**OHRLLS** Office of the High Representative for the Least Developed Countries, Landlocked Developing Countries and Small Island Developing States
**DSS** Department of Safety and Security
**UNODC** United Nations Office on Drugs and Crime

**UNOG** UN Office at Geneva
**UNOV** UN Office at Vienna
**UNON** UN Office at Nairobi

*Source:* from United Nations Department of Public Information 06–39572–August 2006–10,000–DPI/2431, copyright 2006 United Nations. Reprinted with the permission of the United Nations.

**NOTES:** Solid lines from a Principal Organ indicate a direct reporting relationship; dashes indicate a non-subsidiary relationship.
1 The UN Drug Control Programme is part of the UN Office on Drugs and Crime
2 UNRWA and UNIDIR report only to the GA
3 The United Nations Ethics Office and United Nations Ombudsman's Office report directly to the Secretary-General
4 IAEA reports to the Security Council and the General Assembly (GA)
5 The CIBIO Prep.Com and ORCW report to the GA
6 Specialized agencies are autonomous organizations working with the UN and each other through the coordinating machinery of the ECOSOC at the intergovernmental level, and through the Chief Executive Board for coordination (CEB) at the inter-secretariat level
7 UNFIP is an autonomous trust fund operating under the leadership of the United Nations Deputy Secretary-General UNDEF's advisory board recommends funding proposals for approval by the Secretary-General.

Global bureaucracy at work. Examine the organisations that have been developed within the United Nations. You can track the detailed reports of many of these through the UN website at www.un.org. You can watch the UN at work on YouTube: search 'United Nations'

**Key to map**
(7.8) population figures in millions
(2.8) % GDP growth/decline 1990–2001

open elections    least corrupt    more equal
                  moderately corrupt    less equal
fixed elections   most corrupt    very unequal

(X.X) ARMENIA (3.4)
(-0.3) AZERBAIJAN (8.1)
(-0.8) BELARUS (10.1)
(-1.2) BULGARIA (7.80)
(1.2) CZECH REP. (10.3)
(0.2) ESTONIA (1.4)
(X.X) GEORGIA (5.2)
(1.9) HUNGARY (9.9)
(-2.8) KAZAKHSTAN (16)
(-2.9) KYRGYZSTAN (5)
(-2.2) LATVIA (2.4)

(-2.2) LITHUANIA (3.7)
(-8.4) MOLDOVA (4.3)
(4.5) POLAND (38.5)
(-0.4) ROMANIA (22.3)
(-3.7) RUSSIA (143.8)

(2.1) SLOVAKIA (5.4)
(-8.5) TAJIKISTAN (6.2)
(-2.8) TURKMENISTAN (4.9)
(-7.9) UKRAINE (48.7)
(0.4) UZBEKISTAN (25.6)

**Map 16.3**

**Life after communism**
When communism collapsed in the late 1980s, a new hope and optimism appeared for the people of the former Soviet Union and eastern Europe. They hoped for freedom, an expanding economy and an end of corruption. None of this has happened. GDP growth has declined in every country but Poland (with Russia, Georgia, Moldova, Ukraine and Tajikistan the worst). Most countries have become poorer (poverty rose from 14 million in 1989 to 147 million in 1998) – indeed the increase in people living on less than a dollar a day has grown faster in the former Soviet republics than anywhere else in the world. There are differences: Slovakia is one of the most equal countries in the world; Russia and Armenia are among the least equal. Map 16.2 charts some of the issues.

*Source*: Adapted from 'Life after communism: the facts', *New Internationalist*, 366, April 2004.

They challenge government to recognise key issues – often linked to how people can gain control over their (personal) lives in a 'runaway world'. They organise global conferences that establish worldwide agendas of rights. Human rights systems now appear across the world.

## The trouble with rights

Although we can find talk of 'citizens and rights' everywhere in contemporary politics, a number of problems have been identified with it.

First is the claim to universalism. When the classic Universal Declaration of Human Rights was adopted, most Third World or low-income societies were still under colonial rule, and even today many remain suspicious of it. 'Human rights' can easily become a euphemism for Western intervention in other countries. It is often a universality of the privileged. Many of the rights claims just do not ring true in many parts of the world. The right to a paid vacation, for instance, makes no sense in most of the world where sweatshop labour conditions apply; and women's rights

LIVING IN THE C21ST

# Human Rights Bills and Acts

## The Human Rights Act 1998

This came into force in the UK on 2 October 2000. It was the first time that the UK had enforceable official human rights protection. Drawing from the European Convention on Human Rights, the Act now means that old common law in the UK will have to change if it does not respect the rights enshrined in the convention, and that all legislation must now comply with these rights. The main rights are as follows.

## Article

2   The right to life*
3   Freedom from torture, inhuman and degrading treatment
4   Freedom from slavery
5   Freedom from arbitrary arrest and detention
6   The right to a fair trial
7   Freedom from retrospective penalties
8   The right to privacy and family life
9   Freedom of religion
10  Freedom of expression
11  Freedom of assembly and association
12  The right to marry and found a family
13  Prohibition of discrimination
14  Restrictions on political activity of aliens
15  Prohibition of abuse of rights
16  Limitation on use of restrictions on rights

In addition, the Act stipulates, among other things:

• The right to peaceful enjoyment of property
• The right to education
• The right to free elections
• Abolition of the death penalty
• Preservation of the death penalty in times of war.

The full text can be downloaded from www.direct.gov.uk.

\* Article 1 is missing as it does not list a right.

## Other Bills and Acts

**The Bill of Rights, 1689**: www.constitution.org/eng.

**The Declaration of the Rights of the Citizen**, approved by the French Assembly of France, 26 August, 1789: www.hrcr.docs/index.html.

**The United States Bill of Rights, 1791**: www.usconstitution. net.

**United Nations Universal Declaration of Human Rights**: www.un.org/rights.

*See*: Human and Constitutional Rights Documents: www.hrcr.docs/index.html.

become a serious problem when there are major clashes of cultural and religious expectation around family and gender.

Secondly, even if there could be agreement, many of the rights claims are almost completely unenforceable pragmatically. There is evidence from international organisations such as Amnesty International and Human Rights Watch that these 'rights' are incessantly violated around the world. In wars of liberation, for example, one finds gross violations both by the oppressors as well as by the liberators. Rights regimes are often so private that they become unenforceable even with goodwill.

Finally, much rights talk is too individually based. There is a focus on individual rights as opposed to group rights. Collective human rights differ from individual rights. Human rights theory has traditionally focused on the rights of the individual, independent of social groupings, and advocates for individual human rights seek redress mainly through the nation-state system or through intergovernmental structures, such as the United Nations. The focus of collective human rights, on the other hand, is on the rights of social groups, and proponents seek to create an innovative framework independent of nation-states to enhance and protect these rights.

# SUMMARY

1   Politics is the major social institution by which a society distributes power and organises decision-making. Max Weber explained that there are three ways to transform coercive power into legitimate authority: through tradition, through rationally enacted rules and regulations, and through the personal charisma of a leader.

2   Four clusters of government can be roughly outlined. Monarchy is based on traditional authority and is common in pre-industrial societies. Although constitutional monarchies persist in some industrial nations, industrialisation favours democracy based on rational–legal authority and extensive bureaucracy. Authoritarian political regimes deny popular participation in government. Totalitarian political systems go even further, tightly regulating people's everyday lives.

3   The world remains divided into between 190 and 200 politically independent nation-states; one dimension of an emerging global political system, however, is the growing wealth and power of multinational corporations. Additionally, new technology associated with the Information Revolution means that national governments can no longer control the flow of information across national boundaries.

4   The dramatic growth of democratic governments in much of Europe during the past two centuries goes far beyond mere population increase; it reflects wider government involvement in the economy and all of society.

5   The traditional left (socialists) and right (conservatives) take different positions on economic and social issues. The left calls for government regulation of the economy and action to ensure economic equality; conservatives believe the government should not interfere in these arenas. Conservatives, however, do support government regulation of moral issues such as abortion, while the left, along with liberals, argue that government should not interfere in matters of conscience.

6   The pluralist model holds that political power is widely dispersed; the power elite model takes an opposing view, arguing that power is concentrated in the hands of a small, wealthy segment of the population. The Marxist or ruling class model argues that this elite is in fact an economic class.

7   Revolution, terrorism, corruption and war take power outside the normal workings of a political order. Revolution aims to radically transform a political system. Terrorism uses violence in pursuit of political goals. States as well as individuals engage in terrorism. War is armed conflict directed by governments. The development and proliferation of nuclear weapons have increased the threat of global catastrophe. Enhancing world peace ultimately depends on resolving the tensions and conflicts that fuel militarism.

8   A social movement entails deliberate activity intended to promote or discourage change. Social movements vary in the range of people they seek to engage and the extent to which they strive to change society. A typical social movement proceeds through consecutive stages: emergence (defining the public issue), coalescence (entering the public arena), bureaucratisation (becoming formally organised) and decline (brought on by failure or, sometimes, success).

9   At the start of the twenty-first century, the issue of global 'human rights' has been placed firmly on the political agenda.

CONNECT UP: Turn to Part 6 of this book for key resources and link up
with the book's website, which links to these resources
SEE: www.pearsoned.co.uk/plummer

## MYTASKLIST

# Ten suggestions for going further

## 1 Connect up with Part Six and the Sociology Web Resources

As you work through ideas and think about the issues raised in this chapter, look at the accompanying website and the resource centre at the end of this book which connects to it. There is a lot here to help you move on. To link up, see: www.pearson.co.uk/plummer.

## 2 Review the chapter

*Briefly summarise (in a paragraph) just what this chapter has been about.* Consider: (a) What have you learned? (b) What do you disagree with? Be critical. And (c) How would you develop all this? How could you get more detail on matters that interest you?

## 3 Pose questions

(a) How is politics changing in the twenty-first century? What are the problems posed by the developing arguments around 'human rights'?
(b) In what respects do some recent social movements (those concerned with the environment or animal rights) differ from older crusades (focus on, say, civil rights and gender equality)?
(c) Do you think that the dangers of war in the world are greater or less than in past generations? In what ways has war changed? Are there 'new wars'?
(d) Examine the causes and consequences of any one 'crisis spot' in the world today. Do you have any suggestions that could lead to any kind of resolution?

## 4 Explore key words

Many concepts have been introduced in this chapter. You can review them from the website or from the listing at the back of this book. You might like to give special attention to just five words and think them through – how would you define them, what are they dealing with, and do they help you see the social world more clearly or not? Maybe look at:

Martin Smith, *The New Penguin Dictionary of Politics* (2008).

Frank Barnaby, *The Future of Terror: A 21st Century Handbook* (2007): provides a quick guide to the current conflicts.

## 5 Search the Web

Be critical when you look at websites – see the box on p. 940 in the Resources section. For this chapter look at the following:

Political sources on the net
www.politicalresources.net
Useful worldwide listings.

Stockholm International Peace Research Institute
www.sipri.org
Details global military resources.

Freedom House
www.freedomhouse.org
Freedom House charts the state of the world's democracies in its annual volume *Freedom in the World*. It is accused of very clear Western bias.

Transparency International
www.transparency.org
Charts the corruption of governments around the world.

Parties and Elections
www.parties-and-elections.de.
The latest European political parties and parliamentary groups in the European Union.

The UK government and its cabinet
www.cabinetoffice.gov.uk
Provides insight into the workings of the UK government.

Open Democracy
www.opendemocracy.net/about
A human rights and democracy website.

Clausewitz homepage
www.clausewitz.com/index.htm
Clausewitz is seen as a major theorist of war and his book
*On War* the key text.

## Social movements

List of social movements
There have been a number of attempts to create a list of
social movements but it is proving impossible to construct a
full list. We suggest you search with the phrase '*list of social
movements*' and you will soon find more than you can
handle!

## Human rights

On human rights, some of the key documents from the
United Nations Universal Declaration of Human Rights
(1948) to the Beijing Declaration on Women's Global Rights
(1995) have been usefully gathered in M. Ishay, *The Human
Rights Reader* (1997). A useful listing of all documents
linked to human rights across the world can be found at:
www.hrcr.org. See also the TIP box on *Human Rights Watch*
(p. 567).

# 6  Watch a DVD

- Michael Moore's satire *Fahrenheit 9/11* (2004) received
  much praise as a critique of the Bush administration and
  the Iraq invasion. Some find it over the top!
- The Greek director Costa-Gravas made a reputation for
  himself in the 1970s with a series of probing political
  films, such as *Z* (1969), *The Confession* (1970) and *State
  of Siege* (1972). His *Missing* (1981) dealt with Allende's
  Chile and is a powerful moral and political drama.
- Stanley Kubrick's *Dr Strangelove: Or How I Learned to Stop
  Worrying and Love the Bomb* (1964), Gillo Pontecorvo's
  *The Battle of Algiers* (1965), Alan Parker's *Midnight
  Express* (1978), which deals with drugs and prison in
  Turkey, and Oliver Stone's *JFK* (1991) are all worth
  looking at.
- Classic films dealing with war include: Lewis Milestone's
  *All Quiet on the Western Front* (1930), Stanley Kubrick's
  *Paths of Glory* (1975), Michael Cimino's *The Deer Hunter*
  (1977), Oliver Stone's *Born on the Fourth of July* (1989),
  Steven Spielberg's *Saving Private Ryan* (1998) and
  Kathryn Bigelow's *The Hurt Locker*.

- On twenty-first-century terrorism, there are now a
  number of striking films. Adam Curtis's *The Power of the
  Nightmare* (2005) is a telling documentary from the BBC.
  Michael Winterbottom's (with Mat Whitecross) *The Road
  to Guantanamo* (2005) shows how three Muslims from
  Tipton in the West Midlands are arrested as al Qaeda
  suspects and treated barbarously in prison.

# 7  Think and read

John Hoffman and Paul Graham, *Introduction to Political
Theory* (2nd edn, 2009). An excellent introductory
text which covers the wide range of classical and
contemporary accounts of politics.

John Baylis and Steve Smith (eds), *The Globalization of
World Politics* (5th edn, 2010). This is a wide-ranging
textbook which is kept up to date with new revisions.
An excellent and much-used source book.

Anthony D. Smith, *Nationalism* (2001). Provides a succinct
guide to the nature of nations and nationalism. His
recent study, *The Cultural Foundations of Nations* (2008)
is a lively account of the relationship between nations
and modernity.

Charles Tilly, *Social Movements 1768–2004* (2004). Provides
a concise history of the rise of social movements in the
modern world.

Darren J. O. Byrne, *Human Rights: An Introduction* (2003).
Established textbook with full discussion of all matters
linked to human rights.

Penny Green and Tony Ward, *State Crime: Governments,
Violence and Corruption* (2004). Details the corruption
of governments.

Martin Shaw, *War and Genocide: Organized Killing in Modern
Society* (2003). A very readable and important text. It is
also linked to Shaw's website. See: www.martinshaw.org

The work of Mary Kaldor is also very significant here:
see *New and Old Wars* (2007).

On terrorism, see Gus Martin, *Understanding Terrorism*
(3rd edn, 2010).

Andrew Heywood, *Global Politics* (2011). Wide-ranging and
up-to-date global account.

## More information

For recent political data on the UK, see *The Guardian
Political Almanac* (annually).
Key magazines include: *New Statesman* (UK) and *Foreign
Policy* (USA).
See also the student magazine *Politics* (Blackwell publishers).

## 8 Relax with a novel

Classic works on the political world include:

George Orwell, *Animal Farm* (1945).

Edmund Wilson, *To the Finland Station* (1940).

Gunter Grass, *The Tin Drum* (1959).

Isabel Allende, *Of Love and Shadows* (1987).

J. Coetzee, *Waiting for the Barbarians* (1980).

Leo Tolstoy, *War and Peace* (1869).

## 9 Connect to other chapters

- Link back to Marx and Weber in Chapter 3, and clarify how their theories of power link to social change.
- For more on genocide, see Chapter 11.
- For more on wars and conflicts to science and the risk society, see Chapter 23.
- Consider how gender may be linked to power – see Chapter 12.
- To see how the ideas of the surveillance society and the work of Foucault are relevant to the discussion of power, refer to Chapter 17.

## 10 Engaging with THE BIG DEBATE

### Are we moving beyond left and right? The politics of difference

Industrialisation, the emergence of modern nation-states and revolutionary movements on behalf of democracy have brought people together under the labels 'left' or 'right' for the past 200 years. (The terms originated in the French revolutionary assembly of the 1790s, where radicals sat on the left and moderates sat on the right.) For most of the twentieth century, the political divides have been very sharply drawn on these lines: capitalism versus communism, right versus left, the East versus the West. The demise of the Cold War between the United States and what Reagan called the 'evil empire' of the USSR (dominated by Russia) was spectacularly symbolised at the end of the 1980s by the fall of the Berlin Wall. At the time there was much jubilation. But the problem now – in the twenty-first century – is: where is all this heading? For many of the old communist countries, a kind of chaos has ensued. For much of the old West, a kind of directionlessness has happened. If the old divides are crumbling, what is politics about in the twenty-first century?

One response was to see the end of these conflicts as the end of history. The fall of the Berlin Wall symbolised the final victory of capitalist democracy: this was the way of the world from now on. Francis Fukuyama (1989) sees 'the end of history' as nothing less than the worldwide triumph of modernity, capitalism and liberal democracy. The ideological battles are now over, and there are no alternatives. Fukuyama sees the 'universalisation of Western democracy as the final form of human government' (1989): monarchism, fascism and communism have been rendered indefensible for all but a few extreme groups.

But not all agree with Fukuyama. Many new 'politics' are being suggested. For instance, in Chapter 25 we document the degradation of our environment; here many argue for the worldwide development of a green politics. Others, such as the English social theorist Anthony Giddens, are arguing for a 'democratic life politics' – a global politics which rethinks how we are to live and how we are to revitalise democracy through dialogue in a world which is changing globally at an accelerating rate. Arguing that both 'socialism and conservatism have disintegrated' (1994: 9), Giddens champions a 'dialogic democracy' where importance is given to dialogues and the many different voices arguing for different ways to live. He seeks a radical rethinking of democracy – in opposition to fundamentalism of all kinds (see the box on p. 568).

Others see these 'fundamentalisms' as the very basis of conflicts in the future. Benjamin Barber (1995) argues that the world is no longer divided between left and right. Instead the divide has shifted globally to one between consumerist capitalism (symbolised by a global McDonald's, or McWorld) and religious and tribal fundamentalisms (symbolised by the Islamic *jihad*). The former saw rapidly dissolving nation-states and political boundaries, leading to the triumph of individualism and the marketplace all over the world. At the same time, the latter is forcing ethnic, religious and tribal conflicts into politics everywhere. This tension may be seen as one which goes to the heart of global modernity, and its manifestations in 'tribal warfare' have become increasingly apparent. Indeed, after the Twin Tower attacks in New York in September 2001, many argue that such conflicts and wars are now well under way.

Jubilation at the fall of the Berlin Wall, November 1989

*Source*: Tom Stoddart/Hulton Archive/Getty Images.

This is an important debate for contemporary sociology. Some argue that the old left and right positions of the twentieth century need a clear reasserting: they are still relevant. Others argue that we have reached 'the end of history' and we are now, more or less, stuck with capitalist liberal democracies which in the twenty-first century will rule the world. Still others see distinct dangers emerging in the continuing clashes between ethnic and religious fundamentalism and the free-for-all marketplace of consumer capitalism – the clash of civilisations. And still more are looking to the creation of new political forms with social movements and new issues – green politics, lifestyles politics, differences – at the forefront. There is a new political scene in the making at the start of the twenty-first century which is far removed from the Cold War of the twentieth.

### *Continue the debate*

1 Have we really reached 'the end of history' and the triumph of liberal capitalism?
2 If fundamentalism is on the increase, will this not result in more and more bloody wars and conflicts?
3 How might sociological analyses of power, ethnicity (see Chapter 11) and religion (see Chapter 19) assist in understanding the war between the United States and its allies and 'terrorism'?
4 Is a politics based on lifestyle not just an indulgence of the over-rich West?
5 How central do you think social movements around 'green politics' will become in the twenty-first century?

*Source*: Fukuyama (1989); Giddens (1994); Barber (1995); Heywood (2011).

# CHAPTER 18

# FAMILIES, PERSONAL LIFE AND LIVING TOGETHER

IT IS NOW 30 YEARS SINCE CHINA BEGAN implementing a strict birth control policy of one child per couple. The government argued that its policy would avoid a population explosion, and indeed it has prevented some 400 million births, which would have stretched China's resources and prevented its growth. The policy has also resulted in a skewed age structure (it is getting older: in 2009, 13 per cent were over 60) and gender structure (many more boys have been born as girls have been aborted). There has also been a proliferation of forced abortions and sterilisations; newborn children have been abandoned or killed. Heavy fines are still imposed on those with more than one family. Along with this, a hidden population of children, whose birth had to be concealed for fear of reprisals, has appeared. The average size of Chinese families has dropped from over 3 in 1980 to 1.8 in 2008. Recently, some flexibility has been brought into the system (parents outside the cities are often allowed to have a second child if the first-born was a girl).

Meanwhile, in Japan, women are simply not having children – not enough, at least, to replace adults of child-bearing age. Since 1950, in fact, the average number of children born to a Japanese woman during her lifetime has tumbled from 3.65 to 1.3. This precipitous decline is no indication that the Japanese have lost their love for children. Quite the contrary. Virtually all young Japanese couples claim to want children, and even screaming babies on a bus or train elicit smiles and sympathy from fellow travellers. The reason for the declining birth rate is that Japanese women display unprecedented reluctance to marry. Back in 1970, only 20 per cent of Japanese women reaching the age of 30 had yet to wed; today, that share has doubled to 40 per cent.

Why the second thoughts about marriage? For one thing, Japanese culture defines motherhood as a full-time responsibility, which precludes a career. Just as important, the typical Japanese husband works long hours – half are away from home at least 12 hours a day. When he is at home, moreover, the typical Japanese man performs almost no housework and spends little time with his children. To young women in Japan, therefore, marriage commonly amounts to a daily round of housework, doting on youngsters and shuttling older children to special 'cram' schools where they prepare for all-important college entrance examinations. Faced with such prospects, more women are opting to stay single, live with parents, work and enjoy plenty of free time and spending money. Business and governments are alarmed by this. New laws are being made to encourage women to have more children and some businesses are offering up to £6,000 to employees to have children.

See: Susan Greenhalgh, *Just One Child: Science and Policy in Deng's China* (2008); Marcus Rebick, *The Chinese Japanese Family* (2009).

*There is no such thing as the family – only families.*

Diana Gittins (1993: 8)

*The normal family is not normal. Family diversity has always been normal and it is here to stay.*

Judith Stacey (2011: 191)

## In this chapter, we ask:

- What is personal life and the nature of family life?

- What are the key changes in modern lives and families?

- How can we explain key changes? The main theories of families

(Left) Carl Larsson, *My Loved Ones*

See: http://www.clg.se and http://www.carllarsson.se.

Source: The National Museum of Fine Arts, Stockholm © the Nationalmuseum, Stockholm.

Photographer: Sven Nilsson.

**Q** Carl Larsson is one of Sweden's most famous painters. Here, the image of family life perhaps anticipates the homely style indicated these days in the furnishings of IKEA. What do you think? What is his image of family life about? How might it fit with the opening quote?

The state of the family is a 'hot topic' all around the world, not just in Japan and China, where policies on families are very different. In many countries across the world, the traditional image of a married or cohabiting couple with children is less strong than it was. In the UK fewer than one in four households now conform to this standard; and the often presumed model of the traditional nuclear family is now more likely to be found in the UK among households in Bangladeshi and Pakistani communities. In the United States the situation has developed further: one sociologist has suggested that even by 1986 'only 7 per cent of households conformed to the "modern" pattern of breadwinning father, homemaking mother and one to four children under the age of eighteen' (Stacey, 1996: 133). In many countries across the world, there are new laws and key debates emerging around gay marriages, same-sex registered partnerships and queer families as well as controversies about 'arranged marriages' and 'forced marriages' and the position of women in many families. And 'assisted conception', which ranges from 'test-tube babies' to 'surrogate motherhood' and 'baby selling' on the internet (to be discussed in Chapter 23), also brings new issues (Becker, 2000). Alongside all this there has been the growth of **individualisation** as a *process which gives more and more importance to the choices we can make about the personal life we wish to have*. All taken together, an important point is made: personal life in the twenty-first century is changing dramatically; and with it the nature of our 'families'.

These various family structures and changes are the key topics of this chapter. In it we will highlight

# Global patterns of marriage – and its terminologies

**GLOBAL FAMILIES: 1**

Cultural norms, as well as laws, identify people as desirable or unsuitable marriage partners. Some marital norms promote **endogamy**, *marriage between people of the same social category*. Endogamy limits marriage prospects to others of the same age, race, religion or social class. By contrast, **exogamy** mandates *marriage between people of different social categories*. In rural India, for example, young people are expected to marry someone of the same caste (endogamy), but from a different village (exogamy).

Throughout the world, societies pressure people to marry someone of the same social background but of the other sex. The logic of endogamy is simple: people of similar social position pass along their standing to offspring, thereby maintaining traditional social patterns. Exogamy, by contrast, helps to forge useful alliances and promotes cultural diffusion.

In industrial societies today, laws prescribe **monogamy** (from Greek meaning 'one union'), *a form of marriage joining two partners*. The high level of divorce and remarriage, however, suggests that serial monogamy is a more accurate description of much western marital practice. While monogamy is the rule throughout the Americas and in Europe, many pre-industrial societies – especially in Africa and southern Asia – prescribe **polygamy** (from Greek meaning 'many unions'), *a form of marriage uniting three or more people*. There are two types of polygamy. By far the more common is **polygyny** (from Greek meaning 'many women'), *a form of marriage uniting one male and two or more females*. Islamic societies in Africa and southern Asia, for example, permit men up to four wives. In these societies, however, most families are still monogamous because few men have the wealth needed to support several wives and even more children. **Polyandry** (from Greek meaning 'many men' or 'many husbands') is *a form of marriage joining one female with two or more males*. This pattern appears only rarely. One example can be seen in Tibet where agriculture is difficult. There, polyandry discourages the division of land into parcels too small to support a family and divides the work of farming among many men. Polyandry has also been linked to female infanticide – the aborting of female foetuses or killing of female infants – because a decline in the female population forces men to share women.

Historically, most world societies have permitted more than one marital pattern; even so, most actual marriages have been monogamous (Murdock, 1965; orig. 1949). This cultural preference for monogamy reflects two key facts of life: the heavy financial burden of supporting multiple spouses and children, and the rough numerical parity of the sexes, which limit the possibility of polygamy.

the variety of ways of living together and some of the important recent changes in personal life and the way we organise families and households. It offers some insights to explain these trends. Yet, as we shall also point out, changing family patterns and personal lives are nothing new. Nearly two centuries ago, for example, as the Industrial Revolution propelled people from farms to factories, there was much concern over the decline of the family. Today, of course, many of the same concerns surround the rising share of women working, whose careers draw them away from home. In short, changes in other social institutions, especially the economy, keep shaping ways of living together, including marriage and family life.

## What are 'families'?

Let's start with the basics. What is family? For a long while in sociology, the **family** has been seen as *a key social institution, found in all societies, that unites individuals into cooperative groups that oversee the bearing and raising of children*. Most families are built on **kinship**, *a social bond, based on blood, marriage or adoption, that joins individuals into families*. Although all societies contain families, just who is included under the umbrella of kinship has varied through history, and varies today from one culture to another. During the twentieth century, most members of society regarded a **family unit** *as a social group of two or more people, related by blood, marriage or adoption, who usually live together*. Initially, individuals are born into a family composed of parents and siblings (a *family of orientation* central to socialisation) and in adulthood, people have or adopt children of their own (a *family of procreation*). Throughout the world, families form around **marriage**, *a legally sanctioned relationship, involving economic cooperation as well as normative sexual activity and child-bearing, that people expect to be enduring*. Embedded in our language is evidence of a cultural belief that marriage alone is the appropriate context for procreation: traditionally, people have

attached the label of *illegitimacy* to children born out of wedlock; moreover, *matrimony*, in Latin, means 'the condition of motherhood'. This link between child-bearing and marriage has weakened, however, as the proportion of children born to single women has increased (noted to be nearing one in four).

But sociologists – looking at history and watching the changes around them – now find the very idea of 'family' much more complicated. Many now object to defining as 'families' only married couples and children because that implies that everyone should embrace a single standard. As more and more people forge non-traditional family ties, which we will discuss later, many are now thinking of kinship in terms of *families of affinity* or **families of choice** (Weston, 1991), *people with or without legal or blood ties who feel they belong together and wish to define themselves as a family*. What does or does not constitute a family, then, is a moral and political – as well as a legal – matter that lies at the heart of the contemporary 'family values' debate, raised in box *Global families 2*.

Sociologist Christopher Carrington, however, puts this somewhat differently: 'I understand family as consisting of people who love and care for one another' (Carrington, 1999: 5). Carrington's own family research was not with conventional kin, but involved conducting participant observation research within lesbian and gay families in California. He does not approach the family through ideas of kinship or institutions (which implies something too static) but instead as a series of activities: 'People', he says, ' "do" family.' The chapters of his book reflect this as he looks at just how families are achieved through various forms of work: *feeding work* (who cooks, shops, plans); *house work* (who cleans, washes, looks after plants and pets, does the household repairs); *kin work* (looking after the children, visiting parents, etc.); *consumption work* (including watching TV, arranging holidays, purchasing clothes and household goods); and what we might also call *care work* (looking after partners, children and others). All of this implies some continuing divisions of labour within the family and we shall return to this later in the chapter.

GLOBAL FAMILIES: 2

# A report from Sweden

Sweden is burdened with few of the social problems that are often identified with modern capitalism: in urban Sweden, there is little of the violent crime, drug abuse and grinding poverty that have blighted many other places. This Scandinavian nation seems to fulfil the promise of the modern welfare state, with an extensive and professional government bureaucracy that sees to virtually all human needs.

But Sweden also has very different kinds of family. Because people look to the government – not to spouses – for economic assistance, Swedes are less likely to marry than members of any other industrialised society. For the same reason, Sweden also has a high share of adults living alone (more than 20 per cent). Moreover, a large proportion of couples live together outside marriage (25 per cent) and half of all Swedish children (compared to about one in three in Europe) are born to unmarried parents. Average household size in Sweden is also the smallest in the world (2.2 persons). Finally, Swedish couples (whether married or not) are more likely to break up than partners in any other country. US sociologist David Popenoe sums up by claiming that the family 'has probably become weaker in Sweden than anywhere else – certainly among advanced Western nations. Individual family members are the most autonomous and least bound by the group' (Popenoe, 1991: 69).

Popenoe contends that a growing culture of individualism

and self-fulfilment, coupled with the declining influence of religion, began to 'erode' Swedish families back in the 1960s. The movement of women into the labour force also plays a part. Sweden has the lowest proportion of women who are homemakers (10 per cent versus about 25 per cent in Europe) and the highest percentage of women in the labour force (77 per cent versus 59 per cent in Europe).

But, most important, according to Popenoe, is the expansion of the Swedish welfare state, one of the most far-reaching schemes of its kind. The Swedish government offers citizens a lifetime of services – and high taxes. Swedes can count on the government to give them jobs, sustain their income, deliver and educate their children, provide comprehensive healthcare and, when the time comes, pay for their funeral.

Many Swedes supported this welfare programme, Popenoe explains, thinking it would strengthen families. But with the benefit of hindsight, he concludes, we see that proliferating government programmes have actually been replacing families. Take the case of childcare. The Swedish government operates public childcare centres open to all. As officials see it, this system puts care in the hands of professionals, and makes this service equally accessible regardless of parents' income. At the same time, however, the government offers no subsidy for parents who want to care for children in their own home. In effect, then, government has taken over much of the traditional family function of child-rearing.

If this system has solved so many social problems, why should anyone care about the erosion of traditional family life? For two reasons, says Popenoe. First, government can do only at great cost what families used to do for themselves. Recently, Swedes voted to cut back on their burgeoning welfare system because of skyrocketing costs.

Secondly, can government employees in large childcare centres provide children with the level of love and emotional security they would receive from two parents living as a family? Unlikely, claims Popenoe, noting that small, intimate groups can accomplish some human tasks much better than formal organisations can.

David Popenoe uses the case of Sweden as part of his claim for a return to traditional families. We return to this issue in the *Big debate* at the end of this chapter.

*Source*: Popenoe (1991, 1994).

**COUNTRY FACT FILE**

SWEDEN

| | |
|---|---|
| Population | 9.2m |
| Urban Pop | 8.47m |
| Per capita GDP | $51,950 |
| Life expectancy | Men 79.6 |
| | Women 83.6 |
| Major city | Stockholm |
| Key religions | Lutheran (87%) |
| Key language | Swedish |
| Human development index | 9th (0.885) |

*Sources*: Economist World in Figures, 2011.

# Family, history and world forms

When we look at the debate among historians and sociologists over just how the family has changed over time, one thing is clear. The notion of an 'ideal' nuclear family of two parents and two children has, historically, been rare. Throughout history, there have been all kinds of combination – shaped by age cycles, class, region, ethnicity and the like – which have made families very varied and complex. And at any one historical period, we would not expect families to be all the same. Jean-Louis Flandrin (1979) has shown how, for example, a whole array of family types existed at the same time in different parts of France. And British historian Peter Laslett (1972) studied parish records of English country villages from 1564 to 1821 and found that extended families were rare because of late marriage and shorter lives. But there were also large households – where the richer would take in the poorer as labourers and domestic servants.

Lawrence Stone, in a classic study, has charted three phases of the family in western Europe between 1500 and 1800: the first was 'open lineage' and involved a lack of close relations and lack of privacy, but extensive kin. The second was 'restricted patriarchy' (1530–1640), where there were increased loyalties to state and church and less to kin and community. The final stage of 'closed domesticated' families highlights privacy, bonds between children and parents, and 'affective individualism'. It was 'an open ended, low keyed, unemotional, authoritarian institution' (Stone, 1977).

The English sociologists Michael Young and Peter Willmott have traced the changing form of families in modern Britain. In the 1950s they studied the very strong traditional family ties in 'traditional' Bethnal Green in East London and traced how they weakened as the families moved out to new housing estates such as Greenleigh in outer London (Young and Willmott, 1957). The three-generation (grandparents, parents and child) and larger family is replaced with a smaller nuclear pattern where the relationship between husband and wife becomes more intense. In a later study, Young and Willmott (1973) suggested that these newer families were becoming more 'symmetrical'. That is, the relationships were becoming increasingly equal with husband and wife spending more and more time together. These kinds of change have become a common theme in much of the writing on the family – one expects to find shifts from an extended and often patriarchal form of family to a more nuclear and symmetrical form. However, it must be remembered that this is only one pattern – a largely traditional, working-class one. Families vary and change with class and environment.

## Family in the world: 1900–2000

The leading Swedish sociologist Göran Therborn has written a major account of the family and social change across the world in the twentieth century. For Therborn (2004), there are three key elements shaping family structures and he studies each in detail. These are:

1 *Degree of male dominance (patriarchy)* (see Chapter 12). In the twentieth century there has been a major weakening of patriarchy in some countries (notably Western ones), which has been accompanied by the growth of schooling and education for girls – a factor which Therborn sees as crucial (p. 74). At the same time, in many cultures this has not happened. Two key periods of change are noted: the First World War and Russian Revolution – producing a need for women to work – and the sexual revolution of the 1970s.

2 *The need for marriage in sexual regulation.* What has been found quite widely in the West, but not elsewhere, is what has been called the 'detraditionalising of the family'. Western countries have become more open and intimate, and less bound by tradition. This has led to a proliferation of new forms. But it is important to see that this is not spreading globally: there is no globalisation of the family. For example, Muslim cultures remain even more strongly committed to the holy family, and in sub-Saharan Africa polygamy remains common. In Asia, most countries are committed to monogamy.

3 *Fertility and birth control.* The core development here has been the falling birth rate in many countries – again notably in the West. And with this comes a major change in the age structure, as populations become older. All this is linked to what has been called the demographic transition and the growth of family planning. (See the box, and we discuss this further in Chapters 13 and 24.) Again, there are many variations: in the West the trend is stronger, but with major exceptions – such as population in sub-Saharan Africa.

# The demographic transition

## Two waves of fertility decline

### 1850s–1960s

The move to the 'two-to-three child norm' worldwide starts in France (by 1900), in England and Wales (by 1914), and in Australia, USA, Belgium and central Europe by 1930, and in the rest of Europe, the USSR, Japan, the USA, Australia and Canada by 1965.

### 1980s–2000

Initially Ireland, New Zealand, Chile, Cuba, China and Taiwan; later, by 2000: Argentina, Colombia, Cost Rica, Mexico, Israel, Iran, Thailand and Vietnam.

*Source:* Abridged from Therborn (2004: 238).

These three key factors are at the heart of Therborn's account. From these detailed analyses of many cultures, he is able to suggest five major family types (and a few lesser ones) that have emerged:

1 *The West Asia/North Africa Family (Islamic)* is where Islam is at the centre. Here marriage and theology are deeply interconnected. This is a patriarchy strongly engaged with the veiling and sexual control of women. Family matters are of great importance.

2 *The Sub-Saharan African Family (Animist)* combines a strong gender hierarchy but with some female autonomy. Mass polygyny is quite common with several wives serving a common patriarch. Conjugal relations are hence 'thinner' than in the Asian families, but great importance is attached to fertility.

3 *The South Asian Family* (Hindu) is more religious and shaped by religious rituals (e.g. the caste system). It is again characterised by strong patriarchy, but here also is to be found female seclusion. Marriage is regulated by strict rules of endogamy and exogamy.

4 *The East Asian (Confucian) Family* (e.g. China) is strong, central and unchanging. It has an explicitly patriarchal structure, with duty being honoured to both father and patrilineal ancestors. 'Filial piety' – the son's duty – is a core value. Marriage is universal; the husband dominates; fertility

reproduces the male bloodline. As religion is often weaker in such Confucian cultures, the family becomes the moral stronghold.

5 *European/North American (Christian)* is the least patriarchal family, even as it is regulated by the rules of the Catholic Church. Marriage is by 'consent'; monogamy is prized; fertility decisions are in the hands of the couples. In recent times, it has become the family system that is most open to change. It is the main focus of this chapter (Therborn, 2004: 297–301).

## Thinking about families: theories and ideas

As in earlier chapters, several theoretical approaches offer a range of insights about the family.

## 1 The classic approach – the functions of the family

As we would expect, functionalism suggests we look for the functions of the family. Social scientists have produced long lists of functions, and then debated how they have changed over time. You may like to try to create your own list – what are the tasks of families? – before moving on. Below is a fairly standard listing.

1 *Socialisation.* As explained in Chapter 6, the family is the first and most influential setting for socialisation. Ideally, parents teach children to be well-integrated and contributing members of society (Parsons and Bales, 1955). Of course, family socialisation continues throughout the life cycle. Adults change within marriage, and, as any parent knows, mothers and fathers learn as much from raising their children as their children learn from them.

2 *Regulation of sexual activity.* Every culture regulates sexual activity in the interest of maintaining kinship organisation and property rights. One universal regulation is the **incest taboo**, *a cultural norm forbidding sexual relations or marriage between certain kin*. Precisely which kin fall within the incest taboo varies from one culture to another. The matrilineal Navajo, for example, forbid marrying any relative of one's mother. Our bilateral society applies the incest taboo to both sides of the family

but limits it to close relatives, including parents, grandparents, siblings, aunts and uncles. But even brother–sister marriages found approval among the ancient Egyptian, Incan and Hawaiian nobility (Murdock, 1965; orig. 1949). Reproduction between close relatives can adversely affect the mental and physical health of offspring. But this biological fact does not explain why, among all species of life, only human beings observe an incest taboo. The key reasons to control incest, then, are social. Why? First, the incest taboo minimises sexual competition within families by restricting legitimate sexuality to spouses. Secondly, it forces people to marry outside their immediate families, forging broader alliances. Thirdly, since kinship defines people's rights and obligations towards each other, forbidding reproduction among close relatives protects kinship from collapsing into chaos.

3 *Social placement.* Families are not *biologically* necessary for people to reproduce, but they do provide for the *social* placement of children. Social identity based on race, ethnicity, religion and social class is ascribed at birth through the family. This fact explains the long-standing preference for so-called legitimate birth. Especially when parents are of similar social position, families clarify inheritance rights and allow for the stable transmission of social standing from parents to children.

4 *Material and emotional security.* People have long viewed the family as a 'haven in a heartless world', looking to kin for physical protection, emotional support and financial assistance. To a greater or lesser extent, most families do provide all these things, although not without periodic conflict.

When all these functions are taken together, families are often seen as 'the backbone of society'.

## Critical comment

This approach dominated thinking for much of the early part of the twentieth century – from this point of view, it is easy to see that society as we know it could not exist without families. But this approach seriously overlooks the great diversity in ways people can live together in the modern world, the frequent conflicts that families generate, and the different interests they harbour. Children now are often socialised outside the traditional family; many people now have sexual relations outside the family; and there is a lot of evidence of abuse and violence within the family that makes it clear that families can be extremely dysfunctional places. Moreover, functionalism pays little attention to how other social institutions (say, government) could meet at least some of the same human needs. Finally, it minimises the problems of family life. Established family forms reinforce patriarchy and incorporate a surprising amount of violence, with the dysfunctional effect of undermining individual self-confidence, health and well-being, especially of women and children.

# 2 Inequality and the family: conflict theory

Rather than concentrating on ways that kinship benefits society, other theorists investigate how families may perpetuate social inequality. The role of families in the social reproduction of inequality takes several forms.

1 *Property and inheritance.* As noted in Chapter 12, Friedrich Engels (1902; orig. 1884) traced the origin of the family to the need to identify heirs so that men (especially in the higher classes) could transmit property to their sons. Families thus support the concentration of wealth and reproduce the class structure in each succeeding generation.

2 *Patriarchy.* Engels also emphasised how the family promotes patriarchy. The only way men can know who their heirs are is to control the sexuality of women. Thus, Engels continued, families transform women into the sexual and economic property of men. A century ago in Europe, most wives' earnings belonged to their husbands. Although this practice is no longer lawful, men still exert power over women. Despite moving rapidly into the paid workforce, women continue to be paid less, work in more marginal occupations and still have to bear major responsibility for child-rearing and housework. As we shall see from the work of Delphy and Leonard below, patriarchal families offer considerable benefits to men. They also deprive men of the chance to share in the personal satisfaction and growth derived from close interaction with children.

3 *Race and ethnicity.* Racial and ethnic categories will persist over generations only to the degree that people marry others like themselves. Thus endogamous marriage also shores up the racial and ethnic hierarchy.

# A radical feminist approach to the family

Many of the arguments above have been significantly developed by many feminists who see the family as the central location of women's oppression. They argue that men generally benefit greatly from families while women often do not. Until recently, men have nearly always been head of the household and made the key decisions about the family allocating rewards (often payment in kind, such as holidays): even when women work, they often have little decision-making autonomy.

In the 1990s, Christine Delphy and Diana Leonard's *Familiar Exploitation* (1992) was very influential. It argues that the family is an economic system, where men benefit from the work of women (and in many countries the work of children too). This is not just the work in the labour market (of which they do increasing amounts), but also the work they do at home. Family members work for the head of the household. As they say, it is 'the work women do, the uses to which our bodies can be put, which constitutes the reason for our oppression'.

Many studies suggest that women still do more housework than men, still spend more time looking after the children (especially in the more mundane and humdrum ways) and are much more likely to have to look after the sick and the elderly (Finch, 1989; Hochschild, 1989). They are also much more likely to have to give moral support to men (who often make little contribution to their wife's work).

These feminist arguments are strong claims and a careful evaluation of the evidence is needed to make sense of this. For instance, in modern families, there are now many single-parent households where women are alone; further, women are increasingly choosing not to marry, to get divorced once married and not to have children. Twenty per cent of women remain childless, by choice.

## Critical comment

Some sociologists show how family life maintains social inequalities. During his era, Engels condemned the family as part and parcel of capitalism. Yet non-capitalist societies have families (and family problems) all the same. Kinship and social inequality are deeply intertwined, as Engels argued, but the family appears to carry out various societal functions that are not easily accomplished by other means. And the arguments produced by radical feminists usually fail to take into account the growing trends towards equality in decision-making between men and women.

# 3 The family at the intersection of class, ethnicity and gender

Dimensions of inequality – social class, ethnicity and race, and gender – are powerful forces that shape marriage and family life.

## Class

Families can vary enormously across social class (see Chapter 10). Not only does class shape a family's financial security and range of opportunities, it can also affect the family size and shape. For instance, in the UK, families are still likely to be larger among the working class, who also have higher rates of divorce.

In an influential North American study, Lillian Rubin (1976) found that working-class wives deemed a good husband to be one who refrained from violence and excessive drinking and held a steady job. Rubin's middle-class informants, by contrast, never mentioned such things; these women simply *assumed* a husband would provide a safe and secure home. Their ideal husband was a man with whom they could communicate easily and share feelings and experiences.

Such differences reflect the fact that people with higher social standing have more schooling, and most have jobs that emphasise verbal skills. In addition, middle-class couples share a wider range of activities, while working-class life is more sharply divided along gender lines. Conventionally masculine ideas of self-control, Rubin explains, can stifle emotional expressiveness on the part of working-class men, prompting women to turn to each other as confidantes.

Clearly, what women (and men) can hope for in marriage – and what they end up with – is linked to their social class. Much the same holds true for children in families; boys and girls lucky enough to be born into more affluent families enjoy better mental and physical health, develop higher self-confidence, and go on to greater achievement than poor children do (Komarovsky, 1967; Bott, 1971; Rubin, 1976; Fitzpatrick, 1988).

## Ethnicity

But it is not just social class that shapes families. As Chapter 11 indicates, ethnicity and race are powerful social forces. The effects of both surface in family life. We must beware of stereotyping: just as there is enormous diversity behind the label 'white families', so there is great variety among ethnic families. But some differences do seem striking. Ethnic family forms in the UK have been subject to change over the past 40 years: in the early days of mass migration (1950–70), there was often a severe dislocation of family life, as patterns found in the former homes were disrupted. But subsequently new forms of stability emerged.

## Asian families

The Asian population across the world generally has a very strong family system (Fukuyama, 1995). The first contact by Asians with UK culture after migration therefore often came as a culture shock. In the main, Asian culture has continued to assert the importance of family life.

The village model of India was for a while transferred to the UK, with a complex network of kin and responsibilities. In some ways this is the classic 'extended family' model. On arrival initially in the UK, these traditional family structures were disrupted: there were smaller houses, there was less support and women became more isolated from other women. Chain migration eventually restored this as families were reunited. English families were often seen as 'morally bankrupt' (Elliot, 1996: 52).

In Asian families there are usually more people per household than in white families: three-quarters of Pakistani and Bangladeshi households have an average of five members, and three-fifths of Indian households contain four or more people, compared with a quarter of white households (Skellington, 1996: 62, 49).

An ideal type would suggest a value that places family before individual self-interest, and one that is patrilineal, patrilocal and with a strong gender hierarchy. Marriage is a contract between two families, not two individuals.

It is important to recognise again major differences between Asian communities (see Chapter 11). These can be compounded by gender. For instance, while east African and Indian women often work, taking them out of the house, Bangladeshi and Pakistani women's lives – more restricted by Islamic rules which do not permit women to be in close proximity to non-family men – lead to a much stronger home-based commitment, including 'homework'. Likewise, Muslims can marry close kin but this is not permitted for Sikhs and Hindus. *Purdah* is strong in Islam and restricts Islamic women more.

Sallie Westwood and Parminder Bhachu (1988) nevertheless see these traditions as evoking changes. Again, families do not remain static, but respond to current circumstances. Some become more nuclear and a diversity of Asian families starts to appear.

**Families around the world: Asian**
Tibetan family dressed up for a visit to the Labrang Monastery during the Tibetan New Year

*Source:* © Wong Adam/Redlink/Corbis.

### Afro-Caribbean families

These account for less than 1 per cent of all families in the UK (Skellington, 1996: 50). Thirty-seven per cent were headed by a female (compared with 9 per cent of white families). Marriage is often weaker, women-headed households are more common, and the husband/father role is likely to be less strong. In a curious fashion, there is a resemblance to the situation in the United States, where African-American families are also like this. Jocelyn Barrow explains this form of family by linking it to Caribbean society. Originally, while marriage is much valued in Caribbean societies, other patterns of sexual union were possible. There were common-law family households with unmarried cohabitation, as well as women-headed households (Barrow, 1982).

In the main, extended kin units have not reappeared among Afro-Caribbean families in the UK. One study suggested that fewer than 1 per cent of children are cared for by grandmothers as the 'grandmother family' disappears. The families often tend to be matrifocal, even though Afro-Caribbean women are more likely to be working and have less support than in the Caribbean. Men often become marginal to family life.

Lone-parent families are highest among West Indian families (43 per cent in the 1991 Census) but lowest for Asian: the figures were 6 per cent for Indian and Pakistani, 5 per cent for Bangladeshi and 11 per cent for white families (Skellington, 1996: 50, 60).

### Gender

Among all races, Jessie Bernard (1982) asserts, every marriage is actually two different relationships: a woman's marriage and a man's marriage. Although the extent of patriarchy has diminished with time, even today few marriages are composed of two equal partners. Studies in the UK suggest that although there have been some moves towards equality, and that families do come in many forms, it remains the case that men still make most of the major decisions, and that wives generally are economically dependent upon husbands and are more likely to take responsibility for childcare and the housework within the family (Pahl, 1989; Devine, 1992).

## 4 Interaction and the micro-sociology of the family

We saw in Chapter 7 how some sociology works not just at the grand macro-level but at the level of the situation. Micro-sociology would explore how individuals shape and experience family life. Seen from the inside, family life amounts to individuals engaging one another in a changing collage of meanings and work. People construct family life, building a reality that differs from case to case and from day to day. As we saw in Christopher Carrington's (1999) work on lesbian and gay families above, 'people do families'. It is work – caring work, feeding work, kin work and so on (Carrington, 1999: 6).

Family living also offers an opportunity for intimacy, a word with Latin roots meaning 'sharing fears'. That is, as a result of sharing a wide range of activities over a long period of time, members of families forge emotional bonds. Of course, the fact that parents act as authority figures often inhibits their communication with younger children. But, as young people reach adulthood, kinship ties typically 'open up' as family members recognise that they share concern for one another's welfare. They also engage in emotional work (see Chapter 7 and Hochschild, 1983; Macionis, 1978a).

### Social-exchange analysis

An early approach to the dynamics of the family came with social-exchange analysis. It depicts courtship and marriage as forms of negotiation (Blau, 1964). In the case of courtship, dating allows each person the chance to assess the likely advantages and disadvantages of taking the other as a spouse, always keeping in mind the value of what one has to offer in return. In essence, exchange analysts contend, individuals seek to make the best 'deal' they can in selecting a partner. Physical attractiveness is one critical dimension of social exchange. In patriarchal societies around the world, beauty has long been a commodity offered by women on the marriage market. The high value assigned to beauty explains women's traditional concern with physical appearance and their sensitivity about revealing their age. For their part, men have traditionally been assessed according to the financial resources they command. Recently, however, because increasing numbers of women are joining the labour force, they are less dependent on men to support them and their children. Thus, the terms of exchange have been converging for men and women.

### Critical comments

Micro-level analysis offers a useful counterpoint to functionalist and conflict visions of the family as an institutional system. Adopting an interactional or exchange viewpoint, we gain a better sense of the individual's experience of family life and appreciate how people creatively shape this reality for themselves.

Using this approach, however, we run the risk of missing the bigger picture: namely, that family life is similar for people affected by any common set of economic and cultural forces. UK families vary in some predictable ways according to social class and ethnicity, and, as the next section explains, they typically evolve through stages linked to the life course.

# 5  Newer developments: 'doing families', 'family practices' and personal life

More recently, there have been a number of new ways of thinking about families and we will consider some of these here. First, the English sociologist David Morgan has suggested that families can be analysed as a set of 'practices'. At the start of the twenty-first century, most people no longer follow fixed paths for living in families. Like Carrington, he suggests that people are *doing family* rather than simply being in one. Family has come to signify a sense of intimate connections, and much less the formal legal ties of marriage. We are talking now about the multiple ways of doing families. But all this fluidity is not really random: people live their life through a regular set of practices. Rather than simply viewing the family as a fixed 'thing', it is now seen as a set of relationships built around such things as housework, caring, being a mother, being a child, or having sex. These practices highlight:

- *The doing of families*: what actually goes on and gets done in families. This is an active image of activities.

- *The everyday life of families*: we are more concerned with the relatively routine and trivial. David Morgan writes: 'what you had for breakfast today and how you consumed your breakfast may tell the observer as much about your routine understandings of family living as the more dramatic [rituals] such as weddings and funerals' (Morgan, 1999: 17).

- *The processes and fluidity of family life*: practices ebb and flow into each other and one set of practices mixes and merges with others.

- *Regularities*: even if active, people develop patterns, such as 'breakfasting', 'watching television', 'washing baby' or 'having sex'.

- *Interplay of biography and history*: lives are woven together and develop a sense of the past.

- *Interplay of positions*: there are many ways of viewing from the family – children, mothers, fathers, grandparents, visitors, friends, etc. (Morgan, 1999: 17–18).

## *Personal life*

Carol Smart (2007) has taken all this further in a major way. She has studied families in their various patterns for a quarter of a century and has found sociology lacking. Many of the studies look at the wrong things; many of them take too pessimistic a view of change. Smart is critical of the more general and abstract theories which seem in despair about the 'individualisation' and 'chaos' of contemporary families. This is found in a lot of media reporting and gets support from the unresearched theories of Ulrich Beck, Zygymunt Bauman and others. As she says: 'their ideas run directly counter to most empirical sociological studies of family and kinship in Britain' (2007: 20). More than that, they offer very little evidence for their assertions. In particular, they ignore the continuing significance of class, gender inequality, power and intergenerational relationships which is found in the research of Jane Ribbens McCarthy, Lynn Jamieson, Graham Crow, Ros Edwards and others.

Carol Smart prefers a focus on personal life: an 'area of life which impacts closely on people and means much to them, but which does not presume there is an autonomous agency'. It does not mean an individual isolated and with free will. It is rather a term which, whilst it allows for the fact that human beings have agency and make choices, indicates that their lives are always bound up with the presence of others. A personal life charts the ways we connect and link to other people. The personal life is always 'embedded in the social' (Smart, 2007: 29). For Carol Smart, the sociologist's task is to 'map personal lives into their social context and into their specific history or spatial location'. Usually within a life, we can study the 'life projects' of how people make plans and organise their lives. This personal life is always on the move – changing, growing and evolving with all the relations around it. The study of the 'personal life' allows us to look at a whole array of areas that sociologists have hitherto neglected and to bring them to the forefront in our thinking: areas like love, emotions, sexuality, bodies, intimacies. To help in these explorations, Smart suggests five key concepts:

1  *Biography*: how we live our lives over time with many other people. We have personal histories of our own which give meaning to our lives over time, and many of these meanings – and our sense of agency and actions – are located within the family. We become individuals and tell the stories of our lives through the families we live in (and see the interlude at the end of Part Four).

2  *Memory*: how families play a key role in the shaping of 'social memories': they provide key contexts for what we know and can recall. There is now much work on the sociology of memory which suggests that it is not merely a psychological matter – of recalling something from a memory box in the brain. Rather we remember with and through other people: memory is something which is shaped and fashioned by the social. *Memories are collective, shared and social.* Family spaces are particularly important places for organising our memories – often through things such as family photographs and albums. Our social memories speak to our childhoods; they generate contexts in which we recount the meanings of our lives; and they change as our families change.

3  *Embeddedness*: how people become woven together and how this keeps changing and emerging. Here the focus is concretely on what families actually do on a day-to-day basis: from meals and holidays, to the family crises and troubles which all families confront.

4  *Relationships*: how people connect to each other. Here we are concerned with the differing and changing quality of the texture of how people relate to each other, and the emotions that are woven and constructed into these relationships.

5  *Imaginary*: how we come to think and even dream about our personal lives. Often we think more about what we want to be rather than what we actually are. This dreaming and reflection on families and personal life is a very important part of life – and, again, it is collective and cultural. And as the famous adage goes: we should be careful what we dream, for our dreams may come true.

In all of this, then, Carol Smart suggests some key features of this 'personal life' which we all know about but which have been so rarely studied and understood. This includes the 'secrets and lies' found in every family and rarely discussed. It includes the ways in which possessions and things are shared and owned. It looks at the need to understand the anxieties, disrespect and hurts that are found in most relationships and families at all ages and across all members – and, dare we say, across all cultures. These are what make personal relationships – at the extremes there is violence and abuse, but there are surely also everyday troubles in the 'families we live with'. And then there is the significance of love, sex and other kinds of emotions which are fostered in families and personal life.

At the heart of Smart's approach is the need to get close to families and personal lives, to study them in their local contexts and to use autobiographical understandings in particular. There have been sweeping statistical generalisations and quite a lot of grander theorising, but very little close attention to the close living of lives through families and what it means to people. She wants to get away from grand theories of the family and crude statistical abstractions, and wants more research on the family to get closer to real 'families' and what is actually going on. When this happens, she claims we will find that multiple different families are amazingly resilient and strong – even in the face of the many changes they have to confront.

# Some practices of family life

## Practising care

One of the key 'practices' of families is 'caring': caring for partners, caring for children and caring for parents. This is a three- or four-generational span of care. And there is an important distinction to be made here between *caring about*, which is about love, feelings and emotions, and *caring for*, which is an active form of work – a 'labour of love' which involves looking after someone (Ungerson, 1987). They may, of course, be deeply interwoven, but they need not be. Overwhelmingly, this latter care process falls upon the women in the family, although it is usually invisible. Although there are signs that some men are playing a small role in it, feminist research has generally shown that the caring process is closely linked in modern societies to what it means to be a woman. Recall in Chapter 12 how Nancy Chodorow suggested that the social process of becoming a woman was closely linked to the social process of becoming a mother. It is the extension of this 'social mothering' that makes women more prone to look after the array of people within the family – and also outside it.

There has been quite a lot of research on 'care'. It suggests that these commitments are rarely straightforward and always negotiated – often over long periods of time and implicitly. Sometimes there is an unwillingness to engage in care. Often the array of family members that will be carers is narrowly defined: usually from spouse, to daughter, to daughter-in-law and son. There is a hierarchy of care: sons and daughters define their care duties primarily to their own children and partners, only secondarily to their parents. Older people usually do not want to give up their independence – and so are looked after 'at a distance' ('intimacy at a distance'). Nevertheless, research strongly suggests that there is a great deal of care taking place among families today. But when governments cut back on public care, this can hit many families very hard, as they are already engaged in a great deal of unpaid care (Finch and Groves, 1983; Finch, 1989; Elliot, 1996: 122–40).

## Housework practices

Closely linked to the caring tasks of the household is the challenge of who does the household work. Traditionally, and in many countries around the world today, this is usually seen as women's work. The man is the provider and the woman is the home maker. As women now routinely go out to paid employment everyday, and most women in low-income societies have always had to work, this seems a very uneven division of labour.

With the recent change in status of women in some societies, it is often claimed that men now contribute more to the housework. Research generally suggests not – and that women now do a 'double shift' (working both in and out of the home). The men do more than in the past, and women do less – but not significantly; and it varies a great deal from country to country as Table 18.1 shows.

## Doing violence

In Chapter 12 we saw the significance of violence in women's lives. Much of this takes place within the family. The ideal family, of course, is seen as a haven from the dangers of the outside world; the reality is that many families are exceedingly dangerous places. From the biblical story of Cain killing his brother Abel to the horror stories of child abuse that we hear in the

| Table 18.1 | The percentage of people daily involved in housework across Europe | | | |
|---|---|---|---|---|
| Country | Sex respondent | | Total | Female-Male difference |
| | Male | Female | | |
| Finland | 64% | 95% | 79% | 31% |
| Sweden | 65% | 90% | 77% | 25% |
| Romania | 60% | 93% | 76% | 33% |
| Denmark | 65% | 86% | 74% | 21% |
| Hungary | 46% | 93% | 70% | 47% |
| Slovakia | 47% | 92% | 70% | 45% |
| Luxembourg | 44% | 92% | 69% | 48% |
| Belgium | 44% | 91% | 68% | 47% |
| Estonia | 53% | 84% | 68% | 31% |
| Bulgaria | 33% | 95% | 66% | 62% |
| Lithuania | 44% | 90% | 66% | 46% |
| Netherlands | 47% | 86% | 66% | 39% |
| Germany | 36% | 90% | 64% | 54% |
| Latvia | 43% | 85% | 64% | 42% |
| Portugal | 27% | 96% | 62% | 69% |
| France | 32% | 86% | 61% | 54% |
| Slovenia | 30% | 96% | 61% | 66% |
| Austria | 28% | 89% | 59% | 61% |
| Greece | 18% | 94% | 59% | 76% |
| UK | 36% | 80% | 58% | 44% |
| Italy | 26% | 88% | 57% | 62% |
| Turkey | 15% | 91% | 57% | 76% |
| Ireland | 33% | 78% | 56% | 45% |
| Malta | 21% | 91% | 54% | 70% |
| Cyprus | 19% | 80% | 53% | 61% |
| European average* | 35% | 88% | 62% | 53% |

* The sample was weighted according to the population size of each country.

The sample included 26,245 respondents from 25 European societies. See http://iriss.ceps.lu/documents/irisswp75.pdf.

*Source*: 'Engendered housework: a cross-European analysis'; Bogdan Voicu, Malina Voicu and Katarina Strapcov No. 2007-07, IRISS Working Paper Series, from IRISS at CEPS/INSTEAD.

news regularly, we see that the disturbing reality of many homes has been **family violence**, *emotional, physical or sexual abuse of one family member by another*. Some time back, sociologist Richard J. Gelles pointed to a chilling fact:

> **The family is the most violent group in society with the exception of the police and the military. You are more likely to get killed, injured or physically attacked in your home by someone you are related to than in any other social context.**

(quoted in Roesch, 1984: 75)

How does this violence work?

## Violence against women

During the 1970s a seemingly new 'family problem' was discovered: men's violence against women. The women's movement responded by actively establishing women's refuges and also through a critical analysis of men's violence towards women (which often connected it to the rape and power debate discussed in Chapter 12). In England, Erin Pizzey set up the first women's refuge in Chiswick in 1972 (Pizzey, 1974), and today they are common in many large cities throughout the world (though usually, to avoid male harassers, they are kept fairly anonymous). A study by Jayne Mooney (2000) in north London found that about half of all women surveyed had experienced threats of violence or actual violence, although many of these women had not told anybody. In the 1990s, the United Nations recognised domestic violence as a human rights abuse.

It has been claimed that between 1 in 4 or 5 women will be a victim of domestic violence in their lifetime – many of these on a number of occasions. Like most such statistics, they are notoriously difficult to verify, as such events are seriously underreported (see Chapter 17). Women may be ashamed, feel they are to blame, be too frightened to tell anyone, or love their partner and not want him to be criticised or punished for what he did. Whatever the case, we know that such violence is widespread. Reports from around the world show different rates of violence – but its presence seems to exist in families everywhere and many women live in fear because of it. In ten countries surveyed in a 2005 study by the World Health Organization, more than 50 per cent of women in Bangladesh, Ethiopia, Peru and Tanzania reported having been subjected to physical or sexual violence by intimate partners, with figures reaching a staggering 71 per cent in rural Ethiopia. Only in one country (Japan) did less than 20 per cent of women report incidents of domestic violence (Garca-Moreno et al., 2005).

There are a number of factors that help shape domestic violence across the world. The leading researchers in this area, Rebecca and Russell Dobash, highlight 'men's possessiveness and jealousy, men's expectations concerning women's domestic work, men's sense of their right to punish "their" women, and the importance to men of maintaining and exercising their authority' (Dobash, 1992: 3). At the heart of the problem is usually masculinity. The family is usually a place where certain levels of violence will be tolerated and the very intensity of family ties makes it a very emotional place. The violence of the family can become routine. Recently, there has been growing research into the children of such families, who often become the 'hidden victims' of domestic violence (Harne and Radford, 2008).

In the past, the law regarded domestic violence as a private, family matter. Now, even without separation or divorce, a woman can obtain court protection from an abusive spouse. Anti-stalking laws (which prohibit people from following or threatening ex-partners), such as the 1997 Harassment Act in the UK, are now found in many countries. Finally, communities across Europe have established shelters that provide counselling as well as temporary housing for women and children driven from their homes by domestic violence. The analysis has shifted from being based on individuals,

## Spotlight

### What do we mean by violence against women?

The United Nations claims that 'It is estimated that one in every five women faces some form of violence during her lifetime, in some cases leading to serious injury or death.' Gender violence has been identified as a key issue of our times. Below, a United Nations report outlines its key forms.

- *Physical violence* means a woman has been: slapped, or had something thrown at her; pushed, shoved, or had her hair pulled; hit with a fist or something else that could hurt; choked or burnt; threatened with or had a weapon used against her.

- *Sexual violence* means a woman has been: physically forced to have sexual intercourse; had sexual intercourse because she was afraid of what her partner might do; or forced to do something sexual she found degrading or humiliating.

- Though recognized as a serious and pervasive problem, *emotional violence* does not yet have a widely accepted definition, but includes, for example, being humiliated or belittled; being scared or intimidated purposefully.

- *Intimate-partner violence* (also called 'domestic' violence) means a woman has encountered any of the above types of violence, at the hands of an intimate partner or ex-partner; this is one of the most common and universal forms of violence experienced by women.

*Source*: www.who.int/gender/documents/MDGs&VAWSept05.pdf.

to being based on the power relations – patriarchy – between men and women (see Chapter 12).

## Violence against children

Family violence also victimises children. In the United States upwards of 3 million children – roughly 4 per cent of all youngsters – suffer abuse each year, including several thousand who die as a result. Child abuse entails more than physical injury because abusive adults misuse power and trust to undermine a child's emotional well-being. Child abuse is most common among the youngest and most vulnerable children (Straus and Gelles, 1986; Van Biema, 1994).

In the UK several noticeable cases have galvanised action and thinking. In 1973, the seven-year-old Maria Colwell was beaten to death by her stepfather after social workers had allowed her to return to her family from foster care. It led both to a moral panic (see Chapter 22) and to the development of a public awareness of abuse. Later, in 1985, the death of Jasmine Beckford also served to highlight the

continuing problem. The most recent controversy was in 2009 over Baby P., a 17-month-old boy who died in London after some 50 injuries. As a consequence of such cases, social work intervention increased, and registers of children at risk (now Children's Plans) were created. In 2010, there were 46,709 children registered in the UK. Still, the plight of abused children continues: many suffer in silence, believing during their formative years that they are to blame for their own victimisation. The initial abuse, compounded by years of guilt, can leave lasting emotional scars that prevent people abused as children from forming healthy relationships as adults.

About 90 per cent of child abusers are men, but they conform to no simple stereotype. As one man who entered a therapy group reported, 'I kept waiting for all the guys with raincoats and greasy hair to show up. But everyone looked like regular middle-class people.' Most abusers, however, share one trait: they were abused themselves as children. Researchers have discovered that violent behaviour in close relationships is learned. In families, then, violence begets violence.

GLOBAL FAMILIES: 3

# The modern family in the UK around 2008

## Households

There are three main types: a married couple, a cohabiting couple and a lone-parent family. An increasing trend towards smaller household sizes has seen the average household size in Great Britain fall from 3.1 people per household in 1961 to 2.4 people in 2009. There are more lone-parent families, smaller family sizes and, in particular, more one-person households (see Table 18.2).

## Partnerships

In 2007, the majority of the adult population in England and Wales were living as part of a couple, either cohabiting or married. Types of partnership vary according to age group: adults aged 16 to 29 were the least likely age group to be living with a partner; in comparison, almost three-quarters (71 per cent) of adults aged 30 to 44 and just over three-quarters (76 per cent) of adults aged 45 to 64 were living with a partner, as either a married or a cohabiting couple (see Figure 18.1).

## Marriages

Between 1950 and 2005, there was a marked decrease in the number of first marriages. In 1950, more than 300,000 couples married for the first time; this was less than 200,000 in 2005. But remarriage was common – more than 40 per cent of marriages are remarriages, compared with 21 per cent in 1971. People are also marrying later in life. Marriage is by far the most common partnership type. In 2007 more than half (55 per cent) of adults aged 30 and over were married. The number of

marriages in England and Wales fell for the third consecutive year in 2007, to around 231,500.

## Cohabitation

This has risen significantly. Cohabitation among non-married people is now very common: in 2005, 23 per cent of men and 28 per cent of women were cohabiting. Cohabitation is often found among the divorced and frequently ends through remarriage.

## Divorces

The peak period for divorce was in the 1970s. It is now more stable, at around 150,000 a year. Since 1971, marriages have fallen one-fifth and divorces have doubled. Almost half of marriages end in divorce, and most are sought by women (7 out of 10 petitions), while men are more likely to remarry. Roughly a quarter of children can now expect to find their original parents divorced by the time

GLOBAL FAMILIES: 3

they are 16. The UK has the highest divorce rate in the European Union but it is not as high as it is in the United States. There were around 128,500 divorces in England and Wales in 2007, a fall of 3 per cent compared with 2006. This was the lowest number of divorces in a single year since 1976 (see Table 18.3).

## Step-families

In 2000–1 step-families accounted for 8 per cent of families with dependent children.

## Civil partnership

Despite hotly contested debates all over the world, gay marriages or registered partnerships now exist in many countries. In all the Scandinavian countries and most of Europe, such partnerships are now law. Registered partnerships became law in the UK in 2005. There were 18,059 civil partnerships formed in the UK between December 2005 and the end of December 2006. A fall in the number of civil partnership registrations was recorded in all four countries of the UK in 2008. The largest annual fall was in Scotland (24 per cent) where 525 partnerships were registered in 2008, followed by Northern Ireland (23 per cent) where 86 partnerships were registered. England accounted for around 88 per cent (6,276) of all civil partnerships formed in the UK, a fall of 18 per cent in registrations compared with 2007. The smallest fall was recorded in Wales (4 per cent) where 282 partnerships were registered in 2008.

## Home alone

More people are now living alone. In the UK in 2002, 6.2 million adults were living alone. A quarter of all households are now one-person households. This is double what it was in 1971 (when it was 3 million). In addition, household size fell from 3.09 in 1961 to 2.46 in 1990. Many of these are elderly households (in 2000, 10 per cent of these belonged to elderly women and half of all women over 75 years live alone). A new

| Table 18.2 | Households in Great Britain: by type of household and family (%) | | | | | |
|---|---|---|---|---|---|---|
| | 1961 | 1971 | 1981 | 1991 | 2001[1] | 2009[1] |
| **One person households** | | | | | | |
| Under state pension age[2] | 4 | 6 | 8 | 11 | 14 | 14 |
| Over state pension age[2] | 7 | 12 | 14 | 16 | 15 | 14 |
| **One family households** | | | | | | |
| Couple[3] | | | | | | |
| No children | 26 | 27 | 26 | 28 | 29 | 29 |
| 1–2 dependent children[4,5] | 30 | 26 | 25 | 20 | 19 | 18 |
| 3 or more dependent children[4,5] | 8 | 9 | 6 | 5 | 4 | 3 |
| Non-dependent children only | 10 | 8 | 8 | 8 | 6 | 6 |
| Lone parent[3] | | | | | | |
| Dependent children[4,5] | 2 | 3 | 5 | 6 | 7 | 7 |
| Non-dependent children only | 4 | 4 | 4 | 4 | 3 | 3 |
| **Two or more unrelated adults** | 5 | 4 | 5 | 3 | 3 | 3 |
| **Multi-family households** | 3 | 1 | 1 | 1 | 1 | 1 |
| **All households** | | | | | | |
| (= 100%) (millions) | 16.3 | 18.6 | 20.2 | 22.4 | 23.9 | 25.2 |

[1] Data are at Q2 (April–June) each year and are not seasonally adjusted.
[2] State pension age is currently 65 for men and 60 for women.
[3] These households may contain individuals who are not family members. Couples data for 2009 include a small number of same-sex couples and civil partners.
[4] Children aged under 16 and those aged 16 to 18 who have never married and are in full-time education.
[5] These families may also contain non-dependent children.

*Source*: Census, Labour Force Survey, Office for National Statistics in *Social Trends*, 40 (2010), Table 2.2, p. 15.

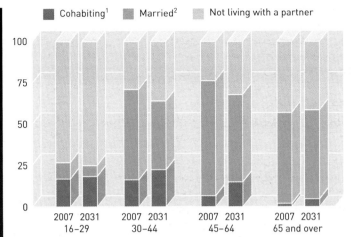

| Cohabiting[1] | Married[2] | Not living with a partner |

Figure 18.1    **Partnerships in England and Wales (%)**

[1] Includes people who are separated and cohabiting.
[2] Includes people who are separated but not cohabiting; projections are not available for this group.

*Source*: Office for National Statistics in *Social Trends*, 40 (2010), Fig. 2.9, p. 19.

trend is for younger men to live on their own (3 per cent in 1971; 10 per cent in 2000; predicted to be 14 per cent by 2021).

## Lone parents

Since 1971, living in lone-parent households has become a more common experience. Almost one in five families with dependent children are lone-parent families. The figures nearly trebled in 25 years from 1 million to 2.8 million. In 1972, 6 per cent of all children grew up in Britain with a single parent, as compared to 22 per cent in 2006. The proportion of living in couple families decreased from 92 per cent to 76 per cent. A large part of this is due to divorce. About 10 per cent of lone-parent families are headed by lone fathers and 90 per cent by lone mothers. Denmark and Sweden have the highest numbers of lone parents in Europe.

## Children

In 1901, 34.6 per cent of the population in the UK were under

16; in 1981 it was 22.3 per cent. The average number of children in a family was 1.8 (including adopted and stepchildren). The birth rate is 1.73 per woman. The number of families with dependent children in the UK in 2009 was around 7.6 million. Of these, 4.6 million (61 per cent) were married couple families. The second most common type was families headed by a lone mother (1.8 million), followed by cohabiting couple families (1.0 million) and lone father families (0.2 million). In the main, children still live in traditional families headed by a couple (78 per cent in spring 2002).

## Birth

The number of births in England and Wales increased for the seventh successive year in 2008, rising from 690,000 in 2007 to 709,000 in 2008. The number of live births is now at its highest level since 1972, when there were 727,000 live births. During this period the average age for women giving birth

the first time has risen from 23.8 years to 27.5 years. Since the 1970s there has been a fall in the proportion of babies born to women aged under 25, from 47 per cent in 1971 (369,600 live births) to 25 per cent in 2008 (180,700 live births).

## The generational gap

There is a large difference in attitude towards 'family' between those born before 1930 and those born since 1950. Older cohorts are firmly against living together before marriage (well over 60 per cent) whereas younger cohorts born since 1950 strongly favour living together before marriage (*British Social Attitudes*, 2004).

## Sexuality

The pill remains the most popular form of contraception with a quarter of all women aged 16–49 using it. In 1971, 21 per cent of births were conceived out of marriage; by 2000, it was over half. There has also been a dramatic decline in the age of first intercourse: the median for young men and women (born between 1966 and 1975) was 17 years. Gay and lesbian sexualities are much more accepted.

## Life expectancy

The twentieth century has seen 25 years added to human life expectancy, shifting the shape of the life cycle.

## Births outside marriage

In the UK, about one-third of all live births occur outside marriage and in nearly all European countries the rate has doubled in the last 30 years.

GLOBAL FAMILIES: 3

| Table 18.3 | Divorces (per 1,000 persons) |

| | 1997 | 1998 | 1999 | 2000 | 2001 | 2002 | 2003 | 2004 | 2005 | 2006 | 2007 |
|---|---|---|---|---|---|---|---|---|---|---|---|
| EU-27 (1) | 1.8 | 1.8 | 1.8 | 1.8 | 1.9 | 1.9 | 2.0 | 2.0 | 2.0 | : | : |
| Belgium | 2.6 | 2.6 | 2.6 | 2.6 | 2.8 | 3.0 | 3.0 | 3.0 | 2.9 | 2.8 | 2.9 |
| Bulgaria | 1.1 | 1.3 | 1.2 | 1.3 | 1.3 | 1.3 | 1.5 | 1.9 | 1.9 | 1.9 | 2.1 |
| Czech Republic | 3.2 | 3.1 | 2.3 | 2.9 | 3.1 | 3.1 | 3.8 | 3.2 | 3.1 | 3.1 | 3.0 |
| Denmark | 2.4 | 2.5 | 2.5 | 2.7 | 2.7 | 2.8 | 2.9 | 2.9 | 2.8 | 2.6 | 2.6 |
| Germany | 2.3 | 2.3 | 2.3 | 2.4 | 2.4 | 2.5 | 2.6 | 2.6 | 2.4 | 2.3 | : |
| Estonia | 3.8 | 3.2 | 3.3 | 3.1 | 3.2 | 3.0 | 2.9 | 3.1 | 3.0 | 2.8 | 2.8 |
| Ireland | 0.0 | 0.4 | 0.6 | 0.7 | 0.7 | 0.7 | 0.7 | 0.8 | 0.8 | : | : |
| Greece | 0.9 | 0.7 | 0.9 | 1.0 | 1.1 | 1.0 | 1.1 | 1.1 | 1.2 | 1.3 | 1.2 |
| Spain | 0.9 | 0.9 | 0.9 | 0.9 | 1.0 | 1.0 | 1.1 | 1.2 | 1.7 | : | : |
| France | 2.0 | 2.0 | 2.0 | 1.9 | 1.9 | 1.9 | 2.1 | 2.2 | 2.5 | 2.2 | : |
| Italy | 0.6 | 0.6 | 0.6 | 0.7 | 0.7 | 0.7 | 0.8 | 0.8 | 0.8 | : | 0.8 |
| Cyprus | 1.3 | 1.3 | 1.7 | 1.7 | 1.7 | 1.9 | 2.0 | 2.2 | 2.0 | 2.3 | 2.1 |
| Latvia | 2.5 | 2.6 | 2.5 | 2.6 | 2.4 | 2.5 | 2.1 | 2.3 | 2.8 | 3.2 | 3.3 |
| Lithuania | 3.2 | 3.3 | 3.2 | 3.1 | 3.2 | 3.0 | 3.1 | 3.2 | 3.3 | 3.3 | 3.4 |
| Luxembourg | 2.4 | 2.4 | 2.4 | 2.4 | 2.3 | 2.4 | 2.3 | 2.3 | 2.3 | 2.5 | 2.3 |
| Hungary | 2.4 | 2.5 | 2.5 | 2.3 | 2.4 | 2.5 | 2.5 | 2.4 | 2.5 | 2.5 | 2.5 |
| Malta | – | – | – | – | – | – | – | – | – | – | – |
| Netherlands | 2.2 | 2.1 | 2.1 | 2.2 | 2.3 | 2.1 | 1.9 | 1.9 | 2.0 | 1.9 | 2.0 |
| Austria | 2.3 | 2.2 | 2.3 | 2.4 | 2.6 | 2.4 | 2.3 | 2.4 | 2.4 | 2.5 | 2.4 |
| Poland | 1.1 | 1.2 | 1.1 | 1.1 | 1.2 | 1.2 | 1.3 | 1.5 | 1.8 | 1.9 | 1.7 |
| Portugal | 1.4 | 1.5 | 1.7 | 1.9 | 1.8 | 2.7 | 2.2 | 2.2 | 2.2 | 2.3 | 2.4 |
| Romania | 1.6 | 1.8 | 1.6 | 1.4 | 1.4 | 1.5 | 1.5 | 1.6 | 1.5 | 1.5 | 1.7 |
| Slovenia | 1.0 | 1.0 | 1.0 | 1.1 | 1.1 | 1.2 | 1.2 | 1.2 | 1.3 | 1.2 | 1.4 |
| Slovakia | 1.7 | 1.7 | 1.8 | 1.7 | 1.8 | 2.0 | 2.0 | 2.0 | 2.1 | 2.4 | 2.3 |
| Finland | 2.6 | 2.7 | 2.7 | 2.7 | 2.6 | 2.6 | 2.6 | 2.5 | 2.6 | 2.5 | 2.5 |
| Sweden | 2.4 | 2.3 | 2.4 | 2.4 | 2.4 | 2.4 | 2.4 | 2.2 | 2.2 | 2.2 | 2.3 |
| United Kingdom | 2.8 | 2.7 | 2.7 | 2.6 | 2.7 | 2.7 | 2.8 | 2.8 | 2.6 | : | : |
| Croatia | 0.9 | 0.9 | 0.8 | 1.0 | 1.1 | 1.0 | 1.1 | 1.1 | 1.1 | 1.1 | : |
| FYR of Macedonia | 0.5 | 0.5 | 0.5 | 0.7 | 0.7 | 0.6 | 0.7 | 0.8 | 0.8 | 0.7 | 0.7 |
| Turkey | : | : | : | : | : | : | 0.7 | 1.3 | 1.3 | 1.3 | : |
| Iceland | 1.9 | 1.8 | 1.7 | 1.9 | 1.9 | 1.8 | 1.8 | 1.9 | 1.9 | 1.6 | : |
| Liechtenstein | 2.1 | : | : | 3.9 | 2.5 | 2.9 | 2.5 | 2.9 | 2.7 | 2.3 | 2.8 |
| Norway | 2.3 | 2.1 | 2.0 | 2.2 | 2.3 | 2.3 | 2.4 | 2.4 | 2.4 | 2.3 | 2.2 |
| Switzerland | 2.4 | 2.5 | 2.9 | 1.5 | 2.2 | 2.2 | 2.3 | 2.4 | 2.9 | 2.8 | 2.6 |

¹ Break in series, 1998.

Source: Eurostat *Europe in Figures: Eurostat Yearbook 2009*, p. 157, Table 3.14 © European Union, 2009.

GLOBAL FAMILIES: 3

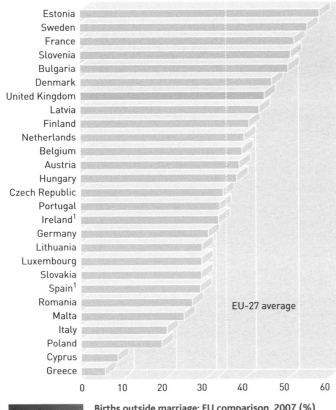

| Figure 18.2 | **Births outside marriage: EU comparison, 2007 (%)** |
|---|---|

[1] Data are for 2006.

*Source*: Office for National Statistics; Eurostat in *Social Trends*, 40 (2010), Fig. 2.19, p. 24.

and women are having children later in the life cycle.

## Forced marriages

In 2009 the UK Forced Marriage Unity (FMU) gave advice or support in 1,682 cases; 86 per cent of these cases involved females and 14 per cent involved males. Forced marriages usually take place to prevent a young woman from marrying someone 'unsuitable' (in terms of class, race, ethnicity, religion or sect); to fulfil a betrothal to a relative; to 'fix' sexual orientation (where either of the spouses is not heterosexual); or to provide a carer for a disabled husband. They often involved abduction abroad, rape or unwanted pregnancy, and have high rates of domestic violence, divorce or abandonment. Girls are being sent at an ever younger age to the family's 'home country' and only returned to Britain once they have been married and become pregnant (see: www.fco.gov.uk/en/travel-and-living-abroad/when-things-go-wrong/forced-marriage/information-for-victims).

## Adoption

The adoption rate has sharply fallen. There were 21,500 adoptions in 1971 and just under 6,000 in 2001.

*Source*: *Social Trends* (mainly the 2010 issue).

Yet most occur in stable relationships outside marriage (in 1992, 75 per cent of registered births included both parents as opposed to 45 per cent in 1971). Birth rate outside marriage is highest in Sweden and Estonia and lowest in Greece. (See Figure 18.2.)

## Women remaining childless

While most women do have children, the number who do not has been growing (20 per cent of those born in 1954 and 25 per cent of those born in 1979 remain childless)

# Twenty-first-century families?

Well into the twenty-first century, families and relationships have continued their path of change – especially in Western societies. True, many of

the older patterns persist, and often mingle with the family patterns of non-Western cultures; but there are certainly some new fashions in the making. We have seen in Chapter 12 the emergence of a new, flexible, highly individualistic, sexually 'plastic', 'pure relationship' where partners are mutually interdependent (Cancian, 1987; Giddens, 1991; Beck and Beck-Gernsheim, 1995). The suggestion is that for some (and it *may* be a blueprint for the future), relationships are emerging where men and women are more interdependent and equal; where their child-rearing is altogether part of a more egalitarian and democratic system; where sexuality and love become more 'plastic', diffuse, open. This is a relationship of choice, closely allied to individualism.

The changes we outline have been taken by many to herald a new form of family relationship. American family sociologist Judith Stacey has argued that we may be discovering the postmodern family. She writes:

> The postmodern family condition is not a new model of family life equivalent to that of the modern family; it is not the next stage in an orderly progression of stages in family history; rather the postmodern family condition signals the moment in history when our belief in a logical progression of stages has broken down . . . The postmodern family condition incorporates both experimental and nostalgic dimensions as it lurches forward and backward into an uncertain future.

(Stacey, 1996: 8)

The box on p. 637 details what the family looks like in one country, the UK, and suggests certain trends – many of which also hold for other Western countries. Recent findings on a range of European families show a number of features in common:

- a reduction in the number of marriages
- an increase in the average age at which people marry
- an increase in the number of divorces
- a smaller average household size
- a higher proportion of people living alone
- the highest proportion of people living alone is found among the elderly.

In what follows, we shall highlight a few features.

## Marriage and divorce

One of the most striking features of modern societies has been the decline in first marriage and the rapid growth of divorce. There were 40 per cent fewer first marriages in the UK in 1994 than there were in 1971 – a steep drop. In 2001, around half of adults in the UK population were married. The age of marriage has also increased – in 2001, it was around 30.6 for men and 28.4 for women (in 1971 it was 24.6 and 22.6 respectively). By contrast, the number of divorces has more than doubled in the same period – a steep rise.

There is also a general drift towards marrying at older ages.

These are trends found throughout Europe and other industrialising societies. Most countries in the European Union have seen a decline in marriage rates, with Sweden having the lowest number of marriages. Taking Europe as a whole, the divorce rate quadrupled between 1960 and 1992, although as Figure 18.3 shows, there are significant differences across all countries. Divorce is highest in the UK and the Nordic countries, and lowest in the Mediterranean regions. US society has the highest divorce rate in the world: double that of Canada and Japan, and seven times as high as Italy (US Bureau of the Census, 2002).

Nevertheless, since the mid-1980s, these rapid rises have stabilised a little, as Figure 18.4 suggests. Although the trend of ending marriage may have slowed for the moment, it does nevertheless seem a stable Western pattern. Far from divorce being an unusual ending to a marriage, it is becoming more and more the norm.

The high UK divorce rate can be traced to a number of factors. The most common reason for women to be granted divorce in the UK is the 'unreasonable behaviour' of the man; for men, it is the adultery of the wife (*Social Trends*, 1997: 48). More broadly, we can see divorce rising because:

1 *Divorce is legally easier to accomplish.* For example, in the UK before 1857, divorces were almost impossible: they were only for wealthy men and required a private Act of Parliament. Legislation over the following century made divorce increasingly easy. But it was the Divorce Reform Act of 1969 (law from 1971) which shifted the grounds of divorce to the 'irretrievable breakdown of marriage' doctrine. Couples could now divorce after two years' separation (five years if the partner objected). From this point onwards, divorces escalated. So there is little doubt that, formally, the changes in the law have made divorce possible. The key peaks of divorces in the UK in the 1970s were almost certainly due to the release of a backlog of long-dead marriages. But since the Matrimonial and Family Proceedings Act 1984, couples no longer have to be married for three years before they can divorce. This has given further impetus for an increasing divorce rate.

2 *Demographic changes.* We commonly exaggerate the stability of marriage in the past, when the early death of a spouse ended as many marriages after a few years as divorce does now. When people lived less long, marriages were of shorter duration.

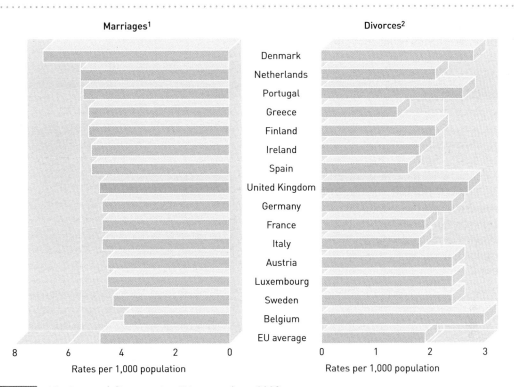

Marriages¹      Divorces²

Denmark
Netherlands
Portugal
Greece
Finland
Ireland
Spain
United Kingdom
Germany
France
Italy
Austria
Luxembourg
Sweden
Belgium
EU average

8   6   4   2   0     0   1   2   3

Rates per 1,000 population     Rates per 1,000 population

**Figure 18.3**    Marriage and divorce rates: EU comparison, 2002

¹ 2001 data for Spain.

² 2001 data for Ireland, Spain, Germany, France, Italy and EU average.

*Source*: Adapted from *Social Trends* (2002: 32); Office for National Statistics; Eurostat.

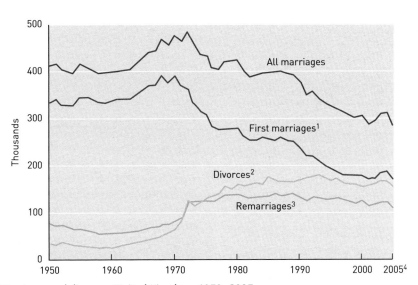

**Figure 18.4**    Marriages and divorces, United Kingdom, 1950–2005

¹ For both partners.

² Includes annulments. Data for 1950–1970 for Great Britain only. Divorce was permitted in Northern Ireland from 1969.

³ For one or both partners.

⁴ Data for 2005 are provisional. Final figures are likely to be higher.

*Source*: *Social Trends* (2007: Fig. 2.9), Office for National Statistics, General Register Office for Scotland, Northern Ireland Statistics and Research Agency.

These days, without divorce most people's marriages could last some 50 years or more – given current life expectancy and marriage rates.

3 *Individualisation is increasing.* Beck and Beck-Gernsheim (1995) see the rise of a modern society where both men and women expect choice and control over their lives, as well as equality. The times are a changing, and we have become more individualistic, seemingly more concerned with personal happiness and success than with the well-being of families and children. Life has become a 'planning project' for many in the West and there are no longer clear guidelines as to who should do what in a family. This makes for more tension and potential conflict as men and women become more individualised, less certain about their roles and more prone to breaking up (Beck-Gernsheim, 2002).

4 *Romantic love often subsides.* Modern cultures emphasise romantic love as a basis for marriage, rendering relationships vulnerable to collapse as sexual passion subsides. There is now widespread support for the notion that one may end a marriage in favour of a new relationship simply to renew excitement and romance.

5 *Women are now less dependent on men and have changed expectations.* Their increasing participation in the labour force has reduced wives' financial dependence on husbands. In addition, women have largely come to expect more from life than being the 'home maker' alone. They are more likely to demand equality from husbands, who may not have recognised the changing role of women. Changing expectations from women, then, may make it easier for them to walk away from unhappy marriages.

6 *Many of today's marriages are stressful.* With both partners working outside the home in most cases, jobs consume time and energy. In the past, wives looked after children, but now (and given the difficulty of securing good, affordable childcare) raising children can be more difficult. Tensions may be increasing between men and women, as women come to demand and expect more. While children do stabilise some marriages, divorce is most common during the early years of marriage when many couples have young children.

7 *Divorce is more socially acceptable.* Divorce no longer carries the powerful, negative stigma it did a century ago. Couples considering divorce typically do not receive the discouragement from family and friends they once did.

## Who divorces?

There is considerable discussion of the factors that put marriages at risk. They are varied but include:

• *Age*: at greatest risk of divorce are young spouses, especially those who marry after a brief courtship and have few financial resources.

• *Class*: those in the highest social class are least likely to divorce and those in the lowest social class are most at risk.

• *Gender*: women who have successful careers are more prone to divorce, partly due to the strains that arise in two-career marriages but, more important, because financially independent women are less inclined to remain in an unhappy marriage.

• *Prior marriage*: men and women who divorce once are more likely to divorce again, presumably because problems follow them from one marriage to another.

Finally, couples who have known their partners for short periods of time before marriage, those who marry in response to an unexpected pregnancy, and people who are not religious divorce more readily than other couples (Coleman and Salt, 1992).

## The experience of divorce

A series of recent studies in the UK have looked at divorce and step-parenting and have persistently found that the decisions taken in these areas are not taken lightly and bring with them major moral concerns. Thus, for instance, the research of Carol Smart and Bren Neal (1999) examines relationships of parenting that are negotiated and renegotiated following a divorce, and are especially concerned with the influence this has on the children. Through their work a complex set of 'post-divorce' relationships, processes, phases and 'practices' come into view. They sense how new roles start to appear: solo parenting, co-parenting, custodial parenting. They find how a complex flow between parenting roles and those of 'others' (grandparents, step-siblings, etc.) surrounds it. And they show new possibilities of 'step-grandparents' emerging. Firmly against the moral traditionalist position – for example, of Patricia Morgan (1995), who is cited as saying that the divorce law 'allies' itself with the spouses who want to break up marriages, and in doing so, rewards selfishness, egoism and destructiveness over altruistic commitment – their focus is much more on the daily moral struggles which are encountered through divorce.

# Muslim families in Niger

Families in Muslim Africa look and feel very different from Western families. To start with, Niger is one of the world's poorest (and hottest) countries in the world, ranking near last on the United Nations Human Development Index. It is a landlocked, sub-Saharan nation, situated on a vast, arid state on the edge of the Sahara desert, and has been under military rule for much of its post-independence history. It has one of the lowest literacy rates in the world, its health system is basic and disease is widespread. A history of colonisation and slavery still shows in its culture: a controversial study suggested

that more than 800,000 people are enslaved (almost 8 per cent of the population). The major groups (90 per cent) share many Muslim beliefs and practices, though there are divides. Niger also has the world's highest infant mortality rate. At the same time, it also has the highest fertility rate in the world (7.2 births per woman). This means that nearly half (49 per cent) of the population is under age 15.

Most typically, in the rural areas, families are composed of a married father and his sons with their wives in a large extended household that is organised around traditional farming labour. Polygamy is authorised by Islam: men can have up to four wives, and more than one-third of married women in Niger are in

## COUNTRY FACT FILE

THE REPUBLIC OF NIGER

| | |
|---|---|
| Population | 15.3 million (UN, 2009) |
| Capital | Niamey |
| Area | 1.27 million square kilometres (489,000 square miles) |
| Major languages | French (official), Arabic, Hausa, Songhai |
| Major religions | Islam, indigenous beliefs |
| Life expectancy | 50 years (men), 52 years (women) (UN) |
| GDP | $700 (2009 est.) |
| Human development index | 182nd (lowest in list) |

**Families around the world: Muslim**
Muslim families at dinner, South Africa.
*Source*: © David Turnley/Corbis.

polygamous unions. Nevertheless many men do not have the economic means to practise this. Although the minimum legal age of marriage is 15, many marry below this age. Marriages are often arranged by the parents in both rural and urban communities. Girls are frequently married off by the age of 12, with half of all girls in Niger married and pregnant by the age of 16, according to a UN report. There is a 76 per cent incidence of child marriage and it is rare to marry someone of whom parents disapprove. Much of this process might be seen by a Western observer as coercive or forced marriage. In addition,

many groups practice patrilineal Islamic-influenced inheritance. There are also bilateral inheritance practices and much informal pre-inherited property in the form of gifts.

The position of women is poor. The Nigerian family code is very unfavourable to women. Female genital mutilation is a common practice, but in decline. There are high levels of obstetric fistula, due to inadequate medical care compounded by the fact that the average age for first pregnancies is 14 years old. There is widespread and often unrecognised domestic violence, marital rape, forced marriage and trafficking in women and children.

Niger is in a process of change but stereotyped and traditional practices persist. A law has been proposed to change the legal marrying age to 18, but has yet to be adopted

See: www.unicef.org/wcaro/ WCARO_Niger_Factsheet-11.pdf; www.forwarduk.org.uk/key-issues/ child-marriage; www.antislavery.org/ includes/documents/cm_docs/2009/f/ full_english_slavery_in_niger.pdf.

 Throughout this chapter, look at the case studies of different families. Research for more data on the internet. The families we briefly introduce come from:

1   China and Japan (introduction)
2   Sweden (p. 626)
3   UK (p. 637)
4   Niger (p. 645)
5   Mexico (p. 650)

Likewise, Jane Ribbens McCarthy and others, in their studies of step-parenting (McCarthy et al., 2000), find an overwhelming sense that 'adults must take responsibility for children in their care, and therefore must seek the needs of the children first'. 'This,' they say, 'is such a strong moral imperative that it seems to have been impossible for anyone to disagree with it in the accounts we have heard' (McCarthy et al., 2000: 16). What we see here, then, is that divorce and step-parenting may lead to a heightened sense of moral decision-making in families. It may be a long process of negotiation, but there are elements of sharedness.

Some writers are starting to suggest that what we are seeing here in families is the emergence of a postmodern morality which is not to be handed down from on high by moralists, but which is instead the very stuff of many people's everyday lives. Children may well now be exposed to a more complex set of relations from an earlier time than perhaps they were in the past. But none of this necessarily means they are open to neglect and indifference.

## Custody residence and parenting

More than half of all divorcing couples must resolve the issue of child custody. Society's conventional practice is still to award custody of children to mothers, based on the notion that women are better parents than men. A recent trend, however, is towards joint custody, whereby children divide their time between the new homes of their two parents. Joint custody is difficult if divorced parents live far apart or do not get along, but it has the advantage of keeping children in regular contact with both parents.

Because mothers usually gain custody of children but fathers typically earn more income, the well-being of children often depends on fathers making court-ordered child-support payments.

## Financial support

In 1991 the UK's Conservative government of the day set up the Child Support Agency (CSA), which aimed to make absent parents (mainly fathers) contribute to their children's upbringing. An agency was set up to administer it and collect money from absent fathers, focusing especially in the first instance on low-income fathers who were easier to locate (through social security offices). It led to considerable controversy and a campaign against the CSA (APART, Absent Parents Asking for Reasonable Treatment). Partly, this was because it did not take into account the obligations a parent may have to a second family, but in addition, it was retrospective, overturning earlier court agreements. Further, if the parent with the child was already on income support, everything collected was recouped by the Benefits Agency.

Controversies still continue, and you can catch up with current controversies by looking at the Child Support Agency website at www.csa.gov.uk.

## Remarriage

Despite the rising divorce rate, marriage – and remarriage – remain as popular as ever. In the UK over one-third of all marriages each year are second marriages. Most people remarry within three to five years. Men, who derive greater benefits from wedlock, are more likely to remarry than women are.

Remarriage often creates *blended families*, composed of children and some combination of biological parents and step-parents. Members of blended families thus have to define precisely who is part of the child's nuclear family (Furstenberg, 1984). Blended families also require children to reorientate themselves; an only child, for example, may suddenly find she has two older brothers. And, as already noted, the risk of divorce is high for partners in such families. But blended families also offer both young and old the opportunity to relax rigid family roles.

## Lone-parent families

Lone-parent households with dependent children more than doubled from 3 per cent of households in 1971 to 7 per cent of households in 2006. As Table 18.2 shows, the number of people in lone-parent households shifted from 4 per cent in 1971 to 12 per cent in 2006. And the proportion of children living in such families more than tripled between 1972 and 2006 to 24 per cent. By any standards, this is a significant growth. Lone-parent families, over 90 per cent of which are headed by a single mother, may result from divorce, separation, death or the choice of an unmarried woman to have a child. Until the mid-1980s, most of the increase was due to divorce, but since then, the proportion of divorced mothers has remained stable, while that of single never-married mothers has doubled. Across Europe the percentage of births outside marriage has been rising significantly. The rate is highest in the Scandinavian countries and lowest in Greece. In the UK it is around 32 per cent, compared with 8 per cent in 1971.

Entering the labour force has bolstered women's financial capacity to be single mothers. But lone

**Figure 18.5**   Lone-parent families by marital status in the UK, 1971–98

*Source*: Adapted from www.statistics.gov.uk, Office for National Statistics.

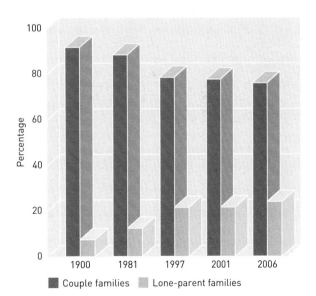

**Figure 18.6**   The shift in household structure, Great Britain, 1972–2006

*Source*: *Social Trends* 37 (2007), Office for National Statistics, www.statistics.co.uk.

parenthood – especially when the parent is a woman – greatly increases the risks of poverty, as it can limit the woman's ability to work and to further her education. Many women in Europe now become pregnant as

**Great Britain**
Percentages

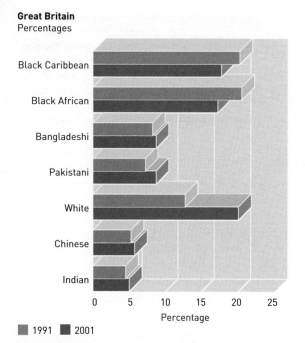

1991    2001

| Figure 18.7 | Ethnic group and lone-parent households, Great Britain, 1991 and 2001 |

*Source:* Census 2001, Office for National Statistics; Census 2001, General Register Office for Scotland, *Social Trends* (2007: Fig. 2.6).

unmarried teenagers, and many decide to raise their children on their own. These young women with children – especially if they have the additional disadvantage of being minorities – form the core of the rising problem of child poverty in Europe.

Some research suggests that growing up in a lone-parent family can disadvantage children. The most serious problem among families with one parent – especially if that parent is a woman – is poverty. On average, children growing up in a lone-parent family start out with disadvantages and end up with lesser educational achievement and lower incomes, and have a greater chance of forming lone-parent families themselves.

## Cohabitation

**Cohabitation** is *the sharing of a household by an unmarried couple.* A generation ago, widespread use of terms like 'living in sin' and 'premarital sex' indicated disapproval of both cohabitation and sex outside marriage. But all this has changed. Attitude surveys find a generational difference, with older people often disapproving of cohabitation, but younger people overwhelmingly in favour of it (*Social Trends*, 2003: 33). Between 1986 and 2005, the proportion of non-married men and women aged under 60 who were cohabiting in Great Britain doubled (from 11 per cent to 24 per cent for men; 13 per cent to 24 per cent for women) (*Social Trends*, 2007: 19). Divorced women and younger women in their twenties were the most likely to cohabit. Cohabitation rarely lasts more than two years, and frequently leads to marriage. In a sense, it has become the new form of 'engagement'.

Cohabitation is common in Europe as a whole. It is most pronounced in Sweden and other Scandinavian societies as a long-term form of family life, with or without children. By contrast, this family form is much rarer in more traditional (and Roman Catholic) nations such as Italy.

## Step-parenting

In 1991 there were around half a million step-families and around 1 million children (step-children and natural children) living in such families in the UK. There were three times as many step-fathers as step-mothers, as children are more likely to stay with their natural mothers (*Social Trends*, 1997: 44). Step-families are growing fast: in 2000, there were some 2.5 million children in step-families, accounting for about 6 per cent of all families in the UK.

## Gay and lesbian couples: 'families of choice', registered partnerships and marriage

Since the 1980s there has been increasing interest in gay and lesbian marriages and partnerships. Kath Weston suggests that these are 'families of choice' as opposed to the more conventional 'families of blood' (Weston, 1991). In 1989, Denmark became the first country to formally recognise homosexual marriages, thereby extending some social legitimacy to gay and lesbian couples as well as conferring legal advantages for inheritance, taxation and joint property ownership. A registered partnership gives two people of the same sex the equivalent rights to heterosexual marriages, except for the rights of adoption or a church marriage.

Versions of registered partnerships are becoming increasingly common throughout many countries

Four same-sex couples celebrate after getting married at the town hall in Mexico City March 11, 2010. The first same-sex couples tied the knot in Mexico City on Thursday under the first law in Latin America to broadly legalize gay marriage. The new law goes beyond previous legislation allowing same-sex couples the same marriage rights as straight couples

*Source*: © Mario Guzman/epa/Corbis.

of the world. The Nordic cultures were first and most prominent: all have registered marriages or partnerships, Denmark in 1989, Norway in 1993, Sweden in 1995, Iceland and Finland in 1996. Most other European countries have followed. In the UK, the Civil Partnership Act 2004 came into effect in December 2005 and in the first nine months, some 15,700 partnerships were formed. In other countries, such as South Africa, Mexico and a few states of the United States (Vermont, Connecticut and Hawaii) laws are being enacted. The pace of change has been significant worldwide, and the trend in public opinion is towards greater support.

Most gay and lesbian couples in households including children raise the offspring of previous heterosexual unions and some couples have adopted children. But many gay parents are quiet about their sexuality, not wishing to draw unwelcome attention to their children. In several widely publicised cases in recent years, courts have removed children from homosexual couples, claiming to represent the best interests of the children (Weeks et al., 2001).

In the United States, while gay people cannot legally marry (although they can adopt children), some cities (including San Francisco and New York) allow 'registered partnerships' that confer some of the legal benefits of marriage. However, it has been estimated that in the United States there are as many as 1 million gay and lesbian couples who are now raising one or more children (Kimmel, 2003).

While this pattern challenges many traditional notions about families in Europe, it also indicates that many gay and lesbian couples perceive the same rewards in child-rearing that 'straight' couples do. There is an irony in all this. As gays and lesbians establish the legal basis for 'marriage' around the world, more and more heterosexuals are running away from it as marriage becomes less popular and divorce increases.

## Singlehood

Living alone is becoming more common in Europe. In 2005, the number of people living alone in Great Britain had more than doubled since 1971, from 3 million to 7 million (*Social Trends*, 2007: 13). Elderly widows have always represented a large share of single people. But a new group of men aged between 25 and 44 have become the second biggest group to live alone: the numbers doubled between 1986 and 2005: 7 per cent to 15 per cent. And it is projected that this group will continue to rise. In the United States, though, the story is somewhat different. Here it is younger women who are staying single. In 1960, 28 per cent of US women aged 20–24 were single; by 2003, the proportion had soared to 74 per cent. Underlying this trend is women's greater participation in the labour force: women who are economically secure view a husband as a matter of choice rather than a financial necessity.

GLOBAL FAMILIES:

# The globalisation and glocalisation of Mexican families

For some time the Mexican family has been seen as a distinctive subject of study by social researchers. Their studies have pointed, for instance, to the centrality of the value of family unity as the unquestionable source of individual and social stability to the historical organisation of family life in Mexico. They have also highlighted cultural tendencies towards strict patriarchal divisions within families: for instance, with regard to fathers' authority over their wives and children, and strict role divisions between men's participation in public life and paid labour and women's confinement to housework, childcare and a largely domestic life. More recently, research has highlighted trends towards more egalitarian forms of family life based on the intimate involvement of spouses and children rather than fixed gendered hierarchies. These trends have been related to factors such as women's massive incorporation into paid labour in the context of the expansion of the modern urban service sector since the 1950s, economic crises requiring both spouses to work to provide for their families, and the advent of easy-to-use contraceptive methods and family planning campaigns reducing women's fertility rates and detaching sexuality from reproduction.

## Diversity and glocalisation

Yet, in spite of these distinctive patterns, 'the Mexican family' in

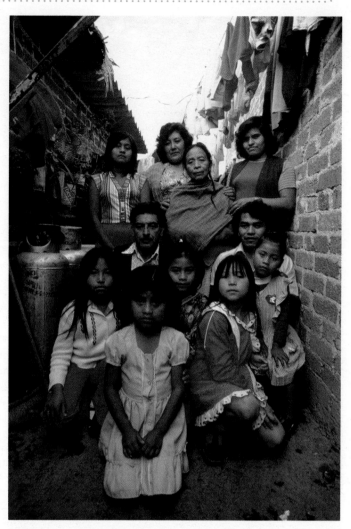

**Families around the world: Mexican**
A family of eleven people poses outside shanty town mexico.
*Source*: © Barry Lewis/Alamy.

a sense does not exist. There is a need to acknowledge the diversity of family relationships that exist in contemporary Mexico (see, again, the opening quote to this chapter from Diana Gittins). In Western popular culture and media, intimate relationships among Mexicans are often portrayed as being shaped by the cultural dynamics of 'machismo'. The concept of machismo refers to extreme forms of masculinity characterised by, among other things, very assertive and

sometimes aggressive behaviour and men's imposition of their authority over their female partners and other female family members. Related to this notion is the image of Mexican families as characterised by clear gendered divisions of power and tasks between a male household head and 'breadwinner' and his submissive wife, limited in her life to housework and childcare.

This imagery has recently been criticised as stereotypical misrepresentation of the empirical diversity of family

GLOBAL FAMILIES

life among Mexicans. The US anthropologist Matthew Gutmann (1996), for example, points to the complex dynamics of family interactions among the residents of a working-class neighbourhood in Mexico City. His findings provide limited empirical evidence of the men's hyper-masculine behaviour in line with notions of machismo. Rather, they point to a variety of understandings and experiences of masculinity, involving fathers actively participating in childcare and loving husbands helping their wives with housework as much as instances of domestic abuse and clear gendered divisions of power and tasks within families. Similarly, the work of the sociologist Gloria González-López (2005) suggests that family relationships among Mexicans are characterised by considerable regional variations in terms of factors such as social class, locally specific political and economic dynamics, culture, and social differences between urban and rural settings. In view of this research, it seems indicated to think about a variety of locally specific 'Mexican families' rather than 'the Mexican family', unchanging and socioculturally homogeneous.

## Global trends and globalisation

Beyond this localised diversity, it is important also to see the ways in which Mexican families participate in processes of social change on a potentially global scale. For instance, in her research on US–Mexican migrant families, Jennifer Hirsch (2003) concludes that factors such as declining fertility levels, women's increasing access to education, and the propagation of egalitarian, individualistic sexual ideals and information about sexuality by the mass media, all contribute to the increasing cultural significance of the mentioned cultural ideal of love-based companionate relationships and family life. It has been concluded (Hirsch and Wardlow, 2006) that such developments reflect a global trend away from traditional patriarchal family life towards alternative modern forms of intimacy. In spite of their distinctiveness, Mexican families thus seem to some extent to be shaped by social forces that are not particular to Mexican society.

Mexican families are both global and local – they participate in social processes that reshape families around the globe in often very similar ways (global), but at the same time they are shaped in a distinctive way by historical forces particular to Mexican society at large, such as the mentioned value of family unity (global and local), and a variety of regionally specific social, economic and political conditions (local).

### Look at

González-López, G. (2005) *Erotic Journeys: Mexican Immigrants and Their Sex Lives*.

Gutmann, M. (1996) *The Meanings of Macho: Being a Man in Mexico City*.

Hirsch, J. (2003) *A Courtship After Marriage: Sexuality and Love in Mexican Transnational Families*.

Hirsch, J. and Wardlow, H. (eds) (2006) *Modern Loves: The Anthropology of Romantic Courtship and Companionate Marriage*.

For a wider look, see also:
Jaipul L. Roopnarine and Uwe P. Gielen (2005) *Families in Global Perspective*.

Prepared for this book by Daniel Nehring.

# Looking ahead: families in the twenty-first century

In recent decades, transformation in family life throughout much of the world has generated controversy, with advocates of 'traditional family values' locked in debate with supporters of new family forms and greater personal choice. Whatever position one takes on the merits of current family trends, change is certain to continue into the coming century. Based on current evidence, we can make five predictions about the future of family life.

First, divorce rates are likely to remain high, even in the face of evidence that divorce can harm children. There may be some erosion of support for easy dissolution of marriage, yet several generations of high divorce rates have seriously weakened the idea that marriage is a lifetime commitment. Looking back through history, marital relationships are about as durable today as they were a century ago, when many marriages were cut short by death (Kain, 1990). But more couples now *choose* to end marriages that fail to live up to their expectations. Therefore, although the divorce rate has stabilised recently, it is unlikely that marriage will regain the durability characteristic of the 1950s. One major reason is that increasing numbers of

A family poses for a very formal portrait on a garden bench, c. 1890

*Source*: © DaZo Vintage Stock Photos/Images.com/Corbis.

women are able to support themselves, and traditional marriages appeal to fewer of them. Men, as well, are seeking more satisfying relationships. Perhaps we should view the recent trend towards higher divorce rates less as a threat to families than as a sign of change in family form. After all, most divorces still lead to remarriage, casting doubt on the notion that marriage itself is becoming obsolete. It is possible, too, that this trend may spread throughout parts of the non-Western world.

Secondly, family life in the twenty-first century will be highly variable. It may become increasingly 'postmodern'. We have noted an increasing number of cohabiting couples, lone-parent families, gay and lesbian families and blended families. Most families may still be based on marriage and most married couples still have children. But, taken together, the variety of family forms observed today represents a new conception of family life as a matter of choice.

Thirdly, men are likely to play changing roles in child-rearing. For much of the nineteenth and early twentieth centuries, men played limited roles in the raising of children. In the 1950s, a decade many people nostalgically recall as the 'golden age' of families, men began to withdraw from active parenting (Snell, 1990; Stacey, 1990). Since then, the share of children growing up in homes without their fathers has passed 25 per cent and is continuing to rise. A countertrend is emerging as some fathers – older, on average, and more established in their careers – eagerly jump into parenting. There has also been the rise of the 'new man', highly involved in child-rearing. But, on balance, the high UK divorce rate and a surge in single motherhood point to more children growing up with weaker ties to fathers than ever before.

Fourthly, economic changes will continue to reform marriage and the family. In many families, both household partners must work to ensure the family's financial security. As Arlie Hochschild (1989) points out, the economy is responsible for most of the change in society, but people *feel* these changes in the family. Marriage today is often the interaction of weary men and women: adults try their best to attend to children, yet often this can become minimal parenting. There are signs, however, that parents are giving increasing attention to their children in the UK.

Finally, the importance of new reproductive technologies will increase. While ethical concerns will surely slow these developments, new methods of reproduction will continue to alter the traditional meanings of parenthood.

# SUMMARY

**1** All societies are built on kinship, although family forms vary considerably across cultures and over time.

**2** In industrial societies such as Europe, marriage is monogamous. Many pre-industrial societies, however, permit polygamy, of which there are two types: polygyny and polyandry.

**3** In global perspective, patrilocality is most common, while industrial societies favour neolocality and a few societies have matrilocal residence. Industrial societies embrace bilateral descent; pre-industrial societies tend to be either patrilineal or matrilineal.

**4** Families in the past were varied, and indeed varied in the same historical period. There is no such thing as one family form.

**5** Functionalist analysis identifies major family functions: socialising the young, regulating sexual activity, transmitting social placement and providing material and emotional support.

**6** Conflict theories explore how the family perpetuates social inequality by strengthening divisions based on class, ethnicity, race and gender.

**7** Micro-level analysis highlights the variable nature of family life both over time and as experienced by individual family members.

**8** Families differ according to class position, race and ethnicity.

**9** Gender affects family dynamics, since husbands play a dominant role in the vast majority of families. Research suggests that marriage provides more benefits to men than to women.

**10** Today's divorce rate is much higher than a century ago; four in ten current marriages will end in divorce. Most people who divorce – especially men – remarry, often forming blended families that include children from previous marriages.

**11** Family violence, victimising both women and children, is far more common than official records indicate. Adults who abuse family members most often suffered abuse themselves as children.

**12** Society's family life is becoming more varied. Lone-parent families, cohabitation, gay and lesbian couples and singlehood have proliferated in recent years across the world.

**13** Although ethically controversial, new reproductive technology is altering conventional notions of parenthood.

CONNECT UP: Turn to Part 6 of this book for key resources and link up
with the book's website, which links to these resources
SEE: www.pearsoned.co.uk/plummer

## MYTASKLIST

# Ten suggestions for going further

## 1 Connect up with Part Six and the Sociology Web Resources

As you work through ideas and think about the issues raised in this chapter, look at the accompanying website and the resource centre at the end of this book which connects to it. There is a lot here to help you move on. To link up, see: www.pearson.co.uk/plummer.

## 2 Review the chapter

*Briefly summarise (in a paragraph) just what this chapter has been about.* Consider: (a) What have you learned? (b) What do you disagree with? Be critical. And (c) How would you develop all this? How could you get more detail on matters that interest you?

## 3 Pose questions

(a)  How has the emerging post-industrial economy affected family life? What other factors are changing the family?

(b)  Why do some analysts describe the family as the 'backbone of society'? How do families perpetuate social inequality?

(c)  Do you think that lone-parent households do as good a job as two-parent households in raising children? Why or why not?

(d)  On balance, are families in Europe becoming 'postmodern'? What evidence supports your contention? When you take the world picture of families, would you also find evidence of major family changes?

(e)  What do you understand by David Morgan's idea of 'family practices'? Keep a diary on your own 'family practices' for a week.

## 4 Explore key words

Many concepts have been introduced in this chapter. You can review them from the website or from the listing at the back of this book. You might like to give special attention to just five words and think them through – how would you define them, what are they dealing with, and do they help you see the social world more clearly or not?

## 5 Search the Web

Be critical when you look at websites – see the box on p. 940 in the Resources section. For this chapter look at the following:

United Nations family development
www.un.org/esa/socdev/family

Introduction to the Focal Point on the Family within the United Nations Secretariat.

Single parents
http://singleparents.about.com
A US website which contains streams of information for single parents.

Gay and lesbian couples
http://buddybuddy.com/partners.html
World details and ongoing debates about gay and lesbian marriages.

Some 'family' research centres in the UK include:

Morgan Centre for the study of relationships and personal life (Manchester)
www.socialsciences.manchester.ac.uk/morgancentre

Families and Social Capital (Southbank)
www1.lsbu.ac.uk/families

Centre for Family Research (Cambridge)
www.ppsis.cam.ac.uk/CFR

Families, Life Course and Generations (FLaG) Research Centre (Leeds)
www.sociology.leeds.ac.uk/flag/about

# 6 Watch a DVD

- Martin Scorsese's *Alice Doesn't Live Here Anymore* (1974) was one of the first 'single mum' films which, for its time, raised a lot of issues. But it now seems a bit old-fashioned.
- There are many Hollywood treatments of classic issues, though they usually deserve very critical viewing. They include Robert Benton's Oscar-winning *Kramer vs Kramer* (1979) on divorce, Robert Redford's *Ordinary People* (1980) on neurotic mothers, and John Lithgow's *Terms of Endearment* (1983) on the importance of family bonds. They make an interesting comparison with films made nearly two decades later, such as Ang Lee's *The Ice Storm* (1997).
- In contrast with many Hollywood films, the films of Mike Leigh in the UK depict family life in tragi-comic tones: see his *Secrets and Lies* (1996), *Life is Sweet* (1990) and *Bleak Moments* (1971).
- See also: Lisa Cholodenko's *The Kids Are Alright* (2010) and Robert Benton's *The Human Stain* (2003).

# 7 Think and read

Jaipaul L. Roopnarine and Uwe Gielen (eds), *Families in Global Perspectives* (2005). Provides case studies of the family in Africa, Asia, the Middle East, Europe and the Americas.

David Cheal, *Families in Today's World: A Comparative Approach* (2008). Provides an introduction.

Carol Smart, *Personal Life, Relationships and Families: New Directions in Sociological Thinking* (2007). Striking new study which rethinks ideas on the ways we live together.

Goran Therborn, *Between Sex and Power: Family in the World* (2004). Major new study which traces the history and patterns of family across the world in the twentieth century.

Graham Allan and Graham Crow, *Families, Households and Society* (2001). Reviews current issues and debates, mainly in the UK.

Judith Stacey, *Unhitched: Love, Marriage and Family Values from Western Hollywood to Western China* (2011). Worldwide empirical research to challenge thinking on one major form.

David Morgan, *Family Connections: An Introduction to Family Studies* (1996). The key book for studying the family as a series of family practices.

Lynn Jamieson, *Intimacy: Personal Relationships in Modern Societies* (1998). Helps establish this as a major new area of enquiry.

Anthony Giddens, *The Transformation of Intimacy* (1992). Written in an accessible way, this book examines the major changes between men and women.

Jeffrey Weeks, Brian Heaphy and Catherine Donovan, *Same Sex Intimacies: Families of Choice and Other Life Experiments* (2001). Provides original UK data on these 'experiments in living'.

Lynne Harne and Jill Radford, *Tackling Domestic Violence* (2008). Recent guide to the issues.

# 8 Relax with a novel

There are many wonderful novels to read about the personal life. Here is a sample of old classics and new ones:

Jane Austen, *Pride and Prejudice* (1813).
Leo Tolstoy, *Anna Karenina* (1877).
Virginia Wolf, *To the Lighthouse* (1927).
Vladimir Nabokov, *Lolita* (1955).
Laurie Lee, *Cider with Rosie* (1959).
Alan Bennett, *Talking Heads* (1988).
Annie Proulx, *The Shipping News* (1993).
Zoe Heller, *Notes on a Scandal* (2003).
Lionel Shriver, *We Need to Talk about Kevin* (2003).

# 9 Connect to other chapters

- An important development – the new reproductive technologies – is discussed in Chapter 23.
- See Chapter 12 for linked discussions of both sexual violence and homosexuality.

# 10 Engaging with THE BIG DEBATE

## What is the future of the family? The family values debate

Are 'traditional families' vital to our way of life? Or are they a barrier to progress? To begin, people typically use the term 'traditional family' to mean a married couple who, at some point in their lives, raise children. But the term is more than simply descriptive – it is also a moral and political statement. That is, support for the traditional family implies that people place a high value on getting and staying married, that parents should place more importance on raising children than on pursuing their own careers, and that society should accord special respect to two-parent families rather than various 'alternative lifestyles'.

*On one side* of the debate, Patricia Morgan, from a conservative view, and Norman Dennis and George Erdos from an ethical socialist view, argue that there has been a serious erosion of the traditional family since 1960. And it is not hard to see that there have indeed been changes from the figures in the *Global families* box on p. 637. There are fewer marriages, fewer children, more divorce, more singlehood, more single parents. Indeed, the number of children born out of wedlock has grown 'from one in ten in the late 1970s to over three in ten in the early 1990s' (Morgan, 1995: 4). And, because of both divorce and increasing numbers of children born out of wedlock, the share of youngsters living with a single parent at some time before age 18 has quadrupled since 1960 to half of all children. Combining the last two facts, just one in four of today's children will grow up with two parents and go on to maintain a stable marriage of their own.

In the light of such data, serious consequences follow. These include the rise of delinquency, the growth of incivility, the huge welfare burden. The family is not just changing, it is heading towards total collapse, and it does not look good for the future of society.

Patricia Morgan suggests that the traditional family of man–wife–children is being replaced by the mother–child state. She deplores the rise of lone-parent families, especially children born out of wedlock, and is very concerned about the growth of 'welfare dependency' for many of these poor lone-parent families. Norman Dennis, with similar arguments, is most concerned with

the ways in which a new family without fatherhood has been created. It is this lack of a father to be an adequate role model for children which has created many problems. In sum, and drawing from research, he suggests that 'on average the life-long socially certified monogamous family of the pre-1960s pattern was better for children than any one of a variety of alternatives' (Dennis and Erdos, 1993: 34).

The same debate is found in the United States. There David Popenoe (1993) describes this breakdown as a fundamental shift from a 'culture of marriage' to a 'culture of divorce'. Traditional vows of marital commitment – 'till death us do part' – now amount to little more than 'as long as I am happy'. The negative consequences of the cultural trend towards weaker families, Popenoe continues, are obvious everywhere: as we pay less and less attention to children, the crime rate goes up along with a host of other problematic behaviours, including smoking, drinking and premarital sex.

As Popenoe sees it, then, we must work hard and quickly to reverse current trends. Government cannot be the solution (and may even be part of the problem): since 1960, as US government spending on social programmes has soared fivefold, the traditional family has grown weaker and weaker. The alternative, Popenoe reasons, is a cultural turnaround by which people will question and ultimately reject the recently popular 'me-first' view of our lives in favour of greater commitment to a spouse and children. (We have seen such a turnaround in the case of cigarette smoking.) Popenoe concludes that we should save the traditional family, and that means we need to affirm publicly the value of marital permanence as well as endorse the two-parent family as best for the well-being of children.

On the other side of the debate, many sociologists argue that the recent changes in the family have mainly been for the good. They are really simply reflections of changes in the wider social world. As people's desire for choice, individuality, freedom, etc. has grown, so has their desire for more control over their personal life. The traditional families desired by the traditionalists are described in too romantic and nostalgic terms. Families of the past often meant that wives were stuck with violent husbands and large families of children lived in abject poverty. Equality was minimal, as was choice.

Instead of returning to a mythical past, a goal now is to achieve democracy in the personal sphere. Equality and choice become key features of modern families. In any event, it is no longer possible to have only one ideal family form – even if we should want it. The world has grown too complex. As Beck and Beck-Gernsheim argue in *The Normal Chaos of Love* (1995), society has become individualised and with that 'It is no longer possible to pronounce in some binding way what family, marriage, parenthood, sexuality or love mean, what they should be or could be; rather they vary in substance, exceptions, norms and morality from individual to individual and from relationships to relationships' (Beck and Beck-Gernsheim, 1995: 5). The traditionalists are looking back to a world that has now gone, and cannot be returned to. They do not paint a rosy picture. They recognise that we are in a transition period, one in which there is likely to be 'a long and bitter battle – a war between men and women' (1995: 5).

Most of our current institutions were designed at a time when there was a sharp division between women in the home and men at work. Now this is changing: work situations, laws, town planning, school curricula all have to be changed.

For Judith Stacey, the traditional family is more problem than solution. Striking to the heart of the matter, Stacey writes (1990: 269): 'The family is not here to stay. Nor should we wish it were. On the contrary, I believe that all democratic people, whatever their kinship preferences, should work to hasten its demise.' The main reason for rejecting the traditional family, Stacey explains, is that it perpetuates and enhances various kinds of social inequality. Families play a key role in maintaining the class hierarchy, transferring wealth as well as 'cultural capital' from one generation to another. Moreover, feminists charge that the traditional family is built on patriarchy, which subjects women to their husbands' authority as well as saddling them with most of the responsibility for housework and childcare. And from a gay-rights perspective, she adds, a society that values traditional families inevitably denies

homosexual men and women equal dignity and participation in social life.

Stacey thus applauds the breakdown of the family as a measure of social progress. Indeed, she views the family not as a basic social institution but as a political construction that serves to elevate one category of people, which she identifies as affluent white males, at the expense of women, homosexuals and poor people who lack the resources to maintain middle-class respectability.

Moreover, Stacey continues, the concept of 'traditional family' is increasingly irrelevant to a diverse society in which people reject singular models of correct behaviour and in which both men and women must work for income. What society needs, Stacey concludes, is not a return to some golden age of the family, but political and economic changes (including income parity for women, universal healthcare, programmes to reduce unemployment and expanded sex education in the schools) that will provide tangible support for children as well as ensure that people in diverse family forms receive the respect and dignity everyone deserves.

## Continue the debate

1  To strengthen families, Popenoe urges parents to put children ahead of their own careers by limiting their joint working week to 60 hours. Do you agree? Why or why not?
2  Judith Stacey urges greater choice and equality in relationships and this means more diverse families. Do you agree?
3  What policies or programmes would you support to enhance the well-being of children?
4  Can you mount a 'defence of single parents', looking at evidence for their 'successes' and 'failures'?

*Source*: Stacey (1990, 1993); Abbot and Wallace (1992); Dennis and Erdos (1993); Popenoe (1993); Beck and Beck-Gernsheim (1995); Council on Families in America (1995); Morgan (1995).

# CHAPTER 19

# RELIGION AND BELIEF

IN 1989 SIR AHMED SALMAN RUSHDIE published his controversial novel *The Satanic Verses* in Britain. One character in the book, the Prophet Mahound, appears as a figure of debauchery, foul language and obscenity. Sensing that this was a thinly disguised, blasphemous attack on Mohammed and the Islamic faith, British Muslims soon expressed their anger and requested a publisher's apology for misrepresenting the Islamic faith. Matters rapidly escalated: the book was ritually burned in Bolton and Bradford; the media accused the Muslims of intolerance; voices were raised against Rushdie in India and Pakistan. On Valentine's Day 1989, the Iranian leader Ayatollah Khomeini issued a *fatwa* – or official call for execution – against Rushdie. Although initially a British affair, *The Satanic Verses* scandal escalated into an international one, symbolising battles between religious institutions and secular cultures, and accompanied by a resurgence of anti-Islamic feeling in the West. Fearing for his life, Rushdie went into hiding, where he stayed for over ten years. Years later, in 2007, he was knighted in the UK. And controversy – though on a much smaller scale – flamed up all over again.

In March 1995, a small group of terrorists released a poisonous gas in Tokyo's underground system, killing 12 but blinding many more and causing complete pandemonium. But this was no ordinary act of terrorism. It was conducted by Aum Shinriyko, a religious sect that claimed 10,000 Japanese members and 20,000 in Russia. Its leader Shoko Asahara had actually created a stockpile of weapons

to kill around 10 million people.

In March 1997, Marshall Applewhite led 39 of his followers to commit suicide as part of the cult Heaven's Gate. Their dead bodies, laid out neatly in bunk beds, were found in Rancho Santa Fe, California. The cult was a distinctly modern group – they wore sneakers and were computer geeks – yet they looked for signs of religious meaning on their computers. They attached enormous significance to the Hale-Bopp comet as a sign that their time to go to heaven had arrived. And when it appeared, they were all led by their cult leader to drink a curious mix of vodka and barbiturates so that their 'earthly vessels' could rise to the heavens.

And on 11 September 2001, in by far the most devastating terrorist action up to that date, four civil airliners were hijacked by suicide bombers and targeted at major US buildings. Two demolished the Twin Towers of the World Trade Center in New York, the third destroyed part of the Pentagon in Washington, and the fourth crashed in Pennsylvania. These were rapidly identified with terrorist attacks, and especially with Osama bin Laden and his al Qaeda international terrorist network. Bin Laden is on record as saying that he is conducting a religious war – an Islamic *jihad* – against America.

It is often argued that religion is in decline in the modern world – in the face of rising rationality and science. And it is true that in many European countries, church going and even Christian beliefs are becoming less common. But, as the cases above well illustrate, in the contemporary world

religion may play as powerful a role as it always has. This chapter will examine the nature and role of religion in the twenty-first century world.

*See:* Salman Rusdie discussing his book and the death sentence on YouTube at: http://fora.tv/2007/05/20/Salman_Rushdie#fullprogram

*There is only one religion, though there are a hundred versions of it.*

George Bernard Shaw: *Plays Pleasant and Unpleasant* (1898), vol. 2 preface

*If God did not exist it would be necessary to invent him.*

Voltaire

---

## In this chapter, we ask:

- **What are the key features and forms of religion?**

- **How are religions organised and why do they exist?**

- **What is the variety of global religions?**

- **How is social change shaping contemporary religions? Is it in decline or not?**

---

(Left) *The Ascent of the Prophet Mohammed to Heaven* by Aqa Mirak, sixteenth-century Persian manuscript

*Source:* OR2265 Ascent of the Prophet Mohammed to Heaven, Mirak, Aqa (FL. c. 1520–76) British Library, London, UK, © British Library Board. All Rights Reserved/ The Bridgeman Art Library.

 Aqa Mirak was a sixteenth-century Persian painter. Think how religious art is shaped by both history and culture.

The twenty-first century world has put religion firmly back on the agenda of sociology as a major area for analysis. For much of the twentieth century, sociologists had argued that religion was in decline, that societies were becoming secularised. But it is now clear that across the globe religion is asserting itself in many ways, and many argue that it is becoming stronger. In this chapter we ask what religion is, explore the changing face of religious belief throughout history and around the world, and examine the place of religion in today's modern, scientific, rational world – as it becomes global, postmodern and digital.

## What is religion?

Throughout most of human history, human beings living in small societies attributed birth, death and even what happened in between to the operation of supernatural forces. Over the course of the last several hundred years, however, science (discussed in Chapter 23) has emerged as an alternative way of understanding the natural world, and scientific sociology offers various explanations of how and why societies operate the way they do.

Yet religion is a matter of **faith**, *belief anchored in conviction rather than scientific evidence*. For instance, the New Testament of the Bible defines faith as 'the assurance of things hoped for, the conviction of things not seen' (Hebrews 11: 1) and exhorts Christians to 'walk by faith, not by sight' (2 Corinthians 5: 7). Some people with strong faith may be disturbed by the thought of sociologists turning a scientific eye to what they hold as sacred. Since religions vary a great deal around the world, with no one thing sacred to everyone on earth, this raises in an acute form *the problem of relativity* and leads to the question: just how can billions of people across the world organise their lives with such profoundly different belief systems, each of which claims its own god or gods? Sociologists recognise that religion appears central to virtually every culture on earth, and they seek to understand just why such religious beliefs and practices assume such importance and what role they play. Because religion deals with ideas that transcend everyday experience, neither common sense nor any scientific discipline can verify or disprove religious doctrine.

## The sacred and the profane

Durkheim (whose ideas were introduced in Chapter 4) claimed that the focus of religion is 'things that surpass the limits of our knowledge' (1965: 62; orig. 1915). As human beings, Durkheim explained, we organise our surroundings by defining most objects, events or experiences as **profane** (from Latin, meaning 'outside the temple'), *that which is an ordinary element of everyday life*. But we set some things apart, Durkheim

Religion is founded on the idea of the sacred, that which is set apart as extraordinary and which demands our submission. Bowing, kneeling or prostrating oneself – each a common element of religious devotion – symbolises this submissiveness
*Source*: Raghu Rai/Magnum Photos.

continued, by designating them as **sacred**, *that which is extraordinary, inspiring a sense of awe, reverence, and even fear*. Distinguishing the sacred from the profane is the essence of all religious belief. **Religion**, then, is *a social institution involving beliefs and practices based upon a conception of the sacred*.

Around the world, matters of faith vary greatly, with no one thing sacred to everyone. Although people regard most books as profane, Jews view the Torah (the first five books of the Hebrew Bible or Old Testament) as sacred, in the same way that Christians revere the entire Bible and Muslims exalt the Qur'an (Koran).

However, a community of believers draws religious lines, Durkheim (1965; orig. 1915: 62) claimed. People understand profane things in terms of their everyday usefulness: we sit down at a computer or turn the key of a car to accomplish various tasks. What is sacred, however, we set apart from everyday life and regard with reverence.

All religions have models of life by which people can organise their activities. Usually these include a **cosmogony**, *a tale about how the world/universe was created*; a theodicy, a tale about how evil and suffering is to be found in the world; and a broad vision of the **ethical life** – *how people should behave*. In addition they are likely to have many rituals: meditations and mantras, worship, festivals, and regulations on hygiene, diet and sex. To make clear the boundary between the sacred and the profane, Muslims remove their shoes before entering a mosque to avoid defiling a sacred place of worship with soles that have touched the profane ground outside. Similarly, every Hindu devotee must engage in ritual washings, while for Jews there are rites of passage such as bar mitzvah for boys and bat mitzvah for girls. The sacred is the focus of **ritual**, which is *formal, ceremonial behaviour*. Holy communion is the central ritual of Christianity; the wafer and wine consumed during communion symbolise the body and blood of Jesus Christ, and are never treated as food.

## Religiosity

**Religiosity** designates *the importance of religion in a person's life*. Years ago, Charles Glock (1959, 1962) distinguished five distinct dimensions of religiosity. *Experiential* religiosity refers to the strength of a person's emotional ties to a religion. *Ritualistic* religiosity refers to frequency of ritual activity such as prayer and church attendance. *Ideological* religiosity concerns an individual's degree of belief in religious doctrine. *Consequential* religiosity has to do with how strongly religious beliefs figure in a person's daily

behaviour. Finally, *intellectual* religiosity refers to a person's knowledge of the history and doctrines of a particular religion. Anyone is likely to be more religious on some dimensions than on others; this inconsistency compounds the difficulty of measuring the concept of religiosity.

## Understanding religion

Although, as individuals, sociologists may hold any number of religious beliefs – or none at all – they all agree that religion has a major importance for the operation of society. Each theoretical paradigm suggests ways in which religion affects social life.

## Religion as ritual: the functions of religion

Emile Durkheim (1965; orig. 1915) maintained that we confront the power of society every day. Society, he argued, has an existence and power all of its own beyond the life of any individual. Thus, society itself is 'godlike', surviving the ultimate deaths of its members whose lives it shapes. Durkheim contended that, in religious life, people celebrate the awesome power of their own society. This insight explains the practice, in every society, of transforming certain everyday objects into sacred symbols of collective life. Members of technologically simple societies, Durkheim explained, do this with the **totem**, *an object in the natural world collectively defined as sacred*. The totem – perhaps an animal or an elaborate work of art – becomes the centrepiece of ritual, symbolising the power of society to transform individuals into a powerful collectivity.

Durkheim pointed out three major functions of religion for the operation of society:

1  *Social cohesion*. Religion unites people through shared symbols, values and norms. Religious doctrine and ritual establish rules of 'fair play' that make organised social life possible. Religion also speaks eloquently about the vital human dimension of *love*. Thus, religious life underscores both our moral and emotional ties to others.

2  *Social control*. Every society uses religious imagery and rhetoric to promote conformity. Societies infuse many cultural norms – especially mores relating to marriage and reproduction – with religious justification. Looking beyond behavioural norms, religion confers legitimacy on the political system.

In medieval Europe, in fact, monarchs claimed to rule by divine right. Few of today's political leaders invoke religion so explicitly, but many publicly ask for God's blessing, implying to audiences that their efforts are right and just.

3 *Providing meaning and purpose.* Religious beliefs offer the comforting sense that the vulnerable human condition serves some greater purpose. Strengthened by such convictions, people are less likely to collapse in despair when confronted by life's calamities. For this reason, major life-course transitions – including birth, marriage and death – are usually marked by religious observances that enhance our spiritual awareness.

## Critical comment

Durkheim's analysis contends that religion represents the collective life of society. The major weakness of this approach, however, is its tendency to downplay religion's dysfunctions – especially the capacity of strongly held beliefs to generate social conflict. During the early Middle Ages, for example, religious faith was the driving force behind the Crusades, in which European Christians sought to wrest from Muslim control lands that both religions considered to be sacred. Conflict among Muslims, Jews and Christians continues as a source of political instability in the world today. The long-standing social divisions in Northern Ireland (now a little abated) are also partly a matter of religious conflict between Protestants and Catholics; Dutch Calvinism historically supported apartheid in South Africa; and religious differences continue to fuel divisions in Algeria, Bosnia, India, Sri Lanka and elsewhere. The map on p. 666 demonstrates this. In short, nations have long marched to war under the banner of their god: differences in faith have provoked more violence in the world than have differences of social class. Indeed, the history of the world may well be written as a history of religious war and conflict.

## Religion as constructed meaning: the power of the symbol

Max Weber's theory is usually considered a prime example of an action theory, and it is discussed elsewhere in this book. He saw religion as sometimes being a major force for change – as we saw in Chapter 3, the Protestant ethic served as a major catalyst for the development of capitalism. But there are many others. 'Society', asserts the Catholic sociologist Peter Berger

(1967: 3), 'is a human product and nothing but a human product, that yet continuously acts back upon its producer.' From an action perspective, religion (like all of society) is socially constructed (although perhaps with divine inspiration!). It is one of the chief mechanisms through which meanings are constructed and people make sense of their lives. It is also one of the areas of life most shot through with symbolism and ritual. Thus, through various rituals, from saying grace before daily meals to annual religious observances such as Easter and Passover, individuals develop the distinction between the sacred and profane. Further, Berger explains, by placing everyday events within a 'cosmic frame of reference', people confer on their own fallible, transitory creations 'the semblance of ultimate security and permanence' (1967: 35–6).

Marriage is a good example. If we look on marriage merely as a contract between two people, we assume that we can end it whenever we want to. But if partners define their relationship as holy matrimony, this bond makes a far stronger claim on them. This fact, no doubt, explains why the divorce rate is lower among people who are more religious.

Especially when humans confront uncertainty and life-threatening situations – such as illness, war and natural disaster – we bring sacred symbols to the fore. By seeking out sacred meaning in any situation, in other words, we can lift ourselves above life's setbacks and even face the prospect of death with strength and courage. Interactionists have researched the ways in which many of the newer religions such as the Moonies and Scientology give people meaning in the face of a modern world which can be deeply stressful (Lofland, 1977; Barker, 1984).

## Critical comment

The action approach views religion as a social construction, placing everyday life under a 'sacred canopy' of meaning (Berger, 1967). Of course, Berger adds, the ability of the sacred to legitimise and stabilise society depends on its constructed character going unrecognised. After all, we could derive little strength from sacred beliefs if we saw them to be mere devices for coping with tragedy. Then, too, this micro-level view pays scant attention to religion's link with social inequality, to which we turn shortly.

## Religion as a chain of memory

The contemporary French sociologist Danièle Hervieu-Leger (2000) sees religion as a kind of memory which provides a chain of connection between individual believers and their communities. In order to understand the changing roles of religious beliefs, we need to trace the historical chains of memory and how they become ruptured by major events (such as the Reformation). Just how the 'memory mutates' becomes of significant interest.

In traditional societies, these memories are very strong indeed. They are supported by all kinds of rituals and strong communities, and are passed from generation to generation. But in modern societies they become much weaker. Hervieu-Leger talks of 'the crumbling memory of modern societies' and sees them as 'amnesic' societies in so far as they tend to forget their traditions and their past (see Davie, 2000).

## Religion as power and inequality: the conflicts of the spirit

Another sociological view of religion is that of Marx, who claimed that religion served ruling elites by legitimising the status quo and diverting people's attention from the social inequities of society. In a famous statement, he saw religion as the 'opium of the people'. It is 'the sign of an oppressed creature, the sentiment of a heartless world and the soul of soulless conditions' (1964: 27; orig. 1848). Religion works both to create and to reinforce systems of stratification, as well as dulling the awareness of it. The caste system, as we have seen in Chapter 8, is a key feature of Hinduism and stratifies into layers of priests, rulers, merchants and servants – with a large 'outcast' group that does not fit (the untouchables). The structure of the Christian church, likewise, has often created considerable wealth for its religious leaders. The extremely wealthy and powerful Vatican City State with it Papal leader has status as an independent country in many international organisations, illustrating the close alliance between religious and political elites.

Gender and ethnicity also figure in religion's tie to social inequality. Virtually all the world's major religions have reflected and encouraged male dominance of social life, as the *World watch* box explains. Many religions predominate in a specific geographical region or society. Islam commands the devotion of most (but not all) people within the Arab societies of the Middle East; Hinduism is closely fused with the culture of India, as is Confucianism with the Chinese way of life. During Marx's lifetime, powerful Christian nations of western Europe justified colonial exploitation of Africa, the Americas and Asia by claiming that they were merely 'converting heathens'. In practical terms, working for political change may mean opposing the church and, by implication, God. Religion also encourages people to look hopefully to a 'better world to come', minimising the social problems of this world.

### Critical comment

Social conflict analysis reveals the power of religion to legitimise social inequality. Yet critics of religion's conservative face, Marx included, minimise ways in which religion has promoted change as well as equality. Nineteenth-century religious groups in the United Kingdom, for example, were at the forefront of the movement to abolish slavery. In the United States, religious organisations and their leaders (including the Reverend Martin Luther King, Jr) were at the core of the civil rights movement and today serve as one of the main lobbies for the needs of poor immigrants from Latin America. There has been a long-standing 'radical' Catholic movement supporting revolutionary change in Latin America and elsewhere (discussed below).

# World religions and patriarchy: do gods favour men?

All world religions seem to be patriarchal. They usually have male gods at the centre of their cosmologies. They favour men to be their officials on earth. And frequently they devise ways of excluding women from their organisations, their power base and the wider society. There is a paradox in all this, though. Just as women are often excluded from the power and influence of religions, so they often display higher levels of religiosity than men. Various surveys have suggested that women are more likely to believe in God than men and that Muslim women were more likely to say that religion was important to them than men (*Social Trends*, Modood).

The pioneering feminist Simone de Beauvoir (in her important book *The Second Sex*, orig. 1949) claimed that 'Man enjoys the great advantage of having a God endorse the code he writes . . . For the Jews, Mohammedans, and Christians amongst others, man is master by divine right; the fear of God will therefore repress any impulse toward revolt in the downtrodden female.' For example, while many Christians revere Mary, the mother of Jesus, the New Testament also contrasts men made in 'the image and glory of God' with

WORLD WATCH

women, made for 'the glory of man', professing: 'For man was not made from woman, but woman from man. Neither was man created for woman, but woman for man' (1 Corinthians 11: 7–9). Likewise, the Qur'an, the sacred text of Islam, contends that 'men are in charge of women' (quoted in Kaufman, 1976: 163). Historically, the major world religions have barred women from serving as priests. Islamic groups, Orthodox Jews and the Roman Catholic Church continue to exclude women from the religious hierarchy.

Still, over the past 50 years many religions have begun to confront the challenges from feminist stances. A growing number of Protestant denominations have overturned historical policies and now ordain women. Since 1993, women have been ordained in the Church of England and around half of those accepted for ordination are now women. There are now 2,000 women clergy in England and around 8,000 worldwide (O'Brien and Palmer, 2007). Reform Judaism has long elevated

women to the role of rabbi (and is the largest denomination to ordain gay and lesbian people). In 1985, the first woman became a rabbi in the Conservative denomination of Judaism.

Challenges to the patriarchal structure of organised religion – from the ordination of women to the introduction of gender-neutral language in hymnals and prayers – has sparked heated controversy, delighting progressives while outraging traditionalists. Propelling these developments is a lively feminism within many religious communities today. Feminist Christians contend that the rigid patriarchal traditions in many churches stand in stark contrast to the biblical image of Jesus Christ as non-aggressive, non-competitive, meek and humble of heart – traits often linked to femininity.

Feminists argue that unless traditional notions of gender are removed from our understanding of God, women will never have equality with men in the church. Theologian Mary Daly (1928–2010) put the matter bluntly:

'If God is male, then male is God.' Mary Daly was a major outspoken feminist critic (and was herself originally a Catholic). She sees Christianity as a patriarchal myth. For her, the Christian story served to eliminate earlier 'goddess' religions and women: 'there is no female presence involved in this Monogender Male Automotherhood', she claims. She then goes on to argue that Christianity is rooted in male 'sado-rituals', with its 'torture cross symbolism', and that it embodies women-hating. This leads her to mount a full-scale critique of male religions (Daly, 1973, 1978).

World religions show few signs of changing their orthodox lines on women. In July 2010, the Pope declared the 'attempted ordination of a woman' to the priesthood as one of the most serious crimes against church law. The Catholic Church teaches that it cannot ordain women as priests because Christ chose only men as his apostles. Of course, feminists and proponents of a female priesthood reject this. The long conflict continues.

## The nature of religious organisations

Sociologists have devised broad schemes to categorise the hundreds of different religious organisations in the world. The most widely used model takes the form of a continuum, with *churches* at one pole and *sects* at the other.

## Church

Drawing on the ideas of his teacher Max Weber, Ernst Troeltsch (1931) defined a **church** as *a type of religious organisation well integrated into the larger society*. Church-like organisations usually persist for centuries and claim as adherents generations of the same family. Churches have well-established rules and regulations, and expect their leaders to undergo approved training before being formally ordained. They have large memberships and tend to be bureaucratic.

While concerned with the sacred, a church accepts the ways of the profane world, which gives it broad appeal. Church doctrine conceives God in highly intellectualised terms (say, as a force for good), and favours abstract moral standards ('do unto others as you would have them do unto you') over specific mandates for day-to-day living. By teaching morality in safely abstract terms, a church can avoid social controversy. For example, many churches that, in principle, celebrate the unity of all peoples, have in practice all-white memberships. Such duality minimises conflict between a church and the surrounding political landscape (Troeltsch, 1931).

A church generally takes one of two forms. Islam in Morocco represents an **ecclesia**, *a church formally allied with the state*. Ecclesias have been common in history; for centuries Roman Catholicism animated the Roman Empire; Confucianism was the state religion in China until early in the twentieth century; the Anglican church remains the official Church of England, as Islam is the official religion of Pakistan and Iran. State churches typically define everyone in the society as a member; tolerance of religious difference, therefore, is severely limited. A **denomination**, by contrast, is *a church, independent of the state, that accepts religious pluralism*. Denominations are sects that have become incorporated into mainstream society. Thus Christian denominations include Baptists, Methodists and Lutherans, among others.

## Sect

At the other end of our continuum is the **sect**, *a type of religious organisation that stands apart from the larger society*. Sect members hold rigidly to their own religious convictions while discounting what others around them claim to be true. In extreme cases, members of a sect may withdraw from society completely in order to practise their religion without interference from outsiders. When cultures view religious tolerance as a virtue, members of sects are sometimes accused of being dogmatic in their insistence that they alone follow the true religion (Stark and Bainbridge, 1979).

In organisational terms, sects are less formal than churches. Thus, sect members often engage in highly spontaneous and emotional practices as they worship, while members of churches tend to be passively attentive to their leader. Sects also reject the intellectualised religion of churches, stressing instead the personal experience of divine power. A further distinction between church and sect turns on patterns of leadership. The more church-like an organisation, the more likely its leaders are to be formally trained and ordained. Because more sect-like organisations celebrate the personal presence of God, members expect their leaders to exude divine inspiration in the form of **charisma** (from Greek, meaning 'divine favour'), *extraordinary personal qualities that can turn an audience into followers*, infusing them with the emotional experience that sects so value.

Sects generally form as breakaway groups from established churches or other religious organisations (Stark and Bainbridge, 1979). Their psychic intensity and informal structure render them less stable than churches, and many sects blossom only to wither and disappear a short time later. The sects that do endure typically become more like churches, losing fervour as they become more bureaucratic and established.

To sustain their membership, many sects rely on active recruitment, or proselytising, of new members. Sects place great value on the experience of **conversion**, *a personal transformation or religious rebirth*. Members of Jehovah's Witnesses, for example, eagerly share their faith with others in the hope of attracting new members. Finally, churches and sects differ in their social composition. Because they are more closely tied to the secular world, well-established churches tend to include people of high social standing. Sects, by contrast, attract more disadvantaged people. A sect's openness to new members and promise of salvation and personal fulfilment may be especially appealing to people who perceive themselves as social outsiders. However, as we shall explain presently, many established churches in the world have lost membership in recent decades. In the process, a number of sects, often global, now find themselves with more affluent members.

## Cult

A **cult** is *a religious organisation that is substantially outside a society's cultural traditions*. Whereas a sect emerges from within a traditional religious organisation, a cult represents something else entirely. Cults typically form around a highly charismatic leader who offers a compelling message of a new way of life. Because some cult principles or practices may seem unconventional, the popular view of cults pictures them as deviant or even evil. Negative publicity given to a few cults has raised suspicion about any unfamiliar religious group. As a result of such aberrant behaviour, some scholars assert that to call a religious community a 'cult' amounts to declaring it unworthy.

Many long-standing religions – Christianity, Islam and Judaism included – began as cults. Of course, not all or even most cults flourish for very long. Cults are more at odds with the larger society than sects, and many demand that members not only accept their doctrine but embrace a radically new lifestyle. As a result, people sometimes accuse cults of brainwashing new members, although research suggests that most people who join cults experience no psychological harm (E. Barker, 1981). The rise in new cults is discussed further below.

## The social shapes of global religions

As we have seen, religion is found in virtually all societies, and the diversity of religious expression is almost as wide ranging as culture itself. In this section, we will look at the range of traditional religions, focusing on some of the major patterns and the societies to which they belong. Map 19.1 provides a view of global state of religions.

# The global state of religions

WORLD WATCH

### INDIGENOUS FAITHS

Many cultures still have their original faiths. There are many of these but they tend to be quite small in size.

### CHRISTIANITY

World's largest religion. Over 2.1 billion adherents and 33,000 dominations (50% Catholic; 20% Independents)

### ISLAM

20% of world's population is Muslim - around 1.4 billion. Islam is a state religion of 25 countries.

### HINDUISM

Third largest world religion. Nearly a billion and primarily in south Asia.

### BUDDHISM

6% of world's population, mainly in southeast Asia (Burma, Thailand, Cambodia; but also Mongolia and Bhutan). Hundreds of smaller groupings worldwide.

### SIKHISM

24 million worldwide, mainly India.

### JUDAISM

There are only 13 million Jews worldwide, more than 5 million live in Israel. 80% live in Israel or the USA.

### NON-BELIEVERS

Both China and Russia - with large populations - have histories of non-belief; but overall the highest concentration is in northern Europe.

### USA

Dominance of Christianity, and also the rise of the Militant Christian right. Dominion Theology and Pentecostalism. Plays an important role in politics with extreme wings of Christian terrorists.

**Majority of population compriesd of:**

- ☐ Roman catholics
- ▨ Protestants
- ■ Christians from various churches
- ☐ Orthodox Christians
- ▨ Churches of Eastern Christianity
- ☐ Mormons
- ▨ Muslims (Sunnis)
- ▨ Muslims (Shiites)

- ☐ Jews
- ▨ Buddhists
- ☐ Japanese Shintoists and Buddhists
- ☐ Hindus
- ■ Sikhs
- ▨ Indigenous religions
- ▨ no dominant religion/ nonreligious
- ☐ unpopulated

**Map 19.1**

*Source*: Adapted from Ninian Smart, *World Atlas of Religions* (1999) and Joanne O'Brien and Martin Palmer, *The Atlas of Religion* (2007).

**EUROPE**

Northern Europe is Christian, but Christianity is often in decline and there are many non-believers. Eastern Europe is a mixture of Muslim and Eastern Orthodox Christian. The faultlines between eastern and western European religion is symbolised by the Turkish application for membership of the EU.

**ISRAEL**

World home for Judaism - often Messianic.

**TIBET**

Conflict over Buddhism and China. 60-plus years under its colonial ruler, the People's Republic of China.

**CHINA**

Weak, outlawed or local, Indigenous religions are now wide open to a multitude of religions for conversion.

**JAPAN**

Primary connections are Buddhism and Taoism, but many new groups: the most famous is Aum Shinrikyo, which believes strongly that the world is full of miracles.

**SOUTH KOREA**

Heartland of the Unification Church (1954).

**AFGHANISTAN**

Islamic Militants: the Taliban is only the extreme of a spectrum of Islamic politics.

**IRAN**

Islamic Republic, Shi'a clerics take a dominant position in politics and nearly all aspects of Iranian life are defined through Muslim faith. Sometimes called a theocracy.

**VATICAN**

One of the world's smallest states - a kind of theocracy with the Pope as its ruler. Embroiled in global scandal about child sex abuse and other issues.

**SRI LANKA**

Main conflict is between borther Tamils and southern Sinhala (with 65,000 dead). Hindus are in the minority. Buddhist activists (of Sinhala variety)

**INDIA**

80% of people in India are Hindu, though the caste system it espouses is officially banned. It has been estimated that by 2050, there will be 1.2 billion Hindus. Clash between Hindu nationalism (the Bharatiya Janata Party) and militant Sikh movements against the secular world as well as the Hindu movement (secular politics is often seen as a form of Hinduism). The Dalits, numbering some 150-250 million, stand on the fringes of Hindu society. Large numbers of Sikhs in the northern parts.

**IRAQ**

Split between Sunnia and Shi'a Muslims dates back to the seventh century.

**LATIN AMERICA**

Strength of Catholic Church, new liberation theologies and Pentecostalism. Brazil is the world's most populous Catholic country. Uruguay has many non-believers.

**SUB-SAHARAN AFRICA**

Christianisation: Striking rise of Christian Pentecostalism and Christian Fundamentalisms. Tensions with Muslims. Conflicts over many issues such as women and gay rights.

**TENSIONS ACROSS RELIGIONS INCLUDE:**

Secular state/all religions
Indigenous religions/all religions
Protestant/Catholic
Christian/Muslim
Muslim/Christian/Jewish
Muslim/Hindu/Sikh
Buddhist/Hindu
Hindu/Buddhist/Christian
Buddhist/Muslim

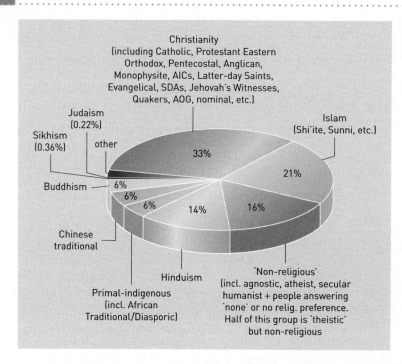

**Figure 19.1** Major religions of the world: by number of adherents

*Note*: Total adds up to more than 100% due to rounding and because upper bound estimates were used for each group.

*Source*: © 2005 www.adherents.com.

Religion predates written history. Archaeological evidence indicates that our human ancestors routinely engaged in religious rituals some 40,000 years ago. Early hunters and gatherers, and some modern non-Western peoples, embrace **animism** (from Latin, meaning 'the breath of life'), *the belief that elements of the natural world are conscious life forms that affect humanity*. Animistic people view forests, oceans, mountains, even the wind as spiritual forces. Hunters and gatherers conduct their religious life entirely within the family. Members of such societies may look to a *shaman* or religious leader, but there are no full-time, specialised religious leaders. Belief in a single divine power responsible for creating the world marked the rise of pastoral and horticultural societies. The Christian view of God as a 'shepherd' may be linked to earlier religions, all of whose original followers were pastoral peoples.

As societies develop more productive capacity, religious life expands beyond the family and priests take their place among other specialised workers. In agrarian societies, the institution of religion gains prominence, as evidenced by the centrality of the church in medieval Europe. Even the physical design of the city casts this dominance in stone, with the cathedral rising above all other structures.

While many of the world's thousands of different religions are highly localised with few followers, there are a number of what we might call *global religions*. These, by contrast, span large areas and often have millions of adherents. We shall briefly describe six of the major world religions, which together claim as adherents some 4 billion people – almost three-quarters of humanity.

# 1 Christianity

Christianity is the most widespread religion, with nearly 2 billion followers, who constitute roughly one-third of humanity. Most Christians live in Europe or the Americas; more than 85 per cent of the people in the United States and Canada identify with Christianity. Moreover, people who are at least nominally Christian represent a significant share of the population in many other world regions, with the notable exceptions of northern Africa and Asia. The diffusion stems from the European colonisation of much of the world during the last 500 years. This dominance of Christianity in the West can be seen in the practice of numbering years on the calendar beginning with the birth of Christ.

Christianity originated as a cult, incorporating elements of its much older predecessor Judaism. Like many cults, Christianity was propelled by the personal charisma of a leader, Jesus of Nazareth, who preached a message of personal salvation. Jesus did not directly challenge the political powers of his day, calling on his followers to 'Render therefore to Caesar things that are Caesar's' (Matthew, xxii: 21). But his message was revolutionary, nonetheless, promising that faith and love would lead to triumph over sin and death.

Christianity is one example of **monotheism**, *belief in a single divine power*. This new religion broke with the Roman Empire's traditional **polytheism**, *belief in many gods*. Yet Christianity has a unique version of the Supreme Being as a sacred Trinity: God the Creator; Jesus Christ, Son of God and Redeemer; and the Holy Spirit, a Christian's personal experience of God's presence. The claim that Jesus was divine rests on accounts of his final days on earth. Tried and sentenced to death in Jerusalem on charges that he was a threat to established political leaders, Jesus endured a cruel execution by crucifixion, which transformed the cross into a sacred Christian symbol. According to Christian belief, Jesus was resurrected – that is, he rose from the dead – showing that he was the Son of God.

The apostles of Jesus spread Christianity widely throughout the Mediterranean region. Although the Roman Empire initially persecuted Christians, by the fourth century Christianity had become an ecclesia – the official religion of what later came to be known as the Holy Roman Empire. What had begun as a cult four centuries before was by then an established church.

Christianity took various forms, including the Roman Catholic Church and the Orthodox Church, centred in Constantinople (now Istanbul, Turkey). Further division occurred towards the end of the Middle Ages, when the Protestant Reformation in Europe sparked the formation of hundreds of denominations. Dozens of these denominations now command sizeable followings in Britain.

## 2  Islam

We have encountered Islam before in Chapter 5. Islam has some 1.1 billion followers (19 per cent of humanity), called Muslims. Like all religions, it is not uniform but made of many schisms – Sunnis, for example, are the more mystical branch of the Muslims. A majority of people in the Middle East are Muslims, which explains our tendency to associate Islam with Arabs in that region of the world. But most Muslims are *not* Arabs. Map 19.1 shows that a majority of people across northern Africa and western Asia are also Muslims. Moreover, significant concentrations of

Muslims are found in Pakistan, India, Bangladesh, Indonesia and the southern republics of the former Soviet Union.

Islam is the second largest faith in Europe, with estimates of 6 million (3 per cent of most western European populations). If eastern Europe were added in, the numbers would be significantly greater. Estimates place the number of British Muslims at 1,200,000 – most concentrated in the Midlands, London, Strathclyde, Yorkshire and Lancashire. British Muslims are predominantly Sunni, with only around 25,000 Shi'as (Storry and Childs, 1997).

As we have seen, Islam is the word of God as revealed to the prophet Mohammed, who was born in the city of Mecca (now in Saudi Arabia) around the year 570 CE. To Muslims, Mohammed, like Jesus, is a prophet, but not a divine being (as Christians define Jesus). The Qur'an (Koran), sacred to Muslims, is the word of God (in Arabic 'Allah') as transmitted through Mohammed, God's messenger. In Arabic, the word 'Islam' means both 'submission' and 'peace', and the Qur'an urges submission to Allah as the path to inner peace. Muslims express this personal devotion in a daily ritual of five prayers.

Islam spread rapidly after the death of Mohammed, although divisions arose. All Muslims, however, accept the Five Pillars of Islam (see Chapter 5). Like Christianity, Islam holds people accountable to God for their deeds on earth. Those who live obediently will be rewarded in heaven, while evil-doers will suffer unending punishment. Muslims are also obligated to defend their faith. Sometimes this tenet has justified holy wars against non-believers (in roughly the same way that medieval Christians joined the Crusades to recapture the Holy Land from the Muslims). Today, one of the world's major conflicts is between 'Western cultures' and fundamentalist Islam (Ahmed, 2007).

Many Westerners view Muslim women as among the most socially oppressed people on earth. Muslim women do lack many of the personal freedoms enjoyed by Muslim men, yet most accept the mandates of their religion. Moreover, patriarchy was well established in the Middle East before the birth of Mohammed. Some defenders of Islam's treatment of women argue that Islam actually improved the social position of women by demanding that husbands deal justly with their wives. Further, although Islam permits a man to have up to four wives, it admonishes men to have only one wife if having more than one would encourage him to treat women unjustly (Qur'an, 'The Women', v. 3). These issues have been raised before in Chapter 11.

# 3 Judaism

Speaking purely in numerical terms, Judaism, with only 15 million adherents worldwide, is among the smallest of the world's religions. Only in Israel do Jews represent a national majority. But Judaism has significance in many countries. The United States has the largest concentration of Jews (6 million people), and the largest European communities are found in France (500,000–600,000) and Britain (300,000) (Davie, 1994: 225).

Jews look to the past as a source of guidance in the present and for the future. Judaism has deep historical roots that extend back some 4,000 years before the birth of Christ to the ancient cultures of Mesopotamia. At this time, Jews were animistic, but this belief was to change after Jacob – grandson of Abraham, the earliest great ancestor – led his people to Egypt. Under Egyptian rule, Jews endured centuries of slavery. In the thirteenth century BCE, a turning point came as Moses, the adopted son of an Egyptian princess, was called by God to lead the Jews from bondage. This exodus (this word's Latin and Greek roots mean 'a marching out') from Egypt is commemorated by Jews today in the annual ritual of Passover. As a result of the Jews' liberation from bondage, Judaism became monotheistic, recognising a single, all-powerful God.

A distinctive concept of Judaism is the *covenant*, a special relationship with God by which Jews became a 'chosen people'. The covenant also implies a duty to observe God's law, especially the Ten Commandments as revealed to Moses on Mount Sinai. Jews regard the Bible (or, in Christian terms, the Old Testament) as both a record of their history and a statement of the obligations of Jewish life. Of special importance are the first five books of the Bible (Genesis, Exodus, Leviticus, Numbers and Deuteronomy), designated as the Torah (a word roughly meaning 'teaching' and 'law'). In contrast to Christianity's concern with personal salvation, Judaism emphasises moral behaviour in this world.

Judaism is composed of three main denominations. Orthodox Jews hold strictly to traditional beliefs and practices, maintaining historical forms of dress, segregating men and women at religious services and consuming only kosher foods. Such traditional practices set off Orthodox Jews as the most sect-like. Hasidism is the most messianic and fosters a strong spiritual devotion to Judaism. In the mid-nineteenth century, many Jews sought greater accommodation to the larger society, leading to the formation of more church-like Reform Judaism. More recently,

Two Jewish boys read the Talmud, the Jewish sacred book
*Source*: Gleb Garanich/Reuters.

a third segment – Conservative Judaism – has established a middle ground between the other two denominations.

All Jews, however, share a keen awareness of their cultural history, which has included battling against considerable prejudice and discrimination. A collective memory of centuries of slavery in Egypt, conquest by Rome and persecution in Europe has shaped Jewish identity. A militant Catholic Church instigated a strong separation of Christian and Jew during the Crusades. Interestingly, the urban ghetto (derived from the Italian word *borghetto*, meaning 'settlement outside the city walls') was first home to Jews in Italy, and this form of residential segregation soon spread to other parts of Europe (Sowell, 1996: Chapter 6). Substantial numbers of Jews have lived in eastern Europe since medieval times (with Poland often being the 'capital').

Around 120,000 Jews came to England as refugees from the pogroms of Russia between 1875 and 1914. Many settled in east London (Castles and Miller, 1993: 55). As larger numbers entered the country during the final decades of the nineteenth century, anti-Semitism increased. During the Second World War, anti-Semitism reached a vicious peak when Jews experienced the most horrific persecution in modern times as the Nazi regime in Germany systematically annihilated approximately 6 million Jews. The history of Judaism is a grim reminder of a tragic dimension of the human record – the extent to which religious minorities have been the target of hatred and even slaughter. Despite all this, anti-Semitism still seems widespread (and some even claim that a new anti-Semitism has emerged to attack Zionism and Israel: but this is another hot debate) (Iganski and Komin, 2003).

# 4 Hinduism

Hinduism is the oldest of all the world religions, originating in the Indus River Valley approximately 4,500 years ago. Hindus number some 775 million (14 per cent of humanity). Map 19.1 shows that Hinduism remains an Eastern religion, the predominant creed of India today, although it does have a significant presence in a few societies of southern Africa as well as Indonesia.

Hinduism differs from most other religions because it did not spring from the life of any single person. Hinduism also has no sacred writings comparable to the Bible or the Qur'an. Nor does Hinduism even envisage God as a specific entity. For this reason, Hinduism – like other Eastern religions – is sometimes thought of as an 'ethical religion'. Hindu beliefs and practices vary widely, but all Hindus recognise a moral force in the universe that imposes on everyone responsibilities known as *dharma*. One traditional example of *dharma* is the need to act in concert with the traditional caste system, described in Chapter 8.

A second Hindu principle, *karma*, refers to the belief in the spiritual progress of the human soul. To a Hindu, all actions have spiritual consequences and proper living contributes to moral development. Karma works through *reincarnation*, a cycle of new birth following death, so that individuals are reborn into a spiritual state corresponding to the moral quality of their previous life. Unlike Christianity and Islam, Hinduism proclaims no ultimate judgement at the hands of a supreme god, although in the cycle of rebirth, each person reaps exactly what the individual has sown. The sublime state of *nirvana* represents spiritual perfection: when a soul reaches this rarefied plateau, it exits the cycle of rebirth.

Looking at Hinduism, we see also that not all religions can be neatly labelled monotheistic or polytheistic. Hinduism may be described as monotheistic because it envisages the universe as a single moral system; yet Hindus perceive this moral order in every element of nature. Rituals, which are central to a Hindu's life, are performed in a variety of ways. Most Hindus practise private devotions, including, for example, ritual cleansing following contact with a person of a lower caste. Many also participate in public rituals, such as *Kumbh Mela*, during which pilgrims flock to the sacred River Ganges in India to bathe in its purifying waters. This ritual, which occurs every 12 years, attracts 15 to 20 million people (Pitt, 1955; Sen, 1961; Schmidt, 1980).

# 5 Buddhism

Some 2,500 years ago, the rich culture of India also gave rise to Buddhism. Today more than 350 million people (6 per cent of humanity) embrace Buddhism, and almost all are Asians. As shown in Map 19.1, adherents of Buddhism are concentrated in parts of southeast Asia – notably Myanmar (Burma), Thailand, Cambodia and Japan. Buddhism is also widespread in India and the People's Republic of China. Of the world religions considered so far, Buddhism most resembles Hinduism in doctrine, but, like Christianity, its inspiration springs from the life of one individual.

Siddhartha Gautama was born to a high-caste family in Nepal about 563 BCE. As a young man, he was preoccupied with spiritual matters. At the age of 29, he underwent a radical personal transformation, setting off for years of travel and meditation. His path ended when he achieved what Buddhists describe as *bodhi*, or enlightenment. Understanding the essence of life, Gautama became a Buddha. During the third century BCE, the ruler of India joined the ranks of Buddhists, subsequently sending missionaries throughout Asia and elevating Buddhism to the status of a world religion.

Energised by the Buddha's personal charisma, followers spread his teachings, the *dhamma*, across India. The Buddhist ethics are found in the five Precepts: do not kill; do not steal; do not lie; do not be unchaste; do not drink intoxicants. Central to Buddhist belief is the notion that human existence involves suffering. The pleasures of the world are real, of course, but Buddhists see such experiences as transitory. This doctrine is rooted in the Buddha's own travels throughout a society rife with poverty. But the Buddha rejected wealth as a solution to suffering; on the contrary, he warned that materialism inhibits spiritual development. Buddhism's answer to world problems is for individuals to pursue personal, spiritual transformation.

Buddhism closely parallels Hinduism in recognising no god of judgement; rather, it finds spiritual consequences in each daily action. Another similarity lies in its belief in reincarnation. Here, again, only full enlightenment ends the cycle of death and rebirth, thereby liberating a person from the suffering of the world (Schumann, 1974).

When Western people perform religious rituals, they typically do so collectively and formally as members of specific congregations. Eastern people, by contrast, visit shrines individually and informally, without joining a specific congregation. (a) Moonie wedding, South Korea; (b) Buddhist monks in Colombo protesting against the war; (c) Kumbh Mela festival in India

*Source*: (a) Reuters/Str Old; (b) Reuters/Str Old; (c) © David Pearson/Alamy.

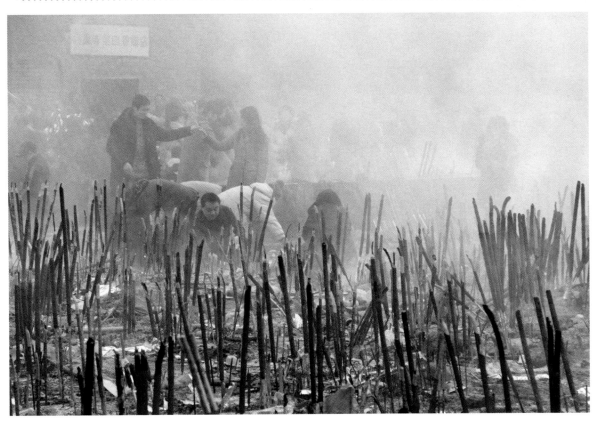

People making offerings of candles, incense sticks and burning paper money to appease the spirits of their ancestors in China
*Source*: © Victor Paul Borg/Alamy.

# 6 Chinese religions and 'Confucianism'

As we saw in Chapter 4, from about 200 BCE until the beginning of the twentieth century, Confucianism was an ecclesia – the official religion of China. Following the 1949 Revolution, religion was suppressed by the communist government of the new People's Republic of China. Although officials provide little in the way of data to establish precise numbers, hundreds of millions of Chinese are still influenced by Confucianism. While almost all adherents to Confucianism live in China, Chinese immigration has introduced this religion to other societies in southeast Asia.

Confucius or, properly, K'ung-Fu-tzu, lived between 551 and 479 BCE. He shared with Buddha a deep concern for the problems and suffering in the world. The Buddha's response was a sect-like withdrawal from the world; Confucius, by contrast, instructed his followers to engage in the world according to a strict code of moral conduct. Thus it was that Confucianism became fused with the traditional culture of China. Here we see a second example of what might be called a 'national religion'. As Hinduism has remained largely synonymous with Indian culture, Confucianism is enshrined in the Chinese way of life.

A central concept of Confucianism is *jen*, meaning humanness. In practice, this means that we must always subordinate our self-interest to moral principle. In the family, the individual must display loyalty and consideration for others. Likewise, families must remain mindful of their duties to the larger community. In this way, layer upon layer of moral obligation integrates society as a whole. Most of all, Confucianism stands out as lacking a clear sense of the sacred. We could view Confucianism, recalling Durkheim's analysis, as the celebration of society itself as sacred. Alternatively, we might argue that Confucianism is less a religion than a model of disciplined living. Certainly the historical dominance of Confucianism helps to explain why Chinese culture has long taken a sceptical attitude towards the supernatural. If we conclude that Confucianism is best thought of as a disciplined way of life, we must also recognise that it shares with religion a body of beliefs and practices that have as their goal goodness, concern for others and the promotion of social harmony (Schmidt, 1980).

## 7  Non-religious: sceptics, agnostics, 'seculars', atheists and humanists

Technically, these beliefs should not be included here. Durkheim and others define religion through 'the sacred', 'things set apart and forbidden'. But throughout history and across the world today, there are very large numbers of people who have doubts about or refuse the dominant worldwide institutionalised faiths. Estimates of world non-believers circulate around the 1 billion figure (i.e. about one-sixth of the world's population). In some countries, such as the former Soviet Union, atheism was the official belief. In others, religion in general is much less organised, as we have seen for China in Chapter 4. Europe has the highest numbers of self-avowed non-religious atheists – around 41 million. Australia and New Zealand also have a relatively high proportion of non-believers. Non-believers can be seen as falling into two broad groups: those who are sceptical about the existence of God (sceptics, agnostics), and those who hold the stronger view that the existence of God can never be proved. Non-believers can be found across all the continents.

In the UK, the British Humanist Association claims that 'Humanism is the belief that we can live good lives without religious or superstititious beliefs. Humanists make sense of life using reason, experiences and shared human values' (*BHA News*, July 2007: 1). The problem with this definition is that history shows a long history of humanisms of all kinds – and that many include a belief in God. Like most religious beliefs, non-religious beliefs are also multiple and often contradictory (Zuckerman, 2005; Dawkins, 2006a; McGrath, 2004).

RESEARCH IN ACTION

# Society without God

Phil Zuckerman is a Californian sociologist who has been researching religions for over 20 years and has written a wonderful introduction to the sociologies of religion – looking at a wide range of them. His most recent study took him to the Nordic countries – and especially Denmark and Sweden. Here he found – as the title of his book puts it – a *Society Without God*.

In Denmark and Sweden, Zuckerman found that most people don't worship or pray, don't give much credence to any religion, and certainly don't believe in a God. He interviewed around 150 Danes and Swedes of all ages and educational backgrounds over the course of 14 months, asking them questions about what it was like to live a life without God. And he found that most of them could lead lives without any worries about an afterlife and were quite contented. Far from being decaying societies of sin and badness, the residents in these countries score top rankings on a number of scales which measure human progress, such as the Human Development Index, which we met in Chapter 9; and the 'happiness index' (see Chapter 26). Their societies have some of the lowest rates of crime in the world, excellent health and educational systems, strong economies, as well as well-supported arts and egalitarian social policies. They stand out as better on most matters of welfare than many countries which are riddled with religious conflicts, wars and genocides. There is no guarantee, it seems, that believing in God will secure you any success on earth!

*See*: Phil Zuckerman, *Society without God: What the Least Religious Countries Can Tell Us about Contentment* (2008). And see an interview with him on YouTube: search *Phil Zuckerman Deadline*.

### COUNTRY FACT FILE

DENMARK

| | |
|---|---|
| Population | 5.5 million |
| Per capita GDP | $36.00 |
| Life expectancy | 78.3 |
| Adult literacy | 100% |
| Key religions | Evangelical Lutheran/ non-believers |
| Key language | Danish |
| Key city | Copenhagen |
| Human development index | 0.866 (19th) |

*Source: Economist World in Figures* (2010).

| Taoism:<br><br>Shit happens. | Protestantism:<br>Let shit happen to someone else. | Catholicism:<br>If shit happens, you deserved it. |
| Judaism:<br>Why does shit always happen to us? | Atheism:<br><br>No shit. | T.V. Evangelism:<br>Send more shit. |
| Buddhism:<br>If shit happens, it is not really shit | Zen Buddhism:<br>What is the sound of shit happening? | Hinduism:<br>This shit happened before. |

**Figure 19.2**   World religions, a humorous view
*Source*: Original design by Barbara Shoolery © Game Plan Design.

# Religion in Europe

Christianity is one of the foundations of European societies. For much of the past two millennia, Christianity has defined life in Europe, dignifying all major actions, from birth and baptism through marriage to death and burial. It has held out the hope of 'salvation'. In pre-Reformation feudal society, the church was unitary – supported by royalty and the entire population. Hamilton says:

> The medieval world was Christian in the sense that everybody shared a common understanding of the world in which they lived based on Christian premises. Only the very learned had full and detailed knowledge of the whole world picture, but everybody understood some part of it.

(Hamilton, 1996: 87)

Yet, while all the countries of Europe make some claim to be Christian and to have Christian values, there are significant religious divides both within and across countries. A potted history would have to include:

- The early combats with both Judaism and Islam in the struggle to establish a dominant religion.
- The fourth-century split of the European Christian Church into Roman Catholicism in the West and Greek Orthodoxy in the East. While Roman Catholicism spread to the Americas, the Eastern Orthodox lost ground in central Europe and Asia to Islam during the eleventh century.
- The long struggles between empires and the papacy. Pope Innocent III (1198–1216) finally established a papal state in central Italy.
- The conflicts within the church itself: the heretical struggles and executions of witches, etc., along with a rather dissolute clergy with an eye on wealth.
- The continuing conflicts with other religions, with high periodic violence (the Spanish Inquisition, the Crusades and the Nazi Holocaust).
- The Reformation: it started in Germany with Martin Luther (1483–1546) when reformists renounced allegiances to Rome in 1520. By 1570, Protestants had established a presence in many places – especially Scandinavia, Britain and 'Baltic Europe', moving later into the Netherlands, France, Spain and even Italy. Calvinism (formed by John Calvin, 1509–64) emerged in France, the Netherlands and Scotland.
- Migration and missionary missions to colonies in the Americas and Africa.

# Religion: East and West

This brief overview of world religions points up two general differences between the belief systems that predominate in Eastern and Western societies. First, Western religions (Christianity, Judaism and Islam) are typically deity-based, with a clear focus on God. Eastern religions (Hinduism, Buddhism, Confucianism) tend to be more like ethical codes that make a less clear-cut distinction between the sacred and secular. Second, the operational unit of Western religious organisations is the congregation. That is, people attend a specific place of worship with others, most of whom are members. Eastern religious organisations, by contrast, are more broadly tied into culture itself. For this reason, for example, a visitor finds a Thai or Hong Kong temple awash with people – tourists and worshippers alike – who come and go on their own schedule, paying little attention to those around them.

These two distinctions do not overshadow the common element of all religions: having a conception of a higher moral force or purpose that transcends the concerns of everyday life. In all these religious beliefs, people of the world find guidance and a sense of purpose for their lives.

- The rise of science, with its claims for rationality, as a serious challenge to Christianity during the Enlightenment and the Industrial Revolution.
- The denial of religion throughout eastern Europe during its communist period, with its attendant struggles from within. (In some countries, such as Poland, religion became a major instigator of change.) Subsequently, there have been major changes: the number of active churches in Moscow, for instance, grew from 50 in 1988 to 250 in 1993.

Today, in Europe, divides and schisms continue, often based on these past conflicts and issues. Indeed, Yugoslavia, torn by divisions between Christians as well as between Christianity and Islam, has dramatically revealed the sharper edge of the continuing conflicts. There have also been deep-seated conflicts between Protestants and Catholics (as in the long conflicts within Northern Ireland) and between religion and humanism (as in the Netherlands). The Christian Democratic parties in many European governments partly base their platforms on Christian principles. In the UK, the Queen is head of both church and state and the two are interconnected. In Germany, the government collects church taxes (*Kirchensteuer*) on behalf of churches and uses it for social services.

Abortion issues continue to preoccupy those countries with a strong Catholic base. The most obvious divides are between the more religious, Catholic countries of southern Europe (Italy, Spain, Greece and Portugal) and the less religious Protestant north. France and Ireland are predominantly Catholic; Belgium, the Netherlands, Britain and the Nordic countries are generally much less religious.

There are also growing populations of Muslims throughout Europe – often with growing tensions. There are three main minority faiths in Europe, and Islam now constitutes the second largest faith in Europe, claiming millions of faithful – around 3 per cent of most European populations. In France, however, the figure is much higher at between 5 and 6 million (nearly 10 per cent of the population): 70 per cent of these have their heritage in former north African colonies of Algeria, Morocco and Tunisia. Estimates place the number of British Muslims at around 1,500,000. When eastern Europe is added in, the numbers are significantly greater. Turkey is 99 per cent Muslim.

Finally, there are possibly around 1 million Jews in post-Holocaust western Europe, concentrated mainly in France (around 500,000) and Britain (300,000). And as we shall see later, there has been a substantial increase in what we can call the new religious movements (NRMs) (Davie, 2000: 13–14).

# How religious are people in the UK?

Note that the statistics in Table 19.1 have been widely quoted but they are based on the 2001 census. A new census is being produced in 2011. There is also evidence from small-scale studies that most religions have been in decline in the UK. See Steve Bruce, *God is Dead: Secularization in the West* (2002). But there is also contrasting evidence that while the Christian faith is in decline, the Muslim faith is growing: with 1,870,000 in 2004 growing to 2,422,000 by 2008 (*Social Trends*, 2010).

| Table 19.1 | UK population by religious identification | |
|---|---|---|
| | Thousands | % |
| Christian | 42,079 | 71.6 |
| Buddhist | 152 | 0.3 |
| Hindu | 559 | 1.0 |
| Jewish | 267 | 0.5 |
| Muslim | 1,591 | 2.7 |
| Sikh | 336 | 0.6 |
| Other religion | 179 | 0.3 |
| All religions | 45,163 | 76.8 |
| No religion | 9,104 | 15.5 |
| Not stated | 4,289 | 7.3 |
| All no religion/not stated | 13,626 | 23.2 |
| Base | 58,789 | 100 |

*Source: Social Trends* (2004).

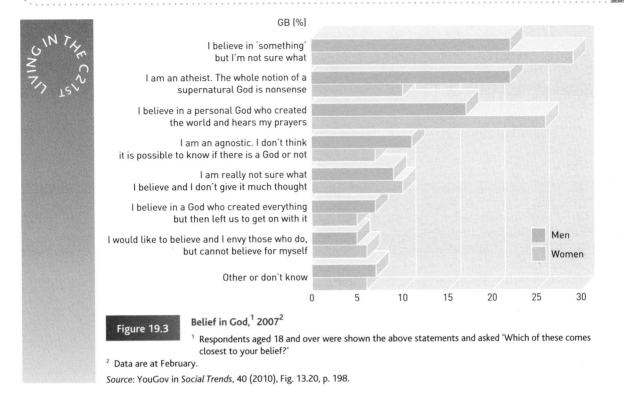

GB (%)

- I believe in 'something' but I'm not sure what
- I am an atheist. The whole notion of a supernatural God is nonsense
- I believe in a personal God who created the world and hears my prayers
- I am an agnostic. I don't think it is possible to know if there is a God or not
- I am really not sure what I believe and I don't give it much thought
- I believe in a God who created everything but then left us to get on with it
- I would like to believe and I envy those who do, but cannot believe for myself
- Other or don't know

Men
Women

0    5    10    15    20    25    30

**Figure 19.3**  Belief in God,[1] 2007[2]

[1] Respondents aged 18 and over were shown the above statements and asked 'Which of these comes closest to your belief?'

[2] Data are at February.

*Source*: YouGov in *Social Trends*, 40 (2010), Fig. 13.20, p. 198.

LIVING IN THE C21ST

# A note on religion in the UK: God is dead

In line with much of Europe, Britain is a relatively non-religious country: when 1,000 people were polled both in the UK and the USA and asked 'Do you believe there is a God?', less than 30 per cent in the UK said yes, compared with 80 per cent in the USA. Indeed, around 60 per cent of the population say they have no connection with any religion or church. Although we can map out the population structure by religious identification – as Table 19.1 does – research generally shows a very low number of people who participate in any kind of religious activity or believe in any kind of God. In 2000, some 60 per cent did claim to be religious and 50 per cent of the population claimed to be Christian. But by 2006 only a third seemed to believe in a God; about 6 per cent went to church; about two-thirds described themselves as not religious.

All major world religions are represented, but the numbers outside Christianity are relatively low: about 6 to 7 per cent. Nearly 40 per cent said they did not consider themselves belonging to any particular religion. The figures for Christian belief also include a lot of non-practising Christians – who may claim the religion but do not take it too seriously in their life.

In Britain, the Churches of England and Wales are formally tied to both Parliament and the monarchy, though the Church of England has shed its image as the 'Tory Party at prayer'. Membership in established, 'mainstream' churches has dwindled. Support for the Anglican, Roman Catholic, Presbyterian and Baptist churches has been declining significantly since the late twentieth century. Nominally, there are around 27 million Anglicans (nearly two-thirds claimed to associate with the Church of England), but only 2 million have officially registered. There are some 5 million Catholics, who are much more likely to attend church (Liverpool is Britain's only mainly Catholic city). Research also suggests that non-religious parents pass on their lack of faith to their children. Two religious parents have roughly a 50–50 chance of passing on their beliefs (Voas and Crockett, 2005: 11–12). That said, the churches do remain involved in the cultural life of the UK, through such activities as playgroups, youth clubs, care for the elderly and community centres. Christianity may now be more of a cultural force than a spiritual one.

As the established Christian churches lose members, however, other religious organisations are showing

LIVING IN THE C21ST

# The god delusion or the twilight of atheism?

In the early twenty-first century, with a major conflict starting to appear between the West and the (fundamentalist) Muslim faith – a conflict with long historical roots – another schism became prominent. This is the divide between believers and non-believers.

There are now a number of countries where over half of the population may be seen as non-believers: Sweden, Denmark, Norway, Japan and much of Europe rank at the top. According to the 2009 *Human Development Report*, the four highest ranked nations in terms of human development were Norway, Australia, Iceland and Canada. All four have very high degrees of atheism. The Netherlands, Sweden and Japan – also with low religion – were in the top ten.

There are deep historical roots into non-believing: from Socrates' refusal to acknowledge Greek gods to Copernicus' heretical idea that the earth revolved around the sun; from Darwin's huge controversy over our evolution from the apes to Freud's understanding of our unconscious. The modern world can indeed be seen as a long battle between 'science' and 'religion' (see Chapter 23).

Recently, there have been a number of spokespeople emerging to make claims for non-belief, and to criticise religions. They have become 'best-sellers' and have attracted wide attention and a not inconsiderable 'following'. In the USA, Sam Harris has published *The End of Faith* (2006), *Letter to Christian Nation* (2007) and *The Moral Landscape* (2010). In the UK, the leading spokesperson has been the scientist Richard Dawkins with his book *The God Delusion* (2006) (as well as the commentator Christopher Hitchens' *God is not Great* (2007) and the philosopher A. C. Grayling's *Against all Gods* (2007) and *The Good Book* (2011)).

In all these books, God is seen as a superstition that the modern world can no longer afford. For progress, we must look for the evidence. We must follow the scientific road. For Dawkins, the highest impulses – empathy, charity – can be found to emerge in natural selection. We are instinctively drawn to acts of human kindness and generosity from our own interests.

As a social movement, atheism is generally quite small and moves under a plethora of names. American Atheists, for example, have only about 2,500 members and a budget of less than a million dollars. In the UK, the British Humanist Association and the National Secular Society are also quite

small. Alistair McGrath suggests that far from witnessing the growth of atheism, at the start of the twenty-first century we are experiencing its twilight (McGrath, 2004).

To most cultures, 'atheists' are seen as a threat to their established order. But for some, like John Gray, humanism is in fact simply a 'mirror image of monotheism'. Indeed, for Gray it is an episode in the decline of Christianity. Atheism has the same key features as most religions: the dogmatism of faith – though in this case it is the dogmatism of non-faith.

Amongst the core religious controversies of our times which humanists debate with believers are:

- Role of women
- Homosexuality and gay marriage
- Abortion and reproductive rights
- Euthanasia
- The family
- Contraception
- Stem cell research
- Dress codes
- Punishments

And at the broadest level: the conflict over science and religion, modernity and tradition. Atheists tend to take liberal views on most of these matters.

 On YouTube you can find Richard Dawkins and Alistair McGrath in debate with each other.

surprising strength. The UK now has substantial populations of Muslims, Sikhs, Hindus and Jews, which, in contrast to the Christian faiths, have generally grown significantly in recent years. Immigration initially underpinned the numbers of Muslims, Sikhs and Hindus, who have established large communities to be found in London, the Midlands, West Yorkshire and Strathclyde, were born in the UK. The one religion which seems to be on the increase in the UK is the Muslim faith with 1,600,000 in 2001 growing to 2,422,000 by 2008. Britain also has the second-largest Jewish community in Europe.

Despite these general observations, measuring religious involvement in any country can be quite a

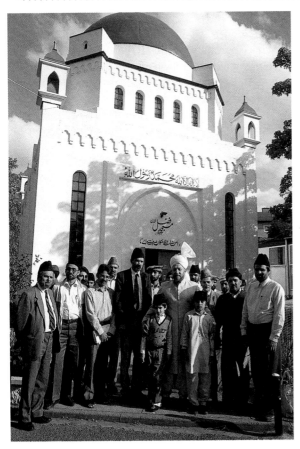

Muslim leaders in front of Britain's oldest mosque, at Earlsfield
*Source*: Paul Popper Popperfoto/getty Images.

# Religion in the twenty-first century

The twentieth century was the age when 'the death of God' was proclaimed. And across parts of the Western world, Christianity was in notable decline. We seemed to be arriving in the Secular Age. But the twenty-first century is beginning to tell a different story. Now, from many angles, there is a resurgence of interest in religion of all kinds. In much of the world, religion is alive and well, even though it is undergoing a number of quite significant changes. In this section we will detect five major trends at work. These are:

1  A limited, partial secularisation that is continuing the twentieth century trend towards a secular age.
2  A resurgence of interest in the mainstream traditional world faiths as they take on new forms and come to attract a wider group of followers.
3  The development of a wide range of new religious movements.
4  The growth of fundamentalisms alongside 'the clash of civilisations', which results in more and more religiously linked conflict, culture wars and even genocide.
5  The development of new institutional (maybe postmodern?) forms of religion, such as cyber-churches and mega-churches.

## 1 Limited and partial secularisation

The first trend regularly discussed among sociologists is **secularisation**, *the historical decline in the importance of the supernatural and the sacred*. For society as a whole, secularisation points to the waning influence of religion in everyday life: we have just seen this in the description of religion in the UK above. And as religious organisations become more secular, they direct attention less to other-worldly issues (such as life after death) and more to worldly affairs (such as sheltering the homeless, feeding the hungry and raising funds). In addition, secularisation means that functions once performed mostly by the church (such as charity) are now primarily the responsibility of businesses and government. More, it means that people are less likely to view the world in spiritual terms and are more likely to see it in terms of material goods and consumption – a trend detected in Chapter 15.

difficult exercise. Peter Brierley (2000), who has studied this in the UK in some detail, suggests there are three major ways to measure it. First, there is *involvement in religious community*: this would involve anyone associated with religion – through baptism, for example. Second, there is *religious membership* – those who join a religious organisation. Finally, there is *religious attendance* – those who go to religious services. Research suggests that in the twenty-first century, very few attend church, there are declining numbers of members, but a somewhat larger number may well affiliate with religions on particular occasions.

Christianity, then, seems to be on the decline in the UK. Church membership and church attendance have been falling and many are concerned that a whole generation has now been brought up without Christian convictions – a real change over the past 50 years.

Secularisation, with Latin roots meaning 'the present age', is commonly associated with modern, technologically advanced societies (Cox, 1971). Jose Casanova has suggested that the term itself can lead to confusion, as it contains three different strands that need clarifying. The first is 'secularisation as decline of religious beliefs and practices'. This is perhaps the most popular meaning, but it conceals other hidden and deeper meanings. Thus the second is 'secularisation as differentiation of the secular spheres from religious institutions'. It is in Europe that one can find the least differentiation between state and the church. And finally, secularisation may be seen as 'marginalisation of religion to a privatised sphere' (Casanova, 1994: 211). Here, while religion may still be honoured in public, it plays less of a role in the private life of individuals.

Secularisation is often seen as one result of the increasing importance of science in understanding human affairs. Science takes over from religion. In broader terms, people perceive birth, illness and death less as the work of a divine power than as natural stages in the life course. Such events are now more likely to occur in the presence of physicians (scientific specialists) than religious leaders (whose knowledge is based on faith). With the rise of science, religion's sphere of influence has diminished. Theologian Harvey Cox elaborates:

> The world looks less and less to religious rules and rituals for its morality or its meanings. For some, religion provides a hobby, for others a mark of national or ethnic identification, for still others an aesthetic delight. For fewer and fewer does it provide an inclusive and commanding system of personal and cosmic values and explanations.
>
> (Cox, 1971: 3)

If Cox is correct, should we expect that religion will disappear completely some day? Is there a decline in religion? The consensus among sociologists is 'no' (Hammond, 1985; Berger, 1999), for three reasons. If the world is looked at globally, then religion is still an overwhelming and dominant force. It is true that religion holds less sway in Europe (and particularly the Scandinavian countries). It is also true that secular views are common among what may be identified as an international subculture of humanists among academics, whose views do have global significance and influence. But everywhere else, religious fervour seems to be clearly rising. Peter Berger says: 'the world today, with some exceptions, is as furiously religious as it ever was, and in some places more so than ever' (1997: 32).

Even as traditional religious forms flourish and expand, modernity and postmodernity – with their growing disenchantment with the world – create an ongoing requirement for creating meanings that go beyond it. People, it is argued, are desperate for meaning in a meaningless world, and they find it in the new religions (Davie, 1998). Hence we find the development of new religions and a resurgence of interest in older religions – trying to make them sensible for today. We consider this below.

## 2 Resurgence of interest in the mainstream traditional world faiths

Many now argue that Christianity is in fact growing – and becoming global (Jenkins, 2007). What has often been overlooked by sociologists is the southward expansion of Christianity in Africa, Asia and Latin America. Jenkins believes that by 2050, only one Christian in five will be a non-Latino white person. In Africa, Christians grew from 10 million in 1900 to 360 million in 2000. But what is really striking about this change is the way these expanding Christian countries are much more fundamentalist – traditional, morally conservative and evangelical. They are much more inclined to deal with faith-healing, exorcism and mysticism. They often raise huge funds from the relatively poor. A new 'Christendom' is coming to the poorer world in the twenty-first century that could well have major consequences.

### Pentecostalism

Starting in the early twentieth century with William J. Seymour, Pentecostals believe that Jesus will return in their lifetime. God will send a new Pentecost if only people have faith to believe hard enough. Pentecostals differ from evangelicals and others in emphasising the 'Holy Spirit' that can enter ordinary people and give them extraordinary powers. With faith, people could speak in tongues, float in the air, fall in trances: some 80 per cent believe they will be transported to heaven. Today it is estimated that there are at least 500 million 'revivalists' and that this may be one of the world's fastest-growing religions – indeed, they could represent a quarter of the world's Christian population (World Christian Database). They meet in huge arenas and buildings (as large as football stadiums), in shopping malls and 'redemption camps' all over the world. They are most significant in Africa, Latin America and the United States.

Pentecostal meetings are less hierarchical and dogmatic than the formal Christian church. They are more expressive; crowds pursue 'ecstasy' and this taps into emotion. The movement started largely with the poor and black in the USA but has now spread to a worldwide religion. It is populist (anyone can set up a church), innovative and highly emotionally charged. The sociologist Peter Berger says: 'Max Weber is alive and well and living in Guatemala City' (*Economist*, 23 December 2006: 86). Religion here is both premodern and postmodern; it is the 'fiesta', the 'encounter group' and the 'big business'.

# 3 The emergence of new religious movements (NRMs)

While membership in established, 'mainstream' churches may have plummeted, affiliation with other religious organisations (including Seventh-Day Adventists and Christian sects) has risen just as dramatically. Indeed, secularisation itself may be self-limiting. As church-like organisations become more worldly, some people within a religious 'marketplace' may simply abandon them in favour of more sect-like religious communities that better address their spiritual concerns and whose members seem to exhibit greater religious commitment (Stark and Bainbridge, 1981; Iannaccone, 1994). Thus, in the face of secularisation and the seeming decline in religion, many so-called NRMs have appeared. Indeed, one of the most striking developments of recent years has been the proliferation of NRMs. It is estimated that there may now be as many as 20,000 new religious groupings in Europe alone.

One way of thinking about these movements is to see their affinities with the traditional mainstream religions described above. Thus, some are linked to Hinduism (Hari Krishnas and the disciples of Bhagwan Rajneesh); others to Buddhism (various Zen groups); and others to Christianity (the Children of God). Some NRMs are eclectic (the Unification Church), while others have links with the Human Potential Movement (which advocates therapies to liberate human potential, such as transcendental meditation). Many years ago (in 1976), the late Roy Wallis (1945–90) proposed a typology of these growing groups which is still useful. He suggested three main kinds of NRM: world affirming, world rejecting and world accommodating.

## World-affirming groups

The world-affirming groups are usually individualistic and life-positive, and aim to release 'human potentials'. They encourage an active participation in society. Research suggests that these are more common among middle-aged, middle-class groups, who are often disillusioned and disenchanted with material values and in search of new positive meanings. These groups generally lack a church, ritual worship or strong ethical systems. They are often more akin to 'therapy groups' than traditional religions.

A major example of this is the Church of Scientology, founded by L. Ron Hubbard. Hubbard developed the philosophy of 'dianetics', which stresses the importance of 'unblocking the mind' and leading it to becoming 'clear'. Hubbard believed in a rebirthing. His church spread throughout the world (with a base in California) and generated courses (usually expensive) and books galore (see Wallis, 1976).

A second example is transcendental meditation (TM). Brought to the West by the Hindu Mahareshi Mahesh Yogi in the early 1950s, it focuses upon building a personal mantra which is then dwelt upon for periods each day. Again, the focus is upon a good world – not an evil one – and a way of 'finding oneself' through positive thinking. Much of this mode of thinking has helped generate a major new linked movement: that of 'New Age'.

'New Age' is a hybrid mix and match of religions, therapies and astrologies, and has become increasingly important since the 1970s. It is part of what might be seen as the globalisation of modern religion – mixing as it does elements from both Eastern and Western traditions, along with the wider concerns of environment and ecology. Bruce (1996: 197) suggests that these are largely 'audience' or 'client cults'. The former have led to a major market of 'self-help therapy' books with mass distribution; the latter have led to the proliferation of new 'therapists' (from astrological to colour therapists), establishing new relationships between a consumer and a seller. Among the practices involved are tarot readings, crystals, reflexology, channelling and I Ching. Currently, many bookshops devote more shelf space to these sorts of book than to books on Christianity. The fascination with television programmes such as *The X Files* may also be seen as part of this. It brings a new science, a new ecology, a new psychology and a new spirituality. 'New Agers make the monistic assumption that the Self is sacred' (Heelas, 1996: 140).

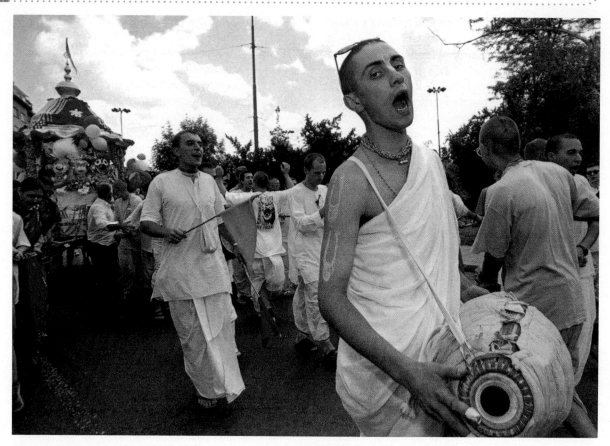

Bulgarian Hare Krishna parade through the streets of Sofia, August 1996
*Source*: Reuters/Alexei Dityakin.

## World-rejecting groups

The world-rejecting groups are like the sects described above. In some ways they are quite like conventional religions in that they may require prayer and the study of key religious texts, and they have strong ethical codes. They are always highly critical of the outside (material evil) world and they demand change of their members through strong communal activities. They are exclusive, share possessions and seek to submerge identities to the greater whole. They are often millenarian – expecting God's intervention to change the world and inspiring activism to make this come about ('millenarian' is derived from the millennium, the 1,000-year reign of Christ). Researchers have suggested that it may well be people who live on the margins who are most attracted to these groups.

Perhaps the most widely cited example of world-rejecting groups is the Unification Church (popularly known as the Moonies), founded in Korea by the Reverend Sun Myung Moon in 1954. It appeared in California in the early 1960s where it was studied by the sociologist John Lofland in his book *Doomsday Cult* (2nd edn, 1977). Later Eileen Barker (1981, 1984) studied it in England. The Unification Church rejects the mundane secular world as evil and has strict moral rules: monogamous heterosexual sex, no smoking, no drinking, etc.

Another example is the Hare Krishna (Children of God, or ISKON – the International Society for Krishna Consciousness). The members are distinguished by their shaved heads, pigtails and flowing gowns; Hare Krishnas repeat a mantra 16 times a day.

These sects are the movements that have come under most public scrutiny in recent years, largely because of the fear of indoctrination and the problems of severe control and even mass suicide. There is a growing list of extreme examples – the mass suicide by Jim Jones's People Temple in Jonestown, Guyana

(Hall, 1987); the Aum Supreme Truth (run by Shoko Ashara), which detonated poisonous gas canisters in the Tokyo underground in 1995, leaving 12 dead and 5,000 sick; and the more recent suicidal death of the 39 members of Heaven's Gate in California when they sighted the Hale-Bopp comet. Heaven's Gate programmers posted a message on their website saying: 'We are happily prepared to leave this world.' While these new religious forms mirror the means and powers that other religions have continued to employ, they are seen by the press and public as deviant, and hence attract more attention.

## World-accommodating groups

World-accommodating religions are more orthodox. They maintain some connections with mainstream religion, but give a high premium to the inner religious life. The Neo-Pentecostals (discussed above) are a good example. The Holy Spirit 'speaks' through them, giving them the gift of 'speaking in tongues'. Such religions are usually dismayed at both the state of the world and the state of organised mainstream religions. They seek to establish older certainties and faith, while giving them a new vitality.

# 4  Religious fundamentalisms and the 'clash of civilisations'

The most extreme version of contemporary developments is the growth of **fundamentalism** across religions. This can be seen as *a conservative religious doctrine that opposes intellectualism and worldly accommodation in favour of restoring traditional, other-worldly spirituality*. Although it is a bit of a rag-bag word – meaning all things to all people – it generally suggests belief in a timeless and absolute value given to sacred writings in all times and places. It is applied to a wide variety of groups: from the 'Moral Majority' in the United States, to Orthodox Jews in Israel and the Islamic government in Iran. In response to what they see as the growing influence of science and the erosion of the conventional family, religious fundamentalists defend their version of traditional values. From this point of view, the liberal churches are simply too tolerant of religious pluralism and too open to change. The enemy of fundamentalism is the 'Great Satan of Modernity' (Bruce, 2000).

A number of features distinguish religious fundamentalists of various stripes.

1   *They interpret 'infallible' sacred texts literally.* Fundamentalists, who see sacred texts as infallible blueprints for life, insist on literal interpretations of the sacred texts as a means of countering what they see as excessive intellectualism among more liberal and revisionist organisations.

2   *They reject religious pluralism.* Fundamentalists maintain that tolerance and relativism water down personal faith, and they harshly judge most modern faiths as illegitimate.

3   *They find a personal experience of God's presence.* Fundamentalists seek to propagate spiritual revival. They define all areas of life as sacred. For example, fundamentalist Christians seek to be 'born again' to establish a personal relationship with Jesus that will shape a person's everyday life.

4   *They oppose secularisation and modernity.* Fundamentalists believe that modernity undermines religious conviction. Secular humanism leads to profane moral corruption.

5   *They promote conservative beliefs, including patriarchal ones.* Fundamentalists argue that God intends humans to live in heterosexual families ruled by men. They blame feminist and gay rights movements for contributing to moral decline. In particular, fundamentalists condemn abortion and decry lesbian and gay relations.

6   *They emerge in response to social inequality or a perceived social crisis.* Fundamentalists attract members by offering solutions to desperate, worried or dejected people.

Taken together, these traits have given fundamentalism a backward and self-righteous reputation. At the same time, this brief sketch also helps us to understand why adherents find such religions an appealing alternative to the more intellectual, tolerant and worldly 'mainstream' denominations.

Fundamentalist religions in the UK and across Europe have recently gained strength, but we must use the term 'fundamentalist' with care. While conservative branches of many religions have turned fundamentalist, the term is often used pejoratively to dismiss religious movements which question the status quo. In particular, as Chapter 11 noted, there has been the development of 'Islamophobia', whereby the label 'fundamentalist' is often used in the West to dismiss the claims of a range of Islamic movements. Even in cases where Islam has evolved into an extreme form, fundamentalist extremism often emerges in response to the capitalist version of modernity that has favoured the West while leaving extreme poverty elsewhere (Esposito, 1992: 14). As we have seen in Chapter 11, it is likely that issues of fundamentalism will become more and more central in the twenty-first century.

Moreover, we should not see fundamentalism as necessarily new. Indeed, Steven Bruce suggests that:

> There is nothing at all unusual in people taking religion very seriously. What we now regard as religious 'extremism' was commonplace 200 years ago in the Western world and is still commonplace in most parts of the globe. It is not the dogmatic believer who insists that the sacred texts are divinely inspired and true, who tries to model his life on the ethical requirements of those texts, and who seeks to impose these requirements on the entire society who is unusual. The liberal who supposes that his sacred texts are actually human constructions of differing moral worth, whose religion makes little difference to his life, and who is not quite happy to accept that what his God requires of him is not binding on other members of his society: this is the strange and remarkable creature.

(Bruce, 2000: 116–17)

## The clash of civilisations

It is precisely this religious conviction that has been behind many historical wars. Yet one of the more dramatic potentials that arise from the spread of fundamentalism may be the increasing risk of major international conflicts based upon religion. Samuel P. Huntington, for instance, sees new fault lines of world conflict arising from religious resurgence across the world in all faiths: 'The unsecularisation of the world is one of the dominant social facts in the late twentieth century' (Huntington, 1996: 96, citing George Wigel). He sees localised *'fault line'* wars breaking out all over the world, especially between Muslims and non-Muslims. At the same time, *'core state'* conflicts are also appearing between the major states of civilisations. A major issue here may be between the Christian West and the Muslim world. In any event, since the breakdown of the Cold War between East and West, the major issues of conflict have returned to all those religious schisms that dominated much of earlier history too.

# 5  The arrival of new religious forms and organisations

One dimension of secularisation is the rise of what Robert Bellah (1975) has called **civil religion**, *a quasi-religious loyalty binding individuals in a basically secular society*. In other words, even if some traditional dimensions of religiosity are weakening, new religious qualities may be found in such things as patriotism, membership in associations, good citizenship and even sports meetings which can retain religious qualities. He conducted research in the United States, where, he argues, religious qualities appear in a range of rituals, from rising to sing the US national anthem at sporting events, to presidential inauguration ceremonies, to sitting down to watch televised public parades several times a year. In England, ceremonies linked to the royal family (coronations, royal weddings, etc.), as well as village fêtes, town parades and similar gatherings, all may serve these same functions.

The enormous outpouring of grief around the death of Diana, Princess of Wales could be taken as further evidence of civil religion. Immediately after her death in Paris on 31 August 1997, hundreds of thousands of people publicly showed their grief by sending flowers, attending the funeral and signing 'commemoration books'. These people came from all walks of life and religions, but created a strong sense of group belonging and national – even international – grief.

## The electronic, 'cyber' and 'mega-church'

In contrast to the small village congregations of years past, some religious organisations – especially fundamentalists – have become electronic churches dominated by 'prime-time preachers' (Hadden and Swain, 1981). Electronic religion has been especially strong in the United States and has propelled charismatic preachers such as Oral Roberts, Pat Robertson, Robert Schuller and others to greater prominence than all but a few clergy have ever enjoyed in the past. About 5 per cent of the US television audience (around 10 million people) regularly tune into religious television, while perhaps 20 per cent (around 40 million) watch some religious programming every week (Martin, 1981; Gallup, 1982; NORC, 1994).

During the 1980s, regular solicitation of contributions brought a financial windfall to some religious organisations. Seen on 3,200 stations in

Indonesia is the world's most populous Muslim nation but Christians account for about 10 per cent of the 226 million population. This is Katedral Mesias in Jakarta, Indonesia: a Chinese–Indonesian multi-million-dollar megachurch that covers 600,000 square feet of land and has two chapels that hold a maximum occupancy of 6,300 people. Here, Christians listen to a preacher during its opening in 2008

*Source*: © Enny Huraheni/Reuters/Corbis.

half the countries in the world, for example, Jimmy Swaggart received as much as $180 million annually in donations. But some media-based ministries were corrupted by the power of money. In 1989, Jim Bakker (who began his television career in 1965 hosting a children's puppet show with his wife Tammy Faye) was jailed following a conviction for defrauding contributors. Such cases, although few in number, attracted enormous international attention and undermined public support as people began to wonder whether television preachers were more interested in raising moral standards or private cash.

Along with the electronic church, we can also find the growth of the 'cyber-church' and the 'mega-church'. The former is easy to find on a website, as all major world religions now have a proliferation of websites, but so too do the multitude of smaller new religious movements. The internet is a prime force for information giving, but it is also an arena for membership recruitment.

'Mega-churches' are very large worship centres – often only loosely affiliated with existing denominations, and more likely to be identified with 'born-again' religions or charismatic Christians. In the United States and all over the world, they can be found in shopping malls and parking lots. Characteristically, they are very large: they house as many as 1,000–3,000 worshippers or more. The Yoido Full Gospel Church in Seoul, South Korea, has six daily services in a facility with 13,000 seats! It has some 700,000 members and reaches 30,000 other worshippers via closed-circuit television. There are 11 choirs and a 24-piece orchestra. In the United States, the largest mega-church is the Lakewood Church, Houston, with 25,060 total weekend attenders in 2003. In 1970, there were just ten such churches; by 2003 there were 740. Many of them function like businesses with their own media (contemporary music, television) technologies and massive budgets (upwards of US$12 million).

# Taking stock and looking ahead

The pace of social change is accelerating. Two contradictory processes are happening at the start of the twenty-first century. On the one hand, the process of 'secularisation' suggests a growing disenchantment with the spiritual and the supernatural and for some a turn to rationality, and science has gained increasing support with many. Secularisation has spread across much of Europe and other Western cultures, with the partial exception of the United States, but remains relatively weak in the rest of the world, where traditional religions hold stronger sway. On the other hand, the growth of religious fundamentalism, the continuing adherence of billions to the 'mainstream' religions, the continuing clash of civilisations over their passionate commitment to their faiths (as in the war in Afghanistan), and the development of more and more 'new religions' all suggest that multiple religions, with all their potential for conflicts, wars and human suffering, will remain a central element of modern society for many years to come. Religion may have been dying in the twentieth century: it seems very alive and well in the twenty-first.

# SUMMARY

1 Religion is a major social institution based on distinguishing the sacred from the profane. Religion is a matter of faith, not scientific evidence, which people express through various rituals. Sociology analyses the social consequences and correlates of religion, but sociology cannot make claims about the ultimate truth or falsity of any religious belief.

2 Emile Durkheim argued that individuals experience the power of their society through religion. Religion promotes social cohesion and conformity by conferring meaning and purpose on life. Max Weber connects religion to meanings and social change: his analysis of Calvinism's contribution to the rise of industrial capitalism demonstrates religion's power to promote social change. Hervieu-Leger has come to see religion as 'chain of memory'. Societies have memories, and as this weakens, so too does religion. Peter Berger suggests that religious beliefs are socially constructed as a means of responding to life's uncertainties and disruptions. Using the social conflict paradigm, Karl Marx charged that religion is the 'opium of the people' and reinforces social inequality.

3 Churches, which are religious organisations well integrated into their society, fall into two categories – ecclesias and denominations. Sects, the result of religious division, are marked by suspicion of the larger society as well as charismatic leadership. Cults are religious organisations that embrace new and unconventional beliefs and practices.

4 Many hunter-gatherer societies are and have been generally animistic, with religious life just one facet of family life; in more complex societies, religion emerges as a distinct social institution. Followers of six world religions – Christianity, Islam, Judaism, Hinduism, Buddhism and Confucianism – represent three-quarters of all humanity. Non-religious groups are about a sixth of the world's population.

5 Five main issues are appearing in contemporary debates over religion: (a) a limited, partial secularisation that is continuing the twentieth-century trend towards a secular age; (b) the resurgence of interest in the mainstream traditional world faiths as they take on new forms and come to attract a wider group of followers; (c) the development of a wide range of new religious movements; (d) the growth of fundamentalisms alongside 'the clash of civilisations', which results in more and more religiously linked conflict, culture wars, and even genocide; and (e) the development of new institutional (maybe postmodern?) forms of religion like cyber-churches and mega-churches.

CONNECT UP: Turn to Part 6 of this book for key resources and link up
with the book's website, which links to these resources
SEE: www.pearsoned.co.uk/plummer

## MYTASKLIST

# Ten suggestions for going further

## 1 Connect up with Part Six and the Sociology Web Resources

As you work through ideas and think about the issues raised in this chapter, look at the accompanying website and the resource centre at the end of this book which connects to it. There is a lot here to help you move on. To link up, see: www.pearson.co.uk/plummer.

## 2 Review the chapter

*Briefly summarise (in a paragraph) just what this chapter has been about.* Consider: (a) What have you learned? (b) What do you disagree with? Be critical. And (c) How would you develop all this? How could you get more detail on matters that interest you?

## 3 Pose questions

(a) In the twenty-first century, is religion becoming more important than ever? If so, how and why?

(b) You can use the website to look at all of the world's major religions as outlined in the text. It is important to note that these 'traditional' religions are using the most up-to-date technologies to spread their word. Consider how modernist tools can be used to bring out traditional ideas of the sacred. What problems and contradictions might this raise?

(c) Using the website, track down the sites of some major new religious movements and inspect what they have to say. Consider the sheer variety of sites and why are there so many.

(d) Use the internet to look for evidence which points to a decline in religion in Europe. Discuss the rise of non-belief and atheism in some parts of the world.

## 4 Explore key words

Many concepts have been introduced in this chapter. You can review them from the website or from the listing at the back of this book. You might like to give special attention to just five words and think them through – how would you define them, what are they dealing with, and do they help you see the social world more clearly or not?

John Bowker, *World Religions* (2006).

John Bowker, *The Concise Oxford Dictionary of World Religions* (2005).

## 5 Search the Web

Be critical when you look at websites – see the box on p. 940 in the Resources section. Look at the following:

Adherents.com www.adherents.com/largecom
Seems to be getting out of date and has not recently been updated. Still, it details some of the largest religious communities of all kinds to be found in the world.

New Religious Movements database
http://religiousmovements.lib.virginia.edu/home.htm
Details more than 200 sites of new religions.

Cult Information Centre www.cultinformation.org.uk
CIC is an educational charity providing advice and information for victims of cults, their families and friends, researchers and the media.

Religious Tolerance www.religioustolerance.org
A website promoting religious tolerance and providing information on different belief systems and surrounding controversies and debates.

## Some specific words to search

All the major religions have their own websites: here are some names to search for:

*World Council of Churches*
*Islam at a glance*
*Judaism*
*Hinduism Today*
*Zen Buddhism*
*Humanism*

## 6　Review a DVD

- Peter Mullan's *The Magdalene Sisters* (2002): shocking true drama about child abuse in the Catholic Church.
- Antonia Bird's *Priest* (1994): a young gay priest confronts his religion.
- Stanley Kramer's *Inherit the Wind* (1960): classic film based on the Scopes 'monkey' trial – science versus religion. Powerful.
- Xavier Beauvois' *Of Gods and Men* (2010): a film about faith and belief – and the murder of monks in Algeria by fundamentalists.
- There is also an online *Journal of Film and Religion* produced by the University of Nebraska, www.unomaha.edu/~wwwjrf

## 7　Read and think

### General introductions

Phil Zuckerman, *Invitation to the Sociology of Religion* (2003). A very general and readable introduction.

Joanne O'Brien and Martin Palmer (2007) *The Atlas of Religion*. Great maps and summaries of all the world's religions.

Grace Davie, *Religion in Modern Europe: A Memory Mutates* (2000). Discusses the diversity of religion in western Europe and follows the theory that religion is a form of collective memory.

## More specific readings

Lester Kurtz, *Gods in the Global Village: The World's Religions in Sociological Perspective* (2nd edn, 2006). Provides a detailed account of all the world's major religions and an analysis of how they are changing under the impact of globalisation and multiculturalism.

Steven Bruce, *Fundamentalism* (2000). Looks at the rise of fundamentalism in the face of modernity, which fundamentalists see as the 'Great Satan'.

Mark Juergensmeyer (2008) *Global Rebellion: Religious Challenges to the Secular State from Christian Militias to Al Quaeda*. Lively account of the twenty-first-century world conflicts over religion.

## 8　Connect and integrate

Many of the ideas in this chapter can also be developed by looking at other chapters. For example:

- For more on the theories of Marx, Durkheim and Weber, see Chapter 4.
- The controversy over ethnicity and the veil is discussed in Chapter 11 (p. 377).
- New religious movements express some of the themes of new social movements, which are discussed in Chapter 16.

## 9　Relax with a novel

Look at Salman Rushdie's *Satanic Verses* (1989), which caused such controversy among the worldwide Muslim community that a *fatwa* was issued on the author. New controversies continue to appear. For a recent illustration amongst Christian groups, see the story writing of Philip Pullman, especially *The Good Man Jesus and the Scoundrel Christ* (2010).

# 10 Engage in THE BIG DEBATE

## Is religion in decline? The death of God or the triumph of religions?

For years now, philosophers like Nietzsche (1844–1900) have proclaimed 'the death of God' and sociologists have talked about the ways in which the modern world is becoming increasingly secularised. After all, as science and rationality become more and more central to the ways in which the modern world works, so the mysteries of the universe, which religion so often had to explain, become demystified. And yet, sociologists increasingly point to the weakness of this secularisation thesis and suggest that, far from becoming less and less religious, the trends actually suggest that we are becoming more and more religious. It is not secularisation that is the issue but desecularisation.

We are talking globally. It is clearly the case that much of northern Europe is becoming less and less religious. But it seems that everywhere else in the world this is not so. Peter Berger suggests that 'on the international religious scene, it is conservative or orthodox or traditionalist movements that are on the rise almost everywhere' (1999: 6). He suggests this is so partly because they are opposed to what they see as developments in the modern world, but also because religion itself is the status quo: it has always been around, and it will continue to be so. What we are witnessing now is an 'Islamic upsurge' alongside a Christian 'Evangelical upsurge'. The Catholic impact can be found from Manila to Krakow, and from Santiago to Seoul (Berger, 1999: 19). With over 1 billion adherents, it is to be found in almost every country, served by some 4,300 bishops and some 404,500 priests. Philip Jenkins looks at the rise of Pentecostalism across the globe – and sees a new Christendom in the making: 'the coming of global Christianity' (2007). At the same time, we see religion fanning wars and civil wars on the Indian subcontinent, in the Balkans, in the Middle East and in Africa. (Look at the map on p. 666). There are disputes in every continent. Everywhere religion is on the rise.

### Continue the debate

1 What evidence is there for desecularisation? For secularisation?
2 Do you believe that the modern and postmodern worlds are showing a decline in religion? Why? Why not?
3 Are the new religious revivals a response to the crises of the modern world?
4 Look at the *Living in the twenty-first century* box on p. 678 and consider the debate over atheism.
5 Look at the map on p. 666 and consider just why so many different religions are in conflict with each other. Might this suggest a coming global war of religions?

# CHAPTER 20

# EDUCATION

**COLIN SAMSON IS A SOCIAL RESEARCHER** who spent years working with the Innu in Labrador in northern Canada. For most of their history, the Innu were a nomadic people, living by hunting. They were independent and self-reliant and had a strong sense of their purpose in the world. When the Canadian government introduced a policy of assimilation, which extinguished their unique identity and their right to the land, their way of life came under severe threat. Samson documents how the changes left the Innu ashamed and confused, and precipitated high rates of suicide, gas sniffing, widespread alcoholism and child abuse. There was a failure to recognise the distinctiveness of the group and its values and history, and in attempting to assimilate them, a crisis developed.

One part of this crisis was to be found in schooling, which the Canadian authorities insisted upon. In a sense the goal was to take on a new generation of Innu and help in the transformation of their culture into a more western European one. In the West, we tend to see formal schooling as a necessity – for the transmission of culture and knowledge, and indeed the preservation of social solidarity, values and order. Education is also one of the major determinants of a person's life chances. But for the Innu, they found this experience of formal schooling an alienating one. It made them apprehensive and worried. They found that schools did not tell the truth about who the Innu were, and did not speak to their values or way of life. Instead they got linear timetables, school discipline, formal lessons and abstractions, and all were alien to them. The school worked to transform them into Akaneshaut (white children). As some Innu commented:

> It made me 'think English' and gave me 'white thoughts' . . . I lost part of my life . . .

The only thing that kids are able to learn in school is to be embarrassed by our culture . . .

I am ashamed to say that I went to the school at all . . . I wasted my years in school . . .

Kids now talk back to their parents. That comes from the school. They don't pay attention at all. They don't listen to parents because in school they get a lot of English. They are gradually losing their language. Kids are starting to talk to each other in English.

(Samson, 2003: 199–201)

Far from providing values and maintaining a way of life, the schools were seen to erode Innu values among the young. School is remembered as a kind of culture shock. Whereas their education before came from living with nature, the landscape and animals, and their values from the persistent need to survive, now they found themselves confronted with abstractions and formalities. More used to lived experience in the past, the abstracted education of the West made them less competent in the world. The values they were now taught were often in terms of money and success – not in terms of spirituality, the hunting way of life and animals.

*Source:* Samson (2003).

*I have never let my schooling interfere with my education.*

Mark Twain

*Give a man a fish and you feed him for a day. Teach a man to fish and you feed him for a lifetime.*

Chinese proverb

## In this chapter, we ask:

- Is all the world becoming educated?

- What are key approaches to studying education?

- How do social divisions perpetuate themselves through education?

- What are key issues being debated in the sociology of education?

(Left) Peter Wagner, Thomas 'Tim' Dyson, George Salmon, Jack Catlin and George Young, outside Lord's, 1937; Jimmy Sime/Getty

Look at this photo and tell what you see. Most frequently, and for over 70 years, this image has been used in both popular and academic writing to tell the same story of educational inequality and social class division. It has become a popular photo – almost a cliché, used by books and newspapers when they want to make the point about inequalities. Here are the smart boys from Eton and Harrow, and the poor boys mocking them: the 'toffs and toughs' in conflict with each other. But recently, a study has suggested that all may not be as simple as the image suggests. Ian Jack researched the history of the photo and its five boys, and suggested all may well not be what it seems. The Harrow schoolboys did not come from elite backgrounds and fared badly in life (one died at 16); the rough boys were not in fact rough and fared better in life. There is, it seems, much more to this picture than meets the eye.

*Source:* Jimmy Sine/Stringer/Hulton Archive/Getty Images.

Look online at the account of this photo: see Ian Jack: Five Boys: The Story of a Picture. *Intelligent Life*. Spring 2010.

Downloadable at: http://moreintelligentlife.com/content/ian-jack/5-boys.

 'The camera never lies'. Trace the social history of this photo and show how the camera often lies.

All societies pay attention to ways of transmitting their cultures and values, and in the modern world these have increasingly become housed in schools and the broader educational process. This chapter spotlights **education**, *the social institution guiding the critical learning of knowledge, job skills, cultural norms and values*. In industrial societies, as we shall see, much education is a matter of **schooling**, *formal instruction under the direction of specially trained teachers*.

## Global education, poverty and literacy

Most people in the Western world spend much of their first 20 years in various kinds of school: nursery, primary, secondary and tertiary. Until recently, formal schooling in all societies was a privilege restricted to a small elite, and so it remains in many poorer societies today.

In hunter-gatherer and small agrarian societies, people's survival depended on learning as much as they could about the plants, animals and landscape in their environment. The Innu were not unusual. Elders devoted much time to passing on both cultural beliefs and knowledge of the natural world to the younger generations. As agrarian societies grew in size and complexity, people needed to learn only specialised knowledge for their field of work, rather than general knowledge. The majority of people in such systems spent most of their time performing physical labour which required little training, while a minority with the greatest wealth and power enjoyed the spare time to study literature, art, history and science. Indeed, the English word 'school' comes from the Greek word for 'leisure'.

We find marked diversity in schooling throughout the world today. In some developing regions, including much of central Asia and central America, religious organisations play a major role in providing education to children. In other regions, particularly eastern Asia,

Open-air classroom in the Primary School, Togo. Togo is a tropical sub-Saharan country with a population of approximately 6.7 million.  It ranks at 139 on the Human Development Index (2010) (see Chapter 9)
*Source:* © Atlantide Phototravel/Corbis.

Europe, the United States, Canada, Australia and New Zealand, the state formally coordinates and regulates the majority of schools. In most high-income societies, a growing number of young people are awarded first degrees: this is much less common in low-income societies, but the numbers are growing rapidly.

All low-income countries have one trait in common: there is limited access to formal schooling. Universal education might seem a relatively straightforward goal, but it has proved as difficult as any to achieve. In the poorest nations, more than 10 per cent of primary-aged children are out of school. At secondary levels, the number attending school is much lower. Table 20.1 provides basic data on school attendance in different regions.

By 2009, low-income countries as a whole had achieved a net enrolment in primary education approaching 90 per cent – higher in east Asia and Latin America, lower in Africa. Likewise, enrolment in secondary education worldwide has expanded tenfold over the past 50 years (from 40 million in 1950 to more than 400 million today), and tertiary education has

| Table 20.1 | School attendance in low-income societies | | | |
|---|---|---|---|---|
| **Countries and territories** | **School net enrolment rate (%) 2003–8** | | **School net attendance rate (%) 2003–8** | |
| | Male | Female | Male | Female |
| **(a) Primary schools** | | | | |
| AFRICA | 79 | 74 | 69 | 66 |
| Sub-Saharan Africa [Sudan, Djibouti] | 76 | 70 | 65 | 63 |
| Eastern and Southern Africa | 83 | 82 | 69 | 70 |
| West and Central Africa | 68 | 58 | 63 | 58 |
| Middle East and North Africa | 92 | 88 | 85 | 81 |
| ASIA | 92 | 89 | 84 | 81* |
| South Asia | 87 | 82 | 83 | 79 |
| East Asia and Pacific | 98 | 97 | 88 | 88* |
| Latin America and Caribbean | 95 | 95 | 92 | 93 |
| CEE/CIS | 92 | 90 | 94 | 92 |
| Industrialized countries | 94 | 95 | – | – |
| Developing countries | 89 | 86 | 80 | 78* |
| Least developed countries | 81 | 76 | 67 | 65 |
| World | 90 | 87 | 81 | 78* |
| **(b) Secondary schools** | | | | |
| AFRICA | 34 | 30 | 32 | 29 |
| Sub-Saharan Africa [Sudan, Djibouti] | 30 | 26 | 27 | 23 |
| Eastern and Southern Africa | 32 | 29 | 20 | 19 |
| West and Central Africa | – | – | 33 | 27 |
| Middle East and North Africa | 63 | 58 | 53 | 50 |
| ASIA | – | – | 55 | 49 |
| South Asia | – | – | 53 | 45 |
| East Asia and Pacific | 61 | 64* | 61 | 65 |
| Latin America and Caribbean | 69 | 74 | 67 | 73 |
| CEE/CIS | 79 | 75 | 79 | 76 |
| Industrialized countries | 91 | 92 | – | – |
| Developing countries | 53 | 52* | 51 | 46 |
| Least developed countries | 31 | 27 | 28 | 26 |
| World | 61 | 60* | 51 | 47 |

* Excludes China.

*Source: The State of the World's Children Special Edition*, UNICEF, Tables 1 and 5.

grown from 6.5 million in 1950 to 88.2 million in 1997. Nevertheless, across the globe it is still the case that some 69 million school age children were not going to school in 2008 (though down from 106 million non-attendees in 1999) (United Nations, Millennium Development Goals Fact Sheet, October 2010).

## The illiteracy question

Despite the world growth in education, illiteracy remains a major issue. A person can be said to be literate 'who can, with understanding, both read and write a short simple statement on his or her everyday life' (UNESCO, 2000: 23). The number of literate adults worldwide has been increasing rapidly. The figure doubled from 1.5 billion in 1970 to 3.4 billion in 2000 (see Table 20.2). This still leaves a huge proportion of the world's population as illiterate. Indeed, at the start of the twenty-first century, by 2005–6 there were an estimated 781 million illiterate adults in the world, about 64 per cent of whom are women. As a consequence, illiteracy disadvantages many.

| Table 20.2 | Literacy rates[1] across the world, 2000 | |
|---|---|---|
| | **Male** | **Female** |
| Sub-Saharan Africa | 69 | 53 |
| Middle East and North Africa | 74 | 52 |
| South Asia | 66 | 42 |
| East Asia and Pacific | 93 | 81 |
| Latin America | 90 | 88 |
| CEE/CIS[2] and Baltic States | 99 | 96 |
| World | 84 | 74 |

[1] Defined as percentage of persons aged 15 and over who can read and write.
[2] Central Eastern Europe/Commonwealth of Independent States.

Source: UNICEF (2004b: 121).

**TOP 10**
**Lowest literacy rates**

| | Adult literacy (%) |
|---|---|
| 1 Mali | 26.2 |
| 2 Burkina Faso | 28.7 |
| 2 Niger | 28.7 |
| 4 Chad | 32.7 |
| 5 Ethiopia | 35.9 |
| 6 Guinea | 38.0 |
| 7 Sierra Leone | 39.8 |
| 8 Benin | 40.8 |
| 9 Senegal | 41.9 |
| 10 The Gambia | 45.3 |

Note: India is ranked 25th with literacy amongst adults of 62.8% and Nigeria is ranked 23rd with a literacy rate of 60.1%.

Source: Pocket World in Figures (2011) Profile Books Ltd.

Even among some high-income countries, illiteracy remains a problem. While the United States opened educational opportunities to all citizens long before most other industrialised countries, some 25 million adults read and write at no more than a fourth-grade level and another 25 million have only eighth-grade language skills. This means that one in four adults in the United States is functionally illiterate, and the proportion is higher among the elderly and minorities. The problem of illiteracy in the United States is most serious among Latinos. In part this is due to a drop-out rate among 14- to 24-year-olds of almost 30 per cent, which is three times the rate among whites or African-Americans. The broader issue is that schools fail to teach many Spanish-speaking people to read and write *any* language very well (Kozol, 1980, 1985a, 1985b).

## The new illiteracy

Even this conceals the real nature of what has been called the 'new illiteracy'. As societies develop and expand their information technologies, so illiteracy will increasingly come to mean the inability to use computers, word processing, email and websites. Although these skills are expanding rapidly across the world, they are still highly selective. There has however been significant growth in low-income societies in recent years, see Table 20.3 which shows the results. In 2004, while there were 750 computers per thousand people in the USA, there were fewer than five per thousand in Cambodia, Uganda, Laos, Niger, Liberia and the Congo (*New Internationalist*, 2007: 60, 6–7). Table 20.3 shows the results of a survey of computer use in primary schools in 11 countries and see Chapter 1, p. 23.

## Resolving illiteracy

Observers such as Ivan Illich (1973) argue that the answer to widespread illiteracy is not to transpose Western-style schools into the rest of the world.

| Table 20.3 | Pupils in schools with computers: a global view 2005–6 | | | | | | | | | | | | | |
|---|---|---|---|---|---|---|---|---|---|---|---|---|---|---|
| | Computer for administrative use | | Computer-based management system | | Website of the school on the Internet | | Intranet site within the school | | Computers for pupils to use without access to the Internet | | Computers for pupils to use with access to the Internet | | Pupils without computers | |
| | % | SE | % | SE | % | SE | % | SE | % | SE | % | SE | % | SE |
| Argentina | 75.3 | 1.61 | 35.5 | 1.60 | 18.0 | 1.40 | 7.7 | 0.91 | 44.0 | 1.75 | 22.9 | 1.34 | 48.0 | 1.73 |
| Brazil | 70.4 | 1.91 | 50.0 | 2.46 | 10.7 | 1.66 | 20.1 | 2.22 | 23.4 | 2.09 | 22.8 | 2.13 | 63.5 | 2.29 |
| Chile | 93.4 | 1.07 | 67.7 | 2.08 | 48.6 | 2.42 | 47.3 | 2.58 | 46.4 | 2.38 | 90.2 | 1.49 | 2.7 | 0.82 |
| India | 12.8 | 1.80 | 9.8 | 1.62 | 2.9 | 1.05 | 5.7 | 1.55 | 9.9 | 1.54 | 8.8 | 1.61 | 85.3 | 1.69 |
| Malaysia | 95.2 | 1.10 | 62.2 | 2.49 | 33.9 | 2.73 | 18.9 | 2.20 | 61.8 | 2.55 | 59.4 | 2.62 | 21.1 | 2.25 |
| Paraguay | 29.0 | 1.71 | 12.6 | 1.36 | 5.0 | 0.81 | 3.2 | 0.64 | 10.4 | 1.14 | 6.5 | 0.92 | 86.2 | 1.27 |
| Peru | 52.7 | 2.00 | 28.2 | 1.92 | 12.1 | 1.78 | 7.8 | 1.23 | 33.5 | 2.04 | 22.1 | 1.86 | 54.5 | 1.95 |
| Philippines | 47.8 | 2.44 | 16.9 | 1.83 | 5.6 | 0.93 | 4.7 | 0.73 | 22.9 | 2.16 | 5.8 | 0.69 | 76.0 | 2.18 |
| Sri Lanka | 21.3 | 2.40 | 5.7 | 1.20 | 2.0 | 0.85 | 8.5 | 1.61 | 18.9 | 2.23 | 3.1 | 0.99 | 79.5 | 2.26 |
| Tunisia | 21.9 | 1.97 | 33.5 | 2.07 | 14.3 | 1.48 | 13.3 | 1.41 | 31.3 | 2.15 | 23.1 | 1.96 | 56.8 | 2.30 |
| Uruguay | 93.4 | 1.00 | 62.4 | 2.01 | 19.9 | 1.62 | 7.9 | 1.09 | 43.1 | 2.16 | 36.8 | 1.88 | 38.5 | 1.96 |

*Source*: *A View Inside Primary Schools* (UNESCO Institute for Statistics, 2008).

THINKERS & THEORY

## Paulo Freire: empowering the poor

The Brazilian educator Paulo Freire (1921–97) used literacy programmes for the poor to enable them to take control of their own lives. He argued that formal education often enabled elites to impose their values on 'developing' peoples. In 1963 he pioneered a literacy project across Brazil for 5 million people, and was supported by a left-wing government. Later, however, he fell out of favour when a new right-wing government came to power. Freire was jailed, before going into exile in Bolivia and Chile. His key book was *Pedagogy of the Oppressed* (1972), and his key idea was conscientisation, where *education becomes a tool to transform the social order*. Ultimately, education struggles for liberation from all kinds of oppression. His work also became part of liberation theology in Latin America. Many of his ideas are used across the world to bring about social change.

Instead of formal degrees on paper, they suggest, people in developing areas need the practical knowledge and skills to provide for their basic life needs in a changing natural environment and to build small businesses that can generate wealth in ways sensitive to local cultural norms. In high-income societies, schooling for everyone serves as the means of training people to participate in democratic political life and apply the economic knowledge and technological skills that are increasingly important in the modern world. At the same time, however, schooling can also serve as a major mechanism for reproducing social inequalities.

# Schooling around the world

In this section, we make a quick tour of some school systems to provide a sense of their variety.

## Schooling in India

India has become a middle-income country, but there are large numbers of families who live in poverty and may depend upon the earnings of children. Many children work up to 60 hours a week and this greatly reduces the time and opportunity for schooling.

Still, about 90 per cent of children in India complete primary schools – typically in crowded schoolrooms where one teacher attends to upwards of 60 children. Children in the poorest families often begin full-time work at an early age to help supplement the family income. Fewer than half of Indian children go on to secondary education.

Pronounced patriarchy also shapes Indian education; 59 per cent of boys but only 49 per cent of girls attend secondary school. While just over one-third of the Indian population is illiterate, two-thirds of women lack basic literary skills. A large majority of the children working in Indian factories are girls. There are economic costs to raising a girl. Parents must provide a dowry, and after the marriage, a daughter's work benefits her husband's family (UNESCO, 2009).

## Schooling in Japan

Before 1872, only a privileged few enrolled in school. But today, Japan is widely praised for producing some of the world's highest achievers. Early grades concentrate on transmitting Japanese traditions, especially a sense of obligation to family. By their early teens, students encounter Japan's system of rigorous and competitive examinations.

The Japanese government invests heavily in the education of students who perform well in these exams, while students performing poorly are pushed out of the system. Understandably, then, around half of Japanese students attend 'cram schools' to supplement their standard education and prepare for the exams. Japanese women, most of whom are not in the labour force, often devote themselves to their children's success in school.

## Schooling in Europe

While all countries in the European Union agree that schooling is highly important, each takes a different approach to education. Luxembourg requires children to attend pre-school. In the Netherlands, primary school begins at four. While the UK introduced compulsory education in 1870, Italy and Greece did not follow suit until the 1950s, and Spain waited until the 1960s. Portugal introduced 6 years of compulsory elementary schooling in 1968, but did not fully implement this requirement until 1986. EU countries also require different minimum periods of study. Portugal, Spain and Italy require only 8 years of schooling; Ireland, Greece, Luxembourg and Denmark require 9 years; France, the Netherlands and Germany, 10 years; the United Kingdom, 11 years; and Belgium, 12 years.

Many European countries have a multi-track secondary education system which channels some students towards university and others towards various levels of vocational training. In Germany, for example, students undertake general secondary education for two years from age 12, then split into the grammar (*Gymnasium*), basic vocational (*Hauptschule*) and higher vocational (*Realschule*) groups. Some countries encourage greater educational specialisation from the secondary level onwards than others. Secondary students in Italy and Germany have more subjects to study at the post-16 level than students in the UK. As with the previous examples, European educational structures also help maintain the social power structures, as we shall now see by looking more closely at the UK.

## Schooling in the UK

During the Middle Ages, schooling was a privilege of the British nobility, who studied classical subjects since they had little need for the practical skills related to earning a living. As the Industrial Revolution created a need for an educated labour force, a rising share of the population entered the classroom. In 1891, the Education Act made elementary education free to all citizens. Three major Acts shaped British education during the twentieth century. These were:

1 *The Balfour Act (1902)*, which established Local Education Authorities (LEAs), and gave these bodies powers over secondary and higher education.

2 *The Butler Act (1944)*, which established a Ministry of Education and set up the tripartite system of three different kinds of school – grammar, technical and secondary modern – to cater to the supposed differing intellectual abilities of students. The Act made education from 5 to 15 free for all people, improved equality of opportunity in education, and offered support services to students from poor families, including free milk, dental check-ups and healthcare.

3 *The Baker Act (1988)*. Following the recommendations of the previous year's Black Report, the British government enacted a series of sweeping and controversial changes in the Education Act of 1988. These included:

| Table 20.4 | Types of school in the U.K. 1970/1–2008/9 | | | | |
|---|---|---|---|---|---|
| | Numbers of students (thousands) | | | | |
| | 1970/1 | 1980/1 | 1990/1 | 2000/1 | 2008/9 |
| Public sector schools[1] | | | | | |
|   Nursery[2] | 50 | 89 | 105 | 152 | 150 |
|   Primary | 5,902 | 5,171 | 4,955 | 5,298 | 4,869 |
|   State-funded secondary[3] of which, admissions policy | | | | | |
|     Comprehensive | 1,313 | 3,730 | 2,925 | 3,340 | 3,243 |
|     Grammar | 673 | 149 | 156 | 205 | 221 |
|     Modern | 1,164 | 233 | 94 | 112 | 142 |
|     City technology colleges | – | – | 8 | 17 | 3 |
|     Academies | – | – | – | – | 122 |
|     Not applicable | 403 | 434 | 298 | 260 | 197 |
| All public sector schools | 9,507 | 9,806 | 8,541 | 9,384 | 8,948 |
| Non-maintained schools | 621 | 619 | 606 | 609 | 621 |
| All special schools | 103 | 148 | 114 | 113 | 107 |
| Pupil referral units | – | – | – | 10 | 16 |
| All schools | 10,230 | 10,572 | 9,260 | 10,116 | 9,691 |

[1] Excludes maintained special schools and pupil referral units.
[2] Figures for Scotland before 1998/9 only include data for local authority pre-schools, data thereafter include partnership pre-schools. From 2005/6, figures refer to centres providing pre-school education at a local authority centre, or in partnership with the local authority only. Children are counted once for each centre they are registered with.
[3] Excludes sixth-form colleges from 1980/1 onwards.
*Source*: Adapted from *Social Trends*, 40, 2010, Table 3.3, p. 29.

- the introduction of the National Curriculum, with achievement targets for students at the ages of 7, 11, 14 and 16
- the right for schools to 'opt out' of the Local Education Authority system if a majority of parents voting in a secret ballot wanted to do so
- devolution of the financial management of schools from LEAs to boards of governors
- the introduction of city technology colleges (15 in 1994).

The arrival of the Labour Government of 1997, with its high priority of 'education, education, education', heralded the passing of an Education Act more or less every year. Between the 1950s and 1970s, the major divide in British education was between the grammar schools and secondary schools, with the former being both more middle class and more successful. The Labour Party of the 1960s had gradually worked to abolish grammar schools and introduce a 'comprehensive' system – ostensibly providing equality of education for all. In practice, some grammar schools remained and comprehensive schools became stratified into

'good' and 'bad'. But when the Labour government of 1997–2010 came to power in 1997, it pledged that education would be a priority. It introduced a wide range of new policies and legislation which included:

- A continuing expansion of education at all levels. In 1970/1 there were 723 state nursery schools in the UK compared with 3,209 in 2008/9. In 2007/8, there were almost 2.5 million students in higher education, nearly four times the total of 621,000 in 1970/1 (*Social Trends*, 2010).
- The development of specialist schools and city academies. These were allowed to specialise but aimed to replace 'failing schools' in disadvantaged areas. The academies programme was introduced in 2000 to promote publicly funded independent schools managed by sponsors from a range of backgrounds, including universities, businesses, faith communities and voluntary groups. These new 'city academies' were allowed to build up their own admission arrangements. There were suspicions that selection might reappear through the back door.

- Education action zones whereby additional funding was given disadvantaged areas to set up breakfast clubs, homework clubs, summer literacy and numeracy schemes.
- A major programme of school regulations through a regulatory body (Ofsted), which aimed to enhance standards by creating a programme of target and monitoring of schools alongside competitive league tables – all of which was widely disliked by teachers.

At the end of the period of Labour government, traditional social distinctions persisted in British education. Many wealthy families still sent their children to independendent *public schools*. Such elite schools not only teach academic subjects, they also convey to children from wealthy families the distinctive patterns of speech, mannerisms and social graces of the British upper class. These schools are far too expensive for most students. Indeed, many prominent members of the Labour government in 1997 sent their own children to grant-maintained schools rather than comprehensives, recognising the continuing difference in standards of education at each level. Moreover, graduates from Oxford and Cambridge, or 'Oxbridge', often enter the core of the British power elite. Research conducted in 2008 showed that although only 7 per cent of the population attended independent schools, well over half of many professions have done so. For example, 75 per cent of judges, 70 per cent of finance directors, 45 per cent of top civil servants and 32 per cent of MPs were independently schooled (Cabinet Office, 2009), as Figure 20.1 shows. More than two-thirds of the top members of the civil service and successive British governments have 'Oxbridge' degrees.

It seems that the new coalition government, which came to power in 2010, is making reforms that may well extend these inequalities; but it is too soon to be clear.

## Understanding education in the modern world

The previous brief comparisons illustrate that education is shaped by other institutions and social forces. Education transmits cultural values and can also contribute to social divisions. In this section we will look briefly at some major approaches to education.

## The functions of education

As we saw in Chapter 2, functionalism highlights the way the institutions of a society are interdependent and interconnect with others. It asks questions about the ways in which institutions work and function in a society – usually to maintain some sense of order (though it can also ask questions about its disruptions and breakdowns – the dysfunctions). Functionalist theories of education can be traced to Emile Durkheim. While Durkheim recognised the wide variety of education practices in all societies across the world, he believed that it usually served a major role of creating a moral bond. Education helped sustain social cohesion.

Contemporary functionalists focus on a number of key functions of schools. The most apparent functions of schools are:

- *Intellectual*: they provide basic thinking skills for analysis and evaluation.
- *Political*: they inculcate people into the norms of their society and train them to be good citizens.
- *Social*: they socialise students into the culture and values of their society.
- *Economic*: they prepare students for later occupational roles and train them for the division of labour.

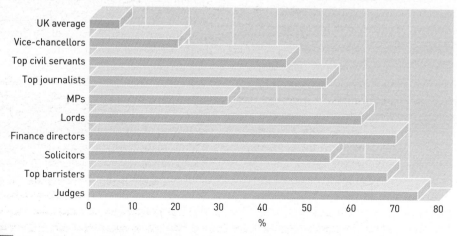

**Figure 20.1**  Proportion of professionals independently schooled: by profession
*Source*: Milsom Report, 2009, The Panel on Fair Access to the Professions, Fig. 1f, p. 18.

But functionalists often take it further than this. They suggest that modern schools are also the means by which modern democratic societies are shaped and maintained by creating conditions for students to achieve academic success. They are institutions which create opportunities for development and success and can help to lead to a more democratic and meritocratic society. Meritocracy implies that success is linked to achievements rather than accidents of birth. (The term 'meritocracy' was first used in Michael Young's 1958 satirical book *Rise of the Meritocracy*. The term was intended to be pejorative.)

## The ethnographic tradition: studying classrooms and cultures

One approach to studying education is to examine first hand what is going on every day, face to face in schools, and this is where fieldwork comes into its own. Researchers, often applying symbolic interactionism (see Chapters 2 and 7) and the method of participant observation (Chapter 3), have documented the *perspectives* of teachers and students, the *labelling* mechanisms within a classroom, the general *processes* through which classes are constructed and negotiated, the different student *roles* and *cultures* which emerge within these classrooms, and the impact of *social divisions* (gender, class, disability and race) on these interactions. There have been many such studies. Good early examples of this are described in the box.

Within school cultures, an 'invisible pedagogy' (Bernstein, 1977), or hidden ranking system, emerges to shape academic performance and the long-term life chances of students. Early studies of classroom interaction in the UK suggest that, while teachers may strive to be impartial, they are culturally conditioned to assess their students' ability by ranking them on a scale

# Studying schools

One focus in the sociology of education has been on the ethnography of schools and classrooms. Often a sociologist enters a school and becomes an observer of school life for a year or so, documenting teaching, the relations between children and teachers, the emergence of different school cultures and their links to the wider school, community and society. Colin Lacey's *Hightown Grammar* (1970), David Hargreaves' *Social Relations in a Secondary School* (1967), Paul Willis's *Learning to Labour* (1976) and Stephen Ball's *Beachside* (1981) were pioneers of this tradition. Stephen Ball was a participant observer of Beachside Comprehensive for three years. A typical approach was that of Colin Lacey (1970), who immersed himself in a school for 18 months, spending a year observing, doing some teaching himself, engaging staff and pupils in informal conversations, sending out

questionnaires to students, and backing all this with material from school records.

Many of these studies point in the same directions. Subcultures emerge in schools for different groups. Kids might conform, rebel, withdraw or develop their own pathways (turning to sports, for example). Most common was the development of a subculture of academic achievement and a subculture of low achievers, often demoralised and bored with school. School structures emphasised competition to the detriment of low achievers (and typically low achievers can be linked to inequalities). There is often a labelling process or self-fulfilling prophecy at work – David Hargreaves and Stephen Ball notably showed how children quickly got classified into types, which are frequently based more on behaviour than ability. Children were often selected from lower streams and indentified as 'louts' and 'trouble makers'. This negative labelling led some kids to resist and fight back. Being 'bad' often gave them an inverse kind of status. Often,

as Paul Willis showed, the disaffected youth of schools simply take this culture with them into the workplace (or more commonly the street culture of no work).

As this kind of study developed, other issues became important. Early work was also carried out on girl cultures (Stanworth, 1983), ethnicity (Sewell, 1996) and sexuality (Mac an Ghail, 1994). Oddly, in recent times, much less research has been conducted which uses this kind of method in the study of schools.

### Classic UK school studies

David Hargreaves, *Social Relations in a Secondary School* (1967)
Colin Lacey, *Hightown Grammar* (1970)
Peter Woods, *The Divided School* (1979)
Stephen Ball, *Beachside* (1981)
Michelle Stanworth, *Gender and Schooling* (1983)
Máirtín mac an Ghail, *Making of Men: Masculinities, Sexualities and Schooling* (1994)
Tony Sewell, *Black Masculinities and Schooling* (1996)

of other characteristics, such as appearance, personality, enthusiasm and conformity, which bear little relation to actual ability (Hargreaves, 1975). In those days, teachers often favoured boys over girls (Stanworth, 1983) and white boys over Afro-Caribbean boys, by tacitly giving them much more attention and opportunities to speak. Likewise, Asian girls were also more likely to be stereotyped as 'passive' (Brah and Minhas, 1988). Here we also see the significance of labelling pupils in certain ways (as 'slow learners' or 'trouble'): this can bring about **self-fulfilling prophecies**, *a prediction that causes itself to become true*, when, for example children defined as low achievers at school actually become low achievers. It is a matter of expectations.

The social background of the students also plays a role in how they experience education. In a major classic study, Paul Willis (1977) looked at a small group of working-class boys and studied their transition from school to work. He found that they generated an anti-school culture heavily focused upon their masculinity. They had little time for the middle-class school values or for posh qualifications, seeing them as boring, effeminate and a waste of time. They castigated other boys who followed the rules as 'ear 'oles' and saw them as sissies. Similar studies found such boys associating good grades with femininity and, to keep face in the eyes of their mates, boys might hand in work that was poor and disorganised. For these 'lads', 'having a laff' was especially important, and it is a value they then took to their workplace. For instance, in class there might be 'a continuous scraping of chairs, a bad tempered "tut-tutting" at the simplest request, and a continuous fidgeting which explores every permutation of sitting or lying on a chair'. They then carried this 'anti-authority', 'anti-achievement' culture to their place of work.

There is much evidence that this pattern continues today. It can be charted from different studies over time. For instance, in the 1990s Mairtin Mac an Ghaill (1994) looked at the construction of gender in classrooms, focusing on a hierarchy of dominant and subordinate masculinities. He observed four major types (there was also a small sub-group of gay male students):

- The '*Macho Lads*' – white, working-class boys who are defiant of the school and disdainful of student achievers (similar to Willis above).

- The '*Academic Achievers*' – boys whose male identities are built out of seeing themselves as future professionals: they take their work and

school seriously, even though they are seen as effeminate 'dickheads' by the Macho Lads.

- The '*New Enterprisers*' – these are less keen on conventional A-levels, but do find a space for work in skills that interest them, such as computer sciences.

- The '*Real Englishmen*' – these see themselves as superior to the teachers, and think they are capable of effortless academic achievement.

## Critical comment

Focusing on classroom interactions is valuable, but it does tend to under-emphasise the relations between the activities within schools and the wider working of society as a whole, as we shall see by looking at a different, more macro approach.

# The critical and conflict traditions: education and social divisions

Another major approach to studying education is through social divisions and social conflict. Education – at all levels – becomes a means for the reproduction of society's inequalities: it can act as a means of social control, reinforcing acceptance of the status quo. In various, sometimes subtle ways, schools operate to reproduce the status hierarchy.

Thus a number of sociologists have suggested that the origins of the UK system in the nineteenth century lay in class issues and control. The public schools came very early for the elite; then in the nineteenth century came the rather limited Sunday schools to provide a basic education for the working classes – often moral education. There was a continuous fear of an insurgent working class rising up once it had too much education.

Samuel Bowles and Herbert Gintis (1976) point out that the clamour for public education in the late nineteenth century arose precisely when capitalists were seeking a literate, docile and disciplined workforce. In many countries with immigrants, but notably the United States, mandatory education laws ensured that schools would teach immigrants the dominant national language as well as cultural values supportive of capitalism. Compliance, punctuality and discipline were – and still are – part of what conflict theorists call the **hidden curriculum**, the *subtle*

SPEAKING LIVES

# A self-fulfilling prophecy: from the autobiography of Malcolm X

Malcolm, a black American, went to school in Lansing, Michigan, in the 1940s. He became leader of the Black Muslims and a spokesperson for many black Americans in the 1960s, and was assassinated in 1965. This is an extract from his autobiography, in which he illustrates the self-fulfilling prophecy at work in his school: think of the power of telling someone 'you're good with your hands'. (See also the film of his life by Spike Lee – *Malcolm X* (1992) with Denzil Washington in the lead role.)

One day something happened which was to become the first major turning point of my life. Somehow, I happened to be alone in the classroom with Mr Ostrowski, my English teacher. He was a tall, rather reddish white man and he had a thick mustachio. I had gotten some of my best marks under him, and he had always made me feel that he liked me.

I know that he probably meant well in what he happened to advise me that day. I doubt that he meant

any harm. It was just in his nature as an American white man. I was one of his top students, one of the school's top students – but all he could see for me was the kind of future 'in your place' that almost all white people see for black people.

He told me, 'Malcolm, you ought to be thinking about a career. Have you been giving it thought?' The truth is, I hadn't. I never have figured out why I told him, 'Well, yes sir, I've been thinking I'd like to be a lawyer.' Lansing certainly had no black lawyers – or doctors either – in those days, to hold up an image I might have aspired to. All I really knew for certain was that a lawyer didn't wash dishes, as I was doing.

Mr Ostrowski looked surprised, I remember, and leaned back in his chair and clasped his hands behind his head. He kind of half smiled and said, 'Malcolm, one of life's first needs is for us to be realistic. Don't misunderstand me, now. We all of us like you, you know that. But you've got to be realistic about being a nigger. You need to think about something you can be. You're good with your hands – making things. Everybody admires your carpentry shop work. Why don't you plan on carpentry? People like you as

**Malcolm X (1925–65)**
*Source*: © Bettmann/Corbis.

a person – you'd get all kinds of work.'

The more I thought afterwards about what he said, the more uneasy it made me. It just kept treading around in my mind.

What made it really begin to disturb me was Mr Ostrowski's advice to others in my class – all of them white. They reported that Mr Ostrowski had encouraged what they had wanted. Yet nearly none of them had earned marks equal to mine.

It was then that I began to change – inside.

I drew away from white people, I came to class, and I answered when called upon. It became a physical strain simply to sit in Mr Ostrowski's class.

*Source*: Adapted from Malcolm X, *The Autobiography of Malcolm X* (1966: 35–7).

*presentation of political or cultural ideas in the classroom.* It teaches young people 'to know their place and sit still in it' and 'reproduces inequality by justifying privilege and attributing poverty to personal failure' (Bowles and Gintis, 1976: 114). In the next section, we will look at just how some of these social divisions work in more detail.

## Class divisions

Schools routinely tailor education according to students' social background, thereby perpetuating social inequality. Indeed, out of all major Western cultures, it has been argued that 'only the Netherlands and Sweden show persistent trends of equalising access

# The Bell Curve debate: are the elite more intelligent?

It is rare that the publication of a new book in the social sciences captures the attention of the public at large. But *The Bell Curve: Intelligence and Class Structure in American Life* (1994) by Richard J. Herrnstein and Charles Murray did that and more, igniting a firestorm of public controversy over why pronounced social stratification divides US society and, just as important, what to do about it. In the first several months of its release, 400,000 copies of the book were sold around the world. Several thousand reviews and commentaries have been written in the short time since the book's publication. Although the book speaks specifically about the USA, its general argument has been made for many countries.

*The Bell Curve* is a long (800-page) book that addresses many critical issues and resists simple summary. But its basic thesis is captured in the following propositions:

1  Something we can describe as 'general intelligence' exists; people with more of it tend to be more successful in their careers than those with less.
2  At least half the variation in human intelligence (Herrnstein and Murray use figures of 60 to 70 per cent) is transmitted genetically from one generation to another; the remaining variability is due to environmental factors.
3  Over the course of the twentieth century – and especially since the

'information revolution' – intelligence has become more necessary to the performance of industrial societies' top occupational positions.
4  Simultaneously, the best US universities have shifted their admissions policies away from favouring children of inherited wealth to admitting young people who perform best on standardised tests.
5  As a result of these changes in the workplace and higher education, US society is now coming to be dominated by a 'cognitive elite', who are, on average, not only better trained than most people but actually more intelligent.
6  Because more intelligent people are socially segregated on the university campus and in the workplace, it is no surprise that they tend to pair up, marry and have intelligent children, perpetuating the 'cognitive elite'.
7  Near the bottom of the social ladder, a similar process is at work. Increasingly, poor people are individuals with lower intelligence, who live segregated from others, and who tend to pass along their modest abilities to their children.

Resting on the validity of the seven assertions presented above, Herrnstein and Murray then offer, as an eighth point, a basic approach to public policy:

8  To the extent that membership in the affluent elite or the impoverished underclass is rooted in intelligence and determined mostly by genetic inheritance, programmes to assist underprivileged people will have few practical benefits.

The book has prompted considerable controversy. Critics

first questioned exactly what is meant by 'intelligence', arguing that anyone's innate abilities can hardly be separated from the effects of socialisation. Of course, rich children perform better on intelligence tests, they explained: these people have had all the advantages! Some critics dismiss the concept of 'intelligence' outright as phony science. Others take a more moderate view, claiming that we should not think of 'intelligence' as the sole cause of achievement, since recent research indicates that mental abilities and life experiences are interactive, each affecting the other.

In addition, while most researchers who study intelligence agree that genetics does play a part in transmitting intelligence, the consensus is that no more than 25–40 per cent is inherited – only about half what Herrnstein and Murray claim. Therefore, critics conclude, *The Bell Curve* misleads readers into thinking that social elitism is both natural and inevitable. In its assumptions and conclusions, moreover, *The Bell Curve* amounts to little more than a rehash of the social Darwinism popular a century ago, which heralded the success of industrial tycoons as merely 'the survival of the fittest'.

Perhaps, as one commentator noted, the more society seems like a jungle, the more people think of stratification as a matter of blood rather than upbringing. But, despite its flaws and exaggerations, the book's success suggests that *The Bell Curve* raises many issues we cannot easily ignore. Can a democratic system tolerate the 'dangerous knowledge' that elites (including not only rich people but also political leaders) may be just a little more intelligent than the

PUBLIC SOCIOLOGY

rest of us? What of *The Bell Curve*'s description that elites are increasingly insulating themselves from social problems such as crime, homelessness and poor schools? As such problems have become worse in recent years, how do we counter the easy explanation that poor people are hobbled by their own limited ability? And, most basically, what should be done to ensure that all people have the opportunity to develop their abilities as fully as possible?

## Continue the debate

1 Do you agree that 'general intelligence' exists? Why or why not?

2 In general, do you think that people of higher social position are more intelligent than those of low social position? If you think intelligence differs by social standing, which factor is cause and which is effect?

3 Do you think sociologists should study controversial issues such as differences in human intelligence? Why or why not? Is *The Bell Curve* ideology or science – and what is the difference?

A useful summary and review of critiques can be found at: *Human Intelligence and the Bell Curve* at www.indiana.edu/~intell/bellcurve.shtml.

---

to education in the course of the twentieth century' (Therborn, 1995: 257). By contrast, education in countries such as the UK has reflected stratification in quality of provision both for individuals and for people of different social classes (Mackinnon et al., 1996: 173).

Table 20.5 shows the differential achievements of children at school from different class backgrounds. *There is no doubt that children from working-class homes consistently under-achieve at every level of the educational system when compared to middle-class and upper-class children.* Why should this be?

Some, like Charles Murray – discussed in the *Public sociology* box – have contended that genetic intellectual potential determines performance in school (Herrnstein and Murray, 1994). Indeed, the tripartite system in Britain gave prominence to the results of

IQ tests given to children at age 11 in helping divide students into their supposedly appropriate schools. The implication of this explanation, however, is that lower-class people generally have lower genetic intellectual abilities. Thus lower-class people could be said to deserve their status because they lack the intellectual ability to compete with people from higher classes.

Many others reject this explanation, however, pointing out that governments have tended not to invest as heavily in the schools attended by the poorest children, and that the less well off also tend to experience greater health problems, which in turn affect their performance at school. Moreover, poorer families cannot afford to send their children to nursery pre-school training and later to cram schools, to hire private tutors, or to purchase items such as books or

---

| Table 20.5 | Attainment of level 2 qualifications[1] at age 16 and 17: by socioeconomic classification of parent,[2] 2008 | | | |
|---|---|---|---|---|
| **England** | **Percentages** | | | |
| | Age 16 | Age 17 | Proportion without Level 2 at 16 but gaining by 17 | Proportion without Level 2 at 17 |
| Higher professional | 81 | 88 | 33 | 12 |
| Lower professional | 75 | 82 | 28 | 18 |
| Intermediate | 61 | 71 | 26 | 29 |
| Lower supervisory | 47 | 58 | 20 | 42 |
| Routine | 43 | 54 | 20 | 46 |
| Other/not classified | 37 | 49 | 19 | 51 |

[1] Attainment of five or more GCSE grades A* to C, National Vocational Qualification level 2, Vocationally Related Qualification level 2, Intermediate General National Vocational Qualification. See Appendix, Part 3: Qualifications.

[2] National Statistics Socio-economic Classification (NS-SEC) of parent.

*Source: Social Trends*, 40 (2010) Table 3.16, p. 38.

personal computers, which give children from more affluent backgrounds an advantage. Additionally, as the Willis (1977) study discovered, poorer children often grow up in environments where people see little hope of upward social mobility and rebel against the system rather than try to conform with it. In such an environment, adults often discourage rather than encourage success at school. To make matters worse, people in different communities within a country often develop distinct dialects and colloquial vocabularies (Bernstein, 1977). While groups across the class divides do this, the dialects and words associated with richer and middle-class communities gain status, while those associated with lower-class communities get judged as 'uneducated'. In consequence, poor children are more likely to be more regularly criticised in school for 'weak' language skills and thus to develop lower educational confidence. These many factors, which have no relation to biological potential, have contributed to the educational class divide in countries such as the UK (see Halsey et al., 1961; Jackson and Marsden, 1963; Douglas, 1964).

# Education as a key reproducer of inequalities

At every level of education the evidence has suggested for a long time that working-class children tend not to do so well in schools as middle-class children. There are many reasons for this and we have already encountered a number of them in earlier chapters – especially in our discussion of education and the reproduction of class (see Chapters 8 and 10). Western educational systems tend to be white, middle-class cultures. In this they support the class and racial systems giving credence to the middle class and often alienating the working class.

In summary, five crucial factors converge in structuring and reproducing social class in education. Early research work has pointed to these processes and later work simply reinforced it.

## 1 The class base of the home

The family is the crucible of education and what goes on there shapes all the child's experiences. At base, working-class homes have less money, low-paid work and unemployment, and much less capital or wealth (see Chapter 10). Early research focusing on working-class families showed how often working-class homes had a lack of books and what is now called 'cultural

capital'. More recent work has shown how middle-class families – usually with more money – have a different language, a different set of values, a different knowledge base, a different set of interests. Stephen Ball has shown how:

> the middle-class family is engaged with its children's education as a family project, and the vast majority of the work is done by mothers. Middle-class parents do not want the child to be 'dragged down' or distracted. These parents fear that, in the 'wrong' context, the child will come under the influence of children with bad attitudes and 'dangerous minds'. They also want the child 'stretched'.
>
> (Ball, 2006)

It is middle-class children who get the early piano lessons, swimming lessons, the extracurricular language lessons and the holidays in cultural places from the earliest of ages.

## 2 The class ecology of the local environment

The geographical catchment areas of the schools reflects a local economic and housing market, along with a local class culture. The opportunities provided by these local communities are very different, and establish different environments for their local schools. A well known 'grapevine' exists which informs parents of where the 'better' schools are; and in turn the parents of middle-class children can afford to move their children into areas with these 'better' schools. The notion of choosing your school makes sense in different ways to different class groups: without adequate financial resources it is not so easy to choose to live in the right catchment area. And this in turn leaves some areas to develop 'sink schools'.

## 3 The culture of the school itself

Research has long shown how the cultures of schools differ greatly – as do their outside reputations. 'Good schools' are formally defined in terms of exam results, but there are other factors at work which are often class located. There is a wealth of studies which suggest the ways in which schools become 'middle-class factories with middle-class teachers cultivating middle-class values'. For many working-class children, schools are alien environments and they cannot wait to leave. Several studies have documented the alienation of young working-class and often 'black' children from this culture (e.g. Willis, 1978).

## 4 The marketplace of schools

Paying for a good education is a key feature of most educational systems. Stephen Ball has studied what he calls 'circuits of schooling' which plug parents from different social classes into different circuits. In the UK, Ball describes three systems:

- a circuit of local, community, comprehensive schools, which recruit from the local community
- a circuit of cosmopolitan, high-profile elite maintained schools, which recruit from outside of the local community
- a local system of day, independent schools, which attract some parents whose children cannot enter the 'cosmopolitan elite' schools, or who are interested in the private system.

Over and above is the private fee-paying school and the public school system. The cost of these is prohibitive for average- and low-income workers: in 2010/11, the school fee at Harrow was £9,890 per term (£29,670 per annum). At the lower end of the scale, in poorer areas, 'sink schools' and slum schools appear. Educational systems depend on financial resources but these are unequally distributed across the classes. Hence more middle-class children go to private schools and the 'elite educational institutions'. They are given more resources and more support. Increasingly, schools are becoming like businesses, and with this come business values.

## 5 Reproducing across generations

Ultimately, this whole system is then reproduced on a daily basis – through economic, cultural and social capital (see Chapter 8). Private education in particular plays a key role in the accumulation of social capital (from private nurseries all the way up to the elite Oxbridge and Ivory Tower systems, where new friendships and networks are developed and often sustained over the cycle.

 On all this, see the work of Stephen Ball, *Education Policy and Social Class* (2006).

## Disability divisions

Historically, children with all kinds of disability and special needs have been socialised into having low expectations of success in both education and work, whilst the 'academic' and the 'normal' are awarded accolades and privileges. In the UK system for many years, this took place largely through a process of exclusion in 'special schools'. There were schools for the 'deaf', schools for the 'blind' and schools for the 'physically handicapped' (all terms that are now often questioned). The 1944 Education Act encouraged disabled children to be educated in mainstream schools, but in practice Local Education Authorities made separate provision. The 1981 Special Education Act abolished the category of handicap, and introduced the category of educational special needs (SEN). Although some say that special schools are needed – how can the deaf learn British Sign Language, and how can they develop positive identities without special schools? – others suggest that special schools actually perpetuate the disabling and stigmatising process (see Chapters 14 and 17). The education experience may remain inferior: disabled students come to have narrower curricula; teachers often have lower expectations; courses are taught in life skills rather than academic knowledge. Often there are disproportionate numbers of immigrant and other 'minority' children are also overrepresented. Children with SEN are at best tolerated, but often abused and excluded. In the climate of 'league tables' introduced into British schools, the disabled seem even less likely to succeed (Tomlinson, 1982). Sustaining the balance of separation and inclusion remains a constant dilemma.

## Ethnic differences

Not every country has adopted the extreme policy of racial segregation in classrooms once practised in the United States and South Africa, but racial differences in educational achievement appear in many countries, and these differences often coincide with social status differences between ethnic groups. Studies in the UK, such as the report of the Swann Committee (Swann, 1985), found that in general West Indian children perform less well than Asian children, and in both cases boys do less well than girls. Asian girls may often do better than white boys, but black boys regularly come out at the bottom of the heap. This pattern continues through higher education. Drawing on the work of David Gilborn (1995), Mairtin Mac an Ghaill (1994) and others, Gail Lewis et al. (2000) have summarised a number of key studies and concluded the following:

- Racial distinctions are applied to pupils of both African-Caribbean and Asian descent but in different ways, leading to divergent expectations of each group . . .

- Such racial distinctions are often based on racial stereotypes of Caribbean and Asian family structures and relationships as, equally but differently, pathological or dysfunctional . . .
- Pupils of Asian descent are characterised as academically able and diligent, if also quiet and docile; and African-Caribbean descent pupils are characterised as academically poor and lazy . . .
- Boys of African-Caribbean descent are assumed to be disorderly and thus to present teachers with behavioural problems.
- There is a high level of conflict between white teachers and African-Caribbean descent pupils . . .
- Teachers and schools themselves often play an active, though unintended part in the creation of this conflict . . .
- There is constant overrepresentation in school exclusions of black pupils . . . of both sexes . . .
- Levels of academic success may be achieved by pupils despite – rather than because of – teacher/school support . . . (Lewis et al., 2000: 269–70)

Some part of all this may be accounted for through links to class – Afro-Caribbean children are more likely to have parents in manual work. Another feature may well be the workings of a self-fulfilling prophecy (described in the *Speaking lives* box, p. 701). Another contributory factor must also be some forms of racism and racialisation at work (see Chapter 11). In addition, part of the explanation may lie in what Smith and Tomlinson (1989) term 'the school effect'. While these authors argue that 'what school a child goes to makes far more difference than which ethnic group he or she belongs to' (1989: 281), they also note that people from ethnic minorities are more likely to be clustered into particular areas, and that their children's educational fate rests in the hands of the schools near where they live. For groups more likely to be poor, or immigrants clustered in poor sections of central cities to cut costs as they adjust to a new culture, this can be bad news.

Since schools tend to reinforce the dominant culture in a society, students from minority communities often face a confusing problem when trying to reconcile differences between their own original culture and that of the larger society in which they live. Children may not feel inclined to sever their roots with their cultural origins, and wish to keep their own language or religion, for example. Often this can initially spark conflict within schools, as schools expect that children should be fully assimilated into the values of the dominant society. With this approach there has often been tacit ethnic discrimination, to which a major response was the promotion of anti-racism strategies in schools, whereby discriminatory practices were more overtly condemned. More recently, multiculturalism is often promoted in the curriculum, allowing the diversity of cultures to be taken more seriously (see Giroux, 1992).

## Gender differences

Peer groups socialise their members according to normative conceptions of gender. A series of feminist researchers in the UK – the late Sue Lees, Christine Griffin and Angela McRobbie among them – have interviewed girls and discovered the ways in which their 'femininity' is shaped from early years. Likewise, some male sociologists – Paul Willis, Mike O'Donnell and Mairtin Mac an Ghaill among them – have studied boys. Reading their studies, it is not hard to sense the overwhelming pressures placed on young boys and girls to conform to gender stereotypes, and to sense the sanctions they will experience if they step out of these roles.

Many of the world's societies have considered schooling more important for boys than for girls. Although the education gender gap has narrowed in Western countries in recent decades, in many low-income societies the divisions remain at a high level. Women still study traditionally feminine subjects such as literature, while men pursue mathematics and engineering. By stressing the experiences of people in traditionally masculine professions, such as the military, while ignoring the lives of other, largely female workforces, such as domestic workers, schools reinforce male dominance in society.

During the 1970s, sociologists discovered how girls were usually disadvantaged at school. Rosemary Deem demonstrated that education for girls in the past largely centred upon how it would prepare them for the family. Dale Spender found curricula riddled with 'sexism' and Sue Sharpe observed that schools steered girls towards 'feminine' subjects. Michelle Stanworth looked at a mixed group of students, finding that teachers gave more attention to boys than to girls. As a result of such experiences, girls learned to lack faith in their abilities (Deem, 1980; Spender, 1982; Stanworth, 1983; Sharpe, 1994). At the same time, Julian Wood (1984) found that there is a general, highly charged, sexual atmosphere in schools – a point that few commentators seem to have noticed before – where there is also a massive amount of sexism among the boys. Boys' cultures regularly derided girls and women as mere body parts. The *Living in the twenty-first century* box on p. 708 highlights how 'homosexuality' appears – or rather does not appear – in this context.

But this was early work. More recently, boys are doing less well and girls doing better. The achievement of girls at all levels of education has overtaken that of boys, though it is often subject-linked. Table 20.6 shows that with one small exception girls now perform better than boys in every subject at every stage of secondary education. And it continues: in 1970/1 males outnumbered females in higher education by at least 2 to 1; by 1996/7 females outnumbered males. There were almost seven times as many female higher education students in 2007/8 (1.4 million) as in 1970/1 (205,000), but only two and a half times as many male students (1.1 million compared with 416,000) (*Social Trends*, 2010). This trend has remained stable now for 20 years.

| Table 20.6 | Pupils reaching or exceeding expected standards in England,[1] by Key Stage and sex (%) | | | |
|---|---|---|---|---|
| | **1999** | | **2009** | |
| | **Boys** | **Girls** | **Boys** | **Girls** |
| **Key Stage 1**[2] | | | | |
| English | | | | |
| Reading | 78 | 86 | 81 | 89 |
| Writing | 75 | 85 | 75 | 87 |
| Mathematics | 84 | 88 | 88 | 91 |
| Science | 85 | 88 | 87 | 91 |
| **Key Stage 2**[3] | | | | |
| English | 62 | 74 | 75 | 84 |
| Mathematics | 69 | 70 | 80 | 80 |
| Science | 75 | 76 | 85 | 87 |
| **Key Stage 3**[4] | | | | |
| English | 55 | 73 | 71 | 84 |
| Mathematics | 63 | 66 | 79 | 80 |
| Science | 59 | 62 | 76 | 79 |

[1] By teacher assessment.
[2] Pupils achieving level 2 or above at Key Stage 1.
[3] Pupils achieving level 4 or above at Key Stage 2.
[4] Pupils achieving level 5 or above at Key Stage 3.

*Source*: *Social Trends*, 40 (2010) Table 3.14, p. 37.

How this shift can be explained is an interesting question. Some suggest that it is to do with the rising expectations placed on girls and women (in turn partly linked to the growth of feminist ideals: see Chapter 12). Girls in the 1990s became less family-focused, attaching more importance to education and work (Sharpe, 1994), whilst a feminist-inspired culture has given many women stronger motivations to succeed. Others suggest it may have much to do with 'the crisis of boys and men', whereby falling expectations are

placed on some boys as they become part of what is commonly called a 'lads culture', and a culture of under-achievement has grown among boys (Willis, 1977; Mac an Ghaill, 1994). Partly too it may be a consequence of a shift in educational policies. The National Curriculum in the UK, for example, insists that all boys have to take a language and all girls have to take a science subject; and almost all schools and universities now have equal opportunities policies.

## Ability or merit? Streaming and teaching

Despite continuing controversy over standardised tests, most schools use them as the basis for **streaming**, *the assignment of students to different types of educational programme*. Streaming, or tracking, is a common practice in many industrial societies, including the UK, the United States, France and Japan. The educational justification for tracking is to give students the kind of schooling appropriate to their individual aptitude. For a variety of reasons, including innate ability and level of motivation, some students are capable of more challenging work than others. Young people also differ in their interests, with some drawn to, say, the study of languages, while others seek training in art or science. Given this diversity of talent and focus, no single programme for all students would serve any of them well.

But critics see streaming as a thinly veiled strategy to perpetuate privilege. The basis of this argument is research indicating that social background has as much to do with streaming as personal aptitude does. Students from affluent families generally do well on standardised, 'scientific' tests and so are placed in university-bound streams, while schools assign those from modest backgrounds (including a disproportionate share of the poor) to programmes that curb their aspirations and teach technical trades. Streaming, therefore, effectively segregates students both academically and socially.

Most schools reserve their best teachers for students in favoured streams. Thus high-stream boys and girls find that their teachers put more effort into classes, show more respect towards students and expect more from them. By contrast, teachers of low-stream students concentrate on memorisation, classroom drill and other unstimulating techniques. Such classrooms also emphasise regimentation, punctuality and respect for authority figures.

In light of these criticisms, schools are now cautious about making streaming assignments and allow greater mobility between streams. Some have even moved

LIVING IN THE C21ST

# Dude, You're a Fag: structuring homosexuality out of education

What is it like to grow up gay? In many countries across the world, it is better to keep quiet: homosexuality is against the law and can even result in the death penalty. But even in countries where homosexuality is more accepted, it can be very hard to come out or be gay at school. Many young people between 14 and 21, who generally seem to know they are gay quite early in life, find their experiences and feelings more or less completely overlooked while they are at school. There are four major ways in which schools make the situation of young gays and lesbians more difficult.

The first is through the hidden curriculum, which not only reproduces conventional gender roles in the classroom, but also reinforces heterosexuality. There have been attempts by some schools to introduce gay texts, but these attempts have caused much controversy.

A second mechanism concerns the absence of lesbian and gay role models in schools. Authorities have objected to gay teachers being 'known about' or teachers openly discussing the issue of being gay. Yet it is precisely the quality of 'being out' that is required in schools if gay teenagers are to have the heterosexual assumption at least punctured and, more practically, if they are to have access to adults who may help them

discuss their gay feelings. There have been some recent changes here, as more celebrities, like Ricky Martin, George Michael and John Barrowman, came out. Indeed, studies show that the age of young people coming out is getting lower and lower, and many schools do now recognise their gay and lesbian youth. A few even integrate 'gay' materials into their curriculums.

A third mechanism, the social operation of youth peer groups, 'structures out' homosexuality. Adolescent culture after the age of ten places much importance on going out with the opposite sex – a key way of validating one's normality.

And there is a fourth and final mechanism that comes into force if all else fails. This entails a direct homophobic response, through the harassment of gay youth by both teachers and other children. In a recent survey, Stonewall – the leading gay and lesbian campaign organisation in the UK – concluded that:

> Homophobic bullying is almost endemic in Britain's schools. Almost **two thirds (65 per cent)** of young lesbian, gay and bisexual pupils have experienced direct bullying. **Seventy-five per cent of** young gay people attending faith schools have experienced homophobic bullying.
>
> **Ninety-seven per cent** of pupils hear other insulting homophobic remarks, such as 'poof', 'dyke', 'rug-muncher', 'queer' and 'bender'. Over **seven in ten** gay pupils hear those phrases used often or frequently. Less than **a quarter (23 per cent)** of young gay people have been told that homophobic

> bullying is wrong in their school. In schools that have said homophobic bullying is wrong, gay young people are **60 per cent** more likely not to have been bullied.
>
> (Hunt and Jensen, 2007)

In her study of an American school, C. Pascoe demonstrates how the 'specter of the fag' becomes a disciplinary mechanism for regulating heterosexual as well as homosexual boys and how the 'fag discourse' is as much tied to gender as it is to sexuality.

As with each of the other mechanisms for making homosexuality invisible, this sort of direct homophobic response occurs in every setting a young person encounters. From mockery and abuse to physical violence, from being rejected by parents to losing one's job, from psychiatric treatment to imprisonment – all these remain distinct possibilities for those who dare to breach the heterosexual assumption.

## Continue the debate

1  Briefly consider your own school experience. Did homosexuality get mentioned at all? If it was mentioned, was this a negative mention or a positive one?

2  Did you know any gays or lesbians when you were at school? If so, how did you respond to them?

3  Are schools changing so that the situation for lesbian and gay youth is no longer as difficult as it was?

*See*: C. J. Pascoe, *Hey Dude, You're a Fag: Masculinity and Sexuality in High School* (2007).

*Source*: Plummer, in Herdt (1989); Hunt and Jensen (2007).

(a) Girls attend lessons in reading and writing at the Zarghona Ana school in Kandahar. After years of being excluded from public education, girls have now returned to schools in Afghanistan
(b) Four schoolboys represent the 'racial scale' in South Africa: black, Indian, half-caste, and white

*Source*: (a) © Thorne Anderson/Corbis; (b) © Alain Nogues/Corbis Sygma.

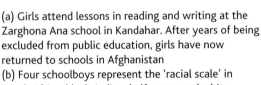

away from the practice entirely. While some streaming seems necessary to match instruction with abilities, rigid streaming has a powerful impact on students' learning and self-concept. Young people who spend years in higher streams tend to see themselves as bright and able, whereas those in lower streams develop lower ambition and self-esteem (Rosenbaum, 1980; Oakes, 1982, 1985).

Just as students are treated differently within schools, schools themselves differ in fundamental ways. One key distinction separates state and public schools in the UK. State schools often have larger class sizes, insufficient libraries and fewer science labs. But money alone does not magically bolster academic quality. Even more important are the cooperative efforts and enthusiasm of teachers, parents and students themselves. In other words, even if school funding were exactly the same everywhere, the students whose families value and encourage education would still

learn more than others (Jencks et al., 1972). In short, we should not expect schools alone to overcome the effects of marked social inequality.

Yet, schools certainly reflect privilege and disadvantage. As educational critic Jonathan Kozol (1992) concludes, 'savage inequalities' in our school system alert young children to the reality that our society has already defined them as winners or losers. And, Kozol continues, all too often the children go on to fulfil this labelling.

Finally, a key theme of conflict analysis deserves to be highlighted: *schooling transforms social privilege into personal merit*. Attending university, in effect, is a rite of passage for people from well-to-do families. People are more likely to interpret university degrees as 'badges of ability' than as symbols of family affluence (Sennett and Cobb, 1973). At the same time, people tend to transform social disadvantage into personal deficiency when they criticise school leavers.

# Education as a major issue of our time: more questions than answers

## Purpose

What is the point of education? This is 'the philosophy of education debate'. Some arguments centre on the value of education for the economy; others upon the need for a critical, thinking citizenship – informed and able to discuss ideas carefully with knowledge, information, etc.

## Economy

Can we afford all this education? This is 'the public spending debate'. The costs of education in all countries throughout the world are spiralling – almost out of control. A key sub-issue here is whether the funding should be private or public, selective or universal. And more, if students are human capital, how should they be seen as investments for the future?

## Hi-tech

Does the new hi-tech Information Revolution mean radically shifting the way we teach and learn? Just as we now look back in horror at the ways children were (not) taught in the nineteenth century, how might we come to see the education of the middle twentieth century? This is the 'e-debate', the educational cyber-world issue. Children will from now on just take for granted the Information Revolution. They live with it from the earliest ages. Children of two or three now use computers;

iPods, YouTube, email and texting have become central to contemporary communication. All educational systems need now to have the new technologies at the very heart of them. The days of changeover – of adjusting to a new system – are over. The new system is here. But what will it be like (Salman, 2004)?

## Populations

Is education now for all across the entire life cycle? Consider the debates over special needs, higher education and third age. Education is not just for children; more and more it is seen as a lifelong process.

## Audit and management

Are we maintaining – or, better still, 'advancing' – with our educational standards? This is the 'quality debate'. Education is in constant fear of being 'dumbed down' and unruly. Systems have been put in place or are being put in place so that schools and universities are well managed and well audited. But often these very systems overreach themselves and there are problems. Teachers may be stripped of their authority by managers and policed by new inspection regimes (see Chapter 6 on audit culture).

## Equity

Are students being treated equally? Are we in a meritocracy? For a long while, there has been a concern over the ways in which certain groups receive such a 'better start in life' through a more priviliged educational route. This used to be the old debate between 'elite/ private' education and mass/ public education. And to some

extent it remains so. The old problems keep reappearing: why do the working class still fail to succeed as well as the middle class in what is mainly a middle-class institution? But now we also have to bring gender (why do girls seem to do better now than boys in schools in the Western world?), ethnicity and disability to the foreground.

## Freedom

What choices do we have in education? There are two kinds of issue here. The first concerns the freedom to learn and teach – much of what is now learnt and taught is restricted to a tightly structured syllabus, and the issue is raised of how far this could or should go. The second concerns parent power – the rights of parents and students to choose their own schools and universities. How far can such 'rights' be extended without creating greater inequalities?

## Local problems

What are the daily 'threats' that schools and even universities now face? Here there are a range of changing issues that confront schools on a regular basis. Day-to-day school life can be challenged by bullying, teacher harassment, unruly behaviour, school meals, truanting, violence.

## Global concerns

What are the issues being posed by globalisation? Now more and more students travel the globe – both in reality and in virtuality. There are increasing concerns about the universal homogenisation of standards (for instance, the 'Europeanisation' of education, and the creation of worldwide league tables for universities).

## Critical comment

This kind of analysis – allied to conflict theory – points up the connection between formal education and social inequality, and shows how schooling transforms privilege into personal worthiness, and social disadvantage into personal deficiency. Critics claim that the approach minimises the extent to which schooling has met the intellectual and personal needs of students, propelling the upward social mobility of many young people in the process. Further, especially in recent years, 'politically correct' educational curricula, closely tied to conflict theory, are challenging the status quo on many fronts.

## Education in the twenty-first century: some current issues

Most Western cultures now place a high premium upon their educational systems. Education debates figure prominently at election times. Perhaps because we expect our educational institutions to do so much – pass on culture and knowledge, equalise opportunity, instil discipline, stimulate individual imagination, provide a labour force, conduct pathbreaking research – education has remained at the centre of controversy for a number of years. In this section, we look at a few recent issues.

## 1 Global inequalities in higher education

Educational inequalities are found at all stages of the educational system throughout the world. At higher levels it is even more marked: out of 100 adults of tertiary age, 69 are enrolled in higher education in North America and Europe, but only five are enrolled in sub-Saharan Africa and 10 in south and west Asia. Nevertheless in recent years there have been more and more students following higher education in lower-income countries and the inequalities are narrowing. Overall during the past 40 years, there has been a massive worldwide increase in the number of students in higher (or tertiary) – fivefold from 28.6 million in 1970 to 152.5 million in 2007. The expansion has been greatest since 2000, and especially in sub-Saharan Africa and much of Asia, including China. Figure 20.2 gives some detail. Figure 20.3 also shows that gender inequalities are taking a new shape. Broadly, in higher-income societies more and more women are following higher education; but they lag behind in much of the rest of the world.

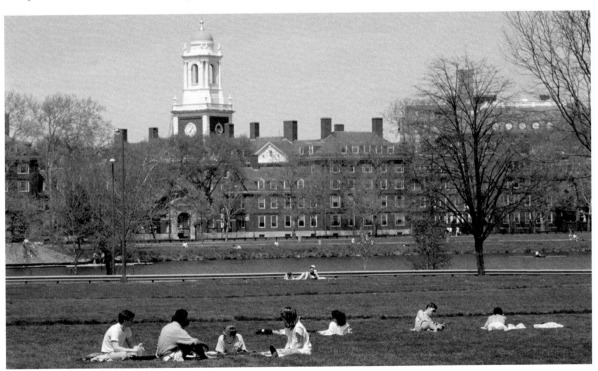

Harvard University, USA
*Source:* © Corbis.

# Higher Education Across the World

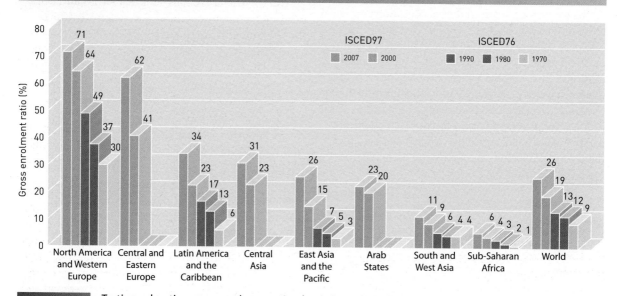

**Figure 20.2** Tertiary education gross enrolment ratios: by region, 1970–2007

*Notes*: ISCED: International Standard Classification of Education. For the purpose of maintaining consistency across the time series, post-secondary non-tertiary (ISCED4) students were included in certain countries. This may lead to an overestimate of the tertiary gross enrolment ratio, especially for central Asia and only slightly for North America and western Europe. Regions are ranked in decreasing order of gross enrolment ratio in 2007.

*Source*: UNESCO Institute for Statistics, Time Series Data, Table 1. *Global Education Digest 2009*, p. 14, Fig. 3.

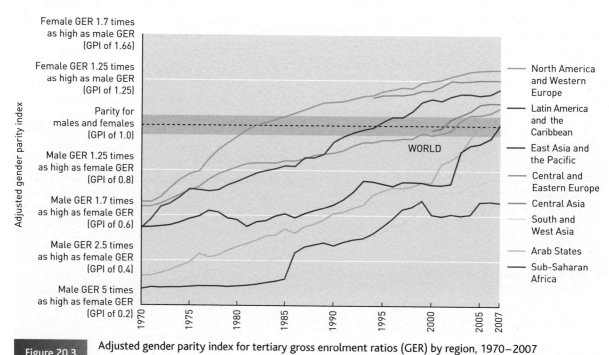

**Figure 20.3** Adjusted gender parity index for tertiary gross enrolment ratios (GER) by region, 1970–2007

*Note*: The adjusted gender parity index provides a comparable scale for both sexes: gender parity indices favouring women are expressed as the ratio of female gross enrolment to male gross enrolment; those favouring males are expressed as the ratio of male gross enrolment to female gross enrolment. The shaded area denotes a gender parity index between 97 per cent and 103 per cent.

*Source*: UNESCO Institute for Statistics, Time Series Data, Table 1. *Global Education Digest 2009*, p. 16, Fig. 4.

**TOP 10**

**Top global universities, 2010**

1  Harvard University, USA
2  California Institute of Technology, USA
3  Massachusetts Institute of Technology, USA
4  Stanford University, USA
5  Princeton University, USA
6  University of Cambridge, UK
7  University of Oxford, UK
8  University of California, Berkeley, USA
9  Imperial College London, UK
10 Yale University, USA

*Source:* Times Higher Education World University Rankings.
http://www.timeshighereducation.co.uk/world-university-rankings.

## Globalisation and education

The twenty-first century is witnessing a significant growth in 'mobile students'. In 2007, over 2.8 million students were enrolled in educational institutions outside of their country of origin. This represents 123,400 more students than in 2006, an increase of 4.6 per cent. The global number of mobile students has grown by 53 per cent since 1999; and the number of female mobile students has increased at an even faster rate.

China sends the greatest number of students abroad, amounting to almost 421,100. Other major countries of origin are: India (153,300), the Republic of Korea (105,300), Germany (77,500), Japan (54,500), France (54,000), the United States (50,300), Malaysia (46,500), Canada (43,900) and the Russian Federation (42,900). These ten countries account for 37.5 per cent of the world's mobile students, reported by 153 host countries with such data.

In contrast, the United States hosts the largest number and share of the world's mobile students at 595,900 and 21.3 per cent respectively. It is followed by the United Kingdom (351,500), France (246,600), Australia (211,500), Germany (206,900), Japan (125,900), Canada (68,500), South Africa (60,600), the Russian Federation (60,300) and Italy (57,300). These 11 countries host 71 per cent of the world's mobile students, with 62 per cent of them studying in the top six countries (UNESCO, *Global Education Digest*, 2009).

## 2  Funding crises, market forces and centralisation

All this significant increase in education – at primary, secondary and tertiary levels – has led to the need for more and more funding. So much so, it is reasonable to

talk of a 'funding crisis' in education across the world. Just how is it all to be paid for?

The United States model suggests the importance of market structures, competition and profit. Unlike the UK and most of Europe, for instance, it has a clear two-tier university system – with the most prestigious colleges and universities (the Ivy League, etc.) being in the private sector, and the rest being run by the public sectors (such as the State of California). In the UK, the Blair–Brown government did not suggest the privatisation of universities but introduced a system of student loans, replacing the previous system of grants. The later coalition government is continuing this – and increasing the size of loans.

In the school system, the Education Act 1988 introduced the devolution of the financial management of schools from Local Education Authorities to boards of governors, and gave schools with over 300 students the right to 'opt out' of the LEA system. They would then become 'grant maintained' – in effect, a business funded from central government. In 1994, 592 of 3,773 secondary schools and 334 of 18,828 primary schools exercised this option.

The main thrust of the 1988 changes was to introduce market forces (supply, demand, competition and choice) into all levels of the education system. By more heavily assessing schools and publishing the results of assessments in 'league tables', the government of the time believed it would instil competition between schools and enable parents and students to make informed choices about where to study.

While the Labour government reversed some aspects of the 1988 policy in 1997, it largely continued the process of marketisation in higher education, introducing student loans and fees in the name of making students keener consumers (and saving public money), and also promoting the repackaging of knowledge into short, non-cumulative 'modules' – often with mass-marketed textbooks, such as this one.

Yet while there is a concern with free markets at one level, at another level there has been increasing central state intervention in matters linked to the syllabus and assessment. A 1992 Education (Schools) Act introduced new centralised arrangements for school inspection (the Office for Standards in Education, Ofsted). Textbooks geared to mass education and new standard curricula may mean much less flexibility.

## 3  'Excellence and quality': the culture of auditing

In many nations, concern has arisen about the standard of education. Some people in many industrialised

# Ethics in educational fieldwork and life stories

Harry Wolcott researches in the field of education. In his book, *Sneaky Kid and Its Aftermath* (2002), he looks at the experience of educational failure, especially how there is so little support for those who are failed by our educational systems. He does this through the life story of Brad, a troubled 19-year-old. The life story is organised by themes, taking us through issues like 'I don't have to steal, but . . .', 'A new life', and 'Being sneaky'. Intriguingly, the book also presents a short dramatic version of the story (with a heavy rock score!) which has been performed in some universities. Ever since its publication, it has been controversial. What is not told in the original story are the background details of how Wolcott met Brad, how Brad lived on his property, and how Wolcott regularly had sex with him. All this happened before he got him to tell his life story. *Sneaky Kid* tells how Brad develops schizophrenia and returns to Wolcott's house and burns it down in an attempt to kill him. Brad is screaming, 'You fucker. I'm going to kill you. I'm going to kill you. I'm going to tie you up and leave you in the house and set the house on fire' (Wolcott, 2002: 74). Luckily, Harry escapes; unluckily, his house does not. It goes up entirely in flames, with all his and his partner's belongings. There is a serious court case, where despite Brad's guilt, Wolcott is himself scrutinised for his relationship with Brad. Brad's family is especially unhappy about the relationship with Wolcott, but so are many academics. Ultimately, Brad is institutionalised.

This life story raises a lot of issues. Most apparently, can there ever be a justification for having sex with a (vulnerable) research subject? It is true that the sex came before the research, but there will also be many who worry about the age difference. Wolcott himself takes a strident tone against his critics. Almost in anger against those who preach at him, he says: 'one can be ethical or one can conduct social research, but one cannot be both ethical and a researcher in such settings. I'll opt for the label of researcher. I'm prepared to take my bumps' (Wolcott, 2002: 145).

This certainly goes against the current tide of work on the need for more ethics in research, not less. All social life is ethical. There is no getting away from how people treat people, and often one makes a mess of it. What Wolcott seems to say is that the mess is one thing and the research is another. Yet, surely, the minute you start meddling around in other people's lives, you develop responsibilities. We have responsibilities as teachers, as friends, as sociologists. We cannot simply shunt them aside, as Wolcott seems to want to do.

In the final chapter of his book, Wolcott reviews ethics and ethics boards. Once again, he does not mince his words. He has no time for them. These Institutional Review Boards are another example of the bureaucratisation of research. Above a simple risk analysis done by the researcher, there is no need for them. As he says:

> Some awfully petty personnel find comfort in enforcing some awfully petty rules, which takes up the valuable time of others from completely closing down the discovery-oriented approach qualitative researchers follow.
>
> (Wolcott, 2002: 148)

In our view, there should be some checks on students. Research training should include ethical dimensions, but so should economics, business studies, social work and psychology. There is no need to separate out social research. We should all become ingrained to take seriously how we conduct our work. What do you think of this case and the issues it raises?

nations fear that schools have done an increasingly poor job of motivating and training students, allowing general intellectual and performance standards to slip. Others, however, argue that the increasing focus on market forces in some countries is itself undermining standards.

Likewise, UK politicians of many colours have expressed alarm that 40 per cent of 11-year-olds and 30 per cent of 14-year-olds were not meeting national numeracy and literacy standards – well below international averages. The Labour government which swept to power in the UK in 1997 claimed in its first White Paper, *Excellence in Schools*, that its main priorities were 'education, education and education'. Following on from the preceding government, Labour has striven to expand monitoring of schools, through an improved Office for Standards in Education (Ofsted). Ministers have proposed testing children from the moment they start school, requiring primary schools to provide an hour a day on literacy and numeracy; weeding out the ranks of so-called incompetent teachers; and setting performance targets for each school, with those that fail to meet targets facing closure.

Some critics of both the former Conservative and the Labour governments have suggested that the language of concern over decline has scapegoated teachers and LEAs for all the wider problems with education. Without a workforce able to feel confidence in itself, they claim, teachers can hardly encourage confidence among children. Some academics at the university level reject Labour's marketisation push as undermining the authority of 'pure knowledge' (Coffey, 2001).

## The culture of auditing

In Chapter 6, we looked at the growth of a culture of auditing – and saw how it has been developed in the field of health, policing and education. In education, debates over standards have become part of a wider movement of auditing, accountability and measuring 'outcomes'. We see it in:

- The creation of targets and tiers: education now has set syllabi, 'key stages' and 'bench marking' for measuring successful outcomes. In universities, the creation of the Research Assessment exercise in 1985 more or less suggests that every tutor should produce at least four good publications in the assessed period, and these are then evaluated by peer review.
- The surveillance of schools and inspection of teachers, largely through Ofsted.
- The creation of published league tables for all stages of education – primary, secondary and tertiary.

All this not only has the outcome of identifying the 'best' schools; it also leads to the phenomenon of the 'failing school'. At their extremes, such schools can be closed down or taken out of the hands of the local authority, or new 'super heads' can be brought in. Such schools seem intensively to encourage a labelling process. As teachers become more and more demoralised, hurt and angry, so children start to find their own experiences invalidated even more. A blame culture weakens both pupils and staff, lowering self-respect and self-esteem, and destroying confidence. This usually means a complete disruption and

discontinuity of schooling, as old teachers leave and new ones are brought in. The schools, in practice, tend to be ones in inner-city areas or areas of significant deprivation.

# 4 Dangerous schools

In recent years, there has been growing concern about levels of violence and misconduct in schools. Thus, for instance, in a few notorious cases in the United States there have been prominent shootings at schools, which have necessitated high-security policing around school buildings. In the most infamous case, at Columbine High School, two boys killed a teacher, 12 students and themselves. Although such killings are very rare, they almost always achieve much publicity and fuel the idea of 'dangerous and violent schools' (*Newsweek*, 23 August 1999).

In April 2007, student Seung-Hui Cho killed 32 people, wounded many more and then killed himself in two separate attacks at Virginia Tech in the United States. It was the deadliest school shooting in US history.

Such shootings have been much less prominent in the UK, though it has been estimated that there are something like three cases of arson per week in UK schools (*Guardian Education*, 30 October 2001: 2). More and more teachers worry about their working conditions when some of their pupils are willing to abuse, fight or even stab them. This seems to be one of the major reasons cited by teachers for leaving the profession.

Linked to this, many children now find themselves outside the educational system, as schools say they cannot cope with 'problem children'. In 2001/2 some 10,000 children were permanently excluded from schools – 4 per cent higher than in the previous year, but lower than in 1996/7 (when 13,000 were excluded). Boys outnumbered girls by nearly five to one; and were highest among some ethnic groupings (Black Caribbean). The age group where exclusions were most common was those aged 13 and 14 (*Social Trends*, 2007: 29).

# 5 Parent power: parentocracy

Education in England and Wales (Scotland and Northern Ireland operate separate education systems) has gone through three phases: a concern for imparting basic information to the working classes, followed by a shift to a meritocratic ideology, followed by a new

The massacre of 12 schoolchildren and one teacher at Columbine High School brought their friends together to consider their emotional and spiritual response to their deaths

*Source*: Rick Wilking/Reuters.

phase labelled **parentocracy**, *a system where a child's education is increasingly dependent upon the wealth and wishes of parents, rather than the ability and efforts of pupils* (P. Brown, 1990).

In part, the emphasis on parental choice in primary schools has fuelled this shift. One study of parents exercising choice over their children's schooling found that class plays a major influence. For working-class parents, school had to be fitted into the demands of work and other family matters, while middle-class parents tended to reorganise their household arrangements to accommodate school. With the ideology of parentocracy, schools may be seen once again to disadvantage the less flexible working classes.

Another aspect of parentocracy is the rise of 'parent power' in the running of schools. Parents are invited to make their voices heard at school governors' meetings and, in the UK, vote on such matters as whether schools should 'opt out' of the LEA system. One study found that 'middle-class white males still dominate the powerful positions in secondary schools governorship', although women have increasing influence at the primary school level (Deem et al., 1995; Deem, 1997: 28). Worryingly, though, the same study found that 'governors may turn out to have quite different characteristics from those of the pupils who attend the school they govern and to have much less interest in

social justice than might be thought appropriate for those overseeing a public education service' (Deem, 1997: 31).

# 6 Credentialism

Randall Collins (1979) coined the term *credential society* for societies where people view diplomas and degrees as evidence of ability to perform specialised occupational roles. As modern societies have become more technologically complex, culturally diverse and socially mobile, a CV or résumé often says more about 'who you are' than family background does.

**Credentialism**, then, is *evaluating a person on the basis of educational qualifications*. Functional analysis views credentialism as simply the way our modern society goes about ensuring that important jobs are filled by well-trained people. But Collins points out that credentials often bear little relation to the responsibilities of a specific job, and maintains that degrees serve as a shorthand way to sort out the people with the manners and attitudes sought by many employers. In short, credentialism operates much like family background as a gatekeeping strategy that restricts prestigious occupations to a small segment of the population. Finally, this emphasis on credentials can encourage *over-education*, by which many workers have more schooling than they need to perform their jobs. As a result, although we see more and more people with degrees, there are relatively fewer jobs calling for highly educated workers, while the proportion of low-skilled service jobs is expanding.

# 7 Education and the Information Revolution

One key trend now reshaping education involves technology. Just as the Industrial Revolution had a major impact on schooling in the nineteenth century, so computers and the Information Revolution are transforming formal education today. At the start of the twenty-first century, all educational institutions require computers and computing skills. It is a major change that has effectively taken one generation – about 20 to 25 years – to more or less complete. But we still cannot quite see where this is leading. The new high-tech world is a world of uncertainty.

The promise of new information technology goes beyond helping students learn basic skills to improving the overall quality of learning. Interacting with computers prompts students to be more active learners and has the added benefit of allowing them to progress at their own pace. For students with disabilities who cannot write with a pen or pencil, computers permit easier self-expression. The introduction of computers into schools at all levels of education appears significantly to increase learning speed and retention of information.

## Looking ahead

This chapter has suggested just how important – and how full of problems – educational systems are across the world. Since the nineteenth century, most countries have seen the provision of education systems as central social institutions. Education can improve literacy, raise general standards of knowledge and awareness, and provide a better-trained workforce. But at the same time it may work to reproduce social divisions across class, gender and ethnicity.

In many low-income countries, children have few opportunities to pursue education beyond a basic level, while in richer countries students are often processed in school via a bureaucratic system, increasingly organised through credentialism, league tables and the 'audit culture'. In all countries there are major problems of funding.

## SUMMARY

1 Education is the major social institution for transmitting knowledge and skills, as well as teaching cultural norms and values.

2 Three classic perspectives can be used to study education. Functional theories examine the functions of a school – such as intellectual, economic and social. Symbolic interactionists search for everyday meanings in schools and have observed classroom interactions often through ethnography. Conflict analysis points out how differences in class, race, gender and sexuality promote unequal opportunities for schooling. Formal education also serves as a means of generating conformity to produce compliant adult workers. When children get labelled as achievers or as failures at school, they learn to become the type of person which the label suggests they are.

3 Five factors serve to perpetuate social inequalities in schools: the home background, the local environment, the culture of the school, the marketplace of schools and the reproduction of class across generations. Streaming, in theory, groups students of similar needs to maximise the appropriateness of teaching materials and the pace of learning. Critics maintain that schools stream students according to their social background, thereby providing privileged youngsters with a richer and more challenging education.

4 Educational inequalities are found at all stages of the educational system right throughout the world. At higher levels it is even more marked. Nevertheless, the twenty-first century is witnessing more and more students across the world in higher education. There is also a significant growth in 'mobile students'.

5 The UK government has introduced market forces into the education system. Some believe that the market will improve services and choice, but others suggest that market forces are increasing inequalities and undermining the traditional principles of education.

6 Many education systems encourage people to get credentials which are not necessarily related to the available jobs.

7 Contemporary issues facing education include funding, auditing, parentocracy, credentialism and the Information Revolution.

CONNECT UP: Turn to Part 6 of this book for key resources and link up with the book's website, which links to these resources
SEE: www.pearsoned.co.uk/plummer

# MYTASKLIST

# Ten suggestions for going further

## 1 Connect up with Part Six and the Sociology Web Resources

As you work through ideas and think about the issues raised in this chapter, look at the accompanying website and the resource centre at the end of this book which connects to it. There is a lot here to help you move on. To link up, see: www.pearson.co.uk/plummer.

## 2 Review the chapter

*Briefly summarise (in a paragraph) just what this chapter has been about.* Consider: (a) What have you learned? (b) What do you disagree with? Be critical. And (c) How would you develop all this? How could you get more detail on matters that interest you?

## 3 Pose questions

(a) Why did widespread schooling develop in Europe only after the Industrial Revolution?

(b) Referring to various countries, including the UK, describe ways in which schooling is shaped by economic, political or cultural factors.

(c) How valuable do you find classroom interaction studies? Do one of your own, looking around your campus and class. Do the themes outlined in the text still apply?

(d) Examine the controversy over why girls seem to be achieving more than boys in UK schools. Consider also how girls 'achieve' in low-income societies. Discuss how cultures may shape such achievement.

## 4 Explore key words

Many concepts have been introduced in this chapter. You can review them from the website or from the listing at the back of this book. You might like to give special attention to just five words and think them through – how would you define them, what are they dealing with, and do they help you see the social world more clearly or not?

## 5 Search the Web

Be critical when you look at websites – see the box on p. 940 in the Resources section. For this chapter look at the following:

### World information

UNESCO
www.unesco.org
The UNESCO website is a useful starting point for world analyses of education.

### UK information

Department for Education and Skills (UK)
www.dfes.gov.uk
For UK government policy and information on funding.

National Literacy Trust
www.literacytrust.org.uk
Covers all aspects of education.

## 6 Watch a DVD

- Laurent Cantent's *The Class* (2008). Teacher and novelist François Bégaudeau plays a version of himself as he negotiates a year with his racially mixed students from a tough Parisian neighbourhood.
- Alan Bennett's play *The History Boys* (2006) becomes a film about grammar school boys and their teacher(s).
- Ken Loach's *Kes* (1969): a classic film set in the 1960s, it is the standard bearer of all flims about education and the working class.
- Peter Weir's *Dead Poets' Society* (1989): Robin Williams in an elite US school challenging his students.

- Mike Newell's *Mona Lisa Smile* (2003): Julia Roberts does the same as the above for girls, but not as well.

## 7 Think and read

Sally Tomlinson, *Education in a Post-welfare Society* (2nd edn, 2007). This is an excellent and critical study of education in the UK over the past 60 years – and has a strong concern with current issues. Her more recent book, *Race and Education* (2008), is another excellent review of this field.

Amanda Coffey, *Education and Social Change* (2001). A lively discussion of the major issues facing education in the contemporary UK (and much of it is relevant to other Western cultures too).

A. H. Halsey, Hugh Lauder, Phillip Brown and Amy Stuart Wells, *Education: Culture, Economy and Society* (1997). A very valuable collection of up-to-date readings which mark out the field of the contemporary sociology of education.

### Gender and schooling

Paul Willis, *Learning to Labour* (1977). The classic UK ethnography: a study of a small group of working-class boys moving from school to work. Its fame may, however, be curiously misplaced: it studies only 12 boys and overlays the observation with a rather dense theoretical Marxism.

Mairtin Mac an Ghaill, *The Making of Men: Masculinities, Sexualities and Schooling* (1994). A vivid study of gender, class and ethnicity in a secondary school.

Sue Sharpe, *Just Like a Girl: How Girls Learn to Become Women* (2nd edn, 1994). Updates her original 1976 study and finds that girls have changed.

 Think about what a university is for. To help you with this, two lively books are:

Mary Evans, *Killing: The Death of the Universities* (2004)

Frank Furedi, *Where Have All the Intellectuals Gone?* (2006)

## 8 Relax with a novel

The classic books on university life include David Lodge's *Small World* and Malcolm Bradbury's *The History Man*. Both are now quite old, but remain very telling about the follies of academic life. Lionel Shriver's *We Need to Talk about Kevin* is ostensibly about a pupil who kills at school, but it is about so much more.

## 9 Connect to other chapters

- To link labelling processes to labelling theory, see Chapters 14 and 17.
- To link education to social class, see Chapter 10.
- To link education to gender and ethnicity, see Chapters 11 and 12.

## 10 Engage in THE BIG DEBATE

### Is education being dumbed down? The case of mass higher education

There has been a marked expansion in numbers going to universities and other institutions of higher education across the world, but especially in the industrialised world. In one sense, 'schooling' has now been extended for many young people to over 20 years of age. It has almost become compulsory for middle-class groups. Figure 20.4 shows figures for 18-year-olds in education for selected countries in 2004.

This change has meant a shift from an *elite system* of higher education (where a very select few went to university, who then automatically got the 'best jobs') to a *mass system* (where a much larger – if still selected – group go to university). Over the past century, the UK has seen a shift from something like 1 per cent to 30 per cent of young people attending university, and a government goal is that some 50 per cent should eventually attain this. In the United States, such a system has existed for a long time, and it is now starting to appear everywhere.

There are many strands of the modern university which we can see as being shaped by some of the themes already discussed in this book. Universities have become large bureaucracies. Standardisation has become the norm for courses and assessments. There has been a *McDonaldisation of the university* as mass textbooks and PowerPoint slides take over from library searching and creative lecturing. Universities have become part of the

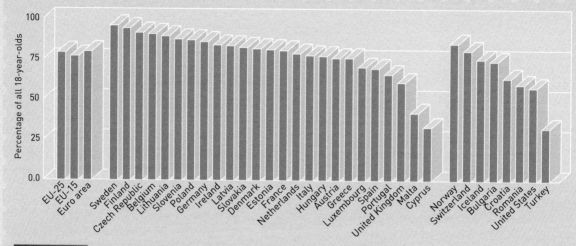

**Figure 20.4**   Percentage of 18-year-olds in education: selected countries, 2004

*Source*: After Eurostat, *Europe in Figures – Eurostat Yearbook 2006–07*, p. 88.

*market*. They are now much more vocational and tied into market forces. Indeed, even within the universities the market dominates so that students now become 'customers'. There is an upside to this in so far as students may now have their immediate demands satisfied: 'We are paying after all!' they say. But there is also a downside: concern over long-term thinking and the values of university life may now have to recede as they are not part of market values. Academics too may come to have more concern with patenting and intellectual property rights than with the search for truth. Instead of the classics of a culture being studied, new courses such as cultural studies, tourism and even golf course studies have appeared in the new curriculum. And the universities have become more and more involved in commercial practices. Contemporary changes in higher education may be closely linked to changes in the work situation. Post-Fordism (discussed in Chapter 15) may now be found in universities. Just as the work system has to become more flexible and adaptable (and this brings growing uncertainty), so too modern university systems need to do this.

Some argue that we are entering the phase of the *postmodern university*. Frank Webster suggests that the idea of 'differences' is central to this. Universities may once have been elite institutions where a common background led to a common search for a common knowledge provided through tutors and libraries. All this has now gone. We have, as Webster says, differences in 'courses, students, purposes, academics and disciplines' (2000: 319). There seem to be very few common traits that now bind the universities together. Along with this, they have declined in general standing: getting a degree has now become a commonplace, and it no longer has a major role in gaining employment or status in society. Elite universities prided themselves on their autonomy and freedom, but mass universities have become much more restrained by business and governments: they have become much more accountable. At the same time, universities have moved from being closed to open – expert knowledge was limited and now there is much more openness.

## Continue the debate

1   Just what is happening to universities today? How have they changed? What do you see as their major problems?

2   Has 'more' meant 'worse'?

*Source*: Evans (2004); Furedi (2006); Smith and Webster (1997); Webster (2000).

# CHAPTER 22

# COMMUNICATION AND THE NEW MEDIA

**SOCIOLOGIST KIRK JOHNSON** spent some years in the small Indian village of Danawli, studying the impact of television. At the time of his research, some 25 of the 104 households in the village had TV sets. The elders of the village worried a great deal about the arrival of this new medium. One, for example, argued that '*TV is the devil . . . It has only caused us pain and is very bad for us.*' Another said: '*Television is ruining our culture . . . People no longer speak like they used to. They all, especially the young people, talk about the life in the cities or in England and America. They don't know anything about own history or traditions. I have heard some even talk about love marriage.*' Another said: '*Children used to come to hear the stories of olden days. Everyone used to listen to me. The young people today only want to watch television and movies and go to Panchgani until late at night*' (Johnson, 2000: 216 and 192).

But for many the television had broadened their horizons into the modern world. They saw a whole array of new experiences: different kinds of gender and class relations; different kinds of marriage and the 'desire for fewer children'; they saw the shift from success by heredity to achievement by merit and a change in the perception of caste relations. Television challenged the positions of traditional leaders. '*We have learned,*' says one man, '*that our leaders are corrupt, even the national leaders are corrupt. On TV they show us about how corrupt our parliament members are . . .*' (Johnson, 2000: 218).

Television promotes a greater receptiveness to new values and an openness to change. Many families may not have had TV in their home, but they would visit the homes of others to watch TV, and it had helped to bring some people together. New kinds of relationship are being formed, and this is particularly noticeable among the young and children.

Danawli reveals a transitional phase in the spread of television in rural India, and Kirk Johnson concludes that 'the one material commodity which has most dramatically influenced social change in rural India has been the television set' (Johnson, 2000: 15). Again, another older man speaks:

There is no doubt about it. You can ask anyone. TV is the one thing that has most changed the way people live. You see how people watch TV. They are also so into TV that nothing else matters. The house could be burning down and no one would realise it. TV is very powerful. Our young people see things on the TV that we never saw, and this has changed the way they behave. They want everything they see. They are not satisfied any more with working the field and providing for the family.

(Johnson, 2000: 213)

*The Medium is the Message: it is the medium that shapes and controls the scale and form of human association and action.*

Marshall McLuhan

## In this chapter, we ask:

- **How has communication changed over time?**

- **How can we think about the way media work; what sorts of question can we ask?**

- **How has globalization changed the contemporary media?**

(Left) Max Ferguson, *News Vendor*, 1986

Max Ferguson's work paints a vanishing world, mainly in New York City. See his website at http://maxferguson.com.

See also: http://www.artnet.com/artist/155558/max-ferguson.html.

*Source*: News Vendor, 1986 (oil on panel), Ferguson, Max (Contemporary Artist)/ Private Collection/The Bridgeman Art Library.

 Old media and new media? What does the image of the news vendor suggest?

# The media age

This is the time of the media. Many of us live our lives increasingly in and through the media. We live what sociologists sometimes call mediated lives – lives immersed in the technologies of media communication. As we have seen (Chapter 1), it has been estimated that in 2010, young people in the USA spent at least seven hours a day hooked up to some kind of electronic communication (Pew Internet and American Life Project, 2010). Similarly, watching television is the most common home-based leisure activity for men and women in the UK. Virtually everyone watches it. Ninety-nine per cent of households in the UK own one television; 86 per cent have a video recorder, renting an average of ten films per year. But this is now almost an older technology: the arrival of digital communications – via websites, iPods, iPhones and iPads – has brought extensive and intensive changes to human social life. Between 1996/7 and 2005/6 the proportion of households owning a mobile

TV watching in outdoor public groups is very popular – as this group of Zambian Soccer fans shows
*Source*: © Gideon Mendel/Corbis.

phone shifted from 17 per cent to 79 per cent. DVD was launched in the UK in 1998 and has become the fastest-selling electronic format of all time – the numbers owning a DVD player grew from 31 per cent in 2002/03 to 79 per cent in 2005/6 – a growth of 48 per cent in three years. In 2010, 19.2 million households in the UK had internet access, or 73 per cent of households. This compares with 57 per cent in 2006, equivalent to 14.3 million households. Similar changes have been happening across the world. Note again, though, that the growth is unequal: in the UK, households in the highest 10 per cent income group were over three-and-a-half times as likely as those in the lowest 10 per cent to have an internet connection: 96 per cent of households compared with 26 per cent (*Social Trends*, 2010).

What is important about the new media technologies is the way in which they have come to play a prominent role in many aspects of our everyday lives. All the institutions discussed in this book have been changed by them. Political elections, for example, are geared up to television and the press; it is hard to imagine elections without the constant 'spin' and 'hype' in all the media. Likewise, religion has its 'televangelical' networks; and business and finance depend upon the new technologies for rapid information as well as a constant stream of advertising. And where would public events – sport or parliament or news – be if they were not relayed in our homes on television? Sports spectacles, from the Olympics and World Cups to golf and racing, depend on the television for their mass audiences.

Even the family has changed dramatically because of television. Until very recently, many homes had a TV centred in their living room, draped with family photos – symbolic of its importance. In the twentieth century, television gradually became a major part of everyday life, marking out family time and routines. It was the intimate machine, giving impressions of talking to you through chat programmes, advice programmes and close-up interviews with all kinds of people. The medium became friend and family. Indeed, much of what is shown on the screen actually depicts friends and families – the most popular programmes remain the 'soap operas', which are always about this (in the UK, *Coronation Street* has been running for over 50 years). But then we take to university or work all the details of the soap lives we have seen on TV and start to discuss them with friends. TV characters invade our lives as new friends. And the taste for 'reality television' over the past decade – from *Survivor* and *Big Brother* to *Strictly Come Dancing* and the *X Factor* – holds large audiences for events that dissolve the boundaries between television and reality. This feature is brought home in films such as *The Truman Show*. Here a man is born on to a massive television set, becomes the focus of a major soap opera, and does not know it (till the end of the film, that is, when he breaks out of the programme to find his 'real' life). We are media saturated. Indeed, one commentator has tellingly remarked that:

> **in one hour's television viewing, each one of us is likely to experience more images than a member of a non-industrial society would in a lifetime. The quantitative difference is so great as to become categorical; we do not just experience more images, but we live with a completely different relationship between the image and other orders of experience.**

(Fiske, 1991: 58)

But now, of course, it has gone much further than just television. As we have seen throughout this book, the twenty-first century has now become the digital, networking and information age. Television is slowly receding into the corner for many, and the new digital technologies are taking over and reshaping life again. As we saw earlier, the Spanish sociologist, Manuel Castells, has argued that 'new information technologies are transforming the way we produce, consume, manage, live and die' (Castells, 1989: 15; see also Chapter 6, p. 200). In this chapter, we will look at some aspects of how our modern mass media system developed and examine some of the theories that have tried to explain how it works. We will show how media research needs to look at what media messages contain, how media messages are made and how they are understood by their audiences. Finally, we will glimpse their importance in the new century, as the media become increasingly globalised. (In the next chapter we will say more about the new digital media.)

# Communications and social change

The history of societies can partially be written as the history of media communications. We have seen in Chapter 4 how social life changed between hunting and gathering societies and industrial society, and how technology is one guiding feature of social change. Technology can do nothing in itself: it takes people to act on the media to bring about change. But without the media themselves, no change would be possible. What we can see is direct one-to-one, face-to-face communication developing into the **mass media**, *any social or technological devices used for the selection, transmission or reception of information.*

One aspect of that technology is the means of communication. As the means of communication change, so do social lives. The major developments in human culture and consciousness are linked to changes in our modes of communication – the evolution from words and primitive speech through writing to typeface and now modern electronic worlds (Ong, 1982).

Our focus here is not upon the content of the media but on their form. In a famous phrase, US media guru Marshall McLuhan proclaimed that *The Medium is the Message* (McLuhan, 1964). What he meant by this is that independently of what is being said, it is the kind of 'medium which shapes and controls the scale of human association and action'. McLuhan sees the history of media as falling into three major periods. The first is an oral culture, where the ear is the important sense. Listening to the words is a harmonious, circular way of thought. The second is the writing and printing culture, where 'the ear' is exchanged for 'the eye'. It brings more linear thought. The third is the electronic culture. And here the media bring radical shifts again.

Consider Table 22.1, which outlines the evolution of the main forms of communication in society. We can return to our image of the world's history scaled to a 24-hour clock starting at midnight and continuing till the next midnight, introduced in Chapter 5. Here, speech is invented around 9.30 in the evening. Writing is not invented till about 8 minutes before midnight. Electronic devices appear some 11 seconds, and digital electronics 2 seconds, before the clock strikes midnight (Neuman, 1991: 7). The *Timeline* box gives some landmarks in media history.

## Oral cultures

For most of our history, then, societies have been entirely dependent upon face-to-face grunts.

| Table 22.1 | Stages in the development of human communication | |
|---|---|---|
| 1 | The Age of Signs | No speech or writing, only sounds and bodily gestures. Maybe 70 million years ago? |
| 2 | The Age of Speech | Oral cultures, pre-literate, started to appear at most 100,000 years ago. Cro-Magnon and other prehistoric cultures. Linguists can identify around 50 prehistoric vocabularies. |
| 3 | The Age of Writing | Writing started to appear around 5,000 years ago. Sumerians, Egyptian civilisation, Turkey, Iraq, Iran. Initially pictographs, hieroglyphics, clay tablets. Later papyrus – a light and portable medium. Alphabets slowly replaced images and songs, and this promoted linear, rational and abstract thought. Problems of censorship started to appear. Chirography – or manuscripts – became the main form in the Middle Ages. |
| 4 | The Age of Print | First printing press in West c. 1445–56 (printing appeared in China nearly 800 years earlier). Gutenberg published Bible. Greatly amplified reach and impact of alphabet. Media censorship by church. Typography dominated. Printing speeded up with the Industrial Revolution. |
| 5 | The Age of Electronics | Electrical and electronic media, from late nineteenth century. Emergence of photography. Rise of recorded music. The Cinema Century. |
| 6 | The Information Age | Digital, high-tech, computing: games playing, mobile phones, iPods, iPhones and iPads. |

## Timeline Some modern landmarks in media history

| 1456 | Gutenberg Press: printing of first book (The Bible) in Western world (but evidence of printing in China some 800 years earlier). |
|---|---|

*17th century* **Press started to develop**

| 1620–1 | Corantos (news sheets) in Holland reporting (with King's authority) on wars. |
|---|---|
| 1665 | Oxford – court news (later *London Gazette*). |
| 1690 | First American newspaper reporting on colonies. |
| 1785 | *The Times* first published, followed by *The Observer* in 1791. |
| 1838 | *The Times* of India founded. Morse code invented. |
| 1839 | First photographs and sales of Daguerrotype camera. |

| *19th century* | Many of today's newspapers started in mid-19th century: *News of the World* in 1843, *The Daily Telegraph* in 1855 (when stamp duties were abolished). *The Daily Mail* was the first million-selling mass circulation newspaper. |
|---|---|
| 1876 | Alexander Graham Bell initiated the telephone. |
| 1877 | Edison patented the phonograph; first replayable recordings. |
| 1891 | Kinematography and 'peep scopes' arrived. |
| 1896 | First permanent cinema: 400-seater Vuitascope Hall, New Orleans. |

| *20th century* | In late 1890s and 1900s, short films like *How Bridget Served the Salad Undressed* and in 1903 *The Great Train Robbery*. |
|---|---|
| 1910 | Nickelodeon – some 10,000 family-orientated exhibition halls existed in the United States. |
| 1915 | *Birth of a Nation*: first 'major' film. |
| 1921 | First US radio station: KDKA Pittsburgh. |
| 1922 | Radio arrived in Britain with the British Broadcasting Company. |
| 1926 | 50 million people per week went to the movies in the United States. |
| 1936 | Television arrived in Britain at Alexandra Palace, for a small audience; but with the onset of the Second World War was not fully developed until the 1950s. ITV came in 1955; BBC2 in 1962; Channel 4 in 1982; Channel 5 in 1997. |
| 1950 | UNIVAC (Universal Automatic Computer): first mass-produced computer. |
| 1952 | First video recorder demonstration in United States. |
| 1960s | Emergence of internet through US Department of Defense; development of global satellite communications. |
| 1967 | First local BBC; first colour TV in UK. |
| 1971 | First successful video game reached United States arcades. |
| Early 1970s | Early development of optical fibre systems of communication. |
| 1981 | MTV first televised (started in United States on 1 August 1981). Developed like a radio station, always on the air, appealing to same market niche; VCR became widespread. |
| 1985 | First 'multiplex' cinema in the UK (The Point in Milton Keynes). |
| 1992 | Internet took off. |
| 1995 | 'Privatised Cyberspace': internet became commercial when United States government pulled out; first commercial DVDs appeared. |
| 1999 | Rapid increase in usage of DVDs. |
| 1990s | Rapid expansion of cell/mobile phones and their development as all-purpose means of communication. |

| *21st century* | The routinisation of hi-technologies globally. Mobile phones, digitalisation, laptops, MP3, iPods, iPads, etc. ubiquitous. |
|---|---|

Language and speech only started to appear with more sophisticated societies, about 100,000 years ago. These were oral cultures, and culture here depended a great deal upon the ability to remember and to tell stories that were passed on from generation to generation. Without such stories, cultures and knowledge would have died out. Certainly, these were 'slow societies' where not a great deal could be retained. For continuity, memory must have been vital. And stories played a crucial role.

## Writing cultures

Significant changes started to happen when the spoken word was written down. This depended upon first, a written language system – an alphabet or code of some kind – and second, a means for writing and an object to write upon. Oral cultures depend upon memory. Poetry and stories became very important in trying to pass on from generation to generation a sense of continuing culture. But writing makes it much easier to pass on this history.

And such a form will depend upon an alphabet or other system of writing. In China, some time around 3,000 years ago, a writing system developed with some 50,000 characters! And with this emerged an elite who could master it: the mandarins. Phonetic alphabets, based on sounds, are more recent and mark a major advance in ease of use.

In some ancient civilisations, writing was carved on stone, which was not at all easily transportable. Stone drawings are hard to change or revise – this medium therefore makes for relatively unchanging and stable societies. In Egypt, the dominance of stone as a medium gave a monopoly to those who owned it. But once papyrus was introduced, it played a major role in communication becoming more flexible.

The next major change came when the churches started to develop significant manuscript writings. The medieval church had a monopoly over religious and all other information, which was controlled in manuscripts by a special class of priests. Again, these were far from available to most people.

## Print cultures

And so we reach a time, just a few hundred years ago, when the method of print was invented. This was truly a revolution. Now the control of the elite church's scribes could be bypassed, because for the first time in history there arose the possibility that large numbers of people could become literate (able to read and write). This brought with it:

- an ability to store and transmit culture much more readily
- the potential to include those people previously excluded from knowledge
- a potentially different way of thinking in which the person 'engages' with a text rather than another person
- the potential for mass culture, mass society and mass education
- the development of new minds in which literate modes of thought become part of our everyday consciousness
- a new sense of 'authorship' and control over the text.

Despite the slow spreading of print, it was really only in the nineteenth century – with the birth of mass newspapers – that whole societies started to become literate (see Table 22.2). And at the same time, a mass education system was required to equip people for the new social order (see Chapter 20). Again, it was also a means of excluding people. There were constant fears of how this new literacy was 'dangerous'.

## Electronic cultures

With the new electronic media, our experiences are no longer limited by where or who we are. Media, and especially television, weaken the strong sense we used to have of being in a place. Limited confines such as the family home, the office or the prison are now invaded by the television, which starts to shift the boundaries of how we experience the world.

In an important study, *No Sense of Place*, Joshua Meyrowitz (1986) looks at how the pattern of information flow changes with television. With television we 'eavesdrop' on a host of different worlds. We can gain access to worlds that in the past were not accessible. Thus, for example, children's worlds and adults' worlds, men's worlds and women's worlds could in the past be kept separate. There were things that adults could talk about when children had gone to bed; things that men could talk about when women were not there. But television cuts out these separate spaces. We now inhabit 'no sense of place'. Our sense of place has changed.

Television weakens the traditional distinction between physical place and social situations. Public spheres now enter the living room; public and private get blurred. Television has changed our way of

| Table 22.2 | Readership of national daily newspapers in Great Britain, 1971–2009 (%)[1] | | | | | |
|---|---|---|---|---|---|---|
| | 1971 | 1978 | 1981 | 1991 | 2001 | 2009 |
| Sun | 17 | 29 | 26 | 22 | 20 | 16 |
| Daily Mail | 12 | 13 | 12 | 10 | 12 | 10 |
| Daily Mirror | 34 | 28 | 25 | 22 | 12 | 7 |
| Daily Telegraph | 9 | 8 | 8 | 6 | 5 | 4 |
| The Times | 3 | 2 | 2 | 2 | 3 | 4 |
| Daily Express | 24 | 16 | 14 | 8 | 4 | 3 |
| Daily Star | . | . | 9 | 6 | 3 | 3 |
| Guardian | 3 | 2 | 3 | 3 | 2 | 2 |
| Independent | . | . | . | 2 | 1 | 1 |
| Financial Times | 2 | 2 | 2 | 2 | 1 | 1 |
| Any national daily newspaper[2] | . | 72 | 72 | 62 | 53 | 42 |

[1] In the 12 months to June each year. Proportion of adults aged 15 and over who have read or looked at the individual newspaper for at least two minutes on the day before interview.

[2] Includes the above newspapers and *The Daily Record* in 1981, and *The Sporting Life* and the *Racing Post* in 2001 and 2009.

*Source*: *National Readership Survey* in *Social Trends*, 40 (2010), Table 13.6, p. 189.

RESEARCH IN ACTION

## Studying micro-media in the world of Goths

The methods of contemporary sociology are less and less dependent upon standard interviews and questionnaires. Access to new media forms has changed all that. Recent work on youth styles, for example, has looked at the significance of such new media in the creation of youth and club cultures. While there may be dominant media forms, club cultures and the like develop their own niche media – in the form of music and style magazines – and micro-media. Thornton defines the latter as: 'Flyers, fanzines, flyposters, listings, telephone information lines, pirate radio, e-mailing lists and internet archive sites . . . an array of media from the most rudimentary of print forms to the latest in digital interactive technologies are the low circulating narrowly targeted micro-media' (Thornton, 1995: 137).

In his research on Goths, Paul Hodkinson (2002) employs a

People often think that the sociological method is about interviewing. But there are many other tools of research – and many new ones in the making. Here are some 'fanzines' that were used in Paul Hodkinson's study of Goths. They tell a great deal about the lifestyles and cultures of Goths

*Source*: © S. L. Hodkinson.

range of research methods, from interviewing and observation to questionnaires and media analysis. He looks, for instance, at various Goth fanzines, analysing their content but also interviewing the producers and readers about them. Fanzines are local, they are not circulated widely, they have no mass distribution. Instead, they are picked up at concerts and have widely dispersed markets. What they do is help construct the values of the Goth scene, creating shared identities.

Fanzines can be very influential. As one interviewee puts it:

> J (female): It has a big role because it's a central point for all the reviews, gig dates, current interviews, where people discover who they like and who they don't. You have to be careful what you put in because to a certain extent you can influence the gothic community as a whole . . . You're in a position where you have a bit of power I guess.
>
> (Hodkinson, 2002: 168)

In addition, Paul Hodkinson looked at Goth websites. Here there were 'pages and pages of relevant sites' (2002: 176). Many Goths had their own home pages and most pages brought with them a cluster of further links. A key aspect of all this was the availability of Goth discussion groups. Groups such as the early *alt.gothic* and *uk.people.gothic* not only attracted local Goths but enhanced worldwide participation.

Consider the use of these new media in your own researches.

---

experiencing the world because it has changed what we know about everything. Television parades before us an array of differences: men can learn about women, children about adult worlds, heterosexuals about gays, whites about blacks, the poor about the rich, the mass about the elite (Meyrowitz, 1986). In earlier times, they could have been kept in separate spheres.

But electronic cultures are now extending way beyond this. Not only do we spend more and more time talking about and living around various media (television, video, DVD), we are shifting our ways of relating, making the PC, the laptop, the mobile phone, text messaging and the full range of new

communications from twitter to YouTube more and more central to our lives. We have seen from Chapter 1 onwards (see the box on p. 24) and in almost every chapter of this book that new technologies are shifting the ways in which we live (for example, in Chapter 7, pp. 226–7; in Chapter 23, pp. 814–18). We now have mediated friends and mediated lives – coming to find our lives in and though the vast array of media communications available to us. We talk to friends and pick up new friends through the media. We watch the media and learn about celebrities. You may like to consider the role of new celebrities and what role they play in your life (see *Living in the twenty-first century*).

---

# Living with a celebrity culture: from Princess Diana to Michael Jackson

The celebrity is a person who is well known for their well knowness.

(Daniel Boorstin, *The Image*, 1961: 58)

The deaths of Michael Jackson (in June 2009) and Princess Diana (31 August 1997) led to mass public displays of affection

across the world. Over a million people lined the four-mile route from Kensington Palace to Westminster Abbey for Diana and there was global television coverage. But many seemingly less prominent celebrities also attract much attention. Until 150 years ago, it was unlikely that we could have many 'celebrities' or stars – if any. But now we live in celebrity times. This is the age of the superstar. We search out the X factor or the winner of *Big Brother*, award endless glittering 'prizes' – for music and sport, for books and philanthropy. Celebrities are found everywhere – in magazines, press, the news and current affairs, on television, in

reality TV, and increasingly in the world of webcam culture (the first, long defunct, being the JenniCam (1996)). We can now become a celebrity overnight with the help of YouTube, Twitter or a blog. And often for the most banal reasons.

For some, this celebrity culture suggests the rise of extraordinary people with extraordinary talents whom we can admire: they excel in sport, have wonderful singing voices, write great novels, do great deeds. For others, it is mere sensationalism – another sign of a 'here today, gone tomorrow' society with a low attention span and a passion for simple momentary heroes.

And sociologists have started to research and ask questions about celebrities in contemporary cultures. They see celebrities as mass media constructs and ask how these come about and what effects they have. Celebrities are cultural forms which serve certain key functions. Sociologists examine how such celebrities are constructed; they develop typologies of celebrities; they ask about the functions they perform in a society. They examine fan cultures and the audiences they create. And they see new forms of 'mediated relationships' in which the media and their celebrities come to play significant roles in our personal lives.

One simple distinction to draw is between the celebrity who is *ascribed* their position (by blood: for example, royalty), one who *achieves* it (for example, in a sports competition) and one who derives it from certain attributes – for example, as a TV personality. For their fame to be developed, they will always need the work of a host of media workers – journalists, photographers, 'publicists'.

Celebrities perform a number of key functions in the modern world. They:

- provide role models and new identities (e.g. sports stars become someone to look up to)

- become scapegoats (someone to hate or blame)
- establish dialogues (the celebrity leads to public debate)
- create new emotional bondings and attachments through which we live our lives – they become our new 'intimate friends'
- facilitate 'parasocial interaction': a one-sided interaction where one person knows a lot about another, who knows nothing about them, which appeals to those who experience loneliness and shyness.

See: Graeme Turner, *Understanding Celebrity* (2004).

# The twentieth century: harbinger of new media

In this section, we briefly trace some of the media developments over the past hundred years.

## The century of film

The twentieth century has been called the century of film. Certainly it was born, grew rapidly across the world and became a dominant form of culture and entertainment during this time. Depositing millions of films of all genres in its wake, the twentieth century also produced a massive worldwide industry.

The film industry came into being through a complex interaction of inventions, and the first movie audience was created in 1895. Initially, the focus was on simple observations, but they soon blossomed into much more complex (but black and white and silent) films that attracted huge crowds (films like D. W. Griffiths' *Intolerance* and the Charlie Chaplin comedies). Sound was invented around 1927 (with Al Johnson in *The Singing Fool*). Colour followed, but did not become widespread until the 1950s. It was an international phenomenon – Germany, France, the UK, India, Russia and Latin America all became major film-makers. Nevertheless, from the 1920s onwards,

Hollywood became dominant. Today the dominant film-making countries are the USA, Japan, South Korea, Hong Kong and India.

In the 1970s, the 'blockbuster' appeared, a film which attracted huge crowds on its opening, achieved massive publicity, developed a merchandise empire around it and 'broke all box office records'. Stephen Spielberg's *Jaws* was probably the very first such blockbuster (in 1975), but it was soon followed by George Lucas's *Star Wars* (1977). Nowadays these 'blockbusters' are a major staple of the American film industry and they have a global impact. They also come in multiples: The *Harry Potter* series, the *Pirates of the Caribbean* series. They need to have a broad family appeal, and must especially appeal to children and teenagers – the largest cinema-going populations.

The top grossing films globally of all time (as of June 2010) are shown in the *Top 10* box. Note that not too much store should be put on these statistics. All amounts are in US dollars and only include theatrical box office receipts (movie ticket sales); they do not include video rentals, television rights and other revenues. Totals may include theatrical re-release receipts. Figures are not adjusted for inflation. The tendency is for this list to become simply a list of recent popular children's films, which tells little about the wider and more complex film industry. *Gone With the Wind*, which was the first major box office runaway success when it was shown in 1939, and which for three

## TOP 10
### All-time worldwide box office hits, 2010

| | | Receipts |
|---|---|---|
| 1 | *Avatar* (2009) | $2,734,434,950 |
| 2 | *Titanic* (1997) | $1,835,300,000 |
| 3 | *The Lord of the Rings: The Return of the King* (2003) | $1,129,219,252 |
| 4 | *Pirates of the Caribbean: Dead Man's Chest* (2006) | $1,060,332,628 |
| 5 | *Alice in Wonderland* (2010) | $1,019,689,394 |
| 6 | *The Dark Knight* (2008) | $1,001,921,825 |
| 7 | *Harry Potter and the Philosopher's Stone* (2001) | $968,657,891 |
| 8 | *Pirates of the Caribbean: At World's End* (2007) | $958,404,152 |
| 9 | *Harry Potter and the Order of the Phoenix* (2007) | $937,000,866 |
| 10 | *Harry Potter and the Half-Blood Prince* (2009) | $933,956,98 |

*Source*: IMDb, the Internet Movie Database.

decades was seen as the top grossing film, now comes in at position 122 (with a gross income of $390,500,000. All these films are from the USA, even though this is a (non-US) world listing, which suggests something of the global power of the American hegemony.

## Broadcasting and television

Broadcasting began life as a 'wireless' version of the telephone. In 1924, in the UK, the British Broadcasting Company (with Lord John Reith at its helm) was licensed by the Post Office to function as a monopoly. Reith saw that the BBC should have a role as 'a trustee of the national interest' and defender of middle-class Christian standards. The aims of the BBC were 'to educate, inform and entertain' (Reith, 1924). The historian Asa Briggs has summarised the BBC as displaying four key characteristics: its programming is for public good, not profit; it should provide a 'national' coverage for a community of the 'British';

## WORLD WATCH

## Bollywood and the diaspora

The Indian film industry is the largest in the world and one of the oldest. In 2010, it was worth about US$1,256 million and nearly one thousand films are produced every year. India's film industry is the largest in the world, both in number of movies produced and in tickets sold. This Hindi film industry is based in Mumbai (Bombay). Much of the music industry is also based in Mumbai.

The film industry fragments into many different forms – from the highbrow and much esteemed films of the intelligentsia, such as the 1950s 'Apu Trilogy' of Satyajit Ray (1921–92), through to a very widespread, popular form which deals with key elements of romance, passion and music in lush settings – they are

(right) Posters for Bollywood films, Bombay, India

*Source*: Corbis © Catherine Karnow.

WORLD WATCH

melodramatic and romantic musicals. This has come to be known as Bollywood (though the Indian film industry predates Hollywood and the first silent feature was made in 1913; maybe Hollywood should be renamed Mumbiwood?). They are available worldwide on DVDs, and they have spawned a large culture and spin-off industry: music albums, international film magazines, worldwide websites, Bollywood stars and celebrities. A 'Bollywood' stage musical *Bombay Dreams* (featuring the lives of Mumbai castrati) opened with moderate success in London in 2002, and in New York in 2004.

In their earliest manifestations, Bollywood films were simply romantic stories of traditional Indian life with music; they grew into lavish romantic musicals. In their more recent manifestations they have become influenced by Western images, music and dance. As Indians have migrated around the world, they have established the Indian film as a major worldwide genre with world appeal. The films are popular in Nigeria, Egypt and Zanzibar. Birmingham in England hosts the 'Bollywood Oscars'. It is estimated that at least 11 million Indian people have migrated around the world, and this diaspora has added to the global impact of these films.

Once the films were watched on large screens in open spaces in small villages (see the opening story to this chapter) and in tattered old cinemas. But as India becomes more and more economically successful, so the films are increasingly shown in Indian multiplexes.

The films have also generated their own UK spin-offs: films like *East is East* (1999) and *Bend it like Beckham* (2002) play jokes with some of the Bollywood forms; in their turn, Bollywood made *Bride and Prejudice*.

### COUNTRY FACT FILE

**INDIA**

| | |
|---|---|
| Population | 1,156.9 million |
| Per capita GDP | $3100 |
| Life expectancy | 65.13 male |
| | 67.13 female |
| Adult literacy | 61% |
| Key languages | Hindi 41%, |
| | Bengali 8.1% |
| Key religions | Hindu 80.5%, |
| | Muslim 13.4% |
| Key city | New Delhi |
| Human development index | 0.519 (119th, 2010) |

In all of this we can see postmodern capitalist hybridic media worlds at work.

*Source*: Rajinder Kumar Dudrah, *Bollywood: Sociology goes to the Movies* (2006).

it should be a monopoly; and it should always provide high moral standards (Briggs, 1961). The BBC came to be seen as part of the 'establishment', embodying the values and power of the dominant class.

After the Second World War, new stations like the 'Third', the 'Light' and the 'Home Services' appeared under the aegis of the BBC, suggesting differences in audience and catering to different classes. The late 1950s and the 1960s brought 'pirate broadcasting' (Radio Luxembourg and offshore broadcasting, which challenged the dominance of the BBC) as well as a more critical and satirical approach to broadcasting that challenged the dominance of Reith's earlier goals. In 1967, it was reorganised (as Radios One, Two, Three and Four) and new commercial services were increasingly facilitated.

Early days of the media which now, a hundred years on, have come to pervade everyday life across the world

*Sources*: Pearson Education Ltd/Photodisc; Pearson Education Ltd/C Squared Studios/ Tony Gable; Pearson Eduction Ltd/ Photodisc/C Squared Studios.

## Timeline Landmarks of British TV, 1990–2010

| | |
|---|---|
| 1990 | Opening of British Satellite Broadcasting (BSB). |
| 1990 | Sky and BSB merged to form BSkyB. |
| 1997 | Start of Channel 5. |
| 1998 | Digital satellite service started. |
| 1998 | Digital terrestrial service started, including widescreen broadcasts. |

| | |
|---|---|
| 2001 | BBC's first digital interactive programme. |
| 2002 | Opening of Freeview digital terrestrial service. |
| 2003 | Regulation of commercial TV passes to Ofcom following merger of ITC with other regulatory bodies. |
| 2004 | BBC Chairman of Governors and Director General both resigned in wake of Hutton Report. |
| 2004 | Merger of Granada and Carlton completed. Merged company called ITV plc. |
| 2006 | Start of high definition service. |
| 2007 | First analogue switch-off: BBC2 signal at Whitehaven, Cumbria. |

*Source:* Adapted from British TV History, Landmark Dates: http://www.tvhistory.btinternet.co.uk/html/landmark.html.

Television started in the UK in 1936 with the BBC in London but was relatively underdeveloped when the Second World War intervened. It was given a boost by the televising of the coronation of Queen Elizabeth in 1953. Independent television with advertising also arrived, with initially an eight-year franchise. In the USA cable started in 1950 (with 625 resolutions for screens) and colour began in 1953. In 1962, Telstar was launched as the first television satellite. Video appeared in 1965, and became popular in the late 1970s and early 1980s (by 2007, it had almost become obsolete). In 1976 the first flat-screen LCD television appeared. The *Timeline* box shows its more recent history.

## Creating popular music recordings

Until the late nineteenth century, most music was live: it played out in small community events, 'bourgeois homes' and, by the eighteenth century, a growing number of theatres and concert halls. But as modern forms of communication started to appear during the nineteenth century, so mediated music became increasingly common. Music popular for its time became 'pop music', and became available first in sheet form and later in electrically recorded forms. The initial recordings appeared at the end of the nineteenth century, but only spread out into the wider Western culture through gramophones and 78 r.p.m. records in the 1920s and onwards. In the 1950s the records technology (their production and the means of playing them) shifted first into vinyl long-playing records (less easy to break and containing much more sound), and then into the relatively short-lived tape. The 1980s and 1990s saw new developments with compact discs (CDs), personal stereo systems and television channels such as MTV. A key time in the development of the music industry was in the post-Second World War period (the 1950s). The pop 'charts' were introduced in 1952, but they had more or less died by 2007 when record sales slumped, musical forms were recognised as very fragmented, and 'play lists' and the iPod had developed.

Musical forms can be traced through an array of genres: jazz, operetta, blues, film scores, song and dance routines, music hall, the dance bands era, crooning, cabaret and 'war songs'. Recently, they have proliferated further: to rock and roll, ballads, reggae, punk, heavy metal, rap, indie, house and 'boy bands'. As the world became more diversified, so too did its musical forms. Although certain stars and music forms dominate the contemporary market, it is now open to a wide range of niche markets – even the young of today can become fans of the Beatles or Elvis from 50 years ago, or the crooner Bing Crosby from nearly 80 years ago. It is the age of a paradoxical mass culture where everyone both listens to the same music and a highly differentiated niche market catering to smaller and smaller groupings. This shift in consumption has generally been called 'the long tail' (Anderson, 2007).

## The growth of digital music

As widespread downloading of music from the internet and the growth of iPod/MP3 technology developed, major changes were needed in the music industry. Eight million people are said to have downloaded illegally in 2004, and annual global music sales started to fall. But the digital music business has continued to expand. In 2008 it had an estimated trade value of some US$3.7 billion – and growing. Recorded music is at the forefront of the online and mobile revolution, generating huge revenue through digital platforms (in percentage terms it is bigger than the newspaper, magazine and film industries combined). Music consumption is becoming far more ubiquitous as companies are expanding and diversifying.

 **tip** To read about the latest issues on the music industry, download the Annual Report of IFPI (International Federation of the Phonographic Industry), which represents the recording industry worldwide with some 1,400 members in 66 countries and affiliated industry associations in 45 countries. See: www.ifpi.org.

# New styles of communications in the twenty-first century

While cinema, television and radio were dominant forms of media in the twentieth century, there are distinct signs of major communication shifts taking place at the start of the twenty-first century that could have radical consequences for social life. As we have seen, mobile phones are now ubiquitous, and have made texting, emailing, photographing, games, audio listening, and film watching something which can now be small, portable and very personal – designer-matched for clothes and lifestyles. IPhones and iPads have become a central accessory for parts of the twenty-first-century world. We have also already seen in Chapter 7 some of the ways in which this is changing our relationships (see pp. 226–7). Table 22.3 suggests some of the key ways in which new and old media differ. We have also seen just how extensive is the penetration of the internet globally. By 2010, nearly 29 per cent of world population (2 billion people) were using the internet. Recent growth has been highest in Africa, the Middle East and Latin America; there are over a billion internet users in developing countries (one-third of these are in China).

## Gaming cultures, YouTube and new entertainment

With the development of new media technologies, new forms of entertainment have also emerged. For example, YouTube, a video-sharing website on which users can upload, share and view videos was formed early in 2005 but by 2010 it claimed to have over 2 billion views a day.

Gaming is another part of the new entertainment world – but has a much longer history. The widespread growth of gaming and gaming cultures have become a key pastime in many countries round the world, initially amongst the young but now across a wider range of ages.

In the UK, 75 per cent of those aged 8 to 11 and 68 per cent of those aged 12 to 15 use the internet to play games (*Social Trends*, 2007: 173). In the 12 months to the end of September 2009, £1.73 billion was spent on video games, according to the data company GFK Chart-Track. The number of games consoles being used in Britain has shot up from 13.5 million in 2008 to well over 25 million in 2010, with enough consoles for nine out of every ten households in the country to have one. Globally, it is reckoned to be a $25 billion industry.

Gaming can be traced through several generations back to the 1940s and 1950s. Periods are often divided into the kinds of platform used: arcade, mainframe, console, personal computer and handheld game. By the 1970s, gaming was to be found in arcades and public places. Soon hand-held games and consoles started to take over; and more recently it has been developed through both the internet and easy downloading on to mobile phones and iPads. The first commercially viable video game was Computer Space in 1971, which laid the foundation for a new entertainment industry in the late 1970s. Arcade games, although still relatively popular in the early 1990s, begin a decline as home consoles became more common. PaRappa the Rapper popularised rhythm or music video games in Japan with its 1996 debut on the PlayStation. Subsequent music and dance games like beatmania and Dance Dance Revolution became ubiquitous attractions in Japanese arcades. Mortal Kombat, released on both SNES and Genesis consoles, was one of the most popular game franchises of its time. In 2009, *Call of*

| Table 22.3 | The movement from old media to new media |
| --- | --- |

| The old media technologies | The new media technologies |
| --- | --- |
| Analog | Digital |
| Corporation based | More and more 'networked' |
| Separate media (e.g. print, computing, photos) | All media converge (e.g. through the iPhone) |
| Separate professions | Increased DIY and blogging |
| Live and lived culture | 'Virtual' culture |

*Source*: Based on Flew (2007).

*Duty: Modern Warfare 2*, was considered the fastest-selling game in history (selling more than 1.2 million units in just 24 hours); it was attacked for encouraging violent behaviour. In 2010, the top console/hand-held games were Wii Play (Wii – 27.38 million), New Super Mario Bros (DS – 24.13 million), Mario Kart Wii (Wii – 24.01 million), Nintendogs (DS – 23.26 million) and Wii Fit (Wii – 22.61 million).

Gaming cultures are part of a new integrated world of entertainment where the differing media converge with each other – video links with YouTube, films with video, music with phones, network groups with photos, books with iPads and Kindles. It becomes difficult to maintain the borders of media that were possible in the twentieth century. Table 22.4 shows the top-selling media in 2009 (note how significant the games culture is).

| Table 22.4 | The Entertainment Chart 2009 | | | | | |
|---|---|---|---|---|---|---|
| Overall position | Sector | Position in sector chart | Title | Artist | Company | 2009 sales total |
| 1 | Game | 1 | Call of Duty: Modern Warfare 2 | | Activision Blizzard | 2,926,637 |
| 2 | Video | 1 | Harry Potter & The Half Blood Prince | | Warner Home Video | 2,193,700 |
| 3 | Game | 2 | FIFA 10 | | Electronic Arts | 2,155,697 |
| 4 | Video | 2 | Quantum of Solace | | 20th Century Fox | 2,040,229 |
| 5 | Video | 3 | Twilight | | E1 Entertainment | 1,815,543 |
| 6 | Album | 1 | I Dreamed a Dream | Susan Boyle | Sony Music | 1,714,369 |
| 7 | Game | 3 | Wii Sports Resort | | Nintendo | 1,488,797 |
| 8 | Album | 2 | The Fame | Lady Gaga | Universal Music | 1,458,289 |
| 9 | Video | 4 | Slumdog Millionaire | | 20th Century Fox | 1,383,838 |
| 10 | Video | 5 | Transformers – Revenge of the Fallen | | Paramount | 1,362,020 |
| 11 | Video | 6 | Micheal McIntyre – Hello Wembley | | Universal Pictures | 1,286,863 |
| 12 | Album | 3 | Crazy Love | Michael Buble | Warner Music | 1,257,292 |
| 13 | Game | 4 | Wii Fit | | Nintendo | 1,246,461 |
| 14 | Video | 7 | Madagascar – Escape 2 Africa | | Paramount | 1,223,805 |
| 15 | Video | 8 | Angels & Demons | | Sony Pictures | 1,153,425 |
| 16 | Album | 4 | The End | Black Eyed Peas | Universal Music | 1,144,722 |
| 17 | Album | 5 | Only By The Night | Kings of Leon | Sony Music | 1,132,483 |
| 18 | Video | 9 | High School Musical 3 – Senior Year | | Walt Disney | 1,084,911 |
| 19 | Video | 10 | Ice Age 3 – Dawn of The Dinosaurs | | 20th Century Fox | 1,074,651 |
| 20 | Album | 6 | Now That's What I Call Music 74 | Various Artists | EMI/Universal | 1,053,574 |

*Source: Era Yearbook 2010 (and online at www.eraltd.org/-attachments/Resources/Yearbook.pdf).*

# Theories of the media

In this section we review a number of the key accounts that have been developed to understand media. We start with the classic hypodermic model, which is rarely taken seriously these days, and end with more recent global theories.

## 1 The classical 'hypodermic' model

The earliest theory of the mass media at the turn of the century – often called the magic bullet theory or the 'hypodermic' model of the media – is the simplest propaganda theory of the media. It assumes that people are passive and that the media message has a direct impact upon them. It suggests the following:

- Media messages are presented to members of a mass society, who receive them more or less uniformly.
- These messages are stimuli which influence the individual strongly.
- The stimuli lead individuals to respond in a similar, uniform fashion.
- The effects of mass communication *are powerful, uniform and direct* (our italics, adapted from Lowery and De Fleur, 1988: 23–4).

Although this theory is still popularly used in everyday discussions (especially among those who see the media as dangerous), such an account has long been discredited. Indeed, each point raised above can be taken as a critical issue of exactly what does not happen with the media! We will now look at some of the theories that have been developed to replace this 'hypodermic syringe' model.

## 2 Functionalist theories of the media

Functionalist theories of the media look at the ways in which the media serve to integrate society in different ways, and examine the role of media effects in doing this. As part of the social system, media can provide information, education, entertainment and diversion. Five functions have been particularly noted:

1  *The surveillance function.* The media provide a continuous flow of data about the world we live in. They can warn us of dangers (from hurricanes to wars to dangerous criminals) and be instrumental in providing information on traffic jams and the stock market, for example, as well as all kinds of information linked to personal welfare. (They can also be dysfunctional – stirring up undue anxiety, for example.)

2  *The status conferral function.* Here, the media give status to people, public issues, organisations and social movements. Enhanced status comes to all who feature in the media – they become more known about, for good or bad. Not only do major events such as political elections or famous criminal trials come to attention, but many minor issues can be accorded status. Thus, a child with a life-threatening illness, an old person on her 100th birthday or environmental activists protesting about a local pollution problem can all be accorded 'status'.

3  *The 'enforced application of social norms' function.* This highlights the public announcement of social norms, and publicity serves to close the gap between 'private attitudes and public morality'. The leading media analyst Dennis McQuail sees the media as fostering public communication values, which stress freedom, equality and order. The media can promote values by dramatising deviance of all kinds. By bringing to our attention 'youth crime', 'rape', 'child sex offenders', 'drugs' or 'serial killers', the community's awareness is heightened and moral boundaries are drawn (see Chapter 17). Later in this chapter we describe how this often works as a 'moral panic'.

4  *The transmission of culture function.* The media have become prime modern agents of socialisation (see Chapter 7). From young children's programmes such as *Teletubbies* to teenage chat shows, the media serve a key role in passing on elements of a society's culture and heritage.

5  *The narcotising function.* This is more of a dysfunction than a function and refers to the way in which a flood of information can lead to superficiality (Lazarsfeld and Merton, 1996: 16–18; see also Wright, 1967; McQuail, 1994).

### Critical comment

Functionalist theories were popular during the mid-twentieth century but have been much in decline since. The above listing suggests why. In many ways, all functionalist theories do is provide a descriptive listing of how an institution works in the current society. The functions listed here may be important, but it is not always clear that they add much depth of understanding.

## 3 Symbolic interactionism

Herbert Blumer, the founder of symbolic-interactionist analysis, was one of the first sociologists to conduct audience research on cinema-going. As part of a widespread concern about the impact of films on young people, a series of investigations were set up in the late 1920s and early 1930s (popularly known as the Payne Studies, they were initiated by a pro-film censorship group, the Motion Picture Research Council). Blumer was involved with one of these that looked at young people. Straightforwardly, he asked some 1,500 young people to write 'motion-picture autobiographies', backed up with more selective interviews, group discussions and observations. He argued that to know what impact media had on young people's lives, it is best simply to ask them. Following on from this, much of his ensuing book *Movies and Conduct* is given over to young people's first-hand accounts of the films they have seen – how they provide the basis of imitation, play, daydreams, emotional development and 'schemes of life'. He let the people speak for themselves. One entry, dealing with stereotypes, reads:

> **Female, 19, white college senior: – One thing these pictures did was to establish a permanent fear of Chinamen in my mind. To this day I do not see a Chinese person but what I think of him as being mixed up in some evil affair. I always pass them as quickly as possible if I meet them in the street, and refuse to go into a Chinese restaurant or laundry.**

(Blumer, 1933: 145)

Quite rightly, others have recently been more critical of his straightforward naiveté of approach. Denzin, for example, has recently been very critical of Blumer, suggesting that the study, while progressive in method, was shrouded with Blumer's assumptions ('pro-middle class and anti-film', Denzin, 1992: 107). It was also open to being used to crusade against film content and viewed texts unproblematically (Clough, 1992). True, Blumer's initial studies in the 1930s now look somewhat simple, but he was the first to take seriously audience responses.

Norman Denzin has focused on the importance of 'the movies' for understanding social life in the twentieth century. He considers the film and going to the cinema to have been the key mode of narrative in that century. Talking of the 'cinematic society', he suggests that watching films shifted much of that century's experience by encouraging a more visual, looking society – a society which he sees as increasingly voyeuristic. Denzin's method is to look at films, ranging from *Blue Velvet* to *Rear Window*, to see how they display the cultural logic of society (Denzin, 1992, 1995).

## The theory of moral panics

Drawing heavily on the symbolic-interactionist tradition, Stanley Cohen investigated an emerging youth phenomenon in the UK in the 1960s: that of the Mods and Rockers (see Chapter 5). These young people appeared on the beaches and around the town centres of several south coast holiday resorts in England (including Clacton) over the Easter holiday of 1964. Although Cohen discovered that the amount of serious violence and vandalism was relatively little, he found that the media 'blew it up out of all proportions'. The media – and other 'moral crusaders' – saw the Mods and Rockers as terrorising the town and being 'hell bent on destruction'. Cohen saw this as a 'moral panic' and defined it in the following way:

> **Societies appear to be subject, every now and then, to periods of moral panic. A condition, episode, person or group of persons emerges to become defined as a threat to societal values and interests; its nature is presented in a stylised and stereotypical fashion by the mass media; the moral barricades are manned by editors, bishops, politicians and other right thinking people; socially accredited experts pronounce their diagnoses and solutions; ways of coping are evolved . . .**

(Cohen, 2003: 28; orig. 1972)

Like Durkheim (in Chapter 4), Cohen argued that when societies entered times of anxiety and crisis, 'folk devils' were created through moral panics to reassert dominant values. For moral panics to exist, these responses have to be out of all proportion to the actual threat or danger. The media played a central role in stirring up concern, often amplifying the problem. From a small initial issue, major hysteria could be created which often served the interest of specific groups worried about specific social issues, such as teenage crime getting out of control.

Since Cohen's influential study, a great many 'folk devils and moral panics' have been identified. The media have mounted major concerns over drugs, mugging, baby battering, granny battering, child abuse of all forms, dole scroungers and welfare cheats, AIDS, video nasties, rapists and serial killers, paedophiles, Satanism and ritual abuse, religious cults, militant trade unionism, 'blacks' and pornography. In some cases the problems behind such issues have been found to be quite major, but in other cases the hysteria is out of all proportion to the actual problem. Phillip Jenkins has shown, for example, that although there is often massive concern over serial killers, they are in fact very rare indeed, and serial killings have remained at roughly the same low rate for the last 100 years (P. Jenkins, 1992).

To understand the workings of a moral panic, it is important to look at the way in which the media – newspapers and TV in particular – come to identify a 'problem' and present it in a particular way, and how this may 'fit' into a particular set of social anxieties or worries. Many moral panics, for example, depict dangerous threats to the traditional moral values of family life. When AIDS first appeared in the early 1980s, the media often handled it in a sensational way, depicting it as a dangerous threat to traditional sexuality (Cohen, 2003, orig. 1972; P. Jenkins, 1992).

# 4 Conflict theories of the media

Much European work on the mass media has adopted a conflict (and often Marxist) approach to the media. Within this paradigm, the media are seen to be owned by dominant classes who use them as a mechanism to serve their own interests. The media thus come to play a major role in the transmission of ideologies. Broadly, conflict theories highlight two important matters. The first concerns the economic base of the media, particularly the ways in which they follow a profit motive and the ways in which big business conglomerates come to shape them. The second concerns the ideological structuring of the media, particularly the ways in which certain conflicting interests – often of class, ethnicity and gender – are 'screened out' of the messages.

## The political economy of the media

This stresses how the major means of communication in society come to be owned by private economic interests. Increasingly, it can be shown that these interests form giant interlocking directorates and are in the hands of powerful tycoons, such as Rupert Murdoch and Silvio Berlusconi. (Berlusconi – who owns Finevest, with a virtual monopoly of Italian commercial television – was elected twice as prime minister after much campaigning on his own television!) It has been true for some time that a country's media have been in the hands of a few powerful economic groups. Table 22.5 shows the approximate concentration of media ownership in the UK in the mid-1990s. But even in the early 1970s, the top five media firms in the UK accounted for 71 per cent of daily newspaper circulation, 78 per cent of admissions to cinemas, 76 per cent of record sales and 74 per cent of homes with commercial television. But what has been happening since that time has been an increasing concentration of ownership globally. Thus Murdoch's transnational company has holdings in the United States, Latin America, Europe (especially the UK and Germany), Australia and Asia. This is discussed further below. Table 22.6 shows circulation figures for the UK press in 2010.

These powerful economic interests work consistently to exclude 'those voices lacking economic power or resources'. All kinds of minority – from ethnic groups to disabled groups, from 'women' to 'gays' – may not be represented in media coverage. But more, much of the media will find that 'the voices which survive will largely belong to those least likely to criticise the prevailing distribution of power and wealth' (Murdock and Golding, 1977: 39).

| Table 22.5 | Ownership of press media in the UK | |
|---|---|---|
| **Approximate share of market** | | |
| News International | 35% | Sun, Times, Sunday Times, News of the World |
| Mirror Group | 23–27% | Mirror, Sunday Mirror, People |
| United Newspapers | 14% (9% for Sundays) | Daily Express, Daily Star, Sunday Express |
| Associated Newspapers | 15% | Daily Mail, Mail on Sunday |
| Hollinger | 7% | Daily Telegraph, Sunday Telegraph |

Note: These figures are approximate and meant only to indicate a broad level of concentration of the media in a few large firms.

| Table 22.6 | National daily newspaper circulation, July 2010 | | | | | | |
|---|---|---|---|---|---|---|---|
| | July 2010 | July 2009 | % change | June 2010 | July 2010 (without bulks) | February– July 2010 | % change on last year |
| Sun | 3,042,406 | 3,121,407 | −2.53 | 2,979,999 | 3,042,406 | 2,983,257 | −1.41 |
| Daily Mirror | 1,242,446 | 1,340,028 | −7.28 | 1,248,919 | 1,242,446 | 1,242,304 | −6.69 |
| Daily Star | 843,229 | 887,106 | −4.95 | 809,992 | 843,229 | 821,448 | −2.14 |
| Daily Record | 324,229 | 343,165 | −5.52 | 323,235 | 322,266 | 328,064 | −6.42 |
| Daily Mail | 2,117,839 | 2,178,640 | −2.79 | 2,092,643 | 2,004,131 | 2,097,778 | −3.75 |
| Daily Express | 663,871 | 734,045 | −9.56 | 664,293 | 663,871 | 666,469 | −8.14 |
| Daily Telegraph | 678,391 | 818,937 | −17.16 | 681,322 | 678,391 | 685,370 | −14.23 |
| The Times | 502,588 | 580,483 | −13.42 | 503,642 | 502,588 | 505,752 | −14.75 |
| Financial Times | 378,497 | 397,600 | −4.80 | 391,865 | 341,457 | 391,702 | −5.60 |
| Guardian | 277,246 | 328,773 | −15.67 | 286,220 | 277,246 | 286,496 | −15.03 |
| Independent | 183,975 | 189,013 | −2.67 | 187,135 | 121,542 | 186,760 | −7.15 |

*Source*: ABCs: National daily newspaper circulation July 2010, Guardian.co.uk, 13 August 2010. Copyright Guardian News & Media Ltd 2010.

## The big media corporations

Although they are constantly merging and buying each other up, the leading media firms in the world are usually said to include TimeWarner (with sales approaching £25.8 billion in 2009), Disney (with £36.1 billion) (see Figure 22.1), Bertelsmann (£19 billion in 2006; the only Europe-based firm), Viacom (£12 billion) and News Corporation (£30.4 billion). Typically, these firms have media holdings in a wide range of enterprises.

For example, News Corporation, owned by Rupert Murdoch, has holdings in Twentieth Century Fox (film, television and video and Fox News), 132 newspapers (in Australia, the UK and the USA), 25 magazines, book publishing, Asian Star Television and BSkyB satellite television. It also has large stakes in Germany's Vox channel, Sky Latin America, Japan Sky Broadcasting, Australian Foxtel Cable, Spanish El Canal Fox, India Sky Broadcasting, Channel V (an Asian music video channel) and Hong Kong Phoenix satellite. As of 30 June 2006, News Corporation owned a particularly large number of subsidiary enterprises in the USA, but equally had a strong presence in Europe, Latin America, Asia and Australia. In the UK, it owns newspapers such as *The Times*, the *Sun*, and the *News of the World*, and it has a large investment in British Sky Broadcasting. Well-known Hollywood film companies it owns include Twentieth Century Fox Film, Searchlight Pictures and numerous others.

Another example is TimeWarner. With an international labour force of around 340,000, it has holdings in 24 magazines (including *Time*), the second largest book publishing business in the world, Warner Bros films, Warner music group, cinemas, comics, Home Box Office (the largest cable channel in the world), Six Flags theme parks, Warner Bros retail stores, several global cable channels including CNN, TBS and TNY, Turner Classic movies, the Cartoon Network and CNN-SI all sports news channel, and on, and on (Herman and McChesney, 1997: Chapter 3). In January 2001, it merged with America Online (AOL), making it the world's biggest media company.

Bertelsmann is one of the largest European media corporations. In 2006, it reported revenues of more than €19 million. It currently owns publishing houses, such as Random House, the RTL television group and many other media companies in different sectors. It is also involved in Sony BMG Music Entertainment, in a joint operation with Sony, which controls well-known labels such as RCA Records and Columbia Records.

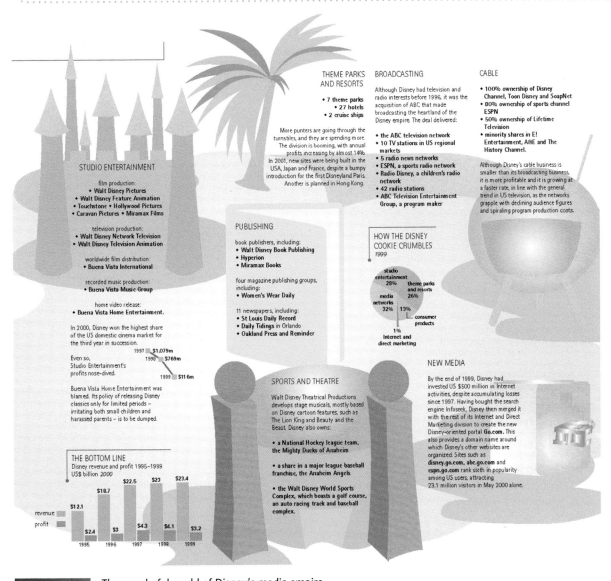

STUDIO ENTERTAINMENT

film production:
• Walt Disney Pictures
• Walt Disney Feature Animation
• Touchstone • Hollywood Pictures
• Caravan Pictures • Miramax Films

television production:
• Walt Disney Network Television
• Walt Disney Television Animation

worldwide film distribution:
• Buena Vista International

recorded music production:
• Buena Vista Music Group

home video release:
• Buena Vista Home Entertainment.

In 2000, Disney won the highest share of the US domestic cinema market for the third year in succession.

| | |
|---|---|
| 1997 | $1,079m |
| 1998 | $769m |

Even so, Studio Entertainment's profits nose-dived.

| | |
|---|---|
| 1999 | $11.6m |

Buena Vista Home Entertainment was blamed. Its policy of releasing Disney classics only for limited periods – irritating both small children and harassed parents – is to be dumped.

THE BOTTOM LINE
Disney revenue and profit 1995–1999
US$ billion 2000

| | | | | |
|---|---|---|---|---|
| $12.1 | $18.7 | $22.5 | $23 | $23.4 |
| revenue | | | | |
| profit | | | | |
| $2.4 | $3 | $4.3 | $4.1 | $3.2 |
| 1995 | 1996 | 1997 | 1998 | 1999 |

THEME PARKS AND RESORTS
• 7 theme parks
• 27 hotels
• 2 cruise ships

More punters are going through the turnstiles, and they are spending more. The division is booming, with annual profits increasing by almost 14%. In 2001, new sites were being built in the USA, Japan and France, despite a bumpy introduction for the first Disneyland Paris. Another is planned in Hong Kong.

PUBLISHING

book publishers, including:
• Walt Disney Book Publishing
• Hyperion
• Miramax Books

four magazine publishing groups, including:
• Women's Wear Daily

11 newspapers, including:
• St Louis Daily Record
• Daily Tidings in Orlando
• Oakland Press and Reminder

SPORTS AND THEATRE

Walt Disney Theatrical Productions develops stage musicals, mostly based on Disney cartoon features, such as The Lion King and Beauty and the Beast. Disney also owns:

• a National Hockey league team, the Mighty Ducks of Anaheim

• a share in a major league baseball franchise, the Anaheim Angels

• the Walt Disney World Sports Complex, which boasts a golf course, an auto racing track and baseball complex.

BROADCASTING

Although Disney had television and radio interests before 1996, it was the acquisition of ABC that made broadcasting the heartland of the Disney empire. The deal delivered:

• the ABC television network
• 10 TV stations in US regional markets
• 5 radio news networks
• ESPN, a sports radio network
• Radio Disney, a children's radio network
• 42 radio stations
• ABC Television Entertainment Group, a program maker

HOW THE DISNEY COOKIE CRUMBLES
1999

studio entertainment 28%
theme parks and resorts 26%
media networks 32%
consumer products 13%
Internet and direct marketing 1%

CABLE

• 100% ownership of Disney Channel, Toon Disney and SoapNet
• 80% ownership of sports channel ESPN
• 50% ownership of Lifetime Television
• minority shares in E! Entertainment, A&E and The History Channel.

Although Disney's cable business is smaller than its broadcasting business, it is more profitable and it is growing at a faster rate, in line with the general trend in US television, as the networks grapple with declining audience figures and spiraling program production costs.

NEW MEDIA

By the end of 1999, Disney had invested US $500 million in Internet activities, despite accumulating losses since 1997. Having bought the search engine Infoseek, Disney then merged it with the rest of its Internet and Direct Marketing division to create the new Disney-oriented portal Go.com. This also provides a domain name around which Disney's other websites are organized. Sites such as disney.go.com, abc.go.com and espn.go.com rank sixth in popularity among US users, attracting 23.1 million visitors in May 2000 alone.

**Figure 22.1** The wonderful world of Disney's media empire

*Source: Reproduced with permission from The Global Media Atlas, p. 64. Copyright © Myriad Editions, www.MyriadEditions.com.*

## The culture industry and ideology

German critical theorists Adorno and Horkheimer saw the development of a 'culture industry' which 'transfers the profit motive naked on to cultural forms'. The multibillion-dollar Hollywood empire sells its wares – from *Star Wars* to *Pirates of the Caribbean* – for huge profits. True 'culture' dissolves in the face of this commercial marketplace. And even 'great culture' will be dug up and recycled for new profits. For instance, the work of the eighteenth-century novelist Jane Austen has been repackaged into films, television

mini-dramas and reworked books. Often this leads to her work becoming 'just like everything else': flattened for profit. Likewise, almost every novel by Charles Dickens has been turned into a musical (*Oliver!* being just the most famous). And every aspect of the media is saturated with this. There are extremes, as in the hype of 'world concerts' by leading rock stars such as Eminem and Madonna. Everywhere, media products 'are commodities through and through' and 'human beings are once more debased'. 'The colour film demolishes the genial old tavern to a greater extent than bombs ever could: the film exterminates its image.' It is 'mass deception', 'anti-enlightenment', and leads to subservience to blind authority (Adorno, 1991: 85–92).

## Ideological state apparatuses

The French Marxist philosopher Louis Althusser (1918–90) saw a number of institutions (the media, but also education, religion, the family) as being independent of the state but functioning to reproduce the dominant ideologies through what he called the **ideological state apparatuses** (or ISAs, as some have called them more popularly). These are *social institutions which reproduce the dominant ideology, independent of the state*. (In contrast, repressive apparatuses such as police and army employ more direct power.) Ideologies construct imaginary relations for people to live in, which help obscure the actual things that are going on (Althusser, 1971).

## Critical comment

Conflict theories are persuasive in alerting us to media capital and bias. There is a growing world concentration of the mass media in the hands of a few major corporations, and the research evidence suggests pervasive biases (especially over what is not allowed to be said in the media). But conflict theories may suffer from exaggeration. People are sometimes seen as being too much like passive victims and capital is seen as moving too coherently in favour of one outcome. In fact, media practices are complex and varied.

# 5  Postmodern media theory

Over the past decade, a group of newer social theorists have come to highlight the centrality of the media in our lives. In particular, they have suggested that we now live increasingly through the products of the mass media, which have come to have an autonomous existence of their own. We are media consumers. And the media messages, from Madonna's video to the soap opera *EastEnders'* murders, become a new form of reality. We are awhirl and awash in signs.

Baudrillard (1929–2007) sees modern societies as concerned with the consumption of signs. While in his earlier work he explored media 'codes', in his later work 'simulation' becomes the core of social life. Broadly, whatever is really happening in the world no longer matters because people are coming to live so

much in a media-mediated world that reality is bypassed. All we are left with are exploding (imploding) signs and **simulacra**, *worlds of media-generated signs and images*. Just what these signs refer to in the world is no longer clearly distinguished.

One of Baudrillard's most famous (and disturbing) remarks concerned the Gulf War (16 January– 28 February 1991). He argued that it was a hyper-real representation on our television screens: the real battlefields were now replaced by media saturation. We can watch the bombings, hear the planning, see the war and all its atrocities from the comfort of our living room. The war is a simulation: we are not there, nor will we ever be there. All we will know is the hyper-reality that media messages convey to us (Baudrillard, 1991).

Once the media tried to provide copies of reality, but now they are their own reality. This is the postmodern world we live in. The masses for Baudrillard are mass media consumers. Everything is now reproduced – be it on video, TV, CDs or film. It comes to us already as a pre-experienced hyper-reality.

## Critical evaluation

This is a fashionable view that certainly places a great deal of importance on media images. But in that lies the critique. For Baudrillard is accused of excess. For him, it is often as if the Gulf War did not really happen, or indeed that any reality outside the media does not really happen. This is a serious problem, not least since large numbers of the world's population are not caught up in the media – millions still have no access to the media. And of those that do, many can clearly distinguish between signs and realities.

News is a central media product in modern societies. Not only was the news press the first major means of mass communication in the nineteenth century, but today most TV channels adopt specific mechanisms for the delivery of news. Many radio stations in the UK punctuate their programmes with hourly or half-hourly news bulletins. And since the 1980s there have been continuous 'wall-to-wall' news channels such as CNN, which circulate around the world. Functionalist analysis may suggest that news serves an important information function. Conflict theories, by contrast, see the media as ideological, mystifying what is really going on. Action theories focus on the ways in which people come to make sense of the media and the ways in which audiences read their messages.

# Three key questions in media analysis

The pioneering media analyst Harold Laswell once said that the goal of media research is to answer the question: *who* says *what*, in *which channel*, to *whom* with *what effect* (Laswell, 1948)? Following this, and putting it simply, we can say that media analysis directs our attention to three broad areas: media texts, media construction and media consumption, which are locatable within codes, encoding and decoding (see Figure 22.2). **Codes** are *rule-governed systems of signs*, **encoding** involves *putting a message of any kind into a language*, and **decoding** is *the process by which we hear or read and understand a message*.

The first area thus highlights the codes in **media texts**: that is *all media products, such as television programmes, films, CDs, books, newspapers and website pages*. We look for the *logics and rules* that pattern these messages, for they are not usually random. The focus here is on the contents of the media and what organises them. It involves looking at specific contents such as chat shows (on television and radio), film genres (for example, comedies or musicals) and 'stars' or 'celebrities' such as Madonna or Brad Pitt. Media texts are analysed for the messages they are trying to get across and their various biases.

A second area concerns the ways in which these media texts are produced. This involves looking at the technologies that emerge to present texts, along with the people who make programmes and their wider social locations. This involves a process of *encoding*, and it enables messages to be put into a language – be they spoken or written, verbal or pictorial. It involves looking at such matters as how journalists produce the news, how specific technologies such as the iPod are manufactured for music production, and the *organisation of finance and the ownership of media*.

A third question looks at how messages are received and consumed. This involves a process of *decoding* and the focus is on ***the audience***. This involves looking at such matters as how families watch television, studying soap opera fans, or looking at the way gender may shape how films are viewed.

All three of these act as a feedback loop.

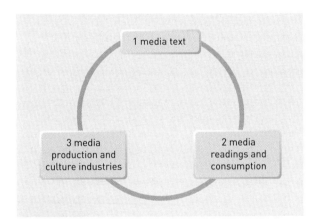

**Figure 22.2**   Questions a media analysis must address

1  What is the nature of the media text to be analysed – a film, a celebrity, a news item, a Facebook entry? How is it coded – what is its message?
2  How is this text consumed by its readers, its audiences, its fans?
3  How is this text produced – what are the organisations, people and corporations behind it? The process and flows of linkage become very important. Here we ask:
   (a)  How does a media text come to be encoded – the link between 1 and 3?
   (b)  How does a media text come to be decoded – the link between 1 and 2?
   (c)  What is the full flow between text, reader and producer?

## 1  Looking at media content

A number of theories have been developed to help us analyse and 'read' the texts and images of the media. We will look at just two: genre theory and semiology. (Others that could be looked at include narrative theory and code analysis.)

### Genre theory

*Genre theory* (from Latin *genus*, meaning 'type') helps us make sense of the seemingly chaotic flux of media programmes by identifying recognisable categories (Table 22.7). Each may then have its own set of rules and codes through which it is turned into a recognisable form.

As an example, consider the soap opera – a very popular topic for media analysis. Whether one is a fan of *EastEnders, Neighbours, Emmerdale, Coronation Street* or countless others, certain broad features make them identifiable as a type of programme. (They all, by the way, have their own elaborate websites as well as fanzines and regular features in soap magazines.) Of course, the specific contents, characters and plots

| Table 22.7 | Genres of television programmes viewed in England:[1] by sex, 2007/8 (%) | | |
|---|---|---|---|
| | Men | Women | All aged 16 and over |
| News[2] | 73 | 71 | 72 |
| Films | 68 | 64 | 66 |
| Comedy | 64 | 54 | 59 |
| Live sport coverage | 72 | 37 | 54 |
| Wildlife | 52 | 50 | 51 |
| Soaps | 29 | 58 | 44 |
| History | 44 | 34 | 39 |
| Food and cookery | 30 | 46 | 39 |
| Contemporary or period drama | 25 | 45 | 35 |
| Quiz shows | 31 | 37 | 35 |
| Current affairs or politics | 36 | 29 | 33 |
| Other sport | 46 | 17 | 31 |

[1] Respondents were asked 'Thinking about when you watch television, what type of programmes do you watch nowadays?'
[2] National or local news.

*Source: Taking Part: The National Survey of Culture, Leisure and Sport,* Department for Culture, Media and Sport, in *Social Trends,* 40 (2010), Table 13.3, p. 187.

will vary. But as a type, soap operas are all likely to have the following:

- *A never-ending story.* Storylines must always carry over to the next episode – there can be no closure, as in a one-hour drama.

- *Regular cliff-hangers.* Each episode must come to some sort of climax. Every hour or half-hour, the programme needs to have a crisis which will make the viewer wish to watch the next episode. The programme has to be a 'tease'.

- *Core characters.* The viewers become very familiar with the characters – they come to know a lot about them through watching many episodes. There are a lot of 'regulars' in soaps.

- *Interweaving storylines.* There are never just one or two plots, but a number. There are always several narrative strands proceeding at the same time.

- *The unfolding text.* Narrative progression has to be fairly slow. Often a storyline unfolds over weeks.

- *A woman's genre.* Women are more likely to feature in soaps, and women are more likely to watch them (see Geraghty, 1991; Allen, 1992, 1995).

 See BARB – British Audience Research Board figures for breakdowns of popular programmes: see www.barb.co.uk.

## Semiology and the study of signs

As we have seen in Chapter 5, semiology is the study of signs. Semiology studies all signs: 'images, gestures, musical sounds, objects and the complex associations of all these, which form the content of ritual, convention or public entertainment' (Barthes, 1967: 9). Signs have no intrinsic or fixed meanings. Instead, their meaning is arbitrary and derived from the way they relate to other words and signs. Language has two components: *langue* (language) and *parole* (speech). The former is the rules and structures of language; the latter is its practice in actual speech and writing. Studying langue would enable the analyst to get at the underlying structures of language. Applied to the media, we become concerned with analysing the content of media as a system of signs, tracing out their relationships to each other – and possibly to an underlying pattern.

## The television message as a code

All the programmes and images on TV can be examined for the kinds of values and messages they get across. Take the example of television news: many of us watch it every day. But 'textual sociologists' attempt to see it as a system of codes and values, and if the news does not fit these values, it will not work. Golding and Elliot, in a classic study, suggest that news values include:

- *Featuring of personalities.* Stories need a human angle – people and personalities who have a story to tell. Abstractions and theories are not favoured, but interesting personal stories are.

- *Elites and celebrities.* The featuring of big or well-known names is better than featuring 'nobodies'.

- *Narrative structures that contain key elements of human drama.* Joy, sorrow, shock, fear: these are the stuff of news.

- *Spectacle, good visuals and aesthetics.* Since television is a visual medium, news stories without good images become less newsworthy than those with good images. Sometimes news stories may be included simply because there are good images!

- *Entertainment value to attract large audiences.* News must provide materials which are captivating, humorous, titillating, amusing or generally diverting.

- *Importance.* The news item must have significance for large numbers of people in the audience.

- *Proximity.* News stories must be recent and relatively local. Foreign news must have local significance. The news in Norway cannot be the same as the news in Brazil.

- *Brevity.* Nothing can last too long and everything must be packed with information. News is part of what has been called the 'three-minute blip culture'.

- *Negativity.* Bad news is good news. It registers potential threats to social order.

- *Recency.* A premium is put on being first with the news. Once a competitor has the story, it becomes less significant (adapted from Golding and Elliott, 1979: 114–23).

Specific forms of news, such as crime news, may also bring other special values. Thus, for example, Pauline Jewkes (2004) suggests that crime newsworthiness increases when it features violence, sex, or threatened or dangerous children, as well as having a strong focus on particular individuals.

## 2 Constructing the message

A second concern of media analysis highlights the ways in which media messages actually get constructed. To take an example: just how is a television 'newscast' made? How is a 'news story' actually produced? Sociologists have done much work on this, and they have highlighted various layers of production.

A first layer looks at the actual *demands of the news programme itself*. Here there is an immediate daily time cycle, a planning structure which creates a routine agenda of predictable stories that provide the background of each day's production requirement (Schlesinger, 1978: 79). Far from being 'news', much of it is planned and routine. Slots need filling: an opening story, a limited number of stories required to fill a 15-minute space, good visuals, all following a regular schedule. Slots must be produced three times a day at the correct time (if there is no news, something has to be found; and if there is too much news, some of it has to be edited out).

A second layer looks at the *day-to-day practices of news journalists*. Here a specific culture of work helps journalists look out for certain kinds of news and not others. It is 'purposive behaviour' (Molotch and Lester, 1974).

A third layer sees the news as being structured by the *organisational demands of a bureaucracy*. We have seen in Chapter 6 how modern organisations tend to be highly rule-governed agencies: news is produced through such rules. Most noticeable are the rules of news production that are tightly linked to a 'stopwatch culture' (Schlesinger, 1978: 83).

Fourth, the news may be linked to wider concerns such as *community needs and dominant ideologies*. The Glasgow Media Group (1982) found that wider influences were at work, such that 'impartial news' often reflected a particular mindset of middle-class values.

Finally, news needs to be seen in the wider context of the *workings of the corporations*. Here such matters as financial structure become important. News that is too offensive or disturbing may lose advertising revenue. News, like all media outputs, becomes part of an industry and can be analysed this way. We looked briefly at the 'business of media' in a previous section (p. 778).

## 3 Looking at media audiences

A final major concern in contemporary approaches to the mass media is that of the audience and the impact of media upon them. Modern audiences differ from those of the past. Once – in theatres and stadia – audiences were linked to a specific public setting, planned, organised and collectively shared. These days, audiences have become much more fragmented and individualised. It is the difference between watching a film in a cinema and watching a video at home. One is public and shared; the other private and personalised.

The main concern of researchers has been to look at the ways in which media impact audiences. One classic study which looked at the impact of television on children's lives gives a typically cautious conclusion:

**For some children under some conditions some television is harmful. For other children under the same conditions, or for the same children under other conditions, it may be beneficial. For most children under most conditions, most television is neither harmful nor potentially beneficial.**

(Schramm, 1961)

Although there has been a long tradition of examining so-called media effects – what the media do to people – it is only fairly recently that researchers have switched the question from what the media do to people to what people do to the media. The classical 'effects literature' has tended to see audiences as fairly passive recipients of media messages. As we have seen above, the most extreme version of this is the hypodermic syringe model – where people are seen to be passively injected with media messages. While no media analyst holds such a view today, it remains popular among public and media moralists. For instance, in the aftermath of the murder of a young child, James Bulger, in the UK in 1993 by two young boys, the video of *Child's Play 3* (in which a similar kind of murder was to be seen) was evoked as a cause of the murder. While it is possible to say that the film may have played a part in the murder – along with many other factors – it cannot be said simply to have caused it.

More recent approaches to the media audience tend to conduct ethnographic research on specific audiences. Thus, the researcher may enter a 'fan group' and see how they watch their favourite star. Or the researcher may observe and interview women as to how they watch soap operas and, indeed, what they like about them. In one celebrated study, David Morley entered families and observed the ways in which they watched the media.

Looking at 18 south London working-class families, Morley observed how they used television. One of his key themes is the way such viewing is structured by gender. Among his findings, which have to be seen as very provisional because of the scale of his study, he suggests:

- Adult men have most control over the programme choice, and the video is more likely to be controlled by 'dad'.
- Women are usually engaged in other domestic activities, and watch television more sporadically (except in 'solo' watching by daytime). Husbands seem to watch more than wives.
- Men are more systematic and focused: they watch more attentively.
- Men prefer sport and news, while women prefer drama and fiction features.
- Women are more likely to express guilt over their viewing habits; they also use it as a conversation piece more (Morley, 1986: Chapter 3).

## The fragmentation of the mass audience

Although many critics have argued that this is the age of 'mass society', others have argued that what we are seeing is a breakdown of the population into hundreds of very different audiences. To take an example: the world of music used to be divisible into a few broad groupings. There was 'classical music', 'popular music', maybe 'jazz' and a few others. Now, as any browser in a record 'megastore' will find, audiences for music have splintered in many directions: New Age, ethnic, rock, classic rock, show tunes, country and western, punk, reggae, folk. But these are broken down into further categories. Show tunes has its Sondheim aficionados who would not go near an Andrew Lloyd Webber score. And there are those who seek out the most obscure musicals that only run for one night. And so on. What has happened is the emergence of many media markets – niche markets. At the same time, some 90 per cent of all albums sold in Europe are for rock or light music, while 5–10 per cent are classical (Therborn, 1995: 224).

This may be depicted, as in Figure 22.3, as a move from media having elite audiences, through those having mass audiences to those having more specialised audiences. When a new medium appears it is usually adopted by an educational elite, before spreading out to a wider mass audience. After a while this splinters into a host of specialist groupings. What this means is that much media expansion takes place through increasingly specialised audiences (Figure 22.4).

## Watching the news

The decoding issue turns to how actual audiences may interpret and watch the news. Here, the task is to get close to actual audiences to see the ways they make sense of the programmes they watch. Often this has a strongly gendered pattern; it may also be shaped by such things as class, age, ethnicity and sexuality. How we 'read' the media is known as *audience ethnography* (see below).

In one celebrated study, the UK media sociologist David Morley examined the audiences of *Nationwide* (a popular UK 1970s news programme). He worked from the premise that the programme can be 'read' or viewed in a number of different ways. The text is *polysemic, open to many interpretations*. He was interested

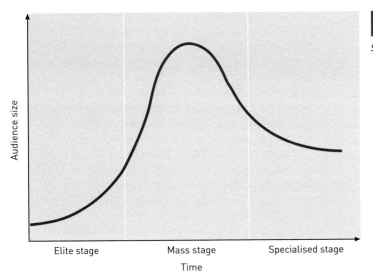

**Figure 22.3**  A model of media specialisation

*Source*: Adapted from Neuman (1991).

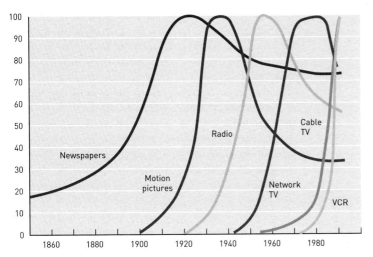

**Figure 22.4**  Size and fragmentation of audiences

*Source*: Adapted from Neuman (1991).

in showing the programme to a range of different groups (university arts students, trade unionists, apprentices, etc.) and getting their feedback. From this, Morley aimed to generate a typology of the 'decodings' made and to analyse their variety.

Broadly, what he found were three main positions in which the 'decoder' stood in relation to the text. For some, the meaning was taken fully within the framework which the message itself suggested (he calls this '*the dominant code*'). For others, the meaning was broadly encoded this way, but through relating it to some specific concrete context that reflected the reader's own position, the meaning was modified ('*the negotiated code*'). For still others, they recognised what was trying to be said, but rejected it and imposed a meaning that worked in an opposite way (an '*oppositional reading*') (Morley, 1992: 89).

What is important about this approach is the way in which it never sees viewers as passive dummies just soaking up the news. Instead, the news is approached actively and audiences have to work to give it meanings.

## The Eurovision Song Contest: globalising music, queering worlds?

Popular music became 'European' somewhere in the mid-1950s, for that was when the European Song Contest came into being. Established in 1956 (at Lugano, Switzerland with 14 delegate countries participating), it was set up by the European Broadcasting Union (EBU) and aimed to be the 'Grand Prix of European Song'. Since then, it has been an annual television event celebrating its fiftieth anniversary in 2006 (with 25 countries in the final, and 38 countries in the semi-final). It has become 'bigger, better and more popular than ever' (O'Connor, 2007: 4). 'The Eurovision Song Contest' is a good example of globalised television. Several sociological issues can be raised.

First, just what does the contest say about musical forms and how a nation's identity presents itself through music? The song contest occupies a curious position with the world of pop music, since very few of its songs ever become 'hits', and usually look way outside the boundaries of what is seen as pop music in Europe. It is usually mocked, for example, by young people who are into other forms of more widespread music. Each country displays a music form which in some way is common to all of Europe while also being very distinctive about its own culture. It is hybridic and glocalised (see Chapter 2).

Secondly, it suggests the political coalitions of Europe. What has become clear over the years is the way in which voting patterns become predictable according to country alignments. Often country proximity shapes the voting: it is not the music that calls the tune, but the politics of each country.

But finally, the contest has generated a cult status among many different groups in each country. One of the most interesting is the way in which gay or 'queer groups' have appropriated much of the style and substance of the programme. The song contest has always been 'camp' – it displays exaggerated musical forms, especially of men and women, and outlandish dress, etc. Abba won in 1974 with 'Waterloo'; Bucks Fizz won in 1981 with a cutish number in which the pretty boys took the pretty girls' skirts off; in 1998 the transsexual Dana International won in Jerusalem (as controversy raged in Israel about her); and in 2007 an out lesbian singer took the stage to win. Queer parties and gay clubs celebrate each year with the Eurovision Song Contest.

*Source*: John Kennedy, O'Connor, *The Eurovision Song Contest: The Official History*, London: Carlton Books (2007).

## The globalisation of the media

As media of various kinds proliferated throughout the world during the twentieth century, the claim was increasingly made that the mass media have become one of the central mechanisms through which globalisation is taking place. Indeed, the vast interconnections across cultures through internet, television satellites and cables have now become a key feature of twenty-first-century life.

We can see the potential of media globalisation across three major areas.

### The globalisation of media content

As internet groups, games, films, music, news and the entertainment industry all come to 'travel' the world, so their languages and images become commonly available across cultures. The *content* of programmes has also become increasingly global. There are 'global totemic festivals' (Barker, 1997: 14) such as the royal marriage of Prince William and Catherine Middleton in April 2011, the World Cup, the Olympics, the funeral of Michael Jackson and earlier the funeral of Diana, Princess of Wales with an estimated 2.5 billion global audience, where it seems as if everyone in the world may be experiencing the same events. This is also true of much live global coverage of many news events:

world disasters like the Asian Tsunami of 2005 and acts of terrorism like the 9/11 suicide bombing of the New York Twin Towers, for example, are screened around the world instantly and simultaneously.

Some commentators have suggested that some genres of television are indeed being recycled everywhere in approximately the same forms throughout the world. Thus, news and soap operas seem to travel very well. There *are* differences across cultures: there are still some 150 cultures to which the Australian soap *Neighbours* has not been exported (Crofts, 1995: 102)! But overall, Barker suggests that a certain kind of international style may be developing. This includes: high production values (glossy and expensive); pleasing visual backgrounds (the landscapes of Australia, the beaches of California); more action than in traditional soaps; a Hollywood-style narrative mode; elements of melodrama over realism (Barker, 1997: 95). Likewise, Barker finds news narration similar. What is news is fairly consistent from country to country, although there are some variations.

## The globalisation of media forms

The new technologies have become more and more pervasive and have started to hook up with each other. During the 1990s, there was a massive shift to 'digital transmission' of all kinds of data, and this, combined with satellite, meant the rapid expansion of the 'information superhighway', with three cores in North America, Europe and east Asia. Nowadays, there is a major convergence of electronic forms – for example, as hand-held mobile phones come to incorporate DVD, CD, news programmes, internet groupings, gaming cultures and other features.

## The rise of super corporations

Traditionally in Europe, radio and television have received *public finance* (via licences and taxes) to provide a *universal service for citizens* by producing programmes which have some form of public *accountability*, some *regulation of content* and some *protection from competition*. The British Broadcasting Corporation (BBC) is one classic instance of this. It used to account for over half of the viewing time, but that proportion is now in serious decline as the new television channels stream online. The BBC World Service, with a long history, is being overtaken by groups such as CNN and MTV. And the story is the same throughout the world. What we are now

seeing is the rise of major mega corporations which dominate media life across the world (see above).

## The myth of media globalisation

Although claims about the importance of the media shaping globalisation are widespread, critics claim that it is overstated. There is much evidence that most cultures have developed their own distinctive major media channels, and although they may 'borrow' from other cultures, they maintain an independence. Bollywood may borrow from Hollywood but it is *not* Hollywood. The China internet blocks the use of much Western material. Muslim television is not the same as Western television. And so on.

Kai Hafez (2007) has made a strong argument against the globalisation of the media. At the very least, he claims, there are three very different responses to cultural change, media and globalisation. These are:

- the adoption of the 'other' culture (this is the globalisation model and often presumes a 'Westernisation' of the media)
- the emergence of 'glocalised' hybrid cultures – in which local and global elements are mixed together
- the revitalisation and reassertion of traditional and other local cultures as a reaction to globalisation (see Hafez, 2007: 14).

## The growth of Al-Jazeera

One interesting 'global' television service (recently much talked about) is that of Al-Jazeera (a term that in Arabic means 'The Peninsula'). Arab television developed from 1996 after the decline of the London-based BBC Arabic network. Based in Qatar (in the Gulf region), it is a state-sponsored Arabic news channel, having (in 2002) a regular audience of 35 million (and being available to some 310 million worldwide). It exists in a region stigmatised for decades and open to huge censorship. After 11 September 2001, this satellite television station became prominent in its coverage of the Afghanistan war, especially exclusive video tapes of Osama bin Laden.

Although the United States has tried setting up its own Arab language news channel in the Middle East, it has not proved popular. Al-Jazeera provides the 'other side of the story', giving global coverage to news that is usually dominated by the English-speaking Western world (especially the USA and the UK) (Miladi, 2003).

## THINKERS & THEORY

# Jürgen Habermas: the changing public sphere

The German sociologist Jürgen Habermas (1929–) is considered one of the world's foremost contemporary social theorists.

Habermas has been concerned with the 'life world' (the immediate environment of the 'social actor'), with knowledge and communication, and how it changes in the modern world. He is concerned with what he calls the changes in the public and private spheres of modern societies. The public sphere is 'a domain of our social life in which such a thing as public opinion can be formed . . . and is open in principle to all citizens' (Habermas, 1989; orig. 1962). The public sphere is an arena where public debate flourishes, and ideas and opinions can grow. Habermas traces its history, suggesting that it was in seventeenth- and eighteenth-century Europe that it developed a clear form. Between the realm of the state (see Chapter 16) and the private sphere of the family, there emerged a new public sphere which allowed people to exercise judgement and to engage critically in public debate. This may have been in the salons and coffee houses of the big European cities.

But nowadays, he worries, such debates have been narrowed by the collapse of this sphere into the mass media. It was originally the newspapers and the mass tabloids that first significantly brought about this change. They developed a much more commercial and consumer-based culture which was linked to the privatised worlds of money and commerce rather than a public forum of debate.

He worries about the future of democracy as the media expand and proposes a theory of communicative action. He sees three forms of knowledge at work in society. First is instrumental knowledge, which is technical and scientific. Much of this has worked against human

Jürgen Habermas
*Source*: © Rex Features/SIPA.

progress and has impoverished human lives. Second is hermeneutic knowledge, where the focus is on understanding. But Habermas looks for a third form of knowledge, which could be 'emancipatory'. Believing in progress and modernity, he argues that societies can move forward only if people can peel away all the irrationalities partially bestowed on them by media messages and arrive at a 'pure speech' situation in which they can understand clearly each other's ideas. At present this is made impossible because of technology.

# Looking ahead: the future of the media

Sociology has come increasingly to recognise that throughout the twentieth century the mass media came to play a growing importance in the lives of societies. This is true not just of the industrial West, but of nearly all cultures. Global 'mediasation' has become a major process in the twenty-first century. The full implications of this have yet to be grasped, but we need to consider at least three questions.

First, it seems likely that more and more of our lives – and those of our children – will come to be lived away from the real world and inside a media-created one. Once the full implications of home multimedia start to be realised, will we spend less and less time in public space confronting real events and more and more time in a virtual space? Is the simulacrum arriving?

Secondly, the media world seems set to become an increasingly commercialised global one, dominated by huge transnational corporations. To the extent that this happens, will this mean not only an increasing homogenisation of different cultures, but also a real threat to democracy as more and more of what we see in the world is regulated by high finance?

But third, the top internet countries are overwhelmingly in the West: 90 per cent of users in 1995 were in North America and western Europe. At least 80 per cent of the world's countries still lack communications technologies. And overwhelmingly, the typical user of the Net is a North American male looking for entertainment. Although globalisation may be taking place, is this a process that will have serious consequences for the wider inequalities in society?

# SUMMARY

1 We live our lives increasingly through the media. Patterns of communication have changed through five main kinds of culture: sign, oral, writing, print and most recently electronic cultures. We now live in a mediated or media-saturated world.

2 Initially, sociologists looked at the media through the hypodermic model: this suggests media messages are presented to members of a mass society, who receive them more or less uniformly and are strongly influenced by them. The stimuli lead individuals to respond in a similar, uniform fashion. The effects of mass communication are powerful, uniform and direct. This view has long been discredited and newer theories show that the reverse of these assumptions is more or less true.

3 There are many theories of the media. Hypodermic theories of simple media cause and effect are generally discredited. Functionalist theories focus on the ways in which media perform key functions. Marxist and conflict theory tends to look at the control function of the media and the concentration of media ownership. Interactionist theories focus on meanings and the interpretations of audiences. And postmodern theories tend to focus on the way media assumes a life of its own in the postmodern world, seeing social life as increasingly dominated by simulacra and signs.

4 There are three main areas for a media analysis: media messages, encoding and decoding. Codes are rule-governed systems of signs, encoding involves putting a message of any kind into a language, and decoding is the process by which we hear or read and understand a message.

5 Media texts are analysed through what the media says, how it is produced and how people (audiences) make sense of it.

6 Although there exist public forms of ownership of the media, such as the BBC in the UK, increasingly the media are concentrated in the ownership of a few major companies, such as TimeWarner, Bertelsmann and Viacom.

CONNECT UP: Turn to Part 6 of this book for key resources and link up
with the book's website, which links to these resources
SEE: www.pearsoned.co.uk/plummer

## MYTASKLIST

# Ten suggestions for going further

## 1 Connect up with Part Six and the Sociology Web Resources

As you work through ideas and think about the issues raised in this chapter, look at the accompanying website and the resource centre at the end of this book which connects to it. There is a lot here to help you move on. To link up, see: www.pearson.co.uk/plummer.

## 2 Review the chapter

*Briefly summarise (in a paragraph) just what this chapter has been about.* Consider: (a) What have you learned? (b) What do you disagree with? Be critical. And (c) How would you develop all this? How could you get more detail on matters that interest you?

## 3 Pose questions

(a) For the next few days, keep a detailed record of 'you and your media'. Keep a detailed log of just when you engage with the mass media, what the kinds of media were, what messages were sent, and how they impinged on your life. Note all the media you use, from papers and magazines to television and film, and from CD and PC to mobile. It may surprise you just how much of your life is now 'mediated'.

(b) Outline the major 'areas of media' study. Select any one media item, such as a TV programme or a film, and examine the kinds of question you would ask about it.

(c) Who owns the media? Using a reference book such as *Who Owns Whom?* examine the ownership of the media and assess the concentration in a few powerful hands.

(d) How far do you think mass media have now become globalised? Discuss the implications of this.

## 4 Explore key words

Many concepts have been introduced in this chapter. You can review them from the website or from the listing at the back of this book. You might like to give special attention to just five words and think them through – how would you define them, what are they dealing with, and do they help you see the social world more clearly or not?

Helpful here are:

Nicholas Abercrombie and Brian Longhurst, *Penguin Dictionary of Media Studies* (2007).

Anne Hill and James Watson, *Dictionary of Media and Communication* (2006).

## 5 Search the Web

Be critical when you look at websites – see the box on p. 940 in the Resources section. For this chapter look at:

OECD and the information economy
www.oecd.org/topic

UNESCO
http://portal.unesco.org

The Blackwell listing for cultural studies
www.blackwellpublishing.com/subjects/SI

The Al-Jazeera television station and its website
http://english.aljazeera.net/HomePage

Al-Jazeera is a 24-hour news and current affairs channel, headquartered in Doha. It provides news in English and Arabic.
Freepress
Working for reform, it documents 'who owns the media'.
www.freepress.net/resources/ownership

## 6 Watch a DVD

- Orson Welles's *Citizen Kane* (1941): classic 'media mogul' story, based on the life of Randolph Hearst.
- Sydney Lumet's *Network* (1976): Peter Finch and Faye Dunaway in a major media battle – a powerful film.
- Peter Weir's *The Truman Show* (1998) and Gary Ross's *Pleasantville* (1998): two films where 'tele-reality' blurs with reality. Very provocative.

- Robert Redford's *Quiz Show* (1994): media corruption around a 1950s quiz show.

## 7  Think and read

Terry Flew, *Understanding Global Media* (2007), Kai Hafez, *The Myth of Media Globalization* (2007) and Tehri Rantanen, *The Media and Globalization* (2005). Good guides to the contemporary debates on the global media.

Kevin Williams, *Understanding Media Theory* (2003) and Denis McQuail, *McQuail's Mass Communication Theory* (5th edn, 2005). Two textbooks: the first is recent, the other classic.

Sue Thornham, Caroline Bassett and Paul Marris (eds), *Media Studies: A Reader* (3rd edn, 2009). A well-established reader which covers the field well (since it was first published, it has developed many rivals).

Joshua Meyrowitz, *No Sense of Place: The Impact of Electronic Media on Social Behavior* (1986). A major, and now classic, study which draws upon Goffman (1959) and McLuhan (1964) to show the way in which television is changing the way we experience the world.

## 8  Relax with a novel

Guy de Maupassant's *Bel-Ami* (1885) is a classic early study of journalism; Evelyn Waugh's *Scoop* (1938) is a classic satire of sensational journalism; and F. Scott Fitzgerald's *The Last Tycoon* is a classic tale of Hollywood.

## 9  Connect to other chapters

- For links to inequalities, see Chapters 8–13.
- For links to globalisation, see Chapter 2.
- For links to functionalist, conflict and interactionist theories, see Chapter 1.
- For links to theories of culture, see Chapter 5; and for links to societal development, see Chapter 4.
- For links to cyberspace media, see Chapters 6 and 23.

## 10  Engage with THE BIG DEBATE

### Are the media destroying social life?

Ever since their inception, the mass media have always been attacked as dangerous. They have been at the centre of controversy. In the very earliest days, when books and novels started to be published, there were worries that these could be corrupting. As the earliest popular literature slowly became available to the 'masses', so it was denounced. In 1806, a Samuel P. Jarvis said that 'The evil consequences attendant upon novel reading are much greater than has generally been imagined' (Starker, 1989: 61). Much later, in the 1930s, radio programmes caused great alarm, and Lyman Bryson wrote:

> All great human inventions, even printing, even language itself, have proved to be two-edged swords. They can do as much evil as good. Radio is as great – and as dangerous – as any . . . and it can broadcast injury and discord and ugliness into the farthest reaches of inhabited space. To be lightminded about the radio is to jig along a precipice . . .
>
> Starker (1989: 115)

These days every new media form comes under attack. When Dungeons and Dragons (D&D) was first marketed in 1973 (with 8 million copies sold by 1985), it was accused of 'dabbling in the demonic' by *Christianity Today*. And attempts were made to link teenage suicides and murders to it. In 1992, the issue became 'rap and race' with the song 'Cop Killer' by Ice-T prompting a boycott of Warner Bros. records by parents anxious about the lyrics. (To see the lyrics, go to www.metrolyrics.com/cop-killer-lyrics-body-count.html.)

This may be extreme. But every form of media has had its critics: the early tabloids and newspapers, Hollywood movies from the start of the twentieth century till now, children's comics, the 'plug-in drug' of television, 'video nasties', pop music, reality TV, 'games', computers. Over and over again, the media have been posed as a threat and a danger.

Media critics have claimed that the media can have serious effects on their audience. Among the many dangers they pose are the following:

- The fostering of passivity: the 'couch potato' syndrome of inertly watching.
- The growth of crime, violence and moral decline: the media shape low values and provide bad role models.

- Trivialisation: we are, in the words of one critic, 'amusing ourselves to death'. Authentic sports, religion and politics get trivialised. Even education becomes 'infotainment'.
- The promotion of materialism and commercial values: most media come with advertising to the forefront and this leads to a 'promotional culture'. Even the weather or the news gets identified with sponsorship.
- Brainwashing, manipulation and mass conformity.
- The 'simulation' of the world, giving us pseudo-images and false realities: at its most extreme we come to inhabit an unreal media world, cut off from more authentic experiences.

In short, mass media lead to a degenerating mass culture. As Bernard Rosenberg says: 'At its worst, mass culture threatens not merely to cretinise our taste but to brutalise our sense, while paving the way to totalitarianism' (cited in Starker, 1989: 13).

In contrast, media defenders reject these criticisms and argue that the media can do the following.

- Increase participation and creativity: viewers can be active and critical and use the media – they respond by writing letters, engaging in debates and the like.
- Enhance the information a society has and help keep us aware of what is going on.
- Increase public debate.
- Extend access to all kinds of information and entertainment that previously were restricted to an elite class.
- Provide diversity.

- Reduce crime and enhance morality through making people more aware of issues.

In short, mass media can enhance a diverse, active and participatory culture.

Some modern media analysts such as Joli Jensen (1990) see the worry over the media as part of a continuing concern over modernity. The 'dangerous media', they suggest, are repeatedly compared with some mythical golden age in the past and taken to symbolise all the dangers of the modern world – rapid change, differences, a loss of clear authority, etc. They are constantly under attack because they are potent symbols of rapid change and a modern world hurtling into an unknown future. But media are in fact human made and here to stay, and we can shape them in the direction that we wish. They cannot in themselves be blamed for anything.

### Continue the debate

1 Do you think that watching soap operas and reality television – the most popular forms of television – can play any useful social role?
2 Do you think 'sport' has been degraded through being turned into a mass media event?
3 Look around you and see what form the attack on the media is currently taking. Dissect this latest example.
4 Look back at earlier forms of media scare. Do the concerns of those times seem tame compared to those of today? Have the media got more outrageous and more threatening?
5 Weigh up the pros and cons of the new global communications systems.

# An Introduction to Irish Society

## Introduction

Speaking to the *Observer* newspaper in 2002, the late Irish writer John McGahern remarked that "Ireland is a peculiar society in the sense that it was a nineteenth century society up to about 1970 and then it almost bypassed the twentieth century" (McCrum 2002). McGahern's observation on the rapid transformation of Irish society – from being underdeveloped, repressed and dependent to becoming one of the most globalised and increasingly secular societies in the world – was well made. Irish society has undergone a radical set of transformations in the last three decades or so. We have moved quickly from being a pre-industrial society to being a post-modern one. These changes are in evidence across most of the ordinary things that we do each day, from consuming fast food, to shopping in malls, to talking to our friends for free in other parts of the world via Skype. Globalisation has impacted on the accents used and the way that many younger people now speak; on the media they consume; and on if, how and where they work in paid employment. While many of the social changes in Irish society are indeed welcome, they are not without their tensions or their costs. Sociologists and others have attempted to explain many

of these changes by addressing critical questions such as our growing dependency on global capital; societal breakdown or anomie; cultural homogenisation and the persistence of class, gender and other forms of inequalities.

In this chapter we highlight a number of areas which we feel will help you have a more critical understanding of the make-up of 21st century Irish society. We focus on the following themes:

> ➤ Ireland's Key Demographic Features
> ➤ Globalisation and Work
> ➤ The Rise and Fall of 'Celtic Tiger' Ireland
> ➤ Social Class and Inequality
> ➤ Racism and Ethnicity
> ➤ Mass Media

Our chapter begins by offering you a clear understanding of the recent demographic features of Irish society. We then consider how economic globalisation has transformed people's working lives. Our discussion of work encompasses such themes as gender, unemployment and emigration. We then look behind the much heralded 'economic miracle' known as the Celtic Tiger and examine how it was responsible for significant social change in Ireland, which was especially manifest in terms of conspicuous consumption. We proceed to discuss how inequality has remained a marked feature of Irish society. Dispelling the myth of a classless Ireland, we examine how class inequalities have persisted and how they are evident, for example, in terms of fair and equal access to education, and in terms of social identity. The first decades of the 21st century have seen inward migration become a distinct feature of Irish society. We examine questions concerning racism and ethnicity in Ireland by reference to the 'New Irish' and also by reference to the experiences of the Irish traveller community. Finally, we discuss the role of the mass media in Irish society by examining how it has been an agent of social change and globalisation. Connecting with some of the chapter's earlier themes we discuss the ownership and control of the Irish mass media, how marginalised groups such as the poor and excluded are portrayed, as well as how the diaspora or 'New Irish' make use of the mass media. The intention of this chapter is to give you an introduction to a number of pertinent areas concerning Irish society. It is, however, merely an introduction and we advise all student readers to make the most of the extensive resource section at the end of our chapter. In addition, we recommend that you use your sociological dictionary to define the words that are in bold lettering throughout the chapter.

# Ireland: Key Demographic Features

Our examination of Irish society commences with an overview of its key demographic features. A basic understanding of recent demographic change is an important prerequisite to appreciating the wider social changes that you will encounter in this chapter. The demographic structure of most industrial countries has been changing very rapidly. In general, people are marrying and having children later in life. Separation and divorce have become much more common and, in many countries, both pre-marital cohabitation and cohabitation as an alternative to marriage have become the norm. When compared to other European countries, Ireland has long been seen as unusual in its demographic trends.

## Stop and Think

> ➤ In what ways do you think the Irish family has changed? Think about your grandparents and how many children they had. Then think about your family.

Irish people have a long history of either marrying late or not marrying at all. Up until 1960, Ireland had the lowest rate of entry into marriage in Europe. In other words, large numbers of Irish men and women never married, nor did they cohabit with a partner. In the 1936 Census of Population a third of men and a quarter of women aged between 45 and 54 had never married. In conjunction with this, Ireland had a higher than average age of marriage. Despite the tendency to marry late, the Irish family was the largest in Europe. In 1960, for example, the mean age of marriage for an Irish man was 30.8 years, compared to a European average of 26.7.[1] In the same year, there were 5.5 marriages per 1,000 of the Irish population compared to the European average of 8.[2] In 1960, Irish women were on average having 2.4 children over their life-course, compared to the European average of 1.8.[3] At that time, Iceland was the only European country to match Ireland's completed fertility rate although Ireland's overall fertility was not especially high by US and other 'new world' standards (see Fahey and Russell 2001). Today, Ireland's demography looks more like that of other European countries.

## Marriages

The marriage rate, or the number of marriages per 1,000 of the population, stood at 4.8 in 2009, compared to a European average (27 countries) of 4.7 (Eurostat 2010). From 1973 onwards, there were over 20 years of steady decline in the proportion of the Irish population marrying. From 1995, the marriage rate increased, which coincided with the economic boom and the introduction of divorce in 1997. The number of marriages rose by 23 per- cent between 1997 and 2001 (see Table 1). The percentage of all marriages that were civil ceremonies (that is, weddings without any religious affiliation) has also increased. In 1996, there were 928 civil marriages (6 per-cent) in Ireland, but this figure increased to 5,127 or just over 23 percent of all marriages in 2006. Recent evidence shows that civil ceremonies are more popular among older couples (CSO 2009). Another indicator of social change is the number of mixed marriages in Ireland. Large-scale immigration into Ireland is a relatively recent development

---

[1] See Eurostat 2000, Table F-8. The European average reported here is the average of the 15 members of the European Union, that is, Belgium, Denmark, Germany, Greece, Spain, France, Ireland, Italy, Luxembourg, The Netherlands, Austria, Portugal, Finland, Sweden and the UK.
[2] See Eurostat 2000, Table F-3.
[3] See Eurostat 2000, Table E-6.

## Table 1 Births and marriages in Ireland, 1950–2009

| Year | Number marriages | Marriage rate | Number births | Birth rate |
|------|------------------|---------------|---------------|------------|
| 1950 | 16,018 | 5.4 | 63,565 | 21.4 |
| 1960 | 15,465 | 5.5 | 60,735 | 21.5 |
| 1970 | 20,778 | 7.1 | 64,382 | 21.9 |
| 1980 | 21,792 | 6.4 | 74,064 | 21.8 |
| 1990 | 17,838 | 5.1 | 53,044 | 15.1 |
| 1991 | 17,441 | 4.9 | 52,718 | 15 |
| 1992 | 16,636 | 4.7 | 51,089 | 14.4 |
| 1993 | 16,824 | 4.7 | 49,304 | 13.8 |
| 1994 | 16,621 | 4.6 | 48,255 | 13.5 |
| 1995 | 15,604 | 4.3 | 48,787 | 13.5 |
| 1996 | 16,174 | 4.5 | 50,655 | 14 |
| 1997 | 15,631 | 4.3 | 52,775 | 14.4 |
| 1998 | 16,783 | 4.5 | 53,969 | 14.6 |
| 1999 | 18,526 | 5 | 53,924 | 14.4 |
| 2000 | 19,168 | 5.1 | 54,789 | 14.5 |
| 2001 | 19,246 | 5 | 57,854 | 15 |
| 2002 | 20,556 | 5.2 | 60,503 | 15.5 |
| 2003 | 20,302 | 5.1 | 61,529 | 15.5 |
| 2004 | 20,619 | 5.1 | 61,972 | 15.3 |
| 2005 | 21,355 | 5.2 | 61,372 | 14.8 |
| 2006 | 21,841 | 5.2 | 65,425 | 15.4 |
| 2007 | 22,544 | 5.2 | 71,389 | 16.5 |
| 2008 | 22,243 | 5 | 75,065 | 17 |
| 2009 | 21,541 | 4.8 | 74,728 | 16.7 |

(Source: CSO 2011)

(see the section on ethnicity and racism later in this chapter). In the 2006 Census, 9 percent of all family units were mixed Irish/non-Irish families indicating more diverse marriage patterns among the Irish population.

The average age at marriage for both brides and grooms has been increasing in recent years. In 2005 almost half (49 percent) of brides were aged 30 or over on their wedding day, compared with 44 percent in 2002 and 28 percent in 1996. Sociologists have argued that the older age at marriage is consistent with women spending longer periods of time in education and men and women establishing a career later in life, before entering marriage.

On average, grooms are still older than brides at marriage. Marriage registration data show that the gender gap in average age of marriage was marginally over two years in 2005, at 33.1 years for men compared to 31.0 years for women (CSO 2007). In 1960, grooms were on average 3.2 years older than brides.

In 2006, the groom was older than the bride in the majority (62 percent) of marriages, the same age in a further 13 percent of marriages and in the remaining 25 percent of cases the bride was older than the groom. The incidence of 'toyboy' marriages in which the man is younger than his bride was similar in the 2002 marriage registration data. This pattern was generally witnessed across all age groups except in the case of males under 25, where in 2006 the bride was older in almost half (46 percent) of marriages, the same in 19 percent and younger in 35 percent of marriages (CSO 2007).

## Stop and Think

> Do you think the Celtic Tiger caused a marriage boom?

> Hint: Do you think people are more likely to marry in an economic boom? Why?

## Cohabitation

Sociologists have debated the role of cohabitation in society. Some argue that cohabitation is a long-term alternative to marriage for some segments of the population while others see cohabitation as a prelude to marriage, implying that most cohabiting couples will either marry or separate. Although cohabitation was relatively uncommon in Ireland in the 1996 Census, the number of cohabiting couples grew fourfold between then and the 2006 Census, rising from 31,300 to 121,800 couples over that period (see Macionis and Plummer 2008, p.597 for a general discussion of cohabitation). The majority of cohabitees, just over 200,000 persons in 2006, are single people for whom cohabitation represents their first entry into partnership (see Lunn *et al.* 2010).

Cohabitation is more popular among the younger population, which is those aged 25–35 in the 2006 Census. Even after taking rising cohabitation and marriage rates into account, there has been a real rise over the past two decades in the incidence of people in their late 20s and early 30s remaining single (Lunn *et al.* 2010). This is consistent with later age at marriage and reflects the fact that, on average, men and women are postponing marriage and having children.

## Divorce/Separation

The present period in Irish demographic history has been labelled 'post-revolutionary' by sociologists Fahey and

Layte (2007, p.157). In 1995, a second national referendum to remove the constitutional ban on divorce was narrowly accepted (the majority in favour was 50.28 percent). This referendum brought to a close three decades of controversy on the 'moral' questions of contraception, abortion and divorce. The divorce bill is, however, quite restrictive by international standards. It allows divorce if the couple have been separated four of the previous five years, and if there is "no reasonable prospect of reconciliation". The new legislation came into force in February 1997.

It appears that there has been a low take-up of divorce after the new legislation came into effect (see Fahey and Field 2008, Lunn *et al.* 2010). In 2007, the divorce rate in Ireland was 0.8 divorces per 1,000 of the population, the lowest rate in the EU (CSO 2010, also see Figure 18.1 in Macionis and Plummer 2008, p.593). The rate of marital breakdown has been increasing since the 1980s. The marriage breakdown rate includes marital separation which has both a common and legal usage; referring both to the *de facto* situation of a married couple who no longer live together and the legal status of a married couple who have a judicial separation agreement.

Between the 1986 and 2006 Census, the total number of people in Ireland whose marriages have broken down increased five-fold, from 40,000 in 1986 to just under 200,000 in 2006 (of the latter, 36,000 were non-Irish nationals). In 2006, non-Irish nationals (measured on a 'usual residence' basis) accounted for 10 percent of the total population (Lunn *et al.* 2010).

---

## A Closer Look

### Marriage and Divorce

The introduction of divorce in 1997 allowed partners in second unions to end their first marriage and formalise their second relationship. One way to assess the degree to which this change may have contributed to the recent marriage boom (in religious and civil ceremonies) is to look at the number of first marriages (the total first marriage rate is the mean number of first marriages per women or men in a given year). In 1997, the total female first marriage rate stood at 0.57 and by 1998, it had increased only slightly to 0.59. First marriage rates after that year are not yet available (see Punch 2007). Fahey (2007), however, concluded that some, but by no means all, of the upward trend in marriage after 1997 was produced by second marriages.

---

## Children

In 1991, for the first time in Ireland's history, Irish fertility finally crossed the below replacement fertility level of 2.1 children per woman. Although the total period fertility rate trend since the late 1990s had been reasonably flat, the number of births increased by 55 percent between 1994 and 2008. By 2008, there were 75,065 births registered. This was the highest number of births recorded since 1896 (CSO 2009). Preliminary evidence from the 2011 Census indicates a continuation of a rise in the national birth rate.

This increase reflects an increase in births to first-time mothers rather than a rise in completed family size. In other words, the large Irish family has become more and more exceptional. In 1960, one third of all births were fifth order or higher, but by 2000, this had fallen to 4 percent of all births. By contrast, the number of first births increased by 19 percent over this period. This represented the highest level of first births in Ireland over the 20th century. Since 2000, the number of first births has remained high. It is possible that the continued rise in the number of births is a Celtic Tiger effect (see the next section) but no research has been carried out on this issue yet.

## Births outside Marriage

Another indicator of social change is the proportion of births occurring outside of marriage, which has increased dramatically. Ireland has moved from being one of the European countries with the lowest extramarital birth rate in 1980, at 5 percent, to join those with the highest rates by 2000, at 32 percent (see Hantrais 2004). Since 2000, the percentage of births occurring outside of marriage has stabilised at about a third of all births. For first births, the proportion has remained around 44 percent in recent years. A large number of these births are to women in relationships. In 2007, just over half of all births outside marriage were to cohabiting parents (CSO 2008).

Since 1980, the average age of mothers at first birth has increased, both within and outside of marriage (see Figure 1). In 2009, the average age of a mother who gave birth to a child within marriage was 33 years, just over five years older than those who gave birth outside of marriage. The age gap between mothers who were having their first children within and outside marriage is even greater (see Punch 2007).

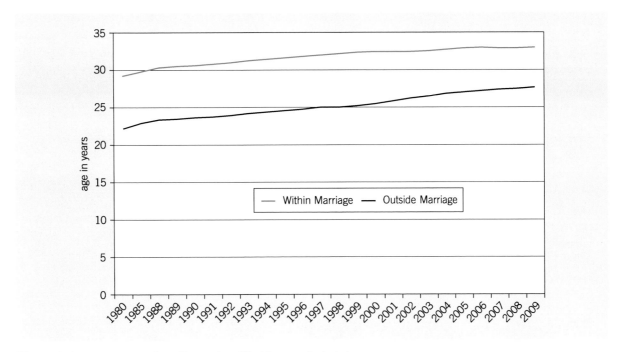

**Figure 1** Average age of mothers classified by marital status
(Source: CSO Principal Statistics 2011)

## Lone Parents

Sociology highlights that inequality is related to families and family structure in a complex way. One such inequality is that lone parents are more likely than any other social group to be living in poverty. As births outside marriage have increased, so has the number of lone parents (see Macionis and Plummer 2008, p.596 for a discussion of lone parents). Female-headed lone parent families grew by an appreciable 3.1 percent per annum between the 1981 and 2006 Census of Population (Punch 2007). In the 2006 Census, never-married lone parents accounted for 36 percent of all lone parent families while in 29 percent of families the lone parent was a widow. In a further 30 percent of families the lone parent was separated or divorced (CSO 2007). In the 2006 Census, 9 percent of lone parents aged 15–59 were lone fathers (see Lunn *et al.* 2010). Current sociological research in this area aims to aid our understanding of lone parent families and how they influence children's development.

## Women Remaining Childless

Childlessness among women has been rising. In 2002, households comprising of childless couples represented the fastest growing category – up 38.7 percent in six years (CSO 2002).

## Living Alone

More people in Ireland are now living alone. One person households accounted for 22.4 percent of all households in the State in the 2006 Census. Over half (56 percent) of one person households were occupied by single (never married) persons. In addition, household size fell to 2.8 compared with 2.94 four years earlier (CSO 2007).

## Gay and Lesbian Couples

In 2010, the Civil Partnership and Certain Rights and Obligations of Cohabitants Act provided an extensive package of rights, obligations and protections for same-sex couples who register as civil partners. The debates surrounding the new law were a surprisingly low-key affair, perhaps reflecting a change in cultural values and behaviour. In April 2011, Barry Dignam and Hugh Walsh became the first male couple in Ireland to avail of the new legislation. The Act also established, for unmarried opposite-sex couples and unregistered same-sex couples, a redress scheme to give protection to a financially dependent person at the end of a long-term cohabiting relationship. The Irish Farmers Association lobbied against the legislation, in part over fears it could lead to the division of family farms. Treoir, a body which promotes the rights of unmarried parents and their children, launched a national information campaign on the new law.

Although still small in absolute number, same-sex couples are becoming more common. Figures from the 1996, 2002 and 2006 Census record a very steep increase in the number of same-sex couples, rising from 150 to 2,090 over the ten-year period. It is likely, however, that a substantial proportion of this increase is due to a change of wording in the question with respect to partnership on the census form.

## Older People

About 11 percent of the population (467,900 persons) were aged 65 and over in the 2006 Census. Ireland has the lowest proportion of its population aged 65 and over among EU countries and is well below the EU average of nearly 17 percent. The number of people aged 65 and over in Ireland has however increased by 54,000 in the last decade (CSO 2007).

## Life Expectancy

Life expectancy for men and women in Ireland has increased. In the four years between 2002 and 2006 life expectancy increased by 1.7 years for males and 1.3 years for females. In 1926, male life expectancy was 57.4 years while it was slightly higher for females at 57.9 years. This gender gap of 0.5 years continued to increase until 1986 when it stood at 5.7 years and has been decreasing gradually ever since (CSO 2009).

## Conclusion

In conclusion, Irish sociology has played an important role in providing a critical perspective on 'moral' issues in relation to the Irish family up to the 1980s. Since then, sociologists have continued to highlight inequalities in family formation and how various inequalities can be reproduced through families. Irish sociologists continue to work with government agencies and policy makers on a number of topics; for example identifying families at risk of poverty or domestic abuse, documenting increasing diversity in family types, and highlighting the continued division of labour or power relations within households. In addition, various private and government funded family organisations continue to highlight the importance of family issues.

> ## Key Questions: Irish Demography
>
> ➤ What factors may explain the low take-up of divorce in Ireland?
>
> ➤ International evidence shows that children in stable two-parent families perform better across a range of educational outcomes compared to children from one-parent families.
>
> ➤ Why might that be the case?

# Globalisation and Work

In the previous section we have seen the types of demographic changes that have shaped recent Irish society. But why have these changes in Irish family size and formation occurred? One contributing factor to this process of social and demographic change is the economic development of Ireland. In this section we will explore this economic development and the impact that the policy of industrialisation and the openness to globalisation has had on shaping Irish society and the working lives of Irish men and women. We will return to the more general theme of globalisation in a later section of the chapter.

Since the mid-20th century, Irish economic policy has embraced a policy of modernisation (Connolly 2003, p.174). This policy shift was as much influenced by the dominance of modernisation theory after the Second World War as by the economic failure of successive Irish governments since the establishment of the Irish Free State in 1922. Even before the War of Independence, Ireland was predominantly an agricultural economy, with industrial development being limited to the textiles industry based predominantly in Belfast. Having missed out on the process of industrialisation (O'Malley 1989 cited in Mahon 1994, p.1282), the newly independent Ireland relied heavily on its agricultural sector to provide economic growth. However, the initial focus on an export based agricultural economy became unstuck as relations soured between Ireland and its main market, Britain, culminating in an Economic War from 1932 to

1938. As a result, a policy of **economic protectionism** was developed whereby high tariffs were placed on all imports in a bid to increase demand for local produce which in turn would increase productivity and competition. Despite initial economic returns, the policy of economic protectionism had the overall effect of stagnating the Irish economy. The extent of the economic depression of the late 1940s and 1950s was exemplified by rising emigration levels, with as many as 400,000 people emigrating from Ireland during the 1950s alone. Faced with such a bleak economic outlook, in 1958 the Taoiseach (Prime Minister) Sean Lemass, influenced by the work of TJ Whitaker, developed an economic development policy that committed the Irish State to the process of industrialisation and modernisation. In the First Programme of Economic Expansion 1958–1963, two aims were established: Firstly, to attract foreign investment into Ireland so as to help establish an export focused industry. This was to be achieved through offering State grants to multinational companies (MNCs), and by offering tax relief, employee grants and other incentives to encourage them to set up in Ireland. Secondly, manufacturing industries were to be promoted as the new base for the Irish economy. This industrialisation policy was further cemented in the subsequent Second Programme for Economic Expansion 1964–1970, and the Third Programme for Economic Expansion 1969–1972.

## Gender and Industrialisation

During the 1960s, Ireland pursued a policy of export-orientated industrialisation through the establishment of multinational corporations in Ireland. A common practice among MNCs is the sourcing of cheap labour, and many of the MNCs were eager to hire Irish women to work in these factories. However, the Industrial Development Authority (IDA), the agency in charge of sourcing and supporting foreign development in Ireland, while initially supportive of this feminising of the industrial labour force issued a policy in 1969 which offered a range of attractive set-up grants all of which were underwritten by the proviso that the workforce employed by the company should be 75 percent male (Mahon 1994, p.1285). Historically, Irish women's participation in industrial work had been one of restrictions. For instance, the Conditions of Employment Act 1935 limited the numbers of hours which women could work in any employment sector (O'Dowd 1987 cited in Mahon 1994, p.1283) as well as restricted women's industrial

employment opportunities to working in textile, shoe production and confectionary companies (Wickham 1982 cited in Mahon 1994, p.1283). Furthermore, a Marriage Ban was introduced in 1932 which prevented married women from working in the Civil Service. As a result, many women had to leave their public sector jobs once they married (Pyle 1990, p.68). This discriminatory IDA employment policy had a direct impact on the composition of the workforce in Ireland. From 1970 to 1974, 74 percent of the Irish workforce was male, with women making up the rest, in the process earning below the national average wage (Mahon 1994, p.1285).

Though Irelands' membership of the EEC in 1972 helped to bring about a decade of equality employment legislation – such as the removal of the Marriage Bar from 1973–77 (Pyle 1990, p.68), the Employment Equality Legislation (equal pay) (1974), the Equal Treatment Act (1977), and the Protection of Employee Act (maternity leave) in 1981 (Mahon 1994, p.126) – women were particularly underrepresented in the work force. Overall the rate of female participation in the workforce rose from 8 percent in 1971 to 14 percent in 1975 and 27 percent in 1987. The numbers of married women in the workforce also rose over the intervening period. In 1971, 13.6 percent of women in the workforce were married, this increased to 30.2 percent in 1982 and 39.6 percent in 1987 (Mahon 1994, p.1286). However, it is important to state that this relatively low increase in female labour participation was not the sole consequence of the implementation of a "**patriarchal** state policy" (Mahon 1994, p.1285) regarding female employment. Rather it was the combination of this discriminatory policy and the lack of jobs available throughout the 1970s and 1980s in Ireland (Mahon 1994, p.1285). This relatively low rate of labour market participation for women coincides with the high marriage rates as evidenced in Table 1.

### Stop and Think

➤ Would you consider the Irish workplace to be patriarchal?

➤ Does it prioritise male workers over female workers? If so, in what ways?

## Unemployment and Emigration

Despite the pursuit of industrialisation the Irish economy has always struggled with an "inadequate rate of employment growth" (Kennedy 1993, p.3) and surplus labour (Kennedy 1993, p.10). The ineffective level of job creation in Ireland can be attributed to Ireland's over-reliance on a foreign investment model of economic development. As a result, too much emphasis was placed on attracting foreign investment at the expense of fostering an indigenous economy. This lack of a home-grown economic base is in turn compounded by the fact that the policy of industrialisation has also contributed to the emergence of an export-orientated economy where industrial goods are sold on the international market. Together, these factors have made the Irish economy particularly vulnerable to international markets, crises and the flows of global economy. For instance, the energy crises of the 1970s and the international economic recession of the 1980s had a devastating impact on the Irish economy with widespread factory closures, unemployment and emigration. Throughout the 1980s Ireland had poor economic performance (Kirby 2004, p.206). In 1985 the long-term unemployment level reached 100,000 and did not fall below that figure for the following decade (O'Connell 1997 cited in O'Hearn 1998, pp.129–130). The number of households in poverty rose from 28.5 percent in 1987 to 34.6 percent in 1994 (Callan *et al.*, 1996 cited in O'Hearn 1998, p.135). Unemployment was considered the biggest obstacle to Irish development in the 1990s (Keane 1992). By January 1993 unemployment reached 300,000, or 21 percent of the domestic labour force (Kennedy 1993, p.1). Equally, emigration levels continued to rise. Between 1991 and 1996, 175,000 people left Ireland, approximately 33,000–35,000 per annum. Interestingly, two thirds of this figure was made up of people between the ages of 15 and 24 years (Corcoran 1998 cited in Share *et al.*, 2007, p.159).

## The Celtic Tiger 1994–2008

The Celtic Tiger boom refers to a period from 1994 to 2008 when the Irish economy underwent a period of unprecedented and rapid economic growth. The ensuing rise in employment, affluence and prosperity of Irish society caused many to reflect that 'traditional' Ireland had become completely modernised and capitalist in outlook.

During the Celtic Tiger years the level of employment rose from 51.7 percent in 1993 to 68.1 percent in 2006. Equally, unemployment fell from 15.6 percent to 4.3 percent over the same period (CSO 2006a cited in Kirby 2008, p.13). This in turn led to Ireland experiencing

employment growth in new employment sectors, especially in the construction, financial and services sectors (CSO cited in Kirby 2008, p.19). One industrial sector which found particular success was the high-tech sector, with Dell, Hewlett Packard and Intel, among others, establishing their European headquarters in Ireland. It has been reported that in 1999, a third of the PCs sold in Europe were manufactured in Ireland (Barry and Curran 1999 cited in Cross and Linehan 2006, p.30). The growth in the services sector had a particular impact on widening female participation in the workplace, especially for married women (O'Hearn 1998, pp.116, 130). In 1993, 435,000 or 38.5 percent of women were in employment. This rose to 787,000 in 2004 (O'Connell and Russell 2007 cited in Kirby 2008, p.20). These increases in employment were also accompanied by an increase in income levels. From 1987 to 1994 average income levels rose by 34 percent. This was followed by a growth in average income of 57 percent from 1994 to 2001. From 2001 to 2005 average income rates began to slow down considerably, only rising by 7 percent over that period (Walsh 2007 cited in Kirby 2008, p.19). As a result, by 2005 Ireland was the second wealthiest country in Europe after Luxembourg in terms of gross domestic product (Kirby 2008, p.19). It was also reported that the rate of **consistent poverty** fell from 15 percent in 1994 to 6 percent in 2000 (Lee 2003, p.57). Following a changeover to a new EU-SILC (European Survey on Income and Living Conditions) **methodology** the rate of consistent poverty rose slightly to 9 percent in 2003 but fell again back to 7 percent in 2005 (Walsh 2007, p.36).

For the first time in the history of the Irish State the shadow of emigration no longer had Ireland in its sights, and inward migration became a newly emerging demographic trend. It wasn't until 1997 that we saw a decline in emigration levels, with 29,000 people emigrating that year (MacEinri 2000 cited in Share *et al.* 2007, p.159). This downward trend continued throughout the Celtic Tiger era – falling to 18,500 in 2004 (Share *et al.* 2007, p.159). Another sign of the economic prosperity of Celtic Tiger Ireland was the increase in inward migration. For instance, during the first four months of 2002, 47,500 people emigrated to Ireland (CSO 2002a cited in Share *et al.* 2007, p.164). The 2006 Census reveals that Ireland was an attractive location for economic migrants during the Celtic Tiger years (Onyeljelem 2005, p.70). Out of a total population of 4,171,203, 3,706,683 declared themselves to be of Irish nationality, leaving 419,733 non-Irish living in Ireland at the time of the Census. According to the statistics, this included 112,548 UK citizens, 163,227 EU citizens, 24,425 from the rest of Europe, 46,952 Asian nationals, 21,124 US nationals, 35,326 African nationals, and 16,131 classed themselves as 'other' nationals. A further 45,597 did not state their nationality (CSO 2006). While many commentators attributed this migratory trend to the process of globalisation in general – as well as to the expansion of the EU to include a number of Eastern European countries (e.g. King-O'Riain 2008, Komolafe 2002 cited in Conlon 2009, p.102) – a particular cohort of these migrants were in fact returning Irish emigrants. Interestingly, returning Irish emigrants made up between 23 percent and 50 percent of net inward migration to Ireland from 1996 to 2006 (CSO 2006; Ni Laoire 2008 cited in Conlon 2009, p.102).

## A Closer Look

### Goodbye to the Celtic Tiger

For an analysis of the causes of the collapse of the Celtic Tiger economy see: Allen, K. (2009) *Ireland's Economic Crash: A Radical Agenda for Change*, Liffey Press: Dublin.

## Evaluating the Achievements of the Celtic Tiger

The sharp reversal of economic fortunes that Ireland experienced thanks to the Celtic Tiger economy led many commentators to remark how beneficial globalisation and foreign direct investment can be for small countries, especially those who modernise late (Kirby 2004, pp.205–206). Here, Ireland's openness to international trade markets and its incentivisation of foreign capital investment was acknowledged for its foresight (e.g. FitzGerald 2000, Sweeney 2003 cited in Kirby 2004, p.207). In fact, O'Riain (2000 cited in Kirby 2004, p.207) considered Ireland to be a "flexible developmental state" and so it was better positioned to benefit from globalisation. In addition to celebrating Ireland's modernisation policy, others highlighted the role played by other factors, such as the availability of an English speaking, highly educated workforce with IT skills, the availability of an educated female pool of labour (O'Connor 1999), the overall stable macroeconomic climate of the late 1990s and early 2000s, and the establishment of a new form of social governance called 'social partnership', which was "a system of negotiated economic and social

governance" (O'Donnell 2000 quoted in Kirby 2004, p.210) where politicians and civil servants met with trade unions, representatives from the community and voluntary sector and the business and agriculture sectors, with the net effect of suppressing wages, reducing the likelihood of industrial disputes and increased labour flexibility (MacSharry and White 2000, Kirby 2004, pp.210–211).

Granted, all of these factors played their part in contributing to the economic success of the Celtic Tiger era. Others, however, like Kirby (2004, 2005), were eager to highlight "the social costs of economic success under these conditions" (Kirby 2004, p.206). Despite the significant economic growth, it was quickly deciphered that the benefits of this growth were unevenly distributed, both spatially and socially, and grossly mismanaged and administered by the Irish State. Despite record levels of employment "at-risk-of-poverty" figures reveal a rise from 19.3 percent in 2000 to 20.8 percent in 2005 (CSO 2006b cited in Kirby 2008, p.21). Households where there was an unemployed, disabled, ill or retired person were more at risk of poverty than any other category from 1994 to 2005 (Murphy 2007 cited in Kirby 2008, p.21). On closer inspection, household poverty rates also rose from 3.2 percent in 1994 to seven percent in 2005 for households where there was employment. In 2001, 23 percent of farmers' households lived in poverty. Clearly, households on a lower income did not fare well in Celtic Tiger Ireland (Kirby 2008, p.22). These income-distribution anomalies highlight the inequalities that underpinned the Celtic Tiger and how it perpetuated a strong trend of polarisation between the working, middle and upper classes. Such a realisation led Smeeding and Nolan (2004 quoted in Kirby 2008, p.22) to remark that "among the richest OECD nations Ireland has the second highest level of inequality". This level of income inequality was compounded by low State investment in public services and a high cost of living which in their sum placed more challenges upon the lives of the marginalised in Irish society (Kirby 2008, p.41).

## Requiem for the Celtic Tiger Economy

The economic prosperity achieved under the Celtic Tiger was lauded as the successful culmination of a process of industrialisation and modernisation that was initially developed in the 1950s. However, with the onset of an international economic recession in 2009, Irish society has learned first hand how mobile and unpredictable global capitalism can be. The contraction of global markets

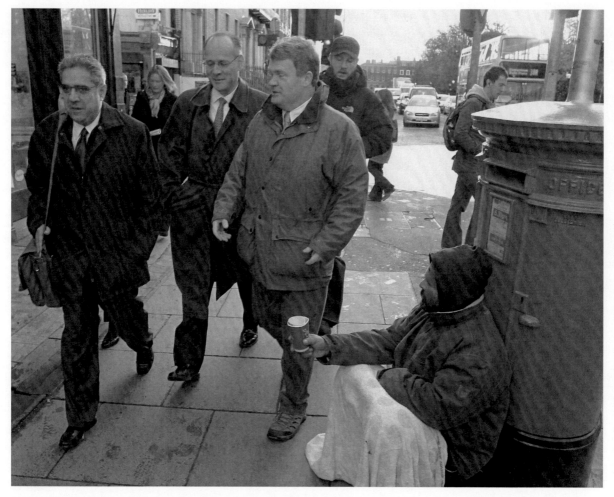

**Figure 2** The International Monetary Fund's Ajai Chopra walks past a homeless man in Dublin on his way to negotiate the IMF 'Bail-Out' of the Irish State in 2010
(Image: Peter Morrison/AP)

revealed the existence of an overheated construction economy and a poorly regulated banking sector, which, in their summation, highlighted a liquidity problem with the State finances as well as in the Irish banking sector as a whole.

As a result, Ireland is experiencing negative economic growth and the collapse of the construction sector contributed to an increase in the numbers of unemployed from 4.4 percent in August 2007 to 13.3 percent in May 2010 (OECD 2010, p.1). In May 2011 the unemployment rate had risen to 14.1 percent (CSO 2011). One group of workers particularly vulnerable to this economic downturn would appear to be young men who previously were employed in the construction sector. Following a general election in February 2011 the Fine Gael/Labour Party coalition government are currently implementing a number of labour market activation polices, such as graduate internship programmes and back to education or

retraining schemes, to address the youthful profile of those unemployed in Ireland. It remains to be seen how successful these initiatives will be, especially when you consider that such strategies do very little to create (sustainable) paid employment for people.

Another indicator of the state of the post-Celtic Tiger economy is our emigration figures. In April 2009, 18,400 Irish people emigrated from Ireland. A year later this figure rose to 27,700 (CSO 21 September 2010). Irish people then represented 42 percent of the 65,300 people who emigrated from Ireland from April 2009 to April 2010. Over the same 12 month period there was a sharp fall in the number of people immigrating to Ireland, from 57,300 in April 2009 to 30,800 in April 2010 (CSO 21 September 2010). Based on these figures it would appear that in April 2010 34,500 more people left Ireland than moved here. This represents the highest level of net outward migration experienced in Ireland since 1989

**Figure 3** An unfinished retail park and a closed factory in Limerick
(Reproduced by kind permission © Martin Power (2011))

(CSO 21 September 2010). It would appear that emigration is again being used as a 'safety valve' for the failures of the Irish economy.

In conclusion, an examination of the economic development of Ireland reveals that as a 'late industrialising peripheral economy' (Mahon 1994, p.1278) Ireland has benefited as well as suffered from its pursuit of an export-orientated, foreign investment directed economy. Once promoted as the 'poster child' for globalisation – the social and economic benefits of the unrestricted movement of capital, resources and people around the globe – the recent demise of the Celtic Tiger economy reveals how 'lopsided' (Bauman 2001, p.7) globalisation is, and the fickle nature of global capital and the prosperity it brings. While many Irish citizens were content with their newly found affluence, and expressed their economic wealth through a process of conspicuous consumption (see Activity: globalisation and consumption for more information), Irish sociologists were more critical of the type of economic growth experienced during the Celtic Tiger years and its effects on Irish society. Interestingly, as Kirby (2005, p.41) remarked, much of this critique remained within academic circles, as it was met with a certain degree of derision and 'ridicule' in the public sphere (in particular some media organisations). It would appear in this instance that Irish society was happy to amuse itself with the idea of personal wealth and possessions rather than adopt a concern for the wider social implications of the Celtic Tiger economy. In the following section we will explore in more detail how possessions intersect with class and class aspirations. But before that there will be a discussion of the role of class in Irish society.

## Table 2 Luxury cars registered from 1990–97

| Year | Audi | BMW | Mercedes |
|------|------|-----|----------|
| 1990 | 648 | 935 | 799 |
| 1991 | 640 | 814 | 804 |
| 1992 | 863 | 744 | 649 |
| 1993 | 635 | 596 | 606 |
| 1994 | 813 | 808 | 1126 |
| 1995 | 1055 | 1052 | 1059 |
| 1996 | 1470 | 1174 | 1452 |
| 1997 | 1563 | 1780 | 1869 |

(Source: adapted from Allen (2000, p.69))

## Key Questions: Globalisation and Work

➤ What actions would you like to see the Irish government take to revitalise the Irish economy?

➤ Should the export-orientated focus of the Irish economy be abandoned? If so, what alternative model of economic policy would you like to see develop?

➤ Do you think that the Irish public sphere is open to sociological perspectives on, and recommendations for, solving the current economic crisis?

## Table 3 Luxury cars registered from 2000–10

| Year | Audi | BMW | Mercedes | Chrysler Jeep | Land Rover | Total new registered |
|------|------|-----|----------|---------------|------------|----------------------|
| 2000 | 2260 | 4005 | 4218 | 231 | 0 | 230,804 |
| 2001 | 2312 | 4043 | 4586 | 245 | 1531 | 164,772 |
| 2002 | 3125 | 4247 | 3882 | 271 | 1346 | 156,115 |
| 2003 | 2999 | 3688 | 4921 | 244 | 1386 | 145,331 |
| 2004 | 3500 | 4820 | 4707 | 353 | 1250 | 154,141 |
| 2005 | 4587 | 5623 | 4875 | 364 | 1449 | 171,732 |
| 2006 | 2880 | 4490 | 4013 | 347 | 1191 | 129,534 |
| 2007 | 5276 | 6952 | 5275 | 296 | 2077 | 186,540 |
| 2008 | 5059 | 5627 | 4056 | 161 | 1402 | 151,607 |
| 2009 | 2388 | 1405 | 1370 | 33 | 89 | 57,460 |
| 2010 | 532 | 538 | 581 | 1 | 29 | 16,595 |

(Source: SIMI New Vehicle Registration Statistics, www.simi.ie)

# Social Class

Sociology is concerned with the issue of social stratification, which can take on a number of forms, either singly or in combination. As an illustration of this we begin by examining social class, before turning to the issue of ethnicity.

Irish society is often self-imagined as a classless society and class-based discourses have historically been frowned upon in the public arena. There is a shared acceptance of neoliberal principles and those ideological differences that do exist between the two main centre-right political parties (Fianna Fáil and Fine Gael) are framed more by Civil War Politics (and therefore competing versions of nationalist **ideologies** which have traditionally shaped public discourse) rather than class-based allegiances (Coakley 1999). Indeed, all mainstream Irish political parties practise a **clientelist politics** (Gallagher and Komito 1999), which individualises problems rather than seeing them in class terms.

Despite the prevalence of common-sense understandings, class inequality has been and remains a significant element of Irish Society (Share *et al.* 2007, p.171). The 'myth of a classless Ireland' was perpetuated most strongly during the Celtic Tiger economic boom. Populist economic commentators such as David McWilliams argued that "the nation is blurring and the most significant aspect of this is in class. Ireland is becoming the most middle-class, suburban nation in Europe and the most startling development . . . has been the rapid **social mobility** the country is experiencing. . . . We are now a middle-class nation" (McWilliams 2005, p.15). But was such social mobility evidence of the '**death of class**' in Irish society?

It is quite true that from the 1970s onwards Ireland experienced considerable mobility into the professional and managerial classes. However, simultaneously Ireland saw the percentage of **working poor** increase from 3.2 percent in 1994 to 7.4 percent in 2000, to 9.8 percent in 2004 (CSO 2005 cited in Murphy 2007, p.119) and to almost 14 percent by 2006 (NESF 2006, p.ix). Moreover, there is strong evidence that the relative advantages enjoyed by the higher socio-economic groups were largely maintained in spite of the social mobility that McWilliams (2005) speaks of. Whelan and Layte (2007) found that while **absolute mobility** increased during the 1990s and early 2000s, "**relative mobility** and **equality of opportunity** stayed stable over time". Tellingly, they reported that disparities in opportunities between those at either end of the socio-economic ladder were "greater in Ireland than in other European countries" (Share *et al.* 2007, p.171). Indeed, the NESF (2006, p.ix) reported that the wealthiest 20 percent of Ireland's "working-age population" earned 12 times more than the poorest 20 percent of the population. Ireland continued to have a comparatively "high degree of economic inequality" in spite of our economic boom, and significant sections of the Irish population "experience deprivation and exclusion as a result of inadequate financial resources" which has a direct connection to social class (Share *et al.* 2007, pp.178–180).

## Class, Meritocracy and Education

In a **meritocracy** the individual alone determines success and failure (Drudy and Lynch 1993; Considine and Dukelow 2009). In essence, it is "a society where ability and effort count for more than privilege and inherited status" (Hurn 1993, p.45). According to this ideology, limitless opportunities exist for all individuals to go as far as their own merit takes them (see Considine and Dukelow 2009, pp.287–299). Proponents of this system argue that a meritocratic society is a more just and productive society, where distinctions based on criteria such as class, race and gender will diminish in time (McNamee and Miller 2004). Ireland has been (self)portrayed as a meritocratic society, but how accurate is this portrayal?

Globally, **neoliberalism** has moulded the education sector to the needs of global capitalism (see Mulderrig 2003, Hirtt 2004). In Ireland (and elsewhere), education now largely determines occupational success. Marxist education theorists hold that it is inevitable that such market-oriented education systems reflect the features of capitalist inequality (Greaves *et al.* 2007). In that context they argue that a meritocratic ideology is very attractive to the dominant classes, as it not alone justifies their privileged position in society, on the basis of their natural "giftedness" (Bourdieu 1977), but it also helps to gain acceptance for this system from the underprivileged classes and effectively absolves the State and wider society of any responsibility for inequality in the education system (see Considine and Dukelow 2009, pp.287–299). So does class impact on educational attainment in Ireland?

By briefly examining the second level education system and access to third level education in Ireland we can clearly see the impact of social class on educational attainment. A small number of Ireland's fee-paying second level schools, for example, have very strong connections to the top of the social hierarchy (see Courtois 2010, Kennedy 2010) and their alumni contain a disproportionate number of individuals in key leadership positions in politics, business and the legal professions (Rice 2006, Flynn 2008, CRO 2009). The "smaller class sizes", extracurricular "innovation" and the "holistic approach to education" offered by these exclusive schools, is said to be responsible for their continued success (Butler 2009). Yet with fees ranging up to €25,000 a year, it is clear that such private education largely remains the preserve of the upper middle classes in Irish society (Walshe and Hickey, 2008). Such fees raise an annual income of €119 million, a bottom line figure which does not include the many other contributions that are sought by these schools to maintain their high standards (Walshe and Hickey, 2008). Despite benefiting from this very healthy income stream, such fee-paying schools also receive a very generous subsidy of taxpayers' money

each year (Special group on public service numbers and expenditure programmes 2009).

What about access to third level education? Is social class a factor here? In 2004 the then Minister for Education and Science, Mary Hanafin, stated that:

> "Equity of access must be an integral feature of our higher education system if that system is to deliver for individuals, society and the economy . . . There is now general agreement that individuals should be able to enter and successfully participate in higher education, regardless of social, economic or cultural background" (Higher Education Authority 2004, p.5).

Such statements were indicative of an evolving Irish government **discourse**. Tackling social exclusion through education, achieving equity of educational opportunity and encouraging access to and successful participation in higher education have all been national policy priorities in Ireland since the mid-1990s (Higher

**Figure 4** Glenstal Abbey: A fee-paying second level school in County Limerick
(Reproduced by kind permission © Martin Power (2011))

Education Authority 2004, p.9). But how successfully have these policy priorities been implemented?

Access to third level education has expanded considerably, but for many working-class children going to college remains an improbable dream. Inequalities in participation ratios show both continuity and change over time (O'Connell, Clancy and McCoy 2006, p.65). Continuity is evidenced in the persistence of class inequalities in access to third level education, while change is indicated in some lower socio-economic groups reducing their disadvantage, partly as a consequence of more advantaged groups reaching saturation point (O'Connell, McCoy and Clancy 2006, p.312). However, it is clear that there remain major differences between socio-economic groups in terms of the levels of participation in higher education in Ireland. Empirical evidence shows that while rising participation rates have assisted all socio-economic groups, working-class groups have not gained any great advantage in relative terms (see ESRI 2006, Action Group on Access 2001, Drudy and Lynch 1993).

At a national level, overall rates of admission to higher education in Ireland rose from 20 percent in 1980, to 44 percent in 1998, and to 55 percent by 2004. It is interesting to note that in 1993 Raftery and Hout suggested growth in the numbers progressing to third level would improve the educational chances of formerly disadvantaged groups. We have seen large increases in participation occurring for those lower socio-economic groups with very low rates in 1980. This is clearly evident in the participation rate of the unskilled manual group, which increased from 3 percent in 1980 to 21 percent by 1998 (Clancy 2001, p.161). The participation rate in third level education for the semi and unskilled socio-economic groups further improved to between 33 percent and 40 percent by 2004, while over the same period the skilled manual socio-economic group almost doubled its participation to a range[4] of 50 percent to 60 percent up from 32 percent in 1998 (ESRI 2006, see also O'Connell, McCoy and Clancy 2006, p.327). However it must also be noted that at the other end of the socio-economic spectrum, the progressive increase in the estimated participation rate of those groups, which were already 'overrepresented' in 1980, is striking. The higher professional group's participation rate reached saturation level, with an estimate of full participation by 1998, up from 85 percent in 1992 (see O'Connell, McCoy and Clancy 2006, p.324; Clancy 2001). The employers and managers group had a participation rate of 84 percent by 1998 (up from 42 percent in 1980), while the farmers group reached a participation rate of 72 percent by 1998 (Clancy 2001, p.161, Action Group on Access 2001, pp.33–34).

In spite of a stated policy priority to increase access to third level education for disadvantaged socio-economic groups, we can see from Table 4 that in 2004 participation ratios in respect of higher professionals, farmers, employers and managers and lower professionals remained above one, illustrating that these groups have advantaged positions in terms of accessing higher education. The share of children of skilled manual workers among new entrants increased and became roughly proportional to their share of the population of college entry age in 2004. A similar improvement in access is evident among the semi-skilled and unskilled manual workers, though these groups remain significantly underrepresented in terms of their proportional share of new entrants to third level relative to their share of the population (O'Connell, Clancy and McCoy 2006, pp.47–51, see also ESRI 2006, O'Connell, McCoy and Clancy 2006, pp.319–322). Therefore, very little has changed since Clancy (2001, pp.158–159) reported that more than 58 percent of third level entrants in 1998 came from just four socio-economic groups (higher professional, lower professional, employers and managers and farmers), in spite of these groups making up just over 37 percent of the relevant national population. All of this has occurred in spite of the abolition of third level tuition fees in Ireland in 1996 (McCoy and Smyth 2003, O'Connell, McCoy and Clancy 2006, p.315), which was designed to remedy this situation.

Moreover, major differences remain between socio-economic groups in terms of the type of college[5] students attend (O'Connell, Clancy and McCoy 2006, p.50, Clancy, 2001). In 2004 we see that 65.1 percent of entrants to university came from just four socio-economic groups (higher professional, lower professional, employers and managers and farmers groups). In addition these four groups made up 51.2 percent of entrants to Institutes of Technology, almost 59 percent of entrants to Colleges

---

[4] The data gathered on who went to college in 2004 had methodological difficulties, with the result that class-specific participation ratios and rates are estimated as ranges. See Chapter 3 in O'Connell, Clancy and McCoy 2006, or O'Connell, McCoy and Clancy 2006, pp.316–318 for a full explanation.

[5] See the Higher Education Authority website www.hea.ie for a list of these colleges. The Universities offer courses up to doctoral level. Institutes of Technology primarily offer courses to certificate and diploma level, though some degree courses are provided. The courses offered in ITs are primarily technical courses. The Colleges of Education prepare individuals for careers as primary school teachers.

**Table 4** Fathers' socio-economic status of entrants to higher education and the adjusted participation ratio for 2004 in comparison to fathers' socio-economic status of entrants to higher education and the participation ratio for 1998

| Socio-economic groups | Higher education entrants in 2004 % | Adjusted participation ratio for 2004 | Higher education entrants in 1998 % | Participation ratio for 1998 % |
|---|---|---|---|---|
| Employers and Managers | 23.1 | 1.2 | 21.6 | 1.46 |
| Higher Professional | 11.1 | 2.5 | 10.1 | 1.94 |
| Lower Professional | 11.5 | 1.2 | 10.1 | 1.31 |
| Non Manual | 8.9 | 0.5 | 9.4 | 0.63 |
| Manual Skilled | 13.5 | 0.9 | 13.6 | 0.71 |
| Semi Skilled | 5.7 | 0.5 | 7.4 | 0.7 |
| Un Skilled | 5 | 0.7 | 3.1 | 0.36 |
| Own Account Workers | 8.2 | 1.2 | 7.2 | 0.92 |
| Farmers | 12.7 | 1.6 | 16.6 | 1.77 |
| Agricultural Workers | 0.4 | 0.3 | 0.7 | 0.35 |
| Total % | 100 | – | 100 | – |

(Sources: O'Connell, Clancy and McCoy 2006, p.47, Clancy 2001, p.159)

of Education and over 61 percent of entrants to other colleges. It is quite profound to note that the employers and managers group made up the highest percentage of new entrants in all four categories of college.

In conclusion, the Irish education system has seen a significant increase in educational attainment across all levels of the system yet class inequalities within the Irish education system have remained relatively unaltered. Indeed, the increased commodification and credential-isation of education when taken together with the role that education plays in the distribution of "social advantage" through the "conversion" of educational qualifications into employment has resulted in the already "advantaged classes" successfully reproducing their dominant positions in Irish society time and time again (Share *et al.* 2007, p.230).

## Stop and Think

➤ Should we be satisfied that the absolute participation rates of lower socio-economic groups in third level education in Ireland have increased considerably over the last number of years, or should relative participation rates be of paramount interest?

➤ Think about the significance of using one set of participation rates rather than the other.

## Class, Identities and Masculinity

Class does not exist in isolation. It intersects with a number of other areas, most notably identity, gender and ethnicity. Those subscribing to the 'death of class' thesis no longer see social class as being an element of our **social identity** that we strongly identify with. Others (see Bourdieu 1979, Skeggs 1997) have reconfigured our understanding of class to focus on the cultural aspect. In doing so they demonstrate that processes of dis-identifying from a (devalued) working-class identity are in fact "the result of class processes" (Bottero 2004, p.989). This, in turn, suggests that class still remains an important ele-ment of our social identity.

The possession of 'valued **cultural capital**' varies according to social class. There is a "class-based prefer-ence in status symbols" (Henslin 2010, p.267) and tastes, with certain types of clothing, cars, bags etc. acting as visible signifiers of a person's class background. This was extremely evident in Ireland during the Celtic Tiger boom when the country was awash with "conspicuous consumption" (Veblen 1899). A person's accent is also identified as an indicator of class and status. Limerick, for example, is regarded as a city in which class divisions are still particularly strongly felt. A strong urban Limerick accent is associated with the stereotypical 'skobe'.[6] In this case, accent or **linguistic capital** is a form of embodied cultural capital, which is devalued because it is decoded as being a cultural manifestation of (devalued) working/under-class identity. As such, our cultural capital, which is shaped by our class origin, in turn impacts upon the class position which we end up in.

In that context it is also interesting to look at how performing **masculinity** is entwined with such classed negotiations of social identity. While the intersection of class and gender has been widely examined in the US (see for example Adair 2001) and the UK (see for example Skeggs 1997) it remains under-researched in an Irish context. A recent study by an Irish sociologist has, however, demonstrated how class and gender identities are performed.

Barnes' (2010) research focused on the daily lives and experiences which structure and shape the understandings and constructions of classed and gendered identities among two groups of young, white, Irish schoolboys, drawn from both working-class and middle-class backgrounds. The key aim of her research was to understand more about how young men construct and define their masculine identities within specific local contexts. **Masculinity** in Ireland is understood primarily in terms of social class, whether or not that is openly acknowledged. The relational nature of masculinities, which sees local context define and demarcate what is appropriate, is clearly evident. The boys in Barnes' study mobilise locally inflected, complex and very different understandings of masculinities around key issues such as the notion of 'trouble', their appearance, and most importantly around the notion of the 'other'. Getting into 'trouble' is viewed as a desirable masculine attribute, but is one that has more resonance for the working-class boys who are, by virtue of where they come from, closer to popular perceptions of the 'dangerous' male youth. Currently, public concerns about what to 'do' with and 'about' young working-class men are couched in and hidden behind the cloaking of gender debates and the '**crisis in masculinity**' (Skeggs 2004, pp.87–88, Walkerdine *et al.* 2001, p.111). There is no crisis for young middle-class men, there is, however, a growing issue whereby public expectations of the role of young working-class men are at odds with the reality of many poor young men's lives. Thus, when middle-class boys behave badly, get into trouble, etc., it is "because this is what young men do". However, when similar 'bad' behaviour is engaged in by males from socially and economically disadvantaged communities, the behaviour is now understood by the middle-class boys and the general public as being dangerous, most often leading to the suggestion that such young men are 'troublemakers' who should be 'locked up'. As it stands, neither group of young men in Barnes' (2010) study knew much about the daily lives, experiences and communities of the other, and both perceived a significant distance between working-class and middle-class lives or, to use their own language, between the lives of 'skobes' and 'pure posh lads'. Both the working-class and middle-class boys position the other as being, respectively, overly masculine (aggressive and dangerous) or as being inadequately masculine (nerdish and 'soft'). The mistrust, fear and lack of knowledge expressed by both in relation to the other is problematic, particularly in a context which seeks greater integration and **social interaction** between what are currently very clearly segregated communities, though they are clearly reflective of the material and structural differences born of social inequalities and economic disadvantage in Irish society.

In conclusion, sociology continues to play a significant role in providing a critical view of social class in Ireland. It has debunked the myth of a classless Ireland and has contributed to illuminating the persistent class inequalities that exist in this state in the areas of education, housing, health and employment. Additionally, Irish sociologists have focused on the cultural manifestations of social class which continue to structure and shape the understandings and constructions of social identities. Indeed, Sociology has contributed handsomely to a body of evidence which shows that class distinctions grew significantly during the boom in Ireland, a process which is continuing unabated in the current economic downturn, with the working classes suffering the greatest hardships.

---

[6] A feckless member of the underclass; an Irish equivalent to the English derogatory term 'chav'.

> # Key Questions: Social Class and Irish Society
>
> ➤ Is Ireland a meritocracy?
>
> ➤ Are we still (or were we ever) a "middle-class nation" (McWilliams 2005, p.15)?
>
> ➤ Social class is a contested concept, but does it offer you insights into how inequality is reproduced in Irish society?

# Racism and Ethnicity

## Irish Ethnicity

Having considered the continued significance of social class in an Irish context we now turn to examine another important aspect of social stratification, namely ethnicity. Like national identity, ethnicity is **socially constructed**. This means it is neither natural, nor static, but constantly being shaped through social interaction. The territorial boundaries of nation states and ethnic groups do not always coincide. For example, consider the collective ritual of identification (Jenkins 2008) that is St. Patrick's Day. On the 17th of March millions of people worldwide celebrate their Irishness. Those celebrating their Irish ethnicity will include people of many different nationalities, not just Irish (as well as people of dual nationality). This group will include children who have been born and raised in Ireland, who may strongly self-identify as ethnically Irish, but because of their ancestry do not have an entitlement to Irish citizenship. For these children there is always the possibility (though the process is not without its difficulties) of naturalisation. However, for some ethnic groups there is no sovereign nation state which corresponds with their ethnicity; for example, the Roma, Kurds, Basques, Irish Travellers and many first peoples.

The concept of the racial state, developed by Goldberg (2002), holds that nation-building involves the conflation or merging of '**race**' and nation in order to construct a **homogenous** population within the national territory. A State may seek to legitimate their own existence by intervening to construct a single dominant ethnic identity among the people within the space they govern, thus associating their claims over a territory with the idea that that territory is occupied by a people who share a common **culture**. For example, historian Eric Hobsbawm (1990) argues that the modern French State preceded French cultural unity. Modern France encompasses the territories of the Basques, Bretons and Alsatians for example. The population governed by the State lacked homogeneity. A French national identity had to be created over time. For example, Hobsbawm (1990, p.60) asserts that the French State did not even have a common language in 1789: "50% of Frenchmen did not speak it [French] at all, only 12–13% spoke it 'correctly' and indeed outside a central region it was not habitually spoken". The State subsequently intervened, installing French as the language of education, officialdom and public life.

Tracy (2000) argues that Irish ethnicity has been associated with a WHISC identity, i.e. historically it has been constructed as inclusive of only those who are white, heterosexual, Irish-born, settled (i.e. not nomadic) and Catholic. Like all social identities, ethnicity is exclusionary as well as inclusionary. We can't construct an 'us' without imagining how we are distinct from 'them'. This particular imagining of Irish ethnicity ignores long-standing diversity among the Irish people, excluding important Jewish, Protestant and nomadic communities, for example. Nonetheless, this homogenising identity was promoted in official discourse and by State-owned media, the education system and the Roman Catholic Church, as part of the new Irish State's process of nation building. Sociologists Tovey and Share (2003) provide a useful overview of research which highlights, for example, the role of the State broadcaster, early in its history, in propagating a particular envisioning of Irish culture through, for example, an overt emphasis on Irish language broadcasting and GAA sports.

## Changing Irish Ethnicity

The WHISC identity, underpinned by political nationalism and the power of the Roman Catholic Church, has in recent years encountered an undeniable surge in the cultural diversity of the Irish population resulting from increased inward migration. The economic circumstances surrounding Ireland's transition to a country of net inward migration are explained in the section entitled 'The Celtic Tiger 1994–2008' in this chapter.

Between 2002 and 2006, the proportion of the population which is composed of non-Irish nationals increased by 87 percent to around 10 percent of the population. Many of these immigrants were perceived as temporary workers, their migration reminiscent of the **guest-worker model** of immigration; an **industrial reserve army** to fuel Ireland's Celtic Tiger. However, in the aftermath of the boom, many immigrants chose to remain, having formed lasting relationships with Ireland both as individuals and through their Irish born children. These 'new Irish' and their children perpetuate pre-existing challenges to the validity of the WHISC identity.

## Anti-immigrant Racism in Ireland

Although Ireland has a long history of outward migration, Gray (2004) argues that shared experiences of emigration are a weak basis for **multiculturalism**. McGinnity *et al.* (2006), of Ireland's Economic and Social Research Institute, conducted a nationally representative **survey** of non-EU adults' experiences of **racism** and **discrimination** in Ireland and found that more than a third of their respondents reported experiencing harassment in public places, including on public transport. A similar proportion of those entitled to work reported harassment at work. Black Africans were more likely to experience discrimination in every sphere.

Research conducted by Trinity Immigration Initiative and Integrating Ireland evidences that young immigrants are also subject to racism. Their **qualitative** research with 169 young migrants found that many of those to whom they spoke had experienced verbal abuse, including in public, at school and at work, and some had been subject to physical violence.

---

### A Closer Look

#### The Fluidity of Ethnicity

The markers of an ethnicity are not static, they are continuously revised. Ethnicity changes over time as groups alter their common understanding of what distinguishes them from other ethnicities, of what marks them out and distinguishes their imagined 'us' from an imagined 'them'.

In a study of primary school children's understanding of Irish national identity Waldron and Pike (2006) found that Irish children continue to define Irishness in terms of the possession of a distinct culture which marks those who are Irish out from other (often stereotyped) national groups. Their research suggests the beginning of a decoupling of Irish ethnicity from Catholicism. However, the children with whom they collaborated still imagined Irish people as ". . . able-bodied, sedentary (non-traveller), and white" (Waldron and Pike 2006, p.247) referring also to birthright as a significant marker.

---

### A Closer Look

#### Racial Discrimination

The United Nations definition of racial discrimination as laid out in the *International Convention on the Elimination of All Forms of Racial Discrimination*, 1966, states that: *". . . any distinction, exclusion, restriction or preference based on race, color, descent, or national or ethnic origin which has the purpose or effect of nullifying or impairing the recognition, enjoyment or exercise, on an equal footing, of human rights and fundamental freedoms in the political, economic, social, cultural or any other field of public life"*.

---

## Anti-Traveller Racism

Of course, racism is not a new phenomenon in Ireland, nor is it dependent on the presence of immigrants. Irish Travellers, an indigenous ethnic minority, are subject to **prejudice** and discrimination on the basis of their ethnicity. Irish Travellers are an ethnic group who are both Irish and Catholic, but are culturally distinctive

**Figure 5** Road signs in Galway: The sign at the top exclaims "Go Home Roma Scum". In response to a request to "Go home please" a second road sign states "This is Home"
(Reproduced by kind permission © Tony Haynes (2011))

**Figure 6** A Traveller driving a 'sulkie' in County Limerick
(Reproduced by kind permission © Martin Power (2011))

by merit, for example, their oral traditions, language (known as Cant or Shelta) and the central place of **nomadism** in their culture.

Factors such as the privatisation of common land and the formalisation of the economy have made it increasingly difficult for Travellers to sustain their nomadic lifestyle. Nonetheless, many choose to live in mobile homes and caravans in order to retain the sense that travel is still a possibility and to maintain contact with extended family. MacLaughlin (1995, p.73) argues that anti-Traveller racism must be understood in the context of the capitalist ideologies discussed earlier in this chapter ". . . anti-Traveller and 'anti-tinker' racism is also traceable to a late nineteenth – and twentieth-century rural fundamentalism which prioritised the values of property-owners over and above those of the propertyless."

Significant obstacles are placed in the paths of Travellers seeking to maintain a nomadic way of life. However, Travellers also experience prejudice and discrimination when they move in to houses alongside settled people. Such experiences are evidence of anti-Traveller racism. Like immigrants, Travellers experience racism across a variety of spheres, including accommodation, employment, health and education.

## A Closer Look

### Cultural Racism

Cultural racism includes incidents where ethnic groups are implied to be innately inferior, possessing static attributes and behaviours or are subjected to discrimination on the basis of their ethnicity.

Irish sociologists have been highly critical regarding the treatment of Irish Travellers not only by the ethnic majority but also by the State. Irish Travellers are recognised as an ethnic group in Britain and Northern Ireland. Irish anti-discrimination legislation defines the Traveller community as "the community of people who are commonly called Travellers and who are identified (both by themselves and others) as people with a shared history, culture and traditions including, historically a nomadic way of life on the island of Ireland." However, the Irish State persistently refuses to explicitly acknowledge their status as an ethnic minority.

The refusal to accept Travellers ethnicity and give them access to the status that this implies can itself be constructed as institutional discrimination on the part of the State. McVeigh (2007) highlights the consequences of this ethnicity denial. He challenges the State's assertion that "separate identification of Travellers in equality legislation guarantees that they are explicitly protected" (Government of Ireland 2004, p.90). While Travellers have been named as a specific group in national legislation, they are not protected by international legislation and policy which seeks to prevent and redress racism since they are not defined as an ethnic group.

## Stop and Think

➤ What do you consider might be the impact of denying ethnic group status to Travellers on the public's perception of Traveller's cultural rights?

## Systems of Immigration and Integration

Irish sociologists also provide an important critical perspective on the State's record with regards to immigration and integration.

Sociological treatments of immigration to Ireland tend to highlight the differences in the rights and responsibilities accorded to EU/EEA citizens, non-EEA migrants and asylum seekers. **Asylum seekers** are housed communally in Direct Provision centres. Denied the right to work, the State provides them with a paltry allowance of €19.10 per adult. In this system of direct provision, most asylum seekers lack the means and facilities to engage in meaningful everyday activities, including cooking for their own families. Loyal (2011) equates asylum seekers' experiences in direct provision with a process of **social degradation** occurring within a **total institution**.

In the mainstream immigration system, non-EEA citizens in particular are subject to the vagaries of a structure which Loyal (2011) refers to as paradoxically characterised both by the complexity of a **bureaucratic iron cage** and the uncertainty of a discretionary system. Within this system, skilled and unskilled migrants experience differential treatment oriented to serving the economic interests of the 'ethnic Irish'.

Although the status of EU/EEA citizens is akin to that of Irish citizens, privileging them above non-EEA migrants, Haynes *et al.* (2010) have highlighted the intervention of the Irish State in the form of a habitual residency clause (HRC), which serves to deny new residents equitable access to the protections of the Irish welfare state.

## A Closer Look

### Migrants

The Crosscare Migrant Project (CMP) have claimed that increasing numbers of migrant workers from new EU states are being unfairly denied access to social welfare payments because the rules governing the HRC are applied inconsistently. They highlighted the case of one Polish migrant worker in Mallow, who was refused supplementary welfare allowance despite having lived and worked in Ireland since September 2004. A copy of a letter of appeal sent by the organisation on the migrant's behalf detailed that he had made a total of 193 paid contributions during his term of employment and was granted jobseeker's benefit before seeking the basic payment. The migrant subsequently won the appeal and received the supplementary welfare allowance (Smith 2010).

Fanning (2010) critiques the construction of categories which legitimate differential treatment of and among migrants, and argues for the explanatory power of ethnic nationalism as a force in shaping Ireland's immigration system. Boucher (2008) too identifies the importance of discourses that purport to protect the nation from migrants. He highlights their role in legitimising State inaction in the field of **integration**, resulting in the delegation by default of integration processes to civil society and private individuals. Haynes *et al.* (2006) attend to the role of the **mass media** in circulating discourses which support very restrictive asylum policies by constructing refugees and asylum seekers as a threat to the financial, bodily and cultural well-being of the 'ethnic Irish'. Haynes *et al.* (2010) assert that political discourses which legitimate State interventions to exclude migrants from the rights and privileges accruing to 'ethnic Irish', are informed by neoliberal interpretations of 'the national interest'.

The 2004 Irish Citizenship Referendum is a prime example of a significant State intervention informed by discourses which appeal to ethnic nationalism. The Referendum removed a pre-existing right to citizenship for children born in Ireland who did not have at least one Irish grandparent, in a development which Loyal (2011) describes as a re-ethnicisation of citizenship; 79.8 percent of voters voted in favour of this constitutional amendment. Lentin (2006) argues that this proactive use of legislation to exclude Irish children of immigrants from Irish citizenship is evidence of a shift from the racial state imagined by Goldberg (2002) to a racist state, in which Irishness is produced through policies and practices that racialise both immigrants and indigenous ethnic groups.

In conclusion, Irish sociology plays an important role in providing a critical perspective on ethnicity and racism in Ireland. It has contributed to illuminating discriminatory State policies and practices; identifying the role of popular and official discourses in legitimating such mechanisms of exclusion; and highlighting the neoliberal interpretation of the national interest which underlies the ethnic nationalism to which many of these discourses appeal. It is important to note that this critical voice is not, however, the exclusive remit of academics. Ireland possesses an array of grassroots anti-racism movements which give testament to the existence of another alternative approach to diversity within Irish society. Haynes *et al.* (2010) have also highlighted that

such voices also exist within the political sphere, although whether they can popularise more critical approaches to diversity is yet to be seen.

# Mass Media in Ireland: From Hall Door to Global Village?

In the 1940s and 1950s it was common for Irish sports fans to gather at houses in local villages and towns whose owners were fortunate enough to own a radio. The broadcast of match commentaries from Dublin (and from further afield) were the reason for such communal gatherings. Radios were sometimes placed outside the house on the windowsill or the doorstep for the ears of avid sports fans. The commentaries provided audiences with mental pictures of distant events and presumably lots of material for post-match discussion and analysis. This historical example reminds us of the importance of understanding the mass media in a social context. It also stands in stark contrast to the radically altered **mediascape** of 21$^{st}$ century Ireland with its seemingly endless array of media choices. Like other **post-modern** societies, Ireland is a media saturated society. Media **globalisation**, technological advancements and the restructuring of media organisations have all contributed to a rapidly changing media environment which has resulted in many social changes. In contrast to those sports fans who gathered around shared radios in the 1940s and 1950s to cheer for their county team, Irish sports fans are now more likely to meet in pubs to view matches broadcast by the global **conglomerate** Sky Sports, whilst wearing official team merchandise. Results and fixtures will be texted by mobile phone. Social media such as Facebook and Twitter may be used to meet up either virtually or in reality in order to discuss favourite sports teams. What both examples have in common, however, are issues concerning access to media technologies; identity formation, as well as the shared aspects of being an audience member. Media globalisation offers Irish and other audiences a tantalising array of technologies and texts about the social world. Recent Irish media history has been characterised by the increased presence of global multimedia conglomerates; by the convergence of 'old' and 'new media' and by a growing range of creative possibilities for many audience members. However, many critical questions remain for the student of Sociology. In briefly examining the many complexities

| **Table 5** Some modern landmarks in Irish media and communications history | |
| --- | --- |
| 1737 | *The Belfast Newsletter* newspaper begins publication. It is the world's longest running newspaper. |
| 1859 | *The Irish Times* commences publication as a daily newspaper. |
| 1866 | First commercial Transatlantic telegraphic communications between Valentia Island (Co. Kerry) and Newfoundland, Canada. |
| 1905 | *Irish Independent* newspaper commences publication. |
| 1909 | The first cinema in Ireland – The Volta – is opened by writer James Joyce and a consortium of Italian businessmen in Mary Street, Dublin. |
| 1916 | First 'pirate radio' broadcast made by Irish revolutionaries from O'Connell Street, Dublin, using a short-wave transmitter. News from the broadcast is carried by US newspapers. |
| 1926 | First Irish radio station 2RN begins broadcasting. Transmits its first sports broadcast in August. |
| 1937 | Radio Eireann starts broadcasting. |
| 1966 | Radio Telefís Éireann (RTE) launches the first Irish television channel in the Republic of Ireland. The President of Ireland Eamonn De Valera warns of its immense power. This was preceded by the launch in Northern Ireland of BBC Northern Ireland (1953) and UTV (1959). |
| 1977–88 | Although there were a small number of predecessors, pirate radio stations become a major feature of the Irish broadcasting landscape. |
| 1988 | TV3, the first commercial television station in the Republic of Ireland, goes on air. Its international investors, over time, include CanWest, Granada TV and Doughty Hansen. |
| 1989 | First licensed commercial radio stations start broadcasting. |
| 1994 | Eurovision interval act Riverdance is viewed by over 300 million people across the globe. |
| 2010 | Launch of Google Street View, Ireland. |
| 2010 | Video for The Rubberbandits 'Horse Outside' scores four million hits on Youtube. |

of the Irish mass media we take as our cue Devereux's (2007a) reminder that we need to give equal attention to *media organisations* (production), *media content* (discourses) and *media reception* (audiences). In doing so, our discussion is focused on the following:

➤ changes in the ownership and control of Irish media organisations;
➤ media representations of marginalised groups in Irish Society;
➤ Irish media audiences and agency (with particular reference to audiences as fans; audiences as diaspora and the use of new media technologies).

## Stop and Think

➤ Compare your media life to that of your parents or grandparents.
➤ What key differences exist?
➤ Why?

## Ownership and Control of Irish Media

Many sociologists (and particularly those coming from a **political economy** perspective) have expressed worries about the ownership and control of the media industries. They argue that the media industries are more likely to reproduce a **hegemonic** world-view that is in agreement with powerful (political and commercial) interests in society. Significant changes have occurred in the ownership structure and orientations of both local and national media in Ireland which would seem to add weight to their concerns. Conglomeration, commercialisation, globalisation, rationalisation, tabloidisation and an increasingly competitive media marketplace are all now key features of the Irish media landscape. A media industry which was once dominated by the public service broadcaster Radio Telefís Éireann (RTE) and a locally owned national and provincial press has been radically transformed and has been supplanted by the increased presence of global multimedia conglomerates (such as News Corporation and Liberty Media). Such conglomerates are not only involved in the reshaping of everyday media experiences but are also the source of significant levels of employment in the economy (e.g. Google, Intel and Apple). The production of media content which is distributed and consumed in Ireland is now more likely to be produced and distributed in a context where the ownership and control of the media rests in the hands of global multimedia conglomerates located in Ireland or elsewhere. Such conglomerates – for example, Sky Sports – seek to charge audiences for access to what were once free-to-air events such as soccer or rugby matches. Given the increasingly commercialised context in which media work now occurs, the prospect of the (Irish) mass media possessing any dimensions of Habermas' Public Sphere seem even more remote. With the exception of RTE's radio and television networks (and BBC's Northern Ireland smaller counterparts) the ownership and control of both traditional and newer forms of media rests in private hands. Whether by accident or design it seems inevitable that the content produced by privately owned media organisations will reflect the world-view of the powerful groups in society.

## Stop and Think

> What are the implications of having media monopolies in society?

## Vertical and Horizontal Integration

There has been a particular focus on how the structure of ownership of media organisations has become more concentrated. Such concentrations are usually described as being either *horizontal* or *vertical* (see Doyle, 2002). Horizontal integration refers to "the process by which one company buys different kinds of media, concentrating ownership across different types of media rather than 'up and down through one industry'" (Croteau and Hoynes 2003, p.40). Vertical integration, on the other hand, refers to "... the process by which one owner acquires all aspects of production and distribution of a single type of media product" (Croteau and Hoynes 2003, p.40). Although variations do exist, multimedia conglomerates tend to be horizontal in structure, owning and controlling different types of media organisations as well as being involved in other commercial activities outside of the media. Independent News and Media (INM) is an example of a transnational Irish multimedia conglomerate that is horizontal in structure (See Table 6). INM dominates the Irish newspaper industry in terms of readership and sales. Its key shareholders include the O'Reilly family and Denis O'Brien's Communicorp. Although there are vertical aspects to some of INM's activities (it produces, prints and distributes national and regional newspapers in Ireland, for example) a

**Table 6** A multimedia conglomerate, Independent News and Media is an example of an Irish global media organisation

| | | | |
|---|---|---|---|
| Newspaper Publishing e.g. *Sunday Independent, Irish Independent, Evening Herald*. | Newspaper Publishing e.g. *Belfast Telegraph, Sunday Life*. | Newspaper Publishing | Publication of Daily Newspaper (NZ) |
| Regional Newspaper Publishing. 13 titles including *Bray People*; *Enniscorthy Guardian*. | Commercial Printing | Publisher of Community Newspapers | Regional Newspaper Publishing (10 Titles) (Australia) |
| Wholesaler and Distributor of Newspapers and Magazines | Online Activities Include: | Commercial Printing | Commercial Printing (NZ) |
| Online Activities Include: | > Property Portal | Magazine Publication | Magazine Publication (NZ) |
| | > News Portal | Online Activities Include: | |
| > News Portal | > Recruitment Portal | > News Portal | 13 Radio Stations (Australia) |
| > Property Portal | > Classified Ads Portal | > Property Website | 1 Radio Station (NZ) |
| > Online Directory | 10% share of Truphone (an application which allows users to route phone calls through the internet). | | Outdoor Advertising (Australia) |
| > Recruitment Portal | | | No. 1 News Website (NZ) |
| Other: | | | Group has a 31.6% investment in APN News & Media Limited |
| Independent Colleges | | | |

significant proportion of its overseas activities involves the ownership and control of media companies involved in broadcasting, outdoor advertising and online activities. Its interests also extend to investments in telephony (Northern Ireland) and the provision of university level courses through its network of Independent Colleges in the Republic of Ireland. Ideologically, its main Irish titles (*Irish Independent, Sunday Independent* and *The Evening Herald*) have a right of centre political and economic orientation. In spite of its historical linkages with the Fine Gael party, the *Irish Independent* has publicly aligned itself with the neoliberal economic strategies of other centre-right parties (e.g. Fianna Fail and Progressive Democrats). Indeed, using a Framing Analysis approach, Murphy (2010), for example, argues that the *Irish Independent* reproduces the perspectives of elite groups (e.g. employers' organisations such as IBEC) when writing about public service workers.

## Media Representations of Poor People and Poor Places

One way in which sociologists test the ideological and discursive power of media representations is to closely examine the content produced on specific themes (see Sheehan 1987, Sheehan 2004). In doing content analysis of this kind it is acknowledged that the mass media operates in a very powerful way, disseminating ideologies and discourses which shape public attitudes and beliefs. Earlier, we noted the continuing classed nature of Irish society. Analyses of how the poor and socially excluded are represented by the Irish mass media, for example, have consistently demonstrated that particular categories of the marginalised (e.g. female lone parents, immigrants, welfare recipients, Travellers, etc.) are constructed as the 'Devils' or 'undeserving poor' (Devereux 1998, Haynes *et al.* 2005, Devereux *et al.* 2011).

In addition to the **stigmatising** and 'othering' of members of the **under-class** or poor, sociologists have also sought to understand how the places in which these groups live come to be stigmatised. This body of work has examined how mass media and other social forces contribute to the creation of negative stereotypes, which damage the reputations of the places in which the underclass or poor reside. The research demonstrates that negative reputations

of such places can, in themselves, have a profound effect upon the life chances, experiences and self-image of those who live in neighbourhoods which carry a stigma. Irish sociologists have demonstrated how places (such as Moyross in Limerick) have been consistently stigmatised within mass media coverage (see Devereux *et al.* 2011).

## Audiences and Agency

The control of the mass media by an ever decreasing number of multimedia conglomerates and the dominant position within mainstream media content of dominant or hegemonic discourses would seem to offer little prospect for **audience agency** or creativity. In spite of the very real concerns raised by political economists and others, the Social Constructionist perspective holds that audiences in fact have considerable agency and creative potential. Recent **ethnographic research** on Irish audiences demonstrates how audiences can exercise agency in a media setting. Questions concerning identities are the over-arching themes of Irish audience research. The importance of social class and gender in shaping audience interpretations of media content was stressed by Kelly and O'Connor (1997). MacKeogh's (2001) detailed ethnographic account of Irish family viewing practices demonstrated the high levels of media literacy amongst teenage audience members. Research by Devereux (2006) examined the creativity of and sub-cultures associated with Morrissey fans; O'Connor and MacKeogh (2007) investigated the significance of an online portal (i-Venus) for female audience members. Both studies demonstrate how some audience members participate in 'imagined communities' which exist in an online or virtual setting. Other work has focused on the importance of gender identities in understanding the relationship between audiences and media texts/practices (see Ging 2007, Kerr 2007). Sociologists have also examined the media uses of immigrant audience members (see Kerr 2007, Titley 2008).

In conclusion, our discussion has highlighted how an understanding of media globalisation is an essential part of understanding recent social change in Irish society. Unlike Cultural Studies, a sociological approach to understanding the social role of the mass media emphasises the need to engage with questions about changes in media ownership and the media industries – the dominant discourses which are found in media content and the relative amount of power which audiences may or may not have.

**Figure 7** The Rubberbandits' parodies of working-class life are best understood in the context of how certain groups such as the long-term unemployed, the underclass or Travellers or the places in which they live are stigmatised by mainstream society

(Reproduced by kind permission. © Rubberbandits (2011))

## A Closer Look

Sociological Research in Practice – Media and Masculinities

In a pioneering research study Ging (2007) undertook audience research focused on masculinities. She used the focus group as her research method and a screening of the film *Intermission* to examine how her male subjects interacted with mediated discourses concerning masculinity. She spoke to men from different backgrounds in terms of their location, their class position (i.e. urban/rural and working/middle-class) and their age. The increased presence within Irish cinema of male characters that embody anti-social and under-class masculinities is interpreted in competing ways. The urban working-class males strongly identified with anti-heroic figures (whom they related to 'real-life' characters such as 'The General' aka Martin Cahill). Their readings of recent Irish cinematic representations of such figures have to be understood in a classed way. The urban professionals and the GAA groups, however, relied more heavily on a gender-based discourse. Their identification with these figures is explained in terms of how they overcome the constraints imposed by adult responsibility and what they perceive as political correctness.

## Key Questions: Mass Media and Irish Society

➤ Does a Public Sphere, as proposed by Habermas, exist in an Irish mass media setting?

➤ What are the implications for the media industry and media audiences arising from the continued conglomeration and rationalisation of the Irish mass media?

➤ Do the Irish mass media portray all citizens equally?

➤ What relative amount of power do you think Irish media audiences possess?

# Activities

1. **Globalisation and Consumption**

A striking feature of the Celtic Tiger years was the increase in personal consumption. According to the CSO, expenditure on personal consumption rose from €37,409 in 1995 to €91,055 in 2008 (CSO website). Consumption was no longer directed towards necessity but became an expression of pleasure, status and lifestyle. Many examples can be furnished to illustrate how consumerist Irish society became during the Celtic Tiger years.

a) Irish society showed a particular predisposition towards car ownership, especially luxury car brands, throughout the Celtic Tiger years. Following on from a consumptive trend identified by Allen (2000, p.69) (see Table 2) the sale of such luxury cars as Audi, BMW and Mercedes continued throughout the 2000s. Perhaps one of the most emblematic cars of the Celtic Tiger era was the Land Rover and Jeep. We first find the sale of Land Rovers being recorded in 2001 with 1,531 models alone being purchased that same year. As a symbol of middle-class distinction Land Rover ownership levels rose to an all time high of 2,077 in 2007. However, once the Celtic Tiger economy began to contract, so too did the numbers of new Land Rovers, falling to just 29 in 2010 (see Table 3).

b) Secondly, while home ownership is a particular cultural feature of Irish society, during the Celtic Tiger years people bought homes for investment and holidaying purposes, both in Ireland and abroad. From 2000 to 2008, 63 percent of net investment in capital stock was in housing (Davy Stockbrokers cited in *RTÉ News*, 19 February 2010). The conspicuous consumption of houses, both for habitation and investment purposes, could also be gleaned from the increase in the number of domestically produced lifestyle and reality shows – holiday travel shows, home build and home improvement shows, interior decorating and garden development shows – that were broadcast over the same period.

c) Another example of Celtic Tiger consumerist excess can be found in the practice of foreign luxury shopping trips. In 2006 alone it was estimated that Irish people spent €25 million in the US shopping for Christmas (*Irish Times* cited in Corcoran 2007, p.244).

2. **Social Class**

Using the following diagram, draw lines to indicate where you think that disadvantage (resulting from one's class situation) in one area might contribute to or compound disadvantage experienced in another area.

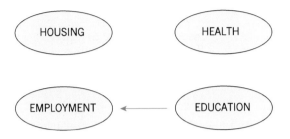

Look at the linkages you have drawn above. Could the same linkages be used to illustrate how advantages in one area, resulting from one's class situation, might contribute to advantage in another area?

3. **Race**

Research the significance of placing the word 'race' in inverted commas. Start here: http://www.enotes.com/oxsoc-encyclopedia/race

4. **Direct Provision**

Research Ireland's direct provision system. Start here: http://www.tcd.ie/immigration/css/downloads/HAPAWeb.pdf

What features of this system might qualify it as a total institution?

Consider the degree of autonomy accorded to asylum seekers within this system. Why might Loyal consider the experience to be degrading?

5. **Irish Ethnic Identity**

Create your own acronym (for example WHISC) to represent your understanding of contemporary Irish ethnic identity. Use this exercise to critically reflect on the degree to which your understanding of Irishness is inclusive or exclusionary. Reflect also on the degree to which you define Irishness in oppositional terms, i.e. in contrast to an imagined Other.

6. **Mass Media**

Try and imagine your everyday life without the mass media.

➤ What sorts of differences would there be in a media-less society?

➤ How would you find out about national and world events?

➤ Where would you get your ideas and opinions about those who are 'different' from you?

➤ How would you know about the views and opinions of the powerful?

➤ Would your conversations with family and friends be any different?

➤ How would you entertain yourself?

➤ How would your use of time be different in your daily life?

Source: Adapted from Devereux (2007, p.12)

7. **Media Ownership**

Do an Internet search on any of the following media organisations in order to establish the range of companies that they own and control. Choose from Johnston Press, Communicorp, UPC, RTE or UTV Media PLC.

Is your selected media organisation engaged exclusively in media activities or does it also have other economic interests?

To what extent is it intertwined with other media conglomerates?

Would you characterise it as being either horizontally or vertically integrated?

8. **Irish Print Media Coverage of Asylum Seekers and Refugees**

Sociologists Breen, Devereux and Haynes have examined the relationship between Irish media coverage of immigration and the shaping of public beliefs (Haynes *et al.* 2008). They note the way in which particular kinds of problematic discourses persist within media coverage. As this sample of newspaper headlines indicates, immigration has been framed as a threat and conflates the terms asylum seekers and refugees.

Write a short newspaper story of your own about immigrants. Think about the implications of the language you might use in your headline and article. What sources would you use? How would you decide on the accompanying images for your newspaper article?

➤ 5,000 Refugees <u>Flooding</u> into Ireland

➤ <u>Floodgates</u> open as a new army of poor <u>floods</u> the country

➤ Demand for curb on <u>tide</u> of 'refugees'

➤ Mother's anguish as junkie daughter marries Nigerian refugee for £5,000 in asylum <u>scam</u>

➤ Blitz on refugees' <u>sham</u> marriages

➤ Refugee <u>rip-off</u> is revealed

➤ Government crackdown on <u>bogus</u> asylum-seeker advisers

➤ Refugees <u>Flooding</u> Maternity Hospitals

➤ Crackdown on 2,000 <u>Sponger</u> Refugees

➤ Inmates lobby to stay in jail as refugees fill up hotels

➤ Refugee <u>Flood</u> to Spark Homes Crisis

➤ Alert on <u>Bogus</u> Refugee Weddings

# Summary

1. The demographic structure of Ireland has been changing, with people marrying and having children later in life. Cohabitation and civil marriages have also increased. Although still small in absolute number, same-sex couples are becoming more common. The rate of marital breakdown has, however, been increasing since the 1980s. In 2006, non-Irish nationals accounted for 10 percent of the total population. Finally, Ireland now has the lowest proportion of its population aged 65 and over among EU countries.

2. Since the mid-20th century Irish economic policy has embraced a policy of modernisation. Historically, Irish women's participation in industrial work had been one of restrictions, though Irelands' membership of the EEC in 1972 helped to bring about a decade of equality employment legislation. The lack of a home-grown economic base and the emergence of an export-orientated economy made the Irish economy particularly vulnerable to international markets, crises and the flows of global economy. The period from the 1970s up to the mid 1990s was characterised by widespread factory closures, unemployment and emigration.

3. The sharp reversal of economic fortunes that Ireland experienced thanks to the Celtic Tiger economy led many commentators to remark how beneficial globalisation and foreign direct investment can be for small countries, especially those who modernise late (Kirby 2004). Others are eager to highlight that despite the significant economic growth, the benefits of this growth were unevenly distributed, both spatially and socially, and grossly mismanaged and administered by the Irish State.

4. Irish society is often self-imagined as a classless society and class-based discourses have historically been frowned upon in the public arena. Yet class inequality continues to be a major component of Irish society. While absolute mobility increased during the 1990s and early 2000s, "relative mobility and equality of opportunity stayed stable over time" (Whelan and Layte 2007). In spite of the portrayal of Ireland as a meritocratic society, in this chapter we have clearly seen the impact of social class on educational attainment in this country.

5. Irish ethnicity has been associated with a WHISC identity. This particular imagining of Irish ethnicity was promoted in official discourse, by State-owned media, the education system and the Roman Catholic Church as part of the process of nation building, ignoring long-standing diversity among the Irish people. The WHISC identity has in recent years encountered an undeniable surge in the cultural diversity of the Irish population resulting from increased inward migration.

6. Racism is not a new phenomenon in Ireland, nor is it dependent on the presence of immigrants. Irish Travellers, an indigenous ethnic minority, are subject to prejudice and discrimination on the basis of their ethnicity. A rejection of nomadism, which is seen as antithetical to capitalist understandings of progress, is core to anti-Traveller racism. The refusal to accept Travellers' ethnicity and give them access to the status that this implies can also be seen as institutional discrimination on the part of the State.

7. Like other post-modern societies, Ireland is a media saturated society. Media globalisation, technological advancements and the restructuring of media organisations have all contributed to a rapidly changing media environment which has resulted in many social changes. Recent Irish media history has been characterised by the increased presence of global multimedia conglomerates, by the convergence of 'old' and 'new media' and by a growing range of creative possibilities for many audience members. Significant changes have occurred in the ownership structure and orientations of both local and national media in Ireland. Conglomeration, commercialisation, globalisation, rationalisation, tabloidisation and an increasingly competitive media marketplace are all now key features of the Irish media landscape. It seems inevitable that the content produced by privately owned media organisations will reflect the world-view of the powerful groups in society.

8. Analyses of how the poor and socially excluded are represented by the Irish mass media have consistently demonstrated that particular categories of the marginalised are constructed as the 'undeserving poor'. Mass media have also contributed to the creation of negative stereotypes, which damage the reputations of the places in which the under-class or poor reside. Tellingly, the control of the mass media by an ever decreasing number of multimedia conglomerates and the dominant position within mainstream media content of dominant or hegemonic discourses would seem to offer little prospect for audience agency or creativity, yet the Social Constructionist perspective holds that audiences in fact have considerable agency and creative potential.

# MyTask List

## Review the Chapter

1. What has the chapter taught you about Irish society that you did not know before?
2. Are there any elements of the chapter that you disagree with? Why? How could you construct an opposing argument to the material that you disagree with?
3. Are there personal examples that you can use to make the content real for you?

## Read a Novel

John McGahern's novels *Amongst Women* and *That They May Face The Rising Sun* offer an insight into Irish rural family life prior to the globalisation of Irish society.

Peter Murphy's novel *John The Revelator* is set in Wexford in the early part of this century. Note how the author writes about recent social change in terms of the presence of African and other immigrants in Ireland.

Frank McCourt's memoir *Angela's Ashes* focuses on poverty and social exclusion in Limerick City. What parallels do you think exist between the poverty of 1950s Ireland and present-day poverty?

Kevin Barry's novel *The City of Bohane* is set in the future. What does it predict about gangs and subcultures in the near future?

Paul Howard's *Ross O'Carroll-Kelly's Guide to (South) Dublin: How To Get By On, Like, €10,000 A Day* is a satirical representation of those residing in affluent addresses in South Dublin. The book is written in a distinct accent (linguistic capital) – commonly referred to as "Dortspeak" – which is the focus of much of the satire. The author of the book – in contrast to his fictional creation – describes himself as being "as working class as curry sauce, processed cheese slices and borrowing money from the credit union." (*Irish Independent*, 31 August 2007).

## Listen

The RTE Radio One Series *The Documentary on One* is freely available as PODCASTS at the following link http://www.rte.ie/radio1/doconone/. You may find the following ones interesting in terms of the contents of this chapter:

➤ Mighty Mac (Sport, Masculinities and Working-Class Life)
➤ The Tatie Hookers (Migration)
➤ Finding Henry (Homelessness)

Damien Dempsey's song 'Celtic Tiger' on the 2003 album 'Seize the Day' offers an excellent insight into the unequal society created in Ireland during the Celtic Tiger era.

[A live recording of the song is available here: http://www.youtube.com/watch?v=TfmAfbqOrP4]

## Watch a Film or Documentary

*Pavee Lackeen: The Traveller Girl* (2005) is a documentary style feature film about a Traveller girl and her family.

*Blood of the Travellers* (RTE 2011) is a documentary which sought to examine the history of Irish Travellers.

*Once* (2006) is a film about a Dublin busker and a young immigrant Czech girl.

*Intermission* (2003) is a fast-moving and revealing film about 21st century Irish crime.

## Search the Web

The Forum on Migration and Communications provides an array of multimedia migration resources including:

➤ Migration Matters (A blog on migration, with a special focus on media and the Irish context) http://www.fomacs.org/blog_detail.php
➤ Candidates (a radio programme in which journalist Colin Murphy follows migrant candidates on the campaign trail during Ireland's 2009 local elections, available as an audio podcast) http://www.fomacs.org/projects/radio/Candidates
➤ A Sikh Face in Ireland (photographic project) http://www.fomacs.org/projects/photography/A-Sikh-Face-In-Ireland

*Metro Éireann* (Irish multicultural newspaper) http://www.metroeireann.com/

Migrant Rights Centre Ireland http://www.mrci.ie/ (also on Facebook)

Irish Travellers Movement www.itmtrav.ie/ (also on Facebook)

Pavee Point www.paveepoint.ie

Exchange House National Travellers Service http://www.exchangehouse.ie/

Irish Refugee Council www.irishrefugeecouncil.ie (also on Facebook)

Doras Luimni www.dorasluimni.org/ (also on Facebook)

## YouTube

Migrant Rights Centre Ireland's YouTube Channel (an excellent source of critical treatments of topical migration issues) http://www.youtube.com/user/migrantrightscentre

Paveepoint's YouTube channel http://www.youtube.com/user/paveepoint

Popular with working and middle-class fans alike, the popularity of the rap act The Rubberbandits is best understood in the context of debates concerning the stigmatisation of specific groups in society (e.g. the underclass and Travellers). 'Horse Outside' is sung in a strong working-class Limerick accent http://www.youtube.com/user/Rubberbandits?blend=1&ob=5#p/u/16/q5aKwSRdr6I

Everybody's Drinkin' by Damo & Ivor – Much like the Ross O' Carroll Kelly books this piece parodies both affluent Southside Dubliners' (middle-class) culture and Northside Dubliners' (working-class) culture primarily through their respective accent, language, clothes, behaviour and mannerisms. http://www.funnyjunk.com/youtube/2039432/Everybody+s+Drinkin+by+Damo+n+Ivor/

## Get Involved

Why not offer to volunteer for your local anti-racism network or migrants support centre, or participate in intercultural activities such as those organised by Show Racism the Red Card?

# Bibliography

Action Group on Access (2001) *Report of the Action Group on Access to Third Level Education*, Dublin: Stationery Office.

Adair, V. (2001) 'Branded with Infamy: Inscriptions of Poverty and Class in the United States', *Signs: Journal of Women in Culture and Society*, 27(2), 451–471.

Allen, K. (2000) *The Celtic Tiger: The Myth of Social Partnership in Ireland*, Manchester: Manchester University Press.

Allen, K. (2004) *Citizenship and Racism: The Case Against McDowell's Referendum*, Policy Contribution.

Allen, K. (2009) *Ireland's Economic Crash: A Radical Agenda for Change*, Dublin: Liffey Press.

Barnes, C. (2010) *Young Masculinities, Class and Community: A Comparative Perspective across Local Boundaries*, Irish Social Sciences Platform Project Report 2008–2010.

Bauman, Z. (2001) 'The Ethical Challenge of Globalisation', *NPQ*, Fall, 4–9.

Bottero, W. (2004) 'Class Identities and the Identity of Class', *Sociology*, 38(5), 985–1003.

Boucher, G. (2008) 'Ireland's Lack of a Coherent Integration Policy', *Translocations*, 3(1), 1–24.

Boucher, G. (2010) 'The Entrenchment of Ireland's Laissez-Faire Integration Policy', *Translocations*, 6(2).

Bourdieu, P. (1977) *Outline of a Theory of Practice*, London: Routledge.

Bourdieu, P. (1979) *Distinction*, London: Routledge and Kegan Paul.

Butler, K. (2009) 'Parent Power', *Sunday Times*, Dublin, 1 March.

Central Statistics Office (2002) *Census 2002, Principal Demographic Results*, Central Statistics Office: Cork.

Central Statistics Office (2007) *Census 2006, Principal Demographic Results*, Central Statistics Office: Cork.

Central Statistics Office (2008) *Vital Statistics 4th Quarter and Yearly Summary 2008*, Central Statistics Office: Dublin.

Central Statistics Office (2009) *Vital Statistics: Yearly Summary 2008*, Central Statistics Office: Cork.

Central Statistics Office (2010) *Population and Migration Estimates. April 2010*, Central Statistics Office: Cork. Available: http://www.cso.ie/releasespublications/documents/population/current/popmig.pdf

Central Statistics Office (2011) *Seasonally Adjusted Standardised Unemployment Rates*, Central Statistics Office: Cork. Available: www.cso.ie/statistics/sasunemprates.htm

Chiyoko King-O'Riain, R. (2007) 'Counting on the "Celtic Tiger": Adding Ethnic Census Categories in the Republic of Ireland', *Ethnicities*, 7(4), 516–542.

Clancy, P. (2001) *College Entry in Focus: A Fourth National Survey of Participation in Higher Education*, Dublin: Higher Education Authority.

Coakley, J. (1999) 'Society and Political Culture', in Coakley, J. and Gallagher, M. (eds) *Politics in the Republic of Ireland*, 3rd edn, Dublin: Routledge.

Companies Registration Office Ireland (2009) Available: http://www.cro.ie

Conlon, D. (2009) '"Germs in the Heart of the Other": Emigrant Scripts, the Celtic Tiger and Lived Realities of Return', *Irish Geography*, 42(1), 101–117.

Connolly, L. (2003) 'Theorizing "Ireland": Social Theory and the Politics of Identity', *Sociology*, 37(1), 173–182.

Considine, M. and Dukelow, F. (2009) *Irish Social Policy: A Critical Introduction*, Dublin: Gill & Macmillan.

Corcoran, M. (2007) 'Review: Consumption and Identity', *Field Day Review*, 3, 239–245.

Courtois, A. (2010) 'The Role of Fee-paying Schools in the Training of the Irish Elites', paper presented at the *Sociological Association of Ireland Annual Conference*, Queens University Belfast, 7–9 May 2010.

Cross, C. and Linehan, M. (2006) 'Barriers to Advancing Female Careers in the High-tech Sector: Empirical Evidence from Ireland', *Women in Management Review*, 21(1), 28–39.

Croteau, D. and Hoynes, W. (2003) *Media Society: Industries, Images and Audiences*, 3rd edn, Thousand Oaks, CA: Pine Forge Press.

Devereux, E. (1998) *Devils and Angels: Television, Ideology and the Coverage of Poverty*, Luton: John Libbey Media.

Devereux, E. (2006) 'Being Wild(e) About Morrissey: Fandom and Identity' in Corcoran, M. and Peillon, M. (eds) *Uncertain Ireland: A sociological chronicle 2003–2004*, Dublin: IPA. Available: www.ul.ie/sociology/Morrissey.pdf.

Devereux, E. (2007a) *Understanding the Media*, 2nd edn, London: Sage.

Devereux, E. (ed.) (2007b) *Media Studies: Key Issues and Debates*, London: Sage.

Devereux, E., Haynes, A. and Power, M. (2011) 'Behind the Headlines: Media Coverage of Social Exclusion in Limerick City – the Case of Moyross', in Hourigan, N. (ed.) *Understanding Limerick: Social Exclusion and Change*, Cork: Cork University Press.

Drudy, S. and Lynch, K. (1993) *Schools and Society in Ireland*, Dublin: Gill & Macmillan.

ESRI (2006) *Who Went to College in 2004? A National Survey of New Entrants to Higher Education* by Philip O'Connell (ESRI), David Clancy (Fitzpatrick Associates) and Selina McCoy (ESRI). The Higher Education Authority [press release], 2 March. Available: http://www.esri.ie/news_events/ press_releases_archive/2006/who_went_to_college_ in_20/index.xml

Eurostat (2010) *European Social Statistics: Demography*, The Statistical Offices of the European Community: Luxembourg.

Fahey, T. (2007) 'How Do We Feel? Economic Boom and Happiness', in Fahey, T., Russell, H. and Whelan, C. (eds), *Best of Times? The Social Impact of the Celtic Tiger*, Dublin: Institute of Public Administration, pp. 11–26.

Fahey, T. and Field, C. (2008) *Families in Ireland: An Analysis of Patterns and Trends*, Dublin: Department of Social and Family Affairs.

Fahey, T. and Layte, R. (2007) 'Family and Sexuality', in Fahey, T., Russell, H. and Whelan, C. (eds), *Best of Times? The Social Impact of the Celtic Tiger*, Dublin: Institute of Public Administration, pp. 155–174.

Fahey, T. and Russell, H. (2001) *Family Formation in Ireland: Trends, Data Needs and Implications*, Dublin: Economic and Social Research Institute Report.

Fahey, T., Russell, H. and Whelan, C. (2007) *Best of Times? The Social Impact of the Celtic Tiger*, Dublin: Institute for Public Administration.

Fanning, B. (2002) *Racism and Social Change in the Republic of Ireland*, Manchester: Manchester University Press.

Fanning, B. (2009) *New Guests of the Nation*, Dublin: Irish Academic Press.

Fanning, B. (2010) 'From Developmental Ireland to Migration Nation: Immigration and Shifting Rules of Belonging in the Republic of Ireland', *The Economic and Social Review*, 41(3), 395–412.

Flynn, S. (2008) 'Subtle Form of Apartheid Permeates School System'. *Irish Times*, 4 April. Available: http://www.irishtimes.com/newspaper/ireland/2008/ 0428/1209158497892.html

Gallagher, M. and Komito, L. (1999) 'The Constituency Role of TDs', in Coakley, J. and Gallagher, M. (eds) *Politics in the Republic of Ireland*, 3rd edn, Dublin: Routledge.

Gilligan, R., McGrath, J., Ní Raghallaigh, M., Scholtz, J., Curry, P., Murphy, D., Rogers, M. and Quinn, A. (2010) *In the Front Line of Integration: Young People Managing Migration to Ireland*, Dublin: Trinity College.

Ging, D. (2005) 'A "Manual on Masculinity"? The Consumption and Use of Mediated Images of Masculinity among Teenage Boys in Ireland', *Irish Journal of Sociology*, 14(2), 29–52.

Ging, D. (2007) 'New Lads or Protest Masculinities?: Investigating Marginalised Masculinities in Contemporary Irish Film', in Horgan, J., O' Connor, B. and Sheehan, H. (eds). Mapping Irish Media: Critical Explorations. Dublin: UCD Press.

Goldberg, D.T. (2002) *The Racial State*, Oxford: Blackwell.

Government of Ireland (2004) First National Report by IRELAND as required under Article 9 of the

Convention on the legislative, judicial, administrative or other measures adopted to give effect to the provisions of the Convention: United Nations International Convention on the Elimination of All Forms of Racial Discrimination, Dublin: Stationary Office.

Gray, B. (2004) 'Remembering a "Multicultural" Future through a History of Emigration: Towards a Feminist Politics of Solidarity across Difference', *Women's Studies International*, 27(4), 413–429.

Greaves, N., Hill, D. and Maisuria, A. (2007) 'Embourgeoisment, Immiseration, Commodification – Marxism Revisited: A Critique of Education in Capitalist Systems', *Journal for Critical Educational Policy Studies*, 5(1).

Hantrais, L. (2004) *Family Policy Matters: responding to family change in Europe*, Bristol: The Policy Press.

Haynes, A. (2007) 'Mass Media Re-Presentations of the Social World: Ethnicity and "Race"' in Devereux, E. (ed.) *Media Studies: Key Issues and Debates*, London: Sage, pp.162–190.

Haynes, A., Breen, M. and Devereux, E. (2005) 'Smuggling Zebras for Lunch: Media Framing of Asylum Seekers in the Irish Print Media', *Etudes Irlandaises*, 30(1).

Haynes, A., Devereux, E. and Breen, M. (2006) 'Fear, Framing and Foreigners: The Othering of Immigrants in the Irish Print Media', *International Journal of Critical Psychology*, 16, 100–121.

Haynes, A., Devereux, E. and Breen, M. (2008) 'Public Exercises in Othering: Irish Print Media Coverage of Asylum Seekers and Refugees' in Faragó, B. and Sullivan, M. (eds), *Facing the Other: Interdisciplinary Studies on Race, Gender and Social Justice in Ireland*, Cambridge: Cambridge Scholars Publishing, 162–181.

Haynes, A., Power, M. and Devereux, E. (2010) *How Irish Politicians Construct Transnational EU Migrants in Ireland*, Limerick: Doras Luimní.

Henslin, J. (2010) *Sociology: A Down-To-Earth Approach*, 10th edn, Boston: Pearson.

Higher Education Authority (2004) *Achieving Equity of Access to Higher Education in Ireland: Action Plan 2005–2007*, Dublin: Higher Education Authority.

Hirtt, N. (2004) 'Three Axes of Merchandisation', *European Educational Research Journal*, 3(2), 442–453.

Hobsbawm, E. (1990) *Nations and Nationalism Since 1780: Programme, Myth, Reality*, Cambridge: Cambridge University Press.

Horgan, J., O'Connor, B. and Sheehan, H. (2007) *Mapping Irish Media: Critical Explorations*, Dublin: UCD Press.

Hurn, C. (1993) *The Limits and Possibilities of Schooling*, Boston: Allyn & Bacon.

Jenkins, R. (2008) *Social Identity*, 3rd edn, Abingdon: Routledge.

Keane, C. (1992) *The Jobs Crisis*, Cork: Mercier Press.

Kelly, M. and O'Connor, B. (1997) *Media Audiences in Ireland*, Dublin: UCD Press.

Kennedy, K. (1993) *Facing the Unemployment Crisis in Ireland*, Cork: Cork University Press.

Kennedy, M. (2010) 'Talking your Way to the Top: A Sociological Examination of the Role of Elite Education in the Reproduction of Privilege in Irish Society', *Socheolas: Limerick Student Journal of Sociology*, 2(1), 70–94.

Kerr, A. (2007) 'Transnational Flows: Media Use by Poles in Ireland' in Horgan, J., O'Connor, B. and Sheehan, H. (eds) *Mapping Irish Media: Critical Explorations*, Dublin: UCD Press.

Kirby, P. (2004) 'Globalisation, the Celtic Tiger and Social Outcomes: Is Ireland a Model or a Mirage?', *Globalisations*, 1(2), 205–222.

Kirby, P. (2005) 'In the Wake of the Tiger: Mapping Anew the Social Terrain', *The Irish Review*, 33 (spring), 40–50.

Kirby, P. (2008) *Explaining Ireland's Development: Economic Growth with Weakening Welfare*, Social Policy and Development Programme Paper No. 37, United Nations Institute for Social Development.

Lee, A. (2003) 'Community Development in Ireland', *Community Development Journal*, 38(1), 48–58.

Lentin, R. (2006) 'From Racial State to Racist State? Racism and Immigration in Twenty First Century Ireland' in Lentin, A. and Lentin, R. (eds) *Race and State*, Newcastle: Cambridge Scholars Press, 187–208.

Lentin, A. and Lentin, R. (eds) (2006) *Race and State*, Newcastle: Cambridge Scholars Press.

Loyal, S. (2011) *Understanding Immigration in Ireland: State, Capital and Labour in a Global Age*, Manchester: Manchester University Press.

Lunn, P., Fahey, T. and Hannan, C. (2010) *Family Figures: Family Types and Family Dynamics in Ireland, 1986–2006*, Dublin: Family Support Agency.

Macionis, J. and Plummer, K. (2008) *Sociology: A Global Introduction*, 4th edn, Harlow: Pearson.

MacKeogh, C. (2002) *Participant Observation: A Case Study of Young People and Television*, Irish Sociological Research Monographs, Vol. 2.

MacLaughlin, J. (1995) *Travellers and Ireland: Whose Country, Whose History?*, Undercurrents, Cork: Cork University Press.

MacSharry, R. and White, P. (2000) *The Making of the Celtic Tiger: The Inside Story of Ireland's Boom Economy*, Cork: Mercier Press.

Mahon, E. (1994) 'Ireland: A Private Patriarchy?', *Environmental and Planning A*, 26, 1277–96.

McCoy, S. and Smyth, E. (2003) *Educational Expenditure: Implications for Equality. Budget Perspectives 2004*, Dublin: ESRI.

McCrum (2002) 'The Whole World in a Community', *Observer*, 6 January.

McCullagh, C. (2002) *Media Power: A Sociological Introduction*, London: Palgrave.

McGinnity, F., O'Connell, P., Quinn, E. and Williams, J. (2006) *Migrants' Experience of Racism and Discrimination in Ireland: Survey Report*, Dublin: ESRI.

McNamee, S. and Miller, R. (2004) *The Meritocracy Myth*, London: Rowman and Littlefield.

McVeigh, R. (2007) '"Ethnicity Denial" and Racism: The Case of the Government of Ireland Against Irish Travellers', *Translocations*, 2(1), 90–133.

McWilliams, D. (2005) *The Pope's Children: Ireland's New Elite*, Dublin: Gill & Macmillan.

Murphy, G. (2010) 'Framing Propaganda: Print Media Coverage of Irish Public Service Workers', *Socheolas: Limerick Student Journal of Sociology*, 3(1), 3–24.

Mulderrig, J. (2003) 'Consuming Education: A Critical Discourse Analysis of Social Actors in New Labour's Education Policy', *Journal for Critical Education Policy Studies*, 1(1).

Murphy, M. (2007) 'Working-aged People and Welfare Policy', in *Welfare Policy and Poverty*, Dublin: Institute of Public Administration and Combat Poverty Agency, 101–138.

National Economic and Social Forum (2006) *Report No. 33: Creating a More Inclusive Labour Market*, Dublin.

O'Hearn, D. (1998) *Inside the Celtic Tiger: The Irish Economy and the Asian Model*, London: Pluto.

O'Connell, P., Clancy, D. and McCoy, S. (2006) *Who Went to College in 2004? A National Survey of Entrants to Higher Education*, Dublin: Higher Education Authority.

O'Connell, P., McCoy, S. and Clancy, D. (2006) 'Who Went to College? Socio-Economic Inequality in Entry to Higher Education in the Republic of Ireland in 2004', *Higher Education Quarterly*, 60(4), 312–332.

O'Connor, B. and MacKeogh, C. (2007) 'New Media Communities: Performing Identity in an Online Women's Magazine', *Irish Journal of Sociology*, 16(2), 97–116.

O'Connor, P. (1999) *Women in Contemporary Irish Society*, Dublin: Institute of Public Administration.

OECD (2010) 'Employment Outlook 2010 – How Does IRELAND Compare?' Available: http://www.oecd.org/dataoecd/14/37/45603074.pdf

Onyeljelem, C. (2005) 'Multiculturalism in Ireland', *Irish Review*, 33, 70–77.

Punch, A. (2007) 'Marriage, Fertility and the Family in Ireland – A Statistical Perspective', Presidential address to the *Statistical and Social Inquiry Society of Ireland*, 31 May.

Pyle, J. (1990) *The State and Women in the Economy: Lessons from Sex Discrimination in the Republic of Ireland*, Albany, NY: State University of New York Press.

Raftery, A. and Hout, M. (1993) 'Maximally Maintained Inequality: Expansion, Reform, and Opportunity in Irish Education, 1921–75', *Sociology of Education*, 66(1), 41–62.

Rice, E. (2006) 'Keep it Private if You Want to End Up on the Judge's Bench'. *The Tribune*, 22 January. Available: https://www.tribune.ie/archive/article/2006/jan/22/keep-it-private-if-you-want-to-end-up-on-the-judge

*RTÉ News* (2010) 'High Incomes "Wasted" in Boom Years'. Available: www.rte.ie/news/2010/0219/economy.html

Share, P., Tovey, H. and Corcoran, M. (2007) *A Sociology of Ireland*, 3rd edn, Dublin: Gill & Macmillan.

Sheehan, H. (1987) *Irish Television Drama: A Society and its Stories*, Dublin: RTE.

Sheehan, H. (2004) *The Continuing Story of Irish Television Drama: Tracking the Tiger*, Dublin: Four Courts Press.

Skeggs, B. (1997) *Formations of Class and Gender*, London: Sage.

Skeggs, B. (2004) *Class, Self, Culture*, London: Routledge.

Smith, J. (2010) 'Migrants from the New EU States Denied Welfare', *Irish Times*, 1 January. Available: http://www.irishtimes.com/newspaper/ireland/2010/0111/1224262053852.html

Society for the Irish Motoring Industry (SIMI). Available: www.simi.ie

Special Group on Public Service Numbers and Expenditure Programmes (2009) *Report of the Special Group on Public Service Numbers and Expenditure Programmes Vol. 1*, Dublin: Government Publications.

Titley, G. (2008) 'Media Transnationalism in Ireland: An Examination of Polish Media Practices', *Translocations*, 3(1).

Tovey, H. and Share, P. (2003) *A Sociology of Ireland*, 2nd edn, Dublin: Gill & Macmillan.

Tracy, M. (2000) *Racism and Immigration in Ireland: A Comparative Analysis*, MPhil Dissertation in Ethnic and Racial Studies, Dublin: Trinity College Dublin.

Veblen, T. (1899) *Theory of the Leisure Class: An Economic Study in the Evolution of Institutions*, New York: Macmillan.

Waldron, F., and Pike, S. (2006) 'What Does It Mean to be Irish? Children's Construction of National Identity', *Irish Educational Studies*, 25(2), 231–251.

Waldron, F. and Pike, S. (2007) 'What Does it Mean to be Irish? Children's Construction of National Identity', *Irish Educational Review*, 25(2), 231–251.

Walkerdine, V., Lucey, H. and Melody, J. (2001) *Growing Up Girl: Psychosocial Explorations of Gender and Class*, Hampshire: Palgrave.

Walsh, J. (2007) 'Monitoring Poverty and Welfare Policy, 1987–2007', in Cousins, M. (ed.) *Welfare Policy and Poverty*, Dublin: Combat Poverty Agency, pp.13–58.

Walshe, J. and Hickey, S. (2008) 'Private School Fee to Soar as State Aid is Cut by €10m'. *Irish Independent*, 28 October. Available: http://www.independent.ie/education/latest-news/private-school-fees-to-soar-as-state-aid-is-cut-by-836410m-1511140.html

Whelan, C. and Layte, R. (2007) 'Opportunities for All in the New Ireland' in Fahey, T., Russell, H. and Whelan, C. (eds) *The Best of Times? The Social Impact of the Celtic Tiger*, Dublin: Institute of Public Administration.